Encyclopedia of the Life Course and Human Development

Encyclopedia of the Life Course and Human Development

VOLUME 2
ADULTHOOD

Deborah Carr
EDITOR IN CHIEF

MACMILLAN REFERENCE USA
A part of Gale, Cengage Learning

GALE
CENGAGE Learning

Detroit • New York • San Francisco • New Haven, Conn • Waterville, Maine • London

GALE
CENGAGE Learning™

Encyclopedia of the Life Course and Human Development
Deborah Carr, Editor in Chief

© 2009 Macmillan Reference USA, a part of Gale, Cengage Learning.

For product information and technology assistance, contact us at
Gale Customer Support, 1-800-877-4253
For permission to use material from this text or product,
submit all requests online at **www.cengage.com/permissions**
Further permissions questions can be emailed to
permissionrequest@cengage.com

Library of Congress Cataloging-in-Publication Data

Encyclopedia of the life course and human development / Deborah Carr, editor in chief.
    v. ; cm.
    Includes bibliographical references and index.
    ISBN 978-0-02-866162-9 (set : alk. paper) – ISBN 978-0-02-866163-6 (vol. 1 : alk. paper) – ISBN 978-0-02-866164-3 (vol. 2 : alk. paper) – ISBN 978-0-02-866165-0 (vol. 3 : alk. paper)
    1. Social evolution—Encyclopedias. 2. Human evolution—Encyclopedias. I. Carr, Deborah S.

HM626.E538 2008
305.203—dc22   2008027490

Gale
27500 Drake Rd.
Farmington Hills, MI 48331-3535

ISBN-13: 978-0-02-866162-9 (set)   ISBN-10: 0-02-866162-1 (set)
ISBN-13: 978-0-02-866163-6 (vol. 1)   ISBN-10: 0-02-866163-X (vol. 1)
ISBN-13: 978-0-02-866164-3 (vol. 2)   ISBN-10: 0-02-866164-8 (vol. 2)
ISBN-13: 978-0-02-866165-0 (vol. 3)   ISBN-10: 0-02-866165-6 (vol. 3)

This title is also available as an e-book.
ISBN-13: 978-0-02-866166-7 ISBN-10: 0-02-866166-4
Contact your Gale sales representative for ordering information.

Printed in the United States of America
1 2 3 4 5 6 7 12 11 10 09 08

Editorial Board

Editorial and Production Staff

Contents

Introduction to Volume 2, Adulthood

What was the moment when you felt that you were really an "adult"? This is a question that I ask students each year, when I teach my graduate seminar Sociology of the Life Course. Without fail, about two-thirds of the fifteen or so students in my class sheepishly respond, "I don't think I'm an adult yet." Each student—most of whom are in their early or mid-20s—then shares the reasons why they feel they're not quite an adult. "I don't own a home." "I'm still in school and don't really have a job." "I live with my boyfriend, but we're not married yet." "I don't have kids." "My parents still pay for my rent and car insurance."

This exercise reveals just how fuzzy the concept of adulthood is; while age 25 would clearly make one a legal adult, few 25-year-olds "feel" adult today. The life stage of adulthood encompasses three distinct and only partially overlapping components: legal, biological, and social. Consistent with this three-prong conceptualization, dictionary definitions of "adult" include: one who has attained maturity; one who is of legal age; and a fully grown, mature organism. Yet these three transitions rarely occur in tandem, thus contributing to the blurry boundaries demarcating adolescence, adulthood, and old age. For example, according to United States law, one becomes a legal adult at age 18. The biological transition to adulthood typically occurs around age 13, when girls and boys reach puberty. The social transition to adulthood is far less clear-cut, although it is typically conceptualized as the age at which one makes transitions into important social roles such as worker, spouse and parent.

Most Americans agree that a particular cluster of social roles signifies the entry to adulthood. Data from the 2002 General Social Survey (GSS), a large national survey of the United States population, revealed that 96% of Americans say financial independence and full-time work are the defining accomplishments of "adult" life, while 94% believe a young person isn't officially an adult until he or she is able to support a family. Yet national data also show that a surprisingly small proportion of young people have actually made such transitions even as late as age 30. The Census Bureau recently calculated the proportion of Americans who have accomplished all of the following transitions by age 30: left their parents' home, finished school, got married, had a child, and achieved financial independence. In the year 2000, just 46% of women and 31% of men had reached all five milestones. In 1960, by contrast, 77% of women and 65% of men had done so (Furstenberg, Kennedy, McLoyd, Rumbaut, & Settersten, 2004).

The entries in this volume provide answers to questions like what is adulthood, and how has adulthood changed over time. Just as importantly, though, the entries in this volume show persuasively that there is not a universal conceptualization or experience of "adult-hood." Adulthood comprises a series of distinctive stages, including early adulthood and midlife. The ways that individuals experience adulthood also vary widely by birth cohort, gender, social class, race, ethnicity, immigrant status, sexual orientation, and geographic region. Finally, one's experiences in adulthood are molded by early life experiences like one's family background, childhood physical and mental health, and educational attainment. One's adult experiences, in turn, set the stage for one's well-being in later life. The life course framework enables scholars to study adulthood using this critically important *whole lives* perspective.

THE STAGES OF ADULTHOOD

Adulthood encompasses the age range of 18 to 64. Persons under age 18 are classified as youths, while the years of 65 and above are typically referred to as later life or old age. In 2000, persons ages 18–64 accounted for 62% of the 281.4 million Americans, while the 0–18 and 65+ populations accounted for 26 and 12% of all Americans, respectively (U.S. Census Bureau, 2001). While demographers define adulthood in terms of chronological age alone, the age range of 18–64 is incredibly broad and encompasses (at least) two distinctive adult stages: young adulthood, and midlife.

Young adulthood is typically conceptualized as ages 18–35, while midlife is typically conceptualized as ages 35–64. However, these boundaries are imprecise and are widely debated. Biologists often define life course stages using *physiological markers*. The transition to young adulthood, in this view, would be marked by puberty, or the point when children's bodies mature physically and are able to reproduce. The transition to midlife, by the same token, is defined in terms of the loss of or declines in reproductive capacity. According to this perspective, the "midlife" stage is demarcated by the transition to menopause for women and andropause or "male menopause" for men. Upon menopause, a woman is no longer physically capable of bearing children, while andropause is a time when men's physical vigor and virility starts to fade (although the very existence of andropause is hotly debated, as the encyclopedia entry reveals).

Other perspectives emphasize *psychological maturation* as the criteria for defining adult stages. Erik Erikson's (1950) classic model of adult development proposes that the transition between life course stages is contingent upon the successful and sequential resolution of a series of "crises." Young adults, defined by Erikson as persons ages 19 to 34, must resolve the crisis of intimacy versus isolation. Intimacy refers to one's ability to relate to another human being on a deep personal level. Before forming a committed romantic relationship or enduring friendship, however, one must develop a sense of their own identity. Young people who fail to achieve an intimate relationship with others are at risk of social and emotional isolation. The distinctive challenge of midlife (defined by Erikson as ages 40–65) is to resolve the conflict between generativity versus stagnation. A midlife adult is expected to avoid the lure of self-absorption and to instead become generative—working to preserve values and opportunities that will benefit succeeding generations.

A complementary perspective holds that an individual must accomplish a set of age-defined developmental tasks in order to make the successful progression through adult life course stages. Robert Havighurst (1971) wrote that the developmental tasks or prerequisites for successful maturation of young adults (defined as ages 18–30) included selecting a mate, learning to live with a partner, bearing and raising children, managing one's home, starting a career, taking on civic responsibilities, and establishing a circle of friends, acquaintances or coworkers. Midlife adults, defined by Havighurst as persons ages 30–60, were expected to raise their teenage children to become responsible and happy adults, to assume social and civic responsibility, to achieve and maintain satisfactory performance in one's career, to participate in rewarding leisure time activities, to develop a strong and understanding relationship with one's spouse, to accept and adjust to the physiological changes of middle age, and to adjust to the challenges experienced by one's aging parents.

Both Erikson and Havighurst proposed stage theories, which are based on the presumption that successful adult development requires the sequential completion of a series of tasks or challenges. Yet life course scholars argue that stage theories do not allow for individual-level innovation nor do they reflect the fact that social and historical context can affect whether, when, and in what order one experiences important role transitions, like marriage, childbearing, and first job. Thus, while life course scholars agree that adulthood should be defined in terms of the social roles one holds rather than one's chronological age, they grant more latitude in how and when adults experiences the stages of young adulthood and midlife.

A LIFE COURSE LENS ON ADULTHOOD: ATTENTION TO DIVERSITY

Life course scholars typically conceptualize life course stages in terms of social roles, as Havighurst did, yet they do not tightly tie their definitions of "adulthood" to chronological age (Riley, Johnson, and Foner, 1972). Rather, they recognize that individual lives reflect the intersection of *biography and history*. As such, the ages at which one achieves particular social roles and statuses—and thus the timing of the transition to both young adulthood and midlife—vary widely across birth cohorts. As noted earlier, in the year 2000, just 46% of women and 31% of men had reached the five milestones believed to define "adulthood." In 1960, by contrast, 77% of women and 65% of men had done so (Furstenberg, Kennedy, McLoyd, Rumbaut, & Settersten, 2004).

Does this mean that younger cohorts of adults, those born in the 1960s, 1970s, and later are less mature than their parents or grandparents? Life course scholars believe the answer is "no." Rather, macrosocial factors including economic restructuring, educational expansion, the advent of effective birth control, and even the recent housing crisis have all contributed to what scholars call the "delayed transition to adulthood." Economic restructuring means that agricultural and manufacturing jobs have disappeared, and have given way to the expansion of the service economy; white-collar and professional jobs require bachelor's and master's degrees, so young people need to remain in school through their 20s and even 30s. Nonmarital cohabitation has become an increasingly acceptable living arrangement, so many young people cohabit with their romantic partner for years before officially tying the knot. The development of effective birth control means that young people can protect themselves against unwanted pregnancy—and the shot-gun, youthful marriages often triggered by such pregnancies. Skyrocketing housing costs mean that many young people can't afford to purchase their own homes, and often must share housing costs with roommates.

It's not just the transition to adulthood that has been delayed in recent years. The transition to midlife also has been delayed, at least if Havighurst's definition of midlife is used as criteria. One reason why the timing of the transition to midlife has been postponed is because this transition is tightly tied to the timing of young adulthood transitions. This pattern reflects the life course theme that the *timing of life events matters* for future transitions and trajectories. For example, life transitions typically viewed as the hallmark of midlife—such as achieving stability in one's career, and launching one's children into adulthood—are happening in one's 50s today, rather than one's 20s. As young people receive more education and enter the job market at later ages, they often do not reach their career peak until their 50s or later. Similarly, parents who have their first child while in their mid 30s do not reach the "empty nest" phase until at least their early 50s, when their 18-year-old child leaves for college. Yet some parents never achieve the empty nest phase, as their children remain in the family home because they cannot afford a place of their own.

Whether, when, and in what order adults experience important life course transitions also varies by social class, race, gender, cultural and geographic context, and immigrant status. For instance, young people from disadvantaged economic backgrounds often cannot afford college, and thus enter into full-time blue-collar or clerical occupations when they are in their late teens. They tend to marry earlier, and have children earlier. As such, they may experience the "empty nest" transition while in their late 30s, while their contemporaries who attended graduate school may be taking care of their newborn babies at that same age.

Social class also affects the timing of midlife and later life transitions. Persons living in economically depressed environments often experience the premature onset of health problems like high blood pressure, heart disease, and diabetes. These health conditions, in turn, can trigger an early transition to retirement or a disability-related departure from the paid work force.

Race also has a powerful effect on the transition to adulthood. Black women are far less likely than their White counterparts to ever marry, and also are more likely to bypass marriage en route to childbearing. For example, while 27% of White women ages 15 and over have never married, this figure is 42% for Black women. Nearly two-thirds of all births to Black women occur out of wedlock, while roughly 35% of White births are nonmarital. However, the meaning of "out of wedlock" birth has changed drastically in recent years, as roughly half of these babies are born to cohabiting couples (Mincieli, Manlove, McGarrett, Moore, & Ryan, 2007). An examination of racial differences in family transitions reveals the life course theme that individuals have *agency and guide their own life course*, within economic and structural constraints. Qualitative research by the sociologists Kathryn Edin and Maria Kefalas shows that young Black women in poor urban neighborhoods recognize that they have very low chances of marrying, and that they intentionally have children at young ages, and out of wedlock—as a way to bring meaning and family relationships into their lives.

ADULTHOOD: THE BRIDGE BETWEEN CHILDHOOD AND LATER LIFE

Although the encyclopedia comprises the three freestanding volumes on childhood/adolescence, adulthood, and later life these three life course stages cannot be understood in isolation from one another. Childhood economic resources, parent-child relationships, the quality of one's schooling, and one's early physical and mental health set the stage for one's adult accomplishments. The broad range of experiences one has in adulthood—attending college, starting a first job, marrying and having children, progressing in one's career (or making major career changes), participating in social and religious activities, maintaining one's health, one's spending patterns, whether or not one relocates their home, and whether one is either a victim of or perpetrator of crime—all reflect, in part, the experiences one had during the formative years. For example, the life course theme of *linked lives* proposes that the fortunes of generations are closely linked. Children often go on to replicate their parents' experiences—either because they have been socialized to hold values and attitudes similar to their parents, or because they and their parents share the social characteristics—like social class or race—that provide either opportunities or constraints as one negotiates adult roles and transitions.

One's adulthood experiences also set the stage for whether one's later life years are marked by poverty, physical disability, cognitive decline, and social isolation—or financial stability, physical vigor, mental acuity, and social engagement. For example, the type of jobs one holds in adulthood may have long-term implications for late-life physical health and cognitive functioning. Physically grueling jobs, fast-paced jobs that place high demands on their workers yet offer them little control over their schedules, and part-time or seasonal jobs that do not offer health benefits all carry potential harmful consequences for health in later life. Interpersonal relationships and community activities also set the stage for successful or problematic aging; friendships, hobbies, family relationships, religion, and workplace relationships all protect against both physical and mental health declines in the long term.

Although the three life course stages are closely intertwined, and each sets the foundation for the successive stages, life course scholars argue strongly that the influences of early life events on adulthood are neither deterministic nor mechanistic. Rather, life course scholars are interested in documenting patterns of both *stability and change*. Resilience is an important theme in life course research, and the encyclopedia entries document those factors that can "undo" or reverse the effects of a particular adversity or resource that one had early in life. For instance, while social class is a strong determinant of college graduation, the strength of this relationship has varied throughout history. Young women from middle class homes during the 1950s and 1960s often attended, but did not graduate, college because strong normative pressures during that time period encouraged early marriage (Goldin, 1990). African Americans, especially those from poor homes, had little chance of attending college during the early half of the 20th century, yet historical changes like the 1960s Civil Rights movement, public policy shifts like the establishment (yet ultimate weakening) of affirmative action programs, and normative shifts, where school teachers and guidance counselors offer encouragement to students of color, have contributed to the steady increase in the number of African Americans who earned bachelor's degrees in the late 20th and early 21st century. Although Blacks' rates of college attendance and graduation still lag far behind Whites, this gap—especially for women—has diminished over the past century (Hacker, 1992).

Taken together, the entries in this volume provide an exciting and thought-provoking glimpse in adulthood. We hope readers come away with an appreciation of the diverse ways that adulthood is experienced in both the United States and throughout the world. The life course lens reveals the ways that adults construct their own lives, yet the influences of time, place, and culture are inescapable.

BIBLIOGRAPHY

Erickson, E. H. (1950). *Childhood and society.* New York: W. W. Norton.

Furstenberg, F. F. Jr., Kennedy, S., McLoyd, V. C., Rumbaut, R. G., & Settersten, R. A., Jr. (2004). *Growing up is harder to do. Contexts,* 3, 33–41.

Goldin, C. (1990). *Understanding the gender gap: an economic history of American women.* New York: Oxford University Press.

Hacker, A. (1992). *Two nations: Black and White, separate, hostile, unequal.* New York: Scribner.

Lachman, M., & James, J. B. (1997). *Multiple paths of midlife development.* Chicago, IL: University of Chicago Press.

Havighurst, R. J. (1971). *Developmental tasks and education,* 3rd ed. New York: Longman.

Edin, K., & Kefalas, M. (2005). *Promises I can keep: Why poor women put motherhood before marriage.* Berkeley: University of California Press.

Minceli, L., J. Manlove, M., McGarrett, K., Moore, & S. Ryan. (2007). The relationship context of births outside of marriage: the rise in cohabitation. Child Trends Research Brief 2007–13. Washington, D.C.: Child Trends. Retrieved on August 20, 2008, from http://www.childtrends.org/Files//Child_Trends-2007_05_14_RB_OutsideBirths.pdf

Riley, M. W., Johnson, M., & Foner, A. (1972). *Aging and society.* (Vol. 3): A sociology of age stratification. New York: Russell Sage.

U.S. Census Bureau. (2001). Age: 2000. Washington, D.C. U.S. Department of Commerce. Retrieved on August 20, 2008, from http://www.census.gov/prod/2001pubs/c2kbr01-12.pdf

Deborah Carr
Editor in Chief

A

ABORTION

Induced abortion (henceforth referred to as abortion) is the voluntary termination of a pregnancy by removing an embryo or fetus from a woman's uterus. Abortion can be performed by either surgical or medical methods. In a surgical abortion, a woman undergoes a procedure called manual or vacuum aspiration that is performed by a trained physician. A medical abortion (or non-surgical abortion) is done early in pregnancy (through 9 weeks gestation) through use of a drug or combination of drugs that first causes the termination of the pregnancy and then causes the contents of the uterus to be expelled out of the body. In the United States, the drugs used for medical abortion (i.e., mifepristone, methotrexate, and misoprostol) must be prescribed by a registered physician. Although a woman usually experiences the actual termination of the pregnancy at home, a follow-up visit to a physician approximately 1 to 2 weeks after taking the medication is required to ensure that the abortion was complete.

It is estimated that over one-third of women in the United States has an abortion in their reproductive lifetime, making it a common life event and an important topic of study because abortion affects the lives of thousands of women each year. The decision to terminate a pregnancy or carry it to term has a significant impact on a woman's life course, physically, emotionally, and financially, and may influence her successful achievement of life goals.

BRIEF HISTORY OF ABORTION IN THE UNITED STATES

Abortion was legal (and quite common) when the United States enacted the Constitution in 1776; but by the early 1900s, it was illegal in all states. In 1973, the United States Supreme Court cases of *Roe v. Wade* and *Doe v. Bolton* declared abortion to be a "fundamental right" rooted in a woman's constitutional right to privacy. In the 1980s and 1990s, the Court recognized the state's interest in "potential life," as evidenced in the cases of *Webster v. Reproductive Health Services* (1989) and *Planned Parenthood v. Casey* (1992), and gave individual states the right to regulate abortion as long as it did not put an "undue burden" on the woman. Since that time, states have introduced and passed several abortion laws that regulate and limit whether, when, and under what circumstances a woman may obtain an abortion (Guttmacher Institute, 2008). State-level laws regulating abortion range from mandatory 24-hour waiting periods, which require a woman to wait a full 24 hours between seeking and obtaining an abortion, information and counseling sessions that sometimes present inaccurate medical information, and restrictions or complete bans on state-level Medicaid funding for low-income women seeking an abortion.

Since 1977, the Hyde Amendment prevents any federal-level Medicaid funds from being used to pay for an abortion unless the pregnancy is the result of rape or incest, or if a woman's life is endangered. In practice, individual states are free to use state-based Medicaid funds to cover abortion, although many choose not to do so. Young women under the age of 18 are particularly affected by state-level restrictions, as many states have either parental consent or parental notification laws in place. These laws severely restrict young women's access to abortion, often resulting in later term abortions or forcing young women to have a child before they are emotionally, financially, or physically prepared to do so.

THE PREVALENCE AND DISTRIBUTION OF ABORTION

Each year, more than 6 million women in the United States—one in every 10 women of reproductive age (between 15 and 44)—become pregnant, and almost half of those pregnancies are unintentional (Finer & Henshaw, 2006). Approximately 48% of unintended pregnancies end in abortion and, as a result, two out of every 100 women aged 15 to 44 have an abortion each year (Finer & Henshaw, 2005). In 2005, 1.21 million pregnancies were terminated by abortion, making abortion one of the most common surgical procedures in the United States (Jones et al., 2008a). The abortion rate, defined as the number of abortions per 1,000 women of reproductive age in a given year, was 19.4 in 2005, which represents a 9% decline over the previous 5 years and was the lowest rate since 1974. The abortion ratio, defined as the number of abortions per 1,000 live births, indicates that 22% of pregnancies (excluding those ending in miscarriages) ended in abortion in 2005 (Jones et al., 2008a). Almost 90% of abortions are performed in the first trimester of pregnancy (i.e., under 12 weeks of gestation) and 6 in 10 abortions are performed within 8 weeks gestation (Strauss et al., 2007). The proportion of abortions performed very early in pregnancy (at 6 weeks or before) increased from 14% in 1992 to 28% in 2004, most likely due to increased access and use of medical abortion, which the U.S. Food and Drug Administration approved for early abortions in 2000. In 2005, medical abortion accounted for 13% of all abortions, an increase from 6% in 2001 (Jones et al., 2008a).

Not all women in the United States are equally likely to obtain an abortion, however. Hispanic and Black women have abortion rates that are 2 and 3 times higher than the rates of White women, respectively (Strauss et al., 2007). The ethnic disparity in abortion rates reflects the fact that Black women and Latinas have higher rates of unintended pregnancy, and that Black women are more likely to resolve an unintended pregnancy through abortion (Guttmacher Institute, 2005). Black and Hispanic women also are at greater risk of poverty than White women, and poverty increases one's likelihood both of having an unintended pregnancy and of resolving the pregnancy through an abortion. Between 1996 and 2000, abortion rates for nearly all subgroups of women fell, yet rates among poor and low-income women increased. Women below the federal poverty level have abortion rates almost 4 times those of higher-income women (Jones et al., 2002).

The likelihood of having an abortion also varies over the life course, reflecting both biological factors (such as one's physical capacity to reproduce) and social factors (such as one's marital and parental statuses). Many people assume unintended pregnancy and abortion are issues confronted by young women or teenagers only, but the majority of women (56%) having abortions are in their 20s, followed by 30- to 34-year-olds (26%), and then 15- to 19-year-olds (16%) (Strauss et al., 2007). Abortion numbers and rates decline with age because fecundity (i.e., the ability to conceive) declines, use of contraceptive sterilization increases, and more women are married—which makes it easier to use contraceptives effectively and to carry an unintended pregnancy to term. Approximately 86% of abortions occur among unmarried women, including both never-married and formerly married women (Strauss et al., 2007). The proportion of unintended pregnancies terminated by abortion ranges from 67% among formerly married women and 57% among never-married women to 27% among currently married women (Finer & Henshaw, 2006). A commonly held myth is that women have abortions before they begin childbearing, but an estimated 6 in 10 women seeking an abortion are already mothers. Approximately half of women seeking an abortion have already had at least one prior abortion (Jones et al., 2002).

When U.S. women having abortions are asked their religious affiliation, 43% say they are Protestant and 27% say they are Catholic (Jones et al, 2002). Statistically speaking, approximately 51% of women between 18 and 44 in the United States identify themselves as Protestant and 28% as Catholics, which means that the abortion rates for these two groups are lower than that of women reporting other religious affiliations (Guttmacher Institute, 2008). Twenty-two percent of women seeking abortions report no religious affiliation and 8% report "other" affiliations, which may include Jews, Muslims, Buddhists, and Mormons, as well as other smaller religious groups (Jones et al, 2002). In the general population, only 16% of women between 18 and 44 report that they have no religious affiliation and 5% report other affiliations indicating that these two groups have abortion rates that are higher than that of Protestant and Catholic women.

Women's reasons for terminating a pregnancy vary, although over 70% of women report doing so out of concern for or responsibility to other people or because they cannot afford a baby at that time (Jones et al., 2008b). Other common reasons are related to an interruption of school or career, not wanting to be a single mother, or having already completed childbearing. These reasons underscore the important role of abortion in a woman's life course. For a young woman, an unwanted or mistimed birth may prevent her from pursuing her educational or career goals. For an older woman, an unwanted or mistimed birth may directly affect her ability to provide for children that she already has.

SHORT- AND LONG-TERM CONSEQUENCES

Abortion is a very safe surgical procedure when performed by a trained medical professional and under sanitary conditions. The risk of death associated with safe abortion is low and the risk of major complications is less than 1% (Grimes, 2006). The earlier in a pregnancy an abortion is performed, the safer the procedure; when an abortion is performed under 12 weeks gestation, the risk of death is 0.4 per 100,000 abortions, but that number dramatically increases to 8.9 deaths per 100,000 abortions when an abortion is performed at 21 weeks gestation or beyond (Bartlett et al., 2004). Fortunately, fewer than 2% of abortions are performed after 20 weeks gestation. The most common causes of abortion-related death are infection and hemorrhage, accounting for over 50% of deaths (Bartlett et al., 2004). On average, eight women each year die in the United States from induced abortion, compared with about 280 who die from pregnancy and childbirth, excluding abortion and ectopic pregnancy.

Since the early 1980s, researchers have investigated the long-term effects of voluntarily terminating a pregnancy. Most research evidence indicates that abortion is safe and carries little or no risk of fertility-related problems, cancer, or psychiatric disorders (Boonstra et al., 2006). Studies indicate that vacuum aspiration—the method most commonly used during first trimester abortions—poses virtually no long-term risks of future fertility-related problems, such as infertility, ectopic pregnancy, spontaneous abortion, or congenital malformation (Hogue et al., 1999). In 1996, a meta-analysis of several studies suggested that there was a significant positive association between abortion and breast cancer; but since then, several reviews by experts concluded that there is not a statistically significant association. In 2003, the National Institute of Health (NIH) declared that the evidence shows that "induced abortion is not associated with an increase in breast cancer risk."

One of the most contested and controversial abortion-related issues is the association between abortion and women's mental health. Opponents of abortion have claimed that abortion is bad for women's mental health and leads to negative psychological outcomes such as depression and anxiety. In 1987, at the request of President Ronald Reagan (1911–2004), Surgeon General C. Everett Koop (b. 1916) reviewed the evidence linking abortion to negative mental health outcomes and stated that he could not come to a conclusion because of the serious methodological flaws of the studies, but that he perceived psychological problems related to abortion to be "miniscule from a public health perspective" (Koop, 1989). Since that time, numerous studies have attempted to link abortion to a range of conditions, including psychiatric treatment, depression, anxiety, substance abuse, and death (Fergusson et al., 2006). Many studies, however, have serious methodological flaws (e.g., failure to take into account important preexisting psychological conditions and other important life factors) that make it impossible to infer any type of causal relationship (Boonstra et al., 2006).

Several well-designed research studies and reviews have found no significant association between abortion and women's long-term mental health (Bradshaw & Slade, 2003). Some of the most conclusive evidence comes from a large-scale, prospective cohort study of 13,000 women in the United Kingdom, which compared women who terminated a pregnancy to women who carried the pregnancy to term. The findings indicate no difference in the psychiatric outcomes between the two groups of women. (Gilchrist et al., 1995).

Although researchers have not found strong evidence linking abortion and women's long-term mental health, opponents of abortion have successfully created the concept of a "postabortion syndrome," suggesting that women who have abortions suffer from symptoms similar to combat veterans and victims of natural disasters, rape, and child abuse (Speckhard & Rue, 1992). As of 2008, postabortion syndrome is neither supported by empirical evidence, nor is it recognized by the American Psychological Association or the American Psychiatric Association. Nevertheless, many antiabortion researchers (and lay people) continue to attribute negative postabortion emotions to the single act of having an abortion instead of taking into consideration the multitude of factors that may affect a woman's emotional adjustment after an abortion, including social stigma, the unintended pregnancy itself, preexisting mental health conditions, and other life circumstances.

The decision to have an abortion is difficult and complex. It occurs in the often-stressful context of experiencing an unintended pregnancy. Sociological research indicates that perceived social support is directly related to feelings of well-being and may reduce or buffer against adverse consequences of a stressful life event (Major et al., 1990). Perceived social support is defined as information or actions (real or potential) leading individuals to believe that they are cared for, valued, or in a position to receive help when they need it. Several studies have found a positive relationship between perceived social support (from partner, family, and friends) and postabortion well-being; women who perceive their family and friends to be supportive of their decision consistently rate higher on measures of well-being than women who perceive their friends and family to be less than supportive (Major et al., 1997). Perceived social support may be particularly important for successful adjustment to abortion because of the strong moral sanctions against abortion in U.S. society. Family members' and friends' attitudes about abortion (as well as those of the general public) have the potential to influence a woman's perceptions of stigmatization, which may influence disclosure about abortion and access to social support.

Some women may feel guilt, shame, or embarrassment after having an abortion, but it is not yet understood whether these feelings are rooted in personal conflict about the abortion or in concerns about how others view her decision (i.e., feeling stigmatized by the abortion). The social stigma associated with abortion, much like stigma attached to other moral issues or behaviors, can have distressing consequences. For women, the stigmatization associated with abortion can confuse or delay an already challenging decision-making process, it can cause unnecessary guilt or remorse, and it can lead to feelings of alienation and isolation.

THE IMPACT OF ABORTION POLICY

Abortion is safe and legal in the United States and it is estimated that one out of every three American women will have at least one abortion in their reproductive lifetime. Despite the legal status and common occurrence, abortion remains extremely politicized with people defining themselves as either pro-choice or pro-life, positions that are often aligned with identifying oneself as a Democrat or Republican. Pro-choice individuals and reproductive rights advocates maintain that women have a fundamental right to decide to carry a pregnancy to term and that the government should not control a woman's right to choose. By contrast, opponents of abortion (often termed *pro-lifers*) usually believe that life begins at conception and that abortion is murder, and thus an immoral and illegal act. Given the controversial nature of abortion, it is sometimes portrayed as a statistically rare and potentially distressing event that requires excessive restrictions and regulations. This depiction can create a hostile environment that fosters judgment and criticism about women who choose to terminate an unwanted pregnancy, and may directly impact the life course of a woman who prefers to terminate an unintended pregnancy but does not have financial, geographic, or social resources to do so.

Having an abortion may also significantly influence a person's life course depending on their own lived experiences. The ability to decide when and how many children to have is crucial to achieving life goals and abortion policies that severely limit whether, when, and under what circumstances a woman may obtain an abortion have the potential to alter a woman or couple's personal, educational, and career goals. Highly restrictive policies that limit access to abortion (geographically and financially) may be particularly injurious to women with the fewest economic resources. Limited access to abortion may force women to carry unintended pregnancies to term, which makes it extremely difficult for women to rise out of poverty and make a better life for themselves and their families.

Conducting rigorous and scientifically objective research on abortion is difficult for several reasons: underreporting of abortion on surveys and questionnaires; stigmatization of the issue that prevents people from talking about it openly; and biased research intended to strengthen arguments in defense of one particular side of the abortion debate. Nonetheless, well-designed abortion research is critical to understanding the role and impact of abortion in women's lives.

BIBLIOGRAPHY

Bartlett, L. A., Berg, C. J., Shulman, H. B., Zane, S. B., Green, C.A., Whitehead, S., et al. (2004). Risk factors for legal induced abortion-related mortality in the United States. *Obstetrics & Gynecology, 103*(4), 729–737.

Boonstra, H., Gold, R. B., Richards, C. L., & Finer, L. (2006). *Abortion in women's lives.* New York: Guttmacher Institute.

Bradshaw, Z., & Slade, P. (2003). The effects of induced abortion on emotional experiences and relationships: A critical review of the literature. *Clinical Psychology Review, 23,* 929–958.

Fergusson, D. M., Horwood, L. J., & Ridder, E. M. (2006). Abortion in young women and subsequent mental health. *Journal of Child Psychology and Psychiatry, 47*(1), 16–24.

Finer, L., & Henshaw, S. K. (2005). *Estimates of U.S. abortion incidence in 2001 and 2002.* New York: Guttmacher Institute.

Finer, L. B., & Henshaw, S. K. (2006). Disparities in rates of unintended pregnancy in the United States, 1994 and 2001. *Perspectives on Sexual and Reproductive Health, 38*(2), 90–96.

Gilchrist, A. C., Hannaford, P. C., Frank, P., & Kay, C. R. (1995). Termination of pregnancy and psychiatric morbidity. *British Journal of Psychiatry, 167*(2), 243–248.

Grimes, D. A. (2006). Estimation of pregnancy-related mortality risk by pregnancy outcome, United States, 1991 to 1999. *American Journal of Obstetrics & Gynecology, 194*(1), 92–94.

Guttmacher Institute. (2008). *An overview of abortion in the United States.* Retrieved July 14, 2008, from http://www.guttmacher.org/media/presskits/2005/06/28/abortionoverview.html

Guttmacher Institute. (2008). *State policies in brief: An overview of abortion laws.* Retrieved July 14, 2008, from http://www.guttmacher.org/statecenter/spibs/spib_OAL.pdf

Hogue, C., Boardman, L., Scotland, N., & Peipert, J. (1999). Answering questions about long-term outcomes. In M. Paul, E. Lichtenberg, L. Borgatta, D. A. Grimes, & P. Stubblefield (Eds.), *A clinician's guide to medical and surgical abortion* (pp. 217–227). New York: Churchill Livingstone.

Jones, R. K., Darroch, J. E., & Henshaw, S. K. (2002). Patterns in the socioeconomic characteristics of women obtaining abortions in 2000–2001. *Perspectives on Sexual and Reproductive Health, 34*(5), 226–235.

Jones, R. K., Zolna, M. R., Henshaw, S. K., & Finer, L. B. (2008a). Abortion in the United States: Incidence and access to services, 2005. *Perspectives on Sexual and Reproductive Health, 40*(1), 6–16.

Jones, R. K., Frohwirth, L. F., & Moore, A. M. (2008b). "I would want to give my child, like, everything in the world": How issues of motherhood influence women who have abortions. *Journal of Family Issues, 29*(1), 79–99.

Koop, C. E. (1989). Letter to President Reagan concerning the health risks of induced abortion. *Medical and Psychological Impact of Abortion*, 68-71. Washington, DC: U.S. Government Printing Office.

Major, B., Cozzarelli, C., Sciacchitano, A. M., Cooper, M. L., Testa, M., & Mueller, P. M. (1990). Perceived social support, self-efficacy, and adjustment to abortion. *Journal of Personality and Social Psychology, 59*(3), 452–463.

Major, B., Zubek, J. M., Cooper, M. L., Cozzarelli, C., & Richards, C. (1997). Mixed messages: Implications of social conflict and social support within close relationships for adjustment to a stressful life event. *Journal of Personality and Social Psychology, 72*(6), 1349–1363.

Speckhard, A. C., & Rue, V. M. (1992). Postabortion syndrome: An emerging public health concern. *The Journal of Social Issues, 48*(3), 95–119.

Strauss, L. T., Gamble, S. B., Parker, W. Y., Cook, D. A., Zane, S. B., & Hamdan, S. (2007). Abortion surveillance—United States, 2004. *Morbidity and Mortality Weekly Review Surveillance Summaries, 56*, 1–33.

Kristen M. Shellenberg

ABSENT FATHERS

SEE Volume 1: *Child Custody and Support;* Volume 2: *Fatherhood; Noncustodial Parents.*

ACTIVITY PARTICIPATION, ADULTHOOD

SEE Volume 2: *Leisure and Travel, Adulthood; Time Use, Adulthood; Volunteering, Adulthood.*

ADOPTION

SEE Volume 2: *Adoptive Parents.*

ADOPTIVE PARENTS

Adoption is the transfer of parental rights and obligations to a person or persons other than the biological parents of a child. Ancient records, including those from Babylonia and China, show that the practice of adoption has existed in various forms throughout history. It has been utilized for reasons as diverse as ensuring family lineage and inheritance, strengthening political and military alliances, and promoting children's well-being. Although adults are sometimes adopted, the vast majority of adoptions today are of minor children for the purpose of family formation.

ADOPTIVE FAMILIES

Adoptive parents assume parental rights and responsibilities for a person who is not their biological offspring. In formal adoption, the parental rights of biological parents are legally severed and the courts oversee an official transfer of parental rights to the adoptive parents. Approximately 127,000 children were formally adopted in the United States during 2000–2001. Census 2000, the first U.S. census to collect data specifically on adopted children, found that there are more than 2.1 million adopted children in the United States, more than 1.6 million of whom were under age 18. According to some estimates, 2 to 4% of American families have an adopted child.

Married couples are the largest percentage of adopters, although adoption rates among unmarried couples and single people are increasing. Adoptive parents are generally older and have been married longer than biological parents. Rates of adoption of unrelated children are higher among Whites than African Americans or, particularly, Hispanics. They are also higher among those with higher levels of education and income. Adoptions of children already related to the adoptive parents before the adoption, however, appear to be higher among persons of color and those with lower levels of education and income. The overall rate of adoption among African Americans is historically higher than that of Whites.

The most common form of adoption (more than 40% of all domestic adoptions) is stepparent adoption. Under the law, a stepparent adoption occurs when the partner of one of the child's biological parents legally replaces the other biological parent as the second parent to the child. The most common scenario is when a biological parent remarries, although cohabiting heterosexual or same-sex partners may qualify in some cases.

Single adults, primarily women, are increasingly becoming adoptive parents. Although studies report outcomes among these adoptions that are comparable with two-parent adoptions, single-parent adopters may still encounter a preference for couple adopters among agency staff or biological mothers seeking to place a child for adoption. One result is that these single adopters may face lengthy waits or end up adopting children who may present particular parenting challenges, such as older, special-needs children. Some single adopters who desire a young child, and who have the financial means to do so, adopt internationally to shorten the wait and increase the likelihood of finding such a child.

Gay and lesbian couples are another kind of adoptive parent. No clear data exist about the number of gay and lesbian adoptive parents, but a small but growing research literature addresses their experiences and family well-being. Evidence suggests these adoptions are as successful in terms of forming well-adjusted, supportive families as adoptive families in general. However, gay and lesbian adoption seekers may still experience resistance by some adoption agency staff, statutory restrictions, or negative public perceptions.

In recent decades, rates of international adoption—that is, adoptions of children born outside the United States—have increased significantly. More than 13% of the adopted children recorded by the 2000 Census were adopted from other countries. The number of immigrant visas issued by the U.S. State Department for international adoptions tripled between 1990 and the mid-2000s. Prior to the 1990s, the majority of international adoptions by U.S. parents were of Asian children, largely from South Korea. By 2008 China, Guatemala, and Russia provided the largest number of children adopted internationally by American parents.

International adoptions have increased in popularity among Americans seeking to adopt infants, to avoid often lengthy waits for children in the United States and to minimize the possibility that birthparents will try to reclaim their child. Age restrictions for adoptive parents vary among countries and may provide more options than some U.S. agencies. Although many countries allow singles to adopt (particularly women), some do not allow same-sex couples to do so. International adoptions can also be expensive relative to domestic adoption, with costs sometimes ranging into the tens of thousands of dollars. In addition to any agency fees and travel costs for the child, adoptive parents may be required to make one or more trips to the country from which their child is being adopted. Children adopted internationally may also have health concerns related to lengthy stays in orphanages, traumas, or illnesses such as HIV/AIDS that add expenses. Whereas most children adopted internationally do well, preadoption experiences such as institutionalization may lead to long-term emotional and behavioral problems or learning deficits. Accordingly, adoptive parents are advised to address potential problems with appropriate pre- and post-adoption support.

ADOPTIVE PARENTS AND THE FAMILY LIFE COURSE

"Adoption is not a one-time event, but a life-long experience" (Palacios, 2006, p. 496). As such, Palacios adds, researchers and practitioners are increasingly taking a family life-course perspective in addressing adoptive families. The circumstances, composition, and experiences of these families vary widely. Some common themes of research on adoptive parents, however, can be identified.

Researchers have long been interested in the decisions, motivations, and preparations to adopt. Most parents adopt because of their love for children and their desire to parent. For some, the decision to adopt is made only after a diagnosis of infertility or failed attempts to become pregnant using assisted reproductive technologies. Adoptive parents experience the scrutiny of investigations and home studies to establish parental suitability as well as the potentially lengthy wait, financial costs, and uncertainties involved in adoption. Although most adoptive parents successfully overcome the challenges involved, this transitional stage can be a stressful time. From the initial phases of the adoption process onward, social supports are important in ameliorating stressors.

Other research has looked at adoptive parents' experiences and concerns. Adopting older children can be particularly stressful. Not only are these parents faced with the challenges of parenting an adolescent, they may be dealing with the child's history of negative experiences in his or her biological or foster family. The strength of parent–child bonding and attachment is a frequent concern, although rates of serious attachment disorders, such as the inability to form close emotional ties, appear to be low.

Most adoptions are successful; family members adjust well and stay together as a family unit. Post-adoption services may provide continued family supports after an adoption is finalized to help ensure this success. Such services may include support groups, access to case workers, and family therapy. Their availability and range varies widely by such factors as state, agency, provider accessibility, and cost. Additionally, adoptive parents may benefit from counseling throughout the adoption process. Counseling may help parents to deal with preadoption issues such as any emotions evoked by their fertility experience, adjustment to parenthood, dealing with moody teens, or other issues that might arise.

Some adoptions are not successful. Estimates suggest that a small percentage (perhaps 15% or less) of all adoption placements disrupt, meaning that the adoption is never finalized in court. Adoption dissolution, when a child is returned to state custody after a legal adoption, is even more rare. Adoptions of teens or of children who exhibit psychological or behavioral problems are most likely to disrupt. Case workers and post-adoption services and supports can be especially crucial in helping avoid disruption and dissolution. When adoptive parents divorce, adopted children are legally treated as biological children would be treated; however, some advocates argue that they may experience especially negative emotional impacts in such an event, reasoning that the adoptive children have already "lost" one set of parents (their biological parents), and this may compound feelings of loss and trauma.

PUBLIC POLICY AND ADOPTIVE PARENTING

Providing homes and post-adoption services for special-needs children have been emphasized in recent research and policy. *Special needs* children are often children in the foster care system who are considered hard to place because of their older age, disability or health issues, race or ethnicity, or wish to stay together with siblings. Research shows that most special-needs adoptions have satisfactory outcomes for both the child and the adoptive parents. However, some adoptive parents of special-needs children will encounter high levels of stress and children's behavioral or educational problems. They may especially benefit from specific support services. Child welfare systems continue to struggle with many policy issues directly related to special-needs adoption to include the provision of adoption subsidies and medical care, legal and process delays in placing children for adoption while they are younger and have spent less time and suffered less potential damage in the foster care system, and recruiting enough adoptive parents (particularly minorities) to meet the needs of children waiting to be adopted.

Although African American families have historically adopted at higher rates than Whites, the high number of African American children in the foster care system overwhelms the number of Black families willing to adopt. Research finds that children adopted interracially generally grow up well adjusted with no racial identity problems. Factors such as the age of the child when adopted and parenting quality have been shown to be more important to outcomes than the racial composition of the family. However, whether African American children should be adopted by White families has been the subject of more than three decades of sometimes contentious debate. In 1972 the National Association of Black Social Workers equated interracial adoption to cultural genocide. Child welfare advocates for the next two decades often supported intraracial placement. It was not until 1997 that federal legislation addressed this issue, prohibiting race from being the sole determining factor in adoption placement.

Recent decades have also seen debate over sharing adoptive familial relationships and information. Depending on the level of "openness" in an adoption, adoptive parents and children may have ongoing contact with the biological parent(s) (*open adoption*), they may share information with the birthparent(s) only through an intermediary such as a social worker (*mediated adoption*), or they may have little or no identifying information about birthparents (*closed adoption*). Closed adoption was widely practiced during the mid-20th century in an effort to protect adopted families from public scrutiny and stigmatization characteristic of the period. Social changes during the 1980s, fed by reduced stigma, growing research on negative effects of secrecy, and activism by birthparents and birth children trying to reunite led to increasingly open adoption practices. By 2000 various types of adoption registries had been established in over half of the states to facilitate the process of adopted children and their birthparents locating each other. Thus, adoptive parents and their children increasingly have access to information about, or a relationship with, the birthparents and can share pertinent information such as health and genetic history.

SEE ALSO Volume 1: *Adopted Children; Foster Care; Parent-Child Relationships, Childhood and Adolescence; Transition to Parenthood;* Volume 2: *Parent-Child Relationships, Adulthood.*

BIBLIOGRAPHY

Atwood, T. C., Allen, L. A., Ravenel, V. C., & Callahan, N. F. (Eds.). (2007). *Adoption factbook IV.* Washington, DC: National Council for Adoption. Available from www.adoptioncouncil.org/documents

Barth, R. P., & Berry, M. (1988). *Adoption and disruption: Rates, risks, and responses.* New York: Aldine de Gruyter.

Carp, E. W. (1998). *Family matters: Secrecy and disclosure in the history of adoption.* Cambridge, MA: Harvard University Press.

Child Welfare Information Gateway, U.S. Department of Health and Human Services, Administration for Children and Families, Children's Bureau. (2008). *Adoption.* Available from http://www.childwelfare.gov/adoption

Festinger, T. (2002). After adoption: Dissolution or permanence. *Child Welfare, 81,* 515–533.

Hill, R. B. (1977). *Informal adoption among Black families.* Washington, DC: National Urban League.

Kadushin, A. (1970). *Adopting older children.* New York: Columbia University.

Kreider, R. M. (2003). *Adopted children and stepchildren: 2000.* Census 2000 Special Report. Washington, DC: U.S. Census Bureau. Available from http://www.census.gov

Palacios, J. (2006). Psychological perspectives on adoption. In K. S. Stolley & V. L. Bullough (Eds.), *The Praeger handbook of adoption* (pp. 494–498). Westport, CT: Praeger.

Simon, R. J., & Altstein, H. (2002). *Adoption, race, and identity.* New Brunswick, NJ: Transaction Publishers.

Stolley, K. S. (1993). Statistics on adoption in the United States. *The Future of Children 3*(1), 26–42.

Stolley, K. S., & Bullough, V. L. (Eds.). (2006). *The Praeger handbook of adoption*. Westport, CT: Praeger.

U.S. Department of State. (2008). *Immigrant visas issued to orphans coming to U.S.* Available from http://www.travel.state.gov/family

Kathy Stolley

ADULT EDUCATION

SEE Volume 2: *Continuing Education.*

AFFIRMATIVE ACTION, IMPLICATIONS FOR ADULTS

SEE Volume 1: *Policy, Education;* Volume 2: *Policy, Employment; Racism/Race Discrimination; Sexism/Sex Discrimination;* Volume 3: *Ageism/Age Discrimination.*

AGENCY

Agency refers to the human capability to exert influence over one's functioning and the course of events by one's actions. The concept of agency is based on a view of human nature that has changed markedly over time. Early and medieval theological thought placed agentive power in a divine being. Following this, evolutionism relocated agentic power in environmental pressures acting on random gene mutations and reproductive assortment of new combinations of genes. This regulatory process is devoid of deliberate plans or purposes. The symbolic ability to comprehend, predict, and alter the course of events confers considerable functional advantages. The evolutionary emergence of language and cognitive capacities provided the means for supplanting aimless environmental selection with cognitive agency. Human forebears evolved into a conscious agentic species (Bandura, 2008). This advanced symbolizing capacity enabled humans to transcend the dictates of their immediate environment and made them unique in their power to shape their circumstances and life courses. Through cognitive self-guidance, humans can visualize futures that act on the present; construct, evaluate, and modify alternative courses of action to gain valued outcomes; and override environmental influences.

CORE PROPERTIES OF HUMAN AGENCY

There are several core properties of human agency (Bandura, 2006). One such property is intentionality. People form intentions that include action plans and strategies for realizing them (Bratman, 1999). The second property involves the temporal extension of agency through forethought. This includes more than future-directed plans. People set goals for themselves and foresee likely outcomes of prospective actions to guide and motivate their efforts anticipatorily. When projected over a long-term course on matters of value, a forethoughtful perspective provides direction, coherence, and meaning to one's life.

Self-reactiveness is the third agentic property. Agents are not only planners and forethinkers, they are also self-regulators. Having adopted an intention and action plan, one cannot simply sit back and wait for the appropriate performances to appear. The translation of plans into successful courses of action requires the self-management of thought processes; motivation to stick with chosen courses in the face of difficulties, setbacks, and uncertainties; and emotional states that can undermine self-regulatory efforts.

The fourth agentic property is self-reflection. People are not only agents of action, they are self-examiners of their own functioning. Through functional self-awareness, they reflect on their personal efficacy, the soundness of their thoughts and actions, the meaning of their pursuits, and can make corrective behavioral adjustments, if necessary, to change existing life course patterns (Bandura, 1986). The capability to reflect upon oneself and the adequacy of one's thoughts and actions is the most distinctly human core property of agency.

MODES OF AGENCY

People exercise their influence through different forms of agency—including personal, proxy, and collective agency (Bandura, 1997). In personal agency exercised individually, people bring their influence to bear on what they can control directly. However, in many spheres of functioning, people do not have direct control over conditions that affect their lives. In such cases, they exercise proxy agency. They do so by influencing others who have the resources, knowledge, and means to act on their behalf to secure the outcomes they desire. For example, children work through parents to get what they want, marital partners through spouses, employees through labor unions, and the general public through their elected officials. However, people often turn to others in areas of functioning where they can exercise direct control but choose not to because they have not developed the competencies to do so, they believe others can do it better, or they do not want to saddle themselves with the work demands, stressors, and onerous responsibilities that personal control requires.

People do not live their lives in social isolation. Many of the things they seek are achievable only by working together. In the exercise of collective agency, they pool their knowledge, skills, and resources, and act in concert to shape their future. In the collective mode of agency, participants have to achieve a unity of effort for a common cause within diverse self-interests. To do so they have to distribute and coordinate subfunctions across a variety of individuals.

Cultures that are individually oriented tend to favor self-initiative and the exercise of personal agency. Those that are collectively oriented place greater emphasis on group interests and collective forms of agency. However, cultures are internally diverse social systems, not monoliths. Diversity in lifestyles and ways of life demands calls for different forms of agentic practices. The distinctive blend of individual, proxy, and collective agency varies cross-culturally. But everyday functioning requires all three forms of agency to make it through the day wherever one lives.

SELF-EFFICACY FOUNDATION OF AGENCY

Among the mechanisms of human agency, none is more central or pervasive than beliefs of personal and collective efficacy (Bandura, 1997; Schwarzer, 1992). This core belief is the foundation of human agency. Unless people believe they can produce desired effects and forestall undesired ones by their actions, they have little incentive to act or to persevere in the face of difficulties. Whatever other factors serve as guides and motivators, they are rooted in the core belief that one has the power to affect changes by one's actions.

Belief in one's efficacy operates through its impact on cognitive, motivational, affective, and decisional processes. People of high efficacy set challenges for themselves and visualize success scenarios that provide positive guides for performance. Those who doubt their efficacy visualize failure scenarios and tend to dwell on things that can go wrong, which undermines performance. A major function of thought is to enable people to predict events and to exercise control over them. People of high efficacy show greater cognitive resourcefulness, strategic flexibility, and effectiveness in managing their environment.

Efficacy beliefs play a central role in the self-regulation of motivation as well. People of high perceived efficacy set motivating goals for themselves, expect their efforts to produce favorable results, and view obstacles as surmountable or as challenges that can be overcome. People's beliefs in their coping efficacy also affect the quality of their emotional life. Those who believe they can manage threats and adversities view them as less inimical, are less distressed by them, and act in ways that reduce their aversiveness, or neutralize them. People have to live with a psychic environment that is largely of their own making. Beliefs about coping efficacy facilitate control over perturbing and dejecting brooding over problems.

People are partly the products of their environments. By choosing their environments and the activities they engage in, people can have a hand in what they become. In self-development through choice processes, destinies are shaped by selection of environments known to cultivate valued potentialities and lifestyles.

INTERPLAY OF HUMAN AGENCY AND SOCIAL STRUCTURE

Personal agency operates within a broad network of socio-structural influences. These social systems are devised to organize, guide, and regulate human affairs in diverse spheres of life by authorized rules, sanctions, and enabling resources. The development of social systems and the way in which they exercise their influence is not disembodied from the behavior of individuals. People are contributors to their lived environment not just products of it.

Social systems are created and changed by human activity (Elder, 1994; Giddens, 1984), largely through the exercise of collective agency. The authorized rules and practices of social systems, in turn, influence human development and functioning. However, as already noted, in agentic transactions people are contributors to their life conditions, not merely conduits through which socio-structural influences exert their effects. These social influences operate, in large part, through psychological mechanisms. Hence, with the societal rule structures, there is a lot of personal variation in the interpretation, adoption, enforcement, circumvention, and opposition to societal prescriptions and sanctions.

EXERCISE OF AGENCY OVER THE LIFE COURSE

Different periods of the life course present new types of competency demands for successful functioning (Bandura, 1997). Changes in roles, aspirations, time perspective, and social systems over the course of life affect how people structure, regulate, and evaluate their lives. Infants' exploratory experiences, in which they see themselves produce effects by their actions, provide the initial basis for the development of a sense of agency (Kagan, 1981). Recognition of personal causation is socially enhanced by linking outcomes closely to an infant's actions, by using aids to channel the infant's attention when there is a temporal disconnect between their actions and the outcomes they are producing, and by heightening the salience and functional value of the outcomes.

There is also a good deal of intentional guidance in fostering young children's agentic capabilities. Parents create highly noticeable proximal effects for their children's actions, segment activities into manageable subskills, and provide their children with objects within their manipulative capabilities that enable them to produce desired outcomes. Through these mastery experiences, young children enlarge their repertoire of basic physical, social, linguistic, and cognitive skills for comprehending and managing the many challenges they encounter daily.

The initial efficacy experiences are centered mainly in the family. But as the growing child's social world expands into the larger community, peers become increasingly important in the formation of a child's sense of efficacy. In the context of peer relations, social comparison comes strongly into play in judging personal efficacy. During the crucial formative period of a child's life, the school functions as the primary agency for the cultivation and social validation of cognitive competencies essential for participating effectively in the larger society. Students' beliefs in their capabilities to regulate their learning activities and to master academic activities affect their academic aspirations, interests, and accomplishments (Pajares & Schunk, 2001).

As adolescents approach the demands of adulthood, they must learn to assume increasing responsibility for themselves in almost every aspect of life. This requires mastering many new skills and the ways of adult society. Learning how to deal with pubertal changes, emotionally invested partnerships, and sexuality becomes a matter of considerable importance. The task of choosing what educational or career paths to pursue also looms large during this period. These are but a few of the areas in which new competencies and self-beliefs of efficacy have to be developed (Pajares & Urdan, 2006). With growing independence during adolescence, some experimentation with risky behavior is not all that uncommon. Adolescents expand and strengthen their sense of efficacy by learning how to deal successfully with potentially troublesome matters in which they are unpracticed as well as with advantageous life conditions.

Adolescence has often been characterized as a period of psychosocial turmoil. While no period of life is ever free of problems, contrary to the stereotype of *storm and stress*, most adolescents negotiate the important transitions of this period without turbulent discord. The ease with which the transition from childhood to the demands of adulthood is made depends on the strength of personal efficacy built up through prior mastery experiences.

In young adulthood people have to learn to cope with many new demands arising from lasting partnerships, marital relationships, parenthood, and occupational careers (Bandura, 1997). Beginning a productive occupational career poses a major transitional challenge in early adulthood. Perceived self-efficacy shapes career paths (Lent, Brown, & Hackett, 1994) and how other evolving demands of young adulthood are managed. By the middle years people settle into established routines that stabilize their sense of personal efficacy in the major areas of functioning. However, the stability is shaky because life conditions do not remain static. Rapid technological and social changes constantly require adaptations calling for reappraisals of agentic capabilities.

The efficacy issues with advanced age center on further self-assessment and misappraisals of personal capabilities. Biological conceptions of aging focus extensively on declining abilities, as many physical capacities do decrease as people grow older. However, psychological functioning follows different trajectories of change for different abilities. Some improve, others remain stable, and still others decline (Baltes & Baltes, 1986). Gains in knowledge, skills, and expertise can compensate for some loss in physical reserve capacity. By its effects on proactive engagement in activities, perceived efficacy contributes to social, physical, and intellectual functioning, as well as to emotional well-being over the adult lifespan.

The course of aging is affected by the societal structures within which it occurs. Older people in the early 21st century are healthier, more knowledgeable and intellectually agile, and more proactively oriented toward life than previous generations. These changes are creating a structural lag in which people are growing older more efficaciously, but in which societal institutions and practices are slow in accommodating their expanded potentials (Riley, Kahn, & Foner, 1994). Hence, some of the declines in functioning with age result from divestment of the social and structural supports for it, as is the case of mandatory retirement and loss of roles that give meaning and purpose to one's life.

GROWING PRIVACY OF HUMAN AGENCY

The revolutionary advances in communications technology are transforming the nature, speed, reach, and loci of human transactions. These transformative changes are creating greater opportunities for people to more effectively shape the courses their lives take. In the past, for example, students' educational development was dependent on the quality of the schools to which they were assigned. Now they have the best libraries, museums, and multimedia instruction at their fingertips through the global Internet. They can educate themselves independently of time and place. The Internet technology similarly gives people a greater chance to participate in social and political activities in their own way at their own time. As these examples illustrate, the exercise of agency takes on added importance in this electronic era.

SEE ALSO Volume 1: *Bandura, Albert;* Volume 2: *Individuation/Standardization Debate; Social Structure/Social System.;* Volume 3: *Self.*

BIBLIOGRAPHY

Baltes, M. M., & Baltes, P. B. (Eds.). (1986). *The psychology of control and aging.* Hillsdale, NJ: Erlbaum.

Bandura, A. (1986). *Social foundations of thought and action: A social cognitive theory.* Englewood Cliffs, NJ: Prentice-Hall.

Bandura, A. (1997). *Self-efficacy: The exercise of control.* New York: Freeman.

Bandura, A. (2006). Toward a psychology of human agency. *Perspectives on Psychological Science, 1*(2), 164–180.

Bandura, A. (2008). The reconstrual of "free will" from the agentic perspective of social cognitive theory. In J. Baer, J. C. Kaufman, & R. F. Baumeister (Eds.), *Are we free? Psychology and free will* (pp. 86–127). New York: Oxford University Press.

Bratman, M.E. (1999). *Faces of intention: Selected essays on intention and agency.* New York: Cambridge University Press.

Elder, G. H., Jr. (1994). Time, human agency, and social change: Perspectives on the life course. *Social Psychology Quarterly, 57*(1), 4–15.

Giddens, A. (1984). *The constitution of society: Outline of the theory of structuration.* Cambridge, U.K.: Polity Press; Berkeley: University of California Press.

Kagan, J. (1981). *The second year: The emergence of self- awareness.* Cambridge, MA: Harvard University Press.

Lent, R., Brown, S., & Hackett, G. (1994). Toward a unifying social cognitive theory of career and academic interest, choice, and performance. *Journal of Vocational Behavior, 45,* 79–122.

Pajares, F., & Schunk, D. H. (2001). Self-beliefs and school success: Self-efficacy, self-concept, and school achievement. In R. J. Riding & S. G. Rayner (Eds), *Self-perception* (Vol. 2, pp. 239–265). Westport, CT: Ablex.

Pajares, F., & Urdan T. (Eds.). (2006). *Self-efficacy beliefs of adolescents* (Vol. 5). Greenwich, CT: Information Age Publishing.

Riley, M. W., Kahn, R. L., & Foner, A. (Eds.). (1994). *Age and structural lag: Society's failure to provide meaningful opportunities in work, family, and leisure.* New York: Wiley.

Schwarzer, R. (Ed.). (1992). *Self-efficacy: Thought control of action.* Washington, DC: Hemisphere.

Albert Bandura

AGGRESSION, ADULTHOOD

SEE Volume 2: *Crime and Victimization, Adulthood; Crime, Criminal Activity in Adulthood; Domestic Violence;* Volume 3: *Elder Abuse and Neglect.*

AIDS

Acquired immunodeficiency syndrome (AIDS) is a disease found worldwide that afflicts both adults and children, has a high degree of mortality, and affects the well-being of families, communities, and entire nations. AIDS is an infectious disease caused by a virus, human immunodeficiency virus (HIV). The virus destroys a person's immune system, thus allowing opportunistic infections to affect his or her body. HIV is found in semen, blood, and vaginal and cervical secretions, with the highest concentrations found in semen and blood. Unprotected vaginal or anal sex places people at a high risk of contracting HIV. AIDS is a fatal disease, and at present there is no cure or vaccine. Thus control of the global AIDS pandemic relies heavily on prevention education, often a formidable challenge.

The HIV and AIDS pandemic is centered in sub-Saharan Africa where it is devastating the population, killing adults in what should be the prime of their lives, and leaving millions of children—some of whom are infected themselves—without parents. Multiple generations in some families have HIV or AIDS in both developed and developing countries. The pandemic has existed since the early 1980s, and the disease itself, as well as the population changes brought about by AIDS deaths, has widespread implications for public health, human rights, development, and national security. HIV and AIDS have proven to be difficult to control through primary and secondary prevention efforts. Primary prevention aims to prevent uninfected individuals from becoming infected whereas secondary prevention seeks to prevent those already infected from infecting others.

Originally AIDS was not a disease that spanned the life course because of its high mortality. Individuals did not live with and experience the disease over their life course. In the early years of the epidemic, persons with HIV or AIDS would usually live 6 to 12 months at most, which led to a heavy demand for hospice care (Stine, 2004). In the early 21st century, advances in antiretroviral therapy for HIV and AIDS allow persons with access to this therapy to have an improved quality of life and increased life expectancy. In the United States, the average time from infection with HIV to an AIDS diagnosis without treatment is 11 years, and this period is longer with treatment (AVERT, 2008). Because of longer life expectancies and a lower death rate, there is less need for hospice care. Drug therapies allow HIV and AIDS to be managed over the life course in a manner similar to the management of chronic diseases. As a result, the HIV and AIDS population has aged over the course of the epidemic in the United States. As the HIV and AIDS population continues to age, there will be a greater need for long-term care. This pattern is specific to the United States and other developed countries in which there is better access to antiretroviral therapies than in sub-Saharan Africa.

AIDS has a long latency from the time of infection with HIV to the onset of symptoms. New AIDS diagnoses do not necessarily represent new infections because people may have actually had HIV for years prior to the onset of AIDS symptoms. This long latency has presented challenges for control because infected, asymptomatic persons may unknowingly infect others. It is estimated that about one-fourth of those infected with HIV do not know it (Macfarlane, 2008). Both primary and secondary prevention are important in the global control of HIV and AIDS.

TRANSMISSION OF HIV AND AIDS

Sexual transmission is the primary means by which people become infected with AIDS throughout the world. Symptoms (which were later retrospectively diagnosed as AIDS) first appeared in gay men in the United States in 1981 (Centers for Disease Control, 1981). From the beginning of the U.S. epidemic, gay men have comprised the largest group of cases. Although homosexual transmission remains the largest route of transmission in the United States, heterosexual transmission has grown over the years. Heterosexual transmission is the more common means of infection in other parts of the world.

Other transmission routes in the United States include infection from sharing drug-injection equipment, contaminated blood products (affecting hemophiliacs and transfusion recipients), contaminated organs (affecting transplant recipients), and needlestick injuries (affecting health care workers). Because blood and blood products have been screened for HIV since 1985, the incidence of cases among hemophiliacs and transfusion recipients is lower compared to the early years of the epidemic.

SOCIAL PATTERNING OF HIV AND AIDS

From the beginning of the epidemic, the majority of U.S. AIDS cases have been male, although women comprise an increasingly larger percentage of cases from heterosexual transmission (Macfarlane, 2008). Women are more vulnerable to HIV infection than men because there are high concentrations of HIV in semen and women have more mucosal area that is exposed for longer periods of time. Heterosexual transmission is the only category in which female cases exceed male cases. This gender difference has existed since the beginning of the epidemic. There is a close tie between transmission by sharing drug-injection equipment and heterosexual transmission, as many people infected through heterosexual transmission are female sex partners of male drug users. There is also a close tie between heterosexual transmission and perinatal transmission, because most infants with HIV or AIDS are infected by their mothers through perinatal transmission. Many infants perinatally infected with HIV, particularly those with access to antiretroviral therapy, have been able to reach adolescence and adulthood.

	Adults & children living with HIV	Adults & children newly infected with HIV	Adult prevalence [%] *	Adult & child deaths due to AIDS
Sub-Saharan Africa	24.7 million [21.8 – 27.7 million]	2.8 million [2.4 – 3.2 million]	5.9% [5.2% – 6.7%]	2.1 million [1.8 – 2.4 million]
Middle East & North Africa	460 000 [270 000 – 760 000]	68 000 [41 000 – 220 000]	0.2% [0.1% – 0.3%]	36 000 [20 000 – 60 000]
South and South-East Asia	7.8 million [5.2 – 12.0 million]	860 000 [550 000 – 2.3 million]	0.6% [0.4% – 1.0%]	590 000 [390 000 – 850 000]
East Asia	750 000 [460 000 – 1.2 million]	100 000 [56 000 – 300 000]	0.1% [<0.2%]	43 000 [26 000 – 64 000]
Latin America	1.7 million [1.3 – 2.5 million]	140 000 [100 000 – 410 000]	0.5% [0.4% – 1.2%]	65 000 [51 000 – 84 000]
Caribbean	250 000 [190 000 – 320 000]	27 000 [20 000 – 41 000]	1.2% [0.9% – 1.7%]	19 000 [14 000 – 25 000]
Eastern Europe & Central Asia	1.7 million [1.2 – 2.6 million]	270 000 [170 000 – 820 000]	0.9% [0.6% – 1.4%]	84 000 [58 000 – 120 000]
Western & Central Europe	740 000 [580 000 – 970 000]	22 000 [18 000 – 33 000]	0.3% [0.2% – 0.4%]	12 000 [<15 000]
North America	1.4 million [880 000 – 2.2 million]	43 000 [34 000 – 65 000]	0.8% [0.6% – 1.1%]	18 000 [11 000 – 26 000]
Oceania	81 000 [50 000 – 170 000]	7100 [3400 – 54 000]	0.4% [0.2% – 0.9%]	4000 [2300 – 6600]
TOTAL	39.5 million [34.1 – 47.1 million]	4.3 million [3.6 – 6.6 million]	1.0% [0.9% – 1.2%]	2.9 million [2.5 – 3.5 million]

* The proportion of adults [15 to 49 years of age] living with HIV in 2006, using 2006 population numbers. The ranges around the estimates in this table define the boundaries within which the actual numbers lie, based on the best available information.

Table 1. *Regional HIV and AIDS statistics and features, 2006.* CENGAGE LEARNING, GALE.

Worldwide, women account for 50% of total HIV and AIDS cases and 60% of cases in sub-Saharan Africa (Macfarlane, 2008). Female inequality, gender power relations, poverty, and economic dependence on men account for the gender balance in infection. Higher rates of sexually transmitted infections in sub-Saharan Africa also contribute to women's vulnerability. Women in sub-Saharan Africa comprise 75% of total female cases worldwide (Macfarlane, 2008). Incidence of AIDS has increased sharply among women and girls 13 years old and under worldwide. Condoms are a major strategy for the prevention and control of the sexual transmission of HIV and AIDS. However, because of gender power relations, women in sub-Saharan Africa are typically not in a strong position to ask their male partners to use condoms. Similarly, traditional heterosexual socialization that promotes promiscuity as a sign of masculinity interferes with safer sex advice to be monogamous. Men often have multiple sex partners, so a single infected man can infect several female partners. There is also a shortage of eligible male sex partners for women. This gender imbalance places women at great risk for HIV.

LIFE COURSE PATTERNS

Since AIDS was first identified in 1981, 65 million people have been infected with HIV and 25 million have died worldwide (Macfarlane, 2008). In the early 21st century 36.5 million people are living with HIV and 24.5 million of them (or 64%) are in sub-Saharan Africa, a region that comprises just 10% of the world's population (Macfarlane, 2008). In the United States more than one-half million people diagnosed with AIDS have died. A majority (around 69%) of these individuals did not live to the age of 45 (AVERT, 2008). In 2005 persons ages 25 to 44 accounted for 39% of the AIDS diagnoses and 41% of AIDS deaths in the United States (AVERT, 2008).

Because AIDS has always led to a high degree of premature mortality, it is associated with a high number of years of potential life lost. AIDS has drastically reduced life expectancy in many countries in sub-Saharan Africa, where the majority of HIV and AIDS cases are found. For example, more than one-third of adults in Botswana have HIV or AIDS. Life expectancy there has dropped from 74 before AIDS appeared to 39 in 2008 (Macfarlane, 2008). Projections for life expectancy in 2010 for nations highly affected by AIDS range from 27 in Botswana to 36 in South Africa, Malawi, and Rwanda (Stine, 2004). Botswana and South Africa will experience more deaths than births by 2010, meaning that populations will begin declining.

Worldwide, the majority of HIV and AIDS cases are adults, but children comprise a substantial number. An overwhelming majority of children with HIV or AIDS and children orphaned by AIDS live in sub-Saharan Africa.

The number of orphans there who have HIV or AIDS is expected to reach 25 million by 2010 (Macfarlane, 2008). Globally, the number of children living with HIV increased from 1.5 million in 2001 to 2.5 million in 2007 (Joint United Nations Programme on HIV/AIDS [UNAIDS], 2007). Although antiretroviral therapy has been available and has proven to be effective in preventing perinatal transmission in the United States and Europe, women in developing countries have not not had the same access to these therapies.

In terms of both prevention and care, inequality underlies the HIV and AIDS pandemic. Worldwide, HIV and AIDS disproportionately affect uneducated, impoverished, and disenfranchised populations. For example, a disproportionate number of U.S. HIV and AIDS cases are found among African Americans and Latinos (Macfarlane, 2008). Poverty, inequality, discrimination, racism, sexism, heterosexism, and ageism are important factors in the spread of the pandemic. Impoverished populations are consumed with daily survival needs such as food and shelter and, as a result, concern about their own risk for HIV may not be a priority in their lives. Unequal access to HIV or AIDS care and unequal quality of care also contribute to the pandemic's powerful impact

HIV AND AIDS RISK

About half of all new HIV infections worldwide are among young people aged between 15 and 24, a majority of whom are women (Card, Amarillas, Conner, Akers, Solomon, & DiClemente, 2007). In the United States, among gay men, younger age is strongly correlated with high-risk sexual behavior (i.e., unprotected anal sex). After a notable decline in U.S. HIV and AIDS cases beginning in 1993, cases began to rise again in 1999, particularly among young gay men. This increase was referred to as the *resurgent epidemic* or the *second wave*. Gay men in the current epidemic differ from those in the earlier wave because they did not have the experience of losing members of their peer group to HIV and AIDS, a common experience for gay men during the 1980s. The introduction of effective antiretroviral therapies in the mid-1990s caused some gay men to see the epidemic as less serious. As a consequence, they relapsed into unsafe behavior.

GENDER AND THE LIFE COURSE

Sociocultural factors play a role in young women's risk. Young women may become dependent on men as a way to achieve independence from their parents. They may become involved in relationships with older men whom they perceive as attractive because of the latter's greater status and wealth. These men, however, also are more sexually experienced and may present a higher risk for

HIV. Girls and young women in developing countries have limited access to education and jobs and may willingly initiate relationships with *sugar daddies*, that is, men who are much older, relatively well-off, and usually married (Card et al., 2007). Some girls may provide sex in order to earn money for school expenses or to help their families. Worldwide, young women's financial vulnerability creates challenges to HIV and AIDS prevention efforts.

In addition to sociocultural factors, physiologic factors play a role in young women's vulnerability to HIV and AIDS. Adolescent women are at heightened risk of HIV infection compared to older women because they have a larger zone of cervical ectopy and their vaginal mucosal lining is thinner. (Cervical ectopy is a condition whereby a small ring of cells extend beyond the normal border of the inner wall of the uterus to the neck of the uterus.) Their immature genital tract can also cause their cervixes to rip or tear during sex, heightening their vulnerability to HIV infection. In addition, vaginal secretions in adolescent women are not fully developed or functional and this physiologic immaturity may play a role in increasing young women's risk for HIV.

Women at the other end of the age spectrum are also vulnerable to HIV infection because of physiologic factors. Women over the age of 45 (perimenopausal women) are at heightened risk because of increased fragility of genital mucosa. In general, all factors, including infectious, traumatic, and hormonal, that impair genital mucosa may increase the risk of HIV transmission. Menopause is associated with a thinning of the vaginal lining and increased vaginal dryness. This can result in small tears and abrasions in the vaginal walls, thereby providing an entryway for HIV.

CAREGIVING ROLES AND ISSUES

HIV and AIDS raise complex caregiving issues. Although gay men have provided a great deal of informal AIDS care to one another, women also have served important caregiving roles. Mothers and sisters of gay men with HIV or AIDS, as well as infected women with children, have provided care for infected persons during the epidemic. Infected mothers often have to plan for the welfare of their children after their own death. Some of these children also are infected with HIV and thus have special needs. Infected mothers who rely on kinship care usually assign the care of their children to their mothers or sisters (or their children's aunts and grandmothers) (Campbell, 1999). In developed countries when informal or kinship care is not available, children will enter a more formal system of foster care. That system in the United States is already overburdened because of foster care needs of children whose parents are addicted to drugs, incarcerated, or dead.

In regions of sub-Saharan Africa, AIDS has taken such a toll that middle-aged adults are virtually absent in many communities. Older parents of adult children with HIV or AIDS often are caring for grandchildren, some of whom are also infected. In those cases when there are no grandparents to provide care, older siblings often provide care to young ones.

AGING AND AIDS

Most of the growth in U.S. HIV and AIDS cases among persons over 50 is because of the aging of persons with HIV and AIDS, rather than new infections. The number of mature adults with HIV and AIDS has grown because of the increasing time between infection, diagnosis, and death. Effective antiretroviral therapy is the primary reason for the growing number of people over 50 with HIV or AIDS. However, some growth in HIV and AIDS cases among persons over age 50 is due to people getting infected for the first time.

In the early years of the U.S. epidemic, most new cases among persons over 50 were caused by HIV-contaminated blood transfusions (Stine, 2004). In the early 21st century most cases are the result of sexual transmission. The number of older adults with HIV or AIDS from sexual transmission is expected to increase as the sexually liberated baby boom generation ages. Compared to previous generations, older people are staying healthier longer and are thus able to enjoy extended sex lives. Older adults are also able to remain sexually active because of hormone therapy and erectile dysfunction drugs. The growth in the baby boom population coincides with the growth in use of these drugs, thus creating a new target group for HIV and AIDS prevention strategies. Exposure to public health messages is critical for this population.

Older adults who have been in long-term relationships and who reenter the dating world after divorce or the death of a spouse may not be aware of how their own behavior puts them at risk for HIV. Because they were in a long-term relationship, they may not have been educated about HIV. Older postmenopausal women, no longer fearing pregnancy, may not think to use condoms for protection against sexually transmitted infections (STIs). A survey of sexual practices among older adults found that just 33% of those who were sexually active in the previous three months used condoms (Gorman, 2006).

In addition to older adults' own perceptions, society often views older persons as asexual. Thus older adults have not been targeted with HIV and AIDS prevention as much as younger age groups. The media have not featured stories about older adults with HIV or AIDS in comparison to stories about younger adults. Physicians and other medical providers may not think to discuss risks of HIV, AIDS, or other STIs with older patients as part of their routine health screening. Nationally, seniors in the United States make up less than 5% of those tested at government funded testing sites (Stine, 2004).

Older adults with HIV and AIDS may experience particular physical and psychological distress. Societal ageism may make the stigma of HIV and AIDS more intense for older adults. Once diagnosed with HIV or AIDS, older adults are less likely than younger age groups to seek out AIDS support groups or other forms of emotional support (Hooyman & Kiyak, 2008). Most of older adults' care comes from friends who also have HIV or AIDS (Shippy, 2007). Older adults with HIV and AIDS are more likely to live alone compared to their younger counterparts, which has important implications for their care (Poindexter & Emlet, 2006). There appears to be a high level of unmet emotional need among older adults with HIV or AIDS.

Although the introduction of antiretroviral therapy in the mid-1990s produced a new optimism, some persons with HIV or AIDS ironically experienced serious side effects more commonly found as age-related conditions in older persons—high blood pressure, heart disease, and diabetes (Stine, 2004). Symptoms of HIV and AIDS are also sometimes confused with the normal effects of aging, because symptoms of HIV and AIDS may mimic those of aging. Some adults may be managing chronic diseases associated with aging, causing them not to recognize symptoms as being associated with HIV or AIDS and to seek treatment. Such symptoms include general aches and pains, headaches, nerve pain, visual problems, chronic cough, lack of energy, loss of appetite and weight, and problems with short-term memory (Hooyman & Kiyak, 2008). Older adults' immune systems are less equipped to combat the effects of HIV, thus allowing the disease to take an accelerated clinical course. The decline in immune system function may explain why the time from infection with HIV to the onset of AIDS is shorter in older adults. In adults over 50, the average time is 5.7 years compared to 7.3 years in people under 50 (Emlet & Farkas, 2002). Older adults are twice as likely as young people to already have developed AIDS by the time that they test positive for HIV (Mugavero, Castellano, Edelman, & Hicks, 2007). Thus early diagnosis in older adults is critical.

FUTURE RESEARCH DIRECTIONS
Age-associated conditions in an aging HIV population present new research questions, such as whether age-associated conditions appear earlier in older adults with HIV or AIDS. Another research area involves interaction between antiretroviral regimens for HIV and treatments for age-associated conditions, particularly unwanted interaction between the two. There are relatively few studies of

how medications for high blood pressure, osteoporosis, and other age-related conditions interact with antiretroviral therapies (Karpiak, 2006). Moreover, clinical AIDS drug trials often exclude older adults precisely because of their age and other health problems. These are among the many challenging research issues in addressing the needs of an aging HIV and AIDS population.

AIDS POLICY ISSUES
A high priority in HIV and AIDS care policy is to assure that persons with HIV or AIDS in developing countries have the same access to antiretroviral drugs as those in developed countries. HIV and AIDS advocacy and activism will need to be unrelenting in its effort to provide this access.

There also are important policy implications of an aging HIV and AIDS population in developed nations. AIDS service organizations (ASOs) will need to retool and restructure services in order to reduce barriers in service delivery to this population. ASOs will need to increase their knowledge of age-related illnesses and the potential complications due to HIV and AIDS and its treatments. As the HIV population continues to age, more support services and long-term care for older adults with HIV or AIDS will be needed. When informal support systems are exhausted, more formal systems of care will be required to meet the needs of older persons with HIV or AIDS. More coordination between HIV and AIDS services and other services for older adults will be necessary for optimal service utilization.

In addition to HIV and AIDS care, the needs of older adults should be recognized in HIV and AIDS prevention education policy. The visibility of older persons with HIV or AIDS must increase and become a major focus of advocacy and activism. More targeted HIV and AIDS prevention education needs to be provided to sexually active older adults. Safer sex messages should continue to target younger persons at high risk for HIV and AIDS but should expand to include older persons at the other end of the age spectrum.

SEE ALSO Volume 2: *Health Differentials/Disparities, Adulthood; Sexual Activity, Adulthood;* Volume 3: *End of Life Decision-Making; Life Expectancy; Mortality.*

BIBLIOGRAPHY
AVERT. *AIDS statistics for USA by age.* Updated April 2, 2008. Retrieved April 4, 2008, from http://www.avert.org/usastata.htm

Campbell, C.A. (1999). *Women, families, and HIV/AIDS: A sociological perspective on the epidemic in America.* Cambridge, UK: Cambridge University Press.

Card, J., Amarillas, A., Conner, A., Akers, D., Solomon, J., & DiClemente, R.. (2007). *The complete HIV/AIDS teaching kit.* New York: Springer.

Centers for Disease Control. (1981, June 5). Pneumocystis pneumonia—Los Angeles. *Morbidity Mortality Weekly Report, 30*(21), 1–3.

Emlet, C.A., & Farkas, C.J. (2002). Correlates of service utilization among midlife and older adults with HIV/AIDS. *Journal of Aging and Health, 14*(3), 315–335.

Gorman, C. (2006, August 14). The graying of AIDS. *Time, 168*(7).

Havlik, R. (2007). Cardiovascular disease and HIV. *HIV Plus, 3,* 5–7 .

Hooyman, N.R., & Kiyak, H.A. (2008). *Social gerontology.* Boston: Pearson.

Joint United Nations Programme on HIV/AIDS (UNAIDS). (2007). 2007 *AIDS epidemic update: Global estimates for adults and children.* Retrieved April 4, 2008, from http://www.unaids.org/

Karpiak, S. (2006). Reality demands change: People over age 50 living with HIV continues to increase. *HIV Plus, 3,* 1–3.

Macfarlane, K. (Ed.). (2008). *Perspectives on diseases and disorders: AIDS.* Farmington Hills, MI: Thomson Gale.

Mugavero, M.J., Castellano, C., Edelman, D., & Hicks, C. (2007). Late diagnosis of HIV infection: The role of age and sex. *American Journal of Medicine, 120*(4), 370–373.

Poindexter, C.C., & Emlet, C.A. (2006). HIV-infected and HIV-affected older adults. In B. Berkman (Ed.), *Handbook of social work in health and aging.* New York: Oxford University Press.

Shippy, R.A. (2007). Who will care for them? *HIV Plus, 3,* 7–8.

Stine, G. (2004). *AIDS update 2004.* San Francisco: Pearson.

Carole A. Campbell

ALCOHOL USE, ADULTHOOD

SEE Volume 2: *Health Behaviors, Adulthood.*

ANDROPAUSE/MALE MENOPAUSE

Andropause, or male menopause, is a set of physical and emotional symptoms that are presumed to result from age-related declines in testosterone levels. Changing views of andropause over time reflect shifting cultural understandings of masculinity, aging, and sexuality. In the post-Viagra climate, with heightened public awareness of the risk of sexual decline with age, the notion of andropause as a widespread disorder has experienced a surge of scientific, commercial, and public interest (Marshall, 2006, 2007).

EARLY RESEARCH AND MEDICALIZATION

Research investigating the male climacteric and its treatment with testosterone first was reported in American medical journals in the 1930s and 1940s. The male climacteric was seen as clinically significant in only a small proportion of aging men and was attributed to a deficiency in the sex glands. Although sexual dysfunction was viewed as a key symptom of the disorder, it was not the main concern in treatment. Although potency treatment might inadvertently be stimulated by testosterone therapy, it was not to be given for this purpose, and at least one researcher suggested that "it is perhaps better for older men if this phase of the reaction does not result" (Werner 1945, p. 710).

The idea of a hormonally treatable male menopause gained little attention from mainstream medicine in subsequent years. Men's midlife problems were viewed as a period of emotional adjustment, or midlife crisis, not a medical problem (Featherstone & Hepworth, 1985, Hepworth & Featherstone, 1998). Only when sexuality reemerged as the key to men's midlife problems in the late 20th century was male menopause, or andropause, remedicalized, that is, conceptualized once again as a medical condition (Marshall, 2006). Since the late 1990s research journals, especially those which focus on urology and impotence, have featured articles on the diagnosis and treatment of andropause or androgen deficiency in aging males.

DEBATES

However, there is a significant gap between andropause as a symptom complex and androgen deficiency—or hypogondadism—as a biochemical state. Research on andropause and its treatment with testosterone remains controversial, and there is more disagreement than agreement on the definition, diagnosis, and treatment of this condition. Researchers and clinicians generally agree that many older men report symptoms such as erectile dysfunction, a decline in libido, and a decrease in strength and energy. They also agree that testosterone declines moderately and gradually as men age but that many men remain within the normal range for younger men.

More contentious are issues such as whether declining testosterone levels have medical implications, whether they are caused by confounding factors such as obesity and inactivity, whether testosterone supplements provide clear benefits, and, if so, whether the benefits outweigh the potential risks. Controversies also remain over how to best measure testosterone levels and how to define what normal levels might be (Bhasin, Cunningham, Hayes, Matsumoto, Snyder, Swerdloff, et al., 2006). Data from the Massachusetts Male Aging Study showed that low libido is a poor predictor of low testosterone levels

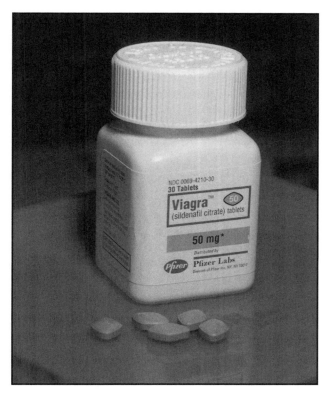

Viagra. *In the post-Viagra climate, with its heightened public awareness of the risk of sexual decline with aging, the notion of andropause as a widespread disorder has experienced a surge of scientific, commercial and public interest.* **AP IMAGES.**

(Travison, Morley, Araujo, O'Donnell, & McKinley, 2006). A meta-analysis suggested that the effects of testosterone supplementation on sexual function may be quite modest and may diminish over time (Isidori, Giannetta, Gianfrilli, Greco, Bonifacio, Aversa, et al., 2005). The National Institute of Health concluded that "the growth in testosterone's reputation and increased use... has outpaced the scientific evidence about its potential benefits and risks" (Liverman & Blazer 2004, p. 11).

A DEBATABLE CONSENSUS

Despite these debates, pharmaceutical companies actively promote an appearance of consensus on the existence, definition, and treatment protocols for clinical entities such as andropause, androgen deficiency in the aging male (ADAM), and symptomatic late-onset hypogonadism. These strategies make use of Web sites, health promotion brochures, articles written or sponsored by pharmaceutical manufacturers that are published in clinical journals, and support to professional and patient groups organized around those disorders. Solvay, the manufacturer of Androgel, a testosterone product, sponsored two studies of primary care physicians' knowledge about andropause (Anderson, Faulk-

ner, Cranor, Briley, Gevirtz, & Roberts, 2002; Pommerville & Zakus, 2006). The studies took as their premise assertions such as "Andropause is a testosterone deficiency that develops gradually over a number of years in all men aged 50 and over" (Anderson, Faulkner, Cranor, Briley, Gevirtz, & Roberts 2002, p. M796) and "The causes, symptoms and treatment options for andropause have been well documented" (Pommerville & Zakus 2006, p. 215) and proceeded to score primary care physicians' responses to questions about the nature of and treatment options for the disorder as correct or incorrect. In light of the lack of scientific consensus on these matters, an exercise of this type should be seen as being in the service of public relations rather than public health.

Mainstream media stories on andropause, usually prompted by press releases from pharmaceutical companies, follow a script suggesting that although the existence of male menopause was a subject of controversy in the past, there is now a scientific consensus that it is a real disorder that is treatable with hormone therapy. Stories of miraculous transformations (weight loss, muscle gain, better sex, better mood, renewed vigor) resulting from testosterone treatment overshadow any mention of possible risks and warnings from skeptical doctors and scientists. In many stories the libido-enhancing benefits of testosterone are added to the already accepted benefits of erectile drugs. Sexual decline and its pharmaceutical reversal are linked clearly with the general restoration of masculine vitality. Not unlike the "feminine forever" message promoted to women by those selling hormone replacement therapy in the 1960s, the newly remedicalized andropause reasserts a hormonal basis for masculinity. Thus, andropause reinvigorates the idea of biologically based lifelong sexual difference (Marshall & Katz, 2006).

Investigators from the Massachusetts Male Aging Study cautioned that viewing normal male aging as a medical problem raises both ethical and public health challenges, especially in the wake of what has been learned about the risks of hormone replacement therapy in women (O'Donnell, Araujo, & McKinley, 2004). It also raises theoretical challenges for those interested in the construction of gender across the life course. Gendered bodies are at the same time sexual bodies and aging bodies. The medicalization of andropause in the late 20th and early 21st centuries illustrates the manner in which such bodies are made and remade at the intersections of science and culture.

SEE ALSO Volume 2: *Menopause; Midlife Crises and Transitions.*

BIBLIOGRAPHY

Anderson, J. K., Faulkner, S., Cranor, C., Briley, J., Gevirtz, F., & Roberts, S. (2002). Andropause: Knowledge and perceptions among the general public and health care professionals. *Journal of Gerontology Series A: Biological Sciences and Medical Sciences, 57A,* M793–M796.

Bhasin, S., Cunningham, G. R., Hayes, F. J., Matsumoto, A. M., Snyder, P. J., Swerdloff, R.S., et al. (2006). Testosterone therapy in adult men with androgen deficiency syndromes: An Endocrine Society clinical practice guideline. *Journal of Clinical Endocrinology and Metabolism, 91*(6), 1995–2010.

Featherstone, M., & Hepworth, M. (1985). The male menopause: Lifestyle and sexuality. *Maturitas, 7*(3), 235–246.

Hepworth, M., & Featherstone, M. (1998). The male menopause: Lay accounts and the cultural reconstruction of midlife. In S. Nettleton & J. Watson (Eds.), *The body in everyday life* (pp. 276–301). London and New York: Routledge.

Isidori, A. M., Giannetta, E., Gianfrilli, D., Greco, E. A., Bonifacio, V., Aversa, A., et al. (2005). Effects of testosterone on sexual function in men: Results of a meta-analysis. *Clinical Endocrinology, 63*(4), 381–394.

Liverman, C. T., & Blazer, D. G. (Eds.). (2004). *Testosterone and aging: Clinical research directions.* Washington, DC: National Academies Press.

Marshall, B. L. (2006). The new virility: Viagra, male aging and sexual function. *Sexualities, 9*(3), 345–362.

Marshall, B. L. (2007). Climacteric redux? (Re)medicalizing the male menopause. *Men and Masculinities, 9*(4), 509–529.

Marshall, B. L., & Katz, S. (2006). From androgyny to androgens: Re-sexing the aging body. In T. M. Calasanti & K. F. Slevin (Eds.), *Age matters: Realigning feminist thinking* (pp.75-97). New York: Routledge.

O'Donnell, A.B., Araujo, A., & McKinlay, J. B. (2004). The health of normally aging men: The Massachusetts male aging study (1987–2004). *Experimental Gerontology, 39*(7), 975–984.

Pommerville, P. J., & Zakus, P. (2006). Andropause: Knowledge and awareness among primary care physicians in Victoria, BC, Canada. *Aging Male, 9*(4), 215–220.

Travison, T. G., Morley, J. E., Araujo, A. B., O'Donnell, A. B., & McKinlay, J. B. (2006). The relationship between libido and testosterone levels in aging men. *Journal of Clinical Endocrinology and Metabolism, 91*(7), 2509–2513.

Werner, A. (1945). The male climacteric (including therapy with testosterone propionate): Fifty-four cases. *Journal of the American Medical Association, 127*(12), 705–710.

Barbara L. Marshall

ATTRACTIVENESS, PHYSICAL

Physically attractive individuals exhibit facial and bodily characteristics that most people perceive as beautiful or handsome. Physical attractiveness influences whether a person is liked or loved irrespective of age or stage in the life course. People recall falling in love not only because of similar interests but also because of their partners' looks. According to the social psychologist Susan Sprecher (2006), passionate love—an intense craving for another—is fueled by physical attraction and is especially strong early in a relationship. In a review of many research studies, Alan Feingold (1990) found that men place a slightly higher value on physical attractiveness than women. Yet gender and sexual orientation have only a limited impact on what is desired in a hypothetical sexual partner. Heterosexual men and women, as well as gay men, all reveal that what they desire most in a short-term sexual partner is physical attractiveness. However, the *matching hypothesis*—that people will actually date persons who are similarly attractive to themselves—is also supported, especially over the length of a relationship.

PHYSICAL ATTRACTIVENESS, EVOLUTION, AND CULTURE

Scholars debate whether physical attractiveness is constant, composed of common elements, or variable over time and place. Based on the Darwinian idea of natural selection, evolutionary theorists believe that attributes thought to signify women's fertility, health, and innocence and men's power and social status are considered attractive across cultures. The psychologist Devendra Singh (2007) noted that what makes women physically attractive includes a low waist-to-hip ratio (e.g., hourglass shape), a combination of childlike (i.e., big eyes, small nose and chin, smooth skin) and sexually mature features (i.e., arched eyebrows, prominent cheekbones), and the overall symmetry of the features. Attractive men display a high waist-to-hip ratio, (i.e., straight torso), dominant features (i.e., prominent cheekbones, large chins) coupled with some "cute" features (i.e., large eyes and small nose), and facial symmetry. Studies in which volunteers rate the attractiveness of a set of faces find composite images (i.e., averaged features of many people) better looking than individual faces, especially when the faces of beauty contestants are averaged. Infants prefer pretty faces, indicated by data showing that they spend more time looking at them. This is important because infants have not yet internalized their cultures' preferences.

In contrast, cultural theorists, such as Lois Banner (1983), argue that physical attractiveness cannot be universal given that standards can and have changed over time. Banner showed that, in the United States, cultural preferences for women's shapes have been quite variable. For example, the ample and buxom "Gibson girl" of the late 1800s made heroic efforts to accentuate a tiny waist (i.e., with tightly laced corsets). Yet in the 1920s the ideal woman was thin, boyish (i.e., flat-chested and straight hips), and clothed in a loose-fitting, light dress. The standard for women in the United States in the early 21st century is a thin and well-muscled habitus that is still buxom. For men, the standards for body shape have varied less than those for women, although the value of muscularity has been variable. The early 21st century standard for men in the United States is trim and toned with discernable musculature.

COSMETIC SURGERY

Cosmetic surgery is a medical and business enterprise whose purpose is to reshape healthy facial and body parts to approximate cultural ideals more closely. Although the techniques used in cosmetic surgery are similar to those used in reconstructive surgery, the former are considered elective rather than medically necessary. Cosmetic procedures grew dramatically in the latter half of the 20th century. Deborah Sullivan (2001) attributed the huge increase between 1992 and 2002 in the number of procedures performed in the United States to several factors, including advances in medical technology, exposure to mass media that upholds a cultural ideal of youthful beauty, and greater public acceptance of cosmetic surgery. By 2003 cosmetic surgery makeover programs were a popular genre of reality television.

Those who take a positive view of cosmetic surgery emphasize how it can be a form of self-healing and personal empowerment. However, critics argue that cosmetic surgery is a symptom of a shallow, media-driven culture that promotes ageism and sexism (i.e., women make up between 80% and 90% of cosmetic surgery patients). The most common procedure performed in the early 2000s was liposuction (i.e., fat is removed from the abdomen, hips, neck, and other bodily areas). Other common procedures for women include breast augmentation, face lift, and thigh lift and, for men, hair restoration, pectoral implants, and rhinoplasty (i.e., nose job).

PHYSICAL ATTRACTIVENESS STEREOTYPING AND THE SELF-FULFILLING PROPHECY

Physical attractiveness confers social status because it triggers expectations that attractive individuals will have more advantageous outcomes. For example, attractive individuals are stereotyped as having greater leadership ability, more sociability, better mental health, greater marriageability, and even better intellectual ability than their less attractive counterparts. Sweeping, positive expectations for this range of capacities is known as the halo effect or the "what is beautiful is good" stereotype (see Dion, 1972, p. 285). However, Alice Eagly and colleagues (Eagly, Ashmore, Makhijani, & Longo, 1991) reviewed many research studies and found that

attractive people are also perceived as having less integrity, less modesty, poorer parenting abilities, and less concern for others than less attractive individuals. Furthermore, attractive women are sometimes stereotyped as incompetent whereas attractive men are not. Sometimes attractive women are believed to have obtained jobs because of their looks rather than their abilities.

Evidence suggests that attractive people are often treated better than unattractive and, in particular, overweight people (Brownell, Puhl, Schwartz, & Rudd 2005). For example, attractive people tend to obtain better jobs, earn more money, be more popular, and have more dates and sexual experiences than unattractive people. Conversely, attractive people experience less loneliness and social anxiety than unattractive people. Juries are usually more lenient toward attractive defendants—who are more likely to be found innocent and less likely to be sent to jail or made to serve long sentences—than unattractive ones. Yet harsher sentences may be issued if jurors perceive that a woman's beauty was used to commit a crime.

Although plenty of studies discuss the stereotyping of attractive people, there is less evidence that attractive individuals actually meet these expectations, a phenomenon known as a self-fulfilling prophecy. Judith Langlois and colleagues (2000) found that attractive people have excellent social skills. Anne Haas and Stanford Gregory (2005) argued that, because social attention is lavished on attractive children, they probably develop good social skills and enhanced interpersonal power. Negative stereotypes about overweight people (e.g., that they lack will power) tend to lower their self-esteem and increase their social anxiety.

PHYSICAL ATTRACTIVENESS OVER THE LIFE COURSE

Physical attractiveness has an impact on people's lives over the entire life course. Evidence that infants recognize beauty suggests that the social status conferred by attractiveness is activated early in life, especially when coupled with evidence that mothers pay more attention to attractive infants. Attractive infants are assumed to be more sociable and competent than less attractive infants, and the stereotyping continues into childhood. Dion (1972) found that bad behavior among attractive 7-year-old children was explained by their having a bad day, or what is known as a situational attribution. Conversely, bad behavior on the part of unattractive children was attributed to major dispositional character flaws.

Little girls are socialized to pay attention to their appearance, which becomes a part of their self-concept. These messages come from their parents, teachers, peers, mass media, and toys. In 2008, a popular toy marketed to 4- to 7-year-old girls were Bratz Babies who, much unlike real infants, wear sexy lingerie and full makeup that accentuates their exaggerated "babyface" features. The dolls also have long highlighted and styled hair, as well as painted finger- and toenails. The only indication that this toy does, indeed, represent a baby is a bottle of milk attached to a thick gold chain around her neck. Feminists believe that a toy that blurs the boundaries between babies and sexually viable women could be harmful. The concern is that girls might internalize the message that their value as women depends on their sexual attractiveness. Toys meant for little boys, on the other hand, draw on popular stereotypes about masculinity. Critics are concerned that representations of "real men" as big, tough, competitive, and warlike could stifle boys' developing nurturing qualities. For example, the popular G.I. Joe action figures have acquired giant muscles in the past 40 years, at the same time that boys have learned that steroids can be used to increase muscle mass.

Appearance takes on still more importance for adolescents and young adults. These are stages in the life course during which young people are susceptible to poor body image and eating disorders, including anorexia nervosa and bulimia nervosa for girls and body dysmorphic disorder for boys. Although the gap is closing, most people with eating disorders (about 85%) are female. It is not uncommon for adolescents to diet, which they are more likely to do if they view idealized and, often digitally altered, images, especially in fashion magazines. As people age, gender plays a role because women are expected to look ageless throughout their lives, which causes depression when their looks, and therefore their feelings of social worth, decline. However, rising rates of cosmetic surgery for men as well as women attest that men also feel cultural pressures to be attractive.

FUTURE DIRECTIONS FOR PHYSICAL ATTRACTIVENESS RESEARCH

Although a great deal is known about physical attractiveness and its effects on life chances, several important gaps remain. More cross-cultural and historical research is needed to understand how different groups of people have defined standards of physical attractiveness. In the United States and other developed societies, most research on physical attractiveness has been done with college-age convenience samples, which means that the results have less generalizability. Older and/or aging samples should be used to determine the relative importance and dimensions of attractiveness over time. In addition, more research is needed on the types and degrees of harm caused by the accentuated value of physical attractiveness in European and American cultures. Finally, there is a dearth of physical attractiveness research about men, racial/ethnic minorities, mature people, and gays and lesbians. For minorities, it remains unclear whether entry into the middle class is associated with assimilating to the physical attractiveness norms of the dominant culture (e.g., regarding body weight).

SEE ALSO Volume 2: *Body Image, Adulthood; Cultural Images, Adulthood; Obesity, Adulthood.*

BIBLIOGRAPHY

Banner, L. (1983). *American beauty.* New York: Knopf.

Brownell, K. D., Puhl, R. M., Schwartz, M. B., & Rudd, L. (Eds.). (2005). *Weight bias: Nature, consequences, and remedies.* New York: Guilford.

Dion, K. K. (1972). Physical attractiveness and evaluations of children's transgressions. *Journal of Personality and Social Psychology, 24,* 207–213.

Eagly, A. H., Ashmore, R. D., Makhijani, M. G., & Longo, L. C. (1991). What is beautiful is good, but … A meta-analytic review of research on the physical attractiveness stereotype. *Psychological Bulletin, 110,* 109–128.

Feingold, A. (1990). Gender differences in effects of physical attractiveness on romantic attraction: A comparison across five research paradigms. *Journal of Personality and Social Psychology, 59,* 981–993.

Haas, A., & Gregory, S. W. (2005). The impact of physical attractiveness on women's social status and interactional power. *Sociological Forum, 20,* 449–471.

Langlois, J. H., Kalakanis, L., Rubenstein, A. J., Larson, A., Hallan, M., & Smoot, M. (2000). Maxims or myths of beauty? A meta-analytic and theoretical review. *Psychological Bulletin, 126,* 390–423.

Sarwer, D. B., & Crerand, C. E. (2004). Body image and cosmetic medical treatments. *Body Image, 1,* 99–111.

Singh, D. (2007). Beauty is in the eye of the plastic surgeon: Waist-hip ratio (WHR) and women's attractiveness. *Personality and Individual Differences, 43,* 329–340.

Sprecher, S. (2006). Sexuality in close relationships. In P. Noller & J. A. Feeney (Eds.), *Close relationships: Functions, forms, and processes* (pp. 267–284). Hove, U.K.: Psychology Press/Taylor and Francis.

Sullivan, D. A. (2001). *Cosmetic surgery: The cutting edge of commercial medicine in America.* New Brunswick, NJ: Rutgers University Press.

Anne E. Haas

B

BABY BOOM COHORT

The term *baby boom* generally refers to a large, usually sudden, increase in the number of births in a population, after which the number of births declines and eventually stabilizes at a lower level. The higher fertility period may last only a few months or persist for a number of years. The birth cohorts born during a baby boom are large relative to those preceding and following them, and the overall population is larger than it would have been had the baby boom not occurred.

Baby boom is also used to refer specifically to the sustained increase in fertility rates experienced in the United States in the decades following World War II (1939–1945). Because of the substantial magnitude and long duration of the postwar baby boom, the baby boom cohorts (composed of *baby boomers* or *boomers*) are especially large relative to other birth cohorts in the U.S. population. Consequently, they have had an impact not only on the size of the population, but also on American social, economic, cultural, and political life.

DIMENSIONS OF THE U.S. BABY BOOM

The U.S. postwar baby boom began in 1946 and lasted until 1964. Following the technical definition of a baby boom, these start and end dates are based on quantitative assessments of postwar fertility trends and reflect the start of the significant fertility increase and the onset of significant decline (O'Connell, 2002). At times, commentators use other dates to demarcate the baby boom cohorts; however, such dates are usually based on criteria other than fertility trends, such as subjective judgments about the extent to which people born in various years share similar cultural or historic experiences.

The baby boom caught scholars and the public by surprise. In the 1930s American fertility rates were at a historic low, as the steady fertility decline that began in the 19th century was exacerbated by the economic difficulties of the Great Depression (1929–1939). In 1936 the total fertility rate (TFR), a measure used by researchers to gauge the level of fertility in a population, reached a prewar low of 2.15 children per woman (Heuser, 1976). The low levels of births led to both popular and scholarly concern about their potential consequences.

The increase in births between 1945 (TFR of 2.42) to 1946 (TFR of 2.86) surprised no one, as people made up births postponed during the war. However, the continuation of the upward trend and the persistence of the higher level for 19 years were indeed surprising. The TFR reached a maximum of 3.68 in 1957, 11 years after the war ended. Shortly thereafter, fertility began its steady decline and by 1964 had reached a TFR of 3.1. The years following are often called the *baby bust*, as fertility continued to decline, reaching a low in 1976 (TFR of 1.76) and then increasing slightly to hover around a TFR of 2.0 through the 1990s and 2000s (National Center for Health Statistics 2008). However, the term baby bust is something of a misnomer, as the decline represents a return to the long-term trend.

A key feature of the U.S. baby boom is that it was pervasive: Births increased among all racial, socioeconomic, and geographic groups. This pervasiveness within the United States was mirrored globally; many developed nations also experienced postwar baby booms (Morgan,

Note: Total fertility rate is the average number of children born per woman given current birth rates.

SOURCE: Coale and Zelnick 1963; Heuser 1976; National Center for Health Statistics 2008.

Figure 1. *Total Fertility Rate, United States 1918–2005.* CENGAGE LEARNING, GALE.

2003). The baby booms were especially pronounced in the United States, Canada (peak TFR of 3.93), and Australia (peak TFR of 3.51).

ORIGINS OF THE U.S. BABY BOOM

The proximate causes of any increase in the yearly number of births in a population are due to one of two things: either an increase in the number of women in the population who are "at risk" of childbearing or an increase in the likelihood that at-risk women will give birth. "At risk" means that one is a potential candidate to give birth; it typically refers to women between the ages of 15 and 45. Because of low fertility in the years prior to World War II, the absolute number of women of childbearing age actually declined during the baby boom. In other words, because birth rates were low in the late 1920s and 1930s, the number of women in their 20s and 30s during the mid-20th century was lower than at other points in recent history. This decline was offset somewhat by younger and more widespread marriage, so that a higher proportion of women were married and

thus at risk of childbearing (childbearing outside of marriage was rare in the United States at this time).

Thus the principal cause of the postwar baby boom was an increase in the likelihood that an at-risk woman would give birth in a given year. Such an increase may be due either to shifts in the *timing* of childbearing, such that women have children earlier rather than later, or to increases in the *total number* of children a woman bears. In a well-known analysis, demographer Norman Ryder (1980) showed that half of the increase in births in the postwar period was because of differences in timing, in particular to women having children at younger ages. The remainder of the increase was due to increases in the average number of children women bore over the life course. However, much of this second component was due to increases in the number of first and second births, not to increases in higher order births. In other words, the baby boom was not caused by some women having huge families, but by nearly all women having at least one, and probably two, children during the baby boom years. Earlier in the century, especially during the Depression, a higher proportion of women remained childless.

ENCYCLOPEDIA OF THE LIFE COURSE AND HUMAN DEVELOPMENT

As Ryder pointed out, identifying the proximate causes of the baby boom helped in the search for the fundamental causes, that is, the broad social and economic forces that encouraged couples who would have had children in any case to have them relatively young and couples who might have otherwise remained childless to have children. The most comprehensive answer to date was provided by sociologist Andrew Cherlin (1992), who argued that the postwar period was characterized by a temporary, and somewhat ahistorical, surge in familistic values. In combination with a robust economy, these values led most people to marry and have children at relatively young ages. For example, in the late 1950s and early 1960s, women typically married at age 19 and had their first child at age 20. Other scholars point to the introduction of the birth control pill in the early 1960s as a factor in the decline in births that heralded the end of the baby boom (Morgan, 2003).

THE BABY BOOM AND SOCIAL CHANGE

The baby boom cohorts have had a significant impact on American society. At the most basic level, the U.S. population is larger than it would have been had the baby boom not occurred, due both to the boomers and to the boomers' children (larger cohorts produce more offspring). Beyond this, however, the large size of the boomer cohorts relative to cohorts born before and after means that the boomers have had a profound effect on American social, economic, cultural, and political life.

First, accommodating these huge cohorts has been a recurrent issue in the United States and the concerns of the age group occupied by the boomers at a given time have tended to dominate national agendas. Thus, as the boomers moved through childhood, to young adulthood, and into midlife, institutions such as schools, universities, and then labor and housing markets were forced to adapt to larger numbers. More recently, a great deal of attention has been directed to the potential impact of aging boomers on the economy, the health care system, and social programs for the aged.

Second, the large size of the boomer cohorts has meant that members of these cohorts faced increased competition for valued resources (e.g., admission to college, or entry-level jobs). This theme was highlighted by economist Richard Easterlin (1980), in the "cohort size hypothesis," which stated that all else equal, the average economic and social outcomes of a cohort will vary inversely with its size. Easterlin suggested that larger cohorts experience, on average, lower quality and levels of education, delayed or forgone marriage and fertility, depressed wages, blocked job mobility, more spells of unemployment, higher levels of daily stress, life dissatisfaction, and even higher suicide rates. Although these patterns are true for the boomer cohort as a whole, the hypothesis has been criticized for ignoring variation within cohorts. In addition, outcomes among members of the smaller baby bust cohorts have not been significantly better than those among the boomers, as the hypothesis predicts. Diane Macunovich (2002) has reformulated Easterlin's hypothesis to account for the different experiences of boomers born early (between 1946 and 1956) and late (between 1957 and 1964).

Third, the boomers played a pivotal role in the social changes that transformed the life course in postwar America (Hughes & O'Rand, 2004). As their lives unfolded, the boomers experienced the profound changes that marked the decades between World War II and the millennium, including a series of economic shifts and shocks, the civil rights movement, a change in U.S. immigration policy that opened the doors to millions of newcomers, a revolution in cultural values that changed the way Americans thought about the individual and society, new perspectives on gender roles, and the sexual revolution. In general, the boomers did not initiate these changes, although they are sometimes credited for doing so. However, because the boomers encountered these shifting social contexts in young adulthood, their lives were disproportionately affected. The choices that boomers made about education, work, and family then reinforced some existing trends and set other new trends in motion. The boomers responded to historical change by living in new ways, ways that set patterns for successive cohorts.

The lives of the boomers thus embody the postwar transformation of American society. Their experiences show some continuity with those of persons born earlier in the century. More noticeable, however, are the ways in which the boomers' lives differ from the lives of their counterparts in earlier cohorts. A key feature distinguishing the baby boom cohorts from cohorts born previously is their heterogeneity: that is, the boomers' experiences are not just different from those of their predecessors; their experiences are different from each other's (Hughes & O'Rand, 2004). For example, boomers are more ethnically diverse than cohorts born previously, and this diversity has increased as immigration swelled the ranks of native-born boomers. Boomers are highly unequal in economic achievements and educational attainments. On nearly every measure, family life among boomers is more heterogeneous; boomers have a wide array of family histories and at midlife live in a wide variety of family situations. Thus the net effect of social change has been to diversify the life course.

The lives of the boomers show clearly how the life course is shaped by the intersection of individual and historical time. As noted above, scholars, policy makers, and the public are increasingly concerned about the impact of the aging of the large boomer cohorts. The heterogeneity of the boomer cohorts suggests that planning for these cohorts' old age will be challenging. At the same time, however, their prior history suggests that in later life the boomers will be able to adapt to social change.

SEE ALSO Volume 2: *Relative Cohort Size Hypothesis;* Volume 3: *Age, Period, Cohort Effects; Cohort; Population Aging.*

BIBLIOGRAPHY

Cherlin, A. J. (1992). *Marriage, divorce, remarriage.* Cambridge, MA: Harvard University Press.

Easterlin, R. A. (1980). *Birth and fortune: The impact of numbers on personal welfare.* New York: Basic Books.

Heuser, R. L. (1976). *Fertility tables for birth cohorts by color: United States, 1917–73.* Washington, DC: U.S. Government Printing Office.

Hughes, M. E., & O'Rand, A. M. (2004). *The lives and times of the baby boomers.* New York: Population Reference Bureau; Russell Sage Foundation.

Macunovich, D. J. (2002). *Birth quake: The baby boom and its aftershocks.* Chicago: University of Chicago Press.

Morgan, S. P. (2003). The post-World War II baby boom. In P. Demeny & G. McNicoll (Eds.), *Encyclopedia of population* (pp. 73–77). New York: Macmillan Reference.

National Center for Health Statistics. (2008). *Vital Statistics of the United States, 2002 Volume I, Natality, Internet Release.* Retrieved 4/2/2008, from http://www.cdc.gov/nchs/data/statab/natfinal2002.annvol1_07.pdf

O'Connell, M. (2002). Childbearing. In L. M. Casper & S. M. Bianchi (Eds.), *Continuity and change in the American family* (pp. 67–94). Thousand Oaks, CA: Sage.

Ryder, N. B. (1980). Components of temporal variation in American fertility. In R.W. Hiorns (Ed.), *Demographic patterns in developed societies* (pp. 15–54). London: Taylor & Francis.

Mary Elizabeth Hughes

BIRACIAL/MIXED RACE ADULTS

In the contemporary United States, multiracial, or mixed race, adults usually are defined as those who self-identify as having two or more racial origins. Although this concept seems straightforward, there are contradictory historical and popular images of what constitutes a mixed race person, and both the criteria for inclusion and the terminology used to describe multiracial populations vary.

DEFINING MULTIRACIAL IDENTITY

Sociologists have long recognized that racial identity is related to but conceptually distinct from racial ancestry. Racial ancestry is an objective measure of the geographic origins of a person's ancestors, whereas racial identities are largely subjective claims of membership within groups that are socially (rather than biologically) defined. Data collection on racial subpopulations usually favors the second concept. For example, the decennial census relies on individuals to identify their race by choosing from a set of listed categories. Individuals also may supply write-ins to provide additional detail (e.g., a specific tribe) or identify with an unlisted category. The 2000 Census was the first to allow multiple responses, and roughly 7 million persons, 4 million of whom were age 18 or older, reported two or more races. Only a small percentage (approximately 3%) of non-Hispanic Blacks and Whites claimed to be multiracial, but 14% of Asians, 40% of American Indians, and 54% of Pacific Islanders listed two or more races, as did 6.5% of Hispanics (people are asked about Hispanic ethnicity in a separate question). Regionally, one-fifth of Hawaiian residents self-identified as multiracial, and 5 to 12% of persons self-identified as multiracial in various counties in the Southwestern states (U.S. Census Bureau, 2001).

Although the official multiracial population includes everyone for whom two or more races are recorded on the census, mixed race persons commonly are viewed as the offspring of interracial unions. Both definitions are problematic. On the one hand, focusing only on persons who are recorded as multiracial excludes the offspring of interracial unions who self-identify or are classified as having only one race. For example, fewer than 55% of children from interracial households are recorded as biracial on the census (Jones & Smith, 2003), and many mixed race children come to identify with only one parent's race as they age (Harris & Sim, 2002); this leads to an even greater underreporting of multiracial ancestry among mixed race adults. On the other hand, limiting attention to the offspring of interracial parents excludes those whose parents are biracial or multiracial (and not necessarily intermarried) as well as those for whom parental data may be incomplete (e.g., single-parent households). Finally, neither definition expressly includes the tens of millions of persons who identify with contemporary racial and ethnic categories that are products of historically admixed (blended) populations (e.g., most Hispanics and Native Americans). As a result, standard reports of the multiracial population underestimate the number of Americans with a complex racial heritage.

A HISTORICAL PERSPECTIVE ON MULTIRACIAL IDENTITY

Although multiraciality often is viewed as a recent phenomenon, historians have noted a rich history of population blending that predates the founding of the United States. Admixed Spanish/indigenous peoples settled in what is now the American Southwest decades before the English landed at Jamestown in the early 17th century (Brading, 1993), and by the 19th century Americans of mixed African/European ancestry had a significant demographic presence in Charlestown, South Carolina; New Orleans; and other Southern cities (Davis, 1991), much like their modern-day equivalents in South Africa and Brazil (Fredrickson, 1981; Telles, 2006). As the 19th century progressed, there was a strong social backlash against intermarriage in the United States, culminating in the rise of antimiscegenation laws throughout the Jim Crow South. Efforts to enforce those bans led to radical changes in the classification of mixed race persons, whose identities were reassigned in accordance with "one drop" ideologies that classified persons with any African ancestry, visible or otherwise, as Black. Those efforts hid much of the nation's multiracial history both by shifting the balance of interracial unions to the illicit, often involuntary variety (Spencer, 2006) and by reallocating untold numbers and future generations of multiracial persons to either the Black or the White community (Piper, 1992).

With the rise of the "color line," multiraciality vanished from American racial consciousness. Before the changes on the 2000 Census there had been few efforts to count persons of mixed ancestry. The 1930 Census was the last to use the mulatto category, which was specifically for persons of mixed African/European heritage. The other major source of diversity—immigration—also fell from the historical highs set in the first two decades of the 20th century to a near trickle after the restrictive quotas set by the National Origins Act of 1924 (Massey, 2002). With the absorption of the children of the Southern and Eastern Europeans who immigrated at the turn of the century, the United States became a predominantly "White" nation with a small (approximately 10%) Black minority, at least according to the official record.

THE OFFICIAL RETURN OF MULTIRACIAL IDENTITY

The situation changed dramatically in the decades after 1970, spurred by liberal immigration reform in the 1960s and the Supreme Court ban on antimiscegenation statutes in the landmark *Loving v. Virginia* ruling. The elimination of legal restrictions coincided with the growing acceptance of interracial unions, and rates of intermarriage for all racial and ethnic groups (Asians and Hispanics in particular) began to trend upward (Qian & Lichter, 2007). These trends have contributed to an increasingly diverse American population and a growing number of children and young adults who claim multiple racial origins.

The official statistical record was slow to record these changes, however. The census and most surveys continued to measure race with mutually exclusive categories despite growing evidence that racial boundaries had become blurred. Defying explicit instructions not to do so, more than 1 million Americans marked or wrote in multiple races on the 1990 Census (Office of Management and Budget, 1995), and during the ensuing decade a small but vocal coalition of multiracial and multiethnic advocacy groups sought and ultimately secured a place for mixed race persons within the federal statistical system (Williams, 2005), which was amended to allow individuals to "mark all races that apply," starting with the 2000 Census and later expanding to other national data sources (Office of Management and Budget, 1997).

With the option to report multiple races, there were reasons to expect that a large number of persons would choose to do so. First, Hispanics had become a sizable and fast-growing panethnic group, and their largely *mestizo* (mixed) heritage seemed difficult to reconcile with mutually exclusive racial categories (Moore, 1976). Second, the population of persons reporting indigenous ancestry on the 1990 Census had ballooned to just under 9 million—nearly five times the number who reported their race as American Indian (1.8 million)—sending a clear signal that the vast majority of persons with indigenous ancestry were of mixed descent (Nagel, 1996; Snipp, 1997). Third, in a striking divergence from the one drop ideology of the recent past, multiraciality had become an increasingly prominent fixture in popular culture. From Keanu Reeves to Tiger Woods and from Halle Berry to Barack Obama, some of the most widely recognized and celebrated Americans proudly acknowledge the complexity of their racial origins.

Although these factors imply that the number of Americans who could have claimed multiple races numbered in the tens of millions, there were indications that the actual count would fall short of those expectations, even substantially, long before the 2000 Census was conducted. Civil rights organizations opposed a stand-alone multiracial category, and Republican-sponsored bills to add an item of that type to the census were defeated. As Kimberly Williams (2005) showed, minority leaders feared that multiple racial identities would reduce the counts and even undermine the legitimacy of their constituencies. Because the government uses census counts to draw electoral districts, allocate Congressional seats, help monitor and enforce civil rights, and provide billions in federal funding to local governments and municipalities, any changes that threatened to reduce the (notoriously undercounted) headcount of minorities even further would not be welcome. Many viewed with suspicion the endorsements of an ostensibly progressive multiracial category by leading conservatives, some of whom expressly championed its existence as proof that race-attentive policy had become unnecessary and unenforceable. The most telling preview of things to come was given by Charles Hirschman, Richard Alba, and Reynolds Farley (2000), who analyzed data from a census pretest that included different multiracial response options. The authors noted that only 1.5 to 2% of respondents reported multiple races, leading them to conclude that the new format probably would have little impact on the racial composition of the United States as a whole.

FINDINGS FROM THE 2000 CENSUS AND 2006 AMERICAN COMMUNITY SURVEY

Their predictions were confirmed when the 2000 Census figures were released and especially when the original count of 7 million was revised downward after a large overcount of multiracial persons was discovered (U.S. Census Bureau, 2005). Later intercensal estimates showed little if any growth in the population of persons reporting two or more races between 2000 and 2006 despite an overall increase of nearly 20 million (mostly minority) persons during that period. As a result, the multiracial population of 6.1 million in the 2006 American Community Survey was nearly 1 million lower than had been enumerated in the census six years earlier (U.S. Census Bureau, 2007).

This trend, like the "disappearance" of mixed-race communities in the nineteenth and early twentieth centuries, cannot be explained by traditional demographic forces such as mortality, fertility, migration, and marriage rates. There is no evidence that interracial marriage declined appreciably in those years or any signs of excessive mortality or emigration among multiracial persons. In fact, every racial and ethnic group grew between 2000 and 2006, especially Asians and Hispanics, who are disproportionately multiracial. The idea that the mixed race population has experienced little if any growth suggests that reluctance to report multiple races has not abated.

Consistent with the perspective that racial identities are sociohistorical constructs, the underreporting of multiple racial origins at once reifies long-held, socially meaningful categories and discredits the notion that those categories represent discrete races with clear boundaries and separate lineages. However, although the lines between racial groups remain blurry, many racial disparities remain. It is certainly telling that even historically fluid and anthropologically suspect racial categories are correlated with so many contemporary life outcomes. Without further reductions in the social and economic inequities that reinforce the differences between racial groups, multiraciality is unlikely to dis-

place discrete racial categorization even if that categorization persists at the expense of nuance and historical accuracy.

SEE ALSO Volume 1: *Socialization, Race;* Volume 2: *Ethnic and Racial Identity; Mate Selection; Racism/ Race Discrimination.*

BIBLIOGRAPHY

Brading, D. A. (1993). *The first America: The Spanish monarchy, Creole patriots, and the liberal state, 1492–1867.* Cambridge, U.K.: Cambridge University Press.

Davis, F. J. (1991). *Who is Black: One nation's definition.* University Park: Pennsylvania State University Press.

Fredrickson, G. M. (1981). *White supremacy: A comparative study in American and South African history.* New York: Oxford University Press.

Harris, D. R., & Sim, J. J. (2002). Who is multiracial? Assessing the complexity of lived race. *American Sociological Review, 67*(4), 614–627.

Hirschman, C., Alba, R., & Farley, R. (2000). The meaning and measurement of race in the U.S. Census: Glimpses into the future. *Demography, 37*(3), 381–393.

Jones, N. A., & Smith, A. S. (2003, May). *Who is multiracial? Exploring the complexities and challenges associated with identifying the two or more races population in Census 2000.* Paper presented at the annual meeting of the Population Association of America, Minneapolis, MN.

Massey, D. S. (2002). The new immigration and ethnicity in the United States. In N. A. Denton & S. E. Tolnay (Eds.), *American diversity: A demographic challenge for the twenty-first century.* Albany: State University of New York Press.

Moore, J. W. (1976). *Mexican Americans.* (2nd ed.). Englewood Cliffs, NJ: Prentice-Hall.

Nagel, J. (1996). *American Indian ethnic renewal: Red power and the resurgence of identity and culture.* New York: Oxford University Press.

Office of Management and Budget. (1995). Standards for the classification of federal data on race and ethnicity. *Federal Register,* August 28 (60 FR 44674–44693).

Office of Management and Budget. (1997). Revisions to the standards for the classification of federal data on race and ethnicity. *Federal Register,* October 30 (62 FR 58782–58790).

Piper, A. (1992). Passing for White, passing for Black. *Transition, 58,* 4–32.

Prewitt, K. (2005). Racial classification in America: Where do we go from here? *Daedalus, 134*(1), 5–17.

Qian, Z., & Lichter, D. T. (2007). Social boundaries and marital assimilation: Interpreting trends in racial and ethnic intermarriage. *American Sociological Review 72,* 68–94.

Snipp, C. M. (1997). Some observations about racial boundaries and the experiences of American Indians. *Ethnic and Racial Studies 20*(4), 667–689.

Spencer, R. (2006). New racial identities, old arguments: Continuing biological reification. In D. L. Brunsma (Ed.), *Mixed messages: Multiracial identities in the "color blind" era* (pp. 83–102). Boulder CO: Lynne Rienner.

Telles, E. E. (2006). *Race in another America: The significance of skin color in Brazil.* Princeton, NJ: Princeton University Press.

U.S. Census Bureau. (2001). *The two or more races population: 2000*. Retrieved May 13, 2008, from http://www.census.gov/prod/

U.S. Census Bureau. (2005). *Notes and errata: 2000 census of population and housing*. Retrieved May 13, 2008, from http://www.census.gov/prod

U.S. Census Bureau. (2006). *2006 American Community Survey*. Retrieved May 13, 2008, from http://factfinder.census.gov/servlet

Williams, K. M. (2005). Multiracialism and the civil rights future. *Daedalus, 134*(1), 53–60.

Anthony Daniel Perez

BIRTH CONTROL

In its broadest scientific scope, birth control may be defined as any attempt to limit the number or control the spacing of births. In this sense, birth control includes a wide variety of modern contraceptive technologies and traditional nontechnological contraceptive methods, male and female sterilization, as well as the postconception birth control methods of abortion and infanticide. Modern contraceptives generally refer to technological methods, from condoms to birth control pills; traditional contraceptives generally refer to nontechnological methods, particularly withdrawal (ejaculation outside the vagina) and the rhythm method (which tries to determine women's fertile periods and avoid intercourse during those times). Although the role of postconception methods of birth control remains significant in both developed and developing nations, this entry will focus solely on birth control methods designed to prevent conception (i.e., contraception).

It should be noted that in common American parlance, birth control often connotes "the pill," whereas contraception connotes condoms or contraceptive technologies. Although the distinction between modern and traditional methods remains important in the study of birth control, the most important distinction in the study of contraceptive technologies is between barrier and hormonal or intrauterine methods of contraception. Barrier methods include condoms, diaphragms, and spermicidal agents and attempt to create a physical barrier between the sperm and the egg to prevent conception. They are coitus dependent, meaning that they are only used during and near coitus (i.e., sexual intercourse), and they are characterized by moderately high efficacy levels in the prevention of pregnancy, although male and female condoms offer extremely effective prevention against sexually transmitted infections (STIs).

Hormonal and intrauterine methods of contraception include oral contraceptive pills (OCPs) and intrauterine devices (IUDs) and are methods that attempt to suppress the release of eggs or create an inhospitable uterine environment for an embryo's development. These methods are used independently of coitus, meaning that they are used essentially at all times, and they are characterized by extremely high efficacy levels in the prevention of pregnancy but offer no protection against STIs. As fertility rates around the world have plummeted, contraception has become a normal part of adolescents' and adults' lives in many countries; meanwhile, fears about the spread of HIV have made condom use a major public health concern.

TRENDS IN BIRTH CONTROL USE ACROSS TIME

Attempts at birth control have been made since ancient times. Such attempts included lambskin condoms and tortoiseshell diaphragms. By far the most successful of these premodern methods was withdrawal, which was an approved Islamic practice for centuries (Santow, 1995). Demographers believe that the first stage of the demographic transition in Europe, the period when birth rates declined sharply, was accomplished primarily through the use of withdrawal. By the late 1800s early versions of condoms and diaphragms had been invented, but the historical accounts suggest that the early formulations of these methods were awkward and that their use was not widespread because of physical discomfort and strong social stigma; the more contemporary versions of these contraceptives were not used until the 1930s.

The modern contraceptive era really began in the early 1960s with the introduction of the OCP, followed several years later by the development of the copper IUD. OCPs, IUDs, condoms, and diaphragms remained the primary methods of contraception from the 1960s to the 1980s. However, since the early 1990s, there has been a proliferation of birth control methods, including new OCP and IUD formulations, as well as hormonal birth control delivery through a patch, a ring, shots, and implants. Emergency contraception (popularly known as "the morning after pill") also emerged in the late 1990s as a method that women could take up to 78 hours after unprotected sex to prevent pregnancy.

Male hormonal methods have been in development for years, but at this writing, none are currently available on the market. Since the 1980s the HIV and AIDS crisis around the world has increased the desirability of condoms as a method of protection and prompted the development of a variety of improved condoms. Among these new condoms are female condoms, which are condoms that are inserted into the vagina and intended to provide a female-controlled method of STI prevention. Unfortunately, their successful use requires male cooperation, which may reduce their usefulness for women. Male condoms remain the standard method of STI prevention. Because male and female condoms possess the dual capacity to prevent pregnancy and STIs, encouraging the use of condoms has become a major public health priority. In order to promote a greater variety of methods of both disease and pregnancy prevention, researchers have been pursuing the development of female-controlled vaginal microbicidal agents, which seek to kill sperm to prevent conception and disease; unfortunately, initial trials have not been promising in effectiveness and women's willingness to use them.

Access to OCPs and IUDs varied greatly among nations for decades, with many predominantly Catholic countries, such as Spain and Italy, not legalizing them until the late 1970s. The last highly developed country to legalize OCPs was Japan, which did so in 1999. However, dates of legalization often do not correspond directly with dates of widespread access. The United States, for instance, legalized OCPs in 1961 but continued to restrict unmarried women's access to them until 1972 when a Supreme Court ruling assured access. Although widespread use of hormonal or intrauterine methods is often still very limited in many developing countries, most new birth control methods—including the first OCPs—were first tested in developing countries.

As of the early 21st century, the most popular method of birth control worldwide is female sterilization, followed by the IUD, although there is significant variation by country. In the United States, for example, the most popular form of birth control is female sterilization, followed closely by OCPs; the pattern is similar in Latin America. Asia, dominated by the contraceptive patterns of China, shows a strong preference for female sterilization and IUDs but not OCPs. Although contraceptive use is uncommon in much of Africa, preference patterns there resemble those in Europe; on both continents, female sterilization is rare, and the favored methods are OCPs and IUDs.

Hormonal or intrauterine methods of birth control are distinguished by their extremely high rates of effectiveness in preventing pregnancy, their independence from coitus, their feminine control, and their medical supervision. In developed countries, where these methods are widely used, the combination of these factors has resulted in women experiencing an increase in control over their reproductive health, while producing a simultaneous increase in medical surveillance over women's bodies. OCPs are generally considered essential in propelling the *sexual revolution* in developed countries during the 1960s and 1970s and disconnecting sexual desire from pregnancy and childbearing, which had traditionally been closely linked, particularly through the institution of marriage. Prior to the post–World War II (1939–1945) baby boom, family size had been steadily declining, and the decline continued after the introduction of hormonal

and intrauterine methods. Scholars generally agree that these contraceptive methods played a significant role in this family size decline but disagree about how large that role really was.

Although the role of hormonal and intrauterine methods in creating smaller families is debatable, the widespread use of these methods undoubtedly helped to create the expectation that the timing and number of births could be easily controlled. This expectation, in turn, allowed women to enter the labor market seeking not merely jobs but careers—that is, jobs that required extensive education and training and that assume a trajectory through promotions. In the early 21st century, many European countries are facing average fertility levels that are well below replacement levels (that is, below 2.1 births per woman), a situation that would probably be impossible without the widespread use of hormonal and intrauterine birth control.

The effect of hormonal and intrauterine birth control methods has been slower to reach many developing countries, where demand for smaller families is often lower and where medical institutions are often poorly equipped to meet existing demands. Scholars continue to debate the extent to which economic development and urbanization drive the demand for smaller families and birth control versus the extent to which smaller families and birth control permit greater development and urbanization. China continues to be the most famous case study for examining this question. Through the imposition of a system of major governmental rewards and penalties, China successfully created a massive demand for contraception (particularly the IUD) and overhauled normative values about family size. The centerpiece of China's population policy is its one-child policy, which penalizes most couples for having more than one child. Although China's population control program would probably not have been possible without hormonal and intrauterine contraceptive technologies, most demographers agree that the existence of birth control cannot in and of itself create a demand for smaller family sizes. Rather, the individual, economic, social, or cultural pressures for family planning must first be in place before birth control is likely to be used. Yet birth control is not always used to create smaller families. Researchers in Africa have documented many cases in which modern birth control methods are desired as a means to accomplish careful birth spacing, which in turn is viewed as a means to attain *larger*, not smaller, family sizes.

BIRTH CONTROL USAGE AND EFFECTIVENESS

Evaluating the efficacy of birth control methods in preventing pregnancy (and to a lesser extent, in curbing

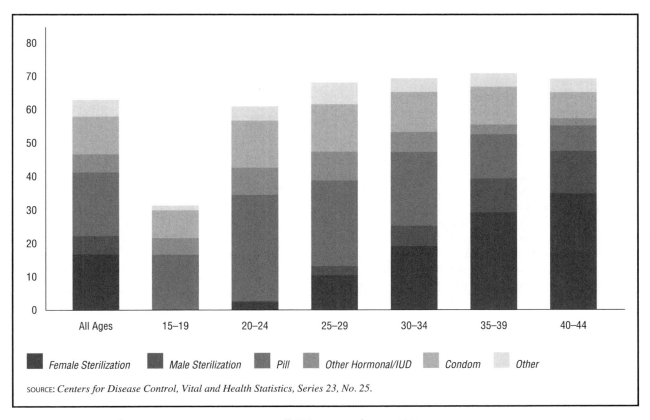

Figure 1. *Perentage of current contraceptive use among all U.S. women, by age, 2002.* CENGAGE LEARNING, GALE.

disease transmission) is one of the major goals in the study of birth control. Clinical studies produce *perfect use* estimates by rigorously monitoring the use of a birth control method according to its instructions and calculating the probability of becoming pregnant while using the method in the first year. Perfect use statistics for most hormonal and intrauterine methods are typically around 99.9%, meaning that in the first year of use, 1 out of every 1,000 women will become pregnant if she uses the method according to directions. Given the millions of women using these methods, however, thousands may become pregnant every year despite these unlikely sounding odds. Perfect use statistics for barrier methods vary widely but are generally around 90%, meaning that in the first year of use, 10 out of every 100 women using them will become pregnant. For short-term methods such as OCPs and barrier methods, the probability of becoming pregnant declines in subsequent years of use (i.e., women are less likely to become pregnant in the second than the first year of use), but for long-acting methods such as IUDs and contraceptive implants, pregnancy is more likely to occur in later years of use.

Perfect use statistics are contrasted with *typical use* statistics, which are derived from surveys conducted with

contracepting women about the actual likelihood of becoming pregnant while using a particular method. These statistics typically make use of questions asking women whether or not they were using a particular method in the month that they conceived and thus may include condom users who only used condoms once among many acts of intercourse during a month. Not surprisingly, typical use efficacy estimates are often much lower than perfect use estimates, with OCP effectiveness down to about 93% (7 in 100 women becoming pregnant) and condom effectiveness down to between 80 and 85% (20 to 15 in 100 women becoming pregnant) in the first year of use. Some researchers argue that the user error—for example, women forgetting to take their pills—should not be considered in evaluating contraceptive effectiveness, but others argue that considering the effectiveness of contraception without clinical assistance is essential to evaluating its real protective capacity.

In keeping with this line of reasoning, it should be noted that the difference between the perfect use and typical use rates of many long-acting methods of birth control, particularly the IUD and birth control implants, is almost nonexistent, meaning that they generally achieve their theoretical effectiveness level in normal use. Birth control researchers are also attentive to socioeconomic differences in method choice (that is, what groups prefer which methods and why) and failure rates, with statistics often indicating that underprivileged women are less likely to use contraceptive methods consistently and more likely to experience contraceptive failures even when they do use them, although the mechanisms behind this trend are not well-understood.

One of the major goals of birth control researchers has been to identify women who say they do not want children in the near future but who are not using a method of birth control; in aggregate, this is referred to as *unmet need*. Numerous criticisms have been leveled against the traditional conceptualization of unmet need, particularly its focus on hormonal and intrauterine methods of contraception. Critics point out that many of these women have valid reasons for not using modern methods of birth control and that portraying these women as traditional or primitive for failing to use appropriate methods ignores the many legitimate objections that women have for avoiding these methods. These objections include the many uncomfortable side effects that arise from hormonal and intrauterine birth control, such as disrupted menstrual cycles and moodiness, diminished pleasure from condoms, and financial expense. Feminist critics have also argued that fertility researchers' almost exclusive emphasis on hormonal and intrauterine methods ignores the problematic implications of widespread medical surveillance of women's bodies and vastly underestimates the health consequences of extended hormonal and intrauterine method use. Researchers have responded to these criticisms in ways that have reshaped the study of birth control.

First, rather than focusing exclusively on women's unmet need, researchers have moved toward a greater focus on the contraceptive needs of women and men, often specifically looking at couples. Whereas earlier research was frequently accused of portraying men as obstacles to women's contraceptive access, recent research has begun to look more broadly at the way that women and men facilitate and deter each other's contraceptive use. Second, in response to the criticism that unmet need did not adequately address the relationship between fertility desires, contraceptive desires, and contraceptive use, researchers have begun to explore the relationship between pregnancy intentionality and birth control use in more depth. *Pregnancy intentionality* refers to women's, men's, and couple's desires and intentions for more children. Research has emphasized the often uncertain nature of pregnancy intentionality, conflicts between partners, and the effects of these patterns on contraceptive use. Both of these changes to contraceptive research have been strongly informed by the contributions from qualitative research (interviews, focus groups, and ethnographies), both in developed

and developing countries. Although the study of contraception continues to be dominated by quantitative research based on surveys, mixed-method studies combining qualitative and quantitative data, as well as qualitative studies on their own, have proliferated in this field. Qualitative contributions have demonstrated the role of social networks in spreading contraceptive use, as well as illustrating some of the social and cultural obstacles people encounter in trying to negotiate contraceptive use with significant others.

Despite these developments, research on birth control use around the world continues to focus disproportionately on adolescents. Critics argue that this focus both reflects and contributes to the problematic aspects of adolescent sexuality, but proponents argue that contraceptive habits formed in adolescence will probably continue into young adulthood. In the U.S. context, at least, the emphasis on adolescent contraceptive use seems perhaps unwarranted because unintended pregnancies are actually most likely to occur to women between ages 18 and 24. Research focusing specifically on adults' contraceptive use has been so lacking that one of the key journals in the field, *Perspectives on Sexual and Reproductive Health*, plans a special issue on the subject. The paucity of research in this area raises many questions about birth control use across the life course, particularly in the face of major fertility-related events, such as abortion, childbirth, marriage, and divorce. Scholars do not know, for example, how women and men decide that they are finished with childbearing, even though they regularly refer to *completed fertility*. Researchers also know that rates of male and female sterilization differ considerably among nations yet know very little about why this is.

Another issue that has been neglected in the study of birth control is the way that considerations of pleasure influence contraceptive use, decision making, and negotiation. Researchers have posited many different reasons why condom use in every society is so much lower than public health officials would like, often emphasizing women's lack of control over male condom use. However, few researchers have addressed the fact that both men and women in many different cultures feel that condoms seriously diminish their sexual pleasure, which may be the most salient reason for not using them. The limited attention the issue has received has almost always been directed toward reductions in men's sexual pleasure, typically ignoring women's lost sexual pleasure from condoms as well as their reduced libido from many hormonal methods.

POLICY ISSUES

Birth control continues to be the subject of religious, policy, and political controversy. The Catholic church still officially condemns all methods of birth control

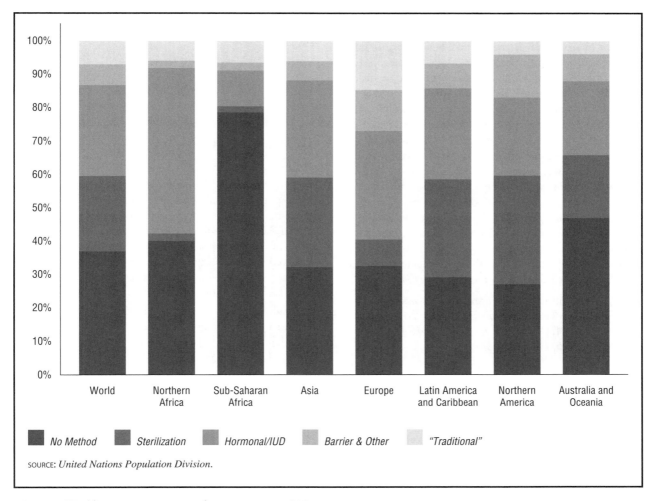

Figure 2. *World contraceptive use trends among women, 2007.* CENGAGE LEARNING, GALE.

other than the natural family planning method it developed based on the rhythm method; yet there is little evidence that most Catholics obey this religious tenet. Other religious groups, such as the Mormons, strongly promote the value of large families while still approving of birth control. National policies likewise range from active government promotion of birth control in China and Iran to government discouragement of population limitation in some African countries.

In general, developing countries frequently struggle with issues of access to, availability of, and acceptability of contraception. One of the greatest obstacles for developing countries is establishing a medical infrastructure capable of managing women's reproductive health care needs, from the safe implantation of IUDs to the timely distribution of OCPs. Normative societal mandates also may prevent unmarried women from obtaining contraceptives, especially in cultures where husbands must approve of their wives' use of contraceptives. Further-

more, distrust of foreign doctors and medicine often make many people in developing countries wary of unfamiliar contraceptive methods. Contraceptive concerns vary widely by region, with some African countries, such as Botswana (where one in three people may be infected with HIV), facing an HIV epidemic that makes condom use seem essential but other methods of birth control superfluous. Meanwhile, many Asian countries, particularly India and China, have made population control a major social priority and have been successful at distributing contraceptives to large swaths of their populations.

Birth control controversy in developed countries also focuses around access but more specifically the issues of adolescents' access and medical intervention. Some countries allow adolescents unfettered access to contraception, whereas others require parental permission for them to obtain it. Even when it is ostensibly available to them, adolescents may have difficulty obtaining contraceptives because of financial, transportation, or confidentiality issues. In many countries, hormonal contraceptives are available without a doctor's prescription (over-the-counter), whereas others, such as the United States, restrict access through medical providers. The United States recently made emergency contraception available to people over 18 over-the-counter, but the issue was clouded in controversy, especially because many view emergency contraception as an abortion-inducing intervention. Political controversy also continues about the extent to which young people should receive formal education about the use of contraception. Research, however, overwhelmingly demonstrates that education about contraceptive methods does not make adolescents more likely to have sex but does make them more likely to use protection when they do. For both adolescents and adults, birth control use is essential in assuring family limitation and the prevention of STIs, and the study of birth control provides insights into the most efficient and user-friendly means to accomplish these ends.

SEE ALSO Volume 1: *Sex Education/Abstinence Education; Transition to Parenthood;* Volume 2: *Abortion; AIDS; Sexual Activity, Adulthood;* Volume 3: *Demographic Transition Theories.*

BIBLIOGRAPHY

Bankole, A., & Singh, S. (1998). Couples' fertility and contraceptive decision-making in developing countries: Hearing the man's voice. *International Family Planning Perspectives, 24*(1), 15–24.

Carrillo, H. (2002). The night is young: Sexuality in Mexico in the time of AIDS. Chicago: University of Chicago Press.

Connelly, M. (2008). *Fatal misconceptions: The struggle to control world population.* Cambridge, MA: Harvard University Press.

Goldin, C., & Katz, L. (2000). *The power of the pill: Oral contraceptives and women's career and marriage decisions.* Cambridge, MA: National Bureau of Economic Research.

Greene, M. E., & Biddlecom, A. E. (2000). Absent and problematic men: Demographic accounts of male reproductive roles. *Population and Development Review, 26*(1), 81–115.

Greenhalgh, S., & Winckler, E. A. (2005). *Governing China's population: From Leninist to neoliberal politics.* Stanford, CA: Stanford University Press.

Hatcher, R. A., Trussell, J., Nelson, A. L., Cates, W. Jr., Stewart, F. H., & Kowal, D. (2008). *Contraceptive technology* (19th ed.). Montvale, NJ: Thomson.

Higgins, J., & Hirsch, J. (2007). The pleasure deficit: Revisiting the "sexuality connection" in reproductive health. *Perspectives on Sexual and Reproductive Health, 39*(4), 240–247.

Johnson-Hanks, J. (2006). *Uncertain honor: Modern motherhood in an African crisis.* Chicago: University of Chicago Press.

Kaler, A. (2003). *Running after pills: Politics, gender, and contraception in colonial Zimbabwe.* Portsmouth, NH: Heinemann.

Santow, G. (1995). Coitus interruptus and the control of natural fertility. *Population Studies, 49*(1), 19–43.

Tone, A. (2001). *Devices and desires: A history of contraceptives in America.* New York: Hill and Wang.

United Nations. (2008). *World contraceptive use 2007.* Retrieved June 19, 2008, from http://www.un.org/esa

Julie Fennell

BODY IMAGE, ADULTHOOD

Although scientists have always regarded body image as more than a mental photograph of oneself, its scientific meaning has evolved over time. In the early 1900s, body schema was a neurological concept—the brain's registration of the body's sensory and motor activities. It emerged in an attempt to understand the *phantom limb* phenomenon, in which patients felt pain or other sensations from amputated limbs.

Subsequently, a psychoanalytic approach to body image was developed. Through the works of Paul Schilder (1886–1940) and Seymour Fisher (1922–1996), body image came to be seen as the complex experience of one's physical being at varying levels of consciousness. Because the body is the boundary between the self and everything outside of the self, one's experience of the body was viewed as the result of early emotional learning. Thus, from a psychoanalytic perspective, body image has less to do with conscious feelings about the body per se than with unconscious feelings about the self. Projective methods (e.g., inkblot and drawing tests) are typically used to study body image from this perspective, albeit with dubious success.

A more recent perspective (e.g., Cash & Pruzinsky, 2002) regards body image as a perceptual representation of the body's size and shape. This view emerged from researchers' attempts to understand the distorted perceptions held by patients with eating disorders, such as anorexia nervosa and bulimia nervosa. However, the empirical meaning of perceptual size distortion is unclear and it represents a very limited conception of body image.

The most contemporary perspective defines body image as a multidimensional attitude toward one's own physical characteristics, especially one's appearance (Cash & Pruzinsky, 2002). Body-image attitudes are evident in people's mostly conscious, body-related cognitions, emotions, and behaviors. A distinction is made between two core dimensions: *Body-image evaluation* pertains to one's feelings about one's looks, such as satisfaction or dissatisfaction, whereas *body-image investment* refers to the psychological importance of one's appearance to one's sense of self and self-worth. Researchers typically use self-report questionnaires to measure body-image attitudes—including evaluations of physical attributes, beliefs about the importance of one's appearance, body-image emotional reactions in everyday situations, and behaviors to manage one's appearance or one's own reactions to it. Popular validated questionnaires include the Body Shape Questionnaire, Multidimensional Body-Self Relations Questionnaire, Body Esteem Scale, and Appearance Schemas Inventory.

Since the late 1980s body-image research has flourished. Thousands of scientific studies and more than a dozen scholarly books have been published on the subject. In 2004, a new journal commenced, *Body Image: An International Journal of Research*. This continuing boom is likely the product of several forces—for example, the recognition of the pivotal importance of body image in the growing prevalence of eating disorders, feminist concerns about how cultures socialize girls and women to overinvest in and loathe their appearance, and an emergent realization that the field must expand to include children and men and to study the body-image issues inherent in many medical conditions or their treatment.

BODY-IMAGE DEVELOPMENT

A person's sense of self is partly rooted in the experience of embodiment, that is, the experience of existing within a physical body. Socialization about the meaning and significance of physical appearance to the self is influenced by the norms and expectations of one's culture, family, and peers. Social learning entails the acquisition of emotion-laden attitudes about one's own body. Largely as the result of explicit and implicit social feedback, people acquire beliefs about the acceptability and attractiveness of their physical characteristics. They develop beliefs about what they look like, and they also internalize standards or ideals about what they should look like and how important these standards are.

An understanding of body image must recognize that the body and its appearance change over the life span. Adolescence is a period that involves increased personal and social emphasis on physical appearance. Appearance-altering conditions such as weight gain or facial acne can diminish a teenager's body satisfaction and sense of social acceptability. These experiences stamp body image in ways that can persist into adulthood. During adulthood, the normal physical changes that come with aging can lead some appearance-invested individuals to worry about losing their youthful looks. For example, common genetic-pattern hair loss can provoke body-image concerns among many men and women. Still, cross-sectional research reveals that older adults do not necessarily have a more negative body image than younger adults. One explanation is that aging tempers one's investment in physical appearance relative to other sources of self-worth, such as family and career roles.

Whereas some physical changes result from the biological aging process, others are precipitated by unforeseen illness or injury, such as traumatic burns, HIV or AIDS, and cancers and their treatment (e.g., chemotherapy or mastectomy). These conditions challenge body-image adaptation, as individuals must integrate their altered appearance into their self-view and manage unwanted social consequences of this altered appearance. Acutely acquired disfigurements are generally more disruptive of body image than are congenital deformities that are incorporated into one's early body-image development.

BODY IMAGE, GENDER, AND CULTURE

National surveys from the 1970s through the 1990s, as well as some meta-analytic research, point to Americans' growing body dissatisfaction, especially among women. Regardless of respondents' age or when the survey was conducted, women consistently report less favorable body-image evaluations than men. For both sexes, body weight, shape, and muscle tone are typically the foci of greatest dissatisfaction. Most weight-dissatisfied women believe that they are too heavy, even if average in weight. By contrast, men who are unhappy with their weight are fairly equally divided into those who believe they are either overweight or underweight. Cross-sectional studies suggest that, despite heavier body weights, college-attending women may have become more accepting of their bodies than was true in the 1990s.

Relative to men, women are more psychologically invested in their appearance and engage in more appearance-management behaviors. These differences mirror European and North American society's greater emphasis on a woman's attractiveness. Considerable evidence points to powerful media influences on societal physical ideals, which if internalized can produce overinvestment in appearance and body dissatisfaction.

To understand the role of cultural differences, body-image researchers have studied various subgroups within European and North American societies. For example, African American women appear to have a more positive body image than European American women, and this is especially apparent at higher body weights. Like various African cultures, African Americans view a more full-figured female shape as feminine and attractive. Individual differences in body image may also depend on sexual orientation (Roberts et al., 2006). Relative to heterosexuals, gay men are more invested in and less satisfied with their appearance. This difference may reflect their inclination to please men who, to a greater extent than women, stress physical attractiveness as a criterion of sexual or romantic desirability. Although not scientifically clear, lesbians may be less appearance-invested and more satisfied with their bodies than heterosexual women.

BODY-IMAGE DISSATISFACTION, DISTURBANCES, AND DISORDERS

Not only is body dissatisfaction a common human experience, for some it can lead to psychosocial problems. Body-dissatisfied individuals are at risk for poor self-esteem, social anxiety, depression, sexual difficulties, and eating disturbances. In turn, these problems can also impair body image satisfaction. However, body-image dissatisfaction is not the same as body-image disturbance. The latter occurs when dissatisfaction entails preoccupation, self-conscious distress, avoidance of situations and experiences that portend such distress, and interference with everyday life.

Substantial research attests to the central role of body-image disturbance in eating disorders. Persons with eating disorders hold an extremely disparaging view of their body weight and shape and overestimate their true size. They are also heavily invested in their appearance as a criterion of self-worth. Prospective studies suggest that these body-image disturbances are precursors to disordered eating and serve to worsen and maintain the behavior once it has begun.

Another severe body-image disorder is body dysmorphic disorder. This disorder was included in the *Diagnostic and Statistical Manual of Mental Disorders* by the American Psychiatric Association in 1994, although it was recognized by Asian and European clinicians long before this time. Comparably affecting men and women, body dysmorphic disorder refers to an excessive preoccupation with a nonexistent or minor physical defect. Persons with this disorder believe that the so-called defect is quite socially noticeable. They spend an inordinate amount of time compulsively inspecting their appearance in mirrors or other reflective surfaces, and they self-protectively avoid ordinary social events because they expect to experience intense self-consciousness and anxiety. Although they may recognize that their perceptions are distorted, they are more likely to consult with a medical or surgical professional to fix the perceived physical flaw than to seek mental-health assistance. A subtype of this disorder is muscle dysmorphia, in which the subjective focus is on perceived insufficient muscularity. This condition is more prevalent among men, who actually may be very muscular and may exercise or use bodybuilding supplements to excess.

BODY-IMAGE IMPROVEMENT

The most common approach to body-image improvement is to alter the body so that it will conform to the person's body-image ideals. Many people pursue weight loss, physical exercise, and cosmetic surgery, as well as aesthetic grooming changes in attempts to create a more personally satisfying appearance. Such body-modifying methods can improve body-image satisfaction. However, critics argue that many of these so-called remedies have inherent health risks and that all ultimately reinforce conformity to unrealistic expectations of physical attractiveness and fail to reduce excessive body-image investment.

Psychotherapeutic interventions have been designed to promote body acceptance without bodily change. Most thoroughly studied is cognitive behavioral therapy (CBT), which has proved effective for a range of psychosocial disorders. It is based on the premise that people can overcome problems by learning more adaptive patterns of thought and action and by eliminating self-defeating patterns. Considerable research supports the effectiveness of cognitive-behavioral body-image therapy with various populations, including body-dissatisfied college students, obese persons, and individuals with eating or body dysmorphic disorders. Such body-image improvement also promotes gains in self-esteem and other aspects of psychosocial well-being. For some people, CBT programs can be successfully implemented as structured, guided self-help via workbooks or Internet-based programs.

SEE ALSO Volume 2: *Attractiveness, Physical; Obesity, Adulthood.*

BIBLIOGRAPHY

Cash, T. F. (2008). *The body image workbook: An 8-step program for learning to like your looks*. (Rev. ed.). Oakland, CA: New Harbinger Publications.

Cash, T. F., Morrow, J. A., Hrabosky, J. I., & Perry, A. A. (2004). How has body image changed? A cross-sectional study of college women and men from 1983 to 2001. *Journal of Consulting and Clinical Psychology*, 72(6), 1081–1089.

Cash, T. F., & Pruzinsky, T. (Eds.). (2002) *Body image: A handbook of theory, research, and clinical practice*. New York: Guilford Press.

Fisher, S. (1986). *Development and structure of the body image* (Vols. 1–2). Hillsdale, NJ: Lawrence Erlbaum Associates.

Grogan, S. (2007). *Body image: Understanding body dissatisfaction in men, women, and children*. New York: Routledge.

Hrabosky, J. I., & Cash, T. F. (2007). Self-help treatment for body image disturbances. In J. D. Latner & G. T. Wilson (Eds.), *Self-help approaches for obesity and eating disorders: Research and practice* (pp. 118-138). New York: Guilford Press.

Jarry, J. L., & Ip, K. (2005). The effectiveness of stand-alone cognitive behavior therapy for body image: A meta-analysis. *Body Image: An International Journal of Research*, 2(4), 317–331.

Morrison, M. A., Morrison, T. G., & Sager, C. L. (2004). Does body satisfaction differ between gay men and lesbian women and heterosexual men and women?: A meta-analytic review. *Body Image: An International Journal of Research*, 1(2), 127–138.

Phillips, K. A. (2005). *The broken mirror: Understanding and treating body dysmorphic disorder.* (Rev. ed.). New York: Oxford University Press.

Roberts, A., Cash, T. F., Feingold, A., & Johnson, B. T. (2006). Are Black-White differences in females' body dissatisfaction decreasing? A meta-analytic review. *Journal of Consulting and Clinical Psychology, 74*(6), 1121–1131.

Rumsey, N., & Harcourt, D. (2005). *The psychology of appearance.* Maidenhead, U.K.: Open University Press.

Sarwer, D.B., Pruzinsky, T., Cash, T. F., Goldwyn, R. M., Persing, J. A., & Whitaker, L. A. (Eds.). (2006). *Psychological aspects of reconstructive and cosmetic plastic surgery: Clinical, empirical, and ethical perspectives.* Philadelphia: Lippincott, Williams, & Wilkins.

Schilder, P. (1950). *The image and appearance of the human body: Studies in the constructive energies of the psyche.* New York: International Universities Press.

Thompson, J. K. (Ed.). (2004). *Handbook of eating disorders and obesity.* Hoboken, NJ: Wiley.

Thompson, J. K., & Cafri, G. (Eds.). (2007). *The muscular ideal: Psychological, social, and medical perspectives.* Washington, DC: American Psychological Association.

Thompson, J. K., Heinberg, L. J., Altabe, M., & Tantleff-Dunn, S. (1999). *Exacting beauty: Theory, assessment, and treatment of body-image disturbance.* Washington, DC: American Psychological Association.

Wertheim, E. H., Paxton, S. J., & Blaney, S. (2004). Risk factors for the development of body image disturbances. In J. K. Thompson (Ed.), *Handbook of eating disorders and obesity* (pp. 463–514). Hoboken, NJ: Wiley.

Thomas F. Cash

C

CANCER, ADULTHOOD

SEE Volume 3: *Cancer, Adulthood and Later Life.*

CARE WORK

SEE Volume 3: *Caregiving.*

CAREERS

In a life course approach careers are defined as observable pathways that consist of patterned trajectories and transitions over time. Although the term *career* most often refers to a series of occupational positions, life course scholars apply it to a range of pathways, such as family careers, mental health careers, and relationship careers.

Research documents the socially patterned timing of career transitions as well as socially patterned career trajectories (or sequences) and the way those patterns differ by gender, age, cohort, social class, race/ethnicity, health, education, occupation, and/or industry. Careers also are studied in terms of people's assessments of their past trajectories, current situation, and prospects for the future. In light of the centrality of paid work in contemporary adult development, this entry focuses on occupational paths and beliefs.

Individuals often assess their occupational careers as coming up short in terms of cultural expectations, making cognitive appraisals of being on or off time in their

occupational careers. Their yardstick is what Phyllis Moen and Patricia Roehling (2005) call the career mystique: ingrained cultural beliefs (institutionalized in rules, regulations, and expectations) about continuous long-hour hard work throughout adulthood as the path to status, security, and satisfaction. In other words, most people have an ideal concept of a career as the path to the American dream of upward mobility, an orderly and hierarchical progression up occupational ladders.

CAREERS AS BLUEPRINTS FOR THE ADULT LIFE COURSE

The idea of a career is a modern invention, having emerged as a social fact only after the development of corporations, bureaucracies, and white-collar employment. As C. Wright Mills (1956) pointed out, before the Industrial Revolution, which occurred in the United States in the second half of the 19th century, most people worked in agriculture or a family business. Though individual farmers, craftspeople, and family entrepreneurs might have had life plans, they did not have careers. It was only after industrialization and in tandem with the Great Depression, two world wars, and a booming postwar economy that a large white-collar and unionized blue-collar workforce experienced the bureaucratization of occupational paths or careers.

Governments, schools, and workplaces developed policies and practices in the 1930s through the 1960s that institutionalized careers as identifiable pathways of full-time employment. Those in white-collar and unionized blue-collar occupations could count on wages and job security increasing with seniority, from entry-level jobs for young people to retirement. Educational, labor market, and retirement policies based on the career mystique produced a three-part life course: full-time education as preparation for employment, an adulthood of continuous full-time employment, and the one-way, irreversible exit to the leisure of retirement, thereby opening job opportunities to younger cohorts of employees. Thus, in the middle of the 20th century most middle-class white men followed a lockstep pattern: a one-way path from schooling through full-time continuous occupational careers to retirement.

A number of life course scholars have pointed to occupational careers as providing an organizational blueprint for the adult life course. Careers embody both structure (relationships between jobs, public- and private-sector policies and practices) and process (moving through identifiable career lines, taking on the occupational identity such as lawyer or doctor). As paid work in corporations and governments replaced farming, the role of the employee became central in contemporary society and the work career came to shape life chances, life quality, and life choices in virtually every arena.

OUTSIDE THE CAREER MYSTIQUE

The lockstep career mystique is a myth and has never been a reality for most ethnic minorities, women, and poorly educated adults. Moreover, the career mystique has become increasingly obsolete even for middle-class men. In a competitive global economy seniority no longer provides protection against job insecurity. Still, this myth is built into the social organization of paid work and continues to shape and define adulthood, life chances, and life quality. Public policies (such as Social Security and unemployment insurance) and corporate policies (hiring, recruiting, firing, promoting, retiring) have reinforced the career mystique by promising rewards to people who work hard, continuously, and full time throughout their adult years in a single organization or "ladder hop" across organizations. Until recently employers have tried to recruit and retain people who are committed to such full-time continuous employment by offering them health insurance and pensions.

One result of this institutionalization of the lockstep career mystique is that individuals who experience uneven or downward career pathways have been seen and often see themselves as deviant. Employers view people moving in and out of the workforce and those employed less than full time as less committed to their jobs, reaping and deserving fewer economic and psychological rewards. Moreover, because a career is equated with occupational history, unpaid work, whether as a participant in a family business, a homemaker, a family care provider, or in formal or informal civic engagement, has been rendered marginal to the real work of society. Individuals who do not or cannot follow this lockstep pattern of continuous full-time

work (e.g., those in insecure jobs, those with family responsibilities) are penalized.

DIVIDING ADULTHOOD BY GENDER

Occupational careers have been fundamental to men's identities—the purported path to security, success, and status—and for their families as well. However, men in the middle of the 20th century were able to lead work-centered lives because their wives took care of their personal and domestic needs and responsibilities and often supported their career progression behind the scenes. By contrast, women's lives have been more contingent and accommodating than lockstep, developing in relation to marriage, motherhood, economic exigencies, and their spouses' occupational careers. However, minorities, the poor, and the poorly educated could follow neither career nor homemaking paths, often moving in and out of jobs that were unrelated (not leading to a particular career pattern) and poorly paid.

Nevertheless, most Americans in the 1950s and 1960s wanted a middle-class lifestyle and worked to achieve it. The breadwinner/homemaker template provided cultural guidelines and clear options related to occupational careers, family careers, and gender that effectively decoupled paid work from unpaid family care work, creating an imaginary divide between them. The ideal-typical "Ozzie and Harriet" family was seen by most Americans in the middle of the 20th century as the ideal arrangement even for those who could not afford or fit its parameters.

Betty Friedan's *The Feminine Mystique* (1963) depicted half of this cultural divide: the belief that women could achieve total fulfillment by devoting themselves to full-time domesticity as homemakers for their husbands and children. However, Friedan paid no (or scant) attention to the career mystique: the belief that most American men could achieve total fulfillment by devoting most of their adulthood and most of their waking hours to their jobs. Though some authors captured the reality of men's lives—C. Wright Mills wrote *White Collar* (1956), William H. Whyte described *The Organization Man* (1956), and Sloan Wilson provided a vivid fictional account in *The Man in the Gray Flannel Suit* (1955)—none of those works had the impact of Friedan's book.

The women's movement of the 1960s and 1970s effectively destroyed the feminine mystique. In rejecting its norms and values, many women in the second half of the 20th century sought equality by embracing the career mystique, wanting men's jobs, salaries, and power and status. Women now constitute nearly half the U.S. workforce, but careers remain designed for those who can focus their time and efforts fully on their jobs. Outdated policies and practices combined with the growing numbers of households with all adults in the workforce have created a fundamental mismatch. Employees struggle with and try to find strategies to adapt to their obligations at work along with the unpaid care work of families, homes, and communities.

In the 21st century most American women have not simply traded one mystique for another, moving from strictures about the good mother or the good wife to the good worker, but instead are trying to fill all three roles. However, the outdated structures and cultures of jobs and career paths make it impossible to do so. Research shows that women who scale back at work, take time off, or shift to jobs that are less time-consuming pay an economic price.

The pervasive gender bias in the ways people think about and study careers also is reflected in the exclusive emphasis on individuals. Dual-earner households have become the norm, and so there are often two occupational paths in a single household. Research shows that couples strategize, prioritizing one person's (typically the husband's) career by having the other person (typically the wife) modify her occupational commitments in light of family considerations as well as considerations of the spouse's career, scaling back to part-time work or leaving the workforce when family care demands are high. Most employees and family members also adjust by modifying the family side of the work-family equation by delaying marriage and/or parenthood and/or having fewer children.

OUT OF STEP

The 20th-century contract between employers and employees that undergirded career paths was based on the seniority system and the notion of a primary and a secondary workforce. Middle-class (mostly White) men with many years of employment were sheltered from economic dislocations. It was the last hired—typically women and minorities—who were the first fired. However, thus far in the 21st century the proportion of workers under union contracts have reached an unprecedented low, and implicit contracts (trading mobility and job security for a continuous commitment to work) have disappeared.

The career mystique vision of orderly careers as the successful path through adulthood has lagged behind 21st-century realities. Unprecedented numbers of Americans are college-educated, expecting to have interesting, challenging, secure jobs but not always finding them. Salaries no longer are sufficient to support families on one income. The amenities of the 1950s—air-conditioning, color televisions, fancy appliances—have come to be viewed by most Americans as necessities. Most workers are part of dual-earner households, married to other workers. Growing numbers of workers are heads of single-parent households, doing all their families'

paid work and unpaid care work. In fact, in 2001 only one in four workers had a full-time homemaker for backup and support. Another challenge looms on the horizon: The workforce is aging as the large boomer cohort moves into and through their fifties and sixties.

Equally consequential, the U.S. economy has become a globalized economy, grappling with new technologies, international workforces, and fast-paced changes, including mergers, buyouts, and acquisitions. The ambiguities and uncertainties in boardrooms, offices, and factory floors affect the sensibilities of workers and their families as they face the realities of frequent employer restructuring, often accompanied by forced early retirements, layoffs, fewer benefits, and greater workloads.

What has not changed is the career mystique: Employers and workers see good employees as those who are willing to make heavy investments of time and energy in their jobs. Not for the U.S. workforce are Western European institutions such as long summer and winter vacations, paid parental leave, and part-time jobs with benefits. Studies show that Americans pride themselves on working hard, taking work home, staying late at the office, and not taking all their vacation time.

SHAPING COGNITIVE BELIEFS, VALUES, AND EXPECTATIONS

The career mystique not only became an organizing principle shaping options and opportunities over the life course, it also shaped people's identities, self-appraisals, and expectations for the future. As Stephen Barley (1989) pointed out, early sociologists acknowledged the "Janus-like" aspects of the career concept as both institutional (a series of structural positions) and subjective (ways employees define and give meaning to their unfolding occupational experiences). Occupational careers as movement through positions also entail changes in peoples' subjective self-definitions, expectations, evaluations, and meaning.

Walter Heinz (1996) pointed out that status passages such as job shifts and retirement "link institutions and actors by defining time-tables and entry as well as exit markers for transitions" (pp. 58–59). However, institutional guidelines for career paths are outdated. Against a backdrop of 21st-century social transformations, even white men with college educations and professional experience are finding fewer career ladders that bring job and income security, much less success.

FUTURE DIRECTIONS

Human development over the life course is shaped by socially patterned expectations related to roles in the form of norms about the right time for adults to begin a career job, get a promotion, or retire, as well as socially structured entry and exit points and durations that shape the opportunity for and reward some pathways and not others. Studying occupational careers involves thinking about and attending to employment over time, referring to, for example, the processes of job development, mobility, and plateauing as well as entries and exits. Three key themes characterize a life course perspective on career development. The first places careers in context, considering the ecology of employees' social location, in terms of their historical cohort, ethnicity, gender, life stage, occupation, and workplace. All these factors shape opportunities and constraints at work and at home. The second is the notion of linked lives, as individuals and couples strategize to synchronize their goals, expectations, and obligations. The third theme is the dynamic notion of pathways, involving transitions, trajectories, and timing.

The term *career* usually refers to recognized patterns of organizational and occupational movement throughout adulthood and the widely accepted career mystique that depicts lockstep careers as the path to the American dream. Even though notions of orderly careers are out of date, government and business rules and regulations continue to reinforce the primacy of full-time continuous employment, rendering marginal all other types of labor force attachment: part-time jobs, temporary work, and intermittent employment. The solution, some scholars have concluded, is to enable customized rather than lockstep career paths, widening the options for employees at different ages and life stages. Research is needed on customized career innovators: both employers and employees who are reshaping possibilities.

The study of careers contributes to the understanding of the dynamic links between lives and organizations as well as the dislocations brought about by both the work-family mismatch and the job security mismatch. In 1977 Seymour Spilerman pointed to the discrepancy between career characterizations and accounts on the one hand and people's actual patterns of job sequences on the other. These discrepancies may have become even more acute. What is required are empirically derived new typologies that capture the experiences of contemporary employees in different employment and home environments, their assessments and strategic responses to those experiences, and the consequences for their health and well-being as well as for business, the family, and society.

A global risk economy, advances in communication and information technologies, an aging workforce, and a workforce with family care responsibilities mean that conventional beliefs about careers are outmoded, with diminishing numbers of workers fitting the traditional orderly career pattern. New public policies and practices and new corporate rules and regulations will be required to widen the career path options and safety nets. However, the concept of careers remains a useful lens with which to view both the dynamic relationship between choice and constraint and the dynamic interplay between organizations and lives that play out over time.

SEE ALSO Volume 2: *Employment, Adulthood; Job Change; Occupations; Social Class;* Volume 3: *Moen, Phyllis.*

BIBLIOGRAPHY

Aldous, J. (1996). *Family careers: Rethinking the developmental perspective.* Thousand Oaks, CA: Sage Publications.

Barley, S. R. (1989). Careers, identities, and institutions: The legacy of the Chicago school of sociology. In M. B. Arthur, D. T. Hall, & B. S. Lawrence (Eds.), *Handbook of career theory* (pp. 41–65). Cambridge, UK, and New York: Cambridge University Press.

Friedan, B. (1963). *The feminine mystique.* New York: Norton.

Han, S.-K., & Moen, P. (1999). Clocking out: Temporal patterning of retirement. *American Journal of Sociology, 105,* 191–236.

Heinz, W. R. (1996). Status passages as micro-macro linkages in life-course research. In A. Weymann & W. R. Heinz (Eds.), *Society and biography: Interrelationships between social structure, institutions, and the life course* (pp. 51–66). Weinheim, Germany: Deutscher Studien Verlag.

Kohli, M. 1986. The World We Forget: A Historical Review of the Life Course. In V. W. Marshall (Ed.), *Later life: The social psychology of aging* (pp. 271–303). Beverly Hills, CA: Sage.

Mills, C. W. (1956). *White collar: The American middle classes.* New York: Oxford University Press.

Moen, P., & Han, S-K. (2001). Reframing careers: Work, family, and gender. In V. Marshall, W. Heinz, H. Krueger, & A. Verma (Eds.), *Restructuring work and the life course* (pp. 424–445). Toronto and Buffalo, NY: University of Toronto Press.

Moen, P., & Roehling, P. (2005). *The career mystique: Cracks in the American dream.* Lanham, MD: Rowman & Littlefield.

Mortimer, J. T., & Borman, K. B. (Eds.). 1988. *Work experience and psychological development through the life span.* Boulder, CO: Westview Press.

Spilerman, S. (1977). Careers, labor market structure, and socioeconomic attainment. *American Journal of Sociology, 83,* 551–593.

Whyte, W. H. (1956). *The organization man.* New York: Simon and Schuster.

Wilson, S. (1955). *The man in the gray flannel suit.* New York: Simon and Schuster.

Phyllis Moen

CHILDBEARING

A life course framework is central to the study of childbearing. Physical maturation is required before women can bear children and before men can impregnate women. This reproductive potential, or fecundity, generally lasts about three decades for women and considerably longer for men. During these fecund years, women could conceivably have a birth each year, but such high levels of childbearing (30+ births per woman) are exceedingly rare. The survival strategy of humans has focused instead on far lower levels of childbearing and intense efforts to increase infant and child survival. The strategies used to limit fertility and aid child survival vary dramatically across societies.

For instance, in many societies marriage norms limit coitus (i.e., sexual intercourse), and therefore childbearing, to particular ages and circumstances. Other norms have specified times when married women should not have coitus or the length of time that they should breastfeed, increasing the interval between births. Thus, at the heart of fertility research is not just the number of births a woman has in her lifetime but the ages at which she has them, their spacing vis-à-vis their siblings, and their sequencing vis-à-vis other life events such as marriage. Childbearing is a prototypical life course event—childbearing is possible for only a segment of the life course, and it is a repeatable event whose timing and sequencing have demonstrable effects on subsequent fertility, other life events, and overall life chances.

Despite the necessary role of males in reproduction, the fertility research literature focuses mainly on women. The reasons are many. First, only women become pregnant and give birth. Thus, the study of maternal and child health closely links women and fertility. Second, women are frequently the primary child caretakers, and, in general, women's lives are more influenced by childbearing and childcare than are men's. These mother–child bonds and interactions generally make mothers more knowledgeable and accurate respondents to surveys that assess matters of childbearing and rearing. As a result of these factors and others, researchers tend to choose women as research subjects. This woman-centered focus does cause some problems, but some of these have been addressed since the late 20th century.

POPULATION-BASED MEASURES OF FERTILITY

Childbearing is generally measured as live births per woman. Miscarriages, abortions, and stillbirths are not counted (live births plus these events equals the number of recognizable pregnancies), but infants who die very early in life (even in the first day of life) are included. Births can be summed across a woman's lifetime to produce the number of children ever born (CEB), and the mean CEB is a useful childbearing measure for a cohort, or study group, of women. However, the most commonly used measures of childbearing are period rates—the ratio of events (births) per years of exposure for a given population in a given time period. The most common period rate is the total fertility rate (TFR), which is an answer to a hypothetical question: If a woman were to experience the age-specific fertility rates of year x, she would have y children. Put a bit more formally, the TFR is the sum of age-specific birth rates from (usually) age 15 to age 45. With the low levels of mortality that characterize contem-

porary industrialized countries, a TFR of 2.1 is replacement level fertility—the level that would lead to long-term stability in the size and structure of the population. Contemporary TFR levels vary from highs of 7.5 in poor countries such as Afghanistan and Niger to below 1.25 in places as varied as South Korea and Poland (United Nations, 2007).

Period fertility rates can be calculated for any population; crucial distinctions from a life course perspective are age, parity (i.e., the woman's number of previous births), and marital/union status (hereafter union status). Fertility rates vary dramatically by these characteristics due to their strong links to the proximate determinants of fertility, which are discussed more fully below. Age can index fecundity or normative ages for childbearing; parity greater than zero provides evidence of fecundity and may indicate that preferred family size has been reached and, thus, could be a signal to use contraception or resort to abortion. Union status can indicate one's likelihood of engaging in coitus or becoming pregnant and is often the preferred relationship status for childbearing. In any given year, the distribution of a population across age/parity/marital status will have an impact on its aggregate level of fertility.

The TFR (as the sum of age-specific rates) accounts for any differences in age structure between populations, which might otherwise distort a comparison of fertility rates if one population has more women of childbearing age than the other. The popularity of the TFR follows from this feature, its interpretability, and widely available data for its calculation. Age-specific rates (the components of TFR) can also be examined to determine if one population has an earlier or later pattern of childbearing. Subsequent sections focus on adolescent childbearing and delayed childbearing—the fertility rates of teenagers or those over the age of 30 (or 35), respectively. This focus is justified because of the implications of childbearing at these ages for the individuals and for their social groups (families, communities, and countries).

Fertility rates are frequently decomposed by parity. A common strategy (largely due to data availability) subdivides the numerator of age-specific rates by parity (while leaving the denominator, years at risk, fixed). Thus, one can sum these parity-specific and age-specific rates to create a set of parity-specific TFR rates ($TFR_i; i = 0, 1, 2, 3+$); this set sums to the original TFR. This is useful because changes in fertility can be concentrated at given parities, or stages of family building. For instance, and as discussed below, the fertility transition (changes in birth rates from high to low) is generally caused by the decline in higher parity births. That is, TFR_0 and TFR_1 change little whereas TFR_{2+} declines dramatically.

Like increasing age and parity, union transitions can have large effects on fertility, but these effects vary greatly by time and place. Preferred measures of childbearing by union status disaggregate the populations into married and unmarried and then calculate fertility rates as discussed above. Fertility rates for married women are generally much higher than for the unmarried, but this differential varies greatly over historical periods and geographic locations.

THE PROXIMATE DETERMINANTS OF FERTILITY

The fundamental challenge in fertility research is to understand the factors that produce variation in fertility across individuals and across populations. There are many reasons; some focus on the proximate determinants of fertility. In a classic typology, Kingsley Davis and Judith Blake (1956) identified variation due to the likelihood of coitus, of becoming pregnant, and of carrying a pregnancy to term. John Bongaarts and Robert Potter (1978) elaborated this typology and then traced most subgroup variation in fertility to four key proximate determinants: (a) marriage or the age at which one becomes sexually active; (b) the length of breastfeeding, which is the primary determinant of the anovulatory (suppressed ovulation) period following a birth; (c) the use of contraceptives; and (d) the use of abortion. A huge body of research accounts for group differences by attributing it to these causes.

However, an important critique of this work is that these proximate answers only beg additional questions: If fertility levels vary because of earlier marriage or greater contraceptive use, then what causes early marriage or greater use of contraceptives? The answers lie in the social environment that constrains and enables action—more fundamental determinants. In sum, there is an important distinction in the fertility literature between proximate and more fundamental determinants (or causes). There is far greater agreement about the former than the latter due to the greater challenges of demonstrating fundamental causes.

With respect to the key proximate determinants listed above, the first two can produce vast variation in fertility across groups (Bongaarts & Potter, 1978). For groups in which contraception and abortion are unknown or rare, fertility has been reliably measured as high as 10 births per woman (among the Hutterites, a religious sect that resides on communal farms in the northern United States and western Canada) and as low as 4 births (among the !kung, a nomadic hunter-gatherer society in the Kalahari Desert). The proximate determinants approach shows that the !kung spend considerably more of their fecund years outside a sexual union (due to widespread union disruption) and that women breastfeed for periods as long as three or four years. As a result, the !kung have long intervals between births. With three fecund decades for childbearing, long intervals imply fewer births. The Hutterites, in contrast,

marry relatively young, remain married throughout the fecund years, and breastfeed for relatively short periods (Bongaarts & Potter, 1983; Howell 1979).

Research shows that other potential proximate determinants generally do not affect fertility levels across time or space. For instance, poor nutrition and disease do not usually cause differences in fertility among populations, although they clearly cause variation within populations (that is, among individuals). Likewise, the frequency of coitus within sexual unions seems not to vary greatly cross-culturally. Age at menarche (i.e., the onset of menstrual periods) does vary across populations and eras, but childbearing at these young ages is rare and thus negates its potential influence on the population level. Age at menopause varies little across populations (Bongaarts & Potter, 1983).

In populations in which birth control (i.e., contraception and abortion) is widely used, these become proximate determinants of overwhelming importance. The acceptability of various contraceptive strategies or techniques (hereafter techniques) varies sharply across populations, and the theoretical and use effectiveness of strategies vary. Theoretical effectiveness, the reduction in fecundity if the technique is properly used, is fixed for a given technique (i.e., for the pill or condom); but use effectiveness (the fecundity reduction achieved in practice) can vary in a population. Condoms have high theoretical effectiveness, but use effectiveness varies because the appropriate regimen (always using them) is sometimes not practiced.

Other important sets of proximate determinants have proven useful in place of those mentioned above or to supplement them. Perhaps the most important is the number of children a woman (or couple) intends to have. Fertility intentions, or the number of children one plans to have in the future, are relatively stable plans of action; they are the cognitive integration of the factors and forces motivating and constraining childbearing. For instance, less educated women might intend more children because their opportunity costs (in terms of lost wages) are lower than are those for more educated women. Fertility intentions, in turn, can be a primary determinant of proximate behaviors (such as use of contraception). Many fertility analyses focus on fertility intentions and the factors that aid or hinder women (or couples) in realizing intentions.

One aspect of the disjuncture between intentions and fertility behavior are unintended births—both mistimed and unwanted. Mistimed births are those that are unintended at the time of conception, but the respondent reports intentions to have a child or children in the future. Again stressing intentions at the time of conception, unwanted births are those that are not intended now nor were intended in the future. Unintended births can result from contraceptive failure or from nonuse of contraception. The latter is related to the important concept of unmet need for contraception. The proportion of sexually active women who do not intend additional children and are not using contraception represent the percentage of women whose need for contraception is unmet. Reducing unintended births and lowering unmet contraception needs are frequent foci of public policy.

WORLD FERTILITY TRENDS AND PATTERNS

Historically, fertility trends are generally couched within the demographic transition framework. Simply stated, the demographic transition is the process of change from high rates of fertility and mortality to low rates. In historical experience, mortality (i.e., the death rate) tends to decline sooner and faster than does fertility, producing a sharp divergence in vital rates—a period with high fertility and low mortality. Thus, the process of demographic transition includes a period of rapid population growth (when vital rates are not in equilibrium).

Much theoretical and empirical work has focused on the demographic transition. Some work has described fertility trends or the trends in proximate determinants that produce the fertility change. As noted earlier, empirical work shows that declines in higher parity births primarily produce the fertility transition. A prototypical case is Taiwan, where Griffith Feeney (1991) showed the fertility transition resulted entirely from declines in births to women with two or more children. Other work has described context-specific mixes of proximate determinants that produce relatively slow or more rapid declines in fertility. Slower declines, for instance, can be produced by increasing contraceptive use that is partly offset by declining duration of breastfeeding; more rapid declines can be produced by simultaneously increasing age at marriage and decreasing the proportion of high parity births.

The more fundamental causes of fertility change have received the greatest attention. Major arguments have stressed cultural/social change, economic change, policy interventions, and other demographic change. Cultural and social change arguments stress the acceptability of fertility control and changes in the importance of children or large families; economic arguments focus on the increasing costs of children due to a changed economic environment, such as a shift from agrarian, or extractive, to manufacturing or service economies. Policy interventions occasionally play a crucial role (e.g., China's one child policy) but more frequently have only a contributing role. Some argue that declining mortality, resulting from

improved living standards or public health efforts (such as those that provide clean water or medical care), has decreased the demand for large families. Specifically, families' fertility desires reflect their wish for *living* children. In periods of high infant and child mortality, individuals need a greater number of births to ensure that the number of surviving children meshes with their initial preference.

Empirical work provides some evidence for all of these claims but demonstrates that when fertility declines take place, various economic and demographic regimes can exist. In Ansley Coale's 1973 classic formulation, fertility declines (a) when control of fertility is legitimate, (b) when individuals are motivated to have fewer children, and (c) when effective contraceptive strategies are available. These preconditions in a population can be attained in a variety of ways and can be encouraged or impeded by a number of factors. Thus, the demographic transition is part of multifaceted social change, including social, economic, demographic, and policy changes. No society develops economically without experiencing the demographic transition; however, the social history of transitions is highly variable in the timing of transition vis-à-vis economic change or in the import of policy interventions. The most attractive explanations focus on changes in (a) the way people live, including increases in education, nonagricultural jobs, and female employment; and (b) how individuals interpret the world around them—what they believe is reasonable, moral, or acceptable.

FERTILITY RATE STATISTICS

Table 1 shows the number (and percentage) of countries by the level and trend in their total fertility rate. Column 1 shows that only 13 countries (7%) have high fertility rates and little evidence of substantial declines over the past 25 years. All but two of these countries are in Africa (Timor and Afghanistan are the exceptions), and all of them are characterized by low levels of socioeconomic development. A larger second set (see Column 2) also have high fertility (mean TFR of 5.1) but show clear evidence of decline—these countries exhibit an average decline of 1.7 births over the past quarter century. These countries are in the earlier stages of the demographic transition.

The third column contains the largest number of countries (77); these countries are in the midst of the demographic transition and show large declines over the past 25 years (average declines of 2.8 births). This tabulation is largely consistent with a global transition toward low levels of fertility—a few countries have yet to begin, some show clear evidence of decline, and a third set is rapidly approaching replacement level fertility. Some

Total Fertility Rate Levels and Trends					
Countries of World	(1) High - Modest Declines* TFR ≥ 4.0	(2) High - Substantial Declines^ TFR > 4.0	(3) Moderate - Mid-Transition 2.1< TFR < 4.0	(4) Low Post-Transition 1.5< TFR < 2.1	(5) Very Low Post-Transition TFR < 1.5
Number (= 195)	13	37	77	37	31
Percent (= 100)	7%	19%	39%	19%	16%
Mean TRF	6.8	5.1	2.9	1.8	1.3
25-year change	-0.2	-1.7	-2.8	-1.3	-1.1

*Rates have declined less than one birth in last 25 years.
^Rates have declined by more than one birth in last 25 years.

SOURCE: Table A.15. UN, 2007.

Table 1. *Countries of the world categorized by 2000–05 total fertility rate levels and trends.* CENGAGE LEARNING, GALE.

interesting questions remain: Will some countries fail to move through the demographic transition? Will the decline of some countries' fertility rates stabilize well above replacement? Only the future can answer these questions, but most demographers would predict *no* to both questions—the transition will be global and the endpoint will be low fertility.

The last two columns of Table 1 show countries that have already completed the demographic transition—the decline of fertility to low levels and, for 31 counties, declines to very low levels. Very low fertility is now reported from a broad array of countries, including South Korea, Japan, Poland, Romania, Italy, Germany, and, according to some sources, China. These fertility levels have raised country-level concerns about both population aging and eventual population decline. Furthermore, as S. Philip Morgan (2003) pointed out, the spread of very low fertility raises the question of whether below-replacement fertility will become a global concern during the 21st century.

ADOLESCENT CHILDBEARING

A focus on adolescent (or teen) childbearing returns the life course perspective to center stage. By definition, teen childbearing occurs relatively early in the life course. Thus, key questions focus on the timing of childbearing vis-à-vis a woman's physical maturity to bear, and her emotional maturity and general resources to rear, a child. Whether teenage childbearing is problematic for mother and child depends on the social setting, including the helpmates available to rear the child and the human capital the child needs to become successful. Frank Furstenberg, Jeanne Brooks-Gunn, and S. Philip Morgan (1987) argued that teenage childbearing in the United States became a major social concern in the 1970s.

Figure 1 shows that this was a period when teen childbearing was actually declining. Heightened concerns were the result of the changing context of teen childbearing, not its increase. First, the human capital demands of the labor force were growing, thus increasing the importance of schooling. Young women were encouraged to postpone childbearing and stay in school to acquire an education and skills that were important for their economic well-being. Increased education also produced more skilled mothers who were deemed important for rearing a future generation of productive citizens. The second major change, also shown in Figure 1, was the increased proportion of teen childbearing that was nonmarital—suggesting the absence of a male helpmate to care and provide for children.

For reasons noted above, adolescent childbearing is considered problematic in industrial and post-industrial society. The attention it receives is linked to its prevalence; generally, its frequency declined in the last two decades of the 20th century and early in the 21st century but varies greatly across societies. In the 1970s, 1980s, and early 1990s the United States stood out as having one of the highest rates of teen childbearing among industrialized countries (Alan Guttmacher Institute, 2002; Jones et al., 1985). This distinction remains, although U.S. teenage birth rates declined substantially in the 1995 to 2005 period. Figure 1 shows the U.S. teen childbearing rate from 1950 to 2005. Overall, the rate declined during this period (although there was an upturn from 1985 to 2001).

In terms of proximate determinants, the high U.S. teen childbearing rate compared to similar countries (e.g., Canada, Great Britain, France, and Sweden) is not due to an earlier age at first intercourse or to a higher frequency of sexual activity. Rather it results from lower levels of

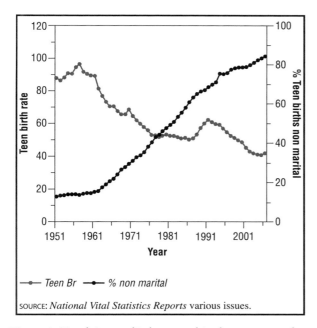

Figure 1. *Trends in teen birth rate and in the percentage of teen births that are nonmarital.* CENGAGE LEARNING, GALE.

contraceptive use and use of less effective contraceptives. In terms of more fundamental causes, these higher rates and the role of these proximate causes can be traced to negative societal attitudes toward teenage sexual relationships. These attitudes, in turn, inhibit access and increase the costs of reproductive health services, and they increase the ambivalence of parents and teens toward contraceptive use by teens. Also, dramatic inequality of opportunity can erode motivation to delay parenthood or to avoid unintended pregnancy. For young women with few promising prospects for education or careers, the potentially detrimental effect of early childbearing may not be considered all that serious (see Alan Guttmacher Institute, 2002; Jones et al., 1985). Recent declines in U.S. teen fertility (1995–2005) have occurred among Whites, Blacks, and Hispanics and have been accompanied by declines in abortions. Thus, there is evidence that increased abstinence and more effective use of contraceptives have both contributed to these sharp declines. The more fundamental causes of this decline remain an unanswered question and an active research area.

The consequences of teen childbearing have been the focus of much research and debate. The dominant view of the 1960s and 1970s is captured by Arthur Campbell's (1968) often quoted statement: "The girl who has an illegitimate child at the age of 16 has 90% of her life's script written. . . . Her life choices are few. And most of them are bad"(p. 238). Purported repercussions of teen childbearing include truncated schooling, poor job opportunities, more rapid subsequent childbearing, larger

completed family size, and few good marriage opportunities. Evidence that teen mothers fared poorly on these dimensions was widespread. Further, "children bearing children" was widely posited as a key mechanism perpetuating poverty and disadvantage.

However, a critique of this view emerged that positioned teen childbearing in a broader context. Specifically, the critique pointed out that those who bore children as teenagers were disadvantaged prior to the birth; they had limitations or constraints that made their educational/economic/marital success less likely (than for others) even if they had postponed childbearing. Thus, their relatively poorer outcomes were due, at least in part and perhaps in their entirety, to these preexisting characteristics. Evidence for this view is impressive and rests on several clever research designs.

One design by Saul Hoffman, E. Michael Foster, and Frank Furstenberg, Jr. in 1993 compared sisters, one having an early birth and one not. This strategy controls for many family characteristics and aspects of the home environment that are shared by the sisters. The effects of teen childbearing estimated from this design are sharply attenuated, compared to the effects detected using more naive research designs. A second strategy by V. Joseph Hotz, Susan Williams McElroy, and Seth Sanders in 2005 used the occurrence of a spontaneous miscarriage as an event or "treatment" that postponed childbearing for a random sample of women. As in the sisters design, effects estimated using this strategy suggest modest impacts of teenage childbearing on many purported consequences. This research places a teen birth in the context of the life course—an important event but one closely connected with prior experience and contributing to subsequent events. In sum, teen childbearing is not nearly as determinative as was often assumed in the 1960s and 1970s.

DELAYED CHILDBEARING

Contrasting delayed childbearing with early (adolescent or teen) childbearing is useful. Clearly delayed childbearing is normative if compared to teen childbearing. Postponing parenthood until one has the physical and emotional maturity to parent well, has established a reasonable level of economic security, and has entered a stable union are frequent normative preconditions for parenthood. That is, social norms encourage that childbearing be timed appropriately and placed in proper sequence in the unfolding life course. Appropriate timing and sequencing are justified by their advantages for the child, mother, and family.

The most common measure of delayed childbearing is change in the mean (or average) age of first births across time periods (or across groups of women defined by successively more recent birth years, i.e., birth cohorts). The 1990s and early 2000s showed remarkably pervasive and consistent increases in the postponement of first births. In many places mean age at first birth has risen by one to two years per decade since the 1980s.

The most proximate determinants for this change are clear: Contraception and abortion are used to postpone childbearing. Women (or their partners) use these techniques to fit their children into a changing life course that includes longer periods of schooling, less secure employment, postponement of marriage, and increased longevity. The process is best characterized by a sequence of decisions to "not have a child now," to allow for greater economic security (a better or more secure job), to accumulate more wealth (e.g., to buy a home), or to build a more secure relationship with a partner. These postponements can be a process that changes goals and intentions. For instance, an interesting career may emerge, and its pursuit may lead to further postponement or a decision to forego childbearing. Postponement allows for the possibility of a union disruption prior to childbearing, and the absence of a partner may lead a woman to postpone or forego childbearing.

The more distal causes are fundamental social and economic changes that have altered the life course centrality of parenthood and the sequencing and duration of other aspects of the life course. Broadly, perceptions of appropriate and advantageous behavior have changed, as have the structural aspects of adolescence and adulthood. Central structural changes have included a declining proportion of manufacturing jobs and increasing proportions of service and white-collar jobs. This shift places a premium on education and training and produces job niches that include many women. The expansion of women's education, now surpassing men's in many places, and the increase in female employment have provided legitimate alternatives to early marriage and the economic independence to realize them. Ideologies that stress the importance of self-actualization and independence encourage a lengthened life course stage for training, experimentation, and emotional maturity. These changes led Ronald Rindfuss (1991) to characterize contemporary late adolescence and early adulthood as a "disorganized" life course period—normative and structural constraints on the transitions from schooling, to work, to marriage, to parenthood have lost their force. As a result, the timing, sequencing, and duration of these events or activities have become uncertain and highly variable.

Although fertility delay is advantageous and normative, repeated delay can have adverse consequences for individuals and populations. For individuals, repeated postponement can lead to unintended childlessness or to smaller than desired family size because of the diminished fecundity that accompanies aging. Repeated fertility postponement can mean that women may try to have a first child at 30, 35, or even 40 years of age. However, fecundity declines with age, with periods of subfecundity (i.e., reduced capacity to reproduce) generally preceding infecundity. Subfecundity does not preclude childbearing but on average increases substantially the time to pregnancy and/or live birth. Precise estimates are not available, but the percentage of women infecund is low at age 20 (perhaps 2 to 3%); this percentage doubles approximately every 5 years.

Thus, at age 40, many women (perhaps one third) are infecund and many more are subfecund (compared to a decade before); by age 50 nearly all women are infecund. Thus, simulations show that some family-building strategies are difficult—for example, a woman marrying at age 35 or 40 and having two children. A substantial proportion of women with such goals will not be successful because they will become infecund before having the second child (see Bongaarts & Potter, 1983, chapter 8). As Sylvia Hewlett (2002) pointed out, some who are unable to realize their strong desire for children may face huge disappointment , which leads them to seek expensive and invasive treatments for infertility. Childbearing at later ages can also carry new and unique risks; some infertility treatments increase dramatically the likelihood of multiple births and associated complications.

At the aggregate level, the increased demand for infertility treatments and the different set of risks experienced by older mothers and their children have consequences for medical provision. Also, later fertility for a birth cohort is strongly associated with lower fertility—"later" translates as "fewer" in the aggregate according to Hans-Peter Kohler, Francesco Billari, and José Antonio Ortega (2002). So to the extent that low fertility in a population is seen as problematic, fertility postponement is clearly part of the problem. Finally, even if women are able to postpone childbearing *and* have all the children they want, Bongaarts and Feeney (1998) pointed out that postponement lowers fertility levels in the current period. A useful way to think about this is that when births are postponed, they are pushed into a subsequent time period. The TFR combines this timing effect with any possible change in the number of births. The implication of this is that when ages at childbearing are increasing, the TFR (as an indicator of long-term or completed fertility) is biased downward. For many countries, Tomás Sobotka (2004) noted, this bias accounts for up to one third of the difference between observed and replacement level fertility (i.e., one third of the difference between 1.5 and 2.1 equals .2 of a birth).

MARITAL AND NONMARITAL CHILDBEARING

The focus on the marital status of the mother (or the legitimate/illegitimate status of the child) has long cultural, legal, and intellectual roots. Details can vary, but cultures have often linked marriage with socially sanctioned sexual intercourse; that is, marriage legitimated sexual intercourse between a husband and wife. In some social contexts the discovery of illicit (premarital or extramarital) intercourse, or even credible rumors of it, could result in strong sanctions, especially for women. Clearly chastity until marriage and sexual exclusivity in marriage would guarantee men of the paternity of their wife's children; paternity in turn linked a man to an identifiable number of children to whom he had rights and obligations. These norms often coexisted with inheritance laws that specified that only children born within marriage were legal (or legitimate) heirs to family rights and property. This recurring attention to offspring legitimacy is reflected in various theoretical attempts to explain its historical and geographic reach by authors such as Bronislaw Malinowski (1964) and Randall Collins (1975).

Twenty-first century attention to marital/nonmarital childbearing has important differences and similarities to this legacy. Differences include the availability of genetic paternity tests that can take the place of marriage in linking men to their progeny. However, as in the past, these links are desired so that responsibility for the support and care of children can be assigned. Other differences include a reduced importance of father's status in determining children's status in contemporary contexts, because contemporary societies are less patriarchal, and status is more often achieved rather than ascribed. Most important, studies, such as those done by Sara McLanahan and Christine Percheski (in press), show residence in a family with both biological parents remains a strong predictor of children's well-being and later life success.

Measurement of marital/nonmarital childbearing is not as straightforward as it might seem. First, there is an issue of the timing and sequencing of the marriage vis-à-vis the conception and the birth. In many contexts, norms specify that marriage precede sexual intercourse and conception. However, in some times/places these norms are frequently violated. They may not produce nonmarital births because premarital conceptions may be "legitimated" by marriage after conception but prior to the birth (these marriages are often in the first three or four months of pregnancy); the prevalence of legitimation varies by social groups and across time (see Parnell, Swicegood, & Stevens, 1994, for U.S. trends and differences). In the United States a birth is considered marital if the mother was married at the birth of the child or at anytime during the pregnancy.

A second definitional issue is posed by marriage—when is someone married? Contemporary definitions of nonmarital births include births to long-term cohabiting couples even if they subsequently marry. Such long-term cohabiters provide the stable family environment thought to advantage children. To the extent that the distinction between cohabiting and marital unions fade, the distinction between marital and nonmarital births should become less important. Such definitional issues must be kept in mind when interpreting data on nonmarital births.

With the above cautions in mind, there are two common measures of nonmarital childbearing: The first is the nonmarital birth rate, and the second is the nonmarital birth ratio (or the percentage of all births that are nonmarital). The first measure treats unmarried women as a separate population and estimates their number of births (b) divided by an estimate of risk (the population of unmarried women [w]). This statistic measures the likelihood that an unmarried woman will have a birth. The second measure, the nonmarital ratio, indicates the proportion of children born in a particular year to unmarried mothers.

In the United States the nonmarital ratio has increased steadily over the past several decades: from 5.3, to 14.3, to 28.0, to 36.9 in 1960, 1975, 1990, and 2005, respectively, according to Stephanie Ventura and Christine Bachrach (2000) and Joyce Martin and colleagues (2007). In 1996 Herbert Smith, S. Philip Morgan, and Tanya Koropeckyj-Cox indicated that the reason for this increase is that the nonmarital ratio has four distinct components: the number of women in the (a) married and (b) unmarried populations and the birth rates for (c) married and (d) unmarried women. Again in the U.S. context, the most important of these factors is the increasing number of unmarried women (and a relative decline in the married). In effect, the postponement of marriage among Whites and the decline of marriage at all ages among Blacks has put more women in the unmarried category and thus at risk of a nonmarital birth. Of secondary importance, an increasing birth rate among unmarried White women (but not Blacks) has contributed to this trend. For both racial groups a decline in the rate of marital childbearing plays a tertiary but significant role.

ADDITIONAL FERTILITY DIFFERENTIALS

Other fertility differences have and continue to attract research attention. The nature of these differences varies over time and place. Four important differences became the focus of U.S. research beginning in the late 20th century.

Fertility differences by education are frequently examined; a common finding is modestly higher fertility for the less educated. A life course perspective helps account for these differences. In the contemporary United States, for example, most young women intend to have small families. Those who do well in school and have high aspirations tend to remain in school and postpone childbearing. Following their investments in higher education, they pursue jobs that have career ladders, which can produce further postponement of childbearing. Thus, those attaining high levels of education are more likely to follow the pattern of delayed childbearing. This results in later and less childbearing. In contrast, those doing poorly in school are less likely to continue their education and are more likely to take jobs seen as less rewarding. These women are also more likely to bear their children early and to have more of them. As noted by some researchers (Rindfuss, Morgan, & Offutt, 1996), the most striking differences by education are in fertility timing with differences in number of children relatively modest.

Racial or ethnic differences receive considerable attention. A first level of explanation is to see if the different socioeconomic standing of the racial or ethnic group accounts for the differences. For instance, does one group have higher poverty or lower educational attainment than another (perhaps due to past or current discrimination)? Such differences are often part of the explanation for overall differences. However, if differences persist after these comparisons, then hypotheses of "minority status" may be employed. The role of minority status depends on the historical context of the race/ethnic group. In a classic formulation, Calvin Goldscheider and Peter Uhlenberg (1969) argued that Jews in the United States reduced their fertility to invest in the education of their children because upward mobility was possible. In contrast, Blacks in the United States faced harsher discrimination such that upward mobility was less promising, and, as a result, fertility limitation was less attractive. Further, in contexts in which racial/ethnic tensions are also political, higher fertility may be encouraged as a means to strengthen the minority group politically.

Differences in fertility by immigrant status are frequently observed; for instance, in the contemporary United States, immigrant Hispanics, especially Mexican immigrants, have higher fertility than do non-Hispanic Whites or Blacks. Assimilation models commonly are invoked to account for these differences. In short, assimilation models posit declining differences across generations as the immigrant group is incorporated into the economic and social fabric of the receiving country. As a result, convergence in behavior is expected in a broad range of behaviors, including speaking the host country language, attaining similar levels of education, and adopting similar marriage and fertility behavior. This assimilation model explains well the fertility and socioeconomic convergence of European

immigrant groups and U.S. natives across the 20th century. Further, when data are appropriately examined, Emilio Parrado and S. Philip Morgan (in press) found evidence that Hispanic/non-Hispanic fertility convergence exists. Nevertheless, some authors, such as Douglas Massey (1995), have questioned whether this model is appropriate for the 21st century flow of Hispanic immigrants and suggested that a continuing influx of immigrants into segregated areas will retard socioeconomic integration and assimilation.

Religious differences may be overlaid on group differences in socioeconomic standing, racial/ethnic composition, and in some cases immigrant status. In their work in 2007, Charles Westoff and Tomas Frejka used the example of Muslim immigrants in Europe and found evidence of all of these factors. In such cases isolating socioeconomic, racial/ethnic, and religious differences can be difficult, impossible, or even inappropriate; these factors can combine in powerful, but historically unique, ways. For instance, different family behaviors (including fertility) may take on significance as markers of identity, for instance in South Asia (Morgan et al., 2002) or India (Dharmaligham & Morgan, 2004). Similarly, in some contexts substantial religious differences persist among groups that are not disadvantaged or identifiable as another race. These differences highlight the importance of religion for maintaining a set of ideas (or an interpretive frame) that privileges certain lifestyles.

In the United States in the 21st century, for instance, primary religious differences are not by denomination (i.e., Protestant versus Catholic) but by measures of intensity of religious belief (i.e., respondents' reports of the "importance of religion in their life"). Those reporting religion as "very important" (as opposed to "not important") have a TFR .5 higher (2.3 versus 1.8). In terms of proximate determinants, this difference can be traced to intentions for larger families among the more religious. Further, this intent to have more children is embedded in a set of ideas that privilege marriage, family, and traditional views of family life. Consistent with this evidence, Ron Lesthaeghe and Lisa Neidert (2006) showed strong state- and county-level associations among levels and timing of fertility, cohabitation and marriage, and political indicators such as the percentage voting for George W. Bush in the 2000 and 2004 presidential elections. They argued that the density of secular versus religious orientations across U.S. states and counties explain these aggregate associations.

FUTURE RESEARCH DIRECTIONS AND ISSUES

In the future, researchers of childbearing will continue to wrestle with all these issues, but important new questions lie ahead as well. Three deserve mention here.

PRONATALIST POLICIES

A growing number of industrialized countries have fertility rates substantially below replacement levels. This low fertility produces aging populations that increase government expenditures for old age financial support and health care. In the long run, very low fertility produces dramatic population decline. One policy response would aim to increase fertility. A major reason for low fertility is fertility postponement due to the competing demands in young adults' life courses. An appropriate intervention would provide high quality, affordable, and widely available daycare, which would allow women to work outside the home or pursue other activities while beginning a family.

Data from Norway (Rindfuss, Guilkey, Morgan, Kravdal, & Guzzo, 2007) showed that state-subsidized childcare reduces age at first birth. However, these effects depend on the systematic placement of daycare centers. Specifically, these centers open in locales where the tension between work and family is greatest (and where fertility is initially lowest). Once daycare placement is completed, the expected pronatalist effects are apparent.

BIBLIOGRAPHY

McDonald, P. (2006). Low fertility and the state: The efficacy of policy. *Population and Development Review*, *32*, 485–510.

Rindfuss, R. R., Guilkey, D., Morgan, S. P., Kravdal, O., & Guzzo, K. B. (2007). Child care availability and fertility in Norway: Pronatalist effects. *Demography*, *44*, 345–372.

First, is the proliferation of very low fertility inevitable? Will its global spread be pervasive? In 2000 to 2005, 31 (17%) had TFR rates below 1.5; another 37 (19%) had below replacement level rates (a TFR < 2.1; see Table 1). These low fertility countries are not confined to one or two geographical regions, nor do they share cultural/historical similarities. Below-replacement fertility exists in China, Japan, South Korea, virtually all of Europe (East and West), Australia, and North America—with the United States above or below replacement depending on the year examined (see Morgan & Taylor, 2006).

This low fertility seems not to be a rejection of children or parenthood but instead is closely linked to delayed childbearing. In industrialized countries men and women intend to have small families (usually a stated intention for two children), but education, careers, leisure pursuits, and economic insecurity conspire to produce a long sequence of postponements. Although many achieve the two children they intend, falling short of this goal is more common than exceeding it. Thus, couples are having fewer children than they intended and fewer than their societies require for long-term population stability. The sidebar discusses possible policy interventions. However, a number of countries are well into their third decade of very low fertility—a low fertility crisis has arrived for these societies. How widespread will low fertility become, and how responsive will it be to pronatalist policy?

A second important question focuses on the role of men in fertility and parenting behavior. Fertility research has focused primarily on women. Some attention is shifting toward men, but some of this new work focuses on the fertility of men and largely ignores women. Instead, what is needed is a focus on the fertility of both married and unmarried couples. Such a focus is challenging because it requires longitudinal life course analysis of both partners. Further, in many contexts, this analysis must include the multiple partnerships that are part of many women's and men's life courses. The previous unions and childbearing of women and men have implications for their subsequent unions and fertility decisions. Early 21st century research on "multipartnered fertility" and "blended families" has begun to address such issues.

Finally, what are the likely impacts of recent and emerging reproductive technology? In general, new technology will be adopted if its use is considered moral and acceptable and if people are motivated to use it. Over the long term, technological advances have increased control over fertility—some methods reduce the likelihood of pregnancy and childbearing whereas others increase the chances. Active debates focus on whether and which methods are considered moral or acceptable. These debates have an impact on the social and political environment in which new technology is developed and deployed. For instance, will the morning-after-pill become more widely available and acceptable? Will assisted reproductive technology (ART) become less expensive?

The fecundity reductions associated with delayed childbearing are increasing the demand for ART. In 2004 the Centers for Disease Control and Prevention reported that more than 45,000 births (more than 1% of all births) resulted from ART. Screening these embryos for healthy genetic predispositions or for their gender (daughters or sons) is possible and will become increasingly affordable and thus will reduce obstacles to their use. Pregnancy and childbirth may be transformed as well; Fay Menacker (2005) noted that cesarean delivery is becoming more common in cases in which it is not a medical necessity. Such changes could fundamentally alter the costs, constraints, and patterns of future childbearing.

SEE ALSO Volume 1: *Breastfeeding; Transition to Parenthood;* Volume 2: *Abortion; Birth Control; Childlessness; Cohabitation; Fatherhood; Infertility; Marriage; Maternal Mortality; Motherhood; Sexual Activity, Adulthood;* Volume 3: *Demographic Transition Theories.*

BIBLIOGRAPHY

Alan Guttmacher Institute. (2002). *Teenagers' sexual and reproductive health: Facts in brief.* New York: Author. Retrieved May 2, 2008, from http://www.guttmacher.org/pubs

Becker, G. S. (1981). *A treatise on the family.* Cambridge, MA: Harvard University Press.

Bongaarts, J., & Feeney, G. (1998). On the quantum and tempo of fertility. *Population and Development Review, 24,* 271–291.

Bongaarts, J., & Potter, R. G. (1983). *Fertility, biology, and behavior.* New York: Academic Press.

Bongaarts, J., & Watkins, S. C. (1996). Social interactions and contemporary fertility transitions. *Population and Development Review, 22,* 639–682.

Campbell, A. A. (1968). The role of family planning in the reduction of poverty. *Journal of Marriage and the Family, 30,* 236–245.

Centers for Disease Control and Prevention. (2004). *2004 assisted reproductive technology report.* Retrieved May 2, 2008, from http://www.cdc.gov/art/

Coale, A. (1973). The demographic transition reconsidered. In *International Union for the Scientific Study of Population Conference* (pp. 53–72). Paris: International Union for the Scientific Study of Population.

Collins, R. (1975). *Conflict sociology.* New York: Academic Press.

Davis, K., & Blake, J. (1956). Social structure and fertility: An analytical framework. *Economic Development and Cultural Change, 4,* 211–235.

Dharmalingam, A., & Morgan, S. P. (2004). Pervasive Muslim/Hindu fertility differences in India. *Demography, 41,* 529–546.

Feeney, G. (1991). Fertility decline in Taiwan. A study using parity progression ratios. *Demography, 28,* 467–480.

Furstenberg, F. F. Jr., Gunn, J. B., & Morgan, S. P. (1987). *Adolescent mothers in later life.* New York: Cambridge University Press.

Goldscheider, C., & Uhlenberg, P. R. (1969). Minority group status and fertility. *American Journal of Sociology, 74,* 361–372.

Hewlett, S. A. (2002). *Creating a life: Professional women and the quest for children.* New York: Mirmax Books.

Hoffman, S. D., Foster, E. M. & Furstenberg, F. F. Jr. (1993). *Reevaluating the costs of teenage childbearing. Demography, 30,* 1–13.

Hotz, J. V., McElroy, S., & Sanders, S. (2005). Teenage childbearing and its life cycle consequences: Exploiting a very natural experiment. *Journal of Human Resources, 40*(3), 683–715.

Howell, N. L. (1979). *Demography of the Dobe !kung.* New York: Academic Press.

Jones, E. F., Darroch Forrest, J., Goldman, N., Henshaw, S. K., Lincoln, R., & Rosoff, J. I. (1985). Teenage pregnancy in developed countries: Determinants and policy implications. *Family Planning Perspectives, 17,* 53–63.

Kohler, H. P., Billari, F. C., & Ortega, J. A. (2002). The emergence of lowest-low fertility in Europe during the 1990s. *Population and Development Review, 28,* 641–680.

Lesthaeghe, R., & Neidert, L. (2006). The second demographic transition in the United States: Exception or textbook example? *Population and Development Review, 32,* 660–698.

Malinowski, B. (1964). Parenthood, the basis of social structure. In R. L. Coser (Ed.), *The family: Its structure and functions* (pp. 3–19). New York: St. Martin's Press.

Martin, J. A., Hamilton, B. E., Sutton, P. D., Ventura, S. J., Menacker, F., Kirmeyer, S., et al. (2007). Births: Final data for 2005. *National Vital Statistics Reports, 56*(6). Hyattsville, MD: National Center for Health Statistics. Retrieved May 2, 2008, from http://www.cdc.gov/nchs

Mason, K. O. (1997). Explaining fertility transitions. *Demography, 34,* 443–454.

Massey, D. S. (1995). The new immigration and ethnicity in the United States. *Population and Development Review, 21,* 631–652.

McLanahan, S., & Percheski, C. (in press). Family structure and the reproduction of inequalities. *Annual Review of Sociology.*

Menacker, F. (2005). Trends in cesarean rates for first births and repeat cesarean rates for low-risk women: United States, 1990–2003. *National vital statistics reports, 54*(4). Hyattsville, MD: National Center for Health Statistics.

Morgan, S. P. (2003). Is low fertility a 21st century demographic crisis? *Demography, 40,* 589–603.

Morgan, S. P., Stash, S., Smith, H. L., & Mason, K. O. (2002). Muslim and non-Muslim differences in female autonomy and fertility: Evidence from four Asian countries. *Population and Development Review, 28,* 515–538.

Morgan, S. P., & Taylor, M. (2006). Low fertility in the 21st century. *Annual Review of Sociology, 32,* 375–400.

Parnell, A. M., Swicegood, C. G., & Stevens, G. (1994). Nonmarital pregnancies and marriage in the United States. *Social Forces, 73,* 263–287.

Parrado, E. A., & Morgan, S. P. (in press). Intergenerational fertility among Hispanic women: New evidence of immigrant assimilation. *Demography.*

Rindfuss, R. R. (1991). The young adult years: Diversity, structural change, and fertility. *Demography, 28,* 493–512.

Rindfuss, R. R., Morgan, S. P., & Offutt, K. (1996). Education and the changing age pattern of American fertility: 1963–1989. *Demography, 33,* 277–290.

Smith, H. L., Morgan, S. P., & Koropeckyj-Cox, T. (1996). A decomposition of trends in the nonmarital fertility ratios of Blacks and Whites in the United States, 1960–1992. *Demography, 33,* 141–151.

Sobotka, T. (2004). Is lowest-low fertility in Europe explained by the postponement of childbearing? *Population Development and Review*, 30, 195–220.

United Nations. (2007). *World population prospects: The 2006 revision, highlights* (Working Paper No. ESA/P/WP.202). Retrieved May 2, 2008, from http://www.un.org/esa

Ventura, S. J., & Bachrach, C. A. (2000). Nonmarital childbearing in the United States, 1940–1999. *National Vital Statistics Reports*, 48(6). Hyattsville, Maryland: National Center for Health Statistics.

Westoff, C. F., & Frejka, T. (2007). Religiousness and fertility among European Muslims. *Population and Development Review*, 33, 785–810.

S. Philip Morgan

CHILDLESSNESS

In general, the term *childless* is used to describe adults who have never had biological or adopted children, and the term *childlessness* is used to refer to this state. These general terms, however, encompass several distinct groups: people who want children but are biologically unable to have them, people who have made a voluntary choice never to have children, people who are postponing parenthood until later in their adulthood, and people who have outlived their children, who are sometimes called "functionally childless" (Dykstra and Wagner, 2007; Rowland, 2007). Researchers who study childbearing and parenthood usually conceptualize childlessness as a lifetime, permanent condition. From this perspective, only members of the first two groups are childless. Although members of the latter two groups are childless in a broad sense (they currently have no living children), they may become parents in the future or they were parents in the past.

The *involuntary childless* are a group of men and women who want and intend to become parents but whose ability (or partner's ability) to reproduce is constrained (biologically or socially) and who have not become parents through other means (e.g., surrogacy, egg or sperm donor, adoption). Note that the label "involuntary" is not necessarily clear-cut. For example, persons unable to conceive and/or maintain a pregnancy can at times become parents by opting for biomedical interventions and/or legal processes (adoption). The decision to parent *exists* for them, but they *choose* to forgo parenthood. From another perspective, however, the inability to reproduce is not a choice, especially if people consider "natural" biological childbearing the only acceptable route into parenthood. With respect to social constraints, some people may want to have children but are selected out of the pool of potential mates because of institutionalization (e.g., incarceration), compromised physical or mental health, or lack of self-sufficiency (e.g., unem-ployed, living with parents, homeless). Although these people may intend to form romantic relationships and have children (with no known biological constraints), their limited ability to marry and work results in social constraints against having children (e.g., remaining unmarried, not qualifying for adoption). The key issue is that people who are involuntarily childless may differ in their fertility intentions and behaviors.

In contrast, *voluntary childlessness* defines a group of women and men who have not become parents either because they made a conscious decision not to have children or made other decisions in life that postponed parenthood repeatedly and, eventually, permanently. The topic of voluntary childlessness thus highlights the question of whether and when people make decisions about childbearing. Many voluntarily childless adults report that they made their decision to be childless during adolescence or childhood (Veevers, 1980). In contrast to people who actively decided early or late in their lives to remain childless are people who become childless by repeatedly postponing childbearing and eventually end their reproductive lives without having had children. The latter type of childlessness unfolds as a series of more or less passive decisions often based on other aspects of the life course, for example timing (e.g., not now) or events (e.g., after I am married). Thus the voluntarily childless is composed of three groups: early deciders, late deciders, and perpetual postponers (Dariotis, 2005). Taking into account this heterogeneity is central to understanding voluntary childlessness because the decision process differs among these types. Note also that the perpetual postponers may be difficult to identify early in the life course because they have not yet made the "decision" to not bear children.

IMPLICATIONS OF CHILDLESSNESS FOR SOCIETIES AND INDIVIDUALS

To continue its existence, a society needs its members to reproduce themselves. This is true not only because new births replace people who have died, maintaining the size of the population, but because societies rely on younger members for certain tasks, for example financially and physically supporting the aged. Because reproduction is essential to societies' survival, societies developed norms, customs and beliefs that, to varying degrees, encouraged and regulated parenthood (for example, by discouraging births outside of marriage or marriagelike unions) and discouraged and stigmatized childlessness (for example, endorsing the motherhood mandate by which every woman was expected to have children as a sign of her womanhood). Some argue that vestiges of pronatalist norms sanction the childless, especially the voluntarily childless, who are viewed as selfish and immature.

Permanent childlessness challenges these societal needs and the pronatalist norms surrounding them. The extent to which they do so, however, depends on the demographic situation of the society. Prior to the widespread use of fertility control, most childlessness was involuntary and the main obstacle to maintaining the size of the population was mortality. Only once mortality rates declined and the use of birth control became widespread could low fertility levels, resulting from both smaller family sizes and increases in voluntary childlessness, be viewed as a threat to a society's continuation. Demographers define "replacement level" fertility as the average number of children women will need to bear in their lifetimes to maintain the size of a population. This number is around 2.1 children per woman. Currently, a number of nations in the developed world are experiencing or approaching below-replacement fertility. For example, between 1995 and 2000 Italian fertility rates were 1.2 children per woman; for Spain and Greece the rates were 1.16 and 1.3, respectively (Morgan and Hagewen, 2005). Although the ultimate concern about low fertility is whether these societies can continue in their present form, the more urgent concern is that low fertility results in an aging population, which in turn raises a host of social, economic and political challenges.

Childlessness has implications for the individual life course as well. Historically (and in many contemporary developing nations), the transition to parenthood marked a rite of passage into adulthood. In modern societies the importance of childbearing as a marker of adulthood has diminished, and the fraction of the life course spent as a parent to minor children is lower (especially with smaller family sizes and longer average lifespan). Nevertheless, the majority of individuals become parents, and the childless need to rely on other transitions to mark their adult status (e.g., self-sufficiency, marriage).

People who are childless may experience different life courses than those in the parent majority. First, people who are childless do not experience the financial and opportunity costs of parenthood. To the extent that they have other resources—temporal, financial, and human—voluntarily childless people may devote these resources to other activities, such as careers, education, charitable causes, or personal development. In fact, the prevalence of permanent childlessness has increased in part because alternatives to parenthood have emerged in modern societies (e.g., careers, educational attainment, self-actualization) and because norms supporting individualized life choices support these alternatives. For other people, not having the financial and time resources (for whatever reason—e.g., poverty, low-paying career choice) to raise children according to societal standards is a motive not to have children.

Second, Heaton, Jacobson, and Holland (1999) found that the decision to have children corresponds with the decision to marry. In other words, voluntarily childless people feel less compelled to marry or to marry during their childbearing years. As a result, they may spend more (or all) of their adult years unmarried. Given that marriage confers health and social benefits to men, this may mean that never-married childless men will experience greater health disparities relative to their married parent counterparts. The extent to which observed disparities are attributable to childlessness per se, to the lack of marriage per se, or to individual characteristics (e.g., low education, unemployment), however, remains to be determined.

Most childless adults are well adjusted and do not report elevated negative mental health outcomes. As Dykstra and Hagestad (2007) report, childless older adults are not "a sad bunch," contrary to popular stereotypes. For example, they found that childless never-married women evidence greater advantages to their female and male parent counterparts in terms of socioeconomic status, educational attainment, and other factors.

TRENDS IN VOLUNTARY AND INVOLUNTARY CHILDLESSNESS

Rates of childlessness in most developing nations are relatively low because of low levels of contraceptive use and large family size norms. Childlessness that does occur in developing nations mostly results from malnutrition, disease-induced sterility, early widowhood, and never marrying. Developed nations have a higher prevalence of childlessness because of widespread use of contraceptive and lower family size norms. In addition, alternatives to childbearing are more pervasive as well as the norms of individualism that make these alternatives viable choices.

In the United States at the turn of the 20th century, childlessness resulted equally from infecundity/sterility and voluntary intentions (Morgan, 1991). Over the second half of the 20th century, this proportion shifted such that two-thirds of childlessness was attributable to personal choice and one-third to infecundity (Houseknecht, 1987; Morgan, 1991; Poston and Trent, 1982; Rowland, 2007). Better nutrition, general medical advances, and new treatments for infertility meant that infecundity was no longer the primary determinant of childlessness. In the early 21st century only 3% of couples experience infecundity (Rowland, 2007). Whereas the incidence of involuntary childlessness declined over time, the incidence of voluntary childlessness increased and accounts for a greater proportion of total childlessness (Houseknecht, 1987). Intentionality, personal choice, life course preferences, and postponed marriage coupled with increased reliance on birth control and voluntary sterility

Characteristic	Number of women	Percent childless
AGE		
Total	61,588	44.6
15 to 19 years	9,964	93.3
20 to 24 years	10,068	68.89
25 to 29 years	9,498	44.2
30 to 34 years	10,082	27.6
35 to 39 years	10,442	19.6
40 to 44 years	11,535	19.3
RACE AND HISPANIC ORIGIN		
White alone		
Total	47,984	45.1
15 to 19 years	7,646	93.9
20 to 24 years	7,790	70.8
25 to 29 years	7,309	45.6
30 to 34 years	7,790	28.4
35 to 39 years	8,212	20.2
40 to 44 years	9,237	19.1
White alone, non-Hispanic		
Total	39,120	47.0
15 to 19 years	6,174	95.5
20 to 24 years	6,252	75.4
25 to 29 years	5,699	49.6
30 to 34 years	6,242	30.9
35 to 39 years	6,784	21.3
40 to 44 years	7,968	20.0
Black alone		
Total	8,798	40.5
15 to 19 years	1,571	90.4
20 to 24 years	1,495	57.0
25 to 29 years	1,370	33.3
30 to 34 years	1,408	18.9
35 to 39 years	1,431	17.0
40 to44 years	1,523	21.3
Asian alone		
Total	3,035	47.2
15 to 19 years	383	94.7
20 to 24 years	443	80.8
25 to 29 years	549	50.4
30 to 34 years	595	40.0
35 to 39 years	559	19.0
40 to 44 years	505	17.8
Hispanic (any race)		
Total	9,618	37.1
15 to 19 years	1,588	87.9
20 to 24 years	1,684	52.8
25 to 29 years	1,744	31.5
30 to 34 years	1,700	18.6
35 to 39 years	1,524	15.1
40 to 44 years	1,378	13.8

SOURCE: U.S Census Bureau.
Current Population Survey. June 2004.

Table 1. Fertility indicators for women 15 to 44 years old by age, race, and Hispanic origin, June 2004. CENGAGE LEARNING, GALE.

remain the primary mechanisms underlying childlessness. National estimates of childlessness range between 10% and 20% of the population, on average, with Australia, England, Scandinavian nations, and the United States having rapidly increasing rates approaching or exceeding 20% (Rowland, 2007). Cross-national comparisons, however, are plagued by differences in reporting biases and sampling issues (Rowland, 2007).

Depending on the definition of childlessness and the sample used, the proportion of childbearing-aged women in the United States who are voluntarily childless ranges from 6.4% (for married couples studied in the 1980s) to 20% (projections for women born in 1962) (Heaton, Jacobson, and Holland, 1999; Houseknecht, 1987; Rovi, 1994). In a nationally representative sample of adolescents aged 16 to 22 in 2001, 17% reported that they intended to be childless (Dariotis, 2005). The fact that Americans have experienced decreased fertility is well documented, and voluntary childlessness has and continues to play a part in that decline (Bianchi and Casper, 2000; Morgan, 1991; Morgan, 1996; Rindfuss and Brewster, 1996; Teachman, Tedrow, and Crowder, 2000). Although this trend is well evidenced, researchers lack a unified explanation for why the decline has occurred (Hirschman, 1994). Such a unified explanation most likely does not exist because of the heterogeneity of motivations across subgroups of people (discussed below).

PATHWAYS INTO PERMANENT CHILDLESSNESS

People can become permanently childless *involuntarily* through a number of means. Some people (or their partners) are subfecund (i.e., their ability to reproduce is impaired), which may result from genetic factors, disease-induced sterility due to untreated infections and conditions, and malnutrition. Others may intend to have children, but have difficulty marrying and mating because others perceive them as low-quality mates (e.g., incarcerated, unemployed, or physically unhealthy people). Other people may marry, become widowed before having children, and never remarry.

Similarly, people become childless *voluntarily* by different paths. *Early deciders* (Houseknecht, 1987; Veevers, 1980) make an active decision to forgo parenthood during their mid- to late adolescence. Retrospective, qualitative studies (Veevers, 1980) suggest that early deciders' decisions stemmed from issues in their families-of-origin, most notably parentification, whereby they were expected to assume parenting responsibilities for younger siblings or siblings with a disability. These early deciders claim that they already completed their parenting duties by rearing their siblings, an experience they do not want to relive. Other commonly reported reasons include the fear of being "bad" parents, de-identification with same-sex parents, incompatibility of parenthood with career and leisure preferences, disinclination toward children, and traumatic early life events—such as experiencing parental divorce during youth and attributing it to parental demands and child presence (Houseknecht, 1987; Veevers, 1980).

Some early deciders remark how negative parenthood was for their parents and believe that parenthood destroyed the quality of their parents' marriages and/or limited their parents' goal achievement. Still others de-identify with the parenting role to prevent "becoming their parents." Hearing negative messages about parenthood and observing parental and marital distress becomes internalized and develops into negative working models of parenthood (e.g., parenthood destroys spousal relations; parenthood precludes freedom and personal growth). These early experiences and rationalizations appear robust and resilient to change (Pol, 1983; Veevers, 1980). Using prospective data, Dariotis (2005) showed that voluntary childless intentions begin in adolescence and that strong predictors included family-of-origin experiences, attitudes toward children, and intentions to remain permanently single.

Late deciders make an active decision, during adulthood, not to have children. Late deciders typically attribute this decision to career and lifestyle factors. For instance, late deciders may perceive parenthood and career aspirations as inconsistent/irreconcilable or believe that parenthood does not offer the same satisfaction as independence. Others may fear that parenthood would compromise their relationship with their romantic partner. Additional reasons include partner choice (becoming involved with a partner who does not want to have children or a partner who they believe will not be a good parent), experience with others' children (observing the demands and related consequences of parenthood for their peers), and health (physical and mental health–related problems that lead the person to doubt his or her parenting capabilities). Still others report philosophical reasons not to have children. For example, people who espouse zero population growth and environmental conservationists want to minimize their contribution to the world's population and depletion of natural resources, respectively.

Perpetual postponers make a sequence of decisions that "the time is not right" to have children because of career, education, and/or marriage (postponement) outcomes. Eventually, they postpone childbearing until a point in their lives when childbearing is not likely (at ages over 40 women are increasingly less likely to conceive) or childbearing is not preferable. Postponement occurs for many reasons. For instance, late nest-leavers may continue to live with parents into their 30s and 40s because they are caring for aging parents, live at home while building human capital (advanced degrees and prolonged workforce participation), or have difficulty finding stable employment. Later onset of independent living and prolonged time pursuing educational and career goals has a ripple effect whereby marriage or stable cohabiting union establishment is postponed. Late union formation, in turn, postpones childbearing. Relationship disruption, via divorce or break-up, perpetuates the ripple effect; it takes time to find another suitable partner, establish a relationship, and con-

sider having children. "Timing out" of the fecund years for women is a product of when they leave home, finish their education, spend enough time establishing a foothold in the workforce, find a mate, stabilize a relationship, and whether the relationship ends prior to having children.

Encouraged Childlessness—a Special Case Yet another group of voluntarily childless individuals are people who experience pressure from family, friends, partners, and health care providers not to have children because of debilitating and/or transmittable conditions (e.g., HIV/AIDS). Even with antiretroviral medications that reduce the chance of disease transference to offspring, HIV-positive women (and men) worry about their own longevity and ability to manage the physical and emotional strains of parenthood. People who suffer from genetic-related conditions (e.g., psychological and/or physical) consider the potential of passing these conditions onto the next generation as well as their likelihood of living long enough to observe their children grow up. Much more research is needed to assess the degree to which disease and genetic conditions contribute to voluntary childlessness intentions.

GAPS IN RESEARCH

Given increasing trends in permanent childlessness, this historically neglected area of study warrants far more attention. Unanswered questions abound, and past findings based on retrospective accounts and limited samples need to be reexamined with improved methods (longitudinal, prospective studies using mixed methods and biological and self-report data). For example, future research needs to examine childlessness among all relationship statuses—not just married couples—and across development. Furthermore, understanding how sex hormones (e.g., testosterone), disease status (e.g., HIV-positive), genetic conditions, and physical and psychological limitations influence the decision to remain childless warrants investigation. Taking a process-oriented approach to the study of permanent childlessness will provide a more in-depth understanding of how and why women and men come to the end of their reproductive lives without bearing or adopting children and how a life without children affects their lives, positively and negatively.

If societies want to maintain or increase total fertility rates (TFRs), pronatal policies need to target alleviating the life-course competition individuals experience with respect to individual goals and parenthood demands (Pierre and Dariotis, 2005). Yet it is not clear such policies will have the desired effect. European nations adopting policies that subsidize childcare costs, provide generous parental leaves, and so on, have not resulted in increased TFRs; instead, TFRs continue to drop in those nations (Pierre and Dariotis, 2005).

SEE ALSO Volume 1: *Transition to Parenthood;* Volume 2: *Birth Control; Fatherhood; Infertility; Motherhood;* Volume 3: *Global Aging; Population Aging.*

BIBLIOGRAPHY

Bianchi, S. M., & Casper, L.M. (2000). American Families. *Population Bulletin, 55*(4), 1–43.

Bongaarts, J. (2001). Fertility and reproductive preferences in post-transitional societies. *Global Fertility Transition: Population and Development Review (supplement), 27,* 260–281.

Bram, S. (1985). Childlessness revisited: A longitudinal study of voluntary childless couples, delayed parents, and parents. *Lifestyles: A Journal of Changing Patterns, 8,* 46–66.

Burman, B., & de Anda, D. (1986). Parenthood or nonparenthood: A comparison of intentional families. *Lifestyles: A Journal of Changing Patterns, 8,* 69–84.

Dariotis, J. K. (2005). Family formation intentions from adolescence to middle adulthood: Emergence, Persistence, and Process. Ph.D. dissertation. Pennsylvania State University.

DePaulo, B. M., & Morris, W. L. (2005). Singles in society and science. *Psychological Inquiry, 16,* 57–83.

Dykstra, P. A., & Hagestad, G. O. (2007). Childlessness and parenthood in two centuries: Different roads—different maps, Pathways to childlessness and late-life outcomes. *Journal of Family Issues, 28,* 1487–1517.

Dykstra, P. A., & Wagner, M. (2007). Pathways to childlessness and late-life outcomes. *Journal of Family Issues, 28,* 1487–1517.

Elder, G. H., Jr. (1998). The life course and human development. In R. L. W. Damon (Ed.), *Handbook of child psychology,* Vol. 1: *Theoretical models of human development* (pp. 931–991). New York: Wiley.

Furstenberg, F. F. (1976). *Unplanned parenthood: The social consequences of teenage childbearing.* New York: Free Press.

Heaton, T. B., Jacobson, C. K., & Holland, K. (1999). Persistence and change in decisions to remain childless. *Journal of Marriage and the Family, 61,* 531–539.

Hirschman, C. (1994). Why fertility changes. *Annual Review of Sociology, 20,* 203–233.

Hoffman, S. R., & Levant, R. F. (1985). A comparison of childfree and child-anticipated married couples. *Family Relations, 34,* 197–203.

Houseknecht, S. K. (1987). Voluntary childlessness. In M. B. Sussman and S. K. Steinmetz (eds.), *Handbook of marriage and the family* (pp. 369–395). New York: Plenum Press.

Langdridge, D., Connolly, K., & Sheeran, P. (2000). Reasons for wanting a child: A network analytic study. *Journal of Reproductive & Infant Psychology, 18*(4). United Kingdom: Carfax Publishing Ltd.

Morgan, S. P. (1991). Late 19th- and early-20th-century childlessness. *American Journal of Sociology, 97*(3), 779–807.

Morgan, S. P. (1996). Characteristic features of modern American fertility. *Population and Development Review, 22*(supplement), 19–63.

Morgan, S. P., & Hagewen, K. (2005). Is very low fertility inevitable in America? Insights and forecasts from an integrative model of fertility. In A. Booth and A. C. Crouter (Eds.), *The new population problem: Why families in developed countries are shrinking and what it means.* Mahwah, NJ: Lawrence Erlbaum.

Pierre, T. S., & Dariotis, J. K. (2005). Understanding low fertility: The impact of life-course competition on fertility behavior in developed nations (pp. 235–250). In A. Booth & A. C. Crouter (Eds.), *The new population problem: Why families in developed countries are shrinking and what it means.* Mahwah, NJ: Lawrence Erlbaum.

Pol, L. G. (1983). Childlessness: A panel study of expressed intentions and reported fertility. *Social Biology, 30,* 318–327.

Popenoe, D. (1993). American family in decline, 1960–1990: A review and appraisal. *Journal of Marriage and the Family, 55,* 527–555.

Poston, Jr., D. L., & Trent, K. (1982). International variability in childlessness: A descriptive and analytical study. *Journal of Family Issues, 3,* 473–91.

Quesnel-Vallée, A., & Morgan, S. P. (2003). Missing the target? Correspondence of fertility intentions and behavior in the U.S. *Population Research and Policy Review, 22,* 497–525.

Rindfuss, R. R., & Brewster, K. L. (1996). Childrearing and fertility. In J. B. Casterline, R. D. Lee, & K. A. Foote (Eds.), *Fertility in the United States: New patterns, new theories.* New York: Population Council.

Rovi, S. L. D. (1994). Taking "no" for an answer: Using negative reproduction intentions to study the childless/childfree. *Population Research and Policy Review, 13,* 343–365.

Rowland, D. T. (2007). Historical trends in childlessness. *Journal of Family Issues, 28,* 1311–1337.

Seccombe, K. (1991). Assessing the costs and benefits of children: Gender comparisons among childfree husbands and wives. *Journal of Marriage and the Family, 53,* 191–202.

Teachman, J. D., Tedrow, L. M., & Crowder, K. D. (2000). The changing demography of America's families. *Journal of Marriage and the Family, 62,* 1234–1246.

Thomson, E. (1997). Couple childbearing desires, intentions, and births. *Demography, 34,* 343–354.

Thomson, E. (1995). Measuring fertility demand. *Demography, 32*(1), 81–96.

Thomson, E., McDonald, E., & Bumpass, L. L. (1990). Fertility desires and fertility: Hers, his, and theirs. *Demography, 27,* 597–588.

Udry, J. R., Morris, N., & Kovenock, J. (1995). Androgen effects on women's gendered behavior. *Journal of Biosocial Science, 27,* 359–369.

Veevers, J. E. (1980). *Childless by choice.* Toronto: Butterworths.

Jacinda K. Dariotis

CHRONIC ILLNESS, ADULTHOOD

SEE Volume 3: *Chronic Illness, Adulthood and Later Life.*

CIVIC ENGAGEMENT, ADULTHOOD

SEE Volume 2: *Political Behavior and Orientations, Adulthood; Volunteering, Adulthood.*

COHABITATION

Cohabitation is defined by social scientists as two adults of the opposite sex living together in an intimate, non-marital relationship. Cohabitation has rapidly become a prominent feature on the landscape of American family life. Using the 2002 National Survey of Family Growth (NSFG), Kennedy and Bumpass (2007) estimated that 58% of women aged between 25 and 29 had cohabited at some point in their lives. Moreover, about 40% of children in the United States will spend some part of their childhood in a cohabiting household (Kennedy & Bumpass, 2007). Young people in the United States approve of cohabitation at much higher rates than their older counterparts, so it is likely that cohabitation rates will continue to rise in the United States (Smock, 2000).

In attempting to understand the causes and consequences of the rise in cohabitation, scholars have tried to identify whether cohabitation is an alternative to marriage, a prelude to marriage, or a convenient dating arrangement. Clearly all three forms of cohabitation exist, but most agree that the most common form, at least among young adults, is as a prelude to marriage. However, consensus is growing that cohabitation is still an *incomplete* institution in the United States with wide variations in the meanings and norms associated with it.

COHABITATION OVER THE LIFE COURSE

The 2000 U.S. Census counted 5.5 million households that are maintained by a cohabiting couple. Although this number reflects a substantial increase in the incidence of cohabitation over the previous 20 years, it still underestimates the true prevalence and impact of cohabitation. The Census figure is an underestimate because cohabitations are usually short-lived, either quickly dissolving or progressing to marriage. Thus, at any given time the number of cohabiting couples is very small relative to the number of people who have ever cohabited. By contrast, examining cohabitation trends across the life course can provide a more accurate account of cohabitation's dramatic increase in frequency and impact.

Young adults increasingly delay marriage and many cohabit in the meantime. Data for 2002 indicate that 62% of women's first marriages are preceded by cohabitation either with their spouses or with someone else. Cohabitation

is even more common following a divorce and may partly account for observed declines in remarriage rates (Kennedy & Bumpass, 2007). Although cohabitation in later life has received substantially less attention than other life course stages, anecdotal evidence and small-scale studies suggest that cohabitation is on the rise among the elderly as well (Chevan, 1996; Brown, Bulanda, & Lee, 2005). Cohabitation, like marriage, tends to cluster with other important life course transitions, such as job changes, residential moves, and breaks in school enrollment (Guzzo, 2006).

These trends among adults have important implications for children's family experiences. According to 2002 data, about one in three births involve an unmarried mother and of these, about half the mothers are cohabiting with the baby's father. In addition, many mothers cohabit with a man who is not the father of their children, for example, following a divorce. The result is that approximately two in five children spend some time living with a cohabiting parent before they reach age 16 (Kennedy & Bumpass, 2007).

DIFFERENCES BETWEEN COHABITATION AND MARRIAGE

The implications of a societal shift from marriage to cohabitation depend partly on how much these arrangements differ and partly on the ways they differ. Scholars have focused on five dimensions along which marriage and cohabitation differ: stability and commitment, relationship quality, economic security, fertility, and cooperation. Starting with stability and commitment, most cohabiters (about 75%) expect to marry their partner (Manning, Smock, & Majumdar, 2004). Of those who expect to marry, most have *definite plans* to do so. Thus, many cohabiting couples are in committed relationships, but a significant minority is not. Despite the high levels of commitment, cohabiting unions are unstable. Among first cohabiting unions in the period from 1997 to 2001, only about one third resulted in marriage and among those who had not married, fewer than two thirds were still together after two years (Kennedy and Bumpass, 2007). When compared with prior estimates (Bumpass & Lu, 2000), these findings suggest that long-term cohabiting relationships are becoming more common, but cohabiting unions continue to be less enduring than marriages.

Cohabiters also are less satisfied with their relationships than married couples. Importantly, the lower average levels of stability and relationship quality among cohabiters are driven largely by the very low stability and quality levels of the minority who do not plan to marry. Cohabiters with marriage plans, especially those who are in their first cohabiting relationship, enjoy similar levels of relationship quality and stability as those who are married (Brown & Booth, 1996; Teachman, 2003).

	1960	1970	1980	1985	1990	1992	1994	1996	1998	2000
Total number of unmarried couple households (000s)	439	523	1.589	1.983	2.856	3.308	3.661	3.958	4.236	4.736
Number of unmarried couple households with children under 15 years	197	196	431	603	891	1.121	1.270	1.442	1.520	1.675
Percent total unmarried couples households with children under 15 years	44.9%	37.4%	27.1%	30.4%	31.3%	33.8%	34.6%	36.4%	35.9%	35.4%

SOURCE: U.S Census Bureau. *Current Population Reports*, P20-537. Table UC-1. Washington, DC.: U.S. Census Bureau, 2001 in (2002). *Father Facts 4*. Gaithersburg. MD: National Fatherhood Initiative. Pg 76.

Figure 1. *Number of unmarried couple households by presence of children under age 15, 1960–2000.* CENGAGE LEARNING, GALE.

Other important dimensions along which marriage and cohabitation differ are economic potential and employment security. Generally, cohabitation is more common among couples with lower socioeconomic status. Among men, higher levels of education and earning potential are associated with a lower likelihood of forming a cohabiting union and a higher chance of marrying (Thornton, Axinn, & Teachman, 1995; Xie, Raymo, Goyette, & Thornton, 2003). Further, men's job instability is associated with a couple's decision to cohabit rather than marry (Oppenheimer, 2003). Both qualitative and quantitative accounts of cohabiting families describe economic insecurity as a key factor blocking marriage (e.g. Smock, Manning, & Porter, 2005).

In some European countries, Sweden for example, cohabitation is viewed as an alternative form of marriage (Heimdal & Houseknecht, 2003). One reason why Swedes tend to see cohabitation as similar to marriage is because most children in that country are born to cohabiting couples. In the United States, however, an increasing proportion of children are born outside of marriage. Given the steep rise in cohabitation among single adults, many of these births occur in cohabiting couples, leading some researchers to question whether fertility continues to distinguish marriage and cohabitation. On the one hand, the proportion of pregnant cohabiters who marry before the birth of their children is declining, suggesting that cohabitation is becoming an acceptable context for childbearing. On the other hand, there is no growth in the likelihood that cohabiting couples will become pregnant, indicating that cohabitation is not becoming a preferred arrangement for parenthood. Mexican-American women are an exception to this general pattern. Among cohabiting women, levels of fertility for Mexican Americans are much higher than for Anglo-Americans, suggesting that for this group

cohabitation may be a preferred and accepted arrangement (Wildsmith & Raley, 2006). In other words, fertility continues to distinguish marriage from cohabitation, but marriage is becoming less distinct from cohabitation along this dimension, perhaps especially for Mexican Americans.

Two of the foundations of marriage are economic cooperation and specialization. That is, married couples tend to pool resources and, although there is some overlap, husbands typically do different tasks than wives, which may include differential involvement in paid work. The interdependence that specialization creates may serve as a barrier to divorce. This is one way that marriage is distinct from cohabitation. Whereas among spouses having similar incomes is positively associated with the risk of divorce, among cohabiters having similar incomes is associated with stability (Brines & Joyner, 1999). Research on housework provides further evidence that specialization and cooperation are less evident in cohabitation than marriage. The difference in time spent on housework performed by husbands and wives is greater than the difference between cohabiting partners (South & Spitze, 1994). This is not because cohabiting women do less housework than their married counterparts; cohabiting men do more housework than married men do (Davis, Greenstein, & Marks, 2007). In addition, cohabiting couples with a more traditional division of labor move more quickly to marriage (Sanchez, Manning, & Smock, 1998). Taken together, this research supports the idea that specialization and economic cooperation distinguish marriage from cohabitation. This distinction may arise because cohabitation, at least in the United States, is a relatively short lived and sometimes tentative arrangement, which reduces the benefits of specialization and increases the risks associated with pooling economic resources.

THE IMPACT OF COHABITATION ON ADULTS AND CHILDREN

Scientists and policy makers alike are interested in the long-term ramifications of the rise in cohabitation rates. This impact is difficult to study for a number of reasons. First, as indicated already, the meaning of cohabitation is unclear and different groups are likely to understand and be affected differently by it. Second, cohabitation is a *moving target* with the norms and meanings associated with it rapidly shifting over time. Third, many of the purported effects of cohabitation may be due to social selection. In other words, the kinds of people who enter cohabiting relationships may also be disposed to other kinds of behavior so that, for example, what seems to be an effect of cohabitation on relationship quality is actually caused by the characteristics of people who choose to cohabit. Despite these limitations, scholars have compiled an impressive trove of information about the outcomes associated with cohabitation for both adults and children.

As already mentioned, cohabiting relationships in the United States tend to be unstable compared with marital relationships. One way in which the instability associated with cohabitation affects cohabiters is the quality and availability of resources from kinship networks. Some evidence suggests that young adult cohabiters reap fewer benefits from parents compared with married young adults (Eggebeen, 2005). Cohabiters also differ from married adults in the impact of relationship dissolution. Although formerly married men tend to be better off after a divorce, formerly cohabiting men experience little financial change after dissolution and formerly cohabiting women suffer about the same financial loss as formerly married women (Avellar & Smock, 2005). Cohabiting relationships also tend to be more violent than married relationships although this is likely the result of the least violent cohabiting couples choosing to marry and the most violent married couples choosing to divorce (Kenney & McLanahan, 2006). Entering a cohabiting relationship appears to have some risk-reducing benefits, especially for men. Men experience similar reductions in marijuana use and binge drinking whether they enter cohabitation or marriage (Duncan, Wilkerson, & England, 2006).

Cohabiters are less healthy than their married counterparts, likely because cohabiters have fewer coping resources and lower relationship quality (Marcussen, 2005). For example, among older adults, cohabiting men experience significantly poorer mental health compared with married men, but cohabiting and married women have similar levels of mental health. Scholars hypothesize that, among older adults, a population for whom caregiving roles are highly gendered, married men benefit from the security of having a caregiving wife, whereas cohabiting women may benefit from having fewer caregiving obligations (Brown et al., 2005). So overall, although some of the differences between cohabitation and marriage in adult outcomes appear to be due to selection, the relative instability of cohabitation may also contribute to some negative outcomes.

An increasing number of children spend part of their childhoods in households headed by a cohabiting couple. Social scientists have developed a modest literature investigating how children fare in cohabiting households. Cohabitation appears to be a significant source of instability in the lives of some children in the United States. This is especially true when a child's mother (or father) moves in and out of several cohabiting relationships while the child is living in the parental home (Raley & Wildsmith, 2004). Several studies indicate that children (and adolescents) in cohabiting households exhibit more behavioral, health, and educational problems than children living in married households.

What is less clear is whether the presence of two adults in a cohabiting household is better for children than a single-parent household is. Most evidence suggests that factors such as instability, lower socioeconomic status, and poorer mental health among mothers in cohabiting relationships offset any potential gains that children may accrue from having a second adult in the household. Indeed, as some research on stepfamilies has shown, the presence of an adult who is not a biological parent may be a stressor for children (Manning & Brown, 2006; Raley, Frisco, & Wildsmith, 2005; Artis, 2007; Ginther & Pollack, 2004; Brown, 2004; Manning, et al. 2004; Manning & Lamb, 2003). Selection is probably responsible for many of the differences between child outcomes in cohabiting households versus findings in married households. Instability, however, may also contribute to poorer childhood outcomes in cohabiting households.

COHABITATION OUTSIDE THE UNITED STATES

Cohabitation is on the rise in many parts of the world. As in the United States, the role of cohabitation in the family systems of many of these nations is unclear. In a few countries, such as Sweden, cohabitation appears to be a stable and entrenched alternative to marriage (Heimdal & Houseknect, 2003). In others, such as New Zealand, cohabitations are short lived and unstable, similar to cohabitations in the United States. Cohabitation has spread rapidly throughout much of Europe, including the United Kingdom, but the practice has been slow to spread in Italy and Spain (Heuveline, Timberlake, & Furstenberg, 2003; Heuveline & Timberlake, 2004; Seltzer, 2004). In Latin America, cohabitation has a long history, because *informal unions* have long existed as an alternative to marriage. Some evidence, however, suggests that in countries such as Mexico, cohabitation is becoming a normative precursor to marriage as well as an alternative (Heaton & Forste, 2007). Less research has been conducted on cohabitation in Asia, where rates have been generally lower. Some evidence in Japan indicates that increases in cohabitation may be forthcoming, as Japanese young people report accepting cohabitation as a legitimate precursor to marriage at much higher rates than older people do (Rindfuss, Choe, Bumpass, & Tsuya, 2004). Little is known about cohabitation in the Middle East, although it is presumably low in traditionally Muslim countries. Cohabitation rates have risen in sub-Saharan Africa in recent years, with some countries, such as Botswana, exhibiting dramatic growth (Mokomane, 2007).

POLICY IMPLICATIONS AND OPPORTUNITIES FOR FUTURE RESEARCH

High rates of cohabitation have a number of policy implications. Lawmakers and business leaders will need to formulate policies that account for cohabitation. Some states and many large corporations already allow adults to nominate domestic partners as beneficiaries and, as cohabitation rates climb, access to health benefits for cohabiters is likely to increase. The welfare of children in cohabiting relationships is another important policy issue. Research showing that children fare worse in cohabiting relationships than marital relationships has been used by some lawmakers to help pass marriage promotion policies. Some scholars are skeptical about marriage promotion legislation, contending that the negative association between cohabitation and child well-being is largely due to the characteristics of people who decide to cohabit. They argue that simply getting cohabiters married will not solve children's' problems and the money would be better spent on addressing underlying problems such as poverty, poor health care, and substandard education (Smock & Manning, 2004). These and other issues will continue to be debated as cohabitation rates rise.

Future research will demonstrate whether cohabiting unions in the United States become stable like the unions observed in parts of Europe and, if so, whether more stable cohabiting unions produce better outcomes for adults and children. Researchers will also find fruitful ground for investigation in the cohabiting unions of older adults, especially if current youth maintain their positive attitudes toward cohabitation as they age. Although it is often assumed that cohabitation fits somewhere between marriage and noncoresidential romantic relationships (or *dating*), very little is known about the diversity and character of modern noncoresidential

romantic relationships. As researchers fill this knowledge gap, scientists will be able to make valid and useful comparisons between cohabitation and dating. Finally, there is much more room for understanding how the forms of cohabitation vary by socio-economic status and race and ethnicity.

CONCLUSIONS

Cohabitation rates are rising around the world, prompting some scholars to suggest that a major demographic transition is underway, one in which cohabitation will become a normative alternative to marriage (Van de Kaa, 1988). In the United States, the most recent evidence suggests that cohabitation is mostly a prelude to marriage and is still far from the stable alternative to marriage observed in some European nations. The relative instability of cohabiting relationships in the United States likely contributes to poorer outcomes for both adults and children in cohabiting households compared with married households. After nearly 30 years of rapidly rising cohabitation rates, cohabitation has become an important family form with potential impacts at every stage in the life course.

SEE ALSO Volume 1: *Transition to Marriage;* Volume 2: *Dating and Romantic Relationships, Adulthood; Divorce and Separation; Family and Household Structure, Adulthood; Gays and Lesbians, Adulthood; Marriage; Mate Selection; Remarriage;* Volume 3: *Singlehood; Widowhood.*

BIBLIOGRAPHY
Artis, J. E. (2007, February). Maternal cohabitation and child well-being among kindergarten children. *Journal of Marriage and the Family*, 69, 222–236.

Avellar, S., & Smock, P. J. (2005). The economic consequences of the dissolution of cohabiting unions. *Journal of Marriage and Family*, 67(2), 315–327.

Briner, J., & Joyner, K. (1999). The Ties That Bind: Principles of Cohesion in Cohabitation and Marriage. *American Sociological Review*, 64(3): 333–355.

Brown, S. L. (2004). Family structure and child well-being: The significance of parental cohabitation. *Journal of Marriage and the Family*, 66, 351–367.

Brown, S. L., & Booth, A. (1996). Cohabitation versus marriage: A comparison of relationship quality. *Journal of Marriage and the Family*, 58, 668–678.

Brown, S. L., Bulanda, J. R., & Lee, G. R. (2005). The significance of nonmarital cohabitation: Marital status and mental health benefits among middle-aged and older adults. *Journals of Gerontology Series B-Psychological Sciences and Social Sciences*, 60, S21–S29.

Bumpass, L. L., & Lu, H. (2000). Trends in Cohabitation and Implications for Children's Family Contexts. *Populations Studies*, 54 (1), 29–41.

Chevan, A. (1996). As cheaply as one: Cohabitation in the older population. *Journal of Marriage and the Family*, 58, 656–667.

Davis, S. N., Greenstein, T. N., & Marks, J. P. G. (2007). Effects of union type on division of household labor: Do cohabiting men really perform more housework? *Journal of Family Issues, 28,* 1246–1272.

Duncan, G. J., Wilkerson, B., & England, P. (2006). Cleaning up their act: The effects of marriage and cohabitation on licit and illicit drug use. *Demography, 43,* 691–710.

Eggebeen, D. J. (2005, March). Cohabitation and exchanges of support. *Social Forces, 83,* 1097–1110.

Ginther, D. K., & Pollak, R. A. (2004). Family structure and children's educational outcomes: Blended families, stylized facts, and descriptive regressions. *Demography, 41,* 671–696.

Guzzo, K. B. (2006). The relationship between life course events and union formation. *Social science research, 35,* 384–408.

Heaton, T. B., & Forste, R. (2007). Informal unions in Mexico and the United States. *Journal of Comparative Family Studies, 38,* 55–70.

Heimdal, K. R., & Houseknecht, S. K. (2003). Cohabiting and married couples' income organization: Approaches in Sweden and the United States. *Journal of Marriage and the Family, 65,* 525–538.

Heuveline, P., & Timberlake, J. M. (2004). The role of cohabitation in family formation: The United States in comparative perspective. *Journal of Marriage and the Family, 66,* 1214–1230.

Heuveline, P., Timberlake, J. M., & Furstenberg, F. F., Jr. (2003). Shifting childrearing to single mothers: Results from 17 western countries. *Population and Development Review, 29,* 47–71.

Kennedy, S., & Bumpass, L. (2007) Cohabitation and children's living arrangements: New estimates from the United States. [Working Paper] Madison, WI: Center for Demography and Ecology.

Kenney, C. T., & McLanahan, S. S. (2006). Why are cohabiting relationships more violent than marriages? *Demography, 43,* 127–140.

Manning, W. D., & Brown, S. (2006, May). Children's economic well-being in married and cohabiting parent families. *Journal of Marriage and the Family, 68,* 345–362.

Manning, W. D., & Lamb, K. A. (2003). Adolescent well-being in cohabiting, married, and single-parent families. *Journal of Marriage and the Family, 65,* 876–893.

Manning, W. D., Smock, P. J., & Majumdar, D. (2004, April). The relative stability of cohabiting and marital unions for children. *Population Research and Policy Review, 23,* 135–159.

Marcussen, K. (2005). Explaining differences in mental health between married and cohabiting individuals. *Social psychology quarterly, 68,* 239–257.

Mokomane, Z. (2006). Cohabiting unions in sub-Saharan Africa: Explaining Botswana's exceptionality. *Journal of Comparative Family Studies, 37,* 25–42.

Oppenheimer, V. K. (2003, February). Cohabiting and marriage during young men's career-development process. *Demography, 40,* 127–149.

Raley, R. K., & Wildsmith, E. (2004). Cohabitation and children's family instability. *Journal of Marriage and the Family, 66,* 210–219.

Raley, R. K., Frisco, M. L., & Wildsmith, E. (2005, April). Maternal cohabitation and educational success. *Sociology of Education, 78,* 144–164.

Rindfuss, R. R., Choe, M. K., Bumpass, L. L., & Tsuya, N. O. (2004). Social networks and family change in Japan. *American Sociological Review, 69,* 838–861.

Sanchez, L., Manning, W. D., & Smock, P. J. (1998). Sex-specialized or collaborative mate selection? Union transitions among cohabitors. *Social Science Research, 27,* 280–304.

Seltzer, J. A. (2004, November). Cohabitation in the United States and Britain: Demography, kinship, and the future. *Journal of Marriage and the Family, 66,* 921–928.

South, S. J., & Spitze, G. (1994). Housework in marital and nonmarital households. *American Sociological Review, 59,* 327–347.

Smock, P. J. (2000). Cohabitation in the United States: An appraisal of research themes, findings, and implications. *Annual Review of Sociology, 26,* 1–20.

Smock, P. J., & Manning, W. D. (2004). Living together unmarried in the United States: Demographic perspectives and implications for family policy. *Law & Policy, 26,* 87–117.

Smock, P. J., Manning, W. D., & Porter, M. (2005). Everything's there except money: How money shapes decisions to marry among cohabitors. *Journal of Marriage and the Family, 67,* 680–696.

Teachman, J. (2003). Premarital sex, premarital cohabitation, and the risk of subsequent marital dissolution among women. *Journal of Marriage and the Family, 65,* 444–455.

Thornton, A., Axinn, W. G., & Teachman, J. D. (1995). The influence of school enrollment and accumulation on cohabitation and marriage in early adulthood. *American Sociological Review, 60,* 762–774.

Van de Kaa, D. J. (1988). Europe's second demographic transition. *Population Bulletin, 42.* Washington, DC: The Population Reference Bureau.

Wildsmith, E., & Raley, R. K. (2006). Race-ethnic differences in nonmarital fertility: A focus on Mexican American women. *Journal of Marriage and the Family, 68,* 491–508.

Xie, Y., Raymo, J. M., Goyette, K., & Thornton, A. (2003). Economic potential and entry into marriage and cohabitation. *Demography, 40,* 351–367.

Charles E. Stokes
R. Kelly Raley

COMMUNITARIANISM

Communitarianism is a sociopolitical philosophy that views individual character virtues and social bonds as central to the lives of social actors. Communitarians believe that social groups—particularly communities—must strive to balance individual freedoms and the welfare of the collective. Elements of communitarian thinking can be found in sociological, philosophical, and political writing and teaching. Contemporary proponents of this movement include Amitai Etzioni (b. 1929), Robert Bellah (b. 1927), Philip Selznick (b. 1919), and Daniel Bell (b. 1919), but aspects of communitarianism are traceable to earlier theorists such as Karl Marx (1818–

1883), Emile Durkheim (1858–1917), and Ferdinand Tönnies (1855–1936). Furthermore, particular facets of communitarian thought such as identity formation, value internalization, and generativity, are exceptionally useful for understanding different stages of the life course and human development.

DEFINING COMMUNITARIANISM

Balance is a consistent theme within communitarianism. Etzioni (1993), in particular, states that the movement is concerned with society's ability to balance the needs of individuals with the collective good. These opposing goals represent the centripetal and centrifugal forces (Etzioni, 1996). According to physicists, centripetal forces sustain a body's circular path at a consistent speed. Similarly, in the communitarian sense, these forces are the resources that individuals provide to the community that enhance the collective good. By contrast, centrifugal forces are the rotational forces that are oriented *away* from the axis of rotation and therefore, according to communitarians represent individuals' quests for independence from the collective. Communitarianism argues that all social groups, especially communities, are pulled in opposing directions by these competing forces. Communitarians therefore envision a sociopolitical environment where individuals are given a particular level of freedom and rights to seek their autonomy at the same time as they work for the common good and to uphold their social responsibilities.

D. R. Karp (2000) argues that communitarianism reflects a struggle with the conditions of modern societies and, in particular, contemporary societies' overt focus on individual liberties. He notes that communitarians believe that modern societies separate individuals from communities, cause a subsequent decline in community life, and promulgate personal independence and individuality. Therefore, according to communitarians, fundamental aspects of modernity destroy communal bonds and shared values and stifle the social obligations and voluntary activities that contribute to the common good.

CLASSIC AND NEW
COMMUNITARIAN THOUGHT

The classic and new forms of communitarianism must be distinguished. Although the term *communitarianism* was not used until the last few decades, basic elements of communitarian thought can be found in the writings of classical sociological theorists such as Tönnies, Durkheim, and Marx. The primary distinction between classic communitarian thought and the new communitarianism is that the latter is more concerned with the balance between the *person* and the community, whereas the classic sense focuses almost entirely on the importance of social forces and social bonds.

For example, O. Newman and R. de Zoysa (1997) suggest that communitarianism bears a conceptual resemblance to Tönnies' models of *Gemeinschaft* and *Gesellschaft*. *Gemeinschaft* is a German word that in this sense refers to social life within small-scale communities that emphasize shared social values and an active voluntary approach to social responsibilities. By contrast, *Gesllschaft*, as used sociologically, characterizes communities with weaker civic bonds, strained social relations, and a heightened sense of self-interest. The distinction between *Gemeinschaft* and *Gesllschaft* mirrors Etzioni's contemporary concepts of *authentic* and *distorted* communities. Within the new communitarian approach, the ideal community—that is, the *authentic* community—is responsive to the *true needs* of all its members, respecting and maintaining the balance of centripetal and centrifugal forces. Such a community allows individuals to flourish creatively and separately, while providing moral and social boundaries that reflect the responsibility to the common good.

According to Etzioni (1996), the term *communitarian* was adopted for the social philosophy to emphasize the necessity of individuals to acknowledge and engage in their responsibilities to the community. He states that since the 1950s, developed society has not heeded the "moral voice" and has therefore experienced the faltering of the traditional family structure, the diminishing role of schools in transmitting moral and social values, and the erosion of confidence in institutional leaders (Etzioni, 1995).

CRITIQUES OF
COMMUNITARIANISM

D. E. Pearson (1995) argues that Etzioni's vision of an authentic community is impractical, unattainable, and does not fully take into account that humans are naturally motivated to strive for status and power through competition, and are not motivated through compassion and altruism for others within their community. S. Prideaux (2002) states that communitarian leaders such as Etzioni employ a restricted and short-sighted view of community in that he has confined his analysis to American social relations. Others contend that the whole communitarian movement is overly nostalgic, longing for a past that was not as pleasant as memory leads one to recollect.

COMMUNITARIANISM
AND THE LIFE COURSE

According to communitarians, it is the individual's duty to fulfill his or her social responsibilities actively at all stages of the life course. Individuals should have the rights to express their individuality, but be grounded by the moral and ethical requirements necessary to reproduce society. This line of thinking echoes Erik Erikson's (1950) lifespan theory of human development and the concept of *generativity*, which consists of actions taken to benefit society through guiding younger people to become custodians of society.

Aspects of communitarianism are also present in literatures emphasizing agents of socialization (e.g., family and schools), as well as the timing and sequencing of individuals pathways through the life course (e.g., becoming a parent, spouse, or worker). Institutions within communities such as families, schools, and groups provide the frameworks upholding social values and order. Furthermore, individual identities are developed and formed within these frameworks of understandings and values (Sayers, 1999). It is the balance of social order and the individual's quest for independence that not only propels the community but also yields a more fruitful environment for individual identity formation. Thus the tension between the individual and society central to communitarian thought is also central to analyzing and understanding the life course.

SEE ALSO Volume 1: *Social Capital;* Volume 2: *Individuation/Standardization Debate; Social Structure/Social System.*

BIBLIOGRAPHY

Erikson, E. H. (1950). *Childhood and society.* New York: Norton.

Etzioni, A. (1993). *The spirit of community.* New York: Crown.

Etzioni, A. (1995). *Rights and the common good.* New York: St. Martin's.

Etzioni, A. (1996). *The new golden rule.* New York, NY: Basic Books.

Etzioni, A. (1996). The responsive community: A communitarian perspective. *American Sociological Review, 61,* 1–11.

Holmes, S. (1993). *The anatomy of antiliberalism.* Cambridge, MA: Harvard University Press.

Karp, D. R. (2000). Sociological communitarianism and the just community. *Contemporary Justice Review, 3,* 152–174.

Newman, O., & De Zoysa, R. (1997). Communitarianism: The new panacea? *Sociological Perspectives, 40,* 623–638.

Pearson, D. E. (1995). Community and society. *Society,* July/August, 45–50.

Prideaux, S. (2002). Note on society. *Canadian Journal of Sociology, 27,* 69–81.

Sayers, S. (1999). Identity and community. *Journal of Social Philosophy, 30,* 147–160.

Barret Michalec
Corey L. Keyes

CONSUMPTION, ADULTHOOD AND LATER LIFE

Consumption is a diverse set of practices at the intersection of human life and the material world. In its everyday meaning, consumption is about individuals satisfying needs and doing so as a private matter. However, as soon as one inquires how individuals come to understand both their needs and the resources that would meet them, consumption becomes a public and social matter. The study of consumption is about acts of using and using things up, but also necessarily about the way such acts come about. In this regard, age and life course change are more than mere contexts for consumption; they in fact propel it.

Researchers who study consumption approach it from many different points of view. One perspective focuses on the stages of consumption, the number of which, in turn, depends on whether people or objects are the primary focus. A tendency to focus on the person—the consumer—sets out stages such as acquisition (by purchase, gift, or creation), transient use or extended possession, and eventual disposal. A focus on objects or commodities may raise questions about their origin (i.e., their production) and, preceding that, their extraction from the environment. The complete cycle thus runs from extraction to disposal. For example, this encyclopedia, in its print or electronic form, is an object that will have had a multistage career, but it is of only present interest to consumers (readers) who have little regard for its origin or fate.

Another way to think about consumption practices is with an emphasis on either the collective or the individual. At the former, *macro* level, what comes to the fore are the enterprises, industries, and social institutions that drive the consumption cycle. At the *micro* level, the consumer and his or her outlook and behavior are central; for example, what are the individual's motives for acquiring or keeping things? The reasons for consumption—retail purchase being a huge topic here—are many but they can be reduced to two: things are practical (they serve some useful function) or things are symbolic (they communicate something about oneself and others) (Belk, 1988). The reasons for having a single thing can be mixed and they can shift over time. Eyeglasses, for example, assist vision but they also adorn the face. A particular pair of glasses is an object worth having, at least until one's prescription changes or fashion renders them outdated or obsolete.

Human development and aging lend a dynamism to the ways that the material world furnishes daily life. Across the years of adulthood, bodily changes occasion alterations in the way that needs are defined and met. The progression of life circumstances and the role sequences of family and work careers likewise bring shifts in the provisioning of everyday activity. At the aggregate level, cohorts of (aging) consumers are also moving through the life course, replacing one another at various stages of life, thus layering the consuming public with different tastes and habits shaped by cohorts' unique historical experience.

Given the wide array of consumption practices, almost every branch of knowledge and scholarship can contribute perspectives on this subject. This article considers consumption as a social activity and addresses how consumption unfolds over the course of adulthood, how marketers supply both goods and models of consuming, and whether some age groups consume at the expense of others.

CONSUMERS AT DIFFERENT AGES

Theorists of consumer culture maintain that, in the modern world, people's values and identities are defined in relation to what they consume (Giddens, 1991; Slater, 1997). Whereas traditionally people may have derived a fixed sense of themselves from religion, work, or family, the dominant resources for identity construction are now to be found in the materials and symbols of the marketplace. Moreover, the self-representations of consumer culture are a fluid, emergent, and ongoing, thus contributing to an unsettledness in modern life. The desirable and undesirable aspects of this condition have generated much social criticism.

The fluidity of identity only accentuates the adult experience of time's passing. To some extent, aging already schedules the obligation to reinvent oneself. Against a backdrop of culturally given age-related norms, expectations, and roles, people use the material world to manage age-appropriate presentations of themselves. As the body changes, consumption changes. Continuing with habits learned in youth and adolescence, adults employ grooming, clothing, and projects of self-care to stage and restage the apt appearance of their person. Fitness routines, lifestyle regimens, cosmetics, and drugs may be deployed to delay, resist, or mask the signs of aging (Katz & Marshall, 2003). Also pacing bodily change, the consumption of health care rises inexorably with advancing age.

Consumption abets not only the long arc of adulthood, but also the recurring events that mark time. For example, anniversaries of birth and marriage are unthinkable without greeting cards, gifts, and festive meals—commodities all. Not to shop on behalf of birthdays and anniversaries is to let these events pass unremarked.

The social roles comprising the life course and the transitions between them are enacted with goods and services. When young adults establish independent residence, perhaps with a partner, living areas and kitchens will need to be stocked. Acquiring a house will extend the task of homemaking to an entire property. Homes, however, are rarely bought outright. Rather, the funds are purchased at extra cost—a mortgage—over a long period of time. Work roles compel the acquisition of specialized clothing, tools, transportation, and self-care materials. Upon changing jobs, these materials may need to be refreshed. Daily and weekly release from work—leisure—

is the occasion for lifestyle explorations via entertainment and recreational consumption.

Parenthood multiplies the obligation to consume, but with a new wrinkle. Parents undertake surrogate consumption for dependent children who are themselves on developmental timetables with their own requirements for types, sizes, and styles of commodities as well as their own projects of identity construction. For all the attention to children and youth as a consumer market, it is primarily parents who choose and buy on behalf of the young, from baby rattles to braces to college tuition.

Having homes and responsibility for others orient adults to maintain their employability and well-being. They purchase insurance of various kinds to minimize the risk of property or income loss. When possible, they also save for old age, which is deferred consumption, but also present consumption to the extent that they pay fees for financial services. With a nest egg (e.g., retirement savings or a 401[k] plan), workers are eventually permitted the leisure of a self-indulgent retirement. Retirement, in fact, can be regarded as an item of consumption, perhaps the largest of a lifetime, and the reformation of identity that it permits is what makes it alluring, delightful, and worth saving for over so many years (Ekerdt, 2004). Another open-ended role of later life—grandparenthood—has few norms for performance, but the bestowal of gifts and experiences on grandchildren is common. Finally, survival into later life will almost certainly involve the continued use of health services and perhaps long-term care, though the ability to consume these goods may need subsidizing by government or the family.

As adults acquire consumer resources in order to enact the sequential roles and stages of life, the goal is not merely to use or have things but also to *be* someone—a homeowner, a hunter, a hostess. Consumption assembles a story about oneself and it is often the means by which to evaluate how well life is going. Two life course transitions merit special mention as market-mediated events: marriage and death (i.e., the funeral and body disposition). Both transitions typically entail extraordinary expenditures for short-term celebrations that are undertaken to honor the social significance of the particular lives in passage.

Recalling the consumption cycle, possession is a life course constant along with acquisition. People proceed through adulthood accompanied by a convoy of material support. Some items are transient (children's toys) and some endure (major furniture, photographs). Goods flow in and out during daily life, but some stick and this residue accumulates over time. The resulting possessions are not mere inert lumps of matter. What is kept must be placed, stored, arranged, maintained, cleaned, insured, emotionally invested, and even animated in the sense that the possessor attributes to them an inner life. People

Eaton Center Mall in Toronto. © RICHARD T. NOWITZ/CORBIS.

cultivate their holdings, taking mass-produced goods such as cars or cookware and make them over as their own (McCracken, 1988). Some things are special, but a lot of personal property is mundane. Out of intergenerational responsibility, individuals adopt family items—curios, heirlooms—as a way to preserve a collective family identity. There has been some research suggesting that younger adults value possessions more for their usefulness, whereas older adults prize symbolic value, but life course differences in the quality of attachment to possessions are not well understood (Kleine & Baker, 2004).

The conclusion of the consumption cycle—disposal—also has life course dimensions. Possessions become candidates for disposal for many reasons, including when their total volume grows too large over time. The imperative to downsize is a staple of popular media, giving rise to the anti-clutter industry that is, ironically, another form of consumption. Life course change is one circumstance that invites disposal, for example, when people exit social roles, become disabled, or need to manage age-related vulnerability, perhaps by moving to a smaller residence. Upon the death of older adults, it may fall to survivors to disassemble the household and discard things.

If keeping things is work, then so is disposal. Whether people give, sell, donate, or discard possessions, the process often involves social calculation and strategizing, efforts to make things presentable, contracting with others, and emotional management. The convenience of storage may well outweigh the inconvenience of disposal, especially if rising affluence across adulthood allows trading up to larger homes.

AGE SEGMENTATION OF CONSUMER MARKETS

A market is a system or structure for exchange, such as commercial exchange between buyers and sellers. A market also denotes a category of the population grouped according to some characteristic, such as geography, to which things might be sold. Grouping by age yields such target segments as the *youth* market or the *mature* market.

It is a chicken-and-egg question whether merchants induce the demand for goods or consumers create it. In consumption studies, competing viewpoints about the priority of supply and demand generate competing portraits of the consumer (Gabriel & Lang, 1995). On the one hand, consumers are compliant dupes, their desires manipulated by seductive marketing. On the other hand, they are creative agents of self-expression, rationally choosing what and when to consume. Over various moments of adulthood, consumers are likely to evince both ideal types and every gradation in between.

Marketers offer goods, but they also cultivate the market for those goods, predisposing consumers of different ages to understand their welfare in relation to certain products. Each wave of young adults arrives from adolescence already socialized to the idea that every generation has its own music, fashion, and pastimes. The next-stage task is to lead maturing adults to shift their tastes from the things of youth to the goods of grown-ups (e.g., the cut of clothes, breakfast cereal, or real estate). The matter is tricky, however, because advertisers will also want to preserve brand loyalty. Life stages such as motherhood or retirement can be portrayed as important aspirations. At the same time there are products that stand for rebellion against age, such as sports cars and motorcycles for middle-aged men. The marketplace deals in discrete commodities but also suggests entire careers of consumption. The American Dream is a standard life course script that implies a sequence of successively richer goods and experiences (the home is iconic), culminating in residential, familial, and occupational contentment at midlife. Adopting this ideal, people then conduct their lives to bring it about.

Marketers have long concentrated on consumers younger than 50 and especially coveted those aged 18 to 34 in order to "get them young." But companies are awakening to the potential of middle-aged and older buyers. Household income increases with age to peak in the 50s, and wealth rises to peak in the 70s. Compared to preceding generations, current cohorts over the age of 50 (now including the baby boom) are more affluent and more willing to endure debt. The rising wealth of older adults and, not incidentally, the post–World War II (1939–1945) habits of consumerism they have brought along with them, portend a shift in the image of later life (Gilleard & Higgs, 2000). Rather than being viewed as dependent and needy, elders will increasingly be courted for their market power. The models of maturity already advertised include the fun grandparent, the foresighted financial planner, the restlessly active retiree, and the rational, discriminating consumer of senior housing.

Age-based or cohort-based marketing has various guidelines (Moschis & Mathur, 2007). Most important of these guidelines is being cognizant that age groups are not homogeneous. A small industry has arisen to advise companies how, depending on product, to subdivide age categories by values and lifestyles, shopping behaviors, and service and price consciousness. For example, what product qualities, promotion strategies, and retail arrangements would beckon larger consumer outlays? Do buyers prefer a sales force that is younger, of the same age, or older? In advertising, direct appeals to, or reminders about, chronological age are unwelcome. Rather, the pitch works better when made indirectly, to life circumstances or cohort experiences. For example, a gray-haired model or spokesperson in an ad can convey the intended audience, but is acceptable only if somewhat younger than the target demographic. Finally, an age or cohort link may be inadvisable for some products and services, which are better marketed with an intergenerational appeal.

FAIRNESS

Consumption is necessarily threaded with ethical issues because the definition of needs and ways to meet them have implications for the common good. Moral and polit-ical discourses have long addressed whether resources are justly allocated; whether the values of consumerism are constructive; the environmental costs of the consumption cycle; and whether markets are conducted with fairness (Wilk, 2001). What is ostensibly an activity of the private sphere—satisfying one's needs—raises very public questions about economic, political, and cultural institutions.

Fairness debates have been a life course issue since the 1980s in most of the advanced economies (Moody, 2006). In the United States, the question has been posed under the heading of *generational equity*. Observing that the aggregate economic well-being of children has fallen while that of elders has risen, some quarters of the policy community have asked whether federal old-age programs deprive families with young children of their fair share of social resources. It is a fair observation that old-age entitlement programs such as Social Security and Medicare transfer, via taxation, buying power from younger cohorts to older citizens. At the same time, it is far from assured that any retrenchment in these programs would benefit the neediest children. Intense discussion has surrounded proposals for age-based rationing of health care. Older cohorts consume a disproportionate amount of health care, which is subsidized by public funds, and costs are always rising. Might age be used as a criterion for allocating and limiting health care? Debates about generational fairness are likely to continue, being sometimes philosophical and often sharply ideological. Against the contention that one age group consumes at the expense of another, others have argued for the essential interdependence of generations in furnishing one another's needs across the life course.

SEE ALSO Volume 1: *Identity Development;* Volume 2: *Cultural Images, Adulthood; Debt; Leisure and Travel, Adulthood; Relative Cohort Size Hypothesis; Saving; Time Use, Adulthood;* Volume 3: *Leisure and Travel, Later Life; Time Use, Later Life.*

BIBLIOGRAPHY

Belk, R. W. (1988). Possessions and the extended self. *Journal of Consumer Research, 15*(2), 139–168.

Ekerdt, D. J. (2004). Born to retire: The foreshortened life course. *The Gerontologist, 44*(1), 3–9.

Gabriel, Y., & Lang, T. (1995). *The unmanageable consumer: Contemporary consumption and its fragmentations.* Thousand Oaks, CA: Sage.

Giddens, A. (1991). *Modernity and self-identity: Self and society in the late modern age.* Stanford, CA: Stanford University Press.

Gilleard, C., & Higgs, P. (2000). *Cultures of ageing: Self, citizen, and the body.* New York: Prentice Hall.

Katz, S., & Marshall, B. (2003). New sex for old: Lifestyle, consumerism, and the ethics of aging well. *Journal of Aging Studies, 17*(1), 3–16.

Kleine, S. S., & Baker, S. M. (2004). An integrative review of material possession attachment. *Academy of Marketing Science*

Review, 1. Retrieved April 4, 2008, from http://www.amsreview.org/articles/kleine01-2004.pdf

McCracken, G. (1988). *Culture and consumption: New approaches to the symbolic character of consumer goods and activities.* Bloomington: Indiana University Press.

Moody, H. R. (2006). *Aging: Concepts and controversies.* (5th ed.). Thousand Oaks, CA: Pine Forge Press.

Moschis, G. P., & Mathur, A. (2007*). Baby boomers and their parents: Surprising findings about their lifestyles, mindsets, and well-being.* Ithaca, NY: Paramount Books.

Slater, D. (1997). *Consumer culture and modernity.* Cambridge, MA: Blackwell.

Wilk, R. (2001). Consuming morality. *Journal of Consumer Culture, 1,* 245–260.

David J. Ekerdt

CONTINGENT WORK

SEE Volume 2: *Flexible Work Arrangements; Self-Employment.*

CONTINUING EDUCATION

Continuing education is a term used by policy makers and educators in many countries. It refers to any form of educational provision for people who have completed their initial fulltime education and entered the adult stage of their life course, which usually involves entering employment. This is a broad definition of continuing education since it includes liberal adult education, professional updating, vocational training, and regular degree or other award-bearing courses that are undertaken by mature students. However, the term is also sometimes used in a narrower sense—to refer only to short courses provided for adults who have completed their substantive formal education.

Several other terms are related to the concept of continuing education. *Recurrent education* carries the implication that an individual alternates formal education with employment across the life course, rather than completing his or her formal education before entering into adult life. Thus, like the broad concept of continuing education, recurrent education seeks to move away from a "front-end" model of education, which takes education in adulthood to be an indulgent or a remedial "add on" to the main education obtainable in compulsory schooling. The term *adult education* also rejects the front-end model; it implies that there are forms of knowledge and ways of learning distinctive of adulthood.

In the late 20th and early 21st centuries, the term *lifelong learning* became increasingly prominent and influential in research and policy making. For example, the 1990s saw the publication of many national policy papers and influential reports from the Organisation for Economic Co-Operation and Development (OECD), the European Commission, the Group of Eight (G8) governments for the eight largest economies, and from United Nations Educational, Scientific, and Cultural Organization (UNESCO), thus bringing in many non-European countries. Lifelong learning is connected to the notion of cradle-to-grave educational provisions and to the idea that education must meet the needs of rapidly changing modern industrial democracies.

Lifelong learning includes vocational and professional updating, liberal education for personal development, and political education for good citizenship. A "learning society" is one that values a broad range of learning and is organized to provide maximum learning opportunities for its members across the life span. Like continuing education and adult education, the concept of lifelong learning recognizes formal, nonformal, and informal learning as worthwhile and valuable to both the individual and to society. (Formal education refers to courses provided by formal educational institutions, such as colleges or universities. Nonformal learning encompasses educational programs provided by organizations whose primary purpose is not education, such as voluntary organizations, churches, or synagogues. Informal learning is learning that takes place in daily life, ranging from watching TV documentaries to holding conversations with friends).

Further education refers to full-time and part-time education provided by educational institutions for persons over compulsory school age. It carries a vocational emphasis and is often referred to as "further education and training." Higher education refers to more academic (university) provision.

The key point is that there are several distinguishable but overlapping terms used to refer to various forms and stages of education beyond formal schooling in childhood and adolescence. In terms of the life course, it is extremely important to recognize the validity and value of education throughout life, up to and including old age.

VALUES IN AND THE VALUE OF CONTINUING EDUCATION

The concept of continuing education values education beyond school and assumes that there is worthwhile learning appropriate to all stages of the life course. For example, people begin to gain skills for the world of work in early adulthood, but the idea of continuing education suggests that adults should continue to gain in competence, broadening and deepening their understanding and skills across their working lives. Parents and children gain from the provision of parental education and also from family learning where children and parents can learn together. In adulthood and later life, too, people may become part of communities where continuing education may be both politically and personally important. The educational awareness gained by women through the women's movement in the 1960s and 1970s is a good example of this sort of continuing education. Retirement also may bring the opportunity to engage in learning of interest to the individual, an engagement that is known to have both health and social benefits.

The value of continuing education is immense. Levels of education and engagement in learning have been linked to enhanced physical and mental health, as well as economic prosperity. Learning has both intrinsic value, in that it provides satisfaction to the learner, and extrinsic rewards, in that it leads to better employment opportunities, health benefits, and correlates to levels of income.

Educators involved in continuing education, aware of its value and power, are often highly committed to widening access to post-school educational opportunities. "Widening" in this sense means not only increasing the number of people who participate, but also increasing proportional participation by members of disadvantaged social groups.

EQUITY AND CONTINUING EDUCATION

The issue of equity and continuing education is multi-dimensional, dynamic, and complex. However, many research studies have shown that social groups that face prejudice and systematic individual and institutional discrimination have fewer educational opportunities and obtain fewer educational qualifications than more advantaged members of the population. Thus, for example, many minority ethnic groups and physically disabled persons suffer educational disadvantage across the life course. Moreover, specific forms of knowledge possessed by such groups, such as cultural art forms, tend to be undervalued.

The OECD's work on equity and education includes comparisons across countries, by gender, social class, ethnicity, and disability levels of participation in continuing education (OECD, 1993). Such research supports the general consensus that major gaps persist between social groups in educational access and participation. Further rigorous research to refine our broad understandings about equity and education would be welcome.

Because knowledge, the process of learning, and educational qualifications are all highly valuable to individuals and to communities, there are implications for policy makers and funding organizations that seek to establish more equitable opportunities. The movement to lifelong learning

has encouraged efforts to reach underrepresented groups but there remains cause for concern. A tendency to concentrate on employment-related education, for example, excludes retired people and the long-term unemployed. Narrow forms of assessment might penalize the disabled, and barriers remain. For example, problems related to information flow are particularly acute for minority ethnic groups (Field and Leicester, 2000).

THEMES AND THEORIES

The study of continuing education is multidisciplinary—drawing on established disciplines including psychology, social psychology, sociology, and philosophy. From psychology and social psychology much has been discovered about how adults learn and social studies have shown why, where, and when such learning occurs. Because education is value-laden and the provision of opportunities for continuing education involves political decisions, and because education involves the development of knowledge, philosophical and epistemological analyses have also contributed to understanding continuing education.

Learning is a central component of human life, and thus occurs across the lifespan as individuals change and develop. Knowles's theory of androgogy, or adult learning, has been particularly influential for adult educators and rests on four major assumptions:

- a change in self concept, because adults need to be more self-directive;

- experience, because mature individuals accumulate and expand a reservoir of experience that becomes an exceedingly rich resource in learning;

- readiness to learn, because adults want to learn in the problem areas they confront and that they regard as relevant;

- orientation toward learning, because adults have a problem-centered orientation and are less likely to be subject-centered (Knowles, 1984).

Compared to Knowles's, Freire's ideas, arising out of his experience of the oppression of the masses in Brazil, focus to a lesser degree on the study of how individuals learn and to a greater degree on a more radical form of education to promote active political participation in the wider world. Education in adulthood should raise the level of the consciousness of oppressed groups so that the operation of the economic, political, social, and psychological forces of oppression can be understood and opposed. These political ideas have been influential in encouraging community education, prompting community educators to develop and deliver forms of education that benefit communities and disadvantaged communities in particular.

Research on continuing education conceptualizes post-compulsory education as a social commodity, requiring policy decisions and implementation, funding and administration—practical aspects that also require monitoring and analysis. This research is also itself imbued with implicit value judgments and philosophical and political assumptions.

POLICY ISSUES IN THE NEW MILLENNIUM

Given the prominence of lifelong learning in the first decade of the new millennium, it seems likely that learning across the life course will continue to be an important educational goal with important policy implications. In the rapidly changing modern world, updating skills and acquiring new ones makes economic sense for individuals and for their societies. And if good teaching is to be offered to students of all ages, the professional development of educators themselves needs to become a matter of career-long learning (Day, 1999). In schools, the curriculum needs to include equipping children with the skills and commitments to become lifelong learners.

Cross-generational learning—in which individuals at different phases of the life course learn with and from each other—has been relatively neglected. Within the movement toward lifelong learning there has been some development of family learning. A key issue for the future will be to monitor and identify good practice in this kind of cross-generational educational provision. Parental education and health education also are crucial areas in connection with individual flourishing and well-being. These forms of education might (and should) be given increasing support. Citizenship education to equip people to be active good citizens is currently receiving attention. This meets the political aspect of lifelong learning and also might (and should) become increasingly supported. A future issue that requires both scholarly and public attention is how to find ways to interrelate these three strands of lifelong learning (vocational/professional, individual/liberal, political/citizenship) in order to provide education across the life course that meets all three of these crucial learning needs.

CONTINUING EDUCATION AND THE LIFE COURSE

The voluntary nature of post-school learning is important. Adults must be free to choose what kinds, and how much, educational provision in which to participate. However, a corresponding ethical requirement is, surely, that all citizens have an equal opportunity to genuinely choose to partake. OECD studies indicate that more than 10% of 30- to 39-year-olds in Australia, Finland, New Zealand, Sweden, and the United Kingdom are enrolled in continuing education (full- or part-time) compared to the OECD country mean of 4.8%. Similar patterns, although with lower overall rates,

are found for persons ages 40 to 49 (Schuller, 2006). Such cross-national differences challenge the notion of free choice and have policy and funding implications.

In schools, lifelong learning implies a need for further curriculum development to increase the agency of pupils by giving more extensive career education and by equipping children with the skills and commitments that will help them to become lifelong learners. Perhaps the most important point is that, given the importance of worthwhile learning to human flourishing across the life course, it is imperative that societies do indeed seek to provide appropriate continuing education. This entails encouraging and supporting learners from all social groups to partake in good quality educational provision at all stages of their lives.

SEE ALSO Volume 1: *College Enrollment;* Volume 2: *Educational Attainment;* Volume 3: *Lifelong Learning.*

BIBLIOGRAPHY

Day, C. (1999). *Developing teachers: The challenges of lifelong learning.* London: Falmer Press.

Field, J., and Leicester, M. (2000). *Lifelong learning: Education across the lifespan.* London: Routledge.

Freire, P. (1972). *Pedagogy of the oppressed,* trans. M. B. Ramos. Hamondsworth, U.K.: Penguin.

Jarvis, P. (1998). *Adult and continuing education: Theory and practice,* (3rd ed.). London: Routledge.

Knowles, M., et al. (1984). *Androgogy in action.* San Francisco: Jossey-Bass.

Organisation for Economic Co-operation and Development (OECD). (1993). *Education at a glance.* Paris: Author.

Schuller, T. (2006). *Education and equity: Perspectives from the OECD.* In J. Chapman, P. Cartwright, and E. J. McGilp (Eds.), *Lifelong learning: Participation and equity.* Dordrecht, Netherlands: Springer.

Mal Leicester

CONTRACEPTION

SEE *Birth Control.*

CRIME, CRIMINAL ACTIVITY IN ADULTHOOD

Criminologists have long recognized a strong life course pattern in criminal activity. Involvement in crime increases dramatically during the teen years, peaks at around age 20, and then declines steadily over the rest of the life course, with very low levels observed after age 65. This general pattern is observed regardless of time period, place, and type of crime. However, rates of violent crime appear to peak a bit later (around age 25) than do those for property crimes (around age 20).

This pattern holds whether one considers official statistics (crimes reported to police), self-report data (respondents' reports of their own criminal activity), or victim reports of offender characteristics. Each type of data has limitations—official statistics are subject to vagaries as a result of selective enforcement and underreporting, and self-report and victim data may be biased because of sampling errors and both over- and underreporting—yet all sources confirm the general age–crime relationship. Indeed, the association is so robust that some scholars have referred to the relationship as invariant.

CRIME ACROSS THE LIFE COURSE

Differences in criminal involvement by gender and race are well documented, with males and minority group members exhibiting higher rates of crime, particularly violent offenses, than females and Whites. For example, the 2006 male arrest rate of 10.8 per 1,000 for the eight most serious crimes reported to the police (homicide, rape, robbery, assault, burglary, larceny, arson, and motor vehicle theft) was almost three times higher than the corresponding rate for females. Similarly, African Americans tend to exhibit higher levels of criminal involvement, with arrest rates about three times those of Whites. These figures should be interpreted with caution because of the possibility that police enforcement practices and biases may distort actual levels. However, self-report data obtained from offenders tend to corroborate these general patterns.

Despite these stark gender and race differences in levels of criminal involvement, the age–crime relationship is apparent within gender and racial groups. For example, female age-specific rates for the eight most serious crimes rise dramatically during the early teen years, peaking at about age 16 and declining steadily afterward. For males the pattern is similar, although rates tend to peak a bit later, at age 18, and rise to dramatically higher levels. Both first arrest and recidivism (or subsequent arrest) rates are considerably higher for males than for females. Aggregate arrest rates are much higher for Blacks than for Whites, yet there is little difference between the two racial groups in recidivism rates. Racial differentials result more from differences in patterns of criminal participation than from differences in the frequency or duration of individual offending.

The age–crime relationship could indicate that criminal activity declines with age among all individuals. However, it also could reflect other scenarios. For example, the

same pattern would be observed if the majority of individuals stopped criminal activity once they reached adulthood even though a minority continued to participate actively in crime through adulthood. Alternatively, the age pattern may reflect declines over time in the frequency with which active offenders commit crime or declines over time in the number of active offenders as a result of incarceration, death, or declining health (because of substance abuse or the natural aging process). These scenarios are all consistent with the observation that criminal activity declines with increasing age in a population.

There has been debate about these issues in the field of criminology. One argument suggests that the relationship between age and criminal involvement does not exist for all types of criminals. Terrie Moffitt (1993), for example, classified offenders into two distinct categories: "adolescence limited" and "life course persistent." An adolescence-limited offender engages in delinquent and criminal behavior during adolescence and stops after reaching adulthood. Criminal activity is confined to a relatively short period, and a clear decline in crime with increasing age is observed among this group. The vast majority of delinquent adolescents can be characterized this way. Criminal activities among life course persistent offenders, or so-called career criminals, are marked by considerable frequency, seriousness, and a long duration. Moffitt suggested that offense and arrest rates in this group remain fairly constant over the life course. Other scholars have included additional types of criminals in this categorization, noting the presence of a low-level chronic group whose members continue to offend but with less frequency through adulthood (Nagin & Land, 1993).

One frequently cited statistic that supports the contention that criminal behavior is concentrated heavily among a few individuals with criminal careers comes from a 1972 study titled *Delinquency in a Birth Cohort* (Wolfgang, Figlio, & Sellin, 1972). Researchers found that although a significant proportion of the young men in that birth cohort had had at least one run-in with police, only 6% of them were responsible for the majority of crime in that cohort. A 1979 study by Alfred Blumstein and Jacqueline Cohen focused on serious offenders in Washington, D.C., and showed that the relationship between age and crime disappeared when cohorts were followed over time, with rates of criminal involvement for these serious offenders remaining fairly constant with age.

Other scholars disagree with that characterization. Travis Hirschi and Michael Gottfredson (1983) argued that the relationship between age and crime is explained by biological (e.g., hormones or physical characteristics) rather than social factors and supported their thesis by showing that the relationship between age and crime does not vary across persons, time periods, place, and type of crime. Other researchers have noted that studies supporting the notion of a career criminal tend to be limited by several design flaws. First, these studies typically follow offenders for a relatively short period and certainly not through midlife and later life. Second, types of criminals tend to be identified retrospectively rather than prospectively, and thus this approach by definition observes only high-level criminals who have not desisted (Laub & Sampson, 2003).

Certainly, some research shows that even among career criminals, involvement in crime seems to diminish with age. For example, retrospective self-reports by incarcerated offenders indicate that involvement in crime declines as offenders age. Independent evidence supports this notion. John Laub and Robert Sampson (2003) found in their sample of highly delinquent boys who were followed up to age 70 that offenses eventually declined among all groups of offenders. The peak age of offending varied, as did the rate of decline with age, but the results clearly showed that the age–crime relationship holds even among the most serious, persistent, and frequent offenders.

LIFE COURSE THEORIES OF CRIMINAL BEHAVIOR

Most theories of crime focus on explaining differences in criminal behavior among individuals. Strain theory emphasizes economic disparities among individuals as a key reason for differential criminal involvement, whereas social disorganization theory focuses on environmental factors. Such explanations are static in nature rather than dynamic and do not attempt to explain the extent to which the criminal behavior of an individual may change over time.

Developmental or life course explanations for criminal behavior focus on this question, asking how criminal behavior develops and changes over the life course. Although there are a number of variants of developmental criminological theories, they all recognize that life events and circumstances can alter criminal behavior. Specifically, these theories focus on three primary issues: identifying factors that explain the initiation and development of antisocial and criminal behavior, documenting risk factors for crime at various ages, and determining the degree to which life events alter the trajectories of those engaged in crime.

FACTORS EXPLAINING THE INITIATION AND DEVELOPMENT OF CRIMINAL BEHAVIOR

Numerous studies indicate that problematic childhood behavior such as temper tantrums, poor school performance, and bullying are linked to antisocial behavior in adulthood. Furthermore, those who initiate delinquent

behavior at an early age tend to commit crimes more frequently and for a longer duration than do those with a later onset. Indeed, early antisocial behavior often is viewed as the single best predictor of antisocial behavior in adulthood. A review of studies exploring this topic reported a substantial positive correlation (0.68) between early aggressive behavior and later criminality (Olweus, 1979). This stability in antisocial behavior has been demonstrated by using data from different countries and varied methods of assessment, including official records as well as teacher, parent, and peer reports of aggressive behavior (Caspi & Moffitt, 1993).

What causes the early propensity among some to engage in aggressive behavior? Gottfredson and Hirschi (1990) and others have argued that personal characteristics such as lack of self-control and a tendency toward impulsivity explain an early onset of antisocial behavior. Other research points to the importance of family factors in predicting problematic behavior in childhood and adolescence, in particular, low levels of parental supervision and involvement, a disciplinary approach that is both erratic and harsh, and weak attachment to parents (Loeber & Stouthamer-Loeber, 1986). Other possible explanations relate to school involvement and attachment, neighborhood factors (e.g., poverty), parental criminal involvement, and heredity.

Antisocial behavior in childhood may influence later behavior though multiple mechanisms. To the extent that personal traits such as low self-control do not change over time, they continue to affect behavior in later life (Gottfredson & Hirschi, 1990). Other researchers note that prior behavior may increase the probability of future problematic behavior either by weakening inhibitions or by increasing motivations (Nagin & Paternoster, 1991). For example, the process of being apprehended and officially sanctioned or labeled for antisocial behavior at a young age may propagate problematic behavior in the future by removing opportunities. Devah Pager (2003) documented the "mark of a criminal record," demonstrating that arrest and incarceration negatively affect future employment prospects.

All this research pointing to stability in antisocial behavior over time seems inconsistent with the notion that individuals desist from crime as they age. Yet stability and desistance are not mutually exclusive patterns. A substantial body of literature reveals that most antisocial children do not manifest similar problematic behavior in adulthood (Robins, 1978). These seemingly contradictory statistics can be reconciled by returning to the research design problem mentioned above: Most studies have been retrospective in design, beginning with adult criminals and tracing their behavior and experiences back in time. That approach excludes delinquent adolescents who eventually desist from

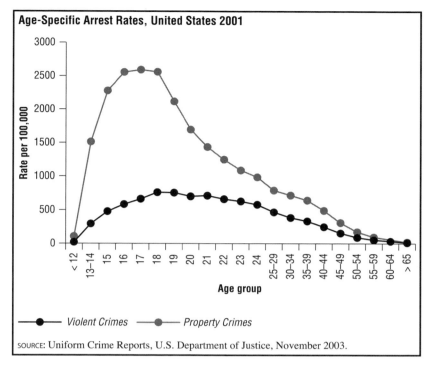

Age-Specific Arrest Rates, United States 2001

SOURCE: Uniform Crime Reports, U.S. Department of Justice, November 2003.

Figure 1. CENGAGE LEARNING, GALE.

crime. Although virtually all adult criminals experienced severe problems as children, most antisocial children grow up to become law-abiding adults.

FACTORS THAT EXPLAIN DESISTANCE FROM CRIME WITH AGE

What factors determine whether antisocial children desist from or persist in criminal behavior in adulthood? Some argue that the causal mechanisms underlying criminal behavior differ in important ways for those whose problematic behavior is confined to late adolescence and early adulthood as opposed to those who persist into later adulthood. Moffit (1993), for example, argued that those on a career criminal path offend because of what she terms "early neuropsychological deficits" such as hyperactivity, impulsiveness, and low self-control. These qualities, which may be inherited or acquired, are exacerbated by poor family relationships and other environmental features but are largely immutable. In contrast, the motivation for offending among adolescent-limited offenders is rooted in peer influences or "social mimicry," forces that lose their sway once individuals reach adulthood.

However, evidence is accumulating that shows that criminal trajectories are not predestined in this way. Instead, certain key life events or turning points explain how and why many antisocial children and delinquent

adolescents are able to change their life trajectories and desist from criminal behavior. Perhaps most influential in this regard is the work of Sampson and Laub (1993, 2005), which demonstrates how informal social controls that are exerted through institutions such as marriage, employment, education, and military involvement can promote changes in problematic behavior. Such turning points separate past history from the present, offer both supervision and monitoring, and provide structure, social support, and economic opportunities. These transformative events are linked closely to age and hence offer an explanation for the declining rate of criminal involvement with age.

Sampson and Laub's study resurrects life histories originally gathered by two Harvard researchers, Sheldon Glueck and Eleanor Glueck, between 1940 and 1965. The Glueck team gathered data on 500 highly delinquent youth and 500 control participants in the Boston area, matching them on several characteristics, including age, IQ, socioeconomic status, and ethnicity (Glueck & Glueck, 1950). The participants originally were followed from age 14 to age 32. Sampson and Laub tracked down some of those men and updated their life histories to age 70.

The analyses conducted by Sampson and Laub provide support for the stability of antisocial behavior. Men who experienced difficulties in childhood and adolescence were most likely to report problematic behavior in adulthood.

For example, 55% of those with an official record of delinquency before age 14 reported at least one arrest in midadulthood (between ages 32 and 45) compared with 16% of those without a record of official delinquency. However, the analyses also revealed that high-quality social bonds to important institutions, such as a close attachment to a spouse and expressed commitment to a stable job, are effective in promoting change. About a third of men who reported stable jobs and strong marital attachments at ages 17 to 25 were arrested between ages 25 and 32 compared with about three-quarters of men with low job stability and weak marital attachments.

Other research has led to similar conclusions. One study (Horney, Osgood, & Marshall, 1995), using retrospective survey data on more than 600 serious offenders, found that school attendance and living with a wife reduced the chances of reoffending in the short term in a sample of male felons. Another study, using prospective panel survey data gathered in the United Kingdom, indicated that delinquent youths who largely were reformed by adulthood had work records and marital relationships that were substantially better than those of chronic offenders. However, those individuals continued to report noncriminal deviant behavior such as heavy drinking and physical disputes (Hagan, 1993; Nagin, Farrington, & Moffitt, 1995).

Of course, an important question is whether such life events actually cause people to desist or whether the individuals most likely to desist anyway are those who obtain good employment and/or choose a stable, supportive partner. In other words, can it really be concluded that such life events actually cause desistance? Sampson and Laub (2003) provided evidence that suggests that the answer is yes, showing that the same person is less likely to offend when married than when unmarried even after controlling for age.

Christopher Uggen (2000) approached this issue by examining data gathered from a national work experiment for individuals with a criminal record. Offenders were assigned randomly to either a treatment group or a control group; those in the treatment group were offered minimum-wage jobs, and random assignment ensured that the nature of employment was not associated with personal traits such as work ethic and commitment level. The results revealed that participants age 27 or older in the treatment group were less likely to report crime and arrest than were those in the control group. However, for younger offenders marginal job opportunities elicited little change in criminal behavior. This study provides convincing evidence that, for older offenders at least, employment is in fact an effective turning point.

FUTURE RESEARCH DIRECTIONS

Past research on adult criminal activity, which is quantitative in nature and typically relies on official statistics (arrest data) or self-report data, has provided much information about how childhood circumstances and key life events such as employment and marriage affect criminal trajectories. What is less well understood is the role of human agency—the degree to which individuals actively make their own decisions about the course of their lives—and how those individual decisions interact with environmental factors to affect criminal trajectories (Sampson & Laub, 2005). Qualitative research would complement quantitative data in this regard. Moreover, future research that attempts to incorporate both self-reports and official measures of offending and considered other types of deviant behavior, such as domestic violence, would further understanding of adult criminal activity (Piquero & Mazerolle, 2001). Also, the degree to which other life events such as the discovery of religion affect criminal involvement is not well understood, nor are the main life events that contribute to persistence in rather than desistance from crime.

INTERVENTION STRATEGIES

The mechanisms through which crime begins and persists suggest two alternative paths for intervention and prevention. To the extent that problematic behavior in childhood contributes to difficulties in adulthood, one set of strategies focuses on targeting youths and their families as early as possible. Programs such as the Seattle Social Development Project, which promotes strong bonds between children, families, and schools, and the Montreal Longitudinal-Experimental Study, which focuses on parent training (e.g., literacy, effective discipline strategies), have had success. Youths participating in those programs exhibited significantly lower levels of delinquency and substance abuse at older ages than did similar youths not involved in the programs (Hawkins, Kosterman, Catalano, Hill, & Abbott, 2005; Tremblay et al., 1992). Nurse home visitation during pregnancy and continuing through infancy also proved effective: Fifteen-year follow-up results show that adolescents from single-parent, economically disadvantaged homes who received nurse home visits report lower levels of official delinquency, substance abuse, and truancy than do those in control groups (Olds et al., 1998).

The other strategy for reducing criminal activity focuses on adults to ensure that protective social bonds are not severed. Community-based corrections, such as residential community institutions, home confinement programs, and day reporting centers, may be most successful in this regard. Laub and Allen (2000) argued that such community incarceration programs emphasize surveillance but also recognize the importance of treatment, such as job training and employment, education, and family counseling. Evidence shows that education and vocational training improve the prospects of employment and reduce reoffending rates. The participants in one such program, the Court Employment Project, could have their criminal charges dropped if they completed 90 days of a job training and placement program. Offenders who successfully completed the program did appear somewhat less likely to reoffend (Bushway & Reuter, 1997). These community-based strategies are in direct contradiction to the current emphasis in the U.S. criminal justice system on incarceration, which may increase the likelihood of crime by severing social ties to family and work, which are important for changing criminal trajectories over the life course.

SEE ALSO Volume 1: *Child Abuse; School Violence;* Volume 2: *Crime and Victimization, Adulthood; Domestic Violence; Incarceration, Adulthood;* Volume 3: *Elder Abuse and Neglect*

BIBLIOGRAPHY

Blumstein, A., & Cohen, J. (1979). Estimation of individual crime rates from arrest records. *Journal of Criminal Law & Criminology, 70*(4), 561–585.

Bushway, S., & Reuter, P. (1997). Labor markets and crime risk factors. In L. W. Sherman, D. Gottfredson, D. MacKenzie, J. Eck, P. Reuter, & S. Bushway (Eds.), *Preventing crime: What works, what doesn't, what's promising: Report to the United States Congress.* Washington, DC: U.S. Department of Justice, Office of Justice Programs.

Caspi, A., & Moffitt, T. E. (1993). The continuity of maladaptive behavior: From description to understanding in the study of antisocial behavior. In D. Cicchetti & D. Cohen (Eds.), *Developmental psychopathology.* New York: Wiley.

Farrington, D. P. (2003). Developmental and life-course criminology: Key theoretical and empirical issues—the 2002 Sutherland Award address. *Criminology, 41*(2), 221–255.

Glueck, S., & Glueck, E. (1950). *Unraveling juvenile delinquency.* New York: Commonwealth Fund.

Gottfredson, M. R., & Hirschi, T. (1990). *A general theory of crime.* Stanford, CA: Stanford University Press.

Hagan, J. (1993). The social embeddedness of crime and unemployment. *Criminology, 31*(4), 465–491.

Hawkins, J. D., Kosterman, R., Catalano, R. F., Hill, K. G., & Abbott, R. D. (2005). Promoting positive adult functioning through social development intervention in childhood: Long-term effects from the Seattle Social Development Project. *Archives of Pediatrics & Adolescent Medicine, 159*(1), 25–31.

Hirschi, T., & Gottfredson, M. (1983). Age and the explanation of crime. *American Journal of Sociology, 89*, 37–55.

Horney, J., Osgood, D. W., & Marshall, I. H. (1995). Criminal careers in the short-term: Intra-individual variability in crime and its relation to local life circumstances. *American Sociological Review, 60*(5), 655–673.

Laub, J. H., & Allen, L. C. (2000). Life course criminology and community corrections. *Perspectives, 24*(2), 20–29.

Laub, J. H., & Sampson, R. J. (2003). *Shared beginnings, divergent lives: Delinquent boys to age 70.* Cambridge, MA: Harvard University Press.

Loeber, R., & Stouthamer-Loeber, M. (1986). Family factors as correlates and predictors of juvenile conduct problems and delinquency. In M. Tonry & N. Morris (Eds.), *Crime and justice* (Vol. 7, pp. 29–149). Chicago: University of Chicago Press.

Moffitt, T. (1993). "Life-course persistent" and "adolescent-limited" antisocial behavior: A developmental taxonomy. *Psychological Review, 100*, 674–701.

Nagin, D. S., Farrington, D. P., & Moffitt, T. E. (1995). Life-course trajectories of different types of offenders. *Criminology, 33*(1), 111–139.

Nagin, D. S., & Land, K. (1993). Age, criminal careers, and population heterogeneity: Specification and estimation of a nonparametric, mixed Poisson model. *Criminology, 31*(3), 327–362.

Nagin, D. S., & Paternoster, R. (1991). On the relationship between past and future participation in delinquency. *Criminology, 29*, 163–189.

Olds, D., Henderson, C. R., Cole, R., Eckenrode, J., Kitzman, H., Luckey, D., et al. (1998). Long-term effects of nurse home visitation on children's criminal and antisocial behavior. *Journal of the American Medical Association, 280*(14), 1238–1244.

Olweus, D. (1979). Stability of aggressive reaction patterns in males: A review. *Psychological Bulletin, 86*, 852–875.

Pager, D. (2003). The mark of a criminal record. *American Journal of Sociology, 108*(5), 937–975.

Piquero, A., & Mazerolle, P. (Eds.). (2001). *Life course criminology: Contemporary and classic readings.* Belmont, CA: Wadsworth Thomson Learning.

Robins, L. N. (1978). Sturdy childhood predictors of adult antisocial behavior: Replications from longitudinal studies. *Psychological Medicine, 8*, 611–622.

Sampson, R. J., & Laub, J. H. (1993). *Crime in the making: Pathways and turning points through life.* Cambridge, MA: Harvard University Press.

Sampson, R. J., & Laub, J. H. (2005). A life-course view of the development of crime. *Annals of the American Academy of Political and Social Science, 602*, 12–45.

Tremblay, R. E., Vitaro, F., Bertrand, L., LeBlanc, M., Beauchesne, H., Boileau, H., et al. (1992). Parent and child training to prevent early onset of delinquency. In J. McCord & R. E. Tremblay (Eds.), *Preventing antisocial behavior: Interventions from birth through adolescence* (pp. 117–138). New York: Guilford Press.

Uggen, C. (2000). Work as a turning point in the life course of criminals: A duration model of age, employment, and recidivism. *American Sociological Review, 65*, 529–546.

Wolfgang, M. E., Figlio, R. M., & Sellin, T. (1972). *Delinquency in a birth cohort.* Chicago: University of Chicago Press.

Julie A. Phillips

CRIME AND VICTIMIZATION, ADULTHOOD

Although victimization has a clear reality in the public mind, efforts to provide a coherent and comprehensive definition have proved notoriously difficult. Most social scientists view victimization in the context of physical attacks on individuals (e.g., assaults, sexual assaults, and murders), the destruction or unwanted removal of property (e.g., vandalism, theft, break and enters), or some combination of the two (e.g., robbery, kidnapping). Still, such definitions are almost always incomplete or contested as seen in descriptions of emotional abuse, pet abuse, or stalking, to name only a few.

Nevertheless, for the most part, victimization (as it is generally measured) is a rare event. Only a select segment of any population is victimized in any given year and fewer, still, experience more frequent or severe incidents such as violence. Thus viewing victimization as a random and perhaps fleeting occurrence is natural. However, the age grading of victimization risk is very strong and the extent and type of this risk is closely connected to adult social roles. Moreover, the experience of victimization may in turn affect how an individual's life course unfolds, with negative consequences for his or her life chances.

LIFE COURSE ANTECEDENTS OF VICTIMIZATION

Research consistently shows that the likelihood of criminal behavior increases steadily through the teenage years, peaks in late adolescence or early adulthood, and then declines steadily with advancing age. Whether this age pattern is the same across times and places has been hotly debated (Blumstein, Farrington, & Cohen, 1988); however, the age grading of crime seems indisputable.

The relationship between age and victimization is much more complex, however. Both social science and public discourse focus considerable attention on specific types of victims defined largely in terms of age. The victimization of children and the elderly is the subject of a great deal of this attention. Likewise, laws often target age-specific victimizations; Megan's Law, for example, requires the identity of persons convicted of sex offenses against children to be made public. Similarly, the Texas Penal Code, like other states, specifically criminalizes someone who "intentionally, knowingly, recklessly, or with criminal negligence, by act or intentionally, knowingly, or recklessly by omission, causes to a child, elderly individual, or disabled individual … serious bodily injury, serious mental deficiency, impairment, or injury, or bodily injury." In light of such interest, it is not surprising that organizations, such as the National Center for Missing and Exploited Children or the National Center on Elder Abuse, exist to increase public awareness and advocate on behalf of young and old victims of crime.

The difference between age patterns of crime and age patterns of criminal victimization reflect the fundamental belief that *vulnerability* is key to understanding victimization. The assumption is that people are victimized because they lack the personal and social resources to prevent their

victimization. Yet, this perception ignores the importance of factors that put potential offenders and potential victims together in time and space. Sociologists Larry Cohen, James Kluegel, and Kenneth Land (1981) describe an opportunity model of crime victimization that emphasizes the importance of *proximity, exposure, guardianship,* and *attractiveness* as key determinants of victimization. Proximity refers to an individual's distance to pools of potential offenders, whereas exposure refers to activities that put potential offenders and potential victims in the same place. Guardianship, a potentially countervailing influence, is the capacity of individuals or their circumstances to prevent victimization by increasing resistance, difficulty, or the likelihood of detection. Finally, attractiveness is the relative symbolic or material value of a given target for a potential offender. An attractive target may simply be someone who looks like they have more money or a nicer house or car. Some even speculate that the overall volume of attractive targets has increased in recent decades with the literal explosion of portable electronic devices such as cell phones, BlackBerries, iPods, and so forth. Importantly, age and life course stage shape these determinants in complex ways, which makes predicting the age pattern of victimization difficult. Still, a number of key themes are important in understanding victimization.

If the risk of victimization increases when potential victims share time and space with potential offenders, then people who are close in age or share a similar lifestyle with potential offenders should be at greatest risk. Given the age pattern of crime, a natural expectation is that people in the age group at which crime rates are highest are most at risk of victimization and indeed considerable research bears this out. In 2007, the Bureau of Justice Statistics reported that rates of violent victimization increased from 47.3 per 1,000 for those aged 12 to 15 to 52.3 for those aged 16 to 19 but then declined steadily with advancing age (Rand & Shannan, 2007). People ages 50 to 64 had a rate of violent victimization approximately one-quarter (13.1 per 1,000), while persons age 65 or older had a rate almost one-fifteenth of those in their teenage years (Rand & Shannan, 2007). When considering property victimization, the story is the same. Heads of households between the ages of 12 and 19 have victimization rates of 370 per 1,000 compared with only 70.3 for heads of households 65 or older. In general, data from a wide variety of sources, time periods, and countries show that victimization is strongly concentrated in the adolescent years.

However, the story does not begin and end with adolescent victimization risk. Also important is how unfolding social roles shape victimization risk over time. Such a view is anticipated in one of the earliest statements of victimization risk, where Michael Hindelang, Michael Gottfredson, and James Garofalo (1978) argued that the idea of *lifestyle* is the key determinant of victimization. In their view, lifestyle refers to the broad pattern of relationships and activities that constitute the core features of an individual's everyday life. Lifestyle is strongly connected to the social roles that people occupy, especially to those that signal the transition to adulthood and give shape to the unfolding life span. How and when people exit from schooling, enter the workforce, get married or begin cohabiting, have children, and leave the parental home all have an impact upon their likely exposure to crime by virtue of the lifestyles they promote. These factors also influence proximity and exposure to potential offenders, as well as guardianship and attractiveness.

Educational roles are a good example. The number of years spent in formal education has increased in the United States. For many, this involves movement into and through higher education and the completion of two- and four-year degrees in the early to mid-20s. For others, schooling is less linear and involves movement into and out of educational institutions, often switching programs and colleges, throughout one's 20s and even into one's 30s. Although the extension of formal schooling has many life course implications, a particularly important one is that the period in which individuals are proximate and exposed to potential offenders also is extended. Although institutions of higher learning are quite safe in comparison to other social spaces, despite recent high-visibility campus shootings, there is also evidence that college students have higher than expected risks. College worlds seem particularly conducive to alcohol related assaults, date rape, and various forms of personal theft.

Another key feature of adulthood is the movement into full-time work. Work is related to victimization in a variety of ways, the two most significant being work-related victimization and socioeconomic inequality in victimization risk. In the former case, considerable violence actually occurs in and around workplaces. Data from the National Crime Victimization Survey (NCVS) indicates that 8% of rapes, 7% of robberies, and 16% of assaults occurred while victims were working or on duty (Bachman, 1994). Moreover, a person's type of work also matters, in that victimization rates appear particularly high in restaurant, bar, and nightclub settings. More generally, criminologist James Lynch (1987) concluded that jobs that involve high amounts of face-to-face contact, the handling of money, and mobility between locations were particularly conducive to victimization. Not surprisingly, research on homicide shows that the risk of being murdered is significantly elevated among cab drivers, bartenders and waitresses, and clerks in convenience stores.

In addition to shaping the kinds of activities in which individuals are involved, jobs are a foundation of socioeconomic status. As such, jobs affect the likelihood

of victimization by shaping the types of neighborhoods people live in, the types of housing they have, the private or public transportation available to them, and their capability to buy protections helping prevent their victimization. However, the relationship between socioeconomic status and victimization risk is complicated. In terms of proximity, money should be able to buy distance and those with more resources should be better able to insulate themselves from potential offenders. Similarly, greater resources should also increase guardianship, as those with more resources are better equipped to purchase protections such as private parking or home security. At the same time, people with more resources usually have more valuable possessions, which increases their attractiveness to potential offenders. More resources also increase people's ability to purchase leisure, increasing exposure as well. These countervailing forces play out differently for various types of victimization risk, so that the relationship between risk of victimization and socioeconomic status varies by type of victimization. For example, the risk of rape victimization is particularly high among those who earn less than $15,000 per year (U.S. Department of Justice, 2003). The pattern is even more pronounced for robbery and assault; those with incomes of less than $7,500 per year have double the risk of victimization of the next highest income group. In contrast, there is no clear relationship between socioeconomic status and risk of personal theft; victimization rates are similar across income categories.

Marital status has a complicated relationship to victimization risk. On one level, being married is generally associated with lower risk of predatory crimes, such as stranger assaults, robberies, and personal theft. According to data from the NCVS, married persons have one-quarter the risk of violent victimization compared with persons who never married (Catalano, 2006). Similar, if not more extreme, differentials appear for rape, robbery, aggravated assault, and personal theft. The complexity of the relationship is revealed by examining the risk of separated and divorced persons, whose risk of victimization for rape, robbery, or aggravated assault is similar to the risk of persons who never married, even though the former are typically much older than the latter and presumably have less exposure to potential offenders.

The question of why formerly married people have such high rates of victimization highlights the unique opportunities and circumstances of marriage that might foster violence between partners, violence that is typically not well-measured in national crime surveys such as the NCVS. As a result, researchers often turn to studies that focus on violence among intimate partners: Studies such as the National Violence against Women Survey (NVAWS), for instance, reveal that there is considerable violence between intimate partners, that women have considerably higher rates of victimization than those shown in traditional crime victimization surveys, and that women who are leaving or have left a relationship are particularly likely to experience violence (Tjaden & Thoennes, 2000). Thus, whereas marriage decreases some forms of victimization by altering individuals' lifestyles and routine activities, it also increases other forms of victimization by situating individuals in a unique social relationship with norms, expectations, and practices that may elicit, and perhaps even allow and encourage, the use of violence.

LIFE COURSE CONSEQUENCES OF VICTIMIZATION

Although life course events affect the risk of victimization, experiences of victimization are nevertheless concentrated in adolescence and early adulthood. The experience of violence, both social and psychological, has the potential to shape life course outcomes by altering the ways in which individuals approach the world and its challenges and opportunities and even the extent and type of relationships that one has (Macmillan, 2001). One particularly prominent vein of research focuses on exposure to violence in early life, be it violence from strangers, peers, or kin, and the likelihood of it resulting in mental distress and poor psychological well-being. Indeed, a core explanation of mental distress focuses on the presence of life stressors of which exposure to violence is a salient theme, regardless of whether the focus is on broad life course linkages such as that between early childhood and later adulthood (Kessler & Magee, 1994) or on life stages such as adolescence (Hagan & Foster, 2001) or old age (Harrell et al., 2002).

An equally provocative literature focuses on the relationship between victimization and offending. Although it is well-established that involvement in crime and deviance dramatically increases risks of victimization, there is also compelling work that views victimization as a precursor to crime. Some suggest that victimization produces the impetus for revenge, whereas others speculate that victimization may induce nihilistic or anomic feelings that neutralize anticrime values (Singer, 1986). Still, there is much more work to be done given the problem of embeddedness where those whose lifestyles involve crime may be more likely to offend and be victimized by virtue of how they spend their time and who they spend it with. Yet what seems clear is a strong association between victimization and offending over the life span (Macmillan & Hagan, 2004).

With effects on mental health and involvement in crime and deviance, it is not surprising to imagine further effects victimization has on other life course trajectories. Recent years have seen the emergence of two streams of work. One area of study is the impact of victimization on social relationships. Constance Fischer (1984), for example, argues that victimization upsets and undermines

people's world views and helps foster mindsets where individuals are seen as predators rather than allies and sources of threat rather than safety. Although the social network implications of this are largely speculative, some work by Andrew Cherlin and colleagues (2004) suggests that physical and sexual abuse in relationships has important effects on the character and likelihood of subsequent relationships. Although further study is clearly necessary, evidence is emerging that victimization shapes social relationships in profound ways.

A final area of study examines the relationship between victimization and trajectories of educational and occupation success. Building off the work of Fischer and others, Ross Macmillan (2000; 2001) proposed a theoretical model that viewed the immediate consequences of victimization as threats to agency and long-term orientations and investments. From these consequences stemmed lower aspirations and less investment in educational endeavors such as homework. This further leads to poorer educational performance and lower grades and lower educational attainment in general. As educational attainment is the lynchpin of socioeconomic attainment, victimization ultimately undermines labor force participation, occupational prestige, income, homeownership, and risk of poverty. Indeed, analysis of high-quality data showed widespread socioeconomic consequences of adolescent victimization in the transition to adulthood (Macmillan & Hagan, 2004).

Although studies of the consequences of victimization are comparatively new relative to studies of victimization risk, there is an impressive and increasing body of evidence that shows victimization in adolescence to be part of a chain of adversity where early experiences shape the character and content of later experiences, with exposure to violence being a recurring feature of an individual's life course and thus dramatically diminishing quality of life. In some respects, early adversity puts people at risk for victimization, which contributes to cycles of disadvantage. In other respects, victimization may constitute a turning point in the life course and derail trajectories of success. In both respects, it appears an important element in the structuring of the life course.

SEE ALSO Volume 1: *Child Abuse; School Violence;* Volume 2: *Crime, Criminal Activity in Adulthood; Domestic Violence; Incarceration, Adulthood;* Volume 3: *Elder Abuse and Neglect.*

BIBLIOGRAPHY

Bachman, R. (1994). *Violence and theft in the workplace.* Washington, DC: Office of Justice Programs, Bureau of Justice Statistics. Retrieved April 27, 2008, from http://www.ojp.usdoj.gov/bjs/pub/pdf/thefwork.pdf

Blumstein, A., Farrington, D., & Cohen, J. (1988). Criminal career research: Its value for criminology. *Criminology, 26,* 1–36.

Catalano, S. (2006). *Criminal Victimization, 2005.* Washington, DC: U.S. Department of Justice, Office of Justice Programs.

Cherlin, A. J., Burton, L. M., Hurt, T. R., & Purvin, D. M. (2004). The influence of physical and sexual abuse on marriage and cohabitation. *American Sociological Review, 69,* 768–789.

Cohen, L., Kluegel, J., & Land, K. (1981). Social inequality and predatory criminal victimization: An exposition and test of a formal theory. *American Sociological Review, 46*(5), 505–524.

Fischer, C. (1984). A phenomenological study of being criminally victimized: Contributions and constraints of qualitative research. *Journal of Social Issues, 40*(1), 161–178.

Greenberg, D. (1985). Age, crime, and social explanation. *American Journal of Sociology, 91*(1), 1–21.

Hagan, J., & Foster, H. (2001). Youth violence and the end of adolescence. *American Sociological Review, 66*(6), 874–899.

Harrell, R., Toronjo, C., McLaughlin, J., Pavlik, V., Hyman, D., & Dyer, C. B. (2002). How geriatricians identify elder abuse and neglect. *American Journal of the Medical Sciences, 323*(1), 34–38.

Hindelang, M., Gottfredson, M., & Garofalo, J. (1978). *Victims of personal crime: An empirical foundation for a theory of personal victimization.* Cambridge, MA: Ballinger.

Hirschi, T., & Gottfredson, M. (1983). Age and the explanation of crime. *American Journal of Sociology, 89*(3), 552–584.

Hirschi, T., & Gottfredson, M. (1985). Age and crime, logic, and scholarship. *American Journal of Sociology, 91*(1), 22–27.

Kessler, R., & Magee, W. (1994). Childhood family violence and adult recurrent depression. *Journal of Health and Social Behavior, 35*(1), 13–27.

Lynch, J. (1987). Routine activity and victimization at work. *Journal of Quantitative Criminology, 3*(4), 283–300.

Macmillan, R. (2000). Adolescent victimization and income deficits in adulthood: Rethinking the costs of criminal violence from a life course perspective. *Criminology, 38*(2), 553–587.

Macmillan, R. (2001). Violence and the life course: The consequences of victimization for personal and social development. *Annual Review of Sociology, 27,* 1–22.

Macmillan, R., & Hagan, J. (2004). Violence in the transition to adulthood: Adolescent victimization, education, and socioeconomic attainment in later life. *Journal of Research on Adolescence, 14*(2), 127–158.

Piquero, A., Farrington, D., & Blumstein, A. (2006). *Key issues in criminal career research: New analyses of the Cambridge study in delinquent development.* New York: Cambridge University Press.

Rand, M., & Shannan, C. (2007). *Criminal victimization, 2006.* Washington, DC: US Department of Justice, Office of Justice Programs. Retrieved April 27, 2008, from http://www.ojp. usdoj.gov/bjs/abstract/cv06.htm

Sampson, R., & Laub, J. (1993). *Crime in the making: Pathways and turning points through life.* Cambridge, MA: Harvard University Press.

Singer, S. (1986). Victims of serious violence and their criminal behavior: Subcultural theory and beyond. *Violence and Victims, 1*(1), 61–70.

Tjaden, P., & Thoennes, N. (2000). *Full report of the prevalence, incidence, and consequences of violence against women: Findings from the National Violence against Women Survey.* Washington, DC: U.S. Department of Justice, Office of Justice Programs, National Institute of Justice.

Ross Macmillan

CULTURAL CAPITAL, ADULTHOOD

SEE Volume 1: *Cultural Capital.*

CULTURAL IMAGES, ADULTHOOD

Cultural images of adulthood, or the prevailing ideas about what it means to be an adult in a particular society, have not been researched systematically by social scientists. Knowledge of these images might provide a framework in which to monitor social change in a variety of areas, including intergenerational relations, age consciousness, lifestyles, gender and ethnic inequalities, and the life course.

The few historical analyses of these images are impressionistic rather than being based on rigorous statistical techniques. Cultural images could be studied by using content analyses of the depiction of adults on television, in movies, and in novels, but no studies of this type have been reported in the literature. Nonetheless, the impressionistic reports are a useful point of reference. Perhaps the best place to start in understanding the evolution of cultural images of adulthood is with an examination of the etymology of the word *adult.*

ETYMOLOGICAL ANALYSIS

An etymological analysis suggests that adulthood as it is known in Western countries is a cultural artifact. This is demonstrated by the fact that in most languages the idea is not important enough in cultural life to require a word to express it. Even among the European languages only English has a specific word designating a distinct stage of the life course as adulthood. In fact, it appears that the differentiation of the life course that occurred in the modern period created the need for a lexicon to describe it, with the term *adult* following a similar etymological path to that of other terms that represent the life course. For example, the word *adult* first appeared in the language in 1656, but it is instructive to note that it is derived from the Latin *adultus* (grown), which is the past participle of *adolescere* (to grow up, mature). The term *adolescent* came into English usage in the 1400s, a half century earlier than the word *adult,* whereas *adulthood* did not appear until 1870 (Côté, 2000; Merser, 1987).

This etymological analysis suggests that historically, people did not make the age distinctions that Anglophones and others do now. These age distinctions appear to be the result of the rise of modernity: the massive social, economic, and technological transformations of the last several hundred years. Those transformations altered social institutions, and as those institutions changed, so did people's lives: People lived longer and were healthier, and adults were less likely to raise large numbers of children. Those changes led to the formation of age groups whose members were similar to one another but distinct from the members of other age groups. Thus, people of different ages became different in terms of social roles and responsibilities as well as social expectations about cognitive and emotional attributes.

According to Cheryl Merser (1987), the relatively recent appearance of a word to describe adulthood suggests that people needed a way to depict the new social conditions they faced, especially increasing uncertainty and the need to make life-altering choices. Traditionally, most people had little choice about how their lives played out. Regardless of their age, people were bound by duties and obligations to fulfill ascribed family and community roles. Young and old alike were expected to work for a common welfare regardless of their personal preferences. However, Merser argued, the rise of uncertainty and the consequent need to know more about the world to be able to make choices gave new meaning to the notion of maturity and widened the gap between those with little experience (children) and those with more experience (adults). The process was hastened by the decline of absolute religious authority and the rise of secular authority; people increasingly were seen as responsible for their own destinies and choices.

CHANGING IMAGES OF MATURITY

In a 1978 essay about the study of adulthood, "Searching for Adulthood in America," Winthrop Jordan explored the changing meaning of adulthood in the United States. In his search of the archives that chronicled early English settlers in the United States, Jordan found little evidence that people held images of different stages of the life course. Instead, he found references to the roles and duties assigned to husbands, wives, children, and servants. Within those roles there was no reference to growth, maturing, or psychological needs and preferences. Among Puritans, for example, people were compelled to know their existing conditions, not to change those conditions. Jordan argued that the decline of patriarchy made way for binary ideas about personality characteristics such as maturity-immaturity and mastery-dependence. Increasingly, family members other than the dominant male gained status and rights, and so people were defined less in terms of their roles and duties and more as individuals with needs and potentials.

In addition, Jordan argued, in the past concern about gender roles overrode age roles in the sense that the dominant images were of manhood and womanhood as distinct but complementary states. Accordingly, it was more important to distinguish males from females than to distinguish children from adults. Over time that changed, with age roles and distinctions gaining importance in relation to gender distinctions. In other words, in early American history it appears that women and men had more in common with those of the same sex regardless of age; over time adult men and women came to have more in common with one another than with children of the same sex.

Complementing those trends was a fall in both fertility and mortality rates. When there were fewer children to raise, each child could receive more attention. At the same time more parents lived to see their children leave their homes. Therefore, a period of the life course without dependent children became common and people could turn their attention to themselves and reflect on their psychological states and needs. Jordan argued that with the rise of the social sciences in the 20th century a technical language emerged that labeled the life stages of childhood, adolescence, and adulthood as real rather than as historically produced and changeable cultural experiences.

From Jordan's historical analyses of the changing ideas of adulthood it is possible to trace the emergence of the fault lines associated with contemporary age consciousness, especially in terms of being a nonadult ("becoming" and "incomplete") versus an adult ("arrived" and "complete") (Wyn & White, 1997). Cultural images of the differences between these age statuses now apparently vary by dimensions such as immature-mature, selfishness-selflessness, and ignorant-knowledgeable.

IMAGES IN THE MASS MEDIA

With the rise of the mass media in the 20th century social scientists were drawn to study various forms of (mis)representations of men and women (Lindsey, 2005) and various ethnic groups (Basow, 1992). For example, men are overrepresented in the proportion of characters, especially those who play a significant role in the outcome of plots, and both males and females are depicted in gender-stereotyped manners: Adult females tend to be linked to home and family roles, whereas adult males are linked to more power-oriented roles and goals, including self-indulgence, wealth, and revenge.

However, little attention has been paid to the representations of adults per se as characters in the mass media, perhaps because adulthood is taken for granted as a self-evident phase in the life course. Still, one can find evidence of the new age consciousness being fed by media that target different age groups. For example, programming directed at young people, especially in forms such as MTV, can depict adults as boring, stupid, and pretentious. Mark Crispin Miller (2001) argued that in rock video imagery

The Cosby Show. *Bill Cosby, as Dr. Cliff Huxtable of "The Cosby Show," listens to a point made by his grandson Gary Gray, as his granddaughter played by Jessica Vaughn looks on.* AP IMAGES.

"parents are creeps, teachers are nerds and idiots, [and] authority figures are laughable."

Taking this line of thinking further, Marcel Danesi (2003) contended that some of the mass media have encouraged a "dumbing down" of cultural images as a way to appeal to the rising youth market and that this approach influences self-conceptions among narcissistic adults who do not want to grow up. In the youth-oriented television programming of the 1980s and 1990s parents were caricatured in ways that corresponded to rebellious adolescent views: shallow in their self-absorption and inept in their ability to make decisions for the family. These images stand in sharp contrast to programming of the 1950s, in which parents were depicted as firm, caring, and ultimately knowing best. These more recent forms of mockery became possible, according to Danesi, because of the overall obsession of contemporary culture with youthfulness and attempts by adults to avoid the commitments and duties attached to their adult roles, including controlling the media images that influence their children. Juliet Schor (2004) attributed some of these changes to marketers who have created "a sophisticated and powerful 'antiadultism' within the com-

mercial world" (Schor, 2004, p. 51) by depicting adults as forcing "a repressive and joyless world" on children who just want to be left in peace to play with their newly acquired consumer items.

However, television programming in the early 21st century has been replete with heterogeneous images of adults depicted for other adults. It has become commonplace for adults to remain happily unmarried (*Friends*), gay relationships are depicted openly (*Will & Grace*, *Desperate Housewives*), and single women take on the predatory role in dating that men once were shown to hold (*Sex and the City*, *Desperate Housewives*). In addition, there have been more depictions of married couples in egalitarian relationships (*Medium*) and a trend toward showing wives who are more educated and successful than their spouses (*Commander in Chief*).

FUTURE RESEARCH

These historical and impressionistic analyses suggest that the study of adulthood and its cultural images is a potentially rich area of research awaiting more rigorous techniques such as content analysis of contemporary mass media and archival material from past eras in the form of diaries, literature, plays, and fine art. Adulthood as it is socially constructed is the longest and least studied portion of the life course. The 21st century probably will see increased research efforts devoted to helping people understand the images they hold of adults, especially as those images contrast with images of other age groups.

SEE ALSO Volume 1: *Age Norms; Cultural Images, Childhood and Adolescence; Identity Development;* Volume 2: *Consumption, Adulthood and Later Life;* Volume 3: *Cultural Images, Later Life.*

BIBLIOGRAPHY

Basow, S. A. (1992). *Gender: Stereotypes and roles*. Pacific Grove, CA: Brooks/Cole.

Côté, J. E. (2000). *Arrested adulthood: The changing nature of maturity and identity*. New York: New York University Press.

Crispin Miller, M. (2001). Interview. In D. Rushkoff (producer), *The merchants of cool* (Video documentary). U.S. distributor: PBS.

Danesi, M. (2003). *Forever young: The teen-aging of modern culture*. Toronto and Buffalo, NY: University of Toronto Press.

Jordan, W. D. (1978). Searching for adulthood in America. In E. H. Erikson (Ed.), *Adulthood: Essays* (pp. 189–199). New York: Norton.

Lindsey, L. L. (2005). *Gender roles: A sociological perspective* (4th ed.). Upper Saddle River, NJ: Pearson Prentice Hall.

Merser, C. (1987). *"Grown-ups": A generation in search of adulthood*. New York: Putnam.

Schor, J. (2004). *Born to buy: The commercialized child and the new consumer culture*. New York: Scribner.

Wyn, J., & White, R. (1997). *Rethinking youth*. St. Leonards, New South Wales, Australia: Allen & Unwin.

James E. Côté

D

DATA SOURCES, ADULTHOOD

This entry contains the following:

I. GENERAL ISSUES

Much of what social scientists know about the life course has been learned from social surveys. Family formation, employment, political preferences and behavior, health and psychosocial adjustment, housing preferences, and health and well-being have all been studied by asking people questions in the context of sample surveys. A sample survey is defined as a formal questionnaire (the survey) that is administered to a group of individuals selected in a statistically valid way (the sample). The goal of a sample survey is to not only obtain answers to questions from the respondents (as the individuals who answer survey questions are called) but also to have these answers represent the answers of the larger group of people from which the sample is drawn (the population). This is possible because when certain methods of selecting respondents are used, researchers can utilize the respondents' answers to estimate (or infer) the answers for all members of the population. This procedure is called *statistical inference*.

Several types of survey designs are useful in life-course research, particularly repeated cross-sectional surveys and longitudinal (sometimes called panel) surveys. The dense sets of personal events that characterize adulthood are often difficult to capture using a questionnaire, but modern advances in survey technology, such as using personal computers or the World Wide Web, have improved researchers' capabilities. In all steps in the survey process, there are also many sources of error that can affect both the accuracy of the information gathered and the validity of inferences made from respondents to a population.

SAMPLE DESIGN, SAMPLING FRAMES, AND METHODS OF COLLECTING DATA

Most sample surveys rely on the science of statistics to ensure that the respondents chosen for the survey represent the population of interest. Probability samples are defined as those survey samples in which the probability of selection into the survey is known for every respondent. There are many types of probability samples, including simple random, stratified, and clustered samples. Stratified samples are used for a variety of purposes, the most important of which is to ensure that a sufficient number of individuals with characteristics relatively rare in the population are included. Most of the large surveys conducted by the federal government of the United States use stratified sampling techniques to ensure adequate representation of ethnic and racial minority populations. Research comparing people with different characteristics requires adequately sized samples of all groups. Thus, stratified sampling is an important tool for making research successful.

To ensure that survey respondents are selected with a known probability, survey professionals must have some method for knowing the potential universe of respondents available to be surveyed. This universe is called a *sampling frame*. A sampling frame should be as complete a listing of the entire study population as possible. Individuals are then selected from this list with some known probability depending on the sampling strategy. *List frames* are simple lists of individuals generated from some source. State driver's licenses, birth and death certificates, mailing lists, and lists of postal addresses are all used by the survey staff to generate a sampling frame. An *area frame* is based on geography rather than a listing of names. Within census groupings such as county, census tract, and census block group, households are listed and then selected using a sampling technique. *Nonlist frames* are used in the case of random digit dial phone surveys. In this case, all households with telephones are considered eligible for interview and are selected with known frequency using random digit dialing technology.

Not all surveys are designed to be representative of the population or to allow for valid inference to a more general population. In nonprobability sample surveys, respondents are chosen by methods other than scientific sampling. These methods include, among others, *convenience* and *snowball sampling*. Convenience sampling means selecting respondents who are close at hand, whereas snowball sampling uses social networks of friends and neighbors to identify respondents. There are many good reasons to use nonprobability samples, including the relatively low cost and studying a population that is difficult to list. Inference about more general population trends from answers to these types of surveys, however, should be limited.

Finding and selecting respondents are the first two steps in survey design. These two steps affect how representative respondents are of the population. The third step is to choose the method of data collection used to gather the information, which includes the means used to ask questions and the technology used to record answers. Interviewer-administered questionnaires can be delivered in person or over the phone. Computers can be used to record the answers and help improve data collection and data quality. Self-administered questionnaires can be on paper, in e-mail, or on Web-based forms. The different methods of collecting data have different strengths and weaknesses.

Three main criteria are used to select a method for administering a questionnaire; the first is cost consideration. Interviewer-administered questionnaires are expensive yet likely to yield higher response rates and more accurate data. The second criterion is the complexity of the questionnaire. For data on the life course, such as that involving complex employment or marital histories, interviewer-administered instruments tend to be more successful because respondents are guided through questions in a systematic way. The third criterion for selecting a data-collection method is the sensitivity of the topic matter. Respondents are often more at ease when allowed to answers questions about sensitive topics such as drug and alcohol use, sexual history, or illegal activity without the intervention of an interviewer (Groves et al., 2004).

In all stages of the survey process, error is introduced, which affects both the quality of the data and the statistical inference for which it is used. Much of survey design and administration are focused on reducing error in all aspects of data collection. Three types of error, in particular, affect most inference and analysis of survey data. *Sampling error* is the error introduced into inference by collecting data on only a subset of the population of interest. The smaller the subset of the population drawn, the larger the sampling error. The importance of sampling error is that it diminishes the precision with which conclusions from survey data can be drawn. In studies of the prevalence of particular characteristics, diseases, or opinions, the concern is how precise the estimates of these characteristics are; thus, the size of the underlying sample is highly relevant. *Nonresponse error* arises when the chosen respondents do not return a survey or ignore repeated attempts to be interviewed. Nonresponse error is critically important when those who do not respond to the survey request are different than those who do. For instance, a survey of mothers of young children about attitudes toward the transition to motherhood that yields a much higher response rate among women who stay at home with their first child might well give a biased understanding of the feelings of new mothers because of the preponderance of women who are home in the sample (Groves, 2006). *Measurement error* is another important source of error in survey data. This type of error arises when the questions asked do not capture the concept of interest.

STUDYING ADULTHOOD THROUGH DIFFERENT FORMS OF SURVEY DESIGN

Surveys are often specifically designed to address the issues associated with adult life transitions. Two survey designs, in particular, are often used to understand how individuals move through the life course. *Cross-sectional surveys* are designed to take a "snapshot" of a large group of individuals in a single time period. To understand different life stages, individuals from different age groups at the time of the survey are used to represent those life stages. For instance, to understand how marital quality changes with age, responses in a cross-sectional survey from people of different ages are used to represent how feelings about marriage change with aging. *Repeated cross-sectional surveys*, in which different individuals are asked the same questions in more than one time period, allow expanding the understanding of life transitions by introducing the effect of historical period. In the above example, perhaps the same marital quality questions were asked in 1985 and 2005; then the way aging effects marital quality in the two time periods could be compared to see if changes in social norms influence how marriage quality varies with age. The difficulty with using either cross-sectional or repeated cross-sectional data to understand adult transitions is clear. Individuals in different age groups with very different life experiences are used to represent the biography of a typical person. Cross-sectional data confuses the process of individual aging with the experience of a cohort in history.

Another method of collecting data to understand the life course of adults is a longitudinal (panel) study. In this case, respondents are interviewed more than once. In some of the large longitudinal studies conducted by the U.S. government, respondents have been followed for more than 30 years. The ability to follow individuals through the life course has greatly enhanced the understanding of adulthood. However, the methodological difficulties of longitudinal data collection do cause some inferential problems for life course analysis. Differential panel attrition—that is, the loss of people who cannot be found after one or more panels—can bias inference because individuals who stay in a survey tend to be different from the ones who leave. Studying marriage with longitudinal data, for instance, is made difficult because those who divorce are much less likely to be found in the next wave of data collection. Those persons who remain are then less likely to represent the original population. Nevertheless, longitudinal data provide important insights into the dense processes of employment, marriage, and family formation in the adult life course (Singleton & Straits, 2005).

BIBLIOGRAPHY

Groves, R. M. (2006). Nonresponse rates and nonresponse bias in household surveys [Special issue]. *Public Opinion Quarterly*, *70*(5), 646–675.

Groves, R. M., Floyd, J., Fowler, M. P., Jr., Couper, J. M., Lepkowski, E. S., & Tourangeau, R. (2004). *Survey methodology*. Hoboken, NJ: Wiley.

Singleton, R. A., Jr., & Straits, B. C. (2005). Elements of research design. In R. A. Singleton & B. C. Straits (Eds.), *Approaches to social research* (4th ed.). New York: Oxford University Press.

Felicia B. LeClere

II. AMERICANS' CHANGING LIVES (ACL)

The Americans' Changing Lives (ACL) study has been an important source of data for understanding the structural and psychosocial context of life course processes. This four-wave panel survey of a nationally representative sample of U.S. adults was conducted under the direction of sociologist James S. House at the University of Michigan and was funded by the National Institute on Aging. Beginning in 1986, face-to-face interviews were conducted with 3,617 men and women between the ages of 24 and 96. Blacks, adults ages 60 and older, and married women whose husband was over age 64 were oversampled. Follow-up interviews were conducted in 1989 ($n = 2,867$), 1994 ($n = 2,562$), and 2001, 2002, or 2003 ($n = 1,787$).

Among the broad range of topics addressed, several are particularly relevant to life-course development and change. These include mental and physical health (self-assessed health, mortality, health behavior, health-care utilization, depressive symptoms), social relationships (quantity and quality), and stress exposure. Also included are sociodemographic characteristics such as household composition, marital status, sex, race/ethnicity, employment, income, and religious practices.

The ACL data have made substantial contributions to the literature on social processes and health over the life course. An influential body of work by House and colleagues uses the ACL to examine the age patterning of socioeconomic disparities in health (House et al, 1990; House, Lantz, & Herd, 2005; House et al, 1994; Lantz, House, Mero, & Williams, 2005; Robert & Li, 2001). The data have also been used to identify life-course variation in a range of outcomes, including depressive symptoms, personal control, volunteering and other productive activities, and the nature and quality of marriage and other personal relationships.

BIBLIOGRAPHY

House, J. S., Kessler, R. C., Herzog, A. R., Mero, R. P., Kinney, A. M., & Breslow, M. J. (1990). Age, socioeconomic status, and health. *Milbank Quarterly, 68*(3), 383–411.

House, J. S., Lantz, P. M., & Herd, P. (2005). Continuity and change in the social stratification of aging and health over the life course: Evidence from a nationally representative longitudinal study from 1986 to 2001–2002 (Americans' Changing Lives Study). *Journals of Gerontology, Series B: Psychological Sciences and Social Sciences, 60B,* 15–26.

House, J. S., Lepkowski, J. M., Kinney, A. M., Mero, R. P., Kessler, R. C., & Herzog, A. R. (1994). The social stratification of aging and health. *Journal of Health and Social Behavior, 35*(3), 213–234.

Lantz, P. M., House, J. S., Mero, R. P., & Williams, D. R. (2005). Stress, life events, and socioeconomic disparities in health: Results from the Americans' Changing Lives study. *Journal of Health and Social Behavior, 46*(3), 274–288.

Robert, S. A., & Li, L. W. (2001). Age variation in the relationship between community socioeconomic status and adult health. *Research on Aging, 23*(2), 233–258.

Kristi Williams

III. CURRENT POPULATION STUDY (CPS)

The Current Population Survey (CPS) is a nationally representative study of households in the United States that has been conducted monthly since 1940. In addition to providing the government's official statistics on unemployment, the survey examines many key features of the life course, including schooling, marriage, fertility, and civic involvement. As a long-standing panel study, the CPS is particularly useful for describing time and cohort trends.

The CPS has a panel structure with an embedded longitudinal component. Each month, a new panel of 60,000 households is selected and surveyed for two periods of 4 months each with an 8-month interval between surveys (U.S. Census Bureau, 2006). The survey is most commonly used for time-series analysis of monthly panels across years, but individual-level longitudinal analysis can also be conducted by matching respondents across months.

Basic questions about household structure and employment are asked of all members of the household over the age of 15 years. In certain months, supplemental data are collected on such wide-ranging topics as fertility, voting, and tobacco use. The most used supplement is the Annual Social and Economic Supplement on employment, income, and health insurance conducted in March.

Many key demographic shifts have been documented and explained using CPS data, including increased returns to schooling and wage inequality (e.g., Juhn, Murphy, & Pierce, 1993), female labor force participation and the gender gap in wages (e.g., O'Neill & Polachek, 1993), and the growth of single parenthood (e.g., Eggebeen & Lichter, 1991). Other studies have used the CPS to identify the determinants of adolescent smoking (e.g., Farkas, Distefan, Choi, Gilpin, & Pierce, 1999), children's health insurance coverage (e.g., Dubay & Kenney, 1996), and preschool enrollment (e.g., Bainbridge, Meyers, Tanaka, & Waldfogel, 2005).

The Census Bureau provides CPS data and extraction software at no cost (http://www.census.gov/cps/). Unicon Research Corporation sells *CPS Utilities,* a version of the data formatted for time-series analysis (http://www.unicon.com).

BIBLIOGRAPHY

Bainbridge, J., Meyers, M. K., Tanaka, S., & Waldfogel, J. (2005). Who gets an early education? Family income and the enrollment of three- to five-year-olds from 1968 to 2000. *Social Science Quarterly, 86,* 724–745.

Eggebeen, D. J., & Lichter, D. T. (1991). Race, family-structure, and changing poverty among American children. *American Sociological Review, 56,* 801–817.

Dubay, L. C., & Kenney, G. M. (1996). The effects of Medicaid expansions on insurance coverage of children. *Future of Children, 6,* 152–161.

Farkas, A. J., Distefan, J. M., Choi, W. S., Gilpin, E. A., & Pierce, J. P. (1999). Does parental smoking cessation discourage adolescent smoking? *Preventive Medicine, 28,* 213–218.

Juhn, C., Murphy, K. M., & Pierce, B. (1993). Wage inequality and the rise in returns to skill. *Journal of Political Economy, 101,* 410–442.

O'Neill, J., & Polachek, S. (1993). Why the gender gap in wages narrowed in the 1980s. *Journal of Labor Economics, 11,* 205–228.

U.S. Census Bureau. (2006). *Current population survey design and methodology.* (Technical Paper 66). Washington, DC: Author.

Heather D. Hill

IV: GENERAL SOCIAL SURVEY (GSS)

The National Data Program for the Social Sciences (NDPSS) has been conducted since 1972 by the National Opinion Research Center (NORC)/University of Chicago, with the support of the National Science Foundation. Its two main goals are to conduct basic scientific research on the structure and development of American society and to distribute up-to-date, important, high-quality data to social scientists, students, policy makers, and others.

These goals are carried out by a data-collection program that monitors societal change within the United States using the General Social Survey and compares the United States with other nations as part of the International Social Survey Programme. The NDPSS is directed by James A. Davis (NORC/University of Chicago), Tom W. Smith (NORC/University of Chicago), and Peter V. Marsden (Harvard University).

Data on societal change in the United States is collected as part of the General Social Survey (GSS). The GSS has been conducted 26 times from 1972 to 2006. It is the only full-probability, personal-interview survey designed to monitor changes in both social characteristics and attitudes in the United States. More than one thousand trends have been tracked since 1972. Age groups can be compared across time; changes within birth cohorts across the life cycle can be analyzed. Among the many topics covered are civil liberties, crime and violence, intergroup tolerance, morality, national spending priorities, psychological well-being, social mobility, and stress and traumatic events.

Cross-national data are collected as part of the International Social Survey Programme (ISSP). ISSP was established in 1984 by NORC and other social science institutes in the United States, Australia, Great Britain, and what was then West Germany. The ISSP collaboration has grown to include 43 nations. ISSP is the largest program of cross-national research in the social sciences. More information on ISSP is available at its Web site.

The GSS has carried out an extensive range of methodological research designed both to advance survey methods in general and to ensure that the GSS data are of the highest possible quality. More than 110 papers have been published in the GSS Methodological Report series. GSS data and documentation are available at the GSS Web site.

BIBLIOGRAPHY

General Social Survey (GSS). Retrieved April 8, 2008, from http://www.gss.norc.org

International Social Survey Programme (ISSP). Retrieved April 8, 2008, from http://www.issp.org

Tom W. Smith

V. LONGITUDINAL STUDY OF GENERATIONS (LSOG)

The Longitudinal Study of Generations (LSOG) provides life course scholars the unique opportunity to explore intergenerational relationships as experienced by four distinctive cohorts of men and women. The LSOG began in 1971 as a cross-sectional study of 358 three-generation families, comprising more than 2,000 individuals in southern California. This initial sample was obtained through a multistage stratified sample of grandfathers enrolled in a large, southern California health maintenance organization (HMO), as well as the men's descendants. Each three-generation family included grandfathers (then in their 60s), their middle-aged children (then in their early 40s), and their young adult children (then ages 16 to 26). These three generations are referred to by the study investigators as G1, G2, and G3, respectively. Spouses of family members in each generation also were surveyed. The study was unique at the time of its inception, because respondents were linked to each other on the basis of their shared family membership, and thus data analysts could examine parent-child, grandparent-grandchild, sibling, and spousal relationships. As a result, the LSOG's measures are considered the gold standard for studying family solidarity and intergenerational relationships.

Since 1985, interviews have been conducted at 3-year intervals with persons from G1, G2, and G3. In 1991, a fourth generation (G4) of Generation X young adults (i.e., those born between 1960 and 1979) was added to the study and followed up on at 3-year intervals. An extensive collection of LSOG materials is available at the University of Southern California Web site or at the Inter-university Consortium for Political and Social Research (ICPSR) at the University of Michigan Web site.

BIBLIOGRAPHY

Bengtson, V.L., Biblarz, T.J., & Roberts, R.E.L. (2002). *How Families Still Matter: A Longitudinal Study of Youth in Two Generations*. Cambridge, UK: Cambridge University Press.

ICPSR: Inter-University Consortium for Political and Social Research. Retrieved July 15, 2008, from http://www.icpsr.umich.edu

Longitudinal Studies of Generations: Home. Retrieved July 15, 2008, from http://www.usc.edu/dept/gero/research/4gen/index.htm

Merril Silverstein

VI. MIDLIFE IN THE UNITED STATES (MIDUS)

In 1995–1996, the MacArthur Midlife Research Network carried out a national survey of more than 7,000 non-institutionalized Americans in the contiguous United States, aged between 25 to 74 years old, called the National Survey of Midlife Development in the United States (MIDUS). The purpose of the study was to investigate the role of behavioral, psychological, and social factors in understanding age-related differences in physical and mental health. The study was innovative for its broad scientific scope, its diverse samples (which included twins and the siblings of main sample respondents), and its creative use of in-depth assessments in key areas (e.g., daily stress, cognitive functioning).

With support from the National Institute on Aging, a longitudinal follow-up of the original MIDUS samples: core sample ($N = 3,487$), metropolitan over-samples ($N = 757$), twins ($N = 998$ pairs), and siblings ($N = 950$), MIDUS 2 was conducted between 2004 and 2006. The foci and content of the MIDUS and its affiliated studies are shaped by the guiding hypothesis that behavioral and psychosocial factors are consequential for physical and mental health. MIDUS 2 respondents were aged between 35 and 86 years old. Data collection largely repeated baseline assessments (e.g., phone interview, extensive self-administered questionnaire), with additional questions in selected areas (e.g., cognitive functioning, optimism and coping, stressful life events, caregiving).

To enhance the diversity of the MIDUS 2 sample, an additional African-American sample ($N = 592$) was recruited from Milwaukee, Wisconsin. Participants completed a personal interview and a self-administered questionnaire that paralleled the MIDUS 1 and 2 content. In an effort to capture those people who might have been missed in earlier waves of the study, MIDUS 2 also administered a modified form of the mail questionnaire, using the telephone, to respondents who did not complete a self-administered questionnaire. Overall, complete data were collected from nearly 5,900 people in the follow-up. To date, more than 200 studies based on the MIDUS data have been published in medical, psychological, sociological, gerontological, and epidemiological scholarly journals. See Brim, Ryff, and Singer (2004) for an overview of the study. An extensive and growing collection of MIDUS materials is available at the Inter-university Consortium for Political and Social Research at the University of Michigan (www.icpsr.umich.edu).

BIBLIOGRAPHY

Brim, O. G., Ryff, C. D., & Kessler, R. C. (2004). The Midus National Survey: An Overview. In O. G. Brim, C. D. Ryff, & R. C. Kessler (Eds.), *How healthy are we?: A national study of well-being at midlife* (pp.1–36). Chicago: University Of Chicago Press.

Inter-University Consortium for Political and Social Research. Retrieved April 7, 2008, from http://www.icpsr.umich.edu

Midlife in the United States: A national study of well-being and aging. Retrieved April 7, 2008, from http://www.midus.wisc.edu

Barry T. Radler

VII. NATIONAL LONGITUDINAL SURVEYS (NLS) OF MATURE MEN AND WOMEN

The National Longitudinal Surveys (NLS) of Older Men and Mature Women represent two cohorts of the larger NLS project: a group of longitudinal studies sponsored by the U.S. Bureau of Labor Statistics.

Interviews of 5,020 American men ages 45 to 59 began in 1966, with data collection focused on work experiences, retirement planning, health conditions, insurance coverage, and leisure-time activities. Interviews with the men continued at regular intervals until 1981. A follow-up interview took place in 1990 with information collected from the men or their widows. The 1990 data include information of cause of death collected from vital records. During the regular 1966–1981 data collection period, a cohort of younger men (ages 14 to 24) was interviewed as well.

Interviews started in 1967 for the NLS mature women, a group of 5,083 American women ages 30 to 44. Much of the information gathered over the years included issues for women reentering the labor market at middle age after child rearing, along with retirement decisions and health issues. Extensive information about pension plans also was gathered, including characteristics of each pension provider and each plan. The mature women were interviewed a total of 20 times; data collection ended in 2003. During roughly the same period a group of younger women (ages 14 to 24 in 1968) also was interviewed. Many of the individuals in that group were the daughters of the mature women, and a series of questions about intergenerational transfers was asked of both groups so that for a subsample the NLS has reports about such transfers that were provided by both the mothers and their daughters.

Data collection continued for two younger mixed-gender NLS groups: one initiated in 1979 (known as the NLSY79) and one begun in 1997 (known as the NLSY97). In addition, age-eligible children of the female respondents in the NLSY79 group have been interviewed since 1986. The NLS database containing data from all cohorts can be accessed free of charge at the web site of the U.S. Bureau of Labor, Bureau of Labor Statistics. The *NLS Annotated Bibliography*, a comprehensive record of research based on NLS-related data, also is available online from the Bureau of Labor Statistics.

BIBLIOGRAPHY

Hayward, M. D., & Gorman, B. K. (2004). Long arm of childhood: The influence of early life social conditions on men's mortality. *Demography. 41*(1), 87–108.

Light, A. L, & McGarry, K. (2004). Why parents play favorites: Explanations for unequal bequests. *American Economic Review. 94*(5), 1669–1682.

Long, J. S., & Pavalko, E. K. (2004). Life course of activity limitations: Exploring indicators of functional limitations over time. *Journal of Aging and Health. 16*(4), 490−517.

Steckel, R. H., & Jayanthi, K. (2006). Wealth mobility of men and women during the 1960s and 1970s. *Review of Income and Wealth. 52*(2), 189−212.

Teachman, J. D., & Tedrow, L. M. (2004). Wages, earnings, and occupationsl status: Did World War II veterans receive a premium? *Social Science Research. 33*(4), 581−605.

Zagorsky, J. L. (2003). Husbands' and wives' view of the family finances. *The Journal of Socio-Economics. 32*(2), 127−146.

Randall J. Olsen
Kathryn Dawson Moneysmith

VIII. PANEL STUDY OF INCOME DYNAMICS (PSID)

The Panel Study of Income Dynamics (PSID) is a longitudinal study of a representative sample of U.S. individuals and the families in which they reside. The PSID emphasizes the dynamic aspects of family economics, demography, and health. Data have been collected since 1968 and continues to be collected as of 2008, making the PSID the longest running panel on family and individual dynamics. It has consistently achieved response rates of 95 to 98%, and as of 2005, 8,041 families were currently participating in the survey. Over the years the PSID has collected information on nearly 70,000 individuals spanning as much as four decades of their lives.

Through multiple waves collected over long time periods, these data are the only data ever collected on life course and multigenerational health, well-being, and economic conditions in a long-term panel representative of the full U.S. population. The PSID has collected data on employment, income, housing, food expenditures, transfer income, and marital and fertility behavior annually between 1968 and 1997, and biennially between 1999 and 2005. Additionally the PSID collects data on health status, health behaviors, health care utilization, health insurance, and philanthropy. Beginning in 1985 comprehensive retrospective fertility and marriage histories of individuals in the households have been assembled.

The PSID sample, originating in 1968, consists of two independent samples of the U.S. population: a cross-sectional national sample and a national sample of low-income families. The Survey Research Center (SRC) at the University of Michigan drew the cross-sectional sample, which was an equal probability sample of households from the 48 contiguous states designated to yield about 3,000 completed interviews. The second sample came from the Survey of Economic Opportunity (SEO) conducted by the Bureau of the Census for the Office of Economic Opportunity. In the mid-1960s the PSID selected about 2,000 low-income families with heads under the age of 60 from SEO respondents. The PSID core sample combines the SRC and SEO samples.

From 1968 to 1997 the PSID interviewed individuals from families in the core sample every year, whether or not they were living in the same dwelling or with the same people. Adults have been followed as they have grown older, and children have been interviewed as they advance through childhood and into adulthood, forming families of their own. In 1997 the PSID changed from every-year interviewing to every-other-year interviewing. Moreover, a sample of 441 immigrant families was added to enhance the representativeness of the sample.

In 1997 and again in 2002, the PSID supplemented its main data collection with information on PSID parents and their children in order to study the dynamic process of early life experiences. The supplement, called the Child Development Supplement (CDS), included a broad array of development measures such as (a) age graded assessments of cognitive, behavioral, and health status of children obtained from the caregivers and the child; (b) a comprehensive accounting of parental, or caregiver, time inputs to children as well as other aspects of the ways in which children and adolescents spend their time; (c) teacher-reported time use in elementary school; and (d) other-than-time use measures of additional resources such as the learning environment in the home, teacher reports of school resources, and decennial-census-based measurement of neighborhood resources. In 1997 CDS-I collected data on 3,563 children aged 0 to 12 in 2,394 families. Five years later, CDS-II reinterviewed 2,021 of the CDS-I families, providing data on 2,907 CDS children and youth.

Since its inception, more than 2,000 journal articles, books, book chapters, and dissertations have been based on the PSID, and in 2008 a paper is published in a peer-reviewed outlet roughly every 4 days. The study was named one of the National Science Foundation's (NSF) *nifty fifty*, which refers to the most notable NSF-funded inventions and discoveries in NSF history between the years 1950 and 2000.

It is difficult to briefly summarize the scientific impact of the PSID. Areas of significant contribution include intergenerational transmission of economic status, children's time use, the dynamics of poverty and economic status, resource sharing among extended family members, the interconnection between well-being and marriage and fertility, and neighborhood effects on individual social and economic outcomes.

BIBLIOGRAPHY

Altonji, J. G., Hayashi, F., & Kotlikoff, L. (1992). Is the extended family altruistically linked? Direct tests using micro data. *The American Economic Review, 82*(5), 1177–1198.

Brooks-Gunn, J., et al. (1993). Do neighborhoods influence child and adolescent development? *American Journal of Sociology, 99*(2), 353–395.

Gottschalk, P., & Moffitt, R. (1994). The growth of earnings instability in the U.S. labor market. *Brookings Papers on Economic Activity, 2*, 217–272.

Hofferth, S. L., & Sandberg, J. F. (2001). How American children spend their time. *Journal of Marriage and the Family, 63*(2), 295–308.

McLanahan, S., & Sandefur, G. (1994). *Growing up with a single parent: What hurts, what helps.* Cambridge, MA: Harvard University Press.

Panel Study of Income Dynamics. Retrieved June 18, 2008, from http://psidonline.org

Solon, G. (1992). Intergenerational income mobility in the United States. *The American Economic Review, 82*(3), 393–408.

Robert F. Schoeni

IX. U.S. (DECENNIAL) CENSUS

Every 10 years since 1790, the Census of the United States has tried to count everyone in the country and note several of his or her characteristics. The enumeration is done by contacting someone in every household—by mail since 1960, in person previously—and asking respondents to describe themselves and also the people living with them. Characteristics of the population accumulated in this way are selected to be most widely useful in the society. They include questions such as age, sex, relationship in family, and marital status; questions about education and work; and questions about race, ethnicity, and geographic origin of the person and his or her ancestors. Some questions appear only in some decades as policy interests wax and wane. Some of the questions are asked only in a sample of these households, often 15 or 20%, so the samples are quite large. Although not perfect, census data have an extremely high response rate by survey standards. More is known about the magnitude and pattern of errors in the Census than in any other social science data set.

Census data are especially useful for describing the social and demographic context, often as part of a research presentation, as the introduction to a paper, or to describe a problem generally. They are useful as a benchmark against which to check the representativeness of data collected from another source, for example an independent and more detailed sample survey. Because data for everyone in the households are collected, census data can yield a lot of information about the living arrangements and the family context of the population. Because of the large sampling fraction and very detailed geographic coding, the Census can provide information about relatively small geographic areas—down to city blocks for some characteristics. The large sampling fractions also mean that the Census is particularly good for obtaining data about numerically small subgroups of people living in the United States. Census data can be used to investigate historical trends over a longer time span than any other kind of data.

Census data are unlikely to provide the researcher with exactly the variable needed to test a detailed hypothesis. Inventive scholars, however, have managed to investigate a remarkable number of issues using data from the Census. For example, a good deal of what is known about ethnicity in the United States is derived from census questions on the immigration status of people and their parents. In the early days of the cohabitation trend, census data on persons of the opposite sex sharing living quarters gave an early indication of the prevalence and trend of this cultural change.

The age variable in census data, however, can present difficulties. For many older people, age is reported by someone else in the household, and that person may not answer accurately. In some decades the Census Bureau has chosen to top-code age (that is, classify the oldest persons into an aggregated subgroup, such as "85 or older") because of concerns about its reliability at the oldest ages.

One can access census data in many ways, from generating a statistic interactively on the Census website to acquiring sample data from many decades to use in a detailed statistical analysis. The official website (http://www.census.gov) provides access to many pages that provide considerable detail on specific topics.

The Public Use Sample Files are samples of census households designed to preserve the confidentiality of the respondents. The result is usually a 1% sample of the total population. The Public Use Sample Files can be acquired in original census form from the Inter-University Consortium for Political and Social Research (http://www.icpsr.umich.edu). Historic census data and data reflecting questions matched across decades (useful for trend analyses) can be obtained from http://www.ipums.org.

BIBLIOGRAPHY

Anderson, M. J., (Ed.). (2000). *Encyclopedia of the U.S. census.* Washington, DC: CQ Press.

Lavin, M. R. (1996). *Understanding the census: A guide for marketers, planners, grant writers, and other data users.* Kenmore, NY: Oryx Press.

National Research Council. (2004). Panel to review the 2000 Census. In C. F. Citro, D. L. Cork, & J. L. Norwood (Eds.),

The 2000 Census: Counting under adversity. Washington, DC: National Academies Press.

Hal Winsborough

DATING AND ROMANTIC RELATIONSHIPS, ADULTHOOD

Broadly defined, dating refers to social activities between individuals romantically interested in each other. However, there is wide variation among scholars and in popular culture as to what dating entails. Finding a long-term partner, entertainment, and increasing social status are among the many reasons that adults give for dating and engaging in romantic relationships. It is not surprising, then, that dating has many outcomes; it can be a satisfying endeavor, increasing the quality of life for individuals, or it can lead to violent or coercive interactions. Although dating may seem trivial or unimportant, the scientific study of dating attitudes and behaviors is vital to promote healthy relationships and prevent or intervene in harmful ones.

HISTORICAL CONTEXT

In the United States, modern dating did not emerge until the 1950s and 1960s. Before then, couples engaged in courtship practices. Courting was a public activity exclusively focused on finding a marriage partner. Although arranged marriages per se were not standard practice, familial input into courtship limited young people's partner choices. In the 19th century it was customary for parents (especially a woman's parents) to give their consent before their children began courting.

Because of heavy parental involvement and the public nature of courting, couples would attend social events in the community, where family members could monitor the young people's activities. Should a more serious interest develop, young men could "call on" young women in their homes, but only if a woman or her mother issued an invitation. Thus, women and their families controlled and initiated courtship situations.

Perhaps in reaction to the rigid rules of courting, later in the 19th century, couples themselves began to have more control over their correspondence and social activities. Enjoyment, rather than marriage, became a central motivation for romantic relationships. Peers, instead of parents, defined conventions concerning these relationships; couples had more freedom and privacy.

Control and initiative in the romantic relationship also changed. Rather than waiting for an invitation to call, men asked women out socially, and planned and paid for activities. Women served as the gatekeepers to affection and sexual activity; however, without parental monitoring, barriers to sexual behaviors were weaker.

Several cultural transformations in the early 20th century shaped modern dating patterns. Affluence and mass consumption turned attention from working to consuming (Whyte, 1992). Increasing numbers of telephones in homes allowed people to formulate plans, connect, and have private conversations more easily. The advent of the automobile gave people the means to leave home and seek recreational activities, as well as providing a private space for romantic and sexual activities.

By the 1920s and 1930s, going out romantically more closely resembled modern dating. Going on dates was no longer directly tied to marriage; rather, there were several steps in between to denote levels of commitment, such as going steady (i.e., dating exclusively), receiving a high school ring or pin, and becoming engaged. Individuals dated for a variety of reasons; enjoyment and romance was a main motivation, but people also dated to gain experience, to experiment, and to enhance their social status.

DATING SCRIPTS IN THE LATE 20TH AND EARLY 21ST CENTURIES

Late in the 20th century, scholars began to theorize about the behaviors and meanings in romantic relationships. Within a society, people develop cognitive schemas, or mental representations, of various scenarios. In the 1980s and 1990s researchers began to study *dating scripts*, defined as the expected behaviors and events for a typical date (Alksnis, Desmarais, & Wood, 1996). Dating scripts are shaped through peer and parental interactions, media outlets, and popular culture. Although individuals have varied dating experiences, people have surprisingly similar ideas of what dating should encompass.

People in the early 21st century are more likely to report egalitarian values than in the past, with a balance of power between members of a couple, but research suggests that women and men have distinct dating scripts that mirror traditional gender roles. One way researchers measure dating scripts is by asking people about hypothetical first dates. Christine Alksnis, Serge Desmarais, and Eileen Wood (1996) asked a primarily White sample of college students to report events that occurred on good, bad, and typical dates. Overall, males and females agreed about what makes a good or a typical first date; however, some gender differences existed regarding appropriate sexual behavior. These findings suggest that gendered dating scripts are particularly salient for sexual events; men may have a greater expectation of sexual activity, whereas women may deter those behaviors.

Other researchers have found support for expectations in which men are the initiators of dating activities, and women are responsible for the emotional aspects of the date (Bartoli & Clark, 2006). These scripts also exist within homosexual dating couples. In response to hypothetical and actual dating scenarios, gay men, like heterosexual men, tended to emphasize sexual aspects of dating and taking initiative for sexual behaviors and date activities. Like heterosexual women, lesbian women tended to focus more on the emotional aspects of the dating experience, such as evaluating feelings about the date. Whereas dating behaviors and partner selection may look different for heterosexual and homosexual dating couples, dating scripts appear similar within gender regardless of sexual orientation.

DATING SCRIPTS FOR DIFFERENT CULTURAL GROUPS

Great variability exists within different cultural and ethnic minority groups regarding attitudes about dating. However, some scholars theorize that there is conflict between dominant culture (White) dating scripts and minority cultural values. Some research has suggested that Latino Americans and Asian Americans adhere more closely to traditional gendered dating scripts (Anderson & Johnson, 2003), compared to Whites. Among African-American dating couples, there is evidence of both traditional gender roles, such as women seeking successful male partners, and more egalitarian relationships, in which women may be the successful partner, for example (Ganong, Coleman, Thompson, & Goodwin-Watkins, 1996). However, the African-American community faces unique dating challenges. High rates of incarceration and mortality for Black men limit the number of potential dating partners available for Black women. Additionally, Black women are more likely to attain a college education and achieve economic success than Black men (Kurdek, 2008). Because of this discrepancy, some Black women may find it difficult to find a compatible partner within the African-American community. Increasingly, both men and women may choose to date interracially (Wilson, McIntosh, & Insana, 2007).

THEORETICAL APPROACHES TO DATING RELATIONSHIPS

Equity Theory and Investment Models Equity theory is one lens through which dating outcomes can be viewed. This approach focuses on the balance between relationship contributions and outcomes, in addition to an individual's characteristics. Relationships in which both individuals experience equal benefits and rewards, such as trust, intimacy, and companionship, have the highest relationship quality and satisfaction (Hatfield et al., 1979). Individuals who contribute more than their partner and receive fewer rewards are likely to experience the most relationship dissatisfaction. People who receive more benefits than they should, based on their contributions, are not as dissatisfied as their partners, but they are not as happy as couples with equal contributions. In general, individuals in unequal relationships report that their relationships are less satisfying, less stable, and individuals are less committed (Sprecher, 2001).

Investment models illuminate the power dynamic in relationships. Power and control in a relationship are determined by the individuals' comparative reliance on each other. Author Willard Waller (1938) first explained "the principle of least interest," in which the person who is the least invested in the relationship will have the most power or control. The more invested person, in trying to maintain the relationship, will concede to their partner's demands. Investment by either partner may be affected by a number of factors. The level to which individuals find their partner rewarding and attractive is primary, as well as the assessment of alternative partners. Individual characteristics, such as physical attractiveness, intelligence, personality, wealth, or popularity, can affect both one's desirability and investment, and thus the power dynamics of a relationship.

Biosocial Models Biosocial perspectives, which draw from many disciplines, including evolutionary psychology, biology, and anthropology, help to explain the motivations underlying dating behavior. Evidence suggests that biological mechanisms may facilitate relationship continuation; levels of testosterone, estrogen, dopamine, nonrepinephrine, serotonin, oxytocin, and vasopressin have been linked to various relationship stages (Bancroft, 2005). For example, in the beginning stages of a relationship, both men and women experience higher levels of oxytocin, known as the *love hormone*, because it produces euphoric effects (Buss, 2004).

Attachment Models Attachment theory has evolved out of John Bowlby's (1982) idea of an attachment system, where attachment to another person, an attachment figure, provides one with a sense of physical closeness and comfort, a safe place or safe haven when one is upset, a secure base from which to draw strength and security, and feelings of sadness, loneliness, and longing when the attachment figure is not present. Bowlby theorized that this system is necessary for survival in infancy, but it also appears to be necessary during adulthood; and, most often, attachment bonds between adults take the form of romantic relationships. Attachment bonds do not form instantaneously, however. They take time. Dating provides the time and interpersonal experience to form attachment bonds. Across age cohorts (from ages 18 to 82), Cindy Hazan and Debra Zeifman (1999) found that it took an average of 2 years for romantic relationships to become bonded, or attachment, relationships.

Ecological Models The nature of dating and relationships is shaped by its context. Societal norms, cultural values, political and historical contexts, technology, and media are only a few of the overarching frameworks that impact the way in which individuals date, as well as the meaning and expectations of the relationship (Bronfenbrenner, 1979). For example, increased casual sex portrayal in popular television shows and movies coincides with the acceptance and higher levels of casual sex among generations X and Y.

FUTURE DIRECTIONS

Advances in modern technology have created new opportunities and challenges for dating. Increasingly, young and older adults alike are using the Internet as a way to meet people, as evidenced by the popularity of social networking sites and online dating services. Researchers have started investigating online relationships (sometimes referred to as computer mediated relationships). Some have argued that online relationships are problematic because interpersonal connection is lost, whereas others suggest that the Internet may be helpful to shy or anxious people that find it hard to meet potential partners. Erich Merkle and Rhonda Richardson (2000) synthesized studies of computer mediated relationships and found that compared to traditional dating relationships, people disclosed and came to know their partner intimately more quickly over the Internet. They also suggested that it may be harder to be committed to an online dating partner or maintain a relationship without face-to-face interaction. How the Internet is used in face-to-face relationships has yet to be examined. Additionally, future research should examine how online communication shapes notions of intimacy, commitment, and fidelity.

Globalization is another force changing dating. In a globalized community, the behaviors, meanings, and scripts associated with dating are likely to be transformed. Cell phones and the Internet allow individuals to connect to virtually anyone at anytime, and advances in transportation give people the opportunity to travel great distances with comparative ease. Long-distance dating is becoming more common, particularly for dual professional couples. However, researchers have yet to examine this trend.

The aging of the U.S. population also means that dating may be transformed in future years. The dating needs of older adults are different from those of younger or middle-aged adults. Kris Bulcroft and Margaret O'Connor (1986) interviewed a group of adults aged 60 or older for their study. Older adults' narratives highlighted companionship aspects of dating; loneliness was a common concern. Additionally, older men accentuate their need to have a confidante. Interestingly, older women associated prestige with dating. This may be due to the unequal male to female ratio among older adults, as women tend to live longer than men. Older adults, compared to their younger cohorts, face obstacles such as diminished social support and more health difficulties. Because of such obstacles, companionship can be that much more vital to an older person's quality of life. Future research could and should give more attention to the impact of elderly dating relationships.

The changing cultural landscape has an influence on dating relationships. Future researchers investigating these trends may also develop innovative methodology, especially with the constant technological advances being made. As children grow up with modern technology in a globalized community, the behaviors, meanings, and scripts associated with dating are likely to be transformed.

SEE ALSO Volume 2: *Marriage; Mate Selection*

BIBLIOGRAPHY

Alksnis, C., Desmarais, S., & Wood, E. (1996). Gender differences in scripts for different types of dates. *Sex Roles*, *34*(5-6), 321–336.

Anderson, S. J., & Johnson, J. T. (2003). The who and when of "gender-blind" attitudes: Predictors of gender-role egalitarianism in two different domains. *Sex Roles*, *49*(9–10), 527–532.

Bancroft, J. (2005). The endocrinology of sexual arousal. *Journal of Endocrinology*, *186*(3), 411–427.

Bartoli, A., & Clark, M. D. (2006). The dating game: Similarities and differences in dating scripts among college students. *Sexuality & Culture*, *10*(4), 54–80.

Bowlby, J. (1982). *Attachment and loss*. New York: Basic Books.

Bronfenbrenner, U. (1979). *The ecology of human development: Experiments by nature and design*. Cambridge, MA: Harvard University Press.

Bulcroft, K., & O'Connor, M. (1986). The importance of dating relationships on quality of life for older persons. *Family Relations*, *35*(3), 397–401.

Buss, D. (2004). *Evolutionary psychology: The new science of the mind*. (2nd ed.). Boston: Pearson; Allyn and Bacon.

Ganong, L. H., Coleman, M., Thompson, A., & Goodwin-Watkins, C. (1996). African-American and European-American college students' expectations for self and for future partners. *Journal of Family Issues*, *17*(6), 758–775.

Hatfield, E., Utne, M. K., & Traupmann, J. (1979). Equity theory and intimate relationships. In R. L. Burgess & T. L. Huston (Eds.), *Social exchange in developing relationships* (pp. 99–133). New York: Academic Press.

Hazan, C., & Zeifman, D. (1999). Pair bonds as attachments: Evaluating the evidence. In J. Cassidy & P. R. Shaver (Eds.),

Handbook of attachment: Theory, research, and clinical applications. New York: Guilford Press.

Hrdy, S. B. (2000). *Mother nature: Maternal instincts and how they shape the human species.* New York: Ballantine Books.

Klinkenberg, D., & Rose, S. (1994). Dating scripts of gay men and lesbians. *Journal of Homosexuality, 26*(4), 23–35.

Kurdek, L. A. (2008). Differences between partners from black and white heterosexual dating couples in a path model of relationship commitment. *Journal of Social and Personal Relationships, 25*, 51–70.

Laner, M. R., & Ventrone, N. A. (2000). Dating scripts revised. *Journal of Family Issues, 21*(4), 488–500.

Merkle, E. R., & Richardson, R. A. (2000). Digital dating and virtual relating: Conceptualizing computer mediated romantic relationships. *Family Relations, 49*(2), 187–192.

Seal, D. W., Wagner-Raphael, L. I., & Ehrhardt, A. A. (2000). Sex, intimacy, and HIV: An ethnographic study of a Puerto Rican social group in New York City. *Journal of Psychology & Human Sexuality, 11*(4), 51–92.

Serewicz, M. C., & Gale, E. (2008). First-date scripts: Gender roles, context, and relationship. *Sex Roles, 58*(3), 149–164.

Sprecher, S. (2001). Equity and social exchange in dating couples: Associations with satisfaction, commitment, and stability. *Journal of Marriage and Family, 63*(3), 599–613.

Waller, W. (1938). *The family: A dynamic interpretation.* New York: Cordon.

Whyte, M. K. (1992). Choosing mates—The American way. *Society, 29*(3), 71–77.

Wilson, S. B., McIntosh, W. D., & Insana S. P. (2007). An examination of African-American Internet personal advertisements. *Journal of Black Studies, 37*(6), 964–982.

Rachel M. Holmes
Katherine C. Little
Deborah P. Welsh

DEBT

Debt is money owed to a lender, and *credit* is an authorization to incur debt given by a lender (the creditor) to an individual, couple, or business. The amount of a debt is a function of the original amount borrowed (the principal), the interest charged, and any fees assessed by the creditor. Creditors typically set interest rates based on their estimated likelihood of being repaid. In modern economies, credit bureaus generate scores for individuals based on their personal characteristics, including past debt history, to estimate the probability the borrower will repay a loan.

Every society experiences tension between classes of debtors and classes of creditors. Legal institutions usually reinforce creditors' rights, and debtors in many societies are cruelly treated: Slavery, prison, transportation to colonies, debt peonage, and even execution have been employed to punish debtors in different times and

BANKRUPTCY

Bankruptcy is a legal proceeding for restructuring or eliminating debt and adjudicating multiple creditors' interests. U.S. law recognizes six types of bankruptcy, identified by chapter number corresponding to the chapter in the U.S. bankruptcy code in which each type of bankruptcy is described in detail. Approximately 99% of the bankruptcies filed annually are consumer or personal bankruptcies filed either in Chapter 7 or in Chapter 13. Chapter 9 is for municipalities, Chapter 11 is for large corporations, Chapter 12 is reserved for family farmers, and Chapter 15 involves international cases.

Consumers who file Chapter 13 bankruptcy keep their assets but devote their disposable income to repay a portion of their debts over a period of not more than five years. Only about one-third of all Chapter 13 filers are able to successfully complete their repayment plan. Chapter 7, the most commonly filed, requires consumers to liquidate their nonexempt assets; proceeds are distributed to creditors. In Chapter 7 most unsecured debts, such as credit card and medical bills, are discharged; student loans, taxes, and child support must be repaid. Layoffs and unemployment, divorce, and medical problems are the most common triggers for consumer bankruptcy.

In 2005 Congress amended the Bankruptcy Code to require that debtors seeking Chapter 7 pass a means test and receive consumer credit counseling. Debtors who earn more than the median income of their state are directed to Chapter 13.

places. In the United States, historic institutions such as share-cropping and company stores used debt to limit employee turnover and to control workers. In share-cropping the landowner lent money to the workers who farmed his land. In the case of the company store, employers allowed workers to buy goods on credit, but only at stores owned by the company. In both cases, workers routinely became heavily indebted to the land and store owners and were therefore often unable to leave for other employment.

In the contemporary United States, the extension of credit is a highly profitable business and central to the economy. The marketing of many goods and services is successful because customers can finance the purchases over time. Some level of debt is widespread in all social classes, so that social class tensions are muted. Between 1989 and 2007 the revolving consumer credit outstanding among residents of the United States soared from 18.9 billion dollars to 97.2 billion dollars. Certain points in the life cycle are associated with greater consumption, such as beginning a household or having children, and for this reason debt patterns can be expected to have a relationship to the life cycle (Kish, 2006).

Credit card debt is one of the largest components of personal debt in the United States in the early 21st century (the others include home mortgages, automobile loans, and loans for purchases of major consumer durables). Credit cards are convenient because nearly every vendor accepts them and consumers can make purchases without cash in person, by phone, or online. Credit purchases constitute borrowing when the consumer *revolves* the card's balance, making a partial payment each month and incurring interest and fees. The minimum payment required each month to keep the account current is not sufficient to liquidate the debt unless continued for months. The very convenience and ubiquity of the credit card may encourage customers to charge more than they can readily repay. Because credit cards are a profitable business for financial institutions, they are aggressively marketed. Credit cards first saturated the United States, but are now marketed worldwide, with substantial penetration of the markets in Europe and Canada. In Japan, by contrast, credit cards are used much less often (Mann, 2006).

Research about debt has been difficult because the most accurate information about debt and credit scores is proprietary and so unavailable for research purposes. The federal government makes available to researchers some debt information collected through surveys such as the Survey on Consumer Finance. Bankruptcy filings are public data with detailed debt listings. Other research findings come from interviews with consumers, credit counselors, bankruptcy trustees, and attorneys. A small body of experimental evidence examines credit card use in various situations.

DEBT ACROSS THE LIFE COURSE

Although the exact method used to score credit is proprietary, age is believed to affect the score because of its association with other characteristics that are positively valued in the credit formula, such as years of schooling, employment seniority, and residential stability. In addition, a characteristic age profile of expenditures has been observed. For example, young people often borrow money for a college education or a first car. Because their credit scores may not yet be high, and borrowers with lower credit scores are typically charged higher interest rates, young people may end up paying more in credit costs than middle-aged customers (Draut, 2007).

Although the legal age of contract is 18, credit cards are marketed to younger teenagers, usually with a parent as a cosigner. Credit cards are heavily marketed to college students, and several small studies of college graduates have indicated that college graduates' credit card debt may average several thousand dollars (Manning, 2000). One incentive for targeting young people is that consumers keep their original credit card for an average of fifteen years.

Many college students take out loans to pay for their tuition and other educational expenses. Some college loans are federally subsidized to keep the interest rates modest. Unsubsidized college loans are easy to obtain because lenders believe the future earnings of college graduates will be much higher than the earnings of high school graduates.

By the time of marriage, both spouses may have substantial debts, including credit card debt, college loans, and perhaps financing for cars or furniture. Early in a marriage, couples commonly pursue joint expenditures, often for a home or consumer durables. Unless the couple has substantial savings, financing major purchases through credit is commonplace.

Middle-aged consumers typically have higher incomes and potentially have better credit scores because of their greater job seniority, but they also have substantial expenditures for their children and perhaps for their elderly parents. Middle-aged consumers are likely to pay regular monthly debt service for home mortgages and perhaps for cars and consumer durables. Some also have remaining college debts to repay and may be cosigning college loans for their own children. Some borrowing is usually considered prudent, assuming that monthly income is stable or rising. But middle-aged consumers may experience sudden drops in income through unemployment, injury, or illness, leading to missed payments, which in turn lead to increased interest rates, especially on credit cards (Sullivan, Warren, and Westbrook, 2000).

People aged 65 and older are the fastest growing segment of the population in bankruptcy, countering a stereotype that the elderly are the most reluctant to incur debt (Sullivan, Thorne, and Warren, 2001). One factor is the cost of medical and long-term care among sick people. Even with Medicare, senior citizens may face unexpected expenditures for medicine, long-term care, medical equipment, and insurance company copays. Conversely, many senior citizens own their homes without a mortgage, have adequate retirement income, and enjoy relatively low rates of interest if they do seek to borrow money.

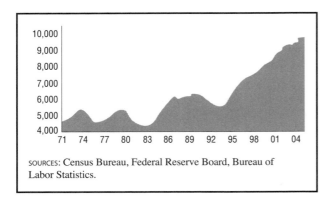

SOURCES: Census Bureau, Federal Reserve Board, Bureau of Labor Statistics.

Real Consumer Credit Growth. *Real consumer credit outstanding per American age 18 and older, 2004.* CENGAGE LEARNING, GALE.

Patterns of debt also vary by gender and by race/ethnicity. United States law provides for equal credit opportunities for women, especially married women, and for racial and ethnic minorities. In part because of their lower earnings and in part because unmarried women may have expenditures for children and other dependents, women appear to have higher debt levels relative to their earnings. Racial and ethnic minorities may also be subjected to higher interest rates because of their choice of lenders and because of practices such as redlining, a practice that charges borrowers high interest rates if they live in neighborhoods with characteristics considered to increase risk of default.

PROBLEMATIC DEBT LEVELS

Both debtors and lenders assume that the debtors' income will continue uninterrupted. This assumption is potentially problematic. Unemployment or layoffs are a factor in 60% of consumer bankruptcies. Small business owners may receive too little profit as a result of a downturn in the business cycle or industry restructuring. A divorced person may lose income, take on additional expenses (e.g., child support, alimony), or both. People who become sick or injured may be unable to work, losing their income even if their medical expenditures are insured.

Moreover, debtors' other expenditures may exceed the anticipated level. Some expenses may simply be due to money mismanagement, but expenditures can rise for reasons beyond the borrower's control, resulting in further debt. Consumers may find themselves with involuntary debts, as when they are judged at fault in an accident. People without medical insurance may find that even the most minor illness or injury leads to serious debt. Failure to pay rent, utilities, or child support results in debt that accumulates interest. Finally debt itself is

stressful and may lead to depression, marital strain, divorce, and other consequences that are in themselves costly (Sullivan, Warren, and Westbrook, 1995; Warren and Tyagi, 2004).

Debtors who are unable to repay have several options. Creditors may be willing to consider debt forbearance, such as a postponement of a payment schedule or even a reduction in the interest rate. Consumer credit counseling may be helpful in rebudgeting the debtor's income and teaching money management skills. At the extreme, the debtor may declare bankruptcy

Some debts are secured by collateral, so that failure to repay the debt results in the creditor taking ownership of the collateral. 68.2% of U.S. families have a home mortgage, which is a type of secured debt Reclaiming the home because of mortgage default is called foreclosure, and between January 2007 and January 2008 the number of foreclosures rose by 57%. Repossession is claiming a car or major appliance for failure to repay. In some states, creditors may also claim (*garnish*) a portion of the paycheck of a defaulting debtor.

SUBPRIME LENDING

Subprime lending targets people whose credit history or income levels indicate that repayment is high risk (and therefore subprime), an assumption used to justify higher interest rates. *Usury* is defined as charging an illegally high rate of interest. Since U.S. usury laws were repealed in the 1970s, the amount of interest a lender may charge has been unregulated, so that market competition sets interest rates. Subprime borrowers, however, are considered such high-risk candidates that few will lend to them at regular interest rates. Beginning in the late 1980s, some lenders began aggressively marketing to the subprime market, which includes large numbers of people who are members of racial minority groups, have low incomes, or have histories of job instability. Subprime lenders may also use redlining, in the presence of characteristics such as high residential mobility, high unemployment rates, low levels of education, low incomes, and low levels of homeownership.

During the 1990s subprime mortgage lending, or making home loans to individuals and couples who did not qualify for conventional mortgages, grew increasingly common. Subprime mortgages often feature adjustable interest rates, with initially low (*teaser*) interest rates, even rates of 0%, which later increase to double-digit rates. Subprime mortgages may have prepayment penalties to discourage efforts to refinance the loans on terms more favorable to the borrower. Subprime lending has been implicated in the high rate of foreclosures in the early 21st century. It has also led to serious dislocations in the financial market, because bundles of subprime mortgages were sold to third-party investors, and these investments have lost value as the subprime mortgages have failed.

FRINGE BANKING

As many as 20% of residents in the United States have no regular banking arrangement and are instead served by lending institutions that charge high interest and market their services principally to the poor, to immigrants, and to racial minorities. These arrangements include pawn shops, title shops, rent-to-own, and payday loans. Pawn shops and title shops are somewhat similar to secured loans in that borrowers allow the lender to hold goods they own (anything of value for a pawn shop; a car title for the title shop) until the debt is repaid. Rent-to-own is superficially similar to ordinary consumer financing of household goods, except that the interest rates are much higher. Payday loans are a cash advance against a paycheck, and thus more similar to unsecured loans, again with a higher interest rate.

REASONS FOR THE INCREASE IN DEBT IN THE UNITED STATES

An argument has been advanced that the current rise in debt results from a decline of the stigma attached to indebtedness, but the evidence for this hypothesis has not been compelling. An alternative hypothesis is that increased debt has risen as a result of consumer industries and the credit industry seeking to expand their markets. The profitable debt business has expanded to include even people who cannot readily repay, either through subprime lending or through the alternative fringe banking institutions. This alternative hypothesis sees the increase in debt as a corollary of advanced capitalism. The advanced capitalism hypothesis typically sees stagnant or declining real wages as an additional corollary to capitalism.

SEE ALSO Volume 2: *Consumption, Adulthood and Later Life; Home Ownership/Housing; Income Inequality; Saving;* Volume 3: *Wealth.*

BIBLIOGRAPHY

Callis, R. R. & Cavanaugh, L.B. (2007, October 26). U.S. Census Bureau News. Retrieved June 26, 2008, from http://www.census.gov/hhes/www/housing/hvs/qtr307/q307press.pdf

Draut, T. (2007). *Strapped: Why America's 20- and 30-somethings can't get ahead.* New York: Anchor Books.

Federal Reserve Statistical Release. G19, Consumer credit. Retrieved July 7, 2008, from http://www.federalreserve.gov/releases/g19/hist/cc_hist_r.html

Kish, A. (2006, June). Perspectives on recent trends in consumer debt. Federal Reserve Bank of Philadelphia. Retrieved July 5, 2008, from http://www.philadelphiafed.org/pcc/papers/2006/D2006JuneConsumerDebtCover.pdf

Mann, Ronald J. 2006. *Charging ahead: The growth and regulation of payment card markets.* Cambridge, U.K.: Cambridge University Press.

Manning, R. D. (2000). *Credit card nation: The consequences of American's addiction to credit.* New York: Basic Books.

Foreclosure activity increases 8% in January. Retrieved July 7, 2008 from http://www.realtytrac.com

Sullivan, T. A., Thorne D., & Warren, E. (2001, September). Young, old, and in between: Who files for bankruptcy? *Norton Bankruptcy Law Adviser,* 1–11.

Sullivan, T. A., Warren, E., & Westbrook, J. L. (1995). Bankruptcy and the family. *Marriage and Family Review, 21,* 193–215.

Sullivan, T. A., Warren, E., & Westbrook, J. L. (2000). *The fragile middle class: Americans in debt.* New Haven, CT: Yale University Press.

Warren, E., & Tyagi, A. (2004.) *The two-income trap: Why middle-class mothers and fathers are going broke.* New York: Basic Books.

Teresa A. Sullivan
Deborah Thorne

DISABILITY, ADULTHOOD

Disability can occur at any age and anyone, at any time, can enter the ranks of "the disabled." Conditions such as blindness, deafness, mobility impairments, and mental retardation are commonly accepted (by the general public) as disabilities. However, in the United States, government definitions of disability include chronic illnesses such as diabetes and multiple sclerosis. Those with psychiatric disabilities, such as depression and mental illnesses, are also eligible for government disability services and benefits. Disabilities that are present at birth are termed congenital disabilities and the individual never develops an identity as a person without a disability. For individuals with congenital disabilities, disability is "normal." In contrast, disabilities either acquired or diagnosed in adulthood presents challenges because adults are faced with the developmental tasks of marriage, establishing a home, developing a career, and financial independence. With an adult-onset disability, often the spouse or partner (of the person with a disability) is involved in responding to the disability. Functional losses may be considerable when an individual acquires a disability in adulthood simply because these years are the period in which most individuals are at the peak of their professional lives.

The disability experience is unique to each person, even among individuals with the same type and severity of disability. The type of onset, the developmental stage when the disability is acquired, the visibility of the disability, the environmental resources available, and personal characteristics and values specific to each individual make every disability experience different. Nonetheless, for purposes of organization and conceptualization, some sort of categorization is necessary. Categorization of disabilities is also necessary in order to provide government benefits and services to those who need them.

CATEGORIZATION OF DISABILITIES

Two disability scholars (Smart, 2001, 2004, 2005 a, b; Vash, 1981) have categorized disabilities into three general types: physical disabilities, cognitive disabilities, and psychiatric disabilities. *Physical disabilities* include mobility impairments, such as quadriplegia (paralysis in both upper and lower extremities) and paraplegia (paralysis in trunk and lower extremities) (Crewe & Krause, 2002); neurologic impairments such as cerebral palsy and seizure disorders (epilepsy); sensory loss (blindness, deafness, and deafness/blindness); musculoskeletal conditions such as muscular dystrophy and chronic illnesses or conditions such as heart disease, autoimmune diseases such as lupus, and the various types of diabetes. Many injuries, after medical stabilization, result in long term disabilities. Often, the general public considers physical disabilities to be the only type of disability. *Cognitive disabilities* include mental retardation, Down syndrome, developmental disabilities such as autism, and learning disabilities, such as dyslexia. *Psychiatric disabilities* include affective disorders such as depression, and mental illnesses such as schizophrenia, alcoholism, and chemical and substance abuse.

An individual may experience a single disability or a combination of two or three disabilities. For the purposes of service provision, one of the disabilities is designated as the primary disability. The three classifications are organized by *symptoms* of disabilities, not by the *cause* (etiology). Often, the causes of disabilities are not known or understood, or there may be multiple causes. More important, the chief purpose of these categorizations is to devise treatment and service plans; therefore, the symptoms are of the greatest interest. Interestingly, there are known physical and organic causes for each type of disability and, therefore, if disabilities were categorized according to cause, all disabilities would be physical disabilities.

Categorization of disabilities also exerts a powerful influence on the degree of prejudice and discrimination directed toward people with disabilities and their families. Typically, those with physical disabilities experience the least degree of stigma and prejudice, probably because these types of disabilities are the easiest for the general public to understand. Persons with cognitive disabilities are subjected to more prejudice and stigma than those with physical disabilities, and individuals with psychiatric disabilities have historically been the targets of the greatest degree of prejudice and discrimination. The history of the provision of government services and financial benefits in the United States closely parallels this categorization of disabilities. Those civilians with physical disabilities received services in 1920 (Vocational Rehabilitation Act of 1920); those with cognitive disabilities received services in 1943 (Vocational Rehabilitation Act Amendments of 1943); and those with psychiatric disabilities in 1965 (Vocational Rehabilitation Act Amendments of 1965). The history of government service provision illustrates that laws and policy are legalized and systematic expressions of public opinion.

RISING DISABILITY RATES ARE ADVANCES FOR SOCIETY

Disability is both common and natural and, furthermore, a larger proportion of the population has disabilities than ever before. Experts expect that this proportion will continue to increase. These rising rates of disability reflect an improvement in social conditions from both individual and societal perspectives because, in most cases, the alternative to the acquisition of the disability would be the individual's death. Innovations in neonatal medicine have allowed more babies to survive; but many are born with a disability. Likewise, advances in emergency medicine have saved the lives of many accident victims; but these survivors often have a disability, such as a spinal cord injury or a traumatic brain injury. Advances in medicine have led to longer life spans and rate of disability is positively correlated with age. For example, at present, there are more people who are blind in the United States than ever before due to the aging of the population. This is due to the higher rates of diabetes, sometimes a condition considered to be associated with old age. Medical progress also has increased the life spans of people with disabilities who, in the past, often did not survive to adulthood because of infections secondary to their disability.

The increase in the number of people with a disability may also reflect a statistical artifact. In recent decades, social and medical scientists have developed more accurate and complete counting of people with disabilities. Further, the definition of disability has been broadened. For example, over the last 25 to 30 years, alcoholism, learning disabilities, and mental illness were not considered to be disabilities. Before these conditions were considered to be disabilities, no services or treatment were provided and, further, these conditions were

Disability Demonstration. *Members of the Americans Disabled for Attendant Programs Today, (ADAPT) take part in a protest outside the White House to protest cuts in funding for community based services.* **AP IMAGES.**

considered personal and moral failures, thus evoking a great deal of prejudice and discrimination.

THE INDIVIDUAL'S RESPONSE TO DISABILITY

Most people with disabilities do not want to be viewed as tragic victims or heroes. Rather, they would like to be considered ordinary people. After their initial physical symptoms stabilize, people with disabilities do not view their disability as their primary identity; but they also understand that society often considers a disability to be the individual's most important characteristic. (This view is captured in widely used phrases such as "the person is not the disability" or disability is not the "master status.") People with disabilities and their families do not deny the presence of the disability, nor do they fail to manage and make accommodations for the disability; they simply consider the many other identities, roles, and functions of an individual with a disability. Often, both people with disabilities and their families are proud of their mastery of the disability and experience satisfaction in negotiating life's demands. Indeed, many people with disabilities consider societal lack of awareness and

prejudice to be more limiting and demanding than the disability.

Someone's response to a disability is influenced by factors in the disability including the type and time of onset. Types of onset may be congenital (present at birth) or acquired. Other types of onset include sudden, traumatic onsets, such as a stroke or an accident. In contrast, other onsets are slow and insidious, such as many types of mental illness or autoimmune diseases. The individual's developmental stage at the time of onset may influence his or her responses. The individual with a congenital disability, such as cerebral palsy, has no identity or memory of being a person without a disability. With a congenital disability, it is the parents, siblings, and grandparents who must negotiate the stages of acceptance. Conversely, someone in middle age, who has an established identity of success and achievement, will experience the onset of a disability very differently, considering the losses to be substantial. Research has shown that older persons tend to accept disability better than do younger persons. Researchers have posited three reasons for this acceptance: The functional demands facing older adults, such as working or raising children, are decreased;

AMERICANS WITH DISABILITIES ACT

∎

The Americans with Disabilities Act (ADA), which was signed into law in 1990, is the civil rights law for people with disabilities. Much of its wording was taken from the Civil Rights Act of 1964.

The ADA has five main sections or titles, each addressing a particular issue and each with different enforcing bodies. Title I is Employment; Title II is Transportation; Title III is Public Accommodations and Services (restaurants, theaters, art galleries, libraries, and so on); Title IV is Telecommunications; and Title V is Miscellaneous and includes guidelines for historical and wilderness sites.

The passage of the ADA in 1990 has facilitated the access of people with disabilities into many aspects of American life and has contributed to the collective identity of people with disabilities. The act also has spurred many advances in telecommunications, assistive technology, and job restructuring.

Despite these accomplishments, some political experts believe that the reforms have not produced much change in the overall social position of Americans with disabilities and that the gap between Americans without disabilities and Americans with disabilities has continued to grow.

many of the individual's age peers experience disability and, therefore disability seems *normal,* and people who are older typically have had a great deal of experience and expertise in responding to life's demands and the acquisition of a disability is simply thought to be another challenge. Interestingly, most, if not all, of the major developmental theories are silent on the issue of disability.

The course of a disability is the way in which the disability advances or progresses. There are three basic courses: stable, progressive, and episodic; each requires a different response from the individual. A stable course, such as would be expected with many types of blindness or spinal cord injury, presents fewer adjustment demands simply because the individual understands with what he or she is dealing. Progressive course disabilities (sometimes referred to as chronic degenerative disorders) require adjustment and response at each level of loss. Often, this includes a change in self-identity. Disabilities

with an episodic course are probably the most difficult to deal with and the most stressful. Obviously, the individual feels a loss of control because he or she cannot predict when an episode will occur.

Some disabilities are visible and others are invisible. Diabetes and some types of mental illness are considered invisible while paralysis and blindness are visible disabilities. Often, it is not the disability itself which is visible, but rather assistive technology such as hearing aids or a wheelchair. For example, although diabetes is considered an invisible disability, those who wear insulin pumps on their belts are considered to have a visible disability. The individual with an invisible disability will be required to consider issues of disclosure. In addition, research has shown that there is a great deal more prejudice and stigma directed toward those with invisible disabilities than those with visible disabilities. Although no correlation exists between degree of visibility and degree of impairment, if the individual wishes to receive accommodations under the Americans with Disabilities Act (ADA), he or she must disclose the disability. Disclosure of disability in social situations, including the timing of the disclosure, is fraught with difficulty. If the individual discloses early in the relationship, the friend, associate, or romantic partner may terminate the relationship. Disclosure late in a relationship may be perceived as a lack of trust and a betrayal.

Not all disabilities involve disfigurement, but those that do, such as amputations, burns, and facial bodily disfigurements, elicit a great deal of stigma. These types of disfigurements do not hinder their activities; but service providers regard disfigurements as limiting simply because of the prejudice and discrimination in the general society. Therefore, we can see that it is society's prejudice, and nothing in the individual or the disability itself, which hinders the individual from full social integration. Obviously, disfigurements acquired in adolescence can undermine self-confidence in peer relationships and romantic and sexual partnerships.

People with disabilities must negotiate all of the developmental stages and, at the same time, respond to and manage both the disability and society's prejudice and discrimination. Adults with disabilities tend to marry at the same rate as those without disabilities; however, the average age at which a person with a disability enters a first marriage is higher.

CURRENT TRENDS IN VIEWING DISABILITY

Until very recently, the *biomedical model of disability* dominated definitions of disability, provision of services and treatment, the public's conceptualization of disability, and the self-identity of people with disabilities. This model defines disability in the language of medicine, lending scientific credibility to the idea that the cause and the management of the disability lie wholly within the individual, often called the *personal tragedy of disability*. Holding the individual responsible is also referred to as the *individualization* and *privatization* of disability. Underlying this model are the assumptions that deficit and loss are present and that disabilities are objective conditions that exist in and of themselves. This *objectification* process opens the door to the possibility of dehumanization because attention is focused on the supposed pathology.

The biomedical model is relatively silent on issues of social justice and one's interaction with the social and physical environment. This lack of awareness of society's collective responsibility to provide accommodations is termed the *medicalization* of disability. Certainly in the biomedical model, the emphasis is on the rehabilitation of the individual, rather than society's responsibility to provide accommodations to such people.

The biomedical model has a long history and, because of this, training in disability issues has been limited to medicine and other medically related fields. This is another example of the *medicalization* of disability. Furthermore, the history, values, and experiences of people with disabilities and their families have not been considered to be part of the general educational curriculum. Indeed, physicians have been the cultural translators of the disability experience. Rather than people with disabilities speaking and writing about the lived experience of disability, it is medical personnel who have described and explained disability to the general public.

The *sociopolitical model of disability* calls for a radical shift in perspective as to the location of the definition of disability from being almost exclusively that of the individual to a collective responsibility as is, for example, communicated in Canadian law. The Canadian Bill of Human Rights of 1960 defines the legal rights of all Canadians and states that it is the responsibility of all Canadians to provide equal opportunities to Canadians with disabilities. The sociopolitical model is an interactional model because it takes into consideration both the person with the disability and that person's unique situation. In this model, policy makers, professional service providers, and the general public become part of the issue of disability or stated differently, if disability is a collective concern, then the response is a collective responsibility. This model defines disability as a social and civil construction because there is nothing inherent in a disability that warrants prejudices or stereotypes and that reduces opportunity. The sociopolitical model has been called the *minority group model* and has fostered the involvement of many people with disabilities in advocacy movements such as the independent living movement and the disability rights movement. Given that the sociopolitical model considers disability a collective concern,

advocates view disability studies and disability history as integral components of sociology, psychology, political science, and history curriculums.

SEE ALSO Volume 3: *Assistive Technologies; Sensory Impairments.*

BIBLIOGRAPHY

Akabas, S. H. (2000). Practice in the world of work. In P. Allen-Meares & C. Garvin (Eds.), *The Handbook of Social Work Direct Practice* (pp. 499–517). Thousand Oaks, CA: Sage.

Albrecht, G. L. (Ed.). (1981). *Cross national rehabilitation policies: A sociological perspective.* Beverly Hills, CA: Sage.

Americans with Disabilities Act of 1990, 42 U.S.C. 12101 *et seq.*

Batavia, A. I., & Shriner, K. (2001). The Americans with Disabilities Act as an engine of social change: Models of disability and the potential of a civil rights approach. *Disability Policy Studies Journal, 29,* 690–702.

Becker, G. S. (1999). Are we hurting or helping the disabled? *Business Week 3635,* 9.

Bickenbach, J. E. (1993). *Physical disability and social policy.* Toronto, ON: University of Toronto.

Bluestone, H. H., Stokes, A., & Kuba, A. (1996). Toward an integrated program design: Evaluating the status of diversity training in a graduate school curriculum. *Professional Psychology: Research and Practice, 27,* 394–400.

Charlton, J. I. (1998). *Nothing about us without us: Disability oppression and empowerment.* Berkeley: University of California Press.

Conrad, P. (2004). The discovery of hyperkinesis: Notes on the medicalization of deviant behavior. In S. Danforth & S. D. Taff (Eds.), *Crucial readings in special education* (pp. 18–24). Upper Saddle River, NJ: Pearson-Merrill, Prentice Hall.

Crewe, N. M., & Krause, J. S. (2002). Spinal cord injuries. In M. G. Brodwin, F. Tellez, & S. K. Brodwin (Eds.), *Medical, psychosocial, and vocational aspects of disability* (2nd ed., pp. 279–291). Athens, GA: Elliott & Fitzpatrick.

Dart, J. (1993). Introduction: The ADA: A promise to be kept. In L. O. Gostin & H. A. Beyer (Eds.), *Implementing the Americans with Disabilities Act* (p. xxii). Baltimore, MD: Paul H. Brookes.

Davis, L. J. (Ed.). (1997). *The disability studies reader.* New York: Routledge.

DeJong, G., & Batavia, A. I. (1990). The Americans with Disabilities Act and the current state of U.S. disability policy. *Journal of Disability Policy Studies, 1,* 65–75.

Fleischer, D. Z., & Zames, F. (2001). *The disability rights movement: From charity to confrontation.* Philadelphia, PA: Temple University.

Fries, K. (Ed.) (1997). *Staring back: The disability experience from the inside out.* New York: Plume.

Hahn, H. (1997). Advertising the acceptable employment image: Disability and capitalism. In L. J. Davis (Ed.), *The disability reader* (pp. 172–186). New York: Praeger.

Hahn, H. (2005). Academic debates and political advocacy: The U.S. disability movement. In G. E. May & M.B. Raske (Eds.), *Ending disability discrimination: Strategies for social workers* (pp. 1–24). Boston: Pearson.

Harris, L. (1994). *The ICD III: Employing disabled Americans.* New York: Louis Harris.

Linton, S. (1998). *Claiming disability: Knowledge and identity.* New York: New York University.

Longmore, P. K. (1995). Medical decision making and people with disabilities: A clash of cultures. *Journal of Law, Medicine, and Ethics, 23,* 82–87.

May, G. E., & Raske, M.B. (Eds.) (2005). *Ending disability discrimination: Strategies for social workers.* Boston: Pearson.

Olkin, R., & Pledger, C. (2003). Can disability studies and psychology join hands? *American Psychologist, 58,* 296–298.

Rossides, D. W. (1990). *Social stratification: The American class system in comparative perspective.* (2nd ed.). Englewood Cliffs, NJ: Prentice Hall.

Scotch, R., & Shriner, K. (1997). Disability as human variation: Implications for policy. *The Annals of the American Academy of Political and Social Science, 549,* 148–160.

Smart, J. F. (2001). *Disability, society, and the individual.* Austin, TX: Pro-Ed.

Smart, J. F. (2004). Models of disability: The juxtaposition of biology and social construction. In T. F. Riggar & D. R. Maki (Eds.), *Handbook of rehabilitation counseling* (pp. 25–49). New York: Springer.

Smart, J. F. (2005). Challenges to the Biomedical Model of Disability: Changes in the practice of rehabilitation counseling. *Directions in Rehabilitation Counseling, 16,* 33–43.

Smart, J. F. (2005). The promise of the International Classification of Functioning, Disability, and Health (ICF). *Rehabilitation Education, 19,* 191–199.

Smart, J. F. (2008). *Disability, society, and the individual.* (2nd ed.) Austin, TX: Pro-Ed.

Stefan, S. (2001). *Unequal rights: Discrimination against people with mental disabilities and the Americans with Disabilities Act.* Washington, DC: American Psychiatric Association.

Thomson, R. G. (1997). Integrating disability studies into the existing curriculum. In L. J. Davis (Ed.), *The disability studies reader* (pp. 295–306). New York: Routledge.

Vash, C. L. (1981). *The psychology of disability.* New York: Springer.

Vocational Rehabilitation Act of 1920, 41 Stat. 374.

Vocational Rehabilitation Act Amendments of 1943, 68 Sta. 652.

Vocational Rehabilitation Act Amendments of 1965, 79 Stat. 1282.

Julie Smart

DISCRIMINATION, WORKPLACE

SEE Volume 2: *Racism/Race Discrimination; Sexism/Sex Discrimination; Ageism/Age Discrimination.*

DIVORCE AND SEPARATION

Individuals rarely enter into serious relationships, especially marriage, with thoughts about how the relationship might end. However, the prevalence of divorce and separation ensures that virtually everyone will have some experience with relationships ending in this manner either personally or by observing others. Most social scientists agree that divorce and separation represent points in a process of marital breakdown rather than isolated events. Therefore, for the purpose of this entry, *divorce* is defined as the legal termination of marriage and is discussed within the context of a series of events, of which separation may be a part. *Separation* refers to the point in a relationship when spouses choose to live apart due to problems in the marriage. The term *marital dissolution* is used to describe the overall process of marital breakdown. The legal status awarded to marital unions sets these relationships apart from dating, cohabiting, and same-sex couples, and, consequently, the processes and implications of relationship dissolution are also somewhat different. Although much of what is said here may apply to these other relationship forms, the primary focus of this entry is married, heterosexual couples.

THE PREVALENCE OF DIVORCE: PATTERNS AND TRENDS

The fact that divorce and separation are frequent experiences in contemporary U.S. society is widely accepted. The most commonly cited statistic is that about 50% of marriages will end in divorce, with other estimates as low as 44% or as high as 64%. One could easily wonder which number is the most accurate and why there is such variability in reports. A few considerations are important in determining the most accurate statistic. First, does the number refer to all marriages or only to marriages that were begun in a certain year? Second, are first marriages the focus or does the number include remarriages? Third, is the intent to describe the entire adult population or a specific subpopulation (e.g., race or age group) only?

One way demographers calculate the divorce rate is by documenting the number of divorces per 1,000 married women age 15 and above for a given year, using data from the census or from marriage and divorce records (Cherlin, 1992). As of 2008, this figure hovers around 20%, or 200 divorces per 1,000 married women in a year. Another way to determine the divorce rate is to estimate the percentage of first marriages begun in a particular year that will end in divorce at some point during the couples' lifetimes—this is the source of the 50% figure so often cited. Individuals who are in their second or later marriages are more likely to divorce than are those in first marriages; about 60% of remarriages end in divorce. Rates also differ by race and ethnicity such that Hispanics have the lowest rates of divorce, followed by Whites, whereas Blacks have the highest rates.

The rising divorce rate occasionally provides fodder for political, media, and even social science debates about the changes occurring in family structures. Some reports discuss the ways in which divorce is causing the decline of the family and the detrimental effects this has on society (Popenoe, 1993). Examination of the longer-term trends in marital dissolution makes apparent that the level of divorce and separation seen in the early 21st century is not new or unusual. The reference period for those who make arguments about the decline of the family is often the late 1950s and 1960s, a time in which divorce rates dropped sharply following a spike after World War II (1939–1945). In fact, observing the trend in divorce from the late 1800s forward shows the 1960s to be a blip in what has otherwise been a fairly steady increase in divorce over time. Additionally, as Andrew Cherlin (1992) notes, the overall rate of marital dissolution has remained generally stable since 1860, but the way in which marriages end has changed. That is, life expectancy has increased over time, reducing the proportion of marriages in a given year that ended due to the death of a spouse so that, since 1970, marriages are more likely to end in divorce than in death. Moreover, separation is not a new phenomenon, although it is perhaps better documented in the recent past than was the case previously. For example, in the past, it was not uncommon for men who had difficulty providing for their families to simply desert them, yet these marriages were never officially recorded as having been ended.

Marital dissolution is one of life's transitions that is important to social scientists both in and of itself and because of its consequences for other family behaviors, including cohabitation, childbearing, and childrearing. Similarly, separation and divorce generally occur at a point in the life course during which the consequences are significant not only for the members of the couple themselves but also for those around them—namely their children, parents, and friends. For example, children must adjust to different living arrangements, either with a single parent (or alternating between both parents), a parent in a cohabiting union or remarriage, or perhaps in a multigenerational home in which grandparents help with childcare. Rising rates of divorce also influence the nature of family formation because individuals change the ways they think about getting married and beginning childbearing (Smock, 2004). That is, the fact that cohabitation and divorce represent options to getting into and remaining in a marriage that may not be ideal appears to be leading individuals to wait longer to marry, waiting until they are sure that the high expectations they have for marriage can be met with a particular partner.

THE CAUSES OF SEPARATION AND DIVORCE

A vast literature describes various causes and factors related to divorce. This work typically stems from several broad theories that help explain changes in patterns of family formation and dissolution over time. The major theories relate changes in the family to (a) secular and demographic trends, (b) stages in the life course, and (c) (inter)personal factors.

Secular and demographic trend theories focus on "big picture" factors that relate to changes in the ways in which families function. For example, a societal shift from an agricultural to industrial economy, and the resulting urbanization, is cited as one of the leading contributors to increasing marital dissolution in European and North American nations (Goode, 1993). Decreased reliance on the family is fostered when schools, jobs, and other nonfamily institutions usurp functions formerly relegated to the family, creating a sense of independence, rather than interdependence, on the part of family members (Nimkoff, 1965). According to the theory, this decreased dependency on other family members reduces familial bonds, and divorce or separation become more likely. Similarly, rising labor force participation and increasing levels of education, particularly among women, are believed to increase marital instability and dissolution by giving women higher status or "bargaining power" in relationships (White & Rogers, 2000).

It should be noted, however, that the relationship between education and divorce is not always straightforward. Women with college educations have experienced a declining divorce rate, whereas the rate continues to rise for those without a college education (Cherlin, 2005). Additionally, individuals are better able to visualize alternatives to their current marriage when more time is spent outside of the family. Alternatives might include a potential partner who appears more desirable than one's current spouse, a new option for childcare, or an alternative income source to offset the possible loss of a spouse's income contributions. Other societal factors such as the percentage of the population that is urban versus rural, changes from fault-based to no-fault divorce laws, and cultural shifts in attitudes toward reduced stigma and increased acceptance of divorce have also been used to contextualize changes in rates of divorce.

Life course theories emphasize characteristics of the marriage that have been consistently related to marital dissolution. First, lower average ages at first marriage, and individuals who marry younger than their peers, predict greater marital dissolution. Age at marriage has even been suggested to be the strongest predictor of divorce in the early years of marriage, possibly because individuals who marry young are less educated and less financially stable or are more likely to be marrying to legitimize a premarital pregnancy than their older counterparts. Second, duration of marriage is important, as about half of all divorces occur within the first 7 years of marriage (Cherlin, 1992). Third, as noted above, individuals in remarriages show higher rates of divorce than those in first marriages. Fourth, the presence of children reduces the likelihood of divorce, at least initially, and childlessness is related to higher rates of divorce. It appears that the presence of children in a family slows the process of marital dissolution so that couples who are prone to divorce will take longer to complete the divorce process (Gottman & Levenson, 2000).

Finally, life course theory suggests that divorce rates have increased as mortality rates declined because individuals grow apart in their interests and goals as they age. Individuals' interests and abilities continue to expand and move in new directions as they mature, and many couples find that, whereas the spouses may have shared much in common in the early years of their marriages, they begin moving in different directions later. In some cases, spouses amicably choose to move in their own directions, whereas in other cases, partners almost seem to weigh the option of ending the relationship against the amount of time they may have to spend living with a partner who is no longer meeting their intellectual and emotional needs. In the past, one partner may have been deceased before the couple really began to feel pulled in separate directions.

Explanations of separation and divorce also consider personal and couple characteristics. For example, evidence consistently shows that religious affiliation and participation is a buffer against divorce. Two common explanations are that (a) some denominations, particularly Catholics and evangelical Christians, are opposed to divorce and their adherents' attitudes and behaviors follow the religious proscriptions and (b) being a member of a religious community offers social integration and social support that promote marriage and family. Couples in which spouses are similar in terms of education level, age, race, and religion, for example, are less divorce-prone than those in which there are large differences between spouses on these characteristics. Likewise, communication style and marital satisfaction have been shown to predict divorce. (However, there are a relatively small percentage of marriages that continue for long durations even though the spouses report low levels of marital satisfaction and low-conflict marriages that dissolve.)

Factors that serve to reduce the risk of divorce are a feeling of commitment to the relationship as expressed by an identity as a member of the couple; a sense that one should stay in the relationship for the sake of the children, because friends or family might disapprove of separation, or for some other reason; or a perceived lack of alternatives (Johnson, 1991). Couples who have many

shared assets may find it more difficult to separate; and overall, good economic circumstances reduce the risk of divorce. Finally, attributes or the behavior of one's spouse (such as alcoholism, domestic violence, infidelity, psychological problems, division of household labor, and so forth) are often cited by the other partner as having led to separation or divorce.

Scientists use census data as well as data from national and smaller-scale surveys to test and refine these theories. Many of the studies are cross-sectional, meaning that data are collected at one point in time, so that trends are deduced by comparing younger and older respondents and those who have experienced a particular event, such as divorce, to those who have not. Cause-and-effect relationships must be inferred. Longitudinal studies, however, collect data from individuals or couples at multiple points in time and allow a clearer picture of the mechanisms relating causes and outcomes. The most sophisticated studies of divorce and separation are prospective studies in which married individuals are sampled and followed over time so that comparisons can be made between those who separate or divorce and those who remain married.

CONSEQUENCES OF DIVORCE AND SEPARATION

Just as theories describing the causes of separation and divorce are varied, so too are assessments of the consequences of these events. Because of differences in perspectives, data collection method, and study samples used, scholars are not in complete agreement about the consequences of divorce, but some strong patterns have emerged.

Undeniably, individuals experience significant changes in their economic status following a divorce. Divorced women's precarious economic well-being is a key factor underlying concerns about high levels of divorce in the contemporary United States. Numerous studies have documented the severe economic consequences of divorce for women (Smock, 1994). For example, in 1996 the median family income of divorced mothers was about $20,000, compared to more than $50,000 for married mothers. By contrast, most studies find that men do not experience the same drops in economic status and in some cases even gained economically following separation or divorce. Patricia McManus and Thomas DiPrete (2001) suggest that this trend may be changing, however, as they found that most of the men in their nationally representative sample did lose economic status because of the loss of their partner's income and an increase in support payments. Other stressors following divorce or separation, such as the need to downsize residences or relocate to be near family and a drop in standard of living to which one has become accustomed, can be directly or indirectly related to this drop in income. The combined effects of various stressors can have large negative effects on the adjustment of both adults and children experiencing divorce.

In addition to changes in economic status, divorce precipitates strains in many types of relationships. When animosity exists between the separating spouses, this may extend to other family members and friends. Depending on the level of conflict between spouses, for example, in-laws may have difficulty maintaining quality relationships that have developed over the course of the marriage. This is especially important for grandparents who may lose contact with their grandchildren if their child is not the custodial parent; conversely, the custodial parent loses this set of grandparents as a source of help with childcare and support. Separating spouses must also adjust to the potential loss of friendships as they find themselves left out of couple activities or because their friends feel it is appropriate only to correspond with the member of the couple to whom they are closer. As there is often animosity between separating spouses, staying friendly with both members of the couple could be perceived as an act of betrayal. Relationships are strained when custody battles are intense or when the noncustodial parent becomes withdrawn from the child's life. Evidence suggests that both the parent and the child suffer when the parent withdraws. Changes in interpersonal relationships such as these increase the negative effects of divorce significantly by adding stress while removing potential sources of social support.

Certainly, the picture of postdivorce adjustment for children is not nearly as grim as it once was—neutral and even beneficial effects of separation have been cited. In general, it appears that many factors beyond the divorce event itself influence the way its effects will be played out for children. For example, if the parents' marriage is one in which little conflict is evident, the effects of the divorce on children appear to be negative, whereas if much conflict has been displayed, the effects are generally positive (Booth & Amato, 2001). A child's age and developmental stage at the time of divorce, gender, and quality of the predivorce parent–child relationships also have an impact on the way the consequences are felt. Scientists find negative consequences to be quite varied, ranging from behavioral problems in children (although some are likely to have been present prior to the divorce), to issues in psychological development and adjustment, to changes in levels of social support received from family and peers, and, later, to difficulties in the offsprings' own marriage(s).

Emerging research is beginning to examine when and how divorce or separation is beneficial to individuals, such as by giving members of unhappy couples a second chance at happiness or removing individuals from environments fraught with conflict, dysfunction, or abuse. Life cycle approaches and theories of adjustment to stress are also being employed to determine the ways in which people adjust to the negative effects of separation or divorce and whether those effects are short lived or long term, or both.

THE STUDY OF DIVORCE AND SEPARATION: BEYOND CAUSES AND CONSEQUENCES

Research on divorce and separation has expanded greatly in the past few decades to include topics not previously examined in any depth. For example, social scientists are beginning to focus on smaller subgroups of the population, such as members of different racial or socioeconomic groups or individuals who divorce at later points in their marriage(s), with an additional focus on how the dissolution of nonmarital unions is similar or different from that of marital unions. Others are making strides in documenting relationships between biological factors and relationship behaviors, including divorce. These studies include the observation of levels of hormones such as testosterone and cortisol among those who divorce (and at various points in the dissolution process) and those who do not, as well as examining whether genetics might play a role in relationship stability. Remarriages and stepfamilies have been explored in the past, but much is left to learn about these complicated family forms.

Along with the expansion of topics of study, new data collection strategies and methods are emerging. Survey data remains the primary source of data in this area, but researchers are employing other methods as well. Focus groups and in-depth interviews provide rich detail about individual couples' experiences, and videotaped interactions allow researchers to examine the ways in which communication patterns and interaction styles predict marital success years later. Biological markers (e.g., measures of hormones, DNA) are being included with survey data for later exploration, and social network analyses and sophisticated statistical techniques allow investigators to fully appreciate the complexity of personal and family relationships.

The field is moving in many new directions, and each step forward uncovers a host of opportunities for further study. Much of the focus to date has been on the effects of divorce and separation on the immediate family, the couple, and their children. Research is just beginning to address how other relationships (e.g., grandparents or grandchildren) are affected in the long term. Another gap that remains in the study of divorce and separation is an evaluation of the various intervention strategies (such as therapy, mandatory mediation, and education-based programs) available for couples and their children at various stages in the divorce process.

POLICY IMPLICATIONS

The continuing concern over contemporary rates of separation and divorce is evident in family policy enacted in the late 20th and early 21st centuries. Marriage-promotion programs have been put into place by state and local governments in order to help families avoid divorce. The ongoing focus on marital unions as the preferred family form means that individuals experiencing dissolutions of other types of relationships—cohabiting unions or same-sex relationships, for example—are not entitled to the same limited resources (e.g., mandated support payments) as divorcing couples, even though the effects of the dissolution may be quite similar. The large body of research summarized here suggests that public policy is not meeting all of the needs of families experiencing the declines in economic circumstances and social support that accompany separation or divorce.

SEE ALSO Volume 1: *Child Custody and Support;* Volume 2: *Cohabitation; Family and Household Structure, Adulthood; Marriage; Noncustodial Parents; Remarriage.*

BIBLIOGRAPHY

Amato, P. R. (2000). The consequences of divorce for adults and children. *Journal of Marriage and the Family*, *62*(4), 1269–1287.

Booth, A., & Amato, P. R. (2001). Parental predivorce relations and offspring postdivorce well-being. *Journal of Marriage and the Family*, *63*(1), 197–212.

Booth, A., Johnson D. R., White, L. K., & Edwards, J. N. (1985). Predicting divorce and permanent separation. *Journal of Family Issues*, *6*(3), 331–346.

Cherlin, A. J. (1992). *Marriage, divorce, and remarriage.* Cambridge, MA: Harvard University Press.

Cherlin, A. J. (2005). American marriage in the early 21st century. *The Future of Children*, *15*(2), 33–55.

Goode, W. (1993). *World changes in divorce patterns.* New Haven, CT: Yale University Press.

Gottman, J. M., & Levenson, R. W. (2000). The timing of divorce: Predicting when a couple will divorce over a 14-year period. *Journal of Marriage and the Family*, *62*(3), 737–745.

Johnson, M. P. (1991). Commitment to personal relationships. In W. Jones & D. Perlman (Eds.), *Advances in personal relationships* (Vol. 3, pp. 117–143). Greenwich, CT: JAI Press.

McManus, P. A., & DiPrete, T. A. (2001). Losers and winners: The financial consequences of separation and divorce for men. *American Sociological Review*, *66*(2), 246–268.

Nimkoff, M. F. (Ed.). (1965). *Comparative family systems.* Boston: Houghton Mifflin.

Popenoe, D. (1993). American family decline, 1960–1990: A review and appraisal. *Journal of Marriage and the Family*, *55*(3), 527–542.

Smock, P. J. (1993). The economic costs of marital disruption for young women over the past two decades. *Demography*, *30*(3), 353–371.

Smock, P. J. (1994). Gender and the short-run economic consequences of marital disruption. *Social Forces*, *73*(1), 243–262.

Smock, P. J. (2004). The wax and wane of marriage: Prospects for marriage in the 21st century. *Journal of Marriage and the Family*, *66*(4), 966–973.

Waite, L. J., & Lillard, L. A. (1991). Children and marital disruption. *American Journal of Sociology*, *96*(4), 930–953.

White, L. K., & Rogers, S. J. (2000). Economic circumstances and family outcomes: A review of the 1990s. *Journal of Marriage and the Family*, *62*(4), 1035–1051.

Lynette F. Hoelter

DOMESTIC LABOR

SEE *Housework.*

DOMESTIC VIOLENCE

Domestic violence research has expanded substantially since the 1970s, as scholars, activists, and policy makers have explored the many facets of this social problem. Research tends to focus primarily on the prevalence, causes, and consequences of intimate partner violence and on the effectiveness of prevention and intervention services for victims and perpetrators. On the one hand, the increase in this line of study has fundamentally changed social perceptions and knowledge about domestic violence and has led to increased resources for victims. On the other hand, the plethora of research makes it apparent that creating a universal definition of domestic violence, particularly of intimate partner violence, is challenging and becoming progressively more difficult. This complexity is essentially the result of typology scholarship that has empirically shown that intimate partner violence is not a unitary phenomenon and that more than one type exists. These new advances have challenged previous conceptualizations of the issue and compelled researchers, activists, and policy makers to reevaluate to whom research findings can be generalized and the appropriateness of "one-size-fits-all" models of understanding, preventing, and ending partner violence. By better understanding why individuals choose to use violence against family members, and by becoming more aware of its differing effects on victims' short- and long-term health and well-being, more can be done to effectively prevent violence, intervene on behalf victims and hold violent partners accountable for their behaviors.

DEFINING DOMESTIC VIOLENCE

Domestic violence or intimate partner violence is typically thought of as a person's use of physical, emotional, or sexual abuse against an intimate partner. Though widely used, this simplistic definition masks the intricacies of this social problem and essentially fails to recognize the complexity of the issue. Mounting evidence suggests that intimate partner violence research explores a wide range of qualitatively distinct types of violence that, without making proper distinctions, can be misinterpreted and contradictory. Depending on the sampling strategy used (i.e., who is being studied and how they were recruited to participate), researchers may uncover very different types of intimate partner violence and subsequent findings about its prevalence, characteristics, and outcomes for victims.

Murray Straus, Richard Gelles, and Suzanne Steinmetz (1980; see also Straus, 1979, 1990, 1999) have contributed significantly to the field by employing large surveys that examine partner violence among the general population of heterosexual couples. This research has tended to focus primarily on the incidence and frequency of partner violence within the U.S. population. Their findings show that partner violence is relatively common in the United States, with about 12% of married couples reporting that at least one partner used an act of physical violence in the past year and about 30% reporting such violence over the course of the relationship. Their findings also suggest that women are as likely as men to use a violent act against an intimate partner, referred to as *gender symmetry*. Steinmetz's controversial 1977–1978 article, "The Battered Husband Syndrome," ignited an ongoing, rancorous debate concerning the issue of intimate partner violence gender symmetry. Steinmetz argued that "An examination of empirical data on wives' use of physical violence on their husbands suggests that husband-beating constitutes a sizable proportion of marital violence" (p. 501).

Straus and colleagues' findings largely contradict those of other researchers who have relied on samples of victims seeking services through the police, divorce courts, hospitals, and battered women's shelters. Data from these agency-based samples consistently show that in heterosexual relationships, it is unequivocally men using violence against women—violence that tends to be severe, frequent, escalating, and largely embedded in a pattern of power and control. Based on such research, the National Coalition Against Domestic Violence (2005) defines intimate partner violence or battering as

a pattern of behavior used to establish power and control over another person with whom an intimate relationship is or has been shared through fear and intimidation, often including the threat

or use of violence. . . . Intimate partner violence [is] intrinsically connected to the societal oppression of women.

Victim advocates and activists, therefore, conceptualize intimate partner violence as one of many types of violence against women (other types include rape, stalking, and sexual harassment) and consider it a social problem rooted in gender-based hierarchies and institutions that "support and reinforce women's subordination" (Goodman & Epstein, 2008, p. 2). This framework draws heavily from the Duluth Domestic Abuse Intervention Project, also known as the Duluth Model, which is considered the most well-known coordinated agency effort to confront the problem of men's violence toward their partners (Pence & Paymar, 1993).

Michael P. Johnson (1995, 2005, 2008) is one of several researchers (see also Holtzworth-Munroe, Meehan, Herron, & Stuart, 1999; Jacobson & Gottman, 1998) who have attempted to resolve the ongoing gender symmetry debate by arguing that more than one type of partner violence exists depending on the sampling strategy used. Johnson (2008) defined *intimate terrorism* as violence in which one partner (almost always the man in heterosexual relationships) uses physical violence to create and maintain general control over his partner. As such, physical and often sexual violence are part of a larger context of coercive control, which likely includes isolation, economic abuse, threats, using male privilege (e.g., treating the woman like a servant whereas the man acts like the master of the house), and using children. The motivation to use violence is essentially to demonstrate and reinforce control over a partner. This is the type of violence that comes to mind for most people when they think about or hear the term *domestic violence*, and victims of intimate terrorism generally show up in agency-based samples such as battered women's shelters and hospitals because of the severe physical and psychological harm that it causes. Sometimes women subjected to intimate terrorism will physically fight back in an attempt to defend themselves or their children. This type of violence is referred to as *violent resistance* (Johnson, 2008).

Intimate terrorism differs dramatically from situational couple violence, which is physical violence that erupts between partners and results more from a specific argument that has "gotten out of hand" with one partner striking out physically against the other (Johnson, 2008). This type of violence is not rooted in a general motivation to control one's partner; rather, it is a situationally specific response to some type of conflict. This is likely the type of violence exposed by Straus and colleagues, who rely on general population-based survey data, and it is arguably the most common type of intimate partner violence (Johnson, 2008).

To date, most research does not clearly distinguish between types of violence, and the field has come to include data representing intimate terrorism, situational couple violence, and violent resistance with dramatically different findings concerning the nature and meaning of each form of violence. Unfortunately, all three of these types are often referred to generically as *domestic violence, domestic abuse, intimate partner violence,* or even *battering,* and often researchers will mix and match statistics from different types without specifically informing the reader which type of violence their study is about or to whom findings can be generalized. Different sampling frames yield different violence prevalence rates and differences concerning factors associated with violence. Moreover, each type of sampling method tends to be biased in its own way. For example, it is unlikely that situational couple victims would be in agency samples such as violence shelters or court samples because they are unlikely to experience a level of danger requiring such intervention. At the same time, intimate terrorism victims might not respond to general population surveys for fear that the abusive partner would find out and retaliate physically (Johnson, 1995).

IMPLICATIONS FOR LIFE COURSE DEVELOPMENT

Depending on the type of violence used, violent partners can cause major psychological and physical harm to victims. The most common physical consequences of partner violence include injuries such as bruises, lacerations, broken bones, concussions, burns, miscarriages, and bullet wounds and also other noninjury-related health problems such gastrointestinal problems, chronic headaches and back pain, and general poor health. Intimate terrorism victims suffer significantly more severe physical consequences compared to situational couple violence victims, which is not surprising given the greater severity and frequency associated with intimate terrorism (Johnson & Leone, 2005).

Research shows that male partner violence is the primary cause of traumatic injury to women and is one of the leading causes of death for pregnant women (Griffin & Koss, 2002). Violence before pregnancy is a strong predictor of violence during pregnancy, whereas for other women violence increases or starts during pregnancy. Women's perceptions of violence during pregnancy indicate that power and control are central to this form of violence and cite their partner's jealousy of the unborn child, anger about the pregnancy, belief that the child is not his own, and/or anger about her lack of sexual interest as causes of the abuse. In some cases, a violent

partner's anger and jealousy will drive him to attempt to cause a miscarriage by direction blows to the pregnant woman's abdomen (Campbell, Oliver, & Bullock, 1993). Approximately 1,300 women are killed each year by an intimate partner, comprising 34% of the murders of women (Rennison, 2003). Male partners are most likely to kill a female partner when she attempts to escape the relationship.

Jacqueline Golding's (1999) meta-analysis of the prevalence of health consequences of violence among female victims of partner violence supports this assertion. She found that about 60% of women studied through agency samples report symptoms of depression compared to 44% in general population samples; between 20% and 55% of women in agency samples report suicide attempts compared to 7% of women in general population samples; and about 33% of agency samples report alcohol abuse or dependence compared to 19% of general population samples. Finally, about 64% of agency samples of women meet the clinical criteria for posttraumatic stress disorder.

Some researchers have examined the association between growing up in a violent home and subsequently becoming involved in a violent marital relationship, the so-called *intergenerational cycle of abuse.* The vast majority of men who experience childhood family violence, however, do not grow up to be violent in their own families (Straus et al., 1980). A meta-analysis by Sandra Stith et al. (2000) found a weak to moderate relationship between the two, with the greatest effect among young males growing up in homes in which the father used highly controlling, often severe physical violence against the mother. These findings potentially support a learning model of male intimate terrorism perpetration and not necessarily one for victimization.

INTERVENTIONS FOR VICTIMS/ PERPETRATORS

Intervention programs for violent partners (typically referred to as *batterer intervention programs*) have been shown to be minimally successful and tend to have low completion rates (i.e., few participants remain in the program for its full duration). For example, a review of effectiveness among both quasi-experimental and experimental studies estimated that 40% of treatment participants are successfully nonviolent compared to 35% of nontreatment participants (Babcock, Green, Webb, & Yerington, 2004). It is also important to note that program "success" is often equated to a cessation in the use of physical violence, which is problematic because many violent partners, particularly intimate terrorists, will likely continue to use coercive control tactics such as emotional abuse, stalking, and threats to use physical or sexual violence even after a victim has escaped (Dobash & Dobash, 2000).

Contrary to common belief, partner violence victims seek help to end the violence against them, and within 2 years nearly half of victims experiencing controlling, severe physical violence escape and two-thirds no longer experience violence (Campbell, Rose, Kub, & Nedd, 1998). Intimate terrorism victims are more likely than situational couple violence victims to seek help from formal help sources (e.g., police, medical agencies, counselors) but are equally likely to seek help from informal help sources (e.g., family, friends; Leone, Johnson, & Cohan, 2007). Although research has not tested the effectiveness of different intervention programs among victims experiencing different types of violence, programs demonstrate relatively short- and long-term success for victims of controlling, physical violence—particularly when it is a part of a community-based advocacy program or a coordinated response. Chris Sullivan and Deborah Bybee (1999) used an experimental design to test the effectiveness of a 10-week post-shelter intervention with trained advocates and found that women who worked with advocates reported less violence and a higher quality of life and social support, and they were more likely to secure community resources over a 2-year period. These findings underscore how important social programs are in not only protecting victims from continued violence and abuse but also helping them secure the social and economic resources needed to recover from the trauma that they have endured.

SEE ALSO Volume 1: *Aggression, Childhood and Adolescence; Child Abuse; Crime, Criminal Activity in Childhood and Adolescence;* Volume 2: *Crime and Victimization, Adulthood; Mental Health, Adulthood; Stress, Adulthood; Trauma;* Volume 3: *Elder Abuse and Neglect.*

BIBLIOGRAPHY

Babcock, J. C., Green, C. E., Webb, S. A., & Yerington, T. P. (2005). Psychophysiological profiles of batterers: Autonomic emotional reactivity as it predicts the antisocial spectrum of behavior among intimate partner abusers. *Journal of Abnormal Psychology, 114,* 444–455.

Campbell, J., Oliver, C., & Bullock, L. (1993). Why battering during pregnancy? *AWHONN's Clinical Issues in Perinatal Women's Health Nursing, 4,* 343–349.

Campbell, J., Rose, L., Kub, J., & Nedd, D. (1998). Voices of strength and resistance: A contextual and longitudinal analysis of women's responses to battering. *Journal of Interpersonal Violence, 13,* 743–762.

Dobash, R. E., & Dobash, R. P. (2000). Evaluating criminal justice interventions for domestic violence. *Crime and Delinquency, 46,* 252–270.

Golding, J. M. (1999). Intimate partner violence as a risk factor for mental disorders: A meta-analysis. *Journal of Family Violence, 14,* 99–132.

Goodman, L. A., & Epstein, D. (2008). *Listening to battered women: A survivor-centered approach to advocacy, mental health, and justice.* Washington, DC: American Psychological Association.

Griffin, M. P., & Koss, M. P. (2002). Clinical screening and intervention in cases of partner violence. *Online Journal of Issues in Nursing, 7*(1), 52–62.

Holtzworth-Munroe, A., Meehan, J. C., Herron, K., & Stuart, G. L. (1999). A typology of male batterers: An initial examination. In X. B. Arriaga & S. Oskamp (Eds.), *Violence in intimate relationships* (pp. 45–72). Thousand Oaks, CA: Sage.

Jacobson, N. S., & Gottman, J. M. (1998). *When men batter women: New insights into ending abusive relationships.* New York: Simon & Schuster.

Johnson, M. P. (1995). Patriarchal terrorism and common couple violence: Two forms of violence against women. *Journal of Marriage and Family, 57,* 283–294.

Johnson, M. P. (2005). Domestic violence: It's not about gender—or is it? *Journal of Marriage and Family, 67,* 1126–1130.

Johnson, M. P. (2008). *A typology of domestic violence: Intimate terrorism, violent resistance, and situational couple violence.* Boston: Northeastern University Press.

Johnson, M. P., & Leone, J. M. (2005). The differential effects of intimate terrorism and situational couple violence: Findings from the National Violence Against Women Survey. *Journal of Family Issues, 26,* 322–349.

Leone, J. M., Johnson, M. P., & Cohan, C. L. (2007). Victim help seeking: Differences between intimate terrorism and situational couple violence. *Family Relations, 56,* 427–439.

National Coalition Against Domestic Violence. (2005). *The problem.* Retrieved June 16, 2008, from http://www.ncadv.org/learn

Pence, E., & Paymar, M. (1993). *Education groups for men who batter: The Duluth Model.* New York: Springer.

Rennison, C. M. (2003, February). *Intimate partner violence, 1993–2001* (Bureau of Justice Statistics Crime Data Brief, Publication No. NCJ 197838). Retrieved June 16, 2008, from http://www.ojp.usdoj.gov/bjs

Steinmetz, S. K. (1977–1978). The battered husband syndrome. *Victimology, 2,* 499–509.

Stith, S. M., Rosen, K. H., Middleton, K. A., Busch, A. L., Lundeberg, K., & Carlton, R. P. (2000). The intergenerational transmission of spouse abuse: A meta-analysis. *Journal of Marriage and Family, 62,* 640–654.

Straus, M. A. (1979). Measuring intrafamily conflict and violence: The Conflict Tactics (CT) Scales. *Journal of Marriage and Family, 41,* 75–88.

Straus, M. A. (1990). Social stress and marital violence in a national sample of American families. In M. A. Straus & R. J. Gelles (Eds.), *Physical violence in American families: Risk factors and adaptations to violence in 8,145 families* (pp. 181–201). New Brunswick, NJ: Transaction.

Straus, M. A. (1999). The controversy over domestic violence by women: A methodological, theoretical, and sociology of science analysis. In X. B. Arriaga & S. Oskamp (Eds.), *Violence in intimate relationships* (pp. 17–44). Thousand Oaks, CA: Sage.

Straus, M. A., Gelles, R. J., & Steinmetz, S. K. (1980). *Behind closed doors: Violence in the American family*. Garden City, NY: Anchor Press/Doubleday.

Sullivan, C. M., & Bybee, D. I. (1999). Reducing violence using community-based advocacy for women with abusive partners. *Journal of Consulting and Clinical Psychology, 67*, 43–53.

Janel M. Leone

DRINKING, ADULTHOOD

SEE Volume 2: *Health Behaviors, Adulthood.*

DRUG USE, ADULTHOOD

SEE Volume 2: *Health Behaviors, Adulthood.*

DUAL CAREER COUPLES

The term *dual career couples* captures the life-course concept of linked lives: Contemporary households increasingly must coordinate and strategize around two employment pathways (his and hers) along with their family pathway.

Some people define dual career couples as those in which both partners hold professional jobs. However, defining the term more broadly (as dual *earner* couples) is useful for understanding continuity and change in the family and occupational circumstances of all employed women and men who are married (or in marriage-like relationships), not just professionals. Dual earner households are now the norm. Only 6% of wives in the United States were employed outside the household in 1900, growing to only one in five by 1950. By contrast, in the early 21st century more than three in five wives are in the workforce. Investigations of dual earner couples are thus key to understanding the changing nature of families, work, and gender relationships.

Research shows that, given the mismatch between jobs designed for single (male breadwinner) earners without family responsibilities and the actual circumstances of their lives, dual earner couples engage in a range of adaptive strategies to coordinate their two occupational pathways and to manage the family side of their work-family equation. They also must adapt to inevitable crises (unemployment, an automobile accident, an unplanned birth, a geographical career move for one spouse) and contradictory gender norms and expectations. For example, many American women have been socialized to believe (a) they can (and should) pursue and move up career ladders and (b) they can (and should) simultaneously have a successful marriage and family life. Similarly, many new age American men have come to believe (a) they can (and should) continue to be the family breadwinners, following the traditional linear, male career path and (b) they can (and should) actively participate in child-rearing and domestic work on the home front.

However, both men and women find these goals difficult to reconcile. Occupational career paths remain designed around the career mystique (a lockstep path of full-time, continuous employment as the only blueprint for good jobs, typical of middle-class men with home-making wives in the 1950s). A global information economy means many jobs now demand far more than the traditional 40-hour workweek, making it difficult for wives and husbands to meet two sets of job demands and goals, along with their family demands and goals.

Life-course scholars examine the ways gender, relationships, and roles intersect and change, studying the interdependence between husbands' and wives' work and family obligations, couple divisions of both paid and unpaid labor, and immediate as well as long-term rewards and costs of various adaptive strategies. Research documents that, even though they may endorse and strive for gender equality in their relationship, couples tend to make strategic occupational and family decisions under the constraints of gender expectations that perpetuate gender stereotypes and inequalities (prioritizing the husbands' jobs, for example, or having the wife "opt out" of the workforce for a time). The fact that women are less likely to earn as much or to advance as far as their husbands colors couples' decisions about how to manage two jobs per household in a world that is organized to accommodate one job per household. The result of women scaling back as a strategy to achieve, retain, or aim for a better life course "fit" in the multiple dimensions of their lives perpetuates gender divisions in the amount of time each partner spends in paid work, home-making, and the care of children and infirm parents or other relatives.

Demographic trends provide evidence that most couples also follow strategies that bend their personal lives to their occupational careers, rather than vice versa. Consider, for example, family strategies that have been adopted culture-wide: postponing marriage or childbearing, reducing family size, or remaining childless. All serve to reduce the family demand side of the dual career-family equation.

Research shows that couples pursue a variety of gender-based strategies around each spouse's paid work. First, a considerable minority of couples have both spouses highly invested in their jobs (the dual committed). Both spouses in this arrangement can be expected to put in long hours on the job, hold high-status (professional or managerial) jobs, and accord high priority to each of their jobs. Evidence shows that these couples are less likely to have children than those pursuing other work arrangements.

A second strategy is to put both partners' occupational careers on the back burner, giving primacy to the private aspects of their lives (those with alternative commitments). This can be either a deliberate choice or a situation in which members of the couple lack the education, skills, or opportunity to do otherwise. This category includes couples in nonprofessional occupations as well as those in a variety of jobs who deliberately choose to work (at most) a regular full-time workweek. Couples with alternative commitments may see both spouses' jobs as having equal (low) priority in their lives. However, studies show this option is likely to be rare, given the ways jobs, careers, pay scales, and consumption patterns are structured.

Often only one partner scales back on career investment and objectives. This compensatory strategy occurs when one spouse invests more in paid work while the other spouse invests more in the domestic aspects of their lives. A modified form of the traditional breadwinner-homemaker model (the neo-traditionalists) occurs when husbands are heavily invested in their jobs and their wives are not. This model perpetuates classic gender inequalities and differences. By contrast, when wives are the ones exclusively on a demanding occupational career track, couples are very much at odds with contemporary gender norms (those with crossover commitments).

The evidence suggests that many dual earner couples (e.g., 38% of the couples in the Ecology of Careers Study; Moen, 2003) follow the neo-traditional strategy. For example, husbands with highly time-consuming or psychologically draining jobs are apt to have wives who carry more of the emotional burden at home, which conforms to evidence on the gendered division of household labor and theories about the social construction of gender. Some research shows that when both spouses work regular full-time hours (39 to 45 hours per week), rather than long hours (more than 45 hours per week), both husbands and wives report higher life quality. This suggests the potential value of a more equal but, at the same time, reasonable division of paid work.

It is increasingly evident that work-life strategies are typically made by couples as couples, not as individual workers, and that they are fluid and dynamic processes. A focus on couple-level adaptations and how they shift over the life course provides a useful way of thinking about and studying gender, jobs, and families, along with the occupational paths of women and men. To do so requires recognition of (a) the value of using couples (rather than individuals) as the theoretical unit of inquiry; (b) possible life-stage variations in dual earner couples' adaptive strategies as couples set up a joint household; children are born, go to school, and grow up; aging parents (or spouses' or personal) health issues emerge; and couples plan for and negotiate two retirements; and (c) the continuing salience of existing gender norms and prepackaged career clocks, calendars, and expectations that privilege and reward the lock-step career mystique. These choices often serve to reconstruct and exacerbate gender inequality in a cumulative process of advantage and disadvantage over the life course.

Examining couples' occupational career development as a joint process illustrates a key policy challenge of modern times—the need for, and the opportunity to develop, new institutional arrangements that expand occupational career options, including opportunities for entries, exits, reentries, and scaling back that are not simply prescriptions for future disadvantage. Moving to greater, "no cost" career customization would enable dual-earner couples to better manage at home and work, improving the life quality of employees, couples, and families.

SEE ALSO Volume 2: *Careers; Employment, Adulthood; Gender in the Workplace; Housework; Marriage; Time Use, Adulthood; Work-Family Conflict;* Volume 3: *Moen, Phyllis.*

BIBLIOGRAPHY

Bianchi, S. M., Robinson, J. P., & Milkie, M. A. (2006). *Changing rhythms of American family life.* New York: Russell Sage Foundation.

Brines, J. (1994). Economic dependency, gender, and the division of labor at home. *American Journal of Sociology, 100*(3), 652–688.

Feldberg, R. L., & Glenn, E. N. (1979). Male and female: Job versus gender models in the sociology of work. *Social Problems, 26,* 525–535.

Hertz, R. (1986). *More equal than others: Women and men in dual career marriages.* Berkeley: University of California Press.

Hochschild, A. (1997). *The time bind: When work becomes home and home becomes work.* New York: Metropolitan Books.

Jacobs, J. A., & Gerson, K. (2004). *The time divide: Work, family, and gender inequality.* Cambridge, MA: Harvard University Press.

Moen, P. (Ed.). (2003). *It's about time: Couples and careers.* Ithaca, NY: ILR Press.

Moen, P., & Roehling, P. (2005). *The career mystique: Cracks in the American dream.* Boulder, CO: Rowman & Littlefield.

Moen, P., & Yu, Y. (2000). Effective work/life strategies: Working couples, work conditions, gender, and life quality. *Social Problems, 47*(3), 291–326.

Stone, P. (2007). *Opting out? Why women really quit careers and head home*. Berkeley: University of California Press.

Sweet, S., Swisher, R., & Moen, P. (2005). Selecting and assessing the family-friendly community: Adaptive strategies of middle-class, dual earner couples. *Family Relations, 54*(5), 596–606.

Phyllis Moen

DURKHEIM, ÉMILE
1858–1917

Émile Durkheim is widely recognized as the father of sociology, and is credited with transforming sociology into a rigorous social science. His seminal writings on suicide, social integration, criminality, and religion have had a profound influence on life course sociology. Durkheim's works focused on the broad question of what makes a society stable and cohesive. He concluded that social integration, or the extent to which norms and shared beliefs hold members of a society together, has powerful influences on the health, stability, and efficiency of a society.

Durkheim was born in the Lorraine province in France on April 15. Following in the footsteps of his forefathers, he spent his childhood years preparing himself for the rabbinate. As an adolescent he discovered that teaching was his calling and moved to Paris to prepare for the École Normale, which he entered in 1879. Durkheim was inspired by his teacher, the classicist Numa-Denis Fustel de Coulanges (1830–1889). From Fustel he learned that the sacred could be studied rationally and objectively. He also read the pioneering work of early empiricists Auguste Comte (1798–1857) and Herbert Spencer (1820–1903), whose ideas shaped the philosophical and methodological foundations of Durkheim's work.

From 1882 to 1885 Durkheim taught philosophy in France. He took a leave of absence in 1885 and 1886, at which time he studied under the psychologist Wilhelm Wundt (1832–1920) in Germany. In 1887 he was named a lecturer at the University of Bordeaux, a position raised to a professorship in 1896, the first professorship of sociology in France.

The 1890s were a period of tremendous creativity and productivity for Durkheim. In 1893 he published *The Division of Labor in Society,* and in 1895 he published *Rules of the Sociological Method*, a manifesto stating what sociology was, and how sociological research and theorizing should be done. In 1898 he founded the scholarly journal *L'Année Sociologique*; his goal was to provide a venue for growing numbers of students and research collaborators to publish and publicize their cutting-edge work. He also had a broader mission: to bring the social sciences together and to demonstrate that sociology was a collective, not a personal, enterprise.

In 1902 Durkheim was named to a professorship at the Sorbonne. Because French universities historically served as training grounds for secondary school teachers, his position afforded him great influence; his lectures were the only ones that were required of all students. In 1912 he was assigned a permanent position of chair. Three years later, he published his last major work, *Elementary Forms of the Religious Life* (1915).

His personal and professional successes reached a tragic turning point during World War I (1914–1918). His son, as well as several of his former students, whom he had trained to become social scientists, were called to fight in the war and ultimately died. Rampant nationalism among the French right made Durkheim's leftism a target of criticism and attack. Emotionally devastated, he died from exhaustion on November 15, 1917, at age 59.

DURKHEIM'S CONTRIBUTIONS TO LIFE COURSE RESEARCH

Durkheim's development of rigorous research methods and his attention to social integration are two of his key contributions to the study of life course. Durkheim proposed that a social system could only be understood through the analysis of social facts, and that contributing to the fund of reliable social facts was the key task of the sociologist. *Social facts* are social patterns that are external to individuals. For example, customs and social values exist outside of individuals, whereas psychological drives and motivation originates within people. Although social facts exist outside individuals, they nonetheless pose constraints on individual behavior. As Durkheim observed, "The individual is dominated by a moral reality greater than himself: namely, collective reality" (Durkheim 1997 [1897], p. 38).

The concept of social fact is exemplified in Durkheim's seminal work *Suicide* (1897); here he revealed that suicide is not necessarily a product of psychological demons, or a biological predisposition to sadness. Rather, Durkheim found that suicide rates were socially patterned: "A victim's act which at first seems to express only his personal temperament is really [caused by] a social condition." He conducted a rigorous analysis of official statistics, and compared and contrasted the suicide rates of diverse social groups across several nations. His analyses revealed that suicide rates were typically higher for men, Protestants, wealthy persons, and unmarried persons, whereas rates were lower for women, Catholics, Jews, and poorer persons. *Suicide* encapsulates a key concept upon which life course sociology is built: the sociological imagination, or the ability to seek the link

Émile Durkheim. ©BETTMANN/CORBIS.

society. Durkheim argued that through the processes of modernization and urbanization, individuals would lose long-standing attachments and social ties that were a trademark of traditional rural villages. He noted that rapidly changing societies would suffer from anomie, or a condition of normlessness. People would not know what the norms (or behavioral expectations) were, and even if they understood the prevailing social rules, they may not obey them if they were not bound by a sense of moral obligation to others. Durkheim argued that in modern urban societies, individuals are without social ties and thus "no force restrains them."

Durkheim's development of the social fact concept has influenced empirical life course sociologists, who meticulously document the ways that social group memberships, such as race, class, gender, religion, and birth cohort, shape personal trajectories. His theorizing on social integration has shaped scholars' thinking about the ways that family, peers, religion, neighborhoods, and other social ties affect individuals at every stage of the life course. As Durkheim observed, such social classifications have an existence of their own and are themselves forces as real as physical forces (Durkheim 1997 [1897], p. 309).

SEE ALSO Volume 2: *Social Integration/Isolation, Adulthood; Social Support, Adulthood; Suicide, Adulthood;* Volume 3: *Social Integration/Isolation, Later Life; Social Support, Later Life; Suicide, Later Life.*

between individualized thoughts and behaviors, and macrosocial patterns or influences.

Perhaps the most important conclusion of *Suicide,* however, was that social integration is critical for individual well-being over the life course. In interpreting his study findings, Durkheim highlighted that married persons and women tend to be embedded in more tightly-knit social networks than single persons and men. Similarly, both the social practices and belief structures of Catholicism and Judaism emphasize social integration, whereas the Protestant tradition upholds the traditions of individuality and personal choice.

Levels of social integration affect more than suicide rates, however; other important life course outcomes such as deviance are also shaped by the level of integration in a

BIBLIOGRAPHY

Durkheim, É. On the normality of crime. (1961). In T. Parsons, E. Shils, K.D. Naegele, & J.R. Pitts (Eds.), *Theories of society: Foundations of modern sociological theory* (pp. 872–875). New York: The Free Press. (Original essay published 1895)

Durkheim, É. *Rules of sociological method.* (1982). New York: The Free Press. (Original work published 1895)

Durkheim, É. *The elementary forms of the religious life.* (1995). New York: The Free Press. (Original work published 1915)

Durkheim, É. *The division of labor in society.* (1997). New York: The Free Press. (Original work published 1893)

Durkheim, É. *Suicide: A study in sociology.* (1997). New York: The Free Press. (Original work published 1897)

Deborah Carr

E

ECONOMIC RESTRUCTURING

Economic restructuring refers to a global change in the nature of labor markets that began in the late 1970s. The restructuring of economies across the globe generally took two forms: (a) declines in manufacturing or goods-producing industries and growth in service and information industries; and (b) increases in the transfer of business activities to external service providers (outsourcing), in contracting others for specialized jobs (subcontracting), and in temporary and part-time work contracts. These industry shifts altered the fundamental nature of work as firms, seeking to attain or maintain their competitive advantage in increasingly global markets, reduced their reliance on skilled workers by fragmenting work-related tasks and increasing their use of technology in the workplace. The result, as noted by Harry Braverman (1974), is what sociologists call *deskilling*, or the downgrading of jobs and occupations. At the same time, firms exercised cost-reduction practices such as mass layoffs, outsourcing, and substituting full-time with part-time workers to make themselves competitive. These demand-side changes in the labor market resulted in higher unemployment, lower wages, larger income disparities, and a dwindling supply of jobs with promotion ladders. Economic restructuring thus changed the context in which people's work lives unfolded over the life course.

CAUSES OF ECONOMIC RESTRUCTURING

The restructuring of labor demands occurred throughout the 1980s and 1990s in countries across the world.

Altough the causes of this restructuring have been debated, one causal factor that scholars agree on is globalization, or the flow of capital, goods, and people across national boundaries. Globalization facilitated the spread of technologies that were instrumental in the production of new ideas and innovations. Embodied in new products, new production processes, and new ways of organizing work, as Manuel Castells (1989) points out, the spread of technologies contributed to the growth of new economic activities. China, India, South Korea, and Japan, in particular, accelerated the pace of technology and scientific advances to improve their capacity to innovate.

A second important factor that fueled the restructuring of labor markets in industrialized nations is the state. National governments, in partnership with financial institutions, designed and implemented industrial policies to improve competitiveness in global markets. As Michael J. Piore and Charles F. Sabel (1984) explain, a number of countries adopted neoliberal economic policies, or strategies based on principals such as free trade in goods and services, free circulation of capital, and freedom of investment. In other words, countries sought to promote economic development by minimizing government regulation in the market in order to increase international trade relationships and manipulate industries and labor markets. For example, the Mexican government implemented a series of policies, endorsed and supported by international financial institutions and the U.S. government, that allowed the country to move away from its model of nationalized industrialization toward a market-driven model of competition and exports. By implementing new economic growth strategies, according to Alejandro Portes and Kelly Hoffman (2003), Mexico was able to manipulate its industry base by trading its low labor costs for capital investments with countries like the United States.

The combination of globalization and state actions profoundly and fundamentally altered the economies of a number of countries. Globalization opened up new markets, industries used technological advancements to improve product designs and the quality of services, and national governments rearranged and reorganized the labor market through trade policies. Economic restructuring can thus be seen as a form of structural change because it systematically and widely changed employment and production processes, with long-term consequences for nations, firms, and the lives of individuals.

UNEVEN CONSEQUENCES OF ECONOMIC RESTRUCTURING

Throughout the 1980s and 1990s, as Saskia Sassen (1991) notes, new economies were taking shape, showing rapid growth in financial and business services and sharp declines in manufacturing industries. These industry shifts generated global cities connected to each other by technology, trade, and production. New York, Tokyo, and London, for example, evolved into centers of finance and top management in part because most financial transactions between Japan, the United States, and the United Kingdom were concentrated in these cities.

At the same time, economic restructuring had devastating effects on some nations. Barry Bluestone and Bennett Harrison (1982) indicate that countries such as Sweden, the United Kingdom, and the United States witnessed growing class inequality. Much of this inequality was directly linked to the disappearance of blue-collar manufacturing jobs that required full-time workers, provided on-the-job training, and offered job mobility. Massive layoffs contributed to high unemployment rates among skilled blue-collar workers who faced shrinking job opportunities. Other blue-collar workers experienced underemployment because low-skill jobs in the growing service sector offered much lower wages, little opportunity for career advancement, and modest training. As manufacturing jobs continued to fade in a labor market with shifting priorities, traditional blue-collar workers and workers without a college degree were vulnerable. Overall, as Emilio A. Parrado and René M. Zenteno (2001) point out, the decline of manufacturing industries left workers facing stagnant career opportunities, weak attachments to the labor market, and downward mobility.

At the other end of the employment spectrum, economic restructuring stimulated unprecedented job growth in professional and managerial occupations. Frank Levy (1998) points out that employees with high levels of

education saw their wages increase and unemployment levels drop. Individuals in these occupations benefited greatly from the reorganization of the economy. Changes in technology and information systems made it possible for highly educated workers to bargain with employers for flexibility, often through telecommuting, home-share work, and job-sharing, according to Leslie McCall (2001).

The consequences of restructuring went beyond falling wages at the bottom of the labor market, rising wages at the top of the labor market, and consequent increases in income inequality. Economic restructuring produced changes in the organization of work that had contradictory effects on women's work lives. On the one hand, the new organization of work undoubtedly shaped women's career choices. For example, the growth of part-time work allowed many women to enter the labor force (McCall, 2001). On the other hand, as Barbara Reskin and Patricia A. Roos (1990) note, occupations that were once predominantly male, such as nursing and clerical jobs, resegregated as they became predominantly female.

As Maria Charles (2005) observes, occupations in a number of industrialized nations were often influenced by cultural beliefs about what men and women are good at. For example, Mary Brinton (2001), in her comparison of Taiwan and Japan, found that large firms in Japan have mobility ladders for men but not women; in contrast, small, family-owned firms in Taiwan create opportunities for female family members to participate in the management of the firm. For women, the downside of economic restructuring was twofold. First, industry changes that encouraged women's labor force participation and new occupations contributed to "mommy tracks" in corporate environments. Second, growing income inequality adversely affected low-wage women as their wages fell and because they did not benefit from the flexibility that high-wage earning women did (McCall, 2000).

Another consequence of economic restructuring is the growth of "under the table" or "off the books" work, or economic activity that occurs outside the formal economy, which is regulated by economic and legal institutions. In the 1980s labor unions were hit hard by the rise in international trade, policies that favored employers, and economic restructuring. The power and protection that labor unions once provided workers withered away as new economic activities emerged. Facing rising unemployment rates and falling wages, workers in many countries turned to informal work for additional sources of income. For example, garment workers in industrialized and nonindustrialized nations saw their wages fall and jobs transformed into informal and home-based work that is neither recognized nor protected by law. With no formal employer, these workers get their own materials, make the garments, and find markets to sell their goods.

UNRESOLVED ISSUES

Although social scientists have documented the extent to which economic restructuring has fragmented and stratified groups by gender, income, and race, there are issues that remain unresolved. First, sociologists do not yet fully understand why economic restructuring has resulted in greater disparity among women. McCall (2001) argues that if the goal is to move toward equitable economic growth and higher wages for women across the board, gender scholars must continue to investigate the causes of rising income inequality among women. These investigations should explore the consequences of labor market policies that shape the career trajectories of men and women. For instance, research on company decisions and policies regarding gender equity would be helpful for understanding whether organizational change subordinates equity issues or enhances women's careers (McCall, 2001).

A second unresolved issue connected to economic restructuring relates to marriage and family life. Since the late 1990s research has shown that declines in marriage among low-educated women have been shaped by the eroding labor market opportunities for low-educated men, who thus appear to be poor prospects for marriage. In contrast, as Daniel T. Lichter and Diane K. McLaughlin (2002) observe, for highly educated women the retreat from marriage is less about the earning power of men and more about rising female earnings, which permit greater independence. To understand the relationship between the labor market and marriage, sociologists continue to debate why growing income inequality, a change produced by economic restructuring, has led to the retreat from marriage across the board.

Finally, because researchers have focused much of their attention on the patterns of wage and income inequality, less is known about how economic restructuring has affected the work histories of individuals. For example, questions remain about the rate of job change that individuals experience and how the sequence of job changes unfold over the life course.

SEE ALSO Volume 2: *Employment, Adulthood; Globalization; Income Inequality; Occupations; Policy, Employment.*

BIBLIOGRAPHY

Bluestone, B., & Harrison, B. (1982). *The deindustrialization of the United States.* New York: Basic Books.

Braverman, H. (1974). *Labor and monopoly capital: The degradation of work in the twentieth century.* New York: Monthly Review Press.

Brinton, M. (2001). *Women's working lives in East Asia.* Stanford, CA: Stanford University Press.

Castells, M. (1989). *The informational city.* Cambridge, MA: Basil Blackwell.

Charles, M. (2005). National skill regimes, postindustrialism, and sex segregation. *Social Politics: International Studies in Gender, State and Society, 12*(2), 289–316.

Levy, F. (1998). *The new dollars and dreams.* New York: Russell Sage Foundation.

Lichter, D. T., & McLaughlin, D. K. (2002). Economic restructuring and the retreat from marriage. *Social Science Research, 31,* 230–256.

McCall, L. (2001). *Complex inequality: Gender, class, and race in the new economy.* New York: Routledge.

Parrado, E. A., & Zenteno, R. M. (2001). Economic restructuring, financial crises, and women's work in Mexico. *Social Problems, 48*(4), 456–477

Piore, M. J., & Sabel, C. (1984). *The second industrial divide: Possibilities for prosperity.* New York: Basic Books.

Reskin, B., & Roos, P. A. (Eds.). (1990). *Job queues, gender queues: Explaining women's inroads into male occupations.* Philadelphia, PA: Temple University Press.

Sassen, S. (1991). *The global city: New York, London, Tokyo.* Princeton, NJ: Princeton University Press.

Jacqueline Olvera

EDUCATIONAL ATTAINMENT

Educational attainment has been of long-standing interest to life course scholars. That interest results from several factors, including the role of education in nation-state development (Meyer, Tyack, Nagel, & Gordon, 1979), children's socialization (Sewell & Hauser, 1980), and adults' earnings (Card, 1999). As educational attainment has risen since the middle of the 20th century, the modal trajectory of the life course has changed, and researchers have tried to document the amount of schooling in populations and key subpopulations and to identify the determinants of educational attainment.

MEASUREMENT AND TRENDS IN EDUCATIONAL ATTAINMENT

Analysts measure educational attainment in two ways. One approach involves counting the years of school a person completes. To document the educational attainment of a population, analysts report the mean (i.e., average) or median years of school completed. A second approach entails recording whether a person has attained certain key markers, such as a high school diploma, a bachelor's degree, or entry to advanced degree study. One then may calculate the proportion of persons in a

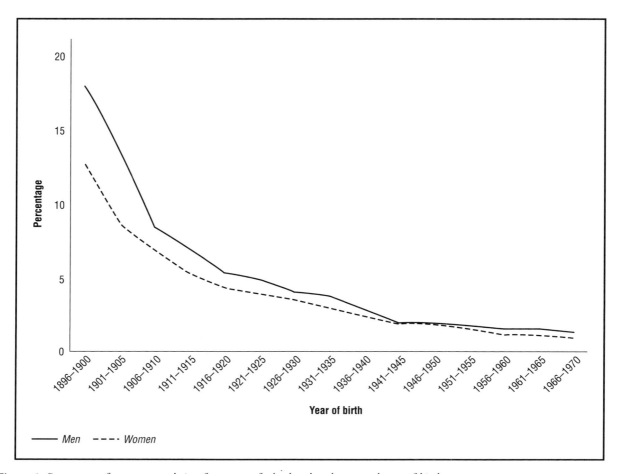

Figure 1. *Percentage of persons completing four years of school or less, by sex and year of birth.* CENGAGE LEARNING, GALE.

population or subpopulation who have reached those thresholds.

By any measure, the level of educational attainment rose between 1901 and 2000. Throughout the 20th century in the United States the mean years of schooling increased for each succeeding cohort (Snyder & Hoffman, 2001). Further, the century witnessed a sharp decline in the proportion of persons with very low levels of education (Mare, 1995); corresponding increases in the proportions graduating from high school, entering college, and completing a bachelor's degree also were observed (Mare, 1995). The United States was not alone, as levels of educational attainment rose throughout the world during the 20th century (Shavit & Blossfeld, 1993).

Historically in the United States women have equaled or surpassed men's likelihood of completing high school, whereas men have exceeded the college attendance rates of women. With the birth cohorts of the mid-1950s, however, women surpassed men in the likelihood of college entry, and by the birth cohorts of the early

1960s women equaled men in the likelihood of obtaining a bachelor's degree (Mare, 1995). Thus, there are complex relationships among gender, cohort, and educational attainment.

Race/ethnicity is another sociodemographic factor that is associated with educational attainment. As of 2007, 93.4% of White persons 25 to 29 years old had completed high school, whereas for African Americans and Hispanics only 86.3% and 63.2%, respectively, had completed high school (Snyder, Dillow, & Hoffman, 2007). However, many Hispanics age 25 to 29 may not have obtained their schooling in the United States; consequently, the extent to which the completion rate reflects the operation of education systems in the United States is not clear.

An additional complexity concerns African Americans. When researchers control for (or hold constant) socioeconomic factors, the Black–White high school completion gap disappears (Bauman, 1998; Lucas, 1996). Researchers routinely find that those of higher socioeconomic status (SES) go further in school. The robustness of this finding has motivated ongoing efforts to explain why SES matters.

UNDERSTANDING THE CAUSAL EFFECT OF INDIVIDUALS' SES

Most educational attainment research is based on the presumption that well-developed educational systems exist. However, an individual cannot enter school, stay in school longer, or pursue postsecondary education unless educational institutions are constructed, expanded, and maintained. The historical process through which schools were constructed and expanded is contested. Key explanations that have been offered characterize the development of educational institutions as a nation-building activity (Meyer & Rubinson, 1975), a result of diffusion processes linked to the world system (Meyer, Ramirez, Rubinson, & Boli-Bennett, 1977), and a tool used by capitalists to create disparate forms of consciousness to slot persons into different—and unequal—positions in the economy (Bowles & Gintis, 1976). A full consideration of the institutional underpinnings of educational attainment must consider theories such as these, which view education from the macrosocial perspective. However, most research centers on explaining individual differences in educational attainment within a single institutional context.

The Wisconsin Social-Psychological Model of Status Attainment (the Wisconsin model) offers a social-psychological explanation for differences in educational attainment (Hauser, Tsai, & Sewell, 1983; Sewell & Hauser, 1980). The original work used Wisconsin Longitudinal Study data on Wisconsin high school graduates of 1957, but replications have extended the model nationwide (Alexander, Eckland, & Griffin, 1975) and beyond (Hansen & Haller, 1973; Nachmias, 1977).

The key factor in the Wisconsin model is the influence of significant others—encouragement by parents, teachers, and peers—as perceived and reported by the child. The higher their SES or academic performance, the greater the encouragement children perceive. The influence of significant others directly affects a child's educational aspiration and occupational aspiration, and educational aspiration affects educational attainment.

The Wisconsin model offers a powerful explanation of observed variation in attainment. The model explains 45% of the variation in significant others' influence, 74% of the variation in educational aspirations, and 68% of the variation in educational attainment. Further, it explains 73% of the variation in early career occupational status and 69% of the variance in occupational status at midlife (Hauser et al., 1983). By any estimation, this theoretical model provides a robust explanation of the process of educational attainment.

However, there are other explanations of the relationship of SES and educational attainment, although none provides the level of explanatory power of the Wisconsin model. The Wisconsin model contrasts sharply with the biogenetic explanation of variation in educational attainment. Biogenetic theorists see ability as the driver in educational attainment; ability is viewed as largely determined by one's genes, and genes are determined by one's parents. To complete the circle, assortative mating on educational attainment and other markers of social class reinforce distinctions of ability (Herrnstein & Murray, 1994).

Genetic explanations of educational attainment differentials have been refuted on scientific grounds. In *Inequality by Design: Cracking the Bell Curve Myth*, Claude Fischer and colleagues (1996) provided a thorough refutation of the biogenetic explanation of social inequality, including inequality in educational attainment. Additional authors, motivated perhaps by the apparent staying power of the biogenetic thesis in the popular imagination, have provided additional refutations (Devlin, Fienberg, Resnick, & Roeder, 1997; Jencks & Phillips, 1998).

Education researchers have found more support for human capital theory, which has affinities with the Wisconsin model. According to human capital theory, adults' productivity is a function of two factors: ability and investment. Individuals invest in their productivity in various ways, such as by acquiring skills through education. With all else equal, the more are able to invest more. However, ability is not completely free to develop, as many individuals face credit constraints and thus cannot make investments they otherwise would make (Becker, 1962). Hence, the socioeconomic gradient in education is due partly to credit constraints that prevent the poor from obtaining levels of education consonant with their ability (Becker & Tomes, 1986; Tomes, 1981). Thus, human capital theory suggests and explains a high association between parent and child educational attainment.

In *Reproduction in Education, Society, and Culture*, Pierre Bourdieu and Jean-Claude Passeron (1977) provided another theoretical explanation for the association between parental status and educational attainment. They contended that schools reward behavior that complies with the norms and standards of the dominant group in a society, yet those authors also noted that one's core (or habitus) develops in the family, is difficult or impossible to change, and directly affects one's likelihood of educational success. Bourdieu (1986) allowed one to interpret the association between parental status and educational attainment as resulting from gatekeeper exclusion, arbitrarily selected criteria of evaluation that advantage the previously advantaged, and parent–child interaction.

These broader theories highlight the ways individuals navigate systems of education by using their personal

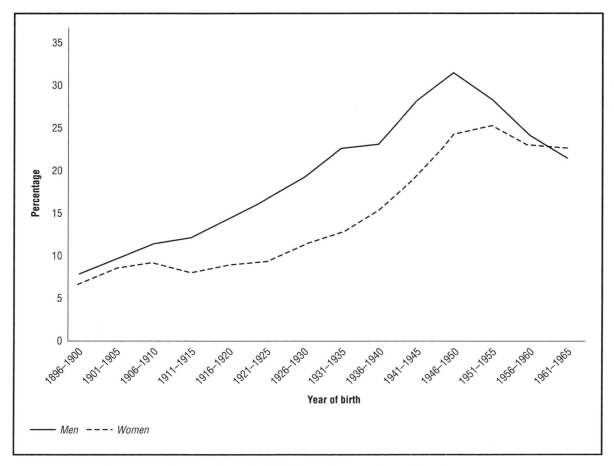

Figure 2. *Percentage of persons completing at least a bachelor's degree, by sex and year of birth.* CENGAGE LEARNING, GALE.

resources as well as those provided by their families. More recent research highlighting cross-national comparisons has moved toward integrating macro-level considerations into the understanding of the production of educational attainment.

INDIVIDUAL-LEVEL FACTORS IN THE CONTEXT OF MACRO-LEVEL DEVELOPMENTS: THE DIFFERING SOCIOECONOMIC GRADIENTS OF EDUCATIONAL ATTAINMENT

Cross-national comparative research has deepened analysts' understanding of educational attainment. The move to cross-national comparative research led researchers to recognize a problem with studying years of schooling. In response, Robert D. Mare (1980, 1981), following the work of Stephen E. Fienberg and William M. Mason (1978), observed that a person's years of schooling reflects a series of separate decisions to stop or continue schooling. Mare proposed that scholars could resolve the challenge

raised by studying years of schooling by investigating the sequence of transitions instead. This education transitions approach (the Mare model) has become the standard for studies of educational attainment. The Mare model allows social scientists to observe (a) the changing association between socioeconomic background and educational attainment across transitions, (b) the different association between socioeconomic background and any particular transition across nations, and (c) the different association between socioeconomic background and any given transition across birth cohorts.

In his original research, Mare (1980) discovered a pattern of waning associations across transitions. Subsequent research replicated that finding with data from Israel (Shavit, 1993), France (Garnier & Raffalovich, 1984), Japan (Treiman & Yamaguchi, 1993), Sweden (Jonsson, 1993), Taiwan (Tsai & Chiu, 1993), and many other countries (Shavit & Blossfeld, 1993). Researchers also have detected stable associations across cohorts in the same country. Analysts have offered several theories to explain one or both of these patterns.

Mare (1980) originally proposed that selective attrition explained the waning association pattern. Fundamentally a statement of the statistical relations underlying the observed pattern, this explanation was revealed to be insufficient when the implications for the pattern of socioeconomic effects across cohorts were not observed (Shavit & Blossfeld, 1993) and when the statistical relations were shown to hold in a cohort even when the pattern of waning associations did not (Lucas, 1996).

Walter Müller and Wolfgang Karle (1993) proposed a life course perspective (LCP) to explain the pattern of waning associations between social background and educational attainment across successive transitions. They noted that students, older at each transition, depend less on their parents both socially and economically with each passing year. Hence, changes in the parent–child relation make parental characteristics decline in importance as a child matures.

Adrian Raftery and Michael Hout (1993; see also Hout, Raftery, & Bell, 1993) provided a further explanation for waning associations across transitions and changing associations across cohorts. They postulated four tenets of maximally maintained inequality (MMI). First, expansion of secondary and higher education reflects increased demand generated by population increase and the rising level of parents' education caused by earlier education expansion and other factors. Second, if enrollment rises faster than demand, the socioeconomically disadvantaged obtain more schooling. Even so, the socioeconomic association is unchanged. Third, if completion of a level of education becomes universal for higher SES persons, the effect of social background on that transition declines but only if educational expansion cannot be maintained otherwise. Fourth, falling SES can reverse and become rising effects; for example, if government support for educational attainment is reduced, socioeconomic effects will increase.

The fourth claim is a key difference between MMI and LCP. LCP emphasizes that as children age, they become increasingly independent of their parents and thus socioeconomic effects inexorably decline across transitions. MMI implies that adolescents' independence itself depends on the sociopolitical context and the resulting social support for particular levels of education.

Richard Breen and John H. Goldthorpe (1997) offered a rational choice model of relative risk aversion (RRA) to explain stable class differentials across cohorts, declining class effects across transitions, and rapidly changing gender effects. RRA draws on the Wisconsin model by highlighting perceptions of likelihood of educational success that are driven in part by ability and draws on human capital theory by highlighting cost constraints. However, Breen and Goldthorpe added the proviso that persons are risk-averse and seek to attain a social class at least equal to that of their parents.

RRA interprets MMI as a special case in which costs decline across the board for all classes. RRA claims that if costs decline differentially for different classes, the patterns highlighted by MMI will not occur. RRA points to rapid decline in the gender effect owing to changes in perceptions of appropriate roles, and thus likely levels of educational success. In Sweden, a rare case occurred in which class effects did decline with expansion owing to effective support for the education of disadvantaged children.

Although RRA is generally applicable to any choice set, both LCP and MMI explicitly concern attainment only. This is important because the traditional Mare model ignores potentially important qualitative differences in schooling. Richard Breen and Jan O. Jonsson (2000) found that the power of socioeconomic background varied with the path students took to their completed educational attainment. They concluded that suppressing qualitative distinctions weakens the understanding of the role of social background in educational transitions.

Consistent with that insight, Samuel R. Lucas (2001) proposed the theory of effectively maintained inequality (EMI), which considers both qualitative and quantitative dimensions of inequality. Lucas contended that socioeconomically advantaged actors secure for themselves and their children advantage wherever advantages are commonly possible. If quantitative differences are common, the socioeconomically advantaged obtain quantitative advantage. If qualitative differences are common, the socioeconomically advantaged obtain qualitative advantage.

Articulated as a general theory of inequality, EMI explained socioeconomic effects on educational attainment in one of at least two ways. When a particular level of schooling is not universal (e.g., high school completion throughout the first half of the 20th century in the United States), the socioeconomically advantaged use their advantages to secure that level of schooling. However, once that level of schooling becomes nearly universal, the socioeconomically advantaged seek out whatever qualitative differences there are at that level, using their advantages to secure quantitatively similar but qualitatively better education (e.g., qualitatively better, more challenging curricular tracks). EMI notes that actors' foci may shift as qualitative differences supplant quantitative differences in importance; alternately, actors may care about qualitative differences even when quantitative differences are common. Either way, EMI claims that the socioeconomically advantaged will use their advantages to secure both quantitatively and qualitatively better outcomes.

Each theory considers individual-level differences in larger dynamics—family dynamics, population dynamics, or power dynamics—all of which potentially differ across time and place according in part to social and political factors. In this way these theories provide resources for integrating macro-level narratives of the development of education systems with the micro-level narrative of persons' navigation of those systems.

FUTURE RESEARCH

LCP implies an inexorable pattern of declining social background effects regardless of the situation. As researchers have found that this pattern reverses at times (Lucas, 1996), the claim of inexorable forces pushing weaker social background effects at older ages cannot be sufficient. However, it remains unclear whether MMI, RRA, or EMI best explains the pattern of socioeconomic background effects on educational transitions. Evidence consistent with each of the remaining three theories has been found. However, rarely have multiple theories been considered simultaneously. Hence, most studies are demonstrations of empirical patterns consistent with a focal theory, not efforts to test multiple theories on the same phenomenon to eliminate some from consideration. Future progress requires analysts to test the existing theories against one another under different conditions.

The effort to evaluate the theories is not aided by MMI and EMI sometimes being confused with each other (Tolsma, Coenders, & Lubbers, 2007). Some analysts fuel the confusion by merging EMI and MMI into one theory (Hout, 2006). Merging EMI and MMI, however, makes little sense because the two theories fundamentally disagree. Notably, MMI claims that socioeconomic inequality will be reduced through educational expansion, whereas EMI states unequivocally that education expansion need not reduce socioeconomic inequality. Thus, MMI points the way to a simple public policy response to socioeconomic inequality in education: expand schools. EMI maintains that expanding schools is insufficient because a plethora of qualitative differences in education can sustain inequality.

The reasoning behind this disagreement is that MMI states that for a transition made by every student or nearly every student the socioeconomic association will be zero and thus social conflict will be zero too. EMI directly contests this claim, explicitly stating that conflict may occur at universal transitions, may be intense, and will concern qualitative dimensions that matter for ultimate attainment. EMI points directly to the contestation around high school tracking as one example of intense class-based contestation at a nearly universal transition (Lucas, 2001; Wells & Serna, 1996). Consequently, MMI and EMI disagree on the crucial sociological point of what occurs when a transition is universal, suggesting that any merger of the theories can only produce an ad hoc melange.

Indeed, Hout's (2006) proposed merger appears ad hoc, as indicated by the statement that "MMI and EMI predict slow and contingent change over time in how strongly family background affects educational opportunity" (p. 239). Although MMI makes this prediction owing to its emphasis on slow-moving population dynamics such as changes in levels of parents' education, EMI suggests that the pace and pattern of change, if any, depend on the mix of qualitative and quantitative goods and thus need not be slow. As another example, Hout stated, "As post-secondary education expands, we can expect the association between family background and educational attainment to weaken....I will propose an appropriate statistical model, fit it in each...country, and assess MMI/EMI in light of the results" (p. 240). Although MMI explicitly argues that large-scale educational expansion will lower the effect of background on educational attainment, the definitive claim of EMI is that educational expansion may fail to alter the effect of social background because the existence of qualitative positions may undermine the egalitarian impact of educational expansion. Thus, Hout's amalgam of EMI and MMI actually reflects only MMI.

In the few studies that have considered multiple theories, the empirical evidence contradicts MMI but is consistent with EMI, suggesting that any synthesis faithful to one will shortchange the other and any synthesis faithful to both will be incoherent. In the original paper on EMI, Lucas (2001) found support for MMI over LCP but support for EMI over both for 1980 U.S. sophomores. Hannah Ayalon and Yossi Shavit (2004) considered MMI and EMI in analyzing reforms of the Israeli educational system. They found that EMI offers a better explanation than MMI. Further work in Israel that focused on higher education institutions and field of study also preferred EMI (Ayalon & Yogev, 2005). If two theories disagree and analyses support one over the other, merging them is likely only to obfuscate matters.

The unhappy marriage of EMI and MMI may stem from the generality of EMI. Although EMI researchers have focused on education, EMI offers a general theory of inequality that is applicable beyond education. In contrast, MMI tenets pertain narrowly to education. Hence, pushing EMI and MMI together undermines both the reach of EMI beyond education and the utility of EMI for studies of education, a utility that has been proven in straight-up comparisons of EMI and MMI in existing research. For these reasons, combining the theories is unwise.

More research is needed to determine which of the existing theories, MMI, RRA, or EMI, best explains patterns of socioeconomic effects on education transitions and under which conditions one theory is preferable. The selection of a theory has ramifications for the understanding of how educational attainment works and for the prospects of and methods for altering the patterns of social background effects. Thus, it is important to keep the theories distinct so that researchers can understand the dynamics of socioeconomic inequality and educational attainment.

SEE ALSO Volume 1: *Cultural Capital; High School Dropout; School Transitions; Socioeconomic Inequality in Education; Stages of Schooling;* Volume 2: *Continuing Education; Social Class.*

BIBLIOGRAPHY

Alexander, K. L., Eckland, B. K., & Griffin, L. J. (1975). The Wisconsin model of socioeconomic achievement: A replication. *American Journal of Sociology, 81*(2), 324–342.

Ayalon, H., & Shavit, Y. (2004). Educational reforms and inequalities in Israel: The MMI hypothesis revisited. *Sociology of Education, 77*(2), 103–120.

Ayalon, H., & Yogev, A. (2005). Field of study and students' stratification in an expanded system of higher education: The case of Israel. *European Sociological Review, 21*(3), 227–241.

Bauman, K. J. (1998). Schools, markets, and family in the history of African-American education. *American Journal of Education, 106*(4), 500–531.

Becker, G. S. (1962). Investment in human capital: A theoretical analysis. *Journal of Political Economy, 70*(Suppl.), 9–49.

Becker, G. S., & Tomes, N. (1986). Human capital and the rise and fall of families. *Journal of Labor Economics, 4*(3), S1–S39.

Bourdieu, P. (1986). The forms of capital. In J. G. Richardson (Ed.), *Handbook of theory and research for the sociology of education* (pp. 241–258). New York: Greenwood Press.

Bourdieu, P., & Passeron, J-C. (1977). *Reproduction in education, society, and culture.* (R. Nice, Trans.). (2nd ed.). London: Sage Publications.

Bowles, S., & Gintis, H. (1976). *Schooling in capitalist America: Educational reform and the contradictions of economic life.* New York: Basic Books.

Breen, R., & Goldthorpe, J. H. (1997). Explaining educational differentials: Towards a formal rational action theory. *Rationality and Society, 9*(3), 275–305.

Breen, R., & Jonsson, J. O. (2000). Analyzing educational careers: A multinomial transition model. *American Sociological Review, 65*(55), 754–772.

Card, D. (1999). The causal effect of education on earnings. In O. C. Ashenfelter & D. Card (Eds.), *Handbook of labor economics* (Vol. 3, pp. 1801–1863). Amsterdam, the Netherlands: North-Holland.

Devlin, B., Fienberg, S. E., Resnick, D. P., & Roeder, K. (1997). *Intelligence, genes, and success: Scientists respond to* The Bell Curve. New York: Springer.

Fienberg, S. E., & Mason, W. M. (1978). Identification and estimation of age-period-cohort models in the analysis of discrete archival data. *Sociological Methodology, 10,* 1–67.

Fischer, C., Hout, M., Sánchez Jankowski, M., Lucas, S. R., Swidler, A., & Voss, K. (1996). *Inequality by design: Cracking the bell curve myth.* Princeton, NJ: Princeton University Press.

Garnier, M. A., & Raffalovich, L. E. (1984). The evolution of educational opportunities in France. *Sociology of Education, 57*(1), 1–11.

Hansen, D. O., & Haller, A. O. (1973). Status attainment of Costa Rican males: A cross-cultural test of a model. *Rural Sociology, 38*(3), 269–282.

Hauser, R. M., Tsai, S-L., & Sewell, W. H. (1983). A model of stratification with response error in social and psychological variables. *Sociology of Education, 56*(1), 20-46.

Herrnstein, R. J., & Murray, C. (1994). *The bell curve: Intelligence and class structure in American life.* New York: Free Press.

Hout, M. (2006). Maximally maintained inequality and essentially maintained inequality: Cross-national comparisons. *Sociological Theory and Methods, 21*(2), 253–278.

Hout, M., Raftery, A. E., & Bell, E. O. (1993). Making the grade: Educational stratification in the United States, 1925–1989. In Y. Shavit & H.-P. Blossfeld (Eds.), *Persistent inequality: Changing educational attainment in thirteen countries* (pp. 25–49). Boulder, CO: Westview Press.

Jencks, C., & Phillips, M. (Eds.). (1998). *The Black–White test score gap.* Washington, DC: Brookings Institution Press.

Jonsson, J. O. (1993). Persisting inequalities in Sweden. In Y. Shavit & H.-P. Blossfeld (Eds.), *Persistent inequality: Changing educational attainment in thirteen countries* (pp. 101–132). Boulder, CO: Westview Press.

Lucas, S. R. (1996). Selective attrition in a newly hostile regime: The case of 1980 sophomores. *Social Forces, 75*(2), 511–533.

Lucas, S. R. (2001). Effectively maintained inequality: Education transitions, track mobility, and social background effects. *American Journal of Sociology, 106,* 1642–1690.

Mare, R. D. (1980). Social background and school continuation decisions. *Journal of the American Statistical Association, 75*(370), 295–305.

Mare, R. D. (1981). Change and stability in educational stratification. *American Sociological Review, 46*(1), 72–87.

Mare, R. D. (1995). Changes in educational attainment and school enrollment. In R. Farley (Ed.), *State of the union: America in the 1990s,* Vol. 1: *Economic trends* (pp. 155–213). New York: Russell Sage Foundation.

Meyer, J. W., Ramirez, F. O., Rubinson, R., & Boli-Bennett, J. (1977). The world educational revolution, 1950–1970. *Sociology of Education, 50*(4), 242–258.

Meyer, J. W., & Rubinson, R. (1975). Education and political development. *Review of Research in Education, 3,* 134–162.

Meyer, J. W., Tyack, D., Nagel, J., & Gordon, A. (1979). Public education as nation-building in America: Enrollments and bureaucratization in the American states, 1870–1930. *American Journal of Sociology, 85*(3), 591–613.

Müller, W., & Karle, W. (1993). Social selection in educational systems in Europe. *European Sociological Review, 9*(1), 1–23.

Nachmias, C. (1977). The status attainment process: A test of a model in two stratification systems. *Sociological Quarterly, 18,* 589–607.

Raftery, A. E., & Hout, M. (1993). Maximally maintained inequality: Expansion, reform, and opportunity in Irish education, 1921–75. *Sociology of Education, 66*(1), 41-62.

Sewell, W. H., & Hauser, R. M. (1980). The Wisconsin Longitudinal Study of social and psychological factors in aspirations and achievement. *Research in Sociology of Education and Socialization, 1,* 59–99.

Shavit, Y. (1993). From peasantry to proletariat: Changes in the educational stratification of Arabs in Israel. In Y. Shavit & H.-P. Blossfeld (Eds.), *Persistent inequality: Changing educational attainment in thirteen countries* (pp. 337–349). Boulder, CO: Westview Press.

Shavit, Y., & Blossfeld, H.-P. (1993). *Persistent inequality: Changing educational attainment in thirteen countries.* Boulder, CO: Westview Press.

Snyder, T. D., Dillow, S. A., & Hoffman, C. M. (2007). *Digest of education statistics, 2007.* Washington, DC: National Center for Education Statistics. Retrieved June 30, 2008, from http://www.nces.ed.gov/pubsearch

Snyder, T., & Hoffman, C. (2001). *Digest of education statistics, 2000.* Washington, DC: National Center for Education Statistics. Retrieved June 30, 2008, from http://www.nces.ed.gov/pubsearch

Tolsma, J., Coenders, M., & Lubbers, M. (2007). Trends in educational inequalities in the Netherlands: A cohort design. *European Sociological Review, 23*(3), 325–339.

Tomes, N. (1981). The family, inheritance, and the intergenerational transmission of inequality. *Journal of Political Economy, 89*(5), 928–958.

Treiman, D. J., & Yamaguchi, K. (1993). Trends in educational attainment in Japan. In Y. Shavit & H.-P. Blossfeld (Eds.), *Persistent inequality: Changing educational attainment in thirteen countries* (pp. 229–249). Boulder, CO: Westview Press.

Tsai, S.-L., & Chiu, H.-Y. (1993). Changes in educational stratification in Taiwan. In Y. Shavit & H.-P. Blossfeld (Eds.), *Persistent inequality: Changing educational attainment in thirteen countries* (pp. 193–227). Boulder, CO: Westview Press.

Wells, A. S., & Serna, I. (1996). The politics of culture: Understanding local political resistance to detracking in racially mixed schools. *Harvard Educational Review, 66,* 93–118.

Samuel R. Lucas

EMPLOYMENT, ADULTHOOD

Employment as a distinct sphere of life that entails significant training and expertise is unique to the modern world. When humans were hunters and gathers, work was not separated from leisure. People gathered or hunted food, made tools, cooked, relaxed, made shelters, and tended children in a fluid mix throughout the day. With the development of agriculture, work became more separate from leisure because tilling the fields required long and hard labor. Under classical empires such as the Mayan, Aztec, and Egyptian, many agriculturalists were enslaved and became subject peoples who worked as slaves or bonded laborers. Leisure was reduced to a minimum or disappeared. In contemporary societies, work, organized as paid employment, and leisure are highly distinct, with people working specific hours of the day and having leisure at home or in other settings different from the places where they work.

Work in modern society primarily takes the form of paid employment. Employment provides earnings that people use to buy the goods and services they once produced themselves, such as food and clothing. Modern society, however, provides a much richer set of goods and services than was available in earlier periods. An equally diverse set of industries and occupations produces those goods and services.

DEFINING EMPLOYMENT

Employment generally is defined as work that generates earnings: either pay or, in the case of someone who is self-employed, profit. This definition highlights the modern orientation toward work as a means to acquire money. The definition of employment as paid work also necessitates the concept of unpaid work. Many household activities, such as cooking, cleaning, and mowing the lawn, require significant effort. These tasks typically are performed as unpaid labor. However, they also can be hired out to a maid, a repair person, or a lawn service company. Most people work for earnings, do quite a bit of unpaid labor, and sometimes hire out activities that they cannot do because of limited time or lack of skills. By contrast, leisure is composed of activities that people do purely for pleasure. There is a gray area, however, between unpaid work and leisure. For a parent, child care often seems like work, but it is also one of life's pleasures. Preparing a meal can be both work and a leisure activity. Shopping is a necessity and therefore is unpaid labor, but some people shop for fun. There is thus a continuum— complete with gray areas between these concepts—from leisure (activities purely for fun) to unpaid work (the chores of life) to paid employment (work for earnings). This entry focuses solely on paid employment. It is useful, however, to bear these related categories of activity in mind to understand the place of employment in people's lives.

Not everyone who would like to have a job is employed. People who lack employment but are looking actively for a job are considered unemployed. The labor force is the sum of these two groups: the employed and the unemployed. The labor force is the pool of people currently at work or available for work. The commonly reported unemployment rate is the number of unemployed (active job seekers) divided by the total labor force.

EMPLOYMENT DEFINES PEOPLE

People's jobs define them in contemporary society. Gainful employment is a key marker of adult status. It allows financial independence and the establishment of one's own household. Someone who is financially dependent often is treated by others as less than a full member of society with equal status and rights. Employment is thus the key to adult status.

Employment also defines people's friendship networks. Early in life people's networks are defined by their families; later they are defined by their schoolmates. After people enter the world of employment, their networks quickly shift to their work associates. This process is often accelerated by a geographic move, as in the case of a college graduate who relocates to start his or her career. However, even if new labor force entrants stay near home, they may spend so much time at work that their colleagues on the job become their new families. Old friends may slip away as one finds new friends, often with similar interests, in one's field of work.

Employment also defines a person's place in society through the level of earnings generated. In general, those in well-paid jobs live in larger homes in more exclusive neighborhoods, take more frequent and exotic vacations, and are able to send their children to expensive schools and colleges. Those who have jobs with lower earnings rent apartments or live in homes in more modest neighborhoods, take fewer and more local vacations (e.g., to visit relatives), and may struggle to help their children through college. Even politics follows employment. Many well-paid persons find sound reasoning behind Republican calls for low taxes and support of business. Those who are less well paid find greater resonance in Democratic calls for educational support, improved social services, and full employment.

Perhaps even more than friends and politics, employment defines people's identity and gives meaning to their lives. The best hours of the day, five or more days a week, and the best years of people's lives are spent working. When people introduce themselves, they most frequently say something about their work, such as, "I work at company X." Work is a foundation for identity because people get meaning and purpose from their productive activity and because many jobs in the contemporary economy are engaging or even fascinating. Practicing the skills of a doctor, lawyer, engineer, teacher, or carpenter can be rewarding. Who is a person as an adult? Most fundamentally a person is his or her job. The only status with comparable power is one's family, but with fewer children and more frequent divorce, the battle for identity increasingly is won by career rather than by family.

Along with its greater importance in people's lives, employment can bring great pressures. To the extent that others define people by their employment, people are more vulnerable to problems at work. If a person loses a job, that person may lose his or her friends, social class

position, and economic security. In this context work-related problems can become major stressors in life. Fears of layoffs plague many people's lives. Bosses who bully their employees can make work unbearable; coworkers who gossip and slander can make it a nightmare.

THEORIES OF EMPLOYMENT

Sociology has long been concerned with employment and its discontents. Karl Marx wrote eloquently on the plight of the working classes in early industrial society and provided important theoretical tools for the study of exploitation, inequality, and alienation. Émile Durkheim examined the same issues, also with great empathy, but came to different conclusions. He interpreted contemporary problems as transitory, arising from an increasing division of labor and rapid change. Those changes did divide society into warring classes, but the tension would be overcome by the emergence of new norms and values that would provide safeguards against abuse and exploitation. The new norms and values would be hammered out in employer, trade, professional, and employee associations arising from the new and more complex division of labor.

Max Weber focused less on inequality and more on the fact that in modern society people increasingly work in large bureaucratic organizations. Before the 20th century most companies were relatively small, employing at most a few dozen workers. The advent of modern industrial society has meant not only the emergence of new class conflicts but also the emergence of the modern bureaucratic form of organizing work on the basis of written rules and formal criteria for hiring and promotion. Weber recognized the immense efficiencies emerging from such regularized procedures, especially relative to earlier forms of organization that were based on nepotism and cronyism. However, he also gave voice to those who experienced bureaucracy as stifling. Prior systems were inefficient and corrupt, but bureaucracy was rigid and ungainly. Weber feared that the efficiencies of bureaucracy would lead to its inevitable spread and the eventual universal dominance of bureaucratic procedures, with the attendant stifling of creativity and initiative. Workplace innovations that allow greater initiative among self-monitoring teams are the latest response to the rule-driven nature of modern work. Their limited success in reducing bureaucracy speaks to the potency of bureaucracy and people's continuing struggles to tame it.

Modern theories of work often are grounded explicitly or implicitly in the writings of Marx, Durkheim, and Weber. However, contemporary theories have added to those broad models of societal conflict and change in at least two major areas, both of which involve a more detailed examination of the employment experience.

Sociotechnical theories focus on social interactions at work, both those between bosses and workers and those among coworkers, and on the technical and physical conditions of work. These theories grew out of the observation that employees respond much better to encouragement and humane direction than to bullying. Because of their focus on workplace social relations, these theories sometimes are called human relations approaches.

A related set of theories grew out of the observation that the formal world of bureaucratic rules and shouting bosses is often only a small part of what constitutes the lived experience of work. Employees constantly maneuver, interpret, and respond to the formal employment situation and in so doing develop their own interpretations of work. This focus on the negotiated order of the workplace highlights the constantly negotiated and renegotiated nature of work life. Even more than the human relations approach, it recognizes the employee as an active coparticipant in the employment relationship.

METHODS OF STUDY

The methods by which contemporary sociologists learn about employment are as diverse as the topic and theories of employment. These methods can be grouped into three categories: surveys, ethnographies, and the use of archival data. All three methods rely heavily on empirical data and are thus part of the general movement in social sciences toward empiricism and away from broad social theories and philosophies.

Social surveys focus on individuals as respondents, most typically employees but also potentially managers or even chief executives. Given the chance, people love to talk about their work. Common survey themes include job satisfaction, autonomy at work, relations with management, coworker relations, job insecurity, stress, and burnout. Surveys are the major source of information about contemporary employment. In an effort to protect their interests or their self-respect, however, survey respondents are not always forthcoming about their experiences. At a minimum their responses to questions about work are filtered to be consistent with their broader sense of identity before being shared with an interviewer.

Accordingly, researchers sometimes seek more personal contact with employment situations rather than taking reports about work at face value. Such a type of contact can be obtained by shadowing a group of workers over time (nonparticipant observation) or by gaining employment in a workplace and experiencing its joys and burdens directly (participant observation). Such studies are called ethnographic accounts. Workplace ethnography is a significant genre of workplace studies and makes for interesting reading because of the details it provides about the dignity, tragedy, and humor that

pervade work life. A classic example is Alvin Gouldner's (1954) *Patterns of Industrial Bureaucracy.*

The third major approach to empirical studies of the workplace uses prerecorded or archival data. Employment records; government reports on occupations, enterprises, and industries; discrimination cases; and any other event or activity that leaves a recorded trace can supply data for these studies. Archival data are particularly useful for extending observations across a range of employment situations and a greater time span, avoiding the significant limits of survey and ethnographic methods. The information from such studies has been foundational for the study of employment trends, occupational growth and decline, globalization, the spread of technology, and other pressing employment issues of the 21st century.

EMPLOYMENT TRENDS

Two major forces drive both overall employment levels and the nature of employment in the 21st century: technology and globalization. Technological advances in recent decades built around the microprocessor and the attendant ability to collect and access information not only have created new high-technology industries but have revolutionized production across almost all industries, resulting in dramatic changes in employment. Sophisticated mechanical devices from previous waves of automation are driven by computer technologies that allow much more flexible applications. These technologies have displaced manufacturing workers, with manufacturing in the United States employing under 15% of the labor force in the first decade of the 21st century—reduced by almost half from its historical peak of 28% in 1960. Information technologies also have been applied to other industries, increasing efficiency by providing more precise information. For example, the driving routes of package delivery companies are arranged and plotted by computer at the beginning of the day. Packages are delivered quickly and precisely, but the efficiencies reduce the number of drivers needed and add to economy-wide downward pressures on employment.

Globalization contributes to these pressures through the outsourcing of lower-paid work to poorer nations. A car or computer in the early 21st century is made of components manufactured across many continents, assembled in one of them, and potentially sold in another. Companies search relentlessly for the cheapest labor, sometimes inadvertently finding that their quest undercuts the market for the goods they are producing because their own employees cannot afford those products.

As a result of the combined pressures of technology and globalization, employment in industrially advanced nations is relatively stagnant, particularly in middle-class and working-class jobs that face automation and outsourcing. Growth areas include professional occupations

Take Our Children to Work Day. *Dawn Sciabaras and her daughter Torie, 7, work on Dawn's computer during Sears' 'Take Our Children to Work Day' event at its world headquarters.* **AP IMAGES.**

such as law, medicine, and engineering and low-wage service work such as fast-food preparation, which cannot be outsourced. However, even fast food can be automated in vending machines. Downward pressures on middle- and working-class jobs in the industrialized nations have created an increasingly divided class structure of well-paid professional and managerial workers and poorly paid service workers chronically at risk of displacement by automation and globalization.

GLOBAL EMPLOYMENT

Americans dominate their hemisphere and have world military supremacy. The 20th century often is referred to as the American century. Futurists, however, are calling the 21st century the Asian century. Globalization thus poses a clear challenge to the era of American and perhaps even Western dominance.

European and North American industrialized nations are struggling with the problems of downward employment pressures for the working and middle classes and increasing inequality in society. However, they are man-

aging to stay even. Incomes are stagnant, at least in the aggregate, although they are increasingly unequal. The reason for this stagnation is that increasing productivity in these nations resulting from new technologies balances the downward pressures on incomes from automation and globalization. The result is stagnation that is seen as starting as far back as the 1970s.

The rest of the world is extremely diverse. Terms such as *less developed* belie this diversity. The least developed parts of the world, such as parts sub-Saharan Africa, basically play little or no role in the world economy. They cannot compete technologically with the European and North American nations or with developing nations such as China and India. The employment situation in such nations is dire, with unemployment rates of 50% or more in some cases. In contrast, the unemployment rate in the United States hovered around 6% in the first decade of the 21st century, whereas the Great Depression of the 1930s saw U.S. employment rates of 20% or more. Such situations are ripe for civil wars and conflicts, which are prevalent in many of the least developed nations.

In developing nations such as China and India the situation is different. Stable political situations with varying levels of democracy have provided a setting for economic growth and development. The jobs lost to outsourcing in the Western nations are reborn there, at wages that are lower than those in Europe and North America but are attractive to workers forced out of agricultural pursuits by increasing mechanization. The prospects for these nations are reasonably favorable. Earnings, at least in the aggregate, are rising, although poverty is still pervasive in many rural areas. It is easy for those in Europe and North America to think of workers in India and China as competitors who now have "their" jobs and to forget that they are paid substantially less for doing them than Westerners once were paid. It is unlikely, however, that these jobs will ever return to the West, and in the current global economy the fate and earnings of these workers are linked closely to those of people in the West. Their success in winning a bigger share of the economic pie may be a precondition for the stabilization of employment in the Western nations.

GENDER, RACE, AGE, AND EMPLOYMENT

In addition to the class inequalities arising from employment, jobs are differentiated by the groups that typically occupy them. Thus, women, members of racial and ethnic minorities, the young, and the elderly often face additional employment challenges that are changing rapidly, only sometimes for the better.

In recent decades women have experienced significant gains in employment, especially in the Western nations, and now have at least some representation across all occupations. These gains rest on federal legislation such as the Civil Rights Act of 1964, which made discrimination against women and minorities illegal. Somewhat ironically in light of the primary focus of the legislation on minorities, women have been the primary beneficiaries of this law. Women are distributed equally across the class structure, and many are able to attain college educations and take advantage of new employment opportunities. Women of poorer and working-class origins have been less advantaged by these opportunities because their class origins create barriers to securing the higher education credentials necessary for better-paid employment.

At least two fundamental challenges remain for women. First, women still have a very limited presence in engineering and related fields. Available cultural scripts for women do not support the occupational choice of engineering, and as a result few women enter these relatively well-paid professions. Second and more fundamental, cultural norms and business practices create serious hurdles to combining work and family. Job expectations,

especially in the professions and management, often involve open-ended commitments of 60 to 70 hours or more per week. Jobs of this sort allow little time for raising children. The most popular current solution is to delay childbearing. Society is in an important transition period between the breadwinner-and-housewife employment model and the two-earner model.

Ethnic minorities also have benefited from the increased opportunities afforded by antidiscrimination legislation. However, their gains have been more limited, leaving many behind. Many minority group members have not been in a position to take advantage of the new employment opportunities. Decades or even centuries of discrimination have produced stark inequalities of wealth and income. In combination with residential segregation, these inequalities mean that many members of minority groups attend poorly funded public schools and thus lack the background or finances necessary for success in college. Affirmative action programs intended to lower those barriers have provided educational and employment opportunities for many minority group members. The accumulated depth of poverty in many minority neighborhoods, however, remains a formidable barrier.

There also are age barriers to employment. In the United States the wide availability of bottom-rung jobs in retail and fast food means that young people often gain some employment experience, although the skills obtained may be minimal. In other Western nations more restrictive job markets often mean lengthy training and waiting periods for employment, resulting in high youth unemployment and careers that may not start until one's middle or late twenties.

Older people also face serious employment problems. Senior employees who are laid off, often because their earnings are high relative to those of younger coworkers, may have difficulty finding comparable employment and may end up underemployed in fast-food or retail service jobs. In other parts of the world these problem are even more serious. In China, for example, the generation of 50-year-olds often is called the unlucky generation. In their youth this generation experienced a violent civil war followed by the disruptions of the Cultural Revolution. By midlife they settled into what was destined to be a very brief period of stability, only to be turned out of their employment in state-owned enterprises as those companies downsized to become more market-oriented. Older workers in many nations are targeted during downturns and in reorganizations.

EMPLOYMENT POLICY

The most important current employment challenges are the promotion of full employment and the provision of living wages for all workers. Most employment policies involve tax subsidies to businesses or public provision of supporting infrastructure such as utilities and roads for business parks to encourage growth. Industry-specific policies also are used to incubate new industries and product lines that can be competitive in the global market. Japan and some other developing Asian nations have used such programs to break into world markets for automobiles, electronics, and steel.

Policies for living wages are always subjects of contention because businesses do not want to pay a living wage if they can hire workers for less and argue that they will be able to hire fewer workers if they have to pay them more. The empirical support for this position is mixed. Living wages for low-wage workers mean that they can spend more, thus producing more employment as a ripple effect.

Another challenge is to develop employment practices that are family-friendly. This can mean onsite day care or flexible hours. Fundamentally, it means fewer hours of paid work. Many contemporary jobs require too many hours of work to allow for family life, leaving children to be raised in after-school programs. The insight that shorter workdays could mean more employment is not lost on policy makers, as can be seen if one considers the consequences of breaking one 70 hour per week job into two 35 hour per week jobs. Many Western European nations have promoted reduced workweeks with this rationale. In the United States, where employment policy is left almost totally in the hands of employers, such policies have not been received warmly.

FUTURE DIRECTIONS FOR EMPLOYMENT RESEARCH

Future directions for employment research closely parallel the policy challenges noted above. Important topics include the success of competing strategies for dealing with job creation, employment discrimination, and work–family tensions. Multimethod approaches involving combinations of survey, observational, and archival data have emerged as important research strategies. When information from a variety of methods is triangulated, the limitations of any single method can be offset. Comparative research is growing in importance. In essence, the world is engaged in a massive experiment to develop effective responses to the employment challenges of the 21st century. Social science researchers thus have both a laboratory for their studies and an important role to play in identifying employment problems and developing effective policy options. The life course of adults has become more variable and uncertain as a result of the employment of the late 20th and early 21st century. New

and developing methods of study have the potential to provide important guidance for developing meaningful policies to assist people in finding new pathways to stable and productive lives during these times of dramatic and continuing change.

SEE ALSO Volume 1: *Maternal Employment;* Volume 2: *Careers; Economic Restructuring; Gender in the Workplace; Globalization; Income Inequality; Job Change; Job Characteristics and Job Stress; Leisure and Travel, Adulthood; Occupations; Policy, Employment; School to Work Transition.*

BIBLIOGRAPHY

Abbott, A. (1988). *The system of professions: An essay on the division of expert labor.* Chicago: University of Chicago Press.

Adler, W. M. (2000). *Mollie's job: A story of life and work on the global assembly line.* New York: Scribner.

Appelbaum, E., Bailey, T., Berg, P., & Kalleberg, A. L. (2000). *Manufacturing advantage: Why high-performance work systems pay off.* Ithaca, NY: Cornell University Press.

Barker, J. R. (1999). *The discipline of teamwork: Participation and concertive control.* Thousand Oaks, CA: Sage.

Bills, D. B. (2004). *The sociology of education and work.* Malden, MA: Blackwell.

Bluestone, B., & Harrison, B. (2000). *Growing prosperity: The battle for growth with equity in the twenty-first century.* Boston: Houghton Mifflin.

Fine, G. A. (1996). *Kitchens: The culture of restaurant work.* Berkeley: University of California Press.

Gouldner, Alvin W. (1954). *Patterns of Industrial Bureaucracy.* New York: Free Press.

Hodson, R. (2001). *Dignity at work.* Cambridge, U.K.: Cambridge University Press.

Hodson, R., & Sullivan, T. A. (2008). *The social organization of work.* (4th ed.). Belmont, CA: Wadsworth.

Jackall, R. (1988). *Moral mazes: The world of corporate managers.* New York: Oxford University Press.

Kalleberg, A. L. (2006). *The mismatched worker.* New York: Norton.

Lee, C. K. (1998). *Gender and the south China miracle: Two worlds of factory women.* Berkeley: University of California Press.

Lopez, S. H. (2004). *Reorganizing the rust belt.* Berkeley: University of California Press.

Rinehart, J., Huxley, C., & Robertson, D. (1997). *Just another car factory? Lean production and its discontents.* Ithaca, NY: ILR Press.

Romero, M. (1992). *Maid in the U.S.A.* New York: Routledge.

Smith, V. (2001). *Crossing the great divide: Worker risk and opportunity in the new economy.* Ithaca, NY: ILR Press.

Sullivan, T. A., Warren, E., & Westbrook, J. L. (2000). *The fragile middle class: Americans in debt.* New Haven, CT: Yale University Press.

Tilly, C. (1996). *Half a job: Bad and good part-time jobs in a changing labor market.* Philadelphia: Temple University Press.

Randy Hodson

EMPLOYMENT PATTERNS AND TRENDS

SEE Volume 2: *Employment, Adulthood; Flexible Work Arrangements; Gender in the Workplace; Job Change.*

EMPTY NEST

SEE Volume 2: *Midlife Crises and Transitions.*

ETHNIC AND RACIAL IDENTITY

What does the term *racial and ethnic identity* mean? Briefly, when something is an identity, it is a part of self-concept. When something is part of self-concept, it influences how people make sense of themselves, what their goals are and how they try to achieve them, as well as the interpretations they give to others' responses to them. Racial and ethnic identity includes three basic components: (a) membership—knowledge that one is a member of particular racial and ethnic groups; (b) beliefs—beliefs about how the groups one is a member of fit into broader society and how members of these groups act, what they believe in, what their goals and values are, and the strategies they use to attain these goals; (c) action readiness—readiness to act in ways that are congruent with beliefs about group membership.

Race and ethnicity can be distinguished in theory: Racial categorization is often associated with beliefs about common physical characteristics that are thought to distinguish groups; these beliefs are often associated with power structures within a society. In contrast, ethnic categorization is often associated with assumed immigration histories and beliefs about shared nationality, history, language, and traditions. However, for a number of reasons, it may not be useful in practice to distinguish them. First, race and ethnicity are both social constructs, that is, their meaning is based on socially agreed-on categorizations, rather than on biologically meaningful categorizations. Second, both involve "imagined communities," groups with which one feels a sense of common fate or allegiance and a sense of common ancestry or kinship, whether or not one personally knows many group members. Third, in modern societies race and ethnicity intermingle. Therefore, this entry discusses

racial-ethnic identities rather than attempting to separate the two concepts artificially.

Race and ethnicity are not always part of self-concept, but they often are because race and ethnicity carry social meaning and therefore are useful in making sense of oneself and one's experiences with others. As noted in the three-part operationalization of racial-ethnic identity, racial-ethnic identity includes more than simple knowledge of group membership, it includes both beliefs about one's group and readiness to take action congruent with these beliefs (see three-part operationalization, above). In this way, people's life courses will in part reflect their racial-ethnic identities.

SELF-CONCEPT AND IDENTITY

The self is a basic cognitive structure; distinguishing self from non-self is an early developmental milestone. Self-concept is a theory about oneself, what one thinks about when one thinks about oneself; the self is experienced as content (who one was, is, and may become, how one fits in); and process (what one's goals are, what one is trying to do). The three basic self-processes are self-protection, self-improvement, and self-maintenance. Self-protection is involved when one's goal is to feel as good about oneself as possible given circumstances. Self-improvement is involved when one's goal is to critically focus on one's limitations in order to make changes for the better. Self-maintenance is involved when one's goal is to provide a stable anchor of self-knowledge from which to make predictions about self and others. A person's self-concept is involved in both intrapersonal processes (e.g., memory, motivation, and self-regulation) and interpersonal processes (e.g., interpretation of social contextual cues, reactions to feedback, relational style).

The idea of self-concept originates in the early theorizing of psychologist William James (1890). Within sociology, the term *identity* is more commonly used. However, modern usage of both terms overlaps in that individuals are assumed to define themselves with a multiplicity of self-descriptions. Thus, self-concept and identity are now seen as multidimensional, multifaceted, and dynamic structures, rooted in and sensitive to social contexts. For clarity, in this entry we operationalize the self-concept as containing diverse, potentially conflicting personal and social identities and self-schemas (cognitive generalizations about the self derived from past experience). Identities can encompass personal traits, feelings, images, and knowledge about the self as well as social memberships, social roles, and social statuses. Some of these identities are more central or "salient" to one's self-concept, while others are less central.

Irish Step Dancers. *Irish step dancers performing in a St. Patrick's Day parade.* © BLAINE HARRINGTON III/CORBIS.

RESEARCH ON RACIAL-ETHNIC IDENTITY

Theoretical development and empirical assessment of racial-ethnic identity draws on social identity theory. According to this perspective, social identities are the parts of self-concept derived from group memberships and adherence to group values (Tajfel, 1981). Social identities include at least three parts: information about group membership (that one is a member of one group and not of another), information about the nature of group boundaries (how permeable is membership, can one quit the group, how do others view one's group), and information about what it means to be a group member (including the norms, values, goals, and attitudes of one's group). From this perspective, racial-ethnic identities may influence behavior by providing information about group norms and expectations and by shaping a person's interpretation of social and contextual feedback (Oyserman, 2007). Perceived group norms can be positive. For example, Oyserman, Gant, and Ager (1995) found that when reminded of their racial-ethnic identity, African American students persisted more at math tasks if they believed that doing well in school was an in-group expectation. Per-

ceived group norms are not always positive though. For example, Oyserman, Fryberg, and Yoder (2007) found that middle school, college-aged, and adult participants were less likely to believe that engaging in a healthy lifestyle is beneficial to one's health if they were reminded of their racial-ethnic identity and believed that people in their in-group did not engage in these behaviors.

Follow-up research suggests that among adult currently smoking African American women, smoking is more likely to be perceived as racial-ethnic identity congruent than it is among non-smokers. That is, smokers are more likely to believe that smoking was in-group normative, something that African Americans commonly do.

Social interactions are central in shaping both personal and social identities, including racial and ethnic identities (e.g., Turner, Oakes, Haslam, & McGarty, 1994). Most generally, who one is in the moment is defined in part by how one's interaction partner makes sense of oneself. In some sense, people have as many versions of themselves as they have interaction partners because different partners facilitate, encourage, and provide role models for different ways of being a self. Although active exploration of one's identity is considered a primary developmental task during adolescence and young adulthood, self-concept and identity are not simply formed at this time and stable thereafter. Rather racial, ethnic, gender, and social class identities begin to develop in early childhood, and changes in social contexts influence identities throughout the lifespan (Demo, 1992). Whether race and ethnicity are part of identity and what this entails is likely to shift as well.

Early research on racial-ethnic identity focused on its content and possible implications for self-esteem (Clark & Clark, 1947; Proshansky & Newton, 1968). In the United States and elsewhere, this line of research focused on historically stigmatized groups (in the United States, African Americans and Jewish Americans). Researchers assumed that the experience of racism, hatred, or disdain from others toward one's racial-ethnic group would be internalized and result in self-hatred and self-disdain (Grambs, 1965; Nobles, 1973). However, the data did not support this idea, so conceptual and empirical models were refined to distinguish a sense of in-group (that is, persons sharing one's social group) worth and knowledge about out-group (that is, persons belonging to other social groups) responses (Cross, 1991). These newer models emphasized the importance of feedback from close, supportive in-group others (e.g., family, kin networks) for feelings of worth, as separate from racial-awareness, which focused on the negative attitudes and beliefs of out-group members (Gray-Little & Hafdahl, 2000; Phinney, 1996). As would be predicted by social identity theories, researchers demonstrated that a positive sense of self-worth was associated with feelings of in-group connection or pride. After the resolution of this conceptual debate, researchers developed new lines of inquiry, focused on identifying consequences of the content and structure of racial-ethnic identity for action, mood, and cognitive processes more generally.

Some evidence suggests that content of racial-ethnic identity matters in that how one describes one's racial-ethnic identity predicts behavior over time. In particular, how the connection between in-group membership and membership in broader society is described seems to influence how much individuals engage in the institutions of broader society. In terms of academic outcomes, teens who describe themselves only in terms of in-group memberships (e.g., American Indian, Black, Latino) were less likely to persist in academic tasks than teens who both described themselves in terms of in-group memberships and saw in-group members as integral members of broader American society, not as separate from broader American society (Oyserman, Kemmelmeier, Fryberg, Brosh, & Hart-Johnson, 2003). Similarly, in terms of health outcomes, women who described themselves as African American were more likely to obtain a mammography than women who described themselves as Black

(Bowen, Christensen, Powers, Graves, & Anderson, 1998). In each case, it seems to be that identity terms convey beliefs about how much the in-group fits into broader society.

Research examining the content of racial-ethnic identities has shown that not all persons incorporate race-ethnicity into their identity (Oyserman et al., 2003). For some individuals, membership in a racial-ethnic group is simply a social fact about oneself, something that may be true but is not self-defining. However, in societies in which race-ethnicity is used by others to make predictions about what one is like and one's skills and abilities, not including race-ethnicity in identity is likely to leave one open to the negative psychological consequences of negative stereotypes. Race-ethnicity is likely to be incorporated into one's self-concept when it feels meaningful—when race-ethnicity has an impact on how in- and out-group others respond to oneself. Like other social identities, racial-ethnic identities are multidimensional; that is, one knows many things about oneself as a group member, not all of which are salient at any moment in time. Moreover, like other aspects of self-concept, racial-ethnic identities can contain competing or conflicting information. Which aspects of racial-ethnic identity are salient and influential at any moment in time will depend on social contextual cues. For example, in academic contexts, content and identity-relevant questions focused on academics (do "we" do well in school?) are likely to come to mind.

Research on racial-ethnic identities explores the ways that such identities affect well-being, motivation, goal pursuit, and behavior. Of particular interest are dimensions of identity including sense of connection to in-group, beliefs about the relationship between in-group and broader society, and beliefs about the goals, activities, and strategies effectively used by in-group members (Oyserman, 2007, in press). Sense of connectedness to the group focuses on the extent to which individuals perceive in-group membership to be central to their self-concept. Identities that are not central are less likely to be activated so are less likely to have an impact on behavior. Beliefs about the relationship between in-group and broader society are sometimes described in terms of the perceived boundaries between in-group and other groups and awareness of the attitudes of others toward one's racial or ethnic group. Knowing how others view one's in-group can provide important information about likely responses of others to oneself. More broadly, this dimension involves perceptions about the connections (or lack thereof) between in-group and broader society. The third dimension of racial-ethnic identity focuses on beliefs about in-group goals, attitudes, norms, values, and strategies. These beliefs are not necessarily accurate, but because they provide standards that are assumed to be accurate and self-relevant, they are likely to influence one's own goals, attitudes, norms, values, and strategies. These beliefs can have powerful effects. For example, if one believes that people from one's own racial-ethnic group gain weight in middle age, one's own heavy future will feel inevitable, and, because effort to lose weight is assumed to be futile, individuals are less likely to expend effort to do so.

Once the in-group is a salient part of identity, then the other two dimensions of identity—being able to gauge how others may respond to the in-group and what in-group members are like—are more likely to shape individual behavior, perception, and motivation. Researchers differ in which of these dimensions they focus on, and individuals are likely to differ in the extent that each of these dimensions is a focus of identity (Cross, 1991; Jenkins, 1982; Sellers, Smith, Shelton, Rowley, & Chavous, 1998). When in-group membership is made situationally salient (e.g., being the only African American at a work conference), both similarity to the in-group (e.g., other African Americans) and the related meanings associated with that group identity will become prominent (Haslam, O'Brien, & Jetten, 2005; Sidanius, Van Laar, & Levin, 2004). Effects are also likely to be linked to salience of one's group in a location, profession, or social institution.

Because most research on racial-ethnic identity has focused on stigmatized groups, an important question is the extent that racial-ethnic identity predicts success across important life domains. Thus, researchers have asked about the relationship between content and structure of racial-ethnic identity and academic success in the adolescent and college years. Oyserman (in press) finds that effect of racial-ethnic identity depends on content. Simply feeling connected to in-group or being aware of racism are not sufficient to improve academic effort and outcomes; rather it is necessary to also believe that in-group members value and engage in effort to do well in school. With regard to engagement healthy lifestyle behaviors in the college years and beyond, Oyserman and colleagues (2007) find that when comparison between in-group and broader society is made salient, minority group members are less likely to believe in the efficacy of preventive health measures such as exercising as an adult if they believe that members of their group do not engage in them (or think that members of their in-group engage in risky health behaviors such as smoking cigarettes). Although research often focuses on a particular group, making sense of commonalities in impact of racial-ethnic identities across groups is beginning to be the focus of more research attention.

FUTURE DIRECTIONS AND GAPS IN THE CURRENT LITERATURE

Literature on racial-ethnic identity has focused primarily on childhood, adolescence, and the early years of adulthood. Thus a major limitation of the research literature is the lack of attention to when and how racial-ethnic identity should matter beyond the college years. Although the previously described research gives some sense that racial-ethnic identity is likely to matter for engagement in health and health care, more needs to be done to conceptualize how racial-ethnic identity should matter to health and other aspects of adult life and to document effects over time and in real-world situations.

IMPLICATIONS FOR POLICY

Research on racial-ethnic identity provides several implications for program development and public policy. First, this research suggests that programs and policies should highlight belongingness and connections between broader society and members of diverse racial-ethnic groups. That is, important social goals and values—including healthy lifestyle and civic engagement, education and career advancement, and effective strategies for obtaining these goals—should feel relevant to all racial-ethnic groups within a society. Second, to the extent that identities continue to be shaped over the lifespan, resources for engagement should be tailored across developmental phases. Globalization and international migration mean that societies across the world, including the United States, are becoming more diverse. Americans now reaching retirement face both the challenges of aging and the challenge of remaining engaged in an increasingly racially and ethnically diverse world.

SEE ALSO Volume 1: *Biracial Youth/Mixed Race Youth; Identity Development; Immigration, Childhood and Adolescence;* Volume 2: *Racism/Race Discrimination.*

BIBLIOGRAPHY

Bowen, D. J., Christensen, C. L., Powers, D., Graves, D. R., & Anderson, C. A. M. (1998). Effects of counseling and ethnic identity on perceived risk and cancer worry in African American women. *Journal of Clinical Psychology in Medical Settings, 5,* 365–379.

Clark, K. B., & Clark, M. P. (1947). Racial identification and preferences in Negro children. In T. M. Newcomb & E. L. Hartley (Eds.), *Readings in social psychology* (pp. 169–178). New York: Holt.

Cross, W. E. (1991). *Shades of black: Diversity in African American identity.* Philadelphia: Temple University Press.

Demo, D. H. (1992). The self-concept over time: Research issues and directions. *Annual Review of Sociology, 18,* 303–326.

Grambs, J. D. (1965). The self-concept: Basis for reeducation of Negro youth. In W. C. Kvaraceus, J. S. Gibson, F. K. Patterson, B. Seasholes, & J. D. Grambs (Eds.), *Negro self-concept: Implications for school and citizenship* (pp. 11–51). New York: McGraw-Hill.

Gray-Little, B., & Hafdahl, A. R. (2000). Factors influencing racial comparisons of self-esteem: A quantitative review. *Psychological Bulletin, 126,* 26–54.

Harter, S. (1992). Visions of self: Beyond the me in the mirror. In J. E. Jacobs (Ed.), *Nebraska Symposium on Motivation; Vol. 40: Developmental perspectives on motivation* (pp. 99–144).Lincoln: University of Nebraska Press.

Haslam, S. A., O'Brien, A., Jetten, J., Vormedal, K., & Penna, S. (2005). Taking the strain: Social identity, social support, and the experience of stress. *The British Journal of Social Psychology, 44,* 355–370.

James, W. (1890). *The principles of psychology* (2 vols.). New York: Holt.

Jenkins, A. H. (1982). *The psychology of the Afro-American: A humanistic approach.* New York: Pergamon Press.

Nobles, W. W. (1973). Psychological research and the black self-concept: A critical review. *Journal of Social Issues, 29,* 11–31.

Oyserman, D. (2007). Social identity and self-regulation. In A. W. Kruglanski & E. T. Higgins (Eds.), *Social psychology: Handbook of basic principles* (2nd ed., pp. 432–453). New York: Guilford Press.

Oyserman, D. (in press). Racial-ethnic self-schemas: Multidimensional identity-based motivation. *Journal of Research in Personality.*

Oyserman, D., Fryberg, S., & Yoder, N. (2007). Identity-based motivation and health. *Journal of Personality and Social Psychology, 93,* 1011–1027.

Oyserman, D., Gant, L., & Ager, J. (1995). A socially contextualized model of African American identity: Possible selves and school persistence. *Journal of Personality and Social Psychology, 69,* 1216–1232.

Oyserman, D., & Harrison, K. (1998). Implications of cultural context: African American identity and possible selves. In J. K. Swim & C. Stangor (Eds.), *Prejudice: The target's perspective* (pp. 281–300). San Diego, CA: Academic Press.

Oyserman, D., Kemmelmeier, M., Fryberg, S., Brosh, H., & Hart-Johnson, T. (2003). Racial-ethnic self-schemas. *Social Psychology Quarterly, 66,* 333–347.

Phan, T., & Tylka, T. L. (2006). Exploring a model and moderators of disordered eating with Asian American college women. *Journal of Counseling Psychology, 53,* 36–47.

Phinney, J. S. (1996). When we talk about American ethnic groups, what do we mean? *American Psychologist, 51,* 918–927.

Proshansky, H., & Newton, P. (1968). The nature and meaning of Negro self-identity. In M. Deutsch, I. Katz, & A. R. Jensen (Eds.), *Social class, race, and psychological development* (pp. 178–218). New York: Holt, Rinehart and Winston.

Sellers, R. M., Smith, M. A., Shelton, J. N., Rowley, S. A. J., & Chavous, T. M. (1998). Multidimensional model of racial identity: A reconceptualization of African American racial identity. *Personality and Social Psychology Review, 2,* 18–39.

Sidanius, J., Van Laar, C., Levin, S., & Sinclair, S. (2004). Ethnic enclaves and the dynamics of social identity on the college campus: The good, the bad, and the ugly. *Journal of Personality and Social Psychology, 87,* 96–110.

Tajfel, H. (1981). *Human groups and social categories: Studies in social psychology.* Cambridge, U.K.: Cambridge University Press.

Turner, J. C., Oakes, P. J., Haslam, S. A., & McGarty, C. (1994). Self and collective: Cognition and social context. *Personality and Social Psychology Bulletin, 20,* 454–463.

Daphna Oyserman
Diane Oliver

F

FAMILY PLANNING

SEE Volume 2: *Birth Control.*

FAMILY AND HOUSEHOLD STRUCTURE, ADULTHOOD

Everyone has or at least had a family, and people live most of their lives in households, but the terms are complexly interrelated, in some ways very similar and in others very different. *Families* are people related by blood, marriage, or adoption; *households* are people who live together in a separate housing unit, defined by various criteria of use and privacy (and hence excluding group quarters such as hotels, college dormitories, and military barracks). Because so many close family relationships are contained within a single household, however, the two concepts are sometimes confused. Most households are still family households, that is, they include people who are related to each other, which reinforces their connection. Many other households, however, are nonfamily households, consisting of either one person or unrelated persons, such as roommates. Further, many family relationships transcend households, particularly those between generations (e.g., between parents and their adult children after they leave home). Hence these terms are related, although distinct, constructs.

HOW CHANGING LIVING ARRANGEMENTS SHAPE FAMILIES AND HOUSEHOLDS

Both families and households changed rapidly, both in size and in composition, in the post–World War II (after 1945) period. In some ways, their changes are closely parallel. When parents have many children, households are large; when they have few children, households are small. This seems obvious, but it depends on a related concept, that of *living arrangements*. Changes in family and household size move together in response to changes in the numbers of children because in nearly every society, the vast majority of minor children live with their parents. A decline in birth rates immediately leads to smaller average household size. But for family relationships other than those of parents and young children, living arrangements can differ substantially, and hence, family changes can have very different effects on households. Further, as is discussed later, declines in fertility in the longer run have even stronger effects on reducing household size than does the immediate reduction in the number of children in households.

Consider a relatively recent change in living arrangements—the increase in independent living among unmarried persons. As recently as the period between 1940 and 1960, in the United States the increase in marriage rates among young adults meant that rates of household formation increased. By the 1970s, however, the increases in the divorce rates also meant that household formation increased. The conundrum is resolved by realizing that in the earlier period, the majority of unmarried adults (including the previously married) lived either with their parents, other relatives, or nonrelatives; by 1970 a

133

majority lived in independent households, often alone (Kobrin, 1976b, p. 237). Marriage was the usual route to residential independence in a separate household until 1970; since that time it has become normal for the unmarried to live independently.

Living arrangements, or who lives with whom, given the choice, are hence an important factor affecting the relationship between the numbers and structure of families and households. The rise of independent living among the unmarried has reduced household *extension* (another term that indicates whether a family household contains relatives other than a couple and their children) and increased the number of households. The people who used to live together in a single household are now spread across a greater number of households.

WHY LIVING ARRANGEMENTS MATTER

Most research on the family pays relatively little attention to living arrangements. Studies of the likelihood of marriage are often vague about where the unmarried live before they marry or if they do not marry. Some researchers studying marriage patterns among women interpret their results as if the contrast were between getting married and remaining with parents (Michael & Tuma, 1985). By contrast, others interpret their findings to suggest that unmarried women are enjoying new opportunities of independent adulthood (Becker, 1991). Those studying men normally do not comment on alternative living arrangements to marriage at all (Hogan, 1981).

Similarly, studies of the consequences of widowhood rarely consider whether the widow(er) has remained independent or gone to live with relatives, normally children. The major change in living arrangements that has gained the attention of family scholars is more closely tied to central family processes: the rise in cohabitation. The question of whether or not it is a "family process" has received considerable attention. For example, is cohabitation an alternative to marriage with many marriage-like qualities, such as joint children? Or is it perhaps a prelude to marriage, a testing of compatibility? Or is it not a family process at all but only an economic arrangement to share living expenses, like roommates, but, as they say, "with benefits"? Or does it mean different things in different countries or at different stages of the life course (e.g., before and after divorce)? The jury is still out on this recent and dramatic change in the living arrangements of the unmarried.

Even beyond cohabitation, however, living arrangements matter a great deal. Clearly they are not the only factor shaping relationships, which can remain warm and supportive, sometimes even warmer, between those not living together. Also, as cohabiting couples normally dis-

cover, their lives change when they marry, even if they remain in the same home, because the institutionalization of marriage and the expectations of others, as well as their own expectations, reshape how they relate to each other. Nevertheless, living in the same household with another person has a major impact on any relationship, affecting as it does the sharing of space and tasks, gaining companionship, and losing privacy.

Household Tasks A historical perspective is important here, as not so long ago agriculture dominated most of the world's economies and the household was the center of economic production. Even in North America and the industrialized countries of western Europe, a majority of households were agricultural as recently as the beginning of the 20th century, and this state lasted even longer in the more recently industrialized countries of southern and eastern Europe, Asia, and Latin America. Married couples depended on each other's productive activities and no less on those of their children.

Although much work has left the household with the growth of the industrial and service economy, the need for other important activities persists. Even in the early 21st century, when fully independent adults decide to live together, whether for practical or romantic reasons, there are many productive activities that take place in households. Except for the very few households that can pay servants or fully outsource, there is food to be bought, prepared, and the results cleaned up; clothes to be washed and mended; and rooms to be straightened and cleaned or even sanitized, depending on the room. The benefits of shared finances still entail organizing bill-paying and account-monitoring, whereas the benefits of a shared social life still entail planning, gift-buying, and maintaining contact.

Further, the amount of work increases dramatically when the household includes dependents, such as small children or disabled adults. As noted earlier, no one questions that infants should live with parents or parent-like adults. Research on child development suggests that there are limits on the number of hours infant care that can be outsourced to institutions without there being at least some negative impact on the child (Belsky, 2001), with perhaps coresident or non-coresident nannies excepted. In addition, the demands of providing care for the elderly or disabled at home are also enormous.

Deciding who cooks, shops, does the dishes, and cleans is often a major problem for adults sharing a home, and the needs of dependent children and adults require deciding who does even more tasks. Living together does, indeed, matter. Some scholars, such as Thomas Burch and Beverly Mathews (1987), have suggested that all people would be happiest if they lived alone, coming together to share social events and occasional one-on-one time. What motivates this approach to living arrangements is that even if all tasks (including meeting all dependents' needs) could be outsourced, there is still the matter of privacy, which for some, trumps companionship.

Privacy and Companionship Living with others undoubtedly reduces privacy. For those in a dependent position—adolescents vis-à-vis their parents, for example—living at home means that parents can monitor closely who their friends are, how they spend their time, and how they are feeling. This is much less of a problem for those in the less dependent position, in this case the parents, because the adolescent's knowledge of their behavior provides much less leverage (except perhaps for telling the neighbors about extreme or embarrassing behaviors or authorities about abuse); adolescents rarely have much power over their parents.

So the power differential matters. For such hierarchal relationships—whether for (near) adult children vis-à-vis their parents, the retired and perhaps disabled elderly vis-à-vis their employed midlife children, or even housewives vis-à-vis their provider husbands—having additional resources often allows the more dependent member to establish an independent residence, gaining privacy and autonomy. For the more powerful members, gains in resources simply allow them to continue to enjoy companionship and services with no loss of privacy and even more relative power. For trusting, equal relationships, however, the reduction in privacy linked with coresidence is much less of a problem. This is why many choose companionship, despite their having enough resources to live alone.

HOW CHANGING DEMOGRAPHIC AVAILABILITY SHAPES FAMILIES AND HOUSEHOLDS

It is not always possible, however, to coreside with preferred others. An important consideration that limits who lives with whom is whether or not the person knows anyone who would be a compatible living partner. Some situations impair the formation of families, such as when there are too few young adults of a given gender relative to the numbers of their potential romantic partners. This normally occurs in situations of extensive sex-selective migration, such as when the movement of men to North America in the 19th century left many unmarried women behind, although the development of sex-selective abortion is also creating marriage market imbalances in societies with strong son preference, such as China. Large imbalances are rare, however, although even small imbalances are likely to have an effect. The marriage markets (or the pool of eligible potential spouses) for educated women, and particularly educated Black women, have narrowed (Tucker & Mitchell-Kernan, 1995).

Another change in availability, one that is the result of the demographic transition from high to low mortality and fertility, has had a more massive effect, this time on intergenerational living arrangements, sharply reducing household size. A major factor behind the increase in independent living arrangements among the unmarried—typically widowed—elderly is the result of a shift in the relative sizes of the generations: the number of children who are available for them to live with and the number of younger families who have elderly relatives available to live with them. This shift has confused analysts for a long time, particularly those studying family extension, and attaining a better understanding of it has come with difficulty (Kobrin, 1976a).

Declines in fertility and mortality, which on average have lengthened lives and reduced the number of children families have, have also reshaped generational relationships because of their effects on the relative sizes of the generations. When fertility was high, even though mortality was also high, populations were dominated by young people, both children and their relatively young parents, with few elderly. This meant that nearly all elderly persons could live with one of their children, but relatively few families would be extended by including a grandparent—there were simply too few elderly relatives to go around, and they did not live very long. In any cross-sectional count of families, very few would be extended.

Once fertility declined to approximately two children per couple, however, an increasing proportion of elderly began to have no children or grandchildren at all. Even among those who do have children, for all widows and widowers to live with a child would mean that as many as half of all families with children would experience family extension, and given the increase in longevity, this extension could last for many years. Scholars who studied trends in the proportion of families with elderly relatives living with them saw fairly stable, low levels of family extension (Laslett, 1972). Because they did not study those who did not live in families, they did not notice, as did those who studied living arrangements, that the proportion of widowed elderly living alone was skyrocketing and hence the proportion living with their adult children was falling rapidly. In the United States this revolution in the living arrangements of the elderly took place in the early 1940s. The elderly during this period had borne their children in an era of relatively high fertility in the last years of the 19th century and the early years of the 20th century. Later in the 20th century, however, the majority of elderly were the parents of relatively few children as a result of the fertility declines that followed (and even the baby boom of the 1950s did not produce large families, mostly just very young families). The ratio of middle-age to widowed elderly women (the daughter-mother ratio) had decreased sharply, from 2.7 in 1930 to 1.2 in 1973, with much slower declines

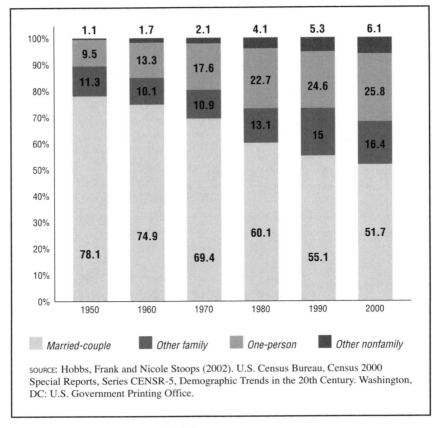

Figure 1. Distribution of households by type, 1950-2000. CENGAGE LEARNING, GALE.

before and since (Kobrin, 1976a). Similar rapid declines occurred in Europe (Wolf, 1995).

ETHNICITY, FAMILIES, AND HOUSEHOLDS

A particularly interesting phenomenon in the decline in household and family size in the United States is that racial and ethnic minorities, and particularly African Americans, have contributed much less to the decline than Whites. There has been an ethnic crossover in household size and structure. Prior to the rapid overall decline in household size that began in the 1940s, Black families had been less likely to include extended family members, and young Black adults had left home younger (and married earlier) than otherwise comparable Whites. By about 1970, these differences had reversed (Goldscheider & Bures, 2003). The growth in living alone was much less marked among African Americans.

Finding answers as to why the growth was less marked is a major challenge for understanding ethnic differences in family and household change in the United States. The much later move out of agriculture (in the South) and the move into the high-rent inner cities, which matched economic opportunities only for a short while in the years immediately after World War II, has meant that young African American adults have experienced extraordinarily high rates of unemployment, so that living with other family members appears to provide a financial safety net for those who need it. However, given that poverty was at least as great in rural areas, a full understanding of these ethnic differences in living arrangement trends remains elusive. Some scholars argue that higher levels of coresidence among African Americans are due to stronger kin obligations and relationships among African Americans than among Whites, but this cultural explanation has not been fully tested and in any case does not explain why extended families were less common among African Americans prior to the racial crossover.

CONSEQUENCES OF FAMILY AND HOUSEHOLD CHANGE

An additional focus of current concern about family change is the consequences for children of experiencing alternative parental structures, whether cohabiting parents, stepparents, or single parents. This is an important concern; however, there are several other issues regarding living arrangements that are underresearched—these include the consequences for families of the strengthened privacy preferences that have emerged with the growth in nonfamily living as well as the consequences for the environment of the more rapid growth in the numbers of households, despite slowing population growth.

Scholars studying the growth in separate living arrangements tend to celebrate it, reflecting the idea that privacy is, in economists' terms, a *normal good* or one that is consumed more as income rises. Journalists write with horror of the growth in living with or returning to live with parents among young adults (Gross, 1991). The values of companionship, and of helping out family members in need, are much less celebrated. The assumption is that these will take care of themselves.

There is evidence, however, that this is not the case. People who had the experience of having a grandparent living with their childhood family were considerably more positive about the phenomenon, so that as this experience becomes rarer, the need for outsourcing care in old age may grow. Further, women (but not men) who lived independently of family in young adulthood were less supportive of providing housing room for young adults who were struggling economically (Goldscheider & Lawton, 1998), reducing young adults' opportunity to leave an inappropriate job or relationship by returning to their parents' home.

In another study, women who had lived independently in young adulthood were considerably less approving of traditional marriage (Goldscheider & Waite, 1991). This finding should put pressure on marriage-minded young men to become more egalitarian as well. However, the alternative of nonfamily living means that the pressures for change that emerge within a loving relationship are not brought to bear on gender relationships.

Hence, the growth in the need for privacy and the reduction in willingness to use the family as an economic safety net for semidependent adults (early and late in adulthood) means that the new phenomenon of nonfamily living may have become a very expensive innovation. It is proving expensive on another dimension, as well—its impact on the environment. Coresidence leads to economies of scale; more households means that more furniture and appliances must be produced and electrified and more public rooms (the shared kitchens, bathrooms, living rooms, and dining rooms) must be heated. These costs of separate living are not trivial. The fall in household size has important implications for both families and the global environment.

SEE ALSO Volume 2: *Cohabitation; Divorce and Separation; Dual Career Couples; Marriage;* *Remarriage;* Volume 3: *Demographic Transition Theories; Singlehood; Widowhood.*

BIBLIOGRAPHY

Attané, I. (2006). The demographic impact of a female deficit in China, 2000–2050. *Population and Development Review, 32*(4), 755–770.

Becker, G. (1991). *A treatise on the family.* Cambridge, MA: Harvard University Press.

Belsky, J. (2001). Developmental risks (still) associated with early child care. *Journal of Child Psychology and Psychiatry, 42*(7), 845–859.

Burch, T., & Mathews, B. (1987). Household formation in developed societies. *Population and Development Review, 13*(3), 495–512.

Cherlin, A. (1992). *Marriage, divorce, remarriage.* (Rev. ed.). Cambridge, MA: Harvard University Press.

Goldscheider, F., & Bures, R. (2003). The racial crossover in family complexity in the United States. *Demography, 40*(3), 569–587.

Goldscheider, F., & Lawton, L. (1998). Family experiences and the erosion of support for intergenerational coresidence. *Journal of Marriage and the Family, 60*(3), 623–632.

Goldscheider, F., & Waite, L. (1991). *New families, no families? The transformation of the American home.* Berkeley: University of California Press.

Gross, J. (1991, June 16). More young single men hang onto apron strings: Recession and pampering keep sons at home. *The New York Times, 140,* 1, 18.

Guttentag, M., & Secord, P. (1983). *Too many women? The sex ratio question.* Beverly Hills, CA: Sage.

Heuveline, P., & Timberlake, J. (2004). The role of cohabitation in family formation: The United States in comparative perspective. *Journal of Marriage and Family, 66*(6), 1214–1230.

Hogan, D. (1981). *Transitions and social change: The early lives of American men.* New York: Academic Press.

Koball, H. (1998). Have African-American men become less committed to marriage? Explaining the 20th century racial crossover in men's marriage timing. *Demography, 35*(2), 251–258.

Kobrin, F. (1976a). The fall in household size and the rise of the primary individual in the United States. *Demography, 13,* 127–138.

Kobrin, F. (1976b). The primary individual and the family: Changes in living arrangements in the United States since 1940. *Journal of Marriage and the Family, 38,* 233–239.

Laslett, P. (1972). *Household and family in past time.* Cambridge, U.K.: Cambridge University Press.

Litwak, E., & Kulis, S. (1987). Technology, proximity, and measures of kin support. *Journal of Marriage and the Family, 49*(3), 649–661.

Michael, R., & Tuma, N. (1985). Entry into marriage and parenthood by young men and women. *Demography, 22*(4), 515–544.

Modell, J. (1989). *Into one's own: From youth to adulthood in the United States, 1920–1975.* Berkeley: University of California Press.

O'Neill, B., MacKellar, L., & Lutz, W. (2001). *Population and climate change.* New York: Cambridge University Press.

Ruggles, S. (2007). The decline of intergenerational coresidence. *American Sociological Review, 72*(6), 964–989.

Thornton, A. (2005). *Reading history sideways: The fallacy and enduring impact of the developmental paradigm on family life.* Chicago: University of Chicago Press.

Tucker, M. B., & Mitchell-Kernan, C. (Eds.). (1995). Trends in African-American family formation: A theoretical and statistical overview. In *The decline in marriage among African Americans: Causes, consequences, and policy implications* (pp. 3–26). New York: Russell Sage Foundation.

Wolf, D. (1995). Changes in the living arrangements of older women: An international study. *The Gerontologist, 35*(6), 724–731.

Frances Goldscheider

FATHERHOOD

The term *fatherhood* can mean both fertility status (i.e., whether a man has biological or adopted children) and the "behavior and identity enacted by men who have children" (Pleck, 2007, p. 196). Joe Pleck suggested that the term *fathering* may be more accurate for describing the behavior and identity aspects of fatherhood.

FERTILITY STATUS VERSUS BEHAVIOR AND IDENTITY

Fatherhood as indicated by fertility status is achieved through one's recognition of having fathered a child, that is, by establishing the paternity of a particular child with a specific female partner. Because paternity establishment sets in motion a number of significant obligations to the child and mother, such as paying child support when fathers do not reside with their children, social scientists have paid considerable attention to this aspect of fatherhood. In contrast, fatherhood defined as an identity and a set of behaviors can apply to men in various types of relationships with a child. Stepfathers, adoptive fathers, grandfathers, and uncles may assume fathering responsibilities for a child. These men sometimes are referred to as social fathers. The links between fatherhood as indicated by fertility status and fathering behavior are also of interest. For example, several studies in nations with low fertility rates have found an association between fathering behavior and fertility: Couples are more likely to have a second child when fathers are more involved in domestic tasks (Olàh, 2003; Ronsen, 2004).

CHANGES IN DEFINITIONS OF FATHERHOOD

A long tradition of research has examined what it means to be a father (i.e., beyond procreation) in different times and places. Margaret Mead (1969) argued that father-

hood has always been a social construction, that is, what it means to be a father varies historically and culturally.

Historians have documented how definitions of fatherhood have changed over time in the United States (LaRossa, Jaret, Gadgil, & Wynn, 2000). During the colonial era in the United States, fathers were responsible for instructing children in basic literacy, craft skills, and religion (Mintz, 1998). Fathers also were responsible for children's moral upbringing and had almost complete authority to make decisions about children's marriages, occupations, discipline, and behavior. The emergence of the Industrial Revolution in the 19th century resulted in greater separation of work and family life. Fathering during that period increasingly was viewed as a breadwinning role. At the turn of the 20th century there was a cultural and normative shift toward viewing fathers as companions to their children (Griswold, 1993). The shift occurred partially because of increasing concern that sons raised primarily by their mothers were at risk of becoming overly feminized (Mintz, 1998). The latter part of the 20th century and the early 21st century witnessed a shift toward defining fathers as nurturers (Morman & Floyd, 2006). Fathers no longer were expected to be only providers and friends to their children; they also were expected to participate in all facets of childcare and child rearing.

In some cultures the role of the father has been assumed by several males. In traditional Dakota families, the role of the father was assumed by both the biological father and *tiyospaye* fathers (paternal uncles), whose role was to teach their *tiyospaye* sons (nephews) about a man's responsibilities to his family, tribe, and nation (White, Godfrey, & Moccasin, 2006). The biological father provided nurturance but never disciplined his children. Having more than one father is not uncommon in the modern era; children may relate on a regular basis to both a stepfather and a biological father. Although the role responsibilities of stepfathers and nonresident biological fathers are not clearly defined, these men often communicate with each other about their respective responsibilities to the child (Marsiglio, 2006).

Michael Lamb (2000) suggested that although the definition of fathering has changed over time, there is much more consensus in any historical period on what it means to be a mother than on what it means to be a father. In most societies the mother has assumed the primary caregiving role, and the definition of her role has remained fairly constant. Feminists argue that because most societies are patriarchal, men determine who assumes privileged roles such as provider and who assumes low-status roles such as caregiver. Others argue that social and economic forces have had a strong influence on expectations for fathers (Doherty, Kouneski, & Erickson, 1998). For example, in

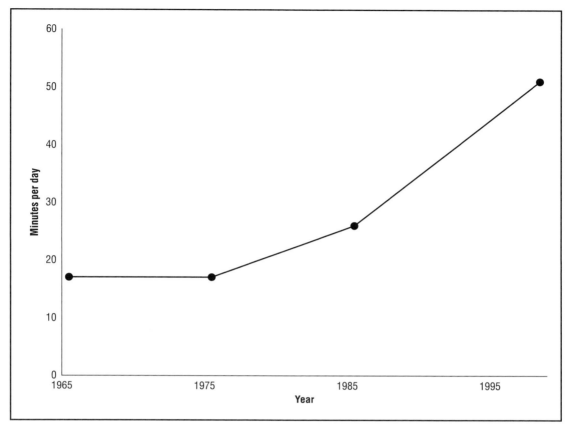

Figure 1. *Married fathers' time spent on child care activities in U.S.* CENGAGE LEARNING, GALE.

the United States during most of the 20th century, fathers' economic responsibilities and military obligations often kept them on the outskirts of family life and minimally involved in the care of their children even though experts in child rearing encouraged fathers to become more involved in their children's daily lives (Neumann, 1926).

TRENDS IN FATHERING

There has been considerable debate among researchers about how best to measure trends in fathering over time. One study (Lamb, Pleck, Charnov, & Levine, 1987) suggested that fathering behavior has three dimensions: (a) engagement, or fathers' shared interactions with their children; (b) accessibility, or a father's availability to a child whether or not he is directly engaged with that child; and (c) responsibility, or a father's organizing and planning activities in relation to a child and provision of resources to that child. These dimensions have been used in many cross-cultural studies. Although each of these dimensions of fathering is important throughout a child's development, fathers' engagement, accessibility, and responsibility vary within each developmental stage. For

example, researchers have found that fathers' engagement with children increases between infancy and preschool. Trend studies most frequently examine levels of fathers' engagement with and accessibility to their children; few have focused on responsibility.

The research literature has documented a clear increase during the last three decades of the 20th century and the first decade of the 21st in the degree to which fathers who coreside with their children in the United States are actively involved with their children (see Figure 1). However, there has been considerable debate among researchers about the extent to which this change is meaningful. Findings from time diary studies reveal that between 1965 and 1998 married fathers engaged more frequently in childcare activities and spent more time in those activities each day (Sayer, Bianchi, & Robinson, 2004). About 40% of fathers reported providing childcare (including daily care, teaching, and play) on any specific day in 1965, whereas more than one half of fathers reported childcare activity in 1998. In addition, the amount of time married fathers spent in childcare activities increased from 17 minutes per day in 1965 to 51 minutes in 1998.

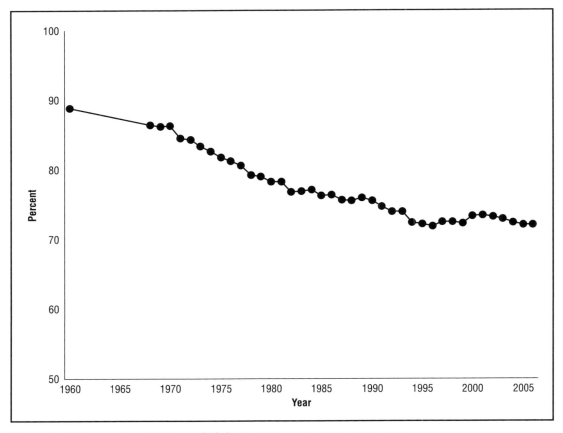

Figure 2. *Children under 18 living with father in U.S.* CENGAGE LEARNING, GALE.

Several researchers have argued that the increase in fathers' involvement should be viewed within the context of mothers' time spent providing childcare to children, which also increased considerably in that period (Sayer, Bianchi, & Robinson, 2004). Married and cohabiting mothers who are employed full-time in the labor force spend about the same amount of time in direct childcare activity per day as did married and cohabiting mothers who were not in the labor force in the 1960s (Bianchi, Robinson, & Milkie, 2006, Gauthier, Smeeding, & Furstenberg, 2004). Annette Lareau (2003) suggested that a culture of concerted cultivation of children explains why parents maximize the time they spend with their children. In addition, critics of research documenting increasing levels of father involvement with children point out that the additional three quarters of an hour per day of childcare is trivial in light of the considerable increase in mothers' participation in the labor force during that period.

The increase in involvement with children has taken place primarily among residential fathers. However, during the same period the proportion of children who do not reside with their fathers has increased (see Figure 2). Approximately 72% of U.S. children under age 18 lived

with their fathers in 2006, compared with 89% in 1960 (U.S. Census Bureau, 2006, 2008). Data from the 1999 National Survey of America's Families revealed that 34% of children living with single mothers who were not married at the time the child was born did not visit their nonresident fathers in the previous year (Koball & Principe, 2002). Taken together, the findings suggest an upward trend for residential fathers' involvement with their children and a downward trend for nonresidential fathers' involvement.

Various explanations have been provided for this phenomenon. Ralph LaRossa and colleagues (2000) suggested that cultural norms often change more quickly than does actual behavior. This suggests that there may be some unevenness in behavioral change, with some groups of fathers (residential fathers) showing evidence of increased involvement with their children and other groups of fathers (nonresidential fathers) showing no change or even less involvement. Other researchers have suggested that although the norms for father involvement have changed, situational factors often interfere with fathers' ability to stay involved with their children (Marsiglio, Roy, & Fox, 2005). For example, whether

STAY AT HOME DADS

Although fathers constitute only a small proportion of primary caregiver parents in the United States (less than 1.5% in 2006), the number of fathers who cared for children at home for a full year while their spouses were in the labor force increased nearly two and a half times between 1995 and 2006—from 64,000 to 159,000 (U.S. Census Bureau, 2007). Primary caregiver fathers challenge traditional ideas about masculinity and gendered family roles. In a study of at-home fathers in Australia, Belgium, Sweden, and the United States, Laura Merla (in press) found that men dealt with their primary caregiving role by adapting traditional definitions of masculinity. Some fathers rejected the importance of paid work and integrated their childcare role into a masculine self-definition. Other fathers developed an alternative form of masculinity that incorporated a feminine side or rejected traditional masculinity in favor of "androgyny." Andrea Doucet (2004) found that many Canadian fathers who were primary caregivers retained close ties to paid work and contributed to the family income, reinforcing their masculinity. In addition to identity issues, at-home fathers face problems such as social isolation. Web sites and blogs attempt to link at-home fathers with one another.

the father ever resided with the child is an important influence on nonresidential father involvement. Fathers are likely to form bonds with their children when they reside in the same household. The father's bond to the child and the child's attachment to the father can have a strong influence on fathers' continued involvement with the child after the father leaves.

On the basis of findings suggesting that a father's residence with a child is critical for his active presence in the life of the child, researchers sometimes have concluded that parental marriage is better for father–child relationships than is cohabitation (i.e., unmarried residential arrangements). Although a substantial body of literature has documented that marital relationships are more stable than cohabiting relationships (Seltzer, 2000), researchers seldom have been able to isolate the effects of these relationship patterns on paternal involvement with children. However, a study using the Fragile Families and Child Well-Being data, a longitudinal study of a cohort of children born in large U.S. cities between 1998 and

2000 primarily to unmarried couples, examined father involvement among a subset of fathers who previously were married or cohabitating with the mother when the child was an infant but no longer were living together or romantically involved when the child was 3 years old (Laughlin, Farrie, & Fagan, 2008). Mothers reported that previously cohabiting fathers were more competent fathers and had more contact with their children after separation. Marriage may benefit families in some ways, but cohabitation may provide unique benefits that are not well understood.

THEORETICAL APPROACHES

Four theoretical perspectives are important for understanding fathering: life course theory, developmental theory, the ecological perspective, and sociological theory. The life course perspective highlights individuals' trajectories of social roles and transitions and the implications of those trajectories for those individuals (Elder, 1998). In addition to acquiring a major social role with associated expectations and obligations, a man making the transition to fatherhood may experience life-altering changes in other areas of his life, including employment, his relationship with the child's partner, his own social behaviors, and his identity as a father. Depending on social and historical circumstances, these life transitions may be stressful or exciting and may lead to positive or negative changes that can set the father on a trajectory of more or less involved parenting (Elder, 1998). The life course perspective also suggests continuity over time in family relationships. For example, noncustodial fathers' commitment to their adolescent children was associated strongly with father–child relationships in early adulthood (Aquilino, 2006). The life course perspective also emphasizes the ways in which individuals' lives are linked to the lives of others, especially others within the family. Thus, events in a father's life such as losing a job reverberate in the life of his child and affect the child's wellbeing. In the same way, events in a child's life such as a critical illness affect the life of the child's father.

Central to the life course perspective is the concept of the timing of life events (Elder, 1998). Being involved early in the transition (at birth) gives a man the opportunity to develop a relationship with his unborn child, and that may strengthen his commitment and engagement over time (Cabrera, Fagan, & Farrie, in press). It is also important to consider timing in terms of the age at which a man becomes a father. Fathering a child during adolescence can have detrimental consequences for the father's life experiences, including lower educational attainment (Rhein et al., 1997), higher rates of drug use and engagement in illegal activities (Fagot, Pears, Capaldi, Crosby, & Leve, 1998), and more psychological problems (Vaz, Smolen, & Miller, 1983) compared with the father's peers. Early fatherhood may have a negative effect on the social and emotional development of the child as adolescent fathers' exposure to these risk factors may lead to decreased involvement with their children over time (Farrie, Lee, & Fagan, 2008).

Developmental theory based on Erik Erikson's (1950) stages of psychosocial development has been used to understand fathering across the life course (Snarey, 1993). In Erikson's theory, a mature young adult is one who has a psychological and social need to nurture the next generation. Fathering is not seen simply as a social role defined by external forces; instead, generative fathering is considered a developmental process that requires continuous efforts to move toward mastery of parenting (Hawkins & Dollahite, 1997). Fathering is viewed as a process of growth and development within the man. The father's sense of well-being is closely tied to his involvement with his children in meeting their developmental needs. The value of the generative fathering framework is that it deemphasizes thinking about fathers as deficient and emphasizes fathers' potentials for growth.

The ecological systems perspective refers to the multiple influences on fathers' behavior and stresses the interrelatedness among those influences (Bronfenbrenner, 1986). A father's behavior is structured by his individual characteristics and his relationships with other members of his immediate social circle as well as by the larger structures (political, economic) in which individuals operate. However, rather than focusing on the interplay among these roles, most research has focused on fathers in relation to their close social relationships. For example, an increasing number of studies have shown the significance of the father–mother dyad relationship in relation to the father–child relationship (Doherty & Beaton, 2004). Recent studies also have addressed structural-level influences (the role of governmental and social policy). For example, research has shown that stricter child support enforcement policies in the United States have been associated with increased father involvement with children in the households of never-married mothers (Huang, 2006). An important contribution of the ecological systems perspective is the finding that fathering appears to be more sensitive to environmental influences (e.g., marital stress) than is mothering (Doherty, Kouneski, & Erickson, 1998).

Sociological theory focuses on fathers' personal and interpersonal resources. A person's set of skills and knowledge, such as educational attainment, personality traits, work habits, and occupational skills, is referred to as human capital (Coleman, 1990). Fathers who have made investments in their personal success have a positive influence on their children's outcomes. Studies have shown that fathers' educational achievement is significantly correlated with children's academic success (Amato, 1998). Social capital

theory suggests that the resources that are generated as a result of relationships between people can affect a father's influence on his children (Amato, 1998). Fathers who have a diverse set of friends and acquaintances can expose their children to a wide variety of experiences and perhaps garner resources to aid in their development. Social capital studies have revealed more positive child outcomes when fathers are more engaged with their children and when the quality of their interactions with their children is high (Marsiglio, Amato, Day, & Lamb, 2000).

FUTURE DIRECTIONS FOR RESEARCH

Early studies of fathers' influences on children made some of the same mistakes that were made in research on mothers' influences on children: The mother–child or father–child relationship was examined without regard for the impact of the other parent or the larger family and social context. Recent studies have begun to address this oversight by including both mothers and fathers (Davidov & Grusec, 2006). The potential for researchers to examine child outcomes within the context of the entire family and the larger social context has increased with the availability of large longitudinal data sets such as the Early Childhood Longitudinal Study: Birth Cohort and the Early Head Start Research and Evaluation Project: Fathers' Study (Cabrera et al., 2004).

Little research has examined fathering across the life course. Few studies have addressed the effects of having children on men from the time when they become fathers though older adulthood. Research on men tends to examine their development in the context of work, relationships, communities, and families (Levinson, 1986) but seldom in relation to fathering; an exception is the work of Rob Palkovitz (2002). For example, there has been little research on how men's development is affected by raising children during adolescence, which can be a difficult time for many parents. Also, little is known about the development of men who do not reside with their children. A fruitful area for research would be the development of men in different types of relationships with their children.

Finally, few studies have examined the ways in which social policies affect fathers' relationships with their children. Fathering-related policies in the United States have focused on low-income nonresidential fathers. The 1996 Personal Responsibility and Work Opportunity Act, which requires parents (mostly mothers) receiving public assistance to be gainfully employed within 2 years after first receiving assistance, specified as one of its major objectives increasing children's access to both parents. The Act allows states to use federal money to develop programs that increase the employability of fathers. One assumption guiding this policy is that low-income

Fathers Taking Leave. *Tim Waddill changes Chase, his newborn twin son's diaper, left, as Stephanie Waddill, back, gives a bottle to their other twin boy, Connor, at their home in Irving, TX.* **AP IMAGES.**

nonresidential fathers who are more employable are likely to provide financial support to their children, stay involved in their children's lives, and lift their children out of poverty. Research is needed to examine the influence of this policy initiative on fathers and children.

SEE ALSO Volume 1: *Parenting Style; Socialization, Gender; Transition to Parenthood;* Volume 2: *Motherhood; Noncustodial Parents; Roles.*

BIBLIOGRAPHY

Amato, P. R. (1998). More than money? Men's contributions to their children's lives. In A. Booth & A. Crouter (Eds.), *Men in families: When do they get involved? What difference does it make?* (pp. 241–278). Mahwah, NJ: Lawrence Erlbaum.

Aquilino, W. S. (2006). The noncustodial father–child relationship from adolescence into young adulthood. *Journal of Marriage and the Family, 68,* 929–946.

Bianchi, S. M., Robinson, J. P., & Milkie, M. A. (2006). *Changing rhythms of American family life.* New York: Russell Sage Foundation.

Bradford, K., & Hawkins, A. (2006). Learning competent fathering: A longitudinal analysis of marital intimacy and fathering. *Fathering, 4*(3), 215–234.

Bronfenbrenner, U. (1986). Ecology of the family as a context for human development: Research perspectives. *Developmental Psychology, 22,* 723–742.

Cabrera, N., Brooks-Gunn, J., Moore, K., Bronte-Tinkew, J., Halle, T., Reichman, N., et al. (2004). The DADS initiative: Measuring father involvement in large-scale surveys. In R. D. Day & M. E. Lamb (Eds.), *Conceptualizing and measuring father involvement* (pp. 417–452). Mahwah, NJ: Lawrence Erlbaum.

Cabrera, N., Fagan, J., & Farrie, D. (in press). Explaining the long reach of fathers' prenatal involvement on later paternal engagement with children. *Journal of Marriage and the Family.*

Coleman, J. S. (1990). *Foundations of social theory.* Cambridge, MA: Belknap Press of Harvard University Press.

Davidov, M., & Grusec, J. E. (2006). Untangling the links of parental responsiveness to distress and warmth to child outcomes. *Child Development, 77,* 44–58.

Doherty, W. J., & Beaton, J. M. (2004). Mothers and fathers parenting together. In A. L. Vangelisti (Ed.), *Handbook of family communication* (pp. 269–286). Mahwah, NJ: Lawrence Erlbaum.

Doherty, W. J., Kouneski, E. F., & Erickson, M. F. (1998). Responsible fathering: An overview and conceptual framework. *Journal of Marriage and the Family, 60,* 277–292.

Doucet, A. (2004). "It's almost like I have a job, but I don't get paid": Fathers at home reconfiguring work, care, and masculinity. *Fathering, 2,* 277–303.

Elder, G. H., Jr. (1998). The life course as developmental theory. *Child Development, 69*(1), 1–12.

Erickson, E. (1950). *Childhood and society.* New York: Norton.

Fagot, B. I., Pears, K. C., Capaldi, D. M., Crosby, L., & Leve, C. S. (1998). Becoming an adolescent father: Precursors and parenting. *Developmental Psychology, 34*(6), 1209–1219.

Farrie, D., Lee, Y., & Fagan, J. (2008). *The effect of cumulative risk on paternal engagement: Examining differences among adolescent and older couples.* Manuscript submitted for publication.

Gauthier, A. H., Smeeding, T. M., & Furstenberg, F. F., Jr. (2004). Are parents investing less time in children? Trends in selected industrialized countries. *Population and Development Review, 30*(4), 647–671.

Griswold, R. L. (1993). *Fatherhood in America: A history.* New York: Basic Books.

Hawkins, A. J., & Dollahite, D. C. (1997). *Generative fathering: Beyond deficit perspectives.* Thousand Oaks, CA: Sage.

Huang, C.-C. (2006). Child support enforcement and father involvement for children in never-married mother families. *Fathering, 4*(1), 97–111.

Koball, H., & Principe, D. (2002). *Do nonresident fathers who pay child support visit their children more?* National Survey of America's Families, Series B, No. B-44. Retrieved June 6, 2008, from http://www.eric.ed.gov/ERICDocs

Lamb, M. E. (2000). The history of research on father involvement: An overview. *Marriage and Family Review, 29,* 23–42.

Lamb, M. E., Pleck, J. H., Charnov, E.L., & Levine, J. A. (1987). A biosocial perspective on paternal behavior and involvement. In J. B. Lancaster, J. Altmann, A. Rossi, & L. Sherrod (Eds.), *Parenting across the life span: Biosocial dimensions* (pp. 111–142). New York: de Gruyter.

Lareau, A. (2003). *Unequal childhoods: Class, race, and family life.* Berkeley: University of California Press.

LaRossa, R., Jaret, C., Gadgil, M., & Wynn, G. R. (2000). The changing culture of fatherhood in comic-strip families: A six-decade analysis. *Journal of Marriage and the Family, 62*(2), 375–387.

Laughlin, L., Farrie, D., & Fagan, J. (2008). *Father involvement with children following marital and non-marital separations.* Manuscript submitted for publication.

Levinson, D. (1986). A conception of adult development. *American Psychologist, 41*(1), 3–13.

Marsiglio, W. (2006). *Stepdads: Stories of love, hope, and repair.* Lanham, MD: Rowman & Littlefield.

Marsiglio, W., Amato, P., Day, R. D., & Lamb, M. E. (2000). Scholarship on fatherhood in the 1990s and beyond. *Journal of Marriage and the Family, 62*(4), 1173–1191.

Marsiglio, W., Roy, K., & Fox, G. L. (2005). *Situated fathering: A focus on physical and social spaces.* Lanham, MD: Rowman & Littlefield.

Mead, M. (1969). A working paper for man and nature. *Natural History, 78*(4), 14–22.

Merla, L. (in press). Determinants, costs, and meanings of stay at-home Belgian fathers: An international comparison. *Fathering.*

Mintz, S. (1998). From patriarchy to androgyny and other myths. In A. Booth & A. Crouter (Eds.), *Men in families: When do they get involved? What difference does it make?* (pp. 3–30). Mahwah, NJ: Lawrence Erlbaum.

Morman, M. T., & Floyd, K. (2006). Good fathering: Father and son perceptions of what it means to be a good father. *Fathering, 4*(2), 113–136.

Neumann, H. (1926). The father's responsibility in the training of his children. In *Intelligent parenthood: Proceedings of the Mid-West Conference on Parent Education* (pp. 222–232). Chicago: University of Chicago Press.

Olàh, L. S. (2003). Gendering fertility: Second births in Sweden and Hungary. *Population Research and Policy Review, 22*(2), 171–200.

Palkovitz, R. (2002). *Involved fathering and men's adult development: Provisional balances.* Mahwah, NJ: Lawrence Erlbaum.

Pleck, J. H. (2007). Why could father involvement benefit children? Theoretical perspectives. *Applied Developmental Science, 11*(4), 196–202.

Rhein, L. M., Ginsburg, K. R., Schwarz, D. F., Pinto-Martin, J. A., Zhao, H., Morgan, A. P., et al. (1997). Teen father participation in child rearing: Family perspectives. *Journal of Adolescent Health, 21*(4), 244–252.

Ronsen, M. (2004). Fertility and public policies: Evidence from Norway and Finland. *Demographic Research, 10*(6), 143–170.

Sayer, L. C., Bianchi, S. M., & Robinson, J. P. (2004). Are parents investing less in children? Trends in mothers' and fathers' time with children. *American Journal of Sociology, 110,* 1–43.

Seltzer, J.A. (2000). Families formed outside of marriage. *Journal of Marriage and the Family, 62*(4), 1247–1268.

Snarey, J. (1993). *How fathers care for the next generation: A four-decade study.* Cambridge, MA: Harvard University Press.

U.S. Census Bureau. (2006). *Statistical abstract of the United States: 2006.* Retrieved June 6, 2008, from http://www.census.gov/compendia

U.S. Census Bureau. (2007). *Parents and children in stay-at-home parent family groups: 1994 to present.* Retrieved May 17, 2008, from http://www.census.gov/population

U.S. Census Bureau. (2008). *Families and living arrangements.* Retrieved June 8, 2008, from http://www.census.gov/population/

Vaz, R., Smolen, P., & Miller, C. (1983). Adolescent pregnancy: Involvement of the male partner. *Journal of Adolescent Health Care, 4*(4), 246–250.

White, J. M., Godfrey, J., & Moccasin, B. I. (2006). American Indian fathering in the Dakota nation: Use of *Akicita* as a fatherhood standard. *Fathering, 4*(1), 49–69.

Jay Fagan
Danielle Farrie

FLEXIBLE WORK ARRANGEMENTS

The term *flexible work arrangements* describes a number of alternative work options (including flextime and telecommuting) that allow work to be done at times and in places outside the standard workday. These arrangements are especially important to workers at different stages in the life course, particularly dual-career couples and single working parents with young children. The related term *flexibility*, however, also characterizes the wide range of employment arrangements that exist outside the standard full-time, continuous-employment contract. These arrangements include temporary, contingent, seasonal, and contracting work. Unlike the first type of flexibility, these arrangements benefit not so much employees as the needs of employers to cut labor and benefit costs.

Although it is doubtful that the majority of workers in industrial economies such as the United States ever worked the so-called standard full-time workday, there is evidence that even fewer did so in the period from the early 1980s into the first years of the 21st century. "Flexibility" has been called the slogan of the emerging postindustrial economy and associated life cycle. Flexible work arrangements are contrasted with the "rigid" work arrangements of industrial economies (e.g., assembly line manufacturing, or clerical office work) and with "linear" life-cycle stages—that is, the assumption of lockstep progression through school, work, and retirement. In the new, flexible arrangements individuals may experience all three of these stages simultaneously.

Rigid work arrangements were best suited to the mass production of consumer goods where markets for the goods and for the workers producing them remained relatively stable from year to year, such as the U.S. auto and home appliance industries of the 1950s and 1960s. Such stability led firms to hire workers on a semipermanent basis, thus allowing within-firm career mobility paths and generous health and retirement benefits for workers. In contrast, the postindustrial economy is based on providing rapidly changing consumer services within globally competitive markets with a demographically diverse workforce. Increasing the flexibility of work arrangements, including legal definitions of who is eligible for work, is argued to be better suited for this new system by advocates for both employees and employers, although the two sides emphasize different forms of flexibility.

Employee preferences for more flexible work arrangements are strongly related to one's stage in the life course. The increasing presence of married women, especially those with young children, in the labor force has led many employers to initiate family-friendly work-flexible programs, such as flextime, compressed workweeks, reduced hours, and telecommuting, in order to attract and retain highly skilled and valued workers, especially professional women. Working mothers with young children also are the demographic group that is most likely to prefer nonstandard weekday shifts (e.g., evenings, nights, weekends), for personal and family reasons, such as childcare. The

combination of workers retiring at younger ages but living longer has increased preferences among retirement-age workers for jobs that allow them to reenter or continue in the labor force, often on a less than full-time basis.

Some firms have addressed these preferences by allowing workers to "phase down" to retirement by reducing their job duties and responsibilities before retirement. Older workers without such arrangements often take new jobs at or after retirement, such as greeters at retail stores. These jobs bridge the financial gap between career and complete retirement. Also, as flatter, less hierarchical organizational structures have reduced traditional "intrafirm" (internal labor market) career paths, many younger, Generation X workers, especially those with highly sought-after professional or technical skills, have developed preferences for inter-firm or "portfolio" careers as self-employed independent contractors who sell their skills to firms for a set period of time or for a particular product. Flexibility is considered a characteristic of a "good" job, when it is sought out as a way for employees to meet their personal and family needs.

The origins of employer preferences for flexible work arrangements are quite different. Although some employers have embraced programs such as flextime and phased retirement to respond to employee preferences, the primary employer motivation for initiating work flexibility has been to better cope with rapidly changing technological changes and consumer preferences that characterize many new product and service markets, such as the computer software and hardware markets. Many firms also seek flexible staffing to cope with the profit squeeze created by increased foreign competition and rising costs of employee health care and pension benefits. In such cases, the flexibility stems from how employers staff jobs, rather than when and where the work is done. Thus, many employers have developed flexible strategies that externalize employee contracts and benefits via the use of temporary agencies or by hiring independent contractors. Other employers have replaced their employees with part-time or contingent workers (or redefined them so), and such workers have no psychological or legal expectations for continued employment.

These trends have been aided by the decline in union membership and influence, which has enabled employers to undo the collectively bargained fixed work rules and defined benefits that were common in industrial production. More flexible staffing arrangements are also consistent with new managerial theories and practices that cut costs by eliminating middle-management positions and thus "flatten" organizational hierarchies. In turn, these changes have reduced intra-firm job mobility while making employees more responsible for their own training and career, using the disincentive of job insecurity. In this context, flexibility is associated with bad jobs.

SHIFT WORK

The most common alternate, if not flexible, work arrangement involves the wide variety of times when workers do their jobs. A worker's job shift defines both the number of hours worked in a week and which hours and days are worked. In the United States, the standard shift is considered to be a fixed daytime, 35 to 40 hours per week, 5 days per week, Monday through Friday schedule. However, according to data from the 1997 Current Population Survey (CPS) of the U.S. Census Bureau and the Bureau of Labor Statistics, by the end of the 20th century fewer than half of adult workers (43%) worked the standard 35 to 40 hours per week. Another 25% worked more than 40 hours, and 22% worked part-time—that is, fewer than 35 hours per week. In addition, in terms of which hours and days one worked, only 3 in 10 adult U.S. workers were employed on the standard weekday shift. Nonstandard shifts include evenings, nights, rotating shifts, being on call, compressed hours, weekends, and multiple combinations of different days and times, including flexible work schedules. The most common nonstandard arrangement was weekend work; 23% of all workers worked at least one weekend day. Weekend work was slightly more common among part-time workers (24%) and was especially common among those working more than 40 hours (30.5%). The most common nonstandard hourly shift was fixed evenings, worked by 6% of all full-time workers and 14% of part-timers.

Men were somewhat more likely than women to work both nonstandard hours (21.1% vs. 18.6%) and nonstandard days (40.3% vs. 38.9%, respectively). Men were more likely to work fixed nights (between midnight and 8 a.m.), weekends, and on rotating shifts in which the shift times change periodically. By contrast, women were more likely to work fewer than 5 days per week because of the higher percentage of women working part-time (30% to 14%). African Americans and Hispanics were more likely than Whites to work nonstandard shifts, whereas increasing age and years of education reduced the likelihood of doing so. Married workers with a coresidential spouse were less likely to work nonstandard shifts than workers in other marital categories. Having school-age or younger children also reduced the likelihood of women, but not men, working nonstandard shifts.

Work shifts, however, are primarily determined by the occupation and industry in which one works. Those working in retail sales and personal services were most likely to work nonstandard shifts, especially waiters/waitresses, cashiers, and supervisors and proprietors in these industries. Well over half of workers in these categories worked nonstandard hours and especially nonstandard days. For example, a full 84% of male waiters and 76% of female waitresses worked weekends. Just 10 specific occupations accounted for one-third of all nonstandard workers, and 8 of the 10 were jobs in the retail and personal services. The other 2 occupations were truck drivers and nurses. Professional and administrative support workers were least likely to work nonstandard shifts (especially hours), particularly if they were government employees.

Most workers—two-thirds of male and half of female employees—cited job requirements as the reason why they held nonstandard shifts. Family considerations and day-care arrangements were also a chief concern among mothers (but not fathers) of preschool-age children. Thus, at least for one sizable segment of the workforce, shift work may be used as a strategy for balancing work and family demands. Likewise, three-fourths of part-time workers kept their reduced hours voluntarily, although an increasing number reported working part-time because they had been unable to find full-time work. For most other workers, shifts appear more fixed than flexible.

Since the 1970s most research on shift work has centered its effects on the well-being of workers and their families. In this area, there is one key question: Is nonstandard work a strategy for balancing work–family demands or a cause of work–family conflict and instability? This question is particularly salient when attempting to understand the work choices of the current cohorts of adults, given the increases in women's labor force participation and the overall number of hours worked by Americans at their jobs. Given these shifts, workers have far less time available for family and leisure activities. The evidence is mixed but does suggest that working nonstandard shifts—especially rotating and weekends—reduces interaction among spouses and their children and interferes with family obligations.

An even longer standing concern, dating back at least to the 1950s, is the health effects of nonstandard shifts. Working nonstandard hours, especially nights and rotating shifts, is thought to create physiological and psychological adjustment problems by disrupting human circadian rhythms and sleeping and eating patterns. As a result, some research shows that workers of nonstandard schedules have elevated risks for cardiovascular and coronary problems, diabetes, gastrointestinal and digestive problems, on-the-job injuries, depression, and alcoholism. The overall results, however, are mixed and inconclusive.

Research is also inconclusive with respect to the prevalence of nonstandard shifts. Although the assumption is that the growth of service industries and the globalization of markets has created a 24/7 economy

Working at Home. *Technology has made it easier for parents to balance time between home and work.* © **STEFANIE GREWEL/ ZEFA/CORBIS.**

necessitating round-the-clock operations, there is no direct evidence that nonstandard shifts are more common in the early 21st century than they were during the 1950s or 1960s. The exception is the expansion of part-time work, which increased from 13% of the workforce in the 1950s to 22% in 1997. Data limitations have prevented the systematic study of nonstandard work over recent decades. Although the CPS has periodically included supplements with questions on work schedules since 1973, the survey questions on specific work hours are not asked consistently. Questions regarding specific workdays were not introduced until 1991. The assumption of increased nonstandard schedules rests primarily on the relative growth rates of jobs with high rates of nonstandard workers and demographic projections for continued rapid growth, such as nursing, food preparation and serving, retail sales security guards, and waitresses/waiters.

FLEXTIME

Flextime is a type of work schedule that allows employees to vary the times they work on a periodic basis, by starting and ending the workday early or late, or by compressing weekly work hours into fewer days (e.g., working 10 hours per day for 4 days). Flextime may be a formal company policy establishing the limits of flexibility. For instance, workers may have the option of starting work within the 2-hour window of 7 to 9 a.m. and ending the workday between 4 and 6 p.m., provided they put in a full day of work. By contrast, flexible hours may be an informal attribute of a job, such as with college professors, who often choose their own work hours. In both formal and informal flextime there are likely to be core times in which employees must be at their jobs.

Since the early 1990s employers have increasingly adopted flextime policies. According to a 2001 survey, 59% of employers offered flextime to some or all of their employees, an increase of 21% since the early 1990s. In a separate 2001 survey of employees, however, only 29% reported working on flexible schedules. This disparity between employer-reported availability and actual use points to the major issue in the flextime literature: the mismatch between its availability and its use. Many workers who have access to flextime may not need it, such as older workers who are not caring for young children or elderly parents. Other workers who could use flextime often do not take it because of informal employer or coworker pressures not to, or because they fear it will negatively affect their career advancement by signaling that family obligations are more important than work obligations, as in the case of the "mommy track."

Surveys of employee preferences have consistently found that working a flexible schedule is a highly desired job characteristic, primarily because it helps balance work and family demands. Out of all working parents, 80% regarded it as an important and sought-after job attribute; 80% of those who lacked access to flextime desired it; 25% said they were considering changing jobs or employers in order to work on a more flexible schedule, even if it would reduce their opportunities for career advancement. Conversely, working inflexible schedules is second only to number of hours worked as a reason for not spending more time with family.

Employers also see the benefits of flextime in reducing job stress, employee turnover, absenteeism, and tardiness while increasing satisfaction and morale, as well as the ultimate benefits of recruiting and retaining highly skilled workers, thus improving organizational performance. Nevertheless, although some evidence shows that flextime improves employee morale and reduces absenteeism, there is no consistent evidence that it increases employee productivity or organizational performance. Moreover, flextime may be of limited practical use to employers because, unlike many job benefits such as health insurance or pensions, it is best suited to the idiosyncratic needs of particular individual workers, regardless of job, such as mothers of young children or those caring for elderly parents, rather than all workers in particular jobs, such as all female lawyers.

The result, as pointed out above, is underutilization of flextime and a mismatch between those who would benefit most and those who have access and use it. As with job shifts in general, flextime is characteristic of the job and not of the demographic characteristics of workers. Although women and African American workers express the strongest desire for flextime, those with greatest access include males, especially married males with children; college-educated, professional, managerial, and sales workers; workers in private household and agricultural occupations; and both those working more than 40 hours per week and those working fewer than 40 hours. Actual use of flextime is greatest among married, high-income, professional, managerial, and sales workers. Age, race, and having school-age children, however, did not increase use of flextime, even when available. Finally, and perhaps because of the disparity between preferences for flextime and who has access to and uses flextime, the

evidence is only mixed as to whether these work arrangements actually help workers balance work and family demands.

HOME-BASED WORK AND TELECOMMUTING

Working at home is not a new work arrangement; indeed, it dates back to the old "putting out" or "cottage" system of the late Middle Ages (and much farther back if one considers agrarian economies). What is new and potentially flexible is the form known as telecommuting. This is an arrangement that allows workers to do work from home or other locations away from the normal work site. Advances in technology, such as computers, fax machines, and cell phones, facilitate communications between off-site workers and a central office, or a "virtual office" in the extreme case in which there is no longer a physical central office.

The term *telecommuting* was introduced and first used by firms in 1970s as a way to make them less vulnerable to fuel shortages during the oil embargo imposed by the Organization of Petroleum Exporting Countries (OPEC). Estimates of the number of workers who telecommute in the United States vary greatly, as such estimates depend on the frequency with which an employee works from home. By the early 1990s it was estimated that between 3% and 8% of workers worked from home at least 1 day per week. The raw number of telecommuters had increased from 1 million in the mid-1970s to more than 8 million by the early 1990s and has continued to grow by roughly 20% per year. In 2000 the U.S. Department of Labor estimated that between 13% and 19% of U.S. workers telecommuted on a regular basis.

As with flextime, the benefits of telecommuting for workers are thought to include increased control over job schedules, which helps balance work–family demands. Telecommuting also reduces commute-related stress and time and saves on fuel and other transportation costs. In addition, telecommuting allows the employer to cut costs related to office space and energy use. Also, because employees no longer have to live within physical commuting distance, companies may hire from a wider pool of potential talent. Society also benefits through reduction of air pollution, fuel use, and traffic congestion.

Telecommuting, however, also has potentially serious drawbacks. For the telecommuter, there is the isolation from coworkers and professional networks and the loss of both a social support system and career contacts and mentors. Working from home also may increase family demands, particularly if one has young children, or other competing family obligations. It can also increase work demands. The technology that facilitates telecommuting also can make the worker "available" to the employer 24/7. For employers, the major drawback is the challenge telecommuting poses for monitoring the work of off-site employees. This is an important issue for employers, especially in the absence of definitive data comparing the productivity of telecommuters with that of on-site workers.

The characteristics of workers who telecommute are generally similar to those who have access to flextime. College-educated, professional, managerial, and sales workers and, to a lesser degree, private household workers were more likely to telecommute, as were married workers, especially if they had a spouse at home. Unlike with flextime, however, women were more likely to telecommute than men, as were both mothers and fathers of preschool children. Working long hours, especially more than 50 per week, substantially increased the likelihood of telecommuting. Such trend data are difficult to interpret, however. It is unclear whether those who work long hours use telecommuting as a strategy for balancing work and family demands or at least meeting work demands, or whether the telecommuting technology makes them available to work longer hours. Telecommuting is also strongly related to working a flexible schedule, particularly having the ability to adjust one's schedule on a daily basis.

FLEXIBLE EMPLOYMENT STAFFING ARRANGEMENTS

Flexible employment relations, also commonly referred to as nonstandard, alternative, or market-mediated work arrangements, consist of temporary, contingent, seasonal, and contract (consulting) work. These diverse categories share one common factor: Employees are not continuous employees for the firm for which their work is done. For the most part, these arrangements are structured by the preferences of employers and not employees.

Temporary, Contingent, and Seasonal Employment

In contrast with part-time employment, which may be regular, long-term employment, temporary, contingent, and seasonal employment is by definition short-term employment. Most temporary employment arrangements involve externalization of responsibility and control of labor through third-party temporary help agencies. Although they have been around since the 1920s, it was only after 1972 that employment through these agencies experienced rapid growth, at more than 11% per year, from 0.3% of the U.S. workforce in 1972 to 2.5% by the late 1990s. Since the mid-1990s, however, the growth rate has slowed considerably. The primary impetus for growth appeared to come from employer strategies of meeting cyclical changes in staffing needs; hiring through

temporary employment agencies allows firms to add or reduce staff on an as-needed basis. Firms also use temporary agencies to lessen their recruitment and training costs and to externalize employee benefits, which are provided by the agency.

Temporary help agency employees are more likely to be women, Black or Hispanic, and under the age of 35. They are most likely to be hired for work in manufacturing and service industries and in administrative support and labor occupations. Of all temporary employees, 60% are involuntary in that they prefer permanent employment with a firm but have been unable to secure such employment. Some employees use temporary agencies to acquire job skills and experience in order to find permanent employment. Data are mixed as to how successful they are able to do so. One study using national CPS data found that 52% of temporary workers had changed employers 1 year later; the data do not reveal, however, whether they had found permanent employment or changed agencies. Temporary workers are paid an average of one-third less than regular employees; however, temporary engineers and technicians often earn more than their counterparts in regular jobs. Even among higher paid temps, fringe benefits are fewer and more limited than those of regular workers.

The Bureau of Labor Statistics defines contingent employment arrangements, including seasonal and on-call employment, as those having no implicit (or explicit) long-term contract. They involve fixed-term contracts or no contracts at all. Unlike temporary workers who are employed by third-party help agencies, most contingent workers are hired and paid directly by the firm for which they will do the work. Based on these characteristics, in 2001 about 5% of the U.S. workforce was contingent. Almost 40% of U.S establishments use contingent workers, most commonly in industries with low-cost production strategies. The most common reason for hiring contingent workers is to meet seasonal demands, such as retail workers during holiday seasons, summer workers in tourism, or farm workers during harvests. Seasonal farm laborers make up 42% of all contingent workers. Contingent workers also help employers with special projects and unexpected increases in demand and fill in for regular workers who are absent. Although there is a lack of good data on overall trends in contingent employment, a decline in nonfarm contingent workers during the late 1990s appeared to be related to the expansion of the U.S. economy and a tightening of the labor market. The need for seasonal farm labor, in contrast, has remained stable.

Contracting and Consulting Work

Contracting or consulting workers may be employed by a firm or they may be self-employed. Contracting firms operate like temporary help agencies except much of the work done for clients may be done off-site, in which case it is labeled "subcontracting." Since the 1980s the use of contract firms has spread throughout U.S. industries, from business consulting firms to data processing to janitorial services, as more firms have sought to externalize labor and production costs by outsourcing these activities.

Contracting may also be done by independent, self-employed workers. Unlike employees, whose work and compensation is defined by the amount of labor expended, independent contractors are generally given specifications for a final product and they decide how best to accomplish it. Thus, independent contractors enjoy greater autonomy over their work, but they bear the economic risk of their employment, while providing their own benefits and being solely responsible for paying Social Security and unemployment compensation taxes. Moreover, many independent contractors are really not that "independent" because much of their work comes from one firm rather than from many.

There are no definitive data on the number of independent contractors in the United States, but according to 1997 CPS data, 7% of workers self-identified as such. Another 5% to 6% of workers identified themselves as self-employed but not as independent contractors. Despite the lack of objective data on employment trends for independent contracting, researchers assume that this type of employment substantially increased since the 1970s because of changes in the U.S. tax code that facilitated and even required some categories of workers, such as real estate agents, to become independent contractors. It has also been assumed that many younger professional and technical workers have been drawn to independent contracting because of the promise of greater flexibility of these work-project-oriented arrangements and portfolio or "boundaryless" careers, especially during a period in which traditional intra-firm career paths were disappearing.

The evidence is mixed, however, as to whether independent contracting is more beneficial than regular employment. Most independent contractors prefer this type of arrangement to traditional employment. Many earn higher wages than comparable workers in traditional employment arrangements. This has been especially true in many professional and technical occupations, particularly during the economic boom and tight labor market of the late 1990s, as epitomized by the software industry in Silicon Valley. Yet, an important disadvantage is that independent contractors are less likely to be covered by health insurance and pensions.

DIRECTIONS FOR FUTURE RESEARCH

Given the great variety of work arrangements that are defined as flexible, each with its own research gaps and needs, it is difficult to summarize overall suggestions for future research. Nevertheless, researchers are in agreement about the following needs. First, future research would benefit from greater clarification and agreement on terminology with respect to terms such as *flexible, alternative, nonstandard, contingent, temporary,* and *contract* work. As noted above, not all alternative or nonstandard arrangements are flexible; examples include shift work or temporary work. Likewise, researchers must clarify how much schedule flexibility constitutes flextime and how much off-site work constitutes telecommuting and, more importantly, who makes the decisions as to where and when to work: Is this a choice of employers or employees? Are flextime and telecommuting considered flexible work arrangements if they occur within strict employer-defined limits? What makes these arrangements flexible is the control employees have over where and when they work.

Second, researchers agree that, once defined, more valid and reliable measures of these work arrangements are needed. Researchers need to go beyond measures that are based on self-identification, as in CPS measures of shift work or independent contracting, yet the measures must still be amenable to survey research. Likewise, because flexible work arrangements are organizational as well as individual, better measures of the organizational characteristics that are associated with both "good" and "bad" flexibility are needed. Such organizational attributes may include departmentalization, formalization, authority structure, and the presence of work teams.

In terms of outcomes, more research is needed that examines the effects of flexible work on the physical and emotional well-being of workers and their families. Outcomes could be expanded to include the distribution of household labor and other responsibilities among dual-earner couples. Research along these lines is most developed in studies of shift work and flextime, but even here more valid and reliable outcome measures are needed.

Other research needs to look at the long-term effects of flexible work arrangements on workers' careers and retirement. Do flexible arrangements hinder upward mobility by creating more interruptions in workers' job histories? What are the implications for postretirement well-being and pension eligibility if workers continually change employers and their employment status? This is an especially critical question in an era of increasing individual responsibility for pensions, as in 401(k) plans.

POLICY IMPLICATIONS

The major policy implications of flexible work arrangements involve labor, health, pension, and family policies. Current U.S. labor laws were crafted during the early

1930s and 1940s and continue to be premised on standard employment arrangements. Thus, workers in flexible arrangements are less likely to have protections provided by various federal occupational safety and antidiscrimination laws. They are also less likely to be covered by employer-provided medical and pension plans. Indeed, the growth of many forms of flexible work arrangements have been spurred by employer efforts at reducing the regulatory and benefit costs of these programs. Thus, many scholars have argued for the development or expansion of benefit programs that are not funded primarily through employer contributions. These would include universal health care and expansion of Social Security eligibility and credits to cover all workers regardless of changes in employer and employment status.

Rapidly increasing health care and pension costs have also limited employers' offerings of family-friendly benefits, particularly paid maternity leave and on-site day care. As employers cut these benefits, it is likely that employee preferences for less costly alternatives such as flextime and telecommuting will grow. Other pressures that could lead to expansion of these flexible arrangements are an aging population and the increasing need for elder care and increasing energy costs and environmental concerns. As these pressures build, scholars need to develop data strategies that answer employers' concerns about the effect of flexible job arrangements on worker productivity and firm profitability. Policy makers need to develop programs that better target flexible work arrangements to work with families and those relatively deprived of flexibility, such as lower income single mothers, African Americans, and those working standard fixed shifts, especially night and rotating shifts. Likewise, they will need to develop alternatives to meet the needs of workers in jobs such as public safety that are not amenable to flexible scheduling or work-site arrangements.

All evidence suggests that both "good" and "bad" flexible work arrangements will become even more common in the future, whereas workers with standard, full-time arrangements will become an even smaller minority. However, because many social benefits such as health insurance, pension funds, and unemployment compensation are tied to full-time status and the number of years worked for the same employer, the growth of work flexibility could create serious problems for the well-being of workers, especially in later life. One general solution is to "decouple" benefit eligibility from employment status and tie it to more universal characteristics, such as citizenship.

At the same time, employers offering benefits such as flextime or telecommuting to one worker in a particular job category are generally required to offer it to all in that category. However, because the use of these benefits is based on individual, nonwork needs, employers are reluc-

tant to provide them, especially in the absence of data on how these benefits will affect their bottom line. This suggests a solution opposite to the more universal provision of health care and pension benefits: that certain flexible benefits be targeted to individual workers based on their personal, nonwork needs. Beyond this difference, however, future policies that address both more universal and more personalized benefits need to take into consideration how workers' progressions through their life courses affect their needs for different types of benefits and different types of flexible work arrangements.

SEE ALSO Volume 2: *Employment, Adulthood; Job Characteristics and Job Stress; Occupations; Policy, Employment; Work-Family Conflict.*

BIBLIOGRAPHY

Berg, P., Appelbaum, E., Bailey, T., & Kalleberg, A. L. (2004). Contesting time: International comparisons of employee control of working time. *Industrial and Labor Relations Review, 57,* 331–349.

Bond, J. T., Galinsky, E., & Swanberg, J. E. (1998). *The 1997 National Study of the Changing Workforce.* New York: Families and Work Institute.

Cappelli, P., Bassi, L., Katz, H. C., Knoke, D., Osterman, P., & Useem, M. (1997). *Change at work.* New York: Oxford University Press.

Evans, J. A., Kunda, G., & Barley, S. R. (2004). Beach time, bridge time, and billable hours: The temporal structure of technical contracting. *Administrative Science Quarterly, 49,* 1–38.

Fenwick, R., & Tausig, M. (2004). The health and family-social consequences of shift work and schedule control: 1977 and 1997. In C. F. Epstein & A. L. Kalleberg (Eds.), *Fighting for time: Shifting boundaries of work and social life* (pp. 77–110). New York: Russell Sage Foundation.

Golden, L. (1996). The expansion of temporary help employment in the U.S., 1982–1992: A test of alternative economic explanations. *Applied Economics, 28,* 1127–1141.

Golden, L. (2008). Limited access: Disparities in flexible work schedules and work-at-home. *Journal of Family and Economic Issues, 29,* 86–109.

Hill, E. J., Hawkins, A. J., & Miller, B. C. (1996). Work and family in the virtual office: Perceived influences of mobile telework. *Family Relations, 45,* 293–301.

Hochschild, A. R. (1997). *The time bind: When work becomes home and home becomes work.* New York: Metropolitan Books.

Hyland, M. (2003, September). Flextime. In *Work and family encyclopedia.* Retrieved June 17, 2008, from http://wfnetwork.bc.edu

Jacobs, J. A., & Gerson, K. (2004). *The time divide: Work, family and gender inequality.* Cambridge, MA: Harvard University Press.

Kalleberg, A. L. (2000). Nonstandard employment relations: Part-time, temporary, and contract work. *Annual Review of Sociology, 26,* 341–365.

Kalleberg, A. L., Reskin, B. F., & Hudson, K. (2000). Bad jobs in America: Standard and nonstandard employment relations and job quality in the United States. *American Sociological Review, 65,* 256–278.

Kunda, G., Barley, S. R., & Evans, J. A. (2002). Why do contractors contract? The experience of highly skilled technical professionals in a contingent labor market. *Industrial and Labor Relations Review, 55*, 234–261.

Kurland, N. B., & Egan, T. D. (1999). Telecommuting: Justice and control in the virtual organization. *Organizational Science, 10*, 500–513.

Marler, J. H. (2004, September). Alternative work arrangements. In *Work and family encyclopedia*. Retrieved June 17, 2008, from http://wfnetwork.bc.edu/

Myles, J. (1990). States, labor markets, and life cycles. In R. Friedland & A. F. Robertson (Eds.), *Beyond the marketplace: Rethinking economy and society* (pp. 271–298). New York: Aldine de Gruyter.

Presser, H. B. (2003). *Working in a 24/7 economy: Challenges for American families*. New York: Russell Sage Foundation.

Purcell, P. J. (2000). Older workers: Employment and retirement trends. *Monthly Labor Review, 123*(10), 19–30.

Rau, B. (2003, October). Flexible work arrangements. In *Work and family encyclopedia*. Retrieved June 17, 2008, from http://wfnetwork.bc.edu/

Ruhm, C. J. (1990). Bridge jobs and partial retirement. *Journal of Labor Economics, 8*, 482–501.

Schor, J. B. (1991). *The overworked American: The unexpected decline of leisure*. New York: Basic Books.

Smith, V. (1997). New forms of work organization. *Annual Review of Sociology, 23*, 315–339.

Tausig, M., & Fenwick, R. (2001). Unbinding time: Alternate work schedules and work–life balance. *Journal of Family and Economic Issues, 22*, 101–119.

Tilly, C. (1996). *Half a job: Bad and good part-time jobs in a changing labor market*. Philadelphia: Temple University Press.

U.S. Department of Labor, Bureau of Labor Statistics. (1998). Workers on flexible and shift schedules in 1997. *BLS News* (USDL 98-119). Washington, DC: U.S. Government Printing Office.

U.S. Department of Labor, Bureau of Labor Statistics. (2002). Workers on flexible and shift schedules in 2001. *BLS News* (USDL 02-225). Washington, DC: U.S. Government Printing Office.

Rudy Fenwick

FRIENDSHIP, ADULTHOOD

Friendship is one of the few relationships that can begin in childhood and endure for the entire life course. It is also a uniquely voluntary relationship that is influenced by choice more than by ties such as kinship. Nevertheless, social statuses and contexts determine the set of acquaintances from which people choose friends, and so the pool of potential friends usually is constrained by factors such as age, gender, race and ethnicity, social class, geographic location, and personal interests. Like other close relationships, a friendship may change over time, reflecting the developmental characteristics of the friend pair as well as their lifestyle choices. Friendships are subject to the joys and frustrations inherent in any strong emotional bond.

DEFINITION AND FUNCTIONS OF ADULT FRIENDSHIP

Adults typically define friends as persons with whom one is intimate and caring, whose company one enjoys, and whom one can trust. Friends are people whom one can depend on, who accept one as is, and who share similar interests. Most friends are similar to each other in characteristics such as age, sex, race, and class.

The definition of friendship is tied closely to the purposes friendship serves in adult life. Friends are valued for companionship, practical assistance, and advice. They provide emotional support, affirm one's worth as a social being, serve as role models, and make life interesting. Friends who share a long and meaningful history help sustain one another's self-identity and provide opportunities for pleasant reminiscing. Some people purposely seek out friends who will stimulate them by introducing them to activities they might not try on their own or involving them in different social networks. Research reviewed by Beverley Fehr (1996) shows that those who are socially integrated with friends (and relatives) are happier and healthier—and even live longer—than social isolates.

HISTORICAL PERSPECTIVES AND DEMOGRAPHIC TRENDS IN ADULT FRIENDSHIP

Interest in friendship dates back to ancient times. Plato, Aristotle, and Cicero described the qualities of ideal friendship, identified categories and functions of friendship, and analyzed the role of friendship in maintaining a stable society. Their conceptions were rooted in philosophical questions about the relationship between social justice and personal happiness and in the conviction that wholesome biological and psychological development results in a spiritual or moral character.

Historical analyses show that until medieval times people spent their daily lives in close association with many community members, not just family members, and presumably found opportunities for friendship across age, sex, and class distinctions in social activity in streets and markets. With the separation of work from the home during the Industrial Revolution and the rise of the nuclear family, friendships became less central to everyday life and tended to be restricted to persons of the same age, sex, and class. Factory and office workers spent more time away from home and had less time for leisurely pursuits, perhaps diminishing the importance of friendship for some. Nevertheless, friendship is considered an important part of social life for both workers and nonworkers in contemporary society. Spouses are supposed to be friends, employees expect to have friendly relations at work, and most people place a high value on friendship despite the demands of work and family responsibilities.

A 2002 survey of a nationally representative sample of 1,000 American adults revealed some interesting features of adult friendship. Many friendships are long-lasting. In fact, 65% of Americans have known their best friend for at least 10 years and only 15% have known their best friend for fewer than 5 years. (In this survey a spouse was not eligible as a best friend.) Most adults share social characteristics with their best friends. Specifically, 92% of women and 88% of men have a best friend of the same sex, 73% of adults have a best friend within 5 years of their own age, 73% of married adults have best friends who are married, and 70% of unmarried adults have best friends who are unmarried.

The survey also revealed that contemporary adult friends are in frequent contact and enjoy spending time together. Among the respondents 45% meet with their best friend at least once per week, 23% talk to their best friend on the phone daily, 40% of online adults exchange e-mail and 23% exchange instant messages with their best friend weekly, and 41% send letters or cards, although the frequency is less than once a month. The survey also showed that 91% said they would enjoy going on vacation with their best friend. Age and sex influence the mode of interaction. Younger adults are most likely to send e-mail or instant messages to their best friend. Older adults are most likely to send handwritten cards and letters, but younger adults do so more often than middle-aged adults do. Women are more likely to phone their best friend or send e-mail or instant messages, whereas men are more likely to meet their best friend in person.

STRUCTURAL FEATURES
OF ADULT FRIENDSHIP

Friendship structure refers to the characteristics of the people who become friends and of the ties linking individuals to their friends. One structural feature of friendship is homogeneity, that is, whether friends are of the same sex and race and are similar in age and social class. Another is hierarchy. Often friends have equal power and social status, but sometimes people choose to be friends with someone who is more or less influential or of a different status. Friendships also vary in terms of the degree of intimacy (which researchers refer to as solidarity) experienced within them. In addition, personal

preferences combined with the context in which friendship occurs influence whether a person cultivates few or many friendships (network size) and whether a person's friends know one another (network density and configuration).

Friendship does not occur in a vacuum; rather, persons who are available to become friends and the functions and activities associated with friendship are influenced by contextual factors that include historical period, social structure, culture, geographic and spatial location, and temporal patterns related to schedules and routines in everyday life. These external elements intersect with one another and change over time, leading to virtually limitless complexity in the range of influences on friendship.

During the high school and college years, many people are friends with others near their age and similar in other personal characteristics because those are the people they know; from this group of available social contacts, they find friends with whom they feel comfortable and share interests. Employment may bring chances to become friends with people from many age groups, as the workplace offers chances to interact with them regularly. Outside work, young adults tend to be close friends with others of the same marital status, and to find friends through sports, church, volunteering, and neighborhood groups. Middle-aged people are sometimes so busy with work and family demands that they have little time for friends and interact mainly with their best friends. Upon retirement, older adults often have time to add to their friendship circle through their leisure pursuits. Many seek friendships with younger persons because they realize they are at risk of losing their same-age friends to old-age-related illness and death.

ADULT FRIENDSHIP
INTERACTION PROCESSES

The interactive aspects of friendship consist of behavioral, cognitive, and affective responses that occur among friends. Behavioral processes include communication, which often takes the form of self-disclosure as well as assistance and advice; shared activities; conflict; and many other forms of interaction. Cognitive processes signify the internal thoughts that partners have about themselves, friends, and friendships. They include evaluations of each person's performance in the friend role, an assessment of the stability of the friendship, perceptions of similarity on psychological attributes, judgments of the friend's character, explanations of events occurring within the friendship, and interpretations of each partner's intentions and needs. Affective processes include emotional responses to friends and friendships. Both pleasant and unpleasant emotions can be involved in friendship, ranging from love and satisfaction to jealousy and anger.

PHASES OF FRIENDSHIP IN ADULTHOOD

Friendships are not static but have multiple possible phases. Friendships begin when acquaintances have opportunities to know one another better, reveal personal information about themselves, and discover shared interests and values. Friendships continue through a sustaining phase, which can be long-lasting and can encompass increasing, decreasing, or fairly stable levels of closeness and interaction over time. Some friendships end, often by fading as friends drift apart because of changes in lifestyle and interests, geographic separation, or competing demands. On rare occasions people terminate a friendship purposely, typically as a result of betrayal or irresolvable conflict. The phases of friendship are not necessarily linear. For example, high school friends who have drifted apart may renew their friendship in adulthood if they resume regular interaction.

NEW DIRECTIONS IN ADULT FRIENDSHIP RESEARCH

Although early research on friendship tended to highlight the positive aspects of interactions among friends and the benefits of friendship, later studies documented the potential for disappointment and conflict in friendship as well. Studies show that some adults tolerate characteristics that are less than desirable if the friend and the friendship fill important needs. However, certain behaviors are likely to lead to strife and the dissolution of a friendship, including criticism, jealousy, and disputes over matters such as business affairs. More research is needed on the extent to which adults experience friendship dissolution, the effects of conflict between friends on personal health and well-being, and the strategies adults use to resolve friendship problems.

Research on friendship among college students and older adults is more prevalent than studies of friendships among middle-aged adults and among young adults who do not attend college. A fuller understanding of friend-

ship structure, interactive processes, and phases could be obtained from studies of the latter groups. In addition, comparative studies of friendship across subcultural and national groups are needed for a comprehensive understanding of friendship. In light of the ubiquitous nature of friendship in adulthood and its important contributions to well-being, increasing the range of information would enable professionals to develop plans to foster the establishment of meaningful friendships, advise people about the best ways to sustain satisfactory friendships, and aid those with friendship troubles.

SEE ALSO Volume 2: *Sibling Relationships, Adulthood; Social Integration/Isolation, Adulthood; Social Support, Adulthood.*

BIBLIOGRAPHY

Adams, R. G., & Allen, G. (Eds.). (1998). *Placing friendship in context.* Cambridge, U.K., and New York: Cambridge University Press.

Blieszner, R., & Adams, R. G. (1992). *Adult friendship.* Newbury Park, CA: Sage.

Fehr, B. (1996). *Friendship processes.* Thousand Oaks, CA: Sage.

Fetto, J. (2002, October 1). Friends forever. *American Demographics* (Article 117). Retrieved June 22, 2008 from http://findarticles.com/p/articles/mi_m4021/is_2002_Oct_1/ai_92087421

Nardi, P. M. (Ed.). (1992). *Men's friendships.* Newbury Park, CA: Sage.

O'Connor, P. (1992). *Friendships between women: A critical review.* New York: Guilford Press.

Rawlins, W. K. (1992). *Friendship matters: Communication, dialectics, and the life course.* New York: Aldine de Gruyter.

Ueno, K., & Adams, R. G. (2006). Adult friendship: A decade review. In P. Noller & J. A. Feeney (Eds.), *Close relationships: Functions, forms, & processes* (pp. 151–169). New York: Psychology Press.

Werking, K. (1997). *We're just good friends: Women and men in nonromantic relationships.* New York: Guilford Press.

Rosemary Blieszner

G

GAMBLING

Gambling is a behavior in which a person puts something of value at risk. When gambling is offered as a commercial product, a person risks money on the outcome of some event, with the possibility of receiving a monetary return if a certain outcome occurs. Governments at the state level offer some forms of gambling and regulate all others. Casinos typically offer slot machines, video poker machines, and a variety of table games (e.g., blackjack, craps, baccarat). Many state governments in the United States offer lotteries, in which people buy tickets with a very small chance of winning a very large jackpot. Other forms of gambling (e.g., betting on horse racing and greyhound racing) are available in several states. Online casino gambling and poker have become very popular in recent years. Some forms of gambling represent games of skill (e.g., casino table games, poker), whereas others are purely games of chance (e.g., lotteries, slot machines).

People who gamble typically see it as a form of entertainment. Gambling is an *experience good* such as watching a movie or a football game, and not a *tangible product*, such as computers or shirts. People are willing to pay for experience goods because the experience itself provides benefits. For example, casino games may be fun to play, often have a social aspect, and offer a chance to win money. Many casinos are built with amenities such as hotels, live theater shows, and restaurants that gamblers also can enjoy. Lotteries offer a chance to win a very large amount of money (usually millions of dollars); many people enjoy thinking about what they would do if they won a large jackpot.

However, by their nature, gambling products have a negative *expected value* for the player. This means that, on average, the players of such games are expected to lose. Casino games typically have an expected value of around -5%, depending on the game, whereas lotteries have an expected value of around -50%. This means that for each $100 bet placed at a casino, the casino keeps an average of $5; for each $100 of lottery tickets purchased, the government selling the lottery keeps an average of about $50. Typically the Website hosting a poker game will keep a small percentage of each hand's total bets. The *house* is able to keep these amounts, on average, and this represents the income they receive for providing the games, facilities, and other costs of doing business. Some players *will* win, but most gamblers understand that casino games and lotteries have, on average, a negative expected value. For people to be willing to gamble, then, they must expect the benefits of playing (e.g., the chance of winning, the enjoyment, any social interactions) to exceed their expected losses, which can be thought of as the *price of gambling*. Just as a person must pay $10 or more to watch a movie at the theater, he or she expects to lose some money to the casino for playing its games.

GAMBLING OVER THE LIFE COURSE

Research by psychologists has focused on gambling among adolescents, adults, and senior citizens. This research is still in its infancy, but rates of gambling participation are a major focus of researchers. Lifetime participation rates are often estimated at more than 70% for all age groups—a majority of people, including adolescents, have gambled at some point in their lives. The gambling participation rate varies by demographic group, geographical location, legal restrictions, and other variables. For example, in Australia, gambling is a much more common and acceptable form of

155

Slot machines. *Casino games are an "experience good" because they may be fun to play, often have a social aspect to them, and offer a chance to win money.* **FIELD MARK PUBLICATIONS.**

entertainment than in the United States. Therefore, the participation rate in Australia is expected to be higher than in the United States where casino gambling is a relatively new phenomenon except in New Jersey and Nevada.

Many adolescents gamble but not always in market-based gambling such as casinos and lotteries. Students may bet on sporting events, play poker, or other social forms of gambling. Such activities are counted in participation rates. Few adolescents develop gambling problems, but still, such gambling is viewed with concern, to the extent that it may lead to problem gambling as an adult. However, for most people, gambling represents a harmless form of entertainment.

PROBLEMATIC GAMBLING

A small portion of gamblers develop what has been termed *pathological gambling*, in which an individual damages his or her personal and professional life because of an unhealthy amount of or a preoccupation with gambling. In 1994, the American Psychiatric Association (*DSM-IV*) suggested that the prevalence of pathological gambling was around 1% of the population. Psychologists, psychiatrists, and medical researchers are interested in understanding the causes of problematic gambling behavior. Among the issues related to pathological gambling are the rate of the affliction (prevalence), how it affects different demographic groups differently, different rates of severity, and the types of behavior that result from or characterize it. Some researchers have focused on youth gambling behaviors and effects, whereas others have focused on gambling among members of minorities, gambling in various cultures, and society as a whole. Different samples of the population may be affected by pathological gambling in different ways.

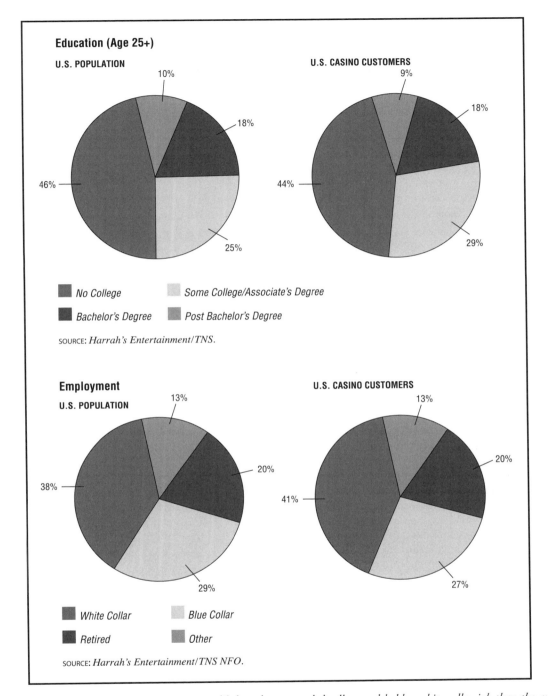

Education (Age 25+)

U.S. POPULATION

10%
18%
46%
25%

U.S. CASINO CUSTOMERS

9%
18%
44%
29%

■ *No College*　　□ *Some College/Associate's Degree*

■ *Bachelor's Degree*　　■ *Post Bachelor's Degree*

SOURCE: *Harrah's Entertainment/TNS.*

Employment

U.S. POPULATION

13%
20%
38%
29%

U.S. CASINO CUSTOMERS

13%
20%
41%
27%

■ *White Collar*　　□ *Blue Collar*

■ *Retired*　　■ *Other*

SOURCE: *Harrah's Entertainment/TNS NFO.*

Figure 1. *The average U.S. casino customer is more likely to have attended college and hold a white collar job than the average American.* **CENGAGE LEARNING, GALE.**

The results of such studies depend on the sample being studied, cultural idiosyncrasies, legal restrictions, research methodology, and other factors. The newest and most promising area of research related to pathological gambling deals with the neuroscience of addiction (Ross, Sharp, Vuchinich, & Spurrett, 2008). This research examines the role of processes inside the brain in initiating and sustaining addiction and promises to improve prevention and treatment strategies. This area of research overlaps with research on other addictions, such as alcoholism and drug abuse. Some researchers have suggested that all forms of addiction, and related behaviors, are not medical issues, but are instead nothing other than very strong preferences (Becker 1996; Schaler 2000).

CONSEQUENCES OF THE GAMBLING INDUSTRY

The other major research interest with respect to gambling is involved with the social and economic effects of the gambling industry. Many governments (local, regional, and national) have either adopted or are considering the adoption of gambling as a public policy tool, primarily to raise tax revenues. Economic studies of the effects of gambling have become more common in recent years, focusing on cost-benefit considerations.

On the *cost* side of gambling adoption are issues of pathological gambling and related behaviors. As psychologists, sociologists, and others attempt to measure the prevalence and severity of such behaviors, economists attempt to quantify these costs. This area of research has been fraught with methodological problems, particularly related to how to define *social costs* and how to measure them in monetary terms (Walker, 2007). No reliable estimates of the social costs of pathological gambling yet exist.

On the benefit side of the equation, most advocates of legalized gambling argue that there are significant consumer benefits, tax benefits, and economic development effects, particularly owing to large casinos. Perhaps the most important and sizable of these benefits is the consumer benefits received from the availability of gambling. If consumers did not enjoy gambling, they would not do it. The facts that casinos earn profits and lotteries continue to raise revenues indicate that people do enjoy gambling. Aside from these consumer benefits, the most common benefits derived from legalized gambling appear to be tax revenues from lotteries and casinos, and economic development, in the case of casinos.

Overall, results of existing research suggest that the economic benefits of legalized gambling (including consumer benefits, development and tax effects) probably outweigh the costs of pathological gambling. However, such economic and medical research is still in its infancy. Before researchers can develop reliable monetary estimates of costs and benefits, many conceptual and methodological issues need to be sorted out. As gambling expands, the gambling industry and government are beginning to offer more help for problem and pathological gamblers. Such programs will become more effective as researchers develop a better understanding of problem gambling behaviors.

SEE ALSO Volume 2: *Debt; Mental Health, Adulthood; Risk.*

BIBLIOGRAPHY

American Psychiatric Association. (1994). *Diagnostic and statistical manual of mental disorders* (4th ed.). (*DSM-IV*). Washington, DC: Author.

Becker, G. (1996). *Accounting for tastes.* Cambridge, MA: Harvard University Press.

Schaler, J. (2000). *Addiction is a choice.* Chicago: Open Court.

Ross, D., Sharp, C., Vuchinich, R., & Spurrett, D. (2008). *Midbrain mutiny: The picoeconomics and neuroeconomics of disordered gambling.* Cambridge, MA: MIT Press.

Walker, D. (2007). *The economics of casino gambling.* New York: Springer.

Douglas M. Walker

GAYS AND LESBIANS, ADULTHOOD

The adult life course of men and women who report same-sex attraction must be considered in the context of social and historical change. Following social theorist Karl Mannheim (1993 [1928]) and sociologist Glen Elder (2002), persons born within adjacent birth years comprise a generational cohort and are subject to many of the same social influences at about the same ages. At the same time, there is considerable intra-cohort variation based on such factors as geography, social status, ethnicity, or sexual orientation. This entry focuses on the interplay of social change and the life course among men and women in contemporary American society who seek others of the same sex for social and sexual ties. Social and historical change interplay with life history in determining the meanings that men and women construct about their sexuality and this is reflected in the distinct identity cohorts that have emerged from the context of social change.

Discussion of the life course of men and women expressing same-sex desire must be understood in terms of three aspects of their sexuality: sexual orientation, sexual behavior, and sexual identity (Savin-Williams, 2005). Sexual orientation refers to awareness of a preponderance of desire for social and sexual encounters with others of the same sex. Desire must be distinguished from sexual behavior, which is the realization of desire in action. Sexual orientation and behavior must in turn be differentiated from sexual identity, that is, the label that men and women use in portraying their sexuality. Biologist Alfred Kinsey et al. (1948), psychologist Ritch Savin-Williams (2005), and philosopher of science Edward Stein (1999) maintain that sexual attraction cannot be viewed as either straight or gay but that sexual attraction instead ranges from complete affinity for the opposite sex to that for one's own sex. This perspective has been supported in Lisa Diamond's (2006) study of young adult women and in Stein's (1999) careful review of quantitative findings regarding homosexuality.

Across generational cohorts in contemporary American society, the narrative of sexuality told by men is most often that of an awareness of same-sex desire that reaches back into childhood or early adolescence and that remains fixed across the life course. Women are more likely than men to portray a variable sexuality across the course of life, involving partners of both the same and the opposite sex. Reviewing findings regarding the expression of same-sex awareness among men and women, Phillip Hammack (2005) has described the life course of women with awareness of same-sex attraction as one of sexual fluidity in which the primary focus is on relationships and a "sex-unspecific pattern of erotic preference" (p. 271).

Understanding of self and sexuality among men and women coming to adulthood and aware of same-sex desire varies across generations because it is closely tied to social and historical change. As historian George Chauncey (1994) has shown in his discussion of the definition of same sex-desire across the past century, the very terms used to portray this desire have changed over time. Within contemporary European and North American society, men and women presently entering late life and aware of same-sex attraction were born in the years preceding World War II (1939–1945) and came to adulthood in the conservative postwar era. With same-sex desire stigmatized by the larger society, to the extent that these men and women even sought social and sexual contact with others of their own sex, meetings were furtive in bars and other venues and were always in danger of exposure with the possibility of criminal sanctions.

Some men aware of their same-sex desire joined the clandestine Mattachine Society, while women seeking same-sex ties joined the Daughters of Bilitis. These homosocial groups were increasingly active in the advent of the civil rights movement in the 1960s. These men and women had often chosen solitary or low-key occupations, such as that of an accountant or librarian, where they could keep "below the social radar," and be able to avoid discussion of their personal life with work colleagues. These men and women often define their sexual identity as *homosexual*, a term common in a time that still viewed same-sex desire as evidence of personal maladjustment.

Sexual orientation, conduct, and identity within generational cohorts born later in the 20th century have been significantly influenced by social and historical change. Men and women born in the immediate postwar period came to adulthood in the turbulent years of the 1960s and 1970s. Often aware from childhood of same-sex desire that was regarded at the time as a source of shame and stigma, many of these men and women were emboldened by the civil rights movement and the tentative social activism of the preceding decade to seek tolerance from the larger society. This generation came to

adulthood at a time of dramatic social change and at a time when membership in a sexual minority group was becoming recognized as one of a number of sexual lifeways. Much of this activism was mobilized in the aftermath of patron resistance to a June 1969 police raid on the Stonewall Inn, an establishment frequented by men and women seeking same-sex camaraderie. This raid galvanized young adult patrons and their friends to demand an end to police raids and inspired visible social activist groups nationwide across the following decade. This activism marked the advent of the gay rights era and resulted in ordinances prohibiting discrimination on the basis of sexual orientation in many cities nationwide. For the first time it was possible for men and women to enjoy same-sex companionship in now visible bars and other spaces. It was also possible to publish newspapers reporting on the activities of the community, which included advertisements for bars and for men and women seeking others as social and sexual partners. Men and women within this cohort often chose the label *gay* and *lesbian* to describe their identity. This generation eschews the term *homosexuality*, because to them it associates awareness of same-sex attraction with psychiatric illness.

The very social changes that made possible socially visible spaces in which to find other men and women with same-sex desire led to anonymous and casual sexual partners. These practices increased the possibility of transmitting a virus that silently destroyed the immune system over a number of years, which became manifest in the following decade as a fatal disease. First reported in the *New York Times* in the summer of 1981 as a rare cancer striking a group of men in San Francisco acknowledging same-sex conduct, the means of transmission and tests for AIDS were available by the mid-1980s. Between 1980 and 1995, when the first medications were discovered that would turn AIDS into a chronic rather than life-threatening illness, several hundred thousands of men had died from complications associated with AIDS. By the mid-1980s most school sex education programs featured the importance of practicing safer sex; men and women coming to adulthood, then, better understood the implications of risky sexual practices.

This young adult generation of self-identifying gay men and lesbians made their community through their activism, and later assisted by the Internet, were able to help other men and women aware of their same-sex desire to learn that they were not alone. Even in high school these young adults had been able to "come out" without the opprobrium that had greeted previous generations. Forming an identity cohort characterized by demand for respect for their sexuality, this generation now in middle adulthood presumes their right to make their own life free from stigma or legal restriction.

The most recent generation of adults coming to adulthood, who follow the activism of preceding generations, presumes that there is little relationship between sexual orientation or sexual desire and conduct and other aspects of their life as they emerge into adulthood. Many of these men and women maintain that their sexual preference for same- or opposite-sex partners has little relevance to who they are as persons. These young adults either identify themselves as *queer* or as *spectrum* (meaning other than completely heterosexual on the six point Kinsey scale of same-sex attraction) or, more often, explicitly reject any sexual or other identity labels (Cohler & Hammack, 2007). Whereas Anthony D'Augelli (2002) has portrayed the struggle of young adults in previous generations to deal with their same-sex desire when faced with shame or hostility at home and in the community, Bertram Cohler and Hammack (2007) observe that changing social circumstances have shifted the narrative of young adulthood among more recent young adults from a narrative of struggle and suppression to a narrative of emancipation. To an even greater extent than youths in the preceding generation, these young adults presume that their sexuality is not relevant to their accomplishments at school and work or their participation in the larger community. Research confirms this presumption: There are few socio-demographic differences in sexual orientation (Badgett, 2001), although these findings are based largely on studies of convenience samples.

Accompanying the social and historical change that has been the background for personal development across these generational cohorts in American society, each generational cohort has been challenged by unique developmental tasks that may not be generalized to later cohorts moving across the course of life from early adulthood to later life. Further reciprocal socialization means that cohort effects across generations shaped the subsequent course of life for each generation in a manner unique to a particular time and place. For example, the very success of current young adult and middle-aged generations in charting a new path in society has led many formerly hidden elders to come out and to found new homophilic organizations such as Senior Action in a Gay Environment (SAGE), which lobbies for quality senior housing for older same-sex attracted men and women no longer able to live alone. A lifetime of increasing competence in dealing with stigma has equipped these older adults to manage the dual prejudices of their aging and their sexuality. At the same time, the lifelong experience of sexual minority stress and stigma has taken its toll on the morale of members of this generation (Meyer, 2003), a toll that is unique to this generation of elders with same-sex orientation and cannot be assumed to characterize

AIDS Quilt. A view from the Washington Monument on Oct. 11, 1996, shows the huge AIDS Quilt laying on the ground, stretching from the monument to the U.S. Capitol. AP IMAGES.

later cohorts of men and women with same-sex attraction. It is important to distinguish between the effects due to aging from those due to membership in a particular cohort.

The present generation of men and women in settled adulthood has participated in much of the social change since the emergence of the gay rights era of the 1970s. Many of these adults still grieve the death of romantic partners and friends from the AIDS pandemic. Viewing the AIDS Memorial Quilt composed of squares memorializing the lives of those who died from AIDS, it is striking how many of these squares are for men born in the 1950s and dying in the time between the mid-1980s and the mid-1990s. Members of this generation experienced loss and mourning more characteristic of later life within the heterosexual world. Despite these experiences of grief, Cohler and Robert Galatzer-Levy (2000), in their review of studies of the association of sexual orientation and mental health, report few differences in well-being among persons who report primarily same- or opposite-sex attractions. However Ilan Meyer (2003) has shown that greater prejudice due to sexual minority orientation experienced in childhood and adolescence is associated with lower morale experienced across the adult years.

Current cohorts of midlife adults also belong to the first generation for which the normative adult role transitions of legally recognized romantic relationships or marriage and parenthood are available as choices. While the desirability of same-sex marriage as an option continues to be controversial among both men and women with same-sex attraction and also within the larger community, several states have accorded legal protection for two men or two women entering into long-term sociosexual relationships. The state of Massachusetts and entire countries such as Canada and the Netherlands explicitly sanction same-sex marriage (see sidebar).

Chauncey (1994) views both legal protection for same-sex romantic unions and legal protection for parenthood among men or women open about their same-sex attraction as the outcome of a process of social change over the postwar period. This is nowhere more evident than in the enhanced opportunity for men and women open about their same-sex desire to adopt children. About one-third of women forming a same-sex relationship have children from a previous heterosexual relationship. Most states permit single men or women to become foster parents and to legally adopt the children in their case. Advances in reproductive technology have made it possible for women to share biological parenthood in which the baby is the product of one partner's egg, sperm donation from either a man who is a friend of the couple or an anonymous donor, and carried to term by the other partner. The birth mother in these same-sex couples reports less stress than her heterosexual counterparts as the other partner is much more involved in child care than men in traditional heterosexual marriages. Men may call upon a friend to serve as a surrogate mother with sperm from either or both partners fertilizing the egg.

Early studies of the effect of parental sexual orientation on child outcomes were based on convenience groups using same- and opposite-sex parents agreeing to a comparative study of children in the classroom and the playground. More recent studies have been based on large-scale national surveys. Taken together, these studies reveal that children raised by same-sex couples do not differ in their adjustment and subsequent life course from children growing up in traditional heterosexual families (Patterson, 1995), although they tend to be particularly tolerant in their social attitudes. When same-sex couples, particularly men, elect to adopt, agencies may still offer the most desirable children to heterosexual couples. Chil-

SAME-SEX MARRIAGE
■

Same-sex (or equal) marriage refers to a union between two persons of the same sex that provides the same legal status and protection that is provided to married heterosexual couples. Belgium, the Netherlands, Canada, Spain, and South Africa currently recognize same-sex unions as a marriage. Some nations such as Israel offer formal recognition for same-sex unions. Whereas one state in the United States (Massachusetts) allows same-sex marriage and eight states provide the same protection for same-sex domestic partnerships as for heterosexual unions, 26 other states explicitly ban using the term *marriage* to refer to the union of a same sex couple. Historian George Chauncey (2004) traces the demand for same-sex marriage to the gay rights era beginning in the 1970s, which by the 1990s led both to many employers offering domestic partnership benefits, and to a series of court decisions regarding the protection of privacy. Opponents of gay marriage maintain that marriage presumes procreation and that persons of the same sex cannot produce offspring (Sullivan, 1997). However, that presumption is not a part of federal or state law regarding heterosexual marriage.

dren offered for foster parenthood or adoption for either single men or same-sex men couples may be at higher developmental risk resulting from foreign birth or biological parental pregnancy and childbirth than children raised by heterosexual couples. These children may be born with some developmental infirmity such as fetal alcohol syndrome or may have such developmental disabilities as developmental delay. However, the motivation for generativity or the need to care for the next generation means that these children get unusually good care and may be helped to overcome these developmental problems.

The current young adult generation of men and women aware of same-sex attraction is unique in two respects. In the first place, the generation of youth or emergent adulthood is itself a generation that was not explicitly recognized in American society until the postwar period. In the second place, while previously stigmatized by peers and teachers, adolescents and young adults aware of same-sex attraction have empowered themselves with the support of both peers and adults. They have been supported in their ability to overcome prejudice—prejudice that in earlier youth cohorts led to sexual minority stress by groups at school and college and even in the workforce—with resources available on the Internet and provided by other questioning and same-sex defined peers and elders.

As a consequence, the life story of members of this generation has shifted from one of struggle to overcoming prejudice to one of emancipation with issues of struggle largely irrelevant in urban America. The change is reflected in the reluctance of these youths to adopt identity labels such as *gay* and *lesbian* or even *queer*. The concern of this generation is with their own success in education and work and perhaps with finding a relationship with a like-minded man or woman aware of his or her own same-sex desire. It is common for these men and women aware of same-sex desire to have close friends and to be part of social groups varying in their commitment to same- and opposite-sex social and romantic relationships. For members of this generation of emergent adulthood, concern with issues of sexual identity appears to be much less of a concern than finding satisfying work and meaningful relationships. Cohler (2007) has illustrated this shift in discussing the blog of a Midwestern college student writing about his boyfriend, his straight fraternity friends, and their views regarding work, relationships, and their future prospects.

The life course of present generations of men and women from youth through middle age aware of their same-sex attraction is increasingly similar to that of their heterosexual counterparts. From the experience of social isolation and sexual minority stress due to stigma characteristic of the oldest generation of same-sex attracted men and women, generations of same-sex attracted men and women within present cohorts across the first half of life have become virtually indistinguishable from their opposite-sex attracted peers. Further, this social change is leading to backward socialization among older adults who now see new possibilities for their life as they embrace social activism. Whereas conservative commentator Andrew Sullivan (1996) celebrates this change, radical social commentator Michael Warner (1999) decries the loss of the vibrant culture created by minority sexuality men and women following the gay rights revolution. However, it is clear that sexuality cannot be discussed apart from social change and the impact of this change upon the life courses of the various generational cohorts born in the 20th century.

SEE ALSO Volume 1: *Gays and Lesbians, Youth and Adolescence;* Volume 2: *Dating and Romantic Relationships, Adulthood; Sexual Activity, Adulthood;* Volume 3: *Cohort; Gays and Lesbians, Later Life.*

BIBLIOGRAPHY

Badgett, M.V.L. (2001). *Money, myths, and change: The economic lives of lesbians and gay men.* Chicago: University of Chicago Press.

Chauncey, G. (1994). *Gay New York: Gender, urban culture, and the makings of the gay male world, 1890–1940.* New York: Basic Books.

Chauncey, G. (2004). Why marriage: The history shaping today's debate over gay equality. New York: Basic Books.

Cohler, B. (2007). *Writing desire: Sixty years of gay autobiography.* Madison: University of Wisconsin Press.

Cohler, B., & Galatzer-Levy, R.M. (2000). *The course of gay and lesbian lives: Social and psychoanalytic perspectives.* Chicago: University of Chicago Press.

Cohler, B., & Hammack, P. (2007). The psychological world of the gay teenager: Social change, narrative, and "normality." *Journal of Youth and Adolescence, 36*(1), 47–59.

D'Augelli, A. R. (2002). Mental health problems among lesbian, gay, and bisexual youth ages 14 to 21. *Clinical Child Psychology and Psychiatry, 7*(3), 433–456.

Diamond, L. (2006). What we got wrong about sexual identity development: Unexpected findings from a longitudinal study of young women. In A.M. Omoto & H.S. Kurtzman (Eds.), *Sexual orientation and mental health: Examining identity and development in lesbian, gay, and bisexual people* (pp. 73–94). Washington, DC: American Psychological Association.

Elder, G. H., Jr. (2002). Historical times and lives: A journey through time and space. In E. Phelps, F. F. Furstenberg, Jr., & A. Colby (Eds), *Looking at lives: American longitudinal studies of the twentieth century* (pp. 194–218). New York: Russell Sage Foundation.

Hammack, P. L. (2005). The life course development of human sexual orientation: An integrative paradigm. *Human Development, 48*(5), 267–290.

Kinsey, A., Pomeroy, W. B., & Martin, C. (1948). *Sexual behavior in the human male.* Philadelphia: W. B. Saunders.

Mannheim, K. (1993). The problem of generations. In K. H. Wolff (Ed.), *From Karl Mannheim* (2nd ed., pp. 351–398). New Brunswick, NJ: Transaction Books. (Original work published 1928.)

Meyer, I. (2003). Prejudice, social stress, and mental health in lesbian, gay, and bisexual populations: Conceptual issues and research evidence. *Psychological Bulletin, 129*(5), 674–697.

Patterson, C. J. (1995). Lesbian mothers, gay fathers, and their children. In A.R. D'Augelli & C. J. Patterson (Eds.), *Lesbian, gay and bisexual identities over the life span: Psychological perspectives* (pp. 262–290). New York: Oxford University Press.

Savin-Williams, R. (2005). *The new gay teenager.* Cambridge, MA: Harvard University Press.

Stein, E. (1999). *The mismeasure of desire: The science, theory, and ethics of sexual orientation.* New York: Oxford University Press.

Sullivan, A. (1995). Virtually normal: An argument about homosexuality. New York: Knopf.

Sullivan, A. (1996). *Virtually normal: An argument about homosexuality.* New York: Vintage Books.

Sullivan, A. (Ed.). (1997). *Same-sex marriage, pro and con: A reader.* New York: Vintage Books.

Warner, M. (1999). *The trouble with normal: Sex, politics, and the ethics of queer life.* New York: Free Press.

Bertram J. Cohler

GENDER DISCRIMINATION

SEE Volume 2: *Sexism/Sex Discrimination.*

GENDER IN THE WORKPLACE

Women's rapid movement into the paid labor market over the past century has had an impact on childrearing, marriage, gender equality, and the labor market itself. Whereas in the past most women devoted their time to caring for their families, women's life courses are now shaped by the combined influences of family and work. In the early 21st century, women in the workplace experience many opportunities, but there are still key issues and challenges.

TRENDS IN WOMEN'S LABOR FORCE PARTICIPATION IN THE UNITED STATES

Women's participation in the paid labor market increased dramatically during the 20th century. In 1890 only 18% of women were in the labor force. Women's labor force participation rose slowly but steadily through the early 1900s, reaching 28% in 1940. During World War II women were actively recruited into jobs that supported the war effort, with the result that their labor force participation rates jumped to 36% in 1945. When soldiers returned home after the war, some women returned to homemaking, but the decline in women's labor force participation rates was short-lived. By 1960, 38% of women age 16 and older were in the labor force, and this participation rate increased every decade until it reached 58% in 1990. Women's overall labor force participation rate hovered between 58 and 60% until the early 2000s (Blau, Ferber, & Winkler, 2006). These numbers are even higher among women who have completed their schooling and have not yet retired. For instance, in 1998, 76 to 78% of women age 25 to 34, 35 to 44, and 45 to 54 participated in the labor force

(Fullerton, 1999). The rise in women's employment occurred in most racial groups. For example, Bart Landry (2000) documented that the percentage of married African American women in the labor force increased from 1940 until 1994. The percentage of African American married women in the labor force was higher than that of White married women in each decade among both upper and lower middle class women. In addition to greater financial need, Landry explained that the Black–White difference was due to Black women, particularly Black middle-class wives, embracing a different version of "true womanhood" that included a commitment to both family and career. These racial differences in employment among married women are still evident in the 21st century. Among young single women, however, White women are working at higher rates than both Blacks and Latinas (see Taniguchi & Rosenfeld, 2002).

Women's roles as wives and mothers have typically had an impact on their participation in the paid labor market, but women's approaches to navigating work and family across the life course have changed substantially over time. In the early part of the 20th century, women typically worked when they were young and single, exiting the labor force when they married or had children—if they could afford to live on only their husband's income. However, labor force participation rates for women with young children have increased rapidly since the 1950s. For instance, only 17% of women experiencing their first birth between 1961 and 1965 were working 12 months after the birth. In contrast, between 2000 and 2002, nearly two-thirds (64%) of new mothers were working 12 months after the birth (Johnson, 2008).

The reasons for this dramatic shift have been studied extensively. Economists argue that women's labor market decisions are based on a comparison of the value of market time (or time at work) to the value of nonmarket time (or time at home). According to this theory, people's decisions are based on *opportunity costs*, that is, an assessment of the costs of making one choice relative to the costs of choosing something else. Over the course of the past century, the value of women's market time increased greatly and the value of women's nonmarket time decreased greatly, leading women to spend a larger proportion of their lives employed (Blau et al., 2006).

Increases in women's educational attainment are an important factor underlying shifts in the value of women's market and nonmarket time (Blau et al., 2006). In 1940 only 4% of women had completed a college degree, but by 2007 this had risen to 28% (U.S. Department of Education, 2007). Men's educational attainment also rose over this period, but women closed, and even

OPTING OUT

Since the 1980s, the media have disseminated stories about professional women opting out, or leaving the workforce, to care for their children. The claim that society is experiencing an opt-out revolution (Belkin, 2003) has spurred debates about whether mothers with professional jobs really are opting out and, when they do, about their motivations for doing so. Evidence on the extent of the opt-out revolution is mixed. Studies examining the work decisions of all women tend to show little evidence of an opt-out revolution (Boushey, 2008; Cotter, England, & Hermsen, 2007), but one study indicated that college-educated women in their late 20s are spending less time in the labor market than did earlier cohorts of young educated women (Vere, 2007). Although some mothers who leave their jobs express a clear preference for staying at home, many others feel pushed out of work by the competing demands of an inflexible workplace and motherhood (Stone, 2007).

BIBLIOGRAPHY

Belkin, L. (2003, October 26). The op-out revolution. *The New York Times*, pp. 42–47, 58, 85–86.

Boushey, H. (2008). "Opting out?" The effect of children on women's employment in the United States. *Feminist Economics, 14*(1), 1–36.

Cotter, D., England, P., & Hermsen, J. (2007). *Moms and jobs: Trends in mothers' employment and which mothers stay home: A fact sheet from Council on Contemporary Families.* Washington, DC: Center for Economic and Policy Research and Council on Contemporary Families.

Stone, P. (2007). *Opting out? Why women really quit their careers and head home.* Berkeley: University of California Press.

Vere, J. P. (2007). "Having it all" no longer: Fertility, female labor supply, and the new life choices of Generation X. *Demography, 44*(4), 821–828.

reversed, gender gaps in educational attainment. In 1900 only 19% of college degrees were awarded to women, whereas in 2006 women earned more than half (58%) of all college degrees (U.S. Department of Education, 2007). These changes in educational attainment have led more women to aspire to professional careers than in the past and mean that women face clear losses in earned income and professional advancement if they exit the labor market when they have children.

Indeed, despite the common impression that women with low education and limited labor market skills (who are more likely to be single or partnered with a low earner) are the most likely to work because they need the income, in reality women with higher education levels are most likely to work when they have young children. Of women experiencing their first birth between 2000 and 2002, 62% of women with less than a high school education did not work within a year of their child's birth compared to 40% of women with a high school degree and 27% of women with a college education or higher (Johnson, 2008). In addition to the career aspirations of women with higher education, researchers have identified multiple barriers to the employment of low-educated women. High childcare costs, low childcare quality, lack of access to a car, and health limitations of the mother or the child all contribute to the challenges that mothers with low education

and wages face when trying to combine work and family (Roy, Tubbs, & Burton, 2004; Scott, London, & Hurst, 2005).

A second factor pulling women into the labor market may be changes in the availability of other sources of income, such as their partners' earnings or welfare and other government benefits. Peter Gottshalk (1997) indicated that since the 1970s the earnings of men with the weakest labor market positions (e.g., low education levels, limited job skills) have declined. The level of welfare payments and the ability to collect welfare without working have also declined (Committee on Ways and Means, 2004). These changes should push more women into the paid labor market, particularly women with low education levels and single mothers. Although mothers with low education levels are still less likely to work when their children are young than mothers with higher education levels (Johnson, 2008), in the late 1990s there was a sharp increase in the labor force participation rates of single mothers (Blau et al., 2006).

In addition to the forces increasing the value of women's time in the market, many forces have reduced the value of women's nonmarket time (Blau et al., 2006). Moving from an agrarian society to an industrial society reduced families' dependence on women's domestic labor as families became less likely to produce their own food and clothing. Domestic responsibilities continued to decrease with the advent of dishwashers, laundry machines, and precooked meals readily available for purchase. Families are smaller than in earlier centuries, reducing the time that women spend pregnant or nursing infants. Additionally, the rapid increase in nonmaternal childcare options provides parents with more opportunities to enter the labor market.

KEY ISSUES AND CHALLENGES FACING WOMEN IN THE WORKPLACE

Some of the key issues and challenges facing women in the workplace include the gender wage gap, discrimination, the glass ceiling, and sexual harassment.

The Gender Wage Gap Despite women's increased educational attainment and strengthening attachment to the labor force, women working full-time still earn less than men working full-time. Estimates of the gender wage gap differ somewhat based on whether researchers compare men's and women's annual earnings or hourly wages, because men tend to work more hours than women. Regardless of the measure used, the gender wage gap has closed over time but has not disappeared. From 1979 to 1998 the ratio of women's to men's hourly wages increased from 63% to 80% (Blau & Kahn, 2006). Several factors explain the gender wage gap, including differences in what women and men choose to study in school, the occupations that women and men enter, the number of years women and men spend employed, and discrimination.

As noted earlier, women are now more likely than men to complete a college degree. However, this trend masks variation that is key to understanding the gender wage gap: Women and men choose very different academic majors. In 2000–2001 women earned just 28% of the bachelor's degrees awarded in computer and information sciences, 20% in engineering, and 34% in economics. In contrast they earned 78% of the degrees in psychology, 77% in education, and 84% in health (Blau et al., 2006). Among those with college degrees, these differences in educational choice translate into women and men holding very different jobs—with very different earning trajectories.

Among those without college degrees, women and men also hold different jobs. Different jobs translate into different pay, authority, and social status (Reskin & Padavic, 1994, p. 31). Jobs that are primarily filled by women and/or minorities tend to require lower level skills and, in turn, provide low wages (Tomaskovic-Devey, 1993). In 2000, women represented more than half of the workers in several major occupational groups such as sales and office work, service (Gist & Hetzel, 2005). A greater percentage of men (58.1%) than women

(41.9%), however, held management, business, and financial jobs, which are generally more lucrative and require more training than sales and service positions. Even after controlling for skill demands, "female occupations" (i.e., jobs comprised of mostly women) pay less than "male occupations" (England, Allison, & Wu, 2007; Huffman, 2004). Pay discrepancies rooted in gender-typed career choices are not easily remedied by public policies. The Equal Pay Act of 1963 requires equal pay for equal jobs. This law does not, however, prohibit employers from paying less to all workers in predominantly female occupations than workers in predominantly male occupations (Reskin & Padavic, 1994).

Jobs that women typically hold have been referred to as *women's work*, a derogatory label emphasizing the low status of these jobs (Tomaskovic-Devey, 1993). In particular, care work, which includes jobs such as childcare provider, nurse, and teacher, is synonymous with women's work. Childhood socialization, in which girls and boys are taught normative gender roles, likely plays a large role in the ultimate educational and occupational choices of women and men. Women do the majority of both paid and unpaid care work, because it meshes with gender roles emphasizing women's capacity for nurturing. The low pay and support for these workers, despite the large skill set required for these jobs, leads many to argue that care work is devalued (England, 2005). Despite continuing gender segregation in care work, other industries showed a decline in segregation between 1996 and 2003. This decline was due in part to the rise in service sector jobs, which are less segregated than jobs in other industries (Tomakovic-Devey et al., 2006).

A second factor that explains the gender wage gap is the amount of time men and women spend in the labor force. The time invested in paid employment, in terms of gaining work experience as well as skills relevant to one's own employer, is often called *human capital*, those skills and experiences that a worker "sells" on the market. Men and women follow very different employment trajectories, with men more likely to work continuously and women more likely to follow a variety of paths that include transitions to and from the labor market as well as spells of part-time employment (Hynes & Clarkberg, 2005; Moen & Han, 1999). Researchers estimate that about 11% of the gender wage gap is due to differences in labor force experience (Blau et al., 2006).

Parenting demands are among the key reasons why women have more discontinuous work histories than their male peers, but children play a role in women's earnings beyond differences in labor force participation. Researchers have begun to study differences in earnings between mothers and nonmothers and have found what they now call a *motherhood wage gap*. Compared to nonmothers, mothers experience a wage penalty of about 7% per child. Here too, labor market entrances and exits explain only part of the gap in pay between mothers and nonmothers (about one-third), leaving the remaining two-thirds of the gap unexplained (Budig & England, 2001). Research in this area is still underway, but some of the hypothesized explanations for the unexplained gap include differences between mothers and nonmothers in their productivity and energy while at work, their decisions about whether to take demanding jobs or to select more family-friendly jobs, and discrimination (Budig & England, 2001).

Discrimination Most researchers acknowledge that discrimination is likely to account for some of the gap that remains between men's and women's wages after factors such as occupation and experience are taken into account (Blau & Kahn, 2006; Budig & England, 2001). The Civil Rights Act of 1964 prohibits employers from discriminating on the basis of gender during hiring, promotion, and job assignment. The Equal Employment Opportunities Commission was created to enforce this act, but given the subtlety of many employers' intentional and unintentional actions, Joan Williams (2000) points out, it can be difficult to prove gender discrimination.

In addition to gender-based discrimination, evidence suggests that caregivers also experience discrimination, such as being terminated or denied promotion due to family responsibilities. In one case, female grocery clerks were not promoted to management because their employer believed the clerks' childcare responsibilities would prevent them from working long hours (Williams & Segal 2002). Although caregiving discrimination can happen to men, it is more likely to happen to women as they typically assume more caregiving responsibilities.

Employers may also discriminate by offering women lower wages than men. Although illegal, there are still cases in which employers pay women less than men for performing the same job (see examples in Reskin & Padavic, 1994). For example, in 2001 six women filed a lawsuit claiming, among other issues, gender discrimination in pay decisions at Wal-Mart and Sam's Club. In 2004 the federal court made it a class action lawsuit applying to all female employees at Wal-Mart in the United States. The case has not been tried or settled out of court. Pay discrimination occurs at all levels of the occupation hierarchy and is partly responsible for the increasing gender wage gaps over the life course (Maume, 2004). Pay differences and differences in hiring and promotion can have a cumulative effect over time, with small differences early in a career adding up and leading to larger differences later in the life course (Maume, 2004).

Unfortunately, estimating how much of a pay gap is due to discrimination versus other factors is a difficult task as researchers rarely have information on all factors influencing wages, such as individual productivity, job experience, and whether jobs require comparable skills (Reskin & Padavic, 1994). Experimental studies can help eliminate these challenges by examining how job applicants are rated when the only substantive difference between two workers is their gender or parental status. For instance, Shelley Correll, Steven Bernard, and In Paik (2007) asked college students to rate the application materials of two job candidates for a high-level position. The students were told that their comments would be passed on to a hiring committee and may influence actual hiring decisions. The researchers constructed resumes and other materials making the applications equally qualified for the job, but they experimentally manipulated the parental status of the applicant. Their results showed that mothers were perceived as less competent and less committed to their jobs than nonmothers and that these perceptions translated into lower proposed starting salaries and higher required achievement standards for mothers.

The Glass Ceiling A *glass ceiling* metaphor has been commonly used to describe the invisible barrier that prevents women, particularly minority women, from advancing in organizations (Williams, 2000). Although many women have management positions, the number of women holding top-level positions, such as chief executive officer of an organization, is very small. In 1995 the Federal Glass Ceiling Commission published a report documenting a stark contrast in the number of male and female senior managers in Fortune 1500 companies: 95% of senior managers were men. Furthermore, when Mary Noonan and Mary Corcoran (2004) examined gender differences in promotion among University of Michigan law school graduates from 1972 to 1985, they found that women were less likely to be promoted to partner in law firms than were men, even after accounting for differences between men and women in factors such as grade point average in law school, number of years they had practiced law, and amount of time taken off, if any, from work to raise children. The Federal Glass Ceiling Commission identified three barriers that account for the glass ceiling: (a) societal barriers (differential opportunities for educational attainment, prejudices), (b) structural barriers within the business (initial placement in noncareer track jobs, lack of mentoring), and (c) governmental barriers (lack of consistent monitoring, inadequate reporting; U.S. Department of Labor, 1995).

Although women may have a difficult time "cracking" the glass ceiling, mothers tend to have an even more difficult time, given the time constraints and responsibilities associated with managing a job and motherhood simultaneously. As noted earlier, mothers with low education and few financial resources often struggle to remain attached to the labor market, which can have immediate negative consequences for their own and their children's financial well-being. Taking time out of the workforce can also have consequences for career advancement. For instance, lawyers who took time out of the labor force to care for children were less likely to make partner and earned less if they did become partners (Noonan & Cochran, 2004).

Some accommodations for working mothers, such as reduced work hours, have led to concerns that they place women onto a "mommy track" that then prevents them from maintaining their previous status or from advancing further. Indeed even mothers who are not interested in these accommodations may be viewed differently once they have children and may experience changes in their work arrangements that move them into less prestigious jobs. For instance, the Federal Glass Ceiling Commission reported that upon returning to work after maternity leave, women often received less desirable assignments than they did before giving birth (U.S. Department of Labor, 1995).

Sexual Harassment As women have become a larger part of the American workforce, many have faced sexual harassment in the workplace. The Equal Employment Opportunity Commission (2007a) defines sexual harassment as "unwelcome sexual advances, requests for sexual favors, and other verbal or physical conduct of a sexual nature . . . when this conduct explicitly or implicitly affects an individual's employment." Although sexual harassment is illegal, a 1994 survey by the U.S. Merit Systems Protection Board (1995) found that 44% of women reported experiencing some type of harassing behavior at work during the previous two-year period. The most common behaviors reported are sexual teasing and jokes, but 10% of survey respondents indicated that they received letters, calls, or other sexual material, and 7% reported being pressured for sexual favors. Of those who reported experiencing some type of sexual harassment, only 6% reported making a formal complaint. Only half of those who made complaints reported that this improved the situation (U.S. Merit Systems Protection Board, 1995). It is unclear why more complaints were not filed, but possible reasons include fear of retaliation or job loss.

Sexual harassment can have negative consequences for health, workplace morale and productivity, and victims' career trajectories. For instance, Chelsea Willness, Piers Steel, and Kibeom Lee (2007) show that harassment has been linked to a reduction in mental wellness for female victims and an increase in rates of posttraumatic stress disorder. Sexual harassment has also been linked to heightened stress and physical illness (Rospenda, Richman, Ehmke, & Zlatoper, 2005), which can lead to frequent absences from work, strained coworker relationships, and limited productivity (Willness et al., 2007). Sexual harassment can also have lasting effects on women's careers. Victims are more likely to be dismissed or lose promotions due to absences from work (Willness et al., 2007).

FUTURE DIRECTIONS FOR RESEARCH ON GENDER IN THE WORKPLACE

One of the most promising avenues for future research on gender in the workplace asks the question: What can be done to address the challenges that women are facing? Many scholars have outlined suggestions to eliminate the glass ceiling, reduce sexual harassment, reduce gender inequality in pay, and help individuals meet their work and family responsibilities (e.g., Catalyst, 2000; Moen & Roehling, 2004; Rapoport, Bailyn, Fletcher, & Pruitt, 2002). A wide variety of interventions and changes have been proposed, ranging from workplace policies about flexible scheduling and sexual harassment to government policies about maternity leave and childcare.

One of the challenges in this area is philosophical. A debate has existed for generations about how to define equality between women and men and what the goal of related policies should be (Loutfi, 2001; Vogel, 1993). Does equality mean that women have the same opportunities as men and receive the same penalties as men for factors such as reduced time in the labor market, or does equality mean that women and men have the same outcomes on issues such as time spent in caregiving and occupational attainment?

This controversy is still apparent in policy debates about how to address employees' needs to balance their work and family responsibilities (Lewis & Guillari, 2005). Jennifer Glass (2004) categorizes commonly proposed work–family policies into three groups. The first set promotes reductions in work hours, allowing workers (typically mothers) to reduce their time in the labor market in order to perform caregiving at home. The second set promotes schedule flexibility (adapting the timing and location of work), allowing workers to meet their caregiving responsibilities without minimizing their overall time in the labor market. The third set provides assistance to workers (such as on-site childcare or assistance finding elder care) and helping workers pay others to provide care when it is needed. These policies reflect very different choices (providing care oneself vs. purchasing care in the market) and may have very different effects on the career trajectories and the well-being of workers and their families.

Although addressing the challenges that women face in the workplace involves grappling with the philosophical question about ultimate policy goals, research can greatly inform these debates by providing concrete information about the costs and benefits of various workplace and government policies. These studies need to be complex, because interventions with positive impacts in one domain (e.g., career attainment) may have negative impacts in another (e.g., individual or child well-being). They also need to reflect the reality that policies that are plausible and beneficial to one group of workers (e.g., professional workers, married workers) may be unfeasible or not beneficial to others (e.g., workers in less skilled occupations, single parents).

SEE ALSO Volume 1: *Socialization, Gender;* Volume 2: *Careers; Dual Career Couples; Employment, Adulthood; Job Characteristics and Job Stress; Occupations; Policy, Employment; Sexism/Sex Discrimination.*

BIBLIOGRAPHY

Blau, F., Ferber, M., & Winkler, A. (2006). *The economics of women, men, and work.* Upper Saddle River, NJ: Pearson, Prentice Hall.

Blau, F., & Kahn, L. (2006). The U.S. gender pay gap in the 1990s: Slowing convergence. *Industrial and Labor Relations Review, 60,* 45–66.

Budig, M. J., & England, P. (2001). The wage penalty for motherhood. *American Sociological Review, 66,* 204–225.

Catalyst, Inc. (2000). *Cracking the glass ceiling: Catalyst's research on women in corporate management, 1995–2000.* New York: Author.

Committee on Ways and Means of the U.S. House of Representatives. (2004). *2004 green book.* Washington, DC: U.S. Government Printing Office.

Correll, S., Bernard, S., & Paik, I. (2007). Getting a job: Is there a motherhood penalty? *American Journal of Sociology, 112,* 1297–1338.

England, P. (2005). Emerging theories of care work. *Annual Review of Sociology, 31,* 381–399.

England, P., Allison, P., & Wu, Y. (2007). Does bad pay cause occupations to feminize, does feminization reduce pay, and how can we tell with longitudinal data? *Social Science Research, 36,* 1237–1256.

Equal Employment Opportunity Commission. (2007a). *Sexual harassment.* Retrieved July 7, 2008, from http://www.eeoc.gov/sexual harassment

Equal Employment Opportunity Commission. (2007b). *Sexual harassment charges EEOC and FEPAs combined: FY 1997–2007.* Retrieved July 7, 2008, from http://www.eeoc.gov/stats

Fullerton, H. N. (1999, December). Labor force participation: 75 years of change, 1950–1998 and 1998–2025. *Monthly Labor Review,* 3–12.

Gerson, K. (1985). *Hard choices: How women decide about work, career, and motherhood.* Berkeley: University of California Press.

Gist, Y. J., & Hetzel, L. I. (2005). *We the people: Women and men in the United States. Census 2000 special reports.* U.S. Census Bureau. Retrieved May 23, 2008, from http://www.census.gov/prod

Glass, J. (2004). Blessing or curse? Work–family policies and mother's wage growth over time. *Work and Occupations, 31,* 367–394.

Gottschalk, P. (1997). Inequality, income growth, and mobility: The basic facts. *The Journal of Economic Perspectives, 11,* 21–40.

Han, S. K., & Moen, P. (1999). Work and family over time: A life course approach. *Annals of the American Academy of Political and Social Science, 562,* 98–110.

Huffman, M. L. (2004). Gender inequality across local wage hierarchies. *Work and Occupations, 31,* 323–344.

Hynes, K., & Clarkberg, M. (2005). Women's employment patterns during early parenthood: A group-based trajectory analysis. *Journal of Marriage and the Family, 67,* 222–239.

Johnson, T. (2008). *Maternity leave and employment patterns: 2001–2003.* Current Population Report, P70-113. Washington, DC: U.S. Census Bureau.

Landry, B. (2000). *Black working wives: Pioneers of the American family revolution.* Berkeley: University of California Press.

Lewis, J., & Guillari, S. (2005). The adult worker model family, gender equality, and care: The search for new policy principles and the possibilities and problems of a capabilities approach. *Economy & Society, 34,* 76–104.

Loutfi, M. F. (2001). *Women, gender, and work: What is equality and how do we get there?* Geneva: International Labour Office.

Marshall, A. M. (2005). Idle rights: Employees' rights consciousness and the construction of sexual harassment policies. *Law & Society Review, 39,* 83–123.

Maume, D. J. Jr. (2004). Wage discrimination over the life course: A comparison of explanations. *Social Problems, 51,* 505–527.

Moen, P., & Han, S. (2001). Gendered careers: A life-course perspective. In R. Hertz & N. L. Marshall (Eds.), *Working families: The transformation of the American home.* Berkeley: University of California Press.

Moen, P., & Roehling, P. (2005). *The career mystique: Cracks in the American dream.* Lanham, MD: Rowman & Littlefield.

Noonan, M. C., & Corcoran, M. E. (2004). The mommy track and partnership: Temporary delay or dead end? *The Annals of the American Academy of Political and Social Science, 596,* 130–150.

O'Connor, M., & Vallabhajosula, B. (2004). Sexual harassment in the workplace: A legal and psychological framework. In B. J. Cling (Ed.), *Sexualized violence against women and children: A psychology and law perspective* (pp. 115–147). New York: Guilford Press.

Rapoport, R., Bailyn, L., Fletcher, J. K., & Pruitt, B. H. (2002). *Beyond work–family balance: Advancing gender equity and workplace performance.* San Francisco, CA: Jossey-Bass.

Reskin, B. F., & Padavic, I. (1994). *Women and men at work.* Thousand Oaks, CA: Pine Forge Press.

Rospenda, K. M., Richman, J. A., Ehmke, J. L. Z., & Zlatoper, K. W. (2005). Is workplace harassment hazardous to your health? *Journal of Business and Psychology, 20,* 95–110.

Roy, K., Tubbs, C., & Burton, L. (2004). Don't have no time: Daily rhythms and the organization of time for low-income families. *Family Relations, 53,* 168–178.

Scott, E. K., London, A. S., & Hurst, A. (2005). Instability in patchworks of childcare when moving from welfare to work. *Journal of Marriage and the Family, 67,* 370–386.

Taniguchi, H., & Rosenfeld, R. A. (2002). Women's employment exit and reentry: Differences among Whites, Blacks, and Hispanics. *Social Science Research, 31,* 432–471.

Tomaskovic-Devey, D. (1993). *Gender & racial inequality at work: The sources & consequences of job segregation.* Ithaca, NY: ILR Press.

Tomaskovic-Devey, D., Zimmer, C., Stainback, K., Robinson, C., Taylor, T., & McTague, T. (2006). Documenting desegregation: Segregation in American workplaces by race, ethnicity, and sex, 1966–2003. *American Sociological Review, 71,* 565–588.

U.S. Department of Education. (2007). *Digest of education statistics, 2007.* Washington, DC: National Center for Education Statistics.

U.S. Department of Labor. (1995). *Executive summary: Fact finding report of the Federal Glass Ceiling Commission.* Retrieved July 7, 2008, from http://www.dol.gov/oasam

U.S. Merit Systems Protection Board. (1995). *Sexual harassment in the federal workplace: Trends, progress, continuing challenges.* Washington, DC: U.S. Government Printing Office.

Vogel, L. (1993). *Mothers on the job.* New Brunswick, NJ: Rutgers University Press.

Williams, J. (2000). *Unbending gender: Why family and work conflict and what to do about it.* New York: Oxford University Press.

Williams, J., & Segal, N. (2002). The new glass ceiling: Mothers—and fathers—sue for discrimination. Washington, DC: Program on Gender, Work, & Family, American University, Washington College of Law.

Willness, C. R., Steel, P., & Lee, K. (2007). A meta-analysis of the antecedents and consequences of workplace sexual harassment. *Personnel Psychology, 60,* 127–162.

Kathryn Hynes
Kelly D. Davis

GENETIC INFLUENCES, ADULTHOOD

One of the most influential developments in science is the growing understanding of genetics. During the last half century, the body of knowledge about genes and their consequences has flourished. As scientists' understanding of genetics has increased, the relevance of genetics to the study of a wide variety of issues has been highlighted. In this vein, understanding adult life trajectories requires taking into account individuals' genetic inheritances and their interplay with the social and physical environment.

GENES AND EVOLUTIONARY HISTORY

A gene is a single coding segment of DNA, which is the hereditary material in all organisms including humans. The hereditary directions in DNA are stored in 3 billion bases. The order of these bases provides the blueprint for building and maintaining an organism. Genes are grouped onto chromosomes, of which humans have 23 pairs. The pairing of chromosomes means that humans have two copies of all genes, with the exception that males have only one copy of sex-linked genes (those that occur on the X chromosome and those that occur on the Y chromosome; females have two X chromosomes, males only one). Different forms of a gene are referred to as alleles, and the combination of allele forms for a particular gene are known as a genotype. A genotype corresponds to a particular set of gene products, whereas a phenotype is the observed end result of the gene process.

To understand the nature of genes as well as how they influence human lives, it is important to recognize their evolutionary past. Genes are passed along from parents to child, so a gene's "success" is measured in the number of copies it transmits to future generations. To pass genes on, an individual must reproduce offspring. Thus, genes that increased the reproductive success of an individual were more successful in the course of evolution and are more prevalent today. Conversely, genes that are present today must have been selected for reproductive advantage over evolutionary history. Because the modern world differs dramatically from the circumstances under which these genes were selected, characteristics that were advantageous then may not be advantageous today. For example, humans have evolved excellent physiological mechanisms to store energy when food is abundant, so as to sustain them in times when food is in short supply. Contemporary humans can be considered as selected for genes that favor energy storage and that defend against weight loss. Contemporary industrialized societies, however, are characterized by low levels of physical exercise and abundant food supply. It is this misfit between one's primeval genes and modern lifestyles that accounts for the current U.S. epidemic in obesity at the population level. Individuals differ considerably in the risk of obesity, however, because they are exposed to different sets of genetic and environmental factors. This evolutionary perspective is a helpful way to interpret research on genes and the life course, because it frames the narrative on the origin of a genetic effect.

The effect of genes on complex phenotypes, such as behaviors, has been explored in a number of ways that have evolved as scholars' understanding of biology has increased. Studies on twins and adopted children allowed researchers to explore the heritability (i.e., the degree to which a characteristic is passed from parents to children via genes) of behaviors using known levels of genetic similarity between individuals to disentangle genetic and social effects. For example, in twin studies, differences between pairs of identical (monozygotic) twins and fraternal (dizygotic) twins are compared; because the identical twins are known to share the same genetic material, smaller average differences in behavior between identical twins than fraternal twins suggest that the behavior is influenced by genetics. In adoption studies, adopted siblings are biologically unrelated to any others raised in the same household, so the effect of the family social environment can be observed by comparing the extent to which adopted siblings resemble others raised in the same family. These models do not isolate any particular gene responsible or associated with behaviors; they simply indicate that there is a genetic component to the observed behaviors.

With advances in genetic technology, more sophisticated methods have become available to researchers. Clinical research using animals enables researchers to ascertain the effects of specific genes. The biochemical effects of these genes can be determined, so researchers are able to observe what the genes do and what the consequences of their actions might be. Drawing upon results of these animal experiments to identify genes that may affect some outcome, scientists can then collect both social and genetic data from humans, which allow them to test for associations between these candidate genes and behaviors. Most recently, the development of genome wide association scans has allowed scientists to use large amounts of information from points along the entire genome in order to examine genetic bases of disease and behaviors.

GENETIC INFLUENCES ON THE ADULT LIFE COURSE

Genes play a part in several aspects of the adult life course, including physical and mental health, fertility, and criminal behavior. However, individuals' statuses and trajectories at the start of adulthood are shaped by a vast array of influences, including genetic influences, experienced at younger ages. Thus genes also have an impact on the adult life course through their effects on development during youth and adolescence. Genetic influences highlight the long-term, cumulative view of life events and processes inherent to the life course perspective.

Evidence suggests that genetics shape health during adulthood. The most obvious cases are genetic diseases such as Huntington's disease, sickle-cell anemia, and hemophilia. These diseases are Mendelian in nature; that is, there is a simple, almost deterministic relationship between a certain genotype and having the disease. However, most diseases are complex and involve a number of genes and nongenetic factors. For example, in most cases, obesity is not caused by a single gene. Rather, many genes and a large number of factors related to dietary patterns, exercise, and other health behaviors appear to be involved. Using several large genome wide association studies, work has produced evidence that the FTO gene is associated with an individual's propensity to obesity (Frayling et al., 2007). As alluded to earlier, a genome wide association study is a method used to identify genes involved in human disease by searching the genome for small variations that occur more frequently in people with a particular disease than in people without the disease. The data is then used to pinpoint genes that may contribute to a person's risk of developing various diseases.

Genes also are implicated in alcohol use (Nurnberger & Bierut, 2007). Facial flushing, drowsiness, and other unpleasant symptoms from even light alcohol use are observed much more frequently among East Asians than Europeans. Such symptoms mainly occur to those possessing the ALDH2*2 allele, which is prevalent in East Asians and encodes inactive forms of the ALDH2 gene. ALDH2. Research also shows that the presence of the ADH2*2 allele, which is also more prevalent in East Asians and encodes superactive forms of ADH2, can trigger the responses. Probably because of the unpleasant flushing responses, the ALDH2*2 and ADH2*2 alleles tend to protect those who possess the alleles from developing alcoholism. GABA-A receptors are believed to be involved in alcoholism. Studies suggest that the GABRA2 gene is associated with alcohol dependence (Soyka, Preuss, Hesselbrock et al., 2008).

Reproductive behavior, whether a person has children and, if so, when they have their first and how many they ultimately have, is another area of adult life that appears to have a genetic basis. In addition to fecundity, the biological ability to have children, there are a number of crucial steps that lead to childbearing, each of which could also be influenced by genetic factors. Age of sexual debut has been shown to be related to the dopamine D4 receptor gene (DRD4), a gene that has been hypothesized to be related to risk-taking behavior (Guo & Tong, 2006). Another important component of reproductive behavior, a person's number of sexual partners, has been found to be related to the DAT1 gene among males (Guo et al., 2007).

Preliminary work suggests that a number of genes (DAT1, DRD2, and MAOA) are associated with involvement in delinquent and criminal acts during adolescence and early adulthood (Guo, Ou, Roettger et al., 2008). However, even if a gene does have an effect on a human outcome, the effect is almost never deterministic. Typically, it increases or decreases the probability of an outcome by a moderate amount just like a nongenetic factor. Sometimes, the effect of a gene depends on environmental factors. Avshalom Caspi and colleagues (2002) investigated the role of genotype in violent behavior among individuals who were maltreated in childhood. Males who were maltreated early in life are at risk of becoming violent offenders, but not all males respond to maltreatment in the same way. The study found that a functional polymorphism in the gene encoding the neurotransmitter-metabolizing enzyme monoamine oxidase A (MAOA) modifies the effect of maltreatment. Only maltreated children with a genotype generating low levels of MAOA expression tended to develop the violent behavior problem.

The above examples highlight some specific areas in which researchers are working to untangle the connections among adult outcomes, genes, and social circumstances. However, there are other possible ways to look at the effects of genes on the adult life course. Genetic effects are not necessarily static, as the effects of genes are known to vary across the life course. Because most genes have a number of consequences, a phenomenon called pleiotropy, which aspect of their work that is important can change over time. For example, a gene called p53 suppresses cancer by limiting the proliferation of stem cells (Rodier et al., 2007). Early in life, the consequences of this gene are helpful—a reduced likelihood of developing cancer. However, as the individual ages, the consequence of suppressing the growth of stem cells is a more rapid aging process.

Changes in social environments over the life course also may lead to temporal variation in the effects of genes on behavior. Over time, an individual is exposed to different circumstances, as a result of their age, historical forces, or a combination of the two. These circumstances can alter the way in which genes are expressed. For example, while there appear to be genes associated with drinking behavior, the importance of these genes varies with life course stage. During adolescence, when the individual is subject to strong peer influences about drinking, there is little genetic association between genes and drinking behavior. But later in life, peer group influences are no longer the dominant force in the person's life and the genes become an important predictor of alcohol use (Guo et al., 2007).

FUTURE DIRECTIONS FOR RESEARCH

This entry has examined a number of paths by which genes could affect the life of an individual, and it may seem that scientists are beginning to understand how genes affect the adult life course. However, current understanding is limited by a number of methodological and conceptual concerns.

First, the relationship between genes and behavior is complex. Some of the relationships between genes and behavior discussed above were direct (e.g., a gene variant raises or lowers the probability of having a disease), whereas others were moderated (e.g., a gene product leads to a particular outcome only under certain circumstances, as in Caspi et al. [2002] about maltreated children.). When the circumstances under which a gene leads to a particular outcome are external to the individual, this situation is referred to as a gene-environment interaction. An example is the case of phenylketonuria (PKU), a condition that develops when individuals born with specific genetic markers are exposed to phenylalanine (an amino acid) in their diet (Khoury, Adams & Flanders, 1988). In a gene-environment interaction, the environment may influence how sensitive individuals are to the effects of a genotype and vice versa (Hunter, 2005). The existence of such complicated interactions makes understanding the effects of genes even more difficult for researchers.

Second, researchers lack the data necessary to research the links among genes, environment, and behavior. To unpack all of the complexity of genes and environments, large-scale collection of both social and genetic information is needed. Because certain genotypes are exceedingly rare, large samples are necessary to analyze their effects. To date, no study has been sufficiently large and detailed to truly capture the nuances of genes and environments. Even with such a data set, methodological issues arise, as the sheer volume of information makes the possibility of false positive results very real.

Third, the outcomes that have been studied thus far are limited in scope; there is room to explore what these genetic factors might mean for career and marriage trajectories, for example. However, with complicated outcomes, more genes and environmental factors will be involved. Thus career trajectories will be much more difficult to study than the trajectory of a person's blood pressure. In addition, research thus far has also examined only a small number of candidate genes. Because researchers rely on previous work to establish a plausible mechanism by which a gene leads to behavioral differences, this gap in knowledge has limited the avenues of exploration. Thus further study is needed on the biological effects of genes and how these effects then translate into observed behaviors.

Finally, the adult years represent the longest span of the life course, yet it remains one of the most understudied areas with regards to genetics and their effects on the life trajectories of individuals. Further research in this area is critical.

While a number of paths are open to future research, there are also a number of ethical, legal, and social issues related to genetic research. The implications of understanding an individual's genetic inheritance and the consequences of what that knowledge can shed light on about the person and their life are immense. An obvious example is the effect on insurance and access to health care, should genetic predispositions be known—a concern that drove the passage of the Genetic Information Nondiscrimination Act of 2008, which protects Americans against discrimination based on their genetic information. For example, this Act prohibits health insurers from denying coverage to healthy individuals who may be predisposed to developing certain illnesses in the future and also bars employers from factoring in a person's genetic makeup into hiring, firing, and promotion decisions. At the same time, within the medical community there has been a persistent hope that, with knowledge of a person's genome, medicine might be personally tailored in order to more accurately and safely deal with health problems (Guttmacher & Collins, 2005).

More attention is needed to the ways in which information about individuals is safeguarded to protect the individual. In addition, genetic testing reveals information not just about an individual, but also about his or her family. For example, if a young person was tested and found positive for Huntington's disease, the test result would also provide disease information on his or her siblings. With the current medical and scientific system built on informed consent, how does one deal with the fact that by testing an individual, you indirectly test family members, who may not have consented to having their genes tested?

Knowledge of a link between genes and behaviors could lead to targeted social programs. Given the policy necessity of targeting resources where the leverage is greatest, this could mean that an individual could warrant intervention on the basis of genetic heritage, even when others in similar social situations may not. Most fundamentally, as it is learned how genes influence the way in which people live their lives, people have to ask what it means to be "created equal" if there are inherent differences in people that cannot necessarily be overcome by environment or conscious effort.

SEE ALSO Volume 1: *Genetic Influences, Early Life;* Volume 3: *Genetic Influences, Later Life.*

BIBLIOGRAPHY

Caspi, A., McClay, J., Moffitt, T.E., Mill, J., Martin, J., & Craig, I.W. (2002). Role of genotype in the cycle of violence in maltreated children. *Science, 297*(5582), 851–854.

Frayling, T.M., Timpson, N.J., Weedon, M.N., Zeggini, E., Freathy, R.M., Lindgren, C.M., et al. (2007). A common variant in the FTO gene is associated with body mass index and predisposes to childhood and adult obesity. *Science, 316*(5826), 889–894.

Guo, G., Ou, X.-M., Roettger, M., & Shih, J.C. (2008). The VNTR 2 repeat in MAOA and delinquent behavior in adolescence and young adulthood: Associations and MAOA promoter activity. *European Journal of Human Genetics, 16*(5), 626–634.

Guo, G., Roettger, M., & Shih, J.C. (2007). Contributions of the DAT1 and DRD2 genes to serious and violent delinquency among adolescents and young adults. *Human Genetics, 121*(1), 125–136.

Guo, G., & Tong, Y. (2006). Age at first sexual intercourse, genes, and social and demographic contexts: Evidence from twins and the dopamine D4 receptor gene. *Demography, 43*(4), 747–769.

Guttmacher, A.E., & Collins, F.S. (2003). Welcome to the genomic era. *New England Journal of Medicine, 349*(10), 996–998.

Guttmacher, A.E., & Collins, F.S. (2005). Realizing the promise of genomics in biomedical research. *Journal of the American Medical Association, 294*(11), 1399–1402.

Hunter, D.J. (2005). Gene-environment interactions in human diseases. *Nature Reviews Genetics, 6*(4), 287–298.

Khoury, M.J., Adams, M.J., & Flanders, W.D. (1988). An epidemiologic approach to ecogenetics. *American Journal of Human Genetics, 42*(1), 89–95.

Nurnberger, J.I., & Bierut, L.J. (2007). Seeking the connections: Alcoholism and our genes. *Scientific American, 296*(4), 46–53.

Pennisi, E. (2007). Breakthrough of the year—Human genetic variation. *Science, 318*(5858), 1842–1843.

Risch, N.J. (2000). Searching for genetic determinants in the new millennium. *Nature, 405*(6788), 847–856.

Rodier, F., Campisi, J., & Bhaumik, D. (2007). Two faces of p53: Aging and tumor suppression. *Nucleic Acids Research, 35*(22), 7475–7484.

Soyka, M., Preuss, U.W., Hesselbrock, V., Zill, P., Koller, G., & Bondy, B. (2008). GABA-A2 receptor subunit gene (GABRA2) polymorphisms and risk for alcohol dependence. *Journal of Psychiatric Research, 42*(3), 184–191.

Guang Guo
Brandon Wagner

GIDDENS, ANTHONY
(1938–)

Born in London, Anthony Giddens is a social theorist with an international reputation. In 1985 he was awarded a professorship from Cambridge University and later became the director of the London School of Economics (1997–2003). He was the cofounder of Polity Press, which is now one of the world's foremost publishing companies for the social sciences and humanities. In

Anthony Giddens. JASON BYE/AFP/GETTY IMAGES.

1999 he was invited to present the British Broadcasting Corporations (BBC) Reith Lectures, which he subsequently published in *Runaway World* (1999). He became a member of the House of Lords in 2004. Over the course of his career, he has been awarded 15 honorary degrees. He continues to add to his substantial body of academic writing, which includes more than 40 books. His work has been translated into more than 40 languages.

The theme in much of Giddens's writing is the tension between structure and agency, which culminated in the development of *structuration theory*. This theory was developed incrementally in Giddens's writings that distinguished it from other theoretical approaches such as positivism, interpretivism, structuralism, and functionalism. Giddens (1984) presented a summary in *The Constitution of Society: Outline of the Theory of Structuration*. He proposed that structures consisted of rules and resources, which the agent uses to reproduce social life. *Agency* refers to the ways in which individuals continually monitor, rationalize, and create their social world. Structuration theory moves beyond the polarized positions held by

objectivist and subjectivist approaches to understanding the social world and provides a new way of understanding the basic elements of social reality. It describes the production and reproduction of social structures through social practices across time and space, reconceptualizing structure and agency as a duality. For Giddens, structures do not have an independent existence outside of the individual but are always partially internal to the agent, mediated by experience, and continuously produced and reproduced through social interaction.

Giddens's later work applied structuration to the way in which large-scale historical forces such as globalization, modernity, and politics shaped the perceptions and experiences of individuals, with particular emphasis on the implications for self and identity. In *Modernity and Self-Identity* Giddens (2001) claimed that "modernity radically alters the nature of day-to-day social life and affects the most personal aspects of our experience" (p. 1). The primary characteristics of late modernity that Giddens observes include increasing technological advances, multiplicity of choice, a decline in traditions, and a reorganization of time and space as systemic social activities are "lifted out" from localized contexts. The centrality of experts and symbols in the coordination of social relations, in a way that is disembedded from traditional communal ties, radically alters the nature of experience.

Despite the advances of late modernity, Giddens does not consider these features of modernity as signs of increasing order and stability. Conversely, he views them as responsible for an increasing sense of living in an out of control or runaway world. Late modernity's attempt to gain control and mastery over the external environment relies on individuals' reflexivity and their knowledge of their social world; however, knowledge is itself constantly questioned and potentially revisable. The consequent existential experience of anxiety, uncertainty, and risk, Giddens argued, is also evident in people's relationship with their own bodies and identities. One can see this in the increased significance, prominence, and preoccupation with the body, particularly in regards to its appearance and performance.

Furthermore, anxieties emerging from a perception of increased risk have become a particular feature of late modernity, related to associated declines in tradition, increases in choice, and subsequent self-awareness and reflexivity of lifestyles. Reflexivity involves individuals' ability to rationalize and reason about their actions. Allied to this, Giddens (2001) suggested that lifestyles consisting of the repetition of taken-for-granted practices, serve to maintain a sense of *ontological security*. This psychological mechanism of ontological security plays a fundamental role in creating a "protective cocoon" (p. 3) from existential anxieties threatening the individual's self-identity and the effective functioning of society in general.

In *The Transformation of Intimacy,* Giddens (1992) applied the concepts of choice, control, and self-identity in modernity to the arena of intimate relationships. In conceptualising what he called "the pure relationship," Giddens contended that intimacy, like self-identity, is a reflexive practice no longer defined by tradition and that "plastic sexuality" represents the emancipation of sexual expression from the traditional reproductive constraints. This has led to a restructuring and democratization of intimate relationships, which increasingly become mechanisms for exploration of self-identity. Moreover, changes in intimacy also reflect the increasing uncertainty, risk, and meaning creation in late modernity.

Research and theory on the life course have been significantly influenced by Giddens's contributions. In particular, lifestyle projects involving self-actualization have a major impact on the way individuals subjectively experience aging, the choices they are faced with as they age, and the intimate relationships they encounter. In navigating the life course, the individual is increasingly exposed to a multiplicity of choice about the cultivation and reconstruction of the body and self-identity. The resulting ethical dilemmas are the grounds for a new life politics about how people should live in a post-traditional order.

SEE ALSO Volume 1: *Agency;* Volume 2: *Sociological Theories.*

BIBLIOGRAPHY

Bryant, C., & Jary, D. (Eds.). (2001). *The contemporary Giddens: Social theory in a globalising age.* London: Palgrave Macmillan.

Craib, I. (1992). *Anthony Giddens.* London: Routledge.

Giddens, A. (1976). *New rules of the sociological method: A positivist critique of interpretive sociologies.* London: Macmillan.

Giddens, A. (1984). *The constitution of society: Outline of the theory of structuration.* Cambridge, England: Polity Press.

Giddens, A. (1990). *The consequences of modernity.* Cambridge, U.K.: Polity Press.

Giddens, A. (1992). *The transformation of intimacy: Sexuality, love, and eroticism in modern societies.* Cambridge, U.K.: Polity Press.

Giddens, A. (1994). *Beyond left and right: The future of radical politics.* Cambridge, U.K.: Polity Press.

Giddens, A. (2001). *Modernity and self-identity.* Cambridge, U.K.: Polity Press.

Giddens, A. (2002). *Runaway world.* London: Profile Books.

Giddens, A., & Pierson, C. (1998). *Conversations with Anthony Giddens: Making sense of modernity.* Cambridge, U.K.: Polity Press.

Stones, R. (2005). *Structuration theory.* London: Palgrave Macmillan.

Bethany Morgan

GLOBALIZATION

Globalization has become a central point of reference for the media, politicians, academics, and policy makers to understand social change. Life course studies therefore increasingly focus on the impact of globalization on life courses in various modern societies.

The term *globalization* summarizes four interrelated structural shifts (Blossfeld, Mills, Klijzing, & Kurz, 2005): (a) the swift internationalization of markets after the fall of the Iron Curtain (which divided Europe into two separate areas from the end of World War II until the end of the 1980s) at the end of the Cold War and the growing integration of cheap manufacturers in eastern Europe, China, and India into the world economy; (b) the rapid intensification of tax competition among nation-states, forcing them to introduce labor and welfare state reforms (such as deregulation, privatization, and liberalization); (c) the accelerated diffusion of knowledge and the spread of networks that are connecting global markets and decision-makers via new information and communication technologies (ICTs); and, (d) the rising vulnerability of local markets because of their dependence on random shocks—such as scientific discoveries, political upsets such as wars and revolutions, economic crises, or price shocks—occurring elsewhere on the globe.

Together these changes are generating an unprecedented level of global competition with resulting structurally based uncertainty for individual actors. In short, globalization is making life courses more insecure. For example, layoffs have become increasingly socially acceptable in the corporate world. Major companies have used the threat of relocating jobs to other locations or countries as a way to secure pay and benefit cuts. Weak unions have little choice but to accept wage cuts or else lose jobs by the thousands. Thus falling wages, reduced benefits, and rising job insecurity seem to be increasingly entrenched features of the new uncertain life courses across most of Western Europe, the United States, and other parts of the developed world. In addition, unemployment and the number of insecure freelance positions are rising while stable jobs with good benefits are being cut. Large numbers of laid-off workers do not get their old jobs back; instead, they are having to look for new work, often in entirely new fields. Those who still have jobs are working longer hours with little prospect of meaningful raises.

Although there is increasing uncertainty in the economic and social spheres of advanced economies, it does not affect all individuals and social groups to the same extent. There are institutional settings and social structures that determine the degree to which people are affected by rising uncertainty (see Figure 1).

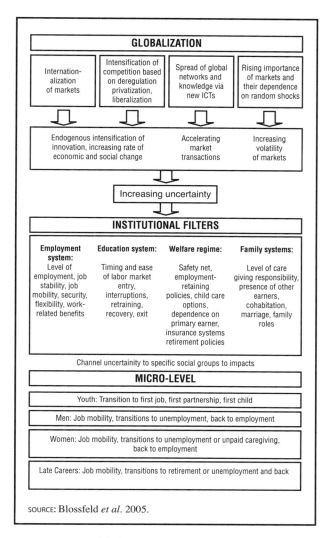

GLOBALIZATION

| Internation-alization of markets | Intensification of competition based on deregulation privatization, liberalization | Spread of global networks and knowledge via new ICTs | Rising importance of markets and their dependence on random shocks |

| Endogenous intensification of innovation, increasing rate of economic and social change | Accelerating market transactions | Increasing volatility of markets |

Increasing uncertainty

INSTITUTIONAL FILTERS

| **Employment system:** Level of employment, job stability, job mobility, security, flexibility, work-related benefits | **Education system:** Timing and ease of labor market entry, interruptions, retraining, recovery, exit | **Welfare regime:** Safety net, employment-retaining policies, child care options, dependence on primary earner, insurance systems retirement policies | **Family systems:** Level of care giving responsibility, presence of other earners, cohabitation, marriage, family roles |

Channel uncertainty to specific social groups to impacts

MICRO-LEVEL

Youth: Transition to first job, first partnership, first child

Men: Job mobility, transitions to unemployment, back to employment

Women: Job mobility, transitions to unemployment or unpaid caregiving, back to employment

Late Careers: Job mobility, transitions to retirement or unemployment and back

SOURCE: Blossfeld *et al.* 2005.

Figure 1. How globalization creates increasing uncertainty, is filtered by domestic institutions, and impacts life course transitions. **CENGAGE LEARNING, GALE.**

FORCES UNDERLYING GLOBALIZATION

The concept of globalization used here summarizes four interrelated structural forces (see Figure 1). First, globalization refers to the internationalization of markets and subsequent decline of national borders. This is connected with changes in laws, institutions, and practices that make various transactions (in commodities, labor, services, and capital) easier or less expensive across national borders. Taxes on imports, for instance, have been greatly reduced under the General Agreement on Tariffs and Trade (GATT), between member states in the European Union (EU), and via the North American Free Trade Agreement (NAFTA). Capital flows are facilitated by new political agreements. In economic terms, the inter-

nationalization of markets is particularly reflected in the rising number of firms conducting business in more than one country, through the presence of multinational corporations (MNCs) and foreign direct investment (FDI). In fact, MNCs are a driving force of the globalization of production and markets because they account for around two-thirds of world trade, 20% of the world's total amount of goods and services, and play a primary role in the diffusion of technology. However, increasingly small and medium-size businesses are also expected to take advantage of cheaper labor in eastern European or Asian countries.

Second, globalization relates to the intensification of competition among nation-states (i.e., the notion that capital and labor, but capital in particular, is increasingly mobile and forcing national economies to compete in attracting global money). Governments are reducing taxes for companies and introducing policy measures designed to improve the functioning of markets, such as the removal or relaxation of government regulation of economic activities (deregulation). Governments are also shifting their policies toward relying more on markets to coordinate economic activities (liberalization), and to transfer the control of assets or enterprises to private ownership that were previously under public ownership (privatization).

A third feature of globalization is the spread of global networks of people and firms linked by ICTs, such as microcomputers and the Internet. These ICTs, together with modern mass media, transmit messages and images instantaneously from the largest city to the smallest village on every continent and allow a faster diffusion of information and knowledge over long distances (Castells, 1996). They increasingly allow people to share information and to connect and create an instant common worldwide standard of comparison. Modern ICTs influence communications between individuals, organizations, and communities by effectively rendering physical space and distance irrelevant. Thus, although the introduction of technology is not unique in itself, recent ICTs have fundamentally altered the scope, intensity, velocity, and impact of technological transformations.

Finally, due to the intensification of competition, globalization also increases the relevance of markets in the coordination of decisions in all modern societies. These developments inherently strengthen the worldwide interdependence of decision-making. As a consequence, market prices and their changes increasingly convey information about the global demand for various goods, services, and assets, and the worldwide relative costs of producing and offering them. These prices increasingly set the standards to which individuals, firms, and nation-states then try to comply. However, globalization does not only mean that actors are increasingly in the hands of anonymous global markets. What is equally important is that the changes in these markets are becoming more dynamic and less predictable. First, the globalization of markets intensifies competition between firms, forcing them to be innovative, to use new technological developments, or to invent new products. This in turn increases the instability of markets.

Second, modern ICTs and deregulation and liberalization measures allow individuals, firms, and governments to react faster to observed market changes and simultaneously accelerate market transactions. This in turn makes long-term developments of globalizing markets inherently harder to predict. Third, global prices tend to become more liable to fluctuations because worldwide supply, demand, or both are getting increasingly dependent on *random shocks* caused somewhere on the globe. Random shocks may include wide-ranging occurrences, such as major scientific discoveries, technical inventions, new consumer fashions, major political upsets such as wars and revolutions, or economic upsets. The accelerated market dynamics and the rising dependence of prices on random events happening somewhere on the globe produce a higher frequency of surprises. In other words, the increasing dynamics and volatility of outcomes of globalizing markets makes it more difficult for individuals, firms, and governments to predict the future of the market and to make choices between different alternatives and strategies.

GLOBALIZATION AND DOMESTIC INSTITUTIONAL FILTERS

Increasing uncertainty is not the most important consideration when studying the consequences of globalization for life courses; rather, it is how rising uncertainty is "institutionally filtered" and channeled toward specific social groups in various countries (Blossfeld et al., 2005). Increasing uncertainty does not affect all regions, states, organizations, or individuals in the same way. There are institutional settings and social structures, historically grown and country-specific, which determine the degree to which people are affected by rising uncertainty (see Figure 1). These institutions have a tendency to persist and act as a sort of intervening variable between global macro forces and the responses at the micro level (Nelson, 1995).

Some have argued that globalization undermines the authority or even heralds the fall of the nation-state. However, new research clearly demonstrates that the nation-state and, in particular, institutions that shape life courses do not lose their significance, but generate country-specific problems that call for country-specific solutions and transformations. Thus, one cannot expect

that increasing uncertainty leads to a rapid convergence of life courses across all modern societies, as claimed, for example, by neo-institutionalists (social scientists who discuss the way modern societies interact and influence each other, e.g., Meyer, Ramirez, & Soysal, 1992) or the proponents of the modernization hypothesis (who describe the mechanisms which contribute to the social progress of modern societies, e.g., Treiman, 1970). Rather, life course research shows that there are unique developments within countries. The institutions that most impact life courses are employment relations, educational systems, national welfare state regimes, and family traditions.

GLOBALIZATION, INCREASING UNCERTAINTY, AND LIFE COURSE DECISIONS

Many decisions in the life course have long-term implications. People choose educational and professional tracks, enter and exit job careers, and make long-term binding family decisions. However, higher levels of uncertainty due to globalization generate insecurity and potential conflict and make it increasingly difficult for individuals to make such choices in ways that maximize their best interest and the best interest of their families. A central issue in modern life course research is therefore to understand how people make life course decisions under conditions of increasing uncertainty. For example, it is important to understand how individuals cope with growing uncertainty in their everyday life and the extent to which their (long-term) decisions are shaped by a specific local social context. As Mario Regini (2000) states: "The institutional context, in fact, provides actors with a set of resources and constraints that they must necessarily take into account when choosing among different alternatives and consequently shapes their actions" (p. 8).

SOME RESULTS FROM THE GLOBALIFE PROJECT

The Globalife project is the first international comparative research project to study the impact of globalization on individual life courses in 23 European and North American societies. It is organized into four volumes that cover the transition from youth into adulthood (Blossfeld et al., 2005), mid-career changes for both men (Blossfeld, Mills, & Bernardi, 2006) and women (Blossfeld & Hofmeister, 2006), and the transition from employment to retirement (Blossfeld, Buchholz, & Hofäcker, 2006) (see Figure 1).

First, this research shows that globalization has influenced young people's ability to establish themselves as independent adults in the workforce, to form romantic partnerships, and to become parents (Blossfeld et al.,

2005). Youth in all studied countries were exposed to dramatically increasing uncertainty at labor market entry in the form of more precarious, lower quality employment (e.g., fixed term contracts, part-time work, lower occupational standing, freelancing, and lower wages). This study also shows that nation-specific institutions clearly shield or funnel uncertainty in unique ways to particular groups of youths. For example, in Italy precarious forms of self-employment among young people have been rising dramatically, or in Spain and Germany the proportion of fixed-term employed young people has been exploding.

The experience of uncertainty is therefore quite unequal among young people, with risk disproportionately accumulating among those in lower-skilled occupations that require little education. There were also clear implications of uncertainty for family formation. Economic, temporal, and employment uncertainties translate into a higher likelihood of postponing or forgoing partnership and parenthood. Thus, globalization contributes to marriage and fertility declines.

Second, Globalife research demonstrates that men in the middle of their careers in countries such as the United Kingdom and the United States, where the labor market is highly deregulated, are also strongly affected by globalization (Blossfeld, Mills, & Bernardi, 2006). In contrast, midlife men in Sweden, Germany, Italy, Denmark, and to a lesser extent Spain and the Netherlands, were more insulated from the negative impacts of globalization. These so-called insider-outsider countries have a history of centralized wage bargaining and restrictions on businesses that mainly protect mid-career men.

Third, Globalife findings demonstrate that globalization has mixed implications for women's employment, largely depending on the welfare state and the country-specific employment regime (Blossfeld & Hofmeister, 2006). In some countries, such as in Germany and the Netherlands, globalization fosters women's employment by allowing more women to (re)enter the labor market than in the past. In these countries, more flexible jobs bring a large group of midlife women into the labor market who previously had no or only marginal difficulty reconciling paid work with unpaid care duties. Yet in other countries that already have achieved higher levels of women's full-time secure employment (e.g., the United States or the Scandinavian countries), employment restructuring due to globalization has the potential to jeopardize that security.

Finally, the Globalife project reveals that older workers are particularly vulnerable in globalized societies because the new type of knowledge-based work in globalized countries puts a huge premium on innovation speed as well as on new technology. New technology and outsourcing renders many established job positions obsolete, in particular the unskilled ones. However, an employer's willingness to invest in retraining older employees is often low because these employees are generally expected to leave the company soon, either due to retirement or poor health. The Globalife project demonstrates great cross-country differences for older workers. In neoliberal countries such as the United Kingdom or the United States, low levels of employment protection foster a relatively high level of labor market mobility among older workers. Low levels of income security provided through public pensions leads to continuous employment even beyond the formal retirement age. In social-democratic countries such as Sweden or Denmark, labor market policies and high emphasis on continuous lifetime education foster older workers' connection to the labor market, while pension systems, to some extent, allow work patterns to remain more flexible. Finally, in conservative and southern European countries, there are relatively high rates of labor market exits through early retirement.

Because of relatively regulated employment relations systems, economic restructuring of work can hardly be achieved by dismissing workers (the so-called insiders). In addition, rigid labor market boundaries created by standardized occupational systems, as in the case of Germany, do not allow the older workforce to move to other jobs easily. In these so-called insider-outsider countries, pension systems therefore provide incentives for an early retirement.

UNRESOLVED ISSUES REGARDING GLOBALIZATION AND THE LIFE COURSE

Globalization is critical to understanding changes in life courses in modern societies. It forces researchers to develop a multilevel conception that links global transformation to impacts at the institutional and individual level. Different experiences and behaviors in these countries led to several interesting findings in the Globalife study. However, one must concede that life course research that incorporates global changes into its analysis is only just beginning. Much more empirical research is necessary because of the complexity of causal mechanisms that work their way through institutions and labor markets to the individual level. However, the results of the Globalife project stimulate discussion, modifications, and new approaches to study these complex and drastic transformations of modern societies. In particular, more life course research in non-Western nations such as India and China would be necessary in the future. Little is known about the life courses of individuals outside the developed world; in addition to having an impact on the life course in developed nations, globalization highlights the importance of considering the contours of life courses throughout the world.

SEE ALSO Volume 2: *Economic Restructuring; Income Inequality; Individuation/Standardization Debate; Occupations; Policy, Employment.*

BIBLIOGRAPHY

Blossfeld, H.-P., Buchholz, S., & Hofäcker, D. (2006). *Globalization, uncertainty, and late careers in society.* New York: Routledge.

Blossfeld, H.-P., & Hofmeister, H. (2006). *Globalization, uncertainty, and women's careers: An international comparison.* Cheltenham, UK; Northhampton, MA: Edward Elgar.

Blossfeld, H.-P., Mills, M., Klijzing, E., & Kurz, K. (2005). *Globalization, uncertainty, and youth in society.* London: Routlegde.

Blossfeld, H.-P., Mills M., & Bernardi, F. (2006). *Globalization, uncertainty, and men's careers: An international comparison.* Cheltenham, UK; Northhampton, MA: Edward Elgar.

Blossfeld, H.-P., & Prein, G. (1998). *Rational choice theory and large-scale data analysis.* Boulder, CO: Westview Press.

Castells, Manuel. (1996). *The rise of the network society, the information age: Economy, society, and culture* (Vol. 1). Oxford, U.K.: Blackwell.

Mayer, K.U. (2001). The paradox of global social change and national path dependencies: Life course patterns in advanced societies. In A. E. Woodward & M. Kohli (Eds), *Inclusions and exclusions in European societies* (pp. 89–110). London: Routledge.

Meyer, J. W., Ramirez, F. O., & Soysal, Y. (1992). World expansion of mass education, 1870–1980. *Sociology of Education, 65*(2), 128–149.

Nelson, R. R. (1995). Recent evolutionary theorizing about economic change. *Journal of Economic Literature, 33*(1), 48–90.

Regini, M. (2000). Between deregulation and social pacts: The responses of European economies to globalization. *Politics and Society, 28*(1), 5–33.

Treiman, D. J. (1970). Industrialization and social stratification. *Journal of Sociological Inquiry, 40*(2), 207–234.

Hans-Peter Blossfeld

H

HEALTH BEHAVIORS, ADULTHOOD

There is growing recognition that the U.S. population is well below the level of health possible given the advanced state of U.S. medical technology. This gap is attributed in part to individual behaviors that contribute to a relatively high population-level risk of disease and ill health (McGinnis, Williams-Russo, & Knickman, 2002). Certain health behaviors may contribute to increases in various cancers, stroke, heart disease, and functional impairment. The two most important negative behaviors for adult health are smoking, which is declining over time, and obesity, which is on the rise. A key positive health behavior is regular exercise. Other important behaviors include diet (as related to body weight) and drinking. In addition, research indicates that health behaviors are interrelated and in particular that negative health behaviors cluster together. For example, individuals who are more sedentary are also more likely to engage in other less healthy behaviors such as smoking (Carlsson, Andersson, Wolk, & Ahlbom, 2006). With adjustments in health policy and medical and educational interventions, these behaviors may be changed to improve health and reduce medical costs.

HEALTH BEHAVIORS AND THE LIFE COURSE

The cumulative impact of lifelong health behaviors on adult health is well established. Many health conditions and mortality in late-middle adulthood are thought to be at least partially the result of the cumulative impact of poor health behaviors (excessively drinking alcoholic beverages, smoking, sedentary lifestyle, high-fat diet, etc.).

Many argue that this connection between negative health behaviors and poor health is also true for older adults. Others argue, however, that poor health and old age mortality are unaffected by current or future health behaviors. In this view, once a person has reached old age, poor health behaviors have little bearing on overall health and mortality. Individuals who have survived despite engaging in poor health behaviors are especially robust or physically strong and resilient. It is likely that both of these scenarios are true, with the latter argument true for only a small fraction of the population.

Health behaviors can be shaped by major life course events. For example, as with many other major historical events, the effects of the Great Depression were felt long after the economy rebounded. Elder (1974) notes that the economic hardship experienced during the Depression "had enduring consequences for life course and values" (p. 3). In particular, those who grew up during this time of uncertainty and deprivation placed high value on the stability of the family as they became spouses and parents. Aside from influencing values about the family, constrained family finances and societal resources not only contributed to poor nutrition during this period but also may have shaped long-term values attached to food and weight management. Research suggests that poor prenatal care or poor childhood nutrition and health conditions may have negative effects on health in adulthood (Johnston, 1985), in particular increased risks of chronic diseases such as coronary heart disease, diabetes, hypertension, and stroke. This negative health impact may have been countered somewhat to the extent that experiencing the Depression led to moderate ideas about food intake and thus better weight management.

179

Other major life events also impact health behaviors; for example, marriage may have a beneficial effect in smoking cessation (Franks, Pienta, & Wray, 2002).

HEALTH BELIEF MODEL

The Health Belief Model (Becker, 1974; Rosenstock, 1974) provides a framework for understanding why some individuals participate in positive health behaviors (healthy diet, moderate alcohol consumption, exercising, and abstaining from smoking) and others do not. A premise of the model is that individuals' decisions to engage in positive health behaviors (or to change their health behaviors) are based on their evaluation of the possible threat posed by a health condition and the perceived benefits and barriers of taking action to prevent getting the health condition. Two factors influence an individual's assessment of the potential threat posed by a health problem: the perceived seriousness of the problem and the perceived susceptibility to it. In the perceived seriousness dimension, the individual considers the potential social, psychological, and physiological ramifications of the problem if left untreated. The greater the perceived severity, the more likely they are to take preventative action. Concerning perceived susceptibility, an individual evaluates the chances of developing the health problem. The greater the perceived susceptibility, the more likely they are to take preventative action. Factors influencing the assessed benefits of taking action include reducing the risk of experiencing negative effects associated with the disease and of contracting the disease, while the perceived barriers include lack of time or resources.

If the sum of the potential threats outweighs the sum of the benefits and barriers to taking action, positive health behavior is likely (Glanz & Rimer, 1997). From this perspective, research on health in adulthood should focus on identifying interventions effective in enhancing perceived benefits and reducing perceived barriers to healthy behaviors. Understanding these determinants has the potential not only to increase the well-being of the adult population but also to decrease the societal costs associated with poor health in this population.

DIET AND BODY WEIGHT

Diet is defined as the quantity and quality of food consumed by an individual. A common way to assess healthy body weight (in part the result of diet) is the body mass index (BMI), an index of the relationship of body weight to height, calculated as weight in kilograms divided by height in meters squared. BMI may be assessed using self-reports of height and weight or by taking physical measurements. The National Heart, Lung, and Blood Institute (NHLBI) has developed a BMI classification scheme commonly used by medical practitioners for the clinical assessment and treatment of problems associated with body weight: underweight = BMI < 18.5; normal weight = BMI 18.5 to 24.9; overweight = BMI 25.0 to 29.9; and obese = BMI 30.0 and over (NHLBI, 1998). Where body fat is stored on the body is also an important predictor of disease and poor health. The waist to hip ratio is a way to assess healthy body fat and can be defined as the ratio of the distance around the waist to that of the hips.

Although BMI is widely used as a measure of obesity and underweight, it is not a perfect measure. First, although self-reported measures of height and weight are considered legitimate ways of defining body weight, they may also result in underestimating BMI because people of short stature tend to overreport height and heavy individuals tend to underreport their weight (Black, Taylor, & Coster, 1998; Kuskowska-Wolk, Bergström, & Boström, 1992). Therefore, self-reported measurements may produce conservative estimates of how obese a society may be. Second, BMI is a measure of excess body weight rather than excess body fat. Because body composition varies with age, race, and gender, people at the same BMI do not necessarily have the same percentage of body fat or the same risk for adverse outcomes (Flegal, 2000). Third, BMI does not indicate how weight is distributed over the body, which may also be an important and independent health risk. For example, previous research suggests that older women with a low BMI but a high waist–hip ratio (abdominal obesity) have a higher risk of death than heavier women who have a lower waist–hip ratio (Folsom et al., 2000).

Rationale for the Study of Diet and Body Weight in Adulthood Social science research on the effects of body weight and health among adults has flourished since the late 1990s. An important health trend has spurred research in this period: Average body weight in the United States has significantly increased over time (He & Baker, 2004), and obesity has become a growing and costly problem. Obese adults have a twofold increase in disease conditions. Disease conditions more prevalent among obese adults include heart disease, diabetes, and certain types of cancers. These national increases in body weight, obesity, and obesity-related health problems likely contribute to elevated medical care costs. One study found that an individual's health care costs are 44% higher when they are obese (Sturm, Ringel, & Andreyeva, 2004). Thus, learning more about body weight, particularly excess weight, could be fruitful in improving quality of life and reducing medical costs among adults.

Life Course Patterns in Weight Individuals tend to gain weight through middle adulthood into early old age and then plateau or decline in weight at very advanced ages, perhaps as a result of disease (Jenkins, Fultz, Fonda, & Wray, 2003). This suggests that middle age is a time of life in which weight management is particularly important to overall health, and especially to health concerns associated with excess weight. In contrast, older age is often marked by weight loss—suggesting a morbid weight loss sometimes related to disease.

Patterns by Sociodemographic Characteristics Body weight in adulthood differs substantially by social and demographic characteristics such as race and ethnicity, gender, and socioeconomic status. A review of studies on body weight patterns among African Americans, Mexican Americans, and other Hispanic groups (versus White Americans) indicates that White men and women have lower average body weight than other racial and ethnic groups, but they tend to gain more weight over their lives. In terms of gender, women tend to gain more weight over the life course than do men (He & Baker, 2004). Although on average women's BMI is lower than men's, at the 75th percentile and above of the BMI distribution, women have higher BMIs than men (Williamson, 1993). That is, the prevalence of BMI $>= 25$ is higher for men than for women, whereas the prevalence of BMI $>= 30$ is higher for women than for men (Flegal, 2000). That BMI varies by race and ethnicity more so for women than for men suggests a stronger association between weight and women's social and cultural roles. Where body fat is typically stored can also vary by certain socioeconomic characteristics such as gender (Flegal, 2000). For example, men tend to carry their weight around their abdomen and women on their hips and thighs.

Socioeconomic factors play a role in body weight, with the incidence of excess weight and obesity generally higher among those with lower education levels and incomes. The educational differential in obesity tends to be highest among young adults and varies by race at older ages. For example, while obesity is more prevalent among older White Americans with lower education, it does not vary systematically by education among older African Americans. Current older cohorts of African-American adults are in general more poorly educated than upcoming cohorts. Because there is little variability in education among current cohorts, the lack of variability in level of education makes it difficult to see changes in obesity by one's education level (Himes, 1999).

Work transitions in adulthood can contribute to a reduction in economic status, resulting in larger weight disparities in adulthood than in other phases in life. Conversely, excess weight related to health declines, which is more common in adulthood, may contribute to the inability to work, resulting in larger economic effects in adulthood than in childhood or retirement. In other words, body weight may be an important predictor of economic advantage or disadvantage in adults, yet these patterns may vary by gender. For older men, obesity may be related to higher socioeconomic status (Fonda, Fultz, Jenkins, Wheeler, & Wray, 2004). Among more recent cohorts of adults, excess weight among men may be a sign of success or a strong work ethic that could provide them with more resources or opportunities (e.g., higher paying jobs).

In sum, excess body weight, a growing concern in the U.S. population, varies by race, gender, age, and education level, with obesity being more common among some subgroups of non-White persons, women, middle-age adults, and the less educated. In addition, sociocultural groups have differing norms about healthy body weights (Chang & Christakis, 2001), and body composition itself suggests the need for varying interpretations of excess weight. To be effective, programs for prevention and treatment of obesity must take into account these differences in developing and targeting interventions (NHLBI, 1998).

Patterns in Diet and Body Weight Internationally Differences exist between lower and higher income countries in the factors associated with body weight. In the United States, lower socioeconomic status is associated with higher BMI, especially among women. In many lower and middle-income countries, the opposite relationship is observed. In these nations, economic development has been accompanied by a transition to a diet high in red meat, saturated fat, sugar, and refined foods—and low in fiber—essentially the "Western diet." This dietary shift emerged after 1950 in East Asia, where an epidemic in excess body weight is starting to emerge. In a lower income country, expanding people's access to money and Western food may actually boost average BMI. For example, in urban India, the affluent are adopting Western dietary patterns and consuming larger quantities of fats, oils, and sugars than are the poor (Chatterjee, 2002). With this nutrition transition (Popkin, 2004) taking hold in lower and middle-income countries, the poorer populations continue to be the most underweight, whereas the affluent have a growing incidence of excess body weight.

The Relationship of Body Weight with Disease, Functional Impairment, and Mortality Both too-low and too-high BMI are associated with health problems that can decrease longevity and quality of life. A too-low BMI (commonly defined as a BMI of less than 18.5) has been suggested as one indicator, along with muscle weakness (Shlipak et al., 2004) and improper immune function (Walston & Fried, 1999), of frailty (Fried et al., 2001), a condition characterized by wasting and a decrease in the body's reserves. Past research indicates that frailty may be a predictor of inability to perform common daily activities such as bathing, eating, and dressing.

Body weight, along with its association with disease, can also affect one's ability to perform basic tasks. Being obese or having a too-high BMI is a contributing factor to a number of chronic medical conditions (Jenkins, 2004) such as hypertension, heart disease, diabetes, stroke, arthritis, and urinary incontinence. Side effects and symptoms of these obesity-related diseases and conditions may themselves contribute to difficulties in doing such things as walking up stairs or getting up from a chair (Himes, 1999; Jenkins, 2004). Being underweight, however, may suggest a concealed disease that would subsequently lead to the diagnosis of a health condition (such as cancer) at a more advanced stage. Side effects and symptoms of certain health conditions can ultimately contribute to impairments.

Even though adults at either extreme in body weight are more likely to have one or more chronic diseases, the same relationship does not hold true for mortality. Individuals who are underweight in middle age and older adulthood are more likely to die than older adults of normal weight. Overweight and obese middle-aged adults are more likely to die than their normal weight counterparts (Adams et al., 2006). In contrast, older adults who are obese have a similar life expectancy to those who are not obese (Reynolds, Saito, & Crimmins, 2005). This finding suggests that there is something unique about older obese adults. They may be particularly robust given that they lived to older age being obese. It is important to remember, however, that their quality of life may still be affected (i.e., they may be more likely to be living with disease and functional impairments) even though their life expectancy may not be affected. Another possibility is that poorer health in midlife contributes to being underweight that then leads to even further health declines.

Several studies have shown that high body weight—beyond its association with debilitating conditions—impairs physical functioning (Clark, Stump, & Wolinsky, 1998; Damush, Stump, & Clark, 2002; Jenkins, 2004). Excess body weight may inhibit functioning in several ways (Launer, Harris, Rumpel, & Madans, 1994). First, excess body weight typically contributes to inflammation of the joint tissues, making walking painful and difficult (Walford, Harris, & Weindruch, 1987). Second, it increases the amount of mechanical stress placed on body joints, elevating the risk for and severity of osteoarthritis (Clark & Mungai, 1997) and increasing functional impairment. Third, excess weight is associated with a sedentary lifestyle, which negatively affects muscle strength and cardiovascular fitness and may eventually

result in difficulties with physical functions such as walking several blocks or climbing flights of stairs (Himes, 2000).

The relationship between diet and body weight and smoking, drinking, and exercising is complex in that body weight may interact with these health behaviors in affecting health and functioning. For example, obesity can contribute to the onset of impairment by restricting one's activities making one less likely to experience the beneficial effects of exercise, and in turn making simple activities difficult. In addition, having a lower BMI is associated with smoking cigarettes (Molarius, Seidell, Kuulasmaa, Dobson, & Sans, 1997), perhaps because smoking acts as an appetite suppressant (Perkins et al., 1991). Smoking, however, can also hamper the body's ability to use oxygen, making daily activities, and indeed breathing, difficult (Stuck et al., 1999). Some research indicates that side effects and symptoms of these obesity-related diseases and conditions may themselves contribute to difficulties in doing such things as walking up stairs or getting up from a chair (Himes, 1999; Jenkins, 2004).

Researchers examining the health status of adults must be attentive to the complex interrelationships among body weight, disease, and functional impairment in this age group. Interventions to encourage healthy weight maintenance and weight management are essential, especially for African-American and Latino adults. Targeting obesity is particularly vital to prevent or delay the onset of disease and functional impairment and thereby improve the quality of life of the adult population.

SMOKING

Smoking in the United States most commonly refers to the consumption of tobacco via cigarettes, but it may also include the use of cigars or a pipe. Like obesity, smoking contributes to a variety of diseases (particularly many cancers and respiratory illnesses), life-threatening health conditions such as heart disease, functional difficulties decreased longevity and higher health care costs. Yet, despite public knowledge of these risks, more than a quarter of the U.S. population continues to smoke (Lahiri & Song, 2000). The proliferation of smoking bans since the late 1990s is likely to have a beneficial effect on the long-term health of society. Among Americans, however, smoking is still considered the most avoidable cause of death (National Cancer Institute, 2007).

Theories about Why People Smoke Given the high incidence of smoking in the face of known health risks and public campaigns against smoking, an important question for researchers and health professionals alike is: What factors motivate people to stop smoking? According to the Health Belief Model (discussed above), an important factor in motivation to change unhealthy behavior is the perceived threat posed by the behavior. Individuals who view their smoking behavior as a threat to their health or life span may be much more motivated to quit smoking than those who do not understand or who underestimate how detrimental smoking is to their lives (Schoenbaum, 1997). Research has shown that smokers know, but tend to underestimate, the dangers of smoking (Schoenbaum, 1997; Smith, Taylor, & Sloan, 2001). A small fraction of smokers may accurately assess the threat posed by smoking, but choose to smoke regardless because they have a high tolerance for risk in this and other areas of their lives (Barsky, Juster, Kimball, & Shapiro, 1997).

Smoking Internationally With the bans on smoking in public areas enacted since the late 1990s, particularly in the United States, smoking in higher income countries is steadily becoming more socially unacceptable. With the loss of revenue from these countries, tobacco companies are more heavily marketing in lower income countries to offset the loss. Compared to higher income countries, the health impact of the increased smoking rates may be even greater in lower income countries, where more highly infectious diseases, such as tuberculosis, are still common. It is projected that by 2030 approximately 80% of annual tobacco use deaths will be from lower income countries (Mathers & Loncar, 2006). Aside from the tremendous health impact that tobacco can have on adults from lower income countries, it also takes a severe economic toll. Individuals from these countries may spend already limited resources on tobacco rather than on education and food (World Health Organization, 2007).

Relationship with Sociodemographic Characteristics Adult smoking varies by education, race/ethnicity, gender, age, and income. Level of education may be particularly useful in helping practitioners to understand patterns and trends in smoking behavior and aiding health professionals in targeting critical subgroups for smoking cessation programs. Adults with lower educational attainment and income are more likely to smoke compared to adults with higher socioeconomic status (Lockery & Stanford, 1996). Smoking also varies by race and ethnicity, with African-American adults having similar smoking rates as White adults, and higher rates than Hispanic and Asian/Pacific Islander adults (Henry J. Kaiser Family Foundation, 2006). In regard to age and gender, adults in their mid-20s have the highest smoking rates, after which rates tend to decline, and men are more likely to smoke than women.

Smoking Cessation Given that smoking contributes to disease, disabling conditions, and decreased longevity, a substantial and growing body of literature addresses smoking cessation. More specifically, one question that is important to study is: What factors may motivate someone to quit smoking? Being diagnosed with a serious chronic condition may motivate an adult to quit smoking. Many older adults do not easily alter lifelong poor health behaviors (Franks et al., 2002). Rather, major health events or transitions spur such changes. This is evidenced by long-term smokers quitting following a cardiac event, such as a heart attack. Higher levels of education may make an older adult even more likely to quit smoking following a health event (Wray, Herzog, Willis, & Wallace, 1998). For example, once an individual is diagnosed with diabetes, they have a higher probability of smoking cessation if they have a college degree compared to having 9 years of education or less (Kahn, 1998). Other life course events, such as having a child, may also prompt an individual to quit smoking.

Another factor that may motivate an individual to quit smoking is the notion that after a number of years, former smoker's health outcomes become similar to those of adults who have never smoked. Smokers are more likely to live more years in failing health. An interesting and optimistic finding, however, is that in regard to the years of healthy life remaining, former smokers (those who stopped smoking 15 or more years ago) were similar to those who never smoked. In order to encourage smoking cessation, health professionals may want to inform patients of the association of smoking with a decrease in living better (Østbye & Taylor, 2004) and educate them on the notion that quitting smoking increases the chances of a healthier life.

Spousal support may also facilitate smoking cessation. At its best, the marital relationship is uniquely intimate and supportive. Individuals also tend to marry people similar to themselves in regard to educational attainment, socioeconomic status, and racial and cultural backgrounds. Thus it is plausible that beneficial changes in smoking behavior may be more likely to be initiated or maintained when both spouses participate in the effort. Clearly, this notion of spousal participation and support has important implications for smoking cessation efforts (Franks et al., 2002).

ALCOHOL CONSUMPTION

Drinking is defined as the consumption of alcoholic beverages such as beer, wine, or liquor. Researchers and medical professionals consider both the quantity and frequency of alcohol consumption in assessing drinking behavior. Moderate alcohol consumption is defined as no more than one drink per day for men 65 years of age and older and for women of any age and no more than two drinks per day for men under 65 years (National Institute on Alcohol Abuse and Alcoholism (NIAAA, 1992). The *Diagnostic and Statistical Manual of Mental Disorders*, 3rd edition, revised (1987), defines alcohol dependence as positive responses to any three of the following four CAGE (derived from the operant word in each of the four screening questions) assessment questions: (a) Have you ever felt that you should cut down on your drinking? (b) Have people ever annoyed you by criticizing your drinking? (c) Have you ever felt bad or guilty about drinking? and (d) Have you ever taken a drink first thing in the morning to steady your nerves or get rid of a hangover? (Ewing, 1984). A positive response to any one of the four CAGE questions could be indicative of an alcohol problem.

Another definition of heavy or problem drinking commonly used in social science and medical research is binge drinking. The NIAAA's National Advisory Council defines binge drinking as behavior that produces a blood alcohol concentration of 0.08-gram percent or above, which is typically having five or more drinks (men) or four or more drinks (women) in about 2 hours. Heavy drinking, a related term, can be defined as five or more drinks per day for men and four or more drinks per day for women.

Historical Patterns in Alcohol Consumption Alcohol use was socially acceptable and increased in popularity starting in the mid-1880s until the prevalence of alcohol-related accidents and illnesses become so widespread and problematic that the social acceptability plummeted, culminating with Prohibition in 1919. Prohibition was revoked in 1933, and a dramatic upswing in the use of alcohol occurred after World War II, followed by a more gradual increase through the 1970s with a peak in 1975 (Nephew, Williams, Stinson, Nguyen, & Dufour, 1999). Recognition of the increase in certain morbidities associated with excessive alcohol use led to a gradual decline in alcohol use until around the late 1990s. Population-based estimates of alcohol use among adults show an increase since the late 1990s (Lakins, Williams, & Yi, 2007).

Characteristics Influencing Alcohol Consumption At the population level, patterns of alcohol use vary by societal, cultural, familial, and sociodemographic factors in part because societies and cultural subgroups vary in their social acceptance of alcohol use. For example, cultural conventions about who consumes alcohol and under what circumstances may at least partly explain why men have a higher percentage of heavy alcohol use than women and why Latino and African-American adults have higher percentages of problem drinking than White adults. Within subgroups, families (via family values) further differentiate individual alcohol behavior (Zucker, 2000).

Biological traits that predispose an individual to alcohol use or abuse further differentiate drinking behavior and should not be ignored when attempting to understand patterns in alcohol use (Anderson, 1998a & b). Someone with a biological predisposition to problem drinking who lives in an environment that has more liberal attitudes about alcohol may be more likely to develop problems with alcohol than someone surrounded by more conservative alcohol attitudes (Elder & Caspi, 1989).

Among individuals, drinking behavior remains relatively stable throughout life. Alcohol consumption can often change, however, in response to major life events. Hospitalization and disease onset can lead to a reduction in alcohol consumption, as side effects of medication, treatment, or the disease itself may make an individual feel too ill to drink. On the other hand, retirement, job loss, and widowhood may result in increased consumption (Perreira & Sloan, 2001). In general, stressful life events are thought to be associated with increased drinking behavior, although marital transitions (getting married or divorced) both increase and decrease alcohol consumption (Perreira & Sloan, 2001). Individuals' perceptions of and the lifestyle changes associated with these marital transitions may influence how an adult may use alcohol (either increasing or decreasing consumption) in managing the transition (Perreira & Sloan, 2001).

Socioeconomic and demographic characteristics also influence alcohol consumption. Adults who have lower educational attainment and reside in more rural areas have higher rates of drinking problems (Dawson, Grant, Chou, & Pickering, 1995). Race and ethnicity also influence alcohol consumption. Specifically, in more recent years, a greater percentage of African-American and Latino adults are abstaining from alcohol, but at the same time a greater percentage among those who drink are drinking heavily (Galvan & Caetano, 2003). Factors such as access to health care and racial discrimination are thought to be important explanations for the racial and ethnic differentials in alcohol use. Health insurance status is thought to be another socioeconomic factor linked to drinking behavior. Individuals with health insurance may be more likely to receive primary, secondary, and tertiary forms of treatment for illness and disease than those without. Regular care is thought to translate into better health and potentially less problem drinking behavior. This insurance–drinking connection is supported by two findings: Compared to adults who are either continuously or intermittently insured, adults who are continuously uninsured are more likely to either drink heavily or abstain from alcohol (Baker, Sudano, Albert, Borawski, & Dor, 2001)—both of which are typically related to poorer health and adults who are continuously uninsured tend to have higher CAGE scores.

Drinking and Health Although the effects of alcohol use on mortality have long intrigued social scientists, health professionals, and policymakers, until more recently, the effects of drinking on disease and morbidity has received much less attention, with the exception of its impact on cardiovascular and liver disease (Perreira & Sloan, 2002). Nevertheless, excessive alcohol use has been shown to have deleterious effects on various aspects of health and functioning in adulthood. Negative health effects include increased risk of onset of functional impairment and increased amount of impairment; greater likelihood of developing depression and disease (particularly some cancers); and increased risk of occupational injury (Ostermann & Sloan, 2001; Perreira & Sloan, 2002; Zwerling et al., 1996). Yet moderate alcohol consumption (not simply red wine consumption) in adulthood may have some beneficial effects on health, particularly cardiovascular disease. Albeit controversial, there is also growing evidence for a beneficial effect of moderate alcohol consumption on cognition, functional limitation, and disability (Kutty, 2000; Ostermann & Sloan, 2001).

In sum, the growing body of work on alcohol consumption's connection with other aspects of health finds that drinking heavily is related to the onset of functional impairment. Having a history of drinking problems is related to the onset of various mental health conditions such as depression. Other studies find that persons who drink in moderation have the lowest rates of disability, with heavy drinkers and those who abstain from drinking each having a greater likelihood of disability. Those who drink heavily, however, also have a greater amount of impairment on their existing activities (Ostermann & Sloan, 2001). To improve overall health and extend active life expectancy, more research is needed in this area to better understand if a relationship exists between moderate alcohol consumption and beneficial health outcomes in various domains of health. It is also important to note that heavy alcohol consumption can have negative effects on other aspects of life besides health, such as marital disruption and unemployment.

ILLICIT DRUG USE

Illicit drug use can be defined as the intake of substances for nonmedical purposes, used solely for recreation and the feeling the substance (or substances) provides. Illicit drugs are typically classified into categories. There are several categories in which governmental organizations and the like commonly collect information. These include prescription-type sedatives, pain relievers, tranquilizers, and stimulants (again used for nonmedical purposes); hallucinogens (e.g., LSD, PCP, and MDMA [also know as Ecstasy]), cocaine (including crack), her-

oin, marijuana (including hashish), and inhalants (e.g., gasoline, glue, and paint).

Characteristics Associated with Drug Use Drug use varies considerably by socioeconomic characteristics. Age, geographic area, gender, educational attainment, race and ethnicity, and employment status are all characteristics in which trends in drug use vary. More specifically, adults who are employed full-time (versus unemployed or employed part-time), live in metropolitan areas, male, American Indian or Alaskan Natives (compared to individuals who are classified as Asian, of two or more races, Black, White, Hispanic, or Native Hawaiian or other Pacific Islander) are more likely to be currently involved in illicit drug use. Interestingly, though, drug use is highest among adults 18 to 20 years of age followed by adults 21 to 25 years of age; after that there is a gradual decline in illicit drug use with increasing age. College graduates have the lowest rate of current illicit drug use (compared to other individuals classified with lower educational attainment). Yet, compared to adults who did not complete high school, college graduates are more likely to have tried an illicit drug at some point in their lives (SAMHSA, 2006).

Gateway Hypothesis The general premise of the gateway hypothesis is that initiation into "harder" classifications of drugs (e.g., cocaine and heroine) is derived from first use (usually in adolescence) of "softer" drugs such as alcohol and cigarettes. There is general support for the gateway hypothesis in the research community. Yet it appears to not be generalizable to all subgroups of the population (e.g., homeless individuals). Certain subgroups seem to follow different substance use trajectories.

Social scientists examine this hypothesis through various lenses, and each contributes unique insights. Economists, for example, typically examine adolescent substance use through the lens of consumer decision-making rather than deviant behavior (Kenkel, Mathios, & Pacula, 2001). Two important economic constructs that contribute to economic modeling of consumer behavior, with alcohol and drug consumption behavior being no different, is the price and availability of goods. Economic theorizing of these two constructs, in regard to the gateway hypothesis, suggests that alcohol and tobacco may serve as gateway drugs in part because of their lower user cost and relatively easy access compared to harder substances. Economic theory argues that the use of these substances varies by gender, race, and ethnicity in part because of accessibility (Kenkel et al., 2001). More specifically, the gateway drug of choice is different for males and females; the two differential initial steps toward illicit drug use appear to be alcohol (for males) and tobacco (for females) (Kandel & Yamaguchi, 1993).

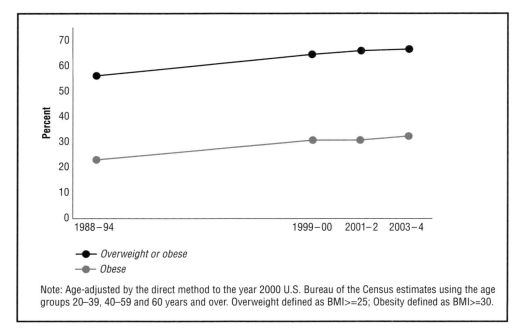

Figure 1. *Trends in adult overweight and obesity, ages 20 years and older.* CENGAGE LEARNING, GALE.

The price and availability of goods as foci in economic modeling of the gateway hypothesis also has important policy implications, particularly in regard to taxation and restrictions of alcohol and drug use. One outstanding policy question for which economic modeling can be particularly useful is: Does a reduction in the use of alcohol or tobacco lead to a reduction in the use of other drugs? There is some evidence to support that indeed higher prices of gateway substances reduce the use of other substances (DeSimone, 1998; Pacula, 1998). With that in mind, taxing the purchase of alcohol and cigarettes and creating stiffer penalties for persons who sell these substances to underage individuals may be some tangible policy-driven methods to reduce substance use problems (Kenkel et al., 2001).

EXERCISE

Defining exercise is complex. One traditional definition of exercise is to physically exert oneself with the intention of benefiting one's health. There are also various dimensions of exercise that one might consider when discussing a definition: frequency, length of participation, and the type of activity in which one engages (e.g., light or vigorous activity). More recently, researchers, health professionals, and policymakers have taken on a more expansive view of exercise and discuss it in terms of being more physically active or having an active lifestyle. This more modern definition deviates slightly from the more traditional one in that the traditional definition of exercise can

be thought of as structured and done with the main purpose of benefiting one's health (e.g., running, bicycling, or swimming), whereas physical activity may or may not be structured and done with the main purpose of having a health benefit. Examples of being physically active are heavy housework, gardening, or dancing. The current recommendation for most adults is 30 minutes of physical activity each day.

The shift from more labor-intensive agricultural and factory jobs to more information management and technical jobs over the past century has contributed to adults being more sedentary. This lack of daily activity on the job is a problem of great public health interest and has made leisure-time physical activity much more important. Lack of exercise is a multifaceted problem that affects many aspects of mental and physical well-being. It has been associated with functional impairment (Jenkins, 2004), depression, survival (Richardson, Kriska, Lantz, & Hayward, 2004), and various diseases such as heart disease, hypertension, cancer, diabetes, and stroke. Because a sedentary lifestyle is an increasing threat to health and longevity, understanding how to incorporate physically active tasks into daily life may prove beneficial in targeting interventions to increase physical activity levels and improve the health of adults.

Differential Patterns in Exercise Evidence suggests that women, racial and ethnic minorities, persons with lower socioeconomic status (Crespo, Ainsworth, Keteyian, Heath, & Smit, 1999), married persons (Pettee et al.,

2006), and rural residents (Arcury et al., 2006) are less likely to participate in physical activities. These are the subgroups most important to target for effective exercise interventions. Research on the determinants of exercise has generally found significant positive effects of both early life and adult socioeconomic status, as measured by parents' education, own education, and economic resources (Wray, Alwin, & McCammon, 2005). Spousal relationships impact health in part because of similarities in both partners' environments. Married couples reside together and therefore are exposed to the same environmental toxins and neighborhood stressors and share household income. With that in mind it is not so surprising that their health behaviors are often very similar. If a husband participates in moderate exercise it is likely that his wife will too. This has important implications for encouraging active lifestyles. Encouraging activities that appeal to both spouses may aid in maintaining health-promoting behaviors (Wilson, 2002).

Exercise, Disease, and Functioning Exercise provides many mental and physical health benefits, and these occur through a variety of mechanisms. Lack of exercise contributes to decreased muscle strength and cardiovascular fitness, which can increase the risk of disease and decrease the ability to perform basic daily activities such as walking or dressing oneself. Adults who participate in regular vigorous physical activity are less likely to experience various diseases and the onset of functional impairment.

Physical exercise has also been shown to have beneficial effects on diverse mental health outcomes, particularly depression (Ruuskanen & Ruoppila, 1995), and has been suggested as a possible treatment for this condition (Barbour & Blumenthal, 2005; Blumenthal et al., 1999). Among adults (60 years of age and older), those who did not need to give up any physical activities and those who found a satisfying replacement for them had lower levels of depressive symptoms (Benyamini & Lomranz, 2004). Several possible linking mechanisms have been suggested for this association including both physiological mechanisms (e.g., central monoamine theory) and psychological factors (e.g., improvements in self-efficacy) (Barbour & Blumenthal, 2005).

Health-promoting behaviors such as exercise are assumed to have the potential to improve quality of life and thus decrease health care costs by preventing disease. Even among older adults this is generally the case—light and heavy long-term exercise does show a slight decrease in health care use (Lee & Kobayashi, 2001). Some empirical evidence, however, supports the opposite patterns for short-term exercise. Short-term light exercise is related to a slight increase in the use of the health care system (e.g., doctor visits or hospital days). One possible reason for this finding is that older adults who initiate only a light exercise regimen but do not maintain it for longer periods may be less healthy. They may view themselves as unhealthy and, knowing the health benefits of exercise, try to engage in a more active lifestyle. Because they do not maintain their exercise regimen, however, they do not reap the health benefits.

It is important to recognize the negative health effects that arise from a sedentary lifestyle. Encouraging routine daily exercise is a significant goal in the effort to improve the health and quality of life of adults. It is also important for policymakers and persons engaged in clinical practice to remember that individuals are more apt to spend time doing what they enjoy and to make time to do such activities, so it is especially important to make physical activities more appealing to certain subgroups of adults who are among the least physically active. More knowledge on the barriers of routine exercise and having an active lifestyle might help both policymakers and researchers target interventions and resources most cost-effectively.

CONCLUSION

Encouraging positive health behaviors early in life is important because health behavior change over the life course is difficult. Positive behavior change, however, even in later life, can be beneficial to overall health. With chronic diseases with long etiologies being common in the United States, a long-term commitment to a healthy lifestyle is encouraged in order to prevent rather than manage such illnesses.

The study of health behaviors is a fruitful area of research for both public health practice and policy. With poor health behaviors, particularly lack of physical activity and excess body weight, being commonplace in the United States, insight on the characteristics that may assist in the development of interventions and educational tools to encourage active and healthy behaviors for adults is important. A better understanding of the relationship between barriers to participating in exercise, maintaining a health body weight, smoking cessation, and responsible drinking will also allow public health policymakers more effectively target resources and interventions to reduce the life-threatening health problems associated with behaviors and improve the health and quality of life of adults.

SEE ALSO Volume 2: *Health Care Use, Adulthood; Health Differentials/Disparities, Adulthood; Obesity, Adulthood; Time Use, Adulthood;* Volume 3: *Cancer, Adulthood and Later Life; Cardiovascular Disease; Health Literacy; Life Expectancy; Mortality; Sleep Patterns and Behavior.*

BIBLIOGRAPHY

Adams, K. F., Schatzkin, A., Harris, T. B., Kipnis, V., Mouw, T., Ballard-Barbash, R. et al. (2006). Overweight, obesity, and mortality in a large prospective cohort of persons 50 to 71 years old. *The New England Journal of Medicine, 355,* 763–778.

American Psychiatric Association (1987). *Diagnostic and statistical manual of mental disorders.* (3rd ed., rev.). Washington, DC: American Psychiatric Press.

Anderson, T. L. (1998a). Drug identity change processes, race, and gender. I. Explanations of drug misuse and a new identity-based model. *Substance Use & Misuse, 33,* 2263–2279.

Anderson, T. L. (1998b). Drug identity change processes, race, and gender. II. Microlevel motivational concepts. *Substance Use & Misuse, 33,* 2469–2483.

Arcury, T. A., Snively, B. M., Bell, R. A., Smith, S. L., Stafford, J. M., Wetmore-Arkader, L. K. et al. (2006). Physical activity among rural older adults with diabetes. *Journal of Rural Health, 22,* 164–168.

Baker, D. W., Sudano, J. J., Albert, J. M., Borawski, E. A., & Dor, A. (2001). Lack of health insurance and decline in overall health in late middle age. *The New England Journal of Medicine, 345,* 1106–1112.

Barbour, K. A., & Blumenthal, J. A. (2005). Exercise training and depression in older adults. *Neurobiology of Aging, 26,* S119–S123.

Barsky, R. B., Juster, F. T., Kimball, M. S., & Shapiro, M. D. (1997). Preference parameters and behavioral heterogeneity: An experimental approach in the Health and Retirement Study. *The Quarterly Journal of Economics, 112,* 537–579.

Becker, M. H. (Ed.). (1974). *The Health Belief Model and personal health behavior.* San Francisco: Society for Public Health Education.

Benyamini, Y., & Lomranz, J. (2004). The relationship of activity restriction and replacement with depressive symptoms among older adults. *Psychology and Aging, 19,* 362–366.

Black, D. R., Taylor, A. M., & Coster, D. C. (1998). Accuracy of self-reported body weight: Stepped Approach Model component assessment. *Health Education Research, 13,* 301–307.

Blumenthal, J. A., Babyak, M. A., Moore, K. A., Craighead, W. E., Herman, S., Khatri, P. et al. (1999). Effects of exercise training on older patients with major depression. *Archives of Internal Medicine, 159,* 2349–2356.

Carlsson, S., Andersson, T., Wolk, A., & Ahlbom, A. (2006). Low physical activity and mortality in women: Baseline lifestyle and health as alternative explanations. *Scandinavian Journal of Public Health, 34,* 480–487.

Chang, V. W., & Christakis, N. A. (2001). Extent and Determinants of Discrepancy between Self-Evaluations of Weight Status and Clinical Standards. *Journal of General Internal Medicine, 16,* 538–543.

Chatterjee, P. (2002, December 14). India sees parallel rise in malnutrition and obesity. *The Lancet, 360,* 1948.

Clark, D. O., & Mungai, S. M. (1997). Distribution and association of chronic disease and mobility difficulty across four body mass index categories of African-American women. *American Journal of Epidemiology, 145,* 865–875.

Clark, D. O., Stump, T. E., & Wolinsky, F. D. (1998). Predictors of onset of and recovery from mobility difficulty among adults aged 51-61 years. *American Journal of Epidemiology, 148,* 63–71.

Crespo, C. J., Ainsworth, B. E., Keteyian, S. J., Heath, G. W., & Smit, E. (1999). Prevalence of physical inactivity and its relation to social class in U.S. adults: Results from the Third National Health and Nutrition Examination Survey, 1988–1994. *Medicine and Science in Sports and Exercise, 31,* 1821–1827.

Damush, T. M., Stump, T. E., & Clark, D. O. (2002). Body-Mass Index and 4-year change in health-related quality of life. *Journal of Aging and Health 14*(2), 195–210.

Dawson, D. A., Grant, B. F., Chou. S. P., & Pickering, R. P. (1995). Subgroup variation in U.S. drinking patterns: results of the 1992 National Longitudinal Alcohol Epidemiologic Study. *Journal of Substance Abuse, 7*(3), 331–344.

DeSimone, J. (1998). Is marijuana a gateway drug? *Eastern Economic Journal, 24,* 149–164.

Elder, G. H., Jr. (1974). *Children of the Great Depression: Social change in life experience.* Chicago: University of Chicago Press.

Elder, G. H., & Caspi, A. (1988). Economic stress in lives: Developmental perspectives. *Journal of Social Issues, 44*(4), 25-45.

Ewing, J. A. (1984). Detecting alcoholism: The CAGE questionnaire. *Journal of the American Medical Association, 252,* 1905–1907.

Flegal, K. M. 2000. In M. B. Goldman, M. C. Hatch (Eds.), *Women and Health* (pp. 830–838). San Diego: Academic Press.

Folsom, A. R., Kushi, L. H., Anderson, K. E., Mink, P. J., Olson, J. E., Hong, C.-P. et al. (2000). Associations of general and abdominal obesity with multiple health outcomes in older women: The Iowa Women's Health Study. *Archives of Internal Medicine, 160,* 2117–2128.

Fonda, S. J., Fultz, N. H., Jenkins, K. R., Wheeler, L. M., & Wray, L. A. (2004). Relationship of body mass and net worth for retirement-aged men and women. *Research on Aging, 26,* 153–176.

Franks, M. M., Pienta, A. M., & Wray, L. A. (2002). It takes two: Marriage and smoking cessation in the middle years. *Journal of Aging and Health, 14,* 336–354.

Fried, L. P., Tangen, C. M., Walston, J., Newman, A. B., Hirsch, C., Gottdiener, J. et al. (2001). Frailty in older adults: Evidence for a phenotype. *The Journals of Gerontology, Series A: Biological Sciences and Medical Sciences, 56,* M146–M157.

Galvan, F. H., & Caetano, R. (2003). Alcohol use and related problems among ethnic minorities in the United States. *Alcohol Research & Health, 27,* 87–94.

Glanz, K., & Rimer, B. K. (1997). *Theory at a glance: A guide for health promotion practice.* Bethesda, MD: National Cancer Institute.

He, X. X. Z., & Baker, D. W. (2004). Body mass index, physical activity, and the risk of decline in overall health and physical functioning in late middle age. *American Journal of Public Health, 94*(9), 1567–1573.

Henry J. Kaiser Family Foundation. (2006). *United States: Smoking rates for adults by race/ethnicity, 2005.* Retrieved December 17, 2007, from http://statehealthfactsonline.org

Himes, C. L. (1999). Racial differences in education, obesity, and health in later life. In N. E. Adler, M. Marmot, B. S. McEwen, & J. Stewart (Eds.), *Socioeconomic status and health in industrial nations* (pp. 370–372). New York: New York Academy of Science.

Himes, C. L. (2000). Obesity, disease, and functional limitation in later life. *Demography, 37*, 73–82.

Jenkins, K. R. (2004). Obesity's effects on the onset of functional impairment among older adults. *The Gerontologist, 44*, 206–216.

Jenkins, K. R., Fultz, N. H., Fonda, S. J., & Wray, L. A. (2003). Patterns of body weight in middle-aged and older Americans, by gender and race, 1993–2000. *Sozial- und Präventivmedizin, 48*, 257–268.

Johnston, F. E. (1985). Health implications of childhood obesity. *Annals of Internal Medicine, 103*, 1068–1072.

Kahn, M. E. (1998). Education's role in explaining diabetic health investment differentials. *Economics of Education Review, 17*, 257–266.

Kandel, D., & Yamaguchi, K. (1993). From beer to crack: Developmental patterns of drug involvement. *American Journal of Public Health, 83*, 851–855.

Kenkel, D., Mathios, A. D., & Pacula, R. L. (2001). Economics of youth drug use, addiction, and gateway effects. *Addiction, 96*, 151–164.

Kuskowska-Wolk, A., Bergström, R., & Boström, G. (1992). Relationship between questionnaire data and medical records of height, weight, and body mass index. *International Journal of Obesity and Related Metabolic Disorders, 16*, 1–9.

Kutty, N. K. (2000). The production of functionality by the elderly: A household production function approach. *Applied Economics, 32*, 1269–1280.

Lahiri, K., & Song, J. G. (2000). The effect of smoking on health using a sequential self-selection model. *Health Economics, 9*, 491–511.

Lakins, N. E., Williams, G. D., & Yi, H. (2007). *Apparent per capita alcohol consumption: National, state, and regional trends, 1977–2005*. Bethesda, MD: National Institute on Alcohol Abuse and Alcoholism. Retrieved December 17, 2007, from http://pubs.niaaa.nih.gov/publications/surveillance82/CONS05.htm

Launer, L. J., Harris, T., Rumpel, C., & Madans, J. (1994). Body mass index, weight change, and risk of mobility disability in middle-aged and older women: The epidemiologic follow-up study of NHANES I. *Journal of the American Medical Association, 271*, 1093–1098.

Lee, M.-J., & Kobayashi, S. (2001). Proportional treatment effects for count response panel data: Effects of binary exercise on health care demand. *Health Economics, 10*, 411–428.

Lockery, S. A., & Stanford, E. P. (1996). Physical activity and smoking: Gender comparisons among older African American adults. *Journal of Health Care for the Poor and Underserved, 7*(3), 232–251.

Mathers, C. D., & Loncar, D. (2006). Projections of global mortality and burden of disease from 2002 to 2030. *PLoS Medicine, 3*(11), e442.

McGinnis, J. M., Williams-Russo, P., & Knickman, J. R. (2002). The case for more active policy attention to health promotion. *Health Affairs, 21*, 78–93.

Molarius, A., Seidell, J. C., Kuulasmaa, K., Dobson, A. J., & Sans, S. (1997). Smoking and relative body weight: An international perspective from the WHO MONICA project. *Journal of Epidemiology and Community Health, 51*, 252–260.

National Cancer Institute. (2007). *Tobacco statistics snapshot*. Retrieved December 17, 2007, from http://www.cancer.gov/cancertopics/tobacco/statisticssnapshot/

National Heart, Lung, Blood Institute. (1998). *Clinical guidelines on the identification, evaluation, and treatment of overweight and obesity in adults: The evidence report*. Bethesda, MD: National Institutes of Health.

National Institute on Alcohol Abuse and Alcoholism. (1992, April). Moderate Drinking. Alcohol Alert. No. 16, PH 315. Retrieved June 12, 2008, from http://pubs.niaaa.nih.gov/publications/aa16.htm

Nephew, T. M., Williams, G. D., Stinson, F. S., Nguyen, K., & Dufour, M. C. (1999). *Apparent per capita alcohol consumption: National, state, and regional trends, 1977–1997*. Bethesda, MD: National Institute on Alcohol Abuse and Alcoholism.

Østbye, T., & Taylor, D. H. (2004). The effect of smoking on years of healthy life (YHL) lost among middle-aged and older Americans. *Health Services Research, 39*, 531–552.

Ostermann, J., & Sloan, F. A. (2001). Effects of alcohol consumption on disability among the near elderly: A longitudinal analysis. *The Milbank Quarterly, 79*, 487–515.

Pacula, R. L. (1998). Does increasing the beer tax reduce marijuana consumption? *Journal of Health Economics, 17*, 557–585.

Perkins, K. A., Epstein, L. H., Stiller, R. L., Fernstrom, M. H., Sexton, J. E., Jacob, R. G. et al. (1991). Acute effects of nicotine on hunger and caloric intake in smokers and nonsmokers. *Psychopharmacology, 103*, 103–109.

Perreira, K. M., & Sloan, F. A. (2001). Life events and alcohol consumption among mature adults: A longitudinal analysis. *Journal of Studies on Alcohol, 62*, 501–508.

Perreira, K. M., & Sloan, F. A. (2002). Excess alcohol consumption and health outcomes: A 6-year follow-up of men over age 50 from the Health and Retirement Study. *Addiction, 97*, 301–310.

Pettee, K. K., Brach, J. S., Kriska, A. M., Boudreau, R., Richardson, C. R., Colbert, L. H. et al. (2006). Influence of marital status on physical activity levels among older adults. *Medicine and Science in Sports and Exercise, 38*, 541–546.

Popkin, B. M. (2004). The nutrition transition: An overview of world patterns of change. *Nutrition Reviews, 62*, S140–S143.

Reynolds, S. L., Saito, Y., & Crimmins, E. M. (2005). The impact of obesity on active life expectancy in older American men and women. *The Gerontologist, 45*, 438–444.

Richardson, C. R., Kriska, A. M., Lantz, P. M., & Hayward, R. A. (2004). Physical activity and mortality across cardiovascular disease risk groups. *Medicine and Science in Sports and Exercise, 36*(11), 1923–1929.

Rosenstock, I. M. (1974). Historical origins of the Health Belief Model. *Health Education Monographs, 2*, 328–335.

Ruuskanen, J. M., & Ruoppila, I. (1995). Physical activity and psychological well-being among people aged 65 to 84 years. *Age and Ageing, 24*, 292–296.

Schoenbaum, M. (1997). Do smokers understand the mortality effects of smoking? Evidence from the Health and Retirement Survey. *American Journal of Public Health, 87*, 755–759.

Shlipak, M. G., Stehman-Breen, C., Vittinghoff, E., Lin, F., Varosy, P. D., Wenger, N. K. et al. (2004). Creatinine levels and cardiovascular events in women with heart disease: Do small changes matter? *American Journal of Kidney Diseases, 43*, 37–44.

Smith, V. K., Taylor, D. H., Jr., & Sloan, F. A. (2001). Longevity expectations and death: Can people predict their own demise? *The American Economic Review, 91,* 1126–1134.

Stuck, A. E., Walthert, J. M., Nikolaus, T., Bula, C. J., Hohmann, C., & Beck, J. C. (1999). Risk factors for functional status decline in community-living elderly people: A systematic literature review. *Social Science & Medicine, 48*(4), 445–469.

Sturm, R., Ringel, J. S., & Andreyeva, T. (2004). Increasing obesity rates and disability trends. *Health Affairs, 23,* 199–205.

Substance Abuse and Mental Health Services Administration (SAMHSA). (2006). *Results from the 2005 National Survey on Drug Use and Health: National findings.* Rockville, MD: Department of Health and Human Services, Substance Abuse and Mental Health Services Administration, Office of Applied Statistics.

Walford, R. L., Harris, S. B., & Weindruch, R. (1987). Dietary restriction and aging: Historical phases, mechanisms, and current directions. *Journal of Nutrition, 117,* 1650–1654.

Walston, J., & Fried, L. P. (1999). Frailty and the older man. *Medical Clinics of North America, 83,* 1173–1194.

Williamson, D. F. (1993). Descriptive epidemiology of body weight and weight change in U.S. adults. *Annals of Internal Medicine, 119,* 646–649.

Wilson, S. E. (2002). The health capital of families: An investigation of the inter-spousal correlation in health status. *Social Science & Medicine, 55*(7), 1157–1172.

World Health Organization and International Union against Tuberculosis and Lung Disease. (2007). *A WHO/The Union monograph on TB and tobacco control: Joining efforts to control two related global epidemics.* Retrieved April 11, 2008, from http://whqlibdoc.who.int/publications/2007/9789241596 220_eng.pdf

Wray, L. A., Alwin, D. F., & McCammon, R. J. (2005). Social status and risky health behaviors: Results from the Health and Retirement Study. *The Journals of Gerontology, Series B: Psychological Sciences and Social Sciences, 60,* S85–S92.

Wray, L. A., & Blaum, C. S. (2001). Explaining the role of sex on disability: A population-based study. *The Gerontologist, 41,* 499–510.

Wray, L. A., Herzog, A. R., Willis, R. J., & Wallace, R. B. (1998). The impact of education and heart attack on smoking cessation among middle-aged adults. *Journal of Health and Social Behavior, 39,* 271–294.

Zucker, R. A. (2000). Alcohol involvement over the life course. In National Institute on Alcohol Abuse and Alcoholism (Ed.), *Tenth special report to the U.S. Congress on alcohol and health: Highlights from current research* (pp. 28–53). Bethesda, MD: U.S. Department of Health and Human Services.

Zwerling, C., Sprince. N. L., Wallace, R. B., Davis, C. S., Whitten, P. S., & Heeringa. S. G. (1996). Risk factors for occupational injuries among older workers: An analysis of the Health and Retirement Study. *American Journal of Public Health, 86*(9), 1306–1309.

Kristi Rahrig Jenkins

HEALTH CARE USE, ADULTHOOD

Health care can be defined as any product or service designed to prevent, treat, or manage illness, or maintain mental and physical well-being. Health care has gone from a relatively minor part of the world's economy, to a sizable proportion of the economies of most developed nations. The United States, for example, spent about $1.9 trillion on health care in 2004, or 16% of its gross domestic product (GDP) (Stanton & Rutherford, 2005). Though the United States spends far more both in absolute and relative terms than any other country (Schoen et al., 2007), the increasing prominence of health care in people's lives and in national budgets is a worldwide phenomenon.

THEORIES OF HEALTH CARE USE

Various aspects of health care, including the determinants and consequences of utilization, are studied across a variety of disciplines, including sociology, economics, and public health. This interdisciplinary field is often referred to as health services research, and several scientific journals are dedicated to the topic. In this literature, two theoretical models, the Health Belief Model (Rosenstock, 1966) and the Behavioral Model of Health Care Use (Andersen, 1968), are commonly used to understand patterns of health care utilization. The Health Belief Model was developed to explain health behavior and use of preventive care, and focuses on one's perceptions, beliefs, and other psychological characteristics that determine whether individuals perceive themselves to have a health problem or are willing to change their behavior or seek care to ameliorate it. The Health Belief Model asserts that the decision to use health care, or to change any health related behavior, is determined by perceptions across the following four dimensions: (a) severity of the illness; (b) susceptibility to the illness; (c) the benefits associated with preventive use or behavioral change; and (d) the barriers to use or behavior.

In contrast, the Behavioral Model takes a systems approach to understanding health care use, categorizing the determinants of use into three groups: (a) factors that predispose individuals to use health care; (b) factors that enable individuals to get care, or impede them from doing so; and (c) factors that relate to the need for health care. Demographic variables such as age, gender, and race are examples of variables usually considered *predisposing* factors; insurance coverage and income are examples of important *enabling* or *impeding* factors; and the presence or absence of specific chronic conditions are examples of *need* factors. Note that the Behavioral Model tends to lump all the social and psychological factors central to the Health Belief Model into the predisposing category.

Though developed in the 1960s, both the Health Belief Model and Behavioral Model are widely used in health services research in the early 21st century. Both are, nonetheless, subject to several critiques. Critics of the Behavioral Model suggest that it places too little emphasis on social, cultural, and psychological factors that contribute to health care use, whereas critics of the Health Belief Model suggest that it places too little emphasis on individual and organizational barriers to obtaining needed health care. Both theoretical frameworks are criticized for being little help in understanding issues regarding the timing of health care utilization, the quality of care, and the continuity of care—all issues that are of growing importance in health services research. It has also been suggested that both the Behavioral Model and the Health Belief Model place too much emphasis on individual decision making, while underemphasizing how social context and social interaction affect beliefs on health and illness and, also, what actions are appropriate and desirable in response to different health conditions (Pescosolido, 1991; Pescosolido, 1992).

From these criticisms, new models are emerging. One example is the Network Episode Model (Pescosolido, 1991; Pescosolido, 1992). Its main focus is how social interaction, structured by social networks, influences the ways individuals recognize and respond to illness. Rather than viewing decisions regarding health care as one-time choices, the Network Episode Model views health care use to be a dynamic process, informed by social interaction both in families and communities and in formal health care settings. Utilization models, like the Network Episode Model, that move away from examining single choices are promising because health care use is increasingly driven by chronic, age- and lifestyle-related conditions. Such conditions often require long-term reliance on formal and informal health care and, therefore, decisions regarding health care use are not one-time occurrences.

DATA ON HEALTH CARE USE AND ACCESS

Data on health care use generally come from two sources: surveys and administrative records. In the United States, for example, the National Health Interview Surveys (NHIS) and the Medical Expenditure Panel Surveys (MEPS) collect information on health insurance coverage, use, expenditures, and attitudes about health care for the noninstitutionalized population; the Medicare Current Beneficiary Survey (MCBS) collects information on enrollees in the Medicare program. The second source of data on health care use, administrative records, makes use of data from hospital discharge records and other records kept by medical practices and institutions. Both survey and administrative data sources have advantages and dis-

---

COMPLEMENTARY AND ALTERNATIVE MEDICINE

■

Complementary and alternative medicine (CAM) is a diverse set of approaches and therapies for treating illness and promoting well-being that generally fall outside of standard medical practices. These approaches are usually not taught in medical schools, and not practiced by physicians or other professionals trained in medical programs. Examples of common CAM therapies include chiropractic, massage, homeopathy, and acupuncture. Complementary medicine is distinct from alternative medicine in that the latter is meant to be used in place of standard medical procedures, while the former is meant to be used in conjunction with medical procedures to increase their efficacy or reduce side effects.

Use of complementary and alternative medicine is common, even in industrialized countries with modern medical systems. For example, a survey in the United States shows that the number of individuals using some form of CAM during 2002 was over 62% (Pagan & Pauly, 2005). Furthermore, the use of CAM has been increasing for at least the late 1980s (Eisenberg, Davis, Ettner, & Appel, 1998).

BIBLIOGRAPHY

Eisenberg, D. M., Davis, R. B., Ettner, S. L., and Appel, S. (1998). Trends in alternative medicine use in the United States, 1990–1997: Results of a follow-up national survey. *Journal of the American Medical Association, 280,* 1569–1575.

Pagan, J., and Pauly, M. V. (2005). Access to conventional medical care and the use of complementary and alternative medicine. *Health Affairs, 24,* 255–263.

---

advantages. The advantage of administrative records is that they usually provide accurate information on the exact type of service used, the date of use, how much was paid, and the source of payment. The disadvantage of this type of data is that detailed information on the characteristics of individuals and households such as income, education, and attitudes about health is limited or nonexistent. Surveys, in contrast, can provide very rich data on individuals, their families, and their attitudes about health, but rely heavily on self-reports for information on health care use and expenditures.

Access to health care, or the ability to obtain needed medical services in a timely manner, is an important concept in health services research, but is difficult to measure. It is frequently measured by health care use, but this is not ideal because use is strongly linked to the need for health care. For example, healthy individuals with jobs that provide generous health benefits may have excellent access to health care, but little or no use. In contrast, unhealthy individuals with poor health insurance coverage may have very high levels of health care use out of medical necessity, but still not be able to get all the care they truly need. Several indicators of access are frequently used to avoid this problem. One approach is to consider hospitalizations for what is termed *ambulatory care sensitive conditions* (Ansari, Laditka, & Laditka, 2006). The underlying idea is that a hospitalization for a condition that could have been avoided or managed better in an outpatient setting is a sign of having poor access to quality health care. This approach to studying health care access often uses administrative records. Other commonly used measures for access are whether someone has a usual source of care, and subjective assessments of the ability to obtain needed medical care (Kirby, Taliaferro, & Zuvekas, 2005; Zuvekas & Taliaferro, 2003). These measures usually come from survey data.

PATTERNS OF HEALTH CARE USE OVER THE LIFE COURSE

Though the amount and intensity of health care use varies widely across individuals, there is a definite pattern of use seen in a typical lifetime, at least in industrialized societies. Health care use is high at the beginning of life, as many births in industrialized countries are now in hospitals and attended by physicians, and continues at a fairly high level into adolescence. Standard medical practice in most industrialized countries consists of frequent visits for very young children, with declining frequency as children age. Health care use declines thereafter and young adults beginning their careers tend to have the lowest health care use of any age group, as they tend to be the healthiest, and are least likely to have the time or money to spend on physician visits. In the United States, these are the years in which individuals are least likely to have health insurance. For women, childbearing prompts an increase in health care use. For both men and women, individuals begin to use more health care services starting in their 40s and 50s and this increases steeply and in a nonlinear fashion with age. Thus, the shape of the health care utilization curve resembles a mortality curve, in that the incidence of use is high at very young ages, declines until early adulthood, and increases thereafter.

A noteworthy characteristic of health care use across the life course is the extent to which it is concentrated toward the end of life. For example, data from the MCBS in the United States suggest that around 27% of all health care expenses among older people go toward care received in the last year of life (Hogan, Lunney, Gabel, & Lynn, 2001). This frequently cited statistic is, however, somewhat misleading. The concentration of usage in the last year of life is often considered the main cause of the high cost of care, but this is debatable. The proportion of medical expenses incurred in the final year of life has not changed much since the 1970s (Hogan et al., 2001), despite the rapid development of expensive new medical technology. Use of inpatient hospital services, the most expensive type of health care, by the terminally ill actually declined beginning in the late 1980s and 1990s (Hoover, Crystal, Kumar, Sambamoorthi, & Cantor, 2002). It is possible that initiatives to promote the use of hospice care and advance directives may have held down end of life expenses. When expenses for decedents are compared to that of survivors with similarly severe conditions, differences in expenses are minimal (Hogan et al., 2001). Thus, what is often termed the *high cost of dying* is really just the high cost of being severely ill.

DISPARITIES IN HEALTH CARE USE AND ACCESS

Health services researchers have documented large and persistent disparities in health care use and access to quality health care by race, ethnicity, and various socioeconomic characteristics, even in nations with universal health care coverage. Racial and ethnic minorities and the poor generally use less care, report more problems with getting care, and have less favorable outcomes from the care they get than others (Agency for Healthcare Research and Quality, 2006). In the United States, for example, Blacks and Hispanics are less likely to have any ambulatory care during a year, are less likely to have a usual source of care, and more likely to report barriers to obtaining care than non-Hispanic Whites (Kirby, Taliaferro, & Zuvekas, 2005). Differences emerge for many specific services too. For example, in the United States, Black children are less likely to have up-to-date vaccination coverage than Whites (Chu, Barker, & Smith, 2004), and Black adults at risk of sudden cardiac death are less likely to have an implantable defibrillator (Stanley, DeLia, & Cantor, 2007). Socioeconomic disparities in access and use are as large as or larger than racial or ethnic disparities. These disparities in health care regarding socioeconomics and race or ethnicity are still not fully understood by researchers. Individual, family, and community characteristics currently thought to affect disparities explain only a fraction of the differences observed (Kirby, Taliaferro, & Zuvekas, 2005).

HEALTH SERVICES RESEARCH AND LIFE COURSE CONCEPTS

Developing a system that organizes, finances, and distributes health care in a financially sustainable and equitable way is a goal that motivates much health services research. To achieve this, a basic understanding of how people perceive and respond to health and illness, and how they interact with various actors in modern health care systems, is essential. To date, life course concepts have been notably lacking in this effort, and have been lacking in health services research in general. This is unfortunate because as populations age and health care utilization is increasingly driven by conditions related to chronic diseases, life course concepts become increasingly relevant. For example, the life course concepts of timing, sequence, and duration applied to different health-related experiences, including interactions with health care systems, could shed light on some of the questions important in health services research. *Linked lives* is another important life course principle that is relevant in the study of health care use. Attitudes about health and health care, and about how best to respond to illness, are formed and influenced by interactions within complex social networks. These and other concepts from the life course perspective are powerful and largely untapped resources in health services research.

SEE ALSO Volume 2: *Health Differentials/Disparities, Adulthood; Health Insurance; Policy, Health;* Volume 3: *Health Literacy.*

BIBLIOGRAPHY

Agency for Healthcare Research and Quality. (2006). *2006 National healthcare disparities report.* Rockville, MD: Author; U.S. Department of Health and Human Services.

Andersen, R.M. (1968). *Behavioral model of families' use of health services.* Chicago: Center for Health Administration Studies; University of Chicago.

Ansari, Z., Laditka, J. N., & Laditka, S. B. (2006). Access to health care and hospitalization for ambulatory care sensitive conditions. *Medical Care Research and Review, 63*(6), 719–741.

Chu, S. Y., Barker, L. E., & Smith, P. (2004). Racial/ethnic disparities in preschool immunizations: United States, 1996–2001. *American Journal of Public Health, 94,* 973–977.

Hogan, C., Lunney, J., Gabel, J., & Lynn, J. (2001). Medicare beneficiaries' costs of care in the last year of life. *Health Affairs, 20*(4), 188–195.

Hoover, D. R., Crystal, S., Kumar, R., Sambamoorthi, U., & Cantor, J. C. (2002). Medical expenditures during the last year of life: Findings from the 1992–1996 Medicare Current Beneficiary Survey. *Health Services Research, 37*(6), 1625–1642.

Kirby, J. B., Taliaferro, G. S., & Zuvekas, S. H. (2005). Explaining racial and ethnic disparities in health care. *Medical Care, 45*(5), 64–72.

Pescosolido, B. (1991). Illness careers and network ties: A conceptual model of utilization and compliance. *Advances in Medical Sociology, 2,* 161–184.

Pescosolido, B. (1992). Beyond rational choice: The social dynamics of how people seek help. *American Journal of Sociology, 97,* 1096–1138.

Rosenstock, I. M. (1966). Why people use health services. *Milbank Memorial Fund Quarterly, 44,* 94–127.

Schoen, C., Osborn, R., Doty, M. M., Bishop, M., Peugh, J., & Murukutia, N. (2007). Toward higher-performance health systems: Adults' health care experiences in seven countries, 2007. *Health Affairs, 26,* w717–w734.

Stanley, A., DeLia, D., & Cantor, J. C. (2007). Racial disparity and technology diffusion: The case of cardioverter defibrillator implants, 1996–2001. *Journal of the American Medical Association, 99*(3), 201–207.

Stanton, M. W., & Rutherford, M. K. (2005). *The high concentration of U.S. health care expenses.* Rockville, MD: Agency for Healthcare Research and Quality.

Zuvekas, S. H., & Taliaferro, G. S. (2003). Pathways to access: Health insurance, the health care delivery system, and racial/ethnic disparities, 1996–1999. *Health Affairs, 22*(2), 139–153.

James B. Kirby

HEALTH DIFFERENTIALS/ DISPARITIES, ADULTHOOD

The term *health disparities* refers to differences in measured mental health, physical health, and death rates (often termed *outcomes*) across meaningful social and demographic groups within a population. While a population can be defined at many different levels (e.g., a hospital population, a clinic population, a city population, or a state population), this entry focuses on health disparities within the working-aged (ages 25 to 64) population of the United States as a whole. Because of the very wide range of health outcomes that can be examined, only the most general of those outcomes will be dissected here. Similarly, because of the breadth of sociodemographic groups for which disparities are measured, this entry will focus on health disparities in adulthood by gender, race and ethnicity, and educational attainment, while recognizing that there are also well-documented U.S. health disparities across income groups, occupational groups, geographic regions, and more.

THE SIGNIFICANCE OF HEALTH DISPARITIES

One of the two overarching goals of the U.S. government's *Healthy People 2010* initiative is to eliminate health disparities among different segments of the population. Specifically, the goal refers to differences that occur by gender, race or ethnicity, education or income, disability, geographic location, or sexual orientation (U.S. Department of Health and Human Services, 2000). The *Healthy People 2010* initiative and the health disparities goal, in particular, have helped create enormous scientific and policy interest on this topic. Scientifically, health disparity studies range across academic disciplines, from public health, medicine, nursing, and biology to economics, geography, sociology, and demography. Indeed, it would be impossible for any review to cover the massive amount of literature on this topic that has been produced in many disciplines since the early 1990s. Policy-wise, the goals and objectives of *Healthy People 2010* have, perhaps most notably, led to significant increases in funding at the federal level for research and programs specifically dedicated toward the better understanding of why health disparities exist and how to eliminate them.

The significance of U.S. health disparities is at least threefold. First, documented health disparities indicate inequalities in well-being across subgroups of a population. Thus, in a society that is striving for both overall excellence as well as excellence in health within all subgroups of the population, disparities in measured outcomes symbolize systematic, unequal access to some of society's most important resources, including the length of life itself. At issue, then, is fairness across population subgroups. Second, continued health disparities in a nation as wealthy as the United States serves as a reminder that even though the overall level of health achievements over the last century or more has been extraordinary, there is still much room for improvement if all groups are to be as healthy as the most advantaged group. Third, individuals in the subgroups who have less favorable health and higher mortality rates experience substantial amounts of human suffering, increased health care costs, and loss of economic productivity that could potentially be alleviated if health disparities did not exist. Together, these add up to some of the most critical social, health, and ethical issues in the 21st-century United States.

Beyond the general significance of health disparities, the topic's significance among the U.S. working-aged population may be especially important. While a great deal of research—and justifiably so—focuses on health disparities among the older population (i.e., age 65 and older) of the United States, measured health disparities by gender, race or ethnicity, and education have often been found to be wider during the working-aged years in comparison to the older adult years (Rogers et al., 2000). Moreover, thinking about health disparities from a life course perspective makes clear that what happens during the working-aged years—such as marriage or divorce, parenting, career trajectories, income trajectories, access to health insurance, and preparation for retirement—is a very important determinant of later life health. Thus, the working-aged years help to structure health disparities during middle and old age. Moreover, life course approaches to health disparities should step back even further—to adolescence, childhood, and even previous generations—to best understand how disparities in the working ages and older adult ages develop.

CURRENT HEALTH DISPARITIES WITHIN THE U.S. WORKING-AGED POPULATION

In this section, disparities will be briefly documented in two general but very important measures of health during the working-aged years—self-reported health and mortality rates—by gender, race or ethnicity, and education. The reasoning for the focus on these two common health outcomes is that, first, self-reported health has been found to be a very strong predictor of subsequent mortality risk, even when other physical health conditions are statistically controlled. Further, it is a standard item on many health surveys. In this case, people who report either fair or poor health are compared to those who report excellent, very good, or good health. Second, mortality rates provide a useful summary indicator of the overall health of a population and its subgroups. There are, of course, many other indicators that could be examined (e.g., activity limitations, presence of hypertension or diabetes, cancer prevalence, measures of mental health, and more). Further, this entry's examination of sociodemographic disparities will be limited to gender, race or ethnicity, and education. The U.S. population clearly continues to be stratified across categories of these sociodemographic factors and this stratification has significant consequences for health outcomes. A more comprehensive documentation would include a full analysis of other sociodemographic characteristics including, but not limited to, sexual orientation, religion, marital status, income, occupation, immigration status, and geographic location.

Nationally representative and publicly available data collected and made available by the federal government are often used to document these disparities. This entry's documentation of disparities in self-reported health specifically draws on nationally representative survey data from the 2004 National Health Interview Survey (NHIS), collected and processed by the National Center for Health Statistics. This annual survey of the U.S. population has collected data from tens of thousands of noninstitutionalized U.S. adults each year since 1957 and is considered to be the nation's core source of information for population-level health and health care trends and disparities. This entry's documentation of disparities in mortality within the working-aged population specifically draws on published data from the National Vital Statistics System, which is also a product of the National Center for Health Statistics. The calculation of mortality rates in this system relies on death counts, taken from U.S. death certificates, as the numerator in the mortality rates and population estimates,

	AGES				
	25–34	35–44	45–54	55–64	Total (25–64)
Gender					
*Men^*	4.61	7.16	12.43	19.13	10.07
Women	6.70	9.58	14.54	20.01	12.11
Race/Ethnicity					
*Non-Hispanic White^*	4.35	7.10	10.58	15.85	9.37
Non-Hispanic Black	9.23	11.45	21.04	29.93	16.37
Mexican	6.69	10.36	20.60	31.90	13.23
Puerto Rican	12.09	16.14	17.96	33.71	17.95
Other Hispanic	4.72	7.62	17.32	24.58	11.40
Asian	2.80	5.66	10.64	16.44	7.90
American Indian	12.93	17.52	30.92	38.73	23.79
Education (Years Completed)					
*17 or more^*	1.37	1.37	4.06	6.33	3.33
16	1.86	3.87	6.44	9.85	4.90
13–15	5.17	7.87	11.49	15.92	9.48
12	6.53	9.32	14.87	19.78	12.19
9–11	11.13	18.26	27.68	36.71	21.60
0–8	10.74	15.13	31.81	45.01	24.81

SOURCE: National Health Interview Survey (2004).
^reference group
*p<.05
**p<.01

Table 1. *Percentage of U.S. working-aged adults who report fair/poor health in 2004 by sociodemographic group.* CENGAGE LEARNING, GALE.

taken from the U.S. Census Bureau, as the denominator of the mortality rates.

Turning first to self-reported health, Table 1 shows the percentage of U.S. working-aged adults who report being in fair or poor heath, by sociodemographic group and by age. Across each sociodemographic group examined, the percentage of individuals reporting fair or poor health is higher in older age categories, as might be expected. By gender, women report worse health than men for all age groups except between 55 and 64; in that interval, there is no statistically significant difference in the percentage of men and women reporting fair or poor health. The overall gender difference in reporting poor or fair health in the full age range of 25 to 64, 12.1% for women versus 10.1% for men, while statistically significant, is not nearly as wide as the disparities by race or ethnicity and educational level.

Table 1 next shows self-reported health disparities across seven self-identified racial or ethnic groups. American Indians have the highest percentage of all the racial and ethnic groups of reporting fair or poor health in each of the 10-year age categories shown, as well as for the entire working-aged population. For the entire age range, 23.8% of American Indians reported poor or fair health, compared to just 9.4% among non-Hispanic Whites. In

contrast, there are no significant differences between Asian Americans and non-Hispanic Whites in reporting fair or poor health. Both non-Hispanic Blacks and Mexican Americans have significantly higher percentages of persons reporting fair or poor health than do non-Hispanic Whites within each 10-year age category, as well as for the entire age range. Puerto Ricans have significantly higher percentages of persons reporting fair or poor health than non-Hispanic Whites for ages 35 to 44 and 55 to 64; these percentages are also higher than those for non-Hispanic Blacks and Mexican Americans.

Table 1 further shows that educational disparities in self-reported health are substantial. Nearly all education levels for all age groups are characterized by a higher percentage of individuals reporting fair or poor health when compared to the reference category of 17 or more years of education; the only exception is that the health reports of persons with 16 years of completed education do not differ from those with 17 or more years in the 25 to 34 age group. Looking within the 10-year age categories, some of these self-reported health disparities by education are very large. For example, within the 35 to 44 age group, 18.3% of people with 9 to 11 years of education reported poor or fair health, compared to just 1.4% of those with 17 or more years of education. Even

	AGES				
	25–34	**35–44**	**45–54**	**55–64**	**Total (25–64)**
Gender					
Men	139.5	243.6	543.5	1,128.8	457.2
Women	63.5	143.5	314.3	707.4	278.6
Total	102.1	193.5	427.0	910.3	367.2
Race/Ethnicity					
Non-Hispanic White	95.9	185.9	400.8	875.1	372.2
Non-Hispanic Black	186.5	332.3	760.8	1,527.9	585.9
Mexican	76.3	133.4	302.2	679.1	195.6
Puerto Rican	101.4	217.0	457.3	931.2	339.5
Other Hispanic	76.3	125.7	285.0	600.9	205.5
Other	58.0	106.6	241.2	521.2	186.1
Education (Years Completed)*					
13 or more	53.4	104.4	257.7	566.3	214.7
12	161.9	282.8	598.3	1,141.5	515.3
0–11	202.2	408.9	850.3	1,588.4	715.2

*Total of 36 States Reporting and the District of Columbia.
SOURCE: Derived from Miniño et al. (2007).
Rates are per 100,000 population in group specified.
Data as of July 1, 2004.

Table 2. *Age-specific mortality rates for US working-aged adults by sociodemographic group.* **CENGAGE LEARNING, GALE.**

at the highest levels of education, there are significant differences between 16 years of education (which is synonymous with attaining a bachelor's degree) and 17 years or more of education (which is any education beyond a bachelor's degree); for example, 4.9% of working-aged adults with 16 years of education reported poor or fair health compared to 3.3% of those with 17 or more years of education.

Table 2 displays age-specific mortality rates (number of deaths per 100,000 persons) for U.S. working-aged adults by sociodemographic group. For all categories of each sociodemographic factor, mortality rates consistently are higher among older age groups, as might be expected. Within each 10-year age category, females have much lower mortality rates than their male counterparts. At the youngest age group (ages 25 to 34), for example, the male mortality rate is more than double that of females. Higher male rates of mortality across the life course result in a life expectancy for men (74.7 years) that is currently more than 5 years less than that of women (80.0 years). This life expectancy disparity by gender is lower than the 8-year disparity observed in the 1970s, but is still very wide (Arias, 2007).

Table 2 next shows age-specific mortality rates for six racial and ethnic groups. Non-Hispanic Blacks experience the highest mortality rate within every age group as well as within the entire 25 to 64 age range. Among the

Hispanic ethnic groups, Puerto Ricans experience the highest mortality rates, whereas Mexican Americans and other Hispanics experience relatively similar and much lower age-specific mortality than Puerto Ricans and non-Hispanic Blacks. Within each age group, Puerto Ricans are the only Hispanic ethnic group to experience a higher mortality rate than non-Hispanic Whites. However, for all ages combined, the Puerto Rican mortality rate is lower than that of non-Hispanic Whites. This reflects the younger average age of the Puerto Rican population compared to the non-Hispanic White population and the fact that mortality rates are lower for younger people.

Mexican Americans and other Hispanics, by contrast, experience mortality rates that are lower than non-Hispanic Whites within each 10-year age group, as well as within the entire working-aged population. The relatively low mortality rates of these Hispanic ethnic groups, in combination with their relatively high rates of poverty and low levels of education, have been termed an *epidemiologic paradox* (Markides & Coreil, 1986). This is in contrast to the very strong correlation between the high rates of poverty and high mortality rates experienced by non-Hispanic Blacks. The epidemiologic paradox among U.S. Mexican Americans is a topic of much scientific research. Current work suggests two clear reasons why Mexican Americans exhibit relatively low rates of mortality in the United States: (a) They are characterized by a high percentage of recent immigrants, who tend to be very healthy when they migrate to the United States; and (b) they exhibit very low levels of negative health behaviors, such as cigarette smoking, heavy alcohol use, and use of illegal drugs.

Turning to educational disparities, it is clear that mortality rates have an inverse relationship with education for each 10-year age group. That is, individuals who attain higher levels of education have much lower rates of working-aged mortality in the United States. For example, the mortality rate for individuals aged 25 to 34 with 0 to 11 years of education is about 4 times as high as the rate for individuals with 13 or more years of education in that age group. Moreover, it is evident that education can protect health not only within a particular age group, but across all age groups. For example, the mortality rate for persons aged 55 to 64 with 13 years or more of education is lower than the mortality rate for persons aged 45 to 54 and 55 to 64 with either 12 or 0 to 11 years of education.

CAUSES OF HEALTH DISPARITIES

Research suggests at least four general sets of factors leading to the development of U.S. health disparities by gender, race or ethnicity, and educational level during the working-aged years: (a) biological factors; (b) behavioral causes; (c) psychosocial factors; and (d) differential access to health-promoting resources across sociodemographic groups.

Biological factors, for example, have been linked to health disparities by gender (Waldron, 1983). The most obvious example is that women are exposed to both common and severe health-related risks associated with pregnancy and childbirth, whereas men are not. Historically, mortality rates among women during the child-bearing ages were strongly influenced by risks associated with pregnancy and childbirth; fortunately, this is no longer the case. Women are also protected, in part, from some infectious diseases and circulatory diseases during early adulthood because of the presence of estrogen, whereas men are more likely to be characterized by the harmful effects of the accumulation of fat in the abdominal region (Waldron, 1993). Biological factors are thought to have much less of an impact on either racial and ethnic or educational disparities in health during the working-aged years.

Behavioral factors across sociodemographic groups can also produce health disparities. Cigarette smoking is an excellent example. Convincing research shows that heavier smoking by men than women had a major impact on gender-specific health disparities in the United States, resulting in much higher male mortality when compared to female mortality throughout the 20th century. The impact of smoking on male-female mortality disparities peaked in the 1970s and has been declining

since (Preston & Wang, 2006). At the same time, smoking is becoming increasingly concentrated among persons with lower education in the United States. Correspondingly, some U.S. health and mortality disparities among the working-aged population appear to have widened quite considerably in more recent years; that is, smoking-related illness and deaths are now much less frequent among the higher educated than the lower educated. Such wide health and mortality differences by educational level are reflected in Tables 1 and 2.

An array of psychosocial factors also affect health disparities during the working-age years. One important example is the experience of racial or gender discrimination—whether racism and sexism are encountered at the individual level, within U.S. social institutions, or both—which can influence the health of racial or ethnic and gender groups. The loss of resources associated with racism and sexism (e.g., lower income) and the psychological stresses of dealing with racism and sexism have been shown to be important in the development of health disparities across U.S. sociodemographic groups (Krieger, Rowley, Herman, Avery, & Phillips, 1993). Another important psychosocial factor that influences health disparities is that higher educated individuals perceive a greater sense of control over their lives than lower educated individuals. A greater sense of control assists highly educated persons in making healthier decisions and in dealing more effectively with life's stresses in comparison to individuals with lower levels of education (Mirowsky & Ross, 2003).

Differential access to health-promoting resources is the fourth set of causal factors underlying U.S. working-aged health disparities (Link & Phelan, 1995). Persons with low levels of education, for example, are less likely to have access to steady, high-paying jobs with health insurance benefits in comparison to persons with low levels of education. Thus, stresses associated with bouts of underemployment or unemployment, less income with which to purchase nutritious food and live in a safe neighborhood, and the lack of health insurance can all lead to lower levels of health and higher levels of mortality among the less educated. Further, differential access to health-promoting resources does not begin in adulthood. For example, non-Hispanic Black, Hispanic, and American Indian children are much less likely to grow up in affluent neighborhoods than non-Hispanic White and Asian-American children in the United States (Massey, 2001). This residential segregation structures the later educational, occupational, housing, and health care opportunities that different sociodemographic groups experience and, thus, can have very important impacts on the development of health disparities throughout the life course.

CONTINUED RESEARCH NEEDS

There is a continuing need to better understand and address U.S. health disparities within the working-aged population. Using the most general measures available, health disparities by gender, race or ethnicity, and education continue to be wide in the United States and have been stubbornly resistant to closing in spite of the priority of this topic set by the U.S. Department of Health and Human Services. Perhaps the greatest challenge for both future researchers and policy makers is not to approach health disparities on an outcome-by-outcome or disease-by-disease basis, but as disparities that are structured in fundamentally social ways, both across generations and over the life course. Given that gender, race or ethnicity, and educational attainment all continue to structure opportunities and constraints in very important ways throughout the life course and even across generations, research and policy priorities in this area might best be focused on how and why these sociodemographic factors continue to have the social impact that they do and what, in turn, can be done to minimize or eliminate the constraints faced by groups that are the most disadvantaged.

SEE ALSO Volume 2: *Health Care Use, Adulthood; Health Behaviors, Adulthood; Health Insurance; Income Inequality; Policy, Health; Poverty, Adulthood; Racism/ Race Discrimination;* Volume 3: *Health Literacy.*

BIBLIOGRAPHY

Anderson, N., Bulatao, R., & Cohen, B. (Eds.). (2004). *Critical perspectives on racial and ethnic differences in health in late life.* Washington, DC: National Academies Press.

Arias, E. (2007). United States life tables, 2003. *National Vital Statistics Reports 54*(14). Retrieved June 6, 2008, from http:// www.cdc.gov/nchs/data/nvsr/nvsr54_14.pdf

Giele, J. Z., & Elder, G. H. (Eds.). (1998). *Methods of life course research: Qualitative and quantitative approaches.* Thousand Oaks, CA: Sage.

Idler, E. L., & Benyamini, Y. (1997). Self-rated health and mortality: A review of 27 community studies. *Journal of Health and Social Behavior, 38*(1), 21–37.

Krieger, N., Rowley, D., Herman, A., Avery, B., & Phillips, M. (1993). Racism, sexism, and social class: Implications for studies of health, disease, and well-being. *American Journal of Preventive Medicine, 9* (Suppl. 6), 82–122.

Link, B. G., & Phelan, J. C. (1995). Social conditions as fundamental causes of disease. *Journal of Health and Social Behavior, 36,* 80–94.

Markides, K. S., & Coreil, J. (1986). The health of southwestern Hispanics: An epidemiologic paradox. *Public Health Reports, 101*(3), 253–265.

Massey, D. S. (2001). Residential segregation and neighborhood conditions in U.S. metropolitan areas. In N. J. Smelser, W. J. Wilson, & F. Mitchell (Eds.), *America becoming: Racial trends and their consequences* (Vol. 1; pp. 391–434). Washington, DC: National Academy Press.

Miniño, A. M., Heron, M. P., Murphy, S. L., & Kochanek, K. D. (2007). Deaths: Final data for 2004. *National Vital Statistics Reports, 55*(19). Retrieved June 6, 2008, from http:// www.cdc.gov/nchs/data/nvsr/nvsr55/nvsr55_19.pdf

Mirowsky, J., & Ross, C.E. (2003). *Education, social status, and health.* New York: Aldine de Gruyter.

National Center for Health Statistics. (2004). *2004 National Health Interview Survey data release.* Hyattsville, MD: Author.

Preston, S. H., & Wang, H. (2006). Sex mortality differences in the United States: The role of cohort smoking patterns. *Demography, 43*(4), 631–646.

Rogers, R., Hummer, R., & Nam, C. (2000). *Living and dying in the U.S.A.: Behavioral, health, and social differentials of adult mortality.* San Diego, CA: Academic Press.

U.S. Department of Health and Human Services. (2000). *Healthy people 2010: Understanding and improving health.* Washington, DC: Author. Retrieved June 6, 2008, from http://www.healthypeople.gov/Document

Waldron, I. (1993). Recent trends in sex mortality ratios for adults in developed countries. *Social Science and Medicine, 36*(4), 451–462.

Robert A. Hummer
Juanita J. Chinn

HEALTH INSURANCE

Health insurance refers to protection against the costs of health care arising from illness or injury. The specific expenses covered by health insurance differ widely, but in general the costs to individuals and families of routine, emergency, and critical health care are covered all or in part by the insurer. In most developed countries, this coverage is mandatory. It can be provided by private companies (operating for profit or not) or by government programs; most countries' health systems rely on a mix of both sources of coverage. Payment for insurance depends on the provider: Private insurers generally collect premiums from individuals and employers, whereas public insurance is often funded through general taxation or salary deductions.

Since the advent of the British National Health Service in 1948, the role of health insurance in producing or ameliorating socioeconomic inequities in health has been of great interest. Based on the widely held assumption that a great part of social inequities in health stemmed from unequal utilization of modern medical care, the most obvious solution to reduce these inequities appeared to be the elimination of inequities in access to medical institutions (Robert & House, 2000). As such, universal, mandatory health insurance coverage and, in certain cases, national health systems were the prime ways by which societies hoped to mitigate the effects of social inequalities on health (Acheson, 1998). While it has since been recognized that health insurance is not a sufficient condition to eliminate socioeconomic inequities in mortality (Townsend, Davidson, & Whitehead, 1992) evidence indicates it keeps them in check. Indeed, in countries such as the United States that still do not guarantee health insurance coverage to all their citizens, social inequalities in health are often amplified, with dire consequences for health across the life course.

PUBLIC AND PRIVATE HEALTH INSURANCE AND INEQUALITIES IN HEALTH

At the national level, the organization of health insurance can affect social inequalities in health through two interrelated mechanisms: whether health insurance is mandatory and the methods for setting rates. By definition, mandatory insurance ensures that no individual is left uninsured, with two important implications for equity: Sick individuals cannot be denied health insurance, and healthy individuals cannot remove themselves from the risk pool. The United States constitutes an exception among developed countries because it does not provide mandatory insurance. Globally, however, the question of how insurance costs are established is the most salient issues for insurance equity across the life course.

The most equitable situation occurs when the cost of health insurance is a function of one's income or salary. This progressive taxation policy favors the most deprived segments of the population, by providing them with the same (or more) services for less money than the wealthiest segments (O'Donnell, van Doorslaer, Wagstaff, & Lindelow, 2008). This is particularly important considering that deprived groups also tend to accumulate the most heath problems and therefore have the greatest need for health services. This type of cost setting is characteristic of public insurance schemes.

At the other end of the spectrum are costs established on the basis of competitive risk rating—that is, according to the relative risk of ill health of the person to be insured. For all but those with the lowest risks, this practice leads to the "inverse coverage law" whereby those who need coverage the most get the least or must pay more for it out of pocket (Light, 1992). Finally, given equal risk, the breadth of coverage can often be increased with higher premiums, meaning that coverage is a function not only of medical characteristics but also of socioeconomic factors. This type of cost setting is characteristic of private insurance schemes.

As such, compared with public insurance, private insurance may contribute to social differentials in health by compounding the positive effects of socioeconomic position on health. In contrast, coverage through public means should mitigate socioeconomic differentials in

health as it can remove—and even reverse through progressive taxation—one pathway whereby advantaged socioeconomic positions may contribute to better health. Theoretically, public insurance should therefore reduce the total effect of social position on health.

EMPIRICAL EVIDENCE

Very few studies have explicitly contrasted the impact of risk rating versus other costing methods on health and social inequalities in health. This question poses the empirical challenge of obtaining data before and after—that is, a "natural experiment" involving a radical change in national health system policy. Unfortunately, there are scant data on such transitions, and they typically are limited to aggregate-level contrasts, as these policies tend to affect whole populations, thus precluding analysis at the individual level. Thus, attributing causality to this specific health policy change is difficult, as it rarely occurs in isolation from other social changes.

The Black Report (Townsend, Davidson, & Whitehead, 1992) probably constitutes the most well-known study to shed some light on this topic. This landmark report revealed that social inequalities in health and mortality had not diminished since the implementation of the National Health Service in the United Kingdom, but had instead increased (Townsend, Davidson, & Whitehead, 1992). Yet part of this growing gap was attributable to improvements in mortality among the wealthier classes, and not to declines among the lower socioeconomic groups. This suggested that the upper classes were making greater (or somehow "better") use of the improved access to medical resources. Note, however, that the Black Report was measuring socioeconomic

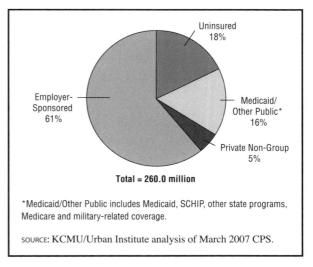

Total = 260.0 million

*Medicaid/Other Public includes Medicaid, SCHIP, other state programs, Medicare and military-related coverage.

SOURCE: KCMU/Urban Institute analysis of March 2007 CPS.

Figure 1. *Health insurance coverage of the nonelderly population (under the age of 65), 2006.* **CENGAGE LEARNING, GALE.**

status through an occupational class schema, and not through income, which precluded the estimation of the aforementioned hypothesized redistribution effects.

In contrast, other studies that made use of the Canadian experience in developing a one-payer public system found that access to care among the poor increased substantially after the introduction of national health insurance (Enterline, Salter, McDonald, & McDonald, 1973; McDonald, McDonald, Salter, & Enterline, 1974). Moreover, it appears that this increase in access also translated into improved health outcomes. Hanratty (1996) found that the introduction of national insurance was associated with a 4% decline in infant mortality rates, coupled with a decrease in the incidence of low birth weight that was particularly marked among single parents. Infant mortality is more sensitive to social inequalities in health than is general, all-cause mortality (Gwatkin, 2001), suggesting that the introduction of a national health insurance system did disproportionately benefit the most destitute in Canada.

Since then a substantial international literature has developed to examine income inequities in access to medical care, to the point where the scholarly journal *Health Economics* even devoted a whole issue to this topic in 2004 (Volume 13, Issue 7). These studies generally found income inequities in access to medical care whereby low-income individuals were less likely to access specialist services, even in countries with universal coverage. The most comprehensive such study found that whereas access to general practitioners was equitably distributed in Organisation for Economic Co-operation and Development (OECD) countries, access to specialists exhibited such a pro-rich gradient that overall access to physicians appeared to favor the wealthiest segments of the population (van Doorslaer, Masseria, & Koolman, 2006). Moreover, this relationship was exacerbated in countries with private health insurance. As the authors themselves point out, however, this research speaks only to access to care, and more research remains to be done to show whether these inequities in access also translate into health differentials.

IN THE ABSENCE OF MANDATORY HEALTH INSURANCE: THE CASE OF THE UNITED STATES

The U.S. health insurance system is unique among developed countries by not providing a guarantee of universal health insurance coverage for its citizens (Fried & Gaydos, 2002). Indeed, the vast majority of the adult population in the United States relies on private coverage through employers, and "holes" still exist that create a substantial—and increasing—uninsured population. Thus, privately insured, publicly insured, and uninsured adults coexist, but the risk of being in any of those groups

is not equally distributed in the population; this has important implications for equity of access to care, and, ultimately, for the elimination of health disparities.

A Growing Uninsured Population After more than half a decade of stable uninsurance rates, the U.S. Bureau of the Census's Current Population Report on health insurance in 2001 reported an increase in the proportion uninsured (Holahan & Pohl, 2002; Mills, 2002), a trend that has since continued unabated (DeNavas-Walt, Proctor, & Smith, 2007). This subgroup continued to grow from 2005 to 2006, reaching an estimated 15.8% of the population, or 47 million Americans (DeNavas-Walt et al., 2007).

Most significantly, these increases were due primarily to a drop among individuals covered by employment-based health insurance (DeNavas-Walt et al., 2007; Mills, 2002; Mills & Bhandari, 2003). Finally, 90% of the growth in the number of uninsured during the early 21st century occurred among low- and middle-income households (Hoffman & Wang, 2003; Holahan & Wang, 2004).

The Unequal Distribution of Risk of Coverage Privately insured individuals are more likely to be employed, to be in good health, and to report higher levels of education and of income (DeNavas-Walt et al., 2007; Institute of Medicine, 2002; Mills & Bhandari, 2003). In contrast, because of the eligibility requirements for this coverage, publicly insured individuals are more likely to have incomes below $25,000 per year (Mills & Bhandari, 2003), and they are often in poor health as well (Institute of Medicine, 2002). The uninsured are a heterogeneous group, composed of a variety of individuals: those just above the eligibility requirements for public insurance, people who would qualify for public insurance but either do not know about it or do not feel that they need it, people temporarily unemployed or working part-time, and those who are working full-time in "bad jobs" that do not offer health insurance (Kalleberg, Reskin, & Hudson, 2000) or in small firms (fewer than 100 employees) that cannot afford health insurance for their employees.

Thus, the young (persons ages 18 to 24) and racial and ethnic minorities are overrepresented among the uninsured (Mills & Bhandari, 2003), chiefly as a consequence of their unfavorable position in the labor market. Nearly two-thirds of the uninsured have low family incomes (i.e., below 200% of the poverty line)—even though about 70% of the uninsured count at least one full-time worker in their household (Hoffman & Wang, 2003). Moreover, the risk of long spells (more than 12 months) uninsured is not uniformly distributed, as it is greater among individuals with low incomes, those in fair or poor health, Hispanics, and young adults (Haley & Zuckerman, 2003).

The Relation between Health Insurance and Health Longitudinal and cross-sectional studies of the effects of health insurance demonstrate a clear link between private health insurance coverage—especially when it is continuous—and more timely and appropriate access to care, better self-rated health, and lower mortality (Ayanian, Weissman, Schneider, Ginsburg, & Zaslavsky, 2000; Baker, Sudano, Albert, Borawski, & Dor, 2002; Hadley, 2003; Institute of Medicine, 2002; Quesnel-Vallée, 2004; Short, Monheit, & Beauregard, 1989; Sudano & Baker, 2003). Uninsured Americans receive fewer services and have lower utilization rates than insured individuals because they generally cannot afford either private health insurance premiums or out-of-pocket medical care costs (Seccombe & Amey, 1995; Short et al., 1989). Moreover, the length of time uninsured is also associated with increasing barriers to access to care (Haley & Zuckerman, 2003).

Thus, it appears that the U.S. exception of not mandating health insurance for all its citizens has a strong potential to put an increasingly large proportion of Americans at risk of ill health. Moreover, as the uninsured tend to come disproportionately from groups that are already socially disadvantaged, this policy also has the potential to contribute to social inequalities in health in the United States.

GAPS IN RESEARCH KNOWLEDGE AND POLICY IMPLICATIONS

The limitations of this emerging body of literature point toward directions for future research. With regard to the contribution of private and public insurance to social inequalities in health, a first limitation is the widespread use of data for countries or geographic units within countries, which limits causal inference and does not usually permit the measurement of within-country inequities. Additionally, many of these studies measure income quite crudely, and often stop at classifications above or below the median country level (e.g., Blendon et al., 2002). This limits the comparison of fine-grained associations between countries as well as the assessment of individuals' life course income trajectories. Another limitation is the tendency to rely on mortality or access to care as measures of health outcomes, instead of morbidity or health-related quality of life. Finally, as highlighted by van Doorslaer and Jones (2004), even state-of-the-art research on these issues has lacked comparative individual-level longitudinal data that would enable the assessment of causal relationships and the evolution of these processes over the life course of individuals.

While the evidence on the public/private mix of insurance and its impact on social inequalities in health has global policy implications for equity, the United States faces the special challenge posed by its lack of mandatory coverage. Indeed, as mentioned earlier the young (ages 18 to 24) and racial and ethnic minorities are overrepresented among the uninsured (Mills & Bhandari, 2003), and this is likely to have a substantial impact on their health. Keppel (2007) identified the ten largest health disparities in the United States, finding that the bulk were related to social inequalities and lack of access to monitoring or testing. Given that the second goal of the federal government's "Healthy People 2010" program is the elimination of health disparities, it appears that ensuring equitable access to care for the uninsured is not simply a lofty ideal, but a pressing necessity.

SEE ALSO Volume 2: *Health Care Use, Adulthood; Health Differentials/Disparities, Adulthood; Income Inequality; Policy, Health; Poverty, Adulthood.*

BIBLIOGRAPHY

Acheson, D. (1998). *Independent inquiry into inequalities in health.* London: Her Majesty's Stationery Office.

Ayanian, J. Z., Weissman, J. S., Schneider, E. C., Ginsburg, J. A., & Zaslavsky, A. M. (2000, October 25). Unmet health needs of uninsured adults in the United States. *The Journal of the American Medical Association, 284,* 2061–2069.

Baker, D. W., Sudano, J. J., Jr., Albert, J. M., Borawski, E. A., & Dor, A. (2002). Loss of health insurance and the risk for a decline in self-reported health and physical functioning. *Medical Care, 40,* 1126–1131.

Blendon, R. J., Schoen, C., DesRoches, C. M., Osborn, R., Scoles, K. L., & Zapert, K. (2002). Inequities in health care: A five-country survey. *Health Affairs, 21*(3), 182–191.

DeNavas-Walt, C., Proctor, B. D., & Smith, J. (2007). *Income, poverty, and health insurance coverage in the United States: 2006* (Current Population Report P60-233). Washington, DC: U.S. Bureau of the Census.

Enterline, P. E., Salter, V., McDonald, A. D., & McDonald, J. C. (1973). The distribution of medical services before and after "free" medical care: The Quebec experience. *The New England Journal of Medicine, 289*(22), 1174–1178.

Fried, B. J., & Gaydos, L. M. (Eds.). (2002). *World health systems: Challenges and perspectives.* Chicago: Health Administration Press.

Gwatkin, D. R. (2001). Poverty and inequalities in health within developing countries: Filling the information gap. In D. A. Leon & G. Walt (Eds.), *Poverty, inequality, and health: An international perspective* (pp. 217–246). Oxford: Oxford University Press.

Hadley, J. (2003). Sicker and poorer—The consequences of being uninsured: A review of the research on the relationship between health insurance, medical care use, health, work, and income. *Medical Care Research and Review, 60*(2 suppl.), 3S–75S.

Haley, J., & Zuckerman, S. (2003, June). *Lack of coverage: A long-term problem for most uninsured.* Washington, DC: Kaiser Commission on Medicaid and the Uninsured. Retrieved March 7, 2008, from http://www.kff.org

Hanratty, M. J. (1996). Canadian national health insurance and infant health. *The American Economic Review, 86*(1), 276–284.

Hoffman, Catherine, & Wang, M. (2003) *Health insurance coverage in America. 2002 data update.* Washington DC: The Henri J. Kaiser Family Foundation.

Holahan, J., & Pohl, M. B. (2002, April 3). Changes in insurance coverage: 1994–2000 and beyond [Web exclusive]. *Health Affairs.* Retrieved March 7, 2008, from http://content.healthaffairs.org/cgi/reprint/hlthaff.w2.162v1

Holahan, J., and Wang, M. (2004, January 28). Changes in health insurance coverage during the economic downturn: 2000–2002 [Web exclusive]. *Health Affairs.* Retrieved April 11, 2008, from http://content.healthaffairs.org/cgi/content/abstract/hlthaff.w4.31

Institute of Medicine. (2002). *Care without coverage: Too little, too late.* Washington, DC: National Academy Press.

Kalleberg, A. L., Reskin, B. F., & Hudson, K. (2000). Bad jobs in America: Standard and nonstandard employment relations and job quality in the United States. *American Sociological Review, 65,* 256–278.

Keppel, K. G. (2007). Ten largest racial and ethnic health disparities in the United States based on Healthy People 2010 objectives. *American Journal of Epidemiology, 166,* 97–103.

Light, D. W. (1992, May 13). The practice and ethics of risk-rated health insurance. *The Journal of the American Medical Association, 267,* 2503–2508.

McDonald, A. D., McDonald, J. C., Salter, V., & Enterline, P. E. (1974). Effects of Quebec medicare on physician consultation for selected symptoms. *The New England Journal of Medicine, 291*(13), 649–652.

Mills, R. J. (2002). *Health insurance coverage: 2001* (Current Population Report P60-220). Washington, DC: U.S. Bureau of the Census.

Mills, R. J., & Bhandari, S. (2003). *Health insurance coverage in the United States: 2002* (Current Population Report P60-223). Washington, DC: U.S. Bureau of the Census.

O'Donnell, O., van Doorslaer, E., Wagstaff, A., & Lindelow, M. (2008). *Analyzing health equity using household survey data: A guide to techniques and their implementation.* Washington, DC: World Bank.

Quesnel-Vallée, A. (2004). Is it really worse to have public health insurance than to have no insurance at all? Health insurance and adult health in the United States. *Journal of Health and Social Behavior, 45,* 376–392.

Robert, S. A., & House, J. S. (2000). Socioeconomic inequalities in health: An enduring sociological problem. In C. E. Bird, P. Conrad, & A. M. Fremont (Eds.), *Handbook of medical sociology* (5th ed., pp. 79–97). Upper Saddle River, NJ: Prentice Hall.

Seccombe, K., & Amey, C. (1995). Playing by the rules and losing: Health insurance and the working poor. *Journal of Health and Social Behavior, 36,* 168–181.

Short, P. F., Monheit, A. C., & Beauregard, K. (1989). *A profile of uninsured Americans: National Medical Expenditure Survey research findings 1* (DHHS Publication No. PHS 89-3443). Rockville, MD: U.S. Department of Health and Human Services, National Center for Health Services Research and Health Care Technology Assessment.

Sudano, J. J., Jr., & Baker, D. W. (2003). Intermittent lack of health insurance coverage and use of preventive services. *American Journal of Public Health, 93,* 130–137.

Townsend, P., Davidson, N., & Whitehead, M (Eds.) (1992). *Inequalities in health: The Black Report; the health divide.* (2nd ed.). Middlesex, U.K.: Penguin.

van Doorslaer, E., & Jones, A. M. (2004). Income-related inequality in health and health care in the European Union. *Health Economics, 13,* 605–608.

van Doorslaer, E., Masseria, C., & Koolman, X. (2006). Inequalities in access to medical care by income in developed countries. *Canadian Medical Association Journal, 174,* 177–183.

Amélie Quesnel-Vallée

HOME OWNERSHIP/ HOUSING

Several key life course transitions, such as leaving home and beginning to cohabit with a partner, also can be considered household transitions because they involve movements between households, the creation of a new household, or the dissolution of a household. Because a household typically is defined as a group of individuals who share a dwelling space, these household transitions are also housing transitions for at least some of the individuals involved. Those persons relocate physically from one housing unit (e.g., an apartment, house, or mobile home) to another. They also may change their housing tenure, that is, whether they own the dwelling, pay rent to live there, or have another arrangement.

In addition to the close practical link between household transitions and housing transitions, housing has a reciprocal relationship with other life course transitions, such as having a child, in that a life course transition may require a change in housing (e.g., to get more space) or may not occur until appropriate housing has been secured. Finally, transitions between housing situations can be considered life course transitions in their own right because they enhance or limit people's opportunities.

HOUSING CHARACTERISTICS

Housing circumstances are differentiated by a variety of characteristics that are influenced strongly by local and national housing policies. One distinction is between institutional or group housing (military barracks, college dormitories, jails, hospitals, monasteries, etc.) and housing that consists of private households. Transitions into and out of group housing can mark important events in the life course, but these transitions usually involve either relatively small proportions of the population or relatively short periods in the life course. In the North American context most housing transitions involve private households.

Tenure Housing consisting of private households can be differentiated by tenure, structure, and neighborhood characteristics. Tenure reflects the social organization of property and establishes rights regarding housing. In North America tenure mostly is divided between rental housing and owner-occupied housing, though there are other categories, including cooperative housing. Those living in rental housing are tenants who pay rent to landlords in exchange for their housing. Depending on local regulations, renters often have limited rights with respect to privacy and few guarantees regarding the stability of their living quarters. However, moving between rental dwellings is relatively easy, leaving renters with more flexibility to move than owners have. Rental housing usually is controlled by the private sector in North America, with considerably smaller ownership by the public (government-run) and nonprofit sectors.

Households that live in owner-occupied housing serve as their own landlords; these owners typically have greater rights to privacy and more stability in their living circumstances than do renters. However, because buying and selling real estate is a much more involved process than renting, there are higher transaction costs associated with moving for owners and correspondingly less flexibility. In the North American context transitions into ownership usually are financed by arranging a loan, or mortgage, from a lender. The dwelling serves as collateral for the loan and may be repossessed if the owner falls behind on the payments (Lea, 1996). Mortgage payments are often higher than rental payments but eventually act as investments, whereas rent does not. As a result of building equity in their housing investment, home owners usually attain wealth faster than renters do. In the United States tax advantages are provided to home owners, further increasing their ability to accumulate wealth relative to renters (Chevan, 1989).

Structure Housing also can be differentiated by structure. Key distinctions based on structure typically relate to the number of households that share the same building and walls. Thus, housing can be detached (or single-family), with one household completely separated from all others; attached or semiattached (e.g., town houses, row houses, duplexes), where dwellings share walls but are otherwise freestanding with separate street-level entrances; or multiunit (apartment buildings). Apartment buildings usually are differentiated into low-rise and high-rise buildings, depending on the number of floors they contain. Other aspects of housing structure also vary, including total floor space, number of bedrooms, number of bathrooms, age, state of repair, and presence and characteristics of kitchens. Some of these aspects, such as number of rooms, are particularly important for the measurement of household-level concepts such as residential crowding (Myers & Baer, 1996).

Neighborhood Housing also can be differentiated by neighborhood. Neighborhood location is a key factor in most housing decisions because neighborhoods differ in distance from work and availability of services and amenities (Dieleman & Mulder, 2002). The structure and costs of different types of housing vary by location, and housing transitions frequently involve movement between neighborhoods. Overall, housing structure is closely related to housing tenure in North America, so that most detached single-family housing is owner-occupied (Rossi & Weber, 1996). Structure of housing also is linked to neighborhood. Roomier single-family housing often dominates low-density rural and suburban neighborhoods, and smaller apartments in multiunit buildings typically predominate in higher-density urban neighborhoods (Rossi & Weber, 1996).

HOUSING, SOCIAL STATUS, AND HISTORICAL TRENDS

Housing structure, tenure, and neighborhood are closely related to social status both in North America (Gans, 1967; Perin, 1977) and elsewhere (Rowlands & Gurney, 2000; Bourdieu, 2005). C. Perin (1977) remarked on the implicit existence of a housing ladder. Individuals are presumed to enter a rental market after leaving the parental home, thus starting at the base of the ladder. Then they gradually climb the ladder, building wealth and status as they obtain owner-occupied housing and move to more desirable neighborhoods. Owner occupation of a detached single-family home in a residential neighborhood is considered the most desirable housing situation (Rossi & Weber, 1996). Consequently, owners often are considered more trustworthy, stable, and responsible than renters (Rowlands & Gurney, 2000). Despite popular perceptions, a review by P. Rossi & E. Weber (1996) found few consistent social benefits (meaning benefits to society) to home ownership.

As a result of the associations between housing and social status, the transition into home ownership is significant for many people. It frequently is viewed as one of the transitions that define responsible adulthood (Henretta, 1984). Policymakers in a variety of contexts also have taken an interest in encouraging home ownership. In the United States tax policies and policies regulating the extension of credit have encouraged transitions into home ownership (Chevan, 1989). Nevertheless, sharp distinctions in access to home ownership remain, separating the economically advantaged from the disadvantaged (Lauster, 2007).

Improvements in Housing Housing conditions and trends differ from place to place, but a few broad historical trends can be identified. Average household size has declined dramatically in North America and Europe over the long term, leaving fewer people sharing the same amount of housing space. According to U.S. Census data, average household size decreased from approximately 4.5 people per private household in 1900 to 2.5 in 2005 (Ruggles, Sobek, Alexander, Fitch, Goeken, Hall et al., 2004). In that period home ownership rose, with an estimated 46% of households owning in 1900, compared with 67% in 2005 (Ruggles et al., 2004). Most of the increase in home ownership in the United States occurred after World War II (Chevan, 1989). The proportion of households living in roomier dwellings and in detached dwellings also rose during that time (Lauster, 2007). All these trends suggest a gradual improvement in North American housing standards, with fewer people living in crowded housing and more people living at the top of the housing ladder.

Unequal Distribution of Housing Improvements in housing standards have not been distributed equally. In the market-dominated model of housing provision that prevails in North America, households with little savings or income have been left without access to more valued forms of housing. Several trends have combined to widen housing disparities since the 1970s. Rising income inequality coinciding with rising housing prices has contributed to widening disparities in access to housing (Piketty & Saez, 2003; Lauster, 2007). At the same time incentives for developers to build new rental housing largely have disappeared, leaving little new housing stock available to those at the lower end of the income range (Erikson. 1994). These trends, coupled with a movement toward deinstitutionalizing those with mental and physical disabilities, have led to a marked rise in substandard housing and homelessness for those marginalized by the market (Burt, 1991).

Estimates of the number of homeless in North America range from hundreds of thousands to several million (Erikson, 1994; Shlay & Rossi, 1992). As the number of homeless people has increased, the composition of the homeless population has changed (Rossi, 1989; Phelan & Link, 1999). Whereas the homeless once were mainly White middle-aged single men (Erikson, 1994; Swanstrom, 1989; Hoch & Slayton, 1989; Cohen & Sokolovsky, 1989), they have become more diverse and include women, children, and families of various ethnic backgrounds (Shlay & Rossi, 1992). The homeless are also more visible throughout cities (Rossi, 1989) as well as being poorer and younger and are affected by various medical, criminal, and social problems (Erikson, 1994; Gelberg & Linn, 1989; Lee & Schreck, 2005). Various life course events influence the likelihood of becoming homeless, but analysts emphasize that the primary cause is the inability of people to compete for

housing in the face of a shrinking supply of low-cost housing (Erikson, 1994). The disadvantages created by homelessness, including loss of opportunities, feelings of helplessness, and general social stigma, have long-term implications for the life course of homeless individuals.

In addition to the ways in which the poor have been disadvantaged by the market provision of housing, other groups have been disadvantaged by direct discrimination. In the United States, historically, Black Americans in particular were often prevented from living outside designated Black neighborhoods. Black Americans also often were denied loans to purchase housing, the major route for building wealth in North America. The Fair Housing Act of 1968 penalized discrimination on the basis of "race, color, religion, or national origin," but few means of enforcement were included in the act (Schill & Friedman, 1999). In 1988 a set of amendments strengthened the act and also barred discrimination against "families with children and . . . persons with physical or mental disabilities" (Schill & Friedman, 1999).

Despite efforts to reduce discrimination in housing in North America and elsewhere, neighborhood segregation is widespread, especially by ethnicity and race (Massey & Denton, 1993; Wilkes & Iceland, 2004). L. Freeman (2000) provided three explanations for the persistence of segregation: the spatial assimilation model, which links segregation to impoverishment and broader lack of housing opportunities (Massey 1985); the place stratification model, which states that direct discrimination continues to limit opportunities for minority group members (Alba & Logan, 1993); and the residential preferences model, which argues that much of segregation can be explained by minority households choosing to live near one another (Schelling, 1971). Freeman found evidence for each of those models.

HOUSING AND LIFE COURSE TRANSITIONS

Housing characteristics, including tenure, structure, and neighborhood, can influence a number of specific life transitions. These effects are often reciprocal, so that life course transitions also influence housing transitions (Mulder & Wagner, 1998; Lauster & Fransson, 2006).

Neighborhood effects on life course transitions have received increased attention (Sampson, Morenoff, & Gannon-Rowley, 2002). For example, neighborhoods influence the likelihood of risky behavior and exposure to violence (Kowaleski-Jones, 2000; Sampson et al., 2002), the timing of first sex (Baumer & South, 2001), and family formation (South & Crowder, 1999).

Life course events also can influence neighborhood choice. For instance, coming out in the life course of gays and lesbians often is accompanied by a choice to live in gay enclaves (Weston, 1991). These communities allow gays and lesbians to share stories and develop histories, feel accepted, exert political and social power, and meet others who are similar (LeVay & Nonas, 1995; Sutton, 1994; Weeks, Heaphy, & Donovan, 2001; Weston, 1991). This process is similar to the residential preference model of segregation discussed by Freeman (2000). In this case the gay community is not necessarily created to separate homosexuals and heterosexuals but is a method for protecting individuals' quality of life.

Similarly, having school-age children can influence neighborhood choice, at least for those with the ability to choose. In addition to neighborhood moves based on minimizing the risks children face, parents may move to further educational achievement and improve social status (Croft, 2004). As J. Holme (2002) noted, these moves often are based on social constructions of school status, combining perceptions of neighborhood class and racial composition with measurements of performance. In turn, neighborhood school status boosts the price of local housing (Kane, Staiger, & Samms, 2003; Croft. 2004), and that also limits neighborhood choice.

Research shows that access to housing, housing tenure, and housing structure are reciprocally related to life course transitions. Access to housing seems to influence both the likelihood that new households will be formed and the form new households take (Mutchler & Krivo, 1989; Hughes, 2003). Some authors argue that limited access to housing increases the likelihood of nontraditional living arrangements, including extended family living and nonmarital cohabitation (Mutchler & Krivo, 1989). Other authors have found evidence that securing high-quality housing serves as a culturally important prerequisite for both traditional (Hughes, 2003) and nontraditional (Lauster & Fransson, 2006) forms of family formation. Increased access to all forms of housing may allow more people to live alone (Kobrin, 1976; Lauster & Fransson, 2006). Securing access to a detached roomy dwelling also may be linked to childbearing in the United States (Lauster, 2007). Conversely, marrying or having children before owning a detached roomy dwelling makes individuals more likely to move to this type of housing (Chevan, 1989; Mulder & Wagner, 1998; Clark, Deurloo, & Dileman, 1997; Lauster & Fransson, 2006).

Although the overall level of mobility between dwellings varies widely across countries, the age pattern of moves is broadly the same (Dieleman & Mulder, 2002). Most housing transitions occur during young adulthood, reflecting the relative instability of the transition to adulthood and its many life course transitions. Rates of residential mobility begin to taper during middle age (Dieleman & Mulder, 2002). Nevertheless, important relationships between housing and later life course transitions remain.

Some researchers have provided evidence that home ownership reduces the risk of divorce, at least on the individual level, because ownership represents a shared investment in a marriage (Murphy, 1985). Others argue that the likelihood of separation is increased in contexts in which single-family homes dominate, preventing the development of supportive communities (Bratt, 2002; Lauster, 2005). Late in life transitions in housing circumstances usually reflect retirement or changes in caregiving arrangements (Dieleman & Mulder, 2002). The move from independent housing to retirement communities or assisted living facilities can be particularly traumatic (Adams, Sanders, & Auth, 2004), leaving many people to age in place (remain in their own homes as they age). However, aging in place may result in deterioration of the dwelling if individuals are unable to make repairs (Golant & LaGreca, 1994).

Housing transitions may lead to or result from a variety of household transitions. Housing serves as one of the key links between life course transitions and the economy. Access to housing is also heavily influenced by policy makers. As a result, housing policy can have large effects on how people proceed through a host of life course transitions. By placing individuals, housing also links the life course to neighborhoods and to the environment. This is important for understanding neighborhood effects on the life course as well as the impacts of life course transitions on the environment. Overall, although most housing transitions take place early in the life course, housing intersects with and shapes the life course at all ages.

SEE ALSO Volume 2: *Consumption, Adulthood and Later Life; Debt; Homeless, Adults; Neighborhood Context, Adulthood; Residential Mobility, Adulthood; Segregation, Residential;* Volume 3: *Wealth.*

BIBLIOGRAPHY

Adams, K., Sanders, S., & Auth, E. A. (2004). Loneliness and depression in independent living retirement communities: Risk and resilience factors. *Aging & Mental Health, 8*(6), 475–485.

Alba, R. D., & Logan, J. R. (1993). Minority proximity to whites in suburbs: An individual-level analysis of segregation. *American Journal of Sociology, 98*(6), 1388–1427.

Baumer, E. P., & South, S. J. (2001). Community effects on youth sexual activity. *Journal of Marriage and the Family, 63*(2), 540–554.

Bourdieu, P. (2005). *The social structures of the economy* (Chris Turner, Trans.). Cambridge, UK, and Malden, MA: Polity.

Bratt, R. G. (2002). Housing and family well-being. *Housing Studies, 17*(1), 13–26.

Burt, M. R. (1991). Causes of the growth of homelessness during the 1980s. *Housing Policy Debate, 2*, 903–936.

Chevan, A. (1989). The growth of home ownership, 1940–1980. *Demography, 26*(2), 249–266.

Clark, W. A. V., Deurloo, M., & Dieleman, R. (1997). Entry to home-ownership in Germany: Some comparisons with the United States. *Urban Studies, 34,* 7–19.

Cohen, C. I., & Sokolovsky, J. (1989). *Old men of the Bowery: Strategy for survival among the homeless.* New York: Guilford Press.

Croft, J. (2004). Positive choice, no choice or total rejection: The perennial problem of school catchments, housing and neighbourhoods. *Housing Studies, 19*(6), 927–945.

Dieleman, F., & Mulder, C. (2002). The geography of residential choice. In J. I. Aragones, G. Francescato, & T. Gärling (Eds.), *Residential environments: Choice satisfaction, and behavior* (pp. 35–54). Westport, CT: Bergin & Garvey.

Erikson, K. (1994). *A new species of trouble: Explorations in disaster, trauma, and community.* New York: W. W. Norton.

Freeman, L. (2000). Minority housing segregation: A test of three perspectives. *Journal of Urban Affairs, 22*(1), 15–37.

Gans, H. J. (1967). *The Levittowners: Ways of life and politics in a new suburban community.* New York: Pantheon Books.

Gelberg, L., & Linn, L. S. (1989). Assessing the physical health of homeless adults. *Journal of the American Medical Association, 262*(14), 1973–1979.

Golant, S. M., & LaGreca, A. J. (1994). Housing quality of U.S. elderly households: Does aging in place matter? *The Gerontologist, 34*(6), 803–814.

Henretta, J. C. (1984). Parental status and child's home ownership. *American Sociological Review, 49,* 131–140.

Hoch, C., & Slayton, R. A. (1989). *New homeless and old: Community and the skid row hotel.* Philadelphia: Temple University Press.

Holme, J. (2002). Buying homes, buying schools: School choice and the social construction of school quality. *Harvard Educational Review, 72,* 177–205.

Hughes, M. E. (2003). Home economics: Metropolitan labor and housing markets and domestic arrangements in young adulthood. *Social Forces, 81*(4), 1399–1429.

Kane, T. J., Staiger, D., & Samms, G. (2003). School accountability ratings and housing values. *Brookings-Wharton Papers on Urban Affairs, 2003:* 83–137.

Kobrin, F. E. (1976). The fall in household size and the rise of the primary individual in the United States. *Demography, 13*(1), 127–138.

Kowaleski-Jones, L. (2000). Staying out of trouble: Community resources and problem behavior among high-risk adolescents. *Journal of Marriage and the Family, 62*(2), 449–464.

Lauster, N. (2005). *Better housing equals stronger families? The impact of housing opportunities on transitions from cohabitation to marriage or separation in Sweden.* Paper presented at the Midwestern Sociological Society Meetings, Minneapolis, MN.

Lauster, N. (2007). *The properly housed family: Status, ownership, and family formation in the US, 1900–2005.* Paper presented at the Family and Residential Choice Workshop, Amsterdam, Netherlands.

Lauster, N., & Fransson, U. (2006). Of marriages and mortgages: The second demographic transition and the relationship between marriage and homeownership in Sweden. *Housing Studies, 21*(6), 909–927.

Lea, M. (1996). Innovation and the cost of mortgage credit: A historical perspective. *Housing Policy Debate, 7*(1), 147–174.

Lee, B. A., & Schreck, C. J. (2005). Danger on the streets: Marginality and victimization among the homeless people. *American Behavioral Scientist, 48*(8), 1055–1081.

LeVay, S., & Nonas, E. (1995). *City of friends: A portrait of the gay and lesbian community in America.* Cambridge, MA: MIT Press.

Massey, D. S. (1985). Ethnic residential segregation: A theoretical synthesis and empirical review. *Sociology and Social Research, 69,* 315–350.

Massey, D. S., & Denton, N. A. (1993). *American apartheid: Segregation and the making of the underclass.* Cambridge, MA: Harvard University Press.

Mulder, C. H., & Wagner, M. (1998). First-time home ownership in the family life course: A West German-Dutch comparison. *Urban Studies, 35*(1), 687–713.

Murphy, M. (1985). Demographic and socio-economic influences on recent British marital breakdown patterns. *Population Studies, 39*(3), 441–460.

Mutchler, J. E., & Krivo, L. J. (1989). Availability and affordability: Household adaptation to a housing squeeze. *Social Forces, 68,* 241–261.

Myers, D., & Baer, W. C. (1996). The changing problem of overcrowded housing. *Journal of the American Planning Association, 62,* 66–84.

Painter, G., Yang, L., & Yu, Z. (2003). Heterogeneity in Asian American home-ownership: The impact of household endowments and immigrant status. *Urban Studies, 40*(3), 505–530.

Perin, C. (1977). *Everything in its place: Social order and land use in America.* Princeton, NJ: Princeton University Press.

Phelan, J. C., & Link, B.G. (1999). Who are "the homeless"? Reconsidering the stability and composition of the homeless population. *American Journal of Public Health, 89,* 1334–1338.

Piketty, T., & Saez, E. (2003). Income inequality in the United States, 1913–1998. *Quarterly Journal of Economics, 118*(1): 1–39.

Rossi, P. H. (1989). *Down and out in America: The origins of homelessness.* Chicago: University of Chicago Press.

Rossi, P. H., & Weber, E. (1996). The social benefits of homeownership: Empirical evidence from national surveys. *Housing Policy Debate, 7*(1), 1–35.

Rowlands, R., & Gurney, C. M. (2000). Young people's perceptions of housing tenure: A case study in the socialization of tenure prejudice. *Housing, Theory & Society, 17*(3), 121–130.

Ruggles, S., Sobek, M., Alexander, T., Fitch, C., Goeken, R., Hall, P. et al (2004). *Integrated Public Use Microdata Series: Version 3.0.* Minneapolis: Minnesota Population Center.

Sampson, R. J., Morenoff, J. D, & Gannon-Rowley, T. (2002). Assessing neighborhood effects: Social processes and new directions in research. *Annual Review of Sociology, 28,* 443–478.

Schelling, T. (1971). Dynamic models of segregation. *Journal of Mathematical Sociology, 1*(2), 143–186.

Schill, M., & Friedman, S. (1999). The Fair Housing Amendments Act of 1988: The first decade. *Cityscape: A Journal of Policy Development and Research, 4*(3), 57–78.

Shlay, A. B., & Rossi, P. H. (1992). Social science research and contemporary studies of homelessness. *Annual Review of Sociology, 18,* 129–160.

South, S. J., & Crowder, K. D. (1999). Neighborhood effects on family formation: Concentrated poverty and beyond. *American Sociological Review, 64*(1), 113–132.

Susser, E., Moore, R. & Link, B. (2002). Risk factors for homelessness. *American Journal of Epidemiology, 15*(2), 546–556.

Sutton, R. (1994). *Hearing us out: Voices from the gay and lesbian community.* Boston: Little, Brown.

Swanstrom, T. (1989). No room at the inn: Housing policy and the homeless. *Journal of Urban and Contemporary Law, 35,* 81–105.

Weeks, J., Heaphy, B., & Donovan, C. (2001). *Same sex intimacies: Families of choice and other life experiments.* London and New York: Routledge.

Weston, K. (1991). *Families we choose: Lesbians, gays, kinship.* New York: Columbia University Press.

Wilkes, R., & Iceland, J. (2004). Hypersegregation in the twenty-first century. *Demography, 41,* 23–36.

Nathanel T. Lauster
Adam Matthew Easterbrook

HOMELESS, ADULTS

Completely accurate and comprehensive documentation of the pervasiveness of homelessness is nearly impossible for many reasons. Not only is the number of individuals who are homeless a matter of contention, but defining homelessness also is a contentious matter. Many studies measure only the *literal homeless*, defined as persons who live in emergency shelters or transitional housing, or those who sleep in places not meant for human habitation (e.g., streets, parks, abandoned buildings, and subway tunnels). Other researchers include in their counts of the homeless those persons who are *precariously housed* or on the brink of homelessness. They may be doubled-up with friends or relatives or may pay extremely high proportions of their resources (more than one-third of monthly income) for rent—thus, they are often characterized as being at imminent risk of becoming homeless (U.S. Department of Housing and Urban Development, 2007). In addition, the population of homeless referred to as the *hidden homeless* further complicates scholars' understanding of the extent of homelessness. The hidden homeless are those who are living in automobiles, campgrounds, abandoned structures, or boxes—that is, places that it would be extremely difficult for researchers to locate.

Enumeration of the homeless is difficult and is usually conducted in one of two ways. One way that the number of homeless persons has been documented is a point in time (PIT) count. The PIT count occurs when the number of persons who are sheltered (in a shelter or transitional housing) or unsheltered (living in the streets,

automobiles, or other public or private place not designed for regular sleeping accommodations) are counted. The problem with this method of documenting homelessness is that a PIT count is representative of individuals and families who were homeless for one specific night and excludes those who may be homeless the next night or the next. Another method of documenting the homeless that is often used is period prevalence counts (PPC). PPCs are counts that determine the number of people who are homeless over a given period of time, utilizing longitudinal data. Longitudinal data are data that are collected over a predetermined amount of time and document unduplicated numbers of persons who have used emergency and/or transitional housing during this time period. This type of enumeration of the homeless provides a more accurate portrait of homelessness than the PIT estimates, because whereas PIT data do capture a higher share of homeless individuals and families who use shelters or transitional housing for long periods of time, PIT estimates underrepresent people whose homelessness is episodic. Using PPC is more costly and takes longer to obtain data, however. So although PPC does provide more information, this method also has limitations.

Despite the many challenges of enumeration, researchers estimate that over the course of a lifetime, approximately 9 to 15% of the U.S. population will experience homelessness (Ringwalt, Greene, Robertson, & McPheeters, 1998; Robertson & Toro, 1999). Homelessness is an event that may occur at any point along the life course with each stage offering a unique set of challenges, depending on how or where one views him/herself on the life-course trajectory. Each year, more than 3 million people are believed to experience homelessness, including 1.3 million children (National Law Center on Homelessness and Poverty, 2008).

WHO IS HOMELESS?

Researchers estimate that on average, single men comprise 53% of the sheltered homeless population (compared to 14% of the U.S. population), single women 17% (compared to 16% of the U.S. population), unaccompanied youth 3% (compared to 5% of the U.S population), adults in households with children 10% (compared to 47% of all U.S. households having children), and children in households with adults 17% (compared to 23% of the U.S. population). Single men, then, are highly overrepresented among the homeless. The sheltered homeless population is estimated to be nearly 44% African American (African Americans represent 13% of total U.S. population), 34% White non-Hispanic (White, non-Hispanic persons represent 66% of total U.S. population), 13% White, Hispanic/Latino (Hispanic and Latino persons represent

15% of total U.S. population), and 9% other (others represent 6% of total U.S. population; U.S. Bureau of Census, 2008b; U.S. Department of Housing and Urban Development, 2008).

SINGLE MEN

Single men (i.e., men who have never been married, divorced, or widowed) who are poor may be particularly vulnerable to homelessness because the largest social programs are targeted toward families, especially mothers and children (Temporary Assistance to Needy Families), or toward the elderly (Social Security). Single men are more likely to have substance abuse problems that make it less likely that friends or family will take them in. Single men also may feel less vulnerable on the streets or in shelters, so they may be less likely to be doubled-up with friends or family to avoid living on the street (U.S. Department of Housing and Urban Development, 2008). Single men also have been found to be socially isolated, transient, and homeless for longer periods of time than other subgroups of homeless (Roth & Bean, 1986). They often have histories of legal problems and marital trouble (First & Toomey, 1989) and often are veterans (U.S. Department of Veterans Affairs, 2008).

About one-third of the adult homeless population in the United States has served their country in the armed services. Current population estimates suggest that about 154,000 veterans (male and female) are homeless on any given night and perhaps twice as many experience homelessness at some point during the course of a year (U.S. Department of Veterans Affairs, 2008). Almost all (97%) homeless veterans are male (just 3% are female); the majority are single, and most come from poor, disadvantaged backgrounds. About 45% of homeless veterans suffer from mental illness and slightly more than 70% experience alcohol or other substance abuse disorders. Currently, the number of homeless Vietnam veterans is greater than the number of service members who died in the Vietnam war. Additionally, a small number of Desert Storm veterans have appeared in the homeless population. The U.S. Department of Veterans Affairs has developed several initiatives to provide services to this population, one of which is the Grant and Per Diem Program, which is offered annually by the U.S. Department of Veterans Affairs to fund transitional housing or service centers for homeless veterans.

SINGLE WOMEN

Another recognized subpopulation of the homeless is single women (17% of sheltered homeless). Single women are generally older, White women with relatively high levels of individual dysfunction such as mental illness, substance abuse, or physical disability (Johnson, 1995; U.S. Conference of Mayors, 2007). Compared to women with children, single childless women are more likely to have been homeless for a longer period of time, more likely to have received mental health services, and more likely to admit to substance abuse problems (Robertson, 1991).

WOMEN WITH CHILDREN

Women with children are considered the fastest growing subgroup of the homeless (National Alliance to End Homelessness, 2007; National Coalition for the Homeless, 2007; U.S. Conference of Mayors, 2007). One of the factors that contribute to this growing subpopulation of the homeless is the poverty rate. Beginning in 2000, the poverty rate rose for 4 consecutive years, from 11.3% in 2000 to 12.7% in 2004. The poverty rate then began to decline slightly, to 12.6% in 2005 and 12.3% in 2006. So although there was a decline in the poverty rate from 2005 to 2006, the change from 12.6% (2005) to 12.3% (2006) was not statistically significant (U.S. Bureau of Census, 2008).

Other characteristics that may contribute to the vulnerability of women include declining wages, a slowing economy, declining welfare rolls (more likely due to the time limits placed on benefits in 1996, rather than an indicator of improvement in the economic well-being of low-income women), loss of social benefits, loss of health insurance, and the limited availability of both affordable housing and subsidized housing. Subsidized housing is so limited that fewer than one in four Temporary Assistance to Needy Families nationwide lives in public housing or receives a housing voucher to assist with rent (National Coalition for the Homeless, 2007). Finally, domestic violence also contributes to homelessness among families. When women leave abusive relationships, often they have no place to go. Due to the lack of affordable housing and limited supply of subsidized housing, many women are forced to choose between the abusive situation or living on the streets. Estimates of rates of domestic violence for homeless women with children range from 12% to 50% (Homes for the Homeless, 2008; National Coalition against Domestic Violence, 2001; U.S. Conference of Mayors, 2007).

CHRONICALLY HOMELESS

Chronic homelessness is described as an unaccompanied homeless individual with a disabling condition who has either been continuously homeless for a year or more or has had at least four episodes of homelessness in the past 3 years. To be considered chronically homeless, a person must have been on the streets or in emergency shelter (i.e., not in transitional or permanent housing) during these stays (U.S. Department of Housing and Urban Development, 2008). The U.S. Department of Housing and Urban Development estimates that approximately

1 in 4 homeless are veterans

In 2006, nearly a half million U.S. veterans spent some time homeless.

Homeless veterans

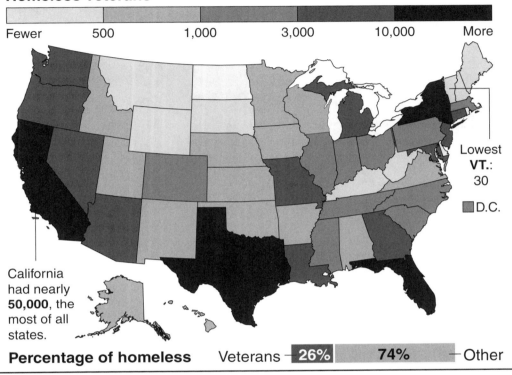

Fewer 500 1,000 3,000 10,000 More

Lowest
VT.:
30

D.C.

California had nearly **50,000**, the most of all states.

Percentage of homeless Veterans — 26% 74% — Other

Source: National Alliance to End Homelessness. AP Image.

Homeless Veterans. U.S. map shows the number of homeless veterans in 2006. **AP IMAGES.**

20% of all homeless persons could be considered chronically homeless. Communities are working to end chronic homelessness by providing services to help meet the needs of this vulnerable population. However, these services—including mental health treatment, substance abuse treatment, intensive medical care, and incarceration—tend to be very expensive.

HOMELESS OLDER ADULTS

The growing consensus is that homeless persons ages 50 and older comprise the "older homeless" category. Homeless persons ages 50 to 65 frequently fall between the cracks in that they are not old enough to qualify for Medicare, therefore many suffer from poor physical health given that they most likely have experienced poor nutrition and severe living conditions (National Coali-

tion for the Homeless, 2007). Increased homelessness among older adults is largely due to the declining availability of affordable housing. Throughout the nation, there are at least nine seniors waiting for every occupied unit of affordable elderly housing (HEARTH, 2008). Many elderly are retired and on fixed incomes, or dependent on Supplemental Security Income for support in their retirement. Still, homeless persons are far less likely than their housed peers to survive until later life. People who experience homelessness for long periods of time do not survive to age 62 as often as persons in the general population; this may account for older adults' relatively small percentage (16%) among the homeless (U.S. Department of Housing and Urban Development, 2008). The average life expectancy of a person without permanent housing is estimated to be between 42 and 52 years, far below the United States' average life expectancy

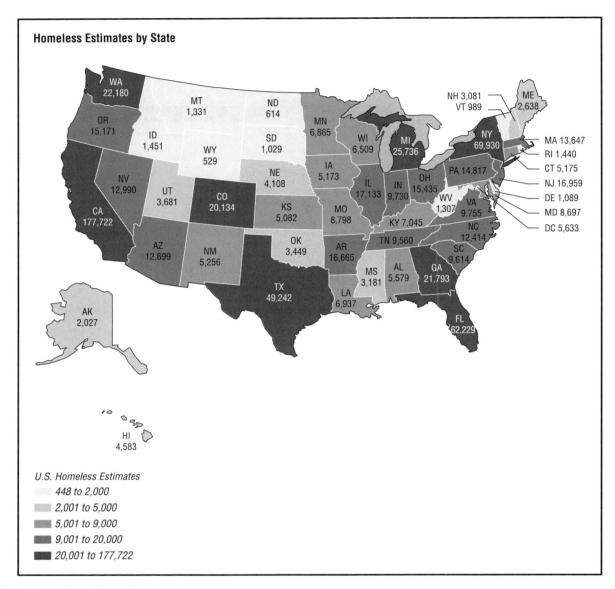

Map 1. *Homeless estimates by state.* **CENGAGE LEARNING, GALE.**

of 80 years. A study by O'Connell (2005) indicated that premature death for older homeless persons most often resulted from acute and chronic medical conditions aggravated by homeless life rather than by either mental illness or substance abuse.

STRUCTURAL FACTORS CONTRIBUTING TO HOMELESSNESS

Lack of Affordable Housing Since the 1970s or so, much of the affordable housing and single room occupancy

(weekly or daily rental of economy motel rooms) housing that had been located in the central part of larger cities has been lost to development or gentrification (e.g., the conversion of rental units to condominiums, historic preservation). Funding for public housing programs has been inadequate. Historically, when money is tight the first programs and services that are cut or eliminated are social service programs. Currently, because housing is not seen as an entitlement, only one in four eligible individuals and families are receiving services from programs such as Housing Choice. Housing Choice, formerly known as Section 8, is a program administered by U.S.

Department of Housing and Urban Development that provides housing vouchers that can be used in partial rent payment for housing. These vouchers may be used for apartments, homes, or mobile homes of the family's choice as long as basic criteria are met. The vouchers also may be used for public housing units (i.e., public housing units are apartment complexes that house large numbers of low-income individuals and families exclusively).

Foreclosure/Subprime Mortgage Crisis Related to the lack of affordable housing is the current foreclosure/subprime lending crisis. Nationally, more than 2 million home foreclosures were reported in 2007. A home foreclosure occurs when an owner is unable to keep up with his or her monthly home payments, which include mortgage, property taxes, and interest. The resulting spiral has resulted in the decline in home values of up to 20%. This decline has perpetuated a plummet in local tax revenues that are based on property taxes (National Coalition for the Homeless, 2007). Congress and state governments are scrambling to provide some stability to the economic crisis that has ensued by crafting legislation to reinforce banks, lenders, and other financial institutions to hold off a recession. Few proposals have been made to provide relief for the homeowners who have lost their homes. Foreclosure has forced many families to move in with friends or relatives, and others have moved into emergency shelters. The National Coalition for the Homeless (2007) conducted a survey of state and local homeless coalitions and asked if they had seen an increase in individuals and families seeking shelter since the crisis began in 2007: 61% of the agencies (71 out of 117) replied that they had indeed seen an increase, which they attributed to the foreclosure crisis. Only five coalitions replied that they had not seen an increase in their area; the remaining respondents were unsure.

Poverty The official poverty rate in 2006 was 12.3%, slightly but not significantly down from 12.6% in 2005. Homelessness and poverty are inextricably linked. Poor people are frequently unable to pay for housing, food, childcare, health care, and education. Difficult choices must be made when limited resources cover only some of these essential necessities (National Coalition for the Homeless, 2007). Often, because housing typically comprises such a high proportion of income, it is at high risk of being dropped from an individual/family's budget. Being poor often means that a person is just a single illness, accident, or a paycheck away from living on the streets.

Health Care The final key issue related to the problem of homelessness is health care. Poor health is both a cause and consequence of homelessness. For individuals and families who are struggling to pay the rent, a health crisis (such as a serious injury or disability) can cause a freefall into homelessness. If an individual is unable to work, once savings (if any) are depleted to pay medical bills or rent, the next step is to double-up, find an emergency shelter, or resort to the streets. Rates of both chronic and acute health problems are extremely high among the homeless population. Conditions that require regular, continuous treatment such as tuberculosis, HIV/AIDS (estimated between 3% and 20% of the homeless population), diabetes, hypertension, addictive disorders, and mental disorders are all extremely difficult to treat or control for those with inadequate housing. Illness may cause homelessness; chronically mentally ill persons or alcoholics who are noncompliant with treatment may be cast out by their families. Alternatively, illness may be a consequence of homelessness and may result from the tough conditions of the street (e.g., inadequate shelter, inadequate diet, or possibly selling sex for money).

In 2006 nearly 47 million Americans under age 65 (15.7%) had no health insurance coverage, an increase of 2.1 million from the previous year (Kaiser Family Foundation, 2007). Further, 38 million people from working families were uninsured in 2005 because not all businesses offer health benefits, not all workers are eligible for health benefits, and many employees cannot afford their share of the health premium.

WHAT THE FUTURE HOLDS

As the number of homeless individuals and families increase in the United States—whether as a result of mental health issues, substance abuse, disability, access to health care, inadequate education and job preparation, or domestic violence—it is clear that the problem of homelessness is a heterogeneous one. However, with all the diversity within this population, there is one thing all members have in common: lack of housing. Since the late 1990s, many pilot programs have been established throughout the United States that advocate a "housing first" approach to eradicating homelessness (Beyond Shelter, 2008). "Housing first" is an alternative to the current system of emergency shelter/transitional housing, which tends to prolong the length of time that families remain homeless. The premise of service delivery is based on the belief that vulnerable and at-risk homeless individuals and families are more responsive to interventions and social services support after they are in their own housing, rather than while living in temporary/transitional facilities or housing programs. With permanent housing, these individuals and families can begin to regain the self-confidence and control over their lives they lost when they became homeless.

SEE ALSO Volume 2: *Family and Household Structure, Adulthood; Home Ownership/Housing; Policy, Health; Poverty, Adulthood.*

BIBLIOGRAPHY

Beyond Shelter. (2008). *Housing first: Ending family homelessness.* Retrieved May 12, 2008, from http://www.beyondshelter.org

First, R. J., & Toomey, B. G. (1989). Homeless men and the work ethic. *Social Service Review, 63*(1), 113–126.

HEARTH. (2008). *Current state of elder homelessness.* Retrieved May 10, 2008, from http://www.hearth-home.org

Homes for the Homeless. (2008). *Facts on family homelessness.* Retrieved May 9, 2008, from http://www.homesforthehome less.com

Johnson, A. K. (1995). Homelessness. In R. L. Edwards & J.G. Hopps (Eds.), *Encyclopedia of social work* (19th ed., pp.1338–1346). New York: National Association of Social Workers.

Kaiser Family Foundation. (2007). *The uninsured: A primer, key facts about Americans without health insurance.* Retrieved June 20, 2008, from http://www.kff.org

National Alliance to End Homelessness. (2007). *Homelessness counts.* Retrieved May 8, 2008, from http://www.naeh.org

National Coalition against Domestic Violence. (2001). *Housing and domestic violence fact sheet.* Retrieved May 7, 2008, from http://www.ncadv.org/files

National Coalition for the Homeless. (2007). *How many people experience homelessness?* Retrieved May 10, 2008, from http://www.nationalhomeless.org

National Law Center on Homelessness and Poverty. (2008). *Homelessness and poverty in America.* Retrieved May 10, 2008, from http://www.nlchp.org/hapia.cfm

O'Connell, J. J. (2005). *Premature mortality in homeless populations: A review of the literature.* Nashville, TN: National Health Care for the Homeless Council. Retrieved May 10, 2008, from http://www.nhchc.org

Ringwalt, C. L., Greene, J. M., Robertson, M., & McPheeters, M. (1998). The prevalence of homelessness among adolescents in the United States. *American Journal of Public Health, 88*(9), 1325–1329.

Robertson, M. J. (1991). Homeless women with children: The role of alcohol and other drug abuse. *American Psychologist, 46*(11), 1198–1204.

Robertson, M. J., & Toto, P.A. (1999). Homeless youth: Research, intervention and policy. In L. B. Fosburg & D. L. Dennis (Eds.), *Practical lessons: The 1998 National Symposium on Homelessness Research.* Washington, DC: U.S. Department of Housing and Urban Development and U.S. Department of Health and Human Services.

Roth, D., & Bean, G. J. (1986). New perspectives on homelessness: Findings from a statewide epidemiological study. *Hospital and Community Psychiatry, 37*(7), 712–719.

U. S. Bureau of Census. (2008a). *Income, poverty and health insurance coverage in the United States.* Retrieved May 10, 2008, from http://www.census.gov

U. S. Bureau of Census. (2008b). *Statistical abstracts.* Retrieved May 20, 2008, from http://www.census.gov

U.S. Conference of Mayors. (2007). *A status report on hunger and homelessness in America's cities: A 23-city survey.* Washington, DC: Author.

U.S. Department of Housing and Urban Development. (2007). *The annual homeless assessment report to Congress.* Retrieved May 10, 2008, from http://www.huduser.org

U.S. Department of Housing and Urban Development. (2008). *The second annual homeless assessment report to Congress.* Retrieved May 10, 2008, from http://www.huduser.org

U.S. Department of Veterans Affairs (2008). *Homeless veterans: Overview of homelessness.* Retrieved May 8, 2008, from http://www.1va.gov/homeless

Carole Zugazaga

HORMONE REPLACEMENT THERAPY

SEE Volume 2: *Menopause.*

HOUSEWORK

Housework is defined by social scientists as unpaid labor that contributes to the maintenance of the household. Studies frequently include as housework tasks such as laundry, cooking, dishwashing, cleaning, shopping for household goods and groceries, and making house repairs. Tasks that involve direct caretaking of family members, such as childcare, are not usually considered housework, even though the distinction between housework and other forms of care is somewhat artificial. Studies of housework not only provide an important window into gender relations in families, housework performance has also been linked to factors including wages, mental health, and relationship quality.

THE EMERGENCE OF MODERN HOUSEWORK

Under the system of subsistence agriculture that was common throughout the world over the past several thousand years, the majority of productive work took place in or near the household. The emergence of the contemporary understanding of housework as distinct from paid employment is the direct result of the separation of paid labor from the household under systems of industrial production. The rise of industrial production during the past two centuries was accompanied by a supporting ideology of "separate spheres." This ideology emphasized the belief that women and men were fundamentally different, and it valorized women in their roles as domestic caretakers and moral guardians. Men, by contrast, were viewed as responsible for the public sphere, and especially market work. A fundamental insight of housework research has been the realization that these two spheres are not separate, but rather are intricately interconnected. Increases in women's employment since the 1950 have heightened awareness of the linkages between paid and unpaid work and collectively demonstrated the false dichotomy that the idea of "separate spheres" represents.

A vast amount of work was required to support families in the pre- and early industrial period. Susan Strasser (1982) points out that this work frequently included making clothes by hand or sewing machine, collecting water, washing clothes by hand, gathering fuel for heating and cooking, producing meals for family members, preserving and storing food, producing sources of lighting, cleaning the house, and a substantial number of related tasks. The sheer volume and physical burden of this work has been gradually reduced by a combination of products available for purchase in the market and the spread of electrical and gas-powered appliances. At the same time, it seems likely that standards of cleanliness rose alongside the availability of such externally powered devices. For example, in 1974 Joann Vanek found little change in the amount of time spent on housework in the United States between 1925 and the mid-1970s despite the increased availability of household appliances over that time.

Although housework is frequently cast as burdensome and unpleasant, scholars increasingly recognize that it serves a dual role. As Marjorie DeVault (1991) explained, housework simultaneously produces goods for individuals and families, such as clean homes and nourished family members, and facilitates the expression of human connection. This dual meaning of housework is reflected in the emergence of the concept of "care work." Despite this dual nature, much housework research has focused on the unpleasant work that tends to be repetitive, to have a relatively rigid schedule for completion, and to be physically demanding. To the extent that such work is unpaid, many scholars have suggested that it is also undervalued socially. Indeed, the purpose of much of this research is to both highlight and recognize the crucial value of such work for the reproduction of families and larger social groups.

STUDYING HOUSEWORK

Two related areas of social research take housework as a central focus. The first is the study of time use. Time spent on domestic labor is a central concern among researchers such as Jonathan Gershuny (2000) and John Robinson and Geoffrey Godbey (1999) who are interested in the contours of human activity across the day, the week, the year, and the life course. Along with paid employment, leisure, and self care, housework constitutes one of four key areas into which researchers generally divide human time use. The second area of research in which housework is examined is the study of gender. In this area, scholars are interested in the role of housework in defining and reflecting role differences between women and men. This second area of study has driven a remarkable increase in research on housework since the 1980s. Housework serves as both a central manifestation of gendered family roles and as a key marker of status. As a result, understanding the factors associated with performing household work as well as the consequences of its performance provides an important indicator through which changes in gender relations may be assessed.

Most studies of housework draw on one of three methodological approaches. The first, and arguably most reliable, technique relies on the completion of "time diaries" by representative samples of specific populations (see Bianchi, Robinson, & Milkie, 2006). With this technique, respondents most commonly report the activities of the previous 24 hours in small time increments. Using this methodology, respondents are generally allowed to report multiple activities performed at the same time (multi-tasking). The disadvantage to this approach is that it is highly resource intensive and is burdensome to study participants, so the collection of data that could be used to explain patterns of time use has often been limited. In the United States the time diary has been utilized to study changes in time use from 1965 into the early 2000s. A growing cross-national time use archive is also available (see Gershuny, 2000).

Two less costly but more common methods for collecting data about time use include "hours estimates" and "stylized" questions about responsibility for household tasks. With the hours-estimates approach, respondents are asked to state the amount of time they spend on particular tasks (laundry, cooking, etc.) in a given day or week. The greatest drawback to this measurement strategy is that respondents tend to overestimate the time they spend on tasks. Among other problems, this approach frequently produces data in which respondents' estimates sum to more than 24 hours per day. With the stylized approach, respondents are asked to describe whether they or their spouses usually perform specific tasks. Although such data may be useful for studies of the way household tasks are divided by gender, they are less useful for studying time allocation.

FINDINGS FROM RESEARCH ON HOUSEWORK

Who Does the Housework? The two most definitive findings to emerge from studies of housework based on time-diary data from the United States are (a) that women spend more time on housework than men, and

(b) that women have substantially reduced the time they devote to housework since the late 1960s (Bianchi et al., 2006. The former finding is reported in almost all studies of housework, and the latter pattern has also been documented in a large number of wealthy nations besides the United States (Gershuny, 2000). Figure 1 presents trends in time spent on meals and cleaning by married mothers and fathers from the United States between 1965 and 2000. This change has occurred over a historical period in which women's rates of employment increased dramatically. Arlie Hochschild (1989) was among the first to note the potential emergence of a "second shift" if women do not reduce their housework time in direct proportion to their time spent in the labor market. Although Bianchi and colleagues (2006) report an hour-for-hour exchange between housework and paid work in the United States, Gershuny (2000) finds that British women reduce their time spent on housework and childcare by only 30 minutes per each additional hour they spend in paid employment. This implies that in Britain women have increased their total working time as their rates of employment have risen.

Closely connected to the debate about the combined burden of paid and unpaid work for women is the issue of the time men spend on housework. In her qualitative study, Arlie Hochschild (1989) framed her findings as reflecting a "stalled revolution" in which men's behavior with regard to unpaid labor had not changed nearly as much as had women's involvement in paid employment. Results from time-diary data suggest, however, that husbands in the United States have increased both the absolute amount of time they spend on housework as well as the amount they spend relative to their spouses. The time married fathers spent preparing meals more than tripled between 1965 and 2000 (from 36 to 126 minutes per week), and their time spent on housecleaning increased by a factor of six (from 18 to 108 minutes per week) (Bianchi et al., 2006). Gershuny, Michael Godwin, and Sally Jones (1994) argue that family behavior can be characterized as reflecting a process of "lagged adaptation" in which men's domestic behaviors are slowly coming in line with contemporary patterns of paid work among women. Nonetheless, with an average of 19.4 hours per week, married mothers now spend just over twice as much time on housework per week as do married fathers (Bianchi et al., 2006).

Children's responsibility for housework declined as education replaced family-based production as the principal use of time during childhood and adolescence. Data on children's housework are scarce, but a study by Bianchi and Robinson in 1997 estimated that children spend an average of 22 minutes per day on housework. Time spent on housework is greater among older children, among girls, and among children from larger families.

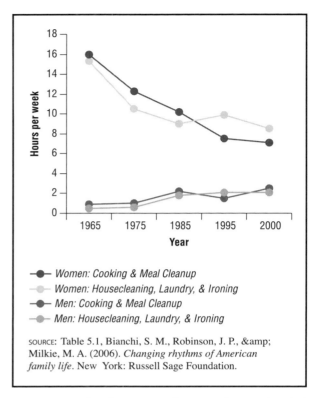

Figure 1. *Trends in hours per week spent on housework tasks by married mothers and fathers in the United States, 1965–2000.* CENGAGE LEARNING, GALE.

One study by David A. Demo and Alan C. Acock published in 1993 reports that children from single-parent families perform more housework than children living with two parents. In support of the life course concept of "linked lives," there is evidence that children's observations of how their parents divide household labor influence their own division of housework in adulthood.

Housework and Life Transitions Participation in housework is closely linked with central transitions in the life course. The transition to marriage is associated with increases in the amount of time women spend on housework and decreases in the amount of time men spend on housework. Although some studies report greater housework sharing among cohabiting couples than married couples, this finding is not universally supported. The transition to parenthood increases time spent on housework for both mothers and fathers (Berk, 1985;), but many studies find that a more strongly gendered division of housework emerges when couples become parents. Couples who become parents at older ages appear to divide housework more equally than couples who have children at younger ages (Coltrane & Ishii-Kuntz, 1992). This finding appears to be the result of greater investments in the father role by men and greater bargaining power among women who delay entry into parenthood.

Changes in women's paid employment are central to explanations of housework allocation, and wives' earnings have frequently been characterized as a resource with which they can bargain to reduce their responsibility for housework. Several researchers suggest that housework serves as an opportunity for the display of gender in addition to the production of household goods (Berk, 1985; Brines 1994). This line of reasoning holds that women who earn more than half of a couple's income may attempt to neutralize this gender "deviance" by performing a larger share of housework, and their husbands may cut back on housework in a similar effort. Recent work by Sanjiv Gupta (2007) casts doubt on this argument by demonstrating that housework performance is best explained by women's absolute earnings, rather than their earnings relative to their spouses'. In addition to women's earnings, several studies have shown that women's employment histories are positively related to their male partners' participation in housework. Research has also demonstrated that causality may move in the other direction, with responsibility for housework decreasing wages (Noonan, 2001). Retirement is another life course transition with implications for housework, and most research suggests that the division of labor remains highly gendered even after both spouses have retired.

A substantial body of research has documented the consequences for individuals of performing housework. For instance, Michelle L. Frisco and Kristi Williams (2003) showed that perceptions of inequity in housework are associated with a higher risk of divorce among women. Housework performance has also been linked to poor mental health, and cross-national studies have recently expanded the understanding of the cultural context of housework (Hook 2006). This research demonstrates how country-level characteristics such as measures of gender empowerment, women's employment, and welfare state policies directly influence the division of labor between spouses and also how they moderate the influence of individual-level characteristics on patterns of housework allocation.

Studies of housework have made important contributions to our understanding of power and exchange in couples' and individuals' time use. Work done at the turn of the 21st century points to the study of the mental, emotional, and even spiritual dimensions of housework. In addition, scholars are paying increasing attention to issues such as paid help for housework, the growing prevalence of shift work, and the emergence of global migration as a significant factor in housework allocation.

Studies of housework continue to document substantial changes in individuals' performance of housework and their perceptions of appropriate patterns of housework for women and men. As such, research on housework will continue to provide important insights into gender and class dynamics across the life course for the foreseeable future.

SEE ALSO Volume 2: *Cohabitation; Dual Career Couples; Gender in the Workplace; Time Use, Adulthood; Work-Family Conflict.*

BIBLIOGRAPHY
Berk, S. F. (1985). The gender factory: The apportionment of work in American households. New York: Plenum Press.
Bianchi, S. M., & Robinson, J. (1997). What did you do today? Children's use of time, family composition, and the acquisition of social capital. *Journal of Marriage & the Family, 59*, 332–344.
Bianchi, S. M., Robinson, J. P., & Milkie, M. A. (2006). *Changing rhythms of American family life.* New York: Russell Sage Foundation.
Brines, J. (1994). Economic dependency, gender, and the division of labor at home. *American Journal of Sociology, 100*, 652–688.
Coltrane, S., & Ishii-Kuntz, M. (1992). Men's housework: A life course perspective. *Journal of Marriage and Family, 54*, 43–57.
Demo, D. H., & Acock, A. C. (1993). Family diversity and the division of domestic labor: How much have things really changed? *Family Relations, 42*, 323–331.
DeVault, M. (1991). *Feeding the family: The social organization of caring and gendered work.* Chicago: University of Chicago Press.
Frisco, M. L., & Williams, K. (2003). Perceived housework equity, marital happiness, and divorce in dual-earner households. *Journal of Family Issues, 24*, 51–73.
Gershuny, J. (2000). *Changing times: Work and leisure in post-industrial societies.* Oxford, U.K.: Oxford University Press.
Gershuny, J., Godwin, M., & Jones, S. (1994). The domestic labour revolution: A process of lagged adaptation? In M. Anderson, F. Bechhofer, & J. Gershuny (Eds.), *The Social and Political Economy of the Household* (pp. 151–197). Oxford, U.K.: Oxford University Press.
Gupta, S. (2007). Autonomy, dependence, or display? The relationship between married women's earnings and housework. *Journal of Marriage and Family, 69*, 399–418.
Hochschild, A. (1989). *The second shift.* New York: Avon Books.
Hook, J. L. (2006). Care in context: men's unpaid work in 20 countries, 1965–2003. *American Sociological Review, 71*, 639–660.
Noonan, M. C. (2001). The impact of domestic work on men's and women's wages. *Journal of Marriage and Family, 63*, 1134–1145.
Strasser, S. (2000). *Never done: A history of American housework.* New York: Henry Holt.
Vanek, J. (1974). Time spent in housework. *Scientific American, 231*, 116–120.

Mick Cunningham

HUMAN CAPITAL

SEE Volume 1: *Human Capital.*

I

IMMIGRATION, ADULTHOOD

Entering the 21st century, the world is becoming increasingly mobile. People frequently cross international borders on daylong excursions or on longer trips as tourists. A few people, who may lack a fixed place of residence and are often referred to as nomads, move across borders in well-established patterns of territorial mobility. Others cross borders, sometimes returning on a daily basis or after a period of time stretching over years, to work or to study abroad. Others cross borders to seek asylum, to exercise their right to establish residence in the receiving country, or to join relatives. All countries of the world are experiencing the movement of people across their borders and available evidence suggests that the phenomenon has been increasing in volume, possibly because of the growing ease of long-range travel.

The complexity of movements across borders and the consequent difficulties in describing and understanding migration flows, monitoring changes over time, and providing governments with a solid basis for formulating policy has led the United Nations to draft several sets of recommendations about the measurement and description of international migration. The United Nations (2006) has recommended that an "international migrant" be defined as "any person who changes his or her country of usual residence" (p. 17). Unlike previous recommended definitions, it does not include a specific time frame. Instead, the United Nations recommends that migrants be classified as *long-term* if they are in the country of destination for at least 1 year and *short-term* migrants if they are in the country of destination between 3 and 12 months.

Much of the data on international migration are gathered at the time migrants enter their destination country via entry and exit permits or visas; by the processing of requests for asylum (thus ignoring what happened before or happens after the crossing of the border); or through population registers, issuance of residence permits, cross-sectional surveys, and censuses of migrants after they arrive in their country of destination (thus including only those who remained there). Unfortunately, these data constraints mean that much of the knowledge about international migrants remains static, ignores how decisions to migrate depend on or vary by life course stage, and ignores how the consequences of migration for the migrants, their families, and the countries involved vary by life course stage. In addition, shifts in the volume and character of international migration and new phenomena, such as remittances, new destinations, and transnational linkages, mean that much of the story is still unfolding.

DEMOGRAPHY OF INTERNATIONAL MIGRATION: TRENDS, GENDER, AND AGE

After compiling the data from national censuses and surveys, the United Nations estimates that there were about 75 million migrants in the world in 1960. By 2005 the number had increased to 190.5 million (see Figure 1). In 1960 about 42% of all migrants were found in the more developed regions of the world. Since then the percentage has been steadily growing; by 2005, 60% of all migrants were living in the more developed regions of the world (United Nations, 2006). The major receiving regions in 2005 were Europe with more than 64 million migrants, Asia with more than 53 million migrants, and North America with 44.5 million migrants. The top three receiving countries in 2005 were the United

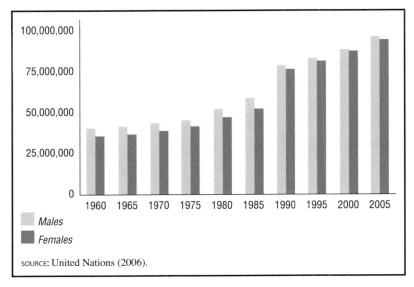

Figure 1. *Estimated numbers of male and female international immigrants in the world.* **CENGAGE LEARNING, GALE.**

States (38.4 million migrants), the Russian Federation (12 million), and Germany (10 million). The three top sending countries were China (35 million), India (20 million), and the Philippines (7 million).

Because of the overwhelming emphasis on economic and occupational incentives and conditions in theories of international migration, typical migrants are often explicitly presumed to be young adult men; yet almost half of the international migrants in 2005, 95 million, were female. In many countries, especially the more developed countries, women constitute the majority of immigrants. In the United States, for example, 57% of the immigrants legally admitted during 2006 were female (see Figure 2). Moreover, although more than half of the newly admitted immigrants were adults in the prime working ages (20–44), about 16% of the newly admitted immigrants were minor children below the age of 15 and about 8% of newly admitted immigrants were over the age of 60 (Office of Immigration Statistics, 2007).

NATIONAL POLICIES

The volume and character of the migration streams reaching across the world lie, to a large extent, under the control of nation-states. A few countries—such as the People's Republic of China and North Korea—limit the emigration (out-migration) of their citizens. In contrast, some countries have reached agreements that allow free movement across their borders. In 1985 five European countries (Belgium, France, Germany, Luxembourg, and the Netherlands) signed the Schengen Agreement, which allowed free movement of persons and commerce across their borders. By December 2007 the agreement had

expanded to include 24 European states and now covers almost all of Europe. (Notably, the United Kingdom and Ireland have only partially implemented the agreement.) The implementation of this agreement means that structure of international migration across almost all European national borders has changed: The movement of people across the shared borders within the Schengen area can no longer be considered international migration. One result is that the focus in European Union countries is now on immigration from countries outside of the Union rather than on what is now being recast as internal migration.

Most countries, however, limit in some way the numbers and characteristics of in-migrants, while not imposing constraints on the emigration of their citizens. Major immigrant-receiving countries, such as Australia, Canada, and the United States, all have immigration policies in place that limit, or attempt to limit, in some way the numbers and types of immigrants allowed into the country. In general, the policies of immigrant-receiving countries focus on numbers (e.g., calculating how many in-migrants the country needs or how many the country can absorb); the potential economic contributions of immigrants; and the social costs (such as the anticipated burdens on the welfare system, health system, and the educational system). However, the details of immigration policies differ greatly from country to country and even within countries across time.

Canada's current immigration policy, for example, uses a point system to rank prospective immigrants with extra points given to those who are younger, well-educated, and know one of the country's official languages. Australia's current system also strongly emphasizes youth, specific occupational skills, and knowledge of English. In the

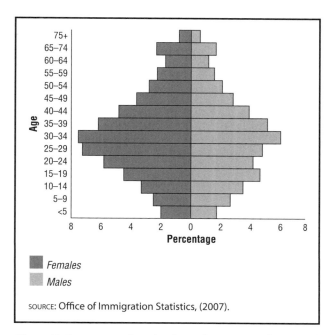

Figure 2. Percentages of newly admitted immigrants by age and sex (U.S.). CENGAGE LEARNING, GALE.

United States, the 1965 Hart-Cellar Act lifted the quotas dating from the 1920s for immigrants from selected countries and established family reunification as the major rationale for the admission of immigrants to the country. But after 1990 the United States immigration policy shifted toward admitting skilled and professional labor and immediate family members. (American immigration policy also includes a provision for admitting citizens from countries that have been less likely to send immigrants to the United States.) At a global level, more and more countries are adjusting their immigration policies to overtly court highly skilled young adult immigrants.

The flip side of encouraging highly skilled immigrants is the discouraging of immigrants who lack the designated educational, occupational, or linguistic skills. Individuals who cannot migrate to specific countries under the auspices of the current policy often resort to migration without appropriate documents. Many immigrant-receiving countries, especially the North American and European countries, have been struggling with the growth in the numbers of undocumented or unauthorized migrants. Unauthorized migrants include those who enter the country without receiving the appropriate visa or official permission under the country's immigration policy and those who enter the country with authorization to stay for a limited time, perhaps as a tourist or student, and then overstay. Estimates in 2006 suggest that about 11 million of 30 million foreign-born people who entered the United States after 1980 are unauthorized migrants (Hoefer,

Rytina, & Campbell, 2007) and that at least 5 million of the 56 million migrants in Europe crossed international borders without authorization (Global Commission on International Migration, 2005).

THEORIES OF INTERNATIONAL MIGRATION

The millions of migrants in the world, who comprise about 3% of the world's population, are engaged in large and patterned flows. Numerous theories of international migration—varying across academic discipline, level of analysis, and data sources—attempt to explain these flows. Economists, for example, focus on wage rates and labor market conditions and thus view migrants, especially young adult males, as prospective workers. Political scientists focus on the role of the state and thus consider how policy shapes the attributes of the incoming migrants. Sociologists focus on the assimilation and integration of immigrants in the country of destination and thus investigate how immigrant children and the children of immigrants fare in the receiving societies. More recently, social scientists are considering global forces shaping international migration.

Neoclassical macroeconomic theory is the oldest and still best-known approach to understanding why some people move from one country to another. The basic assumption is that international migration is caused by national differences in the supply of and demand for labor. Individuals change labor markets if the prevailing wages and other employment conditions are better in the destination country. Neoclassical microeconomic theory presumes that rational actors migrate because they expect an increase in some positive reward, usually higher wages, after taking into account the costs of migration, which include the difficulties of adjusting to a new labor market and a new social environment. The new economics of migration focuses on households rather than on individual workers. Here households are viewed as managing their economic well-being by diversifying the allocation of household resources (and thus minimizing risk) by, for example, sending one or more household members to work in a different economy.

Dual labor market theory, by contrast, argues that international migration is caused by a permanent demand for immigrant labor that is inherent to the economic structure of the more developed nations. The demand for immigrant labor is fed by the need of employers, who have capital at their disposal, to hire workers only when labor is needed to satisfy demand. Immigrants satisfy capitalists' need for temporary labor because immigrants, especially less educated immigrants, are more apt to be satisfied with low-level and unstable jobs than native-born workers.

Doug Massey (2004), a sociologist, offered the theory of cumulative causation to explain why international migrations continue after the initial conditions triggering a migration flow disappear. The basic argument is that the social networks and social institutions that emerge along with a migration stream serve to perpetuate the flow. Scholars such as Alejandro Portes (1999) have argued that contemporary international migration is too complex to be explained by one overarching grand theory. He suggests that scholars consider at least four important dimensions: the origins of immigration, the directionality and continuity of migrant flows, the use of immigrant labor in destination countries, and the integration of immigrants in the receiving societies.

The available theoretical frameworks are limited in many respects. Few consider how gender, age, and life cycle considerations play out in decisions and opportunities to migrate; which migrants countries prefer to encourage under their policies; and how immigrants fare in their country of destination. In particular, there are only piecemeal explanations seeking to understand the migration of people who migrate before or after young adulthood. Young migrant children, for example, are almost always assumed to have migrated with one or both of their parents. Yet this assumption omits the role of international adoption in the migration of orphans, the migration of children who join other family members, and the migration of children who are sent to other countries by their guardians for educational or other reasons. The presumption that minor children always accompany their migrant parents also cloaks the corollary assumption that migrant parents always bring their minor children with them to their country of destination, which is almost certainly not the case. Meanwhile, the preponderance of young adults among recent migrants means that little attention has been paid to the smaller but growing numbers of migrants who move later in adulthood.

Similarly, women are often assumed to migrate with their husbands or other family members but many, in fact, migrate independently of family members. Although many women migrate for economic reasons, some women (and a few men) embark upon cross-national relationships and migrate to join their partners or spouses. This phenomenon, which is fed by countries' worldwide military operations, the growth of multinational businesses, the consequent traveling of employees across borders, and the increasing presence of Internet matchmaking organizations fostering cross-national relationships, appears to be responsible for a growing number of international migrants.

OUTCOMES OF MIGRATION

The effects of international migration are complex, pervasive, and occur at several different levels of analysis. International migration affects both the sending and receiving nations. The lives of migrants are affected by which country they were born in, the timing and reason for migration, and by their country of destination. In addition, migration streams between countries forge social and economic linkages that affect people in both societies.

Between 1990 and 2000, for example, migration accounted for more than half (56%) of the population growth in the developed world, and an astonishing 89% of the population growth in Europe. Many of the major immigrant-receiving countries such as the United States and several countries in the European Union, which are experiencing increases in racial, cultural, and religious diversity because of high levels of immigration, are engaged in heated political discussions about the integration of migrants. In a tightly related phenomenon, because many migrants move in young adulthood, a life stage marked by childbearing and childrearing, migrants in low-fertility regions such as the European Union and North American countries are the parents of a disproportionate number of children. Immigrants in the United States, for example, constitute about 12% of the general American population, but are the parents of about 23% of the nation's children. Many immigrant-receiving countries are thus also engaged in discussions about the added educational needs of the children of immigrant parents—for example, bilingual programs.

Increasingly, international migration is responsible for strong financial linkages between countries. This is clearly seen in the significant growth of remittances from migrants (especially those in the more developed countries) to families in their countries of origin. In 2006 the World Bank estimated that remittances reached a worldwide peak of $258 billion U.S. dollars, most of which was sent to developing countries. These flows of money are widely recognized as among the most stable external sources of money for developing countries and, in the case of countries such as Mexico, the Philippines, and most recently India, constitute a significant fraction of the country's gross domestic product (Chishti, 2007). It is unclear to what extent the levels of remittances are driven by the sheer numbers of international migrants or whether remittances submitted by migrants increase as they age in the destination society (and presumably earn more) or drop as migrants' ties to the sending country fade over time.

Social scientists, especially economists and sociologists, are concerned about the welfare of individual migrants after they arrive in the new country. Economists often track trajectories of earnings over the remainder of the migrants' life cycle in the new country; sociologists have done the same for occupational careers. This research often shows that after controlling for educational attainment and other forms of human capital, migrants' labor force careers are disrupted shortly after migration but often recover as they adapt to the new society.

However, most of this work has concentrated on male migrants who arrive in early adulthood.

Sociologists have also considered how those who migrate in childhood fare in the new society. Very little research has compared how the timing of migration in a migrant's life course, whether in childhood, early adulthood, middle adulthood, or late adulthood, differentially affects a migrant's life trajectory and well-being in the country of destination. But some processes of acculturation may be much more difficult for people who migrate later in life to a new country than for those who migrate earlier in life. The *critical period hypothesis* in second language learning, for example, suggests that age at migration is a potentially important predictor of how well a migrants eventually learn their host society's language and thus of how well they then fare in the labor market (Bleakley & Chin, 2004).

SEE ALSO Volume 1: *Assimilation; Immigration, Childhood and Adolescence;* Volume 2: *Residential Mobility, Adulthood.*

BIBLIOGRAPHY

Bleakley, H., & Chin, A. (2004). Language skills and earnings: Evidence from childhood immigrants. *The Review of Economics and Statistics, 86*(2), 481–496.

Chishti, M. A. (2007). *The phenomenal rise in remittances to India: A closer look* [Policy brief]. Retrieved February 22, 2008, from http://www.migrationpolicy.org/pubs/MigDevPB_052907.pdf

Global Commission on International Migration. (2005). *Migration in an interconnected world: New directions for action.* Retrieved February 22, 2008, from http://www.gcim.org

Hoefer, M., Rytina, N., & Campbell, C. (2007). *Estimates of the unauthorized immigrant population residing in the United States: January 2006.* Washington, DC: Office of Immigration Statistics; U.S. Department of Homeland Security. Retrieved February 22, 2008, from http://www.dhs.gov/xlibrary/assets/statistics/publications/ill_pe_2006.pdf

Massey, D. S., & Taylor, J.E. (2004). *International migration: Prospects and policies in a global market.* New York: Oxford University Press.

Migration Policy Institute. (2007). *Variable impacts: State-level analysis of the slowdown in the growth of remittances to Mexico.* Retrieved February 22, 2008, from http://www.migrationpolicy.org/pubs/FS19_MexicanRemittancesEnglish_091207.pdf

Office of Immigration Statistics. (2007). *2006 Yearbook of immigration statistics.* Washington, DC: U.S. Department of Homeland Security. Retrieved February 22, 2008, from http://www.dhs.gov/ximgtn/statistics/publications/yearbook.shtm

Portes, A. (1999). Immigration theory for a new century: Some problems and opportunities. In C. Hirschman, P. Kasinitz, & J. DeWind (Eds.), *Handbook of international migration: The American experience* (pp. 21–33). New York: Russell Sage Foundation.

United Nations. (2006). *World migrant stock: The 2005 revision population database.* Retrieved February 22, 2008, from: http://esa.un.org/migration/index.asp?panel=1

Gillian Stevens

INCARCERATION, ADULTHOOD

This entry discusses both incarceration and imprisonment. Individuals are considered imprisoned when they have been convicted of a crime and sentenced to more than 1 year. Although some imprisoned individuals are held in local jails, most are transferred to state or federal prisons to serve their sentences. The median sentence for state prisoners, who comprise more than 85% of the American prison population, is 36 months, and the median time served is 17 months. Although an individual must have been sentenced to more than a year to become a prisoner, all an individual must do to be considered incarcerated is be held in a jail—even just for 1 day. The term *incarceration* covers everything from people serving life sentences for murder to people who have been jailed overnight because of disorderly conduct. The term *incarceration* therefore covers a broader range of confinement than does the term *imprisonment.*

THE ERA OF MASS IMPRISONMENT

For the first three-quarters of the twentieth century, the American imprisonment rate hovered around 100 persons per 100,000. Over this period, American imprisonment was noteworthy mainly for its stability; in 1973 the imprisonment rate appeared so immune to social change that researchers doubted it would deviate significantly in the near future (Blumstein & Cohen, 1973). Even the coming and going of two great wars—World War I (1914–1918) and World War II (1939–1945)—had little effect on the imprisonment rate. Starting in the mid-1970s, however, American imprisonment rapidly increased. As of 2008, the imprisonment rate in the United States was more than 500 per 100,000. America's rate of incarceration is closer to those of South Africa, Malta, and the former Soviet Union than to Great Britain, Canada, or other comparable democracies. A high rate of imprisonment has become a distinctive feature of American society since the mid-1980s.

Although researchers debate the causes of the dramatic rise in American imprisonment, there is considerable agreement that the prison boom had political and economic antecedents. Following the presidential campaign of Barry Goldwater (1909–1998) in 1964, crime became a national political issue as it never before had been. For the first time,

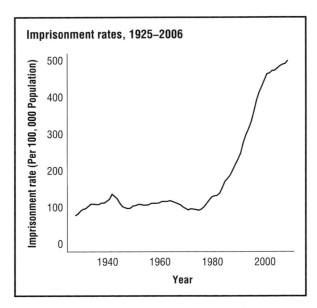

Figure 1. *U.S. Imprisonment rates, 1925–2006.* CENGAGE LEARNING, GALE.

politicians on a grand scale began solidifying public support by sponsoring punitive legislation that was often as predictive as it was reflective of public opinion (Beckett, 1999). The national manufacturing decline and the flight of jobs and people from poor urban neighborhoods to predominantly White suburbs also altered the landscape of opportunities available to the nation's worst off. Crime rates during this period rose, but the connection between rising crime and the use of incarceration is not overwhelmingly strong. The drug trade—and the War on Drugs beginning in the 1980s—hold a particularly important place in the story. Increasing rates of incarceration for drug-related crime explain 45% of the increase in the state prison population (Western, 2006).

The causes of mass imprisonment have received substantial research attention since the 1990s, the consequences of incarceration have also been examined. Rather than focusing solely on the effects of incarceration on crime, this research considers a wider variety of impacts of incarceration on individuals, their families, and society more broadly.

RISKS OF INCARCERATION

The risk of being incarcerated is unequally distributed in America, as elsewhere. The risk of entering prison or jail is highest during the period between a person's late teens and early 30s; before and after this age span, the risk is relatively low (Pettit & Western, 2004). Men are much more likely to be incarcerated than women, although the risk of imprisonment has grown faster for women since the 1980s (Bonczar, 2003). The lion's share of the

growth in female imprisonment is attributable to changes in convictions for drug-related offenses. Individuals with low levels of education—and especially individuals who have not finished high school—are more likely to enter jail or prison than individuals with higher levels of education. Racial inequality in the risk of imprisonment is also substantial: Black men born between 1965 and 1969 were around seven times more likely to have been to prison by 1999 than comparable White men (Pettit & Western 2004, pp. 161–162). Latinos are also at higher risk of imprisonment than Whites, but their risk is much lower than that of comparable Blacks (Bonczar, 2003). Black men who did not finish high school have a 60 percent chance of going to prison in their lifetime (Pettit & Western, 2004, p. 161).

The mass imprisonment of Black men has significant life-course implications. As Table 1 indicates, Black men are more likely to be imprisoned at some point in their lives than they are to earn a college degree or enter military service. The same cannot be said for White men, only about 3% of whom will ever be sent to prison. For Black men with little education, marriage is not even twice as common as imprisonment. White men, by contrast, are 12 times more likely to get married than go to prison.

Large racial and class inequalities in the risk of imprisonment suggest that, even prior to incarceration, the life chances of prisoners are more limited than those of the average individual. Inmate surveys bear this out: Prisoners are more likely than the average citizen to have been abused as children, to suffer some form of mental illness, to have been homeless, and to be addicted to drugs or alcohol (Mumola, 2000). Coupled with histories of criminal activity, unemployment, and residence in poor neighborhoods, most prisoners began life at a significant disadvantage to the general population.

CONSEQUENCES OF INCARCERATION

Research suggests, however, that having been incarcerated may further impede the life chances of formerly incarcerated individuals. Studies conducted since 2000 point to four areas in which incarceration may have consequences for the lives of former prisoners: (a) the labor market, (b) family life, (c) health, and (d) civic participation. This entry does not discuss the effect of imprisonment on crime—a topic that is the subject of much debate—in any detail. One study estimates that the growth in imprisonment rates explains only about 10% of the decline in serious crime at the end of the 1990s, but estimates range from no effect to 40% (Western, 2006).

Of all the consequences of incarceration, its economic effects have probably received the most scholarly attention. Research in this area has focused on three labor market outcomes: (a) getting a job, (b) earnings, and (c)

Life Event	White Men (%)	Black Men (%)
All Men		
Prison Incarceration	3.2	22.4
Bachelor's Degree	31.6	12.5
Military Service	14.0	17.4
Marriage	72.5	59.3
Noncollege Men		
Prison Incarceration	6.0	31.9
High School Diploma/GED	73.5	64.4
Military Service	13.0	13.7
Marriage	72.8	55.9

SOURCE: Pettit and Western 2004:164.

Table 1. *Percentage of non–Hispanic Black and White men, born 1965–1969, experiencing life events and surviving to 1999.* CENGAGE LEARNING, GALE.

wage growth. The most methodologically rigorous study to date of the effects of incarceration on the probability of getting a job showed that having a criminal record drastically reduced the likelihood of receiving a positive response from an employer seeking to fill an entry-level position (Pager, 2003). The study also showed that Black men with criminal records did much worse than White men. White men with criminal records received a positive response 17% of the time; comparable Black men received a positive response 5% of the time (Pager 2003, p. 958). Research on earnings draws similar conclusions, showing that having ever been incarcerated diminishes earnings by as much as 40% (Western, 2006). Other studies suggest that because time out of the labor force may diminish the probability of getting a career job, and thus having substantial wage growth, incarceration may increase economic inequality (Western, 2002). Yet these findings are not without dispute; research using administrative data shows that an additional year of incarceration does not diminish earnings (Kling, 2006).

For individuals attached to families, the experience of imprisonment also appears to weaken family ties. Men who go to jail or prison experience much higher risks of divorce and separation than otherwise comparable men; they also experience much lower rates of marriage than other men when they are incarcerated (Lopoo & Western, 2005). Families of the incarcerated often shoulder burdens of visitation, diminished household earnings, and stigma; mothers tend to suffer psychological distress as a consequence of having their adult sons incarcerated. One study suggests that romantic partners have higher levels of stress and depression because of the incarceration of a loved one (Braman, 2004). Other research, however, reports that the removal of a violent, drug-addicted man from a household may provide temporary respite for women (Comfort, 2008). Substantial differences in inter-

pretations of the effects of incarceration on romantic partners illustrate the need for more research on the collateral consequences of incarceration.

Imprisonment, however, affects more than the life course of incarcerated adults and their families. High levels of imprisonment also have consequences for children. As imprisonment has become common for adults, so also has parental imprisonment become common for children. Christopher Wildeman (in press) estimates that one in four Black children born in 1990 had a parent imprisoned by their 14th birthday; for Black children of high school dropouts, parental imprisonment was modal. These risks are about twice the risk of those for children born 12 years earlier—and drastically higher than the risk for comparable White children. One consequence of high levels of imprisonment—especially female imprisonment—is an elevated risk of children being placed in foster care. Changes in the female incarceration rate account for 30% of the drastic increase in foster-care caseloads between 1985 and 2000 (Swann & Sylvester, 2006). Although other consequences of parental incarceration for children are uncertain, there are reasons to suspect that parental incarceration further disadvantages children. If so, mass imprisonment would contribute not only to social inequality among adults but also to that among children.

Incarceration may additionally worsen the health of former prisoners. Ex-offenders have higher death rates than those who have never been incarcerated after adjusting for age, sex, and race (Binswanger et al., 2007), although it is unclear whether this relationship is causal or spurious. In the latter case, the association may reflect other factors associated with both higher risk of death and incarceration, such as drug abuse. Even if incarceration does not increase mortality risk, research shows that incarceration increases the risk of certain acute health conditions (Massoglia, 2008)—especially those related to stress—and has contributed to racial inequality in HIV and AIDS infection rates for both men and women (Johnson & Raphael, in press). To the degree that mass imprisonment may harm the health of prisoners—and, potentially, their families and children—it is not only a criminal justice concern but also a public health concern.

Finally, incarceration poses formidable legal barriers to political participation, the retention of parental rights, and the receipt of welfare, public housing, and financial aid (Travis, 2002). In all but two states, incarcerated individuals are not allowed to vote, and ex-felons are not allowed to vote in many states. The 1997 Adoption and Safe Families Act speeds the termination of parental rights for children who have been in foster care for 15 of the last 22 months—a duration far shorter than the median prison sentence. An often-overlooked provision of welfare reform permanently prohibits individuals with drug-related felony convictions from receiving federal assistance and food stamps. Statutes enacted in the 1990s give public housing agencies the authority to deny housing to individuals with a wide array of criminal convictions. Also, the Higher Education Act of 1998 renders any individual convicted of a drug-related offense ineligible for student loans. Together, these legal barriers present formidable challenges to individuals seeking to return safely from prison—particularly given their diminished pre-incarceration resources (Travis, 2002).

DOES INCARCERATION REALLY DIMINISH LIFE CHANCES?

Although research on the effects of incarceration on the life chances of individuals points to consistent, negative effects, it is also possible that the poorer life chances of the ever-incarcerated are due to something other than incarceration. The logic for this argument is simple: Because researchers know that individuals likely to go to prison already suffer from diminished life chances, how can they be sure that differences between formerly incarcerated individuals and other individuals are due to incarceration and not something else, such as living in poverty or partaking in crime? Most studies in this area use observational data and therefore have difficulty isolating causal relationships between incarceration and life chances. In order to increase confidence in the foregoing conclusions about the consequences of incarceration, more studies should use experimental or quasi-experimental research designs. Although this type of research is typically more difficult, expensive, and time-consuming to conduct than other types of research, the potential rewards are greater because these experimental studies have less trouble dealing with many of the biases that hinder studies based on observational data.

FURTHER RESEARCH

There are many important areas for future research in the study of incarceration, but two merit special attention because of their potential policy implications. First, researchers should consider situations in which incarceration may *improve* the life chances of incarcerated individuals and those around them. Current research tends to consider incarceration as having only negative effects on the life course of individuals and their loved ones—indeed, this entry suggests just that—but one recent study casts doubt on the claim that incarceration only diminishes life chances (Comfort, 2008). This study is quick to note, of course, that many of the benefits of incarceration exist solely because prisons are one of the only places in which basic social services are readily available to the poor. In order to have a better idea of what the consequences of incarceration are, however, researchers should attempt to determine with greater precision when incarceration harms, helps, and has no effect on individuals.

Second, more research should evaluate programs to help formerly incarcerated individuals successfully return to civic life after leaving prisons and jails. To find out what works, more research should be conducted on which programs—both during and after incarceration—help diminish the probability of recidivism. Research should also consider early intervention programs aimed at decreasing an individual's risk of incarceration. Although the evaluation of programs should not be the sole focus of policy interventions, researchers of the penal state should nonetheless spend more of their time and resources considering how to keep individuals away from crime and out of prison.

SEE ALSO Volume 1: *Juvenile Justice System;* Volume 2: *Crime, Criminal Activity in Adulthood; Employment, Adulthood; Unemployment.*

BIBLIOGRAPHY

Beckett, K. (1999). *Making crime pay: Law and order in contemporary American politics.* New York: Oxford University Press.

Binswanger, I., Stern, M., Deyo, R., Heagerty, P., Cheadle, A., Elmore, J., et al. (2007). Release from Prison—A high risk of death for former inmates. *New England Journal of Medicine, 356*(2), 157–165.

Blumstein, A., & Cohen, J. (1973). A theory of the stability of punishment. *Journal of Criminal Law and Criminology, 64*(2), 198–207.

Bonczar, T. (2003). *The prevalence of imprisonment in the U.S. population.* Washington, DC: U.S. Department of Justice.

Braman, D. (2004). *Doing time on the outside: Incarceration and family life in urban America.* Ann Arbor: University of Michigan Press.

Comfort, M. (2008). *Doing time together: Love and family in the shadow of the prison.* Chicago: University of Chicago Press.

Johnson, R., & Raphael, S. (in press). The effects of male incarceration dynamics on AIDS infection rates among African-American women and men. *Journal of Law and Economics.*

Kling, J. (2006). Incarceration length, employment, and earnings. *American Economic Review, 96*(3), 863–876.

Lopoo, L., & Western, B. (2005). Incarceration and the formation and stability of marital unions. *Journal of Marriage and the Family, 67*(3), 721–734.

Massoglia, M. (2008). Incarceration as exposure: The prison, infectious disease, and other stress-related illnesses. *Journal of Health and Social Behavior, 49*(1), 56–71.

Mumola, C. (2000). *Incarcerated parents and their children.* Washington, DC: Bureau of Justice Statistics. Retrieved June 4, 2008, from http://www.pojp.usdoj.gov/bjs

Pager, D. (2003). The mark of a criminal record. *The American Journal of Sociology, 108*(5), 937–975.

Pettit, B., & Western, B. (2004). Mass imprisonment and the life course: Race and class inequality in U.S. incarceration. *American Sociological Review, 69*(2), 151–169.

Swann, C., & Sylvester, M.S. (2006). The foster care crisis: What caused caseloads to grow? *Demography, 43*(2), 309–335.

Travis, J. (2002). Invisible punishment: An instrument of social exclusion. In M. Mauer & M. Chesney-Lind (Eds.), *Invisible* punishment: *The collateral consequences of mass imprisonment* (pp. 15-36). New York: New Press.

Western, B. (2002). The impact of incarceration on wage mobility and inequality. *American Sociological Review, 67*(4), 526–546.

Western, B. (2006). *Punishment and inequality in America.* New York: Russell Sage Foundation.

Wildeman, C. (in press). Parental imprisonment, the prison boom, and the concentration of childhood disadvantage. *Demography.*

Christopher Wildeman
Christopher Muller

INCOME INEQUALITY

Income inequality can be defined as the amount of variation in the value of goods and services received by individuals in a defined population at a given time. That is, income inequality refers to how income is distributed among members of a population at a point in time. For instance, in the United States, according to Census Bureau estimates for 2006, the poorest 20% of households (those earning $19,178 annually or less) earn just 3.4% of all income earned by households in the United States, whereas the richest 20% of households (those earning over $91,705 annually) earn 50.5% of all income earned by households in the United States. The significance of income inequality for the life course and life course research is difficult to overstate, because life course processes are related to both the causes and the consequences of income inequality. For instance, the degree of variation in income within a society establishes a structure of economic opportunity that constrains economic achievement, and the pursuit of economic well-being itself helps to establish the level of income inequality observed at a particular historical moment. Broadly, the amount of income inequality makes up a central part of an individual's sociohistorical context as that individual navigates the life course.

MEASUREMENT

Researchers have developed a wide array of methods to measure income inequality. One of the most popular is the Gini coefficient, which quantifies the difference between an observed income distribution and a perfectly equal income distribution. The Gini coefficient ranges from a minimum of 0 (or perfect equality, where all income-receiving units receive an equal share of the income produced in a society) to a maximum of 1 (or perfect inequality, where one income-receiving unit receives all the income produced in a society).

The first step in calculating the Gini coefficient and other summary measures of income inequality is thus to define the income-receiving unit. Because incomes are typically shared within households, empirical researchers often designate households as the unit of analysis. The next step is to define income. For instance, one commonly used income measure is *disposable income*, or the sum of all wage and salary income and government income transfers, less direct tax contributions, that is available for spending or saving. Thus disposable income includes income from many sources, not just income from employment. This highlights the important distinction between *income inequality* and *wage inequality*. Income inequality, a broader concept, in addition to wages and salaries also includes money from self-employment; property income; pension, sickness, disability, and unemployment benefits; child support transfers; and a wide range of other government benefits. Because income inequality incorporates information on government taxes and transfers, it is also referred to as *post-fisc inequality*, in contrast to *pre-fisc inequality*, or inequality generated only by the market.

Once the income-receiving unit and income are clearly defined, the Gini coefficient, and other measures of income inequality, can be calculated. The Gini coefficient itself is based on the Lorenz curve, which plots the cumulative share of total income (on the y-axis) against ranked income-receiving units (on the x-axis). For instance, in a society with perfect income equality, the Lorenz curve would be shaped like a straight line tilted at a 45-degree angle, as the lowest 20% of households shared 20% of society's income; the lowest 50% shared 50%; the top 20% shared 20%; and so on. Again, in this perfectly equal society, the Gini coefficient would be 0. By contrast, in the United States, where the bottom 20% of households garner 3.4% of total U.S. income and the top 20% of households garner 50.5% of total U.S. income, the Gini coefficient equals 0.464 (based on Census Bureau estimates for 2006 data).

Other popular summary measures of income inequality include (a) the variance of logged incomes; (b) the coefficient of variation; (c) the Theil index; (d) the Atkinson coefficient; and (e) the relative mean deviation. One popular measure that is especially easy to interpret is the percentile ratio, or the ratio of income received by a household at a percentile rank high in the income distribution to the income of a household at a lower rank. One's location in the income distribution thus refers to how their income ranks relative to others in the United States. For example, a household in the 80th percentile of income distribution is a household whose income is higher than 80% of households in the United States.

In the United States, the ratio of income earned by a household at the 80th percentile of the income distribution

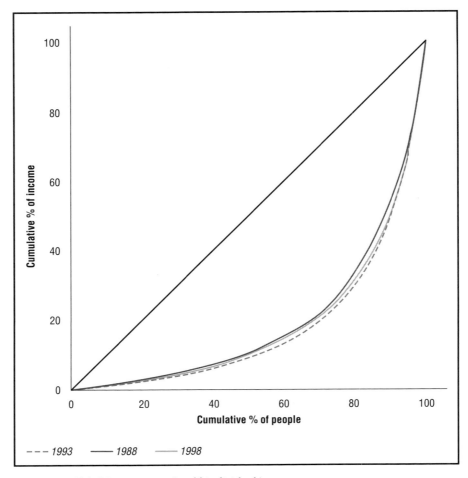

Figure 1. *Global Lorenz curve (world individuals).* **CENGAGE LEARNING, GALE.**

to income earned by a household at the 20th percentile (the 80-20 percentile ratio) was 2.996 in 2000, according to the Luxembourg Income Study (LIS). By contrast, the 80-20 ratio in Canada was 2.524, and in Sweden it was 2.012. The 90–50 percentile ratio—the ratio of the 90th percentile household income to the median household income—was 2.104 in the United States, 1.933 in Canada, and 1.684 in Sweden.

TRENDS

There is a consensus in research literature that income inequality within advanced industrial societies such as the United States has grown since the 1970s. For instance, again according to the LIS, the Gini coefficient for the United States has grown from 0.301 in 1979 to 0.372 in 2004, which is a very large increase as income inequality generally does not exhibit strong trends. (The difference between the LIS estimate and the Census Bureau estimate reflects differences in how the indices are calculated; LIS data are calculated for cross-national comparability.) Even

in egalitarian Sweden, though, the Gini coefficient grew from 0.197 in 1981 to 0.252 by 2000. However, whereas many accept that income inequality has increased in societies such as the United States, there is more debate over (a) the specific timing of the increase; (b) the extent of the increase; (c) the causes of the increase; and (d) the consequences of the increase (Neckerman & Torche, 2007). Arthur Alderson et al. (2005) used LIS data on 16 advanced industrial countries to clarify how inequality has changed. They show that the largest increases in income inequality have been driven more by the rich getting richer (upper polarization) than by the poor getting poorer.

There is also a consensus in this literature that income inequality varies substantially across countries, with the highest levels generally observed in the developing countries of Latin America and sub-Saharan Africa, and the lowest levels generally observed in the advanced industrial countries of Scandinavia and western Europe. Anglo countries such as the United States, the United Kingdom, Canada, and Australia currently exhibit levels of income inequality that are significantly higher than those in western Europe. The trends also differ, with income inequality growing more rapidly in the United States than in western Europe. Of course, whether data are comparable across nations is a key concern when comparing levels of income inequality, but great strides have been made in this regard by data collection and dissemination efforts such as the LIS and the Pitt Inequality Project, which collect comparable data from many nations and make them available to researchers.

If there is general agreement that income inequality has increased in many advanced industrial societies, and has increased especially strongly in the United States, there is much less agreement on how total world income inequality is evolving. (See Kathryn Neckerman's and Florencia Torche's "Inequality: Causes and Consequences" [2007] for an overview addressing this matter and references to key works on the subject.) Total world income inequality is the broadest measure of income inequality, because it is composed of between-country differences in national economic development, and within-country income inequality among individuals. In one influential line of research, sociologist Glenn Firebaugh (2003) argues for a "new geography of global income inequality" based on evidence that total world income inequality is on the decline, because rising income inequality within countries is vastly outweighed by decreasing economic inequality between countries. In direct contrast, economist Branko Milanovic argues that global inequality rose sharply from 1988 to 1993, then declined modestly from 1993 to 1998, based on new evidence from household survey data. This debate is marked by a number of measurement controversies and differences of interpretation, creating a significant opportunity for further research. Moreover, few studies have examined the difference this possible change in the global social context makes for the lives of individuals as they move through the life course.

CAUSES

The relationship between economic development and income inequality has long been a puzzle. In the 1950s, economist Simon Kuznets (1901–1985) conjectured that income inequality has an inverted U-shaped relationship to economic development, rising in the early stages of industrialization and falling at later stages, as people move from the agricultural sector, where wages are lower, to the industrial sector, where wages are higher. This sector dualism causes income inequality to increase at first, purely as a function of the changing composition of the labor force by economic sector. Two other changes associated with economic development can also help to account for the Kuznets curve: the expansion of mass schooling, which decreases the wages of the highly educated by creating a larger pool of highly educated labor, and the demographic transition from a high-fertility, high-mortality regime to a low-fertility, low-mortality regime, which increases income inequality as population growth expands the labor supply at the low end of the income distribution (Alderson & Nielsen, 2002).

Because wage inequality is clearly a significant proportion of income inequality, researchers also look to other aspects of the labor market beyond sectoral composition, skill composition, and demographic composition to explain cross-national differences and trends in income inequality. For instance, a large body of evidence shows that where labor is better organized, inequality will be reduced. Antilabor corporate restructuring and government policies in the United States in the 1980s are often blamed for part of the increase in income inequality in the United States, and cross-national investigations show that unionization rates are highly correlated with income inequality (Alderson & Nielsen, 2002). On the demand side of the labor market, one controversial explanation of increased income inequality in places such as the United States is skill-biased technological change: The argument is that technological shifts have substantially raised the wages of the most highly educated segment of the labor force, which has raised income inequality by increasing inequality in the upper end of the income distribution.

National governments are also critical to any examination of the causes of income inequality. National economic policies, for instance, produce and reproduce social cleavages, as tight monetary policy restricts inflation and benefits the privileged classes, whereas full employment policy benefits the disadvantaged classes. Social policy also affects income inequality directly through income transfers. Other national policies and institutions also affect income inequality: In the United States, laws restricting labor organization, tax policies, infrastructure programs, the declining real value of the minimum wage, and education policies all affect the level of income inequality, by shaping who has access to education and helping to determine which jobs receive what rewards, among other mechanisms.

In response to explanations that center on forces within nations, world systems theory redirected scholarly attention toward international forces during the 1970s and 1980s. World systems theory argues that income inequality in developing countries is worsened by dependence on foreign capital, as (a) the occupational structure is distorted in an expansion of the working class and an internationally oriented elite, and (b) the nation directs its economic and social policy to the advantage of multinational corporations (Chase-Dunn, 1975). In work on advanced industrial societies, there is also evidence that globalization is associated with the recent increase in income inequality that has been dubbed "the Great U-Turn" (Alderson & Nielsen, 2002). New research also shows that other international forces, including the regional integration in western Europe, are also associated with rising income inequality, over and above any relationship between inequality and globalization (Beckfield, 2006). This suggests that regional integration, or the construction of regional political economy that has enjoyed a resurgence around the world, itself may be an important new dimension of the social context that influences the life chances of individuals.

CONSEQUENCES

Whether income inequality has important consequences is an enduring controversy. Neckerman (2004) presents evidence from the Russell Sage Foundation's research program on inequality, focusing on the relationship between growing income inequality in the United States and several other aspects of social inequality, including family and neighborhood life, education and work, health, political participation, public policy, and wealth, while Stephen Morgan, David Grusky, and Gary Fields (2006) review research on the connections between income inequality and social mobility. Although each of these topics is clearly relevant to life course scholarship, the debate over health has been particularly contentious and policy-relevant, and thus warrants a detailed treatment.

Since Richard Wilkinson's pioneering work in the early 1990s, researchers from various disciplines have debated the provocative claim that the level of income inequality in a society is related to the health of its population (Beckfield, 2004; Wilkinson & Pickett, 2006). The theoretical arguments for a negative health effect of income inequality are straightforward. Perhaps most prominently, Wilkinson pursues an approach based on the work of French sociologist Emile Durkheim (1858–1917) that emphasizes social integration. For Wilkinson (1996), income inequality produces social disintegration, which causes unhealthy societies. Disintegration translates into poorer population health as individualism dominates social life and undermines the beneficial health effects of social support. Wilkinson claims that to live in a society characterized by inequality and social disintegration is to "feel depressed, cheated, bitter, desperate, vulnerable, frightened, angry, worried about debts or job and housing insecurity; to feel devalued, useless, helpless, uncared for, hopeless, isolated, anxious and a failure" (1996, p. 215), and that these feelings harm health. This social psychological mechanism may help to account for high correlations between income inequality and measures of population health that are sometimes observed in samples of advanced industrial societies.

Poor health in high-inequality societies has also been explained as a result of societal underinvestment in pro-health physical, human, and cultural capital, including medical services, education, and cultural activities (Lynch & Kaplan, 1997). These claims overlap with Wilkinson's, because they argue that this underinvestment hurts health, in part, because it undermines social cohesion. However,

John Lynch and George Kaplan (1997) focus instead on conditions experienced in everyday life and deemphasize the emotional experience of inequality. Some theorists consider relative deprivation the link between income inequality and health. Relative deprivation theorists generally argue that the perception that one has less than others causes psychological stress, which produces ill health. This reasoning suggests that income inequality harms population health because it intensifies this relative deprivation. Some researchers emphasize both social cohesion and relative deprivation as important determinants of health. Controversies surround the finding of a correlation between income inequality and health, with some researchers questioning the generality of the correlation (Beckfield, 2004; Wilkinson & Pickett, 2006).

Research on income inequality is enjoying a renaissance, and there are a number of opportunities for further work in this theory-rich and policy-relevant area. Research that addresses the debates above is clearly needed, as is further work to address two major gaps in the literature: (a) an inadequate understanding of how inequality among groups within national societies relates to the overall level of income inequality, and (b) an inadequate understanding of how international forces affect income inequality among and within national societies. First, although early-21st-century research on inequality within the United States has focused on the roles of gender discrimination (Correll et al., 2007), racial discrimination (Pager, 2003), social networks (Mouw, 2003), and cultural dynamics of child-rearing strategies (Lareau, 2003) in explaining economic outcomes for different groups within the United States, this work is rarely connected to the level and trend in income inequality. Second, the ongoing formation of international economic and political networks raises new questions about how changes in the scale of social action and institutions affect and are affected by patterns of income inequality.

SEE ALSO Volume 2: *Economic Restructuring; Educational Attainment; Employment, Adulthood; Globalization; Occupations; Poverty, Adulthood; Saving;* Volume 3: *Wealth.*

BIBLIOGRAPHY

Alderson, A. S., Beckfield, J., & Nielsen, F. (2005). Exactly how has income inequality changed? Patterns of distributional change in core societies. *International Journal of Comparative Sociology, 46,* 405–423.

Alderson, A. S., & Nielsen, F. (2002). Globalization and the great U-turn: Income inequality trends in 16 OECD countries. *American Journal of Sociology, 107*(5), 1244–1299.

Beckfield, J. (2004). Does income inequality harm health? New cross-national evidence. *Journal of Health and Social Behavior, 45*(3), 231–248.

Beckfield, J. (2006). European integration and income inequality. *American Sociological Review, 71*(6), 964–985.

Chase-Dunn, C. (1975). The effects of international economic dependence on development and inequality: A cross-national study. *American Sociological Review, 40*(6), 720–738.

Correll, S., Benard, S., & Paik, I. (2007). Getting a job: Is there a motherhood penalty? *American Journal of Sociology, 112*(5), 1297–1338.

Firebaugh, G. (2003). New geography of global income inequality. Cambridge, MA: Harvard University Press.

Fischer, C. S., Hout, M., Sanchez-Jankowski, M., Lucas, S. R., Swidler, A., & Voss, K. (1996). *Inequality by design: Cracking the bell-curve myth.* Princeton, NJ: Princeton University Press.

Lareau, A. (2003). *Unequal childhoods: Class, race, and family life.* Berkeley: University of California Press.

Luxembourg Income Study. Updated April 29, 2008. Retrieved April 30, 2008, from http://lisproject.org

Lynch, J. W., & Kaplan, G. A. (1997). Understanding how inequality in the distribution of income affects health. *Journal of Health Psychology, 2*(3), 297–314.

Morgan, S. L., Grusky, D. B., & Fields, G. S. (Eds.). (2006). *Mobility and inequality: Frontiers of research from sociology and economics.* Stanford, CA: Stanford University Press.

Mouw, T. (2003). Social capital and finding a job: Do contacts matter? *American Sociological Review, 68*(6), 868–898.

Neckerman, K. (Ed.). (2004). *Social inequality.* New York: Russell Sage Foundation.

Neckerman, K., & Torche, F. (2007). Inequality: Causes and consequences. *Annual Review of Sociology, 33,* 335–357.

Pager, D. (2003). The mark of a criminal record. *American Journal of Sociology, 108*(5), 937–975.

Pitt Inequality Project. Retrieved April 30, 2008, from http://www.pitt.edu/inequal/

Wilkinson, R.G. (1996). *Unhealthy societies: The afflictions of inequality.* London: Routledge.

Wilkinson, R. G., & Pickett, K. E. (2006). Income inequality and population health: A review and explanation of the evidence. *Social Science and Medicine, 62*(7), 1768–1784.

Jason Beckfield

INDIVIDUATION/ STANDARDIZATION DEBATE

Social scientists have a long-standing interest in the structure of the life course, that is, in the occurrence, timing, and order of social roles over people's life spans and how these patterns are shaped by sociohistorical conditions. Such interests are two-fold. In one respect, variation in whether, when, and how people move into adult social roles has implications for social achievement, social standing, social experience, as well as one's identity, attitudes, and emotions. For example, the often contentious issue of teen parenthood typically reflects concern about the implications of a major life transition occurring at too young of an age, prior to other life transitions (such

as finishing school), or in the absence of potentially complementary transitions (such as marriage). Yet in another respect, the variable unfolding of human lives is informative about the societies around them. Different societies foster distinctive pathways through life and thus reveal the presence of cultural norms, scripts, and sociostructural contexts that shape how lives unfold. In this regard, the life course is often examined as a window into the modernization and development of societies.

Although analysis of the life course extends back to the 19th century, the dramatic social changes of the 20th and early 21st centuries set the stage for volumes of research. The central issue at hand was how core changes in the nature of society restructured, perhaps even radically so, the individual life course. The empirical aspect of this work is simple in the sense that researchers are largely interested in how, if at all, the life course differs from that of earlier societies or varies across cultures. Yet, the study of the life course is also complex in that there is little agreement on how such comparisons should be made. Available data are often sparse and not well-suited to comparison, and the technological advances in statistical methodology that would allow for systematic comparison are in their infancy.

Nevertheless, contemporary research has done much to increase understanding of social change and the life course and has led an important debate. On one side, some scholars argue that the life course is increasingly *individualized* as pathways through life are increasingly diverse and unanchored from mainstream social institutions and social locations (Buchmann, 1989). Such an argument challenges long-held views that human lives were *standardized* in the 20th century by the increasing importance of institutions such as formal education, work, and law and the emergence of a world society. A number of other terms are used to describe the sides in this debate, including *institutionalization, deinstitutionalization destandardization, differentiation, dedifferentiation,* and *pluralization,* but their distinction from the ideas of individualization and standardization is more subtle than substantive (Bruckner & Mayer, 2005).

THEORIES OF STANDARDIZATION AND INDIVIDUALIZATION

In many respects, arguments for the standardization of the life course are a logical extension of broader arguments about the modernization of societies and their implications for personal and social behavior. Martin Kohli (1986), for example, argued that the modern organization of public services and employment opportunities by age creates a more orderly and homogenous life cycle. Laws regarding age at marriage, mandatory participation in education, and employment establish generic starting lines for life transitions. Likewise, the increased rationality of education and employment in Western nations helped to standardize exits from schooling and thus created similarity in transition ages. Although the evidence to date is thin, there are also grounds to expect that cross-national variation in the life course has diminished with increasing globalization and the emergence of a one-world society linked through shared economies, politics, and social institutions.

The idea of a standardized life course was highly prevalent in the late 1970s and 1980s. This is not surprising given that researchers of the time were typically considering data from the first half of the 20th century and referencing the profound changes in culture and economy that accompanied the post–World War II (1939–1945) era. Specifically, the postwar economic boom led to the regulation of the life course in that males, White males in particular, could finish secondary education (or not), could move into jobs that paid a living wage, and could earn enough to both purchase a house and support a wife and children. Given the emergence of a strong middle class, at least among Whites, it is not surprising that the economic conditions of the era produced a highly regulated life course. Sociologist Dennis Hogan (1978) was among the first to empirically document this *orderly* or *normative* life course whereby people finished school, entered full-time employment, and then proceed to get married and have children, all of which was seen as a rational, almost taken-for-granted response to the economic and cultural conditions of the day.

A view that located the life course in the economic, cultural, and political contexts of society was a logical way of making sense of changes in lives over the 20th century. However, this perspective produced a new set of arguments to accompany the changing conditions of the late 20th century. These arguments emphasized the individualization of the life course and ultimately challenged the earlier standardization thesis. It is difficult to locate exactly where the individualization argument first arose, but it was clearly a reaction to the changing nature of society. Sociologist Michael Shanahan (2000) suggested that an individualization argument had its roots in the decline of family and community, which increasingly freed people from traditional sources of social control and thus allowed them to exercise greater agency in structuring their lives. Likewise, Marlis Buchmann (1989) suggested that the standardized trajectories of the past were "shattered" by structural and cultural change. Among the most significant of these were the increased disconnect between educational attainment and occupational standing, the diminished value of occupational training and expertise, changes in the family involving increased rates of cohabitation and parenthood outside of marriage, and an increase in cultural emphases on emotional well-being through individuality. These forces unanchored the modern life course from regulated and regulating institutions and increased the significance of flexibility, choice, and personality in shaping life paths.

THE STATE OF THE EVIDENCE: WHAT IS KNOWN AND WHAT SHOULD BE KNOWN

Adjudicating among these different arguments is complicated by the fact that there is no agreed-on standard of evaluation and a variety of data has been brought to bear on the issue. Ideally, one would like longitudinal data that covers a number of historical periods. Such data are rare and in many cases nonexistent. As a result, researchers have marshaled data from a wide variety of sources to speak to the key issues. Based on such data, several conclusions can be drawn and several questions remain.

First, it seems clear that the time line for the transition to adulthood became compressed and that standard transitions increased in prevalence through much of the 20th century. John Modell, Frank Furstenberg, and Theodore Hershberg (1976), for example, showed that the time it took 80% of the population to leave their family of origin (i.e., their parents' home), marry, and establish their own household declined significantly between 1880 and 1970. Consistent with this, other research shows that increasing proportions of the population followed a typical or normative life course pattern through the 19th and 20th centuries (Hogan, 1981).

Second, life courses in the late 20th century did have some seemingly unique features. First, the pursuit of higher education became much more prevalent, and thus education characterized a longer period of the life course for a larger percentage of people. Movement into full-time, career-type work was delayed as people increasingly pursued college educations in the hopes of securing better jobs. Yet the labor market itself was less accommodating, which made job entry an even longer and more tenuous process. One corollary to this was an increased overlap between schooling and work, such that full-time students also spent long hours working for pay. At the same time, the age at which people married for the first time increased, in part due to the changes in education and work. In some cases, this produced a re-nesting effect whereby single men and women returned to their parents' home after graduating from college (Goldscheider & Goldscheider, 1999). Coupled with advances in contraceptive technology, later marriage meant that childbearing also occurred later in the life course, creating a phenomenon that sociologists Claude Fischer and Michael Hout (2006) characterized as people having their "third and fourth child" without having their first and second. In addition, new family arrangements became more common—notably cohabitation and nonmarital childbearing—and divorce rates increased sharply. When all these factors are put together, the lockstep, sequential, and orderly life course of the past has given way to an increasingly elongated, increasingly disorderly, and increasingly variable and differentiated process.

Although the demographic reality of the contemporary life course is not strongly disputed, the weight of the evidence supports neither a pure standardization nor a pure individualization perspective. To some extent, this may be because adjudicating between theories, both of which may be partially correct and which concern historically contingent processes, is an unrealistic goal. At the same time, future study could greatly increase understanding of how life courses are constructed, how life courses vary across gender, racial, ethnic, and social class subgroups in society, and whether and how life courses have changed over time. For example, relatively few studies have linked the social psychological processes integral to the individualization thesis to the demographic behavior of the individuals. Future research should focus on opening the "black box" of human agency in the construction of the life course. Several studies have been attentive to the variety of life course pathways, both within and across social groups, yet future research should seek to formally model heterogeneity in pathways through the life span. In the latter respect, social demographer Elizabeth Fussell (2005) has pioneered techniques to systematically document variation in the life course over time, techniques that should lead the way for a new generation of scholarship. Accompanying such work should be systematic comparisons of longitudinal data from comparable samples from different historical periods. Although the latter approach may require unique data collections, as well as creative use of existing data, it could greatly enhance understanding of the past, present, and future of the life course.

Ultimately, the debate over standardization and individualization highlights changes in the life course and provides concepts for making sense of broad and multifaceted change. More research is needed to show how, if at all, the life course has changed and whether it has changed in the ways that individualization advocates argue. Still, it is difficult not to recognize the complexity of contemporary life paths and treat them and their consequences as an important area of study. As Frank Furstenberg, Sheela Kennedy, Vonnie McLloyd, Rubén Rumbaut, and Richard Settersten (2006) provocatively suggest, the contemporary life course, whether truly "individualized" or not, is a time when "growing up is harder to do."

SEE ALSO Volume 2: *Agency; Careers; Globalization.*

BIBLIOGRAPHY

Booth, A., Crouter, A., & Shanahan, M. (1999). *Transitions to adulthood in a changing economy: No work, no family, no future?* Westport, CT: Praeger.

Bruckner, H., & Mayer, K. (2005). Destandardization of the life course: What it might mean? And if it means anything, whether it actually took place? In. R. Macmillan (Ed.), *The structure of the life course: Classic issues and current controversies* (pp. 27–54). Oxford, U.K.: Elsevier.

Buchmann, M. (1989). *The script of life in modern society: Entry into adulthood in a changing world.* Chicago: University of Chicago Press.

Fischer, C. S., & Hout, M. (2006). *Century of difference: How America changed in the last 100 years.* New York: Russell Sage Foundation.

Furstenberg, F. (2007). *Destinies of the disadvantaged: The politics of teenage childbearing.* New York: Russell Sage Foundation.

Furstenberg, F., Kennedy, S., McLloyd, V., Rumbaut, R., & Settersten, R. (2006). Growing up is harder to do. *Contexts, 3*(3), 33–41.

Fussell, E. (2005). Measuring the early adult life course in Mexico: An application of the entropy index. In. R. Macmillan (Ed.), *The structure of the life course: Classic issues and current controversies* (pp. 91–122). Oxford, U.K.: Elsevier.

Fussell, E., & Furstenberg, F. (2006). The transition to adulthood in the 20th century: Race, nativity, and gender. In F. Furstenberg, R. Rumbaut, & R. Settersten (Eds.), *On the frontier of adulthood: Theory, research, and public policy* (pp. 29–75). Chicago: University of Chicago Press.

Golfscheider, F., & Goldscheider, C. (1999). *The changing transition to adulthood: Leaving and returning home.* Thousand Oaks, CA: Sage.

Hogan, D. (1978). The variable order of events in the life course. *American Sociological Review, 43*(4), 573–586.

Hogan, D. (1981). *Transitions and social change: The early lives of American men.* New York: Academic Press.

Kohli, M. (1986). The world we forgot: A historical review of the life course. In V. Marshall (Ed.), *Later life: The social psychology of aging* (pp. 271–303). Beverly Hills, CA: Sage.

Macmillan, R. (2005). *The structure of the life course: Classic issues and current controversies.* Oxford, U.K.: Elsevier.

Mayer, K., & Muller, W. (1986). The state and the structure of the life course. In A. Sørenson, F. Weinert, & L. Sherrod (Eds.), *Human development and the life course* (pp. 217–245). Hillsdale, NJ: Lawrence Erlbaum.

Meyer, J. (1986). The self and the life course: Institutionalization and its effects. In A. Sørenson, F. Weinert, & L. Sherrod (Eds.), *Human development and the life course* (pp. 199–216). Hillsdale, NJ: Lawrence Erlbaum.

Modell, J., Furstenberg, F., & Hershberg, T. (1976). Social change and transitions to adulthood in historical perspective. *Journal of Family History, 1*, 7–32.

National Research Council, Panel on Transitions to Adulthood in Developing Countries. (2005). *Growing up global: The changing transitions to adulthood in developing countries.* Washington, DC: National Academies Press.

Rindfuss, R., Swicegood, G., & Rosenfeld, R. (1989). Disorder in the life course: How common and does it really matter? *American Sociological Review, 52*(6), 785–801.

Shanahan, M. (2000). Pathways to adulthood in changing societies: Variability and mechanisms in life course perspective. *Annual Review of Sociology, 26*, 667–692.

Ulhenberg, P. (1969). A study of cohort life cycles: Cohorts of native-born Massachusetts women, 1830–1920. *Population Studies*, 23(3), 407–420.

Ross Macmillan

INFERTILITY

Infertility is defined as the inability to obtain and sustain a pregnancy after 12 months of regular, unprotected intercourse. Fertility problems are estimated to affect between 15% and 20% of couples of reproductive age (Tierney, McPhee, & Papadakis, 1999, p. 913). Infertility generally affects women and men equally, with approximately one-third of fertility problems in couples being attributed to female factors, close to one-third to male factors, and one-third to both male and female factors or remaining unexplained (Tierney et al., 1999, p. 913).

Infertility is fundamentally physiological, although the physiological condition may have social precursors. In males, the most common fertility problems are *oligospermia*, a deficiency in the number of sperm in the seminal fluid, or *azoospermia*, the absence or near absence of sperm. Until the late 20th century, fertility problems in females were primarily caused by endocrine imbalances or anatomical impairments, such as blocked fallopian tubes or endometriosis. However, since the late 20th century an increasing number of men and women have been choosing to delay parenthood well into their thirties and forties—attempting to fulfill their educational and career aspirations prior to becoming parents.

Despite the growing number of women and men having children at later ages, many who delay parenthood find that they cannot achieve a viable pregnancy. Fertility typically begins to decline for women in their 30s due to changes in endocrine functioning and aging eggs. Also, as a woman ages the risk of spontaneous miscarriage and congenital abnormalities increases, further compromising her chances of a successful pregnancy. There is evidence that as a man ages, his fertility declines as well due to diminished quality of the sperm (Tierney et al., 1999). When the male partner is older, his female partner has a greater risk of miscarriage and there is also a greater risk of genetic disorders in the child (Sloter, Nath, Eskenazi, and Wyrobek, 2004). These facts have contributed to an increase in the number of individuals and couples in their thirties and forties who turn to medical technology in their efforts to produce a child.

The advancement of reproductive knowledge and technologies in the 20th and 21st centuries has provided many couples with an explanation of, and treatment for, their infertility. These technologies include the use of fertility drugs, *in vitro* fertilization (IVF), intracytoplasmic sperm injection (ICSI), egg-freezing, the use of donor sperm and/or eggs, surrogacy, and gestational care (Tierney et al., 1999). The American Society for Reproductive Medicine (ASRM) reported that as of 2002 almost 300,000 babies were born in the United States alone as a result of advancements in reproductive technologies (American Society for Reproductive Medicine, 2008). Despite these advances, medical intervention results in a viable pregnancy for only 30% to 60% of couples using such treatments, depending on the cause of their infertility (Tierney et al., 1999). For a significant number of infertile individuals and couples medical treatment fails, so they face the difficult task of coming to terms with permanent biological childlessness.

THE PSYCHOSOCIAL IMPACT OF INFERTILITY

Most individuals assume they are fertile and have control over if and when they will become parents. Consequently, a diagnosis of infertility is usually met with disbelief. Initially couples may be surprised that they are not getting pregnant, but after several months the idea that they might be infertile seeps into their awareness and they seek medical care. When a diagnosis of infertility is confirmed, couples need to decide whether they want and can afford to pursue fertility treatments, which can cost more than $10,000 per treatment cycle (Garcia, 1998). Because multiple attempts are often required to produce a viable pregnancy, couples must also decide how many treatment cycles they are willing and financially able to undergo and when treatment must be abandoned. They may also face ethically and morally difficult decisions about which treatments they are comfortable pursuing, particularly in the case of third-party options such as donated embryos or surrogacy. In an attempt to make sense of their infertility, many turn inward and wonder what they could have done to cause their infertility.

In most cultures, parenthood is seen as an important benchmark of healthy adult development. Fertility also is associated with femininity and masculinity. Consequently, infertility is a major life crisis for most couples—one that is characterized by multiple losses. Feelings of sadness, grief, anger, inadequacy, and depression are common in response to infertility, according to Judith C. Daniluk (2001b). Caren Jordan & Tracey A. Revenson (1999) indicate this is particularly the case for women, whose bodies bear the primary burden of medical testing and treatments and who tend to be held socially accountable for a couple's infertility. Russell E. Webb and Daniluk (1999) point out that men also struggle with coming to terms with infertility—feeling powerless in being unable to give their partner a child

WOMEN WAITING TOO LONG TO BECOME MOTHERS

■

Increasingly, women in developed nations are delaying motherhood to pursue their educational and career goals and attain stability in their finances and relationships. However, concerns have been raised about the higher risks of birth defects, prenatal complications, and premature births for older mothers, leading some to suggest that delaying motherhood is not advantageous to mothers or their children. Early 21st century advances in reproductive technology, which appear to offer solutions to some of the fertility problems associated with age, may offer women a false sense of security, leaving many to face infertility and childlessness in the future. There has also been considerable debate in the media about the motivations of women who elect to become mothers in their 50s and 60s and about the potential health of these mothers who may not be able, or available, to raise these children. As this debate rages, reproductive technologies continue to advance. Such is the current state of the brave new world of reproductive technologies.

and questioning their own masculinity when faced with a diagnosis of male factor infertility.

Research, such as that done by Frank M. Andrews, Antonia Abbey, and L. Jill Halman (1991), indicates that men's and women's psychosocial distress increases during what are often very time-consuming fertility treatments. The invasiveness of medical tests, assessments, and treatments is emotionally and physically taxing and frequently places considerable stress on both members of the couple and on their relationship (Daniluk, 2001b; Leiblum, 1997). Couples refer to the "emotional rollercoaster" of infertility treatment—feeling hopeful and optimistic at the start of each menstrual and treatment cycle, followed by overwhelming sadness and even despair when they face another month without becoming pregnant. Infertility also takes a tremendous toll on a couple's sexual relationship as sex for pleasure is replaced by sex for procreation, and a once satisfying, spontaneous, and intimate act becomes paired with repeated failure (Leiblum, 1997; Pepe & Byrne, 2005). Patients also describe feeling a loss of control given that fertility investigations and treatments are focused on the most intimate and private parts of their lives and bodies.

If treatment fails or couples reach the end of their emotional or financial resources, they must make the painful transition to biological childlessness (Daniluk, 2001a; Daniluk and Tench, 2007; Leiblum, Aviv, and Hamer, 1998). For Americans this transition occurs in a context where parenthood is seen as central to constructing meaning in one's life and is viewed as a key milestone in adult development. There are few acceptable alternative models of healthy and normative female development for women who are childless, Mardy S. Ireland (1993) explains. In a society where *family* is defined by parental status, those whose biological childlessness is permanent must construct a healthy identity and a meaningful life that does not include the norm of biological parenthood (Daniluk, 2001a). Once treatment fails and the option of parenting their biological progeny is exhausted, couples also must determine which, if any, other parenting options—such as adoption—are available and acceptable to them. Research suggests that in time most couples come to terms with their biological childlessness and live satisfying lives, whether or not they elect to pursue other parenting options such as adoption (Daniluk, 2001a).

POLICY ISSUES

The creation of life outside of the private act of intercourse carries with it considerable ethical, moral, and legal consequences and raises important questions. Reproductive science and technology have advanced and continue to advance at a rate that outpaces society's ability to respond proactively to the potential implications of these newly created family forms. Children can now be born after one or both of their genetic parents have passed away, families can be intentionally created with only one parent, children can be born into families with no knowledge of or information about their genetic fathers or mothers, parents can have their embryos screened to ensure that their children have particular desired characteristics (e.g., gender), children can be created for the express purpose of being tissue or organ donors for a sick sibling, women can gestate and give birth to a child to whom they have no genetic connection, mothers can carry children for their infertile daughters, and women in their fifties and sixties can give birth to children through the use of donated eggs and sometimes sperm. While the governments in many countries of the world (e.g., Australia, the U.K., and Canada) have imposed regulations on the fertility industry, no such national regulations existed in the United States in the early 2000s. Each state had its own laws regarding the acceptability of particular treatments—resulting in reproductive tourism, couples traveling to other states to access treatment options not available to them in their home state.

The issue of cost is also problematic, given that insurance coverage for reproductive treatments is not available through the majority of managed health-care plans. In

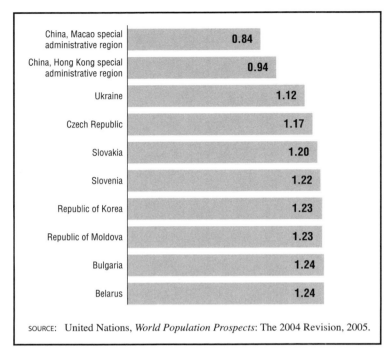

China, Macao special administrative region	0.84
China, Hong Kong special administrative region	0.94
Ukraine	1.12
Czech Republic	1.17
Slovakia	1.20
Slovenia	1.22
Republic of Korea	1.23
Republic of Moldova	1.23
Bulgaria	1.24
Belarus	1.24

SOURCE: United Nations, *World Population Prospects*: The 2004 Revision, 2005.

10 Places with the Lowest Total Fertility Worldwide. Average number of children per woman, 2000–2005. CENGAGE LEARNING, GALE.

1998 Garcia estimated the cost of a live birth through in-vitro fertilization (IVF) to be $66,000, meaning that advanced reproductive technologies are restricted to the economically privileged. Although some fertility centers offer couples who cannot afford treatment the option of cost reduction or deferral if the patient agrees to donate a percentage of her eggs to another couple, serious concerns have been raised about the ethics of this exchange.

Questions also have been raised about the rights of children who are conceived using third-party reproduction to know the circumstances surrounding their conception and to have information about their medical and genetic histories. There is ambiguity and lack of regulatory laws concerning suitable compensation for surrogates and gestational carriers and concern about the economic coercion of young women to become egg donors to offset their personal debts or educational costs. The birth of twins in 2006 to a 67-year-old single woman in Spain has also reignited the worldwide debate about the upper age at which women, and in some cases their male partners, should be able to use technology to pursue a pregnancy. At the heart of the debate is concern about the health and mortality of these older mothers, which may preclude their ability to raise their children to adulthood.

Although the American Society for Reproductive Medicine has created best practice guidelines for the provision of fertility treatments, physicians and health care providers who are not members of ASRM are not bound by these guidelines. Clearly there is much work to be done to deal with the immediate and long-term ramifications for the individuals and families involved in these treatments and for the children created as a consequence.

SEE ALSO Volume 1: *Adopted Children;* Volume 2: *Adoptive Parents; Childlessness; Menopause.*

BIBLIOGRAPHY

American Society of Reproductive Medicine. (2008). *Frequently asked questions about infertility*. Retrieved June 19, 2008, from http://www.asrm.org/Patients/faqs.html

Andrews, F. M., Abbey, A., & Halman, J. (1991). Stress from infertility, marriage factors, and subjective well-being of wives and husbands. *Journal of Health and Social Behavior, 32,* 238–253.

Daniluk, J. C. (2001a). Reconstructing their lives: A longitudinal, qualitative analysis of the transition to biological childlessness for infertile couples. *Journal of Counseling and Development, 79,* 439–449.

Daniluk, J. C. (2001b). *The infertility survival guide: Everything you need to know to cope with the challenges while maintaining your sanity, dignity, and relationships*. Oakland, CA: Harbinger Publications.

Daniluk, J. C., & Tench, E. (2007). Long-term adjustment of infertile couples following unsuccessful medical intervention. *Journal of Counseling and Development, 85,* 89–100.

Domar, A. D., & Boivin, J. (2007, April). Two views: Should mental health professionals encourage infertile patients to try complimentary therapies. *Debate: Society for Reproductive Medicine*, 30–32.

Garcia, J. E. (1998). Profiling assisted reproductive technology: The Society for Assisted Reproductive Technology registry and the rising costs of assisted reproductive technology. *Fertility and Sterility, 69*, 624–626.

Hammer Burns, L., & Covington, S. N. (Eds.). (2006). *Infertility counseling: A comprehensive handbook for clinicians.* (2nd ed.). New York: Cambridge University Press.

Ireland, M. (1993). *Reconceiving women: Separating motherhood from female identity.* New York: Guilford Press.

Jordon, C., & Revenson, T. A. (1999). Gender differences in coping with infertility: Meta-analysis. *Journal of Behavioral Medicine, 22*(4), 341–358.

Leiblum, S. R. (1997). Love, sex and infertility: The impact of infertility on couples. In S. R. Leiblum (Ed.), *Infertility: Psychological issues and coping strategies* (pp. 149–166). New York: Wiley.

Leiblum S. R., Aviv, A., & Hamer, R. (1998). Life after infertility treatment: A long-term investigation of marital and sexual function. *Human Reproduction, 13*(12), 3569–3574.

Martin, J. A., Hamilton, B. E., Sutton, P. D., Ventura, S. J., Menacker, F., Kirmeyer, S., et al. (2007). *Births: Final data for 2005.* Hyattsville, MD: National Center for Health Statistics.

Sloter, E., Nath, J., Eskenazi, B., & Wyrobek, A. J. (2004). Effects of male age on the frequencies of germinal and heritable chromosomal abnormalities in humans and rodents. *Fertility and Sterility, 81*, 925-943.

Pepe, M. V., & Byrne, T. J. (2005). Women's perceptions of immediate and long-term effects of failed infertility treatment on marital and sexual satisfaction. *Family Relations, 40*, 303–309.

Tierney, L. M., McPhee, S. J., & Papadakis, M. A. (1999). *Current medical diagnosis and treatment.* East Norwalk, CT: Appleton and Lange.

Webb, R., & Daniluk, J. C. (1999). The end of the line: Infertile men's experiences of being unable to produce a child. *Men and Masculinity, 2*(1), 6–25.

Judith Daniluk
Emily Koert

J

JOB CHANGE

Over the course of their working lives, individuals often change jobs. Sometimes this mobility is involuntary, as when workers are permanently laid off or fired and must seek new employment. More commonly, workers choose to change jobs in search of better pay or benefits, more interesting work, or to find an arrangement that better accommodates family responsibilities. Job changes play an important role in shaping workers' career trajectories over the life course.

JOB CHANGES OVER
THE LIFE COURSE

Job changing is particularly common during the early career. Economic models suggest that workers will look for new jobs when they believe they can offset the costs of the search by finding a new position that offers higher wages, better working conditions, or other benefits. "Job shopping" is particularly useful for workers who lack experience in the labor market because it helps them discover which jobs will be most rewarding. Over time, workers should improve the quality of their job matches, reducing the likelihood of making gains by switching (Burdett, 1978).

In the period after World War II, ultimately settling down and staying with an employer offered important advantages to a substantial share of workers. Robert Althauser and Arne Kalleberg (1981) explained that in exchange for investing in skills and training of value to their current employer, but not necessarily of value to a wide array of other potential employers, workers were rewarded for seniority, gaining job security and regular pay raises. The ideal-typical pattern of job mobility over the life course was thus one of early job changes succeeded by long-term stable employment with a single employer.

TRENDS IN JOB CHANGING

In recent years, there has been concern that changes in the U.S. economy have weakened bonds between employers and workers, with more and more workers experiencing multiple spells of short-term employment (Baron & Pfeffer, 1998). Studies assessing this possible phenomenon typically measure the flip side of job changes—how long jobs last (job stability). Most commonly, researchers measure trends in job stability by studying changes in tenure distributions (the share of workers who have remained with their employers for different lengths of time) or retention rates (the likelihood that jobs will last for a specified period of time). Although stability has declined in some industrialized countries, a study by the Organisation for Economic Co-operation and Development (1997) showed that this is not a universal trend. In the United States, overall job stability declined between the 1970s and early 1980s, was relatively stable between the 1980s and 1990s, and then declined between the late 1980s and mid-1990s (Neumark, Polsky, & Hansen, 1999).

Although job stability has not declined substantially overall, research by David Neumark, Daniel Polsky, and Daniel Hansen (1999) revealed differences among subgroups. Between the 1970s and 1990s, job stability in the United States declined most sharply for Black workers, both male and female. At the same time, job stability rose

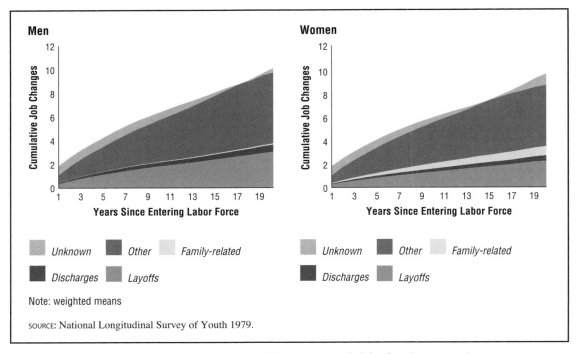

Men

Women

Unknown *Other* *Family-related*

Discharges *Layoffs*

Unknown *Other* *Family-related*

Discharges *Layoffs*

Note: weighted means

SOURCE: National Longitudinal Survey of Youth 1979.

Figure 1. *Cumulative job changes of American workers during the first 20 years in the labor force (1979–2004).* CENGAGE LEARNING, GALE.

among White women as their attachment to the labor market increased. Throughout the 1980s younger workers and those who had started their jobs relatively recently experienced declines in stability, but in the first years of the 1990s job stability declined more among workers who had held their jobs for a relatively long time.

JOB CHANGE PATTERNS

Not all workers follow the same job change trajectories. Workers in European countries and Japan tend to change jobs less frequently than their North American counterparts (Organisation for Economic Co-operation and Development, 1997). Industry, occupation, and worker characteristics all shape the likelihood of job changes in each country. Employers have less incentive to reward worker loyalty with job security or wage premiums when their jobs are not perceived to require specialized skills. In the United States, according to Paul Ryscavage's analysis in 1997, workers are most likely to stay with the same employer in public administration, manufacturing, transportation, communication, and other utilities and least likely to stay with the same employer in entertainment, recreation services, agriculture, forestry, fisheries, personal services, and business services. Worker characteristics are also associated with differences in job change patterns. On average, younger workers, the less educated, and women are more likely to leave their jobs (Ryscavage, 1997).

Workers also differ in the types of job changes they undergo. The best information about these patterns is based on longitudinal data from surveys of younger workers. Among young men, Hyunjoon Park and Gary Sandefur (2003) found that higher turnover among Black and less educated workers is largely a function of their higher likelihood of involuntary job changes. Gender differences in cumulative voluntary job changes and layoffs are not large among younger workers, but Sylvia Fuller (2008) indicated that women are more likely to leave jobs for family-related reasons and are less likely to be discharged. Overall, younger women are less likely than younger men to leave employers for a better job but more likely to experience a period of nonemployment between one job and the next. These differences largely reflect the behavior of less educated women, particularly African Americans and Hispanics (Alon & Tienda, 2005).

CONSEQUENCES OF JOB CHANGES

The consequences of job changes are not inherently positive or negative. Worker flows between jobs are an important mechanism by which labor markets adjust as some occupations, industries, and regions experience faster job growth than others. For employers the ability to change the size of the workforce by hiring or laying off workers provides an important source of flexibility. Changing jobs offers workers the possibility of finding more desirable work. Indeed, for young workers in particular, studies by Robert Topel and Michael Ward (1992) reported a substantial share of wage growth occurs via job mobility.

At the same time, job changing can have a darker side. Whereas voluntary job changes and those whereby a worker moves directly from one job to another typically raise wages; layoffs, discharges, family-related job changes, and changes that involve an intervening period of unemployment or labor force withdrawal usually result in wage losses. Moreover, even the threat of job loss is stressful. Perceptions of job insecurity can negatively affect physical and mental health according to Magnus Sverke, Johnny Hellgren, and Katharina Näswall (2002).

Work by Audrey Light (2005) showed that the outcomes of mobility are also worse for workers who change jobs more frequently. In part this is because workers who experience frequent mobility tend to spend more time not employed (Light, 2005). There is also some evidence for a high-mobility penalty, suggesting that workers who change jobs frequently are stigmatized by employers (Fuller, 2008). High-mobility workers may also experience less social protection because regulatory and welfare systems have been built on a normative model of employment that presumes a relatively stable career. In the United States, for example, job changes commonly result in a loss of employer provided health insurance (Ryscavage, 1997).

FUTURE DIRECTIONS FOR RESEARCH

Contemporary research on job changing largely focuses on isolated or one-time events. More research that investigates patterns and consequences of different types of job changes over the course of workers' careers is needed. Closely attending to how institutional contexts shape job changes is also needed to clarify reasons for cross-national differences in job mobility patterns and trends. Further research is necessary to understand how variation in job mobility norms across occupational and industrial sectors shapes the consequences of job changes.

Job change patterns and their consequences reflect institutionalized opportunity structures arising from the organization of labor markets and households, as well as normative expectations about how careers should unfold for men and women over the life course. For individuals, they are often turning points in career trajectories, shifting the pace or direction of economic mobility.

SEE ALSO Volume 2: *Careers; Economic Restructuring; Employment, Adulthood; Occupations.*

BIBLIOGRAPHY

Alon, S., & Tienda, M. (2005). Job mobility and early career wage growth of White, African American, and Hispanic women. *Social Science Quarterly, 86,* 1198–1217.

Althauser, R. P., & Kalleberg, A. L. (1981). Firms, occupations, and the structure of labor markets: A conceptual analysis. In I. Berg (Ed.), *Sociological perspectives on labor markets* (pp. 119–149). New York: Academic Press.

Baron, J. N., & Pfeffer, J. (1998). Taking the workers back out: Recent trends in the structuring of employment. In B. M. Straw & L. L. Cummings (Eds.), *Research in organizational behavior* (Vol. 10, pp. 257–303). Greenwich, CT: JAI Press.

Burdett, K. (1978). A theory of employer job search and quit rates. *American Economic Review, 68,* 212–220.

Fuller, S. (2008). Job mobility and wage trajectories for men and women in the United States. *American Sociological Review, 73*(1), 158–183.

Light, A. (2005). Job mobility and wage growth: Evidence from the NLSY79. *Monthly Labor Review* (February), 33–39.

Neumark, D., Polsky, D., & Hansen, D. (1999). Has job stability declined yet? New evidence for the 1990s. *Journal of Labor Economics, 17*(4), S29–S45.

Organisation for Economic Co-operation and Development. (1997). *Employment outlook.* Paris: Author.

Park, H., & Sandefur, G. D. (2003). Racial/ethnic differences in voluntary and involuntary job mobility among young men. *Social Science Research, 32*(3), 347–375.

Ryscavage, P. (1997). *Dynamics of economic well-being: Labor force and income, 1991–1993.* Washington, DC: U.S. Census Bureau.

Sverke, M., Hellgren, J., & Näswall, K. (2002). No security: A meta-analysis and review of job insecurity and its consequences. *Journal of Occupational Health Psychology, 7*(3), 242–264.

Topel, R. H., & Ward, M. P. (1992). Job mobility and the careers of young men. *The Quarterly Journal of Economics, 107*(2), 439–480.

Sylvia Fuller

JOB CHARACTERISTICS AND JOB STRESS

For most individuals, working for pay is an important social role during adult life. However, the experiences people have on the job and over the working career vary considerably, due in part to differences in the characteristics of their jobs. Particular job characteristics can contribute to job stress and in turn affect individual well-being and family functioning. Differences in job characteristics and job stress thus help to explain differential life trajectories between socially advantaged and disadvantaged groups.

DEFINING AND MEASURING JOB CHARACTERISTICS AND JOB STRESS

Jobs have been characterized on a variety of dimensions. A key conceptual distinction is between what could be labeled *objective* or *structural* job characteristics—those easily visible to an outside observer and similar for all incumbents in a particular occupation—versus more *subjective* or *psychosocial* job characteristics—those that depend on a worker's interpretation of working conditions. Objective job characteristics that have been linked to job stress include physical and environmental exposures (i.e., heavy labor, hazardous conditions, exposure to loud noise, heat, or fumes), scheduling of work hours (i.e., night hours and shift work), number of hours worked (i.e., part time, full time, or overtime hours), and the type of employment contract held—standard (full time, with expectation of continued employment) versus nonstandard (part-time, temporary, independent contracting, etc.). Robert Karasek's (1979) model of job strain, which posits that jobs that combine low control over tasks with high demands are more hazardous to health than jobs that have one or neither of these conditions, is central to analyses of the psychosocial characteristics of jobs. A related model is Johannes Siegrist's (1996) conceptualization of effort-reward imbalance, which characterizes jobs for which workers expend high effort but receive low rewards. Another important subjective stressor is perceived job insecurity.

Most of these job characteristics can be classified as chronic, or ongoing, stressors. When an individual faces a threatening stressor, the brain and body respond by releasing both adrenaline and adrenocortical hormones in the so-called fight-or-flight response. In the short run, this response can help a person to respond to a stressful situation. However, if a person is persistently exposed to a stressor and does not have the means to cope with it, dysregulation of the body's response system can occur, leading to health problems (McEwen & Seeman, 1999). While the physiological stress response is the same for everyone, it is clear that people exposed to the same job characteristic are not necessarily affected in the same way. Workers appraise conditions differently, and have differential access to coping resources, social support, and mastery (a global sense of control), all of which could protect against negative consequences of job stress (Pearlin & Skaff, 1996). In addition, whereas some negative job characteristics are relatively normative for certain phases of the life course, such as greater job insecurity early in the career, these work-related stressors may be more harmful to well-being if they occur at nonnormative points in the life course, such as among older workers.

Two main approaches have been used to study job characteristics and job stress. Some studies have relied on more objective observational data about the job characteristics of specific occupations, collected by employers reporting on the characteristics of their workers' jobs (i.e., how many are temporary employees); by governments recording occupational exposures, accidents, or fatalities; or by expert raters who observe a job and report

on its characteristics (i.e., the degree to which a worker must work under pressure of time). Other studies have used survey self-reports by workers themselves about their working conditions, such as their perceived job strain, job insecurity, or work-life conflict.

A debate remains about whether objective observational data, collected by an outsider, or more subjective self-reports, collected from surveys of workers, are a better source of information for understanding the consequences of job stress. Workers' self-reports are the most sensitive measures of an individuals' actual experience on the job because conditions vary considerably even within the same occupation, and because workers also have different levels of coping resources, social support, and mastery. However, self-reports are also vulnerable to a worker's reporting style. Some individuals may report negatively about both their job characteristics and their well-being for other reasons, creating an artificial association between the two. For example, people with high levels of neuroticism may evaluate both their job characteristics and their well-being negatively. Using information about job characteristics obtained from someone other than the worker avoids this problem of spurious association, but provides only a rough estimate of conditions experienced by the many different workers in a given occupation. Furthermore, measures based on outsider observation are costly to collect and the information can become out-of-dateif it is collected infrequently because working conditions in a given occupation often change over time.

TRENDS AND PATTERNS IN JOB CHARACTERISTICS

Job characteristics change as economies transition from agricultural, to industrial, to postindustrial forms of production. The relative importance of physical and environmental hazards at work declines as fewer individuals hold agricultural and manufacturing jobs, whereas the importance of psychosocial stressors rises as the dominance of the service sector grows. When wealthier countries transition toward service-based economies, they often export physically and environmentally hazardous jobs to nations with fewer regulations and more workers willing to perform these jobs for low pay. For example, maquiladoras on the Mexico side of the U.S.-Mexico border employ manufacturing workers who earn ten times less than their counterparts in the United States (Frey, 2003). However, increasing globalization also means that psychosocial stressors, notably perceived job insecurity, may rise for workers in wealthier countries. This is true even for higher-status workers, whose job security falls as technological innovation and the push for enhanced flexibility and competitiveness lead to organizational restructuring and layoffs.

The United States labor market at the turn of the 21st century has seen the creation of new jobs that can be divided roughly into a smaller group of *good* jobs with favorable characteristics and a larger group of *bad* jobs with less favorable characteristics and a higher risk of generating job stress. Many so-called bad jobs in the growing service sector are in customer service occupations (i.e., fast-food restaurant worker), and can be characterized by high strain and low pay, job insecurity, nonstandard employment contracts, and few traditional employment benefits. Ethnic minorities, immigrants, and less-educated people are overrepresented among those in bad jobs, perpetuating inequalities over the life course that these groups face. The gap between advantaged and disadvantaged workers in terms of job characteristics appears to be widening in the United States, though risks such as job insecurity are increasing even for many better educated and higher status workers (Sweet & Meiksins, 2008).

CONSEQUENCES OF JOB CHARACTERISTICS AND JOB STRESS

Considerable research has assessed the consequences of job characteristics and job stress for health outcomes or impaired family functioning among workers across the globe. For example, hard physical work and environmental stressors such as noisy surroundings and dangerous conditions are associated with a variety of outcomes, including increased risk of retiring due to disability among Norwegian employees (Blekesaune & Solem, 2005) and greater risk for work-related injuries among Canadian workers (Karmakar & Breslin, 2008). Jobs involving physical labor and noxious environmental stressors often are held by less-educated workers who have fewer options on the labor market, and these experiences contribute to the poorer health profiles overall for people with low education.

Work schedules, hours, and types of contracts are also linked to worker health. For example, shift work is associated with depressive symptoms among Swedish workers (Bildt & Michelsen, 2002), and overtime hours have been associated with poorer perceived health, more work-related injuries and illnesses, and even increased mortality for U.S. workers (Caruso, Hitchcock, Dick, Russo, & Schmit, 2004). Nonstandard contracts have been linked to a higher risk of traumatic and fatal occupational injuries among temporary workers in Spain when compared to their counterparts with standard contracts (Benavides, Benach, Muntaner, Delclos, Catot, & Amable, 2006). However, the consequences of work scheduling, hours, and nonstandard employment contracts may vary depending on the resources and preferences of the job incumbent. In postindustrial economies, for example, overtime work is increasingly performed by highly-educated professionals, so future research is needed to understand how socially advantaged workers manage these conditions.

Turning to the psychosocial stressors, job strain has been linked to higher risk for cardiovascular disease in an array of studies (Belkic, Landsbergis, Schnall, & Baker, 2004), to musculoskeletal symptoms (Smith & Carayon, 1996), and to poorer mental health (Van der Doef & Maes, 1999). Effort-reward imbalance is associated with a similar array of negative outcomes, including increased risk of cardiovascular disease, depression, alcohol dependence, and poor self-rated health (Siegrist & Marmot, 2004). Finally, perceived job insecurity has been linked with self-rated health and psychiatric morbidity in a variety of contexts (Ferrie, Shipley, Stansfeld, & Marmot, 2002). While job strain appears to be more common for less skilled workers, this and other psychosocial stressors are reported by socially disadvantaged and advantaged workers alike.

Work-family conflict is associated with a variety of clinically significant mental health consequences among U.S. workers, but more attention has been directed at the consequences for family functioning. Either mental distress arising from negative job characteristics or a sense of conflict between work and home roles—work and family strains are mutually influential—can lead to poorer family relations and functioning. In particular, work-family conflict has been linked to lower marital dissatisfaction and various measures of family strain (Allen, Herst, Bruck, & Sutton, 2000). Specific job characteristics are also associated with poorer family functioning. Job strain, for example, is associated with more frequent marital disagreements among U.S. workers (Hughes & Galinsky, 1994), and nonstandard schedules are associated with depressive symptoms in parents, hostile and ineffective parenting, and children's emotional and behavioral difficulties in Canadian dual earner families (Strazdins, Clements, Korda, Broom, & D'Souza, 2006). Finally, some studies suggest that families headed by military personnel may be particularly affected by extreme and unusual job stress, such as that arising from exposure to war (Malia, 2007).

Ample evidence reveals that job characteristics and job stress have meaningful consequences for the well-being of workers and their families, yet gaps in understanding persist. First, many studies have relied on data collected at a single point in time. Life course experiences are dynamic, and point-in-time estimates cannot capture the accumulation of exposure to job characteristics that differentiate careers. For example, some individuals stay employed consistently and proceed on a trajectory of improving job characteristics and rewards, whereas others are unable to escape conditions of high job stress. Some studies have showed that stressors such as job strain have a stronger effect when experienced persistently (Chandola et al., 2008), but more longitudinal data collection on a variety of job characteristics is needed to understand how they accumulate and change over the life course. Longitudinal data with repeated measurements of a variety of negative and positive job characteristics would also be useful for understanding whether and how individuals act to change jobs or adjust their careers in response to these stressors, what kinds of workers are able to do so, and how this might affect health and family functioning.

SOCIAL AND POLICY ISSUES

The workplace and the labor force are continuously evolving, and important issues of social inequality and public policy remain. First, social inequality in the distribution of negative job characteristics and job stress has persisted even though labor force composition and workplace organization are changing. Men with high levels of education and skills are generally exposed to fewer onerous job characteristics, whereas many women, ethnic minorities, and people with less education are exposed to more objective or psychosocial stressors on the job. Moreover, people with more education and financial resources may have more stable levels of mastery or other social supports under stressful conditions than people with lower levels of these socioeconomic resources, helping them to manage the stressors they do face. The consequences of these social inequalities in the distribution of desirable jobs are heavily influenced by social contexts. For example, many western European nations provide relatively generous social safety nets and have higher levels of unionization, providing some level of protection for workers from across the social spectrum. By contrast, the United States provides few institutionalized supports for workers, even those in undesirable jobs.

Second, as populations age and life expectancies rise, some older workers are remaining in the workforce longer, whether because they choose to, or because they cannot afford to retire. This will increase their life course exposure to job stress as they reach ages at which health typically begins to decline. Individuals with heavy caregiving responsibilities for children or aging parents are also increasingly working for pay, leading to heightened work-family conflict for many dual earner families and single parents, and perhaps especially for women. These and other contemporary labor force conditions are a poor fit with work policy and social practices developed in the post–World War II (1939–1945) U.S. context of the male breadwinner, manufacturing-centered economy, with a standard retirement age. For example, access to

unemployment insurance and health insurance coverage, on-the-job training, retirement benefits, and other benefits is often limited or absent for the growing number of workers with nonstandard employment contracts. Policies such as the Family and Medical Leave Act (FMLA) of 1993 were enacted to meet the challenges faced by working families in the United States, but many workers are not eligible because of the size or characteristics of their employer, or cannot afford to take advantage of unpaid leave even if they are eligible.

Finally, research must continue to address the issues of intervention and regulation. While the Occupational Safety and Health Administration (OSHA) and similar governmental bodies regulate some of the gross physical and environmental hazards that characterize some jobs, regulatory capacity has weakened in the United States. Moreover, there are few, if any, regulations on psychosocial stressors in the workplace. The appropriate interventions for stressors such as job strain are not entirely clear. Some have argued that it can be difficult to show that psychosocial stressors have a causal effect on well-being, whereas material resource deficits, such as low education or poverty, are more strongly linked to health and well-being. Because in most cases high levels of psychosocial stressors are the burden of people who also have relatively low material resources, this argument suggests that intervention may best be directed at improving the material resources of disadvantaged workers. Such policies would likely include wealth redistribution through progressive taxation. Others argue that restructuring and reorganizing work to reduce job stress could be a useful public health intervention, even apart from supports to improve material conditions for workers (Singh-Manoux, Macleod, & Smith, 2003). Issues of social inequality and questions about appropriate public policy will continue to be central to an understanding of the importance of job characteristics and job stress across the life course.

SEE ALSO Volume 2: *Economic Restructuring; Employment, Adulthood; Health Differentials/ Disparities, Adulthood; Occupations; Policy, Employment; Stress, Adulthood; Work-Family Conflict.*

BIBLIOGRAPHY

Allen, T. D., Herst, D. E. L., Bruck, C. S., & Sutton, M. (2000). Consequences associated with work-to-family conflict: A review and agenda for future research. *Journal of Occupational Health Psychology, 5*(2), 278–308.

Belkic, K. L., Landsbergis, P. A., Schnall, P. L., & Baker, D. (2004). Is job strain a major source of cardiovascular disease risk? *Scandinavian Journal of Work, Environment, & Health, 30*(2), 85–128.

Benavides, F.G., Benach, J., Muntaner, C., Delclos, G. L., Catot, N., & Amable, M. (2006). Associations between temporary employment and occupational injury: What are the mechanisms? *Occupational and Environmental Medicine, 63*(6), 416–421.

Bildt, C., & Michelsen, H. (2002). Gender differences in the effects from working conditions on mental health: A 4-year follow-up. *International Archives of Occupational and Environmental Health, 75*(4), 252–258.

Blekesaune, M., & Solem, P. E. (2005). Working conditions and early retirement—A prospective study of retirement behavior. *Research on Aging, 27*(1), 3–30.

Cappelli, P., Bassi, L., Katz, H., Knoke, P., Osterman, P., & Useem, M. (1997). *Change at work.* New York: Oxford University Press.

Caruso, C., Hitchcock, E., Dick, R., Russo, J., & Schmit, J. (2004). *Overtime and extended work shifts: Recent findings on illnesses, injuries, and health behaviors.* Retrieved June 6, 2008, from http://www.cdc.gov/niosh/docs/2004-143/pdfs/2004-143.pdf

Chandola, T., Britton, A., Brunner, E., Hemingway, H., Malik, M., Kumari, M. et al. (2008). Work stress and coronary heart disease: What are the mechanisms? *European Heart Journal.* Retrieved June 6, 2008, from http://eurheartj.oxfordjournals.org/cgi/content/full/ehm584v1

Ferrie, J. E., Shipley, M. J., Stansfeld, S. A., & Marmot, M.G. (2002). Effects of chronic job insecurity and change in job security on self-reported health, minor psychiatric morbidity, physiological measures, and health-related behaviors in British civil servants: The Whitehall II Study. *Journal of Epidemiology and Community Health, 56*(6), 450–454.

Frey, R. Scott. 2003. The transfer of core-based hazardous production processes to the export processing zones of the periphery: The Maquiladora centers of Northern Mexico. *Journal of World Systems Research 9*(2): 317–354.

Frone, M.R. (2000). Work-family conflict and employee psychiatric disorders: The national comorbidity survey. *Journal of Applied Psychology, 85*(6), 888–895.

Hughes, D., & Galinsky, E. (1994). Work experiences and marital interactions: Elaborating the complexity of work. *Journal of Organizational Behavior, 15*(5), 423–438.

Kalleberg, A. L., Reskin, B. F., & Hudson, K. (2000). Bad jobs in America: Standard and nonstandard employment relations and job quality in the United States. *American Sociological Review, 65*(2), 256–278.

Karasek, R. A. (1979). Job demands, job decision latitude, and mental strain: Implications for job redesign. *Administrative Science Quarterly, 24*(2), 285–308.

Karmakar, S. D., & Breslin, F. C. (2008). The role of educational level and job characteristics on the health of young adults. *Social Science & Medicine, 66*(9), 2011–2022.

Malia, J. A. (2007). A reader's guide to family stress literature. *Journal of Loss and Trauma, 12*(3), 223–243.

McEwen, B. S., & Seeman, T. (1999). Protective and damaging effects of mediators of stress: Elaborating and testing the concepts of allostasis and allostatic load. *Annals of the New York Academy of Sciences, 896*(1), 30–47.

Pearlin, L. I., & Skaff, M. M. (1996). Stress and the life course: A paradigmatic alliance. *Gerontologist, 36*(2), 239–247.

Perry-Jenkins, M., Repetti, R. L., & Crouter, A. C. (2000). Work and family in the 1990s. *Journal of Marriage and the Family, 62*(4), 981–998.

Pflanz, S. E., & Ogle, A. D. (2006). Job stress, depression, work performance, and perceptions of supervisors in military personnel. *Military Medicine, 171*(9), 861–865.

Price, R. H., & Burgard, S. A. (2008). The new employment contract and worker health in the United States. In R. F. Schoeni, J. S. House, G. A. Kaplan, & H. Pollack (Eds.), *Social and economic policy as health policy: Rethinking America's approach to improving health* (pp. 201–227). New York: Russell Sage.

Siegrist, J. (1996). Adverse health effects of high-effort/low-reward conditions. *Journal of Occupational Health Psychology, 1*(1), 27–41.

Siegrist, J., & Marmot, M. (2004). Health inequalities and the psychosocial environment—Two scientific challenges. *Social Science & Medicine, 58*(8), 1463–1473.

Singh-Manoux, A., Macleod, J., & Smith, G. D. (2003). Psychosocial factors and public health. *Journal of Epidemiology and Community Health, 57*(8), 553–556.

Smith, M. J., & Carayon, P. C. (1996). Work organization, stress, and cumulative trauma disorders. In S. Moon & S. Sauter (Eds.), *Beyond biomechanics: Psychosocial aspects of musculoskeletal disorders in office work* (pp. 23–42). London: Taylor & Francis.

Strazdins, L., Clements, M. S., Korda, R. J., Broom, D. H., & D'Souza, M. (2006). Unsociable work? Nonstandard work schedules, family relationships, and children's well-being. *Journal of Marriage and the Family, 68*(2), 394–410.

Sweet, S., & Meiksins, P. (2008). *Changing contours of work: Jobs and opportunities in the new economy.* Thousand Oaks, CA: Pine Forge Press.

Van der Doef, M., & Maes, S. (1999). The job demand-control (-support) model and psychological well-being: A review of 20 years of empirical research. *Work and Stress, 13*(2), 87–114.

Sarah A. Burgard

L

LEISURE AND TRAVEL, ADULTHOOD

The theme of consistency and change underlies the study of leisure over the life course. Individuals start building their leisure repertoires in childhood, and many of these activities remain consistent as people encounter different life stages, even as new ones are added (Kelly, 1982). The everyday definition of leisure is either free time (i.e., time that is not spent at work) or participation in enjoyable activities such as sports, hobbies, or watching television. However, the concept is actually remarkably slippery and complex. As a result, scholars have been debating the definition of leisure for more than 30 years. Leisure, along with work and family roles, is an important aspect of successful adult development and has implications for well-being over the life course.

WHAT IS LEISURE?

Leisure has been defined as free time or, more specifically, residual time, the time left over after all of an individual's daily obligations are met (Neumeyer & Neumeyer, 1958). Some argue that the concept of residual time does not allow for freedom of choice, a central component of leisure, and question whether time is ever completely free from obligations. Thus, the term *discretionary time* was adopted (Murphy, 1974). Over the years, defining leisure in terms of time use worked, because measures of time use are easily quantified. Using time-budget studies, researchers documented differences in time use between men and women (Shaw, 1985), across occupational categories (Burdge, 1969), across countries (Zuzanek, Beckers, & Peters, 1998), and across

historical periods (Schor, 1991). However, in the 1980s scholars increasingly recognized that the concept of leisure as the opposite of work might not be relevant for everyone, particularly the unemployed, stay at home mothers (or fathers), and retired persons. Researchers initially assumed that those not engaged in paid work did not have time off from work and, therefore, could not experience leisure. Thus, scholars moved away from defining leisure as free time.

The definition of leisure as activity, particularly pleasurable activity, developed in parallel with definitions that emphasized time use. This meant that leisure activities were non-work and encompassed such pursuits as hobbies, sports, travel, and outdoor recreation. Defining leisure as activity makes it easy to quantify, so researchers could develop activity inventories to document the most popular activities (Havighurst, 1957) and study participation by gender (Shaw, 1985), race (Floyd, et al., 1994), and age (Witt, 1971). However, if the freedom to choose is a central dimension of leisure, then defining leisure solely in terms of activity obscures the meaning behind the pursuit. This meaning may vary over time and situation. John R. Kelly (1982) points to the differences between playing basketball in a physical education (PE) class as opposed to playing pick-up basketball after school with friends. For some, basketball in a PE class is not leisure because of the obligation associated with it. Feminist scholars also questioned defining leisure in terms of activity, particularly for mothers who are responsible for organizing family activities. Are these family "leisure" activities perceived as leisure by women who organize them, or are they underpinned by a strong sense of obligation? (Shaw, 1992).

Pleasure Cruise. *Ann Duprey feeds squid to sting rays during a shore excursion to Sting Ray City from the cruise ship Norwegian Pearl in the Atlantic ocean during a western Caribbean cruise.* **AP IMAGES.**

Taking the lead from several classic books in the 1960s in which leisure was described as "a state of being" (de Grazia, 1964, p. 5) or "a mental and spiritual attitude" (Pieper, 1963, p. 40), Neulinger (1974) suggested that the central elements of leisure were the *perceived* freedom to choose an intrinsically motivated experience. He proposed that this perception of freedom and motivation could be measured by assessing one's attitudes. In contrast, Kelly (1982) argued that the full array of meanings associated with leisure could not be captured by perceptions and attitudes alone. Rather, he suggested that leisure reflects the quality or meaning of the activity, intrinsic motivation, and *relative* freedom. This latter criterion reflects the recognition that no choice is ever truly free from influence of social constraints or contexts. The concept *relative freedom* was adopted by feminist scholars, such as Erica Wimbush and Margaret Talbot (1988), who felt that it described women's experiences of leisure in relation to the social forces shaping and constraining their lives.

With the advent of the 24-hour, global, technologically-driven society of the 21st century, Kelly (1999) continued to refine his definition of leisure. In postindustrial society, he reasoned, the boundaries between work, family, and leisure were often hard to distinguish. Moreover, psychologists such as Mihály Csikszentmihalyi (1990/1991) found that people often experience "flow" (i.e., a state of feeling fully immersed in and energized by what they are doing) in the work place. To reconcile these psychological and social perspectives, Kelly suggested that leisure as action is existential (in that it is meaningful and produces meaning) and social (in that it is influenced by society as well as frequently experienced with others).

Thus, the dominant definition of *leisure* used by scholars in the early 21st century encompasses more than activity or free time. It is an experience characterized by freedom and meaning that also has social aspects. British scholars of leisure tend to critique this definition as being too individual and psychological. Many U.K. scholars are sociologists, whereas in the United States, social psychology has been the dominant paradigm guiding leisure scholarship (Coalter, 1999). However, a framework that includes both the existential and social qualities captures the essence of leisure and provides a foundation for understanding the role and place of leisure in societies where traditional assumptions about time, space, social structure, and social roles are increasingly blurred.

RESEARCH ABOUT LEISURE

Leisure scholars around the world have amassed a large body of knowledge about leisure as a central life domain as well as its interactions with other life domains such as work or family (Kelly & Freysinger, 2000). In the 1970s and 1980s, researchers examined leisure over the life cycle (Kleiber & Kelly, 1980; Osgood & Howe, 1984), life course (Parker, 1976), or family life cycle (Kelly, 1982; Rapoport & Rapoport, 1975; Witt & Goodale, 1981). A consistent theme in this work is that leisure is characterized by stability and change. Leisure facilitates the completion of specific socio-psychological life tasks, such as finding a partner or maintaining connections with one's community during retirement. At the same time, leisure is shaped by the responsibilities and demands of life stages, events, and transitions. For example, after the birth of children, leisure tends to become more home-centered, and participation in risky activities, particularly adventure sports, is often curtailed.

Some scholars have adopted specific models from life span developmental psychology to examine stability and change in both leisure (Carpenter, 1992; Iso-Ahola, Jackson & Dunn, 1994) and travel choice (Gibson & Yiannakis, 2002). However, whereas some scholars are still proponents of using a life span or life course perspective, most scholars have moved away from this focus and now examine specific life stages such as adolescence (Shaw, Kleiber, & Caldwell, 1995), where leisure provides a context for individuation, identity formation, and experimentation and midlife, where leisure is a context for family bonding and stress relief (Freysinger, 1995).

In addition to investigating leisure in reference to age or life stage, a number of other research foci are evident. In the 1970s and 1980s motivation was a dominant theme. A number of scales were developed, such as Jacob G. Beard and Mounir G. Ragheb's (1983) Leisure Motivation Scale, which identified four sub-dimensions of leisure motivation: competence/mastery, social, stimulus avoidance, and intellectual. The motivations that guide leisure choices are believed to depend on the individual's socio-psychological needs. Conversely, Seppo E. Iso-

Ahola (1980) viewed leisure motivation in terms of optimal level of stimulation (OLS); thus, individuals who are stressed and operating above their preferred OLS seek experiences for escape. By contrast, individuals who feel understimulated may seek out activities that provide challenge, novelty, and social interaction.

Around the world, the study of leisure has been integrally tied to recreation and parks provision and management. In North America much of this research uses a benefits framework. Rather than focusing on motivation, the benefits approach looks at outcomes as a philosophy (i.e. the belief that leisure is positive), a framework for empirically demonstrating these outcomes, and a management strategy (Driver & Bruns, 1999). Four types of benefits have been identified:

1. Personal Benefits are both psychological (e.g., identify affirmation) (Haggard & Williams, 1991) and psycho-physiological (e.g., physical fitness). For example, James F. Sallis and Neville G. Owen (1999) found that people who live in communities with a larger number of recreation facilities are more likely to be physically active.

2. Social and Cultural Benefits are linked to social bonding in families (Orthner & Mancini, 1991) and community satisfaction (Allen, 1990).

3. Economic Benefits, which include monetary gain or value, have been documented by a myriad of economic impact studies. For example, John L. Crompton (2001) found that people who live near parks and trails profit in the form of added value to price of their home.

4. Environmental Benefits take the form of additional green spaces in communities, a justification for conservation, particularly if economic benefits accrue from a park in the form of tourism (Sellars, 1997).

Another issue driven by both academic and practical concerns is access to leisure via public parks, both at the local municipal level as well as at state and national parks and other federal lands. This issue has received attention on both sides of the Atlantic, but from different perspectives. In the United Kingdom research focused on social class differentials in access (Coalter, 1998), whereas in North America, research focused on barriers or constraints to leisure participation. Duane W. Crawford and Geoffrey Godbey (1987) in a seminal paper identified three types of constraints that affect leisure participation: intrapersonal (e.g., attitudes, motives, values), interpersonal (e.g., preferences shaped by family, friends), and structural (e.g., time, money). Prior to this the focus had been largely on structural constraints such as time and money, when in fact researchers found intrapersonal and interpersonal constraints more powerful in shaping leisure participation patterns for both participation or non-participation. This thinking was formalized in the hierarchical model of constraints whereby the three sets of constraints were assumed to be encountered sequentially (Crawford, Jackson, & Godbey, 1991).

However, the hierarchical nature of constraints received little empirical support, particularly as researchers such as Susan M. Shaw, Bonnen, and McCabe (1991) found that the persons with the most constraints participated in leisure activities more frequently and that socio-structural variables were more powerful than previously thought in shaping choices. These findings were supported by others; for example, Tess A. Kay and Guy A. Jackson (1991) found that individuals participate in leisure activities despite constraints, so the idea of constraint negotiation emerged, meaning that "where there is desire an individual will find the way" to take part in preferred leisure activities (Jackson, Crawford & Godbey, 1993). Hubbard and Mannell (2001) established empirically that constraint negotiation has a positive relationship with motivation to participate. This idea receives support from Diane Samdahl and Nancy Jekubovich's (1997) work that indicated people change their routines, such as work schedules, to take part in their favorite activities. In the early 2000s researchers generally believe that constraints are not experienced equally by everybody. While time and money constraints are consistently cited over the life span, this relationship is U-shaped, with people aged 30 to 50 being particularly constrained, whereas cost of participation shows a negative relationship with age, cost being the most important constraint for the younger age groups (Hinch et al., 2006).

Constraints in the form of gender-based inequalities have been the focus of feminist leisure scholars. From the 1980s on, in response to the invisibility of women in previous leisure research (Henderson, 1994), scholars began to identify gender differences in access to leisure, primarily within the context of the family. In North America, working primarily from a symbolic interactionist perspective, researchers suggested that women's leisure was determined by socialization practices, which shaped their activity choices and tended to perpetuate traditional gender roles (Henderson & Bialeschki, 1991). The reinforcement of traditional gender roles was also used to explain why women who are mothers did not enjoy the same assess to leisure as men in terms of time. Shaw (1992) found that women in dual income families spent more time on domestic tasks than their partners, their leisure tended to be family centered, and family leisure was more often work-like than leisure-like. Bella (1992) in a study of family Christmas celebrations found that women often felt obligated to ensure that all of the Christmas rituals were performed, while simultaneously caring for family and children. The ethic of care has been frequently used to explain women's attitudes towards leisure. Learned through socialization, the ethic of care, which emphasizes care of others before self care (Gilligan, 1982), explains why many women do not feel entitled to their own leisure and feel guilty when they take time for themselves (Henderson & Bialeschki, 1991). As feminist research progressed through the 1990s, a shift in thinking focused on leisure as a space where women can resist structural forces and can exercise more control over their lives (Shaw 1994; Wearing, 1998).

Current threads in leisure research reflect recent concerns among both scholars and the public. As immigration becomes a global challenge, the role of leisure in adjustment to life in a new country has received more attention (Stoldolska, 2000). Likewise as different racial and ethnic groups become more prominent in the United States, researchers have begun to examine them. For example, studies have focused on Hispanic leisure (Allison, 2000), whereas in the past most work examined the leisure and recreational experiences of African Americans and whites (Floyd et al., 1994). Another debate centered on the loss of social capital (Putnam, 2001) and stimulated research on the role of leisure and recreation in building social capital (Glover & Hemingway, 2005). A related issue is whether people lack time for leisure and civic engagement (Robinson & Godbey, 1997; Schor, 1991).

This line of research returns to definitions of leisure as free time with all of its disadvantages. However, by providing information that can be compared across different countries and socio-historical periods, time budget data is a good starting point for understanding time pressures and how people deal with them. A portion of this research examines vacation patterns and attitudes to work (de Graaf, 2003). Leisure philosophers studying attitudes towards leisure in different countries and historical periods note that the pervasiveness of the Protestant work ethic explains U.S. attitudes towards leisure and vacation time (Sylvester, 1999); the United States is often cited as one of the most "vacation starved" countries. Taken together, leisure research shows how personal pursuits are molded by larger social, cultural, and economic contexts. Understanding the ways that macrosocial influences and individual preferences shape leisure over the life course is a critically important question that will occupy leisure scholars for decades to come.

SEE ALSO Volume 2: *Consumption, Adulthood and Later Life; Time Use, Adulthood;* Volume 3: *Leisure and Travel, Later Life.*

BIBLIOGRAPHY

Allen, L. (1990). Benefits of leisure attributes to community satisfaction. *Journal of Leisure Research, 22,* 183–196.

Allison, M. (2000). Leisure, diversity and social justice. *Journal of Leisure Research, 32*, 2–6.

Beard, J., & Ragheb, M. (1983). Measuring leisure motivation. *Journal of Leisure Research, 15*, 219–228.

Bella, L. (1992). *The Christmas imperative: Leisure, family and women's work*. Blackpoint, NS, Canada: Fernwood Publishing Company.

Burdge, R. (1969). Levels of occupational prestige and leisure activity. *Journal of Leisure Research, 1*, 262–274.

Carpenter, G. (1992). Adult perceptions of leisure: Life experiences and life structure. *Society and Leisure, 15*, 587–606.

Coalter, F. (1998). Leisure studies, leisure policy, and social citizenship: The failure of welfare or the limits of welfare? *Leisure Studies, 17*, 21–36.

Crawford, D., & Godbey, G. (1987). Reconceptualizing barriers to family leisure. *Leisure Sciences, 9*, 119–127.

Crawford, D., Jackson, E., & Godbey, G. (1991). A hierarchical model of leisure constraints. *Leisure Sciences, 13*, 309–320.

Crompton, J. (2001). Perceptions of how the presence of greenway trails affects the value of proximate properties. *Journal of Park and Recreation Administration, 19*(3), 33–51.

Csikszentmihalyi, M. (1990/1991). *Flow: The psychology of optimal experience*. New York: Harper & Row.

de Graaf, J. (2003). *Take back your time: Fighting overwork and time poverty in America*. San Francisco, CA: Berrett-Koehler Publishers.

de Grazia, S. (1964). *Of time, work, and leisure*. Garden City, NJ: Doubleday.

Driver, B., & Bruns, D. (1999). Concepts and uses of the benefits approach to leisure. In E. Jackson & T. Burton, (Eds.), *Leisure studies: Prospects for the twenty-first century* (pp. 349–369), State College, PA: Venture Publishing.

Floyd, M., Shinew, K., Mcguire, F., & Noe F., (1994). Race, class, and leisure activity preferences: Marginality and ethnicity revisited. *Journal of Leisure Research, 26*, 158–173.

Freysinger, V. (1995). The dialectics of leisure and development for women and men in midlife: An interpretive study. *Journal of Leisure Research, 27*, 61–84.

Gibson, H., & Yiannakis, A. (2002). Tourist roles: Needs and the life course. *Annals of Tourism Research, 29*, 358–383.

Gilligan, C. (1982). *In a different voice*. Cambridge, MA: Harvard University Press.

Glover, T., & Hemingway, J. (2005). Locating leisure in the social capital literature. *Journal of Leisure Research, 37*, 387–401.

Haggard, L., & Williams, D. (1991). In B. Driver, P. Brown, & G. Peterson, (Eds.). *Benefits of Leisure* (pp. 103–120). State College, PA: Venture.

Havighurst, R. (1957). The leisure activities of the middle-aged. *American Journal of Sociology, 63*, 152–162.

Henderson, K. (1994). Perspectives on analyzing gender, women, and leisure. *Journal of Leisure Research, 26*, 119–137.

Henderson, K. A., & Bialschki, M. D. (1991). A sense of entitlement to leisure as constraint and empowerment for women. *Leisure Sciences, 13*, 51–65.

Hinch, T., Jackson, E., Hudson, S., & Walker, G. (2006). Leisure constraint theory and sport tourism. In H. Gibson, (Ed.) *Sport tourism: Concepts and theories* (pp. 10–31). London, UK: Routledge.

Hubbard, J., & Mannell, R. (2001). Testing competing models of the leisure constraint negotiation process in a corporate employee recreation setting. *Leisure Sciences, 23*, 145–163.

Iso-Ahola, S. (1980). *The social psychology of leisure and recreation*. Dubuque, IO: Wm C Brown.

Iso-Ahola, S., Jackson, E., & Dunn, E. (1994). Starting, ceasing, and replacing leisure activities over the human life span. *Journal of Leisure Research, 26*, 227–249.

Jackson, E., Crawford, D., & Godbey, G. (1993). Negotiation of leisure constraints. *Leisure Sciences, 15*, 1–11.

Kay, T., & Jackson, G. A. (1991). Leisure despite constraint: The impact of leisure constraints on leisure participation. *Journal of Leisure Research, 23*, 301–313.

Kelly, J. (1982). *Leisure*. Englewood Cliffs, NJ: Prentice-Hall.

Kelly, J. & Freysinger, V. (2000). *21st Century Leisure*. Boston, MA: Allyn & Bacon

Kleiber, D., & Kelly, J. (1980). Leisure, socialization, and the life cycle. In S. Iso-Ahola (Ed.), *Social psychological perspectives on leisure and recreation* (pp. 91–138). Springfield, IL: Charles C. Thomas.

Murphy, J. (1974). *Concepts of leisure: Philosophical implications*. Englewood Cliffs, NJ: Prentice-Hall.

Neulinger, J. (1974). *The psychology of leisure*. Springfield, IL: Charles C. Thomas Publisher.

Neumeyer, M., & Neumeyer, E. (1958). *Leisure and recreation*, New York: Ronald Press.

Orthner, D., & Mancini, J. (1991). Benefits of leisure for family bonding. In B. Driver, P. Brown, & G. Peterson, (Eds.), *Benefits of Leisure* (pp. 289–302). State College, PA: Venture Publishing.

Osgood, N., & Howe, C. (1984). Psychological aspects of leisure: A life cycle developmental perspective. *Loisir et Société* [Leisure and society], *7*, 175–195.

Parker, S. (1976). *The sociology of leisure*. London: George Allen Unwin.

Pieper, J. (1963). *Leisure: The basis of culture*. New York: Random House.

Putnam, R. (2001). *Bowling alone: The collapse and revival of American community*. Simon and Schuster.

Rapoport, R., & Rapoport, R. (1975). *Leisure and the family life cycle*. London, UK: Routledge & Kegan Paul.

Robinson, J., & Godbey, G. (1997). *Time for life: The surprising ways Americans use their time*. State College, PA: Penn State University Press.

Sallis, J., & Owen, N. (1999). Physical activity and behavioral medicine. London: Sage Publications.

Samdahl, D., & Jekubovich, N. (1997). A critique of constraints theory: Comparative analyses and understandings. *Journal of Leisure Research, 29*, 469–471.

Schor, J. (1991). *The overworked American: The unexpected decline of leisure*. New York: Basic Books.

Sellars, R. (1997). *Preserving nature in the national parks: A history*. New Haven, CT: Yale University Press.

Shaw, S. (1985) Gender and leisure: Inequality in the distribution of leisure time. *Journal of Leisure Research, 17*, 266–282.

Shaw, S. (1992). Dereifying family leisure: An examination of women's and men's everyday experiences and perceptions of family time. *Leisure Sciences, 14*, 271–286.

Shaw, S. (1994). Gender, leisure, and constraint: Towards a framework for the analysis of women's leisure. *Journal of Leisure Research, 26*, 8–22.

Shaw, S., Bonnen, A., & McCabe, J. (1991). Do more constraints mean less leisure? Examining the relationships between constraints and participation. *Journal of Leisure Research, 23*, 286–300.

Shaw, S., Kleiber, D., & Caldwell, L. (1995). Leisure and identity formation in male and female adolescents: A preliminary examination. *Journal of Leisure Research, 27*, 245–263.

Stodolska, M. (2000). Changes in leisure participation patterns after immigration. *Leisure Sciences, 22*, 39–63.

Sylvester, C. (1999). The western idea of work and leisure: Traditions, transformations and the future. In E. Jackson, & T. Burton, (Eds.), *Leisure studies: Prospects for the twenty-first century* (pp.17–33). State College, PA: Venture Publishing.

Wearing, B. (1998). *Leisure and feminist theory.* London: Sage Publications.

Wimbush E., & Talbot, M. (Eds.). (1988). *Relative freedoms.* Milton Keynes, UK: Open University Press.

Witt, P. (1971). Factor structure of leisure behavior for high-school age youth in three communities. *Journal of Leisure Research, 3*, 213–219.

Witt, P., & Goodale, T. (1981). The relationship between barriers to leisure enjoyment and family stages. *Leisure Sciences, 4*, 29–49.

Zuzanek, J., Beckers, T., & Peters, P. (1998). The "harried leisure class" revisited: Dutch and Canadian trends in the use of time from the 1970s to the 1990s, *Leisure Studies, 17* (1), 1–19.

Heather J. Gibson

LIFE EVENTS

Life events are objective experiences that have definable starting and ending points. Formal changes in social roles—for example, getting married, becoming a parent, or retiring from work—represent one type of life event. These are often referred to as *life transitions* because they signal passage from one recognizable social status to another (Moen and Wethington, 1999). Changes in social roles act as markers or placeholders in the life course, positioning individuals at different stages of life (Chiriboga, 1997). Another type of life event is a commonly experienced social milestone, for example, obtaining a driver's license or getting a first job.

Life events may require changes in daily routines and behaviors to accommodate new roles and responsibilities, even those that are an anticipated part of normal daily life. These adjustments may increase the risk of mental or physical illness (Holmes and Rahe, 1967). In addition to physical or behavioral adjustments, life events may initiate psychological adjustments, particularly those that are unexpected; for example, divorce or death of a loved one may initiate changes in the way people see themselves or the world around them. Life experiences that initiate a reevaluation of one's current circumstances or purpose in life are referred to as *turning points*. A turning point alters

the way people perceive themselves, their social roles, and their relationships (Wethington, Brown, & Kessler, 1997). The impact of life events on well-being is often greater when events are perceived as undesirable. *Traumas* are an extreme example of undesirable life events. Traumas are particularly disruptive and shocking life events, for example, experiencing a violent crime, combat duty, or a life-threatening illness. The magnitude and suddenness of these events may disrupt a person's mental and physical well-being long after the occurrence of the event (Pearlin, 1999).

ASSESSING EXPOSURE TO LIFE EVENTS

Checklists are the predominant method for measuring exposure to life events. One of the earliest checklists, the Social Readjustment Rating Scale (SRRS), was developed by stress researchers Thomas Holmes and Richard Rahe (Holmes and Rahe, 1967). Life event checklists consist of an inventory of potentially life-changing situations that may have occurred over a specified period of time, typically over the past 6 months or past year.

Respondents indicate which of the events they have experienced. Some checklist measures tally the responses to estimate total exposure to potentially life-changing events and thus total impact on a person's life. Other checklists weight life events by their normative severity (the degree of disruption for an average person), for example, weighting death of a loved one as more severe than changing employment. This approach, however, does not account for individual circumstances that may alter the impact of the event: For example, death of a loved after a long illness may be experienced as less severe than an unexpected job loss. To account for individual circumstances, some checklists ask the respondent to rate the severity of the event. In this approach, however, respondents may be rating the severity of *consequences* of the event in addition to or instead of the event, for example, financial or relationship difficulties following a job loss. This approach makes it difficult to separate the effects of an event and the response to it.

A limitation of the checklist approach is the need to restrict the number of possible life events that respondents could have experienced. The original SRRS scale, for example, consisted of 43 events. Using the SRRS as a model, life event checklists have been refined to include events relevant to particular life stages, such as adulthood (Paykel, Pursoff, & Uhlenhuth, 1971), or to a common health condition, such as pregnancy (Barnett, Hanna, and Parker, 1983). Another limitation is the inability to distinguish between events and ongoing difficulties that precipitate an event, for example marital strain preceeding a divorce or leading to a job change. Despite these limitations, checklists are a popular and inexpensive way to examine exposure to life events in large and diverse populations.

Investigator-led interviews are an alternative approach to assessing exposure to life events. A personal interview approach involves one-on-one discussions between an investigator (interviewer) and the respondent (the study subject). The interviewer typically begins by asking questions about the respondent's recent experiences in varying domains of life (e.g., births, deaths, employment, health). The investigator probes the respondent for additional information about the circumstances surrounding each event experienced using open-ended questions to obtain in-depth narrative information. The investigator then uses the information to classify experiences into appropriate categories (e.g., life event, health issue, ongoing difficulty), to pinpoint the timing of the event (e.g., June of last year vs. within the past 12 months), and to assess the perceived severity or impact of the event within the context of the respondent's life. The interview approach offers a way to obtain information on a broader range of life events respondents may encounter over the life course. With this approach, the investigator assesses the occurrence of an event and the perceived severity of its impact. Because the interview approach is both expensive and time-consuming, it is most often used in smaller studies, studies that require more accurate timing of events (e.g., for predicting onsets of serious illness), and studies focusing on variations in response to exposure to a specific life event (e.g., death of spouse, retirement) (see Wethington et al., 1997 for a more complete discussion).

THE IMPACT OF LIFE EVENTS ON HEALTH AND WELL-BEING

The foundation for life events research began more than 50 years ago. Early animal laboratory experiments established a biological pathway through which external stimuli initiated a physiological response, commonly referred to as the *fight or flight response* (Cannon, 1939). Subsequent laboratory experiments with human subjects demonstrated that in addition to physical stimuli (e.g., hot, cold, shock), exposure to psychological stimuli (e.g., anticipation of shock) could also initiate physiological changes (Selye, 1956). Life events research emerged from an interest in studying people's responses to the situations of everyday lives (Sapolsky, 1999).

Studies examining the impact of life events on health and well-being may be separated into three types of outcomes: psychological disturbances, physical disorder and disease, and maladaptive behaviors.

Psychological disturbances include a range of effects from minor psychological distress or negative affect, to acute affective disorders, for example, major depression or anxiety disorder. Studies based on both general and clinical populations reveal a strong link between life events, particularly undesirable and uncontrollable events, and increases in psychological disturbances, including distress (Paykel, 1979) depression (Brown & Harris, 1978) (see Tennant, 2006 for a more complete review). The majority of these studies find that it is the perceived severity or significance of an event, rather than the objective occurrence of a particular type of event, that accounts for the impact. Thus, undesirable events impact psychological well-being by threatening individuals' self-image, or sense of control such as unanticipated medical expenses or physical discomfort after a car accident (Thoits, 1983). Consistent findings can be found in studies of older adults (Clémence, Karmaniola, & Green, 2007) and children (Bouma, Ormel, Verhulst, & Oldehinkel, 2008), as well as in international epidemiological (Marmot, Davey Smith, Stansfeld, Patel et al., 1991) and clinical samples (Rojo-Moreno, Livianos-Aldana, Cervera-Martinez, Dominguez-Carabantes et al., 2002).

Studies on the relationship between adverse life events and onset of depression provide the most compelling evidence that exposure to life events directly provokes psychological disturbances (Brown, Harris, & Hepworth, 1994). However, not everyone exposed to a life event, even a very serious event or trauma, responds in the same way. Previous exposure to life events, ongoing life difficulties, and available resources, lifestyle, and genetic factors all contribute to both the risk of experiencing a life event and individual variability in responses to life events as well as to overall vulnerability to subsequent life experiences. Experiencing a major depressive episode, for example, appears to predispose individuals to subsequent depressive episodes, without the occurrence of a subsequent life event (Kendler, Thornton, & Gardner, 2001).

The pathway between exposure to life events and *physical disorder and disease* is more indirect, as changes in physical health occur over long time intervals. Whereas severity of unexpected and undesirable life events most often precede psychological disturbances, total amount of change or cumulative change are more important determinants of disease and physical disorders (McEwen & Seeman, 1999). Recent exposure to life events has been shown to trigger physical disturbances, such as heart attack (Tennant, 1987). Exposure to life events is also associated with increased symptoms of existing physical disorders such as coronary heart disease (see Tennant, 1999 for a review). Exposure to more negative life events is associated with diminished physical functioning and health (Surtees & Wainwright, 2007). Because it takes time for diseases and disorder to develop, life events are not typically the immediate cause of physical disease or disorder but may precipitate acute physical (e.g., heart attack) or mental (e.g. depression) reactions in vulnerable populations.

Exposure to life events may initiate *changes in behavior* to response to changing life circumstances (Cohen & Herbert, 1996). Studies have demonstrated associations between exposure to life events and alcohol addictions (Lloyd & Turner, 2008), eating disorders (Steinhausen, Gavez, & Metzke, 2005) and sleep disturbances (Vahtera, Kivimäki, Hublin et al., 2007). While life events may precipitate behavioral changes, behavioral and life choices may also increase the likelihood of experiencing life events, for example, drinking and driving.

POLICY IMPLICATIONS AND FUTURE DIRECTIONS

Exposure to life events, particularly adverse life events, is not random. Age, gender, and social status influence the type, the frequency, and the impact of life events (Pearlin, 1982), with individuals of lower socioeconomic status at-risk for increased exposure to adverse life events. Without adequate resources to address life's adversities, these individuals are also at increased risk for exposure to subsequent adverse events. This erosion in daily life experiences contributes to the disparity in physical health status and mortality rates by socioeconomic status (Marmot et al., 1991).

The impact of adverse life events on health and well-being is well established, ushering in a new phase in the study of the relationship between exposure to life events and physical and mental health. Health and well-being in adulthood does not result from a single adverse life event; each stage of life is both the consequence of prior experiences as well as the antecedent for subsequent life experiences (Spiro, 2001). A single event may also trigger related stresses that carry additional emotional/physical costs, such as financial difficulties or marital strain following a job loss. The impact of early exposure to adverse life events, such as abuse or parental divorce, may persist well into adulthood.

In addition to the lingering effects of early life events, people's daily lives consist of balancing the demands of interrelated social roles, particularly in adulthood. Disruptions in spouse/partner relationships, parenting, and employment may lead to disruptions in another domain (Pearlin, Menaghan, Lieberman, & Mullan, 1981). The loss of a job, for example, may be followed by ongoing financial instability and subsequent loss of possessions (e.g., car, house) or relationship difficulties leading to an accumulation of difficulties as a consequence of the initial event (Pearlin, Aneshensel, & LeBlanc, 1997). Thus, there is increased need to consider the cumulative impact of life events and other life experiences across the life course (Elder, George, & Shanahan, 1996). Thus, physical and emotional well-being across the life course requires a more complete assessment of both episodic and recurring circumstances of social and environmental of life.

SEE ALSO Volume 2: *Job Change; Midlife Crises and Transitions; Stress in Adulthood; Trauma.*

BIBLIOGRAPHY

Barnett, B. E. W., Hanna, B., & Parker, G. (1983). Life event scales for obstetric groups. *Journal of Psychosomatic Research, 27,* 313–320.

Bouma, E. M. C., Ormel, J., Verhulst, F. C., & Oldehinkel, A. J. (2008). Stressful life events and depressive problems in early adolescent boys and girls: The influence of parental depression, temperament, and family environment. *Journal of Affective Disorders, 105,* 185–193.

Brown, G. W., & Harris, T. O. (1978). *Social origins of depression.* New York: Free Press.

Brown, G. W., Harris, T. O., & Hepworth, C. (1994). Life events and endogenous depression: A puzzle reexamined. *Archives General Psychiatry, 51,* 525–534.

Cannon, W. B. (1939). *The wisdom of the body.* (2nd ed.). New York: W.W. Norton.

Chiriboga, D. A. (1997). Crisis, challenge, & stability in the middle years. In M. E. Lachman & J. B. James (Eds.), *Multiple paths of midlife development* (pp. 293–322). Chicago: The University of Chicago Press.

Clémence, A., Karmaniola, A., Green, E. G. T., & Spini, D. (2007) Disturbing life events and wellbeing after 80 years of age: A longitudinal comparison of survivors and the deceased over five years. *Aging & Society, 27,* 195–213.

Cohen, S., & Herbert, T. B. (1996). Health psychology: Psychological factors and physical disease from the perspective of human psychoneuroimmunology. *Annual Review of Psychology, 47,* 113–142.

Elder, G. H., Jr., George, L. K., & Shanahan, M. J. (1996). Psychosocial stress over the life course. In H. B. Kaplan (Ed.), *Psychosocial stress: Perspectives on structure, theory, life course, and methods* (pp. 247–292). Orlando, FL: Academic Press.

Holmes, T. H., & Rahe, R. H. (1967). The social readjustment rating scale. *Journal of Psychosomatic Research, 11,* 213–218.

Kendler, K. S., Thornton, L. M., & Gardner, C. O. (2001). Genetic risk, number of previous depressive episodes, and stressful life events in predicting onset of major depression. *American Journal of Psychiatry, 158,* 582–586.

Lloyd, D. A., & Turner, R. J. (2008). Cumulative lifetime adversities and alcohol dependence in adolescence and young adulthood. *Drug and Alcohol Dependence, 93,* 217–226.

Marmot, M. G., Davey Smith, G., Stansfeld, S., Patel, C., North F. et al. (1991). Health inequalities among British civil servants: The Whitehall II study. *The Lancet, 337,* 1387–1393.

McEwen, B. S., & Seeman, T. (1999). Protective and damaging effects of mediators of stress: Elaborating and testing the concepts of allostasis and allostatic load. In N. E. Adler, M. Marmot, B. S. McEwen, and J. Stewart (Eds.), *Socioeconomic status and health in industrial nations: Social, psychological, and biological pathways* (pp. 30–47). New York: Academy of Sciences.

Moen, P., & Wethington, E. (1999). Midlife development in a life course context. In S. L. Willis & J. D. Reid (Eds.), *Life in the middle: Psychological and social development in middle age* (pp. 3–23). San Diego, CA: Academic Press.

Paykel, E. (1979). Recent life events in the development of the depressive disorders. In R. Depue (Ed.), *The psychobiology of the depressive disorders: Implications for the effects of stress* (pp. 245–262). New York: Academic Press.

Paykel, E. S., Prusoff, B. A., & Uhlenhuth, E. H. (1971). Scaling of life events. *Archives of General Psychiatry, 25,* 340–347.

Pearlin, L. I. (1982). The social contexts of stress. In L. Goldberger and S. Breznitz (Eds.), *Handbook of Stress* (2nd ed., pp. 303–315). New York: Free Press.

Pearlin, L. I. (1999). The stress process revisited: Reflections on concepts and their interrelationships. In C. S. Aneshensel & J. C. Phelan (Eds.), *Handbook of the Sociology of Mental Health* (pp. 395–415). New York: Kluwer Academic.

Pearlin, L. I., Aneshensel, C. S., & LeBlanc, A. J. (1997). The forms and mechanisms of stress proliferation: The case of AIDS caregivers. *Journal of Health and Social Behavior, 38,* 223–236.

Pearlin, L. I., Menaghan, E. G., Lieberman, M. A., & Mullan, J. T. (1981). The stress process. *Journal of Health and Social Behavior, 22,* 337–356.

Rojo-Moreno, L., Livianos-Aldana, L., Cervera-Martinez, G., Dominguez-Carabantes, J. A., & Reig-Cebrian, M. J. (2002). The role of stress in the onset of depressive disorders. *Social Psychiatry and Psychiatric Epidemiology, 37,* 592–598.

Sapolsky, R. M. (1999). Hormonal correlates of personality and social contexts: From non-human to human primates. In C. Panter-Brick & C. M. Worthman (Eds.). *Hormones, health, and behavior: A socio-ecological and lifespan perspective* (pp. 18–46). New York: Cambridge University Press.

Selye, H. (1956). *The stress of life.* New York: McGraw-Hill.

Spiro, A. III (2001). Health in midlife: Toward a lifespan view. In M. E. Lachman (Ed.), *Handbook of Midlife Development* (pp. 156–187). New York: Wiley.

Steinhausen, H.-C., Gavez, S., & Metzke, C. W. (2005). Psychosocial correlates, outcome and stability of abnormal adolescent eating behavior in community samples of young people. *International Journal of Eating Disorders, 37,* 119–126.

Surtees, P. G., & Wainwright, N. W. J. (2007). The shackles of misfortune: Social adversity assessment and representation in a chronic-disease epidemiological setting. *Social Science & Medicine, 64,* 95–111.

Tennant, C. C. (1987). Stress and coronary heart disease. *Australian and New Zealand Journal of Psychiatry, 21,* 276–282.

Tennant, C. (1999). Life stress, social support and coronary heart disease. *Australian and New Zealand Journal of Psychiatry, 33,* 636–641.

Tennant, C. (2006). Life events, stress and depression. *Australian and New Zealand Journal of Psychiatry, 36,* 173–182.

Thoits, P. (1983). Dimensions of Life events that influence psychological distress: An evaluation and synthesis of the literature. In H. B. Kaplan (Ed.), *Psychological Stress: Trends in Theory and research* (pp. 33–103). New York: Academic Press.

Vahtera, J., Kivimäki, M., Hublin, C., Korkeila, K., Suominen, S., Paunio, T. et al. (2007). Liability to anxiety and severe life events as predictors of new-onset sleep disturbances. *Journal of Sleep and Sleep Disorders Research, 30,* 1537–1546.

Wethington, E., Brown G. W., & Kessler, R. C. (1997). Interview measurement of stressful life events. In S. Cohen, R. C. Kessler, & L. U. Gordon (Eds.), *Measuring stress: A guide for health and social scientists* (pp. 59–79). New York: Oxford University Press.

Joyce Serido

LIVING TOGETHER

SEE Volume 2: *Cohabitation.*

M

MANNHEIM, KARL

1893–1947

Karl Mannheim, a European sociologist, developed the field of the sociology of knowledge. His theoretical work on how people's understanding, ideas, and knowledge of the world are influenced through their membership in generations (or birth cohorts) was an important contribution to the sociology of the life course.

Mannheim was born into a Jewish family in Hungary, where he studied and then taught at the University of Budapest. During his tenure there, Hungary experienced political turmoil from 1918 to 1920: A short-lived Communist government was followed by a military uprising, violence, and the restoration of the monarchy. Mannheim left Hungary, initially moving to Austria and then to Germany, where, in 1921, he married a Hungarian psychologist, Juliska Lang. Mannheim held academic posts in Germany at the universities of Heidelberg and Frankfurt. The rise of Nazism forced Mannheim to leave Germany in 1933. He spent the rest of his academic career in England, working as a lecturer in sociology at the London School of Economics and, later, as a professor of education at the University of London.

Mannheim's (1952) theoretical essay on generations is the most relevant publication for understanding his contribution to the sociology of the life course. For Mannheim, knowledge (defined by him as a style of thought or worldview) is socially conditioned by membership in a generation (or birth cohort). People of different generations therefore have distinct and "definite modes of behaviour, feeling, and thought" (p. 291).

For Mannheim (1952), a person's generational membership arises from the "biological rhythm in human existence—the factors of life and death, a limited span of life, and ageing" (p. 290). Mannheim emphasized, though, the overriding and ultimate influence of social factors, so that biological aging must be understood as embedded within social and historical processes. This view became a foundation of the life course perspective.

In Mannheim's (1952) analysis, it is during the life course stage of youth that experiences, ideas, and impressions gel together, stabilize, and form "a natural view of the world" (p. 298). Individuals then carry this with them throughout the remainder of their life course. People are therefore crucially influenced by the sociohistorical context that predominated during their youth. In this way, adult generations are formed, each with distinctive historically determined worldviews. Mannheim therefore suggests that, at a given point in time, adults in different life course stages will not share the same view of the world because of different formative experiences during their youth.

Mannheim proposed that in order to share generational location in a sociologically meaningful sense, individuals must be born within the same historical and cultural context and be exposed to particular experiences and events during their formative years. More specifically, Mannheim argued that not every member of a generation will be exposed to exactly the same experiences because of variations in geographical and cultural locations during youth. He also recognized that whereas some groups within generations will actively participate in the key social and cultural events of their time, other groups will not. Moreover, among actual (or active) generations, responses to social and cultural events can differ in that they may be oppositional or supportive.

Mannheim's (1952) work on generations also illuminates links between the life course and social change. Mannheim proposed that the likelihood of a youthful cohort developing a distinctive worldview (i.e., of becoming a generation) is dependent on the pace of social change. In turn, generations are regarded by Mannheim as a key element in the production of social change. The "fresh contact" of new adult cohorts with the preestablished social and cultural heritage always means a "changed relationship of distance" and a "novel approach" to doing things (p. 293). The progression of social change is made smoother by the presence of intermediary generations, which act as a buffer between those generations with the greatest difference in worldviews or styles of thought. In times of accelerated social change, however, when the tempo of change quickens, the new generations have even greater opportunity than the natural, gradual changeover allowed by the aging and eventual death of all members of a birth cohort.

Beyond his contribution to life course studies via his work on generations, Mannheim writings engaged more broadly with the social conditioning of knowledge, including the structural positioning of intellectuals and their role in society. Linked to this, Mannheim's work increasingly became concerned with the planned social reconstruction of societies through the application of social policy (including education) to counter both totalitarianism and individualism and sustain democracy.

SEE ALSO Volume 3: *Cohort; Ryder, Norman.*

BIBLIOGRAPHY

Mannheim, K. (1936 [1929]). *Ideology and utopia: An introduction to the sociology of knowledge.* New York: Harcourt Brace.

Mannheim, K. (1952). *Essays on the sociology of knowledge.* (Paul Kecskemeti, Ed.). London: Routledge Kegan Paul.

Jane Pilcher

MARRIAGE

Marriage is a legal contract or socially recognized agreement between two individuals and their families to form a sexual, productive, and reproductive union. Through marriage, a union is recognized by family members, other members of society, religious institutions, and the legal system. Marriage defines the relationship of the two individuals to each other, to any children they might have, to their extended families, to shared property and assets, and to society in general. It also defines the relationship of others, including social institutions, toward the married couple.

The key features of most marriages include a legally binding, long-term contract or socially recognized agreement; sexual exclusivity; coresidence; shared resources; and joint production. In polygamous societies, the circle of sexual exclusivity expands to include multiple spouses, who might have separate residences. Spouses acquire rights and responsibilities with marriage, enforceable through both the legal systems and through social expectations and social pressure. Marriage differs from other, less formal relationships primarily in its legal status and social recognition. Because marriage is a legally or socially recognized contract, the treatment of marriage in the law and custom shapes the institution, and recent changes in family law in some societies appear to have made marriage less stable.

Historically, in the United States and many other countries, both secular and religious law generally viewed marriage vows as binding and permanent. The marriage contract could only be broken if one spouse violated the most basic obligations to the other and could be judged at fault in the breakdown of the marriage (Regan, 1996). Beginning in the mid-1960s, however, states in the United States substantially liberalized and simplified their divorce laws. One of the key features of this change was a shift from divorce based on fault or mutual consent to unilateral divorce, which requires the willingness of only one spouse to end the marriage. Most states also adopted some form of no-fault divorce, which eliminates the need for one spouse to demonstrate a violation of the marriage contract by the other.

The shift to unilateral or no-fault divorce laws was accompanied by a surge in divorce rates in the United States. At least some of the increase in divorce rates appears to have resulted directly from the shift in the legal environment in which couples marry and decide whether to remain married (Friedberg, 1998). The link between divorce rates and laws that permit unilateral divorce has lead several states to develop alternative, more binding marriage contracts, such as covenant marriage, in which partners agree to seek help for marital problems and to a mandatory period of separation prior to the consideration of getting divorced.

Its status as a legal contract and the features of permanence, social recognition of a sexual and childrearing union, coresidence, shared resources, and joint production lead to some of the other defining characteristics of marriage. Because two adults make a legally binding and socially supported promise to live and work together for their joint well-being, and to do so, ideally, for the rest of their lives, they tend to *specialize*, dividing between them the labor required to maintain the family. One person may become an expert at cooking and the other at cleaning or money management. This specialization allows married men and women to produce more than they would if they did not specialize. Any division of labor tends to increase productivity; couples do not need to divide family work along traditional gender lines to reap these benefits. The coresidence and resource sharing of married couples lead to substantial economies of scale; at any standard of living it costs much less for people to live together than it would if they lived separately. Both economies of scale and the specialization of spouses tend to increase the economic well-being of family members living together.

The institution of marriage assumes the sharing of economic and social resources and coinsurance. Spouses act as a small insurance pool against life's uncertainties, sharing responsibility if things go wrong and reducing their need to protect themselves by themselves against unexpected events. Marriage also connects spouses and family members to a larger network of help, support, and obligation through their extended family, friends, and the community. The insurance function of marriage also increases the economic well-being of family members, and the support function improves their economic and emotional well-being.

The institution of marriage builds on and fosters trust. Because spouses share social and economic resources, and expect to do so over the long term, both gain when the family unit gains. This reduces the need for family members to monitor the behavior of other members, increasing efficiency.

The vast majority of adults marry at some point in their lives, both in the United States and in other countries. Most young adults in the United States plan to marry and rank a happy marriage and family life as one of their most important goals (Thornton & Young-DeMarco, 2001). Thus, marriage is a key component

of the life course, and one around which other important transitions, such as moving into the workforce and residential and financial independence, are positioned.

TRENDS, PATTERNS, AND DIFFERENTIALS

Age at Marriage In the United States, age at marriage declined in the first half of the 20th century, but then rose dramatically. Entering the 21st century, men and women in the United States are marrying later than at any other time in past decades (Fitch & Ruggles, 2000). Between 1970 and 2000 the median age of first marriage for women increased by almost 5 years, from 20.8 to 25.1, and for men the median age increased by almost 4 years, from 23.2 to 26.8 (Fields & Casper, 2001). In this same time period, the proportion of women who had never been married increased from 36% to 73% among those 20 to 24 years old and from 6% to 22% among those 30 to 34 years old. Similar increases occurred for men (Fields & Casper, 2001).

For African Americans, the delay of first marriage has been especially striking. The median age at first marriage increased to 28.6 for African-American men, and 27.3 for African-American women (Fitch & Ruggles, 2000). This represents a 6-year increase from about 22 for African-American men and a 7-year increase from about 20 for African-American women since the 1960s. And, in 2000 among those 30 to 34 years old, 44% of African-American women and 46% of African-American men had never married (Fields & Casper, 2001).

Similar changes in marriage patterns have taken place in most European countries; cohorts reaching

	Males			Females		
	Total	Black	White	Total	Black	White
1960	69.3	60.9	70.2	65.9	59.8	66.6
1970	66.7	56.9	68.0	61.9	54.1	62.8
1980	63.2	48.8	65.0	58.9	44.6	60.7
1990	60.7	45.1	62.8	56.9	40.2	59.1
2000	57.9	42.8	60.0	54.7	36.2	57.4
2005[b]	55.0	37.9	57.5	51.5	30.2	54.6

[a]Includes races other than Black and White.
[b]In 2003, the US Census Bureau expanded its racial categories to permit respondents to identify themselves as belonging to more than one race. This means that racial data computations beginning in 2004 may not be strictly comparable to those of prior years.

SOURCE: U.S. Bureau of the Census, Current Population Reports, Series P20-506; America's Families and Living Arrangements: March 2000 and earlier reports; and data calculated from the Current Population Surveys, March 2005 Supplement.

Figure 1. *Percentage of all persons age 15 and older who were married, by sex and race, 1960–2005 United States[a].* CENGAGE LEARNING, GALE.

Year	Males	Females
1960	88.0	87.4
1970	89.3	86.9
1980	84.2	81.4
1990	74.1	73.0
2000	69.0	71.6
2005	66.2	67.2

SOURCE: US Bureau of the Census, Statistical Abstract of the United States, 1961, Page 34, Table 27; Statistical Abstract of the United States, 1971, Page 32, Table 38; Statistical Abstract of the United States, 1981, Page 38, Table 49; and US Bureau of the Census, General Population Characteristics, 1990, Page 45, Table 34; and Statistical Abstract of the United States, 2001, Page 48, Table 51; internet tables (http://www.census.gov/population/socdemo/hh-fam/cps2005/tabA1-all.pdf) and data calculated from the Current Population Surveys, March 2005 Supplement. Figure for 2005 was obtained using data from the Current Population Surveys rather than data from the census. The CPS, March Supplement, is based on a sample of the US population, rather than an actual count such as those available from the decennial census. See sampling and weighting notes at http://www.bls.census.gov:80/cps/ads/2002/ssampwgt.htm

Figure 2. *Percentage of people, ages 35–44, who were married (by sex), 1960–2005.* CENGAGE LEARNING, GALE.

adulthood recently are marrying at older ages and over a wider range of ages than in the past. However, European countries differ substantially in marriage ages. The Nordic countries of Sweden, Denmark, and Iceland show the highest average ages at marriage for women (around age 29), primarily because these countries have high rates of cohabitation, and the eastern European countries of Bulgaria, the Czech Republic, Hungary, and Poland show the lowest (around age 22). Because societies with a relatively high age at marriage also tend to be those in which many people never marry, this diversity suggests that marriage is a more salient component of the family in some European countries than others.

Marriage typically takes place at substantially younger ages in Africa, Asia, and Latin America than in North America and Europe. The average mean age at marriage among countries in the developed regions is almost 28 for men and 25 for women, compared to 25 for men and 21 for women in the less developed regions of the world. Young average ages at marriage are common in some parts of Africa (such as Uganda, Chad, and Burkina Faso), in some parts of Asia (such as India, Nepal, and Indonesia), in the Middle East, and in eastern Europe. Within regions of the world, women and men in developed countries tend to marry at older ages than those living in less developed countries. For example, in Southeast Asia women's age at first marriage is about 27 in Singapore and about 22 in Indonesia. Men tend to marry at older ages than women, but the gender gap in average age at marriage varies quite substantially both within and between regions. The gap tends to be the largest where women marry relatively early

(United Nations, 2000), perhaps because in these countries women are less likely to work for pay and thus depend on their husbands for financial support.

Proportion Married In the United States, age at marriage has risen substantially, divorce rates are high and stable, and rates of remarriage have fallen, so that a larger proportion of adults are unmarried now than in the past. In the United States in 1970, unmarried people made up 28% of the adult population. In 2000, 46% of adults were unmarried. In fact, the shift away from marriage has been so dramatic for Blacks that only 39% of Black men and 31% of Black women were married in 2000, compared to 59% of White men and 56% of White women (Fields & Casper, 2001).

Countries in Europe show a great deal of variation in the proportion of women in marital unions. Marriage is most common in Greece and Portugal, where more than 60% of women ages 25 to 29 are married, and least common in the Nordic countries, Italy, and Spain, where one-third or less are married (Kiernan, 2000).

In spite of increases in the age at first marriage in some countries, the vast majority of adults marry at some time in their lives, with the proportion of those who were ever married by age 50 reaching more than 95% of both men and women. Relatively high proportions of men and women have not married by their late 40s in the Nordic countries, where cohabitation is common, and in Caribbean countries such as Jamaica and Barbados, countries characterized by a long history of informal unions or visiting relationships. In Sweden, for example, 76% of men and 84% of women in their late 40s had ever married, and in Jamaica, 52% of men and 54% of women had ever married by these ages (United Nations, 2000).

Increasingly, couples form intimate unions by cohabiting, with marriage following at some later point unless the relationship dissolves. In the United States, only 7% of the women born in the late 1940s cohabited before age 25 compared to 55% among those born in the late 1960s (Raley, 2000). The percentage of marriages preceded by cohabitation increased from about 10% for those marrying between 1965 and 1974 to more than 50% of those marrying between 1990 and 1994 (Bumpass & Lu, 2000). Cohabitation is especially common among people whose first marriage dissolved (Brien, Lillard, & Waite, 1999).

Although a number of European countries have experienced similar increases in cohabitation, some have experienced much more and some much less. Cohabitation is strikingly common in the Nordic countries of Denmark, Sweden, and Finland, and France also shows fairly high levels, with about 30% of women ages 25 to 29 being in cohabiting unions. In these countries, cohabitation has many of the legal and social characteristics of marriage. A group of countries including the Netherlands, Belgium, Great Britain, West and East Germany, and Austria show moderate levels of cohabitation—between 8 and 16% of women ages 25 to 29 are in this type of union. And in the southern European countries, as well as in Ireland, cohabitation is rare with less than 3% cohabiting among women ages 25 to 29 (Kiernan, 2000). Societies in which cohabitation is rare also tend to have fairly low rates of unmarried childbearing and tend not to recognize cohabiting unions as alternatives to marriage.

Perhaps the most perplexing issue facing researchers studying marriage in the United States revolves around the rapid and dramatic divergence of family patterns and processes between Whites and Blacks. In about 1950, the proportions of Black and White adults who were married was quite similar. Black men and women show little evidence of the substantial decline in age at marriage that characterized the baby boom of the 1950s and early 1960s for Whites in the United States, and show a much more rapid rise in age at marriage since that time (Fitch & Ruggles, 2000). In the mid-1990s, almost twice as many Black men as White men were not married (Waite, 1995), with a similar differential for women. Joshua Goldstein and Catherine Kenney (2001) have found a dramatic decline in the proportion of Black women predicted to ever marry, especially among those who are not college graduates, whereas marriage remains virtually universal among Whites. The proportion of births to unmarried women is three times as high for Blacks as for Whites (Martin, Hamilton, Ventura, Menacker, & Park, 2002). Although numerous hypotheses for this divergence have been put forward, none explains more than a small portion of the racial gap in family patterns.

CHANGES IN THE NATURE OF MARRIAGE

Under the family mode of social organization, which has at its core the married couple, kin groups tend to pool resources, including their labor, specialize in particular tasks, coordinate their activities, and connect to the larger community as a unit. In polygamous societies, the married couple may include a spouse with other wives, with pooling of labor among cowives, or other combinations. In patriarchal societies power often resides in the elders in the family, and in men. The family mode of social organization is often associated with agricultural production, but it appears in a wide range of economic environments (Thornton & Fricke, 1989).

The family mode of social organization has been altered as a result of other, far-reaching social changes, including the rise of the market economy, vast increases in productivity with concomitant increases in real income (Fogel, 2000), urbanization, changes in ideology toward greater individualization (Lesthaeghe, 1995), and changes in the structure of education. All of these changes have shifted decision-making and social control away from the family and toward the individual or other social institutions. As families have less control over the time and resources of children, they are less able to influence marriage choices—whether, when, and whom to wed. As more people support themselves through wage-based employment rather than through work on a family farm or small business, families have less stake in the property and family connections that a potential marriage partner brings, and, accordingly, young adults acquire more autonomy in marriage choices (Caldwell, Reddy, & Caldwell, 1983). Urbanization and electronic communication have made one's spouse and family a less important source of companionship and entertainment now than when most people lived on farms or in villages (Burch & Matthews, 1987).

In developed industrial societies such as the United States, the family retains responsibility for reproduction, socialization, coresidence, and the transmission of property across generations. It is the main unit of consumption and often also produces considerable amounts of goods and services. Families provide care and support for both the young and the old. Although older adults receive financial transfers and access to medical care from the government in many societies, they still receive the vast majority of their help and support from family members (Logan & Spitze, 1996), and children are almost entirely dependent on their families for financial, emotional, and instrumental support. However, the more modern family less often consists of a married couple, their children, and other relatives than in the past.

At the same time, the social and economic bases for marriage have changed, especially in postindustrial societies such as the United States and Britain. Many social thinkers point to a shift toward companionate marriage and intimate relationships, in which the relationship exists primarily to meet the emotional needs of the partners, to be discarded when needs change (Giddens, 1992). Fulfillment of the emotional needs of both partners is a weak reed upon which to build a long-term relationship, making such marriages fragile. The movement of women into advanced education, often at rates equal to men, and into the paid labor force has eroded—but not eliminated—the economic basis for marriage. More women earn enough to support themselves and their children should they be unable or unwilling to marry or stay married (Waite & Nielsen, 2000). Changing attitudes about sex outside of marriage have made some of the services provided by marriage available to those who are not married. And changing gender roles, including rises in women's employment and changing expectations for men's participation in family life, seem to have led to increased conflict in marriage (Amato & Booth, 1995). All these changes have, according to some scholars, weakened the social institution of marriage and made marriages less stable than they were under different conditions.

The married, two-parent family has been the most common family form in the United States and other industrialized countries for some centuries. But even at the height of the married couple family era, many people lived in other types of families, most often due to the death of one member of the couple before all the children were grown (Watkins, Menken, & Bongaarts, 1987). When death ended many marriages relatively early in life, remarriage and stepfamilies were common, as were single-parent families caused by widowhood. High rates of divorce combined with relatively low rates of remarriage, especially for women with children, have been shown to lead to sizable proportions of families with a divorced single mother. The rise of cohabitation and nonmarital childbearing has meant that unmarried-couple families and never-married mother families are now common alternative family forms.

In the United States families consisting of a married couple with children fell from 87% in 1970 to 69% in 2000. The percent of single-mother families rose from 12% to 26%, and that of single-father families rose from 1% to 5%.

One alternative family form consists of two adults of the same sex, sometimes raising children. About 2.4% of men and 1.3% of women in the United States identify themselves as homosexual or bisexual and have same-gender partners (Laumann, Gagnon, Michael, & Michaels, 1994). Although information on the number and characteristics of gay and lesbian couples has not generally been available in the United States, one estimate suggests that in 1990 fewer than 1% of adult men lived with a male partner and about the same percentage of adult women lived with a lesbian partner (Black, Gates, Sanders, & Taylor, 2000). These estimates are based on responses to the unmarried partner question in the U.S. Census and are thus thought to be conservative estimates of the numbers of same-sex cohabitors. This is the case because some of those living in gay and lesbian couples do not identify as such in survey and other data. Legal and social recognition of these unions as marriages is generally not available in the United States. Dan Black and colleagues (2000) have estimated that about 25% of gay men and 40% of lesbian women are currently in or previously were in heterosexual marriages.

MARITAL QUALITY AND DYNAMICS

The life course of marriage has held endless fascination for scholars of the family and for the lay public since research on the family began. This literature points quite consistently to a pattern in which marital happiness was highest at the onset of marriage, with fairly sharp declines over the next few years, followed by further but somewhat slower declines as children were added to the family, grew up, and left home. At this point, most studies showed that marital happiness tended to rebound, although to levels somewhat lower than during the honeymoon phase (Glenn, 1990), so that marital happiness has a sort of U-shaped relationship over the life course: high at the beginning and at the end and low(er) in the middle.

A number of theoretical explanations have been advanced for changes in marital quality over the course of the marriage. One focuses on transitions in family and other roles and structures. Families tend to add children during the early years of marriage, and the presence of young children has been associated with declines in marital quality, perhaps because of conflicts over childrearing, a shift in attention and resources away from the couple toward their children, and increases in stress. Movements of women into the labor force, changes in family income, retirement, and health all may occur over the life of a marriage, perhaps changing the way in which individuals evaluate their marriages.

A second theoretical perspective points to the social psychological processes that take place in any couple, from the bliss of the falling-in-love stage through adaptation, habituation, and disillusionment. Early expectations of lifelong passion run headlong into the realities of getting dinner on the table and the laundry done. In addition, people may change over time in ways that make them less compatible than they were when they married. This developmental perspective on marriage suggests that changes in happiness are a fundamental part of the course of any relationship and are not because of changes in social circumstances, social roles, or family structure.

A third perspective argues that the world has changed in ways that have reduced happiness for all marriages. These include changes in gender relations, especially a shift from breadwinner-homemaker families toward dual earner families, in which both spouses provide income and care; increasing individualism and acceptance of divorce, both of which seem to erode relationship quality and stability by reducing investments in marriage; and an increase in economic uncertainty, especially for those with relatively low levels of education, resulting in increasing stress. In a comparison of marriages in two generations of people, those married during the 1970s and those married during the 1980s, when they had been married for the same number of years, Stacy Rogers and Paul Amato (1997) found that those in the younger generation reported less marital interaction, more marital conflict, and more problems in their marriages than the older generation did at the same points in their marriages.

Research that has tracked marital happiness over the course of the marriage among the same people married to the same spouse shows no support for the U-shaped relationship so common in the literature. Jody VanLaningham and colleagues (2001) found that marital happiness either declines continuously over the course of the marriage or that happiness declines over a long period and then stabilizes, but does not rebound. The authors suggest that the declines in marital happiness they observe are because of a mixture of developmental processes intrinsic to marriage in which spouses become habituated and thereby less happy, and because of shifts in the larger society and culture that have reduced support for the institution of marriage and increased the demands placed upon it, especially the demand to meet the emotional needs of the partners, introducing new sources of stress and instability.

THE CONSEQUENCES OF MARRIAGE

As a result of the characteristics of the institution of marriage discussed above, marriage changes the behavior of spouses and thereby their well-being. The specialization, economies of scale, and insurance functions of marriage all increase the economic well-being of family members, and the increase is typically quite substantial. Generally, married people produce more and accumulate more assets than unmarried people (Lupton & Smith, 2003). Married people also tend to have better physical and emotional health than single people, and at least part of this advantage is attributable to being married—rather than to selection effects (or those preexisting traits of persons who marry versus those who remain single)

(Mirowsky & Ross, 2003). The social support provided by a spouse, combined with the economic resources produced by the marriage, facilitate both the production and maintenance of health.

Lee Lillard and Linda Waite (1995) find that both men and women show declines in the likelihood of dying when they marry, although these effects appear at marriage for men and cumulate with duration of marriage for women. Men who become unmarried show large increases in the chances of dying, net of other characteristics, regardless of whether their marriage ends with divorce, separation, or widowhood. For women, the end of a marriage through divorce or separation increases the risk of death (Hemström, 1996), but the death of the husband does not. Hilke Brockmann and Thomas Klein (2004) find similar results among West German adults; the health benefits of marriage accumulate over time, whereas the negative health consequences of being single, divorced, or widowed attenuate over time. The beneficial effects of marriage are nonlinear; they are most pronounced in the early years of marriage. Men benefit immediately from marriage, whereas women's mortality risk actually increases at first. Researchers find no evidence that these effects differ by marriage order (that is, whether it is a first or later marriage). Theodore Iwashyna (2001) finds that both men and women show increased risks of dying in the year following the death of their spouse.

A number of recent studies have attempted to assess the mental health consequences of marriage, divorce, and widowhood, and to separate these from the selection of emotionally healthy individuals into marriage and distressed or unhealthy individuals out of marriage. These studies followed individuals over time as some marry, some divorce or become widowed, and some retain their previous marital status. Consistently, transitions into marriage improve mental health, on average, for both men and women, and transitions out of marriage decrease it (Horwitz, White, & Howell-White, 1996; Marks & Lambert, 1998; Simon, 2002). It is important to note that although rates of mental illness are quite similar for men and women in the United States in the early 21st century, women show higher rates of affective and anxiety disorders, with symptoms of nonspecific anxiety, distress, and depression, whereas men have higher rates of antisocial personality and substance abuse dependence disorders, which manifest themselves in antisocial behavior and drug and alcohol problems (Kessler, McGonagle, Zhao, Nelson, Hughes, Eshleman et al., 1994).

Robin Simon (2002) finds that divorce increases symptoms of emotional distress among both women and men, but women show greater increases than men in depressive symptoms following divorce and men who marry show greater reductions in alcohol consumption than do women who marry. Both men and women who divorce report a significant increase in alcohol abuse. Simon also finds men and women who divorced reported more depressive symptoms and more alcohol problems earlier than those who remained married, which she interprets as both a cause *and* a consequence of disruption.

Studies that control for the selection of the psychologically healthy into marriage, and also include a wider range of measures of mental well-being, find that although there are differences by gender in the types of emotional responses to marital transitions, the psychological benefits associated with marriage apply equally to men and women (Horwitz, White, & Howell-White, 1996; Marks & Lambert, 1998; Simon, 2002).

Of course, the complete picture is more complicated. Research has extended this line of work to examine differences in the consequences of marital transitions for women and men with various characteristics. This research shows considerable heterogeneity in effects and some surprising similarities.

It seems logical that people who enter marriage disadvantaged in some way, such as ill health, a criminal record, a prior divorce, children from a previous relationship, or poor emotional well-being, bring less to the marriage themselves and are likely to get less out of it than those without these problems. And both scholars and advocates have argued that those in marriages marked by violence, especially women, will gain enormously from leaving those relationships. However neither of these observations seems to find consistent empirical support.

One could argue that those with poor mental health prior to marriage would be less likely to marry and would benefit less from marriage than those with good mental health. Depression in one partner might limit the benefits that person could provide to a spouse, increase the demands on the other spouse, and reduce actual and perceived marital quality. But Adrianne Frech and Kristi Williams (2007) find, instead, that those who were depressed before they married show *larger* gains in emotional well-being than others, and that marital quality plays a similar role in moderating the effect of marriage on mental health for those who were depressed prior to marriage and those who were not. The patterns are similar for men and women. In fact, Frech and Williams find that the psychological benefits of getting married are quite modest for those who were not previously depressed and sizable only for those in poor mental health before marriage. These findings stand conventional wisdom on its head.

Another study does the same for marital violence. Matthijs Kalmijn and Christiaan Monden (2006) find, consistent with previous research, that divorce leads to higher levels of depressive symptoms for women but that men show no change. People who divorce from a marriage characterized by verbal aggression, the authors find, show a *stronger* increase in depressive symptoms than others who divorce. Their results also show that women who divorce from a marriage in which there was physical aggression see a *greater* increase in depressive symptoms than other women who divorce. They suggest that the conflict that characterized the marriage often continues or escalates after the divorce, and so continues to reduce emotional well-being.

To the extent that the benefits of marriage flow from the *state* of being married, then marital disruption, either through divorce or widowhood, interrupts the flow of benefits, which may consist of financial well-being, health, or social connections, remarriage reestablishes the flow of benefits. This suggests that the *duration* of marriage matters. Do transitions into a second or higher-order marriage bring benefits equal to those of a first marriage? In theory, later marriages bring all the same advantages—companionship, economies of scale, trust, social connection, and so on—that come with a first marriage. If later marriages bring the same levels and types of advantages, then spouses in these marriages should show outcomes equal to those of the once-married who had been married the same number of years.

Evidence on the benefits of remarriage is mixed, however. Both Anne Barrett (2000) and Nadine Marks and James Lambert (1998) find that higher-order marriages are less enhancing to mental health than first marriages. However, remarriage seems to undo the negative financial consequences of marital disruption, especially for women (Wilmoth & Koso, 2002).

In most societies, marriage circumscribes a large majority of sexual relationships. Data from the United States show that almost all married men and women are sexually active and almost all have only one sex partner—their spouse. Unmarried men and women have much lower levels of sexual activity than the married, in part because a substantial minority have no sex partner at all. (Just under one-quarter of the unmarried men and one-third of the unmarried women who were not cohabiting at the time of the survey had no sex partner in the previous year.) Men and women who are cohabiting are at least as sexually active as those who are married, but are less likely to be sexually exclusive (Laumann, Gagnon, Michael, & Michaels, 1994).

A key function of marriage is the bearing and raising of children. The institution of marriage directs the resources of the spouses and their extended families, especially time, money, attention, information, skills, and social connections, toward the couple's children, increasing child well-being.

ISSUES REMAINING

Rapid changes in family processes in many postindustrial societies such as the United States mean that researchers studying cohabitation, marriage, or even the family are aiming at a moving target. Defining each of these is both crucial and difficult. Must families be related by blood or marriage? If so, does a cohabiting couple constitute a family? Clearly not, under the current definition, because they share neither a blood nor legal tie. What if they have a child? Blood ties exist between the mother and the child and between the father and the child, so each of these constitutes a family. It becomes difficult to argue that this triad consists of two separate families, and much easier to argue that they form a single family, although the adults do not share a blood or legal tie.

What about a cohabiting couple with a child belonging only to the woman? The mother and child constitute a family, but does it include the man who lives with them but shares no blood or legal ties to either? It is difficult to say. The man has no legal responsibilities to either the woman or her child, and no legal rights as a husband or father. But the three may share powerful social, financial, and emotional bonds.

A central question becomes, "What *is* cohabitation?" Steven Nock (1995) has argued that cohabitation is incompletely institutionalized, leaving partners, their families, and others unsure about the nature of the relationship. Susan Brown and Alan Booth (1996) have suggested that cohabitation may be *several* institutions, each with distinct characteristics. One consists of couples who are engaged, have no children, and no previous marriages. These couples appear to be similar to married couples in their behavior and relationship outcomes. Another type of cohabitation includes couples with no plans to marry, with children (generally from a previous relationship), and at least one divorced partner. These couples seem to differ in important ways from more committed cohabitors and from married couples. So, scholars must ask, and continue asking, "What kind of a relationship is this? What are the rules under which the partners are operating? How does the relationship affect choices made by the members and by others? How does the existence of the relationship and its form affect the well-being of the individuals involved?"

Family scholars face as many questions about marriage. What are the irreducible characteristics of marriage? In the United States, same-sex couples are forbidden to marry, although in a few places they may register a *domestic partnership*. Opponents of granting same-sex couples access to marriage argue that, by definition, marriage must involve a man and a woman. Supporters argue that if marriage provides a wide variety of important benefits to participants, it is discriminatory to deny these to same-sex couples. Does a registered domestic partnership provide same-sex couples with the same benefits as marriage provides heterosexual couples? What *is* marriage?

KEY POLICY ISSUES

Gay and Lesbian Families Historically and traditionally, a family consisted of people related by blood or marriage in a culturally recognized social network of biological and marital relationships. Marriage is a legal relationship between an adult man and an adult woman to form a new family. Gay and lesbian families, sometimes based on socially recognized or legally recognized relationship, challenge these definitions. Attitudes toward sex between two adults of the same sex have become substantially more accepting in the United States during decades leading up to the 21st century. Extension of the definition of *family* and *marriage* to same-sex couples has been hotly contested and fiercely debated. In the United States, many attempts to extend access to marriage and family rights to same-sex couples have been turned back by legislators or voters, with some notable exceptions. Several European countries have moved furthest on these issues. France now allows same-sex couples to register their partnerships, Denmark has extended child custody rights to same-sex couples, and the state supreme courts in Ontario, Canada, and Vermont have both ruled that same-sex couples are entitled to full and equal family rights. And, perhaps most definitively, the Netherlands has granted same-sex couples full and equal rights to marriage (Stacey & Biblarz, 2001).

Current theoretical issues surrounding marriage focus on the elasticity of the definition. Must marriage, by definition, include only adults of opposite sexes? Is it possible for two men to marry? Two women? An adult and a child? Two children? Clearly, in some societies, a husband may have more than one wife, although the reverse is rarely true (Daly & Wilson, 2000). And, theoretically, in countries such as Norway and Sweden, in which the legal distinction between cohabiting and married couples has shrunken to the point of vanishing, have cohabiting couples become *married*? Is this just a return to the common-law marriages of the past, or is it something different?

The forms and patterns of family life have shifted, quite noticeably in some countries and among some groups. But Homo sapiens developed as a species in conjunction with the development of the family, some would argue in conjunction with the institution of marriage (de Waal & Pollick, 2005). Humans' future and the future of the family are inextricably intertwined and always will be.

SEE ALSO Volume 1: *Transition to Marriage;* Volume 2: *Cohabitation; Dating and Romantic Relationships, Adulthood; Divorce and Separation; Dual Career Couples; Family and Household Structure, Adulthood; Gays and Lesbians, Adulthood; Mate Selection; Mental Health, Adulthood; Remarriage;* Volume 3: *Singlehood; Widowhood.*

BIBLIOGRAPHY

Amato, P. R., & Booth, A. (1995). Changes in gender role attitudes and perceived marital quality. *American Sociological Review, 60*(1), 58–66.

Barrett, A. E. (2000). Marital trajectories and mental health. *Journal of Health and Social Behavior, 41*(4), 451–464.

Black, D., Gates, G., Sanders, S., & Taylor, L. (2000). Demographics of the gay and lesbian population in the United States: Evidence from available systematic data sources. *Demography, 37*(2), 139–154.

Brien, M, Lillard, L. A., & Waite, L. J. (1999). Interrelated family-building behaviors: Cohabitation, marriage, and nonmarital conception. *Demography, 36*(4), 535–552.

Brockmann, H, & Klein, T. (2004). Love and death in Germany: The marital biography and its effect on mortality. *Journal of Marriage and the Family, 66*, 582–594.

Brown, S. L., & Booth, A. (1996). Cohabitation versus marriage: A comparison of relationship quality. *Journal of Marriage and the Family, 58*, 668–678.

Bumpass, L., & Lu, H.-H. (2000). Trends in cohabitation and implications for children's family contexts. *Population Studies, 54*(1), 29–41.

Burch, T. K., & Matthews, B. (1987). Household formation in developed societies. *Population and Development Review, 13*(3), 495–511.

Caldwell, J. C., Reddy, P. H., & Caldwell, P. (1983). The causes of marriage change in South Asia. *Population Studies, 37*(3), 343–361.

Daly, M., & Wilson, M. I. (2000). The evolutionary psychology of marriage and divorce. In L. J. Waite, C. Bachrach, M. Hindin, E. Thomson, & A. Thornton (Eds.), *Ties that bind: Perspectives on marriage and cohabitation* (pp. 91–110). New York: Aldine de Gruyter.

de Waal, F. B. M., & Pollick, A. S. (2005). The biology of family values: Reproductive strategies of our fellow primates. In S. M. Tipton & J. Witte, Jr., (Eds.), *Family transformed: Religion, values, and society in American life* (pp. 34–51). Washington, DC: Georgetown University Press.

Fields, J., & Casper, L.M. (2001). America's families and living arrangements: March 2000. Washington, DC: U.S. Census Bureau. Retrieved April 30, 2008, from http://www.census2010.gov/prod/2001pubs/p20-537.pdf

Fitch, C. A., & Ruggles, S. (2000). Historical trends in marriage formation: The United States 1850–1990. In L. J. Waite, C. Bachrach, M. Hindin, E. Thomson, & A. Thornton (Eds.), *Ties that bind: Perspectives on marriage and cohabitation* (pp. 59–90). New York: Aldine de Gruyter.

Fogel, R. W. (2000). *The fourth great awakening and the future of egalitarianism.* Chicago: University of Chicago Press.

Frech, A., & Williams, K. (2007). Depression and the psychological benefits of entering marriage. *Journal of Health and Social Behavior, 48*(2), 149–163.

Friedberg, L. (1998). Did unilateral divorce raise divorce rates? Evidence from panel data. *American Economic Review, 88*(3), 608–627.

Giddens, A. (1992). *The transformation of intimacy: Sexuality, love and, eroticism in modern societies.* Stanford, CA: Stanford University Press.

Glenn, N.D. (1990). Quantitative research in marital quality in the 1980s: A critical review. *Journal of Marriage and Family, 52*(4), 818–831.

Goldstein, J. R., & Kenney, C. T. (2001). Marriage delayed or marriage forgone? New cohort forecasts of first marriage for U.S. women. *American Sociological Review, 66*(4), 506–519.

Hemström, Ö. (1996). Is marriage dissolution linked to differences in mortality risks for men and women? *Journal of Marriage and the Family, 58*(2), 366–378.

Horwitz, A. V., White, H. R., & Howell-White, S. (1996). Becoming married and mental health: A longitudinal study of a cohort of young adults. *Journal of Marriage and the Family, 58*(4), 895–907.

Iwashyna, T. J. (2001). In sickness and in health: Understanding the effects of marriage on health. Chicago: University of Chicago Press.

Kalmijn, M., & Monden, C. W. S. (2006). Are the negative effects of divorce on well-being dependent on marital quality? *Journal of Marriage and Family, 68*(5), 1197–1213.

Kessler, R. C., McGonagle, K. A., Zhao, S., Nelson, C. B., Hughes, M., Eshleman, S. et al. (1994). Lifetime and 12-month prevalence of DSM-III-R psychiatric disorders in the United States. *Archives of General Psychiatry, 51*(1), 8–19.

Kiernan, K. (2000). Cohabitation in western Europe: Trends, issues, and implications. In A. Booth & A.C. Crouter (Eds.), *Just living together: Implications of cohabitation on families, children, and social policy.* Mahwa, NJ: Lawrence Erlbaum.

Laumann, E. O., Gagnon, J. H., Michael, R. T., & Michaels, S. (1994). *The social organization of sexuality: Sexual practices in the United States.* Chicago: University of Chicago Press.

Lesthaeghe, R. (1995). The second demographic transition in Western countries: An interpretation. In K. O. Mason & A.-M. Jensen (Eds.), *Gender and family change in industrialized countries.* New York: Oxford University Press.

Lillard, L. A., & Waite, L. J. (1995). Til death do us part: Marital disruption and mortality. *American Journal of Sociology, 100*(5), 1131–1156.

Logan, J. R., & Spitze, G. D. (1996). *Family ties: Enduring relations between parents and their grown children.* Philadelphia: Temple University Press.

Lupton, J., & Smith, J. P. (2003). Marriage, assets, and savings. In S. Grossbard-Shechtman (Ed.), *Marriage and the economy: Theory and evidence from advanced industrial societies* (pp. 129–152). New York: Cambridge University Press.

Marks, N. F., & Lambert, J. D. (1998). Marital status continuity and change among young and midlife adults: Longitudinal effects on psychological well-being. *Journal of Family Issues, 19*(6), 652–686.

Martin, J. A., Hamilton, B. E., Ventura, S. J., Menacker, F., & Park, M. M. (2002). Births: Final data for 2000. *National Vital Statistics Reports, 50*(5). Hyattsville, MD: National Center for Health Statistics. Retrieved April 30, 2008, from http://www.cdc.gov/nchs/datawh/statab/unpubd/natality/natab97.htm

Mirowsky, J., & Ross, C. (2003). *Social causes of psychological distress.* (2nd ed.). New York: Aldine De Gruyter.

Nock, S. L. (1995). A comparison of marriages and cohabiting relationships. *Journal of Family Issues, 16*(1), 53–76.

Raley, R. K. (2000). Recent trends in marriage and cohabitation. In L. J. Waite, C. Bachrach, M. Hindin, E. Thomson, & A. Thornton (Eds.), *Ties that bind: Perspectives on marriage and cohabitation.* New York: Aldine de Gruyter.

Regan, M. C., Jr. (1996). Postmodern family law: Toward a new model of status. In D. Popenoe, J. B. Elshtain, & D.

Blankenhorn (Eds.), *Promises to keep: Decline and renewal of marriage in America*. Lanham, MD: Rowman & Littlefield.

Rogers, S. J., & Amato, P. (1997). Is marital quality declining? The evidence from two generations. *Social Forces, 75*(3), 1089–1100.

Simon, R. W. (2002). Revisiting the relationships among gender, marital status, and mental health. *American Journal of Sociology, 107*(4), 1065–1096.

Stacey, J., & Biblarz, T. J. (2001). (How) does the sexual orientation of parents matter? *American Sociological Review, 66*(2), 159–183.

Thornton, A., & Fricke, T. E. (1989). Social change and the family: Comparative perspectives from the West, China, and South Asia. In J. M. Stycos (Ed.), *Demography as an interdiscipline* (pp. 128–161). New Brunswick, NJ: Transaction.

Thornton, A., & Young-DeMarco, L. (2001). Four decades of trends in attitudes toward family issues in the United States: The 1960s through the 1990s. *Journal of Marriage and Family, 63*(4), 1009–1037.

United Nations. (2000). Retrieved April 30, 2008, from http://www.un.org/english/

VanLaningham, J., Johnson, D. R., & Amato, P. (2001). Marital happiness, marital duration, and the U-shaped curve: Evidence from a five-wave panel study. *Social Forces, 79*(4), 1313–1341.

Waite, L. J. (1995). Does marriage matter? *Demography, 32*(4), 483–508.

Waite, L. J., & Gallagher, M. (2000). *The case for marriage: Why married people are happier, healthier, and better off financially.* New York: Doubleday.

Waite, L. J., & Nielsen, M. (2000). The rise of the dual career family. In R. Hertz & N. L. Marshall (Eds.), *Work and family: Today's realities and tomorrow's visions.* Berkeley: University of California Press.

Waite, L. J., & Nielsen, M. (2001). The rise of the dual earner family, 1963–1997. In R. Hertz & N. L. Marshall (Eds.), *Working families: The transformation of the American home* (pp. 23–41). Berkeley: University of California Press.

Watkins, S. C., Menken, J. A., & Bongaarts, J. (1987). Demographic foundations of family change. *American Sociological Review, 52*(3), 346–358.

Wilmoth, J., & Koso, G. (2002). Does marital history matter? Marital status and wealth outcomes among preretirement adults. *Journal of Marriage and the Family, 64*(1), 254–268.

Linda J. Waite

MARX, KARL
1818–1883

Karl Marx, a German philosopher, was a pioneer of the sort of interdisciplinary analyses that would later become integral to the life-course perspective. More famously and infamously, his was the voice that both criticized and drew from existing European socialism to define a movement that he called *Communism*. Marx's work derives from two

Karl Marx. AP IMAGES.

additional currents: the philosophy of G. W. F. Hegel (1770–1831) and Ludwig Feuerbach (1804–1872) and the political economy of Adam Smith (1723–1790) and David Ricardo (1772–1823). Marx contributed some of the most enduring notions of social class and social conflict.

Born in Trier, a town near the German border with Luxembourg and France, Marx grew up in an environment heavily influenced by French philosophy and politics. His early life included training in philosophy, history, and law. After receiving his university degree, he founded a series of radical newspapers both at home and abroad that were quickly suppressed. Because of this, Marx returned to his studies of history and political economy.

MARX'S PHILOSOPHIES

Marx's emphasis on the importance of social class derived from these studies, which allowed him to chart the historical transition of the social classes in Europe during the modern period. He argued that a new class, called the *bourgeoisie*, was displacing the European aristocracy as the dominant political class. This often occurred through violent revolution, most notoriously in France. At the same time that the bourgeoisie was seizing political power, a new lower class was developing. Marx called this class the *proletariat*.

Unlike the bourgeoisie, the proletariat did not own any property apart from the capacities of its members to use their bodies to labor for a wage. As the industrial revolution advanced, members of the proletariat grew more numerous and clustered in industrial centers, especially London. Working conditions for the proletariat were deplorable. Marx pointed out that the working conditions of the proletariat poisoned the relationship that members of the proletariat had to their own activity. This proletariat worked only to live, and live minimally, a situation Marx called *alienation*.

Marx expected the proletariat to rise up in revolution against the bourgeoisie that dominated it, and he documented this expectation in his 1848 *Communist Manifesto*. Penned jointly with Friedrich Engels (1820–1895), who would be Marx's lifelong writing partner, the *Communist Manifesto* is one of the most widely dispersed documents of all time and has been read in many global contexts as an essential call of oppressed peoples to action.

Although Marx's attention to social class is both provocative and significant, his philosophy does far more than simply reveal the importance of social class. Marx gave a name to the mode of production developed in the modern European world: *capitalism*. Marx's unfinished *magnum opus*, the work *Das Kapital* (*Capital*), describes capitalism, particularly as it existed in late 19th-century London. *Capital* also presciently forecasts the ways the capitalist mode of production will extend over the whole world. Although some of Marx's analyses in *Capital* bear the historical marks of the era in which they were produced, the work remains salient. Philosophically, *Capital* may even be said to be a work written for and about the future, as it is much more characteristic of subsequent developments than it was of Marx's own time.

Marx's works are voluminous, although only a tiny portion of them was well known prior to Joseph Stalin's death in 1953. The political power of the movements founded under the name of Communism far overshadowed Marx himself and led to the direct suppression of some of his more philosophical or speculative works. Scholars continue to unpack Marx's legacy in the post–cold war era, an era that may allow people to see him clearly for the first time.

Many of Marx's works in addition to the *Communist Manifesto* and *Capital* are worth close study. The most important of these include *The Economic and Philosophical Manuscripts of 1844*, the *Theses on Feuerbach* (1845), *The German Ideology* (1846), *The Eighteenth Brumaire of Louis Bonaparte* (1851–1852), the *Grundrisse* (1857–1858), and the *Preface to the Contribution to the Critique of Political Economy* (1859).

Marx's work has influenced many social, political, and intellectual currents. Leszek Kolakowski's multivo-lume work, *Main Currents of Marxism: Its Rise, Growth, and Dissolution*, remains the best encyclopedic text documenting the various strands of Marxism.

After being expelled from the European continent as a part of the suppression that followed the revolutions of 1848, Marx lived his life from 1849 onward in London. Spending most of his days in the British Museum's Reading Room, Marx drew widely from history, economics, theology, political theory, literature, chemistry, and mathematics. In addition he had access to the new kinds of empirical studies on populations that would later be foundational in the discipline Marx himself was instrumental in crafting: sociology.

SEE ALSO Volume 2: *Social Class; Social Movements; Sociological Theories.*

BIBLIOGRAPHY

Kolakowski, L. (1978). *Main currents of Marxism: Its rise, growth, and dissolution* (Vols.1–3). Oxford, U.K.: Clarendon Press.

Marx, K. (1990). *Capital: A critical analysis of capitalist production*. London and Berlin: Dietz. (Original work published 1887)

Marx-Engels Gesamtausgabe (MEGA2). (2nd ed.). (1990). Berlin: Dietz Verlag.

McLellan, D. (Ed.), & Marx, K. (2000). *Karl Marx: Selected writings*. Oxford, U.K.: Oxford University Press.

Tucker, R. (Ed.), Marx, K., & Engels, F. (1978). *The Marx-Engels reader*. New York and London: W.W. Norton & Company.

Amy Wendling

MATE SELECTION

Almost all young men and women expect to tie the knot, but not all end up getting married according to Daniel Lichter, Deborah Roempke Graefe, and J. Brian Brown (2003). One reason some people never marry is the difficulty of finding the right person. The conventional pattern of mate selection is for men and women to choose a partner with personal characteristics similar to his or her own. Young women usually marry young men, college-educated women tend to marry college-educated men, Black women most likely marry Black men, Catholics prefer to marry Catholics, and so on. This "like marries like" phenomenon is "partly an unconscious result of a process in which many individuals attempt to achieve the best possible bargain for themselves or their children by weighing marital resources and alternatives" (Elder, 1969, p. 519). It effectively diminishes one way of achieving social mobility. Nevertheless, other factors, including shortages of marriage partners in one group and a prolonged search for marriageable partners in marriage markets, may increase the likelihood that a marriage across group lines would occur. The groups people marry into are typically those with shorter social distance from the groups to which they belong. As a result, mate selection patterns help explain relative salience of group boundaries in a society.

THE MARRIAGE MARKET

Social scientists view the mate selection process as analogous to the matching of employers and employees in labor markets. In labor markets, job searchers seek the best job possible, subject both to opportunities (e.g., jobs available) and constraints (e.g., their skills and credentials). Among all potential job offers, some will be acceptable to the job searcher, but others will be unacceptable, failing to meet his or her aspirations regarding work type, pay level, or work condition. Finding the best job among all possible potential job offers is both costly and time-consuming; search activities therefore do not continue indefinitely. Instead, job seekers decide on a minimally acceptable match, the so-called "reservation wage." Searchers reject job offers below the reservation wage and accept the first offer at or above the reservation wage. All else being equal, the lower the reservation wage, the more likely searchers will find a job quickly.

By analogy, in marriage markets, men and women seek the best partner possible given their own opportunities (available partners) and constraints (their own characteristics and preferences). According to Paula England and George Farkas (1986), marriage-seekers have in mind a "reservation quality partner"—analogous to the job seeker's reservation wage. Their minimally acceptable marital partners would be somebody similar to themselves. So when men and women look for the best match in marriage markets, they often end up marrying someone with similar characteristics. Those who set too high a standard for the reservation quality partner prolong the search process. Eventually, they will never marry or will have to "cast a wider net" to lower their reservation quality partner and form mismatched marriages.

HOMOGAMY AND ENDOGAMY

Mate selection processes in marriage markets clarify why people around the world are likely to form homogamous (similar in achieved statuses, such as educational attainment) or endogamous marriages (similar in ascribed statuses, such as race/ethnicity). In traditional societies parents typically play a large role in arranging their children's marriages. The outcome is that their sons and daughters are well matched in socioeconomic status (Goode, 1982). In the United States, young men and women have free choice and prefer to marry someone they fall in love with; however, the mates that young men and women choose based on love are usually much to the liking of their parents. In American society parents no longer arrange marriages for their children—a practice still common in many less developed countries. However, thanks to socialization, American sons and daughters choose mates in the same way their parents would do on their behalf—by finding someone with common interests and backgrounds.

Individuals who are similar in age, belong to the same racial or ethnic group, have the same levels of educational attainment, come from similar family backgrounds, and/or have the same religious beliefs appear to be more "lovable" to each other because of their common interests and backgrounds. Yet an exact match on all those traits is not easy. Certain traits (religion or race) are often more important than others (educational attainment) but, over time, the relative importance of these traits can shift. In the United States, Matthijs Kalmijn (1991) noted that religious boundaries are breaking down, and interfaith marriages have become more common in recent generations. Racially endogamous marriages still are the norm, as Zhenchao Qian and Daniel Lichter (2007) pointed out, but interracial marriages are on the rise, especially among U.S.-born Americans. Meanwhile, educational boundaries have become more rigid, according to Christine Schwartz and Robert Mare (2005). In other words, compared to the past in the United States, marriages involving men and women with similar levels of education have increased whereas those involving men and women who belong to the same racial/ethnic group have declined.

Changes in racial endogamy and educational homogamy reflect changes in social structure and in the openness of American society. Social scientists such as Peter Blau and Otis Dudley Duncan (1967) have argued that, in modern, developed societies, ascriptive traits, such as family and racial background, have become less important than achieved qualities, such as education, in determining economic positions. It makes sense then that in early 21st century marriage markets men and women place more emphasis on educational attainment and less emphasis on race in choosing marriageable partners.

INCREASES IN EDUCATIONAL HOMOGAMY

In the early decades of the 20th century, educational homogamy was high. As shown in Figure 1, in 1940, 59.3% of the husbands and wives had the same level of education. Such a high level of homogamy is not surprising; half of the married men and women had fewer than 10 years of schooling, and there was little variation in educational attainment in the population at that time. Improvements in educational attainment since then initially reduced educational homogamy—the percentage of married couples with the same level of educational

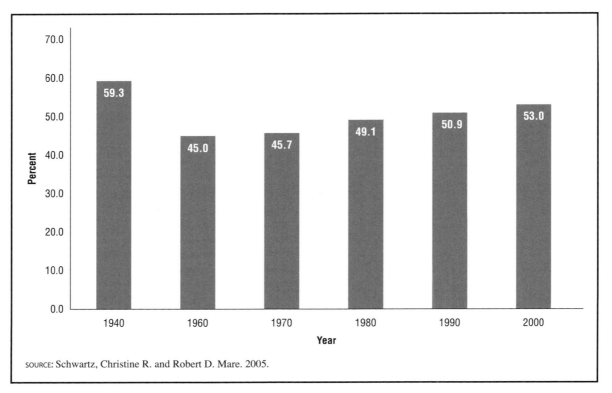

SOURCE: Schwartz, Christine R. and Robert D. Mare. 2005.

Figure 1. *Percent of married couples with same levels of education, 1940–2000.* CENGAGE LEARNING, GALE.

attainment declined to 45% in 1960. At the same time, Richard Rockwell (1976) pointed out that husbands had more education than their wives in an increasing share of marriages. Gary Becker (1981) noted that marriage at that time emphasized spousal complementarity—husbands concentrated their efforts in the labor market, whereas wives specialized in domestic labor. Under these conditions, husbands' earning potentials as measured by educational attainment were more important in the marriage market than wives' educations.

The reversal in educational homogamy started in the 1970s. The percentage of couples with the same educational level increased from 45.7% in 1970 to 53% in 2000. Most of the increase in homogamy is attributable to an increase in marriages in which both the husband and wife have a college education. In large part this is because, according to Claudia Buchmann and Thomas DiPrete (2006), on average, women's educational attainment increased more than men's during this time. This increase closed the gender gap in educational attainment. More women with college educations and more women in the labor force since have moved women's socioeconomic positions upward. Responding to this change, men increasingly find women's socioeconomic resources important in marriage markets. Indeed, Megan Sweeney and Maria Cancian (2004) indicated that women's posi-

tion in the labor market has become more attractive over time as a determinant of their position in the marriage market. Consequently, achieved statuses such as educational attainment have become equally important for men and women in marriage markets.

DECLINES IN RACIAL ENDOGAMY

Levels of racial endogamy depend in part on the size of each racial group. The larger the group, the more likely group members will find marriageable partners of their own race. Thus, Whites, the largest racial group in the United States, have the highest percentage of endogamy. Endogamous marriages accounted for 98% of the White marriages in 1980 and 96% of White marriages in 2000. Endogamy, on the other hand, was much lower for American Indians and Asian Americans, which have much smaller population sizes. Statistical differences in racial/ethnic endogamy are also partly attributable to differences in the size of each group. For example, one Asian-White marriage affects the percentage of endogamous marriages much more for Asians than for Whites because the Asian population is much smaller than the White population. For the same reason, although just 4% of Whites were involved in interracial marriages in 2000, 92% of all interracial marriages include a White partner.

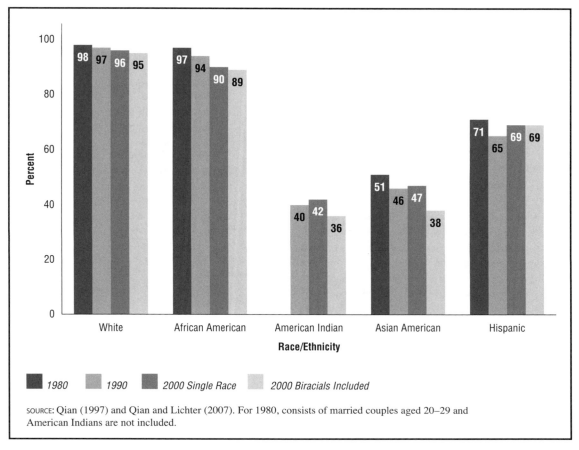

Figure 2. *Percent of racially endogamous marriages among U.S. born couples aged 20–30.* CENGAGE LEARNING, GALE.

Figure 2 shows an overall decline in racial endogamy for all racial/ethnic groups, from 97% to 90% for African Americans and from 51% to 47% for Asian Americans between 1980 and 2000. The trend reversed for U.S.-born Hispanics due to a large influx of immigrants from Latin America; the increase in group size enables greater racial endogamy. Given population size differences, comparing rates of intermarriage among groups can be difficult. Statistical models can account for group size, identify the extent to which any group is marrying another more or less than one would expect given their population group size, and then reveal other factors affecting intermarriage (Qian & Lichter 2007). Results using these models show that racial endogamy among the U.S.-born has indeed declined in the past decades for each racial group.

Racial endogamy has declined for several reasons. First, increases in educational attainment among racial minorities are associated with declines in racial endogamy. College-educated men and women are more likely to marry interracially than those with less education. The fact that Asian Americans attend college at relatively high rates helps explain their low level of racial endogamy. Highly educated minority members often attend colleges,

work in places, and live in neighborhoods that are integrated. They find substantial opportunities for interracial contact, friendship, romance, and marriage.

Second, the growth of the multiracial population has blurred racial boundaries and reduced racial endogamy. The U.S. Census Bureau classifies people into four major race categories: Whites, African Americans, Asian Americans, and American Indians. Hispanics can belong to any of the four racial groups but are considered as one separate minority group. In the 2000 census, Americans could choose more than one racial group for the first time. Most multiracial Americans are part White and part Black, American Indian, or Asian. When biracial Americans are included, Qian and Daniel Lichter (2007) reported, racial endogamy declines even further, especially for American Indians and Asian Americans, who have greater shares of multiracial individuals compared to African Americans.

COHABITATION

In recent decades in the United States, educational homogamy has increased steadily whereas racial endogamy has declined. Clearly, achieved social status and economic positions have become an important mate selection criterion whereas racial barriers have broken down to some extent. These changes also result from the fact that marriage has become more selective, as cohabitation has arisen as a viable alternative to marriage. Cohabitation can serve as a stepping stone to marriage. Debra. Blackwell and Daniel Lichter (2000) call this type of cohabitation a *winnowing process*. Educational homogamy and racial endogamy are relatively low among cohabiting couples but are much greater among those who make transitions to marriage. In other words, those who make transitions to marriage are more likely to share similar racial and educational backgrounds than those who do not.

The connection between cohabitation and marriage, however, is weakening (Cherlin 2004). Fewer cohabiting unions end in marriage. Kathryn Edin (2000) found that lack of economic resources and uncertain labor markets dampened marriage prospects for cohabiting couples. Also in 2000 Larry Bumpass and Hsien-Hen Lu indicated that a large fraction of unmarried births were to cohabiting women. This reduces the likelihood of marriage among unmarried women with children because prospective spouses may be unwilling to assume the economic and parental responsibilities associated with marriage to an unmarried mother. Thus a prior cohabitation may signal a poor "position" in the marriage market. (Qian, Lichter, & Mellott, 2005). However, cohabitation is a short-lived living arrangement. The cohabiting couples that do not make transitions to marriage often end up going their separate ways quickly.

Patterns of mate selections by race and education reflect changes in relative importance of these traits over time. Yet, they also result from increasing selectivity of marital unions—fewer people ever marry and more men and women move from one cohabiting relationship to another. Existing literature on mate selection focuses more on marriages. Future research needs to take into account men and women who are in marriage markets but have not yet formed marital unions.

SEE ALSO Volume 2: *Cohabitation; Dating and Romantic Relationships, Adulthood; Marriage; Remarriage.*

BIBLIOGRAPHY

Becker, G. S. (1981). *A treatise on the family.* Cambridge, MA: Harvard University Press.

Blackwell, D. L., & Lichter, D. T. (2000). Mate selection among married and cohabiting couples. *Journal of Family Issues, 21,* 275–302.

Blau, P. M., & Duncan, O. D. (1967). *The American occupational structure.* New York: Wiley.

Buchmann, C., & DiPrete, T. A. (2006). The growing female advantage in college completion: The role of parental resources and academic achievement. *American Sociological Review, 71,* 515–541.

Bumpass, L. L., & Lu, H.-H. (2000). Trends in cohabitation and implications for children's family contexts. *Population Studies, 54,* 29–41.

Cherlin, A. J. (2004). The deinstitutionalization of American marriage. *Journal of Marriage and the Family, 66,* 848–861.

Edin, K. (2000). What do low-income single mothers say about marriage? *Social Problems, 47,* 112–133.

Elder, G. H. Jr. (1969). Appearance and education in marriage mobility. *American Sociological Review, 34,* 519–533.

England, P., & Farkas, G. (1986). *Households, employment, and gender: A social, economic, and demographic view.* New York: Aldine.

Goode, W. J. (1982). *The family.* Englewood Cliffs, NJ: Prentice-Hall.

Kalmijn, M. (1991). Shifting boundaries: Trends in religious and educational homogamy. *American Sociological Review, 56,* 786–800.

Lichter, D. T., Roempke Graefe, D., & Brown, J. B. (2003). Is marriage a panacea? Union formation among economically disadvantaged unwed mothers. *Social Problems, 50,* 68–86.

Qian, Z., & Lichter, D. T. (2007). Social boundaries and marital assimilation: Interpreting trends in racial and ethnic intermarriage. *American Sociological Review, 72,* 68–94.

Qian, Z., Lichter, D. T., & Mellott, L. M. (2005). Out-of-wedlock childbearing, marital prospects and mate selection. *Social Forces, 84,* 473–491.

Rockwell, R. C. (1976). Historical trends and variations in educational homogamy. *Journal of Marriage and the Family, 38,* 83–95.

Schwartz, C. R., & Mare, R. D. (2005). Trends in educational assortative marriage from 1940 to 2003. *Demography, 42,* 621–646.

Sweeney, M. M., & Cancian, M. (2004). The changing importance of White women's economic prospects for assortative mating. *Journal of Marriage and the Family, 66,* 1015–1028.

Zhenchao Qian

MATERNAL MORTALITY

Maternal mortality refers to death during pregnancy, childbirth, or the postpartum period (defined as 42 days following the termination of pregnancy) from causes directly or indirectly related to the pregnant state. The leading direct cause of maternal mortality globally is hemorrhage (bleeding), with the majority of these deaths occurring in the immediate postpartum period. Other leading direct causes include sepsis (severe blood infection), high blood pressure due to pregnancy, obstructed labor, and induced abortion (with most abortion-related deaths caused from hemorrhage or sepsis). Common indirect causes, which are preexisting conditions made worse by pregnancy, include HIV, malaria, and anemia. The time around delivery is by far the period of greatest risk. Estimates suggest that two-thirds of maternal deaths occur between late pregnancy and within 48 hours after delivery (AbouZahr, 1998).

The estimated number of maternal deaths globally was 536,000 in 2005, with 99% occurring in developing countries. Nearly half of maternal deaths occur in five countries: India, Nigeria, Democratic Republic of the Congo, Afghanistan, and Ethiopia (Hill et al., 2007). The difference in the risk of maternal death between developing and developed countries is greater than that for other common health indicators. For example, the maternal mortality ratio across developed countries is 9 maternal deaths per 100,000 live births, compared to 905 per 100,000 live births in sub-Saharan Africa. Estimates of the maternal mortality ratio for individual countries range as high as 2,100 deaths per 100,000 live births (Hill et al., 2007). Viewed from a life-course perspective, maternal death represents the leading or second leading cause of death among women 15 to 49 years of age in many developing countries. The proportion of deaths due to maternal causes among females ages 15 to 49 ranges from less than 1% in developed countries to 15 to 45% in developed countries (World Health Organization, United Nations Children's Fund, & United Nations Population Fund, 2004).

Measuring maternal mortality is difficult and leads to imprecise estimates. The challenges vary by setting. Even in developed countries with well-established systems for registering births and deaths, maternal mortality has been shown to be underestimated by one-third of the actual maternal mortality ratio on average (Hill et al., 2007). This is primarily due to death certificates that do not specify the pregnant state of the woman at death. Thus, causes of death such as sepsis, embolism (blood clot), or indirect causes of death are not categorized as maternal (AbouZahr, 1998). However, only 26% of the world's population live in countries with complete death reporting via vital registration, and this drops as low as 7% and 1% in Africa and Southeast Asia, respectively (Mahapatra et al., 2007). In these countries, survey or census-based methods are used to estimate maternal deaths in the household or among siblings. Countries with no empirical data must rely on estimates from statistical models. The 2005 series of maternal mortality ratios included 61 developing countries, representing 25% of global births, for which model-based estimates were required (Hill et al., 2007).

Analysis of a time series of global maternal mortality ratios suggests only a 5.4% decrease between 1990 and 2005, with negligible change in sub-Saharan Africa (Hill et al., 2007). This stagnation is in sharp contrast to the historical experience in developed countries. In the early 20th century, maternal mortality ratios in developed countries were similar to those seen in developing countries in the early 21st century, with ratios ranging from 200 to 600 maternal deaths per 100,000 live births. Beginning around 1931, maternal mortality ratios decreased by at least 50% every 10 years over the following 50 years, stabilizing with ratios of 10 maternal deaths or less per 100,000 live births (Loudon, 1992). These declines have been attributed to the discovery of antibiotics, improved procedures for cesarean sections and blood transfusion, as well as the professionalization of midwifery care, which some authors believe explains differences in the pace and timing of the declines (De Brouwere & Van Lerberghe, 2001).

Social and economic factors related to maternal mortality have varied over time, vary currently by setting, and vary when considered at the individual versus population level. Historically, maternal mortality, unlike infant mortality, was not related to the woman's socioeconomic status. During the 19th and early 20th century in Europe and North America, for example, women delivering in a health facility were at substantially greater risk of death from sepsis than women delivering at home because of unsanitary provider practices before recognition and acceptance of germ theory.

At a global level today, although all pregnancies are at risk of obstetric complications, maternal mortality is highly concentrated among the poor. Data from developing countries show risks of maternal death up to 6 times higher for women in the poorest quintile of households relative to the wealthiest (Ronsmans, Graham, & Lancet Maternal Survival Series Steering Group, 2006). By contrast, in the United States, the risk of maternal death varies dramatically by racial and ethnic group, with African American and Hispanic women not born in the United States showing risks 4 times and 1.6 times higher than White women, respectively (Berg, Chang, Callaghan, & Whitehead, 2003). Economic status of the woman does not fully explain these differentials, however. Likewise, wealth at the national level does not fully explain differences in risks of maternal mortality, as there are 40 countries with lower maternal mortality ratios than the United States (World Health Organization et al., 2004); in addition, there are very large differences in maternal mortality at similar levels of per capita income among developing nations (Ronsmans et al., 2006).

Key areas of research regarding maternal mortality encompass clinical research and research into effective service delivery approaches. There is a substantial body of randomized clinical trials assessing the effectiveness of drugs and specific procedures (some but not all of which use risk of maternal death as an outcome), the majority of which were undertaken in developed countries (Ronsmans, Graham, & Lancet Maternal Survival Series steering group, 2006). Examples of such procedures include the use of magnesium sulfate for preeclampsia and eclampsia (a condition in pregnancy characterized by very high blood pressure), the use of active management of the third stage of labor to prevent postpartum hemorrhage, and the use of the partograph for monitoring labor. Only one randomized population-based trial was identified in which maternal death was designed as a primary outcome; in this trial, which assessed the effectiveness of traditional birth attendants for home-based delivery in Pakistan, no significant effect on maternal death was reported (Jokhio, Winter, & Cheng, 2005).

The paucity of population-based trials for maternal death is related to the need for very large sample sizes and the difficulties associated with designing a trial that must assess multiple interventions to address the various causes of maternal death while controlling for confounding factors associated with the social determinants of maternal death, such as women's education, transport, and local infrastructure. Researchers and policy makers continue to debate the acceptability of results from quasi-experimental and other nontrial-based evaluations.

Many questions remain unanswered regarding how to reduce maternal mortality in the countries where 99% of these deaths occur, despite 20 years of advocacy, research, and program implementation by the Safe Motherhood Initiative, the international initiative dedicated to addressing maternal death. As stated above, trend data suggest little improvement in high mortality countries. It is not clear why some countries have succeeded in reducing maternal mortality, where others have not. A key question to answer is this: Where and with whom should women give birth? A systematic review suggests that the use of traditional birth attendants for home-based births has not been effective in decreasing maternal mortality (Sibley et al., 2007). However, the relationship between national rates of use of a medically skilled attendant at birth (which equates to births taking place in a health facility in the vast majority of countries) and national maternal mortality ratios is negative, although weak (Graham, Bell, & Bullough, 2001). Furthermore, although approximately 50% of developing world births report having a medically skilled attendant at birth, there are large areas of South Asia, in particular, where the percentage of births attended by a medical professional is less than 20% (United Nations Children's Fund, 2007).

The inadequate number of skilled health care workers is among the most pressing challenges facing developing countries. It has been estimated that the training of approximately 330,000 new skilled birth attendants would be required for 72% of global births to be assisted by a medical professional (World Health Organization, 2005). Thus, assuring that all births take place with a medically skilled attendant must be viewed as a long-term goal and begs the question of what the most cost-effective, context-specific interventions should be for the immediate future.

SEE ALSO Volume 2: *Abortion; Health Differentials/ Disparities, Adulthood;* Volume 3: *Demographic Transition Theories; Mortality.*

BIBLIOGRAPHY

AbouZahr, C. (1998). Maternal mortality overview. In C. J. L. Murray & A. D. Lopez (Eds.), *Health dimensions of sex and reproduction: The global burden of sexually transmitted disease, HIV, maternal conditions, perinatal disorders, and congenital anomalies* (pp. 110–164). Cambridge, MA: Harvard School of Public Health.

Berg, C. J., Chang, J., Callaghan, W. M., & Whitehead, S. J. (2003). Pregnancy-related mortality in the United States, 1991–1997. *Obstetrics and Gynecology, 101*(2), 289–296.

De Brouwere, V., & Van Lerberghe, W. (Eds.). (2001). Of blind alleys and things that have worked: History's lessons on reducing maternal mortality. In *Safe motherhood strategies: A review of the evidence* (pp. 7–34). Antwerp, Belgium: ITG Press.

Graham, W. J., Bell, J., & Bullough, C. (2001). Can skilled attendance at delivery reduce maternal mortality in developing countries? In V. De Brouwere & W. Van Lerberghe (Eds.), *Safe motherhood strategies: A review of the evidence.* Antwerp, Belgium: ITG Press.

Hill, K., Thomas, K., AbouZahr, C., Walker, N., Say, L., Inoue, M., et al. (2007). Estimates of maternal mortality worldwide between 1990 and 2005: An assessment of available data. *Lancet, 370*(9595), 1311–1319.

Jokhio, A. H., Winter, H. R., & Cheng, K. K. (2005). An intervention involving traditional birth attendants and perinatal and maternal mortality in Pakistan. *The New England Journal of Medicine, 352*(20), 2091–2099.

Loudon, I. (1992). The measurement of maternal mortality. In *Death in childbirth: An international study of maternal care and maternal mortality, 1800–1950* (pp. 11–39). Oxford, England: Oxford University Press.

Mahapatra, P., Shibuya, K., Lopez, A. D., Coullare, F., Notzon, F. C., Rao, C., et al. (2007). Civil registration systems and vital statistics: Successes and missed opportunities. *Lancet, 370*(9599), 1653–1663.

Ronsmans, C., Graham, W. J., & Lancet Maternal Survival Series Steering Group. (2006). Maternal mortality: Who, when, where, and why. *Lancet, 368*(9542), 1189–1200.

Sibley, L. M., Sipe, T. A., Brown, C. M., Diallo, M. M., McNatt, K., & Habarta, N. (2007). Traditional birth attendant training for improving health behaviors and pregnancy outcomes. *Cochrane database of systematic reviews* (3). Retrieved April 27, 2008, from http://mrw.interscience. wiley.com/cochrane

Stanton, C., Hobcraft, J., Hill, K., Kodjogbe, N., Mapeta, W. T., Munene, F., et al. (2001). Every death counts: Measurement of maternal mortality via a census. *Bulletin of the World Health Organization, 79*(7), 657–664.

United Nations Children's Fund. (2007). *UNICEF global database on delivery care.* Retrieved April 7, 2008, from http:// www.childinfo.org/areas/deliverycare

World Health Organization. (2005). *The world health report 2005; make every mother and child count.* Geneva, Switzerland: Author. Retrieved April 27, 2008, from http://www.who.int/whr

World Health Organization, United Nations Children's Fund, & United Nations Population Fund. (2004). *Maternal mortality in 2000: Estimates developed by WHO, UNICEF, and UNFPA.* Geneva, Switzerland: World Health Organization, Department of Reproductive Health and Research.

Cynthia K. Stanton

MEDIA AND TECHNOLOGY USE, ADULTHOOD

Classic mass media (television, radio, newspapers, magazines, movies, and books) and information and communication technologies (ICT) (telephones, mobile phones, and the Internet) play a central role in everyday life. Media and technology use is one of the most important leisure activities and thus accounts for a great deal of time use over the life course. In addition, media and ICT are important in shaping the life course. The technological environment is a critical part of the historical and structural contexts in which people live their lives. For example, people coming of age at the beginning of the 21st century are doing so in the so-called information society, in which mass media and ICT are much more important for individuals, organizations and companies, nations, and global society than they were in the middle of the 20th century.

This fundamental social change has altered many aspects of life; for example, ideas about the speed and frequency of interpersonal communication have been transformed by the availability of cell phones and the Internet. These technologies also are important for the messages they convey about everything from the appropriate timing of life events to the kinds of consumer goods one needs to mark those events (e.g., what new parents need to purchase). Thus, whether or not they represent reality accurately, media and ICT are a means of conveying cultural ideas about the life course and society. ICT in particular have changed the nature of social relationships over the life course in that contemporary people are embedded not only in real social networks but in virtual social networks on the Internet that may span the globe.

ACCESS TO MASS MEDIA AND ICT

Access to mass media and ICT is an indispensable precondition for their use. Research shows that some subgroups of individuals are less likely to have access to these technologies. However, history shows that these access gaps usually diminish or disappear over time as a technology is diffused throughout society. For example, in European and North American societies there are few gaps in access to classic mass media; the U.S. Census estimates that more than 95% of poor households own a color television. When specific types of media are examined, gaps are apparent. Thus, even though television and radio sets are found in well over 90% of households, access gaps arise because not all content is freely available, such as cable and satellite programming. Similar differences can be observed in comparing access to free versus paid newspapers and magazines. This contrast is impor-

---

THE DIGITAL DIVIDE

There are differences in access to and use of mass media and information and communication technologies (ICT) among global regions (e.g., northern hemisphere versus southern hemisphere), countries with different political systems (e.g., democracy versus autocracy), regions within countries (e.g., urban versus rural), social traits (e.g., age, income, education, and ethnicity), and individual characteristics (e.g., literacy, psychological traits). In the case of most media and technologies the ability to afford the cost of the device (television, radio, computer) or the service fee (newspapers, pay television, cinema, Internet) is a precondition for use. The term *digital divide* refers to unequal access to and use of the Internet (Norris, 2002). Therefore, the main digital divide parallels the financial divide. In addition, women in most countries are less likely to have access to the Internet and, if they have access, use it less intensely. However, in 2007 a higher percentage of U.S. women than U.S. men used the Internet (Center for the Digital Future, 2007). Access to the Internet exposes individuals to new information and enables the development of skills. Thus, unequal access to these resources may contribute to further inequalities over the life course.

BIBLIOGRAPHY

Norris, P. (2003). *Digital Divide. Civic Engagement, Information Poverty, and the Internet Worldwide*, Cambridge: Cambridge University Press.

---

tant because of the quality differences between free and paid media.

MOTIVES FOR USE OF MASS MEDIA AND ICT

Research on mass media before the 1970s tended to examine the impact of media on users, viewing them as passive actors causally influenced by powerful media organizations. Beginning in the 1970s, the focus shifted to the motives underlying the use of mass media. The central research question was no longer "What do media do with their users?" but "What do users do with media?" (Rosengren, Wenner, & Palmgreen, 1985). This so-called uses and gratifications approach is still prominent in mass media research.

Researchers categorize the gratifications of using media in various ways, depending on the theoretical approach and research question. One of the most general and widely used categorization distinguishes four gratifications: cognition, affection, social interaction, and integration/habitus. Cognitive gratification refers to the need for information and learning, whereas affective gratification includes aspects such as entertainment, diversion, escapism, and excitement. Social interaction combines two kinds of interaction that are fostered by mass media. On the one hand, mass media provide topics for everyday conversations and therefore for social integration. On the other hand, electronic media such as television and radio can provide parasocial interaction. For example, people may feel personally addressed by news anchors saying "good evening" or "see you tomorrow at the same time" and feel that they are engaging in a social interaction.

The habitus gratification is based on the human need for rituals, stability, and structure. Mass media offer a reliable structure for the rhythm of days, weeks, and years. People often adjust their lives to enable or accommodate their use of media. They may take a different route to work to pick up a free newspaper or buy a magazine, align their dinnertime with the evening news, and not go out when their favorite television shows are screened; major sport events are important landmarks in the yearly calendar. Research has compared the relative importance of these motivations for types of mass media (e.g., television versus newspapers) and examined how the motivations for media use differ from those for other everyday activities (e.g., watching talk shows versus meeting friends). One of the core findings of this line of research is that television outreaches most other mass media on nearly all dimensions. Only newspapers obtain higher ranks on the cognitive function.

PATTERNS OF MASS MEDIA AND ICT USE

In many cases the mass media are financed substantially or solely by advertisements, and the purpose of every advertisement is to reach as many people in a target group as possible. Therefore, media producers want to know in as much detail as possible how many and which people use their products. Thus, a great deal of quantitative research on patterns of media use is conducted by private companies or industry associations. An international comparative analysis showed that nearly every household in the industrialized world has a television set: Central and Eastern Europe 94.1%, Western Europe 95.3%, Japan 99.4%, United States 98.2% (IP/RTL Group, 2007). Even though access to television is widespread, viewing patterns differ significantly between countries and differ within individual countries on the basis of age, gender, race, social class, and other demographic characteristics.

Country	Television[1] Age Group	(2006)	Other Media[2] Newspapers	Radio	Internet	Year
United States	18+	295	28	191	32	2001
United Kingdom	16+	232	30			2005
Spain	16+	228	13	110	27	2005
Germany	14+	227	28	221	73	2005
Japan	20+	213	27	94	71	2003
Switzerland (Italian speakers)	15–74	182				
Switzerland (French speakers)	15–74	175				-
Denmark	12+	160	19	188	18	2004
Norway	12+	156	46	133	30	2005
Switzerland (German speakers)	15–74	147	37	94	43	2005

[1] SOURCE: IP/RTL Group, 2007.
[2] SOURCE: World Association of Newspapers, 2006.

Table 1. *TV, newspaper, radio and internet use in selected countries.* CENGAGE LEARNING, GALE.

Table 1 shows the average number of minutes per individual per working day spent viewing TV in selected industrialized nations. People in the United States spend the most time watching television; Americans spend twice as many minutes per day as do people in the German-speaking part of Switzerland, who spend the least amount of time. Especially in Europe, television use and newspaper reading are inversely related (both on the individual and national level). Whereas newspapers are read widely in middle and Northern Europe (e.g., Switzerland, Germany, Norway), television is the major mass medium in Southern Europe (e.g., Spain).

It is difficult for researchers to make direct comparisons of time spent using specific media because inconsistent measures and operationalizations are used across media types and across contexts. Whereas television use is measured with devices attached to the television set and is therefore reliable, reading time usually is measured by self-reports, which are less reliable. Cultural influences on media use are apparent in Table 1, which shows that the three different language regions of Switzerland have different levels of television viewing. Viewing patterns also vary by cultural and national context. For example, Figure 1 shows the percentage of the audience that watches television throughout the day in Denmark, Japan, and Spain. In Denmark viewing levels are low during the day; the 30% point is reached only with the evening news at

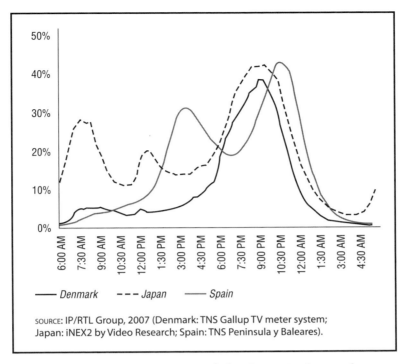

Figure 1. *Daytime TV viewing pattern of selected countries. Percent of population watching television at a particular time on a week day.* CENGAGE LEARNING, GALE.

7:30 P.M. Japan reaches a first peak of 29% audience viewing in the early morning. In Spain there is a clear siesta peak in the late afternoon and a much later prime-time peak, and at midnight 30% of the audience still has the televison on; in contrast, that share is only 10% in Denmark.

Researchers have noted that use of media during recreational time has reached a saturation level; that is, usage rates have reached a ceiling and cannot increase much more. Thus, use of new media devices such as the Internet leads to a reduction in time spent using other media or to a pattern of parallel use: The radio and television are on while people surf the Internet, read a magazine, or do non-media-related activities.

EFFECTS OF MASS MEDIA AND ICT USE

Researchers have long been interested in the effects of mass media use on individuals, social groups, and societies; that interest has extended to ICT. Contemporary research questions cover issues related to entertainment (e.g., "Does violent and pornographic content in movies affect real-life behavior?") as well as news (e.g., "Does the press influence political opinions?") and interpersonal communication devices (e.g., "Are social networks affected by the Internet?").

The most influential theoretical approaches in this field are agenda setting, framing, and cultivation. The agenda setting perspective assumes that mass media do not have a strong influence on what people think but are effective in influencing what people think about. Thus, whether an issue is perceived as important by the public is not just a result of its true importance. Instead, people's perceptions are biased by the mass media, and issues are perceived as more important when they are covered extensively by the media. The framing approach is related to this perspective and can be treated as second-level agenda setting. The media are assumed to influence people by telling them how to think about a certain topic. The same topic can, for example, be framed as an economic, moral/ethical, technical, or conflict issue. Empirical research shows that there are often situations in which these agenda setting and framing effects of mass media can be observed. However the influence of mass media is far away from deterministic and reverse effects in which the public sets the media agenda are observed as well.

Whereas agenda setting and framing refer more to the short-term and medium-term effects of media on users, the cultivation approach studies longer-term effects. In the 1970s George Gerbner and associates coined the term *cultivation approach* to refer to the finding that mass media use evokes a biased perception of the real world by establishing distorted stereotypes (Gerbner, Gross, Morgan, Signorielli, & Shanahan, 2002). Research in this area focused initially on violence but later was applied to gender, minority, age roles, family, and other topics. Findings show that heavy users of television have a more biased perception of the real world. For example, those viewers have a disproportionately high estimate of the number of criminals, police officers, medical doctors, and lawyers in the population because of the overrepresentation of those occupations on television (Gerbner et al., 2002).

In addition to these three approaches there is a more sociologically oriented approach that focuses on the effects of mass media and ICT on social relationships. This perspective emerged in the 1980s and 1990s from concern that heavy use of television and computers would lead to social isolation. As a result of the widespread use of the Internet and its possible interactive use (e.g., instant messaging enables communication between people), the question was reformulated as whether ICT use leads to a shift from offline to online relationships or whether increases in the size of a person's social network facilitate the creation of new relationships and the maintenance of distant relationships. Online communities are often related to hobbies or professions but are used only by a minority (15%) of U.S. Internet users (Center for the Digital Future, 2008). However, among U.S. users who are members of an online community, 43% say that "they feel as strongly about their virtual communities as they do about their real world communities" (Center for the Digital Future, 2007, p. 1). A survey in the United Kingdom showed that students are most likely to make online friends (42%) but that the employed and the retired are more likely to meet those new friends offline (Dutton & Helsper, 2007).

FUTURE RESEARCH

Research linking media, ICT, and the life course is relatively limited because the concept of the life course is not widely known in communication science, and life course research incorporating media and technology use is extremely limited. In light of the increasing importance of ICT and the enduring importance of mass media, an integration of these fields seems overdue. The shortcomings of existing research on media and technology use with regard to the life course lie primarily in their regional focus and their segregation in different scientific disciplines. Cross-national comparative research is very limited because of different research traditions, settings, and methods. Furthermore, research on media and ICT use is biased by the interests of applied research and the focus on target groups of economic relevance.

SEE ALSO Volume 2: *Cultural Images, Adulthood; Leisure and Travel, Adulthood; Time Use, Adulthood.*

BIBLIOGRAPHY
Bryant, J., & Zillmann, D. (Eds.). (2002). *Media effects: Advances in theory and research.* Mahwah, NJ: L. Erlbaum Associates.

Center for the Digital Future. (2007 and 2008). *Digital future project.* University of Southern California. Annenberg School for Communication. Retrieved March 20, 2008, from http://www.digitalcenter.org

Dutton, W. H., & Helsper, E. J. (2007). *The Internet in Britain.* Oxford, U.K.: Oxford Internet Institute.

Elder, G. H., Jr. (1994). Time, human agency, and social change: Perspectives on the life course. *Social Psychology Quarterly,* 57(1), 4–15.

Gerbner, G., Gross, L., Morgan, M., Signorielli, N., & Shanahan, J. (2002). Growing up with television: Cultivation processes. In J. Bryant & D. Zillmann (Eds.), *Media effects: Advances in theory and research* (pp. 43–67). Mahwah, NJ: L. Erlbaum Associates.

IP/RTL Group (Ed.). (2007). *Television key facts 2007.* Frankfurt am Main, Germany: Author. Retrieved May 20, 2008, from http://www.ip-network.com/tvkeyfacts

Rogers, E. M. (1995). *Diffusion of innovations.* New York: Free Press.

Rosengren, K. E., Wenner, L. A., & Palmgreen, P. (Eds.). (1985). *Media gratifications research: Current perspectives.* Beverly Hills, CA: Sage.

World Association of Newspapers (Ed.). (2006). *World press trends 2006.* London: Author. Retrieved May 20, 2008, from http://www.wan-press.org

Thomas N. Friemel

MENOPAUSE

Menopause can be defined as an event, a transition, and a set of stages. As an event menopause is marked by the last menstrual period in a woman's lifetime. Unlike other events, such as a birthday, menopause as a definitive event can be defined only retrospectively. Menopause also represents a transition from menstruating episodically (having periods) to the permanent absence of menstrual cycling. As a transition or passage from one stage of life to another, menopause can be quick, straightforward, easy, and uncomplicated or protracted and disruptive. Although physiologically most women enter a postreproductive, postmenstrual phase of life, societies and cultures assign additional and variable meanings to that phase.

Menopause has been scientifically, though equivocally, demarcated as a set of stages through which women progress. Premenopause is the stage in which most adult women experience regular menstrual cycles. Perimenopause, during which a woman experiences significant changes in menstruation, is characterized by changes in cycle length and the intensity of menstrual bleeding. Postmenopause is the postmenstrual and postreproductive stage. The perimenopausal stage also is referred to as the climacteric and is associated most closely with "the menopause" or, more euphemistically, "the change." Along with unpredictable menstrual bleeding, underlying changes in a perimenopausal woman's endocrine system contribute to hot flashes, a sudden, intense sensation in the face, neck, or upper body of over-heating and sweating. Those symptoms can be a potential source of personal discomfort and social embarrassment. A similar vasomotor symptom (a symptom related to the constriction or dilation of blood vessels) that is attributable to perimenopause, night sweating, is essentially a hot flash that occurs while a person is asleep, often disturbing that person's sleep.

Although menopause can be thought of as a strictly biological phenomenon, it has been culturally imbued with meanings related to associated roles and statuses in women's lives. For example, menopause often is viewed as a marker of aging: Old (i.e., older) women are menopausal. Without social or technological interventions, menopause represents the end of reproduction and the role of a new mother. Although "no more periods" can represent freedom from a periodic persona problem, it also can represent a loss of youthful sexual and reproductive desirability. Both popular and scientific descriptions of menopause are notable for their reliance on analogies to loss, wear, and trouble. These negative connotations coupled with endocrine changes, unpredictable and disruptive bodily sensations (irregular bleeding, hot flashes, and night sweats), and interrupted sleep patterns may contribute to an altered self-concept and depressed psychological well-being among some perimenopausal women.

The solidification of a so-called menopause industry (Coney, 1994) during the 1990s can be regarded as a life course case study of the intersection of age, cohort, and historical time within particular sociocultural contexts. Women born in the post–World War II baby boom entered their mid-forties and early fifties during that period, which coincided with the growth of research on the health of women in midlife. For example, the Office of Research on Women of the U.S. National Institutes of Health, which funded the Women's Health Initiative, was founded in 1990. Public discourse on menopause expanded during the 1990s as well. Particularly focused on the self-help arena, book publication on the change proliferated during that period. Influential books such as Germaine Greer's (1991) *The Change* and Gail Sheehy's (1992) *The Silent Passage* heralded a new area of publishing, including positive approaches; menopause diets; exercise plans; advice books from women physicians and feminist activists; source books and guides for women, for men/husbands, and "for dummies" or "complete idiots"; and a pop-up book. By 2001 *menopause* had become the title of a musical.

EVOLUTIONARY, CLINICAL, AND BIOMEDICAL PERSPECTIVES

A broad bioevolutionary perspective considers whether menopause serves an adaptive purpose. The grandmother hypothesis attempts to explain why, relative to most other mammals, the human female reproductive period ends early in the life span. Prehistoric grandmothers provided assistance to their daughters and their progeny once the grandmothers completed bearing and raising their own children. Thus, grandmothers could invest in the survival of their offspring.

From a clinical vantage point, menopause is inherently pathological and women experiencing menstrual changes are in a diseased or prediseased state. Menopause is defined as functionless or dysfunctional. For example, in the International Classification of Diseases of the World Health Organization, menopause is coded and discussed medically as ovarian failure. In medical textbooks the menopausal stages are portrayed with reference to chronic degenerative diseases such as cardiovascular diseases. A typical analogy is made between menopause and diabetes as hormone deficiency diseases of estrogen and insulin, respectively. Thus, the problem of menopause necessitates medical treatment with estrogen therapies. Hormone therapy—previously termed hormone replacement therapy—includes estrogen medication taken on a continual or daily basis, often combined with progestin. These therapies are prescribed to treat short-term menopausal symptoms such as hot flashes and, more controversially, long-term chronic diseases such as osteoporosis and heart disease. However, estrogen-based hormone therapy is not the only clinically available therapeutic option. Irregular and heavy bleeding associated with the climacteric is addressed medically through hysterectomy. Sexual difficulties among menopausal patients sometimes are treated with estrogen or testosterone. Some depressed and sleep-disturbed patients receive hormone therapy or a variety of psychiatric medications.

Biomedical perspectives are supported in part by empirical findings that the timing of menopause is related to overall health (early menopause may be influenced by poor health practices and can be a marker for subsequent ill health) and longevity (later ages of menopause are positively correlated with longevity). Biomedical research on menopause tends to be conducted on patient populations rather than random samples drawn from the community, and so these perspectives emphasize therapeutic intervention to alleviate the troubles of discomfited patients. However, menopausal patients are not representative generally of menopausal women. Population-based studies of midlife women, by contrast, generally show lower levels of menopause-related sickness and find little evidence for a menopausal syndrome that includes symptoms beyond hot flashes and night sweats (Avis et al., 2001; Rossi, 2004).

FEMINIST AND SOCIAL SCIENTIFIC PERSPECTIVES

Feminist perspectives tend to categorize the medicalization of menopause as a way for the institute of medicine to regulate (Martin, 1987; Zita, 1993). Social scientific perspectives on menopause focus on attitudes and laypersons' understandings of what menopause is and how different women (and men) experience it. Research insights from these perspectives emphasize the diversity of menopause across different sociocultural contexts. For example, anthropological studies document the divergent cultural definitions and consequences of menopause in different countries and geographic regions (Seviert, 2006). Margaret Lock (1993) contrasted the aches, pains, and poor eyesight that tend to characterize the change of life (*konenki*) in Japan to the hot flashes and night sweats considered typical of menopause in North America. Within societies, attitudes toward menstruation influence women's experiences of menopause (Bowles, 1992; Papini, Intrieri, & Goodwin, 2002). Extensive life history data from women enrolled in the Tremin Research Program on Women's Health have helped document many aspects of women's menstrual and menopausal lives, including women's concerns about maintaining self-control and limiting social disclosure during potentially disruptive symptoms and behaviors (Kittell, Mansfield, & Voda, 1998). Applying a biopsychosocial framework to a national study, Alice Rossi (2004) found that somatic amplification—awareness of and sensitivity to one's private bodily functions—influences women's and men's reports of symptoms that often are labeled as menopausal.

RESEARCH DEBATES ON HORMONE THERAPIES

Estrogen, which can help prevent hot flashes, is the most widely used treatment for menopause and, arguably, feminine aging (MacPherson, 1993; McCrea, 1983; Voda & Ashton, 2006). In the 1960s the gynecologist Robert Wilson (1966) advocated estrogen supplementation to help aging women look young and be *Feminine Forever*. By the early 1980s solo estrogen therapy was known to cause uterine cancer. Since that time menopausal hormone therapies for women with intact uteri have combined estrogen with progestin, and during the 1990s those noncontraceptive hormones were prescribed widely for midlife American women. Pharmaceutical companies developed an array of hormone delivery methods, including patches, topical creams, vaginal rings, and low-dose pills. Although those regimes were approved for short-term relief of menopausal symptoms, there was no evidence of long-term benefits. Observational epidemiologic studies found that women who used hormone therapy were healthier and lived longer than other women, but was this because hormones caused better health or because healthier women chose to use hormones (Matthews, Kuller, Wing, Meilahn, & Plantinga, 1996)?

In 1993 the Women's Health Initiative (WHI) was funded to help provide definitive evidence on the relationship between hormone therapies and cardiovascular diseases by enrolling thousands of perimenopausal and postmenopausal women in randomized clinical trials. In 2002, three years before the planned conclusion, the combination hormone therapy component of the WHI was halted when unexpected adverse outcomes were detected. Hormonal treatments increased women's risk of heart attack, stroke, blood clots to the lung, and invasive breast cancer (Rossouw et al., 2002; Voda & Aston, 2006). As a consequence of the WHI, many women stopped taking hormones, contributing to a lower incidence of breast cancer caused by estrogen-sensitive tumors (Ravdin et al., 2007). Some skeptics of the WHI results (Grodstein, Manson, & Stampfer, 2006) advanced a new hypothesis based on the timing of prevention: Hormones benefit only women who start therapy early, and the WHI trials enrolled women who were too old and began hormone therapy too late.

IMPORTANCE TO LIFE COURSE RESEARCH

Research on menopause fits well within life course perspectives. The timing of menopause and cross-cultural menopausal attitudes, beliefs, and practices are important areas of life course studies. In light of the personal and social dimensions of menopause, life course trajectories related to gender, family, and employment may be confounded with menopausal dynamics. The dominant life course model of menopause frames it primarily as an age-related process. Although the sociocultural contexts of menopause have been studied widely, other time dimensions, such as cohort and history, also should be considered within an explicit life course framework.

SEE ALSO Volume 2: *Infertility; Midlife Crisis and Transitions; Sexual Activity, Adulthood;* Volume 3: *Aging; Rossi, Alice.*

BIBLIOGRAPHY

Avis, N. E., Stellato, R., Crawford, S., Bromberger, J., Ganz, P., Cain, V., et al. (2001). Is there a menopausal syndrome? Menopausal status and symptoms across racial/ethnic groups. *Social Science & Medicine, 52*(3), 345–356.

Bowles, C. (1992). The development of a measure of attitude toward menopause. In A. J. Dan & L. L. Lewis (Eds.), *Menstrual health in women's lives* (pp. 206–212). Urbana: University of Illinois Press.

Coney, S. (1994). *The menopause industry: How the medical establishment exploits women.* Alameda, CA: Hunter House.

Greer, G. (1991). *The change: Women, aging, and the menopause.* New York: Knopf.

Grodstein, F., Manson, J. E., & Stampfer, M. J. (2006). Hormone therapy and coronary heart disease: The role of time since menopause and age of hormone initiation. *Journal of Women's Health, 15*(1), 35–44.

Kittell, L. A., Mansfield, P. K., & Voda, A. M. (1998). Keeping up appearances: The basic social process of the menopausal transition. *Qualitative Health Research, 8*(5), 618–633.

Lock, M. (1993). *Encounters with aging: Mythologies of menopause in Japan and North America.* Berkeley: University of California Press.

MacPherson, K. I. (1993). The false promises of hormone replacement therapy and current dilemmas. In J. C. Callahan (Ed.), *Menopause: A midlife passage* (pp. 145–159). Bloomington: Indiana University Press.

Martin, E. (1987). *The woman in the body: A cultural analysis of reproduction.* Boston: Beacon Press.

McCrea, F. B. (1983). The politics of menopause: The "discovery" of a deficiency disease. *Social Problems, 31*(1), 111–123.

Matthews, K. A., Kuller, L. H. Wing, R. R., Meilahn, E. N., & Plantinga, P. (1996). Prior to use of estrogen replacement therapy, are users healthier than nonusers? *American Journal of Epidemiology, 143*(10), 971–978.

Papini, D. R., Intrieri, R. C., & Goodwin, P. E. (2002). Attitude toward menopause among married middle-aged adults. *Women & Health, 36*(4), 55–68.

Ravdin, P. M., Cronin, K. A., Howlader, N., Berg, C. D., Chlebowski, R. T., Feuer, E. J., et al. (2007). The decrease in breast cancer incidence in 2003 in the United States. *New England Journal of Medicine, 356,* 1670–1674.

Rossi, A. S. (2004). The menopausal transition and aging process. In O. G. Brim, C. D. Ryff, & R. C. Kessler (Eds.), *How healthy are we? A national study of well-being at midlife* (pp. 153–201). Chicago: University of Chicago Press.

Rossouw, J. E., Anderson, G. L., Prentice, R. L., LaCroix, A. Z., Kooperberg, C., Stafanick, M. L., et al. (Writing Group for the Women's Health Initiative Investigators). (2002). Risks and benefits of estrogen plus progestin in healthy postmenopausal women: Principal results from the Women's Health Initiative randomized controlled trial. *Journal of the American Medical Association, 288*(3), 321–333.

Seviert, L. L. (2006). *Menopause: A biocultural perspective.* New Brunswick, NJ: Rutgers University Press.

Sheehy, G. (1992). *The silent passage: Menopause.* New York: Random House.

Voda, A. M., & Ashton, C. A. (2006). Fallout from the Women's Health Study: A short-lived vindication for feminists and the resurrection of hormone therapies. *Sex Roles, 54*(5–6), 401–411.

Wilson, R. A. (1966). *Feminine forever.* New York: M. Evans.

Zita, J. N. (1993). Heresy in the female body: The rhetorics of menopause. In J. C. Callahan (Ed.), *Menopause: A midlife passage* (pp. 59–78). Bloomington: Indiana University Press.

Diane S. Shinberg

MENTAL HEALTH, ADULTHOOD

Mental health is a dynamic process that changes over the life course. Although childhood mental health influences mental health during adulthood, mental health in adulthood is also influenced by contextual and historical factors. As people move through the life course, changes in economic circumstances, social roles, social integration, social networks, and personal aspirations affect their mental health trajectories. General social trends such as a globalizing economy, changing marriage and divorce rates, and women entering the work force in increasing numbers as well as historical events, including wars, economic depressions, or terrorist attacks, also can affect adult mental health. The impact of these trends and events varies by the age at which people experience them. Historical and generational trends also affect attitudes toward using mental health services, taking psychotropic medications, and the stigma of mental illness. These processes ensure that mental health is a dynamic rather than static object of study across the life course.

DEFINITIONS OF MENTAL HEALTH AND THEIR RELATION TO THE LIFE COURSE

Mental health has a variety of meanings. On its face, it refers to a general feeling of well-being and an absence of mental health difficulties. Researchers and therapists, however, usually use the term in exactly the opposite sense: the presence of mental health *problems* or mental *illness*. Because mental health is now associated with poor mental health, this is the term that will be used in this chapter.

The initial studies of mental health in the community in the 1950s and 1960s used broad measures that had several characteristics (Langner, 1962). First, they did not distinguish types of disorders, even among those that were viewed as distinct. Instead, they contained a variety of symptoms characteristic of general depressive, anxious, and psychosomatic conditions. Scales combined symptoms of anxiety (e.g., restlessness, nervousness, heart beating hard), depression (e.g., low spirits, feeling apart, nothing seems worthwhile) and various psychosomatic symptoms (e.g., pains in the head, cold sweats, acid stomach). Second, they did not make a sharp distinction between healthy and disordered conditions but viewed mental health as a continuum that moved from mild, to moderate, to severe conditions. Third, they asked about general symptoms such as "do you ever have trouble sleeping," "do you have difficulties in concentrating," or "do you ever feel lonely" that were common in nonclinical community samples. Because they emphasized such ordinary problems, researchers found that the vast majority of respondents reported some mental health problem. Indeed, those who reported no symptoms were the exception rather than the rule in these studies.

General and continuous symptom scales, however, have several weaknesses for the study of mental health.

One is that they do not measure serious mental disorders, which are highly stigmatizing and associated with tremendous suffering, limited role performance, and decreased life chances. A second limitation is that these general measures are not congruent with the discrete conditions that have been the focus of mental health professionals since the development of the *American Psychiatric Association's Diagnostic and Statistical Manual* (*DSM*) in 1980. Since that time, the mental health professions have focused on distinct mental disorders such as major depressive disorder, obsessive-compulsive disorder, posttraumatic stress disorder, and phobias, among many others. Finally, mental health policy is most concerned with serious and persistent mental disorders, not the conditions of generalized distress measured by continuous symptom scales. Although general scales of distress are very useful for uncovering the benefits and flaws of social conditions, they have not proven to be very useful for mental health policy making.

This review provides a general overview of depression, anxiety, phobias (a class of anxiety disorders), and anger during adulthood, as well as the treatment of these conditions. It pays special attention to age differences, changes over the life course, and changes over time in each condition. Full knowledge about how mental health varies across the life course requires long-term prospective studies across many different age cohorts. Because such studies are not available, much of our knowledge about mental health over the life course is provisional and subject to error. This review also discusses some of the major problems that studies of mental health over the life course confront and some of the implications of their findings for public policy.

DEPRESSION

Depression is the single most common diagnosis in psychiatric treatment and one of the most common disorders in the population. It involves states of sad mood, diminished pleasure, sleep and appetite difficulties, fatigue, lack of concentration, feelings of worthlessness, and thoughts of death. Studies in the United States estimate that about 16% of people suffer from major depressive disorder over their lifetime and about 7% have experienced the disorder during the past year (Kessler, Berglund, et al., 2005; Kessler, Chiu, Demler, & Walters, 2005). Major depression disorder is the central disorder in the broader category of mood disorders, which also include bipolar disorder, a serious condition that features mood swings between elation and deep depression, and dysthymia, which features milder but very persistent symptoms of sad mood.

Rates of depression generally decline as people get older. People in their late teens and early twenties consistently report the highest levels of depression. Some studies indicate that middle-age people have the lowest

levels of depression whereas other researchers have found that groups including participants 60 years old or older reported the lowest amounts (George, 2007). These patterns seem to be primarily due to the relationship of age and changing economic status: Young people have the lowest and least stable levels of income, and income in turn is a well-documented correlate of depression. In addition to economic well-being, changing patterns of interpersonal relationships, physical health problems, and discrepancies between aspirations and accomplishments also partially account for age differences in depression. The relationship between age and depression also changes across different generations. For example, growing economic security among recent cohorts of the elderly has improved their mental health status relative to other age cohorts.

Experiences in childhood and adolescence have strong effects on mental health at later stages of the life course. Traumatic childhood experiences such as parental abuse or neglect that lead to a lifelong sense of helplessness and other negative cognitive states often make people prone to develop depressive symptoms as adults (Seligman, 1975). Most studies also show adverse effects of parental divorce, especially when it occurs very early in a child's life, on later rates of depression, although the impact of parental divorce on adult mental health might be declining as divorce becomes more common (Cherlin, Chase-Lansdale, & McRae, 1998). Other studies show that socioeconomic conditions during childhood, especially prolonged states of poverty, are associated with depression during adulthood (McLeod & Shanahan, 1996).

Although early experiences do influence later mental health, they do not determine it, because social changes during adulthood alter life trajectories. For example, finding parental substitutes can mitigate the impact of early parental divorce or death (Brown & Harris, 1978). Likewise, the adverse influence of poor economic circumstances on depression during childhood can be overcome through occupational and educational attainment later in life. In addition, childhood is not the only stage of the life course that influences mental health during later periods. Deborah Carr's (1997) research showed that the occupational aspirations women held during their early 30s influenced their levels of depression when these women entered their middle 50s. Those women who did not meet their earlier aspirations had more distress and less purpose in life than women who achieved the goals they set earlier in life. These processes are also tied to historical contexts. Women who are members of birth cohorts that did not value or have opportunities for achievement outside the home were more content with their statuses as homemakers; conversely, younger cohorts of women were more likely to value pursuing careers and so may be more disappointed when they do not realize their expectations.

The importance of generational differences holds more generally. For example, marriage is especially beneficial and marital loss especially harmful for depression during historical periods when beliefs about the permanence, desirability, and importance of marriage are culturally strong and pervasive (R. W. Simon & Marcussen, 1999). Another example is that having a spouse die is more detrimental to levels of depression among recent cohorts of retired men than women (Umberson, Wortman, & Kessler, 1992). This could stem from the high value these men placed on occupational achievement so that widowhood symbolizes loneliness and the inability to manage daily affairs to them. Conversely, widowhood provides new opportunities for self-sufficiency for older women from the same cohorts.

Several other demographic and social factors are consistently associated with the likelihood of depression. Levels of depression among women are significantly higher than among men, usually about twice as much. This could be because women are more likely to be exposed to the kinds of stressful experiences that are associated with depression, including role overload because of conflicting demands from work and family obligations, and social and economic inequality. These stressors are themselves linked to gender role expectations in particular historical contexts and are not invariant. Alternatively, women might express their distress in forms such as depression whereas men react to similar stressors through substance abuse or violence. The expression of distress also varies across generations and historical periods.

Socioeconomic circumstances also have a consistent relationship with depression among adults. Adults with low incomes, who live in physically and socially hazardous environments, who are unemployed, and who are not well educated have higher levels of depression than individuals who have more resources (Eaton & Mutaner, 1999). The lasting impact of socioeconomic circumstances, however, is influenced by historical context. Glen Elder's classic study, *Children of the Great Depression* (1974), indicated that children who experienced childhood and adolescence during the stressful and economically deprived circumstances of the 1930s suffered adverse mental health effects as adults. However, the experience of the Great Depression did not have a lasting negative impact on the mental health of a somewhat older group in their 20s during this period. Elder's work indicates that the developmental impact of historical events depends on the age when they occur in a person's life.

Another consistent finding is that social and emotional attachments to other people are associated with low levels of depression whereas their absence is related to high levels. For example, married people report less depression than unmarried people (Umberson & Williams, 1999).

This stems from several factors: Married people receive more social support, have stronger ties to community institutions, and display healthier and less risky behaviors. Conversely, divorced and separated people and, to a lesser extent, unmarried and widowed people report more depression. In contrast, ethnicity is one characteristic that does not seem to be associated with depression. Studies report inconsistent relationships between ethnicity and depression but, overall, do not indicate that any ethnic or racial groups are particularly likely or unlikely to become depressed.

Numerous theories have been proposed for why some people but not others become depressed, although no theory has yet been proven. Many studies associate depression with particular clusters of genes; however, it has not been confirmed that genetic dysfunctions cause depressive disorders. Other studies find that people with depression have smaller hippocampuses, a region of the brain that affects memory processes, although it is just as likely that depression itself or the medications that are used to treat it cause differences in brain size instead of the opposite (Sapolsky, 2001). Another popular biologic explanation of depression is the kindling hypothesis, which posits that social stressors trigger first episodes of depression but that stressful events are decreasingly likely to trigger future episodes, which are more likely to arise because of biologic vulnerabilities (Post, 1992). Although genetic and biologic studies have dominated recent research, consensus is growing that no single type of factor, whether genetic, biologic, psychological, or social, can solely cause depression (Kendler, 2005). Instead, researchers increasingly recognize that biopsychosocial explanations emphasizing the interactions between different levels of explanation offer the most adequate causal explanations for this condition.

Finally, rates of depression vary enormously across cultural contexts. One set of studies shows that rates of depression vary from a low of 3% of women in a Basque-speaking rural area of Spain to a high of over 30% of women in an urban township in Zimbabwe in East Africa (Brown, 2002). These disparate rates are directly related to the different numbers of severe losses suffered by people in these countries. Another summary of community surveys in 10 countries found lifetime prevalence rates that ranged from a low of 1.5% in Taiwan and 2.9% in Korea to a high of 16% in Paris and 19% in Beirut in Lebanon (Weissman et al., 1996). A third study found that rates of depression vary by a factor of 15 among primary medical care patients in 14 different countries (G. E. Simon, Goldberg, Von Korff, & Ustun., 2002). These diverse rates could be due to differences in the rates of social stressors leading to depression across cultures, diverse expressions of depression in different cultures, or methodological difficulties in using instruments that are not sensitive to cultural contexts. To the extent that these huge differences in prevalence across cultures are real and not the product of methodological artifacts, they suggest that the early 21st century focus on unraveling the genetic correlates of depression might be misplaced and that more attention should be paid to societal impacts on the development of depression.

ANXIETY

Anxiety disorders involve psychological feelings of worry, nervous tension, foreboding, threat, and alarm; behavioral manifestations such as hyperalertness and excitement; and somatic changes, including increased muscular tension, heart palpitations, difficulties breathing, raised blood pressure, and heavy sweating. Unlike the mood disorders, in which major depressive disorder is clearly the central condition, anxiety disorders are divided into a number of different types (although all generally share the somatic symptoms already mentioned). These include panic disorders that involve sudden and inexplicable episodes in which people lose control of their emotions and often have thoughts of dying (Barlow, 1988); obsessive-compulsive disorders, which feature intrusive, inappropriate, and recurrent thoughts and behaviors; posttraumatic stress disorders, in which the experience of an extreme stressor causes people to experience recurring symptoms of numbing, avoidance, and increased arousal; generalized anxiety disorders with excessive and persistent worries; and phobias, or intense fears of particular objects or situations, which is discussed in the next section.

In contrast to depression, which involves feelings of lethargy, inactivity, and hopelessness, fear and anxiety states are marked by tension, arousal, and alertness. Although depression usually concerns past losses of a love object, important resource, or valued goal, anxiety is directed toward some future threat or danger. Symptoms of anxiety can be normal if they arise in dangerous situations; anxiety disorders exist when people become seriously anxious when they do not face a dangerous situation or their symptoms are disproportionately severe or prolonged relative to their cause.

As a group, anxiety disorders are the most commonly occurring type of mental disorder. Some studies have shown that slightly more than 18% of the American population had experienced an anxiety disorder over the past year and nearly 30% at some point in their lives (Kessler, Berglund, et al., 2005; Kessler, Chiu, et al., 2005). Specific and social phobias are by far the most commonly occurring anxiety disorders, followed by posttraumatic stress disorder, generalized anxiety disorder, separation anxiety disorder, and panic disorder.

As with depression, age and rates of anxiety disorders are inversely related: People over 60 years of age report substantially less anxiety over their lifetimes than those who are younger. The reported age of onset (or first occurrence) for most anxiety disorders is usually during childhood and adolescence, earlier than for depressive disorders. Most people who experience an anxiety disorder at some point in their life report having had their first episode by age 15.

The social correlates of anxiety disorders are comparable with those for depression: being female, unmarried, and of low socioeconomic status, although the relationship of socioeconomic status and anxiety disorders is often not as clear as is the case for depression. Most people who have anxiety disorders also have family members with histories of mental disorder. Most research, however, indicates that little specificity exists in family history: Family members of an affected individual are likely to have some sort of anxiety, mood, or substance use disorder but not necessarily the particular type of disorder that the individual has.

Some researchers have suggested that the social triggers of anxiety and depression are distinct (Finlay-Jones & Brown, 1981). In particular, stressful life events that involve fear generate anxiety whereas events that feature the loss of some valued resource trigger depression. Other scholars, however, suggest that anxiety and depression reflect the same biologic vulnerability to overreactive responses to stressful life events of all kinds (Barlow, 1988). A difficulty in testing these competing explanations is that most major stressful life events involve both fear and loss, so it is difficult to separate these two components. For example, marital dissolution often involves the loss of a valued relationship, but it also may create uncertainties about finances, relationships, children, living conditions, and so on. Few life events solely involve fear or loss, and they typically generate both anxiety and depression.

PHOBIAS

Phobias are a class of anxiety disorders that involve such strong fears of specific objects or situations that people become extremely uncomfortable and even try to avoid the cause of the fears. The two major subtypes of phobias are simple phobias, which involve specific fears such as snakes (ophidiophobia), spiders (arachnophobia), or heights (acrophobia), and social phobias, which feature extreme anxiety and avoidance of situations in which people are exposed to the scrutiny of others, such as when they must speak in public. The sorts of things that most people are phobic about are not the things that are actually most dangerous in modern life, such as automobiles, guns, or electrical outlets. Instead, people seem to be predisposed to fear the sorts of things that were dangerous many thousands of years ago when the human genome was being formed, such as animals, darkness, strange places, and heights.

Phobias are the most commonly occurring specific mental disorder. At any particular time, about 9% of the U.S. population reports having had symptoms of a specific phobia, about 7% of social phobia, and about 3% of agoraphobia (a debilitating and causeless condition that makes those afflicted afraid to leave the home or, in a more general sense, any wider area that does not provide a sense of comfort and ease) in the past year (Kessler, Berglund, et al., 2005). About 13% reports lifetime experiences of some specific phobia, about 12% of social phobia, and about 7% of agoraphobia. The correlates of phobias (e.g., childhood experiences of physical and sexual abuse, parental history of mental disorders, female gender) are comparable with the predictors of other anxiety disorders.

Social phobia has been the subject of intense debates over whether it represents a true disorder or a variant of the normal personality trait of shyness. Social phobia was not even mentioned in psychiatric diagnostic manuals until 1980. When it appeared for the first time, the manual noted that "The disorder is apparently relatively rare" (American Psychiatric Association, 1980, p. 228). Studies of the disorder before 1980 indicated that only about 1 to 2% of the population reported this condition. Yet, more recent studies find that 12% experience social phobia at some point in their lives and about 40% of people report at least one of six social fears, the most common being fear of public speaking (Kessler, Stein, & Berglund, 1998).

Very small changes in the wording used to measure social phobias account for their huge increase. For example, changing the wording of questions that ask about fears of public speaking from having extreme distress when "speaking in front of a group you know" to "speaking in front of a group" doubled the number of positive responses. Likewise, changing the criteria from have "a compelling desire to avoid" fear-inducing situations to having "marked distress" in these situations resulted in a sharp increase in the reported amount of social phobia. The result was that the percentage of the American population with a lifetime experience of social phobia increased from 2% to 3% to 13.3%, a nearly six-fold increase, and has remained at comparably high levels since.

Critics suggest that the extreme growth in rates of social phobia after survey researchers make only minor changes in wording indicates that surveys might create rather than reflect these conditions (Horwitz, 2001). Others note the influence of pharmaceutical companies in defining the normal personality trait of shyness as a mental disorder to increase sales of their products (Lane, 2007). Many of the *symptoms* of social phobia such as apprehension about speaking in public seem to be normal fears and not mental disorders.

In contrast, advocates of viewing social phobia as a true mental disorder cite the distress, hindered educational and occupational performance, and greater levels of substance abuse among people with social phobia (Kessler et al., 1998). They also note that people with social phobia do not prefer to avoid others but intensely desire to have normal social interactions. They are unable to control their fears and so find certain sorts of social interactions intensely uncomfortable. The controversy over the pathology or normality of the symptoms of social phobia illustrates the difficulty of separating ordinary distress from mental disorder.

ANGER

Unlike the vast literature regarding depression, anxiety, and phobia, anger is relatively understudied. It refers to feelings ranging from frustration, irritation, and annoyance to fury and rage. It can remain unexpressed, be manifest verbally, or result in behavioral aggression and violence. Anger is intensely social because it is typically directed at other people or social situations. Often, these feelings involve some sort of perceived unfairness between angry people and the target of their anger

Although the *DSM* defines intermittent explosive disorder (IED), this diagnosis has received far less attention than other common mental health conditions. The *DSM* criteria require several discrete episodes involving failure to resist aggressive impulses that lead to serious assaultive acts or property destruction and are disproportionate to a precipitating psychosocial stressor. The first large population survey that measured the prevalence of IED found that more than 5% of respondents qualified for this diagnosis (Kessler et al., 2006). People seem to get less angry as they grow older: Anger is greatest among young adults, declines in midlife, and is lowest among the elderly. Lifetime prevalence of IED was inversely associated with age so that patients ages 18 to 29, 30 to 44, 45 to 59, and over 60 reported declining levels of 7.4%, 5.7%, 4.9%, and 1.9%, respectively. Although the reasons for this are not clear, it is possible that as people age they become more settled and tolerant of situations that produce anger among younger people, or they simply face fewer situations that they regard as unfair.

Because anger is inherently social, it is related to intense interaction with other people (Schieman, 2006). Parents report more anger than the childless, and people who live alone are less angry than those who live with others. Unlike depression and anxiety, which are primarily disorders of girls and women, most people with anger-related disorders are male. It is not yet clear whether the male predominance in anger disorders reflects biologic and psychological predispositions or cultural expression rules that are more tolerant about male than female displays of anger. Anger is also strongly related to feelings of unfairness: People are angry at those who they believe have received unfair advantages. Workmates who are perceived to have received inequitable economic rewards or promotions, spouses who shirk household and child-care duties, or students who receive unequal treatment are commonly sources of anger. Conversely, situations of social equality are less likely to produce angry emotions.

INCREASING RATES OF MENTAL ILLNESS?

One of the most puzzling aspects about lifetime rates of all of the conditions considered in this entry is that studies at one point in time consistently show that older people have lower rates of lifetime prevalence of each mental illness. Depression illustrates this pattern. About 25% of people between 18 and 29 years old have had a depressive episode compared with 24% of people 30 to 44 years old, 20% among those 45 to 59 years old, and only 13% for those over 60 (Kessler, 2005). This finding, and similar findings for anxiety, phobia, and anger, is unexpected because, the older people get, the more years they have been at risk for developing a disorder. Older people have passed through each earlier stage of the life cycle so that, other things being equal, their lifetime rates of disorders should generally always be higher than those at younger ages. Yet, epidemiological studies show that lifetime rates of all disorders decrease as people age. What factors account for this phenomenon?

One possibility is that social changes have led to increasing rates of mental illness in each succeeding birth cohort. Many researchers have concluded that actual increases in rates of mental disorders have occurred in successive generations (e.g., Klerman & Weissman, 1989). This explanation, however, is not very plausible for a number of reasons.

Studies that measure mental illness prospectively uncover a striking fact about the reporting of mental illness over time. About half of survey respondents who report a mental illness at one point in time cannot recall the episode after as short an interval as 18 months (G. E. Simon & Von Korff, 1995). This could be because they simply forget the episode or because the symptoms were not sufficiently serious to be recalled. These studies also show a consistent inverse relationship exists between the length of time since an episode of depression occurred and people's ability to recall it. Lifetime age of first onset of mental illness reports are about 5 years before an interview, regardless of a respondent's age. These findings have a number of implications for estimating lifetime prevalence across different generations.

First, because most depressive episodes occur during younger ages, older people are more likely to forget previous episodes because longer periods of time have passed since they experienced the episode. Memories naturally fade when the events they refer to are no longer relevant to the individual. Second, current negative states of mind strongly affect people's recall of past negative states. What people remember depends on their current circumstances and mood when they are asked to remember past episodes of mental illness. Because older people are less likely to have current episodes of depression that can serve as reminders for past episodes they are also less likely to report past episodes. In addition, current older cohorts might be more reluctant than younger ones to acknowledge symptoms of mental illness.

Third, no theory about the cause any mental disorder predicts a consistent increase in prevalence over historical time. Genetic and psychological explanations rely on factors that are invariant or change very slowly over time and so are inconsistent with these trends. Although social theories do predict changing rates of mental disorder over time, they cannot account for why trends have increased so steadily and consistently across all types of disorders. Some social predictors of mental disorders such as rates of parental divorce and living alone have become more common, but others such as poverty and education levels have improved; many other trends, including unemployment and crime victimization, are not consistent over time. Finally, most prospective studies of the same people over several decades do not show rising rates of depression among younger cohorts (e.g., Murphy, Laird, Monson, Sobol, & Leighton, 2000).

The consistent finding that increasing age is associated with lower lifetime prevalence of all the disorders considered here is likely to be due to the difficulty people have in remembering and reporting emotional states that occurred in the distant past. It is much less likely that successive birth cohorts have experienced higher lifetime rates of mental disorder. Retrospective reports of subjective feeling states that occurred a long time ago should be viewed with skepticism.

MEDICATIONS AND TREATMENTS

People born at different times have had vastly different experiences with the mental health system. Cohorts who entered adulthood during the 1930s, 1940s, and 1950s faced a mental health system that was largely dependent on large, public inpatient institutions. Since that time, most mental health treatment has occurred in outpatient settings or in private or general hospitals. Older people are more likely to associate mental illness with severe and stigmatizing conditions and are less likely to have favorable attitudes toward using mental health services than younger ones. Conversely, cohorts born more recently have been socialized to a therapeutic culture that emphasizes using mental health services and, especially, taking psychotropic medications. The use of various mental health services, therefore, reflects strong generational effects.

Far more people received treatment for mental health problems in the early 2000s than in the decade preceding. For example, the proportion of people receiving treatment for depression has increased substantially. About 60% of people who report this condition in population surveys now obtain treatment for it, a nearly 40% increase since the early 1980s (Kessler et al., 2003). The percentage of the population in therapy for depression in a given year grew from 2.1% in the early 1980s to 3.7% in the early 2000s, an increase of 76% in just 20 years (Wang et al., 2006). The rate of outpatient treatment for anxiety disorders nearly doubled between 1987 and 1999, from 4.3 of every 1,000 people in 1987 to 8.3 of every 1,000 people in 1999 (Olfson, Marcus, Wan, & Geissler, 2004). Several factors account for rising rates of treatment for depression, anxiety disorders, and phobias, including increased mental health advocacy efforts, the emergence of direct-to-consumer advertisements for psychotropic medications, and growing perceptions of more efficacious and safe medications. People with anger disorders, however, are highly unlikely to seek mental health treatment: not surprisingly, they think that the objects of their anger, not themselves, are the ones at fault for their feelings.

The kinds of treatments people receive for depression and anxiety have also changed dramatically since the 1980s. About 75% of visits to physicians for therapy to resolve mental health problems now involve the use of some medication (Zuvekas, 2005). The most striking change has been the vast increase in the use of antidepressant medications. The use of antidepressants, including fluoxetine (Prozac), paroxetine (Paxil), sertraline (Zoloft), venlafaxine (Effexor), and fluvoxamine (Luvox) nearly tripled between 1988 and 2000; in any given month, 10% of women and 4% of men use these drugs. From 1996 to 2001 alone, the number of patients receiving therapy involving selective serotonin reuptake inhibitors, often called SSRIs, increased from 7.9 million to 15.4 million. Therapy involving antidepressants is especially popular among patients currently in their young adult years, although the rate of increase in the use of these drugs is also striking among the elderly (Crystal, Sambamoorthi, Walkup, & Akincigil, 2003).

The rising use of antidepressant medications has been accompanied by a sharp drop in the use of psychotherapy (treating mental, or emotional, or behavioral disorders, generally by means of extensive talk) since 1990 (Wang et al., 2006). For example, patients treated for anxiety disorders in 1999 were approximately half as likely to receive psychotherapy as they were in 1987. The decline in the use of long-term psychotherapy has been especially sharp (Olfson et al., 2002). For example, although cognitive-behavioral therapy (a type of treatment of mental illness that teaches the patient to try to adapt to stress and the environment by thinking about phenomena using precepts taught by the therapist) is often effective for the treatment of anxiety disorders, psychiatrists rarely use it.

A number of reasons account for the rising rates of drug treatment and falling rates of psychotherapy. One concerns the growing importance of managed health care, which relies on strategies that reduce health care expenditures by supporting the least expensive possible treatments (Mechanic, 2007). Most managed care plans provide more generous benefits for drug than for psychotherapeutic treatments and usually place no barriers on antidepressant use. Conversely, these plans often have severe limits on payments for psychotherapy. The result is that patients themselves prefer drug treatments because they involve lower out-of-pocket costs.

In addition, managed care also encourages the use of general practice physicians, who almost always prescribe medication, instead of mental health specialists who are more likely to use psychotherapy. As a result, most of the expansion of mental health treatment occurred in the general medical sector (Wang et al., 2005). Between the early 1990s and early 2000s, rates of mental health service use increased 159% in the general medical sector compared with 117% in specialty psychiatric services and 59% among other mental health personnel (Wang et al., 2006).

Another major trend leading to the growing use of medications has been the massive use of direct-to-consumer drug advertisements in the popular media. Before 1997, drug advertising could only be directed to physicians. Since that date, drug companies can appeal directly to consumers, who have flocked to physicians with requests for these drugs. Other reasons for the changing patterns of mental health treatment include increased mental health advocacy efforts, often funded by pharmaceutical companies, and the more widespread use of screening instruments aimed at detecting mental illness.

The widespread use of antidepressant medications has raised concerns about the harmful consequences of overmedication. These include potential adverse effects from long-term use of antidepressants and other psychotropic drugs, withdrawal difficulties, and their questionable effectiveness for treatment of mild disorders. In addition, the widespread use of medication as a first-line treatment can preclude consideration of other sorts of treatments, including various forms of psychotherapies as well as self-help alternatives such as changes in diet and exercise and the use of natural networks of social support.

GAPS IN KNOWLEDGE

Many issues about mental health among adults are actively debated. One puzzle regards definitions of mental disorder. Many mental health professionals and researchers assume that any psychological condition that results in negative outcomes must be a mental disorder. The problem with this assumption is that it defines an enormous amount of human behavior as abnormal. Community surveys of mental illness indicate that almost half the general population has a mental illness at some point in their lives and more than one quarter have experienced a mental illness more than the past year. Yet many of these conditions might actually be temporary and understandable responses to distressing events such as romantic breakups, job losses, or receiving news that an intimate (or oneself) has a life-threatening illness (Horwitz & Wakefield, 2007). Feelings of sadness, fear, shyness, and anger can be impairing but are not necessarily indications of disordered depression, anxiety, social phobia, or IED. Even so, researchers assume that acknowledgement of items on self-reported surveys indicate signs of a mental disorder as opposed to natural responses to distressing social contexts. Much work needs to be done in developing techniques that can distinguish appropriate negative emotions from mental disorders.

The separation of normal from disordered emotions is especially important because it has implications for health care policy. Treating normal emotions as if they were disordered can lead to pharmacotherapy that is neither necessary nor helpful. In addition, this point of view can lead to interventions that are based on pessimistic notions of human resilience. For example, shortly after the September 11, 2001, terrorist attacks, the Commissioner of the New York City Health and Mental Hygiene Department told Congress, "We face the possibility of a sharp increase in chronic and disabling mental health problems" (Satel, 2003, p. 1571). Although studies did show sharp increases in rates of mental health problems in the immediate aftermath of the attack, rates had returned to normal within 6 months of that date (Galea et al., 2002). During the same period, rates of use of mental health facilities did not show any substantial increase. In fact, residents of New York City, Washington D.C., and the United States in general showed great psychological resilience. Mental health policy greatly underestimates the ability of people to manage distressing events through self-help, social support, and informal community institutions.

Another puzzle regards the explanation of the young mean age of onset of most mental disorders, which is between 7 and 15 years for impulse control disorders, 6 to 22 for anxiety disorders, and 18 to 43 for depressive disorders (Kessler, Berglund, et al., 2005). In addition, as has been seen, as people grow older their chances of developing a mental disorder decrease. This pattern is exactly the opposite of that for virtually all chronic physical disorders not present at birth. Why mental disorders uniquely arise during the prime reproductive years and then have declining frequency poses a yet unsolved (and rarely addressed) evolutionary puzzle.

A third issue regards whether the current diagnostic system, which sharply distinguishes many distinct disorders from one another, is optimal or whether broader and more continuous categories better fit the underlying reality of most disorders. The bulk of the evidence indicates that many disorders, especially all the anxiety disorders and forms of depression, could be variable expressions of a similar underlying abnormality (Barlow, 1988). Most of the disorders considered here have very high rates of co-occurrence. Patients with one anxiety disorder usually also have additional anxiety disorders: For example, about 80% of patients with generalized anxiety disorder have some additional disorder. Nearly 90% of patients with agoraphobia and more than 80% with simple and social phobias also report at least one other type of mental disorder (Magee, Eaton, Wittchen, McGonagle, & Kessler, 1996).

In addition, anxious people generally have concurrent symptoms of depression whereas depressed people often present concurrent symptoms of anxiety. The causes, prognoses, and treatments for distinct disorders share more similarities than differences, suggesting that the current emphasis on distinct disorders is as much of a product of the social organization of the mental health professions and their desire to receive economic reimbursement for their services as of scientific knowledge. This has led a number of scholars to suggest that the various anxiety and depressive disorders are variants of the same temperamental type that might better be called *neurotic* or irrationally *harm-avoidant* (e.g., Akiskal, 1998). From this viewpoint, people might inherit predispositions to develop anxiety and mood disorders in general, not a particular type of disorder.

A final gap is the lack of knowledge about how mental health has changed over different birth cohorts and historical time. As already suggested, claims of substantial increases in mental health problems in recent decades seem to have more to do with changes in diagnostic criteria and measurement problems than with actual changes in either mental health or the social conditions that give rise to mental health symptoms. Researchers lack the kinds of prospective studies, particular those undertaken over long periods, that can better estimate changes in mental health over time. Similarly, little is known about how large scale historical trends such as the negative effects of globalization of work, macroeconomic changes, changing gender roles, rising income inequality, and other major social changes affect mental health over the life course.

POLICY ISSUES

Almost all mental health treatment now takes place in community settings. Most hospitalization that does occur is usually of brief duration and in general or private hospitals rather than public mental institutions. No indications confirm that the mental health system will return to the widespread use of the large, public inpatient institutions that dominated the system in the 19th and much of the 20th centuries. The challenges for mental health policy lie in delivering the most effective treatment in community-based systems.

One important policy issue regards mental health disorders receiving parity with more clearly physical disorders—that is, the payment for the treatment of mental disorders be seen as on an equivalent basis with physical disorders. At present, long-term treatment, inpatient care, and psychotherapy are reimbursed at lower rates and for shorter periods of time than physical disorders. To date, the many efforts at remedying this situation have not been successful, largely because of fears that parity in payment for mental disorders has the potential to bankrupt the health care system. If the substantial number of people who indicate that they have untreated mental disorders became more likely to seek treatment, it might be impossible for insurance companies or the federal government to cover the costs. Because of these concerns and their implication for mental health parity, it is especially important for the field to develop definitions of mental illness that include conditions that benefit from professional treatment while excluding those that will usually resolve in the absence of professional care. Limiting parity to serious mental disorders may result in a system that is oriented toward treating those conditions that can benefit the most from professional treatment.

The issue of prevention is also critical. Many mental health policies, such as screening for unrecognized mental disorders in primary medical care or in schools or bringing in grief counselors in the immediate aftermath of traumatic events, are based on the assumption that rapid identification and treatment of mental disorders can not only relieve current distress but also prevent more serious disorders from developing in the future. Although prevention has theoretical appeal, it also entails certain costs. Some evidence does suggest that prevention can have positive effects within comprehensive health care settings, but there is no evidence for its efficacy in regular mental health practice. Indeed, evidence is overwhelming that some common forms of prevention, such as single-session debriefings after traumas, are not only ineffective but can be harmful (Rose, Bisson, Churchill, & Wessely, 2002). In addition, given the size of the population with untreated mental disorders, focusing on identifying and treating people with unmet needs for mental health care could overwhelm the health care system. This, in turn, could lead the mental health system away from people with the greatest need for professional services toward those who neither want nor will benefit from treatment.

A final general issue relates to the costs and benefits of subjecting a wide range of human problems to medical care. *Medicalization* refers to defining and treating problems that previously were been outside the medical system as problems to be handled by medical techniques. Normal sadness becomes major depressive disorder, fear is transformed in a variety of anxiety disorders, shyness becomes social phobia, and anger becomes IED. Medicalization promises the benefits of efficient, socially valued, and nonstigmatizing treatment that can often relief the pain of unpleasant emotional experiences. It has the potential costs, however, of neglecting alternative, and sometimes more effective, ways of responding to problems, atrophying self-help solutions, and disregarding the importance of fostering human agency.

SEE ALSO Volume 1: *Attention Deficit/Hyperactivity Disorder (ADHD); Autism;* Volume 2: *Risk; Stress in Adulthood; Suicide, Adulthood; Trauma;* Volume 3: *Dementias; Loneliness, Later Life; Quality of Life; Stress in Later Life.*

BIBLIOGRAPHY

Akiskal, H. S. (1998). Toward a definition of generalized anxiety disorder as an anxious temperament type. *Acta Psychiatrica Scandinavica, 98*(Supp. 393), 66–73.

American Psychiatric Association. (1980). *Diagnostic and statistical manual of mental disorders.* (3rd ed.). Washington, DC: Author.

Barlow, D. H. (1988). *Anxiety and its disorders: The nature and treatment of anxiety and panic.* New York: Guilford.

Brown, G. W. (2002). Social roles, context and evolution in the origins of depression. *Journal of Health and Social Behavior, 43,* 255–276.

Brown, G. W., & Harris, T. (1978). *The social origins of depression.* London: Tavistock.

Carr, D. S. (1997). The fulfillment of career dreams at midlife: Does it matter for women's mental health? *Journal of Health and Social Behavior, 38,* 331–344.

Cherlin, A., Chase-Landsdale, L., & McRae, C. (1998). Effects of parental divorce on mental health throughout the life course. *American Sociological Review, 63,* 239–249.

Crystal, S., Sambamoorthi, U., Walkup, J. T., & Akincigil, A. (2003). Diagnosis and treatment of depression in the elderly Medicare population: Predictors, disparities, and trends. *Journal of the American Geriatric Society, 51,* 1718–1728.

Eaton, W. W., & Mutaner, C. (1999). Socioeconomic stratification and mental health. In A. V. Horwitz & T. L. Scheid (Eds.), *A handbook for the study of mental health: Social contexts, theories, and systems* (pp. 259–283). New York: Cambridge University Press.

Elder, G. H. (1974). *Children of the Great Depression: Social change in the life experience.* Chicago: University of Chicago Press.

Finlay-Jones, R., & G. W. Brown. (1981). Types of stressful life events and the onset of depressive and anxiety disorders. *Psychological Medicine, 11,* 803–815.

Galea, S., Ahern, J., Resnick, H., Kilpatrick, D., Bucuvalas, M., Gold, J., et al. (2002). Psychological sequelae of the

September 11 terrorist attacks in New York City. *New England Journal of Medicine, 346,* 982–987.

George, L. K. (2007). Life course perspectives on social factors and mental illness. In W. S. Avison, J. D. McLeod, & B. A. Pescosolido (Eds.), *Mental health/social mirror* (pp. 191–218). New York: Springer.

Horwitz, A. V. (2002). *Creating mental illness.* Chicago: University of Chicago Press.

Horwitz, A. V., & Wakefield, J. C. (2007). *The loss of sadness: How psychiatry transformed normal sorrow into depressive disorder.* New York: Oxford University Press.

Kendler, K. S. (2005). Toward a philosophical structure for psychiatry. *American Journal of Psychiatry, 162,* 433–440.

Kessler, R. C., Berglund, P., Demler, O., Jin, R., Merikangas, K. R., & Walters, E. E. (2005). Lifetime prevalence and age-of-onset distributions of *DSM–IV* disorders in the National Comorbidity Survey replication. *Archives of General Psychiatry, 62,* 593–602.

Kessler, R. C., Berglund, P. Demler, O., Jin, R., Rotetz, D., Merikangas, K. R., et al. (2003). The epidemiology of major depressive disorder: Results from the National Comorbidity Survey replication. *Journal of the American Medical Association, 289,* 3095–3105.

Kessler, R. C., Chiu, W. T., Demler, O., & Walters, E. E. (2005). Prevalence, severity, and comorbidity of 12-month *DSM–IV* disorders in the National Comorbidity Survey replication. *Archives of General Psychiatry, 62,* 617–627.

Kessler, R. C., Coccaro, E. F., Fava, M., Jaeger, S., Jin R, & Walters, E. (2006). The prevalence and correlates of *DSM–IV* intermittent explosive disorder in the National Comorbidity Survey replication. *Archives of General Psychiatry, 63,* 669–678.

Kessler, R. C., Stein, M. B., & Berglund, P. (1998) Social phobia subtypes in the National Comorbidity Survey. *American Journal of Psychiatry, 155,* 613–619.

Klerman, G. K., & Weissman, M. M. (1989). Increasing rates of depression. *Journal of the American Medical Association, 261,* 2229–2235.

Lane, C. (2007). *Shyness: How normal behavior became a sickness.* New Haven, CT: Yale University Press.

Langner, T. S. (1962). A twenty-two item screening score of psychiatric symptoms indicating impairment. *Journal of Health and Social Behavior, 3,* 269–276.

Magee, W., Eaton, W. W., Wittchen, H. U., McGonagle, K. A., & Kessler, R. C. (1996). Agoraphobia, simple phobia, and social phobia in the National Comorbidity Survey. *Archives of General Psychiatry, 53,* 159–168.

McLeod, J., & Shanahan, M. (1996). Trajectories of poverty and children's mental health. *Journal of Health and Social Behavior, 37,* 207–220.

Mechanic, D. (2007). *The truth about health care: Why reform is not working in America.* New Brunswick, NJ: Rutgers University Press.

Murphy, J. M., Laird, N. M., Monson, R. R., Sobol, A. M., & Leighton, A. H. (2000). A 40-year perspective on the prevalence of depression: The Stirling County study. *Archives of General Psychiatry, 26,* 209–215.

Olfson, M., Marcus, S. C., Wan, G. J., & Geissler, E. C. (2004). National trends in the outpatient treatment of anxiety disorders. *Journal of Clinical Psychiatry, 65,* 1166–1173.

Post, R. M. (1992). Transduction of psychosocial stress into the neurobiology of recurrent affective disorder. *American Journal of Psychiatry, 149,* 999–1010.

Rose, S., Bisson, J., Churchill, R., & Wessely, S. (2002). Psychological debriefing for preventing post-traumatic stress disorder. *Cochrane Database of Systematic Reviews,* issue 2.

Satel, S. L. (2003). The mental health crisis that wasn't. *Psychiatric Services, 54,* 1571.

Sapolsky, R. M. (2001). Depression, antidepressants, and the shrinking hippocampus. *Proceedings of the National Academy of Sciences of the USA, 98,* 12320–12322.

Schieman, S. (2006). Anger. In J. E. Stets & J. H. Turner (Eds.), *Handbook of the sociology of emotions* (pp. 493–515). New York: Springer.

Seligman, M. E. P. (1975). *Helplessness: On depression, development and death.* San Francisco, CA: Freeman.

Simon, G. E., Goldberg, D. P., Von Korff, M, & Ustun, T. B. (2002). Understanding cross-national differences in depression prevalence. *Psychological Medicine, 32,* 585–594.

Simon, G. E., & Von Korff, M. (1995). Recall of psychiatric history in cross-sectional surveys: Implications for epidemiologic research. *Epidemiologic Reviews, 17,* 221–227.

Simon, R. W., & Marcussen, K. (1999). Marital transitions, marital beliefs, and mental health. *Journal of Health and Social Behavior, 40,* 111–125.

Umberson, D., & Williams, K. (1999). Family status and mental health. In C. S. Aneshensel & J. C. Phelan (Eds.), *Handbook of the sociology of mental health* (pp. 225–253). New York: Kluwer/Plenum.

Umberson, D., Wortman, C. B., & Kessler, R. C. (1992). Widowhood and depression: Explaining long-term gender differences in vulnerability. *Journal of Health and Social Behavior, 33,* 10–24.

Wang, P. S., Demler, O., Olfson, M., Pincus, H. A., Wells, K. B., & Kessler, R. C. (2006). Changing profiles of service sectors used for mental health care in the United States. *American Journal of Psychiatry, 163,* 1187–1198.

Wang, P. S., Lane, M., Olfson, M., Pincus, H. A., Wells, K. B., & Kessler, R. C. (2005). Twelve-month use of mental health services in the United States. *Archives of General Psychiatry, 62,* 629–640.

Weissman, M. M., Bland, R. C., Canino, G. J., Faravelli, C., Greenwald, S., Hwu, H. G., et al. (1996). Cross-national epidemiology of major depression and bipolar disorder. *Journal of the American Medical Association, 276,* 293–299.

Zuvekas, S. H. (2005). Prescription drugs and the changing patterns of treatment for mental disorders, 1996–2001. *Health Affairs, 24,* 195–205.

Allan V. Horwitz

MIDLIFE CRISES AND TRANSITIONS

The boundaries of midlife are not well defined; however, the most common conception is that middle age begins at 40 and ends at 65 (Lachman, 2004). This period is characterized by a remarkable complexity of roles, relationships, and resources. Despite the image of midlife as a relatively stable life stage, middle-aged adults typically experience multiple life crises and transitions, many of which pose developmental and social challenges. Important crises and transitions include menopause, parental death, marital dissolution, children leaving home, problems in the lives of adult children, and caregiving responsibilities. These events often entail negative consequences, such as economic hardship, social isolation, psychological distress, and threat to self-concept. Yet these adverse repercussions are often short-lived, and over time individuals may even experience positive consequences, such as wisdom, personal growth, improved coping skills, and stronger interpersonal relationships.

DEFINITIONS OF MIDLIFE CRISES AND TRANSITIONS

Developmental and life span psychologists conceptualize crisis as a normative developmental challenge, a crucial point at which individuals can develop in alternative ways (Lachman & James, 1997). Early work on adult development focused on life stages and orderly transitions. For example, Erik Erikson (1963) placed midlife in the context of eight lifespan stages, whereby each stage encompassed a crisis, or a challenge that needs to be resolved. In midlife, the central challenge is achieving generativity, or moving past a narrow focus on one's self, and instead nurturing and guiding the next generation (Lachman, 2004).

Sociologists, by contrast, conceptualize crises as stressors with potentially adverse consequences for physical and mental health. The meaning of specific stressors is understood from a life course perspective, which places individual development in the context of historical, cultural, and social structures and processes (Bengtson & Allen, 1993). A transition—one of the key concepts in life course research—is a change in status that is discrete and bounded in duration, although it may have long-term consequences (George, 1993). Many transitions are stressors because they threaten well-being and require coping and adjustment (Pearlin, 1999).

Psychological and sociological perspectives on crises and transitions intersect in the notion of a psychological "turning point"—an important life situation or a new insight into one's self that becomes a motive for redirecting and changing one's life (Clausen, 1995). Turning points at midlife can be brought on by both positive and negative experiences.

COMMON CRISES AND TRANSITIONS IN MIDLIFE

One of the most popular images of midlife is the experience of a "midlife crisis." Research and theory in the 1970s described the midlife crisis as an almost exclusively male phenomenon. It was viewed as a crisis of identity that involved increased introspection, a realization of limited time, and a preoccupation with lost opportunities (Rosenberg, Rosenberg, & Farrell, 1999). However, since then researchers have found little evidence to support the idea that the midlife crisis is a universal developmental phenomenon (Wethington, Kessler, & Pixley, 2004). Instead, other crises and transitions appear to have more profound implications for midlife development.

Menopause Menopause has been traditionally viewed as women's midlife crisis because it is a major change in reproductive capacity. Researchers have found no evidence to support the stereotypical view that women hold negative attitudes toward menopause (Avis, 1999). Another notion that persists is that menopause commonly leads to depression. Community-based studies demonstrate that psychological trauma and distress are not typically associated with this normal transition in women's lives (Avis, 1999). The so-called "menopausal syndrome" is more likely explained by personal characteristics and past experiences, such as previous history of depression, than menopause per se (Avis, 1999).

Parental Death The death of a parent during middle age is widely recognized as a life-course marker (George, 1993). Parental death may be less stressful than other types of bereavement, partly because it is considered a normal part of middle age. Still, it is a major turning point for most people. It may compel individuals to confront their own mortality, leading to a reevaluation of identities, values, and behaviors (Kranz & Daniluk, 2002). Losing the buffer of the parent generation may force one to finally "become an adult" and may also promote psychological growth, increased maturity, and a greater appreciation of personal relationships (Aldwin & Levenson, 2001).

Marital Dissolution Spousal death is most likely to occur to adults in their 70s and older, whereas divorce typically occurs during the first decade of marriage in young adulthood. Thus, both divorce and widowhood are "off-time" transitions at midlife. Off-time events, or events that occur earlier or later than expected, may have particularly stressful consequences (Neugarten, Moore, & Lowe, 1965). Middle-aged widows—those widowed before 60—are more likely than their older counterparts to become poor (Holden & Smock, 1991). Similarly, divorced middle-aged women might experience greater financial problems than their younger peers because the most pronounced declines in per capita income are associated with marriages of longer duration (Holden & Smock, 1991), and middle-aged women have been married, on average, for a longer period than women who divorced in young adulthood. Among men, marital dissolution may be associated with social isolation and loss of emotional intimacy (Gerstel, Riessman, & Rosenfield, 1985).

A study of men and women who became widowed or divorced between their mid-50s and mid-60s (Pudrovska & Carr, 2005) showed that recently bereaved and divorced persons report higher levels of depression and alcohol use, even after adjustment for selection factors, health, family characteristics, and social and socioeconomic resources. This effect may reflect the fact that persons who lose a spouse or become divorced in their 50s or early 60s have few peers who share their experiences and may lack institutional supports to help them cope with marital loss, given that most recently divorced persons are young adults under 40, whereas most recently bereaved persons are older adults.

Empty Nest and Problems in the Lives of Adult Children In the family life cycle approach (Glick, 1977) the empty nest following the launching of the last child is a quintessential midlife stage. The launching process minimally extends from the time the first child leaves home for the first time to the time when the last child leaves home for the last time (White, 1994). The empty nest tends to occur later for parents who are in their intact first marriage, are African or Mexican American, and have more children, more sons, more unmarried children, or a higher income (Aquilino, 1990).

The empty-nest stage has been traditionally viewed as a difficult time for midlife women. This transition symbolized the end of women's most intensive years in the mother role, which was usually considered one of the most fundamental sources of a women's identity (Black & Hill, 1984). Although early clinical studies reported depression following the empty-nest transition, more recent studies of the general population revealed positive psychological outcomes for empty-nest parents (White & Edwards, 1990). The empty nest was shown to be associated with improved marital happiness for all parents and increased overall life satisfaction when there was frequent contact with nonresident children (White & Edwards, 1990).

Because of the increased importance of college education, rising ages at marriage, and soaring housing costs, current generations of young adults remain in the parental home longer than prior generations (Aquilino, 1990). These trends have created a demographic context in which the empty nest is no longer a nearly universal experience at midlife. William Aquilino and Khalil Supple (1991) suggested that most parents who coreside with young adult children report high levels of satisfaction with the presence of children at home, particularly when the quality of parent–child relationships is high. Yet parental satisfaction is adversely affected by adult children's inadequate income and inability to maintain an independent household.

Overall, parents are distressed when their adult children have problems—whether children live in the parental household or independently. Adult children's problems, such as illness, unemployment, financial difficulties, and strains in marital relationships, are associated with parents' greater negative affect (Pillemer & Suitor, 1991), lower levels of positive affect, less self-acceptance, and poorer parent–child relationship quality (Greenfield & Marks, 2006).

Caregiving Responsibilities The middle-aged are often viewed as the "sandwich generation" who experience financial, psychological, and physical demands from responsibilities to both younger and older generations while being in the paid labor force, although only a minority of middle-aged adults provide care to their children and parents at the same time (Marks, 1996). Yet more than half of the women with a surviving parent spend at least some time in a caregiving role (Himes, 1994). Women in the middle often face caretaking dilemmas and are more likely than men to sacrifice their careers to take care of spouses and parents (Moen & Wethington, 1999). Caregiving responsibilities often force women to either terminate their employment or reduce work hours, which results in decreased income (Evandrou & Glaser, 2003). As a chronic strain, caregiving may adversely affect caregivers' physical and mental health (Aneshensel, Pearlin, Mullan, Zarit, & Whitlach, 1995). Yet research also reveals psychological benefits from caregiving, such as mastery, self-esteem, and mattering—the sense of being a person of significance to the well-being of loved ones (Moen, Robinson, & Dempster-McClain, 1995).

COPING WITH CRISES AND TRANSITIONS

The challenges of midlife are typically matched by the extensive material, psychosocial, and coping resources of middle-aged adults; thus, most people in midlife successfully adjust to crises and transition and show resilience to burdening and demanding circumstances (Heckhausen, 2001). One of the most consistent findings to emerge from research on crises is that the negative psychological and interpersonal consequences of stressful events are relatively short-lived, and that psychological well-being of individuals who experience even the most disruptive transitions eventually approaches precrisis levels (Booth & Amato, 1991).

Research has increasingly focused on the positive consequences of crises, such as posttraumatic growth (Tedeschi, Park, & Calhoun, 1998) or the perceived benefits of stress (Aldwin & Sutton, 1998). Crises can lead to ego development, wisdom, stronger interpersonal relationships, more effective coping skills, and higher levels of mastery and self-esteem (Aldwin & Levenson, 2001). For example, widowhood and divorce in the long term tend to be accompanied by a positive shift into a new life phase, personal growth, and increased sense of control (Feldman, Biles, & Beaumont, 2001; Umberson, Wortman, & Kessler, 1992).

THE FUTURE OF RESEARCH ON MIDLIFE CRISES AND TRANSITIONS

Although midlife spans 25 to 30 years, little is known about the diversity *within* the middle-aged group with respect to specific periods of midlife, such as early midlife and late midlife (Staudinger & Bluck, 2001). The nature of crises and transitions confronting middle-aged adults is likely to differ by stages of midlife. However, many existing studies that examine such age differences use cross-sectional data and, thus, cannot fully distinguish intrapersonal changes within cohorts from intercohort variation (e.g., Ryff & Keyes, 1995). The use of longitudinal panel data can help to distinguish age-related developmental processes from differences among birth cohorts.

The experiences of members of racial and ethnic minorities at midlife have remained largely unexplored. Yet the nature, antecedents, and consequences of crises confronting middle-aged White persons do not adequately reflect the challenges and circumstances of other racial groups. Detailed racial and ethnic comparisons have not been a prominent theme in the literature.

Finally, demographic trends of recent decades have created a remarkable complexity of family structure and interpersonal relationships. Yet scholars still have limited knowledge about heterogeneity of individual trajectories and the so-called "nonnormative" pathways that become increasingly common, such as having a first child in midlife, choosing to remain single and/or childfree, and being in same-sex relationships and unions. Moreover, despite the trends in men's greater family involvement and women's unprecedented labor force participation (Casper & Bianchi, 2002), the interplay of work and family roles among middle-aged men and women have not been fully explored. Family statuses and transitions matter for midlife men's physical and mental health (Barnett, Brennan, Raudenbush, & Marshall, 1994), whereas career trajectories have profound implications for women's well-being (O'Campo, Eaton, & Muntaner, 2004; Simon, 1995). Given these trends toward increased complexity of family and work arrangements at midlife, public policies should be directed at facilitating work-family balance not only among young adults but also among middle-aged men and women.

SEE ALSO Volume 2: *Divorce; Menopause; Stress in Adulthood; Parent-Child Relationships, Adulthood;* Volume 3: *Caregiving; Retirement; Stress in Later Life.*

BIBLIOGRAPHY

Aldwin, C. M., & Levenson, M. R. (2001). Stress, coping, and health at midlife: A developmental perspective. In M. E. Lachman (Ed.), *Handbook of midlife development* (pp. 188–214). New York: Wiley.

Aldwin, C. M., & Sutton, K. J. (1998). A developmental perspective on posttraumatic growth. In R. G. Tedeschi, C. L. Park, & L. G. Calhoun (Eds.), *Posttraumatic growth: Positive changes in the aftermath of crisis* (pp. 43–63). Mahwah, NJ: Lawrence Erlbaum.

Aneshensel, C. S., Pearlin, L. I., Mullan, J. T., Zarit, S., & Whitlach, C. (1995). *Profiles in caregiving: The unexpected career.* New York: Academic Press.

Aquilino, W. S. (1990). The likelihood of parent–adult child coresidence: Effects of family structure and parental characteristics. *Journal of Marriage and the Family, 52,* 405–419.

Aquilino, W. S., & Supple, K. R. (1991). Parent–child relations and parents' satisfaction with living arrangements when adult children live at home. *Journal of Marriage and the Family, 53,* 13–27.

Avis, N. E. (1999). Women's health at midlife. In S. L. Willis & J. D. Reid (Eds.), *Life in the middle: Psychological and social development in middle age* (pp. 105–146). San Diego, CA: Academic Press.

Barnett, R. C., Brennan, R. T., Raudenbush, S. W., & Marshall, N. L. (1994). Gender and the relationship between marital-role quality and psychological distress: A study of dual-earner couples. *Psychology of Women Quarterly, 18,* 105–127.

Bengtson V. L., & Allen, K.R. (1993). The life course perspective applied to families over time. In P. G. Boss, W. Doherty, R. LaRossa, W. Schumm, & S. Steinmetz (Eds.), *Sourcebook of family theories and methods: A contextual approach* (pp. 469–499). New York: Plenum.

Black, S. M., & Hill, C. E. (1984). The psychological well-being of women in their middle years. *Psychology of Women Quarterly, 8,* 282–292.

Booth, A., & Amato, P. (1991). Divorce and psychological stress. *Journal of Health and Social Behavior, 32,* 396–407.

Casper, L. M., & Bianchi, S. M. (2002). *Continuity and change in the American family.* Thousand Oaks, CA: Sage.

Clausen, J. (1995). Gender, contexts, and turning points in adults' lives. In P. Moen, G. H. Elder Jr., & K. Luscher (Eds.), *Examining lives in context: Perspectives on the ecology of human development* (pp. 365–389). Washington, DC: American Psychological Association.

Erikson E. (1963). *Childhood and society.* (2nd ed.). New York: Norton.

Evandrou, M., & Glaser, K. (2003). Combining work and family life: The pension penalty for caring. *Ageing and Society, 23,* 583–601.

Feldman, S., Byles, J. E., & Beaumont, R. (2000). Is anybody listening? The experiences of widowhood for older Australian women. *Journal of Women & Aging, 12,* 155–176.

George, L. (1993). Sociological perspectives on life transitions. *Annual Review of Sociology, 19,* 353–373.

Gerstel, N., Riessman, C. K., & Rosenfield, S. (1985). Explaining the symptomatology of separated and divorced women and men: The role of material conditions and social support. *Social Forces, 64,* 84–101.

Glick, P. C. (1977). Updating the life cycle of the family. *Journal of Marriage and the Family, 39,* 5–13.

Greenfield, E. A., & Marks, N. F. (2006). Linked lives: Adult children's problems and their parents' psychological and relational well-being. *Journal of Marriage and the Family, 68,* 442–454.

Heckhausen, J. (2001). Adaptation and resilience in midlife. In M. E. Lachman (Ed.), *Handbook of midlife development* (pp. 345–394). New York: Wiley.

Himes, C. L. (1994). Parental caregiving by adult women: A demographic perspective. *Research on Aging, 16,* 191–211.

Holden, K. C., & Smock, P. J. (1991). The economic costs of marital dissolution: Why do women bear a disproportionate cost? *Annual Review of Sociology, 17,* 51–78.

Kranz, K., & Daniluk, J. C. (2002). Gone but not forgotten: The meaning and experience of mother loss for midlife daughters. *Women & Therapy, 25,* 1–18.

Lachman, M. E. (2004). Development in midlife. *Annual Review of Psychology, 55,* 305–331.

Lachman, M. E., & James, J. B. (1997). Charting the course of midlife development: An overview. In M. E. Lachman & J. B. James (Eds.), *Multiple paths of midlife development* (pp. 1–20). Chicago: University of Chicago Press.

Marks, N. F. (1996). Social demographic diversity among American midlife parents. In C. D. Ryff & M. M. Seltzer (Eds.), *The parental experience in midlife* (pp. 29–75). Chicago: University of Chicago Press.

Moen, P., Robinson, J., & Dempster-McClain, D. (1995). Caregiving and women's well-being: A life course approach. *Journal of Health and Social Behavior, 36,* 259–273.

Moen, P., & Wethington, E. (1999). Midlife development in a life course context. In S. L. Willis & J. D. Reid (Eds.), *Life in the middle: Psychological and social development in middle age* (pp. 1–23). San Diego, CA: Academic Press.

Neugarten, B. L., Moore, J. W., & Lowe, J. C. (1965). Age norms, age constraints, and adult socialization. *American Journal of Sociology, 70,* 710–717.

O'Campo, P., Eaton, W. W., Muntaner, C. (2004). Labor market experiences, work organization, gender inequalities and health status: Results from a prospective analysis of U.S. employed women. *Social Science & Medicine, 58,* 585–594.

Pearlin, L. I. (1999). The stress process revisited: Reflections on concepts and their interrelationships. In C. S. Aneshensel & J. C. Phelan (Eds.), *Handbook of the sociology of mental health* (pp. 395–416). New York: Kluwer Academic/Plenum.

Pillemer, K., & Suitor, J. J. (1991). Will I ever escape my child's problems? Effects of adult children's problems on elderly parents. *Journal of Marriage and the Family, 53,* 585–594.

Pudrovska, T., & Carr, D. S. (2005, November). *Psychological well-being of divorced and widowed adults at mid- and later life: Why does marital dissolution matter?* Paper presented at the 58th Annual Meeting of the Gerontological Society of America, Orlando, FL.

Rosenberg, S. D., Rosenberg, H. J., & Farrell, M. P. (1999). The midlife crisis revisited. In S. L. Willis & J. D. Reid (Eds.), *Life in the middle: Psychological and social development in middle age* (pp. 47–73). San Diego, CA: Academic Press.

Ryff, C. D., & Keyes, C. L. M. (1995). The structure of psychological well-being revisited. *Journal of Personality and Social Psychology, 69,* 719–727.

Simon, R. W. (1995). Gender, multiple roles, role meaning, and mental health. *Journal of Health and Social Behavior, 36,* 182–194.

Staudinger, U. M., & Bluck, S. (2001). A view on midlife development from lifespan theory. In M. E. Lachman (Ed.), *Handbook of midlife development* (pp. 3–39). New York: Wiley.

Tedeschi, R.G., Park, C.L., & Calhoun, L.G. (1998). Posttraumatic growth: Conceptual issues. In R.G. Tedeschi, C.L. Park, & L.G. Calhoun (Eds.), *Posttraumatic growth: Positive changes in the aftermath of crisis* (pp. 1–22). Mahwah, NJ: Lawrence Erlbaum.

Umberson, D., Wortman, C. B., & Kessler, R. C. (1992). Widowhood and depression: Explaining long-term gender differences in vulnerability. *Journal of Health and Social Behavior, 33,* 10–24.

Wethington, E., Kessler, R. C., & Pixley, J. E. (2004). Turning points in adulthood. In O. G. Brim, C. D. Ryff, & R. C. Kessler (Eds.), *How healthy are we? A national study of well-being at midlife* (pp. 586–613). Chicago: University of Chicago Press.

White, L. (1994). Coresidence and leaving home: Young adults and their parents. *Annual Review of Sociology, 20,* 81–102.

White, L., & Edwards, J. (1990). Emptying the nest and parental well-being: An analysis of national panel data. *American Sociological Review, 55,* 235–242.

Tetyana Pudrovska

MILITARY SERVICE

Military service entails joining a branch of the armed forces through voluntary enlistment, conscription during a draft, appointment, or in some societies as a mandated duty of citizenship. In the United States, the military services include the Army, Navy, Air Force, Marine Corps, and Coast Guard. Active duty military service refers to full-time engagement in one of these services; it includes members of the Reserve Components when they are serving or in full-time training, but does not include full-time members of the National Guard. Each branch, listed above, has a reserve component. The reserve components of each branch are part-time military personnel who serve a period of active duty after attending basic and job training that usually last several months. Following this active duty training period, reserve personnel return to civilian life; however, for the remainder of their service obligation, they attend trainings and work in their job specialty for their unit one or two days per month. Additionally, they attend a two-week active-duty training each year. After 20 years of reserve service or upon reaching age 60 years, reserve personnel are entitled to a retirement benefit based on reserve pay. Members of the National Guard are under Federal and State jurisdiction, unlike members of the other armed forces, who are under Federal jurisdiction only.

Members of the National Guard can be deployed by the governor of their state or the president. When not deployed on active duty, members of the National Guard are only required to train one weekend per month and during a two-week period each year. Veteran status is conferred upon those who are on active duty or have served previously on active duty and received an other-than-dishonorable discharge. Exposure to combat is not a prerequisite for active duty, veteran status or benefits eligibility. Active duty service encompasses a range of activities, including training, intelligence gathering, conducting maneuvers to ensure preparedness for combat, and serving domestically and overseas in various capacities deemed important for the defense of the Untied States and its allies.

Although there is variation across historical periods, such as when there is an ongoing war, draft, or mobilization of the Reserve Components, persons who serve in the military generally enter service at relatively young ages and exit after only a few years on active duty. From 1941 to 1973, American men of specific ages and a diverse range of personal characteristics were subject to a draft (Flynn, 1993). However, most men and women who have served in the U.S. military in the 20th and 21st centuries have done so voluntarily. Since 1973, the U.S. military has been in what is commonly known as the era of the All-Volunteer Force (AVF).

Military service is selective, reflecting both individual choices to enlist and the military's authority to reject those deemed incapable of serving effectively. To enter the military, people must meet specified eligibility criteria, pass physical and mental health screenings, undergo standardized training regimens, and be willing and able to adhere to the military code of conduct. Each of the military services is organized hierarchically by rank, with enlisted personnel broadly distinguished from officers. Enlisted personnel begin at the lowest rank in the military and serve as the main workforce within it. Enlisted personnel generally have high school educational attainments; with time, good service, training, and education, advancement can be expected. Officers enter a branch of the military services in a supervisory capacity and must have a 4-year college degree in order to be commissioned as an officer. The chain of command is clearly specified and enforced. While there is opportunity for advancement, especially among those who make military service a long-term career, the enlisted and officer ranks select persons with different characteristics and provide members with access to different types of assignments, risks, and rewards.

Researchers who study military service in relation to the life course recognize that the military is a powerful institution whose potential to transform lives for better or worse varies across individual characteristics, the timing of military service in the life course, service experiences,

and historical periods. These insights serve as the foundation for theories about, and empirical life course studies of, the role of military service in men's and, to a lesser extent, women's lives. Taken as a whole, the existing body of life course research on military service succeeds in connecting "the micro- and macro-levels of analysis, thus connecting the soldier's story to that of his [or her] changing society" (Modell and Haggerty, 1991, p. 205).

MILITARY SERVICE AND LIFE COURSE DISCONTINUITY

Studying the role of military service in the life course provides researchers with a rich opportunity to investigate each of the five major principles of the life course paradigm: human agency; location in time and place; timing; linked lives; and lifelong development. Glen H. Elder Jr. is responsible for some of the most influential theorizing about the role of military service in the life course and the importance of military service for life course studies. By focusing age at entry into the military, his work develops and tests two hypotheses: the military as turning point and as life course disruption. Both hypotheses emphasize the potential of military service to produce discontinuity in the life course.

The military as turning point hypothesis focuses on people who enter the military at younger ages, such as persons who enlist right after high school graduation, because the chances for redirection of the life course are maximized and disruption to an established life course is minimized. Elder (1987) argues that early entry into the military enables a pause in individual development, which both delays the transition to adulthood and allows for the maximal utilization of service benefits. Early entrants are often highly disadvantaged with few other options; they see military service as a route out of difficult life circumstances. These are precisely the persons who may benefit most from the health and educational benefits available to veterans.

According to the life course disruption hypothesis, an individual's relatively late entry into the military has the potential to interfere with established marital, parenting, and occupational trajectories, which may have consequences for the subsequent patterning of the life course and for outcomes later in life. Late entrants often come from more advantaged backgrounds than earlier entrants. Moreover, because late entrants are more likely to have completed their educations and will have less time upon completion of their service to take advantage of veterans' educational benefits, they may not experience the gains that accrue to more disadvantaged, earlier entrants. There are several reasons why people enter the military at older ages. Older entrants include people who enlisted or were drafted during a war; delayed entrance in order to complete college or a service academy prior to being commissioned as an officer; entered as physicians to complete a "pay back" after the military paid for their medical education; decided after their transition to adulthood that they were prepared to handle the challenges the military entails or that the military offered them opportunities that were not available in the civilian sector; and responded to incentives for enlistment that the military sometimes offers.

Considerable research shows that early entry into the military can produce a positive turning point in the life course trajectories of initially disadvantaged men. For example, focusing mostly on veterans of World War II, Elder (1986) reports that early entrants had more disadvantaged family backgrounds, poorer grades, and lower feelings of self-adequacy. However, because military service delayed their transition to adult roles and responsibil-

ities, they were able to equal the occupational achievements of, and have more stable marriages and experience larger gains in psychological strength than non-veterans. Early entrants were also much more likely than later entrants to report retrospectively that their lives had followed a different and more rewarding course as a result of their military service. Other studies also support the military as positive turning point hypothesis. For example, Sampson and Laub (1996, p. 364) conclude: "Military service in the World War II era provided American men from economically disadvantaged backgrounds with an unprecedented opportunity to better their lives though on-the-job training and further education" (see also Laub and Sampson, 2003).

Elder, Shanahan, and Clipp (1994) provide direct evidence in support of the life course disruption hypothesis. They report that for each year of delay into military service the economic and job benefits associated with

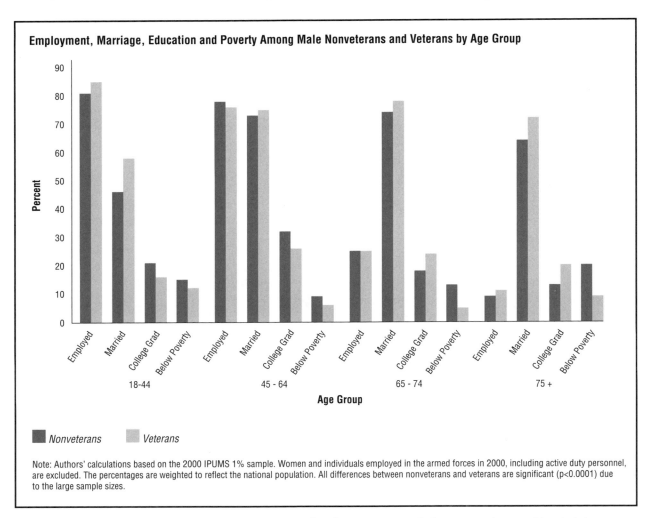

Figure 1. *Differences between veterans and nonveterans across these four age groups, which experienced unique historical circumstances during early adulthood, demonstrate that military service is associated with a variety of social and economic outcomes.* CENGAGE LEARNING, GALE.

G.I. BILL

The Servicemen's Readjustment Act of 1944 (Public Law 346), more commonly known as the G.I. Bill (of Rights), was signed into law by President Franklin D. Roosevelt on June 22, 1944. The G.I. Bill extended numerous social benefits to any veteran of World War II who had served for 90 days or more, except those who received dishonorable discharges. These benefits included unemployment income support for as long as 1 year; guaranteed, low-interest loans to purchase homes, farms, or businesses; and tuition, fee, and living allowances to support education or vocational training. Although all of these benefits were widely used, the education and training benefits were used most frequently. By 1956, 2.2 million veterans had used G.I. Bill benefits to attend college, whereas 5.6 million had obtained noncollege training. Although the G.I. Bill was inclusive and expanded opportunities for Blacks as well as Whites, some Black veterans, particularly in the Deep South, had difficulty accessing or using benefits for which they were eligible.

Overall, the G.I. Bill expanded access to education for veterans of World War II, which transformed their life-course trajectories, the lives of their spouses and children, and the nation as a whole.

BIBLIOGRAPHY

Douglas, D. (1987, February 28). Committees also reject Reagan budget cuts for vets: Highly successful new G.I. Bill. *CQ Weekly*, pp. 364–365.

Mettler, S. (2005). *Soldiers to citizens: The G.I. Bill and the making of the greatest generation.* New York: Oxford University Press.

Onkst, D. H. (1998). "First a Negro…incidentally a veteran": Black World War Two veterans and the G.I. Bill of Rights in the Deep South, 1944–1948. *Journal of Social History, 31*(3), 517–543.

Turner, S., & Bound, J. (2003). Closing the gap or widening the divide: The effects of the G.I. Bill and World War II on the educational outcomes of Black Americans. *Journal of Economic History, 63*(1), 145–177.

military service were reduced and the risk of life disruption and related costs increased. Moreover, partly as a result of the work-life disadvantages they experienced, late-mobilized men were at greatest risk of subsequent downward trajectories in physical health.

MILITARY SERVICE AND SOCIOECONOMIC, MARRIAGE/ FAMILY, AND HEALTH OUTCOMES

Figure 1 uses data from the 2000 U.S. Census to describe how men who have served in the military are different than men who have not served in terms of employment, marriage, college graduation, and poverty statuses. Four age groups are distinguished to highlight persons with different historical experiences during young adulthood: individuals age 75 years or older in 2000 were born in 1925 or earlier and were young and middle-aged adults during World War II; persons in the 65 to 74 age group were born between 1926 and 1935 and became adults around the time of the Korean War; people in the 45 to 64 age group were born between 1936 to 1955 and were subject to the Vietnam War; and persons in the youngest age group were born from 1956 to 1978 and came of age during the All-Volunteer Force era and experienced the first Gulf War. At all ages, veterans are more likely than nonveterans to be married, and they are less likely to be in poverty. In the youngest and oldest age groups, veterans are more likely than nonveterans to be employed,

whereas in the 44–64 age group veterans are less likely than nonveterans to be employed, and in the 65–74 age group the percentage employed is similar among veterans and nonveterans. Differences in marriage and poverty statuses between veterans and nonveterans are larger in the two oldest age categories, suggesting that the social and economic advantages of military service may accumulate over the life course for those who serve in the military as young adults. Differences are also apparent across the age groups in the percentage of veterans and nonveterans who obtained a college degree. Among the two youngest age groups, veterans are less likely to have a college education than nonveterans. But among the two oldest age groups, veterans are more likely than nonveterans to have a college education. These age-based differences likely reflect variation across cohorts in the characteristics of individuals who served, the widespread use of the G.I. Bill among men who served in World War II and Korea, and changes in the terms of the G.I. Bill during the era of the All-Volunteer Force.

Evidence such as this, as well as the foundational work of Elder and his colleagues, point to the importance of military service for socioeconomic, marriage/ family, and health outcomes. Research has addressed a range of questions about how military service in different historical periods has affected outcomes in each of these domains overall and among specific subgroups of veterans.

New Recruit. *At the Military Recruiting Center in Bridgeport, CT, Army Staff Sgt. Jose Cruz shakes hands with 18-year old recruit Camilo Hernandez of Stratford, CT.* **AP IMAGES.**

SOCIOECONOMIC ATTAINMENT

Considerable evidence shows that large numbers of World War II veterans took advantage of the G.I. Bill benefits available to them and enhanced their educational attainments over what they would have been in the absence of military service (Mettler, 2005). While women and Black male veterans, especially those born in the South, were less likely than White male veterans to use these benefits, the post-World War II G.I. Bill significantly increased training and college attendance among the many veterans who took advantage of its generous benefits.

However, researchers who have examined the effect of military service on educational outcomes in other time periods find that veterans have lower educational attainments than nonveterans. For example, during the Cold War period from 1955 to 1965, G.I. Bill benefits were not available. In her analysis of college attendance among veterans who served during this period, MacLean (2005) finds that those who were drafted were less likely to attend college than those who were not drafted and nonveterans. Additionally, she finds that military service redirected academically ambitious men away from college

attendance. Researchers who have focused on Vietnam-era veterans find that veterans have lower educational attainments than nonveterans in the short-term (Teachman and, Call 1996), although they catch up to their non-veteran contemporaries to some extent over time (Teachman, 2005). These differences across and within cohorts may be due in part to variation in enlistment rates between socioeconomic status groups.

Research on the effects of military service during the AVF era on educational attainment also finds negative effects on schooling (Teachman, 2007). This relationship is attributed in part to the reduced availability and value of G.I. Bill benefits in the AVF era. Veterans are now required to contribute some of their earnings in order to access the educational benefit, and many service men and women choose not to do so. However, the effects of military service on educational outcomes are not uniform, as they vary by branch of service and characteristics of veterans. For example, Blacks show increases in schooling reduce the educational deficit they exhibit at the time of discharge.

Other research focuses on occupational attainment and income among veterans and also shows mixed effects depending upon individual characteristics and historical periods. Dechter and Elder (2004) find that officers in World War II were able to convert their service into post-war occupational advancement, whereas other servicemen actually fared worse than nonveterans. Consistent with this finding, Angrist and Krueger (1994, p. 74) conclude that "World War II veterans earn no more than comparable non-veterans and may well earn less," even though they had access to generous G.I. Bill educational benefits. Studies focusing mostly on Vietnam era veterans suggest that military service in a war zone and combat exposure lead to worse labor market experiences and lower earnings. Angrist (1990) finds that White male Vietnam War veterans earned 15% less than the earnings of comparable nonveterans in the early 1980s. The lower earnings of Vietnam-era veterans may in part be attributable to post-traumatic stress and other psychiatric disorders that are more prevalent among such veterans.

Some studies have demonstrated positive effects on earnings for African-American and other non-White veterans who served in World War II (Teachman and Tedrow, 2004) and during the AVF era (Angrist, 1998), which provides evidence of a positive turning point in the earnings trajectories of initially-disadvantaged men. Recently, Teachman and Tedrow (2007) examined income trajectories among those who served in the AVF era and found that men from disadvantaged backgrounds earned more than their civilian counterparts; however, this premium dissipated after discharge.

MARRIAGE AND FAMILY OUTCOMES

Reflecting the life course principle of linked lives, researchers have been attentive to the effects of military service on marriage, divorce, and other family-related outcomes. Considerable attention has been paid to the effects of military service on divorce. The accumulated evidence suggests that veterans are considerably more likely to divorce than comparable nonveterans, although one study that focused on active-duty personnel in the AVF era indicates African-American enlistees have lower divorce rates than comparable White enlistees (Lundquist, 2006).

Considerable evidence across different historical periods shows that combat exposure contributes to marital problems and marital instability (Gimbel and Booth, 1994). However, as was the case with socioeconomic outcomes, these patterns vary across persons and periods. Call and Teachman (1991, 1996) focus on the timing of marriage in relation to military service in order to examine the life course disruption hypothesis. Among White male Vietnam-era veterans, they find that both combat and non-combat veterans were as likely as nonveterans to

marry, and marital stability was no lower among those who had married prior to entering the military than among those who had married during or after military service. Thus, in contrast to findings for World War II veterans (Pavalko and Elder, 1990), they found no support for the disruption hypothesis among these veterans.

A number of studies have addressed the effect of military service on marriage and fertility in general and Black-White differences in these outcomes in particular (Lundquist, 2004; Teachman, 2007). In this literature, a range of arguments are advanced to support the hypothesis that the American military became a relatively "pro-family," "pro-marriage" institution partly to recruit and retain personnel after the AVF replaced the draft in 1973. For example, policies that link coveted opportunities to live off base with a housing allowance to marriage may promote marriage among active-duty personnel. Beyond these inducements, these authors contend that the enforcement of the military's equal opportunity policies sharply reduces racial discrimination in earnings, job advancement, and promotion, thereby reducing one of the key barriers to marriage for many African Americans. Consistent with these arguments, the Black-White difference in marriage, which is substantial in the civilian population, is not present among active-duty military personnel. This fact likely has important implications for the subsequent life course trajectories of Black veterans, as well as those to whom their lives are linked.

Similarly supporting the "pro-family," "pro-marriage" character of the American military, Lundquist and Smith (2005) found that active-duty military women had higher fertility than comparable civilian women. This fertility difference was explained by the earlier and higher rates of marriage among the active-duty women.

HEALTH OUTCOMES

A growing body of research links military service to subsequent health and mortality. This work builds on previous life course research that has shown that military service, in particular combat exposure, has a direct impact on health and health-related resources. These studies suggest that military service may directly expose veterans to circumstances, produce injuries, or engender psychological conditions that have negative implications for physical and mental health trajectories and mortality. As noted previously, military service-related health problems may influence socioeconomic and marital/family outcomes, thereby impacting the lives of persons to whom veterans are linked as well as the veterans themselves.

Building on the life course disruption hypothesis, Elder, Shanahan, and Clipp (1994) posit a stress and health relationship. They hypothesized that late age at mobilization produces life course disruptions, which in turn produce stressful social disruptions, such as separation and divorce, residential changes, emotional distance from children, temporary periods of unemployment and erratic work lives, which have implications for health in later-life. Using data from the Stanford-Terman longitudinal study, which mostly includes World War II veterans, these authors report that late entrants, who are likely to have had the greatest social disruptions, were more likely to experience sporadic health problems, lifetime health declines, and constant poor health after exiting the military. However, social disruption did not fully account for the effect of late entry; rather it was the joint effect of late entry and high levels of social disruption that seemed to adversely affect health. A subsequent investigation by these investigators using the same data (Elder, Shanahan, and Clipp, 1997) found that exposure to combat predicted physical decline or death during the 15-year post-war interval from 1945–1960.

Two studies indicate higher disability and mortality among male veterans decades after the end of their military service. Bedard and Deschênes (2006) found that military service during World War II and the Korean War was associated with higher mortality later in life; 35% to 79% of the excess deaths were due to heart disease and lung cancer. The investigators argue that this excess mortality among veterans is attributable to military-induced smoking resulting from pro-tobacco military policy (i.e., free and reduced-price distribution of cigarettes) in this period. In a sample of men 51 years old and older, London and Wilmoth (2006) found that service in the military led to a greater likelihood of dying compared to those who had not served, even after taking into account early-life circumstances (race and father's education) and mid- to late-life characteristics (marital status, socioeconomic status, health status, and health behaviors). Among the younger cohorts, they found that military service improved the survival of African-American men, which they interpret as evidence of a positive turning point. Such a positive turning point may have occurred because military service afforded these African-American veterans greater access to education, income, family integration, or health care.

CONCLUSION

While the existing research has revealed us a great deal about the ways in which military service affects the life course (MacLean & Elder 2007; Settersten 2006), there is much that remains to be learned. It is critically important that we continue to follow multiple cohorts as they age so that it will be possible to conduct direct cohort comparisions. There is also a need for further research examining the impact of military service on the lives of women who serve, as well as the lives of those to whom

veterans' lives are linked. Finally, as was the case with World War II, the Vietnam War, and the Gulf War, veterans returning from Iraq will face a unique set of challenges. It is important to document how they are faring and how current policies and programs are shaping their life course trajectories in the short- and long-term.

SEE ALSO Volume 1: *Elder, Glen H., Jr.;* Volume 2: *Careers; Employment, Adulthood.*

BIBLIOGRAPHY

Angrist, J. (1990). Lifetime earnings and the Vietnam era draft lottery: Evidence from Social Security administrative records. *The American Economic Review 80*(3), 313–336.

Angrist, J. (1998). Estimating the labor market impact of voluntary military service using Social Security data on military applicants. *Econometrica 66*: 249–288.

Angrist, J., & Krueger, A. B. (1994). Why do World War II veterans earn more than nonveterans? *Journal of Labor Economics 12*(1), 74–97.

Bedard, K., & Deschênes, O. (2006). The long-term impact of military service on health: Evidence from World War II and Korean War veterans. *The American Economic Review 96*(1), 176–194.

Call, V. R. A., & Teachman, J. D. (1991). Military service and stability in the family life sourse. *Military Psychology 3*: 233–250.

Call, V. R. A., & Teachman, J. D. (1996). Life course timing and sequencing of marriage and military service and their effects on marital stability. *Journal of Marriage and the Family 58*: 219–226.

Dechter, A., & Elder, G. H. Jr. (2004). World War II mobilization in men's work lives: Continuity or disruption for the middle class? *American Journal of Sociology 110,* 761–793.

Elder, G. H. Jr. (1986). Military times and turning points in men's lives. *Developmental Psychology 22*: 233–245.

Elder, G. H. Jr. (1987). War mobilization and the life course: A cohort of World War II veterans. *Sociological Forum 2*: 449–472.

Elder, G. H. Jr., Shanahan, M. J., & Clipp, E. C. (1994). When war comes to men's lives: Life-course patterns in family, work, and health. *Psychology and Aging 9*(1), 5–16.

Elder, G. H. Jr., Shanahan, M. J., & Clipp, E. C. (1997). Linking combat and physical health: The legacy of World War II in men's lives. *American Journal of Psychiatry 154*(3), 330–336.

Flynn, G. Q. (1993). *The draft, 1940–1973.* Lawrence: University of Kansas Press.

Gimbel, C., & Booth, A. (1994). Why does military combat experience adversely affect marital relations? *Journal of Marriage and the Family 56*: 691–703.

Laub, J. H., & Sampson, R. J. (2003). *Shared beginnings, divergent lives: Delinquent boys to age 70.* Cambridge, MA: Harvard University Press.

London, A. S., & Wilmoth, J. M. (2006). Military service and (dis)continuity in the life course: Evidence from the health and retirement study and the study of assets and health among the oldest-old. *Research on Aging 28*(1), 135–159.

Lundquist, J. H. (2004). When race makes no difference: Marriage and the military. *Social Forces 83*(2), 731–757.

Lundquist, J. H. (2006). The Black-White gap in marital dissolution among young adults: What can a counterfactual scenario tell us? *Social Problems 53*(3), 421–441.

Lundquist, J. H., & Smith, H. L. (2005). Family formation among women in the U.S. military: Evidence from the NLSY. *Journal of Marriage and Family 67*: 1–13.

MacLean, A. (2005). Lessons from the Cold War: Military service and college education. *Sociology of Education 78*: 250–266.

MacLean, A., & Elder, G. H. Jr. (2007). Military service in the life course. *Annual Review of Sociology 33*: 175–196.

Mettler, S. (2005). *Soldiers to citizens: The G.I. Bill and the making of the greatest generation.* New York: Oxford University Press.

Modell, J., & Haggerty, T. (1991). The social impact of war. *Annual Review of Sociology 17*: 205–224.

Pavalko, E. K., & Elder, G. H. Jr. (1990). World War II and divorce: A life course perspective. *American Journal of Sociology 95*: 1213–1234.

Sampson, R., & Laub, J. (1996). Socioeconomic achievement in the life course of disadvantaged men: Military service as a turning point, circa 1940–1965. *American Sociological Review 61*: 347–367.

Settersten, R. A. Jr. (2006). When nations call: How wartime military service matters for the life course and aging. *Research on Aging 28*(1), 12–36.

Teachman, J. (2005). Military service in the Vietnam era and educational attainment. *Sociology of Education 78*: 50–68.

Teachman, J. (2007). Military service and educational attainment in the all-volunteer era. *Sociology of Education 80*: 359–374.

Teachman, J. D., & Call, V. R. A. (1996). The effect of military service on educational, occupational, and income attainment. *Social Science Research 25*: 1–31.

Teachman, J. D., & Tedrow, L. M. (2004). Wages, earnings, and occupational status: Did World War II veterans receive a premium? *Social Science Research 33*: 581–605.

Teachman, J., & Tedrow, L. (2007). Joining up: Did military service in the early all volunteer era affect subsequent civilian income? *Social Science Research 36*: 1447–1474.

Andrew S. London
Janet M. Wilmoth

MILLS, C. WRIGHT
1916–1962

C. Wright Mills was born on August 28 in Waco, Texas, and was raised in Texas. He earned his Ph.D. from the University of Wisconsin and taught at the University of Maryland and Columbia University. Mills was a public intellectual who was known for motorcycle riding and unconventional dress and for a manner that was consonant with his radical sociology. He used social analysis to shed light on the crises of his time, presenting his analyses in both academic and popular venues. A hero to student movements of the 1960s, Mills continues to be a model

C. Wright Mills. COLUMBIA COLLEGE TODAY.

for academics who see their work as part of political struggles (Gitlin, 2000; Hayden, 2006). He died on March 20 in Nyack, New York.

During the 1950s there was a climate of optimism in American sociology, which was dominated by functionalists who argued that social institutions fulfill specific purposes, all for the general good. Mills's sociology, which was based on conflict theory, challenged that complacency. Although he drew from classic European social theorists such as Karl Marx and Max Weber, Mills had a uniquely American perspective. By orientation and training he rejected disciplinary boundaries (Gerth & Mills, 1953). Mills used case studies of labor leaders, white-collar workers, and the powerful ("elites") to understand the factors that limit people's motivation to work for change. He attempted to understand the conditions that create opportunities and constraints for individuals and institutions and the ways in which power is used.

From his studies of different population segments of the post–World War II United States, Mills developed a theory about the factors that influence the balance of power in a society. He argued that concentrations of power reduce choices for the larger public even as they advance the power of the select few at the top. In *The Power Elite* (1956), he claimed that the United States was controlled by interrelated elite groups in the government, military, and industry, each of which pursued shared self-interested goals. The average American was duped by an illusion of well-being and minimal economic security. Popular culture, which was controlled by the elite, worked to mold a society of what Mills described in *White Collar* (1951) as "cheerful robots" (p. 233; see also Mills, 2000 [1959], pp. 169–176). Absorbed in the pursuit of personal happiness, cheerful robots were apathetic to the political and economic arrangements that limited their autonomy and circumscribed their choices. This depoliticized public included the American working class, which social theorists might expect to be the source of conflict and change.

Mills contended that the power elite, which relied on unchecked military and industrial growth to sustain itself, inevitably would cause a third world war. He did not predict the social and political upheaval of the 1960s, which contrasted with the complacency that made him despair of social change. He did, however, look to nations such as Cuba and the Soviet Union as models. Some claimed that the inaccuracy of Mills's doomsday predictions discredited his analysis. Mills, however, documented particular historical, economic, and social circumstances to understand mechanisms of power and agency. His complex theories included the idea that, under different circumstances, processes and outcomes would change.

Mills called for social theorists and laypeople to critique social institutions and their own choices, arguing that they must examine what people do rather than uncritically accept their words. Mills believed that most individuals, elites or otherwise, are not conscious of societal power dynamics. In *The Sociological Imagination* (2000 [1959]) he noted the difficulty of identifying connections between societal "issues" such as structural unemployment, and private "troubles" such as the loss of a job. In dynamic modern societies it can be difficult to see the historical and biographical circumstances that shape people. In his letters and autobiographical writings Mills acknowledged that those forces shaped him too (Mills with Mills, 2000).

Although Mills believed that the intersection of biography and history provides constraints and opportunities, neither can determine the future. Social analysts and ordinary people use their sociological imagination to transcend their private worlds and connect their personal experiences to the larger stage of history in the "hope to grasp what is going on in the world, and to understand what is happening in themselves as minute points of the intersections of biography and history within society" (Mills 2000 [1959], p. 7). Mills's perspective differs from social theories that focus on the individual as the locus of change or activity and those which focus primarily on the social milieu or institutions. His work affords neither one

primacy and charges social theorists to investigate individual experience and the social environment as well as the reciprocal interplay between them. Mills's ideas were influential in the development of the life course perspective, which emphasizes the links between social forces and individual lives (Elder & Shanahan, 2006).

Mills's social theory has contributed significantly to an understanding of social processes and the interplay among individuals, institutions, and society. He encouraged a critical approach to power, a challenge to complacency, and the expansion of the sociological imagination.

SEE ALSO Volume 2: *Sociological Theories.*

BIBLIOGRAPHY

Elder, G. H., & Shanahan, M. J. (2006). The life course and human development. In R. M. Lerner (Ed.), *Handbook of child psychology* (6th ed.). Vol. 1: *Theoretical models of human development*, ed. W. Damon, R. L. Lerner, & K.A. Renninger (pp. 665–715). New York: John Wiley and Sons.

Gerth, H., & Mills, C. W. (1953). *Character and social structure: The psychology of social institutions.* New York: Harcourt, Brace.

Gitlin, T. (2000). Afterword. In Mills, C. W., *The sociological imagination.* 40th anniversary ed. (pp. 229–242). Oxford and New York: Oxford University Press.

Hayden, T. (2006). *Radical nomad: C. Wright Mills and his times.* Boulder, CO: Paradigm.

Mills, C. W. (1951). *While collar: The American middle class.* New York: Oxford University Press.

Mills, C. W. (1956). *The power elite.* New York: Oxford University Press.

Mills, C. W. (2000 [1959]). *The sociological imagination.* (40th Anniversary ed.). New York: Oxford University Press.

Mills, K., with Mills, P. (Eds.). (2000). *Letters and autobiographical writings/C. Wright Mills.* Berkeley: University of California Press.

Corey S. Shdaimah

MOTHERHOOD

Motherhood represents a distinct aspect of a woman's life course. The beginning of motherhood is defined by pregnancy and childbirth, but when it ends is less clear—a woman does not stop being a mother after her children are grown up. Historically in European and North American societies, motherhood was the final step toward adulthood, closely following marriage. Over the past century the place of motherhood in the life course has significantly changed and, at present, it varies widely. Increasing numbers of women are deciding not to become mothers, many women delay motherhood until later in adulthood, and many become mothers regardless of their marital status.

Mothers provide the vast majority of primary care to their children, and, although they mother in various familial and social structural contexts—married or single, within a nuclear or extended family, in relatively privileged or less-privileged social positions based on class, race, and sexuality—being a mother significantly defines and affects their social and economic positions for the rest of their lifetimes.

SOCIAL ASPECTS OF MOTHERHOOD

Because of women's biological ability to bear children, it is conventionally expected that all women will become mothers. Women's femininity and gender identity are also reinforced by mothering. About 80% of American women become mothers during their reproductive lives. Mothers in the early 21st century, however, spend much less of their life course actively involved in mothering than did women in the past. The average woman spends less than one-seventh of her lifetime doing tasks such as nursing, diapering, or taking care of the everyday needs of a young child (Coltrane & Collins, 2001). The tasks of caring, nurturing, and protecting children are often referred to as *mothering*. They are usually—but not necessarily—performed by mothers; according to some theorists, men or non-mothers also perform mothering tasks when they take care of children (Doucet, 2006; Ruddick, 1995). Even so, motherhood is still seen as the primary purpose of a woman's existence and continues to define and affect women's lives.

Pointing to social, cultural, and historical variations in motherhood roles, norms, and expectations, social scientists argue that motherhood is socially based. The norms of motherhood and defining what a *good* mother is have historically varied and have been applied differentially according to a woman's social status. For example, in the 19th century the belief developed that mothers (rather than wet nurses) were best suited to take care of their babies. American society thus began to expect middle-class mothers to selflessly devote themselves to their children. At the same time, public campaigns, policy measures, and sterilization were used to discourage poor and minority women from becoming mothers at all. Such class differences continue to exist even in the 21st century; middle-class mothers are encouraged to devote as much time as possible to the care of their children, whereas working-class and poor mothers are expected to work outside of the home, leaving their children in the care of others so that they may provide income and even welfare benefits for their families.

The norms and expectations of present-day American motherhood have become more involved and demanding than ever before. The ideology of intensive mothering, as

defined by Sharon Hays (1996), is a child-centered child-rearing approach that requires mothers to spend money, energy, and time to raise their children while following expert advice and being fully tuned in to their child's thinking and emotions. This set of social expectations has become the accepted definition of mainstream American motherhood and has spread from the middle class to other layers of society. Hays showed that intensive mothering is not necessary for the healthy development of children, as expert advice and treatment of children in the past often directly contradict intensive mothering methods, providing further evidence for the social foundations of the motherhood role.

Analysis of media images of mothers and motherhood since the 1970s suggests that the media helps to spread and reinforce the myth of perfect, enjoyable, and fulfilling motherhood, performed to the standards of intensive mothering. Described as *new momism*, the media creates "a set of ideals, norms, and practices . . . that seem on the surface to celebrate the motherhood but which in reality promulgate standards of perfection that are beyond your reach" (Douglas & Michaels, 2004, p. 4). Both academic research and popular writing indicate that it is neither easy nor enjoyable for women to keep up with these expectations. New mothers quickly discover that they are not well-prepared for the reality of motherhood. They realize that the image of motherhood they had—being "brave, serene and all knowing" (Maushart, 1999, p. 2)—was just a mask covering the chaos and complexity of real life. New mothers thus have to deal not only with the social expectations of intensive mothering but also with the process of sorting out expectations from realities and adjusting to the latter. The stress of these adjustments, along with the demands of taking care of the new baby, may be a contributing factor in postpartum depression. Even during their later years as mothers, women with children tend to experience more distress and depression than non-mothers despite the joys and gratifications associated with parenting (Evenson & Simon, 2005).

CHANGING PLACE OF MOTHERHOOD IN WOMEN'S LIFE COURSE: DEMOGRAPHIC TRENDS

Twenty-first century women become mothers at a different point in their life course and under different circumstances than was the case for previous generations. Changes in motherhood are closely related to overall changes in the American family structure and to the position of women in the larger society. Women's increasing education levels, and higher career aspirations and opportunities, and higher rates of labor force participation, as well as increasingly available and improving contraception, contribute to the

MOMMY WARS/IMAGES OF MOTHERHOOD
·

Should mothers stay at home with their children or pursue careers and contribute to family income? This is the main question behind the *mommy wars*—a cultural debate about whether women who stay at home with their children or women who work outside of the home make better mothers. This debate has been played out in the media since the 1970s, with each camp arguing that their choice is right and that children of the mothers in the opposing camp suffer. However, maternal activists point out that working is a necessity rather than a choice for many mothers and that mothers often move between the worlds of family and work. They are asking the media to stop feeding the mommy wars and to focus instead on issues that unite all mothers, such as the implementation of family-friendly public policies, reliable child care, and affordable health care for all families.

changing significance of motherhood and result in changing demographic behavior.

One of the most obvious demographic changes characteristic of today's motherhood is the postponement or avoidance of motherhood. The proportion of women who remain childless nearly doubled between the 1970s and the 2000s. In the 1970s only 10% of women did not have children during their reproductive lives (defined by demographers as ending at age 44); by 2004, 19.3% of women between the ages of 40 and 44 years remained childless (Dye, 2005). Even though improved reproduction technologies and adoption offer women the possibility to become mothers after this age, this increase suggests that more women are postponing and avoiding motherhood than ever before.

Motherhood also occurs at a later stage of life for women who do become mothers, often in their late 20s and, increasingly, in their 30s. The average age of a first-time mother has increased from 21.4 years of age in 1970 to 24.9 in 2000 (Mathews & Hamilton, 2002). In 2004 about 45% of women between 25 and 29 years of age were childless (Dye, 2005).

Concurrent with the trend toward delayed motherhood, women tend to have fewer children than in the past. The average number of children an American woman bears in her lifetime has dropped from 3.5 children during the 1950s baby boom to about 2.1 in 2006

(Centers for Disease Control and Prevention, National Center for Health Statistics, 2007). Having fewer children allows mothers to devote more attention, energy, and resources to each child they have, as required by the ideology of intensive mothering, but it also allows women more time and opportunities to pursue other interests.

Motherhood has also become increasingly disconnected from another important life course transition: marriage. In the early 21st century, about one-third of children are born to women outside of marriage, and this proportion has been increasing. The proportion of childbearing outside of marriage is even higher for African American women, with almost two thirds of their children born outside of marriage compared to one-quarter of White women (Dye, 2005). This is a considerable change from the not-so-distant past of the 1950s, when having a child out of wedlock was quite rare and considered a scandalous, if not socially punishable, offense.

Having children outside of marriage does not necessarily mean that women raise their children without a father. The increasing prevalence of cohabitation—defined as living in a household with a sexual and romantic partner without marriage—has contributed to the increase in nonmarital childbearing. Women are more likely to become first-time mothers while cohabiting than while married. In 2002, 42% of first births were to cohabiting women, whereas only 29% were to married women (Downs, 2003). The trend toward choosing motherhood without marriage is documented both among middle-class women (Hertz, 2006) and poor women (Edin & Kefalas, 2003).

Statistics show that younger and less educated women are more likely to have children outside of marriage than are older women or women with higher levels of education. The proportion of unmarried mothers is highest among teenage mothers—88% of women under 20 were not married when their child was born (Dye, 2005). This stands in stark contrast to the 1950s, when teenage childbearing was at twice the current rate but the majority of young mothers were married.

The life-course stages of teenage mothers are organized differently than those of women who delay childbearing, mostly in respect to completing education and entering marriage. Despite the threat of possible negative outcomes—including lower rates of high school completion, lower incomes, difficulties obtaining and keeping jobs, and lower stability of later marriages—in communities characterized by low life aspirations, a dearth of access to well-paying, stable jobs, and high divorce rates, motherhood represents an alternative strategy for attaining adulthood and social status.

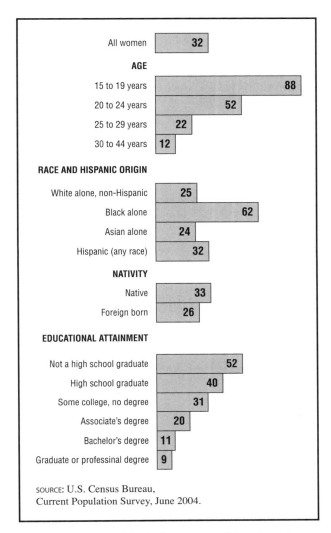

All women — 32

AGE

15 to 19 years — 88
20 to 24 years — 52
25 to 29 years — 22
30 to 44 years — 12

RACE AND HISPANIC ORIGIN

White alone, non-Hispanic — 25
Black alone — 62
Asian alone — 24
Hispanic (any race) — 32

NATIVITY

Native — 33
Foreign born — 26

EDUCATIONAL ATTAINMENT

Not a high school graduate — 52
High school graduate — 40
Some college, no degree — 31
Associate's degree — 20
Bachelor's degree — 11
Graduate or professinal degree — 9

SOURCE: U.S. Census Bureau,
Current Population Survey, June 2004.

Figure 1. Nonmarital births by age, race, Hispanic origin, nativity, and education attainment, June 2004. Percent of births born in the preceding 12 months to women who were never married, divorced, or widowed. **CENGAGE LEARNING, GALE.**

ECONOMIC IMPACT OF MOTHERHOOD

Regardless of social background, motherhood has direct and indirect negative economic implications for women that persist through the life course. Although child care and mothering are often referred to as the most important jobs in the world, mothers receive minimal public support and no economic compensation for their work. The benefits of childrearing are diffuse and shared by the whole society, but mothers are more likely than fathers to carry the negative economic costs of having children as they are more likely to limit their work hours, take time out of the labor force to care for the child, or take jobs compatible with childrearing. Ann Crittenden (2001) referred to the overall impact of motherhood on women's socioeconomic status as *the price of motherhood.*

The economic price women pay to be mothers is most visible in the pay they receive for their work in the paid labor market. Full-time working women made about 81% of men's salary in 2006 (U.S. Bureau of Labor Statistics, 2007). Mothers earn less than women without children, earning 73 cents per a dollar earned by men for the same job, taking into account job-related experience and mother-friendly job characteristics. Researchers find that the first child exacts a 2% to 10% wage penalty and two or more children a 5% to 13% penalty, depending on the children's age and the mother's education and race (Anderson, Binder, & Krause, 2003; Budig & England, 2001; Waldfogel, 1997).

Mothers are also disadvantaged during the hiring process. According to one study, mothers are 79% less likely to get hired if they present the same experiences and resumes as non-mothers and are also offered significantly lower salaries than non-mothers (Correll et al., 2007). The motherhood penalty and hiring discrimination demonstrate that although the labor force has become more equal in the opportunities and pay available for men and women, policies that accommodate employees' family and caregiving responsibilities are insufficient.

Mothers' careers are often interrupted by the needs of their children, limiting their possibilities for career advancement, promotion, and enhanced income. Phyllis Moen and Shin-Kap Han (2001) described gendered career paths characterized as orderly or high-geared for men and intermittent, with delayed entry or steady part-time, for women. This type of career progression is sometimes referred to as the *mommy track,* characterized by slower career advancement but a better ability to combine work and family. Indeed, although the majority of mothers have paid jobs, most of them work less than full time. In 2002, 24.6% of mothers with children under age 18 stayed at home, 38.8% worked full time all year, and 36.7% worked part-time (Lovell, 2003). Part-time work is preferred by 60% of women with minor children (Pew Research Center, 2007), although it has economic disadvantages, such as lower pay and limited benefits. Part-time workers also often work almost full-time hours to maintain their position in the work organization.

Because of the difficulties in balancing work and family, women sometimes leave the workforce altogether. In a widely discussed article, Lisa Belkin (2003) suggested that professional mothers are increasingly leaving the workforce to take care of their children and choosing family over their careers. This is referred to as the *opt-out revolution.* Further research has demonstrated, however, that most of these mothers do not leave the workforce because they want to reestablish traditional family arrangements or have a desire to be full-time mothers as the media has suggested. Instead, they are pushed out from their jobs by inflexible workplaces

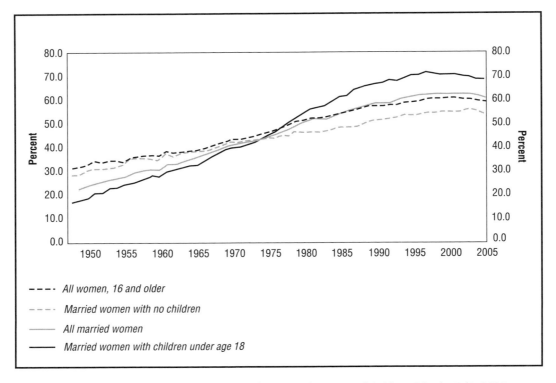

Chart 1. *Labor force participation rates of women by marital status and presence of children, March 1948–2005.* CENGAGE LEARNING, GALE.

that make it difficult or impossible to combine work and motherhood.

Paid labor continues to be structured in a way that disadvantages all caregivers (not only mothers) who cannot perform as ideal workers (i.e., employees fully committed to their jobs and without family impediments to their performance; Williams, 2000). At the same time, cultural expectations for childrearing are still based on the idea that children are better off if cared for and raised by their parents than other caregivers. Therefore, most mothers are socially, culturally, and economically excluded from economically successful roles and forced to opt out or choose mommy track careers. Although women perceive what they do as a choice, it is a choice under the constraints of a social and economic system that is built on the assumption of a division of labor between caregiving and breadwinning. Such a choice is also available only to those who can afford to stay at home, as is clearly shown by the 1996 welfare reform requirements that insist poor mothers work outside of the home to provide for themselves and their families.

The price of motherhood and the economic impact of motherhood on women are not limited to the wage penalty and job discrimination. Indeed, after a divorce, women often slip into poverty because of their limited workforce participation while married, a division of gen-

der roles in the family that is not reflected in the majority of divorce settlements, and their predominant post-divorce care of the children, whereas fathers usually improve their standard of living.

MOTHERHOOD AND PUBLIC POLICY ISSUES

In the contemporary United States, raising children is still primarily considered the mother's responsibility. Comprehensive family-oriented public policies, common in most of the world, such as paid family leave after the birth of a baby and subsidized preschool education, are thus lacking. In fact, the United States is the only industrialized country without a policy that allows mothers to stay home with an infant and maintain an income for the family (some countries even provide paid leave for fathers). The current U.S. policy, the 1993 Family and Medical Leave Act (FMLA), provides unpaid leave to take care of a new baby or sick family member for up to 12 weeks to employees in companies with more than 50 employees. However, even eligible employees often cannot afford to take the unpaid leave. Individual states are therefore passing their own legislation to improve this federal policy.

Similarly, working parents are responsible for providing child care for their children before they achieve school age, as there is no comprehensive, publicly funded preschool system in the United States. Finding good quality and affordable preschool and child care is often very stressful for mothers.

Social movement organizations have been advocating improvement of mothers' and caregivers' social and economic positions, attempting to bring these policy issues to the national consciousness and political debate. Among these are MomsRising.com, Mothers Ought to Have Equal Rights (MOTHERS), the National Association of Motherhood Centers, Mothers & More, Mothers Acting Up, the National Organization of Women (NOW), and many others. They argue that although mothering is a life-changing experience, it should not be a difficult one, much less one that leads to discrimination and poverty.

DIRECTIONS FOR FUTURE RESEARCH

Motherhood and its economic and social value remain highly contested topics in American society. Although much more is known about motherhood and mothers than a few decades ago, changing social, political, economic, and cultural contexts create new challenges for women as they enter motherhood and combine it with other identities and roles. Future research will likely emphasize the diversity of maternal experiences, as women mother under different social, cultural, and economic conditions that are not always reflected in current research. The identities, ideologies, and meanings that women of various backgrounds give to their mothering experiences and the place of motherhood in their life courses are still to be examined in more detail. At the same time, similarities in women's experiences, the issues mothers face, and the prevalence of mainstream motherhood norms across social classes also need to be addressed.

Analyses of the economic implications of motherhood for women and their families are likely to be carried out in the light of new social policies and increased maternal and caregiving activism. Will the new social movements change the way mothers act and organize their family lives and impact the public and corporate family policies? Will this affect the way mothers position themselves in the work-family space? Research into combining work and family obligations will also gain a new dimension as new generations of women enter motherhood. How will these young women, who saw their own mothers juggle work and family obligations, incorporate their experiences into their lives? Will they continue the trend of delaying motherhood into later stages of their life course in order to establish their careers and devote themselves to motherhood afterward, or will they find a way to do both at the same time? Will they continue to follow the expectations and pressures of inten-

sive mothering or will the social expectations on mothers be gradually replaced? There is also a lot to be learned about the long-term life-course implications of the choices previous generations of mothers made on their identities, health, family relations, and overall well-being.

SEE ALSO Volume 1: *Parenting Style; Transition to Parenthood;* Volume 2: *Childlessness; Fatherhood; Infertility; Noncustodial Parents.*

BIBLIOGRAPHY

Anderson, D. J., Binder, M., & Krause, K. (2003.) The motherhood wage penalty revisited: Experience, heterogeneity, work effort, and work-schedule flexibility. *Industrial and Labor Relations Review, 56*(2), 273–294.

Belkin, L. (2003, October 26). The opt-out revolution. *New York Times Magazine.*

Budig, M., & England, P. (2001). The wage penalty for motherhood. *American Sociological Review, 66*(2), 204–225.

Centers for Disease Control and Prevention, National Center for Health Statistics. (2007, December 5). *Teen birth rate rises for first time in 14 years.* Retrieved March 18, 2008, from http://www.cdc.gov/od/

Coltrane, S., & Collins, R. (2001). *Sociology of marriage and the family: Gender, love, and property.* (5th ed.). Belmont, CA: Wadsworth.

Correll, S., Benard, S., & Paik, I. (2007). Getting a job: Is there a motherhood penalty? *American Journal of Sociology, 112*(5), 1297–1338.

Crittenden, A. (2001). *The price of motherhood: Why the most important job in the world is still the least valued.* New York: Metropolitan Books.

Doucet, A. (2006.) *Do men mother? Fathering, care, and domestic responsibility.* Toronto, Canada: University of Toronto.

Douglas, S. J., & Michaels, M. W. (2004). *The mommy myth: The idealization of motherhood and how it has undermined women.* New York: Free Press.

Downs, B. (2003). Fertility of American women: June 2002. *Current population reports.* Washington, DC: U.S. Census Bureau. Retrieved March 18, 2008, from http://www.census.gov/prod

Dye, J. L. (2005). Fertility of American women: June 2004. *Current population reports.* Washington, DC: U.S. Census Bureau. Retrieved March 18, 2008, from http://www.census. gov/prod

Edin, K., & Kefalas, M. (2003). *Promises I can keep: Why poor women put motherhood before marriage.* Berkeley: University of California Press.

Evenson, R. J., & Simon, R. W. (2005.) Clarifying the relationship between parenthood and depression. *Journal of Health and Social Behavior, 46,* 341–358.

Hays, S. (1996). *The cultural contradictions of motherhood.* New Haven, CT: Yale University Press.

Hertz, R. (2006). *Single by chance, mothers by choice: How women are choosing parenthood without marriage and creating the new American family.* New York: Oxford University Press.

Lovell, V. (2003). *Forty-hour work proposal significantly raises mothers' employment standard.* Institute for Women's Policy Research. Retrieved March 18, 2008, from http://www.iwpr.org/pdf

Mathews, T. J., & Hamilton, B. E. (2002). Mean age of mothers, 1970–2000. *National Vital Statistics Report, 51*(1). Retrieved March 18, 2008, from http://www.cdc.gov/nchs

Maushart, S. (1999). *The mask of motherhood: How becoming a mother changes everything and why we pretend it doesn't.* New York: New Press.

Moen, P., & Han, S. (2001). Gendered careers: A life course perspective. In R. Hertz & N. L. Marshall (Eds.), *Working families: The transformation of the American home* (pp. 42–57). Berkeley: University of California Press.

Pew Research Center. (2007.) *Fewer mothers prefer full-time work: From 1997 to 2007.* Retrieved March 21, 2008, from http://pewresearch.org/assets

Ruddick, S. (1995.) *Maternal thinking.* Boston: Beacon Press.

U.S. Bureau of Labor Statistics. (2007). *Highlights of women's earnings in 2006* (Report 1000). U.S. Department of Labor. Retrieved March 18, 2008, from http://www.bls.gov/cps

Waldfogel, J. (1997.) The effect of children on women's wages. *American Sociological Review, 62*(2), 209–217.

Ivana Brown

N

NEIGHBORHOOD CONTEXT, ADULTHOOD

The concept of *neighborhood* refers to an individual's immediate residential community. Research linking characteristics of neighborhoods to adult outcomes reflects a long tradition of sociological research on the role social context has in shaping lives. Results of this research suggest that neighborhoods are more than simply places of residence; they also provide proximate access to opportunities for residents, including employment opportunities, social opportunities, and access to beneficial resources. Just as neighborhoods provide access to positive factors, however, neighborhoods can also negatively affect residents through exposure to crime, social and physical disorder, and environmental and health risks.

THEORETICAL FOUNDATIONS OF NEIGHBORHOOD RESEARCH

The idea of neighborhoods as important social contexts has its origins in the human ecology perspective of the Chicago School of sociology (Park, Burgess, & McKenzie, 1925), which emphasized the interaction between humans and their environments. A key insight of this perspective was that characteristics of residential communities can affect residents' behaviors and beliefs above and beyond their own personal characteristics. In particular, Shaw and McKay (1942) found that neighborhoods with certain characteristics showed higher rates of juvenile delinquency and infant mortality, regardless of the race or ethnic background of the groups living there. Shaw and McKay's *social disorganization* approach focused on three neighborhood characteristics: economic disadvantage, racial and ethnic heterogeneity, and residential instability. These elements were thought to erode a community's capacity for social organization, leading to the cultural transmission of crime and risky behavior with eventual effects on neighborhood crime rates and residents' health.

This insight spurred an interest in the neighborhood as a meaningful locus of intervention: If the problems experienced in disadvantaged neighborhoods were not attributable to the types of people who lived in these neighborhoods, efforts directed at the neighborhood should lift the fortunes of those living there. However, ambitious efforts such as Robert Park's Chicago Area Study, in which he divided the city into a set of community areas and targeted troubled areas for intervention, yielded mixed results (Kobrin, 1959). As a result, by the middle of the 20th century sociological interest in neighborhood research waned.

However, several factors led to a resurgence of interest in neighborhoods in the latter part of the 20th century. First, Kornhauser (1978) critically evaluated and reformulated Shaw and McKay's social disorganization theory, deemphasizing the cultural transmission process, and instead emphasizing the key role of neighborhood social organization. Second, researchers became interested in the causes of observed increases in the spatial concentration of poverty in the United States. By linking the neighborhood to the structure of U.S. society, these researchers addressed a weakness in Shaw and McKay's (1942) work—its inattention to the larger, social structural forces that produced differences in neighborhoods. For example, Massey and Denton (1993) found that the spatial (i.e., geographic) concentration of poverty was intertwined with persistent patterns of residential segregation by race that remained long after the practices that produced them were outlawed (such as *red-lining* primarily minority neighborhoods to indicate their undesirability for mortgage loans). Wilson (1987, 1996) argued that the impact of segregation was compounded by economic changes that eroded job opportunities for low-skilled workers in urban settings, leading to neighborhood decline and the concentration of economic disadvantage in particular urban neighborhoods (Wilson, 1987, 1996). Residents of these neighborhoods were described by Wilson (1996) as *socially isolated*— rooted in their neighborhood contexts, but isolated from mainstream social and employment opportunities.

More recent research on the importance of neighborhood contexts builds on Wilson's (1987, 1996) work, and considers the mechanisms that *link* neighborhood economic, social, and demographic characteristics to neighborhood levels of crime, health problems, and other social ills, as well as the well-being of individual residents (Jargowsky, 1997; Sampson, Morenoff, & Gannon-Rowley, 2002). Consistent with Kornhauser's (1978) reformulation of social disorganization theory, researchers separately examine processes of neighborhood social organization and neighborhood cultural transmission.

LINKS BETWEEN NEIGHBORHOOD CHARACTERISTICS AND OUTCOMES

Social Organization Research on the links between neighborhood social organization and neighborhood and individual outcomes considers how characteristics of neighborhoods can attenuate or promote a community's capacity to regulate the behavior of its residents (Kornhauser, 1978). This research draws on the concept of social capital, the capacity for action on behalf of an individual or group that inheres through networks of social relationships (Bourdieu, 1986; Coleman, 1990). Although social capital is thought of as a good that may be employed for positive goals, it can also have a downside—it may be used, for example, to reinforce social advantage among some groups, to the exclusion of others (Portes, 1988).

Much research on the role of social capital has examined its importance for health and well-being; that is, the way social ties can provide social supports and opportunities to engage in healthy (and health risk) behaviors, as well as the capacity for action that can be employed to lure health-promoting institutions (Lochner, Kawachi, Brennan, & Buka, 2003; Carpiano, 2007). For example, Lochner, Kawachi, Brennan, and Buka (2003) found positive relationships between low levels of social capital and neighborhood total mortality rates, as well as rates of death from cardiovascular disease. Carpiano (2007), however, found that social support was, surprisingly, positively associated with health risk behaviors such as smoking and binge drink-

ing, although informal social control was negatively associated with such behaviors. This research highlights the importance of goal-oriented aspects of social capital—or the ability of a community to employ its social ties for the collective good—and the ways in which social ties supply opportunities for both healthy and health risk behaviors.

Collective Efficacy One important application of social capital theory to the neighborhood context is the concept of *collective efficacy* (Sampson, Raudenbush, & Earls, 1997) that is defined as "the linkage of mutual trust and the willingness to intervene for the common good" (p. 919). Collective efficacy is thus a social good that helps maintain neighborhood order through informal social control. Collective efficacy is goal oriented, and incorporates a neighborhood's capacity for prosocial action.

The structural and demographic characteristics of disadvantaged neighborhoods identified by Shaw and McKay (1942) and by Wilson (1996) serve to limit a community's capacity to achieve collective efficacy, with effects on neighborhood social conditions (e.g., community rates of crime or health risk behaviors) as well as individual outcomes (e.g., victimization or participation in health risk behaviors). Residents of neighborhoods that are residentially unstable, for example, will have difficulty recognizing shared values and may hesitate to intervene in the event of trouble because they cannot be assured that their views are shared by others in the community. Similarly, in some racially and ethnically heterogeneous neighborhoods, hostility among groups may hinder their ability to band together in support of neighborhood goals; moreover, they may not agree on goals for the neighborhood.

Aspects of disadvantage also potentially inhibit neighborhood collective efficacy. In economically disadvantaged neighborhoods, the individual challenges faced by poor residents may not permit residents to engage meaningfully in forms of neighborhood social control. Further, competing allegiances to law-abiding residents and those who are engaged in illegal enterprises, such as the sale of drugs, may restrict residents' willingness to get involved when they recognize illicit activity (Pattillo-McCoy, 1999). Finally, neighborhoods with a high proportion of single-parent families have fewer adult residents available for shared collective supervision of the neighborhood environment.

The emphasis on social control in the concept of collective efficacy has led to a research focus on its effects on child and adolescent outcomes. However, researchers have also found evidence for the importance of collective efficacy for a variety of neighborhood and adult outcomes. Sampson, Raudenbush, and Earls (1997) found that neighborhoods with higher levels of collective efficacy had lower rates of violent crime. Collective efficacy also has been found to be negatively associated with intimate homicide rates and nonlethal partner violence (Browning, 2002).

Neighborhood at War. *North Las Vegas police officers handcuff a suspected gang member during a patrol of a North Las Vegas neighborhood.* AP IMAGES.

Finally, collective efficacy has been found to be positively associated with self-rated physical health (Browning & Cagney, 2002), and negatively associated with obesity (Cohen, Finch, Bower, & Sastry, 2006).

Institutional Resources and Environmental Hazards
Researchers have also identified the importance of social capital as a means to attract and retain institutional resources that are beneficial for neighborhood residents (Elliott, Wilson, Huizinga, & Sampson, 1996). Neighborhoods that are socially organized and able to exploit social ties to decision makers outside the neighborhood may be able to influence the placement of desirable institutions (e.g., health care facilities, community centers, police and fire substations) within the neighborhood. As a result of the proximity of these desirable institutions, the residents' sense of well-being may increase (Leventhal & Brooks-Gunn, 2001). In addition, residents of socially organized neighborhoods may be better able to work together to reduce hazards and risks (Leventhal & Brooks-Gunn, 2001), which include physical disorder (e.g., broken glass, litter, biohazards), social disorder (e.g., public intoxication, prostitution), or the placement and regulation of harmful institutions in or near the neighborhood (industries that pollute).

Skogan (1990) found a positive relationship between aspects of physical disorder and neighborhood levels of crime. Sampson and Raudenbush (1999) found that,

even though physical disorder and neighborhood crime are correlated, the relationship is not causal; rather, both stem from the same set of predictors related to a given neighborhood's high levels of concentrated poverty and low levels of collective efficacy. However, the effects of physical disorder may be perceived through its impact on residents' fear and the effects of that fear on residents' health and well-being (Ross & Mirowsky, 2001). Finally, Altschuler, Somkin, and Adler (2004) examined the effect of neighborhood amenities and liabilities (e.g., pollution, available food stores, effective municipal services) on resident self-rated health. Their findings indicated the importance of goal-oriented social capital for the attraction of neighborhood amenities and the elimination of liabilities.

Routine Activities and Opportunities for Crime Neighborhood social organization may also affect individual opportunities for participation in crime and problem behavior. Cohen and Felson (1979) argued that most societally deviant (i.e., transgressive) behavior, including crime, is a function of an individual's routine, everyday activities. This approach emphasized the unplanned nature of much criminal activity. Using this perspective, neighborhoods may experience increased crime and problem behavior if they have few *guardians*, that is, people who keep watch over the activities of other people and over public and private property; and many vulnerable *targets*, or people who are susceptible to victimization and property that is unsecured or isolated. Although the routine activities framework focuses on deficits in social organization, it shares an emphasis on opportunity with theories of cultural transmission.

Cultural Transmission Differential social organization approaches emphasize the *absence* of social organization and forms of informal social control as key determinants of crime and risk behavior. In contrast, cultural transmission perspectives emphasize the *presence* of problematic behaviors and attitudes in some neighborhoods, and consider how these features also structure residents' opportunities for participation in crime and health risk behavior. These approaches are also called *subcultural* or *epidemic* approaches (Anderson 1990; Crane 1991), and are rooted in early theories of crime and gang delinquency (Short & Strodtbeck, 1965; Cloward & Ohlin, 1960; Smith & Jarjoura, 1988). These perspectives argue that the proliferation of problem behaviors and crime in a neighborhood provides an illegitimate opportunity structure in opposition to mainstream society. In disadvantaged neighborhoods, these illegitimate opportunity structures may present an alternative path for residents who are blocked from mainstream opportunities for success. Ethnographic researchers who studied the lives of adults in disadvantaged settings found evidence to support the cultural transmission of acquired styles that may promote risk or criminal behavior (Liebow, 1967; Duneier, 1992; Anderson, 1978, 1990).

ISSUES OF DEFINITION, MEASUREMENT, AND ANALYSIS

Several methodological considerations arise when examining neighborhood effects. First is the definition of *neighborhood* itself. Researchers have employed different definitions of this term, such as administrative boundaries (census tracts or blocks) (Sastry, Ghosh-Dastidar, Adams, & Pebley, 2006; Hipp, 2007); areas set off by streets, railroad tracks, and other ecological boundaries (Sampson, Raudenbush, & Earls, 1997; Grannis, 1998); social networks (Wellman & Leighton, 1979); and residents' subjective definitions of their sociospatial neighborhood (Lee & Campbell, 1997).

A second consideration is selection bias. The same characteristics that lead individuals to select certain neighborhoods in which to live may also influence their own outcomes. For example, individuals who have a propensity or desire to participate in crime or illicit behavior may seek out contexts that facilitate (or do not inhibit) such criminal or illicit behavior (Stark, 1987). As a result, observed neighborhood effects may be attributable instead to the aggregation of these unmeasured resident characteristics (Duncan, Connell, & Klebanov, 1997). Researchers attempt to address this issue by employing sophisticated statistical models to adjust for individual

characteristics associated with neighborhood selection. An alternative way of dealing with selection is to use data from a quasiexperiment in which people are assigned at random to neighborhoods. Such data usually come from social programs, for example, the "Moving to Opportunity" (MTO) project, sponsored by the U.S. Department of Housing and Urban Development, in which some residents of disadvantaged neighborhoods were given housing vouchers to live in more affluent neighborhoods (Kling, Liebman, Katz, & Sanbonmatsu, 2004).

THE FUTURE OF RESEARCH ON NEIGHBORHOOD EFFECTS ON ADULT OUTCOMES

To date, research on neighborhoods has largely focused on neighborhood level outcomes or children, adolescents, and the elderly, who may have the greatest exposure to the residential neighborhood. In contrast, adults with jobs visit a variety of settings in a given day. They may work outside their neighborhoods, shop outside their neighborhoods, and visit with friends in distant communities. A new direction in research takes into consideration these less geographically rooted existences of adults, and the potential impact of multiple contexts on individual and neighborhood outcomes. For example, Morenoff, Sampson, and Raudenbush (2001) examined spatial interdependencies as determinants of neighborhood variation in homicide rates. Mears and Bhati (2006) examined the social influence of neighborhoods to which residents shared social ties. Using ethnographic data, Pattillo-McCoy (1999) considered the social influence of adjacent neighborhoods on resident outcomes.

More recently, researchers have melded perspectives from geography, sociology, and statistics to consider the importance of individual residents' *activity spaces*, or the potential impact of the characteristics of places residents visit regularly, as well as the aggregate activity space of a neighborhood—the collective span of its residents' activity spaces (Kwan, Peterson, Browning, Burrington, Calder, & Krivo, 2008). These new approaches envision the relationships between adult residents and spatial contexts as dynamic, and move the direction of neighborhood research beyond a narrow, residence-based conception of the neighborhood.

A second new area of research examines neighborhood effects in settings outside the United States. Zhang, Messner, & Liu (2007), for example, who are conducting research in China, are applying collective efficacy theory to residential burglary and theft outcomes there. Wacquant (2007) conducted a study using both qualitative and quantitative data to consider urban social marginality in both the United States and France. Efforts such as these will yield important information about the applicability of theories based on data from the United States in an international context.

Future research on neighborhood effects will be facilitated by recent improvements in both statistical software and survey design. First, researchers are able to account for the clustering of residents within neighborhoods through the use of multilevel statistical models (Raudenbush & Bryk, 2002). Second, surveys of large metropolitan areas, such as the Project on Human Development in Chicago Neighborhoods (PHDCN) and the Los Angeles Family and Neighborhood Survey (LA FANS), have been specifically designed to examine the effects of sociospatial contexts on individual residents (Earls, Raudenbush, Reiss, & Sampson, 2002; Sastry, Ghosh-Dastidar, Adams, & Pebley, 2006). Third, researchers have employed methods of systematic social observation (SSO) to capture both objective and subjective aspects of neighborhood contexts. PHDCN researchers videotaped activities in Chicago neighborhoods in the course of their study and reviewed the tapes to code the extent of physical and social disorder in the neighborhoods (Sampson & Raudenbush, 1999).

In sum, neighborhood effects research helps policymakers understand how neighborhoods can have "good" or "bad" influences on the life chances and outcomes of their adult residents. Detrimental aspects of neighborhood environments are of great concern because they can compound the effects of family poverty on resident outcomes. Programs aimed at reducing the geographic concentration of disadvantage, and community-based efforts to build social cohesion and trust among neighborhood residents, may increase health and well-being, particularly among those residing in urban contexts. For example, the MTO study allows policymakers to assess the potential of voucher programs for reducing the geographic concentration of inequality and increasing access to institutional resources. Other potential interventions include increasing institutional resources within disadvantaged neighborhoods, and reducing the extent to which residents of these neighborhoods are exposed to environmental hazards, and physical and social disorder. An increased understanding of the mechanisms that lead to the spatial concentration of economic disadvantage, crime, poor health, and other social ills, is an important step toward addressing these problems.

SEE ALSO Volume 1: *Neighborhood Context, Childhood and Adolescence;* Volume 2: *Home Ownership/ Housing; Residential Mobility, Adulthood; Segregation, Residential; Social Integration/Isolation, Adulthood;* Volume 3: *Neighborhood Context, Later Life.*

BIBLIOGRAPHY

Altschuler, A., Somkin, C. P., & Adler, N. E. (2004). Local services and amenities, neighborhood social capital, and health. *Social Science & Medicine, 59,* 1219–1229.

Anderson, E. (1978). *A place on the corner: A study of black street corner men.* Chicago: University of Chicago Press.

Anderson, E. (1990). *Streetwise.* Chicago: The University of Chicago Press.

Bourdieu, P. (1986). The forms of capital. In J. G. Richardson (Ed.), *Handbook of theory and research for the sociology of education* (pp. 241–258). New York: Greenwood.

Browning, C. R. (2002). The span of collective efficacy: Extending social disorganization theory to partner violence. *Journal of Marriage and Family, 64,* 833–850.

Carpiano, R. (2007). Neighborhood social capital and adult health: An empirical test of a Bourdieu-based model. *Health and Place, 13,* 639–655.

Cloward, R. A., & Ohlin, L. E. (1960). *Delinquency and opportunity: A theory of delinquent gangs.* New York: Free Press.

Cohen, D. A., Finch, B. K., Bower, A., & Sastry, N. (2006). Collective efficacy and obesity: The potential influence of social factors on health. *Social Science & Medicine, 62,* 769–778.

Cohen, L., & Felson, M. (1979). Social change and crime rate trends: A routine activities approach. *American Sociological Review, 44,* 588–607.

Coleman, J. S. (1990). *Foundations of social theory.* Cambridge, MA: Harvard University Press.

Crane, J. (1991). The epidemic theory of ghettos and neighborhood effects of dropping out and teenage childbearing. *American Journal of Sociology, 96,* 1226–1259.

Duncan, G. J., Connell, J. P., & Klebanov, P. K. (1997). Conceptual and methodological issues in estimating causal effects of neighborhoods and family conditions on individual development. In J. Brooks-Gunn, G. J. Duncan, & J. L. Aber (Eds.), *Neighborhood Poverty: Context and Consequences for Children* (pp. 219–250). New York: Russell Sage Foundation.

Duneier, M. (1992). *Slim's table: Race, respectability, and masculinity.* Chicago: University of Chicago Press.

Earls, F. J., Raudenbush, S. W., Reiss, A. J., Jr., & Sampson, R. J. (1995). Project on Human Development in Chicago Neighborhoods (PHDCN): Systematic social observation, 1995 [Computer file]. ICPSR13578-v1. Boston: Harvard Medical School [producer], 2002. Ann Arbor, MI: Interuniversity Consortium for Political and Social Research [distributor], 2005-07-18.

Elliott, D. S., Wilson, W. J., Huizinga, D., Sampson, R. J., Elliott, A., & Rankin, B. (1996). The effects of neighborhood disadvantage on adolescent development. *Journal of Research in Crime and Delinquency, 33,* 389–426.

Grannis, R. (1998). The importance of trivial streets: Residential streets and residential segregation. *The American Journal of Sociology, 103,* 1530–1564.

Hipp, J. R. (2007). Block, tract, and levels of aggregation: Neighborhood structure and crime and disorder as a case in point. *American Sociological Review, 72,* 659–680.

Jargowsky, P. A. (1997). *Poverty and place: Ghettos, barrios, and the American city.* New York: Russell Sage Foundation.

Kling, J. R., Liebman, J. B., Katz, L. F., & Sanbonmatsu, L. (2004). Moving to opportunity and tranquility: Neighborhood effects on adult economic self-sufficiency and health from a randomized housing voucher experiment. Working Papers 247, Princeton University, Woodrow Wilson School of Public and International Affairs, Center for Health and Wellbeing.

Kobrin, S. (1959). The Chicago Area Project—A 25-year assessment. *Annals of the American Academy of Political and Social Science, 322,* 19–29.

Kornhauser, R. R. (1978). *Social sources of delinquency.* Chicago: University of Chicago Press.

Kwan, M., Peterson, R. D., Browning, C. R., Burrington, L. A., Calder, C. A., & Krivo, L. J. (2008). Reconceptualizing sociogeographical context for the study of drug use, abuse, and addiction. In D. Richardson & Y. Thomas (Eds.), *Geography and Drug Addiction.* Berlin: Springer-Verlag.

Lee, B. A., & Campbell, K. E. (1997). Common ground? Urban neighborhoods as survey respondents see them. *Social Science Quarterly, 78,* 922–936.

Leventhal, T., & Brooks-Gunn, J. (2001). The neighborhoods they live in: Effects of neighborhood residence on child and adolescent outcomes. *Psychological Bulletin, 126,* 309–337.

Liebow, E. (1967). *Tally's Corner.* Boston: Little, Brown.

Lochner, K. A., Kawachi, I., Brennan, R. T., & Buka, S. L. (2003). Social capital and neighborhood mortality rates in Chicago. *Social Science & Medicine, 56,* 1797–1805.

Massey, D. S., & Denton, N. A. (1993). *American apartheid: Segregation and the making of the underclass.* Cambridge, MA: Harvard University Press.

Mears, D. P., & Bhati, A. S. (2006). No community is an island: The effects of resource deprivation on urban violence in spatially and socially proximate communities. *Criminology, 44,* 509–548.

Morenoff, J. D., Sampson, R. J., & Raudenbush, S. (2001). Neighborhood inequality, collective efficacy, and the spatial dynamics of homicide. *Criminology, 39,* 517–560.

Park, R. E., Burgess, E., & McKenzie, R. (1925). *The city.* Chicago: University of Chicago Press.

Pattillo-McCoy, M. (1999). *Black picket fences: Privilege and peril among the black middle class.* Chicago: University of Chicago Press.

Portes, A. (1988). Social capital: Its origins and applications in modern sociology. *Annual Review of Sociology, 24,* 1–24.

Raudenbush, S. W., & Bryk, A. S. (2002). *Hierarchical linear models: Applications and data analysis methods.* Thousand Oaks, London, New Delhi: Sage Publications, Inc.

Ross, C. E., & Mirowsky, J. (2001). Neighborhood disadvantage, disorder, and health. *Journal of Health and Social Behavior, 42,* 258–276.

Sampson, R. J. (1988). Local friendship ties and community attachment in mass society: A multilevel systemic approach. *American Sociological Review, 53,* 766–779.

Sampson, R. J. (2003). Neighborhood-level context and health: Lessons from sociology. In I. Kawachi & L. Berkman (Eds.), *Neighborhoods and Health* (pp. 132-146). Oxford, U.K.: Oxford University Press.

Sampson, R. J., & Groves, W. B. (1989). Community structure and crime: Testing social disorganization theory. *American Journal of Sociology, 94,* 774–802.

Sampson, R. J., Morenoff, J. D., & Gannon-Rowley, T. (2002). Assessing neighborhood effects: Social processes and new directions in research. *Annual Review of Sociology, 28,* 443–478.

Sampson, R. J., Raudenbush, S. W., & Earls, F. (1997). Neighborhoods and violent crime: A multilevel study of collective efficacy. *Science, 227,* 918–923.

Sampson, R. J., & Raudenbush, S. W. (1999). Systematic social observation of public spaces: A new look at disorder in urban neighborhoods. *The American Journal of Sociology, 105*(3), 603–651.

Sastry, N., Ghosh-Dastidar, B., Adams, J. L., & Pebley, A. (2006). The design of a multilevel survey of children, families, and communities: The Los Angeles Family and Neighborhood Survey. *Social Science Research, 35,* 1000–1024.

Shaw, C. R., & McKay, H. (1942). *Juvenile delinquency and urban areas.* Chicago: University of Chicago Press.

Short, J. F., Jr., & Strodtbeck, F. L. (1965). *Group process and gang delinquency.* Chicago: University of Chicago Press.

Skogan, W. G. (1990). *Disorder and decline: Crime and the spiral of decay in American neighborhoods.* New York: Free Press.

Smith, D. A., & Jarjoura, G. R. (1988). Social structure and criminal victimization. *Journal of Research in Crime and Delinquency, 25,* 27–52.

Stark, R. (1987). Deviant places: A theory of the ecology of crime. *Criminology, 25,* 891–907.

Wacquant, L. (2007). *Urban outcasts: A comparative sociology of advanced marginality.* Cambridge; Malden, MA: Polity.

Wellman, B., & Leighton, B. (1979). Networks, neighborhoods, and communities: Approaches to the study of the community question. *Urban Affairs Quarterly, 14,* 363–390.

Wilson, W. J. (1987). *The truly disadvantaged: The inner city, the underclass, and public policy.* Chicago: University of Chicago Press.

Wilson, W. J. (1996). *When work disappears: The world of the new urban poor.* New York: Knopf.

Zhang, L., Messner, S. F., & Liu, J. (2007). A multilevel analysis of the risk of residential burglary in the city of Tianjin, China. *British Journal of Criminology, 47,* 918–937.

Lori A. Burrington
Christopher R. Browning

NONCUSTODIAL PARENTS

A noncustodial parent is a parent who is legally responsible for the support of a dependent minor child and who does not live in the same household as the child. The terms *nonresident parent* and *noncustodial parent* are often used interchangeably. Noncustodial parents may have joint legal custody of their children, but the children's primary residence is with the other parent. The two primary paths to noncustodial parenthood include (a) births that occur outside of a union to parents who are not married or living together, and where one parent, almost always the father, does not live with the child; and (b) noncustodial parenthood resulting from divorce or separation, after which the children live primarily with one parent. The latter may result from the break up of cohabiting unions as well as marriages.

Becoming a noncustodial parent has profound consequences for the adult life course. The transition to parenthood is a vastly different experience when it occurs in the context of not living with the child and the other parent, as when births occur outside of a union. Unmarried, noncustodial parents (most often fathers in this circumstance) will face severe challenges in forming and maintaining close relationships with their children. For example, relationship difficulties with the other parent are likely to constrict noncustodial parents' access to their children.

Noncustodial parenthood following divorce engenders experiences of separation and loss, the possibility of damaging legal battles, and increased ambiguity in the parental role when not residing with children. Often divorce is only the beginning of a series of life-altering transitions for the noncustodial parent, including changes of residence, reduced socioeconomic status, possible new romantic relationships and union formation, and additional childbearing with a new partner. Each of these transitions has implications for relationships with nonresident children. Thus, becoming a noncustodial parent may have a lifelong influence on the quality of a parent's ties to children and on intergenerational relationships in later life.

TRENDS IN NONCUSTODIAL PARENTHOOD

Divorce remains the primary cause of noncustodial parenthood. Estimates by demographers show that about half of all marriages will end in divorce, although the divorce rate has leveled off in the early 21st century. (Raley & Bumpass, 2003). An estimated 47% of White women's and 70% of Black women's marriages will end in divorce. Although mothers typically have physical custody of children following divorce, a growing proportion of fathers have full custody (10%) or shared custody (15% to 20%; Coley, 2001). Thus, there has been a substantial increase in the number of noncustodial mothers in the United States. Marjorie Gunnoe and Eileen Hetherington (2004) estimated that there were 1.2 million noncustodial mothers in the United States in the 1980s, with the numbers increasing during the 1990s. Data from the 2005 and 2006 Current Population Surveys show that about 9.3% of U.S. children under the age of 18 were not living with their biological mother (about 6.8 million children). Only about half of these children were living with their father, whereas the remaining half lived with neither biological parent.

Nonmarital childbearing is a rising cause of noncustodial parenthood in the United States. Since the late 1970s, nonmarital births more than tripled for White women ages 20 to 39 and increased by one-third for Black women (Gray, Stockard, & Stone, 2006). Currently about one-third of all births (and two-thirds of Black births) in

the United States occur outside of marriage. In assessing nonmarital childbearing and its consequences, it is critical to distinguish between births to parents not in a union and births to (unmarried) cohabiting couples. About 40% of nonmarital births are to women who are cohabiting with the baby's father (Woo & Raley, 2005). Thus, in addition to divorce, the break up of cohabiting unions may also lead to noncustodial parenthood.

National survey data from 2002 show that about 40% of American men ages 15 to 44 had fathered a child outside of marriage, with rates higher for Hispanic (50%) and African American (74%) men (Nock, 2007); this included men who were cohabiting with the mother and were therefore resident parents, at least initially. However, national surveys may miss millions of unmarried, nonresident fathers who are not in the household population and difficult to recruit into research studies. Compared to resident fathers, nonresident fathers tend to be younger; have lower levels of schooling, employment, income, and assets; and are more likely to have substance abuse problems (Nelson, 2004). Nearly one-quarter of nonresident fathers are below the poverty line.

RESEARCH ON NONCUSTODIAL PARENTHOOD

The vast majority of empirical studies in this area focus on noncustodial fathers. (The few studies on noncustodial mothers are discussed separately.) Research has shown consistently that noncustodial fathers are less involved with their children than resident, custodial fathers. Fathers after divorce may act more like visitors than parents, emphasizing leisure time with children rather than parenting. Living apart from children because of divorce or nonmarital birth makes it more difficult for men to provide financial and social capital to their offspring. Men in separate households have less income to share with children and have more difficulty in being active parents or active participants in their children's lives. National survey data in the United States show that from 25% to 50% of minor children almost never see their noncustodial fathers, whereas about one-fourth to one-third are in frequent contact with them (Nelson, 2004). Children's contact with noncustodial fathers tends to fade over time. Contact rates may vary across countries. An Israeli study found high levels of father involvement with adolescent children 6 years after divorce (Mandel & Sharlin, 2006). In measuring noncustodial father involvement, the informant matters. Mothers consistently report lower levels of involvement than do the fathers themselves. Interparental conflict leads to greater discrepancies between mothers' and fathers' reports.

To what extent is noncustodial father involvement related to a child's long-term well-being? Research on this linkage has produced mixed results. The clearest findings are that father involvement enhances a child's cognitive development and educational attainment (Coley, 2001), whereas the evidence that fathers affect children's socioemotional development is weak. Analysis of national survey data with children ages 5 to 11 show that positive father–child relationships (e.g., warm, supportive, and responsive fathering behaviors) had modest, negative associations with adolescent internalizing and externalizing problems (King & Sobolewski, 2006). However, a child's relationship with the custodial mother had stronger linkages to well-being. Other research by Valarie King (2006) supported the *primacy of residence* hypothesis, which assumes that the most influential people on an adolescent's well-being are the people with whom he or she lives. Adolescents whose custodial mother remarried benefited from having close relationships with stepfathers and nonresident biological fathers, but relationships with stepfathers appeared to be more influential than relationships with biological fathers. More adolescents reported feeling close to stepfathers (61%) than to biological fathers (41%).

Contact frequency alone is not strongly or consistently associated with a child's adjustment or development. What matters most is what noncustodial fathers do with their children when they spend time together. When noncustodial parents engage in authoritative parenting with their offspring, and when they provide emotional and material support, they likely will contribute to a child's well-being. Contact is a necessary but not sufficient condition for strong relationships between noncustodial fathers and children. More contact leads to more support from fathers to children and more actual parenting as opposed to shared leisure time.

PREDICTORS OF NONCUSTODIAL FATHER INVOLVEMENT

Divorce Versus Nonmarital Birth Children born outside of marriage have less frequent contact with and are less close to noncustodial fathers than children who experienced their parents' divorce. About half of unmarried noncustodial fathers have regular contact in the first years of their child's life, but this drops to about one-third when children are adolescents (Coley, 2001). Laura Argys and Helen Peters (2001) estimated that about 28% of adolescents ages 12 to 16 had weekly contact with nonresident fathers when parents were divorced, but less than 20% had weekly contact if parents had never married. More than 80% of the children of divorced parents had at least one contact with their noncustodial father over the past year, compared to only 57% of the children with unmarried fathers.

Custody Agreement and Payment of Child Support Having joint legal custody has been linked to a noncustodial fathers involvement with and feelings of closeness to his children, compared to fathers without legal custody. Fathers who are more involved with their children prior to divorce are more likely to share custody afterward. Joint legal custody gives fathers an equal say with mothers in decisions regarding the child. Having joint physical custody, whereby children split time between the two parental households, promotes involvement. It is difficult for men to establish and maintain an active father role based on visitation only and without daily involvement with the children. Men may feel they have lost their children because of unfair treatment by the legal system.

Rates of child-support payment by noncustodial fathers are low. About 60% of eligible families have a legal child-support award; among those with a legal award, about 20% of children receive all the financial support they are entitled to (Coley, 2001). Only 13% of unmarried fathers pay formal child support, although some offer informal support by providing goods and services for the child (McLanahan & Carlson, 2004). The longer a father is absent from the home, the less likely he is to pay child support. Nonpayment of mandated child support may weaken a father's connection to his children, resulting in lower levels of visiting the children and less influence over childrearing decisions. Mothers who do not receive mandated child support may impede men's access to their children.

The Coparental Relationship One of the most important barriers to noncustodial father involvement is a poor coparental relationship with the mother. The coparental relationship refers to the ability of the custodial and noncustodial parent to cooperate in childrearing. The coparental relationship tends to deteriorate over time (after the divorce or nonmarital birth), leading to disengagement and a decreased role for fathers in childrearing and decision making about the children. Cooperative coparenting is not common. In a nationally representative sample, about two-thirds of the custodial mothers reported that the noncustodial father had no influence on childrearing decisions (Sobolewski & King, 2005). A cooperative coparental relationship facilitates contact between the noncustodial parent and children, leading to stronger father–child relationships and more responsive fathering and has been linked to a higher probability of joint custody. Conflict between the parents deters men's involvement with their children and makes it harder for them to parent effectively. The most common pattern of nonresident fathering combines nonauthoritative parenting with low levels of interparental cooperation.

Family Composition and Transitions Research has shown that the noncustodial father's remarriage complicates the paternal role and leads to a reduction in contact with his nonresident children. A father's additional childbearing also leads to a drop in visits with nonresident children, as the father may appear to embrace a new set of biological children and concern himself less with his children from previous marriages. The custodial parent's remarriage also may impact the noncustodial parent. When children acquire a stepparent, contact with the noncustodial parent declines.

Fathers' Education and Socioeconomic Status Noncustodial father–child contact is lower in poorer families. Based on research with unmarried fathers, Sara McLanahan and Marcia Carlson (2004) concluded that the male breadwinner role continues to be central to father–child relations. When men are not able to fulfill the breadwinner role for their children, they are more likely to withdraw. Data from a nationally representative sample of adolescents show clear linkages between a noncustodial father's education and their involvement with children (King, Harris, & Heard, 2004). Education was the most influential factor in explaining racial or ethnic differences in father involvement. Lower involvement among Black and Hispanic fathers (compared to White fathers) was explained by lower education levels and a higher probability of having nonmarital births. Education also differentiated the involvement of White fathers. The more educated White fathers (those who attained more than a high school degree) had the highest involvement levels of any ethnic or socioeconomic group, whereas less educated White fathers had the lowest involvement. The work migration of fathers in Hispanic families reduced father involvement in Mexican, Central, and South American families.

Child Gender Father involvement does not appear to vary greatly by the child's gender, although boys have reported somewhat higher involvement with noncustodial fathers than girls (King et al., 2004).

NONCUSTODIAL MOTHERS

The proportion of noncustodial parents who are women has grown in the decades leading up to the 21st century. Nonetheless, research has focused almost exclusively on noncustodial fathers, and relatively little is known about women who occupy this role. This is the largest gap in research concerning noncustodial parenthood. Evidence suggests that sole father custody after divorce is more likely when mothers struggle to fulfill the maternal role because of personal problems (the maternal deficit model) and when mothers enter a new romantic relationship immediately upon separation while fathers remain unattached.

Mothers relinquishing custody of minor children is often viewed as deviant or abnormal. This custody arrangement violates cultural expectations of fathers as breadwinners and mothers as nurturers. Catalina Herrerías (1995)

administered a life history questionnaire and clinical assessments to 130 noncustodial mothers. About 75% of these noncustodial mothers voluntarily gave up custody. Their reasons centered on financial considerations, emotional problems, the threat of a legal custody fight, and having a destructive relationship with the father. Although nearly all the mothers in this sample maintained connections to their children, the societal disapproval they experienced led the women to have negative self-perceptions as mothers. Research in the United States suggests that a noncustodial mother's parenting is more intense and of higher quality than that of noncustodial fathers. Susan Stewart (1999) reported in a national survey that noncustodial mothers were as likely as noncustodial fathers to have face-to-face contact with their children. The noncustodial mothers, however, had significantly higher levels of telephone and letter contact with their children. In contrast to noncustodial fathers, whether or not the noncustodial mothers paid child support did not affect their social contact with children. Noncustodial mothers are more likely than noncustodial fathers to perceive a child support order as fair.

Gunnoe and Hetherington (2004) noted that traditional sex roles encourage mothers more so than fathers to be loving toward and responsible for children. In their research with adolescents, they found that a significantly higher percentage of offspring with noncustodial fathers (52%) had no contact with their noncustodial parent than offspring with noncustodial mothers (31%). Noncustodial mothers exerted a more positive influence on adolescent adjustment than did noncustodial fathers, providing greater social support, engaging in more communication, and knowing more about the children than did noncustodial fathers.

POLICY AND SOCIAL ISSUES

One of the central policy issues of noncustodial parenthood is how child-support awards and their enforcement impact the involvement of noncustodial parents with their children. The majority of noncustodial fathers, especially poor, unmarried fathers, pay no child support at all. Has the stepped-up enforcement of child support orders, including garnishing the wages of parents delinquent in their payments, created a disincentive or barrier to parents in maintaining connections to nonresident children? Men often perceive the child-support order as unfair and are less likely to make the payments when they think the legal system has not been just. One study (Lin & McLanahan, 2007) showed that custodial mothers see paternal obligations and rights as linked and feel that a father's visitation and decision-making rights should be conditional on payment of child support. Men who cannot or will not pay may feel cut off from their paternal role. One family legal scholar has proposed legally requiring nonresident parents to have contact with their children regardless of their ability to pay child support. The aim is to create a norm of involvement for noncustodial parents that is not tied to the economic support of their children. It is not clear whether this controversial proposal will garner support among policy makers.

Rebekah Coley (2001) described the lack of societal norms about the role and responsibilities of noncustodial parents, especially fathers. How do the role expectations for noncustodial parents change as children grow older, when the custodial or noncustodial parent remarries, or when either parent has children with a new partner? Similar to Andrew Cherlin's (1978) description of remarriage, noncustodial parenthood can be viewed as an incomplete institution that lacks clear social and legal guidelines for role performance. The lack of societal expectations for continued involvement with children may make it easier for noncustodial parents to grow less responsible and responsive to their offspring.

A study conducted by William Marsiglio and Ramon Hinojosa (2007) raised the intriguing possibility that the remarriage of the custodial parent could serve to help rather than hinder a noncustodial father's involvement with their children. Based on qualitative research with a broad-based sample of stepfathers, Marsiglio and Hinojosa found that, although many stepfathers have strained relations with the nonresident biological fathers, there are also many cases in which stepfathers seek to facilitate and support the biological father's relationships with his nonresident children. These stepfathers acted as allies to the noncustodial father and developed a cooperative style of interaction. This study offers the possibility that interventions with remarried families could be developed to help stepparents become facilitators of strong connections between children and noncustodial parents.

SEE ALSO Volume 1: *Child Custody and Support; Family and Household Structure, Childhood and Adolescence;* Volume 2: *Cohabitation; Divorce and Separation; Family and Household Structure, Adulthood; Fatherhood; Motherhood.*

BIBLIOGRAPHY

Argys, L. M., & Peters, H. E. (2001). Patterns of nonresident father involvement. In R. T. Michael (Ed.), *Social awakening: Adolescent behavior as adulthood approaches* (pp. 49–78). New York: Russell Sage Foundation.

Cherlin, A. (1978). Remarriage as an incomplete institution. *American Journal of Sociology, 84*(3), 634–650.

Coley, R. L. (2001). (In)visible men: Emerging research on low-income, unmarried, and minority fathers. *American Psychologist, 56,* 743–753.

Gray, J. A., Stockard, J., & Stone, J. (2006). The rising share of nonmarital births: Fertility choice or marital behavior? *Demography, 43*(2), 241–253.

Gunnoe, M. L., & Hetherington, E. M. (2004). Stepchildren's perceptions of noncustodial mothers and noncustodial fathers: Differences in socioemotional involvement and associations with adolescent adjustment problems. *Journal of Family Psychology, 18*(4), 555–563.

Herrerías, C. (1995). Noncustodial mothers following divorce. *Marriage and Family Review, 20,* 233–255.

King, V. (2006). The antecedents and consequences of adolescents' relationships with stepfathers and nonresident fathers. *Journal of Marriage and the Family, 68*(4), 910–928.

King, V., Harris, K. M., & Heard, H. E. (2004). Racial and ethnic diversity in nonresident father involvement. *Journal of Marriage and the Family, 66,* 1–21.

King, V., & Sobolewski, J. M. (2006). Nonresident fathers' contributions to adolescent well-being. *Journal of Marriage and the Family, 68*(3), 537–557.

Lin, I., & McLanahan, S. S. (2007). Parental beliefs about nonresident fathers' obligations and rights. *Journal of Marriage and the Family, 69*(2), 382–398.

Mandel, S., & Sharlin, A. S. (2006). The noncustodial father: His involvement in his children's lives and the connection between his role and the ex-wife's, child's, and father's perception of that role. *Journal of Divorce and Remarriage, 45,* 79–95.

Marsiglio, W., & Hinojosa, R. (2007). Managing the multifather family: Stepfathers as father allies. *Journal of Marriage and the Family, 69,* 845–862.

McLanahan, S., & Carlson, M. S. (2004). Fathers in fragile families. In M. E. Lamb (Ed.), *The role of the father in child development* (4th ed.; pp. 368–396). Hoboken, NJ: Wiley.

Nelson, T. J. (2004). Low-income fathers. *Annual Review of Sociology, 30,* 427–451.

Nock, S. L. (2007). *Marital and unmarried births to men: Complex patterns of fatherhood* (ASPE Research Brief). Washington, DC: Office of the Assistant Secretary for Planning and Evaluation, U.S. Department of Health and Human Services.

Raley, R. K., & Bumpass, L. (2003). The topography of the divorce plateau: Levels and trends in union stability in the United States after 1980. *Demographic Research, 8,* 245–260.

Sobolewski, J. M., & King, V. (2005). The importance of the coparental relationship for nonresident fathers' ties to children. *Journal of Marriage and the Family, 67*(5), 1196–1212.

Stewart, S. D. (1999). Nonresident mothers' and fathers' social contact with children. *Journal of Marriage and the Family, 61*(4), 894–907.

Woo, H., & Raley, R. K. (2005). Costs and rewards of children: The effects of becoming a parent on adults' lives. *Journal of Marriage and the Family, 67*(1), 216–221.

William S. Aqulino

O

OBESITY, ADULT

The world's population is becoming increasingly over-weight. Currently more than 1 billion adults are over-weight, and at least 300 million of them are clinically obese (WHO 2008). Obesity is usually measured by the Body Mass Index (BMI), calculated as weight (in kilo-grams) divided by height (in meters squared). This measure is considered an indicator of body fat. The use of a standard measure is useful for screening patients, for public health interests, and for comparison across time and countries. The National Heart, Lung, and Blood Institute (NHLBI) issued the first federal U.S. guidelines on the evaluation and treatment of obesity in which they adopted the definitions of *overweight,* defined by a BMI of 25 to 29.9 kg/m^2, and *obesity,* defined by a BMI of 30 kg/m^2 or greater. Within the category of obesity further distinctions are made between *class I obesity,* BMI between 30 and 35; *class II obesity,* BMI between 35 and 40; and *class III obesity,* BMI exceeding 40. These guidelines are consistent with those adopted by the World Health Organization (2000) and used in international studies.

TRENDS AND DIFFERENTIALS IN OBESITY

In nearly every nation the proportion of the population considered overweight has increased over the past two decades. This increase in body size is particularly evident in the United States. The proportion of the American population that is overweight and obese has risen dra-matically for all age groups, although there is evidence that this trend may be slowing. Between 1960 and 2004, the proportion of adult men who were overweight rose from 50% to 71%, while the proportion of women who were overweight rose from 40% to more than 62%. The percentage of men who were obese rose from 10% to 31%, and the proportion of women who were obese rose from 15% to about 33% in the same 44-year period (Ogden, Carroll, Curtin, McDowell et al., 2006). How-ever, between 2004 and 2006 there was no significant change in obesity prevalence for either men or women in the United States (Ogden, Carroll, McDowell, & Flegal, 2007). Rates of overweight and obesity generally increase with age until age 75, when there is a small drop (Flegal, Carroll, Kuczmarski, & Johnson, 1998). Men are more likely than women to be overweight, but women are more likely than to be obese, especially with BMIs greater than 35 (Hedley, Ogden, Johnson, Carroll et al., 2004). During the peak years, ages 55 to 74, more than 70% of men and women are overweight and more than 35% are obese. After age 75, the rates drop slightly; just over 60% being overweight and just over 20% classified as obese. Differences in overweight and obesity rates for women vary starkly by race and ethnicity but are not as apparent for men. Across racial and ethnic groups, men have similar prevalences of overweight and obesity (Flegal et al., 1998; Hedley et al., 2004). Black and Hispanic women, by contrast, are much more likely to be over-weight and obese than White women. According to the NCHS analysis of National Health and Nutrition Examination Survey (NHANES) data (Hedley et al., 2004), 77.5% of Black women are overweight, compared to 71.4% of Mexican women and 57% of White women. The prevalence of obesity is similarly skewed with the rates for Black, Mexican, and White women at 49.6%, 38.9%, and 31.3%, respectively. Fully 10% of middle-

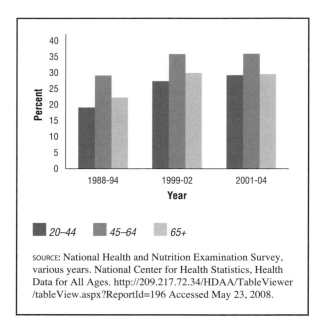

SOURCE: National Health and Nutrition Examination Survey, various years. National Center for Health Statistics, Health Data for All Ages. http://209.217.72.34/HDAA/TableViewer /tableView.aspx?ReportId=196 Accessed May 23, 2008.

Figure 1. *Obesity among adults: U.S., 1988–2004.* CENGAGE LEARNING, GALE.

aged Black women are morbidly obese, with BMIs greater than 40 (Flegal et al., 1998).

HEALTH-RELATED CONSEQUENCES OF OBESITY

Overweight and obesity are significant risk factors for several chronic conditions and may impede proper medical care. Those who are overweight, and particularly those who are obese, are significantly more likely to have diabetes, high blood pressure, high cholesterol, coronary heart disease, and certain types of cancer (WHO, 2008). Because the likelihood of developing diabetes increases significantly as body fat increases, many have attributed the increased prevalence of Type 2 diabetes to the increased obesity of the world's population. According to the *World Health Report 2002*, approximately 58% of diabetes globally is attributable to excess weight (WHO, 2002), while in the United States the prevalence of diabetes rose 120% between 1980 and 2005 (CDC, 2008). Most of the increased risk for chronic diseases is a direct physical result of overweight and obesity, but several authors suggest that the stigma of being overweight is so pronounced in the medical field that many people avoid going to the doctor, complicating the diagnosis of medical conditions and their care (Puhl and Brownell, 2003).

Despite the clear effect of obesity on the development of chronic conditions, the effect of weight on mortality risk is ambiguous. Several studies have shown that being overweight or mildly obese does not increase, and for some may decrease, the risk of dying (Flegal, Graubard, Williamson,

& Gail, 2005; Krueger, Rogers, Hummer, & Boardman, 2004; Reynolds, Saito, & Crimmins, 2005). Others find that obesity increases mortality risks, but the overall magnitude and age gradient is less clear (Fontaine, Redden, Wang, Westfall et al., 2003). The risk seems to be highest for those who have been overweight for longer periods of time and decreases if one does not become overweight or obese until after age 50 (Flegal et al. 2005). In longitudinal analyses, obesity in middle adulthood (ages 30 to 49) has been shown to be associated with an approximately six-year lower life expectancy when compared to normal weight individuals (Peeters, Barendregt, Willekens, Mackenback et al., 2003).

Excess weight creates functional limitations, diminishes mobility, and impairs the ability to exercise at all ages. Those older adults who develop chronic illness due to their obesity still experience functional limitations beyond those created by the illnesses themselves as a result of being overweight (Himes, 2000). The relationship between obesity and disability has important implications for the projection of future disability rates. The rise in obesity may result in higher rates of disability at older ages or increased years of disability in later life (Reynolds, Saito, & Crimmins, 2005). Given the rising rates of obesity at middle ages, it is important to understand how the aging of the obese population may affect disability rates and health care needs in the future.

SOCIAL CONSEQUENCES OF OBESITY

Several studies report economic discrimination against the overweight at all stages of employment. Societal attitudes about being overweight shape employers' attitudes about the abilities of overweight employees. For example, employers often think that overweight employees are slow-moving, have poor attendance, are unattractive, and are not good role models because of negative personality traits (Roehling, 1999). Overweight persons are less likely to be hired than applicants of normal weight. Additionally, overweight and obese people are hired for less prestigious jobs than their normal weight counterparts and have lower occupational attainment (Pagan & Davila, 1997). Overweight and obese employees are paid less than employees of average weight, but the wage penalty varies by gender, race, and age. Women face a greater wage penalty for being overweight than men (Baum & Ford, 2004). Wages of White women are affected by weight more than wages of Black and Hispanic women (Cawley, 2004). Older overweight employees are penalized more than younger workers, and those who gained weight early in life face greater wage penalties than those who gained weight later in life (Baum & Ford, 2004).

Studies suggest that social discrimination continues to occur on the basis of body size. Common stereotypes about overweight persons include laziness, self-indulgence, impulsivity, and incompetence (Rothblum, 1992). People hold overweight individuals responsible for their own condition and often think that if the overweight simply had more willpower, they would reduce their food intake and, thus, lose weight (Puhl & Brownell, 2003; Rothblum, 1992). These stereotypes persist despite evidence that overweight people generally do not have higher caloric intakes than those of average weight (Rothblum, 1992).

In addition to the personal and emotional costs of disability, chronic diseases translate into increased health care and disability costs. Lakdawalla and colleagues (2005) used simulations to calculate that obese 70-year-olds spend an excess $39,000 of health care compared to non-obese 70-year-olds. Society-wide, the direct economic cost associated with obesity has been estimated at 4% to 7% of all health care costs, or about $51.6 billion in 1995. A slightly lower amount, $47.6 billion in 1995, represents the indirect costs of lost economic output caused by morbidity and mortality due to obesity (Allison, Zannolli, & Narayan, 1999).

CAUSES OF OBESITY

Social and environmental factors have been implicated in the global spread of obesity. Body fat is a normal and necessary part of the human body. Fat serves an important function as a store of energy that can be used by the body in response to metabolic demands. At the most basic level, obesity results from an imbalance between energy intake and energy expenditure. However, this imbalance may be the result, individually or in combination, of excess caloric intake, decreased physical activity, or metabolic disorders.

Globally, the obesity epidemic has been attributed to a broader "nutritional transition" in which, with increasing modernization and urbanization, diets have tended to shift from ones consisting of complex carbohydrates to diets with a higher proportion of saturated fats and sugars (Popkin, 2001). The introduction of sweetened beverages and processed foods in low-income countries is one factor contributing to the rapid weight gain. Other dietary changes include the inclusion of more animal-source foods and energy-dense foods. These changes in dietary patterns, combined with a decrease in physically demanding jobs, have created overall weight gain worldwide.

In developed countries, the increase in childhood obesity, in particular, has been linked to declines in physical activity. These declines take the form of reduced time spent in physical education classes and recess time in elementary schools, the increased prevalence of video and computer games as entertainment, and the reduction of family physical recreational activities. Research has pointed to the spread of obesity through social networks.

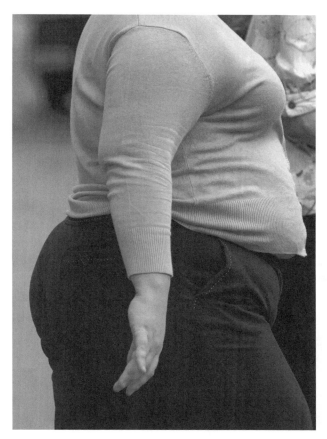

Obesity Crisis. *Obesity raises the risk of a multitude of conditions, especially Type 2 diabetes. Statistics show that 90% of people with the disorder, which causes the body to become resistant to insulin, have a Body Mass Index of more than 23.* AP IMAGES.

Christakis and Fowler (2007) find that, over and above the effects of shared environment, there is evidence that individual weight is affected by the weight of those with whom individuals have close interpersonal relationships. Therefore, as obesity becomes more common it is spread among social networks.

The fight against the spread of obesity is taking place on many fronts. In 2004 the World Health Organization (WHO) issued its statement, *Global Strategy on Diet, Physical Activity, and Health*. Their recommendations cover a broad spectrum of individual and societal initiatives. These include an emphasis on improved school lunch programs and nutrition education for children, and campaigns to increase physical activity among both adults and children. The WHO notes that public policies that influence the pricing of food, either through taxation, subsidy, or direct pricing, need to be considered in ways that will encourage healthy eating. Agricultural policies and food programs are other avenues through which healthy eating and better nutrition can be encouraged. In the United States there has been increased interest in the role of government in nutrition policy. Legislation at the local, state, and national levels has aimed at taxing foods high in calories, fat, and sugar. One proposal would use the revenue generated by these taxes to fund nutrition and physical activity programs (Jacobsen & Brownell, 2000).

The future health and economic impacts of the increased prevalence of obesity in young and middle adulthood are likely to be large. Many diseases associated with obesity, diabetes in particular, have long-lasting impacts on health, health care needs, and the ability to work. The implementation of policies designed to improve nutrition and increase physical activity may be able to reduce these future impacts. Because the longer an individual is obese, the greater the health risk, targeting individuals early in the life course may have life-long effects.

SEE ALSO Volume 2: *Attractiveness, Physical; Body Image, Adulthood; Health Behaviors, Adulthood; Health Differentials/Disparities, Adulthood;* Volume 3: *Cancer, Adulthood and Later Life; Cardiovascular Disease.*

BIBLIOGRAPHY

Allison, D. B., Zannolli, R., & Narayan, K. M. (1999). The direct health care costs of obesity in the United States. *American Journal of Public Health, 89,* 1194–1199.

Baum, C. L., & Ford, W. F. (2004). The wage effects of obesity: A longitudinal study. *Health Economics, 13,* 885–899.

Cawley, J. (2004). The impact of obesity on wages. *Journal of Human Resources, 39*(2), 451–474.

Centers for Disease Control (CDC). (2008). Crude and age-adjusted prevalence of diagnosed diabetes per 100 population, United States, 1980–2005. Retrieved May 20, 2008, from http://www.cdc.gov/diabetes

Christakis, N. A., & Fowler, J. H. (2007). The spread of obesity in a large social network over 32 years. *New England Journal of Medicine, 357,* 370–379.

Flegal, K. M., Carroll, M. D., Kuczmarski, R. J., & Johnson, C. L. (1998). Overweight and obesity in the United States: Prevalence and trends, 1960–1994. *International Journal of Obesity and Related Metabolic Disorders, 22,* 39–47.

Flegal, K. M., Graubard, B. I., Williamson, D. F., & Gail, M. H. (2005). Excess deaths associated with underweight, overweight, and obesity. *Journal of the American Medical Association, 293,* 1861–1867.

Fontaine, K. R., Redden, D. T., Wang, C., Westfall, A. O., & Allison. D. B. (2003). Years of life lost to obesity. *Journal of the American Medical Association, 289,* 187–193.

Hedley, A. A., Ogden, C. L., Johnson, C. L., Carroll, M. D., Curtin, L. R. & Flegal, K. M. (2004). Prevalence of overweight and obesity among US children, adolescents, and adults, 1999–2002. *Journal of the American Medical Association, 291,* 2847–2850.

Himes, C. L. (2000). Obesity, disease, and functional limitation in later life. *Demography, 37,* 73–82.

Jacobsen, M. F., & Brownell, K. D. (2000). Small taxes on soft drinks and snack foods to promote health. *American Journal of Public Health, 90*(6), 854–857.

Krueger, P. M., Rogers, R. G., Hummer, R. A. & Boardman, J. D. (2004). Body mass, smoking, and overall and cause specific mortality among older U.S. adults. *Research on Aging, 26*(1), 82–107.

Lakdawalla, D. N., Goldman, D. P., & Shang, B. (2005). The health and cost consequences of obesity among the future elderly. *Health Affairs.* Web exclusive May 26, 2005.

Ogden, C. L., Carroll, M. D., Curtin, L. R., McDowell, M. A., Tabak, C. J. & Flegal, K. M. (2006). Prevalence of overweight and obesity in the United States, 1999–2004. *Journal of the American Medical Association, 295,* 1549–1555.

Ogden, C. L., Carroll, M. D., McDowell, M. A., & Flegal, K. M. (2007). Obesity among adults in the United States—No change since 2003–04. NCHS Data Brief No.1. Hyattsville, MD: National Center for Health Statistics.

Pagan, J. A., & Davila, A. (1997). Obesity, occupational attainment, and earnings. *Social Science Quarterly, 78*(3), 756–770.

Peeters, A., Barendregt, J. J., Willekens, F., Mackenback, J. P., Mamun, A. A., Bonneux, L. (2003). Obesity in adulthood and its consequences for life expectancy: A life-table analysis. *Annals of Internal Medicine, 138,* 24–32.

Popkin, B. M. (2001). The nutrition transition and obesity in the developing world. *Journal of Nutrition, 131,* 871S–873S.

Puhl, R. M., & Brownell, K. D. (2003). Psychosocial origins of obesity stigma: Toward changing a powerful and pervasive bias. *Obesity Reviews, 4,* 213–227.

Reynolds, S. L., Saito, Y., & Crimmins, E.M. (2005). The impact of obesity on active life expectancy in older American men and women. *The Gerontologist, 45,* 439–444.

Roehling, M. V. (1999). Weight-based discrimination in employment: Psychological and legal aspects. *Personnel Psychology, 52*(4), 969–1016.

Rothblum, E. D. (1992). The stigma of women's weight: Social and economic realities. *Feminism and Psychology, 2*(1), 61–73.

World Health Organization (WHO). (2000). *Obesity: Preventing and managing the global epidemic.* Geneva: World Health Organization.

World Health Organization. (2002). *The world health report 2002—reducing risks, promoting healthy life.* Geneva: World Health Organization.

World Health Organization. (2004). *Global strategy on diet, physical activity, and health.* Retrieved May 15, 2008, from http://www.who.int

World Health Organization. (2008). *Obesity and overweight.* Retrieved May 21, 2008, from http://www.who.int

Christine Himes

OCCUPATIONAL PRESTIGE AND STATUS

SEE Volume 2: *Social Class.*

OCCUPATIONS

Occupation refers to the kind of work usually done by someone to earn a living. The type of work a person does provides one of the best simple summaries of life circumstances available to social scientists, because current occupation reflects past and future opportunities to acquire assets and gain benefits in competition with others. Occupation is a window into social stratification—that is, to the persisting unequal distribution of rank, power, and resources in a society. Although the connection between occupation and inequality is strong, it is also highly nonuniform. Thus, one's occupation is one of the most complex indicators of life circumstances in widespread use.

MEASURING AND CONCEPTUALIZING OCCUPATION

One first issue is what counts as an occupation. Many researchers and most government statistical agencies restrict occupation to work performed for pay outside the home. Unpaid domestic or household labor is thus commonly excluded. Agricultural labor by kin for kin, including work done by children, is also not counted. These activities are excluded because they do not match the idea of *usual occupation* as work involving relatively specialized tasks that are regulated by contract and require formal training, licensing, or previous experience. This model emerged as rural agricultural economies were displaced by urban and industrial alternatives. Relatively unspecialized work gave way to specialized, potentially life-long, vocations that became key determinants of mode and level of living. Eventually the concept of work became equated with labor performed in the formal sector of an industrialized, market economy.

Government concern about ensuring that vocations had adequate supplies of labor is almost as old as urbanism—the Roman emperor Diocletian (245 C.E.–ca. 312 C.E.) decreed that all sons would follow the trade of their fathers, although practical means of enforcement hardly existed. Modern occupational tabulations date from the early industrial era when statistics retained its older meaning of measures created for purposes of state (Desrosiéres, 1998).

Although many terms are used to describe vocations, government tabulations such as the U.S. Census require classifications based on standardized uniform coding rules. From the outset, designers of codes at the U.S. Census Bureau took occupation as a potential master status, "the best single criterion of a man's social and economic status" encompassing "the kind of associates he will have," "the kind of food he will eat," and "the cultural level of his family" (Alba Edwards, in charge of occupational statistics for the U.S. Census Bureau 1920 to 1940 and quoted in Conk, 1980, p 26).

Code creation was an uneven exercise. The scale was daunting. Only government agencies could afford the massive expense of addressing the full range of occupations that individuals report. For the U.S. Census, the raw material was the answers written out in the manuscript census, in which census-takers recorded responses to questions about work usually performed. In the early 20th century, efforts were made to impose a coherent yet detailed classification scheme on such answers. Where possible, code designers relied on folk distinctions among popular trades, such as masonry, which were thought to require special skills. From 1920 on, further job titles were added to accommodate emerging educational specialties in business, engineering, and science. Solid reasons, hunches, and guesswork all played a part. Code designers often rued the lack of reliable information on which decisions could be based. This uncertainty is reflected in the residual categories, such as *Precision Machine Operatives, Not Elsewhere Classified* that are provided as catch-all categories for positions that lack a clear fit.

The result resists easy summary. Many coding schemes implement treelike patterns, in which large coarse classes may be subdivided into finer constituents. The more elaborate catalogues—dictionaries of occupational titles—list upwards of 10,000 distinct categories, whereas survey researchers distinguish at most several hundred down to as few as three. Compromise thus becomes unavoidable.

Categories, although useful, are not intrinsically ranked and thus are ill suited for addressing researchers' questions about occupational change or development. The widely shared intuition that occupation was a master status, however, implied that occupations could be viewed as locations in a social hierarchy.

RANKING OCCUPATIONS

Various techniques for ranking and assessing occupations have been proposed (Nam & Boyd, 2004). Prominent options include ranking by sample surveys of perceptions of desirability (sometimes termed *occupational prestige*; Treiman, 1977), by distance reflected in relative infrequency of social relations such as marriage and inheritance, (Bottero & Prandy, 2003), and by weighted sums of education and earnings' levels typical of incumbents (Nam & Powers, 1983). The most influential has been the *socioeconomic index*, commonly abbreviated SEI, originally developed by sociologist Otis Dudley Duncan (1961). Every occupation is ranked by a weighted sum reflecting incumbents' earnings and level of education (adjusted for age and measuring level as a percentage of incumbents' above-the-population median for education and earnings, respectively, adjusted to some baseline decennial census). An initial motivation was the happy result that the composite based on nearly equal weights for education and earnings correlates well with prestige rankings. However, the details give rise to variants among which researchers must choose, more or less arbitrarily (Hauser & Warren, 1997). Although empirical differences among scales are generally modest, the alternatives draw on conceptions that overlap but have not been reconciled, so that no unified interpretation exists for the difference in values across different scales.

Occupational scales (e.g., the SEI) transform occupations from discrete categories (e.g., professionals, laborers) into a continuum or hierarchy. This provides the key step for addressing occupation as some sequence of levels or ranks that occur over the life course. Blau and Duncan (1967) pioneered such studies of status attainment. They examined statistical models for social mobility based on viewing adult occupation as the culmination of a causal sequence of earlier ranks that occurred as stages over the life cycle.

The initial stage in Blau and Duncan's (1967) life-cycle model was family of origin, represented by the male parent's occupational rank (which required adopting some options for scaling occupation). Possible extensions included fathers' education and attributes of the mother.

The next cluster was schooling, which spawned an entire subfield of educational attainment research, devoted to attempts to assign relative weights to such factors as race, gender, parental background, cognitive ability, school quality, and assorted measures of motivation and encouragement.

The category *completed education* was simplified to *years completed*. This was followed by the rank of the individual's first job. From that point, typically in young adulthood, an occupational trajectory followed, culminating in the current job.

The sequence of origin, schooling, labor market entry, and current job provides a framework that allows abstraction from the detailed statistical results. At each stage, the immediately preceding stage has substantial impact. Thus, social origin influences years of schooling, whereas labor market entry level influences current job. As any further stage is reached, echoes of the past diminish, so that current job reflects origin less than first job or schooling. At every stage, variation that is residual—independent of all earlier factors—is substantial. Hence, the two themes are cumulation, in which every outcome depends on relative success or failure at earlier stages, and decoupling, in which later statuses diverge from earlier ones.

The initial scheme was an open-ended framework. Inserting more measurements between any two stages allows for statistical estimates of the relative contribution of the new factors to the transition. One of the most prominent additions, often called the Wisconsin model after the university and state where the research occurred, emphasized the importance of aspirations in persisting at school and in ending up in a high-ranking job (Sewell, Hauser, Springer, & Hauser, 2003).

Status attainment implies an overall pattern for occupational trajectories. A rough sketch is straightforward. As age-mates advance through young adulthood, a shrinking proportion continues on to the next year of school. The fraction that leaves school then enters the labor market. At each step, those who lasted one more year obtain better jobs than those who left earlier. In the United States, a curvilinear pattern exists in which the bump-up for an added year in school rises sharply with each succeeding year (Hauser & Featherman, 1977, Fig. 5.4). The result is a fan, exposing ever-wider gaps between average rank of first jobs with each increment to education. These initial gaps then widen further because increases in job rank, up to peaks at around 40 years of age, are greater the higher the initial labor market entry point.

An analogy helps shed light on how this unfolds. At issue are differences due to how time is spent during the critical years. A good year is one spent earning top grades at a top school. A bad year is one spent working in a menial position in a fast-food restaurant. One might liken this to drawing cards in a card game. The good year is the equivalent of drawing a top card, such as an ace. Flipping burgers is like losing a turn. These lost turns do not come back, however, and results are cumulative. Only those who collect enough *good cards* in a timely manner are allowed to keep playing when the higher stakes finally come up for grabs.

So who ends up with good cards? Many are already dealt at birth. However, with rare exceptions, birth portions do not directly translate into occupational advantage. High cards, such as birth advantage, only grant access to higher stakes tables, such as better schools, but completing school, and gaining adequate marks, remains an individual accomplishment. These particular achievements (e.g., admission to medical school) are the same in name only, however, because those with better birth portions will require less effort or ability to complete particular achievements. The result is shading—step by step, when higher (versus lower) ranks are examined, the predominance of higher (versus lower) origins is more marked, whereas exceptions are more unusual, but they do occur. In a parallel manner, greater success at school, or labor market entry, favors higher adult occupational rank, but only as increased odds of success and almost never strict certainty.

RACE AND GENDER DIFFERENCES IN OCCUPATIONS

Another source of divergence in occupations and careers are ascribed (or inborn) characteristics, including gender and race. Occupations are strongly influenced by gender. Coarse, medium, or even extremely fine occupational distinctions show strong occupational sex segregation—female workers are heavily concentrated in a relatively small proportion of occupational titles or categories (Jacobs, 1989). This has diminished over time but has hardly disappeared (Queneau, 2006), and it has survived despite the disappearance of any male advantage in overall education (Bae, 2000).

Women are much more likely to work part-time and to leave and rejoin the labor force sporadically, a pattern thought to indicate weak labor force attachment on the part of such employees. This undermines the accumulation of experience and employer willingness to invest in training. Lower wages result (Jacobsen & Levin, 1995). Another consequence is that occupations are more tightly tied to level of education, that is, less open to subsequent career developments (Treiman & Terrell, 1975).

Why this occurs remains open to debate. Reskin and Roos (1990) described the pattern wherein changes in female proportions were restricted to relatively few occupations as due to *queuing*, whereby the less-desired gender is allowed in only after the more desired gender is elsewhere accommodated. Evidence also exists, however, that returns, such as wages, decline *after* feminization and do not precede it, as queuing would require (England, Allison, Wu, & Ross, 2007).

Family pressures, both perceived and real, play a role. Gender is a proxy, an imperfect but inexpensive indicator, of liability to child-bearing and child-care obligations that could compete with work. Trade-offs between job flexibility and lack of career advances might be at work (Bender, Donohue, & Heywood, 2005). However, although women do more unpaid housework than men do and absorb more of the burden of child care when children are young, these differences diminished quite sharply from 1965 to 1995 (Bianchi, Milkie, Sayer, & Robinson, 2000). Meanwhile, evidence remains strong of glass ceilings in which differences in career outcomes are greater toward the top and tend to grow over the length of careers (Cotter, Hermsen, Ovadia, & Vanneman, 2001).

Research on racial differences in careers also focuses primarily on wage levels and only indirectly on the contributions of occupation. Racial differences in careers are marked. Divergence increases over time, and some evidence of glass ceilings has been provided (Maume, 2004). A key debate continues whether differences between races trace back to premarket differences of less effective education and lower cognitive skills (Neal & Johnson, 1996). Much of the racial contrast, however, can be shown to emerge as careers mature and with greater impact among the better educated, showing that the accumulation of assets valued by employers is impeded by apparent discrimination (Tomaskovic-Devey, Thomas, & Johnson, 2005).

LIFE COURSE IMPLICATIONS OF OCCUPATIONS AND CAREERS

The very concept of a career, of a sequence of jobs that progress upward over the life cycle, is likely becoming more restricted to a narrowing slice of better jobs. This corresponds to the concept of dual labor markets, in which low pay, low skill, and absence of advancement contrast with conditions in jobs that offer higher pay, chances to use and accumulate skills, and good chances for promotion. The most recent variant emphasizes computerization as a cause of polarization. Some tasks, such as bookkeeping, are highly routine and subject to direct replacement by information technology. Nonroutine tasks, however, such as writing persuasive legal briefs, cannot be done by computers, even though computers aid in some related tasks, such as legal research. Thus, adding computers has a polarizing effect, undermining the market value of much routine work while enhancing returns to some, but not all, nonroutine jobs. Impacts are apparent within detailed occupations and between major occupational groups—increases in computer use undermine the value of less-skilled occupations but raise both average rewards and internal differences within higher skilled occupations (Autour, Levy, & Murname, 2001) Another factor undermining the relative returns of workers with lower skills is increased international competition (e.g., globalization; Acemoglu, 2003).

The overall pattern is that inequality in earnings began to rise rapidly after 1970. Differences rose between individuals within occupations, as did differences between occupations, and the size of gaps attributable to additional years of schooling (Levy & Murnane, 1992). This is complemented by evidence that more recent cohorts entering the labor force experience polarization in career outcomes that are more dramatic and rapid than in the past (Bernhardt, Morris, Handcock, & Scott, 2001).

This overshadows the longer term tendency in which rising average educational levels translate into occupational upgrading. Ever since continuing economic development began with the emergence of industrialism, the mix of jobs has improved over any decade or longer duration. First, agriculture gave way to industrial jobs, which initially became more common in the latter half of the 19th century. By the 1920s, slightly more than half of all jobs outside agriculture were nonmanual, and the proportion of such nonmanual labor rose to more than 80% by the turn of the 21st century (U.S. Census Bureau, 2008). Although coarse classifications such as manual versus nonmanual only roughly capture the concept of worse-versus-better jobs, as illustrated by contrasting tool-and-die maker (i.e., manual) with food-service worker (i.e., nonmanual), an overall trend to work requiring more training and offering better working conditions and rewards becomes apparent.

Contrasts in rewards due to differences in occupation are not limited to earnings. Morbidity, liability to various causes of ill health, and increased early mortality vary sharply with social rank. Such health gradients are not only apparent within a given country but in comparisons among countries as well (Marmot & Wilkinson, 2006). Whether this is uniform or whether distinct patterns link components of rank, such as education or earnings, to different facets of health is likely to remain a lively source of controversy for the foreseeable future.

SEE ALSO Volume 2: *Careers; Employment, Adulthood; Gender in the Work Place; Military Service.*

BIBLIOGRAPHY

Acemoglu, D. (2003). Patterns of skill premia. *The Review of Economic Studies, 70*, 199–230.

Autour, D. H., Levy, F., & Murname, R. J. (2001). *The skill content of recent technological change: An empirical exploration* (NBER Working Paper Series). Cambridge, MA: National Bureau of Economic Research.

Bae, Y., Choy, S., Geddes, C., Sable, J., & Synder, T. (2000). Trends in educational equity of girls and women. *Educational Statistics Quarterly, 2*.

Bender, K. A., Donohue S. M., & Heywood, J. S. (2005). Job satisfaction and gender segregation. *Oxford Economic Papers, 57*, 479–496.

Bernhardt, A., Morris, M., Handcock, M. S., & Scott, M. A. (2001). *Divergent paths: Economic mobility in the new American labor market.* New York: Russell Sage Foundation.

Bianchi, S. M., Milkie, M. A., Sayer, L. C., & Robinson, J. P. (2000). Is anyone doing the housework? Trends in the gender division of household labor. *Social Forces, 79*, 191–228.

Blau, P. M., & Duncan, O. D. (1967). *The American occupational structure.* New York: John Wiley.

Bottero, W., & Prandy, K. (2003). Social interaction distance and stratification. *British Journal of Sociology, 54*, 177–197.

Conk, M. A. (1980). *The United States Census and the New Jersey urban occupational structure, 1870–1940.* Ann Arbor, MI: UMI Research Press.

Cotter, D. A., Hermsen J. M., Ovadia, S., & Vanneman, R. (2001). The glass ceiling effect. *Social Forces, 80*, 655–681.

Desrosiéres, A. (1998). *The politics of large numbers: A history of statistical reasoning.* Cambridge, MA: Harvard University Press.

Duncan, O. D. (1961). A socioeconomic index of all occupations. In A. Reiss (Ed.), *Occupations and social status* (pp. 109–138). New York: Free Press.

England, P., Allison, P., Wu, Y., & Ross, M. (2007). Does bad pay cause occupations to feminize, does feminization reduce pay, and how can we tell with longitudinal data? *Social Science Research, 36*, 1237–1256.

Hauser, R., & Featherman, D. (1977). *The process of stratification: Trends and analyses.* New York: Academic.

Hauser, R. M., & Warren, J. R. (1997). Socioeconomic indexes for occupations: A review, update, and critique. *Sociological Methodology, 27*, 177–298.

Jacobs, J. A. (1989). *Revolving doors: Sex segregation and women's careers.* Stanford, CA: Stanford University Press.

Jacobsen, J. P., & Levin, L. M. (1995). Effects of intermittent labor force attachment on women's earnings. *Monthly Labor Review, 118*, 14.

Levy, F., & Murnane, R. J. (1992). U.S. earnings levels and earnings inequality: A review of recent trends and proposed explanations. *Journal of Economic Literature, 30*, 1333–1381.

Marmot, M. G., & Wilkinson, R. G. (Eds.). (2006). *Social determinants of health* (2nd ed.). Oxford, U.K.: Oxford University Press.

Maume, D. J., Jr. (2004). Is the glass ceiling a unique form of inequality?: Evidence from a random-effects model of managerial attainment. *Work and Occupations, 31*, 250–274.

Nam, C., B., & Boyd, M. (2004). Occupational status in 2000; Over a century of census-based measurement. *Population Research and Policy Review, 23*, 327–358.

Nam, C. B., & Powers, M. G. (1983). *The socioeconomic approach to status measurement.* Houston, TX: Cap and Gown Press.

Neal, D. A., & Johnson, W. R. (1996). The role of premarket factors in Black–White wage differences. *Journal of Political Economy, 104*, 869.

Queneau, H. (2006). Is the long-term reduction in occupational sex segregation still continuing in the United States? *The Social Science Journal, 43*, 681–688.

Reskin, B. F., & Roos, P. A. (1990). *Job queues, gender queues: Explaining women's inroads into male occupations.* Philadelphia: Temple University Press.

Sewell, W. H., Hauser, R. M., Springer, K. W., & Hauser, T. S. (2003). As we age: A review of the Wisconsin Longitudinal Study, 1957–2001. *Research in Social Stratification and Mobility, 20*, 3–111.

Tomaskovic-Devey, D., Thomas, M., & Johnson, K. (2005). Race and the accumulation of human capital across the career: A theoretical model and fixed effects application. *American Journal of Sociology, 111*, 58–89.

Treiman, D. J. (1977). *Occupational prestige in comparative perspective.* New York: Academic Press.

Treiman, D. J., & Terrell, K. (1975). Sex and the process of status attainment: A comparison of working men and women. *American Sociological Review, 40*, 174–200.

U.S. Census Bureau. 2008. *Historical statistics.* Retrieved May 21, 2008, from http://www.census.gov/statab

Steven Rytina

P

PARENT–CHILD RELATIONSHIPS, ADULTHOOD

The relationship between parent and child is one of the most durable bonds in the family, usually lasting far beyond the offspring's childhood and ending only with the death of parent or child. Once a child reaches adulthood, relationships with his or her parents are no longer driven by the child's dependence and development. Scholars of the family are interested in the characteristics of adult parent–child relationships both because of their implications for individual well-being and because of what they suggest about the institution of the family.

With life expectancy almost doubling in length since the turn of the 20th century, children now commonly reach midlife, and not unusually old age, with at least one parent still alive. Although co-survival of generations may have expanded opportunities to exchange resources across generational lines, other trends, such as geographic mobility, weakening norms of responsibility, and the rise in divorce and remarriage rates, have possibly rendered these relationships less dependable than before.

THEORETICAL AND CONCEPTUAL MODELS

Several different models exist that deal with adult parent–child relationships, including the functionalist, intergenerational solidarity, intergenerational conflict and ambivalence, and intergenerational transfers perspectives.

Functionalist Perspective Early theories of adult parent–child relationships evolved from functionalist perspectives in the social sciences that viewed the unmooring of adults from their families of origin as necessary to societal modernization (Goode, 1963; Ogburn, 1932). In this line of reasoning, extended familism was considered incompatible with an increasingly technocratic and meritocratic society that required a trained, specialized, and geographically mobile labor force. Nuclear families needed to be free from the constraints of older generations to maximize their educational and occupational success and, by extension, the economic vitality of the nation (Parsons & Bales, 1955).

The next generation of theories proposed a more nuanced model. Research revealed that even as opportunities for frequent face-to-face interaction between generations were reduced, relatively rapid transportation and communication technologies allowed the maintenance of strong affective ties, in what came to be described as "intimacy at a distance" (Rosenmayer, 1968). This *modified-extended family* was considered to fit well with the demands of modern economies and served as a corrective to the isolated extended family as a normative family form (Shanas & Sussman, 1977).

During this period, several perspectives emerged to explain the behavior of parents and adult children toward each other. *Task-specific theory* (Litwak, 1985) proposed that adult children were better at performing some tasks than other relatives or friends. For instance, the theory predicted that older adults would receive long-term chronic care from nearby adult children but not from friends and neighbors. Children, unlike friends and neighbors, tend to have the level of commitment necessary to provide intensive care giving but also need to live close to the care recipient. The notion that adult children could relocate on an as-needed basis to meet the challenges of care giving highlighted the flexible nature of family arrangements. A competing theory, the *hierarchical compensatory model*, proposed that older adults turn to others for assistance in a hierarchy based on preferences. Spouses are at the top of the hierarchy, and adult children follow the spouse as preferred providers, but, if children are not available, then other relatives, friends, and finally formal services follow in rank order (Cantor, 1979). Both theories supported the notion that adult children were committed to ensuring the well-being of their older parents and that older parents preferred to rely on their children for help.

Intergenerational Solidarity Perspectives In the 1970s researchers turned toward codifying and classifying the nature of intergenerational relations. Borrowing in part from Emile Durkheim's (1858–1917) concept of social solidarity and Fritz Heider's (1958) and George Homans's (1950) theories of small-group cohesion, David Mangen, Vern Bengtson, and Pierre Landry Jr. (1988) developed the *intergenerational solidarity paradigm*. Both a conceptual scheme and a measurement model, the solidarity paradigm itemized the sentiments, behaviors, attitudes, values, and structural arrangements that bind generations together. Intergenerational solidarity was operationalized along seven dimensions: affectual solidarity (emotional closeness), associational solidarity (social interaction), structural solidarity (opportunity for interaction based mostly on geographic proximity), normative solidarity (filial obligation), consensual solidarity (perceived and actual agreement on values and opinions), and functional solidarity (provisions of material, instrumental, and social support).

Since its development, the solidarity paradigm has been the de facto gold standard for assessing the strength of intergenerational relationships both in the United States (e.g., Lawrence, Bennett, & Markides, 1992) and internationally (e.g., Lowenstein, Katz, & Daatland, 2005). However, research demonstrated that the separate dimensions of solidarity could not justifiably be added together to form a single measure of intergenerational solidarity (Roberts & Bengtson, 1990). More promising were approaches that were relationship centered rather than variable centered, which could group intergenerational relationships based on seemingly antithetical dimensions, such as being geographically distant but emotionally close (Silverstein, Bengtson, & Lawton, 1997).

Intergenerational Conflict and Ambivalence Perspectives Responding to criticism that the solidarity paradigm did not allow for negative emotions and behaviors, researchers subsequently added the dimension of conflict to the model (Clarke, Preston, Raksin, & Bengtson, 1999).

Indeed, challenges to the solidarity model came into high relief by scholars advancing *intergenerational ambivalence theory*, a perspective that focused on mixed feelings—the simultaneous occurrence of affection and hostility—that come from the tension between autonomy and dependence in intergenerational relationships. Although ambivalent feelings are obvious early in the family lifecycle (e.g., adolescents striving for independence), they are evident in older families as well (e.g., aging parents becoming dependent, adult children not living up to parental expectations; e.g., Pillemer & Suitor, 2002). Research has moved toward integrating the solidarity and ambivalence perspectives.

Intergenerational Transfers Perspective A different perspective on adult parent–child relationships is provided by research on intergenerational transfers, which is concerned with identifying motives for providing time and money resources to family members across generational lines. In this line of research, parents and their adult children are considered interdependent actors who provide for each other over the life course.

Findings that transfers tend to be targeted at children with the greatest need offer some evidence that older parents distribute resources altruistically. Research showed that adult children in the lowest income category were more than 50% more likely than those in the highest income category to receive a money transfer from their parents (McGarry & Schoeni, 1997). Similarly, older adults in European nations with relatively generous pension programs are more likely to provide economic transfers to needy children (e.g., Fritzell & Lennartsson, 2005).

Reciprocity has been a consistent theme in the study of adult parent–child relationships. This perspective maintains that the obligation to pay a debt is found in intergenerational family relations as well as market relations. In developed nations, the most commonly tested question is whether adult children who receive more money from their parents provide more instrumental support to them. Several investigations have shown such a pattern (e.g., Caputo, 2002), but others have not or have found substantively small effects (McGarry & Schoeni, 1997).

Several studies found that parents who in middle age provided financial assistance to their young-adult children were more likely to receive social support from them in old age (Silverstein, Conroy, Wang, Giarrusso, & Bengtson, 2002). The obligation to reciprocate is reinforced through norms and emotions; one study found that adult children who felt they owed their aging parents a debt of gratitude were more prolific providers of support to them (Ikkink, Van Tillburg, & Knipscheer, 1999).

It has long been known that the strength of emotional bonds between parents and children is positively correlated with the volume of intergenerational transfers between them (Rossi & Rossi, 1990; Silverstein, Parrott, & Bengtson, 1995). However, motives for transfers are often mixed and not easily distinguished. Transfers of money that stimulate time transfers from children (visiting, social support) may strengthen intergenerational attachment and prompt additional transfers (Attias-Donfut, 2000).

VARIATION IN ADULT PARENT–CHILD RELATIONSHIPS

Several factors have an influence on the nature of parent–child relationships, including family structure, ethnicity, and national contexts.

Family Structure As a result of historical increases in divorce and remarriage, the family has fragmented into myriad family forms that include complex configurations of step- and biological kin (Casper & Bianchi, 2002). Numerous studies have found that parental divorce suppresses transfers of money and time between parents and their adult biological children and that remarriage does the same between stepparents and their adult stepchildren (e.g., Furstenberg, Hoffman, & Shesthra, 1995; Pezzin & Schone, 1999; Silverstein et al., 1997). Divorce has been shown to disrupt transfers by weakening normative beliefs about intergenerational responsibility and by reducing opportunities for interaction and the development of emotional cohesion between generations. Incomplete bonding with a stepparent, competition with stepsiblings, conflict between custodial and noncustodial parents, and the absence of clear institutional rules for establishing normative expectations within stepfamilies conspire to put children at risk of having strained or distant relations with both step- and divorced biological parents (Furstenberg & Cherlin, 1991).

The impact of divorce on intergenerational transfers is greater for fathers, who are less likely than mothers to receive primary custody of their children and more likely to remarry and live with stepchildren. Research by Frank Furstenberg, Saul Hoffman, and Laura Shesthra (1995) suggested that lower levels of intergenerational support received by divorced fathers is not a function of the amount of child support they provided but of the diminished investments of time and emotion they made in their natural children when the children were growing up. Liliana Pezzin and Barbara Steinberg Schone (1999) found that fathers were less sensitive in responding to the needs of their stepchildren than they were to the needs of their biological children, concluding from this that altruism is less a potent social force toward children that fathers did not sire.

An alternative to the support deficit perspective is that marital disruption and remarriage, and the various family recombinations that result, have expanded the kin supply and increased the potential support portfolio of older adults by adding step-relatives to the family network. Taking these social changes into consideration has resulted in the need to develop new models of complex family forms. For instance, the *latent kin matrix* (Riley & Riley, 1993) brings to light how close intergenerational relations are culled from the pool of kin and nonkin associates but also emphasizes greater uncertainty in the stability of these more voluntary family ties.

Ethnic Variation Some scholars posit that elders from minority and traditional cultures have greater opportunities to exchange family support across generations (Angel & Angel, 2006). For example, African Americans are more likely than Whites to reside in extended family households, live close to relatives, and report having "fictive kin" (Chatters & Jayakody, 1995). Latinos also are more likely than Whites to reside in multigenerational households (Himes, Hogan, & Eggebeen, 1996). However, other evidence suggests that economic insufficiency in minority families may suppress their ability to deliver care despite stronger intentions to do so (Silverstein & Waite, 1993).

Older immigrants are more likely to live with kin than their native-born counterparts. This pattern is characteristic of immigrants worldwide. Judith Treas and Shampa Mazumdar (2004) pointed out several unique intergenerational challenges facing older immigrants. First, older immigrants are at elevated risk of social isolation as a result of their limited English proficiency and tendency to subordinate their own needs to those of their families. Second, older immigrants are expected to care for their grandchildren at an age when they are also likely to experience the need for care themselves. Third, they are often called on to sustain the cultural integrity of their native land while their adult children are acculturating into the host society. The popular image of immigrant elders contentedly embedded in family-based support networks is likely an oversimplification.

National Context Formal support mechanisms— government, voluntary organizations, and private enterprises—have become more important in serving the needs of older adults in developed countries. Research finds that the salience of intergenerational relations—as measured by proximity, frequency of contact, and provisions of support—tends to be weaker in nations with more generous public services and benefits to the elderly and less coercive family cultures.

A key question with respect to public policy is whether more liberal social benefits (a) "crowd out" intergenerational family transfers, (b) "crowd-in" intergenerational family transfers, or (c) complement intergenerational family transfers. Evidence shows some support for all three mechanisms (Künemund & Rein, 1999). One study, for instance, found that formal support reduced informal support among older Whites but not among older Blacks (Miner, 1995). However, another found no evidence that more extensive use of formal services was associated with less extensive informal care (Penning, 2002). Similarly, cross-societal research finds that welfare state services tend to be complementary with respect to family care (Attias-Donfut & Wolff, 2000). However, Gerdt Sundstrom, Lennarth Johansson, and Linda Hassing (2002) in an historical analysis found that newly instituted policies restricting eligibility of older adults for home help services in Sweden was followed by increases in family care, providing some evidence that the state had crowded-in adult children.

Complementarity appears to be less true for income transfers. Universal income maintenance programs effectively substitute for financial transfers from adult children, as there are relatively few older adults in need of transfers from children in modern welfare states (Lee, 2000). Net intergenerational financial transfers are decidedly downward—from older parent to adult children—as enabled by generous pension provisions (Fritzell & Lennartsson, 2005; Lowenstein et al., 2005).

In most developing nations, older adults rely almost exclusively on their families for needed support. Time-for-money exchanges between generations describe a common type of mutual aid in the less developed world, where older parents provide household labor and/or childcare services to the families of their adult children in exchange for money or food (Frankenberg, Lillard, & Willis, 2002). However, the primacy of intergenerational relations has declined in rapidly developing nations. In many East Asian nations, filial piety is said to have weakened, altering traditional expectations and social understandings between generations. In the least developed nations of sub-Saharan Africa, adult children have few resources to exchange with their parents and instead devote them mostly to their children, creating a crisis in the support systems of older adults (Aboderin, 2004).

FUTURE DIRECTIONS

Five themes emerge as fruitful directions for future research on adult intergenerational relationships. First, the gerontological implications of family change will soon come to fruition, as those in more complex, less traditional, and smaller families enter old age. How much older parents can rely on their children for support in these "new" family forms remains an open question. Second, increased longevity has verticalized multigenerational families, creating

the possibility that middle-aged individuals may need to support frail older parents, young adult children, and/or grandchildren at the same time. Those in the sandwich generation clearly face difficult challenges if they are simultaneously caring for older and younger generations. Third, the free flow of labor across national borders has made most European and North American nations more culturally heterogeneous. Understanding how immigrants and their descendants negotiate the normative constraints of their native cultures and the forces of assimilation will inform policy makers about the shifting terrain of family life for older and younger generations.

Fourth, public policies, particularly those related to pensions and other benefits will loom large for the well-being of the elderly and their descendants. Postponing age of eligibility for Social Security benefits and reducing the value of European pensions will lower standards of living for older generations and impede transfers received by younger generations. Studies of the impact of public policies on older persons and their family members must account for interdependence between generations. Finally, the concept of ambivalence has taken hold as one of several dominant paradigms guiding research on adult intergenerational relationships. Questions that remain to be answered include how ambivalence is psychologically and socially managed or resolved, how it changes over the life course and varies across social groupings, how emotional and structural ambivalence are connected, and whether ambivalence can be incorporated into the other conceptual models, such as solidarity, or whether it is a unique and independent aspect of intergenerational relations.

SEE ALSO Volume 1: *Parenting Style;* Volume 2: *Fatherhood; Motherhood; Noncustodial Parents; Social Networks; Social Support, Adulthood;* Volume 3: *Intergenerational Transfers.*

BIBLIOGRAPHY

Aboderin, I. (2004). Decline in material family support for older people in urban Ghana, Africa: Understanding processes and causes of change. *Journals of Gerontology: Series-B: Psychological Sciences and Social Sciences, 59B(3),* S128–S137.

Angel, R. J., & Angel, J. L. (2006). Diversity and aging in the United States. In R. L. Binstock & L. K. George (Eds.), *Handbook of aging and the social sciences* (6th ed., pp. 94–110). Amsterdam, the Netherlands: Elsevier.

Attias-Donfut, C. (2000). Cultural and economic transfers between generations: One aspect of age integration. *The Gerontologist, 40,* 270–272.

Attias-Donfut, C., & Wolff, F. (2000). Complementarity between private and public transfers. In S. Arber & C. Attias-Donfut (Eds.), *The myth of generational conflict: The family and state in ageing societies* (pp. 47–68). London: Routledge.

Cantor, M. (1979). Neighbors and friends: An overlooked resource in the informal support system. *Research on Aging, 1,* 434–463.

Caputo, R. K. (2002). Rational actors versus rational agents. *Journal of Family and Economic Issues, 23*, 27–50.

Casper, L. M., & Bianchi, S. (2002). *Continuity & change in the American family.* Thousand Oaks, CA: Sage Publications.

Chatters, L. M., & Jayakody, R. (1995). Commentary: Intergenerational support within African-American families: Concepts and methods. In V. L. Bengtson, K. W. Schaie, & L. M. Burton (Eds.), *Adult intergenerational relations: Effects of social change* (pp. 97–118). New York: Springer.

Clarke, E., Preston, M., Raksin, J., & Bengtson, V. L. (1999). Types of conflicts and tensions between older parents and adult children. *Gerontologist, 39*, 261–270.

Frankenberg, E., Lillard, L., & Willis, R. J. (2002). Patterns of intergenerational transfers in Southeast Asia. *Journal of Marriage and Family, 64*, 627–641.

Fritzell, J., & Lennartsson, C. (2005). Financial transfers between generations in Sweden. *Ageing & Society, 25*, 1–18.

Furstenberg, F., & Cherlin, A. (1991). *Divided families: What happens to children when parents part.* Cambridge, MA: Harvard University Press.

Furstenberg, F. F., Hoffman, S. D., & Shrestha, L. (1995). The effect of divorce on intergenerational transfers: New evidence. *Demography, 32*, 319–333.

Goode, W. J. (1963). *World revolution and family patterns.* New York: Free Press.

Heider, F. (1958). *The psychology of interpersonal relations.* New York: Wiley.

Himes, C. L., Hogan, D. P., & Eggebeen, D. J. (1996). Living arrangements of minority elders. *Journal of Gerontology: Social Sciences, 51B*, S42–S48.

Homans, G. C. (1950). *The human group.* New York: Harcourt, Brace and World.

Ikkink, K. K., Van Tilburg, T., & Knipscheer, K. (1999). Perceived instrumental support exchanges in relationships between elderly parents and their adult children: Normative and structural explanations. *Journal of Marriage and Family, 61*, 831–844.

Künemund, H., & Rein, M. (1999). There is more to receiving than needing: Theoretical arguments and empirical explorations of crowding in and crowding out. *Ageing and Society, 19*(1), 93–121.

Lee, R. D. (2000). Intergenerational transfers and the economic life cycle: A cross-cultural perspective. In A. Mason & G. Tapinos (Eds.), *Sharing the wealth: Demographic change and economic transfers between generations* (pp. 17–56). Oxford, U.K.: Oxford University Press.

Litwak, E. (1985). *Helping the elderly: The complementary roles of informal networks and formal systems.* New York: Guilford.

Lowenstein, A., Katz, R., & Daatland, S. O. (2005). Filial norms and intergenerational support in Europe and Israel: A comparative perspective. In M. Silverstein (Ed.), *Annual review of gerontology and geriatrics*, Vol. 24: *Intergenerational relations across time and place* (pp. 220–223). New York: Springer.

Mangen, D. J., Bengtson, V. L., & Landry, P. H. Jr. (Eds.). (1988). *Measurement of intergenerational relations.* Beverly Hills, CA: Sage Publications.

McGarry, K., & Schoeni, R. F. (1997). Transfer behavior within the family: Results from the Asset and Health Dynamics Study. *Journal of Gerontology, Series B: Psychological Sciences and Social Sciences, 52*, 82–92.

Miner, S. (1995). Racial differences in family support and formal service utilization among older persons: A nonrecursive model. *Journal of Gerontology, 50B*, S143–S153.

Ogburn, W. F. (1932). The family and its functions. In *Recent social trends.* New York: McGraw-Hill.

Parsons, T., & Bales, R. F. (1955). *Family, socialization and interaction process.* Glencoe, IL: The Free Press.

Penning, M. J. (2002). Hydra revisited: Substituting formal for self- and informal in-home care among older adults with disabilities. *The Gerontologist, 42*, 4–16.

Pezzin, L. E., & Schone, B. S. (1999). Parental marital disruption and intergenerational transfers: An analysis of lone elderly parents and their children. *Demography, 36*, 287–297.

Pillemer, K., & Suitor, J. J. (2002). Explaining mothers' ambivalence toward their adult children. *Journal of Marriage and Family, 64*, 602–613.

Riley, M. W., & Riley, J. W. Jr. (1993). Connections: Kin and cohort. In V. L. Bengtson & W. Andrew Achenbaum (Eds.), *The changing contract across generations* (pp. 169–190). Hawthorne, NY: Aldine de Gruyter.

Roberts, R. E. L., & Bengtson, V. L. (1990). Is intergenerational solidarity a unidimensional construct? A second test of a formal model. *Journal of Gerontology: Social Sciences, 45*, S12–S20.

Rosenmayer, L. (1968). Family relations of the elderly. *Journal of Marriage and Family, 30*, 672–680.

Rossi, A. S., & Rossi, P. H. (1990). *Of human bonding: Parent–children relationship across the life course.* New York: Aldine de Gruyter.

Shanas E., & Sussman, M. (1977). *Family, bureaucracy, and the elderly.* Durham, NC: Duke University Press.

Silverstein, M., Bengtson, V. L., & Lawton, L. (1997). Intergenerational solidarity and the structure of adult child–parent relationships in American families. *American Journal of Sociology, 103*, 429–460.

Silverstein, M., Conroy, S., Wang, H., Giarrusso, R., & Bengtson, V. (2002). Reciprocity in parent–child relations over the adult life course. *Journal of Gerontology: Social Sciences, 57B*, S3–S13.

Silverstein, M., Parrott, T. M., & Bengtson, V. L. (1995). Factors that predispose middle-aged sons and daughters to provide social support to older parents. *Journal of Marriage and Family, 57*, 465–475.

Silverstein, M., & Waite, L. (1993). Are Blacks more likely than Whites to receive and provide social support in middle and old age? Yes, no, and maybe so. *Journal of Gerontology: Social Sciences, 48*, S212–S222.

Sundstrom, G., Johansson, L., & Hassing, L. B. (2002). The shifting balance of long-term care in Sweden. *The Gerontologist, 42*, 350–355.

Treas, J., & Mazumdar, S. (2004). Kinkeeping and caregiving: Contributions of older people in immigrant families. *Journal of Comparative Family Studies 35*, 105–122.

Merril Silverstein

PARENTAL BEREAVEMENT

SEE Volume 2: *Midlife Crises and Transitions.*

PERSONALITY

Personality refers to relatively enduring individual differences in patterns of thoughts, feelings, and behavior. A classic definition of personality is provided by author Gordon Allport (1897–1967): "Personality is the dynamic organization within the individual of those psychophysical systems that determine [her or his] characteristic behavior and thought" (1961, p. 28). Embedded in Allport's definition are the ideas that (a) personality attributes are individual difference characteristics; (b) personality attributes partially reflect biological processes (i.e., psychophysical systems); and (c) personality attributes influence patterns of adjustment to the environment.

IDENTIFYING BASIC PERSONALITY TRAITS: THE BIG FIVE

A major task for personality scholars is to identify and classify the many possible personality attributes or traits. One starting point for this task is language itself. According to the *lexical hypothesis*, the most important personality attributes are reflected in the terms used to describe individuals. Using the logic of the lexical hypothesis, many personality psychologists believe that an analysis of how personality-related adjectives (e.g., calm, talkative, dominant, kind) cluster together might provide some insight into the number and nature of the basic units of personality.

In 1936 Allport and psychologist Henry Odbert (1909–1995) attempted to classify the personality trait names in the English language. Since that time, several researchers have engaged in this process, and there is now considerable agreement that five broad domains—the *Big Five*—capture many of the personality adjectives found in the English language. Each factor consists of a cluster of related characteristics: extraversion (traits such as being talkative and energetic); agreeableness (traits such as being cooperative and kind); conscientiousness (traits such as being responsible and dependable); neuroticism (traits such as being tense and nervous); and intellectual or openness to experience (traits such as being curious and artistic). Studies using languages other than English usually find similar dimensions. The exceptions are that an openness dimension sometimes does not appear distinctly in different languages, and that additional dimensions particular to a certain culture will sometimes appear. Nonetheless, the first four dimensions of the Big Five appear to be more or less robust across languages and thus cultures.

There is emerging (but not complete) consensus that the Big Five can serve as a reasonable working model of the basic dimensions of adult personality. Moreover, most of the Big Five traits are evident in adolescents and in children as young as age 5. (Openness, however, may not become clearly evident until late adolescence.) The Big Five also can organize the ways that psychologists have classified the individual differences that are evident in very young children (often called dimensions of temperament). This extension of the Big Five to the very youngest ages helps to focus attention on a core set of personality dimensions that are broadly relevant for functioning and adaptation across the life span.

THE ORIGINS OF PERSONALITY: GENETIC AND ENVIRONMENTAL FACTORS

Consistent with Allport's convictions about the biological basis of traits, researchers are interested in genetic influences on personality. Much of the evidence in support of this idea comes from studies examining personality similarity in twins. One approach is to compare the degree of similarity of identical twin pairs reared in the same household, with the degree of similarity of fraternal twin pairs reared in the same household. If identical twins are much more alike than fraternal twins, then researchers infer that genetic factors must account for some part of personality. This reasoning draws on the fact that identical twins share all of their genes, whereas fraternal twins share, on average, 50% of the same genes. Thus, because both types of twins are living in the same environment, the major explanation for any increased similarity in identical twins is their increased genetic similarity.

A few broad conclusions can be drawn from twin studies. In general, identical twins are more similar in terms of the Big Five than are fraternal twins. Likewise, the few studies that have been able to examine identical twins reared apart indicate that these twins are fairly similar in terms of their personality attributes in adulthood, despite growing up in different circumstances. Thus, genetic factors do account for personality differences between people. However, identical twins are not perfectly alike in terms of their personalities (regardless of where they were reared), indicating that non-genetic factors (called environmental factors in this context) also play an important role in shaping personality. Some examples of environmental factors may include early school experiences and experiences with peers; researchers are currently working to develop a precise understanding of the particular environmental factors that shape personality. In sum, twin studies underscore a point raised by Allport many years ago: "No feature of personality is devoid of both hereditary and environmental influence" (1961, p. 68).

THE DEVELOPMENT OF THE BIG FIVE IN ADULTHOOD

Research that suggests a genetic basis for the Big Five does not exclude the possibility that personality traits change with age or that personality traits can be affected by life experiences. The study of personality development attempts to answer these questions. Researchers examining questions about personality development ideally use longitudinal designs, in which the same group of individuals is followed over a long period of time and assessed repeatedly with the same personality measures. Most of this research is descriptive in that it attempts to quantify the degree of personality stability and change across the life span. A complication in such research is that there are several ways to conceptualize and measure stability. The two most commonly investigated questions have to do with *differential stability* and *absolute stability*.

Studies of differential stability evaluate whether the relative ordering of individuals on a Big Five attribute are consistent over time. A researcher who wants to evaluate the differential stability of extraversion, for example, might investigate whether individuals who are relatively extraverted compared to their peers in their 20s are also relatively extraverted compared to their peers in their 40s. Studies about absolute stability, by contrast, examine the *degree* of stability in the exact amount or level of a personality attribute over time. A researcher who wants to evaluate the absolute stability of extraversion might examine whether, on average, individuals are more extraverted in their 20s compared to their 40s. Alternatively, this researcher might want to know how many members of a sample increased in extraversion from their 20s to their 40s, compared to how many members decreased during that time. Although questions about differential and absolute stability are distinct, both are important questions about personality development.

Research on Differential Stability in Adulthood Differential stability is usually examined by calculating the correlation (a statistic that assesses the degree to which two variables are associated) between the same measures administered on different occasions to a sample followed across substantial intervals of time (e.g., 1 or more years). Because a sizable number of studies have evaluated differential stability, researchers have used a statistical technique called *meta-analysis* to summarize these results. Meta-analytic techniques allow researchers to essentially average results from all available information and then draw quantitative conclusions from an entire research literature.

One prominent meta-analysis summarized correlations from 152 longitudinal studies. The general result was that the Big Five traits showed increasing differential stability with age. Specifically, there was a fairly modest amount of differential stability when individuals were followed during their early childhood years, whereas there was a very strong amount of differential stability when individuals were followed in their 50s

and older. This pattern of differential stability was basically the same for all Big Five traits, and there was little evidence of gender differences in differential stability.

These meta-analytic findings are noteworthy because they confirm that the Big Five traits are relatively enduring characteristics by the time a person reaches adulthood. The current explanation for increasing differential stability with age is that adulthood is a time in the life span when maturational changes are reduced, social roles stabilize, environmental changes are increasingly subject to individual control, and individuals have a more stable sense of self. These conditions tend to promote stability. Even so, the meta-analytic findings also indicate that there is never a time in the life span when personality is set in stone. This seems to contradict a suggestion by the American psychologist William James (1842–1910), who said that personality is "set like plaster" by the age of 30. The Big Five traits do become increasingly stable after age 30; however, there does not appear to be a point when personality is fixed for all people.

Research on Absolute Stability in Adulthood Research on this topic has generally focused on comparing mean levels of traits measured at different ages. In others words, much of this research is useful for answering questions about whether there are differences in average scores on measures of the Big Five for 20-year-olds compared to 40-year-olds. Across studies and meta-analytic results, it appears that average levels of agreeableness and conscientiousness increase with age, whereas average levels of extraversion, neuroticism, and openness decline. Many of the absolute changes in the Big Five tend to be small and gradual when viewed as year-to-year comparisons.

The absolute changes in the Big Five tend to reflect increases in personal qualities that help individuals meet the demands of the adult roles of worker, committed romantic partner, and parent. This trend has been labeled the maturity principle of personality development (i.e., there is increased personality maturity with age). Young adulthood (i.e., the years between the late teens and late 20s) is a time when many absolute changes in personality occur. This is also a time in the life span when individuals gradually start to assume the roles of worker, partner, and parent. Thus, the average absolute changes in the Big Five seem to match the demands of the life course. This finding raises important, but mostly unanswered, questions about the causal connections between adult roles and personality change. For example, it might be the case that assuming the role of a worker or a committed romantic partner creates increases in conscientiousness.

PERSONALITY AND LIFE OUTCOMES

Allport noted that, "personality *is* something and *does* something" (1961, p. 29). Literally hundreds of studies link personality to life outcomes. Fortunately, a number of meta-analyses on these topics provide some of the best evidence that personality differences are associated with important life outcomes, including longevity and health behaviors; crime and aggression; relationship satisfaction and stability; achievement-related outcomes; and overall life satisfaction.

Longevity and Health A life outcome of great importance to individuals and society is longevity. A striking example linking personality with mortality comes from an analysis that followed a group of more than 1,200 individuals from the 1920s through the mid-1980s who were mostly middle class. Study participants who were rated by their parents and teachers as more prudent and conscientious when they were children tended to live longer than participants who were rated as less conscientious. Indeed, conscientiousness appears to be the strongest Big Five personality predictor of longevity based on one meta-analysis and review (Roberts, Kuncel, Shiner, Caspi, & Goldberg, 2007). This report also summarized evidence indicating that people with personality characteristics such as high levels of agreeableness, high levels of extraversion, and low levels of neuroticism lived longer lives.

One potential explanation for the association between conscientiousness and longevity is that conscientiousness statistically predicts many of the behaviors that either promote or hinder physical health. One meta-analysis summarized the results of more than 190 studies on this topic (Bogg & Roberts, 2004). Conscientiousness was negatively associated (i.e., as scores on this trait increased, these behaviors decreased) with drug, alcohol, and tobacco use; risky sexual activity; unsafe driving practices; suicidal ideation; and involvement in violence. As conscientiousness increased, involvement in these sorts of behaviors decreased.

Crime, Delinquency, and Antisocial Behavior Crime and antisocial behavior have enormous consequences for society. One meta-analysis examined the association between personality and crime (Miller & Lynam, 2001). Agreeableness and conscientiousness were negatively associated with antisocial behavior (i.e., as scores on these traits increased, antisocial behavior decreased), and similar results were obtained when researchers examined links between antisocial behavior and comparable traits from other personality models. In short, individuals who engage in criminal behavior tend to

be antagonistic to others and to lack the ability to control impulses or otherwise delay gratification.

Relationship Outcomes Close relationships are valued by most adults, and consistent evidence links personality with relationship satisfaction and stability. One meta-analysis found that neuroticism was negatively associated with marital satisfaction (Heller, Watson, & Ilies, 2004). Agreeableness was positively associated with marital satisfaction, although that relation was examined in 19 studies compared to the 40 studies that examined neuroticism. In fact, there were detectable associations between personality and marital satisfaction for the other Big Five traits, with perhaps the exception of openness. In terms of predictors of divorce, one meta-analysis reported that high levels of neuroticism combined with low levels of agreeableness and conscientiousness were associated with an increased risk for divorce (Roberts, Kuncel, Shiner, Caspi, & Goldberg, 2007). These three individual personality effects were each stronger than the association between socioeconomic status and risk for divorce.

Achievement and Work Outcomes Applied psychologists and organizational scholars have had long-standing interest in the connection between personality and job performance. Meta-analytic findings suggest that conscientiousness is the best overall predictor of job performance out of the Big Five dimensions. Consistent with the effects of conscientiousness on job performance, a series of studies were conducted finding that conscientiousness predicted college grade point average (GPA) even when accounting for achievement test scores such as the Scholastic Aptitude Test (SAT) (Noftle & Robins, 2007). Thus, conscientiousness appears to be a robust predictor of achievement-related outcomes. Personality traits also are associated with ratings of job satisfaction. In particular, low levels of neuroticism and high levels of extraversion are related to job satisfaction, according to a meta-analytic review; however, there are also indications that conscientiousness is also positively associated with job satisfaction.

Life Satisfaction Some people are happier and more satisfied with their lives than others, and these life satisfaction judgments are related to personality dimensions. One meta-analysis from 19 studies involving more than 12,000 participants concluded that all Big Five traits except for openness were related to life satisfaction (Heller, Watson, & Iles, 2004). The strongest predictor was a low level of neuroticism, whereas extraversion, agreeableness, and conscientiousness were all positively related to life satisfaction at about the same degree. In short, personality traits may partially explain why some people are happier with their lives than others.

FUTURE DIRECTIONS FOR RESEARCH

Personality research is an active area that intersects with many disciplines. A considerable amount is known about the structure, development, and correlates of personality traits in adulthood. However, personality is also a contentious research area that can ignite vigorous debates and disagreements. For example, some researchers favor models of personality structure other than the Big Five. In response, other researchers note that the Big Five enjoys a level of support currently unmatched by any other competing model. Some of the debates in personality simply have to do with the topic itself. Personality covers human individuality, and there are always exceptions to every generalization. Thus, there is a wellspring of material for contrary arguments by critics. At the same time, some of the debates in personality psychology occur because the subject raises so many questions that have yet to be fully answered.

Three issues stand out as important directions for future research. First, there will be continued interest in the neurological systems, brain structures, and specific genes that underlie the Big Five. For instance, theoretical and empirical work traces extraversion and its childhood analogues to a biological system that govern one's sensitivity to rewards or incentives. There is also considerable interest in identifying specific genes associated with personality characteristics, and in studying precisely how genes interact with life events to shape life outcomes. All told, future work will continue to evaluate how biological processes and life events work together to shape personality. Research that ignores either of these two major factors will become increasingly less informative.

Second, there will be continued efforts to understand adult personality development. For instance, there is a debate between proponents of the *intrinsic maturational* perspective and proponents of the *social investment* perspective. The intrinsic maturational perspective argues that changes in personality are driven by biological processes, such as changes in the prefrontal lobes of the brain that might lead to increases in conscientiousness in young adulthood. The social investment perspective, by contrast, posits that changes in adult personality are related to involvement in or anticipation of particular roles such as committed romantic partner, worker, and parent. According to the social investment perspective, personality changes are generated by life experiences such as the birth of a child and involvement in steady and satisfying employment, which, for example, may create demands for increased conscientiousness. Future research will determine the level of support for the intrinsic maturation and social investment perspectives, and it is likely that aspects of both perspectives have some merit.

Third, future investigators will strive to identify the processes that link personality to life outcomes. It seems likely that multiple mechanisms will be involved for each broad association. For instance, several potential processes may explain why personality is correlated with job performance. Some mechanisms may involve direct effects, whereby certain people simply perform tasks better than others or have fewer conflicts with coworkers because of their personalities. However, additional and more subtle processes may play out over the life course. For instance, more conscientious individuals might select certain educational or career paths, and conversely, gatekeepers such as employers or college admissions boards might select people based on their personality attributes or motivational tendencies as evidenced in application materials. Nonetheless, involvement in these particular settings may further accentuate conscientiousness and thus promote job performance. Thus, ongoing transactions between social selection and social influence may ultimately help explain the links between personality and life outcomes.

All in all, personality is an active and contentious specialty area in the social and behavioral sciences. Personality is a fertile meeting place of insights from biology, psychology, and sociology, which makes it a vibrant and exciting topic. Despite many unanswered questions, it is clear that personality "is something that does something" when it comes to understanding adaptation across the life span.

SEE ALSO Volume 1: *Identity Development;* Volume 2: *Genetic Influence, Adulthood;* Volume 3: *Self.*

BIBLIOGRAPHY

Allport, G. W. (1961). *Pattern and growth in personality.* New York: Holt, Rinehart, and Winston.

Allport, G. W., & Odbert, H. S. (1936). Trait-Names: A psycholexical study. *Psychological Monographs, 47,* 1–171.

Barrick, M. R., Mount, M. K., & Judge, T. A. (2001). Personality and performance at the beginning of the new millennium: What do we know and where do we go next? *International Journal of Selection and Assessment, 9*(1–2), 9–30.

Block, J. (1995). A contrarian view of the five-factor approach to personality description. *Psychological Bulletin, 117*(2), 187–215.

Bogg, T., & Roberts, B. W. (2004). Conscientiousness and health-related behaviors: A meta-analysis of the leading behavioral contributors to mortality. *Psychological Bulletin, 130*(6), 887–919.

Bouchard, T. J., Jr. (2004). Genetic influences on human psychological traits. *Current Directions in Psychological Science, 13*(4), 148–151.

Caspi, A., Roberts, B. W., & Shiner, R. L. (2005). Personality development: Stability and change. *Annual Review of Psychology, 56,* 453–484.

Costa, P. T., Jr., & McCrae, R. R. (2006). Age changes in personality and their origins: Comment on Roberts, Walton, and Viechtbauer. *Psychological Bulletin, 132*(1), 26–28.

Funder, D. C. (1991). Global traits: A neo-Allportian approach to personality. *Psychological Science, 2,* 31–39.

Goldberg, L. R. (1993). The structure of phenotypic personality traits. *American Psychologist, 48,* 26–34.

Heller, D., Watson, D., & Ilies, R. (2004). The role of the person versus the situation in life satisfaction: A critical examination. *Psychological Bulletin, 130*(4), 574–600.

John, O. P. (2008). The Big Five trait taxonomy: History, measurement, and theoretical perspectives. In O. P. John, R. W. Robins, and L. A. Pervin (Eds.), *Handbook of personality: Theory and research* (3rd ed.). New York: Guilford Press.

Krueger, R. F., Caspi, A., & Moffitt, T. E. (2000). Epidemiological personology: The unifying role of personality in population-based research on problem behaviors. *Journal of Personality, 68,* 967–998.

Markon, K. E., Krueger, R. F., & Watson, D. (2005). Delineating the structure of normal and abnormal personality: An integrative hierarchical approach. *Journal of Personality and Social Psychology, 88*(1), 139–157.

McAdams, D. P. (1995). What do we know when we know a person? *Journal of Personality, 63*(3), 365–396.

McCrae, R. R., & Costa, P. T., Jr. (2003). *Personality in adulthood: A five-factor theory perspective.* New York: Guilford Press.

Miller, J. D., & Lynam, D. (2001). Structural models of personality and their relation to antisocial behavior: A meta-analytic review. *Criminology, 39*(4), 765–798.

Mischel, W. (2004). Toward an integrative science of the person. *Annual Review of Psychology, 55,* 1–22.

Noftle, E. E., & Robins, R. W. (2007). Personality predictors of academic outcomes: Big five correlates of GPA and SAT scores. *Journal of Personality and Social Psychology, 93,* 116–130.

Ozer, D. J., & Benet-Martínez, V. (2006). Personality and the prediction of consequential outcomes. *Annual Review of Psychology, 57*(1), 401–421.

Roberts, B. W., Kuncel, N. R., Shiner, R., Caspi, A., & Goldberg, L. R. (2007). The power of personality: The comparative validity of personality traits, socioeconomic status, and cognitive ability for predicting important life outcomes. *Perspectives on Psychological Science, 2*(4), 313–345.

Roberts, B. W., Wood, D., & Caspi, A. (2008). The development of personality traits in adulthood. In O. P. John, R. W. Robins, and L. A. Pervin (Eds.), *Handbook of personality: Theory and research* (3rd ed.). New York: Guilford Press.

Robins, R. W., Fraley, R. C., & Krueger, R. F. (Eds.). (2007). *Handbook of research methods in personality psychology.* New York: Guilford Press.

Steel, P., Schmidt, J., & Shultz, J. (2008). Refining the relationship between personality and subjective well-being. *Psychological Bulletin, 134*(1), 138–161.

Wiggins, J. S. (2003). *Paradigms of personality assessment.* New York: Guilford Press.

M. Brent Donnellan

POLICY, EMPLOYMENT

Employment policy shapes people's work lives and thus a diverse range of life course outcomes. Along with economic factors such as unemployment rates or industrial trends, policies set the context in which people's work lives unfold by regulating certain aspects of employment and attempting to fix perceived injustices. Employment policies may also involve direct interventions in one's labor market experiences, such as opening career doors to a member of a subgroup who had once been denied entry to a job. It can also refer to macroeconomic policies designed to foster desired conditions for all individuals in a society. Traditionally, employment policies focused on unemployment, often involving financial programs to support individuals during times of job loss.

Although smoothing the transition between employment and nonemployment remains a central goal of some employment policies, policy makers have come to recognize and address other forms of transition that have both short- and long-term consequences for individual well-being. Among the wide range of transitions encompassed by employment policies are (a) ensuring that schools and postschool forms of education prepare younger people adequately for the world of work; (b) enabling workers to manage the simultaneous demands of employment with domestic responsibilities, such as child care or elder care; and (c) easing the transition for older people from employment into retirement through pension policies.

Governments enact employment policies to ensure that the law enforces employment practices that mesh with societal-level values such as equality of opportunity. Specific polices encompass gender equality in terms of income and access to specific occupations, equal access to employment for groups traditionally excluded from particular paid forms of employment, and the protection of workers' health and well-being. An important goal of most employment policies is to eliminate discrimination from the workplace. (To discriminate against someone means to treat that person differently, or less favorably.) Individual employees can be discriminated against by coworkers, managers, or business owners.

The employment policies enforced by different governments (including the United States in particular) are put in place to protect individuals against employment discrimination when it involves (a) unfair treatment because of race, religion, sex (including pregnancy), national origin, disability, or age; (b) harassment by managers, coworkers, or others in the workplace because of one's race, religion, sex (including pregnancy), national origin, disability, or age; (c) denial of a reasonable workplace because of religious beliefs or disability; and (d) retaliation from employers because of worker complaints about job discrimination.

When looking at specific policies, one can see what potentially sweeping impacts they have on both the immediate and future life experiences of workers. The following two examples of the Equal Pay Act (EPA) and affirmative action are indicative of employment policies that seek to minimize disadvantages experienced on the basis of race, class, gender, or religion that historically have impeded one's occupational trajectories over the life course.

THE AMERICAN EQUAL PAY ACT

In 1963 the U.S. Congress (under President John F. Kennedy [1917–1963]) passed the EPA to prohibit discrimination on account of gender in the payment of wages by employers. Within the text of the EPA, Congress included a clear and concise policy statement that briefly described the problems it intended to remedy. The clear statement of congressional intent and policy guiding the EPA's enactment was indicative of the congressional desire to fashion a broad remedial framework to protect employees from wage discrimination on the basis of gender. The Supreme Court has expressly recognized the view that the EPA must be broadly construed to achieve the congressional goal of remedying gender discrimination. Congress passed the EPA out of "concern for the weaker bargaining position of women," as a way to provide a remedy to discriminatory wage structures that reflect "an ancient but outmoded belief that a man, because of his role in society, should be paid more than a woman." The EPA protects both men and women. It also protects administrative, professional, and executive employees who are exempt under the Fair Labor Standards Act.

The EPA is the first law to suggest that the pay of women should be equal to men when their positions are equal. The purpose of the EPA is to secure equal pay for women who have jobs similar to men and to seek to eliminate discrimination and the depressing effects on living standards caused by reduced wages for female workers. Although sources indicate that women's pay is still approximately 25% less than men's pay even in 2008, the EPA is still considered one of the best attempts to help close the gap. At the same time, the EPA has one major practical limitation: It requires that men and women be given equal pay for equal work, yet in practice men and women are rarely employed in the same occupations.

The EPA states that employers may not pay unequal wages to men and women who perform jobs that require equal skill, effort, and responsibility and that are performed under similar working conditions within the same establishment. Among the criteria used to gauge equality are skills required for the job, amount of physical and mental exertion required on the job, degree of accountability required of workers, and physical work conditions such as workplace health hazards.

Despite the establishment of such equal pay policies, gender gaps in earnings persist in the United States and have important implications of gender equality over the life course. For example, there is a 17% gap between men's and women's pay for full-time work in the United States with a woman earning, on average, $80 for every $100 a man earns (Powell, 2006). When accumulated over the life course, these earnings gaps contribute to vast economic disparities in later life. In the United States, women comprise 59% of those age 65 and over; they account for 72% of the older poor (Powell, 2006). Older women's average income is roughly 50% lower than that of their male peers. These disadvantages are particularly pronounced for African American women; in 1990, a stunning 82% of older Black women were classified as poor or "near poor" (Powell, 2006). The case of race and gender disparities clearly illustrates how employment policies targeted toward young or working-age populations have implications for one's well-being over the life course.

AFFIRMATIVE ACTION

A second key theme of employment policy relates to affirmative action. This can be defined as positive steps taken to increase the representation of women and ethnic minorities in areas of employment, education, and business from which they have been historically excluded.

In the United States, the effort to improve the employment and educational opportunities of women and members of minority groups has taken the form of preferential treatment in job hiring, college admissions, the awarding of government contracts, and the allocation of other social benefits. First undertaken at the federal level following the passage of the landmark Civil Rights Act of 1964, affirmative action was designed to counteract the lingering effects of discrimination that had taken place throughout history. The main criteria for inclusion in affirmative action programs are race, sex, ethnic origin, religion, disability, and age. The policy was implemented by federal agencies enforcing the Civil Rights Act of 1964 and two executive orders, which provided that government contractors and educational institutions receiving federal funds develop such programs. The Equal Employment Opportunities Act (1972) set up a commission to enforce such plans.

The establishment of racial quotas in the name of affirmative action brought charges of so-called reverse discrimination in the late 1970s. The U.S. Supreme Court placed important limitations on affirmative action programs in a 1978 ruling (*Regents of the University of*

California v. Bakke). Although the Court accepted such an argument in *Regents of the University of California v. Bakke*, it let existing programs stand and approved the use of quotas in 1979 in a case involving voluntary affirmative action programs in unions and private businesses.

In the 1980s the federal government's role in affirmative action was considerably diluted. In three cases in 1989, the Supreme Court undercut court-approved affirmative action plans by giving greater standing to claims of reverse discrimination, voiding the use of minority set-asides where past discrimination against minority contractors was unproven, and restricting the use of statistics to prove discrimination, because statistics did not prove intent.

The Civil Rights Act of 1991 reaffirmed the federal government's commitment to affirmative action. In the late 1990s, however, in a public backlash against perceived reverse discrimination, California and other states banned the use of race- and sex-based preferences in state and local programs. Several subsequent Supreme Court decisions (e.g., *Adarand Constructors v. Pena* in 1995 and *Hopwood v. Texas* in 1996) imposed further restrictions. A 1995 Supreme Court decision placed limits on the use of race in awarding government contracts; the affected government programs were revamped in the late 1990s to encompass any person who was "socially disadvantaged." In 1996 California voters passed Proposition 209, which prohibited government agencies and institutions from discriminating against or giving preferential treatment to individuals or groups on the basis of race, sex, color, ethnicity, or national origin. Similar measures were subsequently passed in other states. In 2003, in two landmark Supreme Court rulings involving admission to the University of Michigan and its law school, the U.S. Supreme Court reaffirmed the constitutionality of affirmative action but ruled that race could not be the preeminent factor in such decisions.

The effectiveness of affirmative action programs has been widely debated. Conservative scholar and writer Thomas Sowell (2004) asserted that affirmative action policies have not worked. Sowell argued that such programs encourage "nonpreferred" groups to designate themselves as members of "preferred" groups (i.e., primary beneficiaries of affirmative action) in order to take advantage of group preference policies. Further, he argued that such policies tend to benefit primarily the most fortunate among the preferred group (e.g., wealthy Blacks), often to the detriment of the least fortunate among the nonpreferred groups (e.g., poor Whites).

Sowell (2004) further suggested that affirmative action programs reduce the incentives of both the preferred and nonpreferred to perform their best—the former because doing so is unnecessary and the latter because it can prove futile—thereby resulting in net losses for society as a whole. Controversially, Sowell suggested these programs engender animosity toward preferred groups as well as on the part of preferred groups themselves, whose main problem in some cases has been their own inadequacy combined with their resentment of nonpreferred groups who—without preferences—consistently outperform them.

However, the majority of social scientists conducting research point to evidence showing that affirmative action opens professional and educational doors to persons who have historically lacked access to such opportunities. In doing so, these programs allow individuals to explore their untapped talents. Yet society also benefits, by fostering and ultimately utilizing the talents of all persons—regardless of their gender or racial and ethnic background.

The extent to which affirmative action has expanded minority employment in skilled positions is clear (Estes, Biggs, & Phillipson, 2003). The female-to-male ratio of earnings of full-time, year-round workers was roughly stable at around 60% from the early 1900s until the mid 1970s. In 1993 earnings of women who worked full-time, year-round had risen to 72% as much as men. After adjusting for differences in education, experience, and other factors, the wage gap is reduced by about half (i.e., the adjusted ratio is approximately 85; Powell, 2005). An increase in women's work experience and a shift into higher-wage occupations are the major causes of their improved economic position relative to men. The decline in higher-paying manufacturing jobs, which is partly responsible for the decline in the earnings of less-skilled men, has also contributed to the narrowing of the male-female wage gap. Nevertheless, a substantial part of the improved earnings of women cannot be explained by these factors and probably reflects positively how well affirmative action is working (Estes et al., 2003).

Scholars also argue that affirmative action is still needed, yet they also recognize the difficulty in proving beyond a doubt that a worker is the target of unfair or discriminatory practices. Psychological research documents that almost all people have trouble detecting a pattern of discrimination unless they are faced with a blatant example or have access to aggregated data documenting discrimination (Dixon & Rosenbaum, 2004). Affirmative action programs call for the collection of clear data on racial and gendered patterns of hiring and promotion, among other information. These aggregated data, in turn, can help decision makers to avoid or correct imbalances before they become widespread or harmful.

These data are particularly important because it is difficult to document that discrimination is occurring simply by looking at statistics showing that women or ethnic minorities have a poorer quality job or lower earnings than their male and White peers, respectively. For example, Joseph LeFevre (2003) argued that a large proportion of minorities and women are locked into low-wage and low-prestige jobs, yet he attributed this over-representation to a factor other than discrimination: LeFevre reasoned that these two groups have been disproportionately affected by current trends in workforce downsizing. Service-oriented industries disproportionately employ women and minorities, and these industries are particularly susceptible to downsizings and undesirable working and pay conditions. However, many employment policies—taken together—do aim to ensure equality of opportunity and, ultimately, equality of outcome for all workers.

FUTURE IMPLICATIONS OF EMPLOYMENT POLICY

Achieving a balance between economic efficiency and social equity is the ultimate goal of employment policy. Policies are intended to meet the needs of the employers by maintaining economic efficiency yet at the same time must also contribute to social equity by providing workers with fair and equitable benefits so that they can fund and enjoy healthy living. Employment policies also affect adults even after they have exited the workforce and enter retirement. Chris Phillipson (1998) observed that the retirement experience is linked to the timing of economic reduction of wages and that enforced withdrawal from work has made many older people in the United States financially insecure.

It could be argued that the biggest issue affecting employment policy may not come from the nation-state or their policy makers but from global forces. Globalization has created economic conditions that both hinder and facilitate the implementation of employment policies, thus transcending the power of the nation-state (Estes et al., 2003). Phillipson (1998) has noted four ways that globalization shapes both the need for and content of nation-states' employment policy. First, international competition, typically from newly industrialized countries, will cause unemployment growth and increased wage disparity for unskilled workers in industrialized countries. Low-cost imports from low-wage countries exert pressure on the manufacturing sector in industrialized countries, and foreign direct investment is attracted away from the industrialized nations toward low-waged countries. Second, economic liberalization may result in increased unemployment and wage inequality in developing countries. This happens as job losses in uncompetitive industries outstrip job opportunities in new industries. Third, workers may be forced to accept worsening wages

and work conditions, as a global labor market results in a "race to the bottom" (Phillipson, 1998). Finally, globalization reduces the level of autonomy exercised by the nation-state. The reach of globalization is expansive, and virtually no worker is untouched. For example, in industrialized countries, an estimated 70% of workers are employed in the service sector. Ultimately this is a result of changes and trends of employment, an evolving workforce, and globalization that is represented by a more skilled and increasingly more diverse labor force, which is growing in nonstandard forms of employment policy and practice (Phillipson, 1998).

SEE ALSO Volume 2: *Careers; Employment, Adulthood; Racism/Race Discrimination; Sexism/Sex Discrimination;* Volume 3: *Ageism/Age Discrimination.*

BIBLIOGRAPHY

Arber, S., & Ginn, J. (1995). *Connecting gender and ageing: A sociological approach.* Philadelphia: Open University Press.

Dixon, J. C., & Rosenbaum, M. (2004). Nice to know you? Testing contact, cultural, and group threat theories of anti-Black and anti-Hispanic stereotypes. *Social Science Quarterly, 85*(2), 257–280.

Espenshade, T., & Chang C. (2005). The opportunity cost of admission preferences at elite universities. *Social Science Quarterly, 86*(2), 293–305.

Estes, C., Biggs, S., & Phillipson, C. (2003). *Social policy, social theory, and ageing.* London: Open University Press.

Giddens, A. (1993). *Sociology.* Cambridge, U.K.: Polity Press.

LeFevre, J. (2003). The value of diversity: A justification of affirmative action. *Journal of Social Philosophy, 34*(1), 125–133.

Phillipson, C. (1998). *Reconstructing old age: New agendas in social theory and practice.* London: Sage.

Powell, J. (2006). *Rethinking social theory and later life.* New York: Nova Science.

Sander, R. (2004). A systemic analysis of affirmative action in American law schools. *Stanford Law Review, 57,* 367.

Sowell, T. (2004). *Affirmative action around the world: An empirical study.* New Haven, CT: Yale University Press.

Jason L. Powell

POLICY, FAMILY

The goal of family policy is to promote the well-being of families (Zimmerman, 2001). At a minimum, family policy is targeted explicitly at the formation and structure of families (e.g., laws concerning adoption or divorce), family rights, and the functioning and well-being of families. However, because many policies not designed to overtly target families ultimately have implications for families, family policy may be conceptualized in broader terms (Zimmerman, 2001). For this reason, family policy is sometimes considered a policy perspective instead of a specific type of policy (Bogenschneider, 2002). Family policy is pertinent to family members of all stages of the life course (e.g., children, parents, aging and elderly parents) and, as discussed later in this entry, may have important ramifications for a person's progression through his or her life course.

Because of changes in the economy and both family structure and process since the late 1960s, policies aimed at supporting working families and facilitating parents' employment are particularly important in the United States. These work–family policies include federal, state, and local government policies and employers' "family-friendly" policies. The focus here is on the former, specifically federal work–family policies. This review of federal work–family policies emphasizes policies attentive to parents and children, but many of the policies also pertain to elderly parents, sick relatives, and dependents in general.

TYPES OF WORK–FAMILY POLICIES IN THE UNITED STATES

Government work–family policies include family leaves providing employees time off from work for caregiving, publicly supported childcare programs, other forms of support for child and dependent care (e.g., tax breaks), and regulation of work time and work arrangements (Kelly, 2006; Smolensky & Gootman, 2003). Scholars have documented how few policies the United States has in place, particularly in contrast to European countries (e.g., Gornick & Meyers, 2003). Nonetheless, although U.S. policy is relatively limited in this regard, several features of its current work–family policy landscape are important and noteworthy.

FAMILY AND MEDICAL LEAVE

In 1993 the Family and Medical Leave Act (FMLA) was signed into law by President William J. Clinton, following years of Congressional debate and two vetoes by President George H. W. Bush (Elving, 1995). The law requires employers to allow employees (both men and women) to take up to 12 weeks of unpaid leave to recover from their own serious illness or to care for a baby, a newly adopted child, or a seriously ill relative. The law applies to work establishments with at least 50 workers at one site (or within a 75-mile radius), and only employees working at least 1,250 hours over the past year are eligible for FMLA leaves.

Prior to the FMLA, temporary disability insurance policies in some states afforded some mothers partially paid leaves when they were physically recovering from pregnancy and birth; feminists disagreed on whether to pursue maternity leave through sex discrimination

claims, which relied on an analogy between pregnancy and other disabilities, or to advocate for maternity leave on the basis of a mother's need to care for her infant (Williams, 2000). This came to be known as a debate between equal or special treatment strategies. These temporary disability insurance policies remain an option for mothers who are covered by such a plan (Kelly & Dobbin, 1999; Smolensky & Gootman, 2003). Advocates considered the FMLA groundbreaking, however, because it improved job security for employees facing demanding health and caregiving situations and recognized both women's and men's caregiving. Nonetheless, the FMLA has significant limitations.

First, the FMLA does not cover all work establishments and employees. Only 11% of U.S. work establishments are estimated to fall under the FMLA; these establishments, however, employ just over half of the total workforce (Cantor et al., 2001). To help address this shortcoming, legislation in a subset of states extends FMLA's coverage to establishments with fewer than 50 employees (Institute for Women's Policy Research, 2007).

Another concern is that FMLA leaves are unpaid, which reduces the usefulness and value of the law for some workers. Research has shown that the majority of employees in need of a leave cannot afford to go without the pay, and among those who take a leave, a portion have to truncate their leave because of financial constraints (Cantor et al., 2001). Scholars also have raised concerns about the implications of unpaid leave for gender equity because men in general are less likely to take unpaid leave (Kelly, 2006). One state, California, offers its residents a paid family leave program, providing partial paid leave (up to 55% of wages) to an employee for up to 6 weeks to care for a newborn, a newly adopted child, or an ill family member. The benefit is funded through a payroll tax paid by employees contributing to the state's disability program (California Employment Development Department, 2005).

A final limitation to the FMLA concerns employer compliance with the federal law (Albiston, 2005; Kelly, 2004). Employers may violate FMLA's requirements by not allowing an employee to take the full 12 weeks of leave or by not fully or clearly disclosing employees' rights under the law. An employer also may fail to maintain an employee's health insurance coverage during a leave or may somehow penalize workers following a leave. Kelly's 1997 survey of employers found that about a third of workplaces covered by the FMLA violated the law in terms of the length of leave permitted for paternity or maternity reasons (Kelly, 2004). In a survey conducted 3 years later and using a different questionnaire, 13% of covered employers reported that they did not permit up to 12 weeks of leave for any FMLA reason (Cantor et al., 2001). Such violations likely speak to gaps in employers'

FAMILY AND MEDICAL LEAVE ACT

■

The Family and Medical Leave Act (FMLA) was signed into law by President William J. Clinton in 1993 after years of congressional debates and two vetoes by President George H. W. Bush (Elving, 1995). The law requires employers to allow both male and female employees to take up to 12 weeks of unpaid leave to recover from a serious illness or care for a baby or newly adopted child or a seriously ill relative. The FMLA applies to work establishments with at least 50 workers at one site or within a 75-mile radius, and only employees who worked at least 1,250 hours in the past year are eligible for FMLA leaves. Only 11% of U.S. work establishments fall under FMLA; however, those establishments employ an estimated 58% of the total workforce (Cantor et al., 2001). The passage of the FMLA was considered a victory by its advocates because it improved job security for employees with demanding health and caregiving circumstances and recognized both women's and men's caregiving. Nonetheless, the FMLA has significant limitations, including the number of uncovered work establishments and employees, the unpaid nature of FMLA leaves, and employer noncompliance (Kelly, 2004).

understanding of the law as well as their concern that leaves will make it difficult to meet business goals or create burdens for other workers.

Enforcement of the FMLA is limited in that it is largely reactive, focused on responding to reports of potential violations (e.g., employee complaints to the U.S. Department of Labor). Although the FMLA mandates that covered employers maintain records to comply with the law, federal monitoring is minimal because the law does not require employers to submit records to the Labor Department regularly. In fact, employers are not required to submit records unless requested by the department, and without reasonable cause, the department may not ask employers to submit such records more than once during a year (U.S. Department of Labor, 2008).

CHILD/DEPENDENT CARE

Working parents must find care for their children for the hours the parents are at work. Many American parents

rely on family members, such as grandparents or older children, for childcare, or spouses work complementary hours so that a parent is usually with the children (Casper, Hawkins, & O'Connell, 1994; Presser, 1988). Beginning in the 1980s, more parents sought nonfamilial sources of childcare, such as private childcare providers or employer-based centers (Casper & Bianchi, 2002).

With the exception of national emergencies such as the Great Depression and World War II, when the U.S. federal government subsidized childcare centers (Auerbach, 1988; Michel, 1999), the federal government historically has not directly funded childcare for the general public. Instead, the United States provides different types of support for families at different income levels (Kamerman & Kahn, 1987, 1997; Michel, 1999), ranging from family tax abatements, tax reductions for employers who provide childcare benefits to their employees, and subsidies for some low-income families. Given their wide coverage, family and business tax breaks represent the broadest childcare policy in the country. In fact, tax expenditures were the most expensive childcare policy for much of the 1980s and 1990s (Kelly, 2003). Prior to an increase in subsidies for low-income families (discussed more below), the federal government depleted more funds through childcare-related tax reductions than it spent directly funding or subsidizing childcare programs.

Childcare-Related Tax Deductions for Families Federal income tax regulations offer at least two childcare-related reductions to qualifying families. The first is a nonrefundable tax credit, the Child and Dependent Care Credit, aimed at offsetting child/dependent care expenses incurred by working families. A tax credit reduces the amount of tax owed by an individual or family; a nonrefundable tax credit cannot lower the tax below zero and therefore may not result in a refund. Since 1954, federal tax credits have been available for a portion of employment-related child and dependent care expenses. Although income level is not a factor in qualifying for the credit, the amount of the tax credit varies inversely with income to provide more support to low-income households.

Several factors, however, limit low-income families' ability to benefit from the tax credit, and, in fact, the credit is most often used by middle- and upper-income families (Forry & Anderson, 2006). For example, if a family's earnings are so low that it does not have to pay taxes, the tax credit is by definition not available to the family. Further, the nonrefundable nature of the credit prevents low-income families from receiving the benefit if their tax credit exceeds the amount they owe in federal income taxes.

The second childcare-related tax reduction is a Dependent Care Expense Account (DCEA), also known as Section 125 or "cafeteria" plans, dependent-care assistance plans, flexible spending accounts, or tax-free or pretax spending accounts. Such an account is available to individuals whose employers have established a DCEA as an employee benefit and allows employees to set aside a share of their income each year to pay for qualified child- or dependent-care expenses. The funds placed in the account (up to $5,000 per year) are not considered taxable income, which therefore reduces a person's taxable income, resulting in a lower tax burden for participants. Employers also save on their Social Security and Federal Insurance Contributions Act (FICA) contributions, which are calculated based on an employee's taxable earnings (Beam & McFadden, 1996). Access to this tax reduction is contingent on an employer offering the program. An estimated 30% of larger companies (with 50 or more employees) offer these accounts (Kelly, 2006). Although the tax code requires that benefits such as this one be available to all employees (Employee Benefit Research Institute, 2005), higher-income individuals are more likely to benefit from a DCEA, primarily because they are more likely to work for larger employers with more generous benefit packages (Kelly, 2006).

Government Encouragement of Employer-Based Childcare The federal Economic Recovery Tax Act of 1981 was intended to encourage the establishment of employer-based childcare centers by offering tax reductions to employers who provide workplace-based child- and dependent-care benefits. Under this law, employers are allowed to deduct childcare benefit-related expenses from their income tax (Employee Benefit Research Institute, 2005). More recently, the Economic Growth and Tax Relief Reconciliation Act of 2001 granted another tax reduction to employers for providing childcare services or referrals. Employers may earn a tax credit (up to $150,000) for a portion of the expenses incurred in setting up and operating a workplace childcare center for employees (up to 25% of expenses) and providing childcare resources and referrals to employees (up to 10% of expenses). Still, workplace childcare centers continue to be rare in the United States. In a 2005 national survey of employers, only 7% reported a childcare facility at or near the work site (Bond, Galinsky, Kim, & Brownfield, 2005).

Head Start Program The federal government's longest-running involvement with childcare has been via the Head Start program, which during fiscal year 2007 enrolled more than 900,000 children up to age 5 in the United States (Administration for Children and Families [ACF], 2007b). Initiated during President Lyndon B. Johnson's War on Poverty in the 1960s and most recently reauthorized by President George W. Bush in December 2007 for 5 years, Head Start is intended to better prepare low-income and disadvantaged preschool children for school by providing childcare and other services. Head Start's mission is to promote "school readiness by enhancing the social and cognitive development of children through the provision of educational, health, nutritional, social and other services to enrolled children and families" (ACF, 2007a). Historically, Head Start targeted children ages 3 to 5 years. As part of the reauthorization of Head Start in 1994, Early Head Start, a companion component for children younger than 3 years of age was added. Most children in Head Start are enrolled in a full-day or half-day program at a local center or facility (ACF, 2005).

Although Head Start has served a vast number of children—24 million since its inception in 1965 (ACF, 2007b)—the program has its shortcomings. First, not all children who are eligible are served by the program. In 2001 it was estimated that only 50% of eligible children ages 3 and 4 years were being served under Head Start (Currie, 2001). Eligible children may not be enrolled for a number of reasons, including inadequate program funding or program outreach efforts, language/cultural obstacles, or parents' preferences for other early education and childcare providers. Moreover, if the program is a part-year and/or part-day program, it may be only minimally helpful to a working family (Gornick & Meyers, 2003; Smolensky & Gootman, 2003).

Temporary Assistance to Needy Families Program and Other Key Federal Childcare Funding Sources Introduced as part of the 1996 welfare reform legislation, Temporary Assistance to Needy Families (TANF) replaced Aid to Families with Dependent Children and other earlier welfare programs. As part of the reform, the federal government terminated federal entitlement to welfare assistance yet continued to fund welfare assistance to families in need through the new TANF program. Established as a federal grant program for states, TANF is a combined federal and state effort designed to provide temporary income assistance to families. TANF was reauthorized for 5 years by Congress and President George W. Bush in 2006.

The goals of TANF are to (a) assist needy families so that children can be cared for in their homes; (b) reduce the dependency of needy parents by promoting job preparation, work, and marriage; (c) prevent out-of-wedlock pregnancies; and (d) encourage the formation and maintenance of two-parent families (ACF, 2006a). The program provides up to 5 years of income assistance, work opportunities, and other services (including childcare) to qualified families as long as they meet specific employment requirements. TANF has evolved into a significant source of public childcare funding (Smolensky & Gootman, 2003). The program supports childcare in the form of direct expenditures on childcare for families receiving TANF payments and in the form of transfers to the Childcare and Development Fund (CCDF) and Social Services Block Grant, which are additional federal block grants to states that provide childcare services to eligible families.

Although the federal government has increased its childcare funding to low-income families (ACF, 2006b) since 1996, and the reauthorization legislation signed in 2006 further increased this funding, there are several limitations to federal funding of childcare. First, not all eligible low-income children are served. It has been estimated that as few as 10% to 15% of families eligible for CCDF receive benefits (Smolensky & Gootman, 2003), and waiting lists for benefits exist. Second, the payments/vouchers provided to families to pay for care are not necessarily adequate given actual childcare costs. Finally, quality of care is a critical issue. For example, under the CCDF, although providers must meet state health and safety requirements, only a small percentage of CCDF funds must be used toward improvements in the quality of care. The CCDF "does not specify or control the quality of care that children receive" (Smolensky & Gootman, 2003, p. 251).

REGULATION OF WORK TIME AND WORK ARRANGEMENTS

Among work–family policies, work-hour regulation may have the broadest reach because manageable and flexible work hours are important for all families regardless of their specific work and family demands. "[W]orking-time regulations can help allay work–life conflicts that occur across the life course, among parents whose children are young and older, among those caring for ill or disabled relatives, and even among those workers who do not have many family demands" (Kelly, 2006, p. 109).

In the United States, the main law regulating work time is the Fair Labor Standards Act (FLSA) of 1938. Although the law does not overtly define "full-time" and "part-time" work, it implicitly does so by defining overtime as hours worked beyond 40 hours per week. The Fair Labor Standards Act guarantees a higher wage for overtime hours (1.5 times the normal wage) for employees who are covered by the law and work overtime during a given week. The percentage of workers who are exempt from the law, however, has grown (Gornick & Meyers, 2003) due to changes in the law catergorizing more workers as exempt and increases in labor market participation in exempt jobs. Furthermore, the law does not protect workers from mandatory overtime. In contrast, policies elsewhere in the world (e.g., the European

Union) cap working hours, including overtime, and require employers to consider flexible work arrangements for any employee who requests such an arrangement (Kelly & Kalev, 2006).

RESEARCH ON THE IMPACT OF WORK–FAMILY POLICIES ON FAMILIES, PARENTS, AND CHILDREN

As discussed above, work–family policies are intended to facilitate parents' employment and to support members of working families. A growing body of research has examined the effects or consequences of the types of policies described here for families, adults, and children. Research has centered on the impact of work–family policies in several areas: women's employment, wages and equality, and child development.

Research suggests that there is no straightforward relationship between work–family policies and labor force participation among women. Family leaves increase women's employment rates, but, not surprisingly, these findings vary by leave duration (e.g., Gornick & Meyers, 2003). Overall, in the United States, where FMLA leaves are unpaid and short (compared to leaves required in other countries), family leaves have had little impact on overall women's labor force participation (Waldfogel, 1998a). Other U.S. research on maternity leaves has shown that access to such leaves is associated with several employment outcomes among women: the continuation of their involvement in the labor force following childbirth, their retention of the same job following childbirth, and a faster return to work (Estes & Glass, 1996; Glass & Riley, 1998; Hofferth, 1996).

Childcare costs also affect parents' employment decisions. Higher childcare costs are associated with a reduction in women's labor force participation (Gornick & Meyers, 2003). For this reason, the presence of public programs subsidizing childcare costs would be expected to increase women's employment rate, and cross-national research has shown this to be the case (Pettit & Hook, 2005; Stryker, Eliason, & Tranby, 2004).

With regard to women's pay, research has shown that mothers who use work–family policies and stay in the workforce following childbirth have higher wages than mothers who leave the labor force and later return (e.g., Waldfogel, 1998b). Wage consequences from a break in employment are not just short term but continue over time, resulting in a cumulative disadvantage in lifetime income (Jacobsen & Levin, 1995; Noonan, 2001).

Finally, in terms of the impact of work–family policies on children, scholars have examined the effects of policies supporting mother's employment, family leaves, and childcare. Overall, work–family policies have a positive impact on children (Gornick & Meyers, 2003). One study (Kamerman, Neuman, Waldfogel, & Brooks-Gunn, 2003), for example, found that policies supporting mothers' employment had an indirect but significant effect on children's well-being by increasing overall family income. As documented for decades, poverty is associated with a variety of negative child outcomes such as poor health, slower cognitive development, and lower school achievement (e.g., Duncan & Brooks-Gunn, 1997).

Sufficient family leaves following a birth of a child can facilitate breastfeeding and child–parent bonding as well as enhance maternal health (Galtry, 1997; McGovern et al., 1997). Longer family leaves that allow parents to be home with their children or to work part-time during the first year of life also are important because research has shown that children who spend more time with their mothers during the first year score better on cognitive tests (Gornick & Meyers, 2003). For this reason, longer family leaves may be beneficial to children's development and school achievement. Unpaid leaves, however, could be associated with poor outcomes for children if such leaves cause significant financial strain on the family. Finally, for preschool children, studies have highlighted the positive relationship between high-quality childcare and children's development, school readiness, and academic performance (e.g., Kamerman et al., 2003).

FUTURE DIRECTIONS

Research has yielded useful information on the implications of public work–family policies for working families, but important policy and research questions remain. More attention needs to be paid to the linkages between work–family policies and other areas of family policy, including supports for low-income families. How can public policies better support low-wage working parents, who have particular challenges but less access to family leaves, childcare benefits, and flexible work arrangements?

Other questions pertain to the consequences of work–family policies for broader outcomes, such as career advancement, health status and well-being, and community involvement. Beyond wages, are there negative career consequences (e.g., regarding job security and promotion) for using family leaves (e.g., Glass, 2004)? Can public policies be constructed so that workers use the available options without fear of career reprisals? Finally, what is the connection between work–family policies (or the absence thereof) and the health and well-being of parents, caregivers, and their dependents? Research provides some evidence that work–family policies may have benefits beyond the immediate family and work organization because employees with fewer work–family conflicts have better health, are better able to attend to the health and development of their families, and are more likely to be involved in their communities (Bianchi, Casper, & King, 2005; Bookman, 2004).

SEE ALSO Volume 1: *Child Care and Early Education; Child Custody and Support; Policy, Child Well-Being;* Volume 2: *Abortion; Cohabitation; Divorce and Separation; Fatherhood; Motherhood; Noncustodial Parents; Poverty, Adulthood; Work-Family Conflict;* Volume 3: *Long-term Care.*

BIBLIOGRAPHY

Administration for Children and Families, Head Start Bureau. (2005). *Biennial report to Congress: The status of children in Head Start programs.* Retrieved July 7, 2008, from http://www.acf.hhs.gov/programs

Administration for Children and Families, Office of Head Start. (2007a). *About the Office of Head Start.* Retrieved June 16, 2008, from http://www.acf.hhs.gov/programs

Administration for Children and Families, Office of Head Start. (2007b). *Head Start program fact sheet.* Retrieved July 7, 2008, from http://www.acf.hhs.gov/programs

Administration for Children and Families, Office of Public Affairs, Office of Family Assistance. (2006a). *Office of Family Assistance.* Retrieved July 7, 2008, from http://www.acf.hhs.gov/opa

Administration for Children and Families, Office of Public Affairs, Office of Family Assistance. (2006b). *TANF Interim Final Rule: Focus on work and accountability.* Retrieved July 7, 2008, from www.acf.hhs.gov/programs

Albiston, C. R. (2005). Bargaining in the shadow of social institutions: Competing discourses and social change in workplace mobilization of civil rights. *Law and Society Review, 39,* 11–50.

Auerbach, J. D. (1988). *In the business of childcare: Employer initiatives and working women.* New York: Praeger.

Beam, B. T. Jr., & McFadden, J. J. (1996). *Employee benefits.* (8th ed). Chicago: Dearborn Real Estate Education.

Bianchi, S. M., Casper, L. M., & King, R. B. (Eds.). (2005). *Work, family, health, and well-being.* Mahwah, NJ: Lawrence Erlbaum.

Bogenschneider, K. (2002). *Family policy matters: How policymaking affects families and what professionals can do.* Mahwah, NJ: Lawrence Erlbaum.

Bond, J. T., Galinsky, E., Kim, S. S., & Brownfield, E. (2005). *2005 National Study of Employers.* New York: Families and Work Institute.

Bookman, A. (2004). *Starting in our own backyards: How working families can build community and survive the new economy.* New York: Routledge.

California Employment Development Department. (2005). *Paid family leave insurance: Frequently asked questions.* Retrieved July 7, 2008, from http://www.edd.ca.gov/direp

Cantor, D., Waldfogel, J., Kerwin, J., McKinley Wright, M., Levin, K., Rauch, J., et al. (2001). *Balancing the needs of families and employers: Family and medical leave surveys* (2000 update). Washington, DC: U.S. Department of Labor.

Casper, L. M., & Bianchi, S. M. (2002). *Continuity and change in the American family.* Thousand Oaks, CA: Sage.

Casper, L. M., Hawkins, M., & O'Connell, M. (1994). *Who's minding the kids? Childcare arrangements, fall 1991*. Current Population Report No. P70-36. Washington, DC: U.S. Bureau of the Census.

Currie, J. (2001). Early childhood education programs. *The Journal of Economic Perspectives, 15*(2), 213–238.

Duncan, G. J., & Brooks-Gunn, J. (Eds.). (1997). *Consequences of growing up poor*. New York: Russell Sage Foundation.

Elving, R. D. (1995). *Conflict and compromise: How Congress makes the law*. New York: Simon & Schuster.

Employee Benefit Research Institute. (2005). Part four: Other benefits. In *Fundamentals of employee benefit programs*. Washington, DC: Author.

Estes, S. B., & Glass, J. L. (1996). Job changes following childbirth: Are women trading compensation for family-responsive work conditions? *Work and Occupations, 23*, 405–436.

Forry, N. D., & Anderson, E. A. (2006). The child and dependent care tax credit: A policy analysis. In L. Haas & S. K. Wisensale (Eds.), *Families and social policy: National and international perspectives* (pp. 159–176). Binghamton, NY: Haworth Press.

Galtry, J. (1997). Suckling and silence in the USA: The costs and benefits of breastfeeding. *Feminist Economics, 3*(3), 1–24.

Glass, J. L. (2004). Blessing or curse? Work–family policies and mother's wage growth over time. *Work and Occupations, 31*, 367–394.

Glass, J. L., & Riley, L. (1998). Family responsive policies and employee retention following childbirth. *Social Forces, 76*, 1401–1435.

Gornick, J. C., & Meyers, M. K. (2003). *Families that work: Policies for reconciling parenthood and employment*. New York: Russell Sage Foundation.

Hofferth, S. L. (1996). Effects of public and private policies on working after childbirth. *Work and Occupations, 23*, 378–404.

Institute for Women's Policy Research. (2007, August). *Maternity leave in the United States*. Fact Sheet No. A131. Washington, DC: Author. Retrieved May 15, 2008, from http://www.iwpr.org

Jacobsen, J. P., & Levin, L. M. (1995, September). Effects of intermittent labor force attachment on women's earnings. *Monthly Labor Review, 118*, 14–19.

Kamerman, S. B., & Kahn, A. J. (1987). *The responsive workplace: Employers and a changing labor force*. New York: Columbia University Press.

Kamerman, S. B., & Kahn, A. J. (1997). *Family change and family policies in Great Britain, Canada, New Zealand, and the United States*. Oxford, England: Clarendon Press.

Kamerman, S. B., Neuman, M., Waldfogel, J., & Brooks-Gunn, J. (2003). *Social policies, family types, and child outcomes in selected OECD countries*. OECD Social, Employment, and Migration Working Paper No. 6. Paris: Organisation for Economic Co-operation and Development.

Kelly, E. L. (2003). The strange history of employer-sponsored childcare: Interested actors, uncertainty, and the transformation of law in organizational fields. *American Journal of Sociology, 109*, 606–649.

Kelly, E. L. (2004, May). *Explaining non-compliance: Family leave and "the law."* Paper presented at the annual meeting of the Law and Society Association, Chicago.

Kelly, E. L. (2006). Work–family policies: The United States in international perspective. In M. Pitt-Catsouphes, E. E. Kossek, & S. Sweet (Eds.), *The work and family handbook: Multi-*

disciplinary perspectives, methods, and approaches (pp. 99–123). Mahwah, NJ: Lawrence Erlbaum.

Kelly, E. L., & Dobbin, F. (1999). Civil rights law at work: Sex discrimination and the rise of maternity leave policies. *American Journal of Sociology, 105*, 455–492.

Kelly, E. L., & Kalev, A. (2006). Managing flexible work arrangements in U.S. organizations: Formalized discretion or "a right to ask." *Socio-Economic Review, 4*, 379–416.

McGovern, P., Dowd, B., Gjerdingen, D., Moscovice, I., Kochevar, L., & Lohman, W. (1997). Time off work and the postpartum health of employed women. *Medical Care, 35*, 507–521.

Michel, S. (1999). *Children's interests/mothers' rights: The shaping of America's childcare policy*. New Haven, CT: Yale University Press.

Noonan, M. C. (2001, March). *How much does the long-term cost of a work interruption influence women's employment behavior surrounding first birth?* Paper presented at the annual meeting of the Population Association of America, Washington, DC.

Pettit, B., & Hook, J. L. (2005). The structure of women's employment in comparative perspective. *Social Forces, 84*, 779–801.

Presser, H. B. (1988). Shift work and childcare among young dual-earner American parents. *Journal of Marriage and the Family, 50*, 133–148.

Smolensky, E., & Gootman, J. A. (Eds.). (2003). *Working families and growing kids: Caring for children and adolescents*. Washington, DC: National Academies Press.

Stryker, R., Eliason, S., & Tranby, E. (2004, September). *The welfare state, family policies, and women's labor market participation: A fuzzy-set analysis*. Paper presented at the RC-19 annual meeting, Paris.

U.S. Department of Labor, Employment Standards Administration. (2008). *Compliance assistance—Family and medical leave act*. Retrieved April 7, 2008, from http://www.dol.gov/esa/

Waldfogel, J. (1998a). The family gap for young women in the United States and Britain: Can maternity leave make a difference? *Journal of Labor Economics, 16*, 505–545.

Waldfogel, J. (1998b). Understanding the "family gap" in pay for women with children. *The Journal of Economic Perspectives, 12*(1), 137–156.

Williams, J. (2000). *Unbending gender: Why family and work conflict and what to do about it*. New York: Oxford University Press.

Zimmerman, S. L. (2001). *Family policy: Constructed solutions to family problems*. Thousand Oaks, CA: Sage.

Donna L. Spencer
Erin L. Kelly

POLICY, HEALTH

Health policy is a type of social welfare intervention deliberately designed to improve and preserve the health of individuals and populations. Sociologists who study health status and the life courses of individuals and families have documented how experiences that seem far removed from the domain of health policy nonetheless have a profound influence on health-related outcomes. Although health policies formally structure the relationships between individuals and health systems, other institutional realms, such as education, housing, the workplace, and the community, form the context within which good (or ill) health develops and is experienced.

There are two major endeavors governed by health policy. The first is population-level interventions that promote public health. The need for publicly financed health policies is taken for granted, even in the most market-oriented societies. The second health policy endeavor structures national health care systems, shaping the cost, quality, and access to individual health care. Individual entitlement to basic health care is a widely accepted right in both developed and developing nations. Still, national perspectives on what services basic health care covers and how a right to basic care is enacted and paid for create wide variations in the details of national health policies around the world.

DEFINING HEALTH AND HEALTH POLICY

To grasp what constitutes health policy and what does not, it is first important to understand the parameters used to define health. This is because health and health policy, considered broadly, cover such an extensive range of potential actions and interventions that they can be surprisingly difficult to define precisely. In the mid-20th century, physical health and illness were generally viewed as shaped by biological processes and health care. Current definitions are much more complex. For example, one authoritative international source defines health as the state of physical, mental, and social well-being, not just as an absence of disease (World Health Organization [WHO], 1994). In a similar vein, *Healthy People 2010*, a program established by the U.S. Department of Health and Human Services (2000) to minimize or eliminate health disparities in the United States by 2010, notes that the complex factors shaping health disparities demand interventions on multiple fronts, including improved housing, education, employment, and health policies.

Health policy, in the most general sense, is the set of rules, regulations, and procedures that countries use to explicitly coordinate national practices, investments, and systems that are directly health related. Policy makers and stakeholders in the health care system negotiate health policy legislation and the regulations that determine national levels of health expenditure, decide how public and private spending and medical care provision are balanced, and prioritize actions to change health care system arrangements. At the individual level, national health policies determine the cost, quality, and access to health care and medical services faced by individuals and their families. At the population level, health policies govern public health initiatives, workplace and environmental safety regulations, and the specifics of national health care system arrangements and financing. The overarching purpose of health policies is to improve individual well-being and population welfare by enacting programs and practices to preserve health and prevent disease.

Only governments can efficiently undertake collective public health measures on the scale needed to preserve population health. These activities range from ensuring clean food and water supplies, to regulating the safety and efficacy of pharmaceutical products, to implementing population immunization programs and responding to epidemics. Although some countries (especially developing countries) devote more attention and the largest proportion of national expenditures to public health, most citizens in developed countries experience national health policies as individual health care consumers interacting with health care professionals. Most are less aware of public health activities such as safe water supplies and universal vaccination programs, which are collective, behind the scenes, and indirectly experienced.

Despite current definitions of health, which emphasize the importance of policies from other social policy domains in shaping health (such as in *Healthy People 2010*), and despite the emphasis on social inclusion and well-being by the WHO, only policies that directly impact individual, physical, and mental health are conventionally considered within the rubric of health policy. Thus, education, housing, and the workplace factors are not conventionally considered health policies, although such policies would obviously influence individual health status over the life course. Perhaps because the value of most public health measures is taken for granted, or because policy making is most active on the second front, most people who study health policy focus on the relationships between the health care system and individuals accessing medical care.

VALUES AND HEALTH POLICY

Although the purpose of health policy as a way to preserve health and prevent disease seems universal, the specifics of national health policies vary substantially. Each country's health policies reflect its distinctive values and cultural traditions, its unique array of economic, demographic, and political circumstances, and the particular financing and organizational arrangements of health care systems. Nationally, health policies encompass the political decisions that generate health-related laws and regulations, reflecting "more general perceptions about what is fair or important or doable (or all three) in a particular culture, at a particular time, in a particular place" (Stevens, 2006, p. 2). When considering the capacity for health policy to address particular health needs, feasibility depends not only on the concrete resources and infrastructure available for implementation, but on the cultural norms and dominant value systems of the society.

As prominent medical sociologist David Mechanic (who has studied health policy and its outcomes for his entire career), Lynn Rogut, David Colby, and James Knickman (2005) have observed, debates about health policy, regardless of where they occur, are often driven by moral and ideological positions, rather than by evidence about which particular policies could be most effective for the most people. Instead, contests over health policy are often fueled by disagreements over "personal versus collective responsibility, government versus self-help, individual fault versus social causation" and the merits of designing health policies for populations that are regarded as "worthy versus unworthy" (Mechanic et al., 2005, p. 2).

Both the WHO (1994) and the U.S. Department of Health and Human Services (2000) define health and the policies that can influence it based on values of justice, equity, and social inclusion. Yet one of the values reflected in the U.S. health care system is the primacy of individual risk over government responsibility (O'Rand, 2003) and an emphasis on individual fault rather than social causation in explaining illness. Nonetheless, values that presume collective responsibility for public health and individual entitlement to health care are elsewhere widely accepted across the political spectrum and in both the developed and developing world. Broad-based political support for redistributive health policy—whereby resources are redistributed toward the most vulnerable, from the lucky healthy to the unlucky sick—is typically greater than for redistribution in other social policy domains. Regardless of political preferences, most stakeholders and policy makers acknowledge that publicly financed public health measures are essential and that routine access to individual health care should be guaranteed. Still, particular national perspectives on what is appropriate and feasible (given cultural realities and resource constraints) in the realm of public health and what constitutes adequate access to basic individual care is expressed in the myriad variations of health policies observed throughout the world.

One fundamental question that distinguishes how values are expressed differently among national health care systems is, "Who is responsible for paying for and providing health care?" The answer varies cross-nationally, but most developed countries provide universal entitlement to health care for all citizens, from cradle to grave. Some countries, such as the United Kingdom and Spain, have comprehensive national health services that are supported by general taxation; most medical care is delivered by health professionals employed in the public sector. Canada and the Scandinavian countries depend on universal, publicly financed national health insurance, with most health care providers working in the private sector. Other countries, such as France and Germany, complement public programs with mandated employment-based insurance to guarantee universal access.

Alone among developed countries, the United States has no guarantee of universal access to care (see sidebar). Instead, a patchwork of public programs and private insurance structure individuals' access to medical care. Without a national guarantee of health insurance for infants, children, or working-age adults, many nonelderly working individuals and their families depend on private employment-based health insurance; others go without any health insurance at all. Very poor mothers (but not very poor fathers), their infant and preschool-age children, and some segments of the permanently disabled population are covered by Medicaid. Medicaid is a state-federal health insurance program for the poor that applies strict income and asset tests to determine eligibility for coverage. Since the mid-1990s some states have relaxed income eligibility rules and expanded Medicaid insurance coverage to many more low-income children. However, this expansion of public health insurance for children has not occurred evenly across the country, and states encountering fiscal difficulties often withdraw the expanded coverage. Individuals who are over age 65 are eligible for Medicare, a federal program of nearly universal health insurance for the elderly. Medicare covers many of the acute medical care needs for elderly Americans but does not provide long-term care. Thus the United States is unique in the role that life course circumstances—especially the interaction of age with other individual and family characteristics—play in how or whether individuals are likely to gain routine entrance into the health care system and who will pay the bill when they do.

In countries where universal access is guaranteed, the life course basis of health policies may not always be as obvious as in the United States, yet they certainly exist. Countries may enact specialized initiatives to target particular health problems or risks most prevalent at particular life course stages or for particularly vulnerable subpopulations. For example, public health policies may discourage smoking initiation, educate about sexually transmitted diseases, or provide special prenatal care programs for vulnerable pregnant women—policies geared mostly toward the health concerns of teenagers and young adults. Alternatively,

NATIONAL HEALTH INSURANCE

National health insurance (HI) guarantees universal access to basic health care for entire populations. Countries with multi-payer national HI systems, such as Germany, combine compulsory, private insurance (usually employment-based) with public programs for individuals not privately insured. Canada's single-payer HI system provides government-administered coverage for all citizens. Among industrialized democracies, only the United States lacks guaranteed access to health care for all and is distinctive in its heavy reliance on voluntary private HI. Working-age Americans and their families typically are covered by employment-based group HI. Population groups deemed by private insurers as too risky to insure usually rely on public programs for HI coverage: Medicare (HI for the elderly), Medicaid (HI for the poor), and myriad smaller public programs (e.g., coverage under the Veteran's Administration, Indian Health Service, prison health care) account for nearly half of U.S. health care spending. Nearly 47 million Americans lack health insurance coverage. Advocates of national HI note three advantages: (a) everyone has access to basic health care, (b) administrative costs are low, and (c) health costs can be controlled by managing supply. Critics argue that national HI compromises the benefits of private sector HI, including (a) investment in medical innovation, (b) consumer choice, and (c) cost-consciousness that moderates wasteful health care consumption.

policy attention may focus on implementing widespread monitoring of midlife adults to catch the onset of chronic conditions or to preserve mobility or address the risks of polypharmacy among the elderly. In countries where routine access to health care is an entitlement, access to health care in the first place is not shaped by life course influences to the extent that it is in the United States, but the focus of health investments and health policy outcomes certainly are.

THE EFFECTS OF HEALTH POLICY ON LIFE TRAJECTORIES

Historically, the most dramatic improvements to overall population health and to improving and prolonging the lives of individuals were due to advances in public health. Although modern medicine has made stunning advancements that improve health—ranging from the discovery of antibiotics and antivirals, to increasingly effective disease interventions, to organ transplants—the health gains of the most broadly applied medical intervention pale in comparison to the continuing contributions of public health. It is for this reason that, in developing countries, individuals' life chances are often enhanced more by population-level public health policies than by policies relating to individual health care. In developed countries, where public health policies are well-developed and their impact is taken for granted, most health policy attention is usually paid to decisions affecting individual-level interventions and outcomes (such as reforms to spending or arrangements of national health care systems) rather than to population-level initiatives.

Yet precisely how individual-level health policy is implicated in shaping life course trajectories is not entirely clear. It does structure the capacity for individuals to access and benefit from medical advances. Where universal health insurance is provided, there are no financial barriers to accessing medical care, minimizing access and care differences between advantaged and disadvantaged groups. In the United States the fragmented public–private health insurance system multiplies the advantages of some by easing access to health care and reduces the advantages of others by restricting access. Still, in the United States, acute illness and accidents are treated even among the uninsured; it is routine checkups and preventive care that are missed when access to medical care is restricted due to lack of insurance. Yet even elsewhere, where health policies remove financial barriers that impede access to medical care, health disparities begin early in the life course and persist (with rare exceptions) over its span. This emphasizes the complexities of health outcomes, which involve much more than straightforward interactions between individuals and medical care.

Despite significant medical advances throughout the 20th century, low socioeconomic status (SES) is everywhere associated with more adverse health outcomes across all major health conditions. The association between SES and health occurs in both directions. First, an individual's health status impacts his or her ability to work, income level, and wealth built over the life course. Second, increases in income and education are strongly correlated with increases in measured health (Braveman et al., 2005). Research indicates that, in most instances, the impact of SES on health outcomes strengthens across the life course, so that current socioeconomic advantage or disadvantage impacts an individual's immediate and longer-term health. Scholars use this concept of cumulative (dis)advantage to understand how the effects of risk factors for disease accumulate over an individual's life course (Ferraro & Kelley-Moore, 2003).

Many researchers have attempted to determine what specific aspects of SES lead to differential health outcomes. One vehicle through which SES impacts health is individuals' exposure to stress. Individuals with low SES experience, on average, more stressful and negative major life events throughout their lives, and the exposure to such events is associated with higher risks of ill health and death. Bruce Link and Jo Phelan (1995) argue that SES is a fundamental cause of health disparities, because an individual's SES is linked in so many different ways to his or her capacity to gain access to and mobilize resources when needed. Access to important resources, whether knowledge, money, social support networks, or other advantages linked to SES, may explain why the association between SES and health is so persistent across so many different disease outcomes, and why the association between low SES and poor health outcomes persist even when disease risk factors change. The *fundamental cause* perspective explains how an individual's social and economic positions structure access to resources that can either prevent exposure to risks for disease or can be used to shield the effects of disease when it does occur.

Alternatively, lack of resources is implicated in exposure, risk, and shortage of resources to effectively deal with health conditions and setbacks (Link & Phelan, 1995). SES as a fundamental cause of health represents not only a cross-sectional risk but a life course one as well. Most research indicates that low SES (specifically education and income) contributes to cumulative disadvantage over the life course—diverging gaps in physical health among individuals of varying SES at older ages. However, some research indicates that for a handful of conditions, age may be a "leveler" in that some conditions (such as depression) appear to converge across SES groups with increasing age (Kim & Durden, 2007). A tentative explanation for this emphasizes the role of pensions (e.g., Social Security in retirement) in closing some of the gap between incomes and health policy.

According to the *life course health development* model, SES in childhood and early adulthood sets individuals on differing health trajectories (Halfon & Hochstein, 2002). These differing health trajectories differentially expose individuals to experiences that may either buffer or amplify the risks for disease, resulting in greater health disparities as individuals grow older. Children from poor families experience different sets of risks from children in more affluent ones, starting them on a trajectory of life course outcomes that magnify disadvantage over time (Wagmiller, Lennon, & Kuang, 2008). Childhood and family social relationships are associated with later physical and mental health outcomes (Institute of Medicine, 2002), emphasizing the importance of childhood experiences even in mid- and later life health outcomes.

In none of these instances could conventional public health or individual health policies intervene to do much to minimize or ameliorate the life course health risks posed by such early exposures to adverse environments. Rather, Linda George (2005) called for a "simple" health policy approach to "redistribute income and educate children to their maximum potential" (p. S138) and to devote more attention to fixing social institutions than people. Research shows that economic hardship over the life course has cumulative effects on health over time (Hayward, Crimmins, Miles, & Yang, 2000), indicating that alleviating hardship through education (which mitigates health risks and contributes to resilience) and minimizing income inequality may have the most potential to be effective health policies—considered from a life course perspective.

GAPS IN KNOWLEDGE AND ISSUES TO BE RESOLVED

Even when health policies are specifically designed to do so, they do not necessarily benefit the most vulnerable. To the extent that health policies target individuals rather than groups or populations, the initial outcome of a policy intended to improve conditions for the least advantaged may, paradoxically, widen health disparities in the short term. This is because advantaged individuals within any society are nearly always in the best position to take the earliest and greatest advantage of medical innovations that bestow predominantly individual (rather than group) benefits.

Most sociologists of the life course agree that health status is closely related to social status, regardless of the unique risks associated with a particular time period in the life course. Although the risks of particular health statuses and outcomes may change from period to period, an individual's social status is the most fundamental condition in any period. Some health policies, such as effective public health measures, have collective benefits that are quite independent of social status. Adequate sanitation, clean and safe drinking water and food supplies, and immunization programs benefit entire populations and all the groups within them. However, because it is social status that influences whether individuals can access the other kinds of resources they need to maintain health and prevent illness, individuals with more money and social resources have additional capacity to marshal whatever range of resources they need to prevent disease and maintain health, compared to less advantaged individuals.

The *life course health development* framework developed by Neal Halfon and Miles Hochstein (2002) suggests a set of research and health policy goals to improve life course health trajectories and minimize health disparities for vulnerable groups. The authors proposed research that identifies critical and sensitive periods of early health risk and protective factors. By pursuing a developmental approach, they argued that health policy could shift from later interventions focused on ill health to earlier and more effective interventions that could prevent illness and optimize developmental health. Because of the complexity of health development over the life course, Halfon and Hochstein maintained that health disparities can be addressed only within a framework that recognizes the social nature of disparities and cannot be addressed by additional health care access or resources alone. They also argued that successful interventions will depend on reducing inequalities in income and employment benefits and family and social relationships. In this sense, their health policy prescriptions come full circle from the conventional, but restricted, definition of health policy that is most often considered to the more expansive WHO and U.S. Department of Health and Human Services definitions.

Link and Phelan (1995), pioneers of the fundamental cause framework, recommended that health policy initiatives identify strategies that could help individuals who are SES-disadvantaged to compensate by equalizing the coping strategies that now link SES advantages to improved health outcomes. New health advances targeted to individuals, even when targeted especially to disadvantaged individuals, will not necessarily improve health outcomes. In fact, individually targeted health policies may widen disparities, at least initially, because the wealthy are always positioned to take more advantage of innovation. Additional research on life course health trajectories may suggest ways to equalize coping strategies at critical junctures or sensitive turning points in life course trajectories that could inform health policy innovations. The Link and Phelan framework reinforces the importance of broadening the way policy makers think about health policy to address persistent health disparities currently experienced by vulnerable groups.

It seems obvious that health policies that are universal and that minimize dependence on individual resources hold the most promise to smooth health trajectories, address health risks, and minimize health disparities over the life course. Enacting and implementing universalist policies intended to operate at the group or population level—policies resembling public health interventions rather than the dominantly individual medical care preoccupation of current health policy debates—could potentially reduce disparities among the most vulnerable who are unlikely to have their health improved by contemporary health policies that target individuals.

SEE ALSO Volume 2: *Health Care Use, Adulthood; Health Differentials/Disparities, Adulthood; Health Insurance; Policy, Family;* Volume 3: *Long-term Care; Policy, Later Life Well-Being.*

BIBLIOGRAPHY

Braveman, P. A., Cubbin, C., Egerter, S., Chideya, S., Marchi, K. S., Metzler, M., et al. (2005). Socioeconomic status in health research: One size does not fit all. *Journal of the American Medical Association, 294*(22), 2879–2888.

Ferraro, K. F., & Kelley-Moore, J. A. (2003). Cumulative disadvantage and health: Long-term consequences of obesity? *American Sociological Review, 68*(5), 707–729.

George, L. K. (2005). Socioeconomic status and health across the life course: Progress and prospects. *Journals of Gerontology, Series B: Psychological Sciences and Social Sciences, 60,* S135–S139.

Halfon, N., & Hochstein, M. (2002). Life course health development: An integrated framework for developing health, policy, and research. *The Milbank Quarterly, 80*(3), 433–479.

Hayward, M. D., Crimmins, E. M., Miles, T. P., & Yang, Y. (2000). The significance of socioeconomic status in explaining the racial gap in chronic health conditions. *American Sociological Review, 65*(6), 910–930.

Institute of Medicine. (2002). *The future of the public's health in the 21st century.* Committee on Assuring the Health of the Public in the 21st Century, Board on Health Promotion and Disease Prevention. Washington, DC: National Academy Press. Retrieved May 14, 2008, from http://www.iom.edu/Object.File

Kim, J., & Durden, E. (2007). Socioeconomic status and age trajectories of health. *Social Science and Medicine, 65*(12), 2489–2502.

Link, B. G., & Phelan, J. (1995). Social conditions as fundamental causes of disease. *Journal of Health and Social Behavior, 35,* 80–94.

Mechanic, D., Rogut, L B., Colby, D. C., & Knickman, J. R. (2005). Introduction. In D. Mechanic, L. B. Rogut, & D. C. Colby (Eds.), *Policy challenges in modern health care* (pp. 1–12). New Brunswick, NJ: Rutgers University Press.

O'Rand, A. M. (2003). The future of the life course: Late modernity and life course risks. In J. T. Mortimer & M. Shanahan (Eds.), *Handbook of the life course* (pp. 693–701). New York: Kluwer Academic/Plenum.

Singer, B. H., & Ryff, C. D. (Eds.). (2001). *New horizons in health: An integrative approach.* Washington, DC: National Academy Press.

Stevens, R. A. (2006). Introduction. In R. A. Stevens, C. E. Rosenberg, & L. R. Burns (Eds.), *History and health policy in the United States: Putting the past back in* (pp. 1–13). New Brunswick, NJ: Rutgers University Press.

U.S. Department of Health and Human Services. (2000). *Healthy People 2010: Understanding and improving health.* Washington, DC: Author. Retrieved May 14, 2008, from http://www.healthypeople.gov/Document/

Wagmiller, R. L., Lennon, M. C., & Kuang, L. (2008). Parental health and children's economic well-being. *Journal of Health and Social Behavior, 49*(1), 37–55.

World Health Organization. (1994). Constitution of the World Health Organization, 22 July 1946. In *Basic documents* (40th ed., pp. 1–18). Geneva, Switzerland: Author. Retrieved May 14, 2008, from http://www.who.int/gb

Debra Street
Elizabeth Gage

POLITICAL BEHAVIOR AND ORIENTATIONS, ADULTHOOD

Citizen engagement, or the constellation of behaviors that people engage in order to change the political and social world around them, is a multidimensional phenomenon. Despite an early preoccupation with analyzing people's involvement in elections (e.g., political behavior), scholars have come to recognize that citizen engagement extends far beyond the ballot box and encompasses activities such as protesting, volunteering, and even using their power as consumers through engaging in boycotts (not buying certain products, goods, or services) and buycotts (buying only certain products, goods, or services) in order to reward or punish the company that produces them. However, in this entry the focus is on adult political participation, namely voting and a few other behaviors that are centered around elections. In addition to what people *do*, this entry will consider what people *think* about politics. Although studying people's thoughts about politics raises a variety of issues, attention here largely focuses on two indicators related to political orientations—party affiliation and political ideology. (e.g., where one locates oneself along the liberal/conservative continuum).

STABILITY AND CHANGE IN POLITICAL BEHAVIOR AND ATTITUDES ACROSS THE LIFE COURSE

Researchers have long observed increases in political engagement with age (Verba Nie, 1972). For example, one study (Zukin, Keeter, Andolina, Jenkins, & Delli Carpini, 2006) found that political engagement increases with age, reaching a peak at or around age 65 and then falling sharply among individuals near and beyond age 70. The researchers used five indicators to measure political engagement: regularly voting in local and national elections; attempting to persuade others politically around the time of an election; displaying campaign buttons, signs, or sticker;, making a campaign contribution; and volunteering for a candidate or political organization. In the 2004

presidential election, voting turnout followed a similar pattern. Self-reported turnout was the lowest among those between the ages of 18 and 24 (47%) and highest among those older than 55 (73%; Faler, 2005). Turnout increased steadily with age in the intervening years.

It is important to also point out that although youth remain disproportionately absent from participation in electoral politics, the 2008 presidential primaries and caucuses witnessed sizable increases in the number of youth who turned out in predominantly Democratic contests. Inspired by the two historic firsts (Barack Obama as the first viable African American candidate and Hillary Clinton as the first viable female candidate for a major party nomination), and the use of the Internet as a tool for political organizing, young people increased their participation markedly from the 2000 nominating contests (Center for Information and Research on Civic Learning and Engagement, 2008).

Why would voting or volunteering for a campaign be related to age? First, in the words of Sidney Verba and Norman Nie (1972), there is "gradual learning," which refers to the acquisition of political knowledge over the course of one's life that makes navigating the political system easier. Similarly, Steven Rosenstone and John Mark Hansen (1993) suggested a life experience hypothesis, which holds that "people acquire resources that promote participation as they grow older" (p. 137). These resources include political knowledge (regarding parties, candidates, and public affairs more generally), political skills, and denser social networks that increase the likelihood of being asked to take part in public life.

Additionally, the acquisition of new roles and life experiences may account for increases in political participation in adulthood. Once an individual moves beyond young adulthood, responsibilities emerge that can pull him or her toward becoming an engaged citizen. The nomadic existence of youth is now a thing of the past, as adults begin to plant roots upon becoming spouses and parents. Doing so, in turn, helps to foster more political engagement as people come to recognize the importance of politics for concerns such as taxes, public safety, and the quality of schools. One's profession can also play a role in fostering more participation because the workplace is often a site for political discussions and mobilization among peers. Finally, the onset of retirement and widowhood often foreshadows one's declining health and cognitive capacity, which makes active engagement in the polity more difficult than in previous years.

Turning to political orientations, two indicators stand out for their predictable life course patterns: party affiliation and ideology. Party affiliation, or one's willingness to identify with one of the two major parties in the United States (Democrat and Republican), is shaped largely by the nature of the times during which one was being socialized early in life. This means that despite changes in the political environment over the life course, an individual will likely cling to the party that was dominant during the impressionable years of one's youth (Alwin, Cohen, & Newcomb, 1991; Jennings & Markus, 1994; Sears & Funk, 1999). This is not to suggest that the transition to adulthood brings with it virtually no chance of changing one's party affiliation over the life cycle; what it does suggest is that, for example, differences in the party affiliation of those socialized in the 1960s (Baby Boomers) versus the 1980s (Generation Xers) are best explained by generational versus life course effects. (Generational effects refer to the sum of common experiences, opportunities, and situations that help shape an age cohort's behavior and attitudes across the life cycle.) Simply put, Boomers came of age when the Democrats were the dominant party in government, whereas Xers did so during a Republican resurgence led by former U.S. President Ronald Reagan (1911–2004). In short, although change is possible, partisanship tends to remain a stable part of one's identity over the life cycle.

An aspect of party affiliation that does follow a predictable pattern across the life cycle is the strength of partisanship. That is, in addition to asking about a person's party affiliation, pollsters also ask how strongly a person identifies with his or her chosen party. Strong partisanship tends to increase with age, with 41% of those age 55 and older in 2004 identifying themselves as "strong" partisans compared with only 23% of those under 30 (Eriksen & Tedin, 2007). Similar differences have been observed across the life course in previous years. Having had a lifetime to consider whether one is a Democrat or Republican, individuals tend to harden their commitment the closer they get to the end of the life course.

Strength of partisanship is not the only aspect of political orientation that is susceptible to life course effects. Political ideology, or the extent to which a person locates him or herself on a continuum ranging from conservative to liberal, changes in accordance with where he or she is in the life course. The trend in adulthood is to become more conservative with age, and this is true regardless of the time period in which data is collected. Moreover, as Robert Eriksen and Kent Tedin (2007) pointed out, "Each generation starts out with the same level of liberalism and drifts rightward about the same rate" (p. 156).

Underlying the life course effect in political ideology are a variety of factors thought to push one in a conservative direction. The first centers on personal finances. Age brings greater accumulation of wealth, which, in turn, makes conservative economic policies more favorable. Even if the political rhetoric of lower taxes translates into reality for only a small subset of voters, the idea of having more money in one's bank account on payday of course resonates positively with voters.

Canvassing. *Anne Walpole talks to Frank Hill about the gay marriage amendment while canvassing in Richmond, VA.* AP IMAGES.

Additionally, age brings with it a propensity to cling to social norms that were a defining part of one's youth. As is so often the case, social norms are often challenged the most forcefully by young people. Unhappy with the status quo, youth often behave in ways that unsettle older adults who prefer to adhere to established norms of behavior. For example, surveys today reveal a marked age difference in attitudes toward gay rights. Young people are significantly more in favor of allowing gay marriage than are older adults. In one report, 53% of those between the ages of 18 and 29 were in favor of gay marriage, compared with 38% of those age 30 through 49, 30% of those 50 through 64, and only 16% of those 65 and older (Pew Research Center, 2006). Because opposition to the liberalization of marriage laws is most closely associated with conservatism, it is no surprise to see older citizens more closely identified with this end of the ideological continuum than younger adults.

THE CONSEQUENCES OF LIFE COURSE PATTERNS IN POLITICAL BEHAVIOR AND ORIENTATIONS

The disproportionate political activism of older voters compared to younger voters can pose challenges to the crafting of equitable public policies. Naturally, policy makers tend to respond more to those who are politically engaged. At any point in time, policies are likely to be more reflective of the interests of those closer to the end of the life course than the beginning.

For example, the U.S. social welfare policy known as Social Security is facing long-term financial difficulties. Social Security provides retirement income for those age

62 and over. A recent attempt to reform the system by allowing some investment of Social Security contributions in the stock market was met with varying support across the life course. Young people generally favored the plan. A 2002 poll conducted by the *Washington Post*, the Kaiser Family Foundation, and Harvard University estimated support among youth (ages 18 to 24) at 61%. Support dropped off significantly among older adults, and only 24% of those age 65 and older supported such a plan (Zukin et al., 2006). Despite a concerted effort by the White House to rally public opinion behind President George W. Bush's (b. 1946) plan, it was soundly defeated in Congress. Legislators, instead, listened to those who reliably vote—and those who opposed the plan. To *not* have listened would have risked alienating the support of those whom a legislator needs on Election Day.

This example highlights a problem posed by disproportionate activism across the life course. Kay Schlozman, Sidney Verba, and Henry Brady (1999) referred to the "equal protection of interests" rationale for robust citizen engagement, by which they mean the willingness of citizens with conflicting interests to take part in public life. Clearly, different levels of political participation over the life course challenge the ideal of equal protection of interests on any issue in which interests vary by age.

CHALLENGES TO THE MEASUREMENT OF LIFE COURSE EFFECTS ON POLITICAL BEHAVIOR AND ORIENTATIONS

Two issues arise when considering life course effects on political orientations and behavior. The first concerns the use of cross-sectional surveys to measure changes over the life course. Typically, researchers interview different groups of people at different points in time and, by comparing the responses of people born in the same years (a birth cohort) at these different interviews, assess the extent to which individuals alter their behavior or orientations as they age (this design is called a pooled cross-section). Because the same person is not being asked the same question at different times in his or her life, it is difficult to say for certain whether changes in a birth cohort's orientations and behavior are the result of individual maturation. It is likely that these studies reveal a little bit of both—that is, changes that arise over the life course but also stability in some individual behavior, an artifact of cross-sectional data that makes it difficult to measure precisely changes over the life course. A related complication is period effects. These occur when a political or social event, such as the attacks of 9/11, cause an abrupt but temporary change in the behavior of a cohort or cohorts. News interest and political attentiveness were markedly higher among all cohorts in the days after the attacks but returned to their pre-9/11 levels within a year after the event.

Estimating life course effects using cross-sectional data can thus be a limited enterprise. What is needed are more longitudinal data sets from which to gauge changes in adult behavior and orientations with age. This type of survey (a panel or longitudinal survey) tracks the same individuals over the life course and provides more telling insights into how age affects one's orientation to the political world. Unfortunately, longitudinal surveys are few and far between, largely because of cost and an unwillingness or inability of respondents to maintain their participation over many years.

The second issue to complicate the estimation of life course effects on adult political orientations and behavior is the need for more cross-national studies. To say with any certainty how age influences one's political identity requires analyses that extend beyond the United States. However, as Roberta Sigel (1989) pointed out, "We still do not have enough cross-national studies, especially those conducted in the non-Western world.... The importance of obtaining such information is so self-evident as not to require further elaboration here" (p. 469).

Many of the points raised in the preceding analyses are ripe for further elaboration. Scholars in fields such as political science and sociology have developed a rich tradition of inquiry in this area, but there is still much to understand.

SEE ALSO Volume 1: *Identity Development; Political Socialization;* Volume 2: *Social Movement; Volunteering, Adulthood.*

BIBLIOGRAPHY

Alwin, D. F., Cohen, R. L., & Newcomb, T. M. (1991). *Political attitudes over the life span: The Bennington women after 50 years.* Madison: University of Wisconsin Press.

Center for Information and Research on Civic Learning and Engagement. (2008). *The youth vote in the 2008 primaries and caucuses.* Retrieved June 6, 2008, from www.civicyouth.org

Delli Carpini, M. X. (1989). Generations and sociopolitical change. In R. S. Sigel (Ed.), *Political learning in adulthood: A sourcebook of theory and research.* Chicago: University of Chicago Press.

Eriksen, R. S., & Tedin, K. L. (2007). *American public opinion: Its origins, content, and impact.* (7th ed.). New York: Pearson/Longman.

Faler, B. (2005, May 26). Census details voter turnout for 2004. *The Washington Post,* p. A10.

Jennings, M. K., & Markus, G. B. (1984). Partisan orientations over the long haul: Results from the three-wave political socialization panel study. *American Political Science Review, 78*(4), 1000–1018.

Jennings, M. K., & Niemi, R. G. (1981). *Generations and politics: A panel study of young adults and their parents.* Princeton, NJ: Princeton University Press.

Miller, W. E., & Shanks, J. M. (1996). *The new American voter*. Cambridge, MA: Harvard University Press.

Pew Research Center for the People and the Press. (2006, August 3). *Pragmatic Americans liberal and conservative on social issues*. Retrieved June 16, 2008, from http://people.press.org/report/

Rosenstone, S. J., & Hansen, J. M. (1993). *Mobilization, participation, and democracy in America*. New York: Macmillan.

Schlozman, K. L., Verba, S., & Brady, H. (1999). Civic participation and the equality problem. In T. Skocpol & M. P. Fiorina (Eds.), *Civic engagement in American democracy*. Washington, DC: Brookings Institution Press.

Sears, D. O., & Funk, C. L. (1999). Evidence of the long-term persistence of adults' political predispositions. *The Journal of Politics, 61*(1), 1–28.

Sigel, R. S. (Ed.). (1989). Adult political learning—A lifelong process. In *Political learning in adulthood: A sourcebook of theory and research*. Chicago: University of Chicago Press.

Verba, S., & Nie, N. (1972). *Participation in America: Political democracy and social equality*. New York: Harper & Row.

Verba, S., Schlozman, K. L., & Brady, H. (1995). *Voice and equality: Civic voluntarism in American politics*. Cambridge, MA: Harvard University Press.

Zukin, C., Keeter, S., Andolina, M., Jenkins, K., & Delli Carpini, M. X. (2006). *A new engagement? Political participation, civic life, and the changing American citizen*. Oxford, U.K.: Oxford University Press.

Krista Jenkins

POVERTY, ADULTHOOD

Poverty generally refers to individuals residing in households that lack the income to purchase a minimally adequate daily basic "basket" of goods and services. The actual measurement of poverty, however, varies widely across countries. In the United States poverty is officially measured in terms of whether various-sized households fall below specific annual income levels. Considerable debate exists regarding the adequacy of this measure (Blank, 2008; Iceland, 2005). In Europe, poverty is frequently defined as residing in a household that falls below one-half of the national median income. In developing countries the standard often used is living in a family earning less than a dollar per day. The concept behind all of these approaches is that there is a basic minimum amount of income necessary in order for individuals to adequately carry out their day-to-day activities. Households that fail to acquire such income are considered poor. Other measures of poverty (such as those developed by the United Nations) have begun to incorporate aspects of social deprivation into their measurement of poverty, such as shortened life expectancy, illiteracy, and long-term unemployment (United Nations Development Programme, 2007). This entry examines poverty within the context of the life course, and explores the likelihood, consequences, and solutions to poverty from a life course perspective.

THE RISK OF POVERTY ACROSS ADULTHOOD

The social scientific study of poverty across the life course began with Rowntree's (1901) study of 11,560 working-class families in the English city of York. Rowntree estimated the likelihood of falling into poverty at various stages of the life course. His work was seminal in developing the concept of the life cycle, and it demonstrated that working-class families were more likely to experience poverty at certain economically vulnerable stages during their adulthood (e.g., starting a family and during retirement). Since Rowntree's initial work, much has been learned regarding the patterns and dynamics of poverty across adulthood.

Cross-sectional surveys (such as those conducted annually by the U.S. Bureau of the Census) have shown that within the United States, children and young adults are at the greatest risk of experiencing poverty. The risk declines during the prime earning years of the 40s to mid-50s, and then slowly increases as adults reach their retirement years (DeNavas-Walt, Proctor, & Smith, 2007). In addition, cross-sectional analyses indicate that certain characteristics can place individuals at a greater risk of experiencing poverty. These include having low education and few job skills, living in single-parent families, being non-White, residing in economically depressed inner cities or rural areas, and having a disability (DeNavas-Walt et al., 2007). All of these characteristics tend to put individuals at a disadvantage when competing in the labor market.

Comparative analysis using the Luxembourg Income Study (a data source containing income and demographic information on households in approximately 30 industrialized nations) has shown that U.S. poverty rates are among the highest in the developed world. This is true whether one looks at poverty among children, working-age adults, or elderly persons (Smeeding, 2005). Two reasons stand out as to why Americans at the lower end of the income distribution do so badly compared to their counterparts in other countries. First, the social safety net in the United States is considerably weaker than in other industrialized countries, resulting in more households falling into poverty (Alesina & Glaeser, 2004). Second, the United States has been plagued since the early 1980s by relatively low wages at the bottom of the income distribution scale compared to other developed countries (Blank, Danziger, & Schoeni, 2006; Fligstein & Shin, 2004). These factors contribute to both the relative and absolute depths of U.S. poverty in comparison with other industrialized nations.

Beginning in the 1970s, researchers in the United States have increasingly sought to uncover the dynamics of poverty over time. The emphasis has been on understanding the extent of turnover in the poverty population from year to year and determining the length of poverty spells. These studies have relied on several nationally representative panel data sets, including the Panel Study of Income Dynamics, the National Longitudinal Survey of Youth, and the Survey of Income and Program Participation. This work has shown that most spells of poverty are fairly short term (1 to 3 years in length), but that households that experience poverty will often encounter poverty again at some later point in the life course (Duncan, 1984; Stevens, 1994, 1999). In addition, this work has demonstrated that particular events, such as job loss, family breakup, or ill health, are important factors leading households into poverty. This body of work has also shown that a relatively small number of households will experience chronic poverty for years at a time. Such households typically have characteristics that put them at a severe disadvantage vis-à-vis the labor market (e.g., individuals with serious work disabilities, single-headed families with a large number of children, racial minorities living in economically depressed inner-city areas).

An alternative approach for understanding the scope of poverty has been to analyze impoverishment as a life course event. For example, what are the chances that at some point during their adulthood an American will experience poverty? The work of Rank and Hirschl (1999, 2001b) has addressed this question. Their results indicate that between the ages of 20 and 75, nearly 60% of Americans will have spent at least 1 year below the official poverty line, while three-quarters of Americans will encounter poverty or near poverty (below 150% of the poverty line). Consistent with the earlier mentioned studies of poverty dynamics, individuals experiencing poverty throughout the life course often do so for only 1 or 2 consecutive years. Once an individual experiences poverty, however, it is quite likely that the person will encounter poverty again at some later point in his or her life course. This work has indicated that falling into poverty is a common life course event for the majority of Americans.

Rank and Hirschl have also found that the periods of early and later adulthood are characterized by a heightened risk of poverty (as indicated in cross-sectional studies). For example, between the ages of 20 and 40, 36% of Americans experienced poverty; between the ages of 40 and 60, 23%; and between the ages of 60 and 80, 29% (Rank & Hirschl, 2001a). This body of work has also

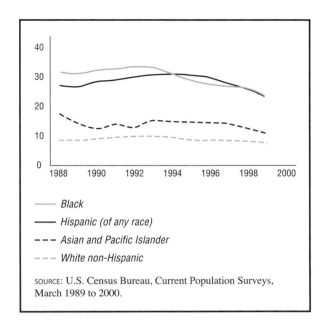

Figure 1. *Poverty rates for individuals by race and Hispanic origin, 1988–1999.* CENGAGE LEARNING, GALE.

shown that the odds of using a social safety net program during adulthood are exceedingly high (Rank & Hirschl, 2002, 2005). Consequently, 65% of all Americans between the ages of 20 and 65 will at some point reside in a household that receives an income-based welfare program (such as food stamps or Medicaid).

THE LIFE COURSE IMPACT OF POVERTY

A second major area of life course research on poverty has been to analyze the impact of poverty on various life outcomes. Two specific areas have received a considerable amount of research attention—intergenerational poverty transmission and the long-term health effects of living in poverty.

Analyses of the American system of stratification show that while some amount of social mobility does occur, social class as a whole tends to reproduce itself (Beeghley, 2008; Fischer et al., 1996). Those with working-class or lower-class parents are likely to remain working or lower class themselves. Similarly, those whose parents are affluent are likely to remain affluent. The reason for this is that parents' economic differences result in significant differences in the resources and opportunities available to their children. These differences, in turn, affect children's future life chances and outcomes (such as the accumulation of skills and education), which in turn affect their economic status (DiPrete & Eirich, 2006; Rank, 2004).

Consequently, growing up in poverty can have a significant impact upon one's later economic well-being (Bowles, Gintis, & Osborne Groves, 2005; Duncan & Brooks-Gunn, 1997). For example, Rodgers (1995) found that of those who experienced poverty as an adult, 50% had experienced poverty as a child, while an additional 38% had grown up in homes that were defined as "near poor" (below 200% of the U.S. poverty line). Research has also shown strong associations between parents' and children's income, wealth, occupational status, and neighborhood status (Beller & Hout, 2006; Shapiro, 2004; Sharkey, 2008). This research illustrates that prior economic advantages or disadvantages can have a profound effect on future life outcomes.

Researchers have also examined the impact that poverty exerts on future health outcomes. One of the most consistent findings in epidemiology is that the quality of an individual's health across the life course is negatively affected by lower socioeconomic status, particularly impoverishment (Mullahy, Robert, & Wolfe, 2004). Poverty is associated with a host of health risks for one's self and one's children, including elevated rates of heart disease, diabetes, hypertension, cancer, infant mortality, mental illness, undernutrition, lead poisoning, asthma, and dental problems. The result is a death rate for the poverty-stricken between the ages of 25 and 64 that is approximately three times higher than that for the affluent within the same age range (Pappas, Queen, Hadden, & Fisher, 1993), and a life expectancy that is considerably shorter (Geronimus, Bound, Waidmann, Colen, & Steffick, 2001). For example, Americans in the top 5% of the income distribution can expect to live approximately 9 years longer than those in the bottom 10% (Jencks, 2002).

LIFE COURSE POLICY APPROACHES FOR ALLEVIATING POVERTY

Although there are a variety of key policy approaches toward poverty alleviation (e.g., macroeconomic policies to stimulate job creation, tax policies such as the Earned Income Tax Credit), a life course approach emphasizes the importance of timing and development across the life span. With this in mind, three such strategies appear critical. First, policies that invest in the well-being and growth of individuals, particularly children, are vitally important. These include increasing access to quality child care, health care, and education. Each of these areas is essential in allowing individuals to fully develop their human and economic potential and thereby reducing their risk of poverty in the future. In addition, such policies have been shown to be quite cost effective in that an investment of resources early in life can produce sizable economic and societal benefits as individuals age

across the life course (Holzer, Schanzenbach, Duncan, & Ludwig, 2007).

A second life course approach to poverty alleviation focuses on asset-building strategies for lower income households and communities (Rank, 2007). Individual asset accumulation provides an effective strategy for coping with economic pitfalls that occur across the life course. A savings account or other source of liquid wealth can allow families to tap into financial reserves during times of economic hardship. Economists refer to this as the ability of assets to protect consumption against unexpected shocks. In addition, wealth and assets can allow individuals to accomplish more of their long-term economic and social goals. For example, financial assets can be instrumental in furthering an education, purchasing a home, or planning for retirement (Schreiner & Sherraden, 2007). Examples of asset-building policies benefiting lower income households include Individual Development Accounts in the United States, Child Trust Funds in the United Kingdom, and the Central Provident Fund in Singapore.

Just as the acquisition and development of assets are important for individuals, they are equally important for the communities in which individuals reside. Poor neighborhoods are often characterized by a lack of strong community assets, such as quality schools, decent housing, adequate infrastructure, economic opportunities, and available jobs. These, in turn, affect the life chances of residents living in such communities. Strengthening the major institutions found within lower income communities is vital because such institutions have the power to improve the quality of life, foster the accumulation of human capital, and increase the overall life course opportunities for community residents (Grogan & Proscio, 2000).

A third life course approach toward poverty alleviation is the strengthening of the social safety net. As noted earlier, a majority of individuals will encounter poverty at some point during their lifetime. Having a strong and effective safety net in place is critical in providing support so that individuals and families are able to get through such difficult economic times. Programs that provide economic relief during times of unemployment, ill health, and family disruption are fundamental to the life course well-being of individuals and families (Esping-Andersen, 2002).

All of these policy approaches recognize the importance of understanding poverty within the context of the life course. Poverty is a life course event that will affect the majority of the population. Effective poverty alleviation policies are those that recognize and confront the life course patterns, dynamics, and effects of poverty for individuals and households.

SEE ALSO Volume 1: *Poverty, Childhood;* Volume 2: *Family and Household Structure, Adulthood; Health Differentials/Disparities, Adulthood; Income Inequality; Social Class; Social Mobility; Unemployment;* Volume 3: *Poverty, Later Life; Wealth.*

BIBLIOGRAPHY

Alesina, A., & Glaeser, E. L. (2004). *Fighting poverty in the US and Europe: A world of difference.* Oxford, U.K.: Oxford University Press.

Beeghley, L. (2008). *The structure of social stratification in the United States* (5th ed.). Boston: Pearson Allyn and Bacon.

Beller, E., & Hout, M. (2006). Intergenerational social mobility: The United States in comparative perspective. *The Future of Children, 16,* 19–36.

Blank, R. M. (2008). Presidential address: How to improve poverty measurement in the United States. *Journal of Policy Analysis and Management, 27,* 233–254.

Blank, R. M., Danziger, S. H., & Schoeni, R. F. (Eds.). (2006). *Working and poor: How economic and policy changes are affecting low-wage workers.* New York: Russell Sage Foundation.

Bowles, S., Gintis, H., & Osborne Groves, M. (Eds.). (2005). *Unequal chances: Family background and economic success.* New York: Russell Sage Foundation; Princeton, NJ: Princeton University Press.

DeNavas-Walt, C., Proctor, B. D., & Smith, J. (2007, August). *Income, poverty, and health insurance coverage in the United States: 2006* (Current Population Report No. P60-233). Retrieved May 19, 2008, from U.S. Bureau of the Census Web site: http://www.census.gov/prod/2007pubs/p60-233.pdf

DiPrete, T. A., & Eirich, G. M. (2006). Cumulative advantage as a mechanism for inequality: A review of theoretical and empirical developments. *Annual Review of Sociology, 32,* 271–297.

Duncan, G. J. (1984). *Years of poverty, years of plenty: The changing economic fortunes of American workers and families.* Ann Arbor: University of Michigan, Institute for Social Research, Survey Research Center.

Duncan, G. J., & Brooks-Gunn, J. (Eds.). (1997). *Consequences of growing up poor.* New York: Russell Sage Foundation.

Esping-Andersen, G. (Ed.). (2002). *Why we need a new welfare state.* New York: Oxford University Press.

Fischer, C. S., Hout, M., Sánchez Jankowski, M., Lucas, S. R., Swidler, A., & Voss, K. (1996). *Inequality by design: Cracking the bell curve myth.* Princeton, NJ: Princeton University Press.

Fligstein, N., & Shin, T.-J. (2004). The shareholder value society: A review of the changes in working conditions and inequality in the United States, 1976 to 2000. In K. M. Neckerman (Ed.), *Social Inequality* (pp. 401–432). New York: Russell Sage Foundation.

Geronimus, A. T., Bound, J., Waidmann, T. A., Colen, C. G., & Steffick, D. (2001). Inequality in life expectancy, functional status, and active life expectancy across selected black and white populations in the United States. *Demography, 38,* 227–251.

Grogan, P. S., & Proscio, T. (2000). *Comeback cities: A blueprint for urban neighborhood revival.* Boulder, CO: Westview Press.

Holzer, H. J., Schanzenbach, D. W., Duncan, G. J., & Ludwig, J. (2007). *The economic costs of poverty in the United States: Subsequent effects of children growing up poor.* Washington, DC: Center for American Progress. Retrieved May 19, 2008, from http://www.americanprogress.org/issues/2007/01/pdf/poverty_report.pdf

Iceland, J. (2005). Measuring poverty: Theoretical and empirical considerations. *Measurement: Interdisciplinary Research and Perspective, 3,* 199–235.

Jencks, C. (2002). Does inequality matter? *Daedalus, 131,* 49–65.

Mullahy, J., Robert, S., & Wolfe, B. (2004). Health, income, and inequality. In K. M. Neckerman (Ed.), *Social Inequality* (pp. 523–544). New York: Russell Sage Foundation.

Pappas, G., Queen, S., Hadden, W., & Fisher, G. (1993). The increasing disparity in mortality between socioeconomic groups in the United States, 1960 and 1986. *The New England Journal of Medicine, 329,* 103–109.

Rank, M. R. (2004). *One nation, underprivileged: Why American poverty affects us all.* New York: Oxford University Press.

Rank, M. R. (2007). *Asset building over the life course.* Report prepared for the U.S. Department of Health and Human Services, Office of the Assistant Secretary for Planning and Evaluation.

Rank, M. R., & Hirschl, T. A. (1999). The likelihood of poverty across the American adult lifespan. *Social Work, 44,* 201–216.

Rank, M. R., & Hirschl, T. A. (2001a.) The occurrence of poverty across the life cycle: Evidence from the PSID. *Journal of Policy Analysis and Management, 20,* 737–755.

Rank, M. R., & Hirschl, T. A. (2001b). Rags or riches? Estimating the probabilities of poverty and affluence across the adult American life span. *Social Science Quarterly, 82,* 651–669.

Rank, M. R., & Hirschl, T. A. (2002). Welfare use as a life course event: Toward a new understanding of the U.S. safety net. *Social Work, 47,* 237–248.

Rank, M. R., & Hirschl, T. A. (2005). Likelihood of using food stamps during the adulthood years. *Journal of Nutrition Education and Behavior, 37,* 137–146.

Rodgers, J. R. (1995). An empirical study of intergenerational transmission of poverty in the United States. *Social Science Quarterly, 76,* 178–194.

Rowntree, B. S. (1901). *Poverty: A study of town life.* London: Macmillan.

Schreiner, M., & Sherraden, M. (2007). *Can the poor save? Saving and asset building in Individual Development Accounts.* New Brunswick, NJ: Transaction.

Shapiro, T. M. (2004). *The hidden cost of being African American: How wealth perpetuates inequality.* New York: Oxford University Press.

Sharkey, P. (2008). The intergenerational transmission of context. *American Journal of Sociology, 113,* 931–969.

Smeeding, T. M. (2005). Public policy, economic inequality, and poverty: The United States in comparative perspective. *Social Science Quarterly, 86,* 955–983.

Stevens, A. H. (1994). The dynamics of poverty spells: Updating Bane and Ellwood. *The American Economic Review, 84,* 34–37.

Stevens, A. H. (1999). Climbing out of poverty, falling back in: Measuring the persistence of poverty over multiple spells. *The Journal of Human Resources, 34,* 557–588.

United Nations Development Programme. (2007). *Human development report, 2007/2008.* New York: Palgrave Macmillan.

Mark R. Rank

R

RACISM/RACE DISCRIMINATION

Racism is an organized system that categorizes, ranks, and differentially allocates societal resources to human population groups (Williams & Rucker, 2000). According to James Jones (1997), racism builds on the negative attitudes arising from prejudice and rests on three broad assumptions: (a) that group characteristics are based on presumed biology; (b) the superiority of one group over others; and (c) the rationalization of institutional and cultural practices that formalize hierarchical domination of one racial group over another.

Racism is thus a complex construct. It is not synonymous with related terms such as prejudice, discrimination, bigotry, or bias that do not necessarily incorporate hierarchical domination in the form of social stratification or power. For example, *prejudice* is "a positive or negative attitude, judgment, or feeling about a person that is generalized from attitudes or beliefs held about the group to which the person belongs" (Jones 1997, p. 10). *Discrimination* involves behavior aimed at denying members of particular groups equal access to societal rewards and, as such, goes beyond merely thinking unfavorably about particular groups.

Racism should not be confused with other forms of oppression such as sexism, heterosexism, or homophobia. Whereas these forms of oppression share a similar root in that one group is viewed as superior to another, racism is distinct because it is founded on cultural conceptions of race. There are important implications of racism for the life course, including negative psychological effects, socioeconomic disadvantage, and racial health disparities.

RACISM AND THE CONCEPT OF RACE

Understanding racism requires an examination of the concept of race and its function in U.S. history and culture. While many have sought a genetic foundation for categorizing population groups, there is no scientific consensus that racialized groups are genetically distinct. Population groups are transformed into races for political purposes on the basis of arbitrary but distinctive phenotypic (i.e., physical appearance) and cultural criteria. The belief that groups of people identified on the basis of these criteria are *also* inherently different and genetically distinct is the unfortunate remnant of an outdated pseudo-scientific idea (Smedley & Smedley, 2005). The ideology of racism is built upon this pseudo-scientific racialization of targeted population groups.

Racism in the United States began during the colonial period, although the exact nature of the historical development of racism has been heavily debated. From one perspective, the ideology of racism is said to be a deliberate invention of early colonists to justify the enslavement of Blacks for economic purposes (Handlin & Handlin, 1947). Others argue that racism developed from preconceived prejudices against African Americans, rooted in early 19th century European biological determinism that classified humans into four hierarchical, mutually exclusive groups—mongoloid, caucasoid, negroid, and australoid—with Blacks at the bottom of the ranking. This categorization was not neutral but characterized physical differences as innate and immutable characteristics. These notions were used to justify slavery and the pseudoscience underlying this classification evolved simultaneously with the development of slavery and legal segregation (Jordan,

357

Hurricane Katrina. *Tangeyon Wall stands by a broken window in her home, which was flooded by Hurricane Katrina in New Orleans. Wall is angry that utility services are returning to her neighborhood of predominantly Black residents much slower than they are to other areas of the city.* AP IMAGES.

1974). Regardless of chronology, racism grew as a system of beliefs and practices that propagated ideas about the inferiority of persons not classified as *White*. While any ethnic group can be the target of racism, in the United States racism is particularly relevant to non-White ethnic minority groups. The lasting effects of the country's racist policies are observable in persistent racial inequities in criminal justice, education, employment, health, health care, housing, income, and other areas. While the emphasis in this entry is the United States, racism occurs in every country throughout the world.

LEVELS OF RACISM

Racism is a process that operates on multiple levels of experience, from the psychological to the social. Racism can be *internalized* when persons accept the ideology of their racial inferiority; *personally-mediated* as when persons are dehumanized or treated differently by others because of their race; or *institutionalized* due to restricted access to material resources and opportunities for empowerment throughout society (Jones, 2000). The various levels at which racism is experienced affect personal stress and life chances, which in turn affect the well-being of individuals, families, and communities.

Institutional racism is a systematic set of procedures, practices, and policies that penalize, disadvantage, and exploit individuals on the basis of race. In addition, institutional racism is the extension of individual beliefs by using and manipulating institutions to restrict the choices, rights,

mobility, and access of certain individuals. Such effects are distributed throughout society through institutional structures, ideological beliefs, and the everyday actions of people (Jones, 1997). Three examples of institutional racism in the United States are chattel slavery, the *Plessy v. Ferguson* decision of the U.S. Supreme Court, which legalized racially separate facilities, and racial residential segregation. These actions were not only associated with an ideology of racism, but they led to policies and practices that unequally distributed resources and opportunities so that people experienced unequal physical environments, educational systems, and economic opportunities.

Structural racism refers to how social structures, historical legacies, individuals, organizations, and institutions interact to disadvantage some racial groups and advantage others. Structural analysis and critical race theory suggest that racism is not an aberrant belief or behavior, but is consistent with U.S. cultural values that tangibly advantage some population groups (Ladson-Billings & Tate, 1995). A structural analysis of racism highlights the important interplay between educational, criminal justice, housing, health, and economic institutions. It is this interinstitutional interaction that distinguishes structural racism from other forms of racism or discrimination.

MEASURING RACISM AND RACIAL DISCRIMINATION

The main challenge of conducting research on racism and racial discrimination lies in the area of measurement. Currently there is little consistency or agreement on how racism or racial discrimination should be measured, much less is there available data on the psychometric properties of current measures. One construct used in research on racism and racial discrimination is perceived discrimination. The construct is based on the process of perception and emphasizes the attributions made by those trying to understand the underlying cause of interpersonal interactions. Perceived discrimination deemphasizes the intention and ideology of the actor and places the subjective interpretation of the observer at the center. In this respect, perceived discrimination is conceptually related to Ellis Cose's (1993) list of race-based daily hassles that take up time and mental energy. Much of this research is based on descriptive survey self-reports. Less empirical information is available on the cognitive processes by which people understand and decide whether or not a particular act is indeed discriminatory. This is an area in need of additional research.

Another approach is to measure experiences of discriminatory behavior. Rebecca Blank and colleagues (2004) provide four types of individual and organizational discriminatory behaviors that can guide measurement and analysis. *Intentional discrimination* is consistent with traditional notions of discrimination whereby people deliberately treat persons of different racial or ethnic groups differently. *Subtle or automatic discrimination* occurs when people unconsciously categorize people based on their race or ethnicity. Similarly, *statistical discrimination* (or profiling) occurs when an individual uses overall beliefs or generalizations about a group to make decisions about an individual in that group. Finally, in addition to the types of discrimination that can be perpetrated by individuals, organizations can reflect the same biases as people who operate within them. This type of discriminatory behavior can be referred to as *organizational discrimination*.

Racism and discrimination have led to residential segregation, exclusionary housing patterns, differential hiring and promotion practices, and other such organizational and institutional practices. Practices and laws that appear to be neutral may, in fact, lead to differential outcomes, regardless of intended impact, and therefore may be considered discriminatory. This also means that the definition of *racism* is unlikely to be universally agreed upon, because different groups will disagree on the inferences made about the causes of observed racial inequalities in income, employment, education, and health. The idea that the consequences of racism need not be intentional suggests that racism is the product of the perception of different observers. Often, terms describing such an idea are used as reactions to institutional and structural conceptualizations of racism that do not require intentionality but illustrate disparate outcomes.

EFFECTS OF RACISM AND DISCRIMINATION OVER THE LIFE COURSE

Numerous personal accounts as well as social scientific research demonstrate the pervasive negative effects of racism on outcomes spanning the entire life course (Collins, David, Handler, Wall, & Andes, 2004). Moreover, while most studies examine racism as though it occurs at a specific point in time, researchers are beginning to argue that racism is a dynamic process (Blank et al., 2004). The consequences of racism range from negative psychological effects, to socioeconomic disadvantages, to health disparities. For example, exposure to racism and racial discrimination has been associated with elevated blood pressure and unhealthy coping behaviors such as smoking or overeating (Krieger & Sidney, 1996), and socioeconomic disadvantage and poor health outcomes during gestation and childhood have been shown to predict chronic diseases in later life (Barker, 1998).

Racism also exerts its toll through suppressed anger and rage and the cognitive burden of dealing with racism on a frequent basis (Feagin & McKinney, 2003). The chronic wear and tear of racism-related stress can alter the body's ability to adapt in a healthy manner over time, thus producing adverse mental, behavioral, and physical health consequences (McEwen, 1998). The impact of racism over the life course is not always linear or continuous. There might be some critical periods, such as early childhood or in old age, where the harmful effects of racism are most intense, or disadvantage at different life stages can have a cumulative dose-response effect (Graham, 2002). Moreover, human agency can moderate the effect of racism exposures at any point during the life course.

SELECTED ISSUES OF DEBATE AND CONTROVERSY

Many provocative issues and questions are the subject of current debates regarding racism. Although there remains disagreement about what race and racism are, what is clear is that these constructs have not been treated with the same care and precision as other key social and scientific variables (LaVeist, 1996). It is common to read studies that carefully define and operationalize each variable in the analysis except race and that conflate racism with discrimination, prejudice, bias, and other related terms.

Many definitions of racism imply that a person or an act is either racist or it is not, but do not distinguish between racism and related terms such as *discrimination* and *prejudice*. Some scholars argue that this duality is a simplistic way to think of racism, which has sparked a variety of new conceptualizations of racism, including *color-blind racism*, *silent racism*, and *liberal racism* (Bonilla-Silva, 2003; Sleeper, 1997; Trepagnier, 2006). Each of these terms suggests that the oppositional categories of *racist* or *not racist* are outdated and should be replaced with a continuum that portrays 21st century racial reality in the United States. However, defining racism as a continuum suggests that just about any statement or behavior can be designated as racist. In addition, reducing racism to a question of individual-level behavior, beliefs, and attitudes clouds the distinction between racism, bias, prejudice, and discrimination.

Prejudice, bias, and discrimination are commonly used to describe the attitudes and behaviors of individuals that are hypothesized to lead to negative interpersonal interactions. Such behaviors are also used to infer the presence of systemic organizational and interrelated social, economic, and political contexts that affect differentially people by race in the absence of identifying individuals who may be biased, ethnocentric, or prejudiced. Hypothesizing racism as the fundamental cause of persistent racial differences in outcomes also can be useful for explaining the differential impact of policies and practices. Inferring the existence of racism neither requires nor precludes individuals who are biased or prejudiced against people of other races.

Sloppiness in use and measurement of the concept of racism raises concerns about how the term can potentially lead to erroneous or misleading conclusions and problems. For example, terminology such as "playing the race card" refers to efforts to infuse social stratification, institutional racism, and structural racism into the discussion of disparate outcomes. The notion that racism is nothing more than an excuse to rationalize personal incompetence or that ethnic minorities cause their own problems is often a result of efforts to discount how cultural and historical institutions advantage some and disadvantage others. Racism is not a proxy for discrimination and prejudice, but a framework for understanding how social stratification advantages some and disadvantages others. The subjective nature of the process employed to identify racism guarantees continuous debate and disagreement about what acts constitute racism and subsequently who is or is not racist. This view accentuates racism as a *process* of understanding how someone is accused of being racist as well as whether that person (or persons) accepts this conceptualization of their behaviors or statements.

The fact that a broad array of behaviors and statements can be, and often are, viewed as racist contributes to a certain degree of cynicism when objectionable discriminatory behavior and bigoted remarks are protested. Some go as far as to argue that racism is no longer a significant problem for people of color (D'Souza, 1995). Like so many contentious political disagreements, what is or is not racist is difficult to prove, except in the legal realm, because labeling something as racist often presumes or requires intention. The objectionable nature of statements, behaviors, or differences in outcomes will continue to be interpreted by many within a framework that views racism as the underlying cause. Certainly not all objectionable statements are worthy of being designated as racist, but it is important for people to understand the complexity of racism that transcends basic notions of prejudice, bias, or discrimination. Racism is an *ideology* that ranks population groups according to a hierarchy of inferiority and superiority and leads to devastating effects on people of color.

Research on racism has had important policy and practice implications. Racism has provided an important perspective for understanding persistent racial differences in such important outcomes as socioeconomic standing, housing patterns, and health. Examining the health of African Americans through the lens of racism highlights how housing policy can lead to racial residential segregation and the unequal distribution of educational and financial resources that affect opportunities for leading long and healthy lives.

SEE ALSO Volume 2: *Gender in the Work Place; Policy, Employment; Stress in Adulthood;* Volume 3: *Ageism/ Age Discrimination.*

BIBLIOGRAPHY

Barker, D. (1998). *Mothers, babies, and health in later life.* Edinburgh, UK: Churchill Livingstone.

Blank, R.M., Dabady, M., & Citro, C.F. (Eds.). (2004). *Measuring racial discrimination.* Washington, DC: National Academies Press.

Bonilla-Silva, E. (2003). *Racism without racists: Color-blind racism and the persistence of racial inequality in the United States.* Lanham, MD: Rowman & Littlefield.

Collins, J. W., David, R. J., Handler, A., Wall, S., & Andes, S. (2004). Very low birth weight in African-American infants: The role of exposure to interpersonal racial discrimination. *American Journal of Public Health, 94,* 2132–2138.

Cose, E. (1993). *The rage of a privileged class: Why do prosperous blacks still have the blues?* New York: HarperCollins.

D'Souza, D. (1995). *The end of racism: Principles for a multiracial society.* New York: Free Press.

Feagin, J. R., & McKinney, K. D. (2003). *The many costs of racism.* Lanham, MD: Rowman & Littlefield.

Graham, H. (2002). Building an interdisciplinary science of health inequalities: The example of life course research. *Social Science and Medicine, 55*(11), 2005–2016.

Handlin, O., & Handlin, M. F. (1947). Commonwealth: A study of the role of government in the American economy. New York: New York University Press.

Jones, C. P. (2000). Levels of racism: A theoretic framework and a gardener's tale. *American Journal of Public Health, 90*(8), 1212–1215.

Jones, J. M. (1997). *Prejudice and racism.* (2nd ed.). New York: McGraw-Hill.

Jordan, W. D. (1974). *The white man's burden: Historical origins of racism in the United States.* New York: Oxford University Press.

Krieger, N., & Sidney, S. (1996). Racial discrimination and blood pressure: The CARDIA study of young black and white adults. *American Journal of Public Health, 86*(10), 1370–1378.

Ladson-Billings, G., & Tate, W.F. (1995). Toward a critical race theory of education. *Teachers College Record, 97*(1), 47–68.

LaVeist, T. A. (1996). Why we should continue to study race . . . but do a better job: An essay on race, racism, and health. *Ethnicity and Disease, 6,* 21–29.

McEwen, B. S. (1998). Stress, adaptation, and disease: Allostasis and allostatic load. *Annals of the New York Academy of Sciences, 840*(1), 33–44.

Sleeper, J. (1997). *Liberal racism: How fixating on race subverts the American dream.* New York: Viking.

Smedley, A., & Smedley, B.D. (2005). Race as biology is fiction, racism as a social problem is real: Anthropological and historical perspectives on the social construction of race. *American Psychologist, 60*(1), 16–26.

Trepagnier, B. (2006). *Silent racism: How well-meaning white people perpetuate the racial divide.* Boulder, CO: Paradigm.

Williams, D. R., & Collins, C. (2001). Racial residential segregation: A fundamental cause of disparities in health. *Public Health Reports, 116,* 404–416.

Williams, D. R., & Rucker, T. D. (2000). Understanding and addressing racial disparities in health care. *Health Care Financing Review, 21*(4), 75–90.

Harold W. Neighbors
Derek M. Griffith
Denise C. Carty

REFUGEES

SEE Volume 1: *Immigration, Childhood and Adolescence;* Volume 2: *Immigration, Adulthood.*

RELATIVE COHORT SIZE HYPOTHESIS

The relative cohort size hypothesis aims to explain changes in birth rates, family formation, and well-being observed in the United States since the mid-20th century. It does so by positing that the economic and social fortunes of birth cohorts stem from their size relative to the size of their parental cohorts. It is also known as the Easterlin hypothesis, named after the economist Richard Easterlin who developed it, and the relative income or relative economic status hypothesis, named after the central concept linking relative cohort size to social and economic outcomes.

Easterlin (1961) first developed the relative cohort size hypothesis to account for fertility rates during the baby-boom years of the mid-20th century and the baby-bust years that followed (Easterlin, 1973). He later applied the argument to trends in marriage, divorce, education, female labor force participation, suicide, homicide, and alienation (Easterlin, 1978, 1987). The originality, insight, and broad scope of the hypothesis have generated a large collection of empirical studies.

THEORY

Relative cohort size has two components: the size of a birth cohort and the size of the parental cohort that produced it. First, like cohort or generational influences more generally, the size of a birth cohort has important implications for the life experiences of its members. The number of persons born during the same year or historical period affects all stages of the life course, including high school graduation, employment, starting salaries, job promotions, salary increases, marriage, childbearing, divorce, retirement, and death. The key mechanism behind these influences of cohort size is income or earnings potential. Members of

smaller cohorts face less crowding in the family and receive more attention from parents, less crowding in schools and more opportunities for educational attainment, and less crowding in the labor market and better job and earnings prospects. Larger cohorts face greater crowding and worse economic prospects.

Second, the size of the parental cohort—those born 20 to 40 years earlier—influences the expected standard of living or material aspirations of a birth cohort. Smaller parental cohorts provide a better standard of living for children, who become accustomed to that standard and develop high aspirations for their own standard of living as adults. Large parental cohorts, in contrast, create a lower expected standard of living among children.

These two components, the income potential or resources of a cohort and their expected standard of living or aspirations, define relative income. Demographic behavior, economic decision making, and social well-being follow directly from this comparison of resources to aspirations. Relative income in turn follows directly from the size of a younger cohort relative to an older cohort. In response to low relative income, members of a large cohort respond to the prospect of a deterioration of their living level relative to that of their parents by making a number of adaptations. They tend to marry late, postpone childbearing, rely on wages of working wives, and experience marital problems. Members of smaller cohorts with higher relative income require fewer such adaptations, more often following traditional norms for early marriage, two or more children, and homemaking roles for women.

The theory nicely fits the fertility swings of the post–World War II baby boom and bust. Cohorts entering young adulthood in the 1950s had been raised by a large parental generation during the poor economic times of the 1930s. Their small size, due to dropping fertility in the 1930s, created economic opportunities during the postwar prosperity. The combination of low aspirations and skyrocketing income led to early marriage, an unexpected burst of childbearing, and adoption of traditional family roles. By the 1970s the course of both relative cohort size and fertility reversed, however. The large baby boom cohorts born after World War II reached childbearing age when the high aspirations generated by the prosperity of their childhood conflicted with an overcrowded labor market and low income prospects. Couples closed the gap between their income and aspirations by avoiding the financial pressures associated with family responsibilities. They delayed marriage, had fewer children, and increased the hours worked by wives.

The logic of the theory also fits other social behaviors. According to Easterlin (1987), the sacrifice of family life and the effort to maintain economic status induce stress among members of large cohorts. This psychological and economic stress may lead to high rates of out-of-wedlock births, suicide, crime, and, homicide—behaviors particularly common among baby-boom cohorts. In contrast, cohorts with smaller relative size and less stress, such as those born during the baby-bust years, experience fewer of these social problems.

Following the implications of his argument, Easterlin (1978) boldly predicted continued changes or reversals in fertility and other social behavior in decades to come. Although many theories predicted the continuation of past trends, the relative cohort size hypothesis posited counter-cyclical change. A small cohort with high relative income has many children, who belong to a large cohort. The large cohort, raised under good economic conditions and developing high expectations, faces crowding in families, school, and work. They then adjust their family behavior to have fewer children. The next smaller generation is positioned for higher relative income and fertility, and so on. Cycles of two decades of good times thus alternate with two decades of bad times. During the 1970s, a period of social and economic malaise, Easterlin predicted a turnaround in the 1980s and 1990s as smaller cohorts entered adulthood.

EVIDENCE

The initial application of the theory to the baby boom and baby bust gave striking evidence of support. Easterlin proposed testing his hypothesis with two measures: the income of younger persons relative to older persons and the number of younger persons relative to the number of older persons. Graphing the total fertility rate by the latter measure—more precisely, the number of persons ages 30 to 64 as a ratio to persons ages 15 to 29—shows a remarkable match from 1951 to 1980 (see Figure 1). The theory does better than others in accounting for the puzzling and unexpected rise in fertility during the 1950s and the sudden and steep drop in the 1960s and 1970s.

However, the vast empirical literature stimulated in more recent decades by this provocative and testable hypothesis has been less clearly supportive. Perhaps most conspicuously, fertility failed to rebound to higher levels in the 1980s and 1990s as relative cohort size increased (see Figure 1). Otherwise, studies have shown much support but also a fair amount of disconfirmation. Interpretations of the diverse evidence have taken three forms.

First, some discount the validity of the theory. In a meta-analysis of 19 studies, Waldorf and Byun (2005) found that only 49 percent of 334 estimated effects of age structure on fertility support the relative cohort size hypothesis. They concluded that "several factors undermine the empirical support of the age structure/fertility link as hypothesized by Easterlin" (p. 36). Others favor competing theories of fertility change. For example, Lesthaeghe and Meekers (1986) and others saw a shift in norms and values as responsible for the

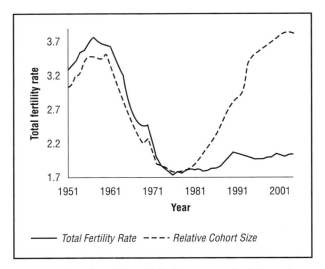

Figure 1. *Trends in the total fertility rate and relative cohort size, 1951–2004.* CENGAGE LEARNING, GALE.

drop and continued low levels of fertility in the United States and Europe. The feminist movement, youth protest, and concern with self-realization during the 1960s and 1970s represented the start of a long-term cultural trend toward individualism and post-materialism that fostered lower fertility and changing family forms. Instead of a component of counter-cyclical fluctuations caused by relative cohort size, such changes may be seen as part of a permanent second demographic transition (van de Kaa, 1987).

Second, defenders of the hypothesis argue that relative cohort size has effects that are clear and consistent, although other factors prove important as well. Macunovich (1998) found that 15 of 22 micro-level fertility studies and 15 of 22 macro-level fertility studies provided significant support for the Easterlin hypothesis. In addition, Macunovich (2002) presented wide-ranging evidence of the influence of relative cohort size on jobs, wages, relative income, female employment, college enrollment, marriage, divorce, fertility, economic demand, goods, and inflation.

Third, an integrative view argues that the influence of relative cohort size proves strong under certain conditions but not others. Easterlin (1987) hinted at this viewpoint by stating, "One would expect cohort size effects to dominate a cohort's experience only when other factors are relatively constant" (p. 3). Waldorf and Byun (2005) and Macunovich (1998, 2002) also recognized the contingent nature of the relative cohort size effects, but Pampel and Peters (1995) and Pampel (2001) presented the most extensive version of the argument. They argued that conditions during the American baby boom and bust such as low immigration, a sexual division of labor in work and family roles, and limited welfare programs intensified the importance of relative cohort size. Since then, rising immigration and movement toward gender equality has weakened the importance of relative cohort size. In a similar way, strong welfare states have limited the importance of relative cohort size for fertility and other outcomes in European nations.

After decades of intense activity, research on relative cohort size has declined to a trickle (the work of Macunovich, 2002, and Waldorf and Byun, 2005, being notable exceptions). The trend no doubt results from the more limited success of relative cohort size in explaining contemporary behavior in contrast to behavior from the 1950s to the 1970s. Yet the potential value of studying the influence of cohort numbers remains. Researchers need to improve on previous work by controlling for factors that attenuate the influence of relative cohort size, improving measures of relative income, and recognizing the contingent nature of relative cohort size effects. With such improvements, the relative cohort size hypothesis may still offer insights into demographic and social behavior.

SEE ALSO Volume 2: *Baby Boom Cohort;* Volume 3: *Age, Period, Cohort Effects; Cohort.*

BIBLIOGRAPHY

Easterlin, R. A. (1961). The American baby boom in historical perspective. *American Economic Review, 51,* 869–911.

Easterlin, R. A. (1973). Relative economic status and the American fertility swing. In E. B. Sheldon (Ed.), *Family economic behavior: Problems and prospects* (pp. 170–223). Philadelphia: Lippincott.

Easterlin, R. A. (1978). What will 1984 be like? Socioeconomic implications of recent twists in age structure. *Demography, 15,* 397–432.

Easterlin, R. A. (1987). *Birth and fortune.* (2nd ed.). New York: Basic Books.

Lesthaeghe, R., & Meekers, D. (1986). Value changes and the dimensions of familism in the European Community. *European Journal of Population, 2,* 225–268.

Macunovich, D. J. (1998). Fertility and the Easterlin hypothesis: An assessment of the literature. *Journal of Population Economics, 11,* 53–111.

Macunovich, D. J. (2002). *Birth quake: The baby boom and its aftershocks.* Chicago: University of Chicago Press.

Pampel, F. C. (2001). *The institutional context of population change: Patterns of fertility and mortality across high-income nations.* Chicago: University of Chicago Press.

Pampel, F. C., & Peters, H. E. (1995). The Easterlin effect. *Annual Review of Sociology, 21,* 163–194.

van de Kaa, D. J. (1987). Europe's second demographic transition. *Population Bulletin, 42*(1), 1–47.

Waldorf, B., & Byun, P. (2005). Meta-analysis of the impact of age structure on fertility. *Journal of Population Economics, 18,* 15–40.

Fred C. Pampel

RELIGION AND SPIRITUALITY, ADULTHOOD

Religion is an important part of adult identity. Almost two-thirds of American adults believe in God without having doubts, and 61% claim membership in a religious organization (Sherkat & Ellison, 1999). In fact, some scholars assert that belief, along with relationships and work, is one of the three pillars of developing an identity as one becomes an adult (Arnett, 2004). Although it is a central component of identity, religiosity is not stable over the course of adulthood. Instead, ebbs and flows in religiosity coincide with major life course transitions. Moreover, historical trends suggest changes in religiosity at the societal level, and there are ongoing scholarly debates about the nature and extent of those changes.

DEFINITIONS AND MEASUREMENT

Religion is an ambiguous term that has been used to describe both personal beliefs and formal organizations. The coming of age of the baby boom generation forced a better articulation of what is meant by religion in the scholarly literature. In their rejection of many formal institutions, baby boomers challenged institutionalized religion. They were among the first to draw a distinction between being religious and being spiritual (Roof, 1999). Being religious meant being associated with formal religious institutions and adhering to doctrinal decrees, whereas being spiritual meant interacting with higher or nonphysical powers that helped in one's search for meaning in life. Spirituality, then, can exist via formal religious institutions but also can exist outside them (Zinnbauer, Pargament, Cole, Rye, Butter, Belavich, et al., 1997). Many baby boomers claimed that they were spiritual, but not religious (Roof, 1999).

This distinction between religiosity and spirituality continues to exist, but because spirituality is more difficult to measure than religiosity, it is less often the focus of study. Religiosity is measured in various ways, including denominational affiliation, service attendance, belief in a deity, and conviction or strength of beliefs. Those measures are relatively common in surveys such as the General Social Survey (GSS), one of the primary sources for tracking aggregate changes in religiosity over time (Sherkat & Ellison, 1991, Firebaugh & Harley, 1991, Chaves, 1991, Hout & Fischer, 2002).

Because of its highly personal nature, spirituality is more difficult to define with simple survey questions. The relatively smaller set of studies that consider spirituality tend to use small sample surveys with open-ended questions (Zinnbauer et al., 1997) or ethnographic methods (Sargeant, 2000) to understand how individuals view the place of spirituality in their lives. Large surveys that take individual spiritual activity into account such as the GSS often use measures such as prayer and meditation, which originate from organized religions. Those measures may overlook new or unique ways of practicing spirituality. A number of religious institutions are incorporating new practices meant to enhance the individual's interaction with a higher power, adding to the difficulty in separating the two concepts. In an age when the boundaries between spirituality and religiosity are being highlighted by some and blurred by others, continued research on individuals' and researchers' definitions of these concepts is important (Roof, 1999).

TRENDS IN RELIGIOSITY OVER TIME

Two main trends in religion dominated the scholarly landscape at the start of the 21st century: the redistribution of individuals among denominations, or switching, and the process of secularization, that is, the process by which U.S. society was becoming less religious and thus more secular. In general the denominational affiliation of a person's parents is highly predictive of that person's affiliation in adulthood. However, a substantial minority of Americans—about one-third—switch affiliations during their lifetimes. Membership in conservative Protestant, Jehovah's Witness, Mormon, and nonreligious categories is growing, whereas mainline Protestant denominations are declining in membership. The denominations that are gaining members are also the ones most likely to retain members, and so their ranks are likely to remain stable or continue to grow (Sherkat & Ellison, 1999). The percentage of Americans who reported no religious preference doubled from 7% to 14% from 1991 to 1998 at the same time that those claiming a conservative Protestant affiliation grew (Hout & Fischer, 2002). This may represent an increasing polarization of belief in the United States, with more people subscribing to no formalized beliefs or strict fundamentalist beliefs.

Whether the United States is secularizing and why are perhaps the most debated questions in the contemporary scholarly study of religion. Whereas some point to the stability of attendance rates at religious services as evidence against secularization, others argue that a process of secularization is taking place nonetheless. This belief stems mostly from changes in common correlates of religious participation, as was shown by Robert Wuthnow in his 2007 book *After the Baby Boom: How Twenty and Thirty Somethings Are Shaping the Future of American Religion*. First, getting married and having children traditionally have been the primary triggers for initiating or reinitiating religious involvement. However, in more recent cohorts of young adults marriage is delayed substantially, and people are starting families later and having fewer children. Moreover, whereas religious involvement increases with educa-

tion, women who earn graduate degrees are less likely to attend services than are those who have only a bachelor's degree. As more women earn advanced degrees, religious involvement among women probably will drop. Thus, although overall service attendance rates have remained stable, rates for young adults have declined and may continue to decline. In fact, the greatest declines have been among those who are not married and those without children, two groups that are increasing in size as a result of the trends in family formation mentioned above.

Although attendance may be declining for recent generations, Wuthnow's (2007) assessment indicates that religious beliefs seem to have remained robust since the 1970s. However, Wuthnow argues that although religious beliefs still are held by many young adults, the content of those beliefs has taken a different form. Instead of doctrinal beliefs, young adults are "tinkering" with a variety of faith traditions, experiences, and resources to build their belief systems. Moreover, belief systems are developed around individual needs as people seek meaning in their lives. Thus, overall attendance rates have not changed in recent decades, but contemporary young adults are less involved in formal religion than were their counterparts in the 1970s; their faith-seeking quests highlight a renewed interest in spirituality.

In a series of studies sociologists have debated the question of why religious attendance rates have been so resilient across decades of major social change (Chaves, 1991, Firebaugh & Harley, 1991, Hout & Fischer, 2002). On the one hand, if marriage and childbearing spur religious involvement, the coming of age and family formation of the baby boomers should have led to increases in church attendance. On the other hand, the previously mentioned rejection of institutions, including formal religion, by the baby boomers should have led to declines in church attendance. Researchers have suggested a number of reasons for this stability. First, a religious revival in the 1980s that increased all cohorts' attendance rates might have masked declining attendance rates across generations. Second, although younger cohorts have lower attendance rates than the older cohorts they are replacing, the large number of baby boomers may be hiding the potential decrease in attendance. Still others feel that life cycle effects remain constant across cohorts and that changes in family structure and cohort size are the key influences on attendance rates.

Regardless of its causes, most researchers agree that the stable attendance and belief rates indicate that secularization has not occurred in the United States, particularly compared with Western Europe, where attendance rates have declined in recent decades. However, the changes in family structure, education requirements, and comparatively low attendance rates among young Americans mentioned above have led some to wonder about the future of organized religion in the United

Buddhist Meditation. *Residents from the Manhattan borough of New York participate in a group meditation session during the sixth annual Change Your Mind Day in Central Park. The free event included meditation teachings from various Buddhist traditions, contemplative exercises, poetry, and music.* **AP IMAGES.**

States. The ability of organized religion to adapt to these changes may determine its staying power in the United States. As Penny Edgell discusses in *Religion and Family in a Changing Society* (2006), the many church programs that were built around the family structure of the 1950s are often ill equipped for the hectic schedules of modern dual-earner and single-parent families. However, she found that innovative congregations are exploring new programs (day care programs, singles groups, intergenerational activities) that are inclusive of all family forms while continuing to provide a moral vision of the "good family" and that those congregations are flourishing. This study illustrates the ability of religion to adjust to a variety of structural changes.

RELIGION ACROSS THE LIFE COURSE

Religiosity is very responsive to life changes triggered by common transitions in the life course. As young people

transition from adolescence to adulthood, religiosity diminishes. There are several reasons for this. First, as Jeffrey Arnett (2004) noted, developing one's own beliefs and values is a core aspect of becoming an adult. Young people want to decide for themselves what their religious beliefs will be, and as they do so, they may relinquish their parents' beliefs at least temporarily. In addition, many young people pursue education beyond high school, and service attendance is noticeably low among college students. This may be due to the freedom college students have to explore their beliefs when separated from their parents and an increased exposure to people from other faith traditions. Another explanation is that college promotes scientific thinking that is at odds with the supernatural beliefs of many religions (Johnson, 1997). Yet others argue that many college students simply "stow" their religion while they are in college because it is not part of mainstream college culture; they maintain their beliefs but do not voice them or outwardly practice their religion (Clydesdale, 2007).

Family formation is generally the first life course event in adulthood that triggers or renews religious participation (Wilson & Sherkat, 1994). Religious involvement increases with both marriage and childbearing (Mueller & Cooper, 1986, DeVaus, 1982, Chaves, 1991). There are several reasons why religious involvement increases with family formation. Parents may be prompted to become involved to socialize their children into a faith tradition. Families may increase their involvement to take advantage of the social support available to them in many religious institutions. However, it appears that these family formation events do not prompt an increase in religiosity among everyone. Rather, increases in religious involvement occur when people make these transitions at normative ages, not early or late (Stolzenberg, Blair-Loy, & Waite, 1995).

Perhaps the social connections available through religion are more accessible if one is of the same age as other adherents who are experiencing these life transitions. It also could be the case that religious involvement is part of a normative script that those making family transitions at the "right" time are more concerned about following. Also, adults who view religion as intimately connected to family life are more likely to return to their religion (Edgell, 2006). Moreover, it is "traditional" family formation, not just any kind of family formation, that induces an increase in religiosity. For example, those who cohabit or who have children outside marriage do not experience the same increase in religious involvement as those who have a child within marriage (Chaves, 1991).

Two less desirable life course events—divorce and death—usually occur after marriage and childbearing. Although less prevalent than marriage or childbearing, divorce is an increasingly common event that triggers changes in religiosity, although in different directions for men and for women. Men who divorce are more likely to drop out of religion, whereas women who divorce are more likely to take up religion. Again, these effects apply to those who divorce at normative ages for divorce: the early thirties (Stolzenberg et al., 1995). Morbidity or impending mortality may prompt increases in religiosity as individuals cope with health problems and contemplate their place in an afterlife (Ellison, 1991).

INFLUENCES OF RELIGION

Religious institutions are family-friendly institutions (Edgell, 2006). D. A. Abbott, M. Berry, and W. H. Meredith (1990) discuss the ways in which marriages and parenting benefit from religious involvement. Religious communities offer families a variety of social supports. Families build friendships with other members that facilitate the exchange of favors such as child care, meal assistance when a loved one is sick, and occasional transportation assistance, all of which are helpful in managing family duties. Some religious institutions provide formal family services such as food pantries, shelters, counseling, and activities for parents, children, and families. Many religions also have teachings about how to treat family members, including directives on respect, selflessness, and forgiveness, all of which should be beneficial for spousal and parent-child relationships. In fact, couples who are more religious report happier and more stable marriages (Call & Heaton, 1997, Scanzoni & Arnett, 1987, Wuthnow, 2007), although it is difficult to know whether religion makes these couples less likely to divorce or if they would be less inclined to divorce even without adult exposure to religion. Finally, religious families may rely on divine intervention to cope with family issues or stress. Believing that there is a higher being guiding family life can relieve pressure in times of strain and help families cope with adversity (Ellison, 1991).

Some researchers argue that various religious traditions may influence family formation in different ways (Wilcox, 2004). For example, conservative Protestant denominations are more likely to promote a male-breadwinner family model that emphasizes the dependence of each spouse on the other, whereas liberal Protestant denominations more commonly emphasize egalitarian relationships. Considerable time is devoted to teachings on parenting in conservative Protestant denominations, which emphasize strict discipline paired with affection and emotional investment (Wilcox, 2004). Although there is debate about which family form and parenting style is most beneficial for families, different religious family directives probably produce different outcomes or different ways of interpreting one's family.

In addition to offering benefits for families, religion can serve other positive purposes for individuals. Specifically, religion and its teachings often make behavioral proscriptions to encourage healthy and lawful behavior.

For example, religions promote health by discouraging smoking and alcohol and drug use (Sherkat & Ellison, 1999). In addition, many religions discourage nonmarital sex, a practice that often increases pregnancy and disease risks if the partners are casual or nonexclusive (Barkan, 2006). Religious involvement and belief have been shown to promote positive psychological well-being as well (Bjorck & Thurman, 2007, Willits & Crider, 1988). As was noted above, religious individuals are better able to cope with stress and strain, in part because they believe life circumstances are out of their control and in the hands of a divine being (Ellison, 1991).

RELIGION AND POLICY ISSUES

Since the year 2000 religion has been granted a greater role in policy debates and federal programs. During his presidency George W. Bush created the White House Office of Faith-Based and Community Initiatives (FBCI), which oversees similarly named centers in eleven federal agencies. The purpose of that action was to "lead a determined attack on need by strengthening and expanding the role of faith-based and community organizations in providing services" (White House, 2007). Particularly relevant to life course transitions, one FBCI center in the Department of Health and Human Services operates the Healthy Marriage Initiative, a program whose goal is to encourage healthy marriages and promote involved, committed, and responsible fatherhood (U.S. Department of Health and Human Services, 2007). Many of the grantees under this federal initiative are faith-based organizations such as Catholic Charities, Lutheran Immigration Refugee Services, Aish HaTorah, and the United Methodist Church. Thus, religious institutions increasingly are playing a role in federal efforts to shape life course events such as marriage.

Immigration is another issue that has generated renewed political interest in part as a result of the faith traditions of recent and future immigrants. The United States has long been a Christian-majority country, with more than 80% of its citizens claiming membership in Christian denominations (Sherkat & Ellison, 1999). However, recent immigrant groups are increasingly non-Christian. Of the top five birth countries of the U.S. foreign-born population in 2000, three were non-Christian nations: China, India, and Vietnam (U.S. Census Bureau, 2003). Moreover, the refugee population in the United States increasingly is coming from predominantly non-Christian nations (U.S. Department of Homeland Security, 2006). The ways in which religion operates in the life course of adults probably will become more variable as the content of Americans' religious beliefs and practices becomes more variable. In addition, the way the new immigrants are incorporated into a very different constituent faith fabric will be a new and stronger test of the American ideal of religious pluralism.

EMERGING QUESTIONS

The destandardization of the life course, particularly delays in marriage and childbearing and increases in cohabitation and nonmarital childbearing, will challenge religious institutions that long have catered to "traditional" families. Research should continue to monitor the relevance of religion to individual and family lives as those lives unfold in less traditional forms. Will religious institutions continue to adapt to bring nontraditional family forms into the fold? If so, how will they do that?

A related topic that merits more attention is the degree to which the faith-seeking quest of individuals will continue to grow. Wuthnow (2007) and others have noted that current generations of young adults are tinkering with many religious and spiritual beliefs and practices in a quest for a more individualized faith that suits their lives. The emergent church movement is an example of how that quest has become formalized. The emergent church gives individuals a space in which to encounter a number of beliefs and views and, through interaction with one another, build their own belief systems. It will be interesting to follow this and other similar movements to discover the ways in which they are addressing particular needs of contemporary adults. Will the individualized faith-seeking quest continue as this new generation of young adults reaches middle age, or is it specific to this particular life stage? Is it simply a form of religious revival or part of a long-term trend toward the deinstitutionalization of religion? Future research should investigate the changing nature of individual beliefs.

Historically, religion and spirituality have occupied a central place in individual identity. They have many documented benefits, including family and social support and physical and psychological health. The importance and usefulness of religion ebb and flow with life course events and across time as the structure and purpose of religious institutions fit more or less with contemporary individual and family life. As the life course undergoes substantial change, religion will have to adapt to remain relevant to future generations of adults.

SEE ALSO Volume 1: *Identity Development;* Volume 2: *Individuation/Standardization Debate; Political Behavior and Orientations, Adulthood; Volunteering, Adulthood.*

BIBLIOGRAPHY

Abbott, D. A., Berry, M., & Meredith, W. H. (1990). Religious belief and practice: A potential asset in helping families. *Family Relations, 39*(4): 443–448.

Arnett, J. J. (2004). *Emerging adulthood: The winding road from the late teens through the twenties.* New York and Oxford: Oxford University Press.

Barkan, S. E. (2006). Religiosity and premarital sex in adulthood. *Journal for the Scientific Study of Religion, 45*(3): 407–417.

Bjorck, J. P., & Thurman, J. W. (2007). Negative life events, patterns of positive and negative religious coping, and psychological functioning. *Journal for the Scientific Study of Religion, 46*(2): 159–167.

Call, V. R., & Heaton, T. B. (1997). Religious influence on marital stability. *Journal for the Scientific Study of Religion, 36*(3): 382–392.

Chaves, M. (1991). Family structure and Protestant church attendance: The sociological basis of cohort and age effects. *Journal for the Scientific Study of Religion, 30*(4): 501–514.

Clydesdale, T. (2007). Abandoned, pursued, or safely stowed? *Social Science Research Council Forum.* Retrieved June 22, 2008, from http://www.religion.ssrc.org/forum/ Clydesdale.pdf

De Vaus, D. A. (1982). The impact of children on sex related differences in church attendance. *Sociological Analysis, 43*(2): 145–154.

Edgell, P. (2006). *Religion and family in a changing society.* Princeton, NJ: Princeton University Press.

Ellison, C. C. (1991). Religious involvement and subjective well-being. *Journal of Health and Social Behavior, 32*(1): 80–99.

Firebaugh, G., & Harley, B. (1991). Trends in U.S. church attendance: Secularization and revival, or merely lifecycle effects? *Journal for the Scientific Study of Religion, 30*(4): 487–500.

Hout, M., & Fischer, C. S. (2002). Why more Americans have no religious preference: Politics and generations. *American Sociological Review, 67*(2): 165–190.

Johnson, D. C. (1997). Formal education vs. religious belief: Soliciting new evidence with multinomial logit modeling. *Journal for the Scientific Study of Religion, 36*(2): 231–46.

Mueller, D. P., & Cooper, P. W. (1986). Religious interest and involvement of young adults: A research note. *Review of Religious Research, 27*(3): 245–254.

Roof, W. C. (1999). *Spiritual marketplace: Baby boomers and the remaking of American religion.* Princeton, NJ: Princeton University Press.

Sargeant, K. H. (2000). *Seeker churches: Promoting traditional religion in a nontraditional way.* New Brunswick, NJ: Rutgers University Press.

Scanzoni, J., & Arnett, C. (1987). Enlarging the understanding of marital commitment via religious devoutness, gender role preferences, and locus of marital control. *Journal of Family Issues, 8*(1): 136–156.

Sherkat, D. E., & Ellison, C. G. (1999). Recent developments and current controversies in the sociology of religion. *Annual Review of Sociology, 25*: 363–394.

Stolzenberg, R. M., Blair-Loy, M., & Waite, L. J. (1995). Religious participation in early adulthood: Age and family life cycle effects on church membership. *American Sociological Review, 60*(1): 84–103.

U.S. Census Bureau. (2003). *The foreign born population: 2000.* Economics and Statistics Administration of the U.S. Department of Commerce. Retrieved June 22, 2008, from http://www.census.gov/pfrod/2003pus./c2kbr-34.pdf

U.S. Department of Health and Human Services. (2007). *The healthy marriage initiative.* Administration for Children and Families. Retrieved June 22, 2008, from http:// www.acf.hhs.gov/healthymarriage/about/mission.html#goals

U.S. Department of Homeland Security. (2006). *Yearbook of immigration statistics.* Office of Immigration Statistics.

Retrieved June 22, 2008, from http://www.dhs.gov/ximgtn/statistics/publications/yearbook.shtm

White House. (2007). *White House faith-based & community initiatives*. Retrieved June 22, 2008, from http://www.whitehouse.gov/government/fbci/president-initiative.html

Wilcox, W. B. (2004). *Soft patriarchs, new men: How Christianity shapes fathers and husbands*. Chicago: University of Chicago Press.

Willits, F. K., & Crider, D. M. (1988). Religion and well-being: Men and women in the middle years. *Review of Religious Research, 29*: 281–294.

Wilson, J., & Sherkat, D. E. (1994). Returning to the fold. *Journal for the Scientific Study of Religion, 33*(2): 148–161.

Wuthnow, R. (2007). *After the baby boomers: How twenty and thirty somethings are shaping the future of American religion*. Princeton, NJ: Princeton University Press.

Zinnbauer, B. J., Pargament, K. I., Cole, B., Rye, M. S., Butter, E. M., Belavich, T. G., et al. (1997). Religion and spirituality: Unfuzzying the fuzzy. *Journal for the Scientific Study of Religion, 36*(4): 549–564.

Ann Meier
Kirsten Bengston O'Brien

REMARRIAGE

Given that roughly one in two marriages is not expected to last a lifetime, it is no surprise that remarriage is an important event in the life course of many Americans. Just under half of all marriages in the mid-1990s involved at least one previously married partner (Clarke, 1995), making remarriage unusually common in the United States relative to other countries. The context in which remarriage occurs differs from that of first marriage in a number of important respects. For example, remarriage tends to occur later in the life course than first marriage. In the mid-1990s women's average age at remarriage after divorce was 39.7 (42.5 years for men), compared to an average age of 26.6 years for first marriage (28.6 years for men; Schoen & Standish, 2001). Remarried individuals bring with them experiences and obligations from at least one prior marriage, which may include changed attitudes about relationships, children, or ongoing interactions with a former spouse. Remarriage often creates complex kinship networks involving parents, children, and siblings with varying relationships to one another. It is also important to keep in mind that remarriage can offer an important route to postdivorce economic recovery for women and children, who tend to experience a substantial drop in standard of living when a marriage ends. Because this entry focuses on remarriage in adulthood rather than later life, the discussion emphasizes remarriage following divorce rather than widowhood. The experience of children living in remarried families is the focus of a separate entry.

REMARRIAGE TRENDS AND PATTERNS

Remarriage is historically common in the United States, although pathways into remarriage have changed substantially over time. Most notably, in the early 21st century remarriage is much more likely to follow divorce than the death of a spouse. Remarriage was more than three times as likely to involve a widowed partner as a divorced partner in 1900 (Jacobson, 1959). By 1990 this pattern had turned on its head, with remarriage more than nine times as likely to involve a divorced partner as a widowed partner (Clarke, 1995). This shift has important implications for the nature of remarried family experiences. For example, in the case of families with children, rather than "substituting" for a parent who has died, a stepparent is often added to an existing set of parental figures in the lives of children (Ganong & Coleman, 2004).

Although remarriage continues to be common in the United States, rates of remarriage declined sharply during the latter half of the 20th century. Between 1970 and 1990, the annual rate of remarriage declined from 123 to 76 marriages per 1,000 divorced women and from 205 to 106 marriages per 1,000 divorced men (Clarke, 1995). Although previously married people are remarrying less, they are no less likely to live with a romantic partner. In fact, the proportion of individuals living with a partner after marital separation increased somewhat between 1970 and the early 1980s (Bumpass, Sweet, & Cherlin, 1991). Cohabitation is more common among separated and divorced people than among the never married, with cohabitation a step along the path to remarriage for the majority of Americans. Indeed, 54% of individuals entering a remarriage during the early to mid-1980s lived with their partner before marriage, compared to only 39% of those marrying for the first time (Bumpass & Sweet, 1989). Cohabiting relationships also tend to be of longer duration among the previously married than among the never married and are more likely to involve children (Bumpass et al., 1991). Thus, nonmarital cohabitation is an important setting for postdivorce family life.

The experience of formal remarriage differs between men and women and across racial and ethnic groups. Estimates for the mid-1990s suggest that just over two-thirds of women but more than three-quarters of men eventually remarry after divorce (Schoen & Standish, 2001). The male advantage in remarriage is even larger after the death of a spouse than after divorce, although this largely reflects gender differences in the likelihood of remarriage at older ages (discussed below). Considerable variation in the likelihood of remarriage also exists across racial and ethnic groups in the United States. Whereas 58% of non-Hispanic White women remarry within 5 years of divorce, the same is true for only 44% of Hispanic women and 32% of non-Hispanic Black women (Bramlett & Mosher, 2001). Reasons for racial and ethnic differences in the likelihood of remarriage are not well understood.

Those who remarry tend to do so relatively quickly, with roughly half remarrying within 3 years of the time a first marriage ends in divorce (Kreider & Fields, 2002). However, because some people never remarry, it takes about 7 years for half of all people experiencing divorce to remarry (Bumpass, Sweet, & Castro Martin, 1990). It is also important to keep in mind that some separated couples may not obtain a legal divorce until at least one partner wishes to remarry, which means that this figure may somewhat underestimate the average total time to remarriage after partners no longer live together (Sweet & Bumpass, 1987). This fact is particularly important when evaluating racial and ethnic differences in patterns of remarriage. Fully 91% of non-Hispanic White women legally divorce 3 years after separating from a first spouse, compared to only 57% of non-Hispanic Black women (Bramlett & Mosher, 2001). For these reasons, family scholars frequently consider the period "at risk" of remarriage to begin when spouses stop living together rather than at the time of legal divorce.

DETERMINANTS OF REMARRIAGE

Although considerably less is known about the process of remarriage than first marriage, a number of studies examine which types of people are more or less likely to remarry after divorce. For example, individuals who are older at the time of separation are less likely to remarry than are individuals who are younger when their marriages end. The relationship between age at separation and remarriage is more pronounced among women than men (Sweet & Bumpass, 1987), perhaps because the pool of available marriage partners declines more rapidly with age for women than for men. This occurs for a number of reasons, including sex differences in life expectancy (women live longer than men) and because men tend to marry women somewhat younger than themselves whereas women tend to marry men somewhat older than themselves (Goldman, Westoff, & Hammerslough, 1984). Individuals who married for the first time at a relatively young age also are more likely than others to remarry after divorce, perhaps because they have an unusually strong desire to be married or because they have less experience with life outside of marriage (Bumpass et al., 1990; Waite, Goldscheider, & Witsberger, 1986).

A number of studies consider how children influence the likelihood that their parents will remarry. Children may constrain their parents' resources and time, affect the desire to remarry, or influence a parent's attractiveness to others as a potential marriage partner. Many studies suggest that having a relatively large number of children or having young children reduces a woman's likelihood of remarriage after divorce (e.g., Bumpass et al., 1990; Koo, Suchindran, & Griffith, 1984). Children place less of a constraint on men's chances of remarriage, perhaps because men are less likely than women to live with their children after divorce. Some research suggests, however, that men who are highly involved with their nonresident children are more likely than other nonresident fathers to enter new unions (Stewart, Manning, & Smock, 2003). One possible explanation for this finding is that the kinds of men who are highly involved fathers may also tend to be more committed to their romantic relationships than other men or tend to have better "relationship skills." Living in an area with relatively stricter enforcement of child support laws is also associated with lower rates of remarriage among low-income fathers (Bloom, Conrad, & Miller, 1998), perhaps because such laws increase the perceived financial obligations of previously married men.

Social scientists have also considered how socioeconomic characteristics such as education and earnings influence the likelihood of remarriage. Relatively higher earnings are generally found to increase remarriage among men, but the nature of this association among women is less well understood (e.g., Glick & Lin, 1987; Morrison & Ritualo, 2000; Wolf & MacDonald, 1979). No association between education and remarriage is found for White women, but among Black women remarriage probabilities are lowest for those with the least education (Smock, 1990). After adjusting for group differences in characteristics such as age at separation and number of children, Black women who are high school dropouts have a 60% lower rate of remarriage than otherwise similar Black women with more education. Although most research reports no overall relationship between men's remarriage and education, little work has investigated racial differences in this association among men.

Finally, prior research also considers whether "initiator status" in divorce has implications for subsequent patterns of remarriage. The nature of the divorce experience may differ considerably depending on whether individuals initiate divorce themselves or end their marriages based on a decision made by a dissatisfied spouse. Diane Vaughan (1986) argued that the initiating partner has a critical advantage over the noninitiating partner with respect to time, such that the initiator has a head start on emotional adjustment to divorce and more time to identify potential alternative marriage partners. Evidence suggests that the availability of new marriage partners is sometimes itself a factor in the decision to divorce (South & Lloyd, 1995). It is thus perhaps not surprising that remarriage tends to occur more quickly for initiating than noninitiating partners (Sweeney, 2002). This difference is most pronounced within the first few years of a marital separation and for women who are relatively older at the time their first marriages end.

THE NATURE OF REMARRIED RELATIONSHIPS

A number of studies explore the nature of remarried relationships, generally defined as marriages involving at least one previously married partner. Outcomes examined include childbearing, marital power and autonomy, and relationship quality and stability. For example, studies suggest that roughly one-half of remarried women bear children within their new unions (Wineberg, 1990), although the presence of stepchildren from a previous relationship reduces the likelihood of childbearing with a new spouse (Stewart, 2002). The association between stepchildren and childbearing intentions is weaker, however, when children are the biological offspring of the husband rather than the wife in a remarried relationship. This again may stem from the increased likelihood of children living with their mothers after divorce rather than their fathers, as the husband's children are relatively less likely to live in the remarried couple's household.

Research suggests that remarriages tend to be more egalitarian than first marriages and are more likely to involve shared decision making, although findings vary across studies (Ganong & Coleman, 2004). Wives tend to do more housework than husbands in all marriages, yet chores tend to be shared more equally in remarriages than first marriages and tasks are less likely to be segregated based on gender in remarriages (Ganong & Coleman, 2004). Some evidence also suggests that remarried families may tend to organize their finances differently than first-married families, with husbands and wives in remarriages being more likely to keep at least some of their money in individual rather than pooled family accounts (Treas, 1993). This may because of a relatively greater desire for financial independence or because of remarried husbands' and wives' greater likelihood of having financial obligations to family members from a previous marriage. Wives in remarried families also tend to perceive themselves as having greater influence over family financial matters than do wives in first-married families (Ganong & Coleman, 2004).

Although most studies report only small differences between remarried families and first-married families with respect to levels of marital quality, remarriages do tend to be less stable than first marriages. Roughly 36% of women entering a second marriage in the early 1980s ended these unions through separation or divorce within 10 years, compared with only 27% of women entering

first marriages during the same period (Kreider & Fields, 2002). The higher instability of remarriages is particularly pronounced within the first few years of a marital relationship (Sweet & Bumpass, 1987). Andrew Cherlin (1978) argued that the lower stability of remarried families may exist because remarriage after divorce is "incompletely institutionalized," meaning that remarriage is not supported by the same laws or shared expectations about social roles and obligations as first marriage. Remarried families have fewer social norms to guide them in making decisions such as which kinship terms to use in reference to individual family members (e.g., should a stepfather be called "Dad" by his wife's children?) or what kind of relationship a stepparent should have with a stepchild (e.g., should a stepparent have the authority to discipline a stepchild?). Remarried families involving stepchildren are also governed by different legal rules than first-married families with only shared biological children. For example, stepparents do not generally have the same legal obligation to provide financial support to a stepchild as a biological child and do not generally have the same presumptive right to visitation with stepchildren after a marriage to the child's biological parent has ended (Mason, Fine, & Carnochan, 2004).

The relatively lower stability of remarriages than first marriages may also result from preexisting differences in the characteristics of people who marry multiple times versus those who marry only once. For example, remarried individuals tend to differ from first-married individuals with respect to divorce risk factors such as level of educational attainment and the perceived ability to cope with divorce (Booth & Edwards, 1992; Castro Martin & Bumpass, 1989). Furthermore, remarried individuals are more likely than first-married individuals to have entered their first marriages as teenagers, which some argue may reflect personality characteristics (e.g., impulsiveness, conscientiousness) or other background factors that make it difficult to choose appropriate romantic partners or maintain relationships throughout the life course (e.g., Castro Martin & Bumpass, 1989).

DISCUSSION

Although almost half of recent marriages in the United States involve a previously married partner, scholars still know considerably less about remarriage than about first marriage. It is important to study remarriage in its own right because of key differences in the context in which remarriage tends to occur. Much of what scholars do know about trends and differentials in patterns of remarriage comes from data collected by the mid-1990s. In the 1970s Cherlin argued that remarriage was "incompletely institutionalized." As increasing numbers of individuals and families have experienced remarriage after divorce, has remarriage become more fully institutionalized? Have the norms, expectations, and determinants associated with the formation and stability of remarriage changed over time? In short, despite a large body of research investigating remarriage, much remains to be learned.

SEE ALSO Volume 2: *Cohabitation; Divorce and Separation; Family and Household Structure, Adulthood.*

BIBLIOGRAPHY

Bloom, D. E., Conrad, C., & Miller, C. K. (1998). Child support and fathers' remarriage and fertility. In I. Garfinkel, S. S. McLanahan, D. R. Meyer, & J. A. Seltzer (Eds.), *Fathers under fire: The revolution in child support enforcement* (pp. 128–156). New York: Russell Sage Foundation.

Booth, A., & Edwards, J. N. (1992). Starting over: Why remarriages are more unstable. *Journal of Family Issues, 13,* 179–194.

Bramlett, M. D., & Mosher, W. D. (2001). *First marriage dissolution, divorce, and remarriage: United States* (Advance Data from Vital and Health Statistics, No. 323). Hyattsville, MD: National Center for Health Statistics. Retrieved June 18, 2008, from http://www.cdc.gov/nchs/

Bumpass, L. L., & Sweet, J. A. (1989). National estimates of cohabitation. *Demography, 26,* 615–625.

Bumpass, L. L., Sweet, J. A., & Castro Martin, T. (1990). Changing patterns of remarriage. *Journal of Marriage and Family, 52,* 747–756.

Bumpass, L. L., Sweet, J. A., & Cherlin, A. (1991). The role of cohabitation in declining rates of marriage. *Journal of Marriage and Family, 53,* 913–927.

Castro Martin, T., & Bumpass, L. L. (1989). Recent trends in marital disruption. *Demography, 26,* 37–51.

Cherlin, A. (1978). Remarriage as an incomplete institution. *American Journal of Sociology, 84,* 634–650.

Clarke, S. C. (1995). *Advance report of final marriage statistics, 1989 and 1990.* (Monthly Vital Statistics Report, Vol. 43, No. 12, suppl.). Hyattsville, MD: National Center for Health Statistics. Retrieved June 18, 2008, from http://www.cdc.gov/nchs/data/

Ganong, L. H., & Coleman, M. (2004). *Stepfamily relationships: Development, dynamics, and interventions.* New York: Kluwer Academic/Plenum.

Glick, P. C., & Lin, S.-L. (1987). Remarriage after divorce: Recent changes and demographic variations. *Sociological Perspectives, 30,* 162–179.

Goldman, N., Westoff, C. F., & Hammerslough, C. (1984). Demography of the marriage market in the United States. *Population Index, 50,* 5–25.

Jacobson, P. H. (1959). *American marriage and divorce.* New York: Rinehart.

Koo, H. P., Suchindran, C. M., & Griffith, J. D. (1984). The effects of children on divorce and remarriage: A multivariate analysis of life table probabilities. *Population Studies, 38,* 451–471.

Kreider, R. M., & Fields, J. M. (2002, February). *Number, timing, and duration of marriages and divorces: 1996* (Current Population Report No. P70-80). Retrieved June 18, 2008, from http://www.census.gov/prod/

Mason, M. A., Fine, M. A., & Carnochan, S. (2004). Family law for changing families in the new millennium. In M. Coleman & L. H. Ganong (Eds.), *Handbook of contemporary families: Considering the past, contemplating the future* (pp. 432–450). Thousand Oaks, CA: Sage.

Morrison, D. R., & Ritualo, A. (2000). Routes to children's economic recovery after divorce: Are cohabitation and remarriage equivalent? *American Sociological Review, 65,* 560–580.

Schoen, R., & Standish, N. (2001). The retrenchment of marriage: Results from marital status life tables for the United States, 1995. *Population and Development Review, 27,* 553–563.

Smock, P. J. (1990). Remarriage patterns of Black and White women: Reassessing the role of educational attainment. *Demography, 27,* 467–473.

South, S. J., & Lloyd, K. M. (1995). Spousal alternatives and marital dissolution. *American Sociological Review, 60,* 21–35.

Stewart, S. D. (2002). The effect of stepchildren on childbearing intentions and births. *Demography, 39,* 181–197.

Stewart, S. D., Manning, W. D., & Smock, P. J. (2003). Union formation among men in the U.S.: Does having prior children matter? *Journal of Marriage and Family, 65,* 90–104.

Sweeney, M. M. (2002). Remarriage and the nature of divorce: Does it matter which spouse chose to leave? *Journal of Family Issues, 23,* 410–440.

Sweet, J. A., & Bumpass, L. L. (1987). *American families and households.* New York: Russell Sage Foundation.

Treas, J. (1993). Money in the bank: Transaction costs and the economic organization of marriage. *American Sociological Review, 58,* 723–734.

Vaughan, D. (1986). *Uncoupling: Turning points in intimate relationships.* New York: Oxford University Press.

Waite, L. J., Goldscheider, F. K., & Witsberger, C. (1986). Nonfamily living and the erosion of traditional family orientations among young adults. *American Sociological Review, 51,* 541–554.

Wineberg, H. (1990). Childbearing after remarriage. *Journal of Marriage and Family, 52,* 31–38.

Wolf, W. C., & MacDonald, M. M. (1979). The earnings of men and remarriage. *Demography, 16,* 389–399.

Megan M. Sweeney

RESIDENTIAL MOBILITY, ADULTHOOD

The United States has long been known, for better or worse, as a nation of movers. According to popular belief, the high geographic mobility rate in American society provides access to opportunity but fosters personal and community disorganization. Social scientific evidence, however, suggests that the truth about the consequences of mobility lies somewhere between these stereotypic extremes. Social scientists also have learned much about why certain segments of the population are disproportionately likely to move. For the type of movement examined here—residential mobility—life course transitions prove crucial. Local changes of address tend to be triggered by a range of events, including school completion, household formation, marriage, parenthood, divorce, widowhood, and ups and downs in financial status. The development of mobility decision-making models represents an attempt to understand how people adjust their housing situations in response to these events.

CONCEPT AND MEASUREMENT

Geographic mobility research focuses on movement involving a permanent or semipermanent change of residence. This definitional criterion excludes a variety of temporary phenomena (e.g., commuting, out-of-town work assignments, extended vacations) from consideration. Among permanent moves, residential mobility is distinguished by its local character. Unlike international or interstate migration, residential mobility begins and ends inside the same community, which might range from a single municipality to a metropolitan-wide housing or labor market. In general, the community should be small enough that moves within it do not require the movers to find new jobs (Clark, 1986).

The U.S. Census Bureau operationally defines residential mobility as *intracounty* mobility. Because counties are recognizable government units with stable boundaries, they provide reasonable approximations of community. The fact that they vary greatly in size and shape, however, leaves room for inconsistencies. Some counties in the Southwest cover thousands of square miles, so that "local" moves within these jurisdictions can be quite long. At the other extreme, the multicounty makeup of a metropolis such as Atlanta means that even short moves may cross one or two county lines—and therefore not count as mobility—despite taking place in the same housing market.

Data on residential mobility are available from censuses, large-scale surveys (e.g., the Current Population Survey conducted by the U.S. Census Bureau), and community case studies. A few nations maintain population registers that contain complete residence histories for all persons. Mobility is typically measured with questions asking whether respondents occupied their current dwelling unit one year or five years earlier and, if not, where the previous unit was located (Long, 1988). As the length of the reference interval increases, so do the risks of recall error (because of faulty memory) and underestimation (because of the comparison of addresses at only two dates, which will miss any moves between those dates). Occasional investigations have measured respondents' mobility desires or expectations rather than actual changes of residence. The preferred approach, though, is to use a *prospective design* in which information gathered about people's residential circumstances, including their thoughts about moving, is supplemented with data from a later time point that indicates whether a move has transpired. In a longitudinal survey such as the Panel Study of Income Dynamics, the same respondents are interviewed repeatedly over many years, facilitating analysis of residential mobility within a larger life course framework.

AGGREGATE PATTERNS

From an international perspective, the footloose reputation of American society appears well deserved. Only a handful of Western countries with large private housing stocks and little tradition of public housing (e.g., Australia, Canada, New Zealand) rival or exceed the United States in overall geographic mobility (Long, 1992). The more modest mobility rates in developing nations can be traced to limited supplies of adequate housing, restricted financing options, and state curtailment of the freedom to move (Huang & Deng, 2006). Few such obstacles exist in the United States, where roughly 40 million people, or 14 to 15% of the total population, have changed addresses annually since 2000, and 120 million (46%) moved at least once between 1995 and 2000. These aggregate mobility levels translate into an average of nearly a dozen moves per person over a lifetime, based on age-specific rates of movement.

About three-fifths of all moves occur within counties, satisfying the definition of residential mobility. Mobility rates vary by region (the West highest, the Northeast lowest) and by state: The percentage of persons moving locally in California, for example, is one-and-a-half times greater than in New Jersey (Berkner & Faber, 2003). An urbanism gradient can also be detected: Central city dwellers are the most likely to make intracounty moves, nonmetropolitan residents are the least likely, and suburbanites rank in between. To some extent these mobility patterns reflect geographic differences in housing market conditions, but they also reflect population composition. Thus, the high percentage of young adults and renters in cities—two especially mobile groups—helps account for higher urban than rural mobility rates.

Although residential mobility is by definition local, its degree of localism remains striking. Intracounty moves cover very short distances on average, with most ending in the neighborhood of origin or no more than a few miles away. This destination proximity makes sense given the limited scope of home seekers' *awareness space*, that portion of the larger community context with which they are

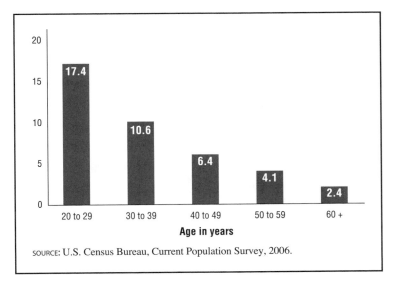

Figure 1. Adult residential mobility rates, 2005–2006. CENGAGE LEARNING, GALE.

most familiar and which shapes their search. The spatially compressed nature of residential mobility is matched by its temporal compression, or seasonality. Local moves occur more often in the summer, even among households without school-age children, and are least common during the winter months, when weather, work and academic schedules, and the holiday season are deterrents.

Despite its still-impressive level in the early 21st century, mobility was much more common in the past (Fischer, 2002). Historical analyses spanning the 1800s through the early 1900s suggest annual rates of residential turnover in excess of 50% for some American cities. The rates were driven in part by large, transient rooming-house populations and a variety of disruptive events (e.g., high mortality among primary-wage earners, economic downturns, natural disasters) that led to moving. As these forces diminished, and as home ownership became accessible to the masses, the annual total (all movement) and local mobility rates dropped to 20% and 14% of all persons, respectively, soon after World War II. Since then, local mobility has fallen further, whereas inter-county movement has remained stable. One plausible explanation for this trend, in addition to the continued rise in ownership, is the outward expansion of commuting ranges. Moves within metropolitan areas now cover greater distances, crossing into neighboring suburban counties and beyond the U.S. Census Bureau's definition of residential mobility.

WHO MOVES?

The intertwining of mobility with other aspects of the life course implies that persons at key transition points should

be the most likely to move. Because these transitions are concentrated in young adulthood, age is a powerful correlate of mobility (see Figure 1). Steps taken by people in their 20s—achieving independence from their parents, pursuing an education, marrying, having a child—frequently trigger a change of address, not only in the United States but also abroad (Long, 1992). By their mid-30s, many have settled down, perhaps after an additional move to accommodate an expanding family or in response to increased earnings. Subsequent transitions, particularly in marital status, increase the odds of moving again. Divorced or separated persons exhibit markedly higher local mobility rates than their married counterparts, as do never-married individuals.

The fact that these single-person and single-parent households are often economically vulnerable suggests another characteristic underlying their high mobility: income. According to 2003 Current Population Survey data, members of households with incomes under $25,000 have mobility rates double those in the $100,000+ category; a similar differential is observed for persons below and above the poverty line (Schachter, 2004). Needless to say, financial hardship makes it difficult to stabilize one's residential situation. The transition in housing tenure (i.e., whether one owns or rents) from renting to owning is a crucial stabilizing force. Renters are four times more likely than owners to move over the course of a year. Owners stay put because, on average, their dwelling units are of better quality, can be altered more easily, and represent a substantial asset. The transaction costs associated with moving from an owned unit are also higher than moving from a

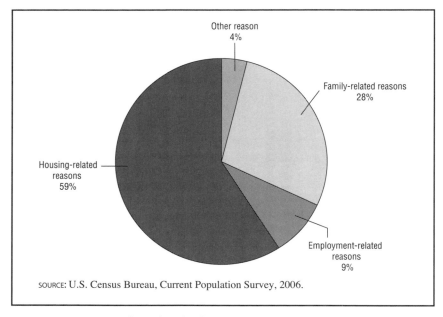

SOURCE: U.S. Census Bureau, Current Population Survey, 2006.

Figure 2. Main reason for making local moves, 2005–2006. **CENGAGE LEARNING, GALE.**

rented unit. Finally, the longer owners remain stable, the stronger their bonds to home and neighborhood become.

Several potential antecedents of residential mobility prove relatively unimportant. Career-based transitions such as transfers or new jobs, for instance, appear more influential in prompting long-distance than short-distance movement. With respect to race, Blacks and Hispanics move locally more often than Whites. The differences are small, however, and they shrink to insignificant once other characteristics that vary by racial group are taken into account. Those characteristics—age, marital status, family size, income, and tenure—tap, at least indirectly, some of the main motivations and resources shaping a household's probability of moving.

Another way to assess the dominant influences on mobility is to ask people why they have moved. In general, the reasons given align well with the demographic correlates already identified (see Figure 2). Three-fifths of respondents to the Current Population Survey, which contains geographic mobility questions in its annual social and economic supplement, cite housing-related factors as their main reason for making a local move. Such factors include preferences for a new or improved unit, home ownership, affordability, and a better neighborhood. A second cluster of reasons, mentioned by more than a quarter of respondents, focus on family or life course transitions, most notably the establishment of a separate household, changes in marital status, and increases or decreases in family size. Work-related reasons, which figure prominently in intercounty and interstate migration, are rarely offered as explanations for residential mobility (Schachter, 2001).

DECISION-MAKING MODELS

Attempts to theorize mobility assume that it represents voluntary behavior designed to avoid confusion with mobility "intention" (see later discussion) to maximize well-being. As a consequence, mobility models emphasize decision making. In his pioneering Philadelphia study, Peter Rossi (1955) argued that life course transitions, especially shifts in family composition, create new housing needs that reduce satisfaction with the current dwelling, setting the decision process in motion. Elaborations of Rossi's approach by sociologists and geographers (e.g., Moore, 1972; Speare, Goldstein, & Frey, 1975) have supplemented the life course variables with other factors hypothesized to influence satisfaction, including housing and neighborhood characteristics, local social attachments, and a person's values and standards of assessment. Only if these factors combine to markedly lower satisfaction does a household develop a desire or intention to move. It then initiates a search for possible destinations, the costs and benefits of which are presumably weighed against those of the origin. The ultimate decision to change addresses depends on whether the anticipated satisfaction associated with the chosen housing unit (discounted by the time, effort, and expense of moving) exceeds what is presently being experienced.

Although generic models of this sort continue to guide research, they are subject to numerous caveats and qualifications. One issue concerns just how pivotal a role residential satisfaction plays in decision making. Satisfaction fails to explain the relationship of housing, demographic, and other variables to mobility, and it rarely has a dominant direct effect itself (Landale & Guest, 1985). More telling is that moves occur despite high levels of satisfaction. People content with their current home might happen onto a "windfall" opportunity that allows them to fulfill long-term housing aspirations. Alternatively, satisfied individuals are sometimes displaced by cost increases, eviction, fire, and the like or feel compelled to leave by events unrelated to housing quality (e.g., divorce or the death of a spouse). Some studies estimate that as many as one-fourth of all local moves are forced or imposed (Sell, 1983). Models that assume the voluntary nature of mobility decisions are less relevant in these cases.

Even when fully voluntary, decision making has been difficult to capture because of its complexity (Michelson, 1977). With the exception of people who live alone, the decision process is collective rather than solitary, involving negotiations among household members at every step. Because members bring their own unique perceptions and standards to the task, they often evaluate the same objective housing circumstances differently. They might also respond differently to stress while contemplating a move. The brief length of many searches, for example, has been attributed to uncertainty about the number of opportunities and competitors, which can pressure home seekers to settle quickly on an acceptable unit (or to stay put) rather than holding out for the ideal destination. Suffice it to say that households vary in how complicated their decision process is.

Households vary in *mobility capital* as well, especially in the United States and other societies with high immigration and growing racial and ethnic diversity. Both ethnographic and quantitative work indicates that English-language ability, time since arrival, citizenship status, and the strength of own-group ties complement more conventional forms of human capital in determining the degree of difficulty newcomers face when navigating the housing market. Their options are further constrained by institutional actors. Despite signs of progress, the 2000 Housing Discrimination Study showed that minority group members (whether foreign- or native-born) still tend to get less favorable treatment from real estate agents and landlords than do comparable Whites (Turner & Ross, 2005). They receive information about fewer units, visit a smaller number, are given less assistance with financing arrangements, and are steered more frequently toward vacancies in minority neighborhoods. Similar discriminatory practices have been documented among lenders and insurers. Thus, the finding that Black and Hispanic households struggle to avoid and escape poor neighborhoods is unsurprising (South, Crowder, & Chavez, 2005).

Such evidence casts doubt on the implicit assumption that households considering a move have complete information about and access to all opportunities. Likewise,

moving should not be regarded as the sole strategy available for reducing residential dissatisfaction. After a fruitless search, some individuals revise their standards of evaluation, bringing aspirations in closer agreement with objective reality. Others elect to voice rather than exit, mobilizing politically in response to neighborhood problems. Finally, because homeowners have a more flexible situation than renters, they may physically modify their units (via repairs, remodeling, or adding on) to alleviate dissatisfaction (Deane, 1990).

What the foregoing critique suggests is that a nontrivial thread of unpredictability runs throughout the mobility decision process. This can be observed in the weak correlations among dissatisfaction, the intention to move, destination selection, and actual mobility, not to mention the variable sequence and time frame in which these decision stages are implemented. The ultimate result is that longitudinal studies identify a large proportion of unexpected movers and even more unexpected stayers, people whose decision making turns out to be somewhat convoluted (Duncan & Newman, 1976). In short, models of residential mobility may overestimate the human capacity for rational, effective planning.

CONSEQUENCES OF MOBILITY

Interest in mobility is motivated in part by the belief that moving is disruptive and therefore harmful to the parties involved. Yet available evidence paints a positive picture with respect to residential consequences. According to 2005 American Housing Survey data, recent movers are far more likely to consider their current dwelling and neighborhood better rather than worse than their previous ones. A parallel finding emerges from research on the concept of the *housing career*, which refers to the succession of units that a person occupies after reaching adulthood and entering the housing market. Most Americans exhibit an upward trajectory over time—toward ownership and higher-quality units and locations—despite occasional setbacks associated with divorce, the loss of a job, or other life events (Clark, Deurloo, & Dieleman, 2003). As already noted, characteristics such as race and nativity can condition how fast and far one's housing career proceeds. Nevertheless, a general pattern of progress holds across all segments of the population.

Nonresidential consequences of mobility have been examined in substantial detail for children, but they remain understudied among adults. Several forms of political participation, including voting, appear depressed in the short run by both local and extralocal moves. This suggests that a practical cost of mobility, the requirement to reregister to vote, rivals social disconnectedness, information deficits, and other explanations of lower civic engagement among movers (Highton, 2000). There are also hints that frequent movement as a child may have long-term (adult) implications for educational attainment, health, and the "inheritance" of a propensity for mobility (Myers, 1999).

These scattered results should be regarded as tentative, however, until their causal basis is more firmly established. *Spuriousness* represents a particularly serious threat to methodological integrity. As an illustration, premove factors (e.g., poverty, domestic violence) might increase the odds of an address change *and* of civic withdrawal or health problems. Moreover, the mechanisms through which mobility influences a given outcome are unclear in most instances, as is the generality of the effect, which could depend on characteristics of both the mover and the move itself (e.g., voluntary vs. involuntary, type of destination). In light of such complications, one should avoid concluding that residential mobility always has harmful consequences or that it affects all individuals in the same manner.

A different way to think about the impact of mobility is at the community level. Criminologists, for example, regularly identify high residential turnover as a significant determinant of neighborhood crime rates, arguing that it undermines social networks, normative consensus, and collective efficacy. Moves also cumulate in urban structural change. The most obvious scenario of this sort entails racial or ethnic transition, when the strength of own-group preferences produces a combination of entries and exits that alters the population composition of a neighborhood. Less visible but more typical is the pairing of high mobility with neighborhood stability. Often the price, size, and style of housing in an area appeals to a narrow market segment, ensuring that arriving households resemble those departing on many social and demographic attributes (Moore, 1972).

Even in the absence of turnover, changes in neighborhood population mix may occur. This counterintuitive notion—that residential *immobility* leads to change—reflects the joint maturation of households and neighborhoods. Imagine that a number of couples move into a new subdivision at roughly the same time and then stay put. Over the life course, they will experience family expansion (and contraction), income growth, and aging, each of which will be manifested in neighborhood-level shifts. Realistically, events such as financial hardship or marital dissolution will necessitate some mobility and thus influence neighborhood change in more conventional fashion. These events, along with immigration and other macro trends, primarily impact neighborhoods via increased demand, but the supply side of the equation also matters. Housing construction, usually concentrated in peripheral locations, can prompt chains of moves that have ripple effects on neighborhoods throughout the metropolis.

THE POLICY DOMAIN

Two basic relationships exist between residential mobility and public policy. The first treats mobility as an outcome and consists of federal, state, and local policies that target discriminatory practices in the real estate market. In the United States, civil rights and fair housing legislation has sought to enhance the residential opportunities available to a range of disadvantaged groups. Current laws prohibit housing and lending discrimination based on race, color, national origin, gender, religion, family status, and physical or mental disability. In terms of race, declines in Black–White residential segregation since 1970 suggest that these laws have had some effect in reducing barriers to mobility. The Housing Discrimination Study results cited above, however, caution against an overly optimistic interpretation.

In the second type of mobility–policy linkage, intervention programs use residential mobility as a means to an end, such as fostering desegregation or reducing concentrated poverty and its consequences. The programs typically provide poor families in distressed neighborhoods with vouchers for relocating to subsidized housing in more advantaged neighborhoods. Whereas certain programs (e.g., Section 8) give participants freedom to choose their new setting, others (such as the Gautreaux and Moving to Opportunity experiments) have stipulated which types of neighborhoods are eligible destinations. Fair-share programs in many American cities pursue similar objectives by redistributing public housing across low- and middle-income residential areas.

Evaluations of these mobility-as-means programs have been mixed, and hence their worth is hotly contested. Generally speaking, comparisons of postmove with premove measures reveal that adult participants report better physical and mental health, improved job opportunities, and lower rates of welfare receipt (Goering & Feins, 2003). Some critics, however, emphasize the limited evidence of actual employment and wage gains, maintaining that policies designed to move poor families into home ownership rather than better neighborhoods would be more effective. Although mobility-as-means programs have so far been tried in only a handful of U.S. metropolises, they are candidates for wider application. Indeed, as housing stocks in European nations and elsewhere increasingly shift from the public to the private sector, such programs have become more germane as a way to alleviate poverty and ethnic concentration.

SEE ALSO Volume 2: *Employment, Adulthood; Home Ownership/Housing; Immigration, Adulthood; School to Work Transition; Transition to Adulthood.*

BIBLIOGRAPHY

Berkner, B., & Faber, C. S. (2003, September). *Geographic mobility: 1995 to 2000* (Census 2000 Brief No. C2KBR-28). Retrieved June 18, 2008, from http://www.census.gov

Clark, W. A. V. (1986). *Human migration*. Beverly Hills, CA: Sage.

Clark, W. A. V., Deurloo, M. C., & Dieleman, F. M. (2003). Housing careers in the United States, 1968–93: Modelling the sequencing of housing states. *Urban Studies, 40*, 143–160.

Deane, G. D. (1990). Mobility and adjustments: Paths to the resolution of residential stress. *Demography, 27*, 65–79.

Duncan, G. J., & Newman, S. J. (1976). Expected and actual residential mobility. *Journal of the American Institute of Planners, 42*, 174–186.

Fischer, C. S. (2002). Ever-more rooted Americans. *City and Community, 1*, 177–198.

Goering, J. M., & Feins, J. D. (Eds.). (2003). *Choosing a better life? Evaluating the Moving to Opportunity social experiment.* Washington, DC: Urban Institute Press.

Highton, B. (2000). Residential mobility, community mobility, and electoral participation. *Political Behavior, 22*, 109–120.

Huang, Y., & Deng, F. F. (2006). Residential mobility in Chinese cities: A longitudinal analysis. *Housing Studies, 21*, 625–652.

Landale, N. S., & Guest, A. M. (1985). Constraints, satisfaction, and residential mobility: Speare's model reconsidered. *Demography, 22*, 199–222.

Long, L. (1988). *Migration and residential mobility in the United States*. New York: Russell Sage Foundation.

Long, L. (1992). Changing residence: Comparative perspectives on its relationship to age, sex, and marital status. *Population Studies, 46*, 141–158.

Michelson, W. (1977). *Environmental choice, human behavior, and residential satisfaction*. New York: Oxford University Press.

Moore, E. G. (1972). *Residential mobility in the city*. Washington, DC: Association of American Geographers, Commission on College Geography.

Myers, S. M. (1999). Residential mobility as a way of life: Evidence of intergenerational similarities. *Journal of Marriage and the Family, 61*, 871–880.

Rossi, P. H. (1955). *Why families move: A study in the social psychology of urban residential mobility*. Glencoe, IL: Free Press.

Schachter, J. P. (2001, May). *Why people move: Exploring the March 2000 Current Population Survey* (Current Population Report No. P23-204). Retrieved May 28, 2008, from http://www.census.gov/prod

Schachter, J. P. (2004, March). *Geographical mobility: 2002 to 2003* (Current Population Report No. P20-549). Retrieved June 16, 2008, from http://www.census2010.gov/prod

Sell, R. R. (1983). Analyzing migration decisions: The first step—whose decisions? *Demography, 20*, 299–311.

South, S. J., Crowder, K., & Chavez, E. (2005). Exiting and entering high-poverty neighborhoods: Latinos, Blacks, and Anglos compared. *Social Forces, 84*, 873–900.

Speare, A., Jr., Goldstein, S., & Frey, W. H. (1975). *Residential mobility, migration, and metropolitan change*. Cambridge, MA: Ballinger.

Turner, M. A., & Ross, S. L. (2005). How racial residential discrimination affects the search for housing. In X. de Souza Briggs (Ed.), *The geography of opportunity: Race and housing choice in metropolitan America* (pp. 81–100). Washington, DC: Brookings Institution Press.

Barrett A. Lee
Matthew S. Hall

RISK

Risk can be defined as "the probability or relative uncertainty of an anticipated opportunity or outcome" (O'Rand, 2000, p. 228). The concept of risk generally has a negative connotation, implying the chance of harm, but risk can also be viewed positively as an opportunity for gain (Giddens, 1999). The study of life course risk is a relatively new area, initially stemming from a dialogue between sociologists and members of other disciplines such as economists, psychologists, anthropologists, and environmentalists, who have historically studied the concept of risk.

One area of research focuses on individual estimations of risk and subsequent decision making in situations involving uncertain outcomes. Research suggests that people are not good at estimating risk and have difficulty understanding information about the probabilities associated with a broad range of activities (such as gambling and financial investment) and behaviors (such as health-related behaviors associated with disease risk; Tversky & Kahneman, 1974, 1981). People's interpretations of risk information are distorted by a number of factors, such as the way risk information is framed by others—leading to individual perceptions of risk that differ from the estimates offered by experts. Building on this work, researchers have begun to examine the effect of social locations (e.g., social class) on perceptions of risk and decision-making processes, focusing on topics such as purchasing health insurance or investing in the stock market (Hardy, 2000; Heimer, 1988).

A second area of study focuses on the social processes involved in the development and identification of risks. Researchers using a social constructionist perspective question an objective model of risk that treats the probability of particular events as knowable and quantifiable. In general, this body of research examines the social and cultural factors that influence perceptions of risk. Researchers seek to understand how social actors (such as government agencies, social movements, and professions) identify and define hazards and risks (e.g., lifestyle risks such as smoking or technological hazards such as chemical pollution) and the role that power plays in framing debates about risks (Adam & van Loon, 2000; Clarke & Short, 1993).

Another body of research strives to understand risk as a function of broader changes within social structures and social institutions. Anthony Giddens's (1991) discussion of the modern self relies heavily on the idea of modernity as a *risk culture* that results from the combination of sophisticated knowledge, a great degree of uncertainty, vulnerability to unrecognizable and uncontrollable risks, and an emphasis on individual choice. Giddens describes modernity as involving the decline in the proportion of risks that are *external risks* (risks that are relatively predictable, easily calculated, and insurable, such as disablement and unemployment) and the growth of *manufactured risks* (new risks that are produced by the progression of science and technology, that are ambiguous in nature, and with which society has little previous experience, such as nuclear power, chemical pollution, global warming, and genetic engineering). Manufactured risk is associated with what Ulrich Beck (1992) described as a *risk society*—a society affected by forces of globalization and techno-science and characterized by an increasing preoccupation with controlling the future and eliminating risk (see Elliott, 2002, for a review).

Angela O'Rand's (2000, 2003) development of the concept of *life course risks* recognizes that the transitions that constitute the life course present individuals with socially constrained opportunities and risks, such as unemployment, poor health or disability, and family disruption. She argues that, in addition to increases in risk stemming from globalization and information technology, demographic trends such as increases in life expectancy influence social policy and lead to individualized risk, as governments devise new solutions to address the challenges of supporting the health and financial security of an aging population.

A central theme within research on risk is that a defining aspect of modern society is the privatization and individualization of risk in all aspects of life. One example is the privatization of economic risk—a process that can be thought of as the *devolution of risk* from the state to the individual. An example of the devolution of risk is change in U.S. pension and health policy, in which collective risk sharing declined and individual responsibility for bearing life course risks related to work and health increased (see O'Rand & Shuey, 2007; Shuey & O'Rand, 2004). Historically, insurance institutions developed as a response to societal perceptions of individual risks of income loss, illness, and death, and these institutions were designed to spread risks across populations, such as those defined by citizenship, employment organization, or profession (see Heimer, 1985; Jacoby, 2001).

The idea of *risk spreading* or *risk sharing* is being replaced, however, by an ideology of *risk embracing* that seeks individualized, market-based solutions for economic risks and shifts the perception of risk from one of individual vulnerability to loss to one of opportunity for accumulation (Baker & Simon, 2002). For example, new pension instruments (such as defined contribution plans) and diverse health management arrangements that minimize employer responsibility and liability (such as HMOs and other forms of managed care) arrived at workplaces in the United States and other Western countries beginning in the early 1980s. Old, occupation-based welfare systems that insured many workers with lifetime pensions and retiree health insurance have declined in prevalence.

The result has been the increasing devolution of labor market risks to households, which then have greater responsibility for planning for and managing expected and unexpected circumstances associated with income loss (such as job loss or stock market volatility) and health problems (O'Rand, 2000, 2003). Shifting corporate and state risks to individuals has the effect of protecting large institutions while exposing individuals to potentially catastrophic results—although, ironically, the discourse surrounding these changes suggests that they represent autonomy, choice, and opportunity for individuals to excel, rather than risks (Dannefer, 2000).

The research discussed above raises many public policy questions and unresolved issues. First, given the rise of new types of risk in modern society, what does the future hold for welfare state policies originally developed as a form of collective risk management to protect individuals from external risks (Giddens, 1999)? What is the effect of increasingly market-based solutions for managing life course risks on levels of inequality? Finally, at the micro level, more research is needed to better understand how individuals and households make decisions across the life course in light of the prevalence of manufactured risks in modern societies.

SEE ALSO Volume 2: *Agency; Economic Restructuring; Health Insurance; Individuation/Standardization Debate;* Volume 3: *Pensions.*

BIBLIOGRAPHY

Adam, B., & van Loon, J. (2000). Repositioning risk: The challenge for social theory. In B. Adam, U. Beck, & J. van Loon (Eds.), *The risk society and beyond: Critical issues for social theory* (pp. 1–31). London: Sage.

Baker, T., & Simon, J. (Eds.). (2002). *Embracing risk: The changing culture of insurance and responsibility.* Chicago: University of Chicago Press.

Beck, U. (1992). *Risk society: Towards a new modernity,* Trans. M. Ritter. London: Sage.

Clarke, L., & Short, J. F., Jr. (1993). Social organization and risk: Some current controversies. *Annual Review of Sociology, 19,* 375–399.

Dannefer, D. (2000). Bringing risk back in: The regulation of the self in the postmodern state. In K. W. Schaie & J. Hendricks (Eds.), *The evolution of the aging self: The societal impact on the aging process* (pp. 269–280). New York: Springer.

Elliott, A. (2002). Beck's sociology of risk: A critical assessment. *Sociology, 36,* 293–315.

Giddens, A. (1991). *Modernity and self-identity: Self and society in the late modern age.* Stanford, CA: Stanford University Press.

Giddens, A. (1999). Risk and responsibility. *The Modern Law Review, 62,* 1–10.

Hardy, M. A. (2000). Control, choice, and collective concerns: Challenges of individualized social policy. In K. W. Schaie & J. Hendricks (Eds.), *The evolution of the aging self: The societal impact on the aging process* (pp. 251–268). New York: Springer.

Heimer, C. A. (1985). *Reactive risk and rational action: Managing moral hazard in insurance contracts.* Berkeley: University of California Press.

Heimer, C. A. (1988). Social structure, psychology, and the estimation of risk. *Annual Review of Sociology, 14,* 491–517.

Jacoby, S. M. (2001). Risk and the labor market: Societal past as economic prologue. In I. Berg & A. L. Kalleberg (Eds.), *Sourcebook of labor markets: Evolving structures and processes* (pp. 31–60). New York: Kluwer Academic/Plenum.

O'Rand, A. M. (2000). Risk, rationality, and modernity: Social policy and the aging self. In K. W. Schaie & J. Hendricks (Eds.), *The evolution of the aging self: The societal impact on the aging process* (pp. 225–249). New York: Springer.

O'Rand, A. M. (2003). The future of the life course: Late modernity and life course risks. In J. T. Mortimer & M. J. Shanahan (Eds.), *Handbook of the life course* (pp. 693–701). New York: Kluwer Academic/Plenum.

O'Rand, A. M., & Shuey, K. M. (2007). Gender and the devolution of pension risks in the U.S. *Current Sociology, 55,* 287–304.

Shuey, K. M., & O'Rand, A. M. (2004). New risks for workers: Pensions, labor markets, and gender. *Annual Review of Sociology, 30,* 453–477.

Tversky, A., & Kahneman, D. (1974, September 27). Judgment under uncertainty: Heuristics and biases. *Science, 185,* 1124–1131.

Tversky, A., & Kahneman, D. (1981, January 30). The framing of decisions and the psychology of choice. *Science, 211,* 453–458.

Kim M. Shuey

ROLES

A *role* is usually defined as a set of expectations for how individuals should behave in certain social situations. It can be thought of as a way of organizing and categorizing social actors. Roles link social behavior, which is easily observed, to social structure and can thus be seen as a link between the individual and society (Goode, 1960). Roles can be used to describe the behaviors and identities of individuals, the social organization of a small group or institution, or the structure of an entire society.

Perhaps because the concept of role has a long history and is used widely across a number of disciplines, the usage of the term varies. *Role* sometimes refers to expectations for behavior, the behaviors themselves, or the social position itself (Biddle, 2000). Although people enact roles but occupy social positions, the term *role* is often used synonymously with *social position.* For example, the social position of "mother" has specific legal definitions in the United States, referring to documents such as birth certificates and adoption papers. This is no guarantee, however, that a person will engage in behaviors that meet society's expectations for "mothering"—the mother may be estranged from her child, or the person doing the mothering may be a sibling or grandparent.

In some situations, the socially constructed demands of a role, an individual's own definition of the role, and the actions of that individual may be highly congruent (Levinson, 1959). In these situations, recognizing the various meanings of role may not be as important. However, in many situations, one or all three of these aspects of roles are in conflict. For example, a member of a particular religious organization may be expected to behave a certain way, but an individual member may not accept all the tenets of the religion and therefore sometimes act in ways that violate the religious expectations.

ROLE THEORY

Role theory developed in two distinct sociological traditions. In functionalist theory, based on the work of sociologist Talcott Parsons (1902–1979), the focus is on how roles help solve problems of social coordination by assigning behavioral expectations to people in particular situations. In functionalist theory, individuals conform to role expectations created by social consensus. The focus is on formal organizations and status networks. Roles, in this view, help define groups and establish hierarchies. Job titles in a large organization are a good example of functional role. People's assigned roles in an organization tells them who they have control over, who has control over them, who they work with on a daily basis, and what tasks they are allowed to do.

In contrast, interactionist theory focuses on how roles are negotiated between individuals engaged in interaction (Mead, 1934). Rather than seeing roles as templates provided through socialization, the emphasis is on how individuals create role expectations through interaction with role partners. An original focus of interactionist theory was on *role taking*, or the ability to take another person's perspective and to use that perspective in making decisions about one's own behavior. This role-taking perspective was also influenced by sociological theorists Everett Hughes (1897–1983) and Erving Goffman (1922–1982) and is a foundation of symbolic interactionism, a major theoretical paradigm in the social sciences (Biddle, 2000). There may be broad agreement, for example, about the expectations for individuals who enact a student role, but the specifics of the expectations and behavior of students in a particular class will depend on their interaction with the teacher. The teacher may also revise his or her behavior and expectations in interaction with the students.

AGE AND ROLES

Traditional role theories have little to say about timing, yet timing is an important aspect of roles. Most roles are

379

associated with age norms, which specify the age range of people expected to fill the role. The *college student* role, for example, carries certain expectations about age, such that the modifiers *traditional* and *nontraditional* clearly express expectations about the normal age range of people who attend college.

If certain roles are appropriate for certain ages, a potential series of role entrances and exits as individuals age is implied. The individual life course is often defined by these role transitions; thus the concept of roles is fundamental to the life course perspective. The transition to adulthood, for example, is marked by maturing into the normal roles of adulthood. Adolescents often look forward to being of legal age to drive, vote, and drink alcohol. Work and family roles both have role entrances that form part of the transition to adulthood—leaving school, entering the full-time workforce, getting married, and becoming a parent.

In contrast, the transition from adulthood to old age is more often marked by role losses and exits rather than the accumulation of new roles (Morgan, 1988). Although older adults may look forward to gaining the role of grandparent, many also exit the work role and experience the death of a spouse. Because the roles that older adults most often enact (grandparent, volunteer) tend to be seen as less demanding than roles characteristic of the middle years (worker, parent), old age has been called a "roleless role" (Burgess, 1960).

Indeed, gerontological theories make explicit claims about the roles that are thought to be best for older adults. Disengagement theory suggests that it would be beneficial, both for individuals and for society, if older adults disengage from the roles associated with the middle years (Cumming & Henry, 1961). By giving up a work role, for example, older adults can focus their efforts on their health and on existential issues and at the same time free up a work position for younger persons just entering the labor force. Activity theory, however, claims that greater well-being in old age is associated with having a greater number and variety of roles (Havighurst, Neugarten, & Tobin, 1968). As a counterpoint, continuity theory argues that it is the continuity of meaningful roles that promote well-being, not the number of roles (Atchley, 1989).

Much of this picture of role accumulation early in the life course and role loss later in life is predicated on what Matilda and John Riley (1994) described as the "three boxes" of the life course. This describes the normative expectations that people will focus on education in their early years, work in their middle years, and leave leisure as the main concern for their later years. This structures age norms for many roles and thus what roles are available to people in different life stages. In contrast

to this age-differentiated social structure, an age-integrated social structure would mean that "role opportunities in work, education, and other structures are more and more open to people of every age" (Riley & Riley 2000, p. 267).

MULTIPLE ROLES

In formal organizations, individuals may be described as having only one role, but most individuals see themselves as occupying multiple social roles, such as worker, parent, spouse, and citizen. The interplay between different roles is a very important stream of roles research. Functionalist role theory suggests that role obligations imposed by society are demanding and that roles are inflexible and difficult to combine (Lynch, 2007). This perspective, then, would tend to view multiple roles in a negative light.

William Goode (1960) defined role strain as the felt difficulty in fulfilling role obligations. In Goode's formulation, individuals are constantly facing choices about which role behaviors to choose, which then necessitates *role bargains*. Role strain might result from individual roles that are difficult to perform or have overwhelming demands; strain might also be a result of role conflict, where the expectations from two or more roles are in opposition to each other. An area of role conflict of interest to many researchers in the early 21st century is that of working parents, who seek to combine roles with very different expectations.

For both men and women, enacting roles many people view as belonging to the opposite gender can create a situation of role conflict. This might be true for women participating in a traditionally male sport or men participating in a traditionally female occupation.

Not all researchers, however, see multiple roles as a problem. In the *role enhancement* perspective, occupying multiple roles improves individual well-being through the accumulation of benefits associated with a variety of roles (Marks, 1977). Paid employment, for example, brings with it the possibility of monetary rewards, feelings of competence, and social rewards. Indeed, satisfaction in one role (perhaps running a successful club) may compensate for problems in another role (such as having an unsatisfying job).

A key resource that may be associated with social roles is social integration. Social integration has been a major theme in sociology since the work of Emile Durkheim (1858–1917) and can be defined broadly to include "both participation in meaningful roles and the network of social contacts" (Pillemer, Moen, Wethington, & Glasgow, 2000, p. 8). Social integration can also be understood in relation to its opposite: social isolation. In the role context, if roles are the link between the

TIME BIND

The "time bind" generally refers to conflict between individuals' work and family roles, especially their competing time demands. Attention to work–family conflict grew in the 1980s as women entered the labor force in large numbers and workers felt pressured by a tougher economic climate. Concerns about the effect of work demands on individuals and families were brought to the public in books such as Hochschild's (1989) *Second Shift* and Schor's (1991) *Overworked American*.

Hochschild's (1997) later book, *The Time Bind*, centers on the paradox that employees generally want more time with their families, but very few take advantage of "family-friendly" options for part-time work, job sharing, and flex time. Barriers to utilizing these policies include a work culture that values work hours as a sign of commitment (Hays, 1998). Although Hochschild suggested that the time bind may be leading to less satisfaction with family life, other research shows that relative satisfaction with work and family has been fairly stable over time (Kiecolt, 2003).

BIBLIOGRAPHY

Hays, S. (1998). Reconsidering the "choice": Do Americans really prefer the workplace over home? *Contemporary Sociology, 27*, 28–32.

Hochschild, A. R. (with Machung, A.). (1989). *The second shift: Working parents and the revolution at home.* New York: Viking.

Hochschild, A. R. (1997). *The time bind: When work becomes home and home becomes work.* New York: Metropolitan Books.

Kiecolt, K. J. (2003). Satisfaction with work and family life: No evidence of a cultural reversal. *Journal of Marriage and the Family, 65*, 23–35.

Schor, J. B. (1991). *The overworked American: The unexpected decline of leisure.* New York: Basic Books.

roles may have a positive effect on older caregivers (Moen, Robison, & Dempster-McClain, 1995).

ROLES AND THE LIFE COURSE

Roles are central to the life course perspective, and the life course perspective has added much to the study of roles. First, the life course emphasis on process suggests that looking at roles cross-sectionally (at one point in time) gives a misleading picture. The impact of being laid off from a job, for example, would be quite different for a seasonal worker compared to an individual who had worked continuously for many years. Viewing roles as part of an ongoing trajectory also broadens the concept of a career beyond the realm of paid employment. The parental career, for example, would connect a variety of family-related role transitions into a meaningful trajectory in the same way that the work career potentially connects and gives context to a large number of individual jobs and transitions into and out of work.

Attention to role trajectories is evident in several areas of current research. Research on care giving is increasingly using the concept of the care-giving career (Lawton, Moss, Hoffman, & Perkinson, 2000). Research in the area of substance abuse is using the concept of the role trajectory to study the development of the drug abuse career (Boeri, Sterk, & Elifson, 2006).

Although research attention is being given to various kinds of role transitions (parenthood and retirement, for example), the impact of timing on these role changes also is being examined. Role transitions that occur during a period in one's life that are not in step with normative cultural expectations may be more stressful than transitions that are. Examples of the importance of timing is evident in research on the transition to adulthood. Early, as opposed to on-time, entry into adult roles is associated with aggressive behavior (Roche, Ensminger, Ialongo, Poduska, & Kellam, 2006) and substance abuse (Krohn, Lizotte, & Perez, 1997), but these negative outcomes are likely both a cause and a consequence of these "off-time" transitions.

Related to the issue of timing is the issue of the sequencing of roles. Again, during the transition to adulthood, the normative sequence of roles is entering the labor force, getting married, and then having children. Pamela Braboy Jackson (2004), however, showed that the role sequences that are associated with positive mental health vary by race, gender, and cohort. Whereas the normative sequence of work, marriage, and children was associated with better outcomes for Whites, African Americans who began work, had children, and then married had better outcomes.

The importance of context is a key component of the life course perspective. One application of the role concept would be to examine the interplay and quality of

individual and society, multiple roles are a measure of social integration.

In general, research generally supports the view of multiple roles as beneficial for individuals. Research links multiple roles to positive physical health outcomes (Verbrugge, 1983) and to reductions in psychological distress for both men and women (Thoits, 1986). Research into multiple roles and care giving suggests that productive particular roles, rather than assuming that all roles contribute equally to either role strain or role enhancement. Research on care giving illustrates the importance of this insight (Edwards, Zarit, Stephens, & Townsend, 2002). Both the work role and the care-giving role can lead to costs and rewards for the individual in these roles. For example, it is not necessarily the case that work is beneficial and care giving is stressful for every individual. Research shows that role occupancy alone is not effective in explaining differences in depressive symptoms, but role quality is (Baruch & Barnett, 1986). Although role quality may be important, few researchers have developed instruments to measure this concept.

Another aspect of role context is role identity. Many people will use roles (mother, engineer, team captain, deacon) to describe themselves, suggesting that adopting the behavior of a particular social role may lead to adopting a corresponding role identity. The salience, or importance, of a particular identity for a particular individual may help explain the effect of role quality on well-being.

Historical and cultural contexts are also key to understanding roles in a life course perspective. Different cultures can define the same role in very different ways. Joel Savishinsky (2004), for example, examined the different meanings of the term *retirement* in the United States and India. Historical changes can also shape the expectations and norms associated with roles. Shin-Kap Han and Phyllis Moen (1999) demonstrated that the timing of retirement has been affected by a number of factors that have changed the average age of retirement and have also increased the variability in the timing of this role transition.

Gender and age, of course, are key contexts influencing role trajectories (Hostetler, Sweet, & Moen, 2007). A count of the total number of roles one holds may not be as important for well-being as having a set of roles that is normative, given an individual's age and gender. Other important ways to contextualize roles are by looking at resources.

GENDER AND ROLES

Gender is a key context influencing role trajectories. Gender is clearly an organizing principle in most societies and shapes the behavior of individuals. Pervasive gender stereotypes both lead to and reflect prevailing gender roles, defined as differing expectations about the behavior of women and men.

In many societies, gender roles assign men primarily to public roles and women primarily to private roles. These behavioral expectations may be formalized in rules and laws, such as early 20th century laws that barred married women from being teachers in most U.S. school districts. Industrialization and modernization, however, led to changes in gender roles. As societies move through the demographic transition from conditions of high mortality and fertility to conditions of low mortality and low fertility, the status of women often undergoes change. Women no longer need to spend most of their lives engaged in bearing and raising children. Along with this demographic transformation comes change in the nature of employment due to modernization, such that more jobs require symbolic skills and are in traditionally female fields such as health and education and fewer jobs require physical strength and are in traditionally male occupations (Kleinfeld & Reyes, 2007).

In modern Western societies, where rules against women's participation in many public domains have been lifted, informal gender roles continue to produce gendered behavior. In many developed countries, for example, women are still primarily responsible for work in the home; this includes the work of care giving, which is still seen as more natural and appropriate for women (Moen, Robison, & Fields, 1994).

Gender roles help determine behavior, such as hours spent on housework, but also shape preferences and beliefs. Prejudice against gays and lesbians, for example, reflects both prejudice against same-sex relationships as well as prejudice against those who violate gender norms such that prejudice is strongest against effeminate gay men and masculine lesbian women (Lehavot & Lambert, 2007).

FUTURE DIRECTIONS

Because of the wide use of the word *role* and its associated concepts such as gender roles and role strain, it is difficult to summarize the state of research in this area. The difficulty is compounded by the use of role concepts without reference to existing theory and research.

Research in several areas of psychology is showing creative uses of the role concept and role theory. A new perspective on multiple roles focuses on the role switching and role overlapping that most people experience in their everyday lives. Because social settings overlap, especially with new forms of communication, social actors are often enacting many roles in a short time frame. Author Karen Lynch (2007) urges scholars to look at the cognitive or mental strategies individuals use to manage multiple roles.

Role concepts are also being used in the study of personality. The Personality and Role Identity Structural Model connects role experiences, role identity traits, and general personality traits (Wood & Roberts, 2006). This positions the role concept not just at the juncture of society and the individual but also at the juncture of psychology and sociology.

Role identities continue to be of interest to researchers, especially in the area of gerontology. A promising intervention for persons with dementia provides individualized activities corresponding with highly salient role identities (Cohen-Mansfield, Parpura-Gil, & Golander, 2006). Those for whom family was paramount might construct family trees; others might engage in activities related to a lifelong interest in sports. Other research in gerontology shows that formal volunteering moderates the negative effect of having few or no role identities in older adults (Greenfield & Marks, 2004).

Finally, several social work practice models have a central focus on social roles. Social role valorization has a long history in the disability field. In the United Kingdom, this model is based on the idea that society tends to identify some people as fundamentally "different" and of less value than others. Analysis of the disability role can be used to counteract the negative impact of the role. This model has been expanded to palliative care and a critique of the role of the dying person (Sinclair, 2007). Social role theory uses the concept of social role to improve adaptation and positive social functioning (Blakely & Dziadosz, 2007). More knowledge in academia about the possible practical uses of role concepts and theories could lead to another step forward in this area.

SEE ALSO Volume 1: *Socialization; Socialization, Gender;* Volume 2: *Careers; Fatherhood; Friendship, Adulthood; Housework; Motherhood; Occupations; Parent-Child Relationships, Adulthood; Sociological Theories; Volunteering, Adulthood;* Volume 3: *Caregiving; Retirement; Theories of Aging.*

BIBLIOGRAPHY

Atchley, R. (1989). A continuity theory of normal aging. *The Gerontologist, 29*(2), 183–190.

Baruch, G. K., & Barnett, R. (1986). Role quality, multiple role involvement, and psychological well-being in midlife women. *Journal of Personality and Social Psychology, 51*(3), 578–585.

Biddle, B. J. (2000). Role theory. In E. F. Borgatta & R. J. V. Montgomery (Eds.), *Encyclopedia of sociology* (pp. 2415–2420). New York: Macmillan Reference.

Blakely, T. J., & Dziadosz, G. M. (2007). Social functioning: A sociological common base for social work practice. *Journal of Sociology & Social Welfare, 34*(4), 151–168.

Boeri, M. W., Sterk, C. E., & Elifson, K. W. (2006). Baby boomer drug users: Career phases, social control, and social learning theory. *Sociological Inquiry, 76*(2), 264–291.

Burgess, E. (1960). *Aging in Western societies.* Chicago: University of Chicago Press.

Cohen-Mansfield, J., Parpura-Gil, A., & Golander, H. (2006). Utilization of self-identity roles for designing interventions for persons with dementia. *Journals of Gerontology, Series B: Psychological Sciences and Social Sciences, 61*(4), 202–212.

Cumming, E., & Henry, W. (1961). *Growing old: The process of disengagement.* New York: Basic Books.

Durkheim, E. (1951). *Suicide: A study in sociology,* Trans. J. A. Spaulding & G. Simpson. Glencoe, IL: Free Press. (Original work published 1897)

Edwards, A. B., Zarit, S. H., Stephens, M. A. P., & Townsend, A. (2002). Employed family caregivers of cognitively

impaired elderly: An examination of role strain and depressive symptoms. *Aging & Mental Health, 6*(1), 55–61.

Goode, W. J. (1960). A theory of role strain. *American Sociological Review, 25*(4), 483–496.

Greenfield, E. A., & Marks, N. F. (2004). Formal volunteering as a protective factor for older adults' psychological well-being. *Journals of Gerontology, Series B: Psychological Sciences and Social Sciences, 59*(5), 258–264.

Han, S.-K., & Moen, P. (1999). Clocking out: Temporal patterning of retirement. *American Journal of Sociology, 105*(1), 191–236.

Havighurst, R. J., Neugarten, B. L., & Tobin, S. S. (1968). Disengagement and patterns of aging. In B. Neugarten (Ed.), *Middle age and aging: A reader in social psychology* (pp. 161–172). Chicago: University of Chicago Press.

Hostetler, A. J., Sweet, S., & Moen, P. (2007). Gendered career paths: A life course perspective on returning to school. *Sex Roles, 56*(1), 85–103.

Jackson, P. B. (2004). Role sequencing: Does order matter for mental health? *Journal of Health and Social Behavior, 45*(2), 132–154.

Kleinfeld, J., & Reyes, M. (2007). Boys left behind: Gender role changes in Alaska. *Journal of Boyhood Studies, 1*(2), 179–190.

Krohn, M. D., Lizotte, A. J., & Perez, C. M. (1997). The interrelationship between substance use and precocious transitions to adult statuses. *Journal of Health and Social Behavior, 38*(1), 87–103.

Lawton, M. P., Moss, M., Hoffman, C., & Perkinson, M. (2000). Two transitions in daughters' caregiving careers. *Gerontologist, 40*(4), 437–448.

Lehavot, K., & Lambert, A. J. (2007). Toward a greater understanding of antigay prejudice: On the role of sexual orientation and gender role violation. *Basic and Applied Social Psychology, 29*(3), 279–292.

Levinson, D. J. (1959). Role, personality, and social structure in the organizational setting. *Journal of Abnormal and Social Psychology, 58*(2), 170–180.

Lynch, K. D. (2007). Modeling role enactment: Linking role theory and social cognition. *Journal for the Theory of Social Behavior, 37*(4), 379–399.

Marks, S. (1977). Multiple roles and role strain: Some notes on human energy, time, and commitment. *American Sociological Review, 42,* 921–936.

Mead, G. H. (1934). *Mind, self, and society.* Chicago: University of Chicago Press.

Moen, P., Robison, J., & Dempster-McClain, D. (1995). Care giving and women's well-being: A life course approach. *Journal of Health and Social Behavior, 36*(3), 259–273.

Moen, P., Robison, J., & Fields, V. (1994). Women's work and caregiving roles: A life course approach. *Journals of Gerontology, Series B: Psychological Sciences and Social Sciences, 49*(4), 176–186.

Morgan, D. L. (1988). Age differences in social network participation. *Journal of Gerontology, Series B: Psychological Sciences and Social Sciences, 43,* 129–137.

Pillemer, K., Moen, P., Wethington, E., & Glasgow, N. (Eds.). (2000). Introduction. In *Social integration in the second half of life* (pp. 1–16). Baltimore, MD: Johns Hopkins University Press.

Riley, M. W., & Riley, J. W. (1994). Age integration and the lives of older people. *The Gerontologist, 34*(1), 110–115.

Riley, M. W., & Riley, J. W. (2000). Age integration: Conceptual and historical background. *The Gerontologist, 40*(3), 266–270.

Roche, K. M., Ensminger, M. E., Ialongo, N., Poduska, J. M., & Kellam, S. G. (2006). Early entries into adult roles: Associations with aggressive behavior from early adolescence into young adulthood. *Youth & Society, 38*(2), 236–261.

Savishinsky, J. (2004). The volunteer and the sannyasin: Archetypes of retirement in America and India. *International Journal of Aging and Human Development, 59*(1), 25–41.

Sinclair, P. (2007). *Rethinking palliative care: A social role valorization approach*. Bristol, England: Policy Press.

Thoits, P. A. (1986). Multiple identities: Examining gender and marital status differences in distress. *American Sociological Review, 51*(2), 259–272.

Verbrugge, L. M. (1983). Multiple roles and physical health of women and men. *Journal of Health and Social Behavior, 24*, 16–30.

Wood, D., & Roberts, B. W. (2006). Cross-sectional and longitudinal tests of the Personality and Role Identity Structural Model (PRISM). *Journal of Personality, 74*(3), 779–810.

Mary Ann Erickson

S

SANDWICH GENERATION

SEE *Caregiving.*

SAVING

Saving is accumulating disposable (after-tax) income that is not used for current consumption (i.e., spending) but set aside for future use. Saved income can be held as cash or in transaction accounts such as checking or savings accounts. Funds being saved also can be invested in stocks, bonds, mutual funds, retirement accounts, and real estate.

Individuals save for several reasons (Bryant & Zick, 2006). First, savings may be used to spread lifetime income evenly over the life course. For most individuals, income is relatively low while young, increases with age during the working years, and falls in later life as individuals work fewer hours or fully retire from the labor force. To avoid large disparities in the consumption standard attainable during different stages of the life course, an individual may borrow against future income while young, save during the peak earning years, and then use income saved in retirement.

Second, saving allows individuals to maximize lifetime consumption, or the spending and purchasing that one does over the life course. The nature of economic cycles is such that both prices and interest rates fluctuate over time. By spending or making purchases when costs are relatively inexpensive (from low prices, low interest rates, or both), an individual can maximize consumption on a given income. Conversely, by saving during periods of high prices or high interest rates, an individual can consume more in the future when consumption is relatively less expensive. At a very basic level, this is achieved when families purchase more of a good (e.g., breakfast cereal) when there is a sale; by purchasing additional units of the good for future consumption while prices are lower (and therefore not purchasing at the higher price), the family maximizes consumption.

Third, saving may be motivated by the desire to transfer wealth to future generations. Transfers may happen after death as bequests to children or grandchildren from estates or insurance. Transfers to children and grandchildren also may be made while an individual is still alive, in the form of funds for higher education or assistance with the purchase of a home.

Finally, savings may be motivated by the desire to minimize economic risk and protect against unexpected financial events. This precautionary saving can act as replacement income in the event of an income loss or reduction or as a buffer against unforeseen expenses such as medical costs due to major illness or injury.

THEORIES AND RESEARCH ABOUT SAVING

Several theories have been proposed to predict saving (and consumption) behavior and explain differences in savings rates over time. Economist John Maynard Keynes proposed the absolute income hypothesis, the first and most basic theory of saving and consumption, in 1936. This theory posits that a positive relationship exists between current income and current consumption and that higher income households will save a greater proportion of their income than lower income households. That is, as income increases, consumption also increases (although not necessarily in exact proportion to increases in income). However, Keynes hypothesized that the proportionate increase in consumption is smaller (and thus savings higher) for households with greater income (on average) because increases in consumption represents a smaller proportion of income for higher income households than for those with lower income. Although subsequent research has supported the absolute income hypothesis using data collected at one point in time, the hypothesis has not been supported when data tracking income and consumption over time are examined.

Two related theories, the permanent (Friedman, 1957) and life cycle (Ando & Modigliani, 1963) income hypotheses were developed to explain individuals' saving and consumption over the life course. According to these hypotheses, individuals allocate their financial resources, including saving and borrowing, over their lifetimes. Saving is motivated by the desire to spread consumption evenly over the life course; although income may vary over time, saving and borrowing based on an individual's projection of his or her lifetime income allows actual consumption to be relatively unaffected by current income. For example, a college student takes student loans to pay for college, anticipating that the increase in after-graduation income will allow the repayment of the loans. In later life, the accumulation of savings during higher income working years enables a relatively stable standard of living in retirement. Although subsequent research supports the idea that saving and borrowing are used to even out lifetime consumption, the positive relationship between current income and consumption indicates that current income, as well as lifetime income, shapes consumption and saving decisions.

TRENDS AND PATTERNS IN SAVING

Although estimates of U.S. personal savings rates (i.e., the fraction of personal income that is not consumed) vary, their downward trend over the past several decades is clear. From an all-time U.S. high of 12.2% in the fourth quarter of 1981, the personal savings rate fell to near zero in the last quarter of 2007, the lowest level since the Great Depression. This decline, at a time when the large baby-boomer generation is aging, exiting the labor force, and consuming out of savings accumulated during previous years may result in a considerable economic downturn due to the inability of families to support current consumption levels. Additionally, the shift in employer-sponsored retirement plans from defined-benefit, in which retirement income was guaranteed, to defined contribution, in which the employee is respon-

sible for saving and investment decisions, may threaten the financial security for many in the future. Taken together, the lower savings rate, relatively large cohort approaching retirement, and changes in pension plan coverage may substantially impact individuals' ability to maintain preretirement consumption levels later in life.

Although the overall saving rate in the United States has decreased, the magnitude of the decline varies across social groups. Of considerable concern is the disparity between the savings of low- and high-income families. In 2003 only 10% of the wealthiest 1% of families in the United States did not save, whereas more than 62% of families in the bottom 25% of the wealth distribution did not save (Kennickell, 2006). Similarly, families in the top percentile of the wealth distribution are more than 2.5 times as likely to have an established savings plan as families in the bottom 25%. There are racial disparities in savings as well; whereas 60% of all American workers are currently saving for retirement, only 45% of Black workers and 34% of Hispanic workers are actively saving for the retirement years (Helman, VanDerhei, & Copeland, 2007). These disparities are likely related to differences in the means and ability to save out of income, individual risk tolerance, and consumption preferences but may also be related to differences in access to formal savings vehicles such as employer-sponsored retirement accounts.

RESEARCH CHALLENGES

One of the critical issues in research on personal savings is the manner in which governmental agencies calculate the average personal saving rate (Reinsdorf, 2007). The National Income and Product Accounts (NIPA) analysis of the National Bureau of Economic Research is a frequently reported source of savings rates. Although these estimates are widely used in literature on personal savings, some researchers argue that these rates underestimate the actual level of savings by omitting capital-gains income (the gain realized from the sale of an asset, such as stocks or bonds, at a higher price than it was originally purchased) and including both working people and retired people (who may be spending out of savings, rather than income resulting in a negative saving rate based on NIPA calculation).

Regardless of the exact rates, the downward trend in personal saving in the United States, as well as some other developed countries including Canada and Australia, is considerable. Scholars have proposed several reasons for this decline, including increases in personal consumption and consumer debt (Parker, 2000), in part due to the increase in the availability of credit card and nontraditional home equity lending (e.g. subprime, adjustable rate mortgages, revolving home equity lines

INVESTMENT

■

Investing involves the purchase of a financial or physical asset with the intention of realizing a future return (i.e., an increase in the asset's value or a monetary payment). Investment can be used to both generate funds for the future and to safely mitigate the impact of inflation on savings. A wide variety of vehicles are used for personal investing, including stocks, corporate and government bonds, mutual funds, and real estate.

Acknowledging the trade-off between risk and return is key to investment decisions. Whereas low-risk investments such as U.S. Treasury bonds are relatively safe from any loss of principal (i.e., the original investment amount), they generate a relatively low level of monetary return. Conversely, a higher-risk asset such as corporate stock is subject to market downturn and principal loss, but has a greater potential return, particularly if held long-term. While a diversified investment portfolio consisting of both low and high-risk assets is generally suggested, the risk-return relationship can be utilized to maximize investment performance based on an individual's position in the life-course.

of credit). Other explanations include the aging of the U.S. population and expectations of continued stable macroeconomic policy (e.g., relatively stable inflation and economic growth) and social program support (such as Social Security) among young households. These factors all help to explain the significant decrease in the personal saving rate in the United States, but no comprehensive theory that sufficiently explains the decrease has been proposed (Guidolin & LaJeunesse, 2007).

Cross-national analyses of personal savings rates are complicated by substantial differences in the financial systems and institutional structures of different countries. For example, research indicates that American households save less than households in some other developed nations but that this decrease is tied to differences in retirement behavior and credit constraints (Kirsanova & Sefton, 2006). This use of individual rather than national data has provided some insight into the diversity in personal saving between citizens of different countries, but direct comparisons remain complicated.

POLICY IMPLICATIONS

As the baby-boomer generation approaches retirement, the importance of saving becomes increasingly important. Several policy implications are related to the current state of personal savings in the United States. The development and implementation of government-sponsored financial education and savings incentive plans has been suggested to increase both awareness of the benefits of saving and the availability of saving options for consumers, particularly for low-income families. The inclusion of mandatory credit counseling for the successful discharge of personal bankruptcy in the Bankruptcy Reform Act of 2005 and the 2003 establishment of the U.S. Financial Literacy and Education Commission are examples of initial steps toward increasing financial education in the United States. To increase the availability of savings vehicles and encourage saving among low-income families, Individual Development Account programs have been established (Comptroller of the Currency Administrator of National Banks, 2005). These programs match the savings of low-income participants, providing additional incentive to save.

Another policy option directed at increasing the personal saving of American families is a shift from income-based to consumption-based taxation. Although a "spending tax," or tax on goods and services consumed rather than on income, could encourage saving by exempting income not used for consumption from taxation, there are several arguments against consumption-based taxes, not the least of which is the potential concentration of wealth among the already wealthy who are able to save and invest more of their income than those with lower incomes.

Although personal savings rates have declined over the past few decades, saving for major life events including retirement remains an important financial issue throughout the life course. Whereas previous generations were able to rely on employer-provided pensions and Social Security for resources in retirement, the shift away from employer pension provision and toward consumerism and easy access to credit creates a challenging environment for saving.

SEE ALSO Volume 2: *Consumption, Adulthood and Later Life; Debt; Poverty, Adulthood;* Volume 3: *Wealth,*

BIBLIOGRAPHY

Ando, A., & Modigliani, E. (1963). The "life-cycle" hypothesis of saving: Aggregate implications and tests. *American Economic Review, 53*(1), 55–84.

Bryant, W. K., & Zick, C. D. (2006). *The economic organization of the household.* (2nd ed.). New York: Cambridge University Press.

Comptroller of the Currency Administrator of National Banks. (2005). Individual development accounts: As asset building product for lower-income consumers. *Community Development: Insights*.

Friedman, M. (1957). *A theory of the consumption function*. Princeton, NJ: Princeton University Press.

Guidolin, M., & LaJeunesse, E. A. (2007). The decline in the U.S. personal saving rate: Is it real and is it a puzzle? *Review— Federal Reserve Bank of St. Louis, 89*(6), 491–514.

Helman, R., VanDerhei, J., & Copeland, C. (2007). Minority workers remain confident about retirement, despite lagging preparation and false expectations. *ERBI Issue Brief*, No. 306, Employee Benefit Research Institute.

Kennickell, A. B. (2006). Currents and undercurrents: Changes in the distribution of wealth, 1989–2004. Accessed June 25, 2008, from http://www.federalreserve.gov

Keynes, N. M. (1936). *The general theory of employment, interest, and money*. London: Macmillan.

Kirsanova, T., & Sefton, J. A. (2006). *A comparison of national saving rates in the U.K., U.S., and Italy*. Working paper, National Institute of Social and Economic Research.

Parker, J. A. (2000). Spendthrift in American? On two decades of decline in the U.S. saving rate. In B. S. Bernanke & J. J. Rotemberg (Eds.), *NBER macroeconomics annual 1999*. Cambridge, MA: MIT Press.

Reinsdorf, M. B. (2007). Alternate measures of personal savings. *Survey of Current Business 87*(2).

U.S. Financial Literacy and Education Commission. (2008). *Providing financial education resources for all Americans*. Accessed June 25, 2008, from http://www.mymoney.gov

Angela Fontes

SCHOOL TO WORK TRANSITION

The transition from school to work (STW) is a critically important juncture in the life course. Socioeconomic attainment is a long-term process starting in adolescence and encompassing achievement in school, the acquisition of educational degrees and other qualifications, and movement through the occupational career. The individual's completed level of schooling and the point of entry into the labor force are major determinants of subsequent occupational and income trajectories. Psychologically, the transition has significant implications for the development of identity. Finishing school and starting full-time work are key markers of the transition to adulthood, signifying adult status and maturity. Young people who have made the transition from *survival jobs* to *career jobs* are more likely to consider themselves adults, and to be viewed, as such, by others.

FEATURES OF THE SCHOOL TO WORK TRANSITION

There are major differences in the character of the STW transition both within and across societies. The transition is facilitated when institutional connections between school and work are strong (Kerckhoff, 2003); these linkages vary considerably in contemporary modern societies. For example, high schools in Japan are linked to employers in the community, and recommend their students for the most desirable jobs in order of their academic performance (Rosenbaum, 2001). The apprenticeship system in Germany similarly functions to link students and jobs, as young apprentices' schooling and employment are effectively coordinated, mutually supporting one another, as the youth prepare themselves for entry into particular occupations (Mortimer & Krueger, 2000). The STW transition is much more difficult and prolonged in North America, where secondary schooling is not vocationally specific, credentials (that is, high school diplomas and BA degrees) are general, and youths are encouraged to go as far as they can in higher education (Kerckhoff, 2002). In these circumstances, attaining the next rung on the educational ladder assumes a much higher priority than vocational preparation.

High school students focus on getting accepted into the best college they can, rather than preparing for entry into the world of work. Their teachers and parents encourage this stance, fearing that premature coursework or other preparatory activities related to work might steer them away from college degrees. While approximately two-thirds of high school graduates enter college, many of these young adults are not successful in completing 4-year degrees. As a result, most young people in the United States enter the labor force (as high school graduates or college dropouts) without an educational credential that would signal to employers their capacity to pursue particular lines of work. Many have difficulties in finding acceptable jobs, and lower their sights as they encounter the realities of the job market (Johnson, 2002). Whereas high school dropouts are the most disadvantaged full-time labor force entrants, even the recipients of college degrees (approximately one-fourth of recent cohorts) often flounder from job to job as they try to obtain a better match between their own interests, occupational values and needs, and the experiences and rewards to be obtained in the labor force.

The term *school to work transition* implies a clear, discrete event: completing school and entering the usually full-time work role. However, as a result of changes in both education and work, as well as cultural shifts in the relative prominence and desirability of the youth and adult phases of the life course (Hartmann & Swartz, 2007), this once clear, predictable, and normative transition has become increasingly delayed and disorderly among recent cohorts of youth in the United States. Instead of full-time immersion in school, followed by similar full-time involvement in work, the lengthy period of transition typically includes long-term involvements in both work and school. Ever-more young people are extending their formal educations through adolescence and into young adulthood. Postsecondary students are becoming older: In 2002, 39% of students who were enrolled in degree-granting institutions in the United States were older than 25 (U.S. Department of Education, 2002). Combining school and work is highly normative throughout the periods of secondary and postsecondary education; most students are employed during the high school years and during college (U.S. Department of Labor, 2000). Shared school and work roles begin in early adolescence—at about age 12 for most of the U.S. youth. Moreover, the transition from school to work is not unidirectional; many young people return to school after leaving and engaging in work full time (Shanahan, 2000). In fact, by age 26, 20% of youths have undergone the transition from school to full-time work at least twice (Arum & Hout, 1998). These trends partly reflect the general nature of educational credentials and the lack of clear connections between employers and schools in the United States, as well as the increasing importance of a college diploma among recent cohorts of youth.

Instead of defining the transition to work as a discrete event, it has come viewed as a long-term process. Patterns of schooling and working during adolescence have long-term implications for postsecondary schooling and wage attainments in early adulthood.

THE SHARING OF SCHOOL AND WORK ROLES AND SOCIOECONOMIC ATTAINMENT

Most prior investigations of occupational attainment assume that young people make a sequential STW transition. The socioeconomic standing of the family of origin, as well as indicators of academic performance and attitudes toward school, are major determinants of a young person's highest level of schooling. Educational attainment, in turn, establishes credentials for more or less prestigious full-time jobs that are held after the completion of school. Yet, as mentioned before, most youths begin working in adolescence and often continue to be both workers and students during the STW transition. In the United States, the average high school graduate acquires nearly 1,500 hours of employment between his or her 16th birthday and graduation from high school, whereas the typical college graduate gains almost 5,000 hours of employment by the time of college graduation (Light, 2001). Students may work to save

money for future education or other purposes, to assert themselves as more "adult-like" in the eyes of parents, teachers, or peers, and to buy clothes, music, or video games. They may also work to pay for educational and living expenses, especially during the college years.

Scholars disagree about the impact of various combinations of schooling and working during the STW transition on future economic attainment (Staff, Mortimer, & Uggen, 2004). One view is that combining work and school, especially during the high school years, ultimately undermines adult attainment because paid work limits time for homework, studying, and extracurricular activities and encourages delinquency and the use of drugs and alcohol. According to this perspective, employment should be discouraged and limited as much as possible prior to full-time entry into the workforce. An alternative view is that longer-term socioeconomic attainment is enhanced when paid work is effectively combined with periods of school attendance. Early work experiences not only benefit adult attainment through on-the-job training and skill development, but also promote *soft skills* that are not learned in the classroom, such as time-management, self-reliance, and other interpersonal skills that facilitate workplace interactions with supervisors, coworkers, and customers.

There is growing consensus that it is the pattern of investment in paid work prior to the completion of schooling that determines its positive or negative influence (Mortimer, 2003). For instance, youths who work intensively (conventionally defined as more than 20 hours per week) during the high school years report fewer hours of homework, lower grade point averages and standardized test scores, and a greater likelihood of dropping out of high school than youths who do not work or who work fewer hours. Research also shows that such intensive work hours during the high school years lessen the likelihood of postsecondary school attendance and the receipt of a college degree in young adulthood.

In contrast, limited involvement in paid work during the STW transition fosters academic progress and longer-term socioeconomic attainment. Moderate work during the high school years is associated with increased grade point averages and greater involvement in school activities than nonemployment. Furthermore, research shows that moderate work hours do not limit time for homework or other extracurricular activities (Schoenhals, Tienda, & Schneider, 1998). Moderate work hours over the duration of high school also increase the likelihood of obtaining a 4-year college degree. Jeremy Staff and Jeylan Mortimer (2007) found this outcome to be linked to continuity in employment patterns. Their analyses of data from the longitudinal Youth Development Study show that a continuous pattern of combining school with low-intensity work throughout the STW transition accrues advantages during high school, postsecondary schooling, and early occupational careers.

It is important to note that preexisting individual differences in school performance, aspirations, socioeconomic background, ability, and motivation shape subsequent investments in paid work and school during the STW transition. For instance, youths from lower socioeconomic backgrounds work more hours when they are employed than their more advantaged peers (Entwisle, Alexander, & Olson, 2000). Moreover, poorly performing students with low educational aspirations have greater workforce involvement in subsequent years of high school than their better performing peers (Bachman, Safron, Sy, & Schulenberg, 2003). Some research suggests that paid work has little effect on school performance once prior differences in grades, aspirations, problem behaviors, and family socioeconomic standing are taken into account (Warren, LePore, & Mare, 2000). Other longitudinal research on young men shows that working during high school has little benefit for adult wages once differences in unmeasured traits (such as ability or motivation) between workers and nonworkers are adequately controlled (Hotz, Xu, Tienda, & Ahituv, 2002).

It is also important to consider whether distinct combinations of schooling and working during the STW transition have different consequences for future attainment, depending on the youth's own interests, motivations, resources, and capacities. In particular, there is evidence that heavy investment in paid work during high school may not be harmful for those youths who come from more disadvantaged backgrounds. Research shows that paid work increases the chances of high school completion for young, economically disadvantaged males (Entwisle, Alexander, & Olson, 2005). Among urban youths residing in impoverished neighborhoods, Katherine Newman (1999) finds that exposure to conventional adolescents and adults at work can serve as an entry to legitimate occupational career paths and may even encourage educational attainment. Similarly, among contemporary rural youth in hard-pressed farm families, early work experiences can build confidence and instill positive work values under conditions of poverty and economic distress (Elder & Conger, 2000). Staff and Mortimer (2007) find that steady work is especially conducive to the attainment of 4-year college degrees for youth who display limited educational promise at the start of high school. Furthermore, Jennifer Lee and Staff (2007) show that high intensity employment during high school does not influence dropout for those who have the greatest propensity to pursue such an employment pattern.

TWO IDEAL TYPICAL SCHOOL TO WORK TRANSITIONS

Based upon what is known about the relations between work and school roles and what is known about how individuals choose various work and school patterns, contemporary young people can be classified into two ideal typical tracks with varying emphases upon school and work. These tracks commence as early as age 14 and 15 and continue as young people make the STW transition. Youths who come from more advantaged backgrounds, and who are more strongly oriented toward schooling, are more likely than their less advantaged counterparts to pursue steady work during high school (i.e., limited hours but near continuous duration) and they invest more in postsecondary education, especially in 4-year colleges (Staff & Mortimer, 2007), during the years following. In contrast, youths from more disadvantaged backgrounds, and those who have poorer grades and lower educational aspirations, are more likely to be employed intensively during high school. These more intensive workers have little likelihood of acquiring 4-year college degrees. These class-differentiated tracks, commencing at the start of high school and persisting through the transition to adulthood, have lasting implications for future socioeconomic attainment. However, when youth from lower socioeconomic backgrounds follow the first track, involving steady work during high school, their educational attainment and longer-term wages are enhanced.

CONCLUSION AND FUTURE DIRECTIONS

In the contemporary United States, where institutional bridges between school and work are notably undeveloped and the sharing of school and work roles often begins in early adolescence, employment experiences appear to be an integral part of human capital acquisition during the STW transition. In decades past, young people typically made a sequential transition from full-time school to full-time work, a transition that could be characterized as a discrete event. There are two ideal typical routes that now characterize the more prolonged STW transition among contemporary cohorts of young people. One route involves less intensive employment during high school, followed by continued part-time employment and postsecondary educational investment, most likely in 4-year colleges. This pathway is more common for youths of higher socioeconomic origins, but is especially beneficial for young people of lower socioeconomic status. A second route involves early intensive work experience during high school that is less conducive to higher educational attainment. These workers are less likely to achieve 4-year degrees, irrespective of their parents'

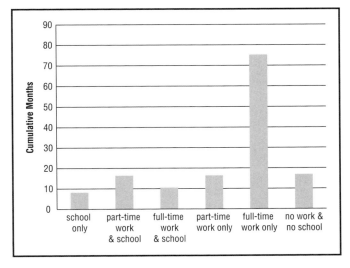

Figure 1. *Cumulative Months of Work and School during the STW Transition (age 18–30).* CENGAGE LEARNING, GALE.

educational backgrounds. When they reach adulthood, these workers begin to show lower hourly wage rates than youths who worked less intensively in adolescence and were more likely to pursue postsecondary schooling in the years immediately following high school.

Whereas this review addresses patterns of temporal investment in work during the STW transition, little is known about the impact of the quality of early employment for educational and wage attainments on the quality of adult work and on adult occupational commitment and job satisfaction. For example, the presence of a supportive supervisor in the workplace may be especially important for youths whose own parents lack the experience and resources to effectively guide them toward higher education and jobs that will sustain a middle-class style of life. Positive work experiences, providing learning opportunities, skill development, and affirming one's role as worker may be especially important for the disadvantaged youth who may have few alternative sources of positive vocational identities, work values, and economic efficacy. Such experiences in the workplace could be particularly important in enabling youths of lower socioeconomic origin to make a successful STW transition, enabling them to find jobs that represent good fits with their interests, values, and capacities. High school guidance and career counselors, parents, and others concerned with the successful development of youth should be aware that early work experience has much to offer young people, particularly if their hours of work are restricted and if they learn to effectively balance schooling and employment through steady participation in the labor force.

SEE ALSO Volume 2: *Careers; Educational Attainment; Employment, Adulthood; Transition to Adulthood.*

BIBLIOGRAPHY

Arum, R., & Hout, M. (1998). The early returns: The transition from school to work in the United States. In Y. Shavit & W. Müller (Eds.), *From school to work: A comparative study of educational qualifications and occupational destinations.* Oxford, U.K.: Clarendon Press.

Bachman, J. G., Safron, D. J., Sy, S. R., & Schulenberg, J. E. (2003). Wishing to work: New perspectives on how adolescents' part-time work intensity is linked with educational disengagement, drug use, and other problem behaviors. *International Journal of Behavioral Development, 27*(4), 301–315.

Elder, G. H., Jr., & Conger, R. D. (2000). *Children of the land: Adversity and success in rural America.* Chicago: University of Chicago Press.

Entwisle, D. R., Alexander, K. L., & Olson, L. S. (2000). Early work histories of urban youth. *American Sociological Review, 65*(2), 279–297.

Entwisle, D. R., Alexander, K. L., & Olson, L. S. (2005). Urban teenagers: Work and dropout. *Youth and Society, 37*(1), 3–32.

Hartmann, D., & Swartz, T. T. (2007). The new adulthood? The transition to adulthood from the perspective of transitioning young adults. In R. Macmillan (Ed.), *Constructing adulthood: Agency and subjectivity in adolescence and adulthood, advances in life course research.* Amsterdam: Elsevier/ JAI Press.

Herman, A. M. (2000). *Report on the youth labor force.* Washington, DC: U.S. Government Printing Office.

Hotz, V. J., Xu, L. C., Tienda, M., & Ahituv, A. (2002). Are there returns to the wages of young men from working while in school? *The Review of Economics and Statistics, 84*(2), 221–236.

Johnson, M. K. (2002). Social origins, adolescent experiences, and work value trajectories during the transition to adulthood. *Social Forces, 80*(4), 1307–1341.

Kerckhoff, A. C. (2002). The transition from school to work. In J. T. Mortimer & R. W. Larson (Eds.), *The changing adolescent experience: Societal trends and the transition to adulthood*. New York: Cambridge University Press.

Kerckhoff, A. C. (2003). From student to worker. In J. T. Mortimer & M. J. Shanahan (Eds.), *Handbook of the life course*. New York: Kluwer Academic/Plenum.

Lee, J. C., & Staff, J. (2007). When work matters: The varying impact of adolescent work intensity on high school dropout. *Sociology of Education, 80*(2), 158–178.

Light, A. (2001). In-school work experience and the returns to schooling. *Journal of Labor Economics, 19*(1), 65–93.

Mortimer, J. T. (2003). *Working and growing up in America*. Cambridge, MA: Harvard University Press.

Mortimer, J. T., & Krueger, H. (2000). Transition from school to work in the United States and Germany: Formal pathways matter. In M. T. Hallinan (Ed.), *Handbook of the sociology of education*. New York: Kluwer Academic/Plenum.

Newman, K. S. (1999). *No shame in my game: The working poor in the inner city*. New York: Knopf and Russell Sage Foundation.

Rosenbaum, J. E. (2001). *Beyond college for all: Career paths for the forgotten half*. New York: Russell Sage Foundation.

Schoenhals, M., Tienda, M., & Schneider, B. (1998). The educational and personal consequences of adolescent employment. *Social Forces, 77*(2), 723–762.

Shanahan, M. J. (2000). Pathways to adulthood in changing societies: Variability and mechanisms in life course perspective. *Annual Review of Sociology, 26*, 667–692.

Staff, J., & Mortimer, J. T. (2007). Educational and work strategies from adolescence to early adulthood: Consequences for educational attainment. *Social Forces, 85*(3), 1169–1194.

Staff, J., Mortimer, J. T., & Uggen, C. (2004). Work and leisure in adolescence. In R. M. Lerner & L. Steinberg (Eds.), *The handbook of adolescent psychology*. (2nd ed.). New York: Wiley.

U.S. Department of Education. (2002). *The condition of education, 2002*. Washington, DC: U.S. Government Printing Office.

Warren, J. R., LePore, P. C., & Mare, R. D. (2000). Employment during high school: Consequences for students' grades in academic courses. *American Educational Research Journal, 37*(4), 943–969.

Jeylan T. Mortimer
Jeremy Staff

SEGREGATION, RESIDENTIAL

Residential segregation refers to the situation in which members of social groups live separately from members of other groups within a larger geographic entity. The term is most commonly used to describe the extent to which groups occupy distinct, separate neighborhoods within a city or metropolitan area. Cities can be segregated along many sociocultural dimensions, including social class, ethnicity, race, and even religion. In the United States, the most important dimension of residen-

tial segregation in terms of both prevalence and consequences is racial and ethnic. Of special interest is the spatial separation of racial and ethnic minority groups from non-Hispanic Whites. The spatial separation of populations can have profound consequences for a group's collective well-being as well as their inclusion or exclusion in the larger society. This is because resources are unevenly distributed across geographic space. Therefore, where one lives determines the safety of neighborhoods, quality of schools and housing, and availability of public amenities such as libraries and police stations.

MEASURES OF SEGREGATION

The idea of residential segregation makes intuitive sense to most people. However, measuring segregation is complex because segregation can be conceptualized in multiple ways. Sociologists Douglas Massey and Nancy Denton (1988) identified five dimensions of residential segregation, each of which provides a different way of thinking about how race and ethnic groups are separated from each other within an area: (a) evenness, (b) exposure, (c) clustering, (d) concentration, and (e) centralization. *Evenness* refers to how groups are distributed over geographic space within an area—for example, the proportions of Whites and Blacks across all neighborhoods in a city. *Exposure* refers to a person's potential for contact with members of other groups. *Clustering* describes spatial distributions in which minority neighborhoods are tightly clustered to form a large contiguous area (as opposed to being dispersed throughout a city). *Concentration*, a closely related concept, captures the degree of crowdedness of a group within an area. Finally, *centralization* assesses whether a minority group is centralized around the urban core or spread out along the periphery of a city. The term *hypersegregated* is used to refer to areas where segregation scores are high on four out of the five dimensions.

Evenness and exposure are the two most commonly measured dimensions of residential segregation. Evenness is typically gauged by a measure known as the dissimilarity index. Values for the dissimilarity index range from 0 to 100, with values of 0 representing complete integration and 100 representing complete segregation. It is interpreted as the proportion of members of one group who would have to move—assuming that members of the other group remain where they are—in order to obtain an even distribution of the groups across an area. Examples of U.S. metropolitan areas where Blacks and Whites are highly segregated on the evenness dimension (values greater than or equal to 80) are Detroit, Chicago, Newark, and New York. Two common measures of contact are the exposure and isolation indices. The exposure index describes the probability that members of group A will come into contact with members of group B. Values for the index also range from 0 to 100, with higher values representing a greater probability of one group coming into contact with a member of another group. Blacks have the least probability of exposure (i.e., exposure values less than 20) to Whites in the Los Angeles, Chicago, Detroit, Miami, New York, and Newark metros. The isolation index assesses the degree to which members of a group live in neighborhoods where the other residents are predominantly of the same racial or ethnic group (i.e., *ghettoization*). Unlike the dissimilarity index, the isolation index is sensitive to group size. Values are low if the minority group is small but high if the group is large. The range for the index is from 0 to 100, with 100 reflecting complete ghettoization. Metros where Blacks are highly ghettoized (values greater than 70) include Chicago, Detroit, Cleveland, and New Orleans.

TRENDS IN RACIAL RESIDENTIAL SEGREGATION IN THE UNITED STATES

American cities were not always characterized by high levels of racial residential segregation. During the 19th century, non-Hispanic Blacks were less segregated from the majority group (i.e., White Anglo-Saxon Protestants) than White European immigrants (Lieberson, 1980). During the 20th century, segregation between Blacks and Whites increased and segregation of European immigrants decreased. By the 1970s and 1980s, Black–White segregation was so high that in some cities, such as Milwaukee, Cleveland, New York, and Los Angeles, the dissimilarity index was in the 80s and 90s (Massey & Denton 1987, pp. 815–816). Hispanic–White and Asian–White segregation have always been much lower than Black–White segregation. In fact, extreme Black–White residential segregation is one of the hallmarks of American society; no other developed, pluralistic society has segregation levels as high as those in the United States.

The overwhelming conclusion from the cross-national literature is that hypersegregation does not exist in the Canadian or European context (Huttman, 1991; Massey, 1985). Although segregation and ethnic clustering can be found in virtually every immigrant-receiving country, segregation levels do not approach those for Blacks and Whites in the United States. Not only is racial residential segregation lower in Europe, but where it does exist, the cleavage is not necessarily between Blacks and Whites. For example, geographer Ceri Peach (1996) examined the residential segregation of six major racial and ethnic minority groups in Great Britain. He found that Bangladeshis and Pakistanis were more segregated from British Whites than were Afro-Caribbeans or Africans. Blacks in

Britain were the least segregated out of all six ethnic minority groups under study. Likewise, in Sweden, White and non-White immigrants have similar degrees of residential separation from Swedes (Linden & Lindberg, 1991). Socioeconomic differences between immigrants and natives, as well as cultural factors, have been posited to explain the patterns observed in Western Europe.

Studies based on the 2000 U.S. Census show that segregation between non-Hispanic Whites and minorities has declined throughout the 20th century. Black–White segregation in 2000 was at its lowest level since 1920 (Iceland, Weinberg, & Steinmetz, 2002). Yet there are regional variations in the decline of Black–White segregation across the United States. The Northeast and Midwest continue to have high levels of Black–White segregation, especially in former manufacturing cities such as Cleveland, Chicago, and New York, where housing is older (Cutler, Glaeser, & Vigdor, 1999). However, in regions with new housing and population growth, particularly the south and southwestern regions of the United States, Black–White segregation has declined markedly. Segregation among Asians and Hispanics has declined as well (Glaeser & Vigdor, 2001).

THE CAUSES OF RESIDENTIAL SEGREGATION

A significant amount of scholarly attention has been given to explaining why residential segregation occurs and persists over time. Spatial assimilation theory is one of the leading frameworks used to understand processes of residential segregation (Alba & Logan, 1993). A central tenet of spatial assimilation theory is that spatial distance equals social distance. In other words, people want to live with others who are like themselves; spatial distance reflects some underlying social chasm between the separated groups that may be purely subjective or based on some real objective difference. The theory outlines a linear progression of spatial integration in which minority groups (and immigrants) initially start out in a state of geographic isolation from the dominant group (i.e., non-Hispanic Whites). Typically, minorities and immigrants will reside in poor central city areas where housing is cheap and one's neighbors are other minorities or immigrants. The theory assumes that this initial state of spatial separation is due to socioeconomic and cultural differences between minorities (or immigrants) and non-Hispanic Whites. Over time as minorities increase their socioeconomic status, they not only become more socially and culturally acceptable as neighbors, but they can also afford housing in predominantly White or racially mixed neighborhoods. These types of neighborhoods are more desirable because they tend to have better public amenities, have lower rates of crime, and are located in resource-rich suburbs. For immigrants, acculturation—particularly the acquisition of the English language—along with increased socioeconomic status helps to diminish the cultural and socioeconomic gaps between native and foreign-born persons, thereby facilitating residential integration.

The spatial assimilation model has been criticized for its failure to explain the persistence of residential segregation among Blacks and darker-skin Hispanics (e.g., Puerto Ricans). Despite increases in income and education or cultural assimilation, Blacks and Puerto Ricans remain segregated from Whites. An alternative, although not necessarily contradictory, theory of residential segregation has been forwarded to explain the persistent segregation of Blacks and darker-skin minorities. Place stratification theory argues that residential patterns of different racial and ethnic groups reflect their relative standing in the larger society. In the United States, Blacks are at the bottom of the hierarchy, and race is a "master status," barring access to desirable, racially integrated neighborhoods (Charles, 2003).

The specific mechanisms for how race constrains the social mobility of Blacks and, by extension, other racial and ethnic minority groups are a hotly contested topic in the residential segregation literature. Three individual-level hypotheses have been influential: in-group preferences, racial proxy, and racial stereotyping. The in-group preferences thesis attributes residential segregation to varying degrees of ethnocentrism between the races. It is argued that all groups exhibit ethnocentrism and preferences for same-race and same-ethnicity neighbors. In the racial proxy hypothesis, it is argued that because Black neighborhoods are often associated with poorer amenities, inferior schools, and high crime, White avoidance of Black neighborhoods is not due to race per se but rather the desire to avoid disadvantaged neighborhoods and poor neighbors. Finally, the racial prejudice or discrimination thesis attributes racial residential segregation to active out-group avoidance or domination. It is believed that White prejudicial attitudes and racial discrimination cause Whites to avoid neighborhoods with Blacks and other racial and ethnic minorities.

THE CONSEQUENCES OF RESIDENTIAL SEGREGATION FOR THE LIFE COURSE

Residential segregation can have negative consequences for individuals' life chances because resources are unevenly distributed across space. In general, majority-White, suburban areas tend to have better public amenities (such as well-maintained parks and playgrounds, safer streets, and high-quality public schools with well-trained teachers and smaller class sizes), economic resources, and higher-quality housing than non-White, central city areas. The

geographic disparity in public resources stems from interactions among social class, race, and geography. Where one resides determines who one's neighbors are, which in turn affects the degree of political power, economic clout, and, ultimately, resources to which one has access. The high correlation between socioeconomic status and race means that middle-class areas will, on average, consist more of Whites than non-Whites. The overlap among race, place, and class means that, irrespective of a family's socioeconomic status, Blacks and other racial and ethnic minorities will, on average, reside in socioeconomically disadvantaged and segregated neighborhoods.

Research has shown that access to resources and amenities can affect health outcomes across the life course. For example, a study of neighborhood drug stores in New York City showed that pharmacies in non-White neighborhoods tend to carry fewer pain medications than those in predominantly White neighborhoods (Morrison et al., 2000). Another study found that grocery stores that stock nutritious food are less easily accessible for residents in segregated neighborhoods (Zenk et al., 2005). Segregated Black neighborhoods bear the burden of housing unhealthy establishments. Black neighborhoods tend to have a disproportionately high density of fast-food restaurants (Kwate, 2008)—no doubt contributing to the obesity epidemic among low-income minorities. Liquor stores and advertisements for unhealthy behavior, such as cigarette smoking and alcohol consumption, are also disproportionately concentrated in low-income, predominantly Black neighborhoods (Hackbarth, Silvestri, & Cosper, 1995).

The physical deterioration of the built environment (e.g., building and physical infrastructure, quality of transportation, and so on) often associated with poor, segregated neighborhoods also can have harmful effects on the health of children and adults. Poor housing conditions, for instance, can expose residents to lead and other harmful elements such as mildew and disease-carrying rodents (Hood, 2005). Residential segregation has also been shown to increase residents' exposure to airborne pollutants (Lopez, 2002), elevate the cancer risks associated with ambient air toxins (Morello-Frosch & Shenassa, 2006), and increase both infant and adult mortality rates (Polednak, 1993). Additionally, physical activity in segregated neighborhoods may be difficult due to the absence of walkable spaces or safe green spaces for children's play and recreation in segregated areas (Holt, Spence, Sehn, & Cutumisu, 2008).

Another way that residential segregation influences life course development is through exposing residents to violence. Violence is a regular feature of life for many residents of segregated urban neighborhoods in the United States. Children living in segregated neighborhoods experience frequent and ongoing exposure to guns, knives, drugs, and random violence (Ofosky, 1999). Additionally, the burden of violence disproportionately falls on the shoulders of Black Americans. The homicide rate for African Americans ages 15 to 24 years in 1999 was 38.6 per 100,000 persons. This was twice the rate for Hispanics (17.3 per 100,000 persons) and 12 times the rate for non-Hispanic Whites (3.1 per 100,000 persons) of similar age (Krug et al., 2002, p. 11). In addition to mortality risks, living in resource-poor, segregated neighborhoods can have adverse effects on transitions into and out of different life stages. For example, ethnographic studies have shown that minority youths living in harsh, segregated neighborhoods where violence is an everyday occurrence may supplant mainstream norms of success with alternative norms such as sexual prowess, teenage pregnancy, and displays of aggression (Anderson, 1999). These alternative markers of social success may bring short-term satisfaction but often derail long-term transitions into adulthood roles, such as steady employment and marriage. Instead, youths may find themselves rotating in and out of prison, navigating the welfare system, and raising children without the support of a partner.

(SUPPOSED) BENEFITS OF RESIDENTIAL INTEGRATION

Implicit in spatial assimilation theory is the idea that spatial propinquity helps to generate meaningful social relationships among neighbors. Coming into contact with people on the streets, on the subway, or at the supermarket does not provide opportunities to develop primary social relationships, nor does living in the same neighborhood guarantee that people would know their neighbors on a more intimate social level. However, coresidence in integrated neighborhoods is assumed to provide opportunities to develop primary social relationships through community activities and organizations. These primary social relationships, particularly with middle-class and non-Hispanic Whites, may have benefits for minorities in the form of job-generating social networks, a wider array of positive adult role models for children, greater social capital, and so on.

Despite the intuitively appealing premise that residential integration may foster beneficial primary social relationships between minority and majority group members and help to bridge social class, racial or ethnic, and cultural divides, the empirical evidence to support this notion is weak. Research shows that people's social support networks are not tied to neighbors within their neighborhood of residence. Neighborhood and family ethnographies from the Three-City Welfare Project show that the social support networks of poor families are not located in their neighborhoods of residence (Matthews, Detwiler, & Burton, 2005). One possible explanation for the lack of within-neighborhood social support networks is the density of multifamily residential units in low-income, segregated neighborhoods. The design of multi-family dwellings can adversely affect interaction patterns by discouraging social interaction and thereby increase residents' feelings of social isolation and impede the cultivation of strong social support networks (Evans, Wells, & Moch, 2003).

POLICY ISSUES

The research evidence suggests that public policy can best ameliorate the negative effects of residential segregation on life course development in the short run by improving the physical conditions of segregated neighborhoods and minimizing public disorder. For instance, greater attention can be given to making segregated neighborhoods health-friendly by investing in safer parks and play-grounds, making streets more walkable for residents, and altering zoning laws such that there is a greater balance of healthy and unhealthy establishments in low-income, Black neighborhoods. Similarly, neighborhood development or renewal projects can improve community cohesion and strengthen within-neighborhood social support networks by directly incorporating building designs and land use that encourage socialization. In the long term, the goal of public policy should be to eliminate racial residential segregation. This would entail targeting the social and institutional mechanisms that perpetuate segregation—a feat that is, at best, daunting given the lack of consensus in the field regarding the root causes of segregation. However, recent declines in segregation are promising and suggest that the United States may potentially achieve low segregation levels on par with other developed, pluralistic countries.

SEE ALSO Volume 2: *Health Differentials/Disparities, Adulthood; Home Ownership/Housing; Immigration, Adulthood; Neighborhood Context, Adulthood; Policy, Health; Poverty, Adulthood; Racism/Race Discrimination; Residential Mobility, Adulthood; Social Integration/Isolation, Adulthood.*

BIBLIOGRAPHY

Alba, R. D., & Logan, J. R. (1993). Minority proximity to Whites in suburbs: An individual-level analysis of segregation. *American Journal of Sociology, 98*(6), 1388–1427.

Anderson, E. (1999). *Code of the street: Decency, violence, and the moral life of the inner city.* New York: Norton.

Charles, C. Z. (2003). The dynamics of racial residential segregation. *Annual Review of Sociology, 29,* 167–207.

Cutler, D. E., Glaeser, E., & Vigdor, J. L. (1999). The rise and decline of the American ghetto. *Journal of Political Economy, 107*(3), 455–506.

Evans, G. W., Wells, N. M., & Moch, A. (2003). Housing and mental health: A review of the evidence and a methodological and conceptual critique. *Journal of Social Issues, 59*(3), 475–500.

Glaeser, E. L., & Vigdor, J. L. (2001). *Racial segregation in the 2000 Census: Promising news.* Washington, DC: Brookings Institution. Retrieved June 24, 2008, from http://www.brookings.edu/es/

Hackbarth, D. P., Silvestri, B., & Cosper, W. (1995). Tobacco and alcohol billboards in 50 Chicago neighborhoods: Market segmentation to sell dangerous products to the poor. *Journal of Public Health Policy, 16*(2), 213–230.

Holt, N. L., Spence, J. C., Sehn, Z. L., & Cutumisu, N. (2008). Neighborhood and developmental differences in children's perceptions of opportunities for play and physical activity. *Health & Place, 14*(1), 2–14.

Hood, E. (2005). Dwelling disparities: How poor housing leads to poor health. *Environmental Health Perspectives, 113*(5), 310–317.

Huttman, E. D. (1991). Housing segregation in Western Europe: An introduction. In E. D. Huttman, W. Blauw, & J. Saltman (Eds.), *Urban housing segregation of minorities in Western Europe and the United States* (pp. 21–42). Durham, NC: Duke University Press.

Iceland, J., Weinberg, D. H., & Steinmetz, E. (2002). *Racial and ethnic residential segregation in the United States: 1980–2000.* Washington, DC: U.S. Census Bureau.

Krenichyn, K. (2006). "The only place to go and be in the city": Women talk about exercise, being outdoors, and the meanings of a large urban park. *Health & Place, 12*(4), 631–643.

Krug, E. G., Dahlberg, L. L., Mercy, J. A., Zwi, A. B., & Lozano, R. (2002). *World report on violence and health.* Geneva, Switzerland: World Health Organization.

Kwate, N. O. A. (2008). Fried chicken and fresh apples: Racial segregation as a fundamental cause of fast-food density in Black neighborhoods. *Health & Place, 14*(1), 32–44.

LaVeist, T. A., & Wallace, J. M. (2000). Health risk and inequitable distribution of liquor stores in African-American neighborhood. *Social Science & Medicine, 51*(4), 613–617.

LeClere, F. B., Rogers, R. G., & Peters, K. D. (1997). Ethnicity and mortality in the United States: Individual and community correlates. *Social Forces, 76*(1), 169–198.

Lieberson, S. (1980). *A piece of the pie: Blacks and White immigrants since 1880.* Berkeley: University of California Press.

Linden, A.-L., & Lindberg, G. (1991). Immigrant housing patterns in Sweden. In E. D. Huttman, W. Blauw, & J. Saltman (Eds.), *Urban housing segregation of minorities in Western Europe and the United States* (pp. 92–115). Durham, NC: Duke University Press.

Lopez, R. (2002). Segregation and Black/White differences in exposure to air toxics in 1990. *Environmental Health Perspectives, 110*(Suppl. 2), 289–295.

Massey, D. S. (1985). Ethnic residential segregation: A theoretical synthesis and empirical review. *Sociology and Social Research, 69*(3), 315–350.

Massey, D. S., & Denton, N. A. (1987). Trends in the residential segregation of Blacks, Hispanics, and Asians: 1970–1980. *American Sociological Review, 52*(6), 802–825.

Massey, D. S., & Denton, N. A. (1988). The dimensions of residential segregation. *Social Forces, 67*(2), 281–315.

Massey, D. S., & Denton, N. A. (1993). *American apartheid: Segregation and the making of the underclass.* Cambridge, MA: Harvard University Press.

Matthews, S. A., Detwiler, J. E., & Burton, L. M. (2005). Geo-ethnography: Coupling geographic information analysis techniques with ethnographic methods in urban research. *Cartographica, 40*(4), 75–90.

Morello-Frosch, R., & Shenassa, E. D. (2006). The environmental "riskscape" and social inequality: Implications for explaining maternal and child health disparities. *Environmental Health Perspectives, 114*(8), 1150–1153.

Morrison, S., Wallenstein, S., Natale, D. K., Senzel, R. S., & Huang, L.-L. (2000). "We don't carry that": Failure of pharmacies in predominantly non-White neighborhoods to stock opioid analgesics. *The New England Journal of Medicine, 342,* 1023–1026.

Ofosky, J. D. (1999). The impact of violence on children. *The Future of Children, 9*(3), 33–49.

Peach, C. (1996). Does Britain have ghettos? *Transactions of the Institute of British Geographers, 21*(1), 216–235.

Polednak, A. P. (1993). Poverty, residential segregation, and Black/White mortality ratios in urban areas. *Journal of Health Care for the Poor and Underserved, 4*(4), 363–373.

Zenk, S. N., Schulz, A. J., Israel, B. A., James, S. A., Bao, S., & Wilson, M. L. (2005). Neighborhood racial composition, neighborhood poverty, and the spatial accessibility of supermarkets in metropolitan Detroit. *American Journal of Public Health, 95*(4), 660–667.

Zoua Vang

SELF-EMPLOYMENT

Self-employed persons are those who earn income from their trade or business, who set the terms of how, when and where they perform their work; and who assume all the risks and responsibilities of their entrepreneurial activities. Thus, self-employed persons include those who own businesses as sole proprietors or in partnerships, those who work as independent contractors, and those who work as consultants. The ranks of the self-employed include lawyers, tutors, plumbers, child care providers, cleaners, wedding planners, and Web site developers. The self-employed are a heterogeneous group, and to complicate matters further, individuals can be both employees and self-employed in different income-generating activities at the same time. Although the self-employed must still meet the demands of clients and contactors and cede some decision making to those with whom they contract, unlike wage work, to be self-employed means that a worker has some autonomy because he or she is not employed by another and that the individual derives an income from his or her own work effort. However, this autonomy can also be a source of instability, because nearly all self-employed workers are not afforded the same protections that are available to wage workers, such as social insurance, including unemployment, health and disability benefits, and labor contracts.

After several decades of decline, self-employment experienced a rebirth in the 1970s in industrialized countries. It is unclear whether the rise in self-employment is the result of a vibrant, entrepreneurial middle class or declining economic opportunities for the working class and those in nonprofessional occupations. The scholarly debate regarding the location of the self-employed in the social class structure is complicated by the heterogeneity of the self-employed. For some, self-employment is a means of obtaining upward mobility. However, the widely varying economic successes of the self-employed are linked to the gender, race/ethnicity, and the professional and nonprofessional status of the worker. It is an empirical question whether self-employment reduces or exacerbates existing inequalities found among wage-employed workers. Therefore, the role of self-employment is important not only for the life course of self-employed individuals, but also for understanding the state of the economy as a whole.

MEASUREMENT ISSUES AND SELF-EMPLOYMENT

Just as defining self-employment is difficult, so is measuring it. Most data gathered on the self-employed in the United States are based on individual self-identification. The Current Population Survey (CPS), a monthly survey of employment and unemployment administered by the Census Bureau, is the most frequently analyzed dataset when it comes to self-employment. The CPS divides workers into four categories: government, private, non-profit, and self-employed. If self-employed individuals indicate that their business is incorporated, they are reclassified as employees of their own company whereas the unincorporated are categorized as self-employed. The introduction of the questions related to incorporation in 1967 has created confusion regarding the accuracy of self-employment measures due to increasing rates of incorporation.

RECENT TRENDS IN SELF-EMPLOYMENT

From the late 1940s to the 1970s, self-employment rates fell dramatically. However, since the 1970s the trend has been reversed in nonagricultural sectors. By 2003, 10.3 million U.S. workers were self-employed, primarily in construction, professional, business, and other services. In 2004 self-employed workers comprised 7.5% of the total U.S. workforce (Hipple, 2004). The incorporated self-employed tend to have advanced degrees whereas the unincorporated self-employed tend to have less than a high school diploma, indicating a large gap in the quality of self-employment. The self-employed also tend to be older than wage workers, with those 65 and over com-

prising 19.1% of the self-employed whereas only 2% of the self-employed are aged 16 and 24 (Hipple, 2004). Unlike older workers, who are more likely to have retired from wage employment, younger individuals typically have not yet acquired the necessary capital and managerial skills to start their own business.

The gender composition of the self-employed is unequal but changing. Although men are more likely to be self-employed, since 1975 women's participation has grown by 60%, compared with men's growth of 20% (Blau, 1998). The factors leading to and the economic returns from self-employment are linked to gender in complex ways. Professional status of the worker is key to understanding these linkages. Among professionals, women receive higher returns for skills if self-employed, compared with findings in wage-employed women. The factors leading to self-employment among professionals do not differ by gender, and women receive the same increase in earnings for becoming self-employed as do men (Budig, 2006). However, self-employment does not appear to reduce the gender gap in earnings that is found among wage-earning professionals. Among nonprofessional workers, the importance of gender is more pronounced (Arum, 1997; Budig, 2006).

The primary causes of women's self-employment in this group are family factors: number of children, marital status, and having a self-employed husband. None of these factors matters for men's self-employment among nonprofessionals. Gender occupational segregation is greatest among self-employed nonprofessionals, as is the gender gap in earnings. In contrast to professionals, among nonprofessionals self-employment appears to exacerbate gender earnings inequality. Thus, family factors powerfully shape women's self-employment in nonprofessional work and gender earnings gaps are largest among nonprofessional self-employment. In contrast, women engaged in professional self-employment are more similar to men and reap similar rewards from self-employment as men do.

Because self-employment is often described as a route to prosperity, understanding race/ethnic differences among the self-employed is important (Bates, 1997). Whites have higher levels of self-employment than Hispanics and African Americans, and this may result from some advantage among whites in asset accumulation and in consumer and lender discrimination. Family background and parental experience with self-employment are among the most important predictors of an individual becoming self-employed (Aldrich, Renzulli, & Langton, 1998). Because African Americans have historically had low levels of self-employment, the likelihood of subsequent generations of African Americans becoming self-employed is reduced. Stratification also appears

Characteristic	Unincorporated Self-employed			Incorporated Self-employed			Wages and Salary Workers'		
	Total	Men	Women	Total	Men	Women	Total	Men	Women
Age									
Total, 16 years and older:									
Thousands	10,295	6,430	3,865	4,956	3,626	1,330	122,358	63,236	59,123
Percent	100.0	100.0	100.0	100.0	100.0	100.0	100.0	100.0	100.0
16 to 19 years	9	10	7	2	2	5	4.7	4.5	5.0
20 to 24 years	2.6	2.8	2.3	1.0	9	1.2	10.7	10.8	10.6
25 to 34 years	15.6	15.3	16.2	11.6	11.5	12.0	23.0	24.1	21.8
35 to 44 years	26.4	25.4	28.0	28.7	29.0	27.8	25.1	25.4	24.8
45 to 54 years	27.1	27.2	27.0	30.8	30.6	31.4	22.5	21.7	23.4
55 to 64 years	18.8	19.1	18.3	20.5	19.9	22.0	11.1	10.7	11.6
65 years and older	8.5	9.2	7.5	7.2	7.8	5.6	2.7	2.7	2.8
Race and Hispanic or Latino ethnicity									
White	88.2	88.7	87.3	90.1	90.5	88.9	82.2	83.6	80.7
Black or African American	5.8	5.6	6.1	4.1	4.2	3.9	11.4	10.0	12.9
Asian	3.9	3.5	4.4	4.6	4.2	5.9	4.2	4.3	4.1
Hispanic or Latino	9.3	10.2	7.7	5.5	5.4	5.9	13.2	15.2	11.0
Country of birth and U.S. citizenship status									
U.S. born	87.2	86.6	88.1	87.0	86.8	87.3	85.5	83.4	87.9
Foreign-born	12.8	13.4	11.9	13.1	13.2	12.8	14.5	16.6	12.2
U.S. citizen	6.4	6.4	6.3	8.6	8.6	8.6	5.5	5.6	5.4
Not a U.S. citizen	6.4	7.0	5.6	4.5	4.6	4.1	9.0	11.0	6.8
Educational attainment									
Total, 25 years and older:									
Thousands	9,936	6,186	3,750	4,896	3,586	1,310	103,454	53,553	49,901
Percent	100.0	100.0	100.0	100.0	100.0	100.0	100.0	100.0	100.0
Less than a high school diploma	10.6	12.7	7.3	4.9	5.1	4.4	9.9	11.8	7.8
High school graduates, no college	31.4	32.4	29.7	23.0	23.0	23.1	30.5	30.6	30.5
Some college, no degree	18.3	17.7	19.2	18.3	17.6	20.2	17.8	17.0	18.5
Associate degree	8.5	7.1	10.8	7.4	7.0	8.6	9.8	8.5	11.1
College graduates	31.2	30.1	33.0	46.3	47.3	43.6	32.1	32.1	32.0
Advanced degree	12.3	12.2	12.5	17.9	18.8	15.5	10.9	11.2	10.6

Data exclude the incorporated self-employed
Note: Detail for the above race and Hispanic or Latino groups will not sum to total because data for the "other races" group are not presented and Hispanics or Latinos are included in both the white and black populationt groups. Detail for other characteristics may not sum to totals due to rounding. In addition, data exclude unpaid family workers.

Table 1. *Unincorporated self–employed, incorporated self–employed, and wage and salary workers by sex and selected characteristics, 2003 annual average.* CENGAGE LEARNING, GALE.

within groups regarding self-employment that could also be attributed to differential treatment in lending and consumer practices. Among Hispanic groups, Mexican Americans have low levels of self-employment whereas Cuban Americans have rates similar to those of whites. Asian Americans also tend to have higher rates of self-employment compared with other groups. Due to economic opportunity in ethnic enclaves, often resulting from discriminatory treatment in business arenas outside the enclave, some immigrant groups therefore tend to have distinctly higher rates of self-employment compared

with the native born (Borjas, 1986). This illustrates how differences in access to economic and social mobility constrain different groups' participation in self-employment.

THEORETICAL EXPLANATIONS

Which factors have contributed to the existence of self-employment and its resurgence over time? The Marxist (Karl Marx, German economist, 1818–1883) school of thought argues that the self-employed are part of the middle class, or petty bourgeoisie, because they own their own businesses. Although some contention remains regarding what classifies an individual as petty bourgeois, Marxists argue that due to the tendency of businesses to concentrate into large firms, the middle class will eventually decline and become part of the working class. However, this is problematized by the resurgence in self-employment (Steinmetz and Wright, 1990). This theory has become less salient and useful over time for explaining the persistence of self-employment.

A second theory addressing the existence of the self-employed argues that capitalist economic systems require a healthy sector of self-employed to provide specialized skills and fill market niches not addressed by larger firms. Along with individual explanations such as the desire for upward mobility, larger structural economic factors also influence the rate of self-employment. The shift to a postindustrial economy has encouraged self-employment as a result of technological change, which allows for more decentralization of firms and increased opportunities for individual entrepreneurial ventures.

Technological change and economic decentralization also may explain increased self-employment rates. Some researchers suggest that the shift from a manufacturing to a service-based economy and the marginalization of nonprofessional occupations has encouraged the growth of self-employment. With the decline of the manufacturing sector in the United States and some countries in Western Europe, self-employment may provide a means of avoiding unemployment for displaced workers. Therefore, with an economic downturn or a rise in the unemployment rate, the number of individuals who become self-employed may increase. This is exemplified by the slight increase of workers becoming self-employed, 6.5% to 6.8%, during the sluggish economic period between 2002 and 2004 in the United States (Hipple, 2004).

Another explanation for the rise in self-employment focuses on the role of politics and the state in supporting small business ownership. Government policies have been increasingly directed at fostering self-employment by providing tax incentives and other programs designed to encourage small businesses. Comparing policies in the United States with those in Germany, McManus (2000) argues that the institutional features of labor markets and welfare states have important implications for quality of self-employment. The provision of social insurance and health care to Germany's small business sector provides more stability for the self-employed than in the United States, where social programs are not available to all.

IMPLICATIONS FOR THE LIFE COURSE

The fate of the self-employed has tremendous significance for understanding economic conditions and their implications for the life course. Most researchers argue

that its existence and size serves as a benchmark for measuring the state of the economy. A rise in the levels of self-employment may coincide with an economic downturn as individuals thrown out of work by recession seek other means for earning income. Others seek to understand the relationship of self-employment and earnings inequality. Under capitalist economic systems, it has been argued that the self-employed have the capacity to provide the economy employment for workers, generate new jobs, and stimulate innovation. The job creation potential of this economic sector has major implications for providing economic opportunities to women and immigrants. The self-employed also play an important political role in society through their general support of the capitalist system and democratic institutions. Although much more research is required to fully understand the role played by self-employment, this sector of employment has significant implications in both the short and long-term for the life course of individuals regarding economic and social mobility and for understanding the level of inequality in the larger economy.

SEE ALSO Volume 2: *Careers; Economic Restructuring; Employment, Adulthood; Flexible Work Arrangements; Job Characteristics and Job Stress; Marx, Karl; Occupations.*

BIBLIOGRAPHY

Aldrich, H. E., Renzulli, L. A., & Langton, N. (1998). Passing on privilege: Resources provided by self-employed parents to their self-employed children. *Research in social stratification, 16,* 291-318.

Arum, R. (1997). Trends in male and female self-employment: Growth in a new middle class or increasing marginalization of the labor force? *Research in Stratification and Mobility, 15,* 209–238.

Bates, T. (1997). *Race, self-employment, and upward mobility.* Baltimore: The Johns Hopkins University Press.

Blau, F. (1998). Trends in the well-being of American women, 1970-1995. *Journal of Economic Literature, 36,* 112–165.

Borjas, G. J. (1986). The self-employment experience of immigrants. *Journal of Human Resources, 21,* 485–506.

Budig, M. J. (2006). Gender, self-employment, and earnings: The interlocking structures of family and professional status. *Gender and Society, 20,* 725–753.

Hipple, S. (2004). Self-employment in the United States: An update. *Monthly Labor Review, 127,* 13–23.

McManus, P. A. (2000). Market, state, and the quality of new self-employment jobs among men in the U.S. and Western Germany. *Social Forces, 78,* 865–905.

Steinmetz, G., & Wright, E. O. (1990). The fall and rise of the petty bourgeoisie: Changing patterns of self-employment in the postwar United States. *American Journal of Sociology, 94,* 973–1018.

Melissa J. Hodges
Michelle J. Budig

SEXISM/SEX DISCRIMINATION

Sexism and sexual discrimination are two of the primary reasons that gender inequality persists in the United States. The U.S. Equal Employment Opportunity Commission (EEOC) received almost 25,000 "charges of sex-based discrimination" in the 2007 fiscal year alone (EEOC, 2008). Sexism refers to attitudes and beliefs about people based on their sex. Often these prejudices are negative, such as the idea that women are incompetent, but these opinions may also be positive, such as the belief that women are nurturing. Sexual discrimination, in contrast, involves treating people differently based on their sex. For example, this may be the preference to hire men instead of women or to allow more women than men to enter a dance club.

These terms are frequently used to refer to the negative treatment or position of women relative to men. This approach makes sense. Because women are subordinate to men in most parts of the world, they are more likely to be the targets of sexism and sexual discrimination. However, men may be the targets as well. Because members of subordinate groups (e.g., women, gay men, and so forth) tend to be victims of gender bias and members of the dominant group tend to be perpetrators, sexism and sexual discrimination help preserve the system of male privilege and the subordination of women and nondominant masculinities.

If someone discriminates based on another person's gender, does that mean that he or she is sexist? The answer is not necessarily. Sexism and sexual discrimination often go together, but not always. Consider a male employer at an electronics store seeking a new salesperson. This employer may know that there are many women knowledgeable about electronics, but if he fears that his clientele will only buy from a man, then he will be hesitant to hire a woman, regardless of her credentials. His behavior, then, is discriminatory, even though he does not consciously hold sexist beliefs. It is possible that a person can have subconscious attitudes (implicit beliefs), which can influence behavior, even without the person being consciously aware of it (Quillian, 2006).

It is worth noting that sexism and sexual discrimination are actually misnomers. The two concepts technically focus on attitudes and behavior based on someone's sex, but what this concept really refers to is a person's gender rather than his or her sex. Sex is biology; gender relates to the meaning and behavior associated with being a man or a woman (Kimmel, 2008). Some of the most frequently measured forms of sexism are beliefs about how women are supposed to behave. For instance, should a mother work outside the home? Is it a woman's responsibility to care for the home? Can a woman be assertive

and still be feminine? These beliefs have nothing to do with a woman's biological sex and everything to do with what it means to be a woman.

But why are some people sexist and why do some people discriminate? The simplest explanation is socialization—that is, the idea that people have been taught that certain behaviors are appropriate for one gender and other behaviors are appropriate for the other gender. (This assumes only two genders, a point that is contested by many gender scholars and intersex advocates; see Kimmel, 2008.) The extent to which one holds sexist attitudes is partly based on age, with people from older generations being more likely to hold "old fashioned" views about women (what is now called sexist) and younger people being likely to hold more egalitarian views. There is evidence for this argument, but the explanation is incomplete.

A related perspective is that people hold views about what is appropriate gendered behavior (i.e., their gender ideology) that agree with how they perceive their own gender (i.e., their gender role identity). This is because disagreement between someone's gender role identity and his or her gender ideology can cause confusion. For instance, if a man believes that masculine men are big and burly but he is small and delicate, does that mean he is not a "real man"? In contrast, agreement between someone's gender role identity and his or her gender ideology is validating. The result is that a masculine man is likely to support behavior that agrees with his ideas of masculinity (such as the male breadwinner role) and is likely to resist behavior that opposes it (such as married women earning an income).

A different set of arguments contend that sexism and sexual discrimination stem from some men's need to protect their position of privilege (Goldin, 2002). This practice may include men protecting their personal status or that of males as a group. Men are in the dominant social position, but not all men are as dominant as others. Masculinity, or manliness, helps determine which men are atop the hierarchy. Because of the privileges that come with appropriate displays of masculinity, some men are concerned that if their masculinity is questioned then they are somehow less of a man. In order to prove their masculinity to themselves and to others, they may denigrate and harass women or less masculine men.

Men as a group are in power; women are not. Sexism and sexual discrimination have been and continue to be used to prevent women from gaining power. From the perspective of those in power, it therefore makes sense to perpetuate gender stereotypes, even when there is overwhelming evidence invalidating those stereotypes. For instance, the common but erroneous stereotype that women are irrational implies that a woman should not

Sexism in Advertising. *Pedestrians walk past large outdoor clothing advertisements.* **SPENCER PLATT/GETTY IMAGES.**

be a boss, a chief executive officer, or the president. If this stereotype is believed, then these positions are preserved for a man. This logic makes women less attractive as employees and keeps men "first in line" for the most desirable jobs (Reskin, 2001).

The consequences of sexism and sexual discrimination are felt by everyone, if for no other reason than that everyone has women in their lives. More specifically, the effects are seen in labor market inequality, such as the devaluation of the jobs predominantly held by women and the work women do, discriminatory hiring practices and job allocation, and different expectations; discrimination against mothers in hiring and promotion; the disproportionate amount of home, child, and elderly care done by women, along with the failure to either compensate workers for their labor or provide affordable alternatives; the medical field's disregard for women, as evidenced by women's exclusion from medical studies and absence from medical texts; and the disproportionate level of violence suffered by women at the hands of their partners. Biased treatment can also impact women's health, causing them to suffer from such ailments as depression, nausea, and headaches (Welsh, 1999, p. 183).

Although sexism and sexual discrimination impact women in all walks of life, the ramifications may be more severe for women of color and of lower socioeconomic status. These women not only face stigma and discrimination because of their gender but also because of their race and class. Oppression based on these statuses is multiplicative, not additive. This means that a Black woman does not face the same gender oppression as a White woman or the same racial oppression as a Black man. Instead, she faces unique experiences because she is Black *and* a woman. For instance, lower-class women of color, particularly immigrants, often work as domestics (lower-class men tend to hold other jobs), positioning

them for exploitation, whereas upper-class women can use their wealth to reallocate their domestic responsibilities to women of lower classes (Amott & Matthaei 1996, p. 15). Young, lower-class Black women have the added stigma of being stereotyped as single mothers. Middle- and upper-class Black workers, in contrast, risk being "isolated" in a "corporate environment...that [is] inhospitable and alien" (Browne & Misra 2003, p. 501). Moreover, Black workers, regardless of age and class, must cope with the consequences of a long history of racial bias in the United States. Class and racial status also influence medical care, with lower-class and non-White patients receiving a lower quality of treatment than their wealthy White counterparts.

Sexism and sexual discrimination primarily impact women, but men can be victims too. For instance, current ideals of masculinity reward acts of risk-taking, aggression, and heterosexual sexual prowess while punishing behavior deemed to conflict with them. As a result, some men feel pressured into pursuing dangerous or even criminal behavior in order to prove their manhood. Men may also be harmed by the sexist belief that women and children deserve to be protected from danger first, leading men to be the last saved and the first to die.

A large proportion of the research on sexism and sexual discrimination considered in the United States focuses on what is going on here. It is therefore tempting to want to know how the situation in the United States compares to that in other countries. However, direct comparisons should be undertaken only with the utmost care. Cross-cultural comparisons are complicated by different definitions, data collection standards, and ethnocentrism.

Varying definitions and data collection standards are problematic because they make it difficult to ensure that measures of sexism and sexual discrimination are consistent and comparable across countries. For example, if country A defines discrimination as anything that creates a negative working environment, whereas country B says that the only thing that qualifies as discrimination is pressure from a superior to have sexual relations (Saguy, 2000, p. 1092), then it is meaningless to compare rates of discrimination across the two countries.

A second issue is how to apply one's own perceptions of sexism to other cultures without being too "ethnocentric." A single example should suffice to illustrate this problem. In 2004 France passed a law banning the wearing of conspicuous religious symbols in state schools. Although the law applied to all religious groups, there was a clear understanding that it was enacted to stop Muslim women from wearing headscarves. Two main justifications were given for the law. The first explanation was that headscarves were emblematic of Muslims' refusal to assimilate to secular French society. The second contention was that headscarves were symbols of Islam's oppression of women. Some Muslim women agreed with this latter assessment, but many did not.

If the headscarf is considered only from a European/North American perspective, one could legitimately argue that it represents Muslim women's subordinate place in Muslim society (if for no other reason than that they are not granted the same freedom in attire as men). But if the decision is considered from the standpoint of many Muslim women, one could possibly see that maybe these women are not oppressed by the tradition. In fact, when asked, some women said that, for them, wearing a headscarf was a personal choice to follow cultural traditions and beliefs about what "was modest and right." This example demonstrates that before attempting to determine if certain cultural behaviors are sexist, it is necessary to have some understanding of that culture.

Even with the caveat that it may be ill-advised to compare sexism and sexual discrimination across cultures, it is clear that the treatment of women varies regionally. Norway, for instance, is known for its progressive policies promoting gender equality, whereas in Saudi Arabia women are forbidden from voting, driving cars, or being in public without a male relation. In many parts of the developing world the situation for women is even worse and is characterized by high rates of female infanticide and sex-selective abortion, poor nutrition, little or no medical care, and low life expectancies for those who survive childhood.

Because sexism and sexual discrimination persists almost everywhere in the world, further research on the subject must continue. Two likely areas of ongoing research are sexual harassment and the intersection of gender, race, and class. The trend of applying paradigms developed outside of gender of research is also likely to continue. Another area that deserves more attention is sexism and sexual discrimination against men. Although men are not the prime targets, to ignore them in favor of women would be both sexist and discriminatory.

SEE ALSO Volume 1: *Socialization, Gender;* Volume 2: *Gender in the Workplace; Policy, Employment; Racism/ Race Discrimination;* Volume 3: *Ageism/Age Discrimination.*

BIBLIOGRAPHY

Acker, J. (1999). Rewriting class, race, and gender: Problems in feminist rethinking. In M. M. Ferree, J. Lorber, & B. B. Hess (Eds.), *Revisioning gender.* Thousand Oaks, CA: Sage.

Amott, T. L., & Matthaei, J. (Eds.). (1996). Race, class, gender, and women's work. In *Race, gender, and work: A multicultural economic history of women in the United States.* (rev. ed.). Boston: South End Press.

Browne, I., & Misra, J. (2003). The intersection of gender and race in the labor market. *Annual Review of Sociology, 29,* 487–513.

Goldin, C. (2002). *A pollution theory of discrimination: Male and female differences in occupations and earnings.* Cambridge, MA: National Bureau of Economic Research. Retrieved May 21, 2008, from http://ssrn.com/abstract=315335

Kimmel, M. S., & Aronson, A. (Eds.). (2008). *The gendered society.* New York: Oxford University Press.

Kington, R. S., & Nickens, H. W. (2001). Racial and ethnic differences in health: Recent trends and their consequences. In N. J. Smelser, W. J. Wilson, & F. Mitchell (Eds.), *America becoming* (Vol. 2, pp. 253–310). Washington, DC: National Academy Press.

Miedzian, M. (2002). *Boys will be boys: Breaking the link between masculinity and violence.* New York: Lantern Books.

Quillian, L. (2006). New approaches to understanding racial prejudice and discrimination. *Annual Review of Sociology, 32,* 299–328.

Reskin, B. F. (2001). Labor markets as queues: A structural approach to changing occupational sex composition. In D. B. Grusky (Ed.), *Social stratification: Class, race, and gender in sociological perspective.* (2nd ed.). Boulder, CO: Westview Press.

Saguy, A. C. (2000). Employment discrimination or sexual violence? Defining sexual harassment in American and French law. *Law & Society Review, 34*(4), 1091–1128.

Toller, P. W., Suter, E. A., & Trautman, T. C. (2004). Gender role identity and attitudes toward feminism. *Sex Roles, 51,* 85–90.

U.S. Equal Employment Opportunity Commission. (2008). *Sex-based discrimination.* Retrieved April 27, 2008, from http:www. eeoc.gov/types

Welsh, S. (1999). Gender and sexual harassment. *Annual Review of Sociology, 25,* 169–190.

Wyatt, C. (2003). *Liberty, equality, and the headscarf.* Retrieved May 21, 2008, from http://news.bbc.co.uk

Judith E. Rosenstein

SEXUAL ACTIVITY, ADULTHOOD

People are born sexual and have the capacity for sexual activity throughout the life course. Sexual activity involves the behavioral expression of erotic feelings, typically for pleasurable or reproductive purposes but in some contexts for power and control. Sexuality is influenced by biological, psychological, sociological, and spiritual factors, within historical, cultural, and developmental contexts. Virtually all societies attempt to regulate sexual activity, with varying degrees of success. Individuals are presumed to be most capable of both fulfilling their sexual potential and conforming to social norms in their sexual behaviors when they are adults; thus, sexual activity is viewed as most acceptable for adults of legal age but before they become too old. This does not mean that children and older adults are not sexual, but it does reveal that sexuality over the life course is socially constructed and socially controlled.

THE NATURE OF HUMAN SEXUALITY RESEARCH

Sexology is the scientific study of sexuality. Given the private nature of human sexual behavior and the ways that societies attempt to control sexuality through laws and social norms, understanding and investigating the complex nature of human sexual activity requires multiple disciplinary perspectives and many types of research methods. Throughout the 20th century, sexologists sought to change the belief that sexuality was not worthy of serious attention by bringing a positivist scientific approach to the study of sexuality. Sexual science introduced survey and interview methods and laboratory research as a way to bring credibility to the investigation of behaviors, such as masturbation, homosexuality, oral sex, and sexual intercourse for purposes other than reproduction that had been condemned as sinful and deviant.

Alfred Kinsey (1894–1956) was the leading figure in conducting research in which Americans were asked about their actual sexual practices. His samples included 20,000 men and women who were surveyed and interviewed in the 1940s and 1950s (Kinsey, Pomeroy, & Martin, 1948; Kinsey, Pomeroy, Martin, & Gebhard, 1953). He demonstrated that people from all walks of life were willing to answer very personal questions about their most intimate behavior, including masturbation, orgasms, sexual intercourse, homosexual behavior, sexual responsiveness, extramarital relationships, and sex with animals. He found that many of the practices previously thought uncommon or perverse were widely practiced by ordinary citizens. His books were instant best-sellers, attesting to the public's keen interest in and desire for sexual knowledge and communication.

Kinsey and his associates also changed the conceptualization of homosexuality. They described sexuality along a continuum, with 0 being exclusively heterosexual, 6 being exclusively homosexual, and 3 being equally heterosexual and homosexual. They reported that 37% of men and 13% of women had experienced at least one sexual experience to orgasm with someone of the same gender and that 4% of men and 3% of women considered themselves lifelong homosexuals. The oft-cited and frequently challenged statistic that 10% of the population is gay came from one of Kinsey's findings, which indicated that 10% of White men had been mostly homosexual for at least 3 years between the ages of 16 to 55 (Carroll, 2007).

William Masters (1915–2001) and Virginia Johnson (b. 1925), a medical doctor and a psychologist, respectively, were among the first modern sexologists to con-

duct observational studies of people who volunteered to engage in sexual activity in their laboratory. In 1966 they published *Human Sexual Response*, in which they reported on their research with 700 volunteers they had studied engaging in sexual activities. Masters and Johnson measured physiological changes in the heart and of the sexual organs to study orgasmic potential and sexual response. Their research resulted in the four-phase sexual response cycle, consisting of the excitement phase, the plateau phase, the orgasm phase, and the resolution phase. They found that women experienced only one type of orgasm, through the direct or indirect stimulation of the clitoris. This finding was in direct contrast to Sigmund Freud's (1856–1939) theory of the vaginal versus the clitoral orgasm, with the vaginal orgasm characterized as a more mature and thus superior version. Masters and Johnson also found that women are capable of multiple orgasms, whereas males experience a refractory stage following ejaculation. That is, a male cannot be restimulated to orgasm for a certain period of time; the length of time is highly dependent on age, with older males experiencing a longer refractory period.

The National Health and Social Life Survey, conducted by Edward Laumann, John Gagnon, Robert Michael, and Stuart Michaels (1994), attempted to provide a more representative sample and thus improve on and update the Kinsey studies. After the U.S. government pulled its funding from this project due to policy makers' reluctance to fund the work, the researchers were forced to reduce the scope of the study. The final sample was much smaller than originally intended. It consisted of nearly 3,500 respondents between the ages of 18 and 59 and revealed that Americans were more sexually conservative in their behavior than Kinsey had reported. For example, Laumann et al. reported that the median number of sexual partners for men since age 18 was six, and, for women, it was two. They also found a smaller portion of married adults reporting infidelity than had been found in the Kinsey data: Only 25% of married men and 20% of married women reported that they had engaged in extramarital sex, whereas Kinsey's findings were 50% of men and 25% of women. Finally, the study challenged the Kinsey statistic about homosexuality: 2.8% of men and 1.4% of women described themselves as homosexual or bisexual. One possible explanation for the more conservative nature of the Laumann et al. findings is that they used a random sample approach, whereas oversampling of particular kinds of respondents, including those who were Northern, educated, White, and Protestant, among other characteristics, may have occurred in the Kinsey studies.

A study conducted by William Mosher, Anjani Chandra, and Jo Jones (2005), however, reported that the incidence of bisexuality is increasing among young and middle-age adults, particularly for women. Eleven percent of women between the ages of 25 and 44 reported having had at least one sexual experience with another woman, and about 6.5% of men reported having oral or anal sex with another man. One conclusion from this study is that it is becoming more socially acceptable to openly discuss and experience bisexuality, particularly among recent cohorts of college-educated women.

Richard Parker and John Gagnon (1995) suggested that since 1980, the scientific study of sexuality has been reconceived by postmodern sex researchers. Several trends have greatly altered the way in which human sexual activity can and should be studied. One major trend is the global pandemic of HIV and AIDS and its disproportionate effect on women and children in developing nations. Another trend is the deconstruction of neat categories of heterosexual versus homosexual, which have been challenged by people who are bisexual, gay, and transgendered (i.e., people whose very identities are fluid and change across gender and sexual categories).

Postmodern sex researchers critique the 20th-century sexologists for their use of traditional scientific research methods (e.g., survey, interviews, and laboratory observations) that upheld conservative political values and normalized heterosexual middle-class behaviors. In contrast, postmodern researchers claim that new theories and methods are needed to account for how power and privilege structure sexual activity. Postmodern researchers critique sexology for its attention only to individual sexuality and its lack of attention to social change (Irvine, 2005). For example, when male pleasure is emphasized and privileged, women's expansive capacity for sexual pleasure is ignored; women learn to fake an orgasm, for example, in the service of male pleasure (Jackson & Scott, 2007). A postmodern feminist approach would reinterpret the Masters and Johnson finding of the myth of the vaginal orgasm by exposing how gender, sexuality, and power are intertwined.

SOCIAL CONTEXTS OF ADULT SEXUAL ACTIVITY

Sexual activity in adulthood involves the variety of individual and relational experiences in which adults engage. People can be asexual and experience no sexual feelings, desires, or behaviors. People can also engage in autoerotic experiences such as fantasy and masturbation. Typically, however, sexual activity is defined relationally, by the partners with whom one engages sexually (Sprecher & Regan, 2000). The most socially acceptable form of adult sexual activity occurs in the context of a marital relationship. In most cultures throughout history, with notable exceptions, a heterosexual partnership is the key way in which people express their sexuality. As noted above, a

significant minority of people also engage in homosexual behaviors and relationships, regardless of how they identify their sexual orientation. Finally, people can have sexual experiences with more than one person. These relationships can be open, in which partners in a primary relationship are allowed to have sexual contacts with others (e.g., polyamorist), or closed. Open relationships are sometimes referred to as *swinging*. A relationship in which secret sexual liaisons occur is characterized as infidelity, adultery, or having an affair.

In most European and North American societies, sexual activity is proscribed in the form of a monogamous relationship. Legal heterosexual marriage is the idealized form of this kind of relationship. Since the industrial revolution of the 19th century, marriage has represented a relationship in which feelings of romantic love and sexual behavior are expected to co-occur, though men were seen as the more sexually desirous and demanding gender. In the 20th century, however, marriage became more companionate and egalitarian, with women becoming freer to discover and express their sexuality.

Throughout history, variations have occurred to the socially and legally proscribed form of sexual activity as only occurring in marriage. For example, polygamy (whereby the husband has more than one wife) is common in many countries in the Middle East and parts of Africa (e.g., Iran, Nigeria, and Kenya) and is associated with the Muslim faith. Gender is an important distinction, though, in polygamous marriages. Although a man may have several wives, a woman's sexual behavior is restricted to her one husband, with severe punishments for transgressions. In European and North American societies, male and female infidelity is more acknowledged and tolerated, but a double standard still exists. Women carry the burden for nonmarital sex and suffer damage to their reputations, whereas men's sexual behavior is not as constricted by behavioral norms (Risman & Schwartz, 2003).

DEVELOPMENTAL CONTEXTS OF ADULT SEXUAL ACTIVITY

By adulthood, most people have experimented with and faced challenges in establishing their sexual identity, orientation, and relational commitments. Sexuality, though, is best conceived of as an emergent process and not one that is settled or achieved by a certain age. The early years of adult life are characterized by initiating and experiencing various forms of sexual intimacy with partners, including dating, courtship, cohabitation, and marriage, as well as establishing one's sexual orientation. About half of the relationships that result in marriage also end in divorce, but most people who divorce also remarry.

Sexual orientation involves a range of feelings, thoughts, and behaviors associated with how people perceive their sexuality. In updating Kinsey's conceptualization, Fritz Klein (1990) described the following seven dimensions: sexual attraction, sexual behavior, sexual fantasies, emotional preference, social preference, self-identification, and lifestyle preference. The dimension of time is also considered in terms of a person's self-categorization in the past, present, and ideally. Thus, sexual orientation is reconceptualized as fluid and changeable over the life course, not a stable or fixed identity resulting merely from self-labeling or sexual behavior.

In addition to issues of sexual pleasure, relational fulfillment, and sexual orientation, there are other serious decisions to be made. Contraceptive and reproductive decisions that affect planned and unplanned pregnancies are central to sexual activity in adulthood. Another key concern is practicing safe sex to avoid sexually transmitted diseases (e.g., bacterial infections such as gonorrhea, syphilis, and chlamydia; viral infections such as herpes and human papillomavirus; and HIV or AIDS). People most likely to avoid making decisions on behalf of their reproductive and sexual health are those in compromised circumstances, including having sex for money, combining sexual activity with alcohol and drug use, having casual and unprotected sex, and experiencing sexual violence (Bowleg, Lucas, & Tschann, 2004).

Although adult sexual activity does not follow a uniform pattern, some research has shown that for married couples, sex is common and prevalent in the early years. Newlyweds report having sex about two to three times per week. The early phases of passion and intimacy in a new relationship can deteriorate over time, however, as the reality of adult life intercedes in the form of multiple and competing role expectations. Sexual activity tapers off when children are being reared and work and family demands compete with sexual desire (Schwartz, 1994). Unless passion is kept alive and rekindled, sexual desire in a committed relationship declines and may disappear altogether, with partners leading separate lives, experiencing infidelity, or divorcing (Schnarch, 1998).

Sexual relationships, then, require attention. This monitoring is especially important as people age and marriage endures. In midlife, menopause changes not only how the female body is capable of sexual response (e.g., vaginal drying), but the loss of hormones can dampen desire. Men also experience decreased desire and the physical changes that accompany aging, such as difficulty in getting and maintaining an erection. The prolonged use of alcohol and drugs also erodes sexual responsiveness and desire. In addition, the physical process of aging, in a society that prizes young, perfect bodies, can lead adults to feel less attractive and desirable as they mature.

Individuals and couples are advised to redefine the nature of sexual intimacy as they age. Sexual intercourse is only one way to express erotic potential. Heterosexual and gay and lesbian couples in established relationships report that deep kissing, hugging, erotic massage, intimate conversations, holding hands, taking showers together, and other established rituals are key parts of their erotic relationships (Sprecher & Regan, 2000). One of the advantages of adult sexual activity in a committed relationship in which couples are able to look each other in the eyes and take the time to fully experience their sensuality is that the culturally prescribed rituals of faking pleasure are no longer necessary (Schnarch, 1998).

Opportunities for partnered sex appear to be one of the biggest issues facing adults. Research also suggests that sexual satisfaction in midlife and beyond is linked to having a partner. Laumann et al. (1994) found that married couples reported higher levels of sexual satisfaction and pleasure than singles or those in extramarital relationships. Individuals who lived alone and those who were unmarried reported the lowest rates of satisfaction.

THE RANGE OF SEXUAL ACTIVITY IN ADULTHOOD

Human sexual activity involves many ways in which adults act on their feelings and thoughts about sexuality. A large portion of adult sexuality is concerned with the reproductive potential within human beings, but sexuality is also about the pursuit of pleasure. Some individuals experience pleasure in socially accepted ways; others' experiences with sexual pleasure are more variant.

Sexually variant behaviors are characterized as *paraphilias*. They involve a desire for an erotic object that is unusual or different, with *different* being defined according to social and historical standards. For example, until 1973 the American Psychiatric Association defined homosexual behavior as a mental disorder. People who were caught engaging in homosexual behavior or diagnosed as homosexual could be arrested and institutionalized. Some stigma may linger about gay and lesbian people, but the myths of homosexuality as mental illness and social deviance have been debunked.

Paraphilias range from innocuous to harmful, that is, from certain behaviors such as having a fetish, in which no one is hurt, to behaviors such as pedophilia, in which there are criminals and victims. Paraphiliacs can be found in every race, social class, or ethnic group and are prevalent among people of every sexual orientation and intelligence level. The one demographic characteristic paraphiliacs have in common, however, is that they are disproportionately male (Carroll, 2007).

Certain paraphiliac behaviors (e.g., fetishes and cross-dressing) are typically harmless, particularly if they do not interfere with normal functioning and do not harm another person. Others, such as exhibitionism and voyeurism, are nonconsensual and do involve a victim. Sexual masochism (feeling sexual pleasure from being humiliated or being forced to experience pain) and sexual sadism (feeling sexual pleasure from inflicting humiliation or pain on another) are experienced along a continuum, from dominance and submission sexual narratives and practices that are eroticized in heterosexual and homosexual relationships to very dangerous activities that could involve torture and death. Sadomasochism (S & M) is the ritualized experience of a master–slave relationship; a couple agrees on the dominance and submission script and uses an exit phrase if the role-play becomes too intense. The purpose of the exit phrase is to ensure that no harm comes to the dominated partner.

Pedophilia is an obsessive and predatory paraphilia, illegal in every country but practiced nonetheless. A pedophiliac is an adult who fantasizes or engages in sexual activity with a child under the age of 13. The typical pedophile is at least 5 years older than the victim. The majority of pedophiles (more than 90%) are males. Pedophilia is very difficult to treat or change (Carroll, 2007).

One of the major issues influencing contemporary sexuality is the way in which societies project values about sexual agency and the social control of sexuality. European and North American society projects an ambivalence that both celebrates and condemns sexuality. The mass media helps to construct and exploit human sexuality and its expression in adult intimate relationships. The media is saturated with contradictory messages and images that alternately take advantage of and repress sexuality. Agentic sexuality, whereby individuals are able to make wise choices on behalf of their own desires and express those desires in authentic relationships, is challenged in a society with such competing messages. How these messages are interpreted and sorted out is an issue for parents, educators, policy makers, and citizens alike.

Comprehensive sexuality education throughout the life course is a key remedy to the contradictory ways in which society exploits and represses sexuality. The scientific study of sexuality reveals that human sexuality is an emergent process, and the thirst for sexual knowledge does not end in childhood. Sexuality is primarily a relational experience, and adults grow and change through their sexual encounters with others. It is important for social institutions to provide all citizens access to new knowledge that has been generated from research so they can incorporate this knowledge into their own quests for sexual agency and authentic relationships.

SEE ALSO Volume 1: *Sex Education/Abstinence Education;* Volume 2: *Abortion; AIDS; Birth Control; Childbearing; Cohabitation; Dating and Romantic Relationships, Adulthood; Gays and Lesbians, Adulthood; Marriage.*

BIBLIOGRAPHY

Adams, B. N., & Trost, J. (Eds.). (2005). *Handbook of world families.* Thousand Oaks, CA: Sage.

Baber, K. M. (2000). Women's sexualities. In M. Biaggio & M. Hersen (Eds.), *Issues in the psychology of women* (pp. 145–171). New York: Kluwer Academic/Plenum.

Bowleg, L., Lucas, K. J., & Tschann, J. M. (2004). The ball was always in his court: An exploratory analysis of relationship scripts, sexual scripts, and condom use among African-American women. *Psychology of Women Quarterly, 28*(1), 70–82.

Carroll, J. L. (2007). *Sexuality now: Embracing diversity* (2nd ed.). Belmont, CA: Thomson.

Crown, L., & Roberts, L. J. (2007). Against their will: Young women's nonagentic sexual experiences. *Journal of Social and Personal Relationships, 24*(3), 385–405.

D'Emilio, J., & Freedman, E. B. (1997). *Intimate matters: A history of sexuality in America.* (2nd ed.). Chicago: University of Chicago Press.

Irvine, J. M. (2005). *Disorders of desire: Sexuality and gender in modern American sexology* (rev. ed.). Philadelphia, PA: Temple University Press.

Jackson, S., & Scott, S. (2007). Faking like a woman? Towards an interpretive theorization of sexual pleasure. *Body & Society, 13*(2), 95–116.

Kinsey, A., Pomeroy, W., & Martin, C. (1948). *Sexual behavior in the human male.* Philadelphia, PA: Saunders.

Kinsey, A., Pomeroy, W., Martin, C., & Gebhard, P. (1953). *Sexual behavior in the human female.* Philadelphia, PA: Saunders.

Klein, F. (1990). The need to view sexual orientation as a multivariable dynamic process: A theoretical perspective. In D. P. McWhirter, S. A. Sanders, & J. M. Reinisch (Eds.), *Homosexuality/heterosexuality* (pp. 277–282). New York: Oxford University Press.

Laumann, E. O., Gagnon, J., Michael, R., & Michaels, S. (1994). *The social organization of sexuality: Sexual practices in the United States.* Chicago: University of Chicago Press.

Masters, W. H., & Johnson, V. E. (1966). *Human sexual response.* Boston: Little, Brown.

Mosher, W. D., Chandra, A., & Jones, J. (2005). Sexual behavior and selected health measures: Men and women 15–44 years of age, United States, 2002. *Advance Data from Vital and Health Statistics, 362.* Hyattsville, MD: National Center for Health Statistics. Retrieved May 14, 2008, from http://www.cdc.gov/nchs/

Parker, R. G., & Gagnon, J. H. (Eds.). (1995). *Conceiving sexuality: Approaches to sex research in a postmodern world.* New York: Routledge.

Risman, B., & Schwartz, P. (2003). After the sexual revolution: Gender politics in teen dating. *Contexts, 1*(1), 16–24.

Schnarch, D. (1998). *Passionate marriage: Love, sex, and intimacy in emotionally committed relationships.* New York: Holt.

Schwartz, P. (1994). *Peer marriage: How love between equals really works.* New York: Free Press.

Sprecher, S., & Regan, P. C. (2000). Sexuality in a relational context. In C. Hendrick & S. S. Hendrick (Eds.), *Close relationships: A sourcebook* (pp. 217–227). Thousand Oaks, CA: Sage.

Katherine R. Allen

SIBLING RELATIONSHIPS, ADULTHOOD

The families of adults in American and European societies frequently are assumed to consist of parents, children, and spouses; siblings have been relatively invisible. As adult baby boomers' family experiences are studied, however, it has become clear that in that generation, with the largest sibships in the 20th century, sibling relationships are also primary. The stability of the sibling tie is emphasized by the fact that boomers will have fewer children to rely on than did their parents, are less likely to have a spouse because of their high divorce rates, and are less likely to have family members nearby because of their high rates of geographic mobility. Further, the need to provide care for frail elderly parents is becoming the norm; that role often reactivates dormant sibling relationships.

Addressing adult sibling relationships also makes visible certain overlooked aspects of adult life. For instance, because siblings are "beyond the bonds of partnering and parenting," they force researchers to focus on a broader social network (Walker, Allen, & Connidis, 2005, p. 167). Siblings link one another to many other relationships, such as those with nephews, nieces, uncles, aunts, and cousins, as well as the network ties those kin make available to their family members (Matthews, 2005). Because relationships among adult siblings usually transcend household boundaries, they highlight family relationships beyond the household.

Before one can address some of the dimensions of sibling relationships, influences on them, and the consequences of those dimensions for the well-being of the siblings, it is necessary to define the sibling relationship. A sibling is a person's brother or sister. A sibling may have the same parents by birth (biological sibling) or through adoption or share only one parent (half-sibling). Some siblings have different parents: parents who may be married to each other in the case of a stepsibling or parents who may be cohabiting with each other in the case of a quasi-sibling. A sibling may be informally adopted in the case of fictive siblings. Most of what is known about adult siblings concerns biological siblings. More than 80% of adults have a living sibling (*General Social Survey Cumulative Datafile*, 1986). Sibships take into account all of a person's brothers and sisters. Sibships vary by number, gender composition (number of brothers and sisters), and birth order (position of each brother and sister relative to the others). Most research on adult siblings focuses on pairs of siblings rather than the whole sibship.

Most studies of siblings in adulthood use relatively small, nonrepresentative samples, with the exception of a few national samples, such as the National Study of Family and Households and the Netherlands Kinship Panel Study. Therefore, their findings rarely can be generalized.

DIMENSIONS OF SIBLING RELATIONSHIPS

Despite the early Freudian emphasis on sibling rivalry, adult sibling relationships have many dimensions. Sibling relationships have been rated on specific emotional qualities such as closeness, conflict, separateness, indifference, and ambivalence. The emotional content of the relationship can be described in terms of its intensity (strength) and valence (positive and negative direction), but much of the research on adult siblings has been limited to feelings of closeness and conflict. The relationship also has been rated on the frequencies of behaviors that are engaged in, such as contact, provision of assistance, and companionship. Sometimes qualities and behaviors have been grouped into types of sibling relationships, such as intimate, loyal, and hostile (Gold, 1989). Various influences on the relationship have been studied. How close siblings live to each other and their frequency of contact with one another can be viewed as dimensions of the relationship but also as influences on it because both facilitate or constrain other aspects of the relationship.

INFLUENCES OF EARLY LIFE-COURSE EXPERIENCES ON ADULT SIBLING RELATIONSHIPS

Adult sibling relationships are shaped by experiences earlier in the life course. For instance, it is known that differential treatment by parents of their children is destructive to the children's sibling relationships. Early differential treatment (parental "favoritism") also has a negative impact on the relationship in adulthood. Young adults whose parents showed different levels of affection toward them were more jealous of their siblings than were those whose parents were perceived to be equal in their affection (Rauer & Volling, 2007). Similar results apply to middle-age adults. In a study of more than 1,000 German men and women ages 40 to 54, the individuals who reported the best sibling experiences also reported that they and their siblings had been treated equally in childhood. The quality of the adult sibling relationship diminished both with increasing favoritism and with "disfavoritism" (Boll, Ferring, & Filipp, 2003).

Another example of the influence of earlier experiences on the adult relationship concerns the rarely studied tie between siblings with different sexual orientations. In one exploratory study, women ages 19 to 74 discussed influences on their feelings of closeness with their siblings. Lesbian women could trace their positive relationships with their straight sisters to having received support from them when faced with parental disapproval after coming out (Mize, Turell, & Meier, 2004).

The death of a parent during a person's childhood also influences adult sibling relationships. Comparing the results of the death of a mother, father, both, and no death in childhood, Kristin Mack (2004) found that the death of parents results in more closeness but not more contact than in intact families. Maternal death in childhood results in less contact between adult siblings than does paternal death, most likely because mothers are typically the family "kinkeepers" who keep family members in contact with one another. The effect of parental death during adulthood is more varied: It draws some siblings closer together, whereas some become more distant.

INFLUENCES OF SOCIAL CONTEXTS ON ADULT SIBLING RELATIONSHIPS

Sibling relationships are shaped by social contexts, both proximate (e.g., family, peer, and friendship groups) and distal (e.g., work organizations, historical setting, demographic conditions, and culture). For instance, in American and European societies the adult sibling tie is considered voluntary at the same time that demands are placed on it: Siblings are expected to be involved in one another's lives, be friends, and feel a sense of family commitment without asking too much of one another (Connidis, 2005). These conflicting expectations can generate feelings of ambivalence toward siblings.

Research on geographic proximity has shown that ethnicity, immigrant status, and education influence how close siblings live to each other, which in general declines through age 50 and then stabilizes. Individuals with more education and recent immigrants are more likely to increase their geographic distance from siblings over the life course. African Americans and people from large families are more likely to remain geographically close to siblings. Marital dissolution also increases geographic closeness to siblings. Contact with siblings follows the same pattern as geographic closeness with one modification: Women and Latinos also increase contact over the life course (White, 2001).

A large body of literature has examined exchanges of support and help between siblings. Shelley Eriksen and Naomi Gerstel (2002) found that race has little effect on the assistance and support siblings provide one another. Instead, gender, age, and social class influence the likelihood of providing care to siblings. Having a living parent also promotes sibling help. Marieke Voorpostel and Rosemary Blieszner (2008) found that when parents provide more emotional support, siblings exchange more

practical and emotional support with one another. More practical support from parents, however, is related only to exchanges of more practical support between the siblings. Siblings also compensate for parents' lack of support when they have poor relationships with their parents. In this case siblings exchange more support with one another than they do when the relationship with parents is better.

Some influences on sibling relationships are the parent and marital status of siblings and the structure of the sibling group (birth order, number of siblings, gender composition), but their effects are observed mostly in early adulthood. In terms of birth order, older siblings are more supportive of their younger siblings than the reverse (Voorpostel, van der Lippe, Dykstra, & Flap, 2007), but this birth order effect disappears by middle adulthood (Connidis, 2005). Also, members of larger sibships exchange more affection, contact, and support within the sibship than do members of smaller sibships (White, 2001). Further, in young adulthood childless adults provide help to their siblings who have children. In regard to advice, in young adulthood it is siblings with children who share more, whereas childless sibling dyads are more likely to give advice later. Whether siblings have spouses or partners does not influence their exchange of support in Holland; it does in the United States, but in complex ways. Among siblings with different levels of education, those with lower levels of education show more interest in their more highly educated siblings than the reverse (Voorpostel et al., 2007).

Exchanges of help among siblings also depend on the type of help required, the gender and age of the siblings, and other characteristics of the sibling relationship. Voorpostel and Blieszner (2008) found that siblings exchange both practical and emotional support when the relationship is more positive and when there is more frequent contact. Voorpostel et al. (2007) found that sister–sister pairs are more likely to help with housework, give advice, and show interest in their siblings than are other gender combinations, but after age 36 those gender distinctions are less apparent.

Although Dutch men exchange practical support with siblings more than Dutch women do, women are more likely to exchange emotional support, but only with their sisters. Further, sibling relationship quality and contact are frequently more important for support among sisters than among brothers (Voorpostel & Blieszner, 2008), suggesting that whether brothers help one another appears to be independent of the relationship context. This seeming contextual detachment of support between brothers may illustrate a profound difference between female and male expressions of closeness (Matthews, 2005). Men may mask their care behaviors intentionally to protect their brothers from breaking the normative "rules" of masculinity, in which men are expected to be strong and independent. Thus, in stories about brothers, men appeared insensitive to brothers who sought support because they asserted a controlling style, particularly when it came to practical support (Bedford & Avioli, 2006). This seeming insensitivity may be an act of caring in itself (Swain, 1989). Little research has been devoted to brothers.

SIBLING INFLUENCES ON PERSONAL DEVELOPMENT

The sibling relationship in both childhood and adulthood influences adult development and well-being. In a prospective study of young non-Hispanic White American men that continued until the individuals were in their 50s, men who had a poor sibling relationship in childhood were more than three times as likely to develop major depression by age 50 than were men with better sibling relationships. This effect was independent of a family history of depression and the quality of relationships with parents (Waldinger, Vaillant, & Orav, 2007).

Siblings also may benefit one another as attachment figures (close others who provide solace in times of stress). Caroline Tancredy and R. Chris Fraley (2006) found that both twin pairs and nontwin pairs met the attachment criteria in young adulthood, although twins were more likely to do so. Also, the same factors contributed to becoming attachment figures among twins and nontwins, such as having spent time together as children and having shared interests, personal lives, or professional lives as adults.

Another sibling effect on well-being in adulthood derives from sharing in parent care. Attempts by individuals to correct sibling inequities in their care of parents resulted in distress to the primary caregiving sibling (Eriksen & Gerstel, 2002). Parent care also can offer opportunities for personal growth by forcing siblings to confront interpersonal issues that may have been avoided earlier through distancing. Sibling conflict in other contexts also offers opportunities for personal growth. Because the sibling tie cannot be dissolved, when faced with high levels of conflict, siblings have to develop strategies for regulating their own as well as another's emotions, including maladaptive expressions of anger and aggression (Bedford & Volling, 2004). In another study the most frequently named benefit stemming from conflicts in adults' sibling relationships was helping one's children and grandchildren manage their own sibling relationships, followed by gains in social competence and gains in one's self-understanding (knowing one's emotional limitations and talents and career choices; Bedford, Volling, & Avioli, 2000).

Siblings also contribute indirectly to the well-being of adults' romantic relationships. Amy Rauer and Brenda Volling (2007) found that young adults who were treated differently by their parents experienced distress in romantic relationships. They found that those adults' models of attachment contained representations of the self and the object of attachment that were more negative than were those of adults who received equal levels of affection from their parents.

FUTURE DIRECTIONS

These research findings illustrate that the life course provides a meaningful framework for viewing sibling relationships. Spanning the whole of life, this relationship demonstrates the continuing interdependence of siblings as they move into and out of one another's inner circles; it also demonstrates how the changing social network of each sibling influences characteristics of the sibling relationship. Timing of events also may have an effect; early influences on the adult relationship, such as the death of a parent, differ when the event occurs later in life. The findings of research underscore the growing realization of the importance of siblings as both actual and potential sources of support in adulthood. In particular, siblings were seen to offer compensatory support in the absence of parental, spousal, or other resources as well as to make unique contributions.

In light of the growing importance of this relationship in later life, future research should focus on ways to maximize its support potential, such as by identifying potential socialization and intervention processes throughout the life course. For instance, it would be instructive to compare sibling support outcomes during various life transitions among different cultures as well as across different sibling constellations. Future research also should target all siblings, not only biological ones.

SEE ALSO Volume 1: *Sibling Relationships, Childhood and Adolescence;* Volume 2: *Friendship, Adulthood; Parent–Child Relationships, Adulthood; Social Networks; Social Support, Adulthood;* Volume 3: *Sibling Relationships, Later Life.*

BIBLIOGRAPHY

Bedford, V. H., & Avioli, P. S. (2006). "Shooting the bull": Cohort comparisons of fraternal intimacy in mid-life and old age. In V. H. Bedford & B. F. Turner (Eds.), *Men in relationships: A new look from a life course perspective* (pp. 81–102). New York: Springer.

Bedford, V. H., & Volling, B. (2004). A dynamic ecological systems perspective on emotion regulation development within the sibling relationship context. In F. R. Lang & K. L. Fingerman (Eds.), *Growing together: Personal relationships across the lifespan* (pp. 76–101). New York: Cambridge University Press.

Bedford, V. H., Volling, B. L., & Avioli, P. S. (2000). Positive consequences of sibling conflict in childhood and adulthood. *International Journal of Aging and Human Development, 51,* 53–67.

Boll, T., Ferring, D., & Filipp, S. H. (2003). Perceived parental differential treatment in middle adulthood: Curvilinear relations with individuals' experienced relationship quality to sibling and parents. *Journal of Family Psychology, 17,* 472–487.

Connidis, I. A. (2005). Sibling ties across time: The middle and later years. In M. Johnson, V. L. Bengtson, P. G. Coleman, & T. B. L. Kirkwood (Eds.), *The Cambridge handbook of age and ageing* (pp. 429–436). Cambridge, U.K.: Cambridge University Press.

Eriksen, S., & Gerstel, N. (2002). A labor of love or labor itself: Care work among adult brothers and sisters. *Journal of Family Issues, 23,* 836–856.

General Social Survey Cumulative Datafile. (1986). Retrieved April 15, 2008, from http://www.sda.berkeley.edu

Gold, D. T. (1989). Sibling relationships in old age: A typology. *International Journal of Aging and Human Development, 28,* 37–51.

Mack, K. (2004). The effects of early parental death on sibling relationships in later life. *Omega, 49*(2), 131–148.

Matthews, S. H. (2005). Reaching beyond the dyad: Research on adult siblings. In V. L. Bengtson, A. C. Acock, K. A. Allen, P. Dilworth-Anderson, & D. M. Klein (Eds.), *Sourcebook of family theory and research* (pp. 181–184). Thousand Oaks, CA: Sage.

Mize, L. K., Turell, S., & Meier, J. (2004). Sexual orientation and the sister relationship: Conversations and opportunities. *Journal of Feminist Family Therapy, 1*(4), 1–19.

Rauer, A. J., & Volling, B. L. (2007). Differential parenting and sibling jealousy: Developmental correlates of young adults' romantic relationships. *Personal Relationships, 14*(4), 475–511.

Swain, S. (1989). Covert intimacy: Closeness in men's friendships. In B. J. Risman & P. Schwartz (Eds.), *Gender in intimate relationships: A microstructural approach* (pp. 71–85). Belmont, CA: Wadsworth.

Tancredy, C. M., & Fraley, R. C. (2006). The nature of adult twin relationships: An attachment-theoretical perspective. *Journal of Personality and Social Psychology, 90,* 78–93.

Voorpostel, M., & Blieszner, R. (2008). Intergenerational solidarity and support between adult siblings. *Journal of Marriage and the Family, 70*(1), 157–167.

Voorpostel, M, van der Lippe, T., Dykstra, P. A., & Flap, H. (2007). Similar or different? The importance of similarities and differences for support between siblings. *Journal of Family Issues, 28*(8), 1026–1053.

Waldinger, R. J., Vaillant, G. E., & Orav, E. J. (2007). Childhood sibling relationships as a predictor of major depression in adulthood: A 30-year prospective study. *American Journal of Psychiatry, 164*(6), 949–954.

Walker, A. J., Allen, K. R., Connidis, I. A. (2005). Theorizing and studying sibling ties in adulthood. In V. L. Bengtson, A. C. Acock, K. A. Allen, P. Dilworth-Anderson, & D. M. Klein (Eds.), *Sourcebook of family theory & research* (pp. 181–184). Thousand Oaks, CA: Sage.

White, K. (2001). Sibling relationships over the life course: A panel analysis. *Journal of Marriage and the Family, 63,* 555–568.

Victoria Hilkevitch Bedford

SIMMEL, GEORG
1858–1918

Georg Simmel was born on March 1 in Berlin and died on September 28 in Strassburg, Germany (now Strasbourg, France). Trained as a philosopher, he also belonged to the first generation of German sociologists. After receiving a doctorate in philosophy at the University of Berlin (now Humboldt University) in 1881, he became a lecturer at that university in sociology, philosophy, ethics, art, and psychology. Not only were his lectures popular in the university, they attracted the intellectual elite of Berlin as well as many students from abroad.

Simmel was a founding member of the German Sociological Society, along with German sociologists such as Max Weber and Ferdinand Tönnies. By 1900 Simmel's work was well known throughout Europe, Russia, and the Americas, but his repeated attempts to gain a formal university position were unsuccessful. In 1901 he was granted an honorary position that placed him above the rank of lecturer but left him out of the mainstream affairs of the university. His Jewish heritage (despite his family's Protestant conversion) and especially his popularity outside of academia made him appear dubious to many of his colleagues and did not help to secure him a formal position early in his career. In 1914, only four years before his death, he became a full professor at the University of Strassburg.

CONTRIBUTIONS TO LIFE COURSE RESEARCH

In contrast to some other sociological approaches, Simmel viewed society as neither an organism nor a convenient label for something that does not exist. Instead, Simmel pictured society as a web of reciprocal interactions (*Wechselwirkung*) among individuals and sometimes between people and the material world. Simmel's core notion of *Wechselwirkung* can be translated as both "reciprocal interaction" and "reciprocal effect and causation." To Simmel all social life consists of reciprocal interaction so that the actions and destinies of each element have an impact on the other elements. That notion allowed him to perceive that the modern individual has a strained relationship between what he called objective culture and subjective culture. Simmel saw the modern concept of individualization—the idea that individual people can and should have power and agency—as a part of subjective culture, but he was aware that the world outside the individual may develop its own dynamics (objective culture). Objective culture can have negative as well as positive unintended consequences for

Georg Simmel.

the life course of the individual. This perspective is echoed in the emphasis in contemporary life course research on the tension between human agency and social structure.

From that perspective Simmel defined the subject of sociology not as the study of society, community, or even groups but as the study of the modes or forms of sociation or, more literally, societalization (*Vergesellschaftung*), by which he meant the ways in which humans associate with one another and become interdependent. Throughout his work Simmel considered social actions not in themselves but in relation to particular structures and processes. For him sociology is the science that studies the processes of societalization.

That definition of sociology was a response to critiques from the historical sciences as well as from psychology that a science of society never would be established because it would fail to have a field of study of its own. To Simmel a sociologist's object of study should not be an entity called society but the intricate connections that give rise to society. As a result of his interest in the forms of association by which a mere sum

of separate individuals undergoes the process of societalization to become something greater than that sum, Simmel was especially interested in the issue of individualization. He also considered historical change in individuals' group affiliations and in the life course stages of individuals' group affiliations. For instance, Simmel often discussed the impact of modern technologies, which in his view allow individuals to master their everyday tasks and help design novel forms of societalization in which individuals can pursue their goals and interests. He exemplified the pressure of objective culture when he discussed how modern technologies such as the telephone and new forms of transportation can become means in what he called the process of superordination and subordination. Essentially, he argued that technologies can end up controlling individuals. Subordination by objective culture in the form of a principle or a technological device can be seen as more disturbing than subordination to a group. To Simmel, subordination to a certain group still allowed a person to develop some form of individuality and express beneficial social bonds.

SIGNIFICANCE OF SIMMEL'S WORK BEYOND LIFE COURSE RESEARCH

In addition to Simmel's contributions to understanding the modern life course and its implications, his work has remained relevant in many other areas in the social sciences. Simmel has been influential in the development of sociology, anthropology, and cultural studies. His ideas on individualization and reciprocal interaction have been critical to the contemporary understanding of modern life in big cities, the phenomenon of strangeness in debates on assimilation, personal and social interaction, modern sexuality, studies of social conflict, exchange theory, and qualitative data analysis in the social sciences.

SEE ALSO Volume 1: *Agency;* Volume 2: *Sociological Theories.*

BIBLIOGRAPHY

Levine, N. Georg Simmel on individuality and social forms. (1972). Trans. D. N. Levine. Chicago: University of Chicago Press.
Simmel, G. The sociology of Georg Simmel. (1950). Trans. K. H. Wolfe. Glencoe, IL: Free Press.
Simmel, G. Conflict and the web of group affiliations. (1955). Trans. K. H. Wolfe. New York: Free Press.

Matthias Gross

SINGLEHOOD

SEE Volume 3: *Singlehood.*

SOCIAL CLASS

Most societies employ some system of hierarchical ranking, whether explicit or implicit, to make distinctions among their members. In stratified societies, individuals who occupy similar positions in the hierarchy are considered members of the same social class. Although the determinants of social class vary across societies, most modern societies base their rankings on some combination of occupation, education, income, and wealth. In addition to possessing greater financial resources, occupants of higher social classes tend to have greater access to power and authority, better living and working conditions, and better physical and mental health. Those who occupy higher-class positions in a given society typically distinguish themselves by adopting particular dialects, dress codes, leisure activities, manners, and other behaviors and traits that both signify and further their prestige. These behaviors and traits are cultivated to contrast with those of the lower classes, which are considered less culturally refined and therefore less desirable (Bourdieu, 1984).

The social class an individual belongs to typically has a great deal of influence on the shape and structure of his or her life course. As Max Weber's (1864–1920) concept of *life chances* implies, class plays a significant role in expanding or limiting access to a wide variety of experiences, goods, and conditions (Weber, 1946). This influence may be direct, such as when limited financial resources constrain an individual's ability to acquire goods or services that could improve quality of life (e.g., health care, legal services, higher education). Similarly, occupations at the higher end of the social hierarchy differ from those at the lower end in that they often offer greater stability of work and greater opportunities for promotion, as well as greater income.

However, the effect of social class on the life course can also be seen in much more subtle and insidious ways. Position in the social structure affects the very ways that people perceive the world, including the values that they emphasize, the opportunities that they encounter or consider feasible, and even the characteristics that they seek to instill in their children. For example, parents of lower-class children have been found to emphasize behaviors, such as obedience and good manners, that reflect the conformity required by their own class positions, whereas middle-class parents are more likely to emphasize self-direction (Kohn & Schooler, 1983). These traits are encouraged in children because they are likely to enable professional success in their respective milieus: Children who become factory workers will be rewarded for following rules, whereas children who become white-collar workers will be rewarded for innovation.

Social class is associated with a variety of outcomes across the life course. For instance, middle-class students often have better educational outcomes than do lower-class students. As Lareau (2003) has shown, this is not only because they have access to greater financial resources but also because they and their families have greater familiarity with the values, language, and culture of educational institutions; consequently, they are more likely to feel as if they *belong* in school (Ostrove & Long, 2007). Even seemingly personal decisions such as those involving marriage and child-bearing are associated with social class. Lower-class women are less likely than their middle-class counterparts to marry, a social fact that at least partly reflects the poor employment prospects of lower-class men in the modern economy (Edin & Kefalas, 2004). Lower-class women are thus more likely than middle-class women to have children out of wedlock; they are also, on average, younger than middle-class women when they become mothers. Indeed, middle-class women in industrialized societies are postponing motherhood longer than they have since at least World War II; they are also having fewer children (Hall, 1999).

Evidence is particularly compelling about the effect of social class on health throughout the life course. As Henry (2001) has noted, social class contributes to health inequalities in a variety of ways, including psychological mechanisms (e.g., cultural norms and habits, dispositions and cognitive styles, health knowledge); behavioral constraints (e.g., economic resources, barriers to access); and physical influences (e.g., environmental conditions, physiological stress, genetics). Further, the complex interactions of these mechanisms do not result in a simple difference between rich and poor. Instead, socioeconomic differences in health are gradational: The highest income group is healthier than the second-highest income group and so on (Marmot, 1999). A considerable amount of policy work has been devoted to finding ways to reduce inequalities in both the health outcomes and the health care experienced by members of different social classes.

DEFINING AND STUDYING SOCIAL CLASS

Despite the importance of class to the organization of social life, no single definition of the term exists. Instead, social class has a number of distinct meanings. In everyday usage, it most closely approximates the idea of social prestige, as indicated by lifestyle and consumption patterns. Researchers, however, may use the term to signify one of three meanings. First, class may be used to describe a system of structured inequality, particularly with respect to economic and power resources. Second, class may mean an actual or potential social and political force, with the power to produce significant social change. Third, similar to the everyday usage of the term, class may be relatively synonymous with prestige, status, culture, or lifestyles (Crompton, 1998). These multiple meanings can be traced back to those developed by Karl Marx (1818–1883) and Max Weber, whose works spawned the theoretical traditions that have been most important to the contemporary study of social class.

Social stratification, the systems of hierarchical ranking employed by societies, has long been a focal point of discussion and debate among intellectuals and philosophers. However, Karl Marx and his literary collaborator, Friedrich Engels (1820–1895), were the first to describe the motivating forces of the new social order that developed in the wake of the industrial revolution of the mid-19th century. Their work emphasized the social relations inherent to industrial production and linked these relations to the dynamics of social change (Rothman, 1999). Marx argued that each period of history was defined by two social classes that were in opposition to each other because of their different relationships to the *means of production* (the tools, equipment, materials, and infrastructure necessary to make products). In feudalistic societies, for example, the two classes were landowners and serfs; in slavery, they were masters and slaves. Under capitalism, the two classes are the *bourgeois*, those who own the economic resources, or capital, and the *proletariat*, workers who own nothing and thus can only survive by selling their labor. The dominant class in any period occupies an extremely advantageous position, which it both maintains and furthers by organizing the *ideological superstructure* (a society's laws, institutions, beliefs, art, values, and so on) to support the status quo.

Despite the considerable disadvantage of the proletariat under capitalism, Marx believed that it would eventually overthrow the capitalist system. To engage in revolution, however, members of the proletariat must recognize their collective predicament. To do so, Marx believed that the proletariat must move from being simply a *Klasse an sich* (a class unto itself) to a *Klasse für sich* (a class for itself), in which its members are not only aware of the interests they share by virtue of their common location within the economic system but are self-consciously acting together to realize those interests. Marx believed that collective action by the proletariat would overthrow the bourgeoisie, resulting first in a temporary, transitional period of socialism and then settling into a permanent state of communism, in which the distribution of goods would be determined by each individual's abilities and needs.

Although class is obviously central to the Marxist conception of history and society, it is not defined clearly in Marx's writings. Wright (1985, pp. 26–38) argued that Marx referenced class in two distinct ways: structurally, as in the relationship to the means of production (i.e., ownership versus lack of ownership), and relationally, in that classes are defined by their opposing interests and antagonistic relationship. The two-class framework

developed by Marx has also been criticized by some because it has been largely unable to account for the marked rise of the middle class(es) during the 20th century. How to incorporate this segment of society, as well as how to account for other developments in modern capitalism, has created considerable debate among neo-Marxist scholars. However, Marx and Engels' work spawned extensive analysis of industrial society, and all scholars of class analysis are thus indebted to them. They introduced many of the key issues on which the study of class and stratification has been based, particularly the concept of class as based on position in a specific productive system and the concept of class-consciousness.

Weber drew on Marx's work to develop a multi-dimensional view of stratification that extended beyond the Marxist emphasis on class relationships alone. Like Marx, Weber viewed social classes as groups of individuals who share a common market situation that significantly influences their life chances. However, he saw three types of market situation: the labor market, which divides individuals into employers and employees; the money market, which distinguishes debtors from creditors; and the commodity market, which distinguishes buyers from sellers. Participation in more than one market can result in simultaneous membership in more than one economic class. Further, Weber recognized that people without property had a range of skills and abilities that can significantly affect their social standing and life chances. In this way, his work allows more room for the incorporation of the middle classes than does the Marxist tradition.

Weber argued that there are actually three forms of social inequality under capitalism: economic inequality, status inequality, and power inequality. Status inequality is conceptually distinct from economic inequality but is often correlated with it, inasmuch as individuals and groups with the most economic resources often enjoy the highest status. What he termed *status honor*, but which is now typically called social status or prestige, reflected and was based on social values and ideals. Communities of people sharing a similar location in the status hierarchy comprise status groups; their commonalities are grounded in consumption patterns and lifestyles, as well as aspects such as ancestry, ethnicity, education, or occupation. Because status groups are aware of their commonalities to at least some degree, higher-ranked status groups develop exclusionary rules and practices to protect their position and maintain their privilege over time. Weber was less explicit about the nature and dynamics of power inequality. However, his identification of this third type of inequality as distinct from (if often overlapping with) economic and status inequality was significant and further contributed to his multidimensional model of social stratification.

Blue-collar. *Assembly line workers install wheel well liners in the Ford F-150 at the Dearborn Truck Plant in Dearborn, MI. Manual laborers are often referred to as "blue-collar" workers.* **AP IMAGES.**

In contemporary social science, analysis of social class has typically assumed one of four forms: (a) the study of the emergence and perpetuation of (dis)advantaged groups within a society, with a focus on understanding and explaining a particular class; (b) the study of the consequences of class location, with a focus on understanding and explaining other phenomena (e.g., voting behavior) by examining the impact of social class; (c) the study of the development of class and status cultures and identities; and (d) the largely theoretical discussion of the significance of class processes, particularly with regard to their role in social change (Crompton, 1998, pp. 203–205). A large literature on social mobility has also emerged that examines the movement of individuals up and down the social class hierarchy, both across generations (intergenerationally) and within a single individual's lifetime (intragenerationally).

THE CLASS STRUCTURE OF POSTINDUSTRIAL SOCIETIES

In some societies, little room is available for subjective interpretation about what constitutes a higher or lower social ranking. For example, the Hindu caste system in India is based on a division of labor and has informed the structure of Indian society for centuries. The caste system has historically determined the social interactions that members can have as well as the occupations they can pursue, although there has been some decline in the rigidity of observance in the modern business environment. However, in societies such as the United States where class divisions are not formalized, ideas about the precise location of class boundaries may vary.

Most models of contemporary stratified societies contain at least three classes: an upper class, a middle class, and a lower class. It is generally agreed that the most powerful and wealthy members of a society comprise the upper class, whereas those who have little to no power and property comprise the lower class. The middle class falls somewhere in between, consisting of those who may or may not exert power over others but who have at least some control over their own destinies through occupation, education, or property ownership. However, both the boundaries and the meaning of these social classes are subject to considerable debate. This is particularly so in societies with great economic, social, and cultural complexity where there are few easily observable breaks in socioeconomic strata, such as the postindustrial United States (Eichar, 1989). Consequently, although most scholars of social class employ somewhat congruent theories, agreement on the proper operationalization of class remains elusive. For instance, some scholars conceptualize class as being primarily defined by relationships to power (e.g., Zweig, 2000), whereas others emphasize sources of income (e.g., Gilbert, 2002) or consumption patterns (e.g., Lury, 1997). This operational imprecision is also reflected in public opinion data. For example, polls have repeatedly shown that 90% or more of residents in the United States believe themselves to be somewhere in the middle of the class hierarchy (see, e.g., Baker, 2003; CBS News, 2007).

Most analysts of the modern U.S. class system divide it into a somewhat more complicated hierarchy, with each of the three main classes further divided into subclasses. The upper class, also sometimes referred to as the capitalist class (Gilbert, 2002), is in various models further subdivided into the super-rich and the rich (Beeghley, 2005) or the upper-upper and the lower-upper (Warner, Mecker, & Eells, 1960), or divided by the provenance of the wealth (i.e., those who were born into wealth, or old money, vs. those who became rich in their own lifetimes, or new money). The middle class is also often divided into two or three subclasses. These subclasses, which are organized roughly by individuals' educational attainment and the degree of autonomy they enjoy in the workplace, include the upper-middle, sometimes also called the professional class (Ehrenreich, 1989), and the lower-middle. Similarly, the lower class is also sometimes further divided, with scholars such as Coleman and Rainwater (1978) making distinctions between the *semipoor*, or unskilled labor and service workers with some high school education, and the bottom, those who are often unemployed and reliant on welfare. Many class analysts also include a fourth major class, the working class, which is located between the middle and the lower classes. This class, which is also sometimes called the upper-lower class (Warner et al., 1960), is typically made up of manual or blue-collar laborers who did not attend college. Some scholars also include workers in predominantly female clerical positions, or *pink-collar* workers, in this class.

As the multiplicity of these models suggests, a great deal of contention remains regarding which typology best captures postindustrial class structure. A similar lack of consensus exists surrounding the question of whether the unit of analysis for social class should be the individual or the family. For example, should a wife be accorded the same status as her husband if she does not work outside the home, or if her own class characteristics (e.g., education, manners) are different from her husband's? Simi-

larly, should minor children be considered lower class, given their lack of power both within and beyond the family home?

Including women in class analysis has posed a significant challenge to social scientists since the 1970s. Prior to that, class analysis and social stratification in the United States and Europe was devoted almost entirely to studies of men (Sørensen, 1994). Women were considered peripheral to the main concerns of stratification theory because of their intermittent employment patterns outside the home and thus were classified according to the characteristics, particularly the occupational status, of their husbands. This conventional approach to class analysis took for granted that the family should be the appropriate unit for class analysis. However, married women's increasing involvement in the labor force led to criticism of the conventional approach's method of determining family class position, as well as its assumption that all members of a given family occupy the same position in the social structure (Acker, 1973). In what became known as the feminist critique of class analysis, some scholars argued for an individualistic model of class analysis in which the class positions of both men and women were determined individually, regardless of their marital status. Instead of conceptualizing the family as the unit of class analysis, then, this approach emphasized the class position of individuals. Although the issue of how the social scientific literatures on social class and stratification should incorporate women remains unresolved, the considerable debate it has generated has contributed to the development of a substantial literature on women's occupational mobility and disadvantage in the labor market, as well as on the status inequality that women may experience within the household.

In the last decades of the 20th century, some scholars began to argue that social class is of decreasing importance in shaping identity. These arguments reflect changes in the structure of work in modern industrial societies, including the decline in workers employed in traditional blue-collar industries such as heavy manufacturing, and the growth of jobs in the service economy (i.e., nonmanual workers in finance and retail services). These scholars argue that this upheaval in traditional class markers (e.g., clear distinctions in the status of white- and blue-collar work) as well as the individualization encouraged by increasing social fragmentation and an unstable labor market, mean that factors other than employment are becoming more relevant as sources of identity and social cleavage. However, other scholars strongly reject such arguments, asserting that social class remains both a salient source of identity and a highly relevant social force.

BIBLIOGRAPHY

Acker, J. (1973). Women and social stratification: A case of intellectual sexism. *American Journal of Sociology, 78,* 936–945.

Baker, C. (2003, November 30). What is middle class? Income isn't necessarily sole measure. *The Washington Times.*

Beeghley, L. (2005). *The structure of social stratification in the United States.* Boston: Pearson, Allyn & Bacon.

Bourdieu, P. (1984). *Distinction: A social critique of the judgment of taste* (R. Nice, Trans.). Cambridge, MA: Harvard University Press.

CBS News. (2007). Survey dated April 9–April 12, 2007. Retrieved February 28, 2008, from the iPOLL Databank, The Roper Center for Public Opinion Research, University of Connecticut. Retrieved May 21, 2008, from http://www.ropercenter.uconn.edu/ipoll.html

Coleman, R. P., & Rainwater, L. (1978). *Social standing in America.* New York: Basic Books.

Crompton, R. (1998). *Class and stratification: An introduction to current debates.* Cambridge, England: Polity Press.

Edin, K., & Kefalas, M. (2004). *Promises I can keep: Why poor women put motherhood before marriage.* Berkeley: University of California Press.

Ehrenreich, B. (1989). *Fear of falling: The inner life of the middle class.* New York: HarperCollins.

Eichar, D. (1989). *Occupation and class consciousness in America.* Westport, CT: Greenwood Press.

Gilbert, D. (2002). *The American class structure: In an age of growing inequality.* Belmont, CA: Wadsworth.

Hall, D. M. B. (1999). Children in an ageing society. *British Medical Journal, 319,* 1356–1358.

Henry, P. (2001). An examination of the pathways through which social class impacts health outcomes. *Academy of Marketing Science Review, 1.* Retrieved March 1, 2008, from http://www.amsreview.org/amsrev

Kohn, M. L., & Schooler, C. (1983). *Work and personality: An inquiry into the impact of social stratification.* Norwood, NJ: Ablex.

Lareau, A. (2003). *Unequal childhoods: Class, race, and family life.* Berkeley: University of California Press.

Lury, C. (1997). *Consumer culture.* Cambridge, U.K.: Polity Press.

Marmot, M. (1999). Epidemiology of socioeconomic status and health: Are determinants within countries the same as between countries? In A. Tarlov & R. St. Peter (Eds.), *The society and population health reader: A state and community perspective.* New York: New Press.

Ostrove, J. M., & Long, S. M. (2007). Social class and belonging: Implications for college adjustment. *The Review of Higher Education, 30,* 363–389.

Rothman, R. A. (1999). *Inequality and stratification: Race, class, and gender.* Upper Saddle River, NJ: Prentice Hall.

Sørensen, A. (1994). Women, family and class. *Annual Review of Sociology, 20,* 27–47.

Warner, W. L., Mecker, M., & Eells, K. (1960). *Social class in America.* New York: Harper & Row.

Weber, M. (1946). *From Max Weber: Essays in sociology* (H. H. Gerth & C. W. Mills, Trans.). New York: Oxford University Press.

Wright, E. O. (1985). *Classes.* London: New Left Books.

Zweig, M. (2000). *The working class majority: America's best kept secret.* Ithaca, NY: Cornell University Press.

Karen Albright

SOCIAL EXCLUSION

SEE Volume 2: *Social Integration/Isolation, Adulthood.*

SOCIAL INTEGRATION/ ISOLATION, ADULTHOOD

Social integration refers to the degree to which an individual is tied to other individuals, organizations and groups, and his or her community. These ties may be formal or informal. They may be objective (i.e., based on actual relationships) or subjective (i.e., based on individuals' perceptions of relationships). People who are not socially integrated often are referred to as socially isolated. Social integration both reflects and shapes the adult life course; social bonds emerge from the events and circumstances of people's lives, and those bonds affect people's lives because of the resources they bring.

EARLY INTEREST IN SOCIAL INTEGRATION

The concept of social integration emerged from the work of the sociologists Ferdinand Tönnies (1855–1936) and Emile Durkheim (1858–1917), who were interested in the ways societies change as they progress from rural to urban. Tönnies used the term *Gemeinschaft* ("intimate community") to describe social integration in rural villages where people are closely tied by kinship and tradition and can be considered members of a single social group. In a Gemeinschaft, relationships are intimate and cooperative and individuals' interactions are guided by the interests of the group. As societies industrialize and urbanize, Tönnies argued, *Gesselschaft* ("impersonal association") emerges and weakens the integrated fabric of family and community. In a Gesselschaft, social bonds and long-lasting social relations are lacking and individuals' interactions are based on self-interest and material accumulation.

For Durkheim persons in both urban and rural areas have social bonds, but those bonds differ. Both types of society have a collective conscience, a system of fundamental beliefs that tie people together and foster social integration. Rural communities are tied together by mechanical solidarity, that is, social bonds and integration based on common sentiments and tasks and shared moral values. Adults in rural societies have a deep and personal involvement with the community and with one another because they perform similar tasks. By contrast, urban communities, which are shaped by industrialization, are based on organic solidarity, in which individuals perform specialized tasks and rely on one another to perform those tasks. Social relationships thus are more formal and functionally determined in urban societies, but those societies still are socially integrated.

In his influential work *Suicide* (1951 [1897]), Durkheim examined the impact of social integration on individual well-being. He argued that geographic variation in suicide rates (high rates in some countries and low rates in others) are due to different levels of social integration and regulation. Insufficient levels of social integration lead to a high degree of individualism, and the consequent isolation results in higher rates of suicide. Durkheim also argued that excessive levels of social integration also lead to higher rates of suicide because individuals who are very highly integrated feel overwhelmed by the demands and regulations of society. However, this idea is largely unfounded because modern societies rarely have excessive levels of social integration (Johnson, 1965).

In a classic study Mark Granovetter (1973) examined the qualitative nature of social integration, emphasizing the importance of weak ties (acquaintances). Strong ties form among people as a result of long-term, frequent, and sustained interactions; by contrast, weak ties result from infrequent and more casual interaction. Granovetter argued that weak ties are more efficient for innovation and knowledge; strong ties include individuals so embedded in interaction that change is hard to come by. If two people have a strong tie, they are also likely to be strongly tied to all the members of each other's networks, and that creates high levels of overlap in their social integration. Weak ties, in contrast, are the building blocks and bridges for social integration between groups.

DEFINING AND MEASURING SOCIAL INTEGRATION

Researchers draw a general distinction between structural (objective) integration and perceived (subjective) integration (Moen, Dempster-McClain, & Williams, 1989). Structural social integration refers to an individual's concrete involvement with other individuals, such as friendships, and with social groups, such as clubs and churches. Perceived integration reflects people's feelings about the depth of their connectedness to others, such as the sense

of belonging. Another distinction is the social context in which integration occurs. N. Lin (1986) classified social integration as occurring at the community level, within social networks, and through intimate and confiding relationships. Another way of conceptualizing social integration is to think about variation across diverse social contexts. Some of the more common contexts are family, friendships, voluntary groups, civic organizations, the workplace, the local neighborhood, and the larger community. It is important to distinguish among these different types of integration because adults may draw on specific resources for different situational needs (Messeri, Silverstein, & Litwak, 1993).

A counterpart to social integration is social isolation, which refers to a lack of social ties, companionship, and connectedness. Like social integration, social isolation may be structural or perceived. Perceived social isolation sometimes is referred to as loneliness (Ernst & Cacioppo, 1999). Using survey information from 1985 and 2004 General Social Survey (GSS) data, M. McPherson, L. Smith-Lovin, and M. E. Brashears (2006) found that social isolation in the United States increased over that two-decade period. For example, the number of adults who said that they had "no one" with whom to discuss important matters nearly tripled. The connection between age and loneliness is contradictory. Some researchers find that loneliness is most intense during adolescence and young adulthood and then declines with age (Rokach, 2000). McPherson and associates (2006), however, found that a person's network size decreases with age; the older people are, the more likely they are to report that they have no discussion partners in their social network.

Research on social integration is confronted by a number of conceptual and measurement issues. First, the field lacks agreed-on measures of social integration; that means that researchers use a wide variety of measures, making comparisons across studies and data sources difficult. Second, this lack of precision in measurement reflects an underlying lack of conceptual precision. The term *social integration* is not used or accepted universally, and the following terms may be used interchangeably: social integration, social support, social networks, social capital, social isolation, social alienation, social ties, social relationships, social attachment, social disorganization, and social engagement. However, many of these terms, in particular *social support* and *social networks*, refer to specific concepts that although closely related to social integration, are distinct from it. This conceptual imprecision arises in part because research about social integration is carried out in several academic disciplines and because within disciplines, different researchers study different aspects of social ties.

A third issue in defining and measuring social integration is that the concept applies to individuals as well as social groups; for individuals, integration may be structural or perceived. Thus, social integration may refer to a structural characteristic of an adult such as social support (House, Umberson, & Landis, 1988), a psychological characteristic of an adult such as social attachment (Kasarda & Janowitz, 1974), a structural characteristic of a small group such as social networks, or a structural characteristic of a geographic space such as social disorganization (Faris, 1955). A fourth issue is that similar concepts often are used to measure levels of integration; for example, higher levels of social ties indicate higher levels of social integration (Pescosolido & Georgianna, 1989).

Further development and refinement of the related concept of social capital eventually may rectify some of this conceptual confusion. The idea of social capital entered popular culture with the publication of *Bowling Alone: The Collapse and Revival of American Community* in 2000 by the political scientist Robert D. Putnam. Putnam argued that traditional forms of social integration—interpersonal ties, voluntary organizations, and civic participation—have had massive declines in involvement. Putnam made a distinction between two types of social capital: Bonding involves integration with individuals who have similar characteristics, whereas bridging involves integration with individuals who have diverse and often dissimilar characteristics. Putnam's work on social capital has been criticized and is not accepted universally in the academic community (Fischer, 2005).

The origin of the term *social capital* is debated (Portes, 1988). Although there is no universal definition of social capital—certainly a limitation of the concept—A. Portes (1988) provided a general definition that is accepted widely: Social capital is the ability of individuals to access and use resources and benefits as a result of their integration in social networks and social structures. Social capital is an extremely popular concept and is used extensively throughout the social sciences: The preface to a widely read edited volume on social capital states that "[s]ocial capital as both a concept and theory has drawn much intellectual interest and research in the past two decades. The attraction of the notion is perhaps in part due to the common understanding that as a social element it may capture the essence of many sociological concepts (e.g., social support, social integration, social cohesion, and even norms and values) and serve as an umbrella term that can be easily understood and transported across many disciplines" (Lin, Cook, & Burt, 2001, p. vii).

CAUSES OF SOCIAL INTEGRATION AND SOCIAL ISOLATION

Social integration is important for well-being throughout the adult life course. However, the causes of adult social integration begin much earlier in the life course, generally during childhood and adolescence. Indeed, early life course experiences have an enduring impact on integration throughout the adult years and in later life. Research has indicated that four childhood and adolescent processes and experiences are reliable predictors of adult social integration. Those processes all limit the ability of children and adolescents to form social bonds, and those limitations persist into the adult years. All the processes generally are called family social capital (Coleman, 1988). Specifically, adults have lower levels of social integration if they experienced any of the following events as children or adolescents: parental divorce, geographic mobility (especially moves that require frequently changing schools), poor parent-child relationships, and socially isolated parents (Myers, 1999).

Although these earlier experiences persist into adulthood and shape social integration, life course variables in adulthood also have contemporary effects on social integration (McPherson et al., 2006). Historically, women always have had greater levels of social integration. This trend has continued, but the differences in social integration between men and women have been shrinking. Other factors important for social integration in adulthood are age (social integration declines in one's older years), education (higher levels lead to greater integration), race (Whites are more socially integrated), and marital status (those who are married are more socially integrated). One's community also influences one's level of adult social integration. Generally, social integration is lower if one lives in a poor neighborhood and a neighborhood with higher crime rates. These factors create stress, fear, and less psychological investment in one's community, all of which are linked to lower social integration.

THE CONSEQUENCES OF SOCIAL INTEGRATION FOR THE ADULT LIFE COURSE

Life course researchers attempt to understand the opportunities, barriers, and social structures that shape individuals' life chances and well-being. The concept of social integration is integral to this understanding because social integration acts as a conduit for both tangible (e.g., money, help) and intangible (e.g., emotional support, intimacy, connections to opportunities) resources. Although measures of social integration and their equivalents are employed in almost all aspects of life course research, three research areas stand out in the importance they place on social integration: health, crime, and immigration.

Research shows that higher levels of social integration are associated with better physical and mental health

(House et al., 1988). This finding holds for diverse outcomes, including diabetes, hypertension, depression, self-rated health, and mortality. In general, higher levels of social integration provide (a) social support, such as information and help with tasks; (b) social influence, which may encourage health-enhancing beliefs and behaviors; (c) social engagement and attachment, for example, with friends and beneficial social institutions; and (d) material resources, which may facilitate preventive care and healthy behaviors (Berkman & Glass, 2000). Critics of research on social integration and health argue that too much attention is focused on structural aspects of integration. They propose that research should be directed at understanding the role of perceived integration and the qualities of relationships.

Building on earlier theories of social disorganization (Shaw & McKay, 1942), the social scientific study of crime emphasizes social integration and support at the individual, family, and structural levels. E. T. Cullen (1994) argued that that social integration and support should be an organizing concept for studies of crime. Social integration may provide a moral compass, an orientation toward family, a set of prosocial behaviors, coping resources, economic resources, and social control. Cullen (1994) argued that crime rates vary inversely with the level of social support across nations and communities. Research supports that statement and also finds that the beneficial effects of social integration on crime accrue to adults who are at the greatest risk of committing crimes: less educated persons and those with lower incomes. Unfortunately, structural and economic inequalities may create barriers to high levels of social integration among those adults who most need those resources to generate institutional controls (Messner & Rosenfeld, 2001).

The study of immigration has long employed concepts similar to social integration, such as assimilation, acculturation, and incorporation. Immigration research generally finds that as adult immigrants socially integrate into the new country, they learn the sociocultural ways of their new communities. As a result, immigrants receive the resources and benefits that social integration provides. Research on the benefits of social integration finds superior occupational, social mobility, and health outcomes for immigrants who can integrate comprehensively into their new communities. Immigrants who do not integrate socially may be viewed as the other group, be assigned to a lower socioeconomic position, and be marginalized and socially excluded.

Some scholars counter that social integration of immigrants does not have to be absolute and complete. Instead, successful social integration involves the combination of involvement in the mainstream institutions and organizations with one's familiar social and cultural practices. From this argument, the concept of social capital has crept into the theories and research on immigration. The benefits of social integration can be realized even when such integration occurs within a specific ethnic immigrant community if that community has established links and integration with mainstream institutions and organizations (Zhou, 2005).

THE FUTURE OF SOCIAL INTEGRATION

Social integration is an important adult characteristic that shapes life course outcomes, such as those associated with health, crime, and immigration. Research also shows that social integration can be a stratifying variable because levels of social integration are not equal across individuals. One's ability to integrate socially in adulthood is the result of a wide variety of adult statuses and characteristics. Research finds that social integration, along with its negative counterpart, social isolation, is a function of a person's physical and mental health; occupational, marital, and economic statuses; race and ethnicity; age; geographic location and mobility; and neighborhood quality.

However, the concept of social integration is broad, and social integration can be measured in numerous ways. Some researchers have abandoned the term in favor of more popular terms such as *social isolation*, *social capital*, and *social networks*. Therefore, much work is needed if social integration is to remain a useful concept for research and not just a broad construct in the social sciences.

Three avenues should be pursued by researchers in the future. First, qualitative research should be conducted on social integration in adulthood to reveal its complex and dynamic causes and consequences. Research that relies on large-scale quantitative surveys often cannot capture the interpersonal and structural processes that shape social integration in adulthood. For example, qualitative methods such as open-ended interviews could help researchers understand fully how individuals weigh the costs (such as time and effort) and benefits (such as friendship and support) associated with social integration. The demographic variables typically used in quantitative research—age, race, education, gender—do not capture these more nuanced processes. Second, much theoretical and empirical work on social integration is focused on the very young (children and adolescents) and the very old. Equal attention should be devoted to adults.

Third, social scientists should address the policy implications associated with social integration and the disparities in them. Policy is a dominant feature of international work on immigration, such as the importance of quickly integrating migrants into their destination communities. In the United States policy efforts are pursued in the educational context, but those efforts are focused mainly on child and adolescent social integration. For example, a review of outreach policies found that parental integration into a child's school and peer-group families is the stated goal of 75% of the federally funded programs that target low-income and racial minority students (Perna, 2002). Utilizing the life course perspective in this policy endeavor could be fruitful because it would show that social integration in adulthood has significant implications for life chances and well-being.

SEE ALSO Volume 1: *Coleman, James; Social Capital;* Volume 2: *Durkheim, Émile; Fatherhood; Motherhood; Neighborhood Context, Adulthood; Religion and Spirituality, Adulthood; Roles; Social Networks; Social Support, Adulthood; Volunteering, Adulthood;* Volume 3: *Loneliness, Later Life.*

BIBLIOGRAPHY

Baum, F. E., & Ziersch, A. M. (2008). Social capital. *Journal of Epidemiology and Community Health, 57,* 320–323.

Blau, P. M. (1960). A theory of social integration. *American Journal of Sociology, 65*(6), 545–556.

Berkman, L. F., & Glass, T. (2000). Social integration, social networks, social support, and health. In L. F. Berkman & I. Kawachi (Eds.), *Social epidemiology* (pp.137–173). New York: Oxford University Press.

Bursik, R. J., Jr. (1988). Social disorganization and theories of crime and delinquency. *Criminology, 26*(4), 519–552.

Coleman, J. S. (1988). Social capital in the creation of human capital. *American Journal of Sociology, 94,* S95–S120.

Cullen F. T. (1994). Social support as an organizing concept for criminology: Presidential address to the Academy of Criminal Justice Sciences. *Justice Quarterly, 11*(4), 527–559.

Durkheim, E. (1951 [1897]). *Suicide: A study in sociology* (J. A. Spaulding & G. Simpson, Trans.). Glencoe, IL: Free Press.

Durkheim, E. (1964 [1893]). *The division of labor in society* (G. Simpson, Trans.). New York: Free Press of Glencoe.

Elder, G. H., Jr. (1985). Perspectives on the life course. In G. H. Elder Jr. (Ed.), *Life course dynamics: Trajectories and transitions, 1968–1980* (pp. 23–49). Ithaca, NY: Cornell University Press.

Elder, G. H., Jr. (1997). The life course and human development. In R. M. Lerner (Ed.), *Handbook of child psychology.* Vol. 1: *Theoretical models of human development* (pp. 939–991). New York: Wiley.

Ernst, J. M., & Cacioppo, J. T. (1999). Lonely hearts: Psychological perspectives on loneliness. *Applied and Preventive Psychology, 8,* 1–22.

Faris, R.E.L. (1955). *Social disorganization.* (2nd ed.). New York: Ronald Press.

Fischer, C. S. (2005). Bowling alone: What's the score? *Social Networks, 27,* 155–167.

Granovetter, M. S. (1973). The strength of weak ties. *American Journal of Sociology, 78*(6), 1360–1380.

Granovetter, M. S. (1985). Economic action and social structure: The problem of embeddedness. *American Journal of Sociology, 91*(3), 481–510.

House, J. S., Umberson, D., & Landis, K. R. (1988). Structures and processes of social support. *Annual Review of Sociology, 14,* 293–318.

Johnson, B. D. (1965). Durkheim's one cause of suicide. *American Sociological Review, 30,* 875–856.

Kasarda, J. D., & Janowitz, M. (1974). Community attachment in mass society. *American Sociological Review, 39*(3), 328–339.

Lin, N. (1986). Conceptualizing social support. In N. Lin, A. Dean, & W. M. Edsel (Eds.), *Social support, life events, and depression* (pp. 17–30). New York: Academic Press.

Lin, N., Cook, K., & Burt, R. S. (Eds.). (2001). *Social capital: Theory and research.* New York: Aldine de Gruyter.

McPherson, M., Smith-Lovin, L., & Brashears, M. E. (2006). Social isolation in America: Changes in core discussion networks over two decades. *American Sociological Review, 71*(3), 353–375.

Messeri, P., Silverstein. M., & Litwak, E. (1993). Choice of optimal social supports among the elderly: A meta-analysis of competing theoretical perspectives. *Journal of Health and Social Behavior, 34,* 122–137.

Messner, S. F., & Rosenfeld, R. (2001). *Crime and the American dream.* (3rd ed.). Belmont, CA: Wadsworth/Thomson Learning.

Moen, P., Dempster-McClain, D., & Williams, R. M., Jr. (1989). Social integration and longevity: An event history analysis of women's roles and resilience. *American Sociological Review, 54,* 635–647.

Myers, S. (1999). Childhood migration and social integration in adulthood. *Journal of Marriage and the Family, 61*(3), 774–789.

Perna, L. W. (2002). Precollege outreach programs: Characteristics of programs serving historically underrepresented groups of students. *Journal of College Student Development, 43,* 64–83.

Pescosolido, B. A., & Georgianna, S. (1989). Durkheim, suicide, and religion: Toward a network theory of suicide. *American Sociological Review, 54*(1), 33–48.

Portes, A. (1998). Social capital: Its origins and applications in modern sociology. *Annual Review of Sociology, 24,* 1–24.

Putnam, R. D. (2000). *Bowling alone: The collapse and revival of American community.* New York: Simon & Schuster.

Rokach, A. (2000). Loneliness and the life cycle. *Psychological Reports, 86,* 629–642.

Shaw, C. R., & McKay, H. D. (1942). *Juvenile delinquency in urban areas: A study of rates of delinquency in relation to differential characteristics of local communities in American cities.* Chicago: University of Chicago Press.

Tönnies, F. (2001). *Community and civil society* (J. Harris & M. Hollis, Trans.). New York: Cambridge University Press.

Zhou, M. (2005). Ethnicity as social capital: Community-based institutions and embedded networks of social relations. In G. C. Loury, T. Modood, & S. M. Teles (Eds.), *Ethnicity, social mobility, and public policy: Comparing the USA and UK* (pp. 131–159). Cambridge, U.K., and New York: Cambridge University Press.

Scott M. Myers

SOCIAL MOBILITY

Social mobility refers to the extent to which the social position attained by adults is linked to the social position of their parents. Research on social mobility illuminates the degree of opportunity in a society, because it shows whether and how advantages or disadvantages in family background contribute to one's adult social position. To that end, studies of intergenerational social mobility generally examine the extent to which *social destinations*, or the social position attained by adult individuals, are similar to or different from *social origins*, the social position of the adults' parents (and, in some studies, grandparents). Although social position can be defined and understood in different ways, the focus in mobility studies is on socioeconomic position (i.e., occupation, education, income, and wealth). The majority of sociological research on social mobility focuses on socioeconomic position as defined by occupational status or class and, in some studies, educational attainment.

For example, one seminal study compared father's occupation to son's occupation, with occupation categorized into the broad categories of farm, manual, or nonmanual, in various nations (Lipset & Zetterberg, 1956), and another investigated the impact of father's occupational status and educational attainment on son's educational attainment, first job, and current occupational status (Blau & Duncan, 1967). A large body of social mobility research has subsequently addressed questions about the linkages between childhood social origins and adult destinations, as well as questions about how these linkages may differ between, for example, nations, time periods, birth cohorts, individuals with different levels of education, racial/ethnic groups, and men and women. In answering such questions, social mobility research illustrates interdependencies between generations as well as some of the ways in which lives are shaped by key life transitions or contexts of time and place.

DISTINGUISHING SOCIAL POSITIONS

The concept of social mobility assumes that societies contain social positions that differ meaningfully from each other. These positions are usually defined in socioeconomic terms, most often by occupation, and are often, but not always, assumed to be ranked in an inherent hierarchy. Social mobility is often described as "upward" or "downward" mobility in reference to comparing higher or lower occupations on this hierarchy. A fundamental theoretical difference among mobility researchers concerns how to distinguish occupations meaningfully.

Pitirim Sorokin (1959), a pioneer in social mobility research, suggested the existence of *vertical channels* of mobility in societies, and much work that followed was influenced by or compatible with this theory. Thus many mobility researchers conceptualized occupations as finely vertically gradated along an inherent hierarchy. For example, some research distinguishes occupations by ranking each one relative to the others in terms of occupational prestige, or similarly, on a vertical scale that measures occupations based on the average job holder's income levels and educational credentials.

In contrast, another approach to distinguishing occupations takes the perspective that mobility occurs within a structure of discrete social classes rather than a finely ranked hierarchy of occupational status or prestige. Proponents of this *class structure* approach generally view occupations as falling into relatively large categories (for an exception, see Weeden & Grusky, 2005). The large categories of occupations represent discrete social classes, the distinctions between which are not necessarily hierarchical. For example, the self-employed class may be distinct from other classes without necessarily being considered a higher or lower class position. Although hierarchy is not the most central concept in the class structure approach, it is still present—some classes are considered "lower" than all others, although the specific positions can vary between perspectives.

Within the class structure perspective, scholars have proposed defining the boundaries of the class categories in different ways. The most commonly implemented approach in current social mobility research is often known as the EGP class schema in reference to an early explication of the schema (Erikson, Goldthorpe, & Portocarero, 1979; see also Erikson & Goldthorpe, 1992). The EGP schema posits that class position distinctly shapes individuals' life chances such as through its association with specific employment conditions. It organizes occupations into class categories such that the occupations held by individuals in a given class involve similar labor market relationships (i.e., being an employer, self-employed, or an employee) and employment conditions. In particular, service or professional occupations, whose incumbents generally experience relative job security, regular advancement opportunities, and employer trust, are contrasted with working-class occupations, whose incumbents generally experience close supervision and earn a specified wage per hour of labor.

Although the EGP class schema is dominant in social mobility research, other researchers have proposed different ways of theorizing class distinctions. One such perspective, associated with the work of Erik Olin Wright (2005) and based on Marxist concepts of class, views classes as not only involving different employment conditions but also distinct and conflicting class interests. In Wright's class schema, occupations are divided into class positions with respect to class exploitation or, more specifically, with respect to incumbents' control of assets that Wright theorizes are the mechanisms of class exploitation—ownership of capital, skills or expertise, and authority. Consequently, employers are distinguished from employees, experts from nonexperts, and managers from nonmanagers (Wright, 2005; see Western & Wright, 1994, for an application to social mobility research).

ABSOLUTE AND RELATIVE SOCIAL MOBILITY

Social mobility researchers generally make a conceptual distinction between *absolute mobility* (also termed *structural mobility*) and *relative mobility* (also termed *social fluidity*). Absolute mobility results from economic change in a society, such as shifts in job growth away from farm employment toward industrial employment. It thus results from changes in the distribution of available occupations between one generation and the next. If the proportion of higher status jobs increases in the children's generation compared to the parents' generation, all individuals in the children's generation, regardless of their class background, have a greater likelihood of upward intergenerational mobility than if the distribution of occupations remained unchanged.

Relative mobility, on the other hand, is the social mobility that remains after adjusting for differences in the distribution of occupations between parents and children's generations (i.e., absolute mobility). Relative mobility is considered a reflection of the degree of equality of opportunity in a society rather than a reflection of societal economic shifts. High relative mobility is thought to reflect a degree of equal opportunity because intergenerational movement between classes occurs when adults' class destinations are not tightly linked to their social class of origin (and the advantages or disadvantages it entails). Researchers in the United States have been most interested in relative as opposed to absolute social mobility. It is worth noting, however, that the destinations and life chances of individuals in a society are more strongly affected by absolute mobility than by relative mobility (see Breen & Jonsson, 2005, for a discussion).

PATTERNS OF SOCIAL MOBILITY

Social mobility researchers may take different theoretical approaches to identifying social positions, but their findings nevertheless concur that significant constraints to relative mobility exist. Regardless of theoretical perspective, studies have demonstrated that the chances of achieving a particular status position as an adult depend significantly on one's social origins after absolute mobility is taken into account. In order to summarize this variation, researchers test statistical models representing various mobility patterns and select the model that they believe best summarizes the actual patterns observed in real-world data. A key pattern consistently identified by scholars is that the farther apart two classes or occupations are in a hierarchy, the lower the chances that individuals will experience mobility between them (whether upward or downward). Research findings also have illustrated a pattern of relatively high immobility in certain class positions; for example, children of the self-

employed are likely to become self-employed adults (see Ganzeboom, Treiman, & Ultee, 1991, for a review).

In addition to the commonly identified hierarchy and immobility patterns, Robert Erikson and John Goldthorpe (1992) identified a pattern they termed *affinity*, in which certain classes have relatively high inter-class mobility whereas other classes have low inter-class mobility. They also identified a sector-based pattern such that mobility between agricultural and nonagricultural classes is unlikely. Erikson and Goldthorpe proposed a mobility model that incorporates affinity and sector in addition to hierarchy and immobility. Their model has been contested by others who argue that it understates the importance of the hierarchical component of social mobility (Hout & Hauser, 1992). Interestingly, regardless of the model of mobility, research suggests that mobility patterns are generally similar across nations. For example, a variety of research has demonstrated the presence of hierarchical mobility patterns across nations, and researchers utilizing Erikson and Goldthorpe's model have also found that it applies cross-nationally (see Hout & DiPrete, 2006, for a review).

EXTENT OF SOCIAL MOBILITY

Although social mobility patterns may be generally similar between countries, the *extent* of mobility (i.e., the likelihood that an individual will experience social mobility or the frequency of social mobility) is a different question and one that has been extensively debated by social mobility researchers. Although many scholars expected the United States to demonstrate high rates of social mobility compared to European countries (due to perceptions that class is less important for life chances in the United States), an early cross-national social mobility study suggested that nonfarm mobility rates were similar among Western industrialized nations. This idea became known as the *Lipset-Zetterberg hypothesis* (Lipset & Zetterberg, 1956). This hypothesis was later reformulated by others to posit that, although absolute mobility rates may differ between industrialized nations, relative mobility rates are basically the same. This became known as the *FJH hypothesis* (Featherman, Jones, & Hauser, 1975). Subsequent research, however, has demonstrated that important differences exist between nations in both absolute and relative mobility rates. Although cross-national rankings comparing more and less mobile countries must be made with caution due to differences in data collection, research findings suggest that the United States falls toward the low end within a group of relatively high mobility countries, in which Israel, Sweden, Norway, Hungary, Poland, the Netherlands, and Canada are some of the more fluid nations. Countries exhibiting lower relative mobility rates include Great Britain, Italy,

Germany, Portugal, and Ireland (Beller & Hout, 2006; Breen, 2004; Breen & Jonsson, 2005).

In addition to addressing cross-national variation in the extent of relative social mobility, researchers also have examined differences in mobility rates within countries, including differences over time that could result either from cohort effects (changes that occur when older birth cohorts leave the workforce and are replaced by younger cohorts with different mobility experiences) or from period effects (changes in mobility that affect individuals of all ages during a given time period, such as a country's transition to post-socialism, for example). In most countries, relative mobility rates appear to have increased with time. Great Britain is an exception to this trend, however, as are Hungary and Russia (Breen, 2004; Breen & Jonsson, 2005; Gerber & Hout, 2004). One explanation for the pattern of increasing mobility over time within many countries concerns expanded access to higher education, thus granting educational opportunities even to persons with humble backgrounds.

EDUCATION AND SOCIAL MOBILITY

Early social mobility researchers showed that educational systems contribute both to intergenerational social mobility and immobility because educational attainment plays a key role in the process of attaining an occupation. Individuals with advantaged social origins have relatively high chances of attaining a postsecondary education and vice versa. Because educational attainment is so important to occupational attainment, this link between social origins and educational attainment largely explains the link between social origins and social destinations. At the same time, however, many factors other than social origins shape educational attainment. The extent to which educational attainment depends on social origins constrains social mobility, whereas the extent to which it does not depend on social origins fosters social mobility.

In part due to its importance in the occupational attainment process, education plays a key role in mobility researchers' understandings of differences in rates of relative social mobility between countries and over time. Greater access to postsecondary education is associated with higher mobility rates in some countries, and the expansion of postsecondary education systems over time within a country can underlie rising social mobility rates over time in that country. Expanded access to postsecondary education increases relative social mobility if the linkage between social origins and destinations is weaker among individuals who achieve a postsecondary education, as research shows is the case in some countries (Breen, 2004; Breen & Jonsson, 2005; Hout, 1988). For example, an individual of disadvantaged social ori-

gins who earns an advanced educational degree is more likely to be upwardly mobile than an individual from the same background without the advanced degree.

Although societies that expand access to higher education tend to experience increased social mobility rates over time, there is evidence that this effect can weaken as more and more people earn a postsecondary degree. Also, whereas greater access to education is associated with higher social mobility in certain countries, other countries (e.g., post-socialist countries such as Poland and Hungary) achieve higher rates of social mobility for reasons not fully understood, despite comparatively low access to postsecondary education. Research also shows that mobility rates tend to be higher in countries with greater equality of educational opportunity (i.e., in countries in which educational attainment depends less on social origins) regardless of the extent of access to higher education. This pattern suggests that either equality of educational opportunity causes higher rates of relative mobility, or the same factors that foster greater equality of educational opportunity in a nation simultaneously foster social mobility (Beller & Hout, 2006).

UNRESOLVED QUESTIONS IN SOCIAL MOBILITY RESEARCH

Many interesting questions about social mobility remain unresolved. One such question concerns how to capture the shared class position of families in measures of class origins and destinations. Although class origins and destinations can be measured in terms of the occupations held by individuals, many researchers theorize that individuals within families share a common class position. Researchers have particularly debated how to define the family-level class positions of married employed women. One position in this debate is that either the husband or the spouse with the dominant class position (i.e., the spouse with the higher position and/or stronger labor force attachment) defines the class position of all individuals in the family, regardless of whether the other spouse also has an occupation. Another view is that the class positions of families are jointly determined by both spouses. These two approaches yield different findings about women's social mobility, and the debate has not been adequately resolved (see Sorenson, 1994).

Although social mobility researchers have mainly debated the problem of determining shared family class positions with respect to class destinations, the problem is equally important when applied to social origins. It is widely accepted that social origins theoretically refer to family class background, not to fathers' class per se. In practice, however, researchers generally define social origins on the basis of a father's or head of household's occupation alone. Although some studies suggest that both parents' positions matter for children's outcomes, the research consequences of measuring social origins without including mothers' positions have been difficult to assess, in part because of inadequate data on mothers' occupations.

The unresolved debate regarding family level class position is only one of many areas of social mobility research in which further progress remains to be made. For example, a number of scholars have called for social mobility researchers to move beyond descriptive research about social mobility processes (e.g., patterns and extent of mobility) toward more complex issues such as why mobility may be high or low in a given context, or the impact of structural factors that may affect mobility such as the clustering of men and women or racial groups within occupations, occupational segregation, labor market segmentation, or national policies. Although much interesting research remains to be conducted, the lessons of social mobility research to date compellingly illustrate the impact of intergenerational linkages for individuals' life chances and likewise illustrate the importance of national context, historical period, and educational attainment in mediating these intergenerational linkages.

SEE ALSO Volume 1: *College Enrollment; Cultural Capital; Family and Household Structure, Childhood and Adolescence; High School Organization; Parental Involvement in Education; School Tracking;* Volume 2: *Agency; Educational Attainment; Income Inequality; Social Class;* Volume 3: *Wealth.*

BIBLIOGRAPHY

Beller, E., & Hout, M. (2006). Welfare states and social mobility: How educational and social policy may affect cross-national differences in the association between occupational origins and destinations. *Research in Social Stratification and Mobility, 24,* 353–365.

Blau, P., & Duncan, O. D. (1967). *The American occupational structure.* New York: Wiley.

Breen, R. (Ed.). (2004). *Social mobility in Europe.* Oxford, U.K.: Oxford University Press.

Breen, R., & Jonsson, J. O. (2005). Inequality of opportunity in comparative perspective: Recent research on educational attainment and social mobility. *Annual Review of Sociology, 31,* 223–243.

Erikson, R., & Goldthorpe, J. H. (1992). *The constant flux.* Oxford, U.K.: Clarendon Press.

Erikson, R., Goldthorpe, J. H., & Portocarero, L. (1979). Intergenerational class mobility in three Western societies: England, France, and Sweden. *The British Journal of Sociology, 30,* 415–441.

Featherman, D. L., Jones, F. L., & Hauser, R. M. (1975). Assumptions of social mobility research in the U.S.: The case of occupational status. *Social Science Research, 4,* 329–360.

Ganzeboom, H. B. G., Treiman, D. J., & Ultee, W. C. (1991). Comparative intergenerational stratification research: Three generations and beyond. *Annual Review of Sociology, 17,* 277–302.

Gerber, T. P., & Hout, M. (2004). Tightening up: Declining class mobility during Russia's market transition. *American Sociological Review, 69,* 677–703.

Hout, M. (1988). More universalism, less structural mobility: The American occupational structure in the 1980s. *American Journal of Sociology, 93,* 1358–1400.

Hout, M., & DiPrete, T. A. (2006). What we have learned: RC28's contributions to knowledge about social stratification. *Research in Social Stratification and Mobility, 24,* 1–20.

Hout, M., & Hauser, R. M. (1992). Symmetry and hierarchy in social mobility: A methodological analysis of the Casmin model of class mobility. *European Sociological Review, 8,* 239–266.

Lipset, S. M., & Zetterberg, H. L. (1956). A theory of social mobility. *Transactions of the Third World Congress of Sociology, 3,* 155–177.

Sorensen, A. (1994). Women, family, and class. *Annual Review of Sociology, 20,* 27–47.

Sorokin, P. A. (1959). *Social and cultural mobility.* Glencoe, IL: Free Press.

Weeden, K. A., & Grusky, D. B. (2005). The case for a new class map. *American Journal of Sociology, 111,* 141–212.

Western, M., & Wright, E. O. (1994). The permeability of class boundaries to intergenerational mobility among men in the United States, Canada, Norway, and Sweden. *American Sociological Review, 49,* 606–629.

Wright, E. O. (2005). Foundations of neo-Marxist class analysis. In E. O. Wright (Ed.), *Approaches to class analysis* (pp. 4–30). Cambridge, U.K.: Cambridge University Press.

Emily Beller

SOCIAL MOVEMENTS

Humans have always found ways to register their discontent, ranging in scope from jokes and complaints to sweeping revolutions. But in the modern world they have unprecedented access to arenas, resources, ideas, and know-how that allow them to form collective efforts known as social movements. Access to all these ingredients differs according to how old people are and when they were born.

Social movements are sustained and intentional efforts to foster or retard social changes, primarily outside the normal institutional channels encouraged by authorities. For instance, gay rights advocates have used a variety of tactics, from monitoring media portrayals of gay men and lesbians to challenging discrimination to pursuing marriage rights in the courts; at the same time, however, their opponents have tried to fight these efforts and roll back any gains resulting from them. Movements are *sustained* in that they differ from single events such as riots or rallies. Their persistence often allows them to develop formal organizations, but they may also operate through informal social networks. The intentionality of these efforts links movements to culture and strategy: People have ideas about what they want and how to get it, ideas that are filtered through culture as well as psychology.

Movements have purposes, even when these have to do with transforming members themselves (as in many religious movements) rather than the world outside the movement. Although many scholars view movements as progressive, dismissing regressive efforts as countermovements, this distinction seems arbitrary and unsustainable. Finally, movements are noninstitutional, distinguished from political parties and interest groups that are a regular part of many political systems, even though movements frequently create these other entities and often maintain close relationships to them. Most movements today deploy some tactics within mainstream institutions, and "noninstitutional" protest itself is often quite institutionalized.

GENERATIONS OF THEORIES

Theories of discontent have always reflected the form a protest was taking at the time, as well as each writer's own sympathies and political participation. In 17th- and 18th-century Europe, thinkers such as John Locke (1632–1704) and Jean-Jacques Rousseau (1712–1778) understood the collective expression of discontent primarily as a battle against tyrannical rulers. The economic and social dimensions of emerging nation-states were not yet distinguished from the political dimensions, so protest was seen as a political act. The concept of the social movement was not yet possible.

With accelerated urbanization in the 19th century, European intellectuals were increasingly alarmed at the regular rebellions of artisans, developing the concept of the *mob*. Crowds came to be seen as a form of madness that caused individuals to act differently than they would when alone. A more sophisticated generation of crowd theorists emerged in the mid-20th century, largely in response to communism and fascism, which were viewed as forms of mass society. Until the late 1960s the dominant view of protest overemphasized the noninstitutional dimension of movements, lumping them together with fads, panics, and other collective behavior. Explicitly or implicitly, crowds remained at the heart of this vision.

Everything changed in the 1960s. Social movements were everywhere, no longer populated by working-class persons but by middle-class faces. Because many of these movements were filled with young people, middle-age scholars often dismissed them as a sign of immaturity or youthful rebelliousness. Many scholars saw these young people as unsure of their identities and in search of an ideology that would provide one (Klapp, 1969). Conservative scholars saw the young populations of less developed nations with even greater alarm, viewing them as potential sources of revolution.

A generation of scholars more sympathetic to protestors prevailed from the 1970s to the late 1990s, highlighting the sustained dimension of movements by linking them to the core political and economic institutions and cleavages of society. No longer grouped with fads, movements were now nearly indistinguishable from political parties. They were thought to reflect deep structural (and objective) interests—especially regarding class, but also gender, race, and (eventually) sexual preference. What mattered most was how they mobilized resources and interacted with government.

Alain Touraine (1977) offered a perspective that linked contemporary movements to social change instead of organizational forms. He proposed that postindustrial societies experienced conflicts over cultural understandings, especially the direction in which a society's increasing self-control would take it. The technocrats of capital and government sought profit and efficiency as ends above all else, whereas protestors viewed these as mere means. They feared that society's goals—democracy, health, quality of life—were being ignored and crowded out. Touraine's vision helped scholars recognize the significance of new social movements, such as ecology, feminism, or gay rights, populated by a political generation less concerned with personal material benefits than its elders.

Inspired by the number of young people involved in the 1960s movements, scholars in the years since have used several different age-related concepts to understand how protest and age are related: youth movements, biographical availability, protest cohorts, and political generations.

YOUTH MOVEMENTS

Young people have been associated with social change throughout human history. They are prominent actors not only in protest but in wars, revolutions, migrations, urbanization, and technological change. They raise anxieties in their elders, who are never sure that young people will be fully and properly socialized into existing norms, roles, and institutions. They are a frequent subject of moral panics, in which they are assailed for their supposedly deviant music, motorbikes, drugs, clothes, and other aspects of youthful lifestyles (Cohen, 1972). The concept of *youth movements* has proven useful for scholars who study anything from scouting to ethnic and religious groups.

With the expansion of higher education in the affluent world during the 1950s and 1960s, the similar concept of *student movement* emerged as a way of understanding youthful political participation (Lipset & Altbach, 1969).

Some analyses emphasized the ideas to which students were exposed, others their physical concentration, and yet others their lack of a direct economic role during a lengthening period of childhood and adolescence.

Placed together in the relatively sheltered environment of colleges and universities, students had what scholars later came to recognize as free spaces in which ideas about goals and tactics could develop while being sheltered from immediate repression by authorities. In such places, people can develop movement cultures, including an ideology, an emotional sensibility, optimism about change, a collective identity and sense of community, and tastes in tactics. Free spaces foster the democratic skills (public speaking, ability to compromise, and a sense of agency) considered vital to civic participation.

There was an echo of these ideas in the theories of *new social movements* (Melucci, 1980). Many activists in these movements were people in their 30s who had been involved in the student movements of the 1960s and were looking for less dramatic ways to pursue their political goals. Others were too young to have been active in the 1960s and were trying to avoid what they saw as the romantic, utopian hopes (and subsequent burnout) of the earlier movements. This new wave of movements tried to avoid creating media stars—by rotating leadership positions, for instance—and they tried to develop group procedures that encouraged input from everyone (sometimes dubbed the *feminist process*) to avoid even informal domination by a handful of leaders.

BIOGRAPHICAL AVAILABILITY

The disproportionate participation by young people in many movements is sometimes interpreted as due to their biographical availability. In other words, they have the free time to participate. They are less likely to have a job from which they might be fired, small children to care for, or a spouse with whom they would like to spend time. Biographical availability implies that a person has few countervailing ties to counteract the pull of mobilization. Others have observed that many movements have a disproportionate number of students and the self-employed.

Such factors do not fully account for life course differences in participation, however. After all, retirees and empty-nesters may have as much biographical availability as young people, but it is not clear that their participation rises as a result (although there has been little research on this). Young people may be more likely than older persons to participate in high-risk, high-cost protest activities that might land them in jail or inspire violence from authorities.

Protestors tend to develop tastes in tactics that remain fairly stable as they change from movement to movement, even as they face successes and defeats that might suggest the need to change tactics (Jasper, 1997, pp. 174, 240). They attach moral worth to tactics; means are never viewed as neutral. Such tastes are often specific to cohorts and generations. College students who joined the U.S. civil rights movement, for example, retained a fondness for the kind of confrontational sit-in that they had pioneered, whereas older participants continued to favor marches and lawsuits.

The contrast between these two kinds of effect reflects the difference between aging life course effects and cohort or generational effects, which need to be combined for more robust models (Braungart & Braungart, 1986). College students in the 1960s may have joined the antiwar movement in part because of their biographical availability, but that participation in turn left them more politically radical than the generations that preceded or followed them.

PROTEST COHORTS

Different people are recruited to movements at different times, forming distinct cohorts that are often age-related. Most protest groups contain rival factions, which may have different goals or different tastes in tactics (Jasper, 1997). Factions often develop as newcomers join a movement, demanding internal as well as external changes. Each new cohort reacts to the existing routines and sensibilities within the movement as well as to problems in the broader society. Movements may grow more radical because of new recruits bringing a more combative mentality to them or because these recruits have identities based on being radical, although other theories emphasize rebuffs by the state as the key source of radicalization. These new radical flanks can have advantages as well as disadvantages.

Nancy Whittier (1995) has described the impact of successive cohorts on the women's movement in Columbus, Ohio:

> Each micro-cohort entered the women's movement at a specific point in its history, engaged in different activities, had a characteristic political culture, and modified the feminist collective identity. Each defined the type of people, issues, language, tactics, or organizational structures that "qualified" as feminist differently. Presentation of self, use of language, and participation in political culture help to identify individuals with their micro-cohorts. (p. 56)

This kind of internal conflict can preoccupy or even destroy a movement, but it can also lead to innovation and clarification.

Anti-war Demonstrators. *Demonstrators carry banners and signs during a protest against the Iraq war.* AP IMAGES.

POLITICAL GENERATIONS

The idea that there are political generations marked by formative events is associated with Karl Mannheim (1893–1947), who was primarily concerned with the sources of human knowledge. The concept has remained useful as a way of understanding cultural meanings and collective memories, as events leave a special mark on those who, in late adolescence and early adulthood, are coming of age politically. Wars, revolutions, economic depressions, and other dramatic upheavals define political generations, as, in more modest ways, do smaller events such as a presidential campaign or the assassination of a significant social or political figure.

Mass migrations can also shape the experience of a generation in ways that affect its politics. For example, in the United States during the early and mid-20th century, African Americans left the rural south in large numbers for industrial cities, most of them in the North, generating resources and autonomy that helped produce the civil rights movement.

One key experience that shapes a generation is its political activity early in life. Considerable research has shown that those who were politically active in the generation that came of age in the 1960s have remained more politically active throughout their life course (Fendrich & Lovoy, 1988; Jennings, 1987; Whalen & Flacks, 1984). They remain more knowledgeable about politics and retain some of their early political leanings. They also are more likely to have personal identities that involve politics, the know-how to participate, and ties to social networks of others who remain politically active. Such networks provide both information and emotional encouragement to continued activism. Often, they move directly from one movement to another, related movement, taking their expertise with them; in other cases they remain active even when their movement is in the "doldrums" (Rupp & Taylor, 1987).

Of course, the existence of this political generation does not preclude age effects as well: Their participation has remained high but may also have been channeled into different mechanisms of action at different ages. The same people who, in 1968, were in the streets trying to shut down their universities might now be trying to bring about change by serving on their local school board. Again, age and generation effects interact.

INTERGENERATIONAL CONFLICT

Although early theories of youth movements tended to see them as the result of immaturity and other psychological dynamics of participants themselves, more recent perspectives find real conflicts between generations. Structuralists tend to emphasize objective conflicts between generations and suggest that age is a core source of inequality in modern societies (Turner, 1989). A number of public policies affect the distribution of rewards and protections to people of different ages. Such policies deal with mandatory retirement ages, pensions, age-related competency, youth unemployment, school spending, and so on. Legislation may prohibit discrimination on the basis of age. Although all societies face issues of how to distribute honor and material benefits across age groups, these issues can inspire mobilization in a world of social movements. In the United States, war veterans and the elderly formed early movements to promote pensions and other welfare-state protections, and they continue to support other groups that pursue their interests.

Attitude surveys have been used in a more cultural approach to intergenerational conflict that emphasizes differences in basic values and political priorities. The largest research project along these lines stems from Ronald Inglehart's (1977) post-materialist thesis that generations of Europeans and Americans born after World War II (1939–1945) developed a feeling of security, or a freedom from warfare and material want, which allowed them to care more about their quality of life. Instead of placing priority on jobs and material well-being, they would criticize industrial society, hierarchy, and pollution in favor of greater political participation, peace, and a cleaner environment. The supposed generation gap of the 1960s and 1970s thus stemmed from differences in basic values. Later generations do not necessarily share the post-materialism of the 1960s generation, however, suggesting that there were special features of the period in which the latter came of age—a generational effect rather than a once-and-for-all change in history.

FUTURE RESEARCH

A number of themes in current research on social movements are linked to life course research. For example, emotions, a popular topic for research, underlie many of the dynamics of age and generational effects. These might involve basic emotional commitments, such as those to families, friends, and fellow participants. They might involve different emotional reactions to grievances, which might differ by age in kind or intensity. Few have tested the popular stereotypes of younger people as having stronger emotional reactions, for instance, or of older

people as more tempered by experience or family obligations. In addition, the events that define political generations are emotional as well as cognitive, often because of the moral shocks they trigger.

Because the current trend in movement research is to emphasize the ways that participants are involved in other institutions, research might investigate how these ties influence protest activities at different ages. Middle-age adults, for instance, might have positions of authority that they can use to further their ends without turning to extra-institutional outlets. The young and the old might lack such positions. The young might also lack resources that would allow them to pursue more institutionalized mechanisms, such as trade unions, again pushing them into noninstitutional means. Young people, however, might be more adept with newer media, such as the Internet, which has proven an efficient means for spreading information and mobilizing people. Research along these lines promises to overcome an unfortunate, inhibiting separation between research on movements and on more institutionalized participation.

Finally, life course research, with its frequent use of robust longitudinal techniques such as panel data, can redress weaknesses in movement research. Much of the latter depends on case studies of movements. When individuals are the unit of the analysis, they are often sampled on the dependent variable: participation. More research is needed comparing those who are mobilized with those who are not, at different points in their lives. Life course and movement research have the potential to interact in promising, fruitful ways.

SEE ALSO Volume 1: *Identity Development; Political Socialization;* Volume 2: *Mannheim, Karl; Political Behavior and Orientations, Adulthood;* Volume 3: *Age, Period, Cohort Effects.*

BIBLIOGRAPHY

Braungart, R. G., & Braungart, M. M. (1986). Life course and generational politics. *Annual Review of Sociology, 12,* 205–231.

Cohen, S. (1972). *Folk devils and moral panics: The creation of the mods and rockers.* London: MacGibbon and Kee.

Esler, A. (1984). "The truest community": Social generations as collective mentalities. *Journal of Political and Military Sociology, 12,* 99–112.

Fendrich, J. M., & Lovoy, K. L. (1988). Back to the future: Adult political behavior of former student activists. *American Sociological Review, 53*(5), 780–784.

Feuer, L. S. (1969). *The conflict of generations: The character and significance of student movements.* New York: Basic Books.

Inglehart, R. (1977). *The silent revolution: Changing values and political styles among Western publics.* Princeton, NJ: Princeton University Press.

Jasper, J. M. (1997). *The art of moral protest: Culture, biography, and creativity in social movements.* Chicago: University of Chicago Press.

Jennings, M. K. (1987). Residues of a movement: The aging of the American protest generation. *American Political Science Review, 81*(2), 367–382.

Klapp, O. E. (1969). *Collective search for identity.* New York: Holt, Rinehart and Winston.

Lipset, S. M., & Altbach, P. G. (Eds.). (1969). *Students in revolt.* Boston: Houghton Mifflin.

Mannheim, K. (1952). The problem of generations. In P. Kecskemeti (Ed.), *Essays on the sociology of knowledge.* London: Routledge, Kegan Paul. (Original work published 1928)

McAdam, D. (1982). *Political process and the development of Black insurgency, 1930–1970.* Chicago: University of Chicago Press.

Melucci, A. (1980). The new social movements: A theoretical approach. *Social Scientific Information, 19*(2), 199–226.

Rupp, L. J., & Taylor, V. (1987). *Survival in the doldrums: The American women's rights movement, 1945 to the 1960s.* New York: Oxford University Press.

Ryder, N. B. (1965). The cohort as a concept in the study of social change. *American Sociological Review, 30*(6), 843–861.

Sherrod, L. R., (Ed.). (2006). *Youth activism: An international encyclopedia.* Westport, CT: Greenwood Press.

Smelser, N. J. (1968). *Essays in sociological explanation.* Englewood Cliffs, NJ: Prentice Hall.

Touraine, A. (1977). *The self-production of society* (D. Coltman, Trans.). Chicago: University of Chicago Press.

Turner, B. S. (1989). Ageing, status politics, and sociological theory. *British Journal of Sociology, 40*(4), 588–606.

Whalen, J., & Flacks, R. (1984). Echoes of rebellion: The liberated generation grows up. *Journal of Political and Military Sociology, 12*, 61–78.

Whittier, N. (1995). *Feminist generations: The persistence of the radical women's movement.* Philadelphia: Temple University Press.

James M. Jasper

SOCIAL NETWORKS

Social network analysis (SNA) provides a direct means for examining the structural foundations of society. A social network is a collection of relationships—referred to as *edges*—connecting individuals, or aggregations of individuals (e.g., schools or businesses)—known as *nodes*. Analyzing social networks allows researchers to shift their focus from nodes and their characteristics to the spaces between them. SNA analysts examine the presence or absence of edges within the spaces between nodes and systematically analyze the patterning of those relationships within a studied population. SNA may include a variety of node types, including people, computers, places, and organizations; they focus on edges including friendship, trade, sex, shared memberships, and conversations. SNA draws on this variety of node and edge types to derive theories and methods that are equally applicable to all potential nodes and edges.

A BRIEF HISTORY

Historically, social network analysis draws its roots from a range of academic disciplines—with mathematics, anthropology, and sociology playing especially important roles. Early research during the 1920s and 1930s in education research and observational developmental psychology began building the language of *sociometry* to describe formal properties of social organization within small groups (Moreno, 1934). Later anthropologists—along with others studying kinship in the 1940s and 1950s—dominated networks research with an aim to provide general models of the patterned relationships in kinship structures across a wide range of societies (White, 1963).

The 1970s saw a rapid increase in studies incorporating network ideas, shaped in large part by Harrison White and his students. Among the foundational pieces from this period was one of the most readily cited sociological findings—the *strength of weak ties* that demonstrated that people are more likely to benefit in job searches from their acquaintances than from their closer relationships. Granovetter (1973) argued the mechanism for this finding is based on strong personal relationships' likelihood of high redundancy. He shows that weak social ties are much less likely to overlap, therefore branching out into wider ranges of the population, and thus are more productive for seeking novel information.

Simultaneous and subsequent developments in network studies also arose in fields such as developmental psychology, education, communications, business, and most recently—physics and biology (Freeman, 2004). The past few decades have seen rapid growth in the volume of network studies produced and the range of topics they address—including the diffusion of innovations, the spread of infectious diseases, friendship and discussion networks, modes of social influence, interlocking boards of directors, and the evolution of academic disciplines. The formation of the *International Network for Social Network Analysis* and founding of the *Social Networks* journal helped consolidate these disparate scholars and range of topics into a relatively cohesive field (Wellman, 2000). Freeman (2004) provides an illuminating historical social network analysis of the development of the SNA field.

A NEW PARADIGM?

Social science is driven primarily by only a few prevailing orientations to research—known as *paradigms*, which provide the frameworks within which scientists can produce individually testable theoretical propositions—referred to as *hypotheses*. Further, a paradigm also generally lays the ground rules for the criteria to evaluate those hypotheses—inferring particular methodological approaches. Network scholars have generated numerous theories that have been readily incorporated into existing models of social science—such as the importance of social capital. Others have suggested that SNA provides only a new methodological tool kit for evaluating the variety of existing social theories. These new methods are important because, although many social theories are fundamentally relational in nature, current methodological approaches focus almost exclusively on individual, independent, unconnected nodes.

However, Wellman and Berkowitz (1988), among others, have consistently argued that SNA provides more than simply new theories and methods. Instead, they contend that the fundamental shift of researchers' focus from nodes to edges lays the foundations for a new research paradigm. Freeman agrees with this notion of networks as a new paradigm for social research, which he outlines as being demarcated by its: (a) focus on the structural properties of patterned links between actors, (b) empirical derivation of those patterns; (c) dependence on the graphical representation of those relationships—both intuitively and illustratively; and (d) use of complex mathematical/computational analytic methods (Freeman, 2004).

GATHERING NETWORK DATA

To incorporate network ideas into traditional research methods, surveys of individuals can gather information about portions of their respondents' networks, simply treating this *local network data* as they would any other individual characteristic. Local network studies generally collect information about the focal individual—known as an *ego*—and their ties, such as the number and types of relationships they have, descriptions of the others—known as *alters*—with whom they have those relationships, and possibly details about the existing relationships between those alters.

Researchers interested in analyzing connections that extend beyond an initially sampled population typically expand their efforts in one of two ways. *Partial network data* not only collects information from index respondents about their alters, but also subsequently recruits those alters into the study and asks about their relationships—a process that can be repeated as many or few times as desired. Alternately, *complete network data* defines the boundaries of the population to be studied, then enumerates and describes all of the relationships within that entire population.

These three data collection strategies require vastly different techniques and amount of resources to gather (Morris, 2004). They each also produce substantially different types of data, which provide different options from the varied analytic strategies described below. The

aims of the research can help the investigators consider these important tradeoffs.

ANALYZING SOCIAL NETWORKS

The techniques available for SNA are numerous but can be classified roughly into measures that focus on node and edge composition, those that describe node position, and those that describe properties of the full network. Several handbooks detail the numerous strategies and the particular individual metrics available for SNA (Carrington, Scott, & Wasserman, 2005; Wasserman & Faust, 1994).

The first set of measures available provide a means for describing the relations between an ego and its alters. These measures capture properties that describe the composition and distribution of the nodes and edges in this bounded set. One such example calculates the density of ties, which compares the number of ties observed to the number possible. These composition measures can be calculated for local, partial, and complete network data, but the additional measures described later in this entry cannot be calculated for local network data.

When examining partial or complete networks, measures exist for describing both the position of an individual node in the network and characteristics of the entire network. Individual positional measures describe how a particular node is connected to all of the others. Centrality is a common class of measures capturing a node's position, which conceptually measures the node's comparative importance in a network. One conceptualization of centrality is based on how many edges a node has. In addition, the edges in a network can be thought of as pipes through which a *bit* can pass—such as an idea, money, or a disease. With this in mind, other variants of centrality determine the likelihood of a particular node being able to pass that *bit* to other members of the network, or the probability of a bit reaching that node (e.g., transmitting or contracting a disease, respectively). A key insight in network studies is that many individual position measures are not directly related to each other, even within a single class of measures such as centrality (i.e., having many friends is not the same as having the *right* friends) (Freeman, 1979).

Additionally, other measures focus on describing the patterns of connectivity in an entire network. One example of this type—*cohesion*—describes methods for identifying subgroups in a network that are more readily connected to each other than to the rest of the nodes in the network.

Another set of measurements assesses local composition patterns that are known to produce an impact on potential full network connectivity patterns. One of the most common of this type—*transitivity*—takes advantage of the insight that a friend (*k*) of a friend (*j*) is likely a friend (of ego–*i*), and calculates the proportion of observed edges for all possible node-pairs (*i*–*k*) in an entire network, given the existence of two edges that share a node (*i*–*j* and *j*–*k*) (Holland & Leinhardt, 1972). Virtually all of the measures described here can be calculated separately for undirected edges (e.g., had a conversation) and directed edges (e.g., gave money to); many vary depending on whether analyzed as directed or not.

NETWORK VISUALIZATION

Network data can be visualized just to illustrate the patterns found in the data, or they can be used as a means to assist in the discovery of those patterns. These visualizations typically use dots to depict nodes and lines connecting those dots to illustrate edges. Early network scholars manually produced visualizations; however, computer routines for producing these representations have become increasingly automated and are even being developed for displaying dynamic networks (Bender-DeMoll & McFarland, 2006). Network visualization techniques employ layout algorithms meant to suppress noninformative patterns, while drawing attention to the meaningful.

NETWORKS AND LIFE COURSE RESEARCH

Many insights available using SNA have been slow to influence research not explicitly focused on developing network methods. This is largely because population-based studies common in social science use strategies to identify samples, which rarely are able to connect study participants to one another with any relationship information gathered. This limits analytic possibilities only to those developed for *local network data*. To overcome this limitation, institutional settings have been particularly attractive for network data collection, disproportionately including young people (e.g., in schools) and the elderly (e.g., in nursing homes or medical facilities). Further, because network data are often more intensive to gather, network data spanning long periods of extended observation are rare. Because of these limitations, existing work incorporating SNA into life course research typically focuses on networks immediately surrounding specific life course events, rather than network trajectories over the passage of time.

In adolescents, existing studies focus on key transitions and turning points that presumptively shape later life trajectories. For example, one substantial area of literature examines the important roles social networks play in teens' uptake and frequency of substance abuse. Network studies have confirmed that peer friendships substantially influence individuals' decisions to begin smoking and to use other substances. Perhaps more important for later health outcomes is the finding that those who do smoke, drink, or take drugs are more likely to subsequently choose friends who share those behaviors than those who do not (Kirke, 2004). As a result, having started, teens are then more likely to spend time with other teens who also abuse substances, thus decreasing their likelihood of quitting.

The time of sexual debut and subsequent sexual activity is another key transition that generally takes place in adolescence; it has been linked to a variety of later life outcomes. Therefore, many studies have examined the role teens' social networks play in determining the timing of sexual debut, and in regulating who might become potential sexual partners. On the latter point, for example, one study demonstrates that high schoolers' sexual partnering behaviors often adhere to unarticulated local configuration prohibitions (e.g., they do not partner with a former partner's current partner's former partner, described as *avoiding closed four-cycles*) (Bearman, Moody, & Stovel, 2004). This effectively creates *spanning-trees* in connecting most of the sexually active population to each other indirectly (through partners' partners' partners, and so on). This structure has direct implications for the potential spread of sexually transmitted infections in high schools, because those pathogens with long infectivity windows (e.g., herpes or human papillomavirus) are more likely to spread within adolescent populations than other pathogens with shorter windows (e.g., human immunodeficiency virus), which are likely to have a more limited spread because the timing of relationships readily breaks apart long singly-connected chains.

Some work addresses how social network patterns change over the life course, particularly in response to specific age-staged events. For example, studies of *dyadic withdrawal* demonstrate that networks of married and cohabiting people are more constricted than those observed before partnering, and likely increasingly overlap with their partner (Kalmijn, 2003). Furthermore, the segregation of social networks into age homogeneous clusters "reflect[s] institutional, spatial and cultural segregation associated with a tripartite life course" (Hagestad & Uhlenberg, 2005). These age configurations are especially exacerbated in nonkin relationships and slightly muted when limited to kin-only ties.

NEW AGENDAS

Two of the most important ongoing areas of SNA work are developing methods for analyzing dynamic networks and generating statistical methods for analyzing network data. In addition to expanding the umbrella of SNA, these efforts are also likely to help bridge some of the gaps to more ready inclusion of network ideas into life course research. They happen to coincide with the completion of additional waves of several ongoing longitudinal studies that have been collecting data for a number of years—such as the National Longitudinal Study of Adolescent Health, which has an explicit focus on gathering network data (Bearman, Jones, & Udry, 1997). Each of these advances combines to provide possibilities for researchers to explore how adolescent social networks contribute to outcomes later in life: both in terms of durability of previously observed behaviors and the contribution of behaviors not observed in respondents' adolescence. These new techniques and newly available data will also provide opportunities to examine how social networks change throughout the life course and the ways those changes differentially influence behavior and trajectories.

USING NETWORKS FOR GOOD

Valente, Hoffman, Ritt-Olsen, Lichtman, and Johnson (2003) demonstrate that health promotion programs can strategically use the observed structure of social networks to enhance the spread of targeted information. However, the research remains inconclusive regarding how readily these strategies can be applied to efforts that are more general and whether they successfully transition from attitudinal shifts to behavioral change. Present uncertainties aside, more explicitly examining individuals' social network properties, and employing that knowledge in outreach efforts, at worst will help researchers better understand the potential that social networks hold for changing the relational contexts within which people experience critical life events. Further, these approaches may also provide key points of entry (relational, not temporal, although given the advances described earlier in this entry, in the best case scenario, perhaps a combination of the two) into individuals' lives to intervene for altering trajectories or providing alternative means for managing experienced events.

SEE ALSO Volume 2: *Friendship, Adulthood; Parent-Child Relationships, Adulthood; Sibling Relationships, Adulthood; Social Integration/Isolation, Adulthood; Social Mobility; Social Support, Adulthood;* Volume 3: *Loneliness, Later Life.*

BIBLIOGRAPHY

Bearman, P. S., Moody, J., & Stovel, K. (2004). Chains of affection: The structure of adolescent romantic and sexual networks. *American Journal of Sociology, 110*, 44–91.

Bearman, P. S., Jones, J., & Udry, J. R. (1997). The national longitudinal study of adolescent health: Research design. Retrieved February 1, 2005, from http://www.cpc.unc.edu/projects/addhealth/codebooks

Bender-DeMoll, S., & McFarland, D. A. (2006). The art and science of dynamic network visualization. [Online] *Journal of Social Structure, 7*(1).

Carrington, P. J., Scott, J., & Wasserman, S. (Eds.). (2005). *Models and methods in social network analysis* (Vol. 27) Structural Analysis in the Social Sciences. Grannovetter, M. (Series Ed.). New York: Cambridge University Press.

Freeman, L. C. (1979). Centrality in social networks: Conceptual clarification. *Social Networks, 1*, 215–239.

Freeman, L. C. (2004). *The development of social network analysis: A study in the sociology of science.* Vancouver, BC, Canada: Empirical Press.

Granovetter, M. (1973). The strength of weak ties. *American Journal of Sociology, 81*, 1287–1303.

Hagestad, G. O., & Uhlenberg, P. (2005). The social separation of old and young: A root of ageism. *Journal of Social Issues, 61*, 343–360.

Holland, P. W., & Leinhardt, S. (1972). Some evidence on the transitivity of positive interpersonal sentiment. *American Journal of Sociology, 72*, 1205–1209.

Kalmijn, M. (2003). Shared friendship networks and the life course: An analysis of survey data on married and cohabiting couples. *Social Networks, 25*, 231–249.

Kirke, D. M. (2004). Chain reactions in adolescents' cigarette, alcohol and drug use: Similarity through peer influence or the patterning of ties in peer networks. *Social Networks, 26*, 3–28.

Moody, J. (2005). Dynamic social balance—Freeman Award Plenary. in *Sunbelt XXV—Annual meetings of the International Network for Social Network Analysis.* Redondo Beach, CA. Retrieved December15, 2007, from http://www.soc.duke.edu/jmoody77/presentations/freemantalk1.ppt

Moreno, J. L. (1934). *Who shall survive?* Washington, DC: Nervous and Mental Disease Publishing Company.

Morris, M. (2004). *Network epidemiology: A handbook for survey design and data collection.* New York: Oxford University Press.

Valente, T. W., Hoffman, B. R., Ritt-Olsen, A., Lichtman, K., & C. Anderson Johnson, C. (2003). Effects of a social-network method for group assignment strategies on peer-led tobacco prevention programs in schools. *American Journal of Public Health, 93*, 1837–1843.

Wasserman, S., & Faust, K. (1994). *Social network analysis: Methods and applications.* Vol. 8: *Structural Analysis in the Social Sciences.* Grannovetter, M. (Series Ed.). New York: Cambridge University Press.

Wellman, B. (2000). Networking network analysts: How INSNA (the International Network for Social Network Analysis) came to be. *Connections 23*, 20–31.

Wellman, B., & Berkowitz, S. D. (1988). *Social structures: A network approach.* Vol. 2: *Structural Analysis in the Social Sciences.* Grannovetter, M. (Series Ed.). New York: Cambridge University Press.

White, H. C. (1963). *An anatomy of kinship.* Englewood Cliffs, NJ: Prentice Hall.

jimi adams

SOCIAL STRUCTURE/ SOCIAL SYSTEM

The concept of the life course is predicated on an age-graded sequence of events and roles that are embodied in social structures; these structures vary from family relations at a personal or individual level to age-graded educational organizations at the wider level. Such social structures can shape life-course experiences over time through such social institutions as marriage to shorter transitions in the life course, including those ranging from educational institutions to paid employment. These popular assumptions regarding the life course are nonetheless embedded in wider theoretical underpinnings developed by sociological approaches related to social systems and structures.

Social structure and the subsequent integration with social systems theory are longstanding sociological tenets. *Structuralism* is widely used in the social sciences and that stresses the causal force of the relations among components of an established *system* or in emerging properties with observable patterns. Its application to the understanding of the life course has, however, been less systematic and susceptible to theoretical discrepancies and unanswered criticism.

Various structural approaches are common to anthropology, sociology, psychology, and linguistics. In the first two disciplines, a distinct doctrine emerged that can be traced back to the work of Emile Durkheim (1858–1917) from the turn of the 20th century onward. Structuralism in anthropology in the 1950s and 1960s were inspired by Claude Lévi-Strauss (b. 1908), who was influenced by Durkheim's (1915) *The Elementary Forms of Religious Life*. Durkheim posited that some cognitive structures have the same forms as the components of social elements in everyday life. With more direct relevance to the life course, Mary Douglas (1921–2007) in her 1966 *Purity and Danger* studied social structures in traditional African societies, in biblical-era Judaea, and in modern society. Douglas also hypothesized that people with strong internal and external structural boundaries were more likely to honor clear rites of passage and the rules of taboo.

In sociology, structuralism has experienced a popularity of notable duration. Nonetheless, the underpinning theoretical frameworks have proved to be divergent. A number of early works from a structuralist approach addressed what is now the largely redundant concept of the life cycle. Compared with modern industrial societies, preindustrial communities were understood as displaying a less complex and relatively undifferentiated *cycle of life* and typically involved merely preadult and adult stages (although frequently subdivided into various age-graded sets)—a simple distinction that endured over generations. This basic differentiation was marked out by the near-universal phenomenon of rites of passage.

Writings that emerged from the structural functionalist school of sociology and anthropology enjoyed a noteworthy influence on the study of preindustrial tribal societies—one that accounted for rites of passage largely

in social rather than psychological terms. Thus, Alfred Radcliffe-Browne (1891–1955), for example, focused on what he called the "ritual" prohibition that surrounded rites of passage in numerous societies and that served a positive function for African kinship systems among other sociocultural orders (Radcliffe-Brown, 1940).

Possibly the most significant framework, albeit with a significant degree of modification, was Erik Erikson's (1902–1994) eight-stage model of the life cycle. Erikson attempted to present the maturational relationship linking the biological, chronological, psychological, and social aspects of human progress through the life cycle as a fairly universal phenomenon. The most important aspect of Erikson's model, however, was the emphasis placed on the social context by way of significant structural relationships and institutions in which individual development occurred at any given stage. For instance, in the first year of life it was vital that the infant forged a bond of trust with his or her mother. In the next stage of life, the child ideally developed a level of self-control, which, according to Erikson, was important in the wider process of socialization and beneficial normative aspect of social control.

By the 1950s the exploration and account of social structures within sociology became connected more closely with systems theories. Such theories are largely differentiated in the extent to which they emphasize human agency and inherent normative structures in understanding the maintenance of sociocultural arrangements, as well as accounting for social change and transformation. However, the dominant sociological perspective in which the theoretical framework of social systems has been elaborated is that of structural functionalism. To be sure, one of the weaknesses of structuralism and social systems theory in its various forms has been its failure to provide a systematic account of the life course. Nonetheless, it has provided a broad framework by which to understand everyday life experiences in a range of institutional settings, including bureaucracies, educational establishments, the professions, and the family and small groups. It has also furnished insights into life experiences in the context of the dynamics of modernization, social evolution, economic change, and social disequilibrium.

Although structural functional theory has taken various forms, a few basic elements are central to its framework. Theorists who adopt this paradigm focus on the origins and maintenance of the integral and indispensable parts, structures, institutions, and cultural patterns that forge elaborate systems of norms, values, and behavior. In the most detailed formulation of social systems, Talcott Parsons (1902–1979) understood social life to be an aggregate of normative social structures and a functioning system that may vary from one society to another according to levels of coherence, integration, and performance (Parsons, 1955).

Parsons's major contribution to the theoretical frameworks was in identifying four universal social functions that he deemed universal and indispensable if any social system was to survive ideally as a coherent and functioning whole: *goal attainment* (political and decision-making institutions that are designed to determine societal goals and priorities), *adaptation* (institutions geared to transforming the material environment), *latency* (institutions of socialization and social control), and *integration* (institutions that manage and coordinate numerous social structures and individual agents).

Although providing little by way of a systematic analysis of the life course, Parsons laid the foundations for further theoretical speculation and empirical work not least of all in identifying specific and universal socio-structural patterns that allowed people to make sense of life events and biographically structure their lives. For example, the family, for Parsons, was one of the most obvious institutions in this respect and provided a site of both latency and integration throughout life. The marriage and the establishment of the family of procreation, alongside the nurturing or early socialization of the child, denoted adult maturity and social responsibility for both genders. This was clear in Parsons's (1955) controversial account of the structuring of gender roles throughout the life course. He also maintained that in nuclear families the feminine role is expressive and the masculine, instrumental. Women thereby fulfill internal familial functions; men provide financial support and provide damilial adaptation to the society. The idea of the modern nuclear family, as well as other social institutions, being underpinned by the dominant value of instrumental individualism inspired other commentators in tracing the implications for declining extended family relationships (Beck & Beck-Gernsheim, 2004).

For Parsons, latency varies according to the evolutional stage of any given society. In premodern societies, this function tends to be carried out informally in everyday life in which typically the young learn by the instruction and examples of their elders. In modern societies, according to Parsons, socialization and social control become the preserve of formal educational institutions.

Parsons's discussion of latency also exemplifies how specific social structures or arrangement shape the life course at certain stages of life. Although clearly demarcated rites of passage take initiates from one stage of life to another and have a certain educational function for new responsibilities in premodern societies, in industrialized societies such responsibilities are more likely to be informed by new rights and duties framed in formal regulation related to specific ages. This clearly includes age restrictions related to voting, the age of consent, and marriage. Duties largely relate to civil responsibility in respect of codify laws.

Structural functionalist theories have also been applied to later life and are characterized by Elaine Cumming and Wiliam Henry's *disengagement theory* (1961) and again can be understood in terms of latency and integration. This theory implies that the major social passage in later life allows society to promote its own orderly functioning by removing older people from productive economic roles; such people welcome the opportunity to disengage at a time of declining physical and mental capacities.

Although the life work of Parsons was dedicated to establishing a coherent structuralist theory, his starting point was a general theory of social action in understanding relationships and behavior. In essence, this meant tracing any meaningful human conduct to four basic elements of ends, means, norms, and conditions that implemented action. Despite the attempt to understand social action, Parsonian and other system theories are relatively weak in conceptualizing and taking into account human agency. Thus were developed actor-oriented and dynamic systems theories, including Buckley's (1967), *modern systems theory*, Archer's (1995) *morphogenetic* theory, and the *actor-system-dynamics* (Burn, Baumgartner, & DeVille, 1985) that sought to rectify the perceived weakness of structural functionalism. In turn, few such alternatives systematically addressed the subject of the life course.

To conclude, the attempt to uncover structural determinants of the life course has been handicapped by disagreements among sociologists and anthropologists over the precise meaning of social structure. Without consensus about the important dimensions along which social structures vary, the focus of scholarship has been scattered and has not given rise to many systematic research traditions regarding the life course (although some works specialize in some aspects of it) or to relevant research in countries outside North America and Western Europe.

Other weaknesses are also observable. One problem highlighted in structuralist/social systems accounts of the life course is neglect of the so-called cohort effect, which points to the historical time and place in which experiences of the life course are forged. Another problem involves underpinning typologies: The "traditional" society amounted to a loose, catch-all typology, ranging from tribal groups, to settled agricultural societies, to large-scale feudal orders. This invariably weakened the opportunity to engage in systematic comparative accounts of particular concrete examples. No less troublesome was the typology of "modernity" in which structural/social systems theory was embedded. It is one that, in the contemporary setting, appears increasingly redundant as a result of the emergence of late or post-modernity that is practically synonymous with the collapse of social structures and increasingly identified with discontinuity, reversibility, and flexible stages of life in respect to the life course.

SEE ALSO Volume 2: *Social Roles; Sociological Theories;* Volume 3: *Theories of Aging.*

BIBLIOGRAPHY

Archer, M. (1995). *Realist social theory: The morphogenetic approach.* Cambridge, U.K: Cambridge University Press.

Beck, U., & Beck-Gernsheim, E. (2004). Families in a runaway world. In J. Scott, J. Treas, & M. Richards (Eds.), *The Blackwell companion to the sociology of families* (pp.499–541). Oxford, U.K: Blackwell.

Buckley, W. (1967). *Sociology and modern systems theory.* Englewood Cliffs, NJ: Prentice-Hall.

Burn, T., Baumgartner, T., & DeVille, P. (1985). *Man, decisions, and society.* London: Gordon & Breach.

Cumming, E., & Henry, W. (1961). *Growing old: The process of disengagement.* New York: Basic Books.

Durkheim, E. (1912, English trans., 1915). *Les formes elementaires de la vie religieuse* [The elementary forms of religious life]. London: Allen & Unwin.

Douglas, M. (1966). *Purity and danger: An analysis of concepts of pollution and taboo.* London: Routledge.

Lévi-Strauss, C. (1958.) *Anthropologie structurale* [Structural anthropology]. (Claire Jacobson & Brooke Grundfest Schoepf, Trans.). New York: Basic Books.

Parsons, T. (1955). *Family, socialization and interaction process.* Glencoe, IL: Free Press.

Radcliffe-Browne, A. (1940). On social structure. *Journal of the Royal Society of Great Britain and Ireland, 70,* 1–12.

Stephen Hunt

SOCIAL SUPPORT, ADULTHOOD

An old Beatles song states, "I get by with a little help from my friends." Most people rely on family and friends for a variety of resources, including help when needed, companionship, and intimacy. Social and behavioral scientists use the term *social support* to refer to the myriad ways that adults rely on and provide assistance to family and friends. The effects of social support on health and well-being have been intensely studied for more than 30 years. Results of those studies generally find that social support benefits physical and mental health and subjective well-being, but there are important definitional and substantive complexities as well.

DEFINING SOCIAL SUPPORT

Defining social support as the ways in which family and friends assist one another is reasonable conceptually but of limited value for measurement. Early research devoted substantial attention to defining the boundaries of social support and developing ways of validly and reliably measuring it. In the early 21st century there is considerable consensus that two major dimensions underlie the many forms and functions of social support.

One dimension concerns the extent to which social support is an objective phenomenon versus a subjective sense that support is available and of high quality, leading to the distinction between received and perceived support (Krause, 2001; Lin, Ye, & Ensel, 1999). *Received support* refers to the forms and amount of support that individuals obtain from their families and friends. Because it refers to actual supportive transactions, received support is an objective measure, to the extent to which individuals are able to report reliably about it. *Perceived support* refers to individuals' evaluations of the support available to them—whether it is sufficient for their needs, whether it is readily available, and how satisfied they are with the amount and quality of support available to them. Most researchers report that the correlations between received and perceived support are very low (Krause, 2001). Thus, receiving large amounts of assistance from family and friends does not ensure that the recipient feels that support is of sufficient amount or quality. Conversely, many people who receive little or no social support nonetheless believe that more than enough high-quality support is available, if needed.

The second major dimension of social support concerns the specific kinds of assistance provided by family and friends. Three major types of support encompass most supportive transactions (Krause, 2001; Lin et al., 1999). *Emotional support* refers to the various ways that family and friends provide comfort, validation, reassurance, and understanding to the support recipient. *Instrumental support* refers to tangible forms of assistance such as help with meals, housework, transportation, and personal care. *Informational support* refers to the knowledge that family and friends provide to the support recipient. Each type of social support can be measured as either received or perceived. For example, emotional support can be measured in terms of the amount of support received in a given period of time or in terms of the individual's perception of the amount and quality of emotional support that would be available if needed.

ANTECEDENTS OF SOCIAL SUPPORT

The primary prerequisite for social support is a network of close relationships from which support may be obtained.

Most adults marry and have children—although rates of both marriage and fertility have declined among recent cohorts and rates of divorce remain at nearly 50% of all first marriages (Bianchi, Robinson, & Milkie, 2006). Nonetheless, the majority of adults have family members who are both potential sources and potential recipients of support. Similarly, most adults report having two to five close friends on whom they can depend and to whom they confide their problems (Fehr, 2000). Thus, adults typically have a sufficient pool of family and friends who serve as potential support providers.

The composition of one's social network also has important consequences for receipt of various kinds of support. Simply stated, social networks can take one of four forms: absence of both family and friends, family-based networks, friend-based networks, and networks that contain both family and friends. Lack of family and friends obviously precludes supportive relationships. Conversely, the most functional networks, for purposes of social support, include both family and friends. The more interesting patterns are the two forms of single-source networks. In general, family-based networks provide support for longer periods of time than friend-based networks. On the other hand, friend-based networks typically have access to a wider range of resources than family-based networks (Fiori, Antonucci, & Cortina, 2006).

Although most adults have sufficient family and friends to lay the foundation for supportive relationships, not all people are able to sustain the close relationships required. A few adults lack social networks because of either external constraints or internal dispositions. External circumstances occasionally intervene to diminish social networks (e.g., deaths) or to produce networks that lack the capacity to provide social support (e.g., network members are too impaired to offer support). A minority of adults lack social networks because of their own inability to sustain close relationships. The inability to develop and sustain close relationships is strongly linked to a variety of psychological and social characteristics including attachment style (i.e., secure with and trusting of others vs. distrusting and insecure with others), narcissism, and lack of social skills (Sharabany & Bar-Tal, 1982).

It also is difficult to sustain supportive social networks if one lacks the capacity to provide support, as well as receive it. The norm of reciprocity that dictates a relative balance between benefits given and received in social relationships is strongly endorsed in Western societies (Uehara, 1995). Imbalances can take two forms: Overbenefited individuals receive substantially more benefits from their family and friends than they provide to them, whereas underbenefited people pro-

vide substantially more benefits to others than they receive from family and friends. Both forms of imbalance generate feelings of injustice. A long-term pattern of giving more than one receives typically generates feelings of resentment. Sustained receipt of more help than one gives leads to feelings of guilt and dependency. A defining characteristic of intimate relationships is that imbalances in benefits given and received are tolerated for longer than is the case in less intimate relationships. Nonetheless, even the closest relationships can be strained—sometimes to the breaking point—by long-term imbalances in receipt versus provision of social support. Unfortunately, individuals who are mentally or physically disabled invariably need more support from family and friends than they can reciprocate—now or in the future. Consequently, the support available to persons with long-term inability to provide support to others tends to dissipate over time.

SOCIAL SUPPORT ACROSS THE LIFE COURSE

Although children can provide social support in only limited ways, important aspects of social support begin in childhood, as children are taught norms of commitment to family, sharing, and reciprocity. Perhaps most important, children observe supportive exchanges in which family members participate. Most children first experience the receipt and provision of social support at school and have peer-based social networks in which supportive exchanges are common by the time they are teenagers (Sharabany & Bar-Tal, 1982). Although relatively little research explores the early origins of social support, it is clear that most individuals are quite conversant in the provision and receipt of social support before adulthood (Gottlieb, 1991).

Although adults of all ages are engaged in complex patterns of providing and receiving support, the three major segments of adulthood are distinctive in the size and direction of supportive transactions (Silverstein, 2006). Young adulthood is typically characterized by high levels of receiving social support and relatively low levels of providing support outside the nuclear family. Although young adults typically do not live with their parents, the major flow of social support remains from middle-age parents to their adult children. Support from grandparents also is common during young adulthood. Both older generations typically send resources down the genealogical ladder to help young adults establish stable families and careers.

Middle age is characterized by very high levels of support provision and low levels of support receipt. During middle age, individuals typically provide more support than they receive to both their young adult children and their aging parents. Health is typically good and resources peak in middle age. As a result, middle-age persons need and receive relatively little social support. During late life, the ratio of support given versus received changes again. Older adults receive more support, especially from their middle-age children, than they did when they were middle-age. Contrary to common stereotypes, however, most older adults remain intensely involved in providing support to younger generations in their families.

In contrast to family-based patterns of social support, patterns of support among friends change little across adulthood (Mulvaney-Day, Alegria, & Sribney, 2007). Support exchanges are more evenly balanced, in terms of the provision and receipt of support, at all adult ages than those observed among family members. The norm of reciprocity is undoubtedly the major explanation for this pattern. Family relationships may become strained if there is a sustained lack of balance between the provision and receipt of social support, but they rarely end as a result of imbalance. In contrast, friendships are less likely to survive when one friend consistently gives more than the other. These patterns reflect the social norms that family ties should persist over the life course—even in the face of long-term imbalanced support. In contrast, friendships are voluntary relationships that can end with relatively few costs.

CONSEQUENCES OF SOCIAL SUPPORT

Massive amounts of research document the generally positive effects of social support for physical health, mental health, and well-being, but important distinctions and qualifications underlie this general conclusion.

Received Support The vast majority of research focuses on the effects of support received from family and friends. Type of support also is important. *Perceived support* and *emotional support* are consistently positively related to better physical and mental health and greater subjective well-being. They also are associated with the prevention of illness and disability (see Cohen, 2004, for a review) and quicker recovery from mental illness (Bosworth, McQuoid, George, & Steffens 2002; Nasser & Overholser, 2005). Evidence about *instrumental support* is more mixed, with effects differing depending on the outcome of interest. Clearly, receipt of instrumental support can be critical in preventing institutionalization of older adults and reducing the need for formal care arrangements (Bharucha, Pandav, Shen, Dodge, & Ganguli, 2004; Gaugler et al., 2000). Long-term receipt of instrumental support, however, has been reported in some

studies to lead to decreased feelings of mastery and control and decreases in subjective well-being (Silverstein, Chen, & Heller, 1996; Wolff & Agree, 2004). Erosion of psychological assets in the face of sustained dependency is congruent with the norm of reciprocity. *Informational support* increases the range of coping resources utilized and thus indirectly benefits health and well-being. It has not been shown to directly benefit health, however (Krause, 1987; Stewart & Barling, 1996).

Providing Support Although the research base is small, evidence consistently demonstrates that providing support to others benefits not only the recipients but also the provider (Krause, Herzog, & Baker 1992; Lu, 1997). To date, studies of the effects of providing support have primarily examined mental health outcomes. When a loved one needs instrumental support for long periods of time and at high levels of volume, the support provider becomes a caregiver. In contrast to more typical patterns of providing support, care giving often harms physical and mental health (see Pinquart & Sorensen, 2007, for a meta-analysis). Thus, providing support to others—but only at moderate levels—benefits health.

Methodological Issues Several important methodological issues must be considered when examining the consequences of social support. First, the effects of social support need to be examined using longitudinal data, or data sources spanning relatively long time periods. Cross-sectional, or single point in time, studies not only fail to provide evidence that social support affects health at a later point in time, but their results are often misleading. It is not unusual, for example, to observe negative correlations between social support and health in cross-sectional studies. This pattern does not mean that support harms health; rather, it reflects the fact that sicker people need more assistance and mobilize their social networks to provide it. Thus, at any point in time, social support is likely to be related to worse health. When longitudinal data are used, however, investigators typically observe that high levels of support protect against the onset of illness and facilitate illness recovery.

Second, and also related to the need for longitudinal data, is the issue of whether social causation or social selection (or both) are responsible for the positive relationships between social support and health. The social causation perspective views social support as the causal agent and health as the outcome. The social selection perspective argues that healthier people are better equipped to develop and sustain supportive relationships. Evidence to date indicates that both processes operate (Johnson, 1991; Wade & Pevalin, 2004). Social selection is reflected in that, as the norm of reciprocity would predict, social support often dissipates in the context of long-term need for it, but the dominant causal direction is from social support to health.

Finally, there has been long-term debate about whether the effects of social support on health are direct or interactive. Advocates for the direct effects hypothesis argue that social support is always an asset—even when it is not acutely needed, the availability of social support promotes health and well-being. The rationale for the interactive hypothesis is that social support is needed only in times of crisis and it is only in those situations that social support benefits health—a perspective known as the stress-buffering hypothesis. Logically, these are not mutually exclusive hypotheses, and research evidence supports both of them (Hays, Steffens, Flint, Bosworth, & George, 2001; Krause, 2006). In most studies, the direct effect of social support on health is positive and significant. The direct effect of social support on health also may mediate the effects of more distal antecedents of health and well-being. Yang (2006) reported that perceived social support partially mediates the effects of disability on depressive symptoms in late life. Similarly, in a longitudinal study of Swedish men, researchers found that neighborhood-based support mediated the effects of low income on ischemic heart disease (Chaix, Isacsson, Råstam, Lindström, & Merio, 2007). Many studies also report a significant interaction between social support and health, indicating that the effects of social support are stronger during times of crisis.

Given the strong relationships between social support and health, adults would be well-advised to sustain close, personal ties with family and friends. Beyond the pleasure involved, these relationships can help protect health and facilitate recovery when ill. From a policy perspective, it is important that policies support, rather than hinder, preexisting social ties.

SEE ALSO Volume 2: *Friendship, Adulthood; Parent-Child Relationships, Adulthood; Sibling Relationships, Adulthood; Social Integration/Isolation, Adulthood; Social Networks;* Volume 3: *Loneliness, Later Life; Social Integration/Isolation, Later Life; Social Support, Later Life.*

BIBLIOGRAPHY

Bharucha, A. J., Pandav, R., Shen, C., Dodge, H. H., & Ganguli, M. (2004). Predictors of nursing facility admission: A 12-year epidemiological study in the United States. *Journal of the American Geriatrics Society, 52,* 434–439.

Bianchi, S. M., Robinson, J. P., & Milkie, M. A. (2006). *Changing rhythms of American family life.* New York: Russell Sage Foundation.

Bosworth, H. B., McQuoid, D. R., George, L. K., & Steffens, D. C. (2002). Time-to-remission from geriatric depression: Psychosocial and clinical factors. *American Journal of Geriatric Psychiatry, 10,* 551–559.

Chaix, B., Isacsson, S.-O., Råstam, L., Lindström, M., & Merio, J. (2007). Income change at retirement, neighborhood-based social support, and ischaemic heart disease: Results from the prospective cohort study "Men born in 1914." *Social Science and Medicine, 64,* 818–829.

Cohen, S. (2004). Social relationships and health. *American Psychologist, 59,* 676–684.

Fehr, B. (2000). The life cycle of friendship. C. Hendrick & S. S. Hendrick (Eds.), *Close relationships: A sourcebook* (pp. 71–82). Thousand Oaks, CA: Sage.

Fiori, K. L., Antonucci, T. C., & Cortina, K. S. (2006). Social network typologies and mental health among older adults. *Journal of Gerontology: Psychological Sciences, 61B,* P25–P32.

Gaugler, J. E., Edwards, A. B., Femia, E. E., Zarit, S. H., Stephens, M. P., Townsend, A., et al. (2000). Predictors of institutionalization of cognitively impaired elders: Family help and the timing of placement. *Journal of Gerontology: Psychological Sciences, 55B,* P247–P255.

Gottlieb, B. H. (1991). Social support in adolescence. M. E. Colten & S. Gore (Eds.), *Adolescent stress: Causes and consequences* (pp. 281–306). Hawthorne, NY: Aldine de Gruyter.

Hays, J. C., Steffens, D. C., Flint, E. P., Bosworth, H. B., & George, L. K. (2001). Does social support buffer functional decline in elderly patients with unipolar depression? *American Journal of Psychiatry, 158,* 1850–1855.

Johnson, T. P. (1991). Mental health, social relations, and social selection: A longitudinal analysis. *Journal of Health and Social Behavior, 32,* 408–423.

Krause, N. (1987). Chronic financial strain, social support, and depressive symptoms among older adults. *Psychology and Aging, 2,* 185–192.

Krause, N. (2001). Social support. In R. H. Binstock & L. K. George (Eds.), *Handbook of aging and the social sciences* (5th ed., pp. 272–294). San Diego, CA: Academic Press.

Krause, N. (2006). Exploring the stress-buffering effects of church-based and secular social support on self-rated health in late life. *Journal of Gerontology: Social Sciences, 61B,* S35–S43.

Krause, N., Herzog, A. R., & Baker, E. (1992). Providing support to others and well-being in later life. *Journal of Gerontology, 47,* 300–311.

Lin, N., Ye, X., & Ensel, W. M. (1999). Social support and depressed mood: A structural analysis. *Journal of Health and Social Behavior, 40,* 344–359.

Lu, L. (1997). Social support, reciprocity, and well-being. *Journal of Social Psychology, 137,* 618–628.

Mulvaney-Day, N. E., Alegria, M., & Sribney, W. (2007). Social cohesion, social support, and health among Latinos in the United States. *Social Science and Medicine, 64,* 477–495.

Nasser, E. H., & Overholser, James C. (2005). Recovery from major depression: The role of support from family, friends, and spiritual beliefs. *Acta Psychiatrica, 111,* 125–132.

Pinquart, M., & Sorensen, S. (2007). Correlates of physical health of informal caregivers: A meta-analysis. *Journal of Gerontology: Psychological Sciences, 62B,* P126–P137.

Sharabany, R., & Bar-Tal, D. (1982). Theories of the development of altruism: Review, comparisons, and integration. *International Journal of Behavioral Development, 5,* 49–80.

Silverstein, M. (2006). Intergenerational family transfers in social context. R. H. Binstock & L. K. George (Eds.), *Handbook of aging and the social sciences* (6th ed., pp. 165–180). Amsterdam: Elsevier.

Silverstein, M., Chen, X., & Heller, K. (1996). Too much of a good thing? Intergenerational social support and psychological well-being of older parents. *Journal of Marriage and the Family, 58*, 970–982.

Stewart, W., & Barling, J. (1996). Daily work stress, mood, and interpersonal job performance: A mediational model. *Work & Stress, 10*, 336–351.

Uehara, E. A. (1995). Reciprocity reconsidered: Gouldner's "moral norm of reciprocity" and social support. *Journal of Social and Personal Relationships, 12*, 483–502.

Wade, T. J., & Pevalin. D. J. (2004). Marital transitions and mental health. *Journal of Health and Social Behavior, 45*, 155–170.

Wolff, J. L., & Agree, E. M. (2004). Depression among recipients of informal care: The effects of reciprocity, respect, and adequacy of support. *Journal of Gerontology: Social Sciences, 59B*, S173–S180.

Yang, Y. (2006). How does functional disability affect depressive symptoms in late life? The role of perceived social support and psychological resources. *Journal of Health and Social Behavior, 47*, 355–372.

Linda K. George

SOCIOECONOMIC STATUS

SEE Volume 2: *Social Class.*

SOCIOLOGICAL THEORIES

A sociological theory is "a systematically developed consciousness of society and social relations" (Smith 1987, p. 2). Sociology is a multiparadigm science, having developed a number of important general theories. The term *general theory* is used to distinguish theories that aim at a full explanation of why and how societies exist from theories of the middle-range that aim to explain a particular phenomenon and theoretical orientations that serve as guides to research (the life course perspective is an example of a theoretical orientation). Sociological theories may be understood in terms of two competing but complementary commitments: A commitment to science and a commitment to justice. Commitment to science theories focus on discovering general principles of social life without assessing whether outcomes are ultimately just. Commitment to justice theories focus on describing, explaining, and critiquing socially produced inequalities and are frequently spoken of collectively as *conflict theory* because they assume that antagonistic interests are a fundamental feature of social life. Within these two commitments, one can identify a number of paradigms or theories grouped around a shared central concern as presented in Table 1. In addition to these two divisions, social theorists tend to describe a theory as macrosocial or microsocial in its orientation, that is, as concerned with large scale anonymous social structures or with individuals in interaction, and as focused either on agency or on structure.

COMMITMENT TO SCIENCE: POSITIVISM

All positivist theories share five assumptions: the possibility of objective knowledge, the existence of universally applicable principles of social life, the unity of scientific method, the need for value neutrality, and the goal of creating formal expressions of social theory. The central problematic mission for modern positivism is to create a formal social theory that explains human social behavior and societal organization. Two key modern positivist paradigms are the primarily macrosocial paradigm of structural functionalism and the primarily microsocial perspective represented by exchange, rational choice, and social network theories.

Structural functionalism Structural functionalism offers a coherent formal theory focused on the relation between structure and agency, emphasizing structure as the shaper of agency and as functioning to ensure group survival. It proposes a triangular linkage of structure, function, and agency, a theme apparent throughout the work of its major modern progenitor, Talcott Parsons (1902–1979), beginning with his first major work *The Structure of Social Action* (1937). In structural functionalism, *structure* refers to collectively created arrangements generated out of ongoing group life, such as family, education, government, the Catholic church, and gender; *agency* (or action) is behavior undertaken by an individual actor, begun in a situation in which the actor is subject to certain conditions but also has some choice of means (Parsons, 1937) and *function* refers to the consequences of social structures for group life. For instance, gender patterns may be seen as functioning to provide a division of labor within the family. Over time, the concept of function has been elaborated to distinguish among manifest functions (the intended consequences of a structure), latent functions (the unintended consequences), and dysfunctions, which are counterproductive for the society (Merton, 1968). Central to the structural functionalist explanation of the relations among agency, structure, and function are the assumptions that the central dynamics of collective social life are those that serve to reproduce that life and that the conditions constraining agency are the dynamics that create conformity with what is already in place.

Commitment to Science Theories			Commitment to Justice Theories		
Paradigms	**Positivist**	**Interpretive**	**Marxian**	**Feminist**	**Africana**
Classical ca.1830–1930	Comte Spencer Durkheim Simmel	Martineau Weber (Max) Mead	Marx and Engels	Martineau Addams Gilman Weber (Marianne)	Douglass Cooper Wells-Barnett DuBois
Modern and Contemporary	**Structural-Functionalism Exchange Rational Choice** Analytic Conflict Macro Systems	**Symbolic Interactionism** *Dramaturgy* Phenomenology **Social Constructionism Ethnomethodology** Post-structuralism Post-modernism	**Neo-Marxian Critical World Systems Theory** Bourdieu	Liberal Cultural Radical **Psychoanalytic Materialist**	Afro-Caribbean World Systems AfricanaTheory
Integrative theories		*Social comparison theory Reference group theory Role theory Structuration theory*			**Intersectionality Theory**

Table 1. *An overview of sociology as a multiparadigm science. Boldface indicates that the theory is discussed in the article; italics indicate a middle-range theory.* CENGAGE LEARNING, GALE.

Parsons and his student and colleague, Robert Merton (1910–2003), offer five concepts essential to an explication of structural functionalist theory: social system, hierarchy of control, the functional prerequisites, institution, and status role. *Social system* describes society in terms of the interrelatedness of its parts or structures (the relationships among key institutions that include economy, politics, law, family, education, and religion). A social system is itself defined in terms of agency as "a plurality of individual actors *interacting* with each other" in a situation within normative limits (Parsons, 1951, pp. 5–6). The social system exists in an environment of other systems that affect action, *the hierarchy of control*, which includes nature, human biology, personality, other societies, and culture. All but the last of these extrasocial forces primarily affect the social system as destabilizers of pattern interaction; only the cultural system, the source of values and beliefs, works as a force for stabilizing those patterns.

Structural functionalists argue that if a social system is to reproduce itself, certain needs of group life—the functional prerequisites—must be effectively addressed. Parsons identifies four prerequisites, expressed in a model widely known by the acronym AGIL: *adaptation* to the physical environment in order to meet material needs; *goal attainment*, or collective agreements about priorities and the dispersal of resources; *integration* to settle con-

flicts between societal members; and *latent pattern maintenance* to transmit knowledge to and manage tensions among group members.

The work of meeting these prerequisites is done by institutions. A pivotal structure that links the social system, the agentic individual, and function, an institution is a complex arrangement of multiple status role sets and of norms, organized around satisfying one or more of the functional prerequisites. The concept of *status-role* incorporates the human actor into the social system. A *status* is a position in a system of relationships, most importantly a position in an institution; and a *role* is the behavior expected of someone in such a position. The interrelation of functional prerequisites, institutional structures, and individual actors in status roles can be conceptualized as shown in Table 2.

Implications for the Study of the Life Course Structural functionalism's emphasis on structure can inform the study of the life course in five ways. First, structural functionalism suggests understanding the life course as an institution meeting certain functions of the social system. The life course as an institution serves to meet the function of adaptation: If the primary structuring principle of trajectories across roles is age, then the institutions of the life course adapt to aging, the physiological change over time (a property of the biological system),

Adaptation	Goal Attainment
Institution: economy Status: worker Role: perform assigned duties Role Set: boss, customers, coworkers	Institution: government Status: legislator Role: to pass laws that will govern the use of society's resources Role Set: fellow legislators, citizen constituents, lobbyists
Institutions: family, religion, education Status: mother Role: producing material and emotional stability in the home Role set: husband, children, extended family, friends	Institution: court Status: judge Role: to determine facts and law in conflict between two parties Role Set: plaintiff, defendant, lawyers, other judges
Latent pattern maintenance	**Integration**

Table 2. *Functions, Structures, and Individual Actors in Structural Functionalism. This table presents the institutions typically associated with meeting key societal functional prerequisites and suggests possible status roles within that institution.* CENGAGE LEARNING, GALE.

and to the functional needs of the social system. Indeed, the life course may be a meta-institution (a structure that transcends and connects existing institutions) linking the status roles a person plays over the lifetime to the four major functional prerequisites—for example, as a worker in the economy (adaptation); as a citizen in government (goal attainment); as a juror or claimant in the law (integration); or as a parent in the family or a student in education (latent pattern maintenance). This orientation allows one to see how an actor's individual choices over the life course sustain the social system.

Second, structural functionalism conceives of constraints on agency as beneficial for individuals rather than as a necessary sacrifice for the collective good. From Émile Durkheim's (1858–1917) classic formulation of *anomie*, or normlessness, as an unhappy condition—"all man's pleasure in acting . . . implies that by walking he advances. However, one does not advance when one proceed toward no goal . . . or the goal is infinity" (Durkheim, 1972, p. 175)—to the present, structural functionalism views socialization, the process of learning to take and play roles, as liberating humans from the chaos of unregulated desires and impulses. This perspective raises important questions about the de-standardization of the life course and whether the opening up of more options necessarily produces greater happiness.

Third, structural functionalism's elaboration of the experience of role-playing conceptualizes several themes in the life course paradigm, including linked lives and transitions. The experience of playing a role exemplifies the creative tensions in structural functionalism between agency and structure and the theory's significant empha-

sis on interaction as the fundamental form of the social. Actors do not perform roles alone; roles exist only in terms of relations to others because they arise out of one's having a position in a system of relationships. Within role theory as developed in structural functionalism, the key relationship is the *role set*, that is, the other persons (or positions) one must interact with in playing one's role. When those expectations come into conflict, the individual experiences *role strain*, the condition in which one cannot easily meet all the varying expectations of one's role set for a given status. *Role conflict* arises when two or more of the many statuses an individual occupies generate conflicting expectations, such as is suggested in the status label *working mother*. The experience of transition may be understood through the concept of *role exit*, the process of leaving a role or identity one has previously held for a significant length of time. Life course scholars see the individual trajectory as an age-linked movement from one role to another; structural functionalism's elaboration of the concept of role reveals complications and conflicts that surround both the experiences of duration and transition.

Fourth, structural functionalism offers a nuanced interpretation of the individual-history problematic through a multilevel analysis of the causes of social change. First, individual action may initiate changes in societal arrangements, when, as Merton (1968) points out in his theory of anomie, the goals of action upheld by the culture are out of alignment with people's access to socially sanctioned means to the goals. For instance, a socially-sanctioned goal is college attendance after high school graduation, the person who lacks the means to go to college at this juncture would experience anomie. This structurally produced stress can produce several kinds of individual nonconformity: improvising unapproved means to the goals (innovation), an empty following of means with no belief in the goal (ritualism), an abandonment of goals and means (retreatism), and an active critique of both goals and norms (rebellion). These various forms of nonconformity leach the system of the energy to reproduce itself, and for life course analysts, suggest an explanation of the ways individuals may repattern their trajectories away from conventional paths.

Fifth, social change occurs as an adjustment to changes in the environment of the social system or in other institutions. These adjustments can have a strong impact on the individual life course. For example, as biological changes lead to longer lives and more diseases of aging, the work of the adult family members is redefined to include caregiving to aging parents.

Structural functionalism argues that while structures change, functional prerequisites are a constant. This insight is useful for the cross-cultural or historical comparative study of the life course, showing, among other things, how valued life skills may change across time and space. For example, to be dyslexic at the court of Charlemagne in the 8th century, where literacy was unnecessary, had little effect on one's life, but to be dyslexic in today's world potentially limits one's access to institutionalized means for achieving success.

Exchange Theory, Network Theory, and Rational Choice Theory Exchange theory, network theory, and rational choice theory share four key qualities, although each perspective is distinctive in important ways. First, they all represent a microsocial positivism, seeing individual action and interaction as the foundation of societal arrangements. Second, each builds on a particular social process or structure identified as critical and ubiquitous to social life. For exchange theory this is exchange, defined as an interaction involving the giving and receiving of tangible and intangible goods and services; for network theory it is social relations, understood as empirically observable ties that bind persons and groups to each other; for rational choice theory, it is the actions of rational actors undertaking projects in order to secure objectives judged important in terms of personal hierarchies of good. Third, all three have a studied indifference to the individual psychic processes of meaning-making, concentrating instead on visible activities common to all social actors. Fourth, they all strive for formal theoretical expression, as exemplified by exchange theorist George Homans's (1910–1989) propositions designed to predict behavioral outcomes, such as the success proposition: "For all actions taken by persons, the more often a particular person is rewarded, the more likely the person is to perform that action" (1974, p. 16).

Each theory elaborates the ways these fundamental processes and structures play out in social life. Rational choice theory generally shows human actors engaged in decision-making, assessing—for alternative courses of action—what resources they have, what costs they will incur, what benefits may accrue, and choosing the course that optimizes desirable outcomes. Exchange theorists argue that exchange shapes social structure by giving rise to norms that promote integration and by creating relations of power (Emerson, 1972; Molm, 2001). Group integration is facilitated by the norm of reciprocity, which makes possible indirect exchanges in which persons give in a context that does not allow for immediate repayment; such exchanges, Peter Blau (1977) argues, are only possible if there is a norm of trust, such as that of reciprocity, which says one will repay or be repaid in some equivalent manner at some future date. Power relations in society arise from situations of unequal exchange, where one actor needs something from another but lacks the resources or cannot afford to incur the costs

to get it. The first actor may offer the second what Blau sees as subordination—an act of exchange Richard Emerson (1972) describes as creating power-dependence relations. An actor's dependence is determined by the extent to which an outcome the actor wants initiates an exchange with the other. For exchange theory, power-dependence relations are a force for social integration.

Rational choice arose out of utilitarian economics, came into sociology initially as a background presence in the assumptions of exchange theory and became institutionalized through the prodigious efforts of sociologist James Coleman who sought, in part, to craft a theory that would allow sociologists to evaluate a social system in terms of how well it met individual needs. Rational choice theory presents a model of the human actor making decisions by weighing the best means to achieve a self-selected goal. Three facts of human existence impinge on this decision-making: scarce resources (people do not have infinite resources in undertaking a course of action), opportunity costs (costs that result from other goals foregone), and institutional constraints (positive or negative sanctions facilitating some actions and hindering other actions).

Rational choice theory builds its analysis of structure through the concept of the aggregation mechanism by which separate actions by individuals combine to produce social outcomes (Friedman & Hechter, 1988)—outcomes that Raymond Boudon (1982) argues may sometimes be "perverse effects," that is, effects different from what the individual actors in their separate reasoning intended. For instance, individual actors rationally deciding to restrict family size and have only one child per couple can produce a demographic situation of an aging population without a sufficient younger generation to provide care and companionship for the older generation who find themselves 1 of 4 grandparents sharing a single grandchild.

Network theory approaches social structure by looking at the pattern of ties linking its members and at the intensity of those ties. These ties are conceptualized in terms of *deep structures*, patterns of relationship not immediately visible from a surface view of social life; *structural holes*, situations in which no connections exist between actors or groups; *social capital* (an idea initially advanced by Coleman), the resource of being connected to people; and *weak* or *strong* measured by time spent together, emotional intensity, degrees of mutual revelation, and exchange of reciprocal services.

Implications for the Study of the Life Course Exchange, rational choice, and network theories offer conceptual frameworks for analyzing the ways individuals make decisions that shape life trajectories—and for analyzing

442

the effects of these decisions on social structure. For example, individual life courses can be charted in terms of the individual's relation to exchange. In childhood, the individual gives affection and obedience in return to for care (material or emotional). The duration of childhood, defined by this exchange position, depends on both the industrial development of the society and the position of the family of origin within that society. The movement to adolescence is signaled by a sense on the part of all parties that the individual can now participate more equally in exchange, as he or she is able to offer labor and more formulated gifts of affection and service (thus, the driver's license becomes a resource in complex processes of exchange, as does access to the family car).

Adulthood is signaled in most societies by the expectation that the person will be a full partner in both economic and social exchange relations. The maintenance of long-term commitments, such as marriage, depends in part on the parties negotiating a mode of continuous exchange. From this perspective, the illness of a spouse is a major life crisis, disrupting agreed upon patterns of exchange. Retirement also creates crisis because as one moves out of formal economic exchange, one must discover new resources for exchange (e.g., grandparenting, hosting traditional events such as Thanksgiving) or risk an imbalance in power-dependence relations.

Applied to the life course, rational choice theory raises the question of whether the individual involved in making life decisions—to end one role, to begin another, to emphasize one role over another—is doing so in a rational manner as defined by the theory. Equally important is the issue of whether the concept of the life course is undergirded by an assumption of rational choice in decision-making processes—and if it is not, discovering what other processes are at work. The concept of the *aggregation mechanism* has important implications for the dialectic between individual action and social structure over the life course. For instance, there are numerous moments in economic history where an oversupply of workers in some employment sectors seems to have been the result of actors individually evaluating opportunities and rationally choosing a similar career (e.g., teaching or engineering). This "perverse effect" affects both individual life courses—for example, in the inability to find employment in what one has trained to do, disappointment, and irregularity in labor market participation—and social structure (e.g., a higher unemployment rate, too many teachers and not enough nurses, the need to offer retraining).

The major contribution of network theory to the study of the life course is the understanding that life course decisions are affected by social networks and the social capital they embody. For instance, labor market entry may be understood through Mark Granovetter's (1973) hypothesis about the strength of weak ties. Nan Lin (1999) shows that one is more likely to have a weak (rather than strong) tie to someone higher in the status hierarchy than oneself and the possession of this weak tie may prove to be the link that opens the possibility of employment.

COMMITMENT TO SCIENCE: INTERPRETIVE THEORY

The central problematic of interpretive theory is to create a sociology that takes into account the distinctive human quality of acting on the basis of meaning. This focus gives interpretive theories a bias toward microsociology, the study of individual actors, which produces a secondary concern of how to relate individual action to macrosocial structure. While interpretive theory does not aim, as positivism does, at the production of formal theory, two theories in the interpretive paradigm, symbolic interaction and social constructionism, offer tightly argued statements linking individual action and societal organization.

Symbolic Interaction Symbolic interactionism has its primary origin in the work of philosopher George Herbert Mead (1863–1931) who was in debate with the radical behaviorism of psychologist John Watson (1878–1958) (which explains human behavior in terms of stimulus-response and conditioning). Mead sought to establish that mind and self can be studied as behaviors and are social in origin. Mead's work was given its formulation as a sociological theory by his student Herbert Blumer (1900–1987) in *Society as Symbolic Interaction* (1969). The foundational principle of symbolic interaction is that people do not simply respond to stimuli as do other animals. Instead, between stimulus and response, people interpret the stimulus—a process that involves taking the stimulus out of its context and making it an object by assigning meanings to it. People then respond to or interact with others on the basis of the meanings they have assigned. Furthermore, people are able to think and have a self by internalizing the social experience of communication; thus without socially experienced communication, thinking and self are not possible. Mead defines *thinking* as an internal conversation (carried on through the socially acquired symbols of language) and the *self* as a subject which is its own object. Both of these phenomena involve the ability of the individual to bring the social experience of other people into his or her own field of consciousness. This is done primarily through the human capacity for *taking the role of the other*, the process of imagining how the world and one's self look to other people. Essentially to have a self is to be able to see one's own person as it is seen by other people; to think is to have a conversation between different parts of the self—an *I* that spontaneously proposes action and a *me* that reflects what others would say.

The ability to take the role of the other is not innate but is acquired through socialization, which occurs in three stages: *imitation*, in which a child mimics others without imagining what the action means for others; *play*, in which the child begins to imagine how he or she and the world actually appear to others and to take over some of others' meanings for action; and *game*, in which the child understands the various positions and attitudes of people involved in an activity and can synthesize those to create a sense of the way the community sees him or her and the world.

Society is composed of people engaged in symbolic interaction with each other: that is, people are always stopping and thinking, indicating to themselves what other people have said or done, and then responding. Because the majority of situations in which this happens are recurring, people build up a repertoire of indications and responses and may only experience "stopping and thinking" when a unique or problematic situation presents itself. Nevertheless, symbolic interactionism argues that the process goes on; it only seems automatic because of repetition.

Social Constructionism The definitive work in the development of social constructionism is Peter Berger's and Thomas Luckmann's *The Social Construction of Reality* (1966), a synthesis drawing especially on the work of phenomenological social theorist Alfred Schutz (1899–1959) and to a lesser degree on Mead and Durkheim. Social constructionism analyzes the paradox that humans produce a social reality that they come to experience as objective and independent of the producer.

Berger and Luckmann begin with an exploration of how people experience "reality" or things as "real." Following phenomenology (the branch of philosophy that deals with how the mind experiences the world), they argue that reality is conferred by the way consciousness *intends* toward—or pays attention to—an object. Different kinds of intention produce different realities—the everyday life world, the world of fantasy, the world of dreams, the world of scientific theorizing—and thus multiple realities are possible for every individual at any point in time. But the reality that concerns sociology is the reality of everyday life world that is produced by people intending toward the world in *the natural attitude of everyday life*. One feature of the intentionality of everyday life is that people are able to move between two states of consciousness: nonreflection, in which they look outward on the world, and reflection, in which they intend toward themselves, that is, toward their own consciousness.

Within the natural attitude of everyday life, people maintain and produce social reality through three moments in a process: externalization, objectivation, and internalization. Human beings externalize themselves—that is, project their thinking into the world—either through individual actions or group efforts. The products of those externalizations become objectivated in the world—experienced as existing as things in themselves independent of the persons who produced them. Those objectivated products are then internalized as independent realities, by their original producers, other people, and even across generations.

These three moments are ongoing and simultaneously occurring and are presented primarily through the medium of language. Primary socialization is thus the internalization of objectivated typifications—symbolic, usually linguistic, expressions of the essential features of a recurring phenomenon. Through socialization one acquires the relevant parts of the society's *stock of knowledge*, the *typifications* of phenomena, and *recipes* for action. Out of these and combined with group and personal experience, the individual creates a personal stock that guides action in a taken-for-granted manner "until further notice." Problems arise when the individual has experiences for which the stock of knowledge seems to lack adequate typifications or recipes.

These processes occur on the microsocial and macrosocial levels and, over time among larger groups and generations, produce *institutionalization*, the establishment of typified actions by typified actors in typified positions. As new generations question these massively institutionalized structures, *legitimations* are offered to explain why something is done the way it is. These legitimations lead to *reification*, the experiencing of a human product as something beyond human control. From a classroom syllabus to the U.S. Constitution, reification produces a situation in which people experience human products as having a reality beyond human control.

Implications of Symbolic Interaction and Social Constructionism for Life Course Study From the perspective of interpretive theory, the individual's negotiation of the life course involves various acts of individual consciousness and interpretation about which six hypotheses seem particularly significant. First, in early socialization the individual needs to acquire a self that has a sense of personal efficacy and achieving this depends in part on the quality of interaction with others. To navigate the life course, people need to see themselves as able to set and execute projects successfully in the world; attaining this self requires that others–particular and generalized–have defined them that way. If one belongs to a category of people defined by others as efficacious—that is, are constantly presented as leaders in cultural expressions such as newspapers—the individual receives a sense that people like him or her can handle things. Conversely, the absence of such images can make the attainment of self-confidence harder.

Second, crises or turning points in the life course may be produced by failure in role-taking and the lack of an appropriate generalized other. Symbolic interactionism assumes that people unproblematically acquire the skill of taking the role of the other. This assumption is questioned by other theorists, most notably Schutz (1967), who argues that the concept of role-taking is based on the assumption of reciprocity of perspectives, which he believes to be flawed because were two persons to trade places, they would not see exactly the same thing due to differences in biography. This means that role-taking must be an imperfect process. Failures and negative experiences at various moments in the life course may have, as one cause, the inability to correctly take the role of a particular other or a generalized other (e.g., the student who finds they have failed to anticipate what would be on an exam). Thus an important consideration in the study of the life course must be the degree to which an individual can or cannot access the appropriate generalized other or has a wrong or inadequate generalized other for a situation. It can be hypothesized that many people's success—and the ability of professional classes to pass on status attributes to their children—results from their sharing the same generalized other as those in control, and, conversely, the failure of lower-class children may be due to a lack of a compatible generalized other.

Third, the model of primary socialization presented in symbolic interactionism may also be usefully applied to secondary socialization experiences. The stages of imitation, play, and game may describe one's initiation in to any new life stage including being a teenager, getting married, starting a new job, immigrating, or retiring.

Fourth, social constructionism urges a consideration of the life course in terms of the workings of consciousness and the organization of knowledge. If an individual is to have any experience of planful competence, he or she must have the time and space to step out of the demands of lived experience (i.e., of nonreflective consciousness) and switch to reflective consciousness, intending toward themselves as actors of a past or future state. (One cannot, by definition, reflect on the present because one only catches it in consciousness in a next moment—an axiom attested to by the experience of being asked if one is happy and having to stop and think.) Thus, planning in itself, which must involve reflection, may be emotionally frightening because it takes one away from living life.

This alternation between reflection and nonreflection affects a person's whole sense of duration. The time between transitions may at some fundamental level be unclear to an individual if these transitions are nonproblematic, because it was largely lived in nonreflection. Hence, older persons' statements that they do not "feel" older in their internal knowledge of themselves are a function of the inability of consciousness to actually reconstitute the lived, nonreflected upon experience of biologically growing old. Knowing where one is in one's life depends on being able to do acts of reflection that coordinate one's own being at a given moment with stages in the life course as outlined in the stock of knowledge of the society.

Fifth, the crisis nature of even happy transitions such as marriage or pregnancy can be conceptualized in terms of people moving into areas where their personal stock of knowledge is incomplete. Part of a transition involves figuring out how to fill in the perceived gaps in one's stock of knowledge. A person in transition may need to externalize with others about what lies ahead—for instance, expectant mothers in a waiting room or new mothers in a park. They will almost certainly try to discover what exists as objectivations in the culture for this moment—hence the enormous popularity of baby books and general self-help books. In addition, part of the stress of transition may be the feeling of needing to internalize too much too fast.

Sixth, the concept of *stock of knowledge*—and the attendant concepts of *typification* and *recipe*—help the life course scholar analyze the importance of birth cohorts, especially in a rapidly changing society. One of the things that happens across generations is that people do not share the same stock of knowledge. This difference intensifies the inherent problem in *the assumption of reciprocity of perspectives*. A knowledge organization approach may explain tensions between generations, such as with adolescents and parents. Entering a series of new worlds, adolescents find themselves lacking appropriate recipes for success and at the same time discover that their parents seem to be utterly clueless. Looked at from the social constructionist perspective, this seems less a baseless complaint than a descriptor; the parents simply do not have the knowledge that is needed. All of this is complicated by the fact that the development of a distinctive set of typifications is one of the ways that adolescents, or other groups, establish their own identity.

COMMITMENT TO SCIENCE THEORIES: THEORIES OF THE MIDDLE RANGE

At least three middle-range theories deal with recurring themes in life course study: role theory, reference group theory, and social comparison theory. What these three theories have in common is that they have been approached from both positivist and interpretive perspectives. The general social theory of ethnomethodology is a useful complement to role theory and has origins in both structural functionalism and social constructionism.

Role Theory (and Ethnomethodology) Role theory focuses on how individuals know what to do in a particular status role, which is a question that can be looked at from the perspective of structural considerations for the society or of interpretive problems for the individual. Role theory is based on the recognition that people spend much of their lifetime playing social roles (Biddle, 1986). From the structural functionalist perspective, *role* is understood as the behavior expected of someone occupying a given status in a system of relationships. In the interpretive view, the sense of one's status and role are much more open for negotiation and depend on signals from other people that have to be interpreted. The general thrust of role theory is more in the functionalist direction of role as a set of expectations that are fairly clearly understood or at least understandable, to which people seek to conform and monitor others and are monitored in terms of such conforminty and which are enforced by social monitoring.

Important work related to the question of how people know how to play roles and how they monitor each other is being done in ethnomethodology, a branch of interpretive theory pioneered by Harold Garfinkel (b. 1917). *Ethnomethodology* means "people's methods" and refers to the ways that people figure out what to do in given situations. According to Garfinkel (1967), the original question came to him when he was studying jurors: How did the jurors know that they were "doing juror"? Ethnomethodology suggests that people in everyday life situations appeal to norms in order to make sense of situations. This action of invoking a rule in a specific situation and holding oneself or others accountable for conforming to it constitutes the creation of social reality. A well-known example of ethnomethodological theory is the 1987 paper *Doing Gender* by Candace West and Don Zimmerman, which argues that while people are born with biological gender in some form, what matters socially is the gender category that is assigned to them, usually at birth. Most people pattern their life course, in part, by trying to engage in behavior that fits their gender category. This attempt to fit gender role behavior to gender category constitutes "doing gender." It is possible to talk about the "doing" orientation for a variety of roles, such as "doing student." The concept of "doing" and its attendant concept of accountability offer an important bridge between the fact of status and the execution of role. "Doing gender" can be seen in situations where groups of young women do "girl talk." There exists in that conversational moment expectations of what topics are appropriate, what tone is to be taken toward those topics, what gestures can be made (and the same is true of a group of young men doing "guy talk"). People occupy many status roles over the course of a lifetime, many of them simultaneously. As they try to meet the role expectations of any particular status, or balance the conflicting expectations of different statuses, people may experience role strain, role conflict, role confusion, role distance, and role exit.

Reference Group Theory Reference group theory dates to the first generation of U.S. sociologists in the work of William Graham Sumner (1840–1910) and Charles Horton Cooley (1864–1929), but it received an expansion and formulation in the 1950s with Merton's and Alice Rossi's (b. 1922) analyses of findings from Samuel Stouffer's (1900–1960) *The American Soldier* (published in 1949). Over its long use as a concept in American social science, the term *reference group* has spawned at least three different definitions (Shibutani, 1972). Essentially, however, all have in common the idea—central also to social comparison theory—that a reference group is a group that a person or another group takes as a standard for comparison in evaluating themselves, locating themselves in the world, and deciding whether to undertake or avoid certain courses of action. Reference groups are often typed in terms of how they are used by actors: A negative reference group is used to indicate conduct or attitudes one wishes to avoid; a positive reference group, to emulate; a comparative reference group, to get information about some significant dimension of one's own life (e.g., opinions, abilities, plans); a normative reference group, to get a guide to appropriate behavior within a given situation; and an aspiration reference group, to engage in anticipatory socialization.

Social Comparison Theory Social comparison theory has focused more on individual motivations and processes in making comparisons. Originally formulated by social psychologist Leon Festinger (1919–1989), social comparison theory began with the proposition that people are impelled to make comparisons in order to understand and evaluate the self, abilities, and opinions. This original concept of motivation has been revised to acknowledge that people may feel so impelled under some conditions, but under other conditions may find themselves presented with comparison data that they do not want (Suls, Martin, & Wheeler, 2000). This latter possibility underscores the enormous power of social comparison. Social comparison theorists have explored the kinds of groups that actors choose to make comparisons to and the conditions under which they choose groups defined as similar to themselves, groups defined as different, groups above themselves in status, and groups below themselves in status. What emerges from the literature is a sense that, when they have the agency to do so, people are calculating and self-protective in their choice of comparisons.

Implications for the Study of the Life course The implications of role theory for the study of the life course have been suggested above: It offers a way to analyze people's experiences of duration and to conceptualize the experience of transition as involving a change in statuses and roles. An additional concept useful in considering the effects of age patterning over the life course is *role distance*, that is, the enactment by an individual in a particular status of behaviors intended to signal that the status does not reflect on her or his true self. The most typical examples of this given in the area's literature involve persons finding themselves momentarily in age-inappropriate roles. Ethnomethodology's concept of "doing" offers a useful lens for describing the work done by people in transition. (One of Garfinkel's first studies was of a young transsexual man in the process of changing himself into a woman.)

Reference group theory and social comparison theory are most significant in attempts to analyze how persons manage transitions. Social comparison theory, in particular, may offer insights into situations that might produce turning points. For example, a person might find themselves confronted with unsought and unwanted data about salary differentials between his or her job and those of another occupation; if the data are forceful enough and perhaps combine with other discontents, the person may feel more impelled toward major change. Reference group theory offers insights into at least one mechanism by which that transition may be planned and accomplished: the selection of an appropriate reference group to provide anticipatory socialization. The classic example is Merton's and Rossi's analysis of Stouffer, which found that enlisted men who eventually gained promotion to officer tended *not* to share the perspective of persons of their own in-group, other enlisted men, but to take on the perspective of the officer class. Changes in reference group may also account for an underexplored phenomenon in the life course—the inability of many immigrants to return to their native countries because their reference group has shifted. Equally problematic is the immigrant experience in which the actor holds to the original, but now irrelevant, reference group.

COMMITMENT TO SCIENCE THEORIES: INTEGRATIVE THEORIES

The structuration theory of Anthony Giddens (b. 1938) is presented here as an attempt to integrate insights from interpretive theory and from structural functionalism.

The concern of structuration theory is to resolve the agency versus structure debate by showing how social analysis can only be effective if both are given equal weight and their relationship understood as a dynamic duality: Social structure enables social action even as social action creates structure.

Structuration theory explores this duality by taking recurrent social practices as its object of study, that is, ongoing social activity patterned across time and space. Social practices are initiated by human actors or agents who are possessed of both consciousness and power. Consciousness is used by social agents not only to monitor the self, but also to monitor the conditions of their activity; power is their capacity for agency, their ability to affect the situations in which they act. But agents for the most part do not create social practices. Much of social practice consists of routines developed over time in response to people's needs for security and efficiency. Most of the time agents perform these actions with a nonreflective mode of *practical consciousness*. Thus, in general, agents reproduce rather than initiate social practices. Agents' actions, however, are always framed by social structures—rules and resources for engaging in practices, so that practices are patterned and similar across time and space.

Giddens (1984) identifies three main types of structures: signification, or the rules and resources of language that make communication possible and both constrain and enable what can be said; legitimation, or rules and resources that produce an ordering of values and standards; and domination, or rules and resources that make possible the exercise of power. These structures, originally arising from agents' needs for routinization, exist only in the moment when they are expressed in social practices, and never as external, determining forces. The concept of *social systems* refers to the most permanent features of social structure, expressed in highly regular and predictable sequences of social practice. Structuration may be seen in the transitional moment of the wedding: The agents (bride, groom, and families), in choosing the pattern of their wedding, even if that choice is to conform to very ritualized traditions, express agency as they reproduce those traditions and may also change structure as they choose to depart from those traditions.

Implications for the Life Course Structuration theory may provide a strategy for life course scholars' analyses of how an individual actor shapes a life course trajectory by exercising agency within the opportunities and constraints presented by social structure. The theory suggests that this analysis might focus on social practices, the recurring activities of actors across time and space; such a focus calls attention not just to moments of transition, when agency is high, but to the long periods of duration when actors enact the life course through the social practices of everyday life, thereby reproducing the social structures that make that life possible. Similar to exchange theory, structuration theory points to the importance of trust in the conduct of social life; *trust* is seen here as an ultimate proof of structure. Action is possible because agents trust that a course of action will in all probability produce a given result, and that trust is based on a sense of prevailing rules and resources. It also seems possible to apply the concept of trust to moments of transition, especially voluntary transition. Here the individual agent must engage in what Giddens calls *discursive consciousness*, that is, one must consider the self as an actor in a situation and calculate what rules may apply and what resources may be forthcoming. This is possible in part because of the transposable rules (structures) that may be applied in a range of situations beyond those in which they were originally learned.

COMMITMENT TO JUSTICE THEORIES (CONFLICT THEORY)

Commitment to justice theories look critically at socially produced inequalities and see theory as a means of creating a more just world. They describe society as an arena of struggle between unequally empowered groups—hence the description of them as conflict theories. This section describes three conflict paradigms: Marxian and neo-Marxian theory, modern feminist theory, and intersectionality theory.

Marxian and Neo-Marxian Theory Focusing critically on material inequality, Karl Marx (1818–1883) and Friedrich Engels (1820–1895) presented a model of society as located in history and divided into a substructure, the material economy of collective human work, and a superstructure, all other social institutions and the body of shared ideas, *ideology*. The substructure gives rise to economic classes, groups with different positions in their work arrangements, and the experiences and interests of classes in turn pattern the content of the superstructure. Throughout history the major classes have been an owner class, which claims as its property *the means of production* (i.e., the resources necessary to make goods and services), and a worker class, which, lacking access to the means of production, survives by selling its labor to the owner class by becoming a means of production. Class struggle between these two groups drives history. In the present historical moment, which is dominated by capitalism, the owner class (or bourgeoisie), in its unending pursuit of wealth through profit, engages in intensifying exploitation of the worker class (the proletariat).

Marx predicted that the revolution of the proletariat was inevitable as capitalists attempted to wring more and more profit out of labor by cutting wages and increasing hours and that such a system would give rise to a new

postcapitalist phase in history. The revolution predicted by Marx and Engels has not happened. The central problematic of neo-Marxian theory is to explain why the revolution of the proletariat did not occur. Two different explanations are offered, one by the critical theorists of the Frankfurt Institute and the other by world systems theorists.

Neo-Marxian critical theory is the work of two generations of scholars. The first generation included Theodor Adorno (1903–1969), Max Horkheimer (1896–1973), and Herbert Marcuse (1898–1979), all of whom worked first in Germany and then in the United States after the rise of Nazism; the second, postwar generation works in Germany and its most prominent member is Jürgen Habermas (b. 1929).

The first generation of critical theorists addresses the lack of revolution by elaborating on Marx's concept of the superstructure. They describe their contemporary world as *an administered society*, that is, a nation-state organized to give the illusion of choice rather than real choice. This illusion is achieved by collaboration between government and capitalism. In classical Marxism, the state was seen as just another institution of the superstructure shaped by capitalism, but in critical theory the state becomes an active ally of capitalism. State and capitalism together employ the pathology of hyperrationality, that is, the use of reason to control rather than liberate people by giving people a false sense of options. Workers' capacity for independent thought is further subverted by the culture industry, the mass media that fills their time so completely that there is a loss of *negative space*, the space where people can imagine a world different from the one they are presented with daily. The ultimate product of the administered society is what Marcuse (1964) terms "one-dimensional man." The concept of one-dimensionality is meant to describe a person who is incapable of critique, who is poised for "the spontaneous acceptance of what is offered" (p. 74).

Adorno's (1950) analysis of the genesis of the authoritarian personality parallels Marcuse, but traces the loss of critical thinking to the disintegration of the family under capitalism. The father, rather than being an independent craftsman, is a wage slave and cannot provide an example of life competence for his children, who increasingly turn to charismatic political leaders to make up for this loss. Thus, for critical theorists, the revolution failed to materialize because the workers lost their capacity to think critically about their condition.

The second generation of critical theorists, lead by Habermas, tries to find some hope for change in this dark picture. Habermas argues that negative spaces, with their possibility for critical thought, persist in the *life world*, the world of face-to-face interactions in which people can know each other directly and arrive at a mutual understanding of their lived experience. He argues that they will increasingly be presented with the *legitimation crises* of the modern democratic state brought on by the contradiction between its claims to aid the people and its structural ties to global capitalism. Legitimation crises may serve as catalysts for the critique and change of the capitalist world in place.

World systems theory shares some of the insights of critical theory, but it answers the question of why history has not evolved, as Marx and Engels predicted, by turning to conditions of the substructure. The primary fact about the organization of the substructure in the early 21st century is that the pattern is global capitalism. Capitalism has experienced unparalleled expansion by reaching out for world exploitation. World systems theory divides the mode of production in global terms, seeing a global division of labor: core areas of capital accumulation that control the means of production; semi-peripheral areas of technically skilled workers who provide the core with certain services; and peripheral areas of low-skilled workers who are used by the core as a source of raw materials and cheap mass labor. This global division of labor is marked by transnational elite solidarity on the one hand and working-class fractures on the other. These fractures are caused partly by a proliferation of organizational positions within production that lead some workers to identify with capitalists and partly by the growth of identity politics, which makes loyalty to other groups (e.g., race, religion) more significant than class identity. Finally, global capital expands markets in three ways: consumerism makes every human being a consumer (even small children); commodification brings value to products, things made to meet the immediate needs of people and not for sale, into the nexus of capitalist production and exchange (such as selling bottled water); and keeps working classes, semi-peripheral, and peripheral areas owing money to capitalists and thus subordinate.

Feminist Sociological Theory Feminist sociological theory derives from feminist theory, which has six broad branches: liberal, cultural, radical, materialist, psychoanalytic, and womanist. What follows draws primarily on materialist feminist and psychoanalytic feminism; the former is a reworking of Marxian theory and the latter of psychoanalytic theory.

All feminist sociological theory attempts to present an analysis of society and social relations from the standpoint of women. The first point that must be made, then, is methodological: Feminist sociological theory uses *standpoint epistemology*, that is, it founds knowledge on the assertion that all accounts of the social world are given from a particular location in society and are affected by that location.

From the standpoint of women, society is organized as patriarchy, a system of power relations designed to

	Local Actuality of Lived Experience—product here is material labor	Extralocal Relations of Ruling—product here is texts that govern production in local actuality
Private	All women doing work of home with only minimal assistance from men even if women also work in public sphere	Ceremonial appearances to enact heteronormativity—wife standing by erring husband is one typical enactment
Public	Most men and many women working but men paid more and have more access to more jobs	A few elite men's special province—very few women allowed entry

Table 3. *The Gender Division of Labor.* CENGAGE LEARNING, GALE.

benefit men in all social arrangements. Feminist sociological theory focuses particularly on the arrangements of production and socialization. Its first approach to the organization of production centers on the everyday, taken-for-granted division of the social world into public and the private spheres—a division traceable historically to the industrial revolution. Social production occurs in both spheres; one key difference between Marxian theory and materialist feminist analysis is the latter's emphasis on the social significance of production done in the private sphere. Both spheres are deeply gendered. The public sphere, where the bulk of paid work occurs, belongs to men as their birthright under patriarchy; women are admitted increasingly but grudgingly as ongoing sexual harassment and pay inequity show. The private sphere, where the bulk of work is unpaid, is assigned to women; they are expected to perform homemaking tasks, which involves housework, reproduction of children, child care, emotional labor, meeting of sexual needs, health care, scheduling, money management, the production of sociality, aesthetic presentations within the house, and so on.

Dorothy Smith (b. 1926) offers a deeper look at this division of production by identifying a second division overlying the public and private division: the division of the world into *the local actualities of lived experience* and *the extralocal relations of ruling.* The local actualities are where material production is actually done and may be public or private; the relations of ruling is where elites interact to produce texts (documents, in the broadest sense) that serve to control the production done in the local actualities; contracts, wage laws, immigration laws, passports, licenses, diplomas, advertisements and so on are all examples of these texts. The relation between private and public and local actualities and relations of ruling may be pictured as shown in Table 3.

This gendered division of labor handicaps women's attempts to move from the private to the public sphere and keeps them at a disadvantage in negotiating for wages. At the same time, the work of the home is at once romanticized and trivialized under patriarchy. The woman who works outside the home ends up doing "the second shift" at home (Hochschild & Machung, 1989).

The persistence of such a materially unfair arrangement is explained by the experience of socialization, which in all feminist sociological theory is understood as a deeply gendered process patterned by norms of patriarchy and by the institution of compulsory heterosexuality—that is, making heterosexuality and the heterosexual household the only acceptable way for persons to form homes and experience intimacy. Feminist psychoanalytic theory sees gender socialization as producing a male personality that is equipped for domination, the relationship in which the superordinate makes the subordinate an instrument of his will, a denial of the subordinate's independent subjectivity, and a female personality lacking the psychic energy to resist domination. This socialization is accomplished through differential experiences of and training in recognition, the process whereby one person acknowledges the agency of the other.

This differential experience results from the facts that "women mother" and social structure values men and women differently (Chodorow, 1978). Males are trained to win recognition; to do this, they must separate from the mother, accepting that they are different from the person who provided them with that earliest life-sustaining recognition. To do their duty by their sons, mothers must encourage them to separate at a very young age, leaving them a lifelong hostility toward women. In contrast, females are trained to give recognition as one way of experiencing agency. In adolescence, they are also encouraged to transform themselves from seekers of agency to objects of male desire—an encouragement their mothers are expected to aid in and that leaves the daughter feeling rejected.

Intersectionality Theory Intersectionality theory emerged from the joining of Feminist and Africana theory, especially in the work of Patricia Hill Collins (b. 1948). Its central problematic is to explain the way stratification works in the contemporary world. Intersectionality theory begins with the Africana theory conceptions that the essential societal unit is the group, understood as individuals who share a common experience that positions them in the system of social stratification, and that the essential dynamic in society is the interactions among such groups. These interactions, the relations between power and difference, shape history. The world today is organized by hierarchical power relations—a constellation of related practices in employment, government education, law,

business, and housing that work to maintain an unjust system for the production and distribution of social resources. These hierarchical power relations reflect and reproduce a matrix of domination, the interaction of multiple practices of stratification, especially among the categories of class, race, gender, age, ethnicity, sexual preference, and global location. Intersectionality is the lived experience of embodying in one's person multiple dimensions of the matrix of domination. Being female and lesbian fundamentally affects the way one can create a family as opposed to the experience of being female and heterosexual; similarly, being female and poor affects the sequence in which one chooses to have children and marry in a way that contrasts with being female and professional class.

Implications of Commitment to Justice Theories for the Study of the Life Course The primary implication of commitment to justice theories for the study of the life course is that inequality matters. Inequality is produced by one's position in the system of production: for Marxian theory, the system of capitalism; for feminist theory, capitalist patriarchy; and for intersectionality theory, capitalist-racist patriarchy. Commitment to justice theories focus attention on the causes and consequences of inequality in the individual life course and the life course mechanisms by which social inequality is reproduced from generation to generation.

Classic Marxian theory would analyze the life course in terms of the individual's position in the substructure, beginning with a child being born into a family that occupies a particular position in the substructure—a position that in classic Marxian theory depends primarily on the father's work. This family position patterns interactions among family members and childhood socialization: Working-class parents value obedience in children because that is their experience of what secures them a place in the means of production; professional-class parents value initiative and verbal skills for the same reasons. The child's relationship to the institution of education will be largely dependent on the class position of the family. Adult experiences of sexuality, marriage, childbearing, transitions into and out of work, residence patterns, and the possibility or impossibility of retirement are shaped by position in the economic substructure.

The life course itself would be viewed as an ideology that bestows distinct life expectations to persons according to their location in the class structure. The purpose of life course ideology is to create a satisfied, nonrebellious working class that accepts that its life is as good as it could have hoped and that others who have better lives are entitled to this preferential outcome. Neo-Marxian critical theory would view many stages in the life course as products of the administered society, especially the illusions of choice about schooling, about workforce entry, and about retirement. Critical theory sees these decisions as managed by a partnership among capitalism, the state, and mass culture to secure a passive workforce.

World systems theory calls attention to both the global nature of the substructural forces shaping individual life courses and the possibility of global mobility as a transition in the life of nearly every person on the planet. A phenomenon once typical of peripheral societies—being born to leave—now is potentially a part of planning in nearly all societies. But all capacity for intelligent individual planning may be corrupted by the erosion of negative space. The culture industry fills people's free time with innumerable images of the life course and becomes a part of many celebrations of life course transitions. For example, movies about weddings constitute an enormous and continuously profitable source of commentary on the life course. This is true not only for commercial films, but of films people make of their own weddings, as if the event would not be real if not captured in a form approved by the culture industry. Finally, life course transitions—birth, birthdays, marriages, anniversaries, graduations, new jobs, retirements, and death—are commodified into occasions to be marked by consumption.

Feminist theory highlights the different life courses of men and women. Under the ideology of patriarchy, women are socialized to a different set of life course expectations than men. Men within patriarchy understand that material success in the world (variably assessed by the classes under capitalism) entitles them and will bring with it the use of a woman. Women are socialized to measure part of their success as having a man who wants them, but that this alone is not connected to their material success—even though relation to a man brings with it a great deal of material responsibility. Men typically experience the self as competent and capable of independent action; women are more likely to experience the self as caring and generous. This means that for a woman, a successful life course requires someone to care for and look after. Women may also experience themselves as less capable of independent action, creating one danger in the female life course—the possibility of an abusive marriage, which the woman hesitates to leave because of lack of material resources, lack of confidence, and concern for how she would care for her children.

Intersectionality theory emphasizes that the life course is determined by the interaction among different vectors in the matrix of domination in an individual life, and that the relative importance of vectors may change over time. Class, gender, race, sexual orientation, and global position are all subject both to change and to change in significance. Gender may become less important as one becomes settled in one's intimate relations; race may affect one's class mobility; and class will almost certainly determine one's old age.

Theory comes from the Greek verb *therein* which means "to look at" or "see" and is also the root for *theater*, a place for viewing. Sociological theory, as a multi-paradigm science, offers a variety of positions from which to view the life course. The structural functionalist position illuminates the way the life course functions as an institutional arrangement in the working of the social system. The micro-positivist perspectives—exchange, rational choice and network theories—depict the individual as a decision-maker navigating this institutional arrangement. The interpretive paradigm allows one to see how the individual subjectively arrives at and processes typified understandings of the life course and of their position in it at any given moment. The commitment to justice theories show how socially produced inequalities shape every moment of the individual's experience of the life course and that any generalization about the life course must be qualified in terms of the dictum that "inequality matters."

SEE ALSO Volume 1: *Coleman, James; Interpretive Theory; Thomas, W.I.;* Volume 2: *Agency; Durkheim, Émile; Giddens, Anthony; Mannheim, Karl; Marx, Karl; Mills, C. Wright; Roles; Simmel, Georg;* Volume 3: *Theories of Aging.*

BIBLIOGRAPHY

Adorno, T., Frenkel-Brunswik, E., Levinson, D.J., & Sanford, R.N. (1950). *The authoritarian personality.* New York: Harper.

Benjamin, J. (1988). *The bonds of love: Psychoanalysis, feminism, and the problem of domination.* New York: Pantheon.

Berger, P., & Luckmann, T. (1966). *The social construction of reality: A treatise in the sociology of knowledge.* Garden City, NY: Doubleday.

Biddle, B.J. (1986). Recent developments in role theory. *Annual Review of Sociology,* 1267–1292.

Blau, P. (1977). *Inequality and heterogeneity: A primitive theory of social structures.* New York: Free Press.

Blumer, H. (Ed.). (1969). Society as symbolic interaction. In *Symbolic interactionism: Perspective and method.* Englewood Cliffs, NJ: Prentice-Hall.

Boudon, R. (1982). *The unintended consequences of social action.* New York: St. Martin's Press.

Burt, R. (1992). *Structural holes: The social structure of competition.* Cambridge, MA: Harvard University Press.

Calhoun, C., & Karaganis, J. (2001). Critical theory. In G. Ritzer & B. Smart (Eds.), *Handbook of social theory* (pp. 179–200). London: Sage.

Chodorow, N. (1978). *The reproduction of mothering: Psychoanalysis and the sociology of gender.* Berkeley: University of California Press.

Coleman, J. (1990). *Foundations of social theory.* Cambridge, MA: Belknap Press of Harvard University Press.

Collins, P.H. (1990). *Black feminist thought: Knowledge, consciousness, and the politics of empowerment.* Boston: Unwin Hyman.

Collins, P.H. (1998). *Fighting words: Black women and the search for justice.* Minneapolis: University of Minnesota Press.

Durkheim, É. (1972). *Émile Durkheim: Selected writings.* (A. Giddens, Ed. & Trans.). Cambridge, U.K.: Cambridge University Press.

Elder, G., Johnson, M.K., & Crosnoe, R. (2003). The emergence and development of life course theory. In J.T. Mortimer (Ed.), *The handbook of the life course* (pp. 3–19). New York: Kluwer Academic/Plenum.

Emerson, R. (1972). Exchange theory, part II: Exchange relations and networks. In J. Berger, M. Zelditch, Jr., & B. Anderson (Eds.), *Sociological theories in progress* (Vol. 2). Boston: Houghton Mifflin.

Friedman, D., & Hechter, M. (1988). The contribution of rational choice theory to macrosociological research. *Sociological Theory, 6*(2), 201–218.

Garfinkel, H. (1967). *Studies in ethnomethodology.* Englewood Cliffs, NJ: Prentice-Hall.

Giddens, A. (1984). *The constitution of society: Outline of the theory of structuration.* Berkeley: University of California Press.

Granovetter, M. (1973). The strength of weak ties. *American Journal of Sociology, 78*(6), 1360–1380.

Habermas, J. (1975). *Legitimation crisis.* Boston: Beacon Press.

Hochschild, A., & Machung, A. (1989). *The second shift: Working parents and the revolution at home.* New York: Viking.

Homans, G.C. (1974). *Social behavior: Its elementary forms.* New York: Harcourt, Brace, Jovanovich.

Lin, N. (1999). Social networks and status attainment. *Annual Review of Sociology, 25,* 467–487.

Marcuse, H. (1964). *One-dimensional man: Studies in the ideology of advanced industrial society.* Boston: Beacon Press.

Mead, G.H. (1934). *Mind, self, and society.* Chicago: University of Chicago Press.

Merton, R. (1968). *Social theory and social structure.* New York: The Free Press.

Molm, L. (2001). Theories of social exchange and exchange networks. In G. Ritzer & B. Smart (Eds.), *Handbook of social theory* (pp. 260–272). London: Sage.

Parsons, T. (1937). *The structure of social action.* New York: McGraw-Hill.

Parsons, T. (1951). *The social system.* Glencoe, IL: The Free Press.

Ritzer, G. (1975). *Sociology: A multiple paradigm science.* Boston: Allyn & Bacon.

Schutz, A. (1967). *The phenomenology of the social world.* Evanston, IL: Northwestern University Press.

Shibutani, T. (1972). Reference groups as perspective. In J.G. Manis & B.N. Meltzer (Eds.), *Symbolic interaction: A reader in social psychology* (2nd ed., pp. 160–170). Boston: Allyn & Bacon.

Smith, D.E. (1987). *The everyday world as problematic: A feminist sociology.* Boston: Northeastern University Press.

Stiles, B., & Kaplan, H.B. (2004). Adverse social comparison processes and negative self-feelings: A test of alternative models. *Social Behavior and Personality, 32*(1), 31–44. Retrieved June 29, 2008, from http://findarticles.com/p/articles/mi_qa3852/is_200401/ai_n9352286/pg_10

Stouffer, S.A. (1949). *American soldier.* Princeton, NJ: Princeton University Press.

Suls, J., Martin, R., & Wheeler, L. (2000). Three kinds of opinion comparison: The triadic model. *Personality and Social Psychology Review, 4*(3), 219–237.

Wallerstein, I. (2000). *The essential Wallerstein.* New York: New Press.

West, C., & Zimmerman, D. (1987). Doing gender. *Gender & Society, 1*(2), 125–151.

Patricia Lengermann
Gillian Niebrugge

SPIRITUALITY

SEE Volume 2: *Religion and Spirituality, Adulthood.*

STATUS ATTAINMENT MODEL

SEE Volume 2: *Social Class.*

STIGMA

SEE Volume 2: *Racism/Race Discrimination; Sexism/Sex Discrimination;* Volume 3: *Ageism/Age Discrimination; Self.*

STRESS IN ADULTHOOD

The term *stress* is widely used in everyday life, and even scholars have defined and used the term in different ways. However, researchers who study stress have arrived at a general consensus in the definition of the concept. *Stressor* refers to life circumstances that disturb or threaten to disturb the patterns of everyday life. Stressors initiate a process of adaptation to the demands of life. The degree of adaptation required depends on characteristics of the stressor, such as its intensity or duration. Adaptations that evoke changes in psychological and physical functioning are referred to as *stress responses*. The *stress process* refers to people's ongoing adaptation (changes in physical, social, and psychological functioning) to the demands of life. In other words, the stress process is an ongoing system of adaptation to the ups and downs of everyday life; stressors are antecedents of the stress process; and stress responses are the outcomes of adaptation.

THEORETICAL PERSPECTIVES ON THE STRESS PROCESS

Theoretical perspectives on the stress process emphasize different aspects of the relationship between an individual and his or her physical and social environment.

Biological Perspective The biological perspective considers the underlying physiological responses people exhibit when exposed to stressors. Author Walter Cannon (1929) wrote that the body physically prepares to handle a stressor by mounting a short-term defensive response to meet an immediate threat to physical safety. When the brain detects a potential threat, it sends an alert through the central nervous system directly to major bodily systems (e.g., circulatory, respiratory). In response to this alert, the systems release hormones, called catecholamines, to help the person defend against the threat. This response is commonly referred to as the fight-or-flight response. The catecholamines (e.g., adrenaline) trigger processes that provide energy needed by the body to protect itself by either fighting off the threat or running away. Once the threat ceases, the brain signals the release of different hormones (e.g., noradrenaline) prompting the body to return to its normal resting state (i.e., homeostasis). This physiological response is adaptive, allowing people to successfully manage short-term physical stressors (e.g., a charging woolly mammoth, pulling a child out of deep water, running a race).

Hans Selye (1956) recognized that psychosocial stressors also could trigger the fight-or-flight response and that many stressors may endure over long time periods. Thus, he hypothesized that the body needs an alternative response to fuel a prolonged defense. Selye proposed that an alternative, neuroendocrine stress response meets this need. The brain initiates the release of a different type of hormone (i.e., glucocorticoids) that actually triggers the breakdown of proteins and excess body fats to fuel the body's longer-term response to stressors. However, without adequate recovery time between stressors, the body cannot replenish its supply of excess fats and proteins and will burn up essential body cells, eventually leading to physical illness.

The current perspective on the biological stress response suggests that the normal state of an individual is ongoing adaptation to his or her environment. Referred to as *allostasis*, this ongoing, self-regulating adaptation promotes a balance between complex bodily systems and the demands of a changing physical and social environment. In this sense, responding to a stressor is a within-person, self-regulating process that brings physiological systems back into balance. However, repeated physiological adjustments in response to a lifetime of physical and psychological stressors exact a physical cost on the body, referred to as *allostatic load* (McEwen & Stellar, 1993). It is the physical wear and tear from prolonged or continuous activation of the stress response that increases the risk of physical and mental disease and disorder (Seeman, McEwen, Rowe, & Singer, 2001). Current depictions of the stress response posit an interrelationship between the central nervous and endocrine systems, providing a more complete picture of the integrated pathway by which stressors affect health outcomes. Essentially, the initial response to a stressor is the activation of the central nervous system, with the endocrine system providing a more protracted response to stressors.

The way an individual interprets the surrounding physical and social environment affects the way he or she feels about the current situation. These feelings may prompt physiological changes through two physiological pathways: the central nervous system and the hormonal system. These feelings may also initiate behavioral changes or coping strategies to adapt to the situation. The physiological changes may initiate a change in the functioning of the immune system, which in turn may increase disease susceptibility.

Sociological Perspective The sociological perspective on the stress process focuses on the naturalistic causes of stress or, more specifically, on the social and environmental conditions that serve as sources of stress that then influence individual well-being (Pearlin, 1999). From this perspective, key questions relate to the social conditions (e.g., social positions, roles, and challenging life course events) that trigger the physiological stress response and how the availability and distribution of resources affect people's ability to successfully manage stressors. Stress is viewed as a dynamic and ongoing set of interrelationships between the individual and his or her social environment. Although unique circumstances do occur and do affect individuals, research into social stress is concerned with the difficult or threatening circumstances confronted by groups of people who share similar social and economic attributes, that is, the social patterning of stress. Research on social stress also examines the consequences of stress for individual well-being, especially for mental health.

Psychological Perspective Whereas the sociological perspective examines the social conditions that create potentially stressful situations and the consequent social patterning of stress and well-being, the psychological perspective emphasizes the internal cognitive and behavioral processes that account for individual variations in response to stressors (Lazarus, 1999). In this sense, the psychological perspective provides a bridge for understanding how life circumstances and physiological responses together affect individual health and well-being. The psychological perspective emphasizes the ways personality and biological factors combine with environmental conditions, allowing people to make meaning of the current situation with respect to individual well-being. Simply put, if an individual perceives a situation as stressful, it is a stressor. Thus, despite similarities among people experiencing a particular stressor, individuals respond uniquely to each situation. A key assumption of psychological perspectives on the stress process is that the ways people think about and interpret the circumstances of everyday life changes their physiological response to those circumstances.

Integrated Perspective Although several perspectives are used to study stress, a common goal for all of them is gaining an understanding of how individuals adapt to the changing circumstances of daily life and the impact of that adaptation on well-being across the life course. Rather than being at odds with each other, integrating findings from different perspectives has the potential to provide a more complete explanation of the stress process and to more effectively delineate the impact of social stress on individual health and well-being (Wheaton, 2001).

TYPES OF STRESSORS AND THEIR EFFECTS ON WELL-BEING

Selye (1956) proposed that anything that initiated a stress response constituted a stressor. Such a broad definition, however, makes it difficult to systematically study the individual components of the stress process. Thus, social stress research categorizes sources of stress to examine their distinct origins and develop better methods for further investigating their consequences. Social stressors are challenging conditions emerging from the social contexts of everyday life, including traumas, life events, chronic demands and strains in specific life domains (e.g., work and at home), and minor interruptions to one's daily routine (daily hassles). Typically, physical stressors (e.g., environmental exposure to hot or cold weather) and psychological stressors that focus largely on one's perceptions of a social stressor (e.g., ruminating and reliving past situations, or catastrophizing about a current situation) are not considered types of social stress.

Trauma Extreme events that both overwhelm a person and disrupt the life course (e.g., a violent crime, war, or a life-threatening illness) are referred to as traumas. The magnitude and suddenness of these events may disrupt a person's mental and physical well-being long after the occurrence of the event (Pearlin, 1999).

One often-studied trauma is combat exposure or war stress. Beginning after World War II (1939–1945), systematic research documented the effects of combat exposure on psychological health. This research led to the establishment of posttraumatic stress disorder (PTSD) as a psychological condition (Fontana & Rosenheck, 1994). PTSD is an anxiety disorder observed in persons who have been exposed to an extreme stressor. In addition to its immediate detrimental impact, war stress has the potential for both ongoing disruption to the life course and onset of PTSD symptomatology late in adulthood. The effects of wartime trauma extend beyond people with direct combat exposure. Similar disruptive and long-term effects have been found in both children of military parents (Shaw, 2003) and nonmilitary rela-

tives of military adults. PTSD and other severe psychological disorders also have been associated with exposure to other trauma conditions, including natural disasters and severe physical injury.

Life Events Life events are discrete, observable, and objectively reportable changes that require some adjustment on the part of the individual experiencing them. Examples include marriage, divorce, death of a loved one, and loss of a job. Exposure to life events, particularly undesirable and uncontrollable events, is associated with increases in psychological distress. A long research tradition linking life events and depression provides compelling evidence for a direct link between life events and onset of major depressive disorder, especially the onset of one's first major depressive disorder (Kendler, Karkowski, & Prescott, 1999). Stressful life events have also been linked to negative physical health outcomes such as coronary heart disease and other physical disorders, including rheumatoid arthritis (Zautra et al., 1998) and AIDS or HIV (Leserman et al., 1999). Although several studies provide strong support for a link between life event stressors and physical disease and disorders, the findings must be interpreted with caution, as it may be the combination of life events with other factors (e.g., ongoing life difficulties, social support, current health status) that influence health outcomes.

Chronic Stressors Chronic stressors are persistent or recurrent life difficulties, including strains in particular areas of life (e.g., job demands and family responsibilities), conflicting social roles (e.g., being a parent and worker), or excessive complexity in everyday life. Chronic stressors activate a prolonged immune response that may lead to physical diseases, including those that suppress immune response (e.g., infection), as well as those that overactivate the immune response (e.g., allergic and autoimmune responses). The open-ended nature of chronic stressors (not knowing when, or if, the stressor will end) may deplete biological, psychological, and social resources and thus be particularly influential in increasing the risk of distress and disease.

Job strain, or the combination of high job demands and low control over those demands, is a typical example of a chronic work-related stressor that contributes to negative psychological and physical outcomes. The effects of job strain may be particularly harmful in high-strain jobs, such as those for service workers and machine-paced operatives (Repetti, 1989).

Caregiving for loved ones is another source of chronic stress. The responsibilities of a primary caregiver include meeting the demands of caring for a loved one with a serious illness as well as the emotional burdens associated with the loved one's increasing physical and mental impairments. Leonard Pearlin, Joseph Mullan, Shirley Semple, and Marilyn Skaff (1990) referred to the cascading burden of caregiver stress as *stress proliferation*, or managing both primary stressors of caregiving (e.g., tending to the patient's meals, medications, and hygiene) and secondary stressors (i.e., additional demands unrelated to the person's illness). Role strains and resentments are examples of secondary stressors that may emerge when children care for an aging parent (Suitor & Pillemer, 1993).

Although chronic stressors are a distinct type of stressor, there is often an interrelationship between types of stressors. Ongoing job strain may lead to an acute life event, such as job layoff. Alternatively, an acute life event such as a divorce may give rise to ongoing financial difficulties. Thus studies that focus on a single type of stressor may understate the harmful effects of stressors.

Daily Hassles Daily hassles are defined as relatively minor events arising out of day-to-day living, such as a last-minute change on a work project or a flat tire. Although they may not have the same impact as a life-altering event, daily hassles do significantly influence daily health and psychological well-being. Studies of daily stress and health provide a unique opportunity to examine the unfolding process of stress adaptation within a person (i.e., how the same person responds to changing conditions) by documenting how a person's reactivity (i.e., how likely he or she is they are to experience distress) fluctuates. Daily diary studies, in which people record their experiences and their reactions to them, offer insight into the dynamic interplay between stressor exposure and reactivity and how the two combine to affect daily health and well-being (Almeida, Wethington, & Kessler, 2002).

To put it another way, everyone has good days and bad days. On good days, a person may be less reactive to experiences; on bad days, he or she may be more reactive. Daily studies also consider how the characteristics of a stressor may trigger different responses, both for the same person and for different groups of people. One study found that the type of daily stressor affected variations in mood (Bolger, DeLongis, Kessler, & Schilling, 1989). Of the 10 categories of stressors studied, interpersonal tensions were the most upsetting for both men and women.

In a follow-up study, David Almeida and Ronald Kessler (1998) found that although exposure to stressors was associated with higher levels of distress for both husbands and wives, wives reported more stressors overall than did husbands. In addition, family demands, arguments with a spouse, arguments with a person besides the spouse, transportation difficulties (e.g., traffic jams, car trouble), and other demands (e.g., those of relatives or friends) were more strongly related to distress for wives than for husbands, whereas work overloads, arguments with children, and financial problems were more strongly related to distress among husbands than among wives.

Associations among Types of Stressors Stressors rarely occur independently; one stressor may trigger a number of subsequent stressful experiences. Chronic stressors may lead to more daily hassles or life events. Even minor stressors can increase in intensity by accumulating and disrupting other aspects of a person's life or usurping resources needed to manage subsequent circumstances. Thus, considering the association among the stressors in a person's life is important to understand the effects of stress on health and well-being. For example, ongoing financial strain following a divorce or job loss may be more damaging to individuals health than the actual event itself.

COPING WITH STRESSORS

Coping typically refers to the things that people do to manage the ups and downs of life. Coping includes both the cognitive and behavioral strategies people use as well as the resources they apply in managing the demands of life.

Coping Strategies There are two primary coping strategies: problem-focused and emotion-focused. Problem-focused coping refers to efforts directed at resolving or removing the source of the stressor—for example, taking an alternate route to work to avoid traffic caused by road construction. In contrast, emotion-focused coping strategies address the negative emotions and feelings of distress triggered by a stressor. Rather than feeling frustrated or angry at traffic delays due to construction, a person may tell him or herself how easy the ride to work will be when the road is finished, or use the time to think about the pleasant things that she or he will do when they arrive at home. In these examples, the stressor is unchanged, but the negative reaction to the stressor dissipates.

Much research on coping examines which emotion-focused and problem-focused strategies are effective at minimizing the impact of stressors. Emotion-focused coping strategies are often associated with *increased* distress (Penley, Tomaka, & Wiebe, 2002). Passive coping strategies—for example, avoiding difficult situations rather than dealing with them—have been found to be associated with higher levels of depression and psychological distress. Denial as a coping strategy (e.g., ignoring worsening symptoms or saying that a personal problem "is not real") also may be maladaptive for chronic illnesses because it does not allow for learning to manage the long-term stressor (Burker, Evon, Losielle, Finkel, &

Mill, 2005). In contrast, however, denial may have positive effects for people dealing with certain short-term stressors by diverting attention from the stressor until it has passed. For example, one study found that avoidant coping was most effective in dealing with the stress of donating blood (Kaloupek, White, & Wong, 1984).

Problem-focused coping strategies, such as seeking social support and problem solving, tend to be favored in individual-oriented Western nations. Problem-focused strategies have been associated with better outcomes for patients dealing with a variety of illnesses and also with helping a patient's partner psychologically adjust to his or her loved one's illness (Chandler, Kennedy, & Sandhu, 2007). In general, however, most effective coping responses, particularly to severe stressors, involve multiple strategies (Folkman, 1997).

Coping Resources Coping resources are assets people have that may alter their reaction to stressful circumstances. In other words, resources are not the things that people do (e.g., strategies) but rather the things they can apply to meet the needs and demands of challenges. Coping resources may be internal (i.e., within the person) or external (i.e., outside of the person).

Internal resources refer to psychological resources that may help or hinder how people cope with stressors. Personality traits are an example of internal resources. Enduring personality traits are typically associated with differing coping strategies. Personality traits are often conceptualized as consisting of five main dimensions: neuroticism, extroversion, openness, agreeableness, and conscientiousness (McCrae & Costa, 1986). In terms of use of coping strategies, emotion-focused coping tends to be used by those with high levels of neuroticism, as well as by those who are open and agreeable. Extroversion and conscientiousness, as well as agreeableness, have been associated with the use of problem-focused coping strategies (Penley & Tomaka, 2002). It is possible that these personality characteristics themselves may serve to either exacerbate or buffer the effects of stress. For example, in an experimental study in which participants were assigned a stressful cognitive task (giving a speech on a controversial topic), people who were extroverted, open, agreeable, and conscientious were more satisfied with their performance on lab tasks than those with high levels of neuroticism. Neurotic individuals also reported more negative emotions such as anxiety, fear, and self-disgust (Penley & Tomaka, 2002). A similar pattern emerges in response to chronic stressors.

Other personality traits also may modify the impact of a stressor. For example, an optimistic disposition buffers the effects of stressors for patients suffering from chronic diseases perceived to be uncontrollable (Fournier, de Ridder, & Bensing, 2002). Whether a person sees events as within his or her control (*internal locus of control*) or outside

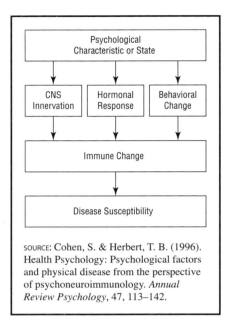

SOURCE: Cohen, S. & Herbert, T. B. (1996). Health Psychology: Psychological factors and physical disease from the perspective of psychoneuroimmunology. *Annual Review Psychology*, 47, 113–142.

Figure 1. CENGAGE LEARNING, GALE.

of his or her control (*external locus of control*) has been shown to affect people's responses to stressors; an internal locus of control is more effective in coping with stressors. Negative events are more strongly correlated with anxiety for people with external, as opposed to internal, locus of control (Sandler & Lakey, 1982).

External resources refer to the available tangible and social assets people can apply to offset the impact of potential stressors, such as money, social characteristics, and social resources. In their seminal work on the structure of coping, Pearlin and Carmi Schooler (1978) found that certain social characteristics had an impact on coping. For example, pronounced differences were found between men and women. Women were more likely to use coping responses that increased distress, such as selective ignoring, whereas men were more likely to use psychological resources that actually diminished stress reactivity in response to life problems, such as optimism. Additionally, lower socioeconomic status was associated with increased exposure to hardships and more reported stressors. People with lower socioeconomic status were also less likely to possess the necessary resources to buffer the negative distress associated with these hardships. The availability and type of social resources also may contribute to coping differences. *Social resources* refer to the people in one's social network, such as family, friends, and coworkers, who may offer tangible assistance and emotional support.

Some evidence suggests that the potential buffering effects of resources depend on the type of stressors being faced. For example, findings from a study conducted in

England examined the links between psychological resources and illness-related death (Surtees, Wainwright, & Luben, 2006). Findings suggested that a strong sense of mastery was associated with lower rates of death due to cardiovascular disease, whereas a sense of coherence, the belief that the things that happen are manageable and meaningful, was associated with lower rates of cancer death. In a separate study conducted in the Netherlands, researchers found that the psychological resource of self-esteem lessened the effects of cancer and arthritis on depressive symptoms, whereas the psychological resource of mastery lessened the effects of only diabetes on depressive symptoms (Bisschop, Kriegsman, & Beekman, 2004). In contrast, having a partner, an important social resource, lessened the negative psychological effects of a variety of chronic diseases.

INTERDEPENDENCE OF SOCIAL RELATIONSHIPS AND THE STRESS PROCESS

Considering the interdependence between individual experiences and the experiences of close others is important for understanding both the stressors that people experience and their responses to those stressors. Most human behavior takes place in the context of relationships with others. In virtually every study examining human happiness, satisfying close relationships are an integral component of well-being (Berscheid, 1999). Glen Elder (1999) referred to the interdependence of social relationships as *linked lives*, where the individual life course is influenced by experiences and life transitions of other social relationships. Because of these interdependencies, social relationships play an important part in the individual stress process. Social relationships make it easier to handle the challenges of life, offering emotional and tangible support during difficult situations. Indeed, supportive relationships are associated with decreased risk for morbidity and mortality (Kiecolt-Glaser, McGuire, Robles, & Glaser, 2002).

Family Relationships Each stage of the life course is both the consequence of prior experiences as well as the antecedent for subsequent life experiences (Spiro, 2001). Thus, early family life is important for understanding people's responses to stressful experiences. Family interactions establish both the initial trajectory of the life course as well as patterns for managing life experiences. First, biological families determine a person's genetic endowment, which lays the foundation for lifelong characteristics such as disposition or temperament and for predispositions to health conditions such as depression or heart disease. Family relationships and family environments influence the individual stress process in other ways as well, including exposure to different types of

stressors, selection of coping strategies, and development of social skills.

Rena Repetti, Shelley Taylor, and Teresa Seeman (2002) considered the long-term effects of growing up in a "risky" family. These authors defined risky families in terms of their relationship interactions, specifically those that have high levels of conflict and aggression or relationships that are cold, unsupportive, and neglectful. Ongoing exposure to conflictual family relationships can literally change the underlying physiological mechanisms for handling even routine challenges by continually activating the stress response. This chronic activation may lead to later deficits in physical health, such as coronary heart disease. These life experiences contribute to early wear and tear on the body, or allostatic load.

Families also may influence the individual stress process by modeling coping strategies and patterns for handling day-to-day life experiences. Once established, coping patterns are difficult to change. Repetti et al. (2002) suggested that growing up in families with high levels of conflict or anger results in the use of less adaptive coping strategies, such as those that focus on reducing tension or escaping from intense emotions rather than dealing with the stressor itself. Although escape from the angry situations in the home may be adaptive for their immediate safety, over the long run these avoidant coping strategies may result in other costs such as social problems with peers and difficulties in problem solving.

Finally, the family environment may influence the development of children's social skills. Repetti et al. (2002) found that children who grew up in risky families had problems processing emotions. Emotion-processing skills are essential for engaging in healthy relationships with others. High levels of conflict in the home may sensitize children to respond to social situations with negative emotions such as anger and anxiety. In adolescence, these children may demonstrate less control over their emotions and less understanding of emotions. Because children model the social behavior that they learn at home, they may develop unhealthy ideas about how relationships work. Indeed, there is evidence that the children of cold, unsupportive, or neglectful parents continued to experience problematic and unsupportive relationships throughout their life (Repetti et al., 2002).

Romantic Relationships Studies often find that married people tend to enjoy physical, emotional, and economic advantage, compared to their unmarried counterparts (Coyne & DeLongis, 1986). Romantic relationships can be an important source of social support. For example, one study found that support from a spouse was more strongly associated with life satisfaction and positive mood than support from friends or family (Walen & Lachman, 2000). This suggests that there may be something unique about the kind of support that a spouse can provide. Unfortunately, interpersonal relationships are not always supportive and may actually be a source of strain. Relationship conflicts are among the most potent of stressors, evoking strong psychological and physiological responses in both men and women (Bolger et al., 1989). Exposure to high levels of stress also may have an impact on the quality of one's relationships. Thus, whereas having a supportive spouse may ameliorate the impact of stress, ongoing exposure to stress may also strain relationships.

Peer Relationships and Friendships Friendships are another type of close social relationship that may modify the individual stress process. Social networks that include supportive friends are one of the best predictors of overall life satisfaction and physical health. The presence of a supportive friend has been associated with lower cardiovascular reactivity in response to acute stressors (Kirschbaum, Klauer, Filipp, & Hellhammer, 1995). Similar to romantic relationships, friendships can be sources of both support and strain. Negative interactions with friends are more predictive of depressed mood than supportive interactions.

Much of the literature on the relation between friends and one's stress level has examined the role of friendships during adolescence and young adulthood, particularly in undergraduate samples. Friendships are particularly important during this time in life—perhaps even more important than family relationships. For example, a study that examined first-year college students adjusting to school life found that increased social support from friends, but not the family, was associated with better adjustment (Friedlander et al., 2007). Thus, friends can be a great source of support for managing stressors.

Epidemiological studies on the health of older adults provide substantial evidence that social integration and social support contribute to longevity. In a review of the protective effects of social support from friends and family and the health of older adults, Seeman (2000) suggested that it is the pattern of support received, rather than the source of support, that contributes most to health outcomes. Thus, social support that is perceived as critical, demanding, or conflictual has a negative effect on both morbidity and mortality rates in older adults.

Research on the influence of friends and well-being during middle adulthood is limited, comparing the influence of friends to the influence of others (e.g., spouse or relatives). For example, Pamela Jackson (1992) found that for married parents who are employed full time,

spousal support lessened the depressing effects of all types of life strain whereas the support of friends was limited to specific domains (i.e., marital, economic, and health). Additionally, under high-stress conditions, such as those for people diagnosed with AIDS, for example, family support was found to be more important than support from friends (Crystal & Kersting, 1998). In summary, although the importance of friendships on individual health and well-being may be an important resource for managing the individual stress process, additional research in this area, particularly during adulthood, is needed.

PHYSIOLOGICAL PATHWAYS BETWEEN STRESSOR EXPOSURE AND DISEASE

As described in part above, psychosocial stressors are risk factors for a broad range of physical diseases. Stress-related illnesses include minor physical ailments, such as colds, allergies, back pain, and headaches, as well as severe diseases such as coronary heart disease and cancer. Research has thus focused on the specific physiological processes linking stress exposure and disease.

The physiological response to stressors involves direct stimulation of the central nervous system and a hormonal relay system among three main organs: the hypothalamus and the pituitary gland, located in the brain, and the adrenal glands, located at the top of each kidney. Both the central nervous system and the hypothalamic-pituitary-adrenal (HPA) axis play a vital role in linking stressor exposure to physical health outcomes (Cohen & Herbert, 1996; McEwen, 1998). Much of the research on the link between psychosocial stress and health has focused on the cardiovascular and immune systems, as these two systems are directly involved in the etiology of several disease processes (Cohen & Manuck, 1995).

Coronary Heart Disease and Stress Coronary heart disease is the leading cause of death in European and North American populations (Brydon, Magid, & Steptoe, 2006) and is gaining momentum in developing countries. Epidemiological evidence suggests that psychological stress has a profound effect on cardiovascular functioning and the development of coronary heart disease globally (Rosengren et al., 2004). A rich literature documents the association between psychosocial stressors and incidence of heart attack in Western countries. However, an increase in both coronary heart disease mortality and psychosocial stress among eastern European populations, especially middle-aged men (Weidner & Cain, 2003), suggests that the health risk of psychosocial stress extends beyond the border of Western societies. An international study on the association between psychosocial stress and heart attack in 24,767 people in 52 countries provides evidence for the association (Rosengren et al., 2004). The study found that for people reporting their first heart attack, stressful life events, general stress, and financial stress were more frequent compared to controls. The findings were consistent across regions, genders, and ethnic groups.

Reactivity to stressors is thought to account for the relationship between exposure to psychosocial stress and coronary heart disease. High stress reactivity increases vascular inflammation (atherosclerosis), which in turn leads to a build up of plaque in the arteries (arteriosclerosis), in turn increasing the likelihood of heart attack (myocardial infarction) and stroke. Stress reactivity also increases production of platelets. Platelet activation releases substances into the blood stream that adhere to arteries, which results in plaque buildup and may also account for the association between reactivity to stressors and coronary heart disease (Brydon et al., 2006). Laboratory studies examining the association between reactivity to acute stressors and atherosclerosis find that people who are more reactive to acute lab stressors demonstrate more evidence of cardiovascular disease (Barnett et al., 1997; Player, King, Mainous, & Geesey, 2007).

Psychoneuroimmunology and Stress The immune system protects the body from foreign materials, such as bacteria and viruses, by releasing antibodies and white blood cells into the circulatory system. Psychological stressors increase the risk of illness and disease by altering the immune response, making the body less able to defend itself against foreign materials. Research examining these associations since the late 1980s has provided a much clearer understanding of the process (Kemeny & Schedlowski, 2007).

The strongest evidence for a direct link between psychosocial stressors and the etiology of physical disease comes from studies on stress and viral infections, such as colds and the flu (Cohen, Tyrrell, & Smith, 1993). In these experimental studies, healthy volunteers answered questions about life stress and were then inoculated with a virus to examine the impact of stressors on health outcomes. After several days, health symptoms evaluated through both self-report and physiological measures (i.e., blood draws) suggested that exposure to psychosocial stressors increased susceptibility to upper respiratory infection. An association between stressor exposure and other infectious diseases has been documented in both laboratory studies (Kiecolt-Glaser & Glaser, 1987) and in studies on the progression of immune diseases, including HIV and rheumatoid arthritis. Findings from these studies support the idea that exposure to both acute and ongoing stressors contributes to a worsening of health conditions and disease symptoms.

CONCLUSION

All people, regardless of age, gender, or social situation, face changing life circumstances and are therefore engaged in a process of ongoing adaptation. A life course perspective suggests that researchers study people of varying social and economic backgrounds at different life stages (e.g., childhood, adolescence, adulthood) to identify the kinds of challenges they are facing and the processes they are likely to use in dealing with those challenges. There are several reasons why this life course perspective is vital in the study of stress. First, adverse early-life circumstances (e.g., poverty, abuse, neglect) have both immediate and long-term effects. Second, adaptation to severe, unexpected events may be very different depending on the timing of the event—consider the implications, for example, of the loss of a job in young adulthood compared to the loss of a job near retirement age. Finally, the frequency and type of life circumstances people face as well as the impact on the life course are likely to vary by age, socioeconomic status, gender, and culture. Thus, the study of stress and the life course emphasizes the importance of examining people engaged in ordinary activities of everyday life, so as to enable the understanding of how life circumstances account for exposure to various types of stressors and, in turn, how the availability of resources to combat these stressors contributes to variability in individual health and well-being.

SEE ALSO Volume 1: *Resilience, Childhood and Adolescence;* Volume 2: *Mental Health, Adulthood; Midlife Crises and Transitions; Roles.*

BIBLIOGRAPHY

Almeida, D. M., & Kessler, R. C. (1998). Everyday stressors and gender differences in daily distress. *Journal of Personality and Social Psychology, 75*(3), 670–680.

Almeida, D. M., Wethington, E., & Kessler, R. C. (2002). The daily inventory of stressful events: An interview-based approach for measuring daily stressors. *Assessment, 9*(1), 41–55.

Barnett, P. A., Spence, J. D., Manuck, S. B., & Jennings, J. R. (1997). Psychological stress and the progression of carotid artery disease. *Journal of Hypertension, 15*(1), 49–55.

Berscheid, E. (1999). The greening of relationship science. *American Psychologist, 54*(4), 260–266.

Bisschop, M. I., Kriegsman, D. M. W., & Beekman, A. T. F. (2004). Chronic diseases and depression: The modifying role of psychosocial resources. *Social Science & Medicine, 59*(4), 721–733.

Bolger, N., DeLongis, A., Kessler, R. C., & Schilling, E. A. (1989). Effects of daily stress on negative mood. *Journal of Personality and Social Psychology, 57*(5), 808–818.

Brydon, L., Magid, K., & Steptoe, A. (2006). Platelets, coronary heart disease, and stress. *Brain, Behavior, and Immunity, 20*(2), 113–119.

Burker, E. J., Evon, D. M., Losielle, M. M., Finkel, J. B., & Mill, M. R. (2005). Coping predicts depression and disability in heart transplant candidates. *Journal of Psychosomatic Research*, *59*(4), 215–222.

Cannon, W. (1929). The sympathetic division of the autonomic system in relation to homeostasis. *Archives of Neurology and Psychiatry*, *22*, 282–294.

Chandler, M., Kennedy, P., & Sandhu, N. (2007). The association between threat appraisals and psychological adjustment in partners of people with spinal cord injuries. *Rehabilitation Psychology*, *52*, 470–477.

Cohen, S., & Herbert, T. B. (1996). Health psychology: Psychological factors and physical disease from the perspective of human psychoneuroimmunology. *Annual Review of Psychology*, *47*, 113–142.

Cohen, S., & Manuck, S. B. (1995). Stress, reactivity, and disease. *Psychosomatic Medicine*, *57*(5), 423–426.

Cohen, S., Tyrrell, D. A., & Smith, A. P. (1993). Negative life events, perceived stress, negative affect, and susceptibility to the common cold. *Journal of Personality and Social Psychology*, *64*(1), 131–140.

Coyne, J. C., & DeLongis, A. (1986). Going beyond social support: The role of social relationships in adaptation. *Journal of Consulting and Clinical Psychology*, *54*, 454–460.

Crystal, S., & Kersting, R. C. (1998). Stress, social support, and distress in a statewide population of person with AIDS in New Jersey. *Social Work in Health Care*, *28*(1), 41–60.

Elder, G. H., Jr. (1999). *Children of the Great Depression: Social change in life experience*. Boulder, CO: Westview Press.

Folkman, S. (1997). Positive psychological states and coping with severe stress. *Social Science & Medicine*, *45*(8), 1207–1221.

Fontana, A., & Rosenheck, R. (1994). Traumatic war stressors and psychiatric symptoms among World War II, Korean, and Vietnam War veterans. *Psychology and Aging*, *9*(1), 27–33.

Fournier, M., de Ridder, D., & Bensing, J. (2002). How optimism contributes to the adaptation of chronic illness: A prospective study into the enduring effects of optimism on adaptation moderated by the controllability of chronic illness. *Personality and Individual Differences*, *33*(7), 1163–1183.

Friedlander, L. J., Reid, G. J., & Shupak, N. (2007). Social support, self-esteem, and stress as predictors of adjustment to university among first-year undergraduates. *Journal of College Student Development*, *48*(3), 259–274.

Jackson, P. B. (1992). Specifying the buffering hypothesis: Support, strain, and depression. *Social Psychology Quarterly*, *55*(4), 363–378.

Kaloupek, D. G., White, H., & Wong, M. (1984). Multiple assessment of coping strategies used by volunteer blood donors: Implications for preparatory training. *Journal of Behavioral Medicine*, *7*(1), 35–60.

Kemeny, M. E., & Schedlowski, M. (2007). Understanding the interaction between psychosocial stress and immune-related diseases: A stepwise progression. *Brain, Behavior, and Immunity*, *21*(8), 1009–1018.

Kendler, K. S., Karkowski, L. M., & Prescott, C. A. (1999). The assessment of dependence in the study of stressful life events: Validation using a twin design. *Psychological Medicine*, *29*(6), 1455–1460.

Kiecolt-Glaser, J. K., & Glaser, R. (1987). Psychosocial moderators of immune function. *Annals of Behavioral Medicine*, *9*(2), 16–20.

Kiecolt-Glaser, J. K., McGuire, L., Robles, T. F., & Glaser, R. (2002). Emotions, morbidity, and mortality: New perspectives from psychoneuroimmunology. *Annual Review of Psychology*, *53*, 83–107.

Kirschbaum, C., Klauer, T., Filipp, S. H., & Hellhammer, D. H. (1995). Sex-specific effects of social support on cortisol and subjective responses to acute psychological stress. *Psychosomatic Medicine*, *57*(1), 23–31.

Lazarus, R. S. (1999). *Stress and emotion: A new synthesis*. New York: Springer.

Leserman, J., Jackson, E. D., Petitto, J. M., Golden, R. N., Silva, S. G., Perkins, D. O., et al. (1999). Progression to AIDS: The effects of stress, depressive symptoms, and social support. *Psychosomatic Medicine*, *61*(3), 397–406.

McCrae, R. R., & Costa, P. T. (1986). Personality, coping, and coping effectiveness in an adult sample. *Journal of Personality*, *54*, 385–405.

McEwen, B. S. (1998). Stress, adaptation, and disease: Allostasis and allostatic load. *Annals of the New York Academy of Sciences*, *840*(1), 33–44.

McEwen, B. S., & Stellar, E. (1993). Stress and the individual: Mechanisms leading to disease. *Archives of Internal Medicine*, *153*(18), 2093–2101.

Pearlin, L. I. (1999). The stress process revisited: Reflections on concepts and their interrelationships. In C. S. Aneshensel & J. C. Phelan (Eds.), *Handbook of the sociology of mental health* (pp. 395–415). New York: Kluwer Academic/Plenum.

Pearlin, L. I., Mullan, J. T., Semple, S. J., & Skaff, M. M. (1990). Caregiving and the stress process: An overview of concepts and their measures. *The Gerontologist*, *30*(5), 583–594.

Pearlin, L. I., & Schooler, C. (1978). The structure of coping. *Journal of Health and Social Behavior*, *19*(1), 2–21.

Penley, J. A., & Tomaka, J. (2002). Associations among the Big Five, emotional responses, and coping with acute stress. *Personality and Individual Differences*, *32*, 1215–1228.

Penley, J. A., Tomaka, J., & Wiebe, J. S. (2002). The association of coping to physical and psychological health outcomes: A meta-analytic review. *Journal of Behavioral Medicine*, *25*(6), 551–603.

Player, M. S., King, D. E., Mainous, A. G., & Geesey, M. E. (2007). Psychosocial factors and progression from pre-hypertension to hypertension or coronary heart disease. *Annals of Family Medicine*, *5*(5), 403–411.

Repetti, R. L. (1989). Effects of daily workload on subsequent behavior during marital interaction: The roles of social withdrawal and spouse support. *Journal of Personality and Social Psychology*, *57*(4), 651–659.

Repetti, R. L., Taylor, S. E., & Seeman, T. E. (2002). Risky families: Family social environments and the mental and physical health of offspring. *Psychological Bulletin*, *128*(2), 330–366.

Rosengren, A., Hawken, S., Ôunpuu, S., Sliwa, K., Zubaid, M., Almahmeed, W. A., et al. (2004). Association of psychosocial risk factors with risk of acute myocardial infarction in 11,119 cases and 13,648 controls from 52 countries (the INTERHEART Study): Case-control study. *Lancet*, *364*(9438), 953–962.

Sandler, I. N., & Lakey, B. (1982). Locus of control as a stress moderator: The role of control perceptions and social support. *American Journal of Community Psychology*, *10*(1), 65–80.

Seeman, T. E. (2000). Health-promoting effects of friends and family on health outcomes in older adults. *American Journal of Health Promotion*, *14*(6), 362–370.

Seeman, T. E., McEwen, B. S., Rowe, J. W., & Singer, B. H. (2001). Allostatic load as a marker of cumulative biological risk: MacArthur studies of successful aging. *Proceedings of the National Academy of Sciences of the United States of America, 98*(8), 4770–4775.

Selye, H. (1956). Stress and psychobiology. *Journal of Clinical & Experimental Psychopathology, 17,* 370–375.

Shaw, J. A. (2003). Children exposed to war/terrorism. *Clinical Child & Family Psychology Review, 6*(4), 237–246.

Spiro, A. (2001). Health in midlife: Toward a life span view. In M. E. Lachman (Ed.), *Handbook of midlife development* (pp.156–187). New York: Wiley.

Suitor, J. J., & Pillemer, K. (1993). Support and interpersonal stress in the social networks of married daughters caring for parents with dementia. *Journal of Gerontology, 48*(1), 1–8.

Surtees, P. G., Wainwright, N. W. J., & Luben, R. (2006). Mastery, sense of coherence, and mortality: Evidence of independent associations from the EPIC-Norfolk Prospective Cohort Study. *Health Psychology, 25*(1), 102–110.

Walen, H. R., & Lachman, M. E. (2000). Social support and strain from partner, family, and friends: Costs and benefits for men and women in adulthood. *Journal of Social and Personal Relationships, 17*(1), 5–30.

Weidner, G., & Cain, V. S. (2003). The gender gap in heart disease: Lessons from eastern Europe. *American Journal of Public Health, 93*(5), 768–770.

Wheaton, B. (2001). The role of sociology in the study of mental health and the role of mental health in the study of sociology. *Journal of Health and Social Behavior, 42*(3), 221–234.

Zautra, A. J., Hoffman, J. M., Matt, K. S., Yocum, D., Potter, P. T., Castro, W. L., et al. (1998). An examination of individual differences in the relationship between interpersonal stress and disease activity among women with rheumatoid arthritis. *Arthritis Care and Research, 11*(4), 271–279.

Joyce Serido
Casey Totenhagen

SUICIDE, ADULTHOOD

Suicide refers to the willful taking of one's life. A life course perspective on suicide helps to address two fundamental questions about the causes of suicide: (a) Are there individual-based factors such as lifelong depression that affect suicide risk independent of stage in the life course, and (b) to what extent do the common transitions in adulthood, such as marriage, parenthood, and employment, predict suicide risk?

THE PSYCHIATRIC PERSPECTIVE ON SUICIDE

The most well-researched area in adult suicide is the linkage between certain psychiatric disorders and suicide risk. Most suicides result, in part, from a serious psychiatric disorder. For example, in a review of 3,275 suicides,

Psychiatric Disorder	Increased Odds of Suicide for Persons With the Disorder vs. Controls	Number of Research Studies	Number of Persons Studied
Eating Disorder	23	13	1,300
Alcohol Dependence and Abuse	6	32	45,000
Opioid Dependence & Abuse	14	9	7,500
Schizophrenia	8.5	38	30,000
Major Depression	20.4	23	8,000
Bipolar Disorder	15.1	14	3,700
Dysthymia	12	9	50,000
Mood Disorders	16	12	10,000
Epilepsy	4.9	12	6,500
Suicide Attempts by self poisoning	40	11	8,000
Suicide Attempts, any method	38	9	2,700

Table 1. *Average risk ratio for selected psychiatric disorders.*
CENGAGE LEARNING, GALE.

researchers found that 87.3% of the victims had been diagnosed with a mental disorder prior to their death (Arsenault-Lapierre, Kim, & Turecki, 2004). Similarly, E. Clare Harris and Brian Barraclough (1997) systematically reviewed 249 research studies. Of the 44 disorders investigated, 36 were found to significantly raise the risk of suicide. Table 1 provides a summary of the average risk for suicide among people experiencing selected psychiatric disorders in which at least nine studies linking the disorder and suicide were available. For example, on average, major depression increases the risk of suicide 20.4 times, whereas schizophrenia increases it 8.5 times.

Substance abuse disorders are among the best-researched disorders. A recent meta-analysis of 42 comparable research studies found that substance abuse disorders increased the risk of suicide above that experienced in the general population as follows: alcohol use disorder 9.7 times, opiate use disorder 13.51 times, intravenous drug use 13.73 times, mixed drug use 16.85 times, and heavy drinking 3.51 times (Wilcox, Connor, & Caine, 2004). A different meta-analysis calculated an annual suicide rate of 193 per 100,000 persons among those with anxiety disorders, including the posttraumatic stress and panic disorders (Khan, Leventhal, Khan, & Brown, 2002). By contrast,

Group	1950	1960	1970	1980	1990	2000	2004
White Males							
25–44	17.9	18.5	21.5	24.6	25.4	22.9	23.8
45–64	39.3	36.5	31.9	25.0	26.0	23.2	26.1
Black Males							
25–44	9.8	12.6	16.1	19.2	19.6	14.3	13.7
45–64	12.7	13.0	12.4	11.8	13.1	9.9	10.1
White Females							
25–44	6.6	7.0	11.0	8.1	6.6	6.0	6.6
45–64	10.6	10.9	13.0	9.6	7.7	6.9	8.5
Black Females							
25–44	2.3	3.0	4.8	4.3	3.8	2.6	2.9
45–64	2.7	3.1	2.9	2.5	2.9	2.1	2.2
Ratio of Male 25–44 to Female 25–44 Suicide Rates	2.7	2.64	1.95	3.0	3.8	3.8	3.6

Table 2. *Suicide rates per 100,000 By gender, race and age group, adult, 25–64 population, USA, 1950–2004.* CENGAGE LEARNING, GALE.

annual suicide rates for the general population in developed nations typically range between 10 and 20 per 100,000 persons.

Schizophrenia, a condition marked by perceptual distortions of reality including auditory and visual delusions, generally begins to take hold in early adulthood. In case-series studies, an investigator follows a group of people diagnosed as schizophrenic and determines the proportion that die through suicide at follow-up some years later. A review of 30 such studies determined that, on average, 37.7% of male and 27% of female schizophrenics had committed suicide by follow-up, typically 5 to 15 years after the onset of the study. In contrast, only 1 to 2% of the population of developed nations dies through suicide (Lester, 2006).

One investigation exploring the relation between various psychiatric factors and suicide risk involved a large, 18-year study that tracked the lives of 444,297 persons in Denmark, including 21,169 who committed suicide during the study period. Researchers found that the group with, by far, the highest risk of suicide was former mental patients during the first 8 days of being discharged. Their risk of suicide was 278 times that of nonmental patients (Qin, Agerbo, & Mortensen, 2003).

That biological factors are involved in the transmission of psychiatric disorders across generations is consis-

tent with findings on suicide risk within families. For example, persons who committed suicide in the Denmark study were 3.5 times more apt to have had a first-degree relative who also had committed suicide, relative to similar people in the general population.

Although the psychiatric perspective explains much of the variation in adult suicide risk, it does not fully explain secondary variation (or subgroup differences) in risk, such as the large gap in suicide rates between men and women, and the considerable variation in suicide rates over time and among geographic units such as cities, states, and nations. Work on other risk and protective factors needs to be considered to fully understand the causes of adult suicide.

INDIVIDUAL-LEVEL RISK AND PROTECTIVE FACTORS

Gender In what approaches something akin to a social science law, adult males tend to have a suicide rate that is between 2 to 4 times that of adult females. Data on U.S. suicide rates between 1950 and 2004 by race or ethnicity and gender are provided in Table 2.

Researchers have advanced many hypotheses to explain the gender differential in suicide, with these hypotheses drawn from prior research on gender differences in behaviors and attitudes. These behaviors include factors such as alcoholism rates, which are higher among men, and men's greater knowledge about and ownership of firearms. There are also gender differentials in help-seeking behavior for mental disturbances, such that females have a greater tendency to seek professional help for psychiatric problems. Females also generally have more extensive support networks than males (Stack, 2000). Although these factors help explain the gender gap at one point in time, additional factors are needed to explain trends.

Table 1 shows that the suicide gender gap in the United States changed between 1950 and 2004. For White persons ages 25 to 44, the male to female suicide ratio decreased from 2.7 in 1950 to 1.95 in 1970. From 1970 it increased to 3.6 in 2004. Sociological analysis of this curvilinear relationship has been done both in the United States and in 17 other developed nations. The main explanation for it is that after a critical mass of women enters the labor force, cultural definitions of women's (and men's) role in society change. Cultural approval of women working while raising children was relatively low in the 1950s and contributed to feelings of role conflict between homemaker and worker. However, as the proportion of working women increased, culture defined the working mother in positive terms, lessening any guilt feelings about tension between the worlds of work and family. There is corresponding growth in supportive cultural institutions and patterns such as day-care centers and greater male involvement in housework and childcare. Unfortunately, male suicide rates have held steady or increased as female rates have decreased. This male response is related to declining opportunity for men to enter and advance in managerial professional careers (Stack, 2000).

Race Whites generally have had a suicide rate that is double that of African Americans. However, this pattern is somewhat weaker for young adults (see Table 2). The best available national database on suicide is the National Mortality Followback Survey (National Center for Health Statistics, 2000). It contains detailed information on 9,869 adult deaths (ages 18 to 64), including 948 suicides. An analysis of this database found that controlling for 18 other contributing factors, including age and depressive symptoms, White adults were 1.85 times more likely than minorities to die through suicide.

Several explanations have been advanced for the race–suicide relationship. The first such argument posits that societal discrimination against African Americans has contributed to a particular response, the externalization of aggression. Given the history of racial discrimination in the United States, Blacks are more apt to blame others than themselves when confronted with stressful life

events. As a consequence, Black homicide rates are five or more times those of Whites. A second argument notes that tolerance of suicide, suicide acceptability, is considerably lower among Blacks than Whites. Finally, religiosity levels are higher among Blacks than Whites. Religions tend to condemn suicide (Stack, 2000).

LIFE COURSE EVENTS AND SUICIDE IN ADULTHOOD

Suicide rates increase from childhood to adulthood. During the adult years there are life events that act as risk and protective factors for suicide. The more well-researched life events include several regarding measures of social integration, an individuals ties, and social and interpersonal networks that provide emotional support and, hence, reduce suicide risk. Marriage, parenthood, living alone, migration, as well as economic strain, which is shown to increase suicide risk in adulthood, are all areas that have been given specific attention in their relation to suicide prevalence (Stack, 2000).

Marital Status During adulthood marriage is a powerful protective factor against suicide. A review of 789 research findings from 132 studies published over 115 years found that 78% demonstrated a link between divorce and increased suicide risk (Stack, 2000). For example, in Austria, divorced persons had a suicide rate of 128.6 per 100,000 compared to 30.5 per 100,000 for married persons. The ratio of the divorced to married rate, the coefficient of aggravation (COA) of 4.22 is in the typical range for adult men in the United States. The COA for men in the United States ranges from 4.58 for men ages 40 to 44 to a low of 3.53 for men ages 60 to 64. For adult American women, the COA varies from a high of 4.15 for women ages 25 to 29 to a low of 2.10 for women ages 60 to 64.

Cohabitation Although there is little research on the protective effect of cohabitation on suicide risk, what does exist suggests that cohabitation does not protect as much against suicide as marriage. For example, in Denmark, cohabitants have a risk of suicide 1.54 times higher than married persons, whereas single persons have a risk 3.17 times higher than that of married persons (Qin et al., 2003).

Living Alone Living alone contributes to suicide through minimizing emotional support from intimate relationships. An analysis of the National Mortality Followback Survey determined that after controlling for depressive symptoms and 17 other predictors of suicide, persons who lived alone were 1.58 times more likely to die through suicide than those not living alone (National Center for Health Statistics, 2000).

Parenthood Dating back to early research conducted by French sociologist Émile Durkheim (1858–1917), sociologists have documented the tendency for married persons with children to have a lower rate of suicide than married persons without children. For example, in Denmark, parents with a young child are 50% less apt to commit suicide than parents without a young child (Qin et al., 2003). Ties to children can increase purpose or meaning in life and increase the odds of going on with life in the face of adversity—for the sake of one's children.

Migration Persons who migrate, especially over long distances, break ties with friends, extended family, coworkers, and other sources of social support. Although not as well-studied as marital ties, migration tends to be related to suicide risk. For example, controlling for depression and 17 other predictors of suicide, an analysis of the National Mortality Followback Survey determined that persons who changed residence in the previous 12 months were 4.32 times more likely to die through suicide than persons who did not move (National Center for Health Statistics, 2000).

Religiosity A large body of sociological research has found that the higher a person's level of religiosity, the lower their suicide risk (Stack, 2000). Religions tend to condemn suicide as a sin, promote social networking and support among coreligionists, and offer a variety of beliefs (e.g., a pleasant afterlife), which can act as coping mechanisms in times of adversity. For example, in the National Mortality Followback Survey, controlling for the effects of 18 other predictors including depression and living alone, persons who reportedly were active in religious activities had an 18% lower probability of dying through suicide (National Center for Health Statistics, 2000).

Socioeconomic Status Measures of economic strain generally raise the risk of suicide by creating an environment marked by hardship and disappointments. Variation in risk of suicide among adults is associated with variation in income levels. For example, a large, over-time study of suicides in Denmark determined that persons in the lowest quartile in income were 5.52 times more apt to die of suicide than persons in the top quartile in income (Qin et al., 2003).

Job Demotions The limited research on downward social mobility indicates that job demotions increase suicide risk. An analysis of the National Mortality Followback Survey determined that persons who were demoted at work had a suicide risk 5.06 times greater than those who were not demoted in the past 12 months (National Center for Health Statistics, 2000).

Unemployment Being out of work raises the risk of suicide independent of depression and other predictors of suicide. For example, marked differences exist in London, England, where the suicide rate of the unemployed was 73.4 per 100,000 compared to 14.1 per 100,000 for the general population. Controlling for 12 other socioeconomic predictors of suicide, unemployed persons in Denmark were 18% more apt to die through suicide than fully employed persons (Qin et al., 2003).

Opportunity Factors Suicide rates reflect contextual factors that provide the opportunity for suicide attempts. For example, an analysis of the National Mortality Followback Survey found that, controlling for depression and 17 other predictors of suicide, persons who had a gun available in their homes were 3.41 times more apt to die through suicide than persons with no gun available (National Center for Health Statistics, 2000).

COMMUNITY-LEVEL PREDICTORS OF ADULT SUICIDE

Many of the individual-level predictors of suicide risk have been used to predict the suicide rates of cities, counties, states, and nations. For example, divorce rates of the 50 American states, in each of five census years during 1940 to 1980, were the single best predictor of state suicide rates (Stack, 2000). At the community level, divorce rates measure not only low levels of social integration among the divorced members of the state but also problems in intimate relationships (including marriage) in general. For example, the classic work of Durkheim (1966/1897) on suicide took divorce as an index of a trend in society toward individualism, where people pursue their own self-interests and are guided less and less by traditional ties to groups such as marriage, religion, and other institutions. It should be noted that divorce rates are often found to be correlated with other characteristics of states such as income level, but the association between divorce rates and suicide rates remains strong even after these covariates are controlled.

Imitation At least 105 studies to date have explored the association between the appearance of widely publicized suicide stories and suicide rates. Evidence supporting the existence of imitation or copycat effects includes a study based in New York City around the time of the publication of Derek Humphry's (b. 1930) *Final Exit* in 1991, a book advocating suicide among terminally ill persons by plastic-bag asphyxiation. Researchers found that suicide by this method increased by 313% and that 27.3% of these suicides were found with a copy of the book next to them. However, many studies report no copycat effect. Among the most likely stories to trigger copycat effects are those concerning well-known celebrities such as entertainers and political officials. A meta-analysis of 419 research studies on copycat suicides determined that investigations that explored the impact of the suicide of a well-known celebrity were 5.27 times more apt than other studies to report a copycat effect (Stack, 2005).

PREVENTION AND TREATMENT POLICY

In 2002 an estimated 877,000 persons committed suicide worldwide. In response to suicides, many countries have developed suicide prevention and treatment programs. Prevention programs include suicide educational programs in the schools, education of primary care physicians regarding suicide risk assessment, and general public education through the media concerning signs of suicide risk. Treatment programs have included pharmacotherapy using antidepressants or antipsychotic drugs and psychotherapy, including alcoholism treatment programs and cognitive-behavioral therapy. Means restrictions programs have attempted to lower suicide rates by limiting access to highly lethal means of suicide (e.g., gun control). The effectiveness of these suicide prevention and treatment programs is rarely evaluated. Based on the limited evaluation research available to date, some of the more promising suicide prevention strategies are further educating primary care physicians so they are more able to detect suicide risk and the restriction of lethal means of suicide (Mann et al., 2005). Evaluation research of media education and school-based suicide prevention programs is needed to fully assess their effectiveness in preventing suicide.

Treatment for suicidal persons with mental disorders, such as schizophrenia and affective disorders, includes both drug and talk therapies. Lithium has been used for more than 50 years as a biochemical treatment for persons with affective disorders (including borderline personality disorder). A meta-analysis of 31 research studies, which collectively covered 85,229 persons, found that the overall risk of suicide among those treated with lithium was 4.91 times less than those not treated with lithium (Baldessarini et al., 2006). A review of 32 of the most comparable and rigorously designed studies (randomized trials) found similar results: 1,389 patients with mood disorders (including forms of depression and manic depression) were randomly assigned into a lithium treatment group and placebo-receiving group. The probability of death through suicide was 74% less in the lithium treatment groups (Cipriani, Pretty, Hawton, & Geddes, 2005). Still, even with lithium treatment, persons with psychiatric disorders had a relatively high suicide rate.

Suicide rates do not vary considerably during the adult years of the life course. However, adults have a much higher rate than children. In turn, midlife male rates are considerably lower than those of elderly males. Within the stage of midlife, however, groups with relatively high suicide risk include persons diagnosed with manic depression or schizophrenia, divorced persons, persons who are demoted in or lose their jobs, persons who migrate long distances, Whites, and males. The average age at suicide is 44. Hence, whereas the elderly have a higher suicide rate, people in midlife account for the majority of suicides in the United States. This social fact is expected to begin to shift as the large cohort of baby boomers enter their retirement years beginning in 2012. As the proportion of elderly approximately doubles over the next generation, the mean age of suicides is expected to be much higher. As a consequence, adults in midlife will account for a lower proportion of suicides than they do at present.

SEE ALSO Volume 2: *Life Events; Mental Health, Adulthood; Risk; Stress in Adulthood; Trauma;* Volume 3: *Mortality.*

BIBLIOGRAPHY

Arsenault-Lapierre, C., Kim, C., & Turecki, G. (2004). Psychiatric diagnoses in 3275 suicides: A meta-analysis. *BMC Psychiatry, 4,* 37–47.

Baldessarini, R. J., Tondo, L., Davis, P., Pompili, M., Goodwin, F. K., & Hennen, J. (2006). Decreased risk of suicides and attempts during long-term lithium treatment: A meta-analytic review. *Bipolar Disorders, 8*(5), 625–639.

Centers for Disease Control. (2006). *Health, United States, 2006: With chartbook on trends in the health of Americans.* Washington, DC: Author. Retrieved May 17, 2008, from http://www.cdc.gov/nchs/

Cipriani, A., Pretty, H., Hawton, K., & Geddes, J. R. (2005). Lithium in the prevention of suicidal behavior and all-cause mortality in patients with mood disorders: A systematic review of randomized trials. *American Journal of Psychiatry, 162*(10), 1805–1819.

Durkheim, E. (1966). *Suicide.* New York: Free Press. (Original work published 1897)

Harris, E. C., & Barraclough, B. (1997). Suicide as an outcome for mental disorders: A meta-analysis. *British Journal of Psychiatry, 170*(3), 205–228.

Khan, A., Leventhal, R. M., Khan, S., & Brown, W. A. (2002). Suicide risk in patients with anxiety disorders: A meta-analysis of the FDA database. *Journal of Affective Disorders, 68*(2-3), 183–190.

Lester, D. (2006). Sex differences in completed suicide by schizophrenic patients: A meta-analysis. *Suicide and Life-Threatening Behavior, 36*(1), 50–56.

Mann, J. J., Apter, A., Bertolote, J., Beutrais, A., Currier, D., Haas, A., et al. (2005). Suicide prevention strategies: A systematic review. *Journal of the American Medical Association, 294*(16), 2064–2074.

National Center for Health Statistics. (2000). *National Mortality Followback Survey, codebook*. Ann Arbor, MI: Inter-University Consortium for Political and Social Research.

Qin, P., Agerbo, E., & Mortensen, P. B. (2003). Suicide risk in relation to socioeconomic, demographic, psychiatric, and familial factors: A national register-based study of all suicides in Denmark, 1981–1997. *American Journal of Psychiatry, 160*(4), 765–772.

Stack, S. (2000). Suicide: A 15-year review of the sociological literature. *Suicide and Life-Threatening Behavior, 30*(2), 163–176.

Stack, S. (2005). Suicide and the media: A quantitative review of studies based on nonfictional stories. *Suicide and Life-Threatening Behavior, 35*(2), 121–133.

Wilcox, H. C., Connor, K. R., & Caine, E. D. (2004). Association of alcohol and drug use disorders and completed suicide: An empirical review of cohort studies. *Drug and Alcohol Dependence, 76*, S11–S19.

Steven Stack

T

TECHNOLOGY USE, ADULTHOOD

SEE Volume 2: *Media and Technology Use, Adulthood.*

TIME USE, ADULTHOOD

Time is an essential resource in modern life. More Americans say they are concerned about the lack of time than say they are about the lack of money. Benjamin Franklin's adage that "Time is money" has taken on a new meaning, with the advantage of time being that it is equally distributed to everyone (at least in the short term). How a society uses its time provides a behavioral window on its values and attitudes, and time use data identify the important lifestyle changes that occur across the life course, especially as one takes on the social roles of spouse, parent, or other caregiver.

MEASURING PEOPLE'S TIME USE

One of the challenges in studying how individuals use their time is measuring the use of time. Researchers use a variety of methods to measure time use: direct observation (shadowing), on-site verification, "beeper" studies, and respondent recall or estimates, among others. Prior to the 1960s most information about time use was obtained from surveys that asked respondents to estimate the hours they typically spend on some activity such as working or watching TV. These self-reported measures were often subject to errors in estimation and recall, and this method provided relatively little information on daily activities not included on the survey.

Researchers thus have begun to depend more on the time-diary method, which enables them to assess more precisely the time one spends in all daily activities. More important, time diaries suggest a somewhat different set of conclusions about almost all aspects of daily life (decreased free time, increased sleep, among many others) than research using time estimates or other measures (see Robinson & Godbey, 1999, for evidence of counterintuitive trends in increased free time, childcare, and fitness activity in society).

In the time-diary method, respondents provide complete accounts of what they do on a particular day and for the full 24 hours of that day. Respondents take the researcher step-by-step through their day, describing everything they did from the time they woke up until midnight of that day. The researcher also learns about where people spent their day, whom they were with, and what other activities they were involved in during their main activities (multitasking). Because these data are intended to represent complete accounts of daily activity, diary data can be used to generate estimates of how much societal time is spent on the complete range of human behavior—from work to free time, from travel to time spent at home. Because they are complete, diary data can address most issues about various policy implications of daily activity in society, from the time children spend doing homework, to the amount of sleep people get, to how much they are working long hours.

Features of the Time Diary The time-diary approach follows from the first American diary study, done as part of the most extensive and well-known of diary studies—the 1965 Multinational Time Budget Study (Szalai, 1972). In that benchmark study, roughly 2,000 respondents ages 18 to 64 in urban employed households from each of 12 different countries kept a diary account of a single day, with each day of the week equivalently represented; in subsequent U.S. studies all seasons of the year were covered as well. The purpose of this research design was to ensure that the data truly were a representative snapshot of American life, both during weekdays and weekends, as well as throughout the calendar year.

Respondents using the time diary sometimes have some recall difficulties, but these are small compared to the task of making estimates of past time use over a long time period. The diary keeper's task is to recall all of one day's activities in sequence, which may be similar to the way most people store their activities in memory. Rather than having to consider a long time period, the respondent need only focus attention on a single day (i.e., yesterday). Rather than working from some list of activities whose meanings vary from respondent to respondent, respondents simply describe their day's activities in their own words. The open-ended nature of activity reporting means that these diaries are also automatically geared to detecting new and unanticipated activities (e.g., in past decades, aerobic exercises and use of e-mail, VCRs, and other new communications technologies).

The diary technique also provides respondents minimal opportunity to distort activities in order to present themselves in a particular light. They are not told about a study's interest in one activity or another, because the diary is a simple record of any and all activity. Some respondents may wish to portray themselves as hard workers or light television viewers, but to do so they must fabricate the activities that precede and follow it. Further, a time-diary represents a one-day account, and on any given day respondents likely realize that on a particular day they may work less or watch television more than usual. Moreover, respondents are not pressured to report an activity if they cannot recall it or do not wish to report it.

In sum, the time diary is a microbehavioral technique for collecting self-reports of an individual's daily behavior in an open-ended fashion on an activity-by-activity basis. In this way, the technique capitalizes on the most attractive measurement properties of the time variable, namely:

- All daily activity is potentially recorded and must sum to 1,440 minutes of the day.

- The "zero sum" property of time is preserved, so that if time on one activity increases, it must be balanced out by decreases in some other activity.

- It uses an accounting variable, time, that is maximally understandable to participants and accessible in memory.

- The open-ended activity reporting allows one to detect new and unanticipated activities.

EARLIER DIARY SURVEYS IN THE UNITED STATES

There have been roughly decade-interval (1965, 1975, 1985, 1992–1995, 2003–2005) time-diary surveys from which to make trend comparisons, although time-diary interviewing has generally moved from face-to-face personal interviews to telephone interviews and from "tomorrow" diaries to "yesterday" diaries (rather than asking participants to keep a leave-behind diary to be filled out tomorrow, asking them simply to recall what they did yesterday).

1965 U.S. Time-Use Study In the fall of 1965, as part of a multinational time-use study, the University of Michigan Survey Research Center (SRC) surveyed 1,244 adult respondents, ages 18 to 64, who kept a single-day "tomorrow" diary. The interviewer visited respondents and explained the procedure then left the diary to be filled out for the following day. The interviewer then returned on the day after the "diary day" to collect the completed diary.

1975 U.S. Time-Use Survey In fall 1975, the SRC surveyed 1,519 adult respondents and 887 of their spouses, who provided retrospective "yesterday" diaries. These respondents were subsequently reinterviewed in the winter, spring, and summer months of 1976, mainly by telephone.

1985 U.S. Time-Use Survey In 1985 the SRC collected single-day diaries from more than 5,300 respondents employing the same basic open-ended diary approach as the 1965 and 1975 studies, using personal, telephone, and mail-back diaries for either yesterday or tomorrow.

U.S. Time-Diary Collections in the 1990s Two diary studies were conducted by the SRC by national random digit dial telephone procedures between 1992 and 1995, one with 9,386 respondents and the second with 1,200 respondents. All interviews in both phases used the retrospective diary (or yesterday) method for the previous day. Two further yesterday studies were conducted by the University of Maryland, one in 1998 ($n = 1200$) and the other in 1999–2001 ($n = 978$).

2003–2005 Bureau of Labor Statistics Diary Study The Bureau of Labor Statistics has collected over 60,000 daily diaries continuously since 2003, using the telephone

PATTERNS OF TV VIEWING

National trend data in the United States indicate that television has had more of an impact on daily time use than any other household technology and that it continues to account for more than half of Americans' free time. Moreover, time spent watching television has been minimally reduced since the advent of the Internet and other new IT. Early multinational data indicated that television initially drew time away from "functionally equivalent" activities such as movies, radio, and print fiction—and more recently from newspapers. It also appears to have drawn time from activities that are less clearly functional equivalents, such as sleep and grooming (see Robinson & Godbey, 1999).

The main increases in viewing time occurred in the 1970s, apparently related to the availability of color television, although television has made persistent but smaller inroads on free time since that time. As was true in that period, time-diary studies show that less television time is correlated with less time working and traveling, so that people who are at home more do more viewing. Television time has been named as the daily activity people would give up if something urgent occurred.

As shown in Table 1, TV viewing is rated as more enjoyable in "real time" in the diaries than in general, and falls in the middle of other leisure activities. However, Kubey (1992) indicated that was not the case the longer TV is viewed. These quantitative results stand alongside other lasting effects of TV outside of time that have been alleged (at least in the United States). These include (1) decreasing the number of manufacturers and producers,

due to the concentration of mass advertising; (2) increasing the fear of crime; and (3) fostering a multitude and democracy of voices that has led to "post modernism." Another cause for concern came from Putnam's (2000) link of TV viewing with long-term declines in social capital in the United States. Other works whose titles give a pessimistic appraisal of TV's effects include Mander's (1978) *Four Arguments for the Elimination of Television* (1977), Postman's *Amusing Ourselves to Death* (1985), and Kubey's *Television and the Quality of Life* (1990). Only the latter is based on actual viewer feedback, finding viewers rated themselves as more passive and using less concentration than for other activities. More upbeat views can be found in Bianculli's *Teleliteracy* (1992), Johnson's *Everything Bad is Good for You* (2004), and Neuman's *The Active TV Audience* (1988), the latter again being the only one based on viewer feedback.

BIBLIOGRAPHY

Bianculli, D. (1992). *Teleliteracy*. New York: Continuum.

Johnson, H. (2006). *Everything bad is good for you*. New York: Riverhead Books.

Kubey, R., & Csikszentmihalyi, M. 1990. *Television and the quality of life: How viewing shapes everyday experience*. Hillsdale, NJ: L. Erlbaum Associates.

Mander, J. (1978). *Four arguments for the elimination of television*. New York: Harper.

Postman, N. (1985). *Amusing ourselves to death*. New York: Penguin.

Robinson, J. P., & Godbey, G. 1999. *Time for life: The surprising ways Americans use their time*. (2nd ed.). University Park, PA: Pennsylvania Sate University Press.

yesterday method and a more detailed set of activity categories, as described at www.bls.gov.

TRENDS AND PATTERNS IN TIME USE

Figure 1 shows a list of the 22 main uses of time recorded in prior research on the right and a standard set of predictor variables on the left that are used in studies of time use. In most studies, the activities or uses of time (such as work or TV viewing) are dependent variables, or the behavior to be predicted, whereas the demographic characteristics (such as gender and marital status) are the independent variables, or the predictive factors. Researchers can the assess the extent to which the six categories of background factors can predict

the four major types of time: contracted (paid work) time; committed (family care) time (mainly divided into core housework and cleaning, childcare, and shopping); personal care (sleeping, eating, and grooming); and the remaining activities that comprise free time (dominated by TV viewing, which takes up almost half, as noted below).

The predictor variables are grouped into six categories in Figure 1:

1. Birth factors: The factors one is born with (e.g., gender, race, and age).

2. Status factors: The factors that reflect one's social standing (e.g., education, income, and occupation).

Demographic/ Background Factors	Time Uses
BIRTH FACTORS	A. CONTRACTED TIME
a) Age	1. Paid Work
b) Gender	2. Work Commute
c) Race	B. COMMITTED TIME
STATUS FACTORS	3. Housework
d) Education	4. Child care
e) Income	5. Shopping
f) Occupation	C. PERSONAL CARE
ROLE FACTORS	6. Sleeping
g) Employment	7. Eating
h) Marriage	8. Grooming
i) Children	D. FREE TIME
LOCATION FACTORS	9. Religion
j) Region	10. Organizations
k) Urbanicity	11. Social events
l) Dwelling type	12. Visiting
TEMPORAL FACTORS	13. Fitness activity
m) Year	14. Hobbies
n) Season	15. TV
o) Day of week	16. Radio/recordings
GEOGRAPHY/CULTURE/ETC.	17. Reading
p) Country	18. Home communication
q) Technology	19. IT
	20. Rest/relax
	21. Free travel
	22. Total travel

Figure 1. *Time/Activity categories and their major background predictors.* CENGAGE LEARNING, GALE.

3. Role factors: The various roles one undertakes and performs (e.g., as an employee, spouse, or parent).

4. Location factors: The effects of where one lives (e.g., by region, living in urban vs. rural areas, type of housing).

5. Temporal factors: What year, season, or day of the week is being reported.

6. Geo-cultural factors: Such as the country lived in or access to technology.

Attention to these six sets of factors demonstrates the ways that time use is powerfully shaped by social factors such as life course stage, gender, and access to social and economic resources. In terms of the main trends in U.S. time use since 1965 (the "year" variable on the left side of Figure 1), most notable overall activity increases are found in childcare, TV viewing (see sidebar), and fitness activities. The most notable decreases are found in paid work for men, housework for women (men's housework, by contrast, has nearly doubled), eating, and reading (mainly of newspapers). The main shifts occurred between 1965 and 1975.

There is little evidence in these diaries of other expected changes—even those considered to be common knowledge, such as historical increases in average paid work hours or decreases in free time, childcare, social

visiting, relaxing, or (non-newspaper) reading—or of age per se as a major predictor of time. Among the key findings obtained are:

1. Age: Between the ages of 18 and 64, the main age differences are predicted by role factors, such as those due to the increase in housework and childcare that accompany marriage and parenthood. One major shift is the decline in paid work time by those ages 55 to 64, many of whom are taking early retirement. Another is that those under age 30 are going to college in greater numbers than in the past.

2. Gender: The largest shift here is the above-noted activity of housework, whereby men's share increased from 15% in 1965 to 35% today (with the notable exception of laundry). This is part of a larger picture of increased "gender convergence" and "time androgyny," in that women are doing more of the activities that men dominated before, primarily for paid work but also for the former "male" activities involving education, TV viewing, and fitness activity. In contrast, the gender gap in childcare, grooming, reading, and hobbies has declined.

3. Race: Since 1965, Blacks have consistently spent more time in grooming, religion, and TV viewing, whereas Whites spend more time in housework, reading, and visiting. Thus there is little closing of the race gap to parallel the closing of the gender gap. Moreover, the above differences by race are not explained by education or other demographic differences between the races.

4. Education: There is an increasing tendency for a greater number of work hours and less sleep for the college educated, along with higher figures for reading and attending social events (such as the arts or sporting events). By far the most dramatic educational difference is for lower levels of TV viewing among the college educated; the amount of time college-educated people spend watching TV is about half of that for those with less than a high school degree.

5. Income: Differences by income parallel those for education and are often a function of education.

6. Occupation: Again, these differences largely reflect related education differences.

7. Employment: Whether one is currently employed is probably the most significant predictor of time use, particularly as work hours increase. Sleep is the major activity affected; housework and childcare are cut by a third, and TV viewing decreases dramatically as well.

8. Marriage: Getting married also reduces most free-time activities, mainly due to increased housework

and other family care activities (but more for wives than for husbands).

9. Parenthood: Surprisingly, having children has less time effect than getting married, but it still means more housework and shopping and less free time and TV viewing.

The other sets of predictor factors on the left of Figure 1 seem to have much less impact than those above, and those that are found tend be a function of them, such as higher TV viewing in the South due to lower education levels there. Few notable regional differences emerge, nor is there much evidence of a more hectic lifestyle in more urban areas. Outside of less housework among dwellers of apartments or trailers, housing type has little relation to ways of spending time little effect of seasonal differences is found, much as for regional differences that may reflect climatic/weather differences. There are major and obvious differences by day of the week, with weekends meaning decreased work and more time for sleep and TV.

Another primary factor that is often linked to time use is technology. Although the development of so-called time-saving appliances in the 20th century might lead one to believe that time use has changed as a result, the few time studies conducted to date suggest that consumers seem to use their "hassle-saving" features instead—that is, to increase outputs from the technology rather than to save time (Robinson & Godbey, 1999).

Cross-National Results Finally, research reveals surprising convergences across most of the more than 30 countries studied (some identified below), although most of them are developed, Western societies in Europe, which can afford to conduct expensive time-diary surveys. For example, Bittman (2000) found similar increases in free time since the 1960s in other countries, much as in the United States. In an analysis of all productive activity (contracted and committed time together) in 12 countries, Goldschmidt-Claremont (1995) found the same basic equality of men and women in overall hours spent on such activities. Another study found the same pattern of increased father childcare across six Western countries since 1990 (France being a notable exception), much as was reported in a 2004 study (Gauthier, Smeeding, & Furstenberg, 2004) for many other countries over this period. Robinson and Godbey (1999) found many similarities in both the trends and predictors of time use in Japan, Russia, and Canada. Gershuny (2000) extended these results to more than 15 other countries.

National trend studies of time use indicate that TV has had a greater impact on daily use of time than any other household technology (see sidebar) and that it continues to consume almost half of free time, at least in the United States. TV use appears to have not been greatly displaced by the Internet and personal computers.

Main gains in viewing time occurred in the United States in the 1970s, coincident with the arrival of color TV, and it has made persistent but smaller inroads on free time since then. As was true in the late 1960s, these diary studies show that lower TV time is correlated with more time at work and more travel and that TV is viewed more by people who are at home and who have more free time. Early casualties of TV, such as sleep and reading, are now correlated with more viewing.

POLICY ISSUES AND TIME

Because time diaries cover all daily activities performed by individuals in a society, they might be thought to have immense policy implications. However, it is often the case that time itself is less the issue than how the time is used or valued. The "fun meter," displayed in Table 1, shows differences in how people rate the enjoyment they get from various daily activities, when asked on the left-hand column "in real time" (when they were doing it in the diary) or when asked to think about a particular activity in general on the right. Although the two ratings correlate highly, there are exceptions (such as the low rating for TV in general vs. its higher rating in real time, as discussed below and in the sidebar).

For example, in the case of the division of housework between men and women, Table 1 shows that both men and women rate housework low in terms of enjoyment, yet women continue to do twice as much of it. However, it is hard to imagine what type of policy would offset this imbalance, outside of providing counselors to help individual couples to make better arrangements for themselves. The "take back your time" movement (de Graff, 2003) has proposed that American workers stop all paid work after mid-October, so that their total annual work hours would be equivalent to those of European workers. Yet Hochschild (1997) found in one company that it was other workers themselves who sabotaged innovative family-friendly policies to reduce work hours. The National Sleep Foundation has raised alarms about sleep deprivation as a national crisis, although time diaries show no decline in sleep since the 1960—which holds steady at the legendary 8 hours per night. The "turn off your TV" movement has designated one week per year for people to leave their sets off and to instead participate in more potentially gratifying activities. However, Table 1 suggests that, although people rate TV in general as relatively low on the fun meter, the programs they watched on the diary day rated far higher in enjoyment.

On a Scale from 10 = Enjoy a Great Deal to 0 = Dislike a Great Deal. (1985 and 1975 National Data from Robinson and Godbey 1999, Appendix O)	
(1985 Diary Average = 7.0)	**1975 General (Average = 6.8)**
9.3 Sex	
9.2 Play sports	
8.7 Playing/reading with children	8.9 Child care
8.5 Church, religion	
8.5 Sleep	8.6 Play with children
8.2 Meals away	8.0 Socializing, talking
8.2 Socialize, visit others	8.0 Work
8.0 Socialize with family	
8.0 Work breaks	
7.9 Reading	7.5 Sleep
7.8 Meals at home	7.4 Eating
7.8 TV	7.4 Washing, dressing
7.4 Hobbies, crafts	7.3 Church, religion
7.2 Exercise	7.0 Reading
7.2 Baby care	
7.2 Organizations	
7.0 Work	
7.0 Bathing	
6.6 Cooking	6.8 Hobbies
6.6 Other shopping	6.5 Play sports
6.4 Child care	6.5 Cultural events
6.4 Help others	6.2 Cooking
6.3 Work commute	
6.1 Dressing	
5.8 Other housework	5.9 TV
5.5 Grocery shopping	
5.5 Home repairs	5.1 Home repairs
5.2 Pay bills, financial etc.	5.0 Organizations
5.0 Yardwork	
4.9 Clean house	4.6 Grocery shopping
4.9 Laundry	4.3 Other shopping
4.8 Health care, doctor	4.2 Clean house
4.7 Car repair	

Table 2. *Activity enjoyment ratings in time diaries vs. in general.* CENGAGE LEARNING, GALE.

Of all the potential policy issues related to time use, perhaps what is most impressive is the largely anecdotal data on the meager, marginal outputs that workers produce and obtain for their inputs of work time. These data largely suggest that the same work productivity can be achieved with 20 to 50% less time spent on the job (Parkinson, 1962; Schor, 1991; Schuman, Walsh, Olson, & Etheridge, 1985) and that many workers put in simple "face time" to impress their employers.

This inability of diary data to speak to the quality of people's lives and to guide policy to improve that life quality remains the major limitation of time use research and a major area for future studies. The findings reported in Table 1 represent an important first step toward gaining more nuanced insights into time-use statistics, but a new study design—such as a representative ethnography that combines observation with representative sampling (Robinson & Meadow, 1982)—could provide more enlightened insights. Diary data allow researchers to document what people are doing, yet scholars need to find out more about why, with whom, for whom, and to what ends adults are using their time.

SEE ALSO Volume 2: *Consumption, Adulthood and Later Life; Housework; Leisure and Travel, Adulthood; Work-Family Conflict;* Volume 3: *Time Use, Later Life.*

BIBLIOGRAPHY

Allen, C. L. (1968). Photographing the TV audience. *Journal of Advertising Research*, 8(1), 8.

Bianculli, D. (1992). *Teleliteracy.* New York: Continuum.

Bittman, M. (2000). Now it's 2000: Trends in doing and being in the new millennium. *Journal of Occupational Science, 7,* 108–117.

deGraff, J. (2003). *Take back your time.* New York: Berrett-Koehler.

Gauthier, A. H., Smeeding, T. M., & Furstenberg, F. F. Jr. (2004). Are parents investing less time in children? Trends in selected industrialized countries. *Population and Development Review, 30,* 647–671.

Gershuny, J. (2000). *Changing times: Work and leisure in postindustrial society.* Oxford, U.K.: Oxford University Press.

Goldschmidt-Claremont, L. (1995). Measures of unrecorded economic activities in fourteen countries. *Human Development Report No. 20.* New York: United Nations Development Report Office.

Harvey, A., & Elliot, D. (1983). *Time and time again.* Ottawa-Hull, Canada: Employment and Immigration Commission.

Hochschild, A., with Machung, A. (1989). *The second shift: Working parents and the revolution at home.* New York: Viking.

Johnson, S. (2006). *Everything bad is good for you.* New York: Riverhead Books.

Juster, T. (1985). The validity and quality of time use estimates obtained from recall diaries. In F. T. Juster & F. P. Stafford (Eds.), *Time, goods, and well-being* (pp. 63–91). Ann Arbor: Survey Research Center, Institute for Social Research, University of Michigan.

Kubey, R., & Csikszentmihalyi, M. (1990). *Television and the quality of life: How viewing shapes everyday experience.* Hillsdale, NJ: Lawrence Erlbaum.

Mander, J. (1978). *Four arguments for the elimination of television.* New York: Morrow.

Parkinson, C. N. (1962). *Parkinson's law.* New York: Penguin.

Postman, N. (1985). *Amusing ourselves to death.* New York: Viking.

Putnam, R. D. (2000). *Bowling alone: The collapse and revival of American community.* New York: Simon & Schuster.

Robinson, J. P. (1977). *How Americans use time: A social-psychological analysis of everyday behavior.* New York: Praeger.

Robinson, J. P. (1985). The validity and reliability of diaries versus alternative time use measures. In F. T. Juster & F. P. Stafford (Eds.), *Time, goods, and well-being* (pp. 33–62). Ann Arbor: Survey Research Center, Institute for Social Research, University of Michigan.

Robinson, J. P., & Godbey, G. (1999). *Time for life: The surprising ways Americans use their time.* (2nd ed.). University Park: Pennsylvania Sate University Press.

Robinson, J. P., & Meadow, R. (1982). *Polls apart.* Cabin John, MD: Seven Locks Press.

Schor, J. B. (1991). *The overworked American: The unexpected decline of leisure.* New York: Basic Books.

Schuman, H., Walsh, E., Olson, C., & Etheridge, B. (1985) Effort and reward: The assumption that college grades are affected by quantity of study. *Social Forces, 63,* 944–956.

Szalai, A. (Ed.). (1972). *The use of time: Daily activities of urban and suburban populations in twelve countries.* The Hague: Mouton.

John P. Robinson
Steven Martin

TRANSITION TO ADULTHOOD

The transition to adulthood is the period in the life course that bridges childhood and adulthood. This transition stage is defined by exits from roles that support and foster childlike dependence (e.g., student), entries into roles that confer adult status (e.g., parent), and the acquisition of stage-specific, developmental skills such as the development of one's personal identity. This stage has been called "demographically dense" (Rindfuss, 1991) because it is defined by a large number of transitions into and out of roles in a relatively short period of time. The transitions are pivotal in individuals' lives, distinguishing it as a stage of life during which individuals are most likely to experience self-described key, turning-point life events that involve family and relationships, education, and work (Elnick, Margrett, Fitzgerald, & Labouvie-Vief, 1999).

Industrialization has influenced the transition to adulthood by increasing society's need for a more highly educated workforce. In turn, in more industrialized countries, education is prolonged and transitions to careers and family roles are delayed. Industrialization has variably influenced the world's nations; in turn, the age span over which the transition to adulthood occurs and the specific criteria that characterize an *adult* vary culturally and historically. This variation principally reflects differences in the degree to which childhood is distinguished from adulthood, the range of opportunities for entry into the labor market, and the availability of resources during this transition stage, in any given culture. In contemporary industrialized nations, this transitional stage spans a wide age range: the later half of the teens, the decade of the twenties, and even into the early thirties. In less industrialized countries, transitions to adulthood are more likely to reflect traditional and homogeneous pathways beginning and ending at younger ages.

DEFINING AND MEASURING THE TRANSITION TO ADULTHOOD

The transition to adulthood is typically defined by a specific set of role transitions: completing formal education, moving out of the parental home, entering the labor force, getting married, and becoming a parent. These events have a normative sequence; for example, young people are expected to finish their education and establish their work lives prior to marrying or having children. Thus, a "successful" transition to adulthood occurs when an individual completes school, moves out of his or her parents' home, establishes employment, gets married, and becomes a parent (Settersten, Furstenberg, & Rumbaut, 2005).

Yet, individuals' transitions to adulthood are influenced by a range of factors beyond macroeconomic forces, including shifts in the roles of social institutions (e.g., family and schools), social norms, and social values that, in turn, determine and constrain role opportunities. Transition to adulthood experiences vary across individuals in whether or not a role transition is completed, the age at which it occurred, the extent to which it occurred at the normatively expected age, and whether or not it occurred in the normative sequence. Variation in the transition to adulthood also occurs because of personal agency; people act in their own behalf to maximize their well-being, weighing the costs and benefits of choices and options (Schwartz, Côté, & Arnett, 2005).

The role-based definition of the transition to adulthood reflects sociological and demographic perspectives. Psychologists offer an alternative definition of transition from childhood to adulthood. Instead of focusing on social roles, this perspective focuses on the specific life skills that individuals acquire at specific stages of life. Drawing from the developmental theory of Erik Erikson (1950), life span psychologists classically view the stages and ages referred to as adolescence and young adulthood, stages 5 (ages 12–17) and 6 (ages 18–35), as the transition to adulthood. Respectively, during these transitional years individuals are confronted with two challenges—the resolution of one's personal identity and the establishment of intimacy with others. A successful transition to adulthood, therefore, results in a personal sense of self and the ability to simultaneously merge and maintain oneself with another in a love relationship.

Contemporary theorists have expanded the psychological perspective on the transition to adulthood to include a stage between adolescence and young adulthood, "emerging adulthood" (Arnett, 2000). This stage of life is defined by individuals' lack of formal commitments to social roles. Rather, the stage is defined by psychological markers of adulthood: accepting responsibility for the consequences of one's actions, deciding on personal beliefs and values independently of parents or other influences, becoming financially independent from parents, and establishing a relationship with parents as equal adults (Arnett, 1997). In other words, the developmental task of this age period is gaining self-sufficiency. Therefore, from a contemporary and psychological perspective, the transition to adulthood is a three-stage process through which individuals move at varying rates and with varying degrees of resolution of the respective life tasks associated with adolescence, emerging adulthood, and young adulthood (Tanner, 2006).

The sociological and psychological perspectives differ in their definitions of the transition to adulthood. From a sociological perspective, role transitions are indicators of becoming an "adult." Some empirical research supports this idea. For example, financial self-sufficiency and taking on family roles (marriage and parent) have been associated with feelings of "being an adult." In addition, expectations for taking on adult roles are associated with increasing age through the twenties. The psychological perspective refutes the position that social role transitions are the sole markers of adulthood. This position is supported by studies that demonstrate that only small proportions of people see role transitions as relevant criteria for adult status, while most people favor psychological criteria of adulthood, such as accepting responsibility for self (Arnett, 1997). Still other research suggests that chronological age, the social roles one holds, and psychological gains each contribute to feelings of being adult. However, it is important to highlight that age, roles, and psychosocial maturation are not independent; rather the three are closely intertwined. For example, the number of roles an individual acquires increases with age; and, as age increases, individuals' perceptions of their psychosocial maturity increases, as well (Galambos, Turner, & Tilton-Weaver, 2005).

HISTORICAL CHANGES IN THE TRANSITION TO ADULTHOOD

The transition to adulthood is different for contemporary cohorts versus prior generations due to changes in the economy and related shifts in social values and norms. The economy defines key dimensions of the school-to-work transition including the types and availability of job opportunities for young people and the education and training requirements for these jobs. In the United States over the past 200 years, the economy shifted from an agrarian to an industrialized economy. In the industrialized nations, economies are increasingly organized around providing services, generating information, and supplying

energy. In response, labor market needs increased the demand for a more educated workforce.

The recent macroeconomic reshaping of the labor market has had specific effects on individuals' transitions into adulthood. First, the time between childhood and adolescence has been elongated. Demands for more education prolong young adults' time spent in the student role, delay entry into labor force, and subsequently postpone entry into marriage and parenthood. Second, the traditional sequence of transitioning from student to worker to spouse and parent no longer defines a normative experience. Holding both "student" and "worker" roles concurrently has become more common. Also, trends indicate that there is an increase in out-of-wedlock childbearing and childbearing within cohabiting unions. The extent to which a group of transition-stage individuals are in different roles, experience transitions at different ages, and go through transitions in different sequences determines the heterogeneity of the transition to adulthood in that population, a measure labeled *entropy* (Billari, 2001). Entropy analyses confirm that transitions to adulthood are growing more heterogeneous and that there is variation in entropy across countries (Fussell, Gauthier, & Evans, 2007).

Changes in social values and social norms have accompanied macroeconomic shifts and have also influenced changes in the transition to adulthood (Smith, 2005). In industrialized countries, social values have come to place a greater emphasis on gender egalitarianism, self-actualization, and self-fulfillment. Contemporary cohorts are less religious, less connected to social institutions, and more pessimistic about society and people in general. All together these changes reveal an *individualization* of life pathways and movement away from proscribed, socially sanctioned transition sequences. Current generations also have a different relationship with the economy than prior generations have; both in their own perceptions and in terms of real dollars, current generations fare financially less well than prior cohorts.

CROSS-CULTURAL VARIATION IN THE TRANSITION TO ADULTHOOD

The contemporary pattern of transitioning to adulthood varies between countries as a function of their economic advancement and other social and political trends. At one end of the continuum, industrialized nations (i.e., United States, Canada, Australia, Japan, and Western Europe) comprise a cluster of countries considered economically advanced and socially and culturally similar. Findings have demonstrated similar entropy patterns across the three countries: very little heterogeneity at ages 17, a quick rise and high heterogeneity through the late 20s, and then a gradual decrease through the late 20s and 30s. Despite the political, social, and economic similarities in these nations, life course researchers have also detected some differences that reflect the nations' distinctive social values and policies. Transition to adulthood patterns in the United States differ from those in Canada and Australia in that marriage occurs at younger ages, and marriage and parenthood remain more closely tied, perhaps due to higher religiosity in the United States. The result is that the transition to adulthood is less variable and more compressed temporally in the United States than in Canada and Australia (Fussell et al., 2007).

The United States is considered a moderate example of the trend in prolonged and non-traditional transitions to adulthood. European countries with advanced economies are the countries with the longest delays in entries into marriage and parenthood (Douglass, 2007). In Italy a relatively old age at first birth has contributed to a below-replacement level fertility trend, perhaps due to the fact that marriage and parenthood remain closely linked. Additional variation arises between Mediterranean and Scandinavian countries in that, similar to in the United States, Scandinavian youth tend to leave home to live alone or cohabitate with roommates. Young adults in Mediterranean nations leave home later and tend to move in with a romantic partner, commonly with intentions to marry and have children. This one difference explains, to some extent, the increased risk for poverty during the transition to adulthood in countries in which a period of time is spent cohabiting between living with parents and living with a marriage partner. The increased risk for poverty is explained by the decreased likelihood of living with a full-time wage-earner, more common among cohabitors who are more likely to be students or employed only part-time. Comparatively, occupational stability and full-time wage earnings accelerate transitions to marriage and parenthood.

In Latin American countries there is also great variation in transitions to adulthood. In Argentina, a country with a developed economy, the delay in transitions has been observed, but is relatively limited to the proportion of the Argentinian population that can afford a college education and thus experience a delayed entry into the labor force. Independent living is relatively rare in Argentina; the majority of transition-stage individuals who are not married or cohabiting live with their parents or families. Reasons for living with family during the transition-stage are rooted in Latino and Catholic traditions placing high value on family responsibility (Galambos & Martinez, 2007).

Evidence for the broad trends depicting contemporary shifts in the transitions to adulthood varies across Asian countries as well. In China, college students' tran-sitions to adulthood resemble transitions to adulthood in the United States. However, very different patterns are evidenced by Chinese young persons who live in rural villages and/or regions with largely agrarian economies. Agrarian-based economies offer young adults opportunities to enter the local labor market via family- or local-owned businesses, primarily requiring manual labor. Providing young people with employment opportunities that favor manual labor and skill over higher-education affords young people an opportunity to earn a living wage, and thus reduces the likelihood of delay in marriage and parenthood associated with educational attainment (Nelson & Chen, 2007).

In less industrialized countries there is a weaker association between prolonged time spent in education and delays in transitions to marriage and parenthood. In Mexico, for example, there is some evidence of a link between college attendance and delayed entries into marriage and parenthood, but the delays are not as long and the pattern reflects the patterns and behaviors of only a minority proportion of the transition-stage population. The rate of college participation for 16- to 29-year-olds is 25% in Mexico, compared to 55% in Spain, two countries considered close in cultural and social values. Despite the similarities in culture, transitions to adulthood in Spain conform to Mediterranean patterns of late home-leaving and delayed transitions into family formation. In contrast, the average age of home-leaving in Mexico is 18 to 19, followed closely, on average, by transitions to marriage and parenthood. One possible reason for early home-leaving and the lack of postponement of family roles is the lack of a shift toward egalitarianism at the cultural–level that has accompanied industrialization in the United States. The result, despite higher levels of educational attainment, without equality afforded to young women to enter the labor market, women do not delay transitions to family roles to pursue education or careers in their 20s (Fussell et al., 2007).

In non-industrialized countries researchers have found high levels of homogeneity in the timing of life course transitions between mid-adolescence and age 30. In six developing countries—the Dominican Republic, Ghana, Columbia, Kenya, Peru, and Cameroon—there is evidence of increasing levels of educational attainment, yet educational attainment does not fully account for the economic forces that are shaping transitions to adulthood in these countries (Grant & Furstenberg, 2007). In developing nations, the move toward a delayed and varied transition to adulthood is shaped by factors other than educational expansion. As is the case with Mexico, lack of movement toward egalitarian gender roles and lack of a labor market that provides rich opportunities to young people has thwarted delays in marriage and parenthood (except for a small proportion) despite increasing rates of participation in college.

WITHIN-CULTURE VARIATION: SOCIOECONOMICS, SOCIAL NORMS AND VALUES, FAMILY RESOURCES, AND CUMULATIVE ADVANTAGE

Within-culture, sub-group and individual-level variation in duration and sequencing of the transition to adulthood exists as a function of access to and involvement in tertiary education and the advanced economy. Within the United States, social class differences have been cited as a key source of variation in pathways through the transition to adulthood. These differences have been observed and reported across countries reflecting different pathways between the middle-class versus working-class, and the college-educated versus high school–educated (Furstenberg, 2008). These observations suggest that the contemporary conceptualizations of transition to adulthood may, at least, neglect the experiences of the poor, less educated, working class.

The labor market currently favors educated young people from higher social class backgrounds, by granting "time off" from labor market participation to build human capital and accumulate education opportunities. In the United States, the half of the population that does not go on to college after high school—the Forgotten Half—not only earn lower salaries when they enter the labor market in their late teens and 20s compared to their college-educated peers, but they also experience slower acceleration in their salaries across their life spans. In addition to the economic inequalities, they miss the normative experiences of the age period that afford freedom from role stress and responsibility if only for a brief period of the life course. Not experiencing a period of being in-between childhood and adulthood for a prolonged period of time may result in different life course pathways for those who delay commitments to adult roles and responsibilities versus those who make commitments early in adulthood, without a period of exploration prior to commitment. For example, it may be the case that spending time exploring a range of professional and personal options during the early adult years before making commitments may lead to better marriage and career choices, and greater preparedness for the parental role. Given the recency of the new transition to adulthood patterns, future studies will be required to test for differences in outcomes associated with different transition to adulthood patterns.

Within countries, sub-groups vary with respect to the access they have to higher education. Across societies, racial and ethnic minorities and non-native born populations typically face the most severe obstacles to high

Graduation Ceremony at Brown University. *A group of Brown University undergraduates cheer as they exit through the Brown University gates prior to Brown's graduation ceremony in Providence, RI.* AP IMAGES.

levels of educational attainment. In the United States, for example, enforcement of Affirmative Action programs decreased in the 1970s and 1980s resulting in large and increasing gaps in educational advancement between whites and African Americans (Corcoran & Matsudaira, 2005). Both high school and college graduation rates are higher for Whites and Asians compared to Hispanic, Black, and Native Americans, resulting in variation in the age of entry into the transition to adulthood.

Sub-group variation also has been attributed to immigration status. Studies of educational trajectories and attainments of immigrant versus native-born students inform our current understanding of processes that may underlie differences in transition patterns between immigrant and native groups. Mollenkopf and colleagues (2005) collected data on a sample of second-generation immigrant and native-born White young adults (i.e., ages 18 to 32) in New York City and surrounding areas. The second-generation immigrants were the children of

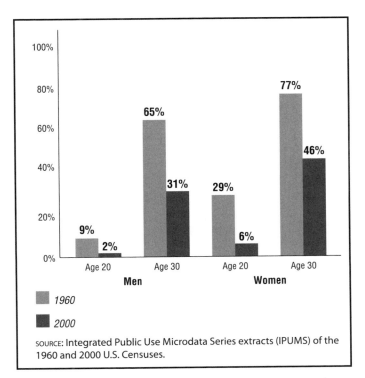

Figure 1. *Percent completing transition to adulthood in 1960 and 2000 using traditional benchmarks (leaving home, finishing school, getting married, having a child and being financially independent).* CENGAGE LEARNING, GALE.

parents who immigrated to the United States after 1965. The research revealed much variation in the rate of college enrollment among these young people; for example, Chinese and Russian immigrants enrolled at higher rates than native Whites. This difference has been attributed to the influence of family value for education attributed to these immigrant groups, manifesting in high parental expectations for achievement, and child adherence to such expectations. Immigration selectivity has also been advanced as a factor leading to these differences; the characteristics of those who immigrate to the United States may be the same factors that lead them to achieve educationally and financially.

Differences between immigrant and native groups of transition-stage adults in the United States are not only reflected in educational attainment, but also in the proportion of each group that makes transitions to marriage and parenthood between ages 22 and 32. As a function of longer periods of time spent as students, the trend demonstrates later ages at marriage and first birth among immigrant Chinese and Russian groups (they are more likely to delay these role transitions). By contrast, Dominican, Puerto Rican, and native-born Black persons made these transitions at younger ages (Mollenkopf, Waters, Holdaway, & Kasinitz, 2005).

Subjective accounts of "success" in the transition to adulthood vary as a function of sub-culture. Native-born Blacks are more apt to describe success in terms of meeting basic needs, staying alive, staying out of jail, having fun, meeting one's material needs, being the boss (having power), and having stability. In contrast, native-born Whites and Chinese and Russian Jewish immigrant groups—those with higher levels of education and upward mobility—reported that success was realized not only through the attainment of education, career, and money, but also the achievement of higher-order human needs such as awareness of future goals, being happy, being a good person, and making the world a better place (Mollenkopf et al., 2005).

Family support for semi-autonomy plays some role in the prolongation of the transition into adult roles of adult children. One key assumption of the sociological perspective holds that family resources provide a safety net during the transition to adulthood and provide for a period of semi-autonomy during which transition-age youth can extend their role as student and delay adult self-sufficiency (Osgood, Foster, Flanagan, & Ruth, 2005). Parental socioeconomic resources affect the timing of a young person's transition to adulthood (Sandefur, Eggerling-Boeck, & Park, 2005). Parental resources operate both directly and indirectly. First, parents with richer economic resources can contribute to their children's educational attainment directly, by paying for tuition. Second, parental socioeconomic resources affect children indirectly, as parent's social background may affect a child's socialization, peer group, and attitudes toward education—each of which contribute to a child's educational trajectory and, in turn, delayed marital and parental transitions (Osgood, Ruth, Eccles, Jacobs et al., 2005). Socioeconomic differences also may be transmitted through parental expectations for secondary education, which explains some variance in post-secondary attainment (Furstenberg, 2008).

FUTURE DIRECTIONS

Contemporary studies of the transition to adulthood indicate that, in many countries, the transitions to adulthood are taking longer and are less likely to reflect the "traditional" sequence of role transitions. The growing complexity in young people's pathways to becoming adult reflects an increasingly composite global economy and world. Consistent with these global changes, life course researchers are embracing theoretical frameworks that capture the multidimensionality of the contemporary transition to adulthood. There is momentum across disciplines to establish a more integrated, less disciplinary-divided definition and theoretical frame for study of this salient period of the life course. As new complex frames and methods evolve, studies of macro–micro forces that shape individual-level transitions, intergenerational and bidirectional shaping of transitions, and integrations of the subjective nature of the transition to adulthood are expected to paint a dynamic portrait of the transition from child to adult (Gauthier, 2007). Some scholars have advocated for a human development framework to integrate multidisciplinary perspectives of the transition to adulthood, and one that bridges theoretical and applied goals (Settersten, 2007; Tanner, 2006).

In sum, the transition to adulthood is a stage of life that, for individuals, varies as a function of a broad range of factors, some macro- (e.g., such as the changing economy) and some micro (e.g., parent financial contributions). For some, the contemporary transition to adulthood reveals great opportunities for growth, development, and the accumulation of resources and attainment of roles. For others, economic and institutional barriers, as well as developmental histories, present challenges to optimizing pathways during these critical years.

SEE ALSO Volume 1: *Age Norms; Identity Development; Transition to Marriage; Transition to Parenthood;* Volume 2: *Cultural Images, Adulthood; Fatherhood; Motherhood; Residential Mobility, Adulthood; Roles;* Volume 3: *Age Identity.*

BIBLIOGRAPHY

Arnett, J. J. (1997). Young people's conceptions of the transition to adulthood. *Youth & Society, 29,* 1–23.

Arnett, J. J. (2000). Emerging adulthood: A theory of development from the late teens through the twenties. *American Psychologist, 55,* 469–480.

Billari, F. C. (2001). The analysis of early life courses: Complex descriptions of the transition to adulthood. *Journal of Population Research, 18,* 119–142.

Corcoran, M., & Matsudaira, J. (2005). Is it getting harder to get ahead? Economic attainment in early adulthood for two cohorts. In R. A. Settersten Jr., F. F. Furstenberg Jr., & R. G. Rumbaut (Eds.), *On the frontier of adulthood: Theory, research, and public policy.* Chicago: University of Chicago Press.

Douglass, C. B. (2007). From duty to desire: Emerging adulthood in Europe and its consequences. *Child Development Perspectives, 1*(2), 101–108.

Elnick, A. B., Margrett, J. A., Fitzgerald, J. M., & Labouvie-Vief, G. (1999). Benchmark memories in adulthood: Central domains and predictors of their frequency. *Journal of Adult Development, 6,* 45–59.

Erikson, E. H. (1950). *Childhood and society.* New York: Norton.

Furstenberg, F. F., Jr. (2008). The intersections of social class and the transition to adulthood. *New Directions in Child and Adolescent Development. Special Issue: Social class and transitions to adulthood, 119,* 1–10. DOI: 10.1002/cd.205.

Fussell, E., Gauthier, A. H., & Evans, A. (2007). Heterogeneity in the transition to adulthood: The cases of Australia, Canada, & the United States. *European Journal of Population, 23,* 389.

Galambos, N. L., & Martinez, M. L. (2007). Poised for emerging adulthood in Latin America: A pleasure for the privileged. *Child Development Perspectives, 1*(2), 109–114.

Galambos, N. L., Turner, P. K., & Tilton-Weaver, L. C. (2005). Chronological and subjective age in emerging adulthood: The crossover effect. *Journal of Adolescent Research, 20*(5), 538–556.

Gauthier, A. H. (2007). Becoming a young adult: An international perspective on the transition to adulthood. *European Journal of Population, 23*(3–4), 217–223.

Grant, M. J., & Furstenberg, F. F., Jr. (2007). Changes in the transition to adulthood in less developed countries. *European Journal of Population, 23,* 415–428.

Mollenkopf, J., Waters, M. C., Holdaway, J., & Kasinitz, P. (2005). The ever-winding path: Ethnic and racial diversity in the transition to adulthood. In R. A. Settersten Jr., F. F. Furstenberg Jr., & R. G. Rumbaut (Eds.), *On the frontier of adulthood: Theory, research, and public policy.* Chicago: University of Chicago Press.

Nelson, L. J., & Chen, X. (2007). Emerging adulthood in China: The role of social and cultural factors. *Child Development Perspectives, 1,* 86–91.

Osgood, D. W., Foster, E. M., Flanagan, C., & Ruth, G. R. (2005). *On your own without a net.* Chicago, IL: Chicago University Press.

Osgood, D. W., Ruth, G., Eccles, J. S., Jacobs. J. E., & Barber, B. L. (2005). Six paths to adulthood: Fast starters, parents without careers, educated partners, educated singles, working singles, and slow starters. In R. A. Settersten Jr., F. F. Furstenberg Jr., & R. G. Rumbaut (Eds.), *On the frontier of adulthood: Theory, research, and public policy.* Chicago: University of Chicago Press.

Rindfuss, R. R. (1991). The young adult years: Diversity, structural change, and fertility. *Demography, 28,* 411–438.

Sandefur, G. D., Eggerling-Boeck, J., & Park, H. (2005). Off to a good start? Postsecondary education and early adult life. In R. A. Settersten Jr., F. F. Furstenberg Jr., & R. G. Rumbaut (Eds.), *On the frontier of adulthood: Theory, research, and public policy.* Chicago: University of Chicago Press.

Schwartz, S. J., Côté, J. E., & Arnett, J. J. (2005). Identity and agency in emerging adulthood. *Youth & Society, 37*(2), 201–229.

Settersten, R. A. (2007). Passages to adulthood: Linking demographic change and human development. *European Journal of Population, 23,* 251–272.

Settersten, R. A., Jr., Furstenberg, F. F., & Rumbaut, R. G. (2005). *On the frontier of adulthood: Theory, research, and public policy.* Chicago: University of Chicago Press.

Smith, T. W. (2005). *Coming of age in 21st century America: Public attitudes towards the importance and timing of transitions to adulthood. GSS Topical Report No. 35.* National Opinion Research Center: University of Chicago.

Tanner, J. L. (2006). Recentering during emerging adulthood. In J. J. Arnett & J. L. Tanner (Eds.), *Emerging adults in America: Coming of age in the 21st century.* Washington, DC: American Psychological Associations.

Jennifer L. Tanner

TRAUMA

Trauma is the extreme psychological distress that a person experiences when exposed to severe adversity. Although experiencing trauma is relatively uncommon for most people over the course of a given day, year, or developmental stage, studies show that the majority of the population experiences trauma at least once over the course of a lifetime. Experiencing trauma can lead to long-lasting, negative consequences for both mental and physical health, yet not everyone who is exposed to trauma suffers equally. The long-term impact of trauma depends on many factors, including the nature of the trauma-inducing event, the developmental stage and coping resources of the person exposed, and the social and cultural context within which the event occurred.

THE DEFINITION AND DISTRIBUTION OF TRAUMA

The term *trauma* originates from the Greek word for "wound." Whereas physical trauma is defined as a wound to living tissue caused by an external force, psychological trauma is the mental and emotional distress that results from experiencing extremely threatening life events. The distress that is associated with trauma is described as an overwhelming sense of fear, helplessness, or horror. Events, or stressors, that can lead to trauma responses are called *traumatic events*. Traumatic events are distinguished from other stressors by their heightened seriousness or severity. According to the *Diagnostic and Statistical Manual of Mental Disorders* (4th edition) of the American Psychiatric Association (1994), a traumatic event is an experience that involves actual or threatened death or serious injury, or a threat to the physical integrity of self or others. The *ICD-10 Classification of Mental and Behavioral Disorders* of the World Health Organization (1992) refers to a traumatic event as that which is of an exceptionally threatening or catastrophic nature, which is likely to cause pervasive distress in almost anyone. The term *trauma* is often used to represent both the traumatic event and the initial distress that it causes.

Examples of traumatic events (or traumas) include sudden events, such as exposure to natural or manmade disaster, or witnessing violent crime, as well as events that are more chronic in nature, such as participation in combat or being the victim of physical or sexual abuse or assault (Wheaton, 1996). Traumas also can be characterized by their scope of influence. For instance, some traumatic events, such as natural disasters, affect entire populations simultaneously, whereas others, such as exposure to physical or sexual assault, primarily affect individuals in isolation.

Traumatic events differ with regard to their prevalence. The most common forms of trauma over a lifetime include witnessing someone being injured or killed, being exposed to a natural disaster, and experiencing a life-threatening accident or illness (Kessler, Sonnega, Bromet, Hughes, & Nelson, 1995; Krause, Shaw, & Cairney,

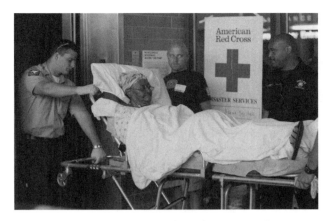

Refugee. *A hurricane Katrina refugee from New Orleans is transported by paramedics to a Dallas shelter. Texans opened their schools, hospitals, and sports arenas to some of Hurricane Katrina's most desperate refugees, offering them a chance to recover from the trauma of the event, regain some normalcy, and decide their next move.* **AP IMAGES.**

2004). Population-based studies of trauma suggest that the lifetime prevalence of exposure to any trauma among adults is more than 50%, with the majority of those who have been exposed actually reporting more than one type of trauma exposure.

The lifetime prevalence of most of the relatively common traumas is higher among men than women; however, some forms of trauma have higher rates among women, including rape, sexual molestation, and childhood abuse and neglect (Breslau et al., 1998; Kessler et al., 1995; Norris, 1992). Evidence of race differences in the prevalence of exposure to traumatic events is mixed, with some data showing higher rates of most traumas among Whites (Norris, 1992), and other data showing no race differences for most traumas, and higher rates among non-Whites for violent assaults (Breslau et al., 1998). Exposure to violent assaults is also more common among persons of low socioeconomic status (Breslau et al., 1998).

Some age differences in the prevalence of exposure to trauma are also apparent. Not surprisingly, lifetime trauma exposure appears to be positively associated with age for young and middle-age adults (Kessler et al., 1995). Among older adults, however, additional years of life do not appear to result in higher levels of lifetime trauma (Krause et al., 2004). Other studies have estimated rates of trauma exposure by age and have found the highest rates between the ages of 16 and 20 years (Breslau et al., 1998). After age 20, exposure rates tend to decline for most forms of trauma; however, rates are stable and actually increase for some forms of trauma, such as the unexpected death of a loved one and natural disaster (Breslau et al., 1998; Norris, 1992).

THE LONG-TERM
IMPACT OF TRAUMA

Virtually everyone exposed to a traumatic event experiences some degree of distress in the immediate aftermath (O'Brien, 1998). This trauma response typically entails intense feelings of fear and helplessness arising from the appraisal that one's life or sense of self has been fundamentally threatened (Resick, 2001). Following this immediate response, however, most people are able to cope effectively and recover satisfactorily. Nevertheless, for a substantial number of people, the distress caused by a traumatic event lingers and can lead to the development of mental, as well as physical, health problems over the life course.

The vast majority of studies of the long-term impact of trauma focus on mental health problems. The mental disorder most commonly associated with trauma is post-traumatic stress disorder (PTSD). PTSD is a pathological stress response syndrome with symptoms that include (a) "re-experiencing" the traumatic event through flashbacks and nightmares, (b) avoidance of stimuli associated with the trauma and a numbing of responsiveness, and (c) excessive arousal (American Psychiatric Association, 1994). In order to meet the threshold for a PTSD diagnosis, these symptoms must persist for at least one month and must cause "clinically significant" impairment in social functioning. In adults, estimates of the prevalence of PTSD among those exposed to a traumatic event range from 8% to 20% (Breslau et al., 1998; Kessler et al., 1995).

Other mental disorders that are associated with exposure to traumatic events include substance abuse, depression, and anxiety disorders. Often, these disorders co-occur with PTSD. Kessler and colleagues (1995) estimated that 79% of women and 88.3% of men with PTSD have at least one other mental disorder.

A growing number of studies have also raised the possibility that trauma has adverse long-term effects on physical health (Krause et al., 2004; Shaw & Krause, 2002). Data from these studies show significant associations between exposure to traumatic events earlier in the life course and subsequent physical health outcomes such as poor self-rated health, acute and chronic illnesses, and functional disability. At least two possible explanations for these associations have been proposed. First, exposure to trauma may impair one's psychosocial resources, such as personal control beliefs and social support, which themselves are strong determinants of physical health (Shaw & Krause, 2002). In addition, exposure to trauma may lead individuals to engage in negative health-related behaviors—such as smoking, substance abuse, or poor weight management—in attempts to cope with the ongoing distress associated with a trauma (Irving & Ferraro, 2006; Resick, 2001).

FACTORS INFLUENCING
THE IMPACT OF TRAUMA

A particular event is traumatic only to the extent that victims appraise the event as extremely threatening (Van der Kolk, McFarlane, & Weisaeth, 1996). Therefore, it is one's interpretations of the meaning of an event that largely dictate its long-term impact. Characteristics of a traumatic event that may influence its interpreted meaning, and thus its long-term impact, include its perceived intendedness and whether the victim is oneself or another person. For example, Kessler and colleagues (1995) found that events that are natural (e.g., natural disasters), unintentional (e.g., accidents), and impersonal (e.g., witnessing death or injury) are less strongly associated with PTSD than are events involving intentional interpersonal violence (e.g., combat, rape, and physical abuse). Therefore, it appears that events that cause people to perceive themselves as deliberate victims may have a stronger long-term impact than events involving immediate harm to others or events that are perceived to be natural or accidental.

Other determinants of the long-term effects of a traumatic event involve characteristics of the victim. Figuring prominently in this regard is the victim's stage in the life course. Both the stage in the life course at which a victim was originally exposed to a trauma, as well as a victim's current life course stage, are important to consider. Research findings regarding which life course stage is associated with the most harmful impacts are somewhat equivocal. Many investigators believe that exposure to trauma during childhood is especially harmful (Irving & Ferraro, 2006; Shaw & Krause, 2002). This is because childhood is viewed as a particularly vulnerable developmental stage, when the foundations for key psychosocial resources that are essential for effective functioning in adulthood, such as perceptions of control over one's environment and the ability to form and maintain meaningful and supportive social relationships, are being developed. The feelings of helplessness and insecurity caused by traumatic events could permanently impair the development of these key psychosocial resources.

Despite evidence of the strong and enduring negative consequences of childhood trauma, however, other research suggests that exposure to trauma at other stages of the life course may be even more damaging. In particular, research by Krause and colleagues (2004) found that traumatic events encountered during young and middle adulthood (i.e., between the ages of 18 and 64) exert the greatest negative effects on health. However, this research does not indicate whether the greater level of harm caused by trauma encountered during these stages is due to something characteristic of these developmental stages or to the particular types of trauma that are likely to be encountered during these stages.

Trauma encountered during old age does not appear to be associated with negative health outcomes. This may be because the extensive life experience of elderly individuals better prepares them to anticipate and cope with the consequences of a traumatic event.

A person's stage in the life course is also important for understanding the long-term impact of trauma because the interpreted meaning of a traumatic event is likely to evolve over time. For instance, the impact of trauma encountered during childhood may not be apparent until much later in the life course because a child may not have the cognitive capacity or life experience to fully appreciate how threatening an event actually was until adulthood. Furthermore, the developmental stages encountered during late life may also influence the effects of trauma encountered many years earlier. For example, many people, as they enter old age, consciously strive to evaluate, integrate, and make sense of the experiences they have encountered over the course of their lives. In the process, they may learn to reconcile or overcome the negative effects of earlier trauma by reaching an understanding of the experiences they have had, and perhaps even forgiving the perpetrators of their traumatic experience. Alternatively, during these final stages of life, some traumatic experiences that have not been effectively coped with previously may resurface and lead to a reoccurrence, or delayed onset, of posttraumatic disorders (Aarts & Op den Velde, 1996).

Finally, the social environment surrounding a trauma victim also influences the long-term impact of the event. For example, the meaning attached to a particular event is heavily influenced by social context. This is evident from changes in the ways in which American society has viewed the use of physical force as a form of discipline by parents. Over the course of the last century, Americans have progressed from viewing corporal punishment as normative and morally sanctioned to viewing it as abusive and condemning it. Therefore, older cohorts who were exposed to childhood physical abuse may have interpreted these events differently than do younger cohorts, and this may influence the long-term psychological impact of such an event (Shaw & Krause, 2002).

Factors in the social and cultural environment are also important for the recovery process. Strong and supportive relationships with others are thought to be a primary defense against the negative long-term effects of trauma (van der Kolk et al., 1996). In addition, the presence of cultural rituals for coping with some forms of trauma (e.g., funerals) are also helpful in the recovery process.

CURRENT RESEARCH AND POLICY ISSUES

Despite the tremendous growth in recent decades in knowledge regarding psychosocial trauma and its potential long-term effects, more research is needed. Exposure to traumatic events is an inevitable part of life. However, the more that is known about how people respond to trauma, the more effective societies will be at promoting healthy recovery.

Several specific issues are high priorities for future research. First, most studies focusing on trauma have been limited to mental health outcomes of traumatic events, such as PTSD and depression. Further examination of the extent to which trauma leads to physical health problems, and how exactly exposure to trauma affects physical health, is greatly needed. Second, although researchers have begun to examine the effects of multiple exposures to trauma throughout the life course (Breslau, Chilcoat, Kessler, & Davis, 1999; Turner & Lloyd, 1995), further investigation into the joint and cumulative effects of multiple exposures to trauma at different points in the life course is critical. Third, a relatively new area that is ripe for further examination is posttraumatic growth. A growing body of research has revealed that for many individuals, the process of struggling with extreme adversity actually leads to improved functioning (Linley & Joseph, 2004). Nevertheless, it remains unclear how common such growth is or what factors are likely to facilitate it. Finally, research is needed to better understand the public health impact of large-scale traumas that affect entire groups of people simultaneously, such as natural disasters, wars, and terrorist attacks. More research is needed to better predict who in the population is most vulnerable to trauma-induced mental and physical health problems in the wake of such events.

Current policy challenges related to trauma involve devising ways to prevent posttraumatic illnesses among those who are exposed. Because exposure to many traumatic events is unavoidable, prevention policies that focus on secondary, rather than primary, prevention are likely to be most productive. For example, policies are needed to ensure that those who must be exposed to trauma (e.g., emergency response personnel) are adequately trained. In addition, following exposure to traumatic events, early intervention with efforts to stimulate healthy coping is thought to be effective at limiting long-term damage. Therefore, policies that reduce barriers to seeking mental health treatment and otherwise facilitate early intervention programs for those who are exposed to trauma are greatly needed. This may be especially true in developing countries that currently lack the critical resources needed to launch extensive prevention efforts but whose rates of exposure to many traumas (e.g., disasters) far surpass those in developed countries (Van de Kolk et al., 1996).

SEE ALSO Volume 1: *Child Abuse; Resilience;* Volume 2: *Crime and Victimization, Adulthood; Domestic Violence; Life Events; Mental Health, Adulthood; Stress in Adulthood;* Volume 3: *Elder Abuse and Neglect; Stress in Later Life.*

BIBLIOGRAPHY

Aarts, P. G., & Op den Velde, W. (1996). Prior traumatization and the process of aging: Theory and clinical applications. In B. A. van der Kolk, A. C. McFarlane, & L. Weisaeth (Eds.), *Traumatic stress: The effects of overwhelming experience on mind, body, and society* (pp. 359–377). New York: Guilford Press.

American Psychiatric Association. (1994). *Diagnostic and statistical manual of mental disorders.* (4th ed.). Washington, DC: Author.

Black, D., Newman, M., Harris-Hendriks, J., & Mezey, G. (Eds.). (1997). *Psychological trauma: A developmental approach.* London: Gaskell.

Breslau, N., Chilcoat, H. D., Kessler, R. C., & Davis, G. C. (1999). Previous exposure to trauma and PTSD effects of subsequent trauma: Results from the Detroit Area Survey of Trauma. *American Journal of Psychiatry, 156,* 902–907.

Breslau, N., Kessler, R. C., Chilcoat, H. D., Schultz, L. R., Davis, G. C., & Andreski, P. (1998). Trauma and posttraumatic stress disorder in the community: The 1996 Detroit Area Survey of Trauma. *Archives of General Psychiatry, 55,* 626–632.

Irving, S. M., & Ferraro, K. F. (2006). Reports of abusive experiences during childhood and adult health ratings: Personal control as a pathway? *Journal of Aging and Health, 18,* 458–485.

Kessler, R. C., Sonnega, A., Bromet, E., Hughes, M., & Nelson, C. B. (1995). Posttraumatic stress disorder in the National Comorbidity Survey. *Archives of General Psychiatry, 52,* 1048–1060.

Krause, N., Shaw, B. A., & Cairney, J. (2004). A descriptive epidemiology of lifetime trauma and the physical health status of older adults. *Psychology and Aging, 19,* 637–648.

Linley, P. A., & Joseph, S. (2004). Positive change following trauma and adversity: A review. *Journal of Traumatic Stress, 17,* 11–21.

Norris, F. H. (1992). Epidemiology of trauma: Frequency and impact of different potentially traumatic events on different demographic groups. *Journal of Consulting and Clinical Psychology, 60,* 409–418.

O'Brien, L. S. (1998). *Traumatic events and mental health.* Cambridge, U.K.: Cambridge University Press.

Resick, P. A. (2001). *Stress and trauma.* Philadelphia, PA: Taylor & Francis.

Shaw, B. A., & Krause, N. (2002). Exposure to physical violence during childhood, aging, and health. *Journal of Aging and Health, 14,* 467–494.

Turner, R. J., & Lloyd, D. A. (1995). Lifetime traumas and mental health: The significance of cumulative adversity. *Journal of Health and Social Behavior, 36,* 360–376.

Van der Kolk, B. A., McFarlane, A. C., & Weisaeth, L. (1996). *Traumatic stress: The effects of overwhelming experience on mind, body, and society.* New York: Guilford Press.

Wheaton, B. (1996). The domains and boundaries of stress concepts. In H. B. Kaplan (Ed.), *Psychosocial stress: Perspectives on structure, theory, life-course, and methods* (pp. 29–70). San Diego, CA: Academic Press.

World Health Organization. (1992). *The ICD-10 classification of mental and behavioral disorders: Clinical descriptions and diagnostic guidelines.* Geneva: Author.

Benjamin A. Shaw

U-Z

UNEMPLOYMENT

Individuals are officially defined as unemployed if they are seeking paid work but are unable to find a job. The unemployment rate is obtained each month from the Current Population Survey of U.S. households, conducted by the Bureau of Labor Statistics. The official unemployment rate is computed by dividing the number of people unemployed during a survey week by the total number of people employed and unemployed during the same week (excluding those under 16 years of age, institutionalized persons, and persons on active duty in the armed forces). The denominator is referred to as the civilian labor force; thus the unemployment rate shows the fraction of the labor force that is unemployed, not the fraction of all people who are unemployed.

UNDEREMPLOYMENT

The unemployment rate is usually considered to be an underestimate of labor market weakness because it does not include people who are underemployed in one of three ways: (a) those who are employed only part-time when they need and desire full-time employment; (b) those who are employed at a low-paying job that requires less skill or training than they possess; and (c) those who have become discouraged workers because of a lack of job opportunities, training opportunities, or services that enable them to work, such as child care and public transportation. Such difficulties lead them to accept economic inactivity rather than to register as unemployed or actively seek jobs because their prospects for regular employment appear to be bleak. Members of the first two groups are included in the labor force, but not counted as unemployed; members of the third group are not counted as a part of the labor force, because actively seeking a job is required for them to be considered unemployed in official statistics.

EXPANDED MEASURES OF LABOR UNDERUTILIZATION

Policy-makers and the public-at-large would benefit from having greater knowledge of the full extent of the level of underutilization of people who are available for work. It is widely acknowledged that the official unemployment rate understates the number of persons who are negatively affected by labor market conditions, and that it is not the best estimate of the nation's economic health. For example, it is likely that in inner city areas with limited job opportunities, the number of discouraged workers is higher among young minority men (Wilson, 1996). The monthly publication of a single unemployment rate fails to report on the rates for different age and racial and ethnic groups, the number of part-time workers who desire full-time jobs, and the duration of unemployment that is experienced. The 2006 Bureau of Labor Statistics, as reported in Nelson (2007), provides six alternative measures of labor underutilization that should be reported along with the official unemployment rate; they include the addition of discouraged workers, involuntary part-time workers, and marginally attached workers (see Figure 1).

CROSS-NATIONAL COMPARISONS OF UNEMPLOYMENT

The unemployment rate is often used as an indicator of a nation's economic health. The U.S. rate is often compared

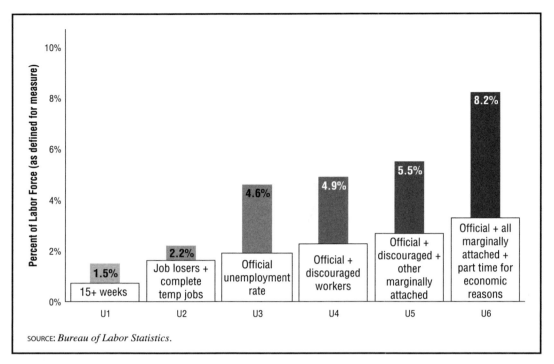

Figure 1. *Alternative measures of labor underutilization, United States 2006.* CENGAGE LEARNING, GALE.

with that of the industrialized countries of Canada, Australia, Japan, France, Germany, and Italy. Since 2001 the United States has had a relatively low rate, coming in either second to Japan, or third behind Australia. The highest rates are for Germany and France. In all these countries, highest rates are for teenagers (Bureau of Labor Statistics, 2007a).

U.S. DEMOGRAPHIC GROUP COMPARISONS

In the United States unemployment rates are calculated for several demographic groups, enabling subgroup comparisons. While unemployment characterizes all age groups to some extent, it is highest for teenagers and young adults aged 20 to 24 years. The unemployment rate is lowest for adults aged 45 to 55 years. In general, women have lower rates than men, but married women have higher rates than married men. With respect to race and ethnicity, Whites have the lowest unemployment rates, followed by Asian Americans, Hispanic or Latino Americans, and African Americans (Bureau of Labor Statistics, 2007b). These differentials are due to a number of factors, such as educational level of each group and job opportunities in area of residence (Wilson, 1996).

CAUSES AND GENERAL EFFECTS OF UNEMPLOYMENT

Unemployment rates largely reflect the workings of a market economy, especially technological changes in

industrial production and corporate reorganization or relocation to minimize costs. It is the unemployed workers, however, who experience income loss, anxiety, reduced self-esteem, loss of social contacts, heightened smoking and alcohol use, lower quality nutrition, postponed health care, family conflicts, and illness.

EFFECTS ON HEALTH

Extensive research has been conducted on the health impact of economic downturns and unemployment (Perrucci & Perrucci, 1990). Research based on state and county unemployment rates and its effects reveals a relationship between economic downturns and aggregate rates of negative health symptoms. Research focused on the link between unemployment and health has been conducted on both broad, general samples of unemployed workers as well as on workers displaced by specific plant closings. For general samples of unemployed workers, studies conducted at one point in time and studies that take repeated measurements across time demonstrate the development of mild levels of distress or increases in levels of psychological distress subsequent to unemployment.

Workers who have been displaced by a specific plant closing in a community experience greater health impacts than workers drawn from a general sample of unemployed persons (Perrucci & Perrucci, 1990). The difference is probably because of (a) the impact that a plant closing has on a community's economy, reducing the chances for reemployment; (b) longer periods of unemployment for workers in a depressed local economy; and (c) greater economic strain resulting from longer periods of unemployment.

EFFECTS ON FAMILIES AND COMMUNITIES

Families with unemployed members have significantly lower marital adjustment, poorer marital communication, and lower satisfaction and harmony in family relations. Also, children whose fathers are unemployed are more likely to experience infectious disease as well as illness of longer duration in comparison with children whose parents are continuously employed. Even for continuously employed fathers, children whose fathers feel considerable job insecurity are more likely to experience illness than children whose fathers feel very secure in their work positions, suggesting that the anticipation of joblessness affects health (Margolis and Farran, 1981).

The effects of unemployment can reach beyond the individual worker to affect entire communities in situations where tax revenues are reduced and needs for additional public social expenditures increase. Several case studies of unemployment indicate that the loss of economic security usually adversely affects the social cohesiveness of communities as the unemployed workers lose faith in the economic system and become dependent, precluding redevelopment of their communities. Cutbacks in public services, such as education and police protection, reduce quality of life and impair the community's ability to attract new families and new employers.

GAPS IN RESEARCH KNOWLEDGE

Research on the way in which unemployment affects health points to three explanatory factors: First, and perhaps most important, is income loss and the threat to future financial security; second, is the loss of meaningful work and self-esteem; third, is the lack of social support from friends, kin, and community. These factors have been studied in the context of the stress process. Learning more about who is vulnerable, when in their lives they are vulnerable, and why some vulnerable people become resilient in the face of stress is an agenda for future research (Broman, Hamilton, and Hoffman, 2001).

UNEMPLOYMENT AND POLICY CONSIDERATIONS

Unemployment is an economic problem and much more. Its impact on individuals, families, and communities results in human and social costs that require a public response. A consideration of the nature and effectiveness of current public policy on unemployment and

assumptions about patterns of economic change in the future also encourage a policy response.

Current policy assumes that unemployment is a normal and unavoidable cost of a growing, changing economy operating in a free market. A growing economy requires change, and change leaves behind those individuals who lack the needed human capital (education and skills) and those firms that cannot compete in the marketplace. The challenge is how to get corporations to accept some of the costs of unemployment that now jeopardize workers and their communities.

There is evidence that current unemployment insurance and severance pay or continuing job-related fringe benefits, especially health insurance, is inadequate for most displaced workers. Also, when unemployment occurs during a recession, or by plant closings by a major employer in a small community, there is also a decline in the availability of community resources to assist displaced workers. Current policy attempts to assist those whose jobs have been moved overseas through the Trade Adjustment Act of 2002 and Title III of the Job Training and Partnership Act of 1983, but both serve relatively few displaced workers. And as corporations continue to move or initiate operations abroad, workers will experience job insecurity as well as loss.

There are at least four general policy initiatives that could be considered. First, a policy initiative should be job-centered, with a focus on creating and maintaining jobs through stronger federal legislation to place the human and social costs of unemployment at the center of economic decision-making. Companies should be required to provide sufficient reason in closing their plant(s) before federal permission is granted to do it, particularly if the closing would devastate the individuals and communities involved.

A second policy initiative should expand unemployment benefits available to displaced workers, and it should set uniform standards for states to follow to deliver benefits. These benefits would be particularly effective if combined with an adequately funded program that coordinates job retraining and relocation expenses.

A third policy initiative should provide social services to unemployed workers and their families while they are participating in retraining and relocation programs. Such assistance would help workers to better cope with job loss, and it would help spouses and other family members to obtain advice, training, and agency referrals to help the entire family deal with unemployment.

Fourth, as the creation and export of jobs overseas continues, the federal government should undertake a jobs program, implemented through state and local governments, to hire the unemployed into meaningful and valued jobs in communities across the country. These workers could assist with vital community services in underserved areas of education, health care, and other community-based services, while benefiting from gainful employment and a sense of contributing to the community.

SEE ALSO Volume 2: *Careers; Policy, Employment;* Volume 3: *Retirement.*

BIBLIOGRAPHY

Broman, C. L., Hamilton, V. L., & Hoffman, W. S. (2001). *Stress and distress among the unemployed: Hard times and vulnerable people.* New York: Kluwer Academic/Plenum.

Bureau of Labor Statistics. (2007a). Employment and unemployment in families by race and hispanic or latino ethnicity, 2005–06 annual averages. Retrieved February 29, 2008, from http://www.bls.gov/NEWS.RELEASE/ FAMEE.T01.HTM

Bureau of Labor Statistics. (2007b). Civilian labor force, employment and unemployment approximating U.S. concepts, 1960–2006. Retrieved February 29, 2008, from http://www.bls.gov/fls/flscomparelf.htm

Caplan, R. D., Vinokur, A. D., Price, R. H., & Van Ryn, M. (1989). Job-seeking, reemployment, and mental health: A randomized field experiment in coping with job loss. *Journal of Applied Psychology, 74*(5), 759–769.

Elder, G. H., Jr., & Liker, J. K. (1982). Hard times in women's lives: Historical influences across 40 years. *American Journal of Sociology, 88*(2), 241–269.

Feather, N. T. (1990). *The psychological impact of unemployment.* New York: Springer-Verlag.

Kessler, R. C., Turner, J. B., & House, J. S. (1989). Unemployment, reemployment, and emotional functioning in a community sample. *American Sociological Review, 54*(4), 648–657.

Margolis, L. H. & Farran, D. (1981). Unemployment and children. *International Journal of Mental Health, 13,* 107–124.

Moore, T. S. (1990). The nature and unequal incidence of job displacement costs. *Social Problems, 37,* 230–242.

Nelson, J. (2007). *Alternative measures of the unemployment rate.* Retrieved February 22, 2008, from http://www.qualityinfo.org

Perrucci, R., & Perrucci, C. C. (1990). Unemployment and health: Research and policy implications. In J. R. Greenley (Ed.), *Research in Community and Mental Health,* Vol. 6, *Mental disorder in social context* (pp. 237–264). Greenwich, CT: JAI Press.

Perrucci, C. C., Perrucci, R., Targ, D. B., & Targ, H. (2005). *Plant closings: International context and social costs.* New Brunswick, NJ: Transaction/Aldine.

Rosen, E. I. (1987). *Bitter choices: Blue-collar women in and out of work.* Chicago: University of Chicago Press.

Targ, D. B., & Perrucci, C. C. (1991). Plant closings, unemployment, and families. *Marriage and Family Review, 15,* 131–145.

Wilson, W. J. (1996). *When work disappears: The world of the new urban poor.* New York: Knopf.

Carolyn C. Perrucci
Robert Perrucci

UNIVERSAL HEALTH INSURANCE

SEE Volume 2: *Policy, Health.*

VOLUNTEERING, ADULTHOOD

Volunteering is a form of altruistic behavior. Its goal is to provide help to another person, group, organization, cause, or the community at large, without expectation of material reward. Volunteer work is not to be confused with informal helping, which is unpaid service people provide on a more casual basis, outside of any organizational context, to someone in need, or care work, which is normally associated with kin relations and consists of face-to-face help provided to an individual toward whom one feels some kind of social responsibility. Volunteer work does, however, include advocacy, which is a form of service that is very close to social activism. Advocacy organizations seek to influence the outcomes of public or private decisions on issues that affect the fortunes of the organization's clients or broader constituencies.

When people think of a volunteer, they almost always imagine someone who is making a sacrifice to help another person, an organization, or a cause. Although most people agree that individuals can benefit from their volunteer work, they must not volunteer for the purpose of gaining those benefits and would, it is assumed, continue to volunteer even if those benefits disappeared. In the public mind, then, volunteer work is not simply unpaid labor but unpaid labor performed for the correct reason. *Good works* are inspired by virtues such as generosity, love, gratitude, loyalty, courage, compassion, and a desire for justice: any benefits are a byproduct.

According to social surveys, just over a quarter of Americans age 16 years or older will have volunteered at some point in the past 12 months, but the likelihood of having done so and the specific volunteer activity in which they engage vary considerably across social groups. Volunteers tend to be more highly educated (about 20% of high school graduates volunteer compared with 43.3% of college graduates); they are more likely to be White, female, working part-time, married, parenting school-age children, and frequent church-goers. Some people volunteer just a few hours in the course of the year, whereas others contribute several hours a week steadily; the latter group is composed disproportionately of those who are not in the labor force, such as homemakers, students, and retirees (U. S. Bureau of Labor Statistics, 2006).

Volunteerism is more common in the United States than most other advanced industrial societies, mainly because of the religiosity of the American people. A comparison of two otherwise quite similar countries substantiates this argument. The volunteer rate in the United States is higher than the rate in Canada. After country-level differences in frequency of attendance at religious services are controlled, however, the Canadian rate exceeds that of the United States. The same could be said for Sweden and Norway because they, too, have higher rates of volunteering than the United States after frequency of religious services attendance is controlled for. This is because much of the volunteer work in the United States is performed on behalf of religious organizations (Curtis, Baer, & Grabb, 2001).

VOLUNTEERING OVER THE LIFE COURSE

Life-course patterns in volunteering are quite evident in Figure 1, which uses Current Population Survey data from 2006 (U.S. Bureau of Labor Statistics, 2006). The columns show the percentage of each age group who volunteered at all during the previous 12 months.

Life-course variation in the number of hours volunteered among those who volunteer follows a different pattern: The number of hours volunteered per year is highest among those age 65 or older, followed by those age 55 to 64 years. Volunteers between 16 and 34 years contribute the fewest hours.

Teenagers and Young Adults Teenagers are often portrayed as rather self-centered, preoccupied with material possessions, and uninterested in community affairs, political activities, or helping others. In addition, many of the voluntary associations that sponsor and organize volunteer work are relatively inhospitable to teenagers, the one major exception being religious organizations. The teenage years would therefore appear to be a wasteland as far as volunteerism is concerned. In the United States, at least, teenagers show considerable interest in volunteering mainly because schools, churches, and other youth-oriented institutions encourage or, in some cases, require community service of their young people. Numerous studies show that the habit of volunteering tends to be passed from one generation to another. The mother's volunteering is more influential than the father's, due partly to her greater efforts to integrate her children into her own activities and partly to the fact that she is more likely to volunteer for child-related activities than the father (Wuthnow, 1995).

By volunteering early in life, people acquire experience and skills that establish the groundwork for volunteering in later life. In many respects, middle-age volunteers are simply young volunteers who have aged. From a human development perspective, it is no surprise that adult volunteers are more likely to say they volunteered in youth. However, young adults in their early 20s experience the time-pressure of multiple commitments and engage vigorously in a wide variety of leisure-time pursuits—a lifestyle not normally associated with doing volunteer work and this stage of the life course tends to mark a low point in volunteering.

The most popular form of volunteering among younger Americans is in connection with youth development organizations, followed by civic and community groups and environmental organizations. They are less interested than are older people in working in connection with a church (Lopez, 2004). Although young people are less interested in more routine forms of advocacy volunteering, they turn out in greater numbers for the kind of "high-risk activism" associated with protest movements. They are more available for this kind of work (their free time is relatively plentiful, social obligations are few, and, for those in school or college, work commitments are flexible), but the thrill of risky volunteering, which appeals to young people, should not be overlooked. They are also more likely than older people to take on high-adrenalin work, such as search and rescue or emergency squad volunteering.

Forming a Family Most Americans get married for the first time in their 20s. When looking at the possible influence of marriage on volunteering, it is important to bear in mind the several different ways people can be single. Compared with married people (and controlling for age), those whose spouses who have died are the least likely to volunteer, followed by those never married and those who are divorced or separated. Significantly, when frequency of religious service attendance is controlled for, the positive effect of marital status disappears, probably because marital status is associated primarily with volunteering in connection with a religious organization (Musick & Wilson, 2008).

Married couples tend to behave similarly when it comes to volunteer work: Freeman (1997) found that 59% of men married to women who were volunteers were volunteers themselves, compared with only 10% of men married to women who were not volunteers. Seventy percent of women married to men who volunteered were volunteers themselves, compared with only 16% of women married to men who did not volunteer. Furthermore, respondents married to spouses who volunteered contributed more hours than respondents married to spouses who did not volunteer (Hook, 2004).

Who Has the Most Influence? Spouses have a reciprocal positive effect on each other's volunteer hours; this influence is stronger when spouses are volunteering in the same domain, and the influence of the wife is stronger than the influence of the husband. Interestingly,

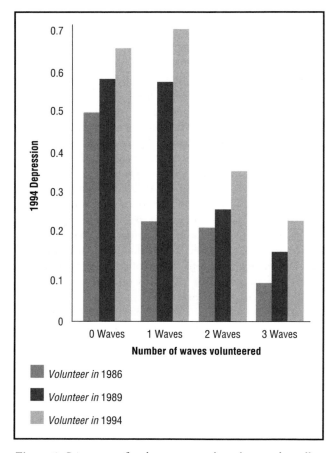

Figure 1. *Percentage of each age group who volunteered at all during the previous twelve months, 2006.* **CENGAGE LEARNING, GALE.**

unmarried couples living together (i.e. cohabiting) have *no* influence on each other's volunteer behavior (Rotolo & Wilson, 2007).

Volunteering with a Spouse Spouses clearly influence each other's volunteer behavior, but it does not necessarily follow that they volunteer together. One survey found that remarkably high proportions of married volunteers (41.4%) were accompanied by their spouses. Husbands were more likely to say they had volunteered with their spouses than wives did. Surprisingly, the tendency to volunteer together did not increase with age. Among the married couples who were volunteering, frequent church-goers were most likely to be volunteering together (Musick & Wilson, 2008).

Becoming Parents Newly married couples tend to have low volunteer rates, but this is mainly due to the fact that any children they have are young and that young children inhibit their parents' ability to do much outside the

household other than paid work. After they reach school age, however, children act as a social magnet for their parents, drawing them into a wider range of activities outside the home, including volunteer work. Parents of school-age children have a stake in maintaining organizations and activities that cater to their children and that, as individuals, they could not provide on their own, such as sports teams and scout troops.

The influence of children on their parents' volunteering is felt most keenly by mothers, who bear most of the responsibility of looking after children. According to Current Population Survey data, both mothers and fathers are more likely to volunteer if their children are between 6 and 13 years of age—and this pattern does not vary based on gender of the child. Compared with findings in parents of children ages 2 years or younger, parents of children between 6 and 13 years of age are much more likely to volunteer—but mothers are especially likely to do so. The influence of children ages 14 to 17 years on educational volunteering is also stronger for mothers than fathers. Both mothers and fathers of children ages 2 or younger are less likely to volunteer than married couples who have no children, but the deterrent effect is stronger for mothers than fathers (Musick & Wilson, 2008). In short, gender makes a difference regarding the influence of children on volunteering: Young children deter their mothers more than their fathers and school-age children involve their mothers more in volunteer work than their fathers.

Parental status and the gender of the parent also make a difference as to what the volunteer does. The Current Population Survey asks volunteers to report their main activity or job as a volunteer. For example, only 5.5% of men without children volunteered as a coach or referee compared with 18.9% of men with children younger than 18, but their volunteer rate for this activity was nevertheless higher for women whether they have children under 18 (4.2%) or not (1.8%).

The positive influence of school-age children on volunteering in midlife is conditioned by available free time. Full-time workers find it more difficult to volunteer than part-time workers; women with part-time jobs are more likely to volunteer and volunteer more hours than women working full-time, especially if they have school-age children. Full-time work, however, lowers the probability of volunteering and the number of hours volunteered but less so for mothers with school-age children (Musick & Wilson, 2008).

Volunteer Work in Later Life People become steadily less likely to volunteer as they enter old age and volunteer for fewer organizations. However, the hours contributed by each volunteer increase until he or she enters the ranks of the *oldest old* (75 years of age or more). According to

2006 Current Population Survey data, among those who volunteer at all, the median annual hours is highest (104) for the over-65 age group and lowest for 25- to 34-year-old age group. This age profile is found in most industrialized societies that gather such volunteer data. Interestingly, older people (i.e., those 65 years old and older) are somewhat more likely to say they became a volunteer by approaching an organization (43.4% compared with 40.8% of volunteers as a whole). Although this difference is small, it suggests that older people are more likely to take the initiative as a way of finding rewarding activities in their old age.

As far as volunteer preferences are concerned, older people favor volunteer activities in which they can help on a one-to-one basis and see the fruits of their labor immediately. Not surprisingly, older people are also drawn to volunteer work that targets other older people. In the 2006 Current Population Survey data, religious volunteering was the most popular choice among older people. Age also positively influenced volunteering for social and community service organizations, health, civic, political, and professional organizations. However, people older than 65 were less likely than younger people to volunteer for education or youth services, environmental or animal care organizations, and public safety organizations (U.S. Bureau of Labor, 2006).

The Effect of Retirement on Volunteering Many Americans plan to take up volunteer work in their retirement. The data suggest, however, that continuity is the predominant pattern: People tend to maintain the habits they had before retirement, but they modify them in light of their new circumstances. If they volunteered in middle age, they volunteer in old age and, in all likelihood, increase the number of hours they contribute. If they did not volunteer in middle age, they are unlikely to take it up when they retire. Those who do begin volunteering after retirement are more likely to be White, highly educated, in good health, and, above all, strongly religious and married to a spouse who is also volunteering (Zedlewski, 2007). Much also depends on what retirement means for the person: Older people who have fully retired volunteer the most hours, followed by older people who have retired but returned to work, followed by full-time workers who have not yet retired (Musick & Wilson, 2008). Once again, the interweaving of influences from several life domains—a hallmark of life-course analysis—helps shape the amount and direction of volunteer work.

THE BENEFITS OF VOLUNTEERING

A growing body of research indicates that volunteering is good for the physical and mental health of the volunteer. Volunteers have lower early mortality rates, possess greater

functional ability, and are less likely to feel depressed. Up to a certain point (around 100 hours per year), more volunteer work means more positive health outcomes. Long-term volunteers also seem to enjoy more benefits. For example, an analysis of the American Changing Lives data over three waves (1989, 1992, and 1994) showed that respondents who volunteered in all waves had fewer depressive symptoms than those who volunteered only once (Musick & Wilson, 2003). From a life-course perspective, it is interesting that older volunteers receive the greatest mental health benefits from doing volunteer work, no doubt because it provides them with physical and social activities and a sense of purpose at a time when they are losing social roles. It is also likely that older volunteers have more discretion over their volunteer work and contribute more of their volunteer time to religious organizations, both of which increase the likelihood of positive health benefits (Musick & Wilson, 2003).

POLICY

In the United States and other countries, such as Canada, the United Kingdom, and Australia, it is official government policy to promote volunteerism. Governments have come to regard volunteer work as a valuable adjunct to publicly provided services such as education, recreation, health care, and social services and an important stimulus for wider engagement in the community through political and civic organizations. In 1993 the United States established the Corporation for National Service to coordinate federal and state organization and promotion of volunteerism. Among the initiatives pursued by the Corporation are Senior Companions, to encourage volunteer work among the elderly, and Americorps, to engage teenagers and young adults in helping others. Service-learning curricula, in which high school students perform community service in return for academic credit, have recently spread throughout the United States, their aim being not only to improve educational quality but also to encourage a long-term commitment to helping out in the community.

SEE ALSO Volume 2: *Fatherhood; Motherhood; Political Behavior and Orientations, Adulthood; Religion and Spirituality, Adulthood; Social Integration/Isolation, Adulthood; Social Movements; Time Use, Adulthood.*

BIBLIOGRAPHY

Curtis, J., Baer, D., & Grabb, E. (2001). Nations of joiners: Voluntary association memberships in democratic societies. *American Sociological Review, 66,* 783–805.

Freeman, R. (1997). Working for nothing: The supply of volunteer labor. *Journal of Labor Economics, 15,* 140–167.

Hook, J. (2004). Reconsidering the division of household labor: Incorporating volunteer work and informal support. *Journal of Marriage and the Family, 66,* 101–117.

Lopez, M. (2004). *Volunteering among young people*. College Park, MD: Center for Information and Research on Civic Learning and Engagement, University of Maryland.

Musick, M., & Wilson, J. (2003). Volunteering and depression: The role of psychological and social resources on different age groups. *Social Science and Medicine, 56*, 259–269.

Musick, M., & Wilson, J. (2008). *Volunteers: A social profile*. Indianapolis: Indiana University Press.

Putnam, R. (2000). *Bowling alone: The collapse and revival of American community*. New York: Simon and Schuster.

Rotolo, T., & Wilson, J. (2004). What happened to the "long civic generation"? Explaining cohort differences in volunteerism. *Social Forces, 82*, 1091–1121.

Rotolo, T., & Wilson, J. (2007). The effects of children and employment status on the volunteer work of American women. *Nonprofit and Voluntary Sector Quarterly, 36*, 487–503.

U. S. Bureau of Labor Statistics. (2006). *Volunteering in the United States*. Washington DC: Government Printing Office.

Wuthnow, R. (1995). *Learning to care: Elementary kindness in an age of indifference*. New York: Oxford University Press

Zedlewski, S. (2007). *Will retiring boomers form a new army of volunteers?* Washington, DC: Urban Institute Retirement Project (Perspectives on Productive Aging).

John Wilson

WORK–FAMILY CONFLICT

Work–family conflict (WFC) refers to the situation in which the responsibilities and expectations of an individual's work roles interfere with the performance of his or her family roles—or vice versa. The work–family literature has burgeoned in the wake of large numbers of women and mothers entering the workforce since the 1970s. This research, which is based largely on the scarcity principle that individuals have finite resources that become overtaxed by multiple role responsibilities, takes one of two broad approaches. The first approach focuses on specific manifestations of WFC, as when employment or job characteristics interfere with specific family activities such as parenting or marital quality. The second approach focuses on experiences of WFC more broadly and the putative causes and consequences of these generalized experiences. This entry focuses on the latter of these two approaches because the full scope and breadth of WFC has direct effects on individuals at most stages in the adult life span, and it has untold potential effects for individuals' children and other family members as well as for coworkers and employers.

WFC: THE EVOLUTION OF A CONCEPT

Jeffrey Greenhaus and Nicholas Beutell (1985) defined WFC as "a form of interrole conflict in which role pressures from work and family domains are mutually incompatible in some respect" (p. 77). Building from this basic definition, a substantial literature in the fields of sociology, psychology, organizational behavior, management, and family studies has conceptualized WFC as a stressor. As such, WFC is believed to interfere with individual health and well-being, marital quality, family functioning, and fulfillment of job expectations.

There have been two primary innovations to the WFC concept since Greenhaus and Beutell's influential definition. The first primary innovation is the idea of directionality. Michael Frone, Marsha Russell, and M. Lynne Cooper (1992) argued that work-to-family conflict, or the extent to which work pressures impinge on family responsibilities, was conceptually and operationally distinct from family-to-work conflict, or the degree to which family responsibilities impinge on work responsibilities. Frone, John Yardley, and K. S. Markel (1997) then demonstrated the empirical distinction between work-to-family and family-to-work conflict and subsequently developed an influential model of the work–family interface, which emphasizes the reciprocal and bidirectional relationship between work-to-family and family-to-work conflict.

The directionality issue is interesting because it is in direct contrast to the original conceptualization of WFC. Greenhaus and Beutell (1985) specifically argued that WFC is inherently nondirectional until a decision is made to resolve one of the pressures contributing to the conflict, at which point directionality takes form, a situation sometimes referred to as work interference with family or family interference with work. This consideration of directionality creates conceptual confusion between WFC, conceptualized as a discrete occurrence of mutually incompatible role responsibilities, and work–family interference. Nevertheless, two separate meta-analyses have concluded that work-to-family and family-to-work conflicts are distinct yet bidirectionally interrelated. It is now standard practice in most research to conceptually and empirically separate work-to-family and family-to-work conflict.

The second primary innovation revolves around typologies of WFC. Greenhaus and Beutell (1985) originally speculated that WFC takes three primary forms: time-based (e.g., missing work because of a sick child or inclement weather keeps a child from school), behavior-based (e.g., treating family members like a subordinate at work), and strain-based (e.g., a person being short-tempered with his or her children following a bad day at work) conflict. However, only recently have researchers given serious consideration to these different types of WFC. Whereas some reviewers of the work–family literature question the utility of different types of WFC (Bellavia & Frone, 2005), others conclude that there is useful evidence supporting the distinction of some types of WFC—particularly time- and strain-based conflict (Geurts & Demerouti, 2003). Some researchers suggest that differentiating time-, behavior-, and strain-based conflict is important because they may have different antecedents and consequences, thereby requiring different intervention strategies (Carlson, Kacmar, & Williams, 2000). Greenhaus, Tammy Allen, and Paul Spector (2006) expanded the original typology to differentiate energy-based conflict from strain-based conflict, whereby the former reflects physical or emotional exhaustion and the latter reflects the transfer of negative emotions or feeling states (e.g., stressed or cranky). The utility of differentiating among different types of WFC is not yet resolved and awaits focused empirical and theoretical analysis.

MEASURING AND STUDYING WFC

In a review of the industrial-organizational psychological and organizational behavior literatures, disciplines central in studying WFC, Wendy Casper, Lillian Eby, Christopher

Bordeaux, Angie Lockwood, and Dawn Lambert (2007) noted that 85% of WFC studies used survey methods. Several studies of WFC have been based on nationally representative samples such as the National Study of the Changing Workforce (NSCW), a sequential panel study that began in 1977 and was refielded in 1992 and 5 years thereafter by the Families and Work Institute. Other national data on WFC come from the Midlife Development in the United States survey, which was originally fielded in 1995. In addition to these nationally representative studies, a large number of studies have been conducted with industry- and company-specific samples of workers.

WFC research is almost exclusively cross-sectional. Casper and colleagues (2007) noted that only 6% of WFC studies conducted in the past 25 years have followed individuals over time. Studies based on longitudinal data have produced results that are consistent with the general view of WFC as a stressor. Frone and colleagues (1997), for example, found that elevated levels of family-to-work conflict predicted the onset of incident hypertension (i.e., high blood pressure) over a 4-year time horizon. Similarly supportive of the stress perspective, other researchers have documented that elevated levels of WFC predicted health declines over time (Grant Vallone & Donaldson, 2001). These few longitudinal

Working Mom. *Kirstie Foster, a corporate public relations manager with General Mills, comforts her 10-month-old daughter Mia as she pays her a visit at the childcare facilities in the company's headquarters in Golden Valley, MN. General Mills is on Working Mother magazine's 19th annual list of the 100 best companies for working mothers.* **AP IMAGES.**

studies notwithstanding, surprisingly little is known about the antecedents and consequences of WFC over time.

Measurement of WFC has relied almost exclusively on self-reports that are either self- or interviewer-administered. Lois Tetrick and Louis Buffardi (2005) identified five to six measures of WFC most commonly used in the literature since the mid-1990s. They pointed out that there is substantial variation in the degree to which self-report measures have demonstrated construct validity, indicating that they actually measure WFC.

Some concern has been expressed that measures of WFC are inherently problematic because they overlap with outcomes of interest such as psychological strain, marital quality, and job satisfaction (MacDermid, 2004). Others question the structure of items assessing work-to-family conflict and family-to-work conflict and raise concerns that the absence of parallelism could create the impression that one direction of conflict is more common than the other (Bellavia & Frone, 2005). Still others have been critical because common measures do not capture the conceptual difference between WFC, such as the simultaneous occurrence of incompatible pressures in work and family domains, from work–family interference or the extent to which experiences in one domain impede activities in the other (Carlson & Grzywacz, 2008). Some investigators have developed proxy reports whereby knowledgeable counterparts report on levels of WFC for a focal individual, such as a spouse (Small & Riley, 1990); however, proxy measures are infrequently used. The infrequent use of proxy measures is driven, at least in part, by the fact that WFC can occur at both the social (and observable) and psychological (and nonobservable) level, suggesting that proxy reports can only capture a portion of WFC.

FINDINGS FROM WFC RESEARCH

The WFC literature is large and spans multiple disciplines. Since the late 1990s, there have been no fewer than 10 narrative reviews of the work–family literature. Most of these reviews provide summaries of the antecedents and consequences of WFC (Bellavia & Frone, 2005; Eby, Casper, Lockwood, Bordeaux, & Brinley, 2005). Additionally, there have been several quantitative reviews of the WFC literature (Allen, Herst, Bruck, & Sutton, 2000; Byron, 2005). Interested readers are encouraged to consult these. In this entry, a few main findings are emphasized that are likely to be of particular interest to life course researchers.

WFC across Time Relatively little research examines WFC across either historical or developmental time. In terms of historical trends, evidence from the NSCW indicates that levels of WFC increased among American workers in the late 20th and early 21st century and that

this increase is not attributed to growth in the proportion of women in the labor force and increases in dual-earner families (Winslow, 2005). On the developmental side, in light of the absence of longitudinal studies of WFC, there is limited ability to determine whether WFC changes across the adult life span. Based on cross-sectional data, Joseph Grzywacz, David Almeida, and Daniel McDonald (2002) reported that both work-to-family and family-to-work conflict increased and then declined across adulthood, with both directions of WFC peaking between the ages of 35 and 44.

Drawing on birth cohort data from Sweden, Gunn Johansson, Qinghai Huang, and Petra Lindfors (2007) reported significant differences in WFC among 43-year-old women, depending on life course employment patterns: Women with more intensive and persistent employment coupled with late childbearing generally reported greater WFC than those who began parenting earlier while working part time. Deborah Carr (2002) reported cohort differences in the effects of work–family trade-offs on psychological well-being. Despite these and other studies using birth cohort studies or a life course approach, there is a substantial need to better understand whether experiences of WFC have changed over time and how the ebb and flow of work and family responsibilities across the adult life span may contribute to age-related differences in WFC.

WFC across Social Groups Gender is a dominant focus of WFC research, both historically and substantively. The historical focus arises from the reality that WFC research is rooted in the large-scale shift of women and mothers of young children into the labor force. Although women and mothers have always been in the labor force, particularly women from minority and working-class families, the substantial increase in labor force participation among White middle-class women stimulated a large amount of research questioning the degree to which problems arise from women's employment. The substantive interest in gender differences in WFC arises from a theory suggesting that the worlds of work and family are inherently gendered and that gender-specific constructions of these worlds would create unequal experiences of WFC. Joseph Pleck's *(1977) asymmetrical boundary hypothesis*, or the view that women and men will have different patterns of WFC because of socialization patterns that assign responsibility for family to women and responsibility for work to men, exemplifies the gender argument made by several researchers.

Despite strong theory that indicates otherwise, there is only mixed evidence of gender differences in WFC. One review concluded that "there is little support for differences across basic characteristics that are typically examined such as gender" (Bellavia & Frone, 2005, p. 118). Likewise, another study reported that "there is no clear pattern in terms of the relative importance of work or family domain predictors for men's and women's work-family conflict" (Eby et al., 2005, p. 181), although those authors did conclude that gender is deeply engrained in work–family relationships. Kristin Byron's (2005) conclusion from a meta-analysis is that there is little evidence that experiences of WFC differ between women and men. Research acknowledging that women are overrepresented in some occupations whereas men are overrepresented in others and that uses gender-neutral measures of WFC are needed to resolve the inconsistent pattern of results observed in the WFC literature.

The WFC literature has been criticized as being overly focused on individuals who are valued by the labor market, that is, White, middle-class individuals working in professional jobs (Lambert, 1999). Little research examines WFC among members of racial and ethnic minority groups or compares experiences of WFC across racial and ethnic groups; such research is sorely needed. Evidence from the 1997 NSCW suggests significant racial and ethnic variation in WFC (Roehling, Jarvis, & Swope, 2005). Research that treats race and ethnicity as more than control variables would improve theoretical understanding of WFC—recognizing that cultural beliefs likely shape the relative salience of work and family and the importance of integrating these domains (Korabik, Lero, & Ayman, 2003). On a more practical level, in light of the growing diversity of the labor force in the United States and around the world, research that documents and seeks to understand racial and ethnic variation in WFC is needed to ensure that all workers benefit from governmental and occupational programs designed to help workers effectively integrate their work and family lives.

Likewise, location in the social hierarchy has not been adequately handled in the WFC literature. Jody Heymann (2000) characterized jobs occupied by lower-class individuals as requiring nonstandard and erratic work hours and lacking necessary benefits (e.g., child sick leave) and argued that these types of jobs create WFCs that exacerbate health disparities. This basic argument has strong face validity, but there is little attempt to document social class or socioeconomic inequalities in WFC or to consider the degree to which WFC contributes to difficulties experienced by lower-status families. The few studies on the topic find that higher-status workers, as indicated by education and occupation, report more rather than less work-to-family conflict (Schieman, Whitestone, & Van Gundy, 2006). Single mothers report high levels of WFC (Avison, Ali, & Walters, 2007), but whether this is attributable to family structure or socioeconomic hardship remains uncertain. More research is needed to firmly determine whether the WFC is unequally shared in the social hierarchy and the potential role of WFC in contemporary social problems such as health disparities.

CONCLUSION

Evidence from the large multidisciplinary literature suggests that WFC is a pressing social problem in need of policy solutions. Diane Halpern (2005), in her presidential address to the American Psychological Association, described WFC as the issue of our time. WFC is an issue confronted by most workers, regardless of whether it is the new parent transitioning back to work, the midlife individuals sandwiched between children and aging parents, or the older worker laying plans for retirement. Echoing Halpern's claim, the National Institute for Child Health and Human Development has created a network of researchers to develop and test policies and organizational practices that reduce WFC. Workplace flexibility, particularly management strategies that give workers control over when and where job-related tasks are performed, is believed to be invaluable for minimizing WFC. Similarly, systematic training of supervisors and managers to help them be more supportive of employees' lives outside the workplace also offers promise for minimizing WFC. These types of strategies help adults respond effectively to legitimate demands that arise in daily life, such as needing to drive an aging parent to a health care appointment or meeting with a child's teacher to resolve a learning or behavioral problem. The short- and long-term consequences of strategies to reduce WFC remain unknown, but researchers and policy advocates believe that they will produce healthier and more content workers, better-functioning families, and more productive organizations.

The WFC literature has developed substantially since the 1980s with contributions from several disciplines. Despite the breadth and depth of the literature, substantial room remains for advancements and new areas of research. Longitudinal research examining WFC over time is needed, as is research devoted to documenting and understanding secular trends in WFC. Advancements in measurement tools are needed to better capture WFC while remaining attentive to problems that arise from exclusive reliance on self-report data. Finally, focused research on understudied segments of the population, such as economically disadvantaged families and members of racial and ethnic minority groups, is needed. Focused research attention in these areas will deepen understanding of WFC and contribute to the creation of workplace and public policies that promote adults' ability to integrate work and family.

SEE ALSO Volume 2: *Fatherhood; Gender in the Work Place; Housework; Motherhood; Policy, Family; Stress in Adulthood; Time Use, Adulthood;* Volume 3: *Caregiving.*

BIBLIOGRAPHY

Allen, T. D., Herst, D. E., Bruck, C. S., & Sutton, M. (2000). Consequences associated with work-to-family conflict: A review and agenda for future research. *Journal of Occupational Health Psychology, 5*(2), 278–308.

Avison, W. R., Ali, J., & Walters, D. (2007). Family structure, stress, and psychological distress: A demonstration of the impact of differential exposure. *Journal of Health and Social Behavior, 48*(3), 301–317.

Bellavia, G., & Frone, M. R. (2005). Work–family conflict. In J. Barling, E. K. Kelloway, & M. R. Frone (Eds.), *Handbook of work stress* (pp. 113–147). Thousand Oaks, CA: Sage.

Byron, K. (2005). A meta-analytic review of work–family conflict and its antecedents. *Journal of Vocational Behavior, 67*(2), 169–198.

Carlson, D. S., & Grzywacz, J.G. (2008). Reflections and future directions on measurement in work-family research. In K. Korabik, D. S. Lero, & D. L. Whitehead (Eds.), *The handbook of work–family integration: Theories, perspectives, and best practices.* San Diego, CA: Elsevier.

Carlson, D. S., & Grzywacz, J. G. (2008). Reflections and future directions on measurement in work–family research. In K. Korabik, D. S. Lero, & D. L. Whitehead (Eds.), *The handbook of work–family integration: Theories, perspectives, and best practices* (pp. 57–73). San Diego, CA: Elsevier.

Carlson, D. S., Kacmar, K. M., & Williams, L. J. (2000). Construction and initial validation of a multidimensional measure of work–family conflict. *Journal of Vocational Behavior, 56*(2), 249–276.

Carr, D. (2002). The psychological consequences of work–family trade-offs for three cohorts of women and men. *Social Psychology Quarterly, 65*(2), 103–124.

Casper, W. J., Eby, L. T., Bordeaux, C., Lockwood, A., & Lambert, D. (2007). A review of research methods in IO/OB work-family research. *Journal of Applied Psychology, 92*(1), 28–43.

Eby, L. T., Casper, W. J., Lockwood, A., Bordeaux, C., & Brinley, A. (2005). Work and family research in IO/OB: Content analysis and review of the literature (1980–2002). *Journal of Vocational Behavior, 66*(1), 124–197.

Frone, M. R., Russell, M., & Cooper, M. L. (1992). Antecedents and outcomes of work–family conflict: Testing a model of the work–family interface. *Journal of Applied Psychology, 77*(1), 65–78.

Frone, M. R., Russell, M., & Cooper, M. L. (1997). Relation of work–family conflict to health outcomes: A 4-year longitudinal study of employed parents. *Journal of Occupational and Organizational Psychology, 70,* 325–335.

Frone, M. R., Yardley, J. K., & Markel, K. S. (1997). Developing and testing an integrative model of the work–family interface. *Journal of Vocational Behavior, 50*(2), 145–167.

Geurts, S. A. E., & Demerouti, E. (2003). Work/nonwork interface: A review of theories and findings. In M. J. Schabracq, J. A. M. Winnubst, & C. L. Cooper (Eds.), *The handbook of work and health psychology* (2nd ed., pp. 279–312). New York: Wiley.

Grant Vallone, E. J., & Donaldson, S. I. (2001). Consequences of work–family conflict on employee well-being over time. *Work and Stress, 15*(3), 214–226.

Greenhaus, J. H., Allen, T. D., & Spector, P. E. (2006). Health consequences of work–family conflict: The dark side of the work-family interface. In P. L. Perrewe & D. C. Ganster (Eds.), *Research in occupational stress and well-being* (Vol. 5, pp. 61–98). Amsterdam: JAI Press/Elsevier.

Greenhaus, J. H., & Beutell, N.J. (1985). Sources of conflict between work and family roles. *Academy of Management Review, 10*(1), 76–88.

Grzywacz, J. G., Almeida, D. M., & McDonald, D. A. (2002). Work–family spillover and daily reports of work and family stress in the adult labor force. *Family Relations, 51*(1), 28–36.

Halpern, D. F. (2005). Psychology at the intersection of work and family: Recommendations for employers, working families, and policy makers. *American Psychologist, 60*(5), 397–409.

Heymann, J. (2000). *The widening gap: Why America's working families are in jeopardy, and what can be done about it.* New York: Basic Books.

Johansson, G., Huang, Q., & Lindfors, P. (2007). A life span perspective on women's careers, health, and well-being. *Social Science and Medicine, 65*(4), 685–697.

Korabik, K., Lero, D. S., & Ayman, R. (2003). A multi-level approach to cross-cultural work–family research. *International Journal of Cross Cultural Management, 3,* 289–303.

Lambert, S. J. (1999). Lower-wage workers and the new realities of work and family. *Annals of the American Academy of Political and Social Science, 562,* 174–190.

MacDermid, S. M. (2004). (Re)considering conflict between work and family. In E. E. Kossek & S. Lambert (Eds.), *Work and life integration in organizations: New directions for theory and practice* (pp. 19–40). Mahwah, NJ: Lawrence Erlbaum.

Pleck, J. H. (1977). The work–family role system. *Social Problems, 24*(4), 417–442.

Roehling, P. V., Jarvis, L. H., & Swope, H. E. (2005). Variations in negative work–family spillover among White, Black, and Hispanic-American men and women: Does ethnicity matter? *Journal of Family Issues, 26*(6), 840–865.

Schieman, S., Whitestone, Y. K., & Van Gundy, K. (2006). The nature of work and the stress of higher status. *Journal of Health and Social Behavior, 47,* 242–257.

Small, S. A., & Riley, D. (1990). Toward a multidimensional assessment of work spillover into family life. *Journal of Marriage and the Family, 52,* 51–61.

Tetrick, L. E., & Buffardi, L. C. (2005). Measurement issues in research on the work–home interface. In F. Jones, R. J. Burke, & M. Westman (Eds.), *Work–life balance: A psychological perspective* (pp. 90–114). East Sussex, U.K.: Psychology Press.

Winslow, S. (2005). Work–family conflict, gender, and parenthood, 1977–1997. *Journal of Family Issues, 26*(6), 727–755.

Joseph G. Grzywacz

ZNANIECKI, FLORIAN
1882–1958

Florian Witold Znaniecki was born on January 15 in Świątniki near Włocławek, Poland; he died on March 23 in Champaign, Illinois. A sociologist, social theorist, and philosopher of culture, he taught at the Poznań University (1920–1939) and the University of Illinois (1940–1958). Together with William I. Thomas of the University of Chicago he published *The Polish Peasant in Europe and America* (1918–1920), considered an early examination of what would later be called the life course. Another of his notable works is *Cultural Reality* (1919/1983), which outlined his theory of human action and values. Recognized as an eminent sociologist of education, he directed the Education and Social Change project at Columbia University's Teachers' College from 1930 to 1933. In 1956 he was elected as President of the American Sociological Association.

Znaniecki was one of the first sociologists to consider the two-way process by which society is maintained through the actions of individuals while, at the same time, the actions of individuals are shaped by society. This duality is central to sociology in general and to the study of the life course in particular. Znaniecki focused on culture and emphasized its construction by individuals as social agents. His work provided the conceptual and empirical foundations for the development of life-course studies.

Znaniecki's approach to understanding the relationship between society and the individual emerged from his theory of cultural systems, which he developed in *The Method of Sociology* (1934), *Social Actions* (1936), and *Cultural Sciences* (1954). In Znaniecki's view, culture encompasses multiple systems—social, economic, hedonistic, technical, cognitive, aesthetic, and religious—that are composed of different values and constructed by human activities. Within the cultural system, social systems are crucial for their perpetuation and development. Social systems encompass social actions, relations, roles, and groups. The "humanistic coefficient" of cultural systems refers to their meaning and axiological significance in the experiences of individuals as members of various groups. To Znaniecki, the individual "self" is not independent but exists with the humanistic coefficient as an object of the active experience of others and of the individual him- or herself. In short, individuals are constructed by their participation in cultural systems as social values and social agents. Znaniecki's works relating to individuals as cultural and social persons include *Wstęp do socjologi* [Introduction to Sociology] (1922), *The Laws of Social Psychology* (1925/1967), *Socjologia wychowania* [The Sociology of Education] (1928–1930), *Ludzie terázniejsi a cywilizacja przyslósci* [People of the Present and the Civilization of the Future] (1934), *The Social Role of the Man of Knowledge* (1940), and *Social Relations and Social Roles* (1965).

Znaniecki combined data from individual life histories and the study of social groups to identify major types of

Florian Znaniecki. COURTESY OF THE AMERICAN SOCIOLOGICAL ASSOCIATION.

social personalities, which are formed through the interactions between individuals and social circles. He argued that three kinds of social circles are particularly relevant in the formation of social personalities: educational, occupational, and companionable. Social personality is the cultural, constructionist view of the individual. Znaniecki distinguished four major components of the social person: the *reflected self*—the way individuals believe members of their social circle view them; the *social position,* including social standing (the rights of being recognized as socially valuable) and economic status; the *social function,* comprised of obligations such as objective tasks and moral integrity; and finally the *reconstructed self,* which is independent from the social circle and is both autobiographical (related to one's memories) and one's ideal (or the desired self that one projects into the future).

Znaniecki believed that social personality evolves throughout the life course, because each new social role introduces new experiences and leads to the development of new active tendencies. The extent to which social tendencies developed early set life trajectories varies across individuals. What develops is the tendency toward either a stable and predictable life course or a changeable and unpredictable one. Personality is conceptualized not as a reflection of one's inborn biological or psychological characteristics but as shaped by social and cultural context. Particularly important in the early part of the life course is the emergence of person-creating tendencies, that is, tendencies to form one's person according to a unique pattern. An individual's social biography is actualized in various social circles through these person-creating tendencies.

Znaniecki conceived of the individual life course very differently from those who built on the basic framework of biological maturation. He took into consideration the influence of social circles and developed a role theory that took into account the dynamic interplay between society and individual, in contrast to those who either emphasized the "self" as the dominant element of roles or who highlighted the social structural aspects. For Znaniecki, the social role is a purely cultural phenomenon, involving the active participation of the performer and other individuals as social agents. An individual's participation in social life in terms of role performance implies four components: the social person, social circle, duties, and rights. Znaniecki's work contributed to the study of the historical evolution of various social roles: of men of knowledge, educators, religious and political personas, as well as to the study of marital and erotic relations, mother–child relations, fraternal relations, and friendships.

SEE ALSO Volume 3: *Lopata, Helena; Self.*

BIBLIOGRAPHY

Hałas, E. (2006). Classical cultural sociology: Florian Znaniecki's impact in a new light. *Journal of Classical Sociology, 6,* no. 3, 257–282.

Znaniecki, F. (1965). *Social relations and social roles: The unfinished systematic sociology.* San Francisco: Chandler.

Znaniecki, F. (1967). *The laws of social psychology.* New York: Russell & Russell. (Original work published 1925)

Znaniecki, F. (1983). *Cultural reality.* Houston: Cap and Gown Press. (Original work published 1919)

Znaniecki, F. (1998). *Education and social change.* (Edited and introduction by E. Hałas). Frankfurt am Main: Peter Lang Verlag.

Elżbieta Hałas